Speakers
of the House
of Representatives

Speakers
of the House
# of Representatives

Mark Grossman

PUBLISHER: Leslie Mackenzie
EDITORIAL DIRECTOR: Laura Mars-Proietti
EDITORIAL ASSISTANT: Kristen Thatcher
COMPOSITION: David Garoogian
MARKETING DIRECTOR: Jessica Moody

Grey House Publishing, Inc.
4919 Route 22
Amenia, NY 12501
518.789.8700
FAX 518.789.0545
www.greyhouse.com
e-mail: books @greyhouse.com

First edition published 2009
Printed in the U.S.A.

Publisher's Cataloging-In-Publication Data
(Prepared by The Donohue Group, Inc.)

Grossman, Mark.
    Speakers of the House of Representatives / Mark Grossman. – 1st ed.

    p. : ill. ; cm.

"A universal reference book."
Includes bibliographical references and index.
ISBN: 978-1-59237-404-5

1. United States. Congress. House–Speakers–Biography. 2. Legislators–United States–Biography. I. Title.

JK1411 .G767 2009
328.73/092

Acknowledgments

This work began as an idea formulated in 1997 while sitting in the British Library in London, England. There, I came across the name of one of the Speakers of the British House of Commons. I wondered, was there a book on the Speakers of the US House of Representatives? Now, 12 years later, the answer is yes.

Much of the research for this book spanned more than a decade, from the smallest note-taking at the Library of Congress in Washington, D.C. to the British Library in London, England, some in person and some on the phone or by mail. I was aided and encouraged by hundreds of people whose assistance I can never fully acknowledge.

I do thank: Dale L. Couch, archivist, State of Georgia legislative archives, Atlanta, Georgia; Brad Vogus, Government Documents librarian at Arizona State University in Tempe, Arizona, as well as the entire staff of the Hayden Library at ASU, where much of the research for this work was conducted; Dale L. Neighbors, Prints and Photographs Coordinator, Special Collections Branch, at the Library of Virginia, Richmond, for his work on obtaining information and images of Thomas S. Bocock; Jeffery A. Jenkins, Associate Professor, Woodrow Wilson Department of Politics, the University of Virginia, for his permission to utilize some of the information from his varied works on the Speakers of the House; the magnificent folks at the Division of Rare and Manuscript Collections, the Carl A. Kroch Library, Cornell University, in Ithaca, New York, especially Ana and Connie, for their work in accessing the Edwin Barber Morgan Papers, as well as the folks at Wells College in Aurora, New York, for finding specific Morgan papers; the Manuscript Department of the University Library at the University of North Carolina at Chapel Hill, for their work in finding specific papers relating to John Rutledge; Elaine Grublin, Reference Librarian, and Tracy Potter, Assistant Reference Librarian, both at the Massachusetts Historical Society, Boston, Massachusetts; the staff of the New York Public Library, Main Branch; the staff of the Bodleian Library at Oxford University in Oxford, England; and the many libraries that sent me items through the Interlibrary Loan (ILL) system.

Finally, this work would not exist without the long hours of dedicated work of Laura Mars-Proietti and Kristen Thatcher, both at Grey House Publishing, who put up for lengthy periods with my mountains of text and images and intolerable e-mails, yet stayed true to their mission of publishing a really great book. Any writer would be fortunate to get two people half as involved as they were.

Mark Grossman
5 March 2009

Table of Contents

Preface

Speaker Sam Rayburn, who served longer in the speakership than any other holder of that office, was once asked about his experiences in serving under eight different Presidents. "No," Rayburn needled the reporter. "I haven't served under anybody. I have *served with* eight Presidents."

It has become almost a given that when the American people are asked who their leaders are - be they members of the cabinet, or the US Senate, or the US House of Representatives - they draw almost a complete blank. Some famous Americans, from Lincoln to Reagan, are remembered, but they are few and far between. Perhaps one of the most neglected leaders in this country, both historically and in contemporary studies, are the Speakers of the US House. It is almost understandable, as many of them served almost in the same anonymity that they are discussed in American history books. However, for the historian, it is the angst in trying to find sources on the lives and services of this unique club - only 53 people have served as Speaker since the First Congress opened in 1789 - that made this book a necessity.

Alexander Hamilton, who served as the first Secretary of the Treasury, once wrote of the US House of Representatives, "Here, sir, the people rule." The names of many important House leaders, from 1789 to the present, emblazon American history. But what of the 52 men and one woman who have served as the leader of the House? Who has even heard of Thomas S. Bocock for example, who served as Speaker of the Confederate House of Representatives, or Bob Livingston, named as Speaker following the 1998 election but who resigned before taking office in January 1999? Both are profiled in this work. Few Americans today can recognize or name their own US Representative or US Senator; even fewer can name any Speaker, present or past. This work is designed to discuss not just who these people were, the lives they led and the work that they did while in the House and as Speaker, but also to give a history of the office, its ties to the speakership of the House of Commons in the United Kingdom, and the unique role of the Speaker in the formulation both of house policy and debate.

In 1851, James Alexander Manning compiled a massive history of the lives of the Speaker of the British House of Commons. In this work, he detailed the finer points on how the "speaker" became such an integral part of the deliberative body which is the lower house of the British Parliament:

> This great officer must have been anciently, as at present, the organ or mouth-piece of the Commons, although in modern times he is more occupied in presiding over the deliberations of the House, than in delivering speeches on their behalf. Amongst the duties of the Speaker, are the following: To read to the Sovereign [those] petitions or addresses from the Commons, and to deliver, in the royal presence, whether at the Palace or in the House of Lords, such speeches as are usually made on behalf of the Commons; to manage in the name of the House, where counsel, witnesses, or prisoners, are at the bar; to reprimand persons who have incurred the displeasure of the House; to issue warrants of committal or release for breaches of privilege; to communicate in writing with any parties, when so instructed by the House; to exercise vigilance in reference to private bills, especially with a view to protect property in general, or the rights of individuals, from undue encroachment or injury; to express the thanks or approbation of the Com-

mons to distinguished personages; to control and regulate the subordinate officers of the House; to entertain the members at dinner, in due succession, and at state periods; to adjourn the House at four o'clock, if forty members be not present; [and] to appoint tellers on divisions. The Speaker must abstain from debating, unless in Committees of the whole House. As Chairman of the House, his duties are the same as those of any other President of a deliberative assembly. When Parliament is about to be prorogued ["to discontinue a session of a parliament or assembly without dissolving it"], it is customary for the Speaker to address to the Sovereign, in the House of Lords, a speech, recapitulating the proceedings of the session.

Writing just eight years earlier in a two-volume history of the House of Commons itself, historian W. Charles Townsend examined the role of the Speaker from the Parliament of 1688-89 to the-then "modern" Parliament which enacted the Reform Bill of 1832:

The first speakers of the House of Commons were chosen from belted knights and commoners of distinction, the choice being made in the House, but in accordance with the previous nomination of the king. Sir Thomas Hungerford, 51 Henry III., in the year of 1376, is the first named as speaker in the parliament roll, and termed parlour, or mouth of the House." [Parlour from Anglo-Norman French: parlur, 'a place for speaking,' from the Latin: parlare, 'to speak.'] More on the origins of the speaker and his office come from "The Parliamentary or Constitutional History of England; From the Earliest Times to the Restoration of King Charles II," published in 1762. In discussing the Parliament of 1376, the writers of this history, not identified, explain, "Another Affair, which we must not omit, is, That this is the first Parliament in which we find a Speaker of the House of Commons expressly named as such; and here Sir Thomas de Hungerford, Knt. [Knight] was appointed Speaker by the Evidence of the Record itself. There is not Doubt to be made that, in former Parliaments, and perhaps in all ever since the Commons were call'd to sit there, a public Orator, or one that was chosen by the rest to deliver their Petitions to the King, was elected; but no one is particularized in the Records, for having that Office, before the last-named Gentleman; tho', for the future, the Records go very regularly on in giving us their Names, even down to the present Times." It is noted by this same work that Hungerford, or de Hungerford, is called in the record "Monsieur Thomas de Hungerford, Chevalier, qui avoit les Paroles put les Communes d'Angleterre." The Oxford English Dictionary denotes a "chevalier" as "a knight," and "a member of certain orders of knighthood or of modern French orders such as the Legion of Honour.

No history of the US House of Representatives can be told without an in-depth examination of the Speaker and the role of the office in the growth and power of the lower house of the US Congress. Nevertheless, these assessments usually appear in dry and ancient works, rarely intended for the wider audience of the American public other than scholars. This work serves to expand the discussion to the layman, to the amateur historian or those who study the House and its celebrated history. It is not just a collection of biographies of those who have served as Speaker of the House; it is also a collection of primary documents dealing with the speakership, essays on the formation of the office and its role in American history, and listings scrutinizing the facts behind the Speakers: who served when as well as other information rarely found in one single volume.

The Congress of the United States, established by the US Constitution, first met in New York City's Federal Hall on 4 March 1789. To this Congress fell the incredible task of enacting the legislation that formed the new nation. To lead this Congress, Frederick A.C. Muhlenberg of Pennsylvania was elected as Speaker. As with his successors, Muhlenberg discovered the limitations of the position he held, as well as the incredible labors the members of the House had to endure. For instance, in the years when Congress met first in New York, then in Philadelphia, and finally in the new national capital of Washington, D.C., travel back to the homes of the congressmen took days by carriage or horse and, while the members were in session, they received only $6 a day in pay.

But just what are the powers of the Speaker? The Constitution that established the office does not specify what its parameters are, only that the House "chuse" its leader. In a 1903 biography of Speaker Nathaniel Macon, who served from 1801 to 1807, it was noted that "Speakers were chosen then for their ability as moderators, for their judicious trend of mind and their knowledge of parliamentary practice..." In an interview with Frank G. Carpenter of *The Washington Post* which appeared in 1891, Speaker John Griffin Carlisle spoke at length about the duties of the office of the Speaker and its role in the inner workings of the House's legislative agenda:

> *The Speakership is certainly a very arduous position, he stated. It entails hard work from the beginning to the end of the session, and taxes the strength and tries the patience of the incumbent to the fullest extent. The work of selecting the committees, determining just what members will deal most intelligently with certain classes of questions, and the naming of chairmen, is perplexing and tedious in the extreme. When this is done the Speaker's work is only begun. He had to pass upon questions of importance almost every hour. He has to be consulted as to the time that shall be given to the various legislative measures; must carry in his mind a panoramic view of the whole legislation of the session, and must understand the merits of each measure and how it should be treated. This, of course, requires a great amount of investigation and study. He must be ready to decide upon all matters the moment they come up, and new questions of procedure and parliamentary law are always being present.*

In 1916, noted American historian De Alva Stanwood Alexander wrote, "The Speaker is the organ of the House. As its executive head he receives its invitations, represents it at public functions, appoints and removes official reporters, names visitors and trustees of public institutions, issues warrants, executes orders, authenticates proceedings, approves bonds, certifies salary accounts of members, controls committee rooms, corridors, galleries, and the House grounds, regulates admission to the floor and to the press gallery, signs all bills that pass, and notifies the proper state official whenever a vacancy in the House occurs." Certainly, this is an accurate list of the duties of the Speaker of the House. But, in a sense, the more modern speakership has endowed the men - and now woman - who have held the post with incredible amounts of power. When the President delivers the State of the Union address, it is the Speaker who sits behind the President, to his left, next to the Vice President. The Speaker is not just the head of the majority party in the House but the face of that body; they also allow (or disallow) for the voting on certain legislation, bring together committees for the passage of legislation or for hearings, and other duties. In a 2007 report by the Congressional Research Service, which provides reports to members of Congress, it was noted:

The Speaker of the House of Representatives is widely viewed as symbolizing the power and authority of the House. The Speaker's most prominent role is that of presiding officer of the House. In this capacity, the Speaker is empowered by House rules to administer proceedings on the House floor, including the power to recognize Members on the floor to speak or make motions and the power to appoint Members to conference committees. The Speaker also oversees much of the non-legislative business of the House, such as general control over the Hall of the House and the House side of the Capitol and service as chair of the House Office Building Commission. The Speaker's role as 'elect of the elect' in the House also placed him or her in a highly visible position with the public.

The Speaker also serves not only as titular leader of the House but as leader of the majority party conference. The Speaker is often responsible for airing and defending the majority party's legislative agenda in the House.

The Speaker's third distinct role is that of an elected Member of the House. Although elected as an officer of the House, the Speaker continues to be a Member as well. As such the Speaker enjoys the same rights, responsibilities, and privileges of all Representatives. However, the Speaker has traditionally refrained from debating or voting in most circumstances, and does not sit on any standing committee of the House.

As the country has grown from 13 small colonies to a Republic in the last years of the 18th century, to the 50 states and massive government that is the United States today, the power of the Speaker has changed and grown exponentially with that growth in the country. General A.W. Greely, in an 1898 article, wrote, "The power of the Speaker of the House of Representatives has steadily increased from the first Congress to the present, and its influence on national legislation is believed by man even to exceed that exerted by the President. Samuel J. Randall, through whom the influence of the Speaker was increased more largely than by other man in this country, once said: 'I came to consider that [the Speakership]...was the highest office within the reach of American citizens; that it was a grand official station, great in the honors which it conferred and still greater in the ability it gave to impress on our history and legislation the stamp of truth, fairness, justice, and right."

The first Congresses were weak in their oversight of the growing Executive branch. The anti-Federalists in the First and Second Congresses, believing that Secretary of the Treasury Andrew Hamilton was not accurately reporting to the Congress on expenditures and other financial matters, argued in the Congress that Hamilton provide detailed and meticulous reports to the Congress, then turned and maintained that he not deliver these reports in person or by delivering them to Congress, in effect forcing him to report and stay quiet at the same time, a seemingly bewildering position to take. On 3 December 1791, Rep. Elbridge Gerry, an anti-administration member from Massachusetts - and later Vice President of the United States - introduced two resolutions from "the committee to whom were referred several motions for obtaining annual and regular statements of the receipts and expenditures of all public moneys." Gerry stated that the House adopt a rule that the Secretary of the Treasury report "regular" and "accurate" statements to the House of Representatives. Rep. Abraham Clark, pro-administration member from New Jersey, maintained that the House had no right to make such a rule, "than they have to say that the Speaker of the next House shall wear a tie-wig." The resolution passed, nevertheless. However, it showed how the office of the Speaker would be shaped not by its constitutional mandate but how those who served in the House would sculpt its contours.

Mary Parker Follett, one of the greatest historians on the speakership, wrote in 1902, "The Speakership had been little discussed outside the House until Mr. [Thomas Brackett] Reed made it famous. But we cannot give either [John Griffin] Carlisle or Reed credit of inventing a political Speakership. The history of the House of Representatives shows that the consolidation of power has been an inevitable development. Individual men have only emphasized and perhaps hastened their development. The Fifty-first Congress, a Republican body, made a new code of rules increasing the Speaker's power; the Fifty-second and Fifty-third Congresses, Democratic bodies, also formally enlarged their chairman's authority, especially by giving very large power to a small committee of five men, the committee on Rules." Historians Joseph Cooper and David Brady noted, "It was with good reason that Speaker of the House in the years between 1890 and 1910 were often referred to as czars. The Speaker appointed the committees. He served as the chairman of and had unchallengeable control over the Rules Committee. He had great, though not unlimited, discretion over the recognition of members desiring to call business off the calendars, to make motions, or to address the House, and absolute discretion over the recognition of motions for unanimous consent and suspension of the rules."

The Speaker of the House is not just the moderator of debate: he (and, with the election of Nancy Pelosi as the first female Speaker, she) is also the chairman of the Committee of the Whole, and, until the revolution against Speaker Joseph G. Cannon in 1910, a member of the Committee of the Rules. Until Cannon, the Speaker also had the authority to name the members of the committees; at the same time, these committee chairmen acted as *de facto* leaders of the House, instead of the positions of Majority Leader and Majority Whip that we have today. In a history of the House Ways and Means Committee written by historians Donald R. Kennon and Rebecca M. Rogers, it was stated:

> [B]ecause of the importance of revenue bills, which under the Constitution must originate in the House, the 19th century chairmen often served as the de facto floor leaders [of the House]. Before the post of majority leader became an official position of party leadership at the turn of the century, the chairman of Ways and Means had most often performed the function of directing floor consideration of legislation. From 1899 to 1919, the chairman was the official majority leader. Chairman such as John Randolph and Thaddeus Stevens before 1899 and Oscar W. Underwood after 1899 were acknowledged masters of legislative influence...in some instances the chairman of the Committee of Ways and Means was selected on the basis of a second-place finish in the speakership election, such as was the case with Millard Fillmore in 1841, while at other times the position was awarded simply as a reward for services rendered to the Speaker. The latter was true in the selection of Democrat Thomas Bayly of Virginia in 1849, who had delivered some key votes for Georgia's Howell Cobb during the heated speakership contest.

The election of a Speaker, until at least within the last 80 years, was a spirited contest that was without a decision until the House itself convened. In four instances in House history, the fight for the speakership went on for a protracted period. Recent history, however, demonstrates the fact that on election night, the leader of the party that garners the majority will become the next Speaker.

When the Thirty-eighth Congress convened in Washington, D.C. on 7 December 1863, the majority Republicans elected Rep. Schuyler Colfax of Indiana as the Speaker of the House. Whitelaw Reid, the Washington correspondent for the *Cincinnati Gazette*, wrote of the election of Colfax to the speakership, while at the same time giving an insight into this rarely-seen (at the time) but exceedingly fascinating process to select the leader of the US House of Representatives:

> *There is a moment of suspense while the lists are carefully footed up; the tellers - [Henry Lauren] Dawes, [George Hunt] Pendleton, [Samuel Clarke] Pomeroy and [William Henry] Wadsworth, a Yankee Radical, a Cincinnati Democrat, a Pennsylvania Republican and a Kentucky pro-slavery Unionist - range themselves before the Clerk's desk, and Mr. Pendleton announces that Colfax has one hundred and one votes, Cox [has] forty-two, and the rest scattering down to two. And the galleries cheer again. He has carried every vote of his party in the House - there is not a bolter or a dodger. It is the sixth time in his political career he has had just such a flattering experience. With what grace he may, the Clerk announces that 'Schuyler Colfax, one of the Representatives from the State of Indiana, having received a majority of the votes given, is duly elected Speaker of the House of Representatives for the Thirty-eighth Congress.' And the galleries cheer again, while the members' faces are wreathed in smiles, and there is a general turning to the medium-sized, brown- bearded, genial-faced man in the midst of the administration members, who has been avoiding the fire of gazes from spectators by bending over a roll-call.*

> *In a moment, at the Clerk's appointment, a couple of Democrats, Dawson and Cox, are coming over from the opposite side to congratulate the Speaker and conduct him to the chair.*

> *And then, under the gaze of all this assemblage of Place and Power, there walks up the aisle, to take the official oath of the third executive office in the nation, the son of a poor widow of New York city, who quit school at the age of ten years to seek his fortune in the West, and since then, thanks to the training of the printing-office to generous talents and a good use of them, has been gradually climbing, climbing, till to-day he stands in this envied position, the unanimous choice of his party for the place; stands where the Fathers who first gathered in our national Congress placed Muhlenberg, where Henry Clay so long shed dignity upon the position, where, in later years, Bell and Polk and Winthrop and Linn Boyd and Banks have deemed it high honor to stand. It is another triumph of the best feature of the institutions we are striving to preserve.*

> *He speaks briefly, gracefully, patriotically; invokes their remembrance of that sacred truth, which all history verifies, that they who rule not in righteousness shall perish from the earth; and, after grateful thanks, turns to take the solemn oath of office, which Mr. Washburne administers. And the galleries ring again with applause as he takes the Speaker's chair, and the House no longer depends on [Emerson] Etheridge, the Clerk.*

A Congressional Research Service (CRS) report on the speakership also noted that the length of House service relative to getting elected as Speaker has changed. "In the 19th century, longevity of House service was not as important a criterion in selecting the

Speaker as it is today. From 1789 to 1899, the average length of House service before a Member was elected Speaker was 7.1 years. In fact, Henry Clay of Kentucky (in 1811) and William Pennington of New Jersey (in 1860) were each elected Speaker as freshmen (the first Speaker, Frederick A. Muhlenberg of Pennsylvania, was obviously a third, albeit special, case)." However, the report notes, "The 19 Speakers elected between 1899 (David B. Henderson) and 2007 (Nancy Pelosi) served an average of 22.9 years in the House prior to their first election as Speaker. The longest pre-speakership tenure in this period belonged to Jim Wright who served for 17 terms before being elected as Speaker."

Alas, the Speaker is also the "water carrier" of the President's programs, both domestic and international. Historians Norman Thomas and Joseph Pika explained:

> The extent to which presidential programs become reality depends to a considerable degree on the president's influence over the party within the government, the officials in the legislative and executive branches who are either elected under a partisan label or appointed primarily of their party activities because it is expected that they will implement party views on public policy matters. A president usually has little control over party activities in Congress. Most senators and representatives are elected independently of the president. Moreover, the president has comparatively little influence over the organization of his party in Congress. Although Thomas Jefferson determined who his party's leaders would be, for the most part American chief executives have been chary of interfering with the right of Congress to choose its own people. Dwight Eisenhower was forced to work with Senate Republican Leader William Knowland, whose views on foreign policy were quite different from his own. During part of John Kennedy's administration, the Democratic Speaker of the House was John McCormack, a political rival from Kennedy's home state.

In 1967, with the passage of the Twenty-fifth Amendment to the US Constitution, the Speaker of the House became the second in line, just behind the Vice President, in succession to the presidency; John W. McCormack became the first Speaker to serve in this line of succession. In 1962, the US House moved to honor three of its former Speakers, one of whom had just passed away the previous year. The Old House Office Building, built in 1908, was renamed the Joseph Cannon House Office Building; the "new" House Office Building, constructed in 1933, was renamed the Nicholas Longworth House Office Building. A third structure, signed into law by President John F. Kennedy on 22 May 1962 and completed three years later, was officially named the Sam Rayburn House Office Building.

Sources: Manning, James Alexander, "The Lives of the Speakers of the House of Commons, From the Time of King Edward III to Queen Victoria, Comprising the Biographies of Upwards of One Hundred Distinguished Persons, and Copious Details of the Parliamentary History of England, from the Most Authentic Documents" (London: George Willis, 1851), i; Townsend, W. Charles, "History of the House of Commons, From the Convention Parliament of 1688-9 to the Passing of the Reform Bill, in 1832" (London: Henry Colburn, Publisher; 2 volumes, 1843), I:1-2: "The Parliamentary or Constitutional History of England; From the Earliest Times, to the Restoration of King Charles II. Collected from the Records, the Rolls of Parliament, the Journals of both Houses, the public Libraries, original Manuscripts, scarce Speeches, and Tracts; all compared with the several Contemporary Writers, and connected, throughout, with the History of the Times" (London: Printed for J. and R. Tonson, and R. Millar, in the Strand; and W. Sandby, in Fleet-Street; 24 volumes, 1762), I:351; Moore, Rev. A.Y., "The Life of Schuyler Colfax" (Philadelphia: T.B. Peterson & Brothers, 1868), 137-39; Dodd, William E., "The Life of Nathaniel Macon" (Raleigh, North Carolina: Edwards & Broughton, Printers and Binders, 1903), 144; Carlisle interview with Frank G. Carpenter in "A Talk with Carlisle: Views of the Kentucky Senator on Problems of the Day," *The Washington*

Post, 27 December 1891, 3; Alexander, De Alva Stanwood, "History and Procedure of the House of Representatives" (Boston: Houghton Mifflin Company, 1916), 41; Greely, A.W., "The Speaker and the Committees of the House of Representatives," *The North American Review*, CLXVI:CCCXCIV (January 1898), 24; "The Speaker of the House: House Officer, Party Leader, and Representative," *CRS Report for Congress*, 29 January 2007, II; Follett, Mary Parker, "The Speaker of the House of Representatives" (New York: Longmans, Green, and Co., 1909), 307; Cooper, Joseph, and David W. Brady, "Institutional Context and Leadership Style: The House from Cannon to Rayburn," *The American Political Science Review*, 75:2 (June 1981), 411-12; Donald R. Kennon and Rebecca M. Rogers, "The Committee on Ways and Means: A Bicentennial History, 1789-1989" (Washington, D.C.: Government Printing Office, 1989), 2, 100; "The Speaker of the House: House Officer, Party Leader, and Representative," *CRS Report for Congress*, 29 January 2007, 3; Thomas, Norman C., and Joseph A. Pika, "The Politics of the Presidency" (Washington, D.C.: CQ Press, 1996), 136.

Introduction and Study Guide

This is the first edition of *Speakers of the House of Representatives 1789 - 2009*. With information that has never before been gathered into one volume, it not only includes detailed biographies of the 53 men and woman who have served as Speaker, but offers a wealth of supportive material that combines for a complete picture of the Speakers and the speakership - the history, the power, and the changes.

With detailed content, thoughtful arrangement, and several "user guide" elements, *Speakers of the House of Representatives* is designed for multiple levels of study.

CONTENT

Speaker Biographies
This major portion of the work - comprises 54 detailed biographies that average 7 pages long. This section is arranged chronologically, beginning with the first Speaker — Frederick Muhlenberg, who began his term in 1789 - and ending with the current Speaker - Nancy Pelosi, who was elected in 2007 as the first female Speaker of the House. Each biography starts off with an image of the Speaker and dates of service, and thoughtfully categorized into logical subsections that guide the reader through the details: *Personal History; Early Years in Congress; The Vote; Acceptance Speech; Legacy as Speaker; After Leaving the Speakership.*

Each biography is strengthened by direct quotations — easily identified in italics — of the Speaker, or influential colleagues of the time. In addition, scattered throughout the biographical section are unique, original graphics - from autographs to personal letters - that not only give the reader an inside look at the Speaker, but also at the times during which he served. Biographies also include Further Reading, and cross references to Primary Documents that appear later in the book.

Historical Essays
Provides in-depth information, at an average of 6 pages each, on the office of the speakership. The topics of these nine essays are far reaching. You will read about the office's early formation in the House of Commons in England, controversial Speaker elections, the role of the Speaker during Presidential Impeachment, and even the difficulty in studying the speakership.

These historical essays are engagingly written, and provide facts and figures that will help give the reader a full understanding of why the office of speakership was created, and how it evolved into what some consider the most powerful in modern politics.

Primary Documents
This is a unique collection of 43 documents. From acceptance and resignation speeches, to articles with titles like "The New Speaker" (1899) and "... the Changing of the Guard" (1989), these documents are reprinted verbatim and fully sourced. The author sets the stage with an individual introduction for each document that gives timing, background and historical significance. Using cross-references, the reader can quickly link these Primary Documents to Speaker Bios, for a more complete understanding of each speaker's struggles and successes.

Timeline 1789 - 2009

This chronology of the speakership begins in 1789, when the House of Representatives met for the first time in Federal Hall in New York City, and ends with the passage of the 2009 American Recovery and Reinvestment Act. It includes significant events — such as the creation of committees, landmark votes, critical arguments, and the passage of laws - all as they relate to not only specific Speakers, but to the office of the speakership. It includes over 120 entries, most of which are not simply dates and events, but lengthy explanations of the "before" and "after" each significant event.

Appendices

These eight Appendices offer a fascinating look at the statistics of the speakership. These tables include: Years Served in Congress before being Elected Speaker; Votes of each Speaker Election; Midterm Election Results; Speakers by State; Congressional Distribution by Congress and Party. Each Appendix also includes a brief description.

Bibliography

More than 300 sources, organized in several categories, including Books, Articles, Unpublished Master's Theses and Dissertations, Official Government Documents.

Subject Index

This detailed subject index helps readers quickly find just what they are looking for, including individuals, places, legislation, publications and areas of significance to the office of the speakership.

Speakers of the House of Representatives 1789 - 2009 is the only resource of its kind. It offers an unequalled look at the men and woman given the distinct honor to work nearly always behind the political scenes, but the power to affect life-altering change for all Americans.

This first edition of *Speakers of the House of Representatives 1789 - 2009* is also available as an ebook. For more information, visit www.greyhouse.com.

Speaker Biographies

Frederick Augustus Conrad Muhlenberg

Served as Speaker:
April 1, 1789 - March 4, 1791
December 2, 1793 - March 4, 1795

Speaker of the House (1789-91, 1793-95), a Lutheran minister whose move into the political arena led to his serving as the President of the Pennsylvania Constitutional Convention (1787), which led to his election to a seat in the first Congress. Muhlenberg, the scion of a famed Pennsylvania family, served as the first Speaker in the first Congress, as well as the Speaker in the Third Congress, alternating in the first years of the legislative branch with Jonathan Trumbull, Jr. (Second Congress) and Jonathan Dayton (Fourth Congress). Speculation on the decision of the members of that first Federal Congress, which met in New York City in 1789, for selecting Muhlenberg for the distinguished post vary, but historians believe that his firm and resolute presiding over the Pennsylvania Constitutional Convention, which ratified the charter, led to his selection as Speaker.

Personal History

Frederick Muhlenberg came from an extremely influential family in early America. According to William Mann, the biographer of Frederick Muhlenberg's father, his ancestors, the von Mühlenbergs, came from

Mühlen (Mann says that the town is Mühlberg, but all other sources name it as Mühlen), the mill town ("muhlen" is German for mill) on the Elbe River in Saxony where the family originated about the tenth century in the form of Ziracka, a prince of the Wendish and Sorbic tribes, who converted to Christianity about 950 AD. Frederick's father, Henry Melchior Muhlenberg (1711-1787), born at Einbeck (also spelled Eimbeck in some source) in the Electoral Principality of Hanover, came to America in 1742 and is called the "Father of American Lutheranism" for his aiding and establishing the German wing of the Lutheran Church in this country. The father of 11 children, Henry saw two of his sons become famous in American history: John Peter Gabriel Muhlenberg (1746-1807), also a minister, sided, against his father's wishes, with the American Revolution in 1776 against the British crown, obtaining a commission with the backing of General George Washington.

In a moment noted by his John Peter's grandson a century later, in 1775 Peter Muhlenberg, in one of his sermons, exclaimed, "There is a time for all things: a time to preach and a time to pray; but there is also a time to fight, and that time has now come." Allegedly, he threw down his robe, revealing a military uniform - although the story is apocryphal and is perhaps myth. Henry Muhlenberg's other famous son, Frederick Augustus Conrad Muhlenberg, was born in the German settlement of Trappe, Pennsylvania, in Montgomery County in the eastern part of that state, on 1 January 1850. His father Henry had married Anna Maria (née Weiser), also a German immigrant, although little is known about her. In 1763, when he was 13, Frederick and his brothers John Peter Gabriel and Gotthilf Henry Ernest (known as Henry) moved to Germany, where they received their education. Frederick attended the Orphan House School of the Franckesche Stiftungen before he completed his education at the University of Halle (now the Martin Luther University of Halle-Wittenberg), in Saxony, where, like his father, he studied theology and became a Lutheran minister. Muhlenberg returned to the colonies with his brother Henry in September 1770 and the following month was ordained as a Lutheran minister by the United Evangelical Lutheran Congregations in Reading, Pennsylvania. From that period until 1773, he preached in several towns in Pennsylvania; in late 1773, he moved to New York City, where he had been invited to minister to the Swamp Church (also known as Christ Church) in what is now Manhattan. In 1771, Muhlenberg had married Catharine Schaefer, and the two had seven children.

During his time in New York, Muhlenberg became a supporter of the cause of those who opposed the British crown and desired to make the American colonies into a separate nation. In the summer of 1776, when the American Revolution exploded and the British prepared to invade New York City, Muhlenberg and his family left to return to Pennsylvania. He settled in Philadelphia, but when British forces moved into Pennsylvania in 1777 he and his family moved again - this time to New Hanover, Pennsylvania. He continued to preach in various churches in that area, but after three years he was compelled to seek employment to earn a better living. He opened a small goods store in Trappe.

Early Service in the Continental Congress
By the end of the 1770s, as the American nation fought a war for independence, Muhlenberg turned from religion to politics. In 1779, he was nominated -

without his approval - by the Pennsylvania Assembly to serve as one of the state's three seats in the Continental Congress. Muhlenberg served on several important committees in the Congress, but because of the dire economic situation in Pennsylvania little could be done; however, he was also optimistic, mixing religion and politics with ease. In a letter to one of his brothers in October 1780, Muhlenberg explained,

> The coffers are empty, the taxes almost unendurable, the people are in a bad humor, the money discredited, the army magazines exhausted, and the prospect to replenish them poor; the soldiers are badly clad, winter is coming...taking this and other things into account, public service might appear undesirable. However, let us one more take cheer and be steadfast, rely on God, and our own strength, and endure courageously, then we shall after be sure of reaching our goal.

Tiring of fighting about these issues, when the Continental Congress adjourned Muhlenberg accepted a seat in the Pennsylvania State Assembly and was elected Speaker. During this period, Muhlenberg wrote a series of articles - some in English, but many in German - defending his service in the Continental Congress and the body itself. By now, Muhlenberg was tiring of politics and was considering re-entering the ministry. In another letter to his family, written in either 1780 or 1781, he penned, "It us settled that I go to The Trappe in April, where I expect to recuperate in the solitude and quiet of rural life. For, believe me, I have become faint in body and soul. Take my remark as you please, I assure you I aim at nothing but the welfare of my country. Popularity I do not seek. The fool's praise or censure I do not mind."

But Muhlenberg remained in politics, and, in 1782, he was re-elected to the State Assembly, and again was elected Speaker. He was elected a member of the Board of Censors, which oversaw the finances of Pennsylvania, and, before that session of the Assembly ended, he was elected as President of the board. In his time outside of politics, he became involved in business matters in Philadelphia, and even served as a justice of the peace for several areas of Pennsylvania.

With the end of the revolution against British rule, the fledgling U.S. government was controlled by the

Articles of Confederation, a ragtag listing of measures that left the government strong in some areas and weak in others. By 1785, the Articles had become such a hindrance that a national movement to enact a federal Constitution began in the country. Frederick Muhlenberg was one of the first in his state to call for such a document to be composed. A convention held in the summer of 1787 drafted a document that was sent to the states for ratification. Both Frederick and Peter Muhlenberg became important figures in Pennsylvania in the effort to ratify the Constitution. Because the Federalists had a commanding control of the state legislation, when the convention set to debate the Constitution met in November 1787 it elected Frederick A.C. Muhlenberg as its president. With Frederick's and Peter's firm support behind the measure, on 12 December 1787 the document was ratified by a vote of 46 to 23. On 15 December, the convention sent a letter, signed by Frederick Muhlenberg as "President of the Convention of Pennsylvania," to the President of the Continental Congress, announcing that the state of Pennsylvania had ratified the Constitution.

Service in the New Federal Congress

Under the Constitution, Pennsylvania was to send eight members to sit in the new Federal Congress, which would not sit until 1789. Frederick and Peter Muhlenberg were selected as two of the eight by the State Assembly. In 1776 Frederick Muhlenberg had been forced to flee from New York City with his family to avoid British troops; now, 13 years later, he was returning to that capital city to sit in the first Federal Congress of the new nation. The controversy over the selection of New York City as the new national capital was widely debated.

In a letter from Thomas Jefferson, possibly to James Madison, and dated 2 November 1793, Jefferson penned,

> H.R. Lewis, [William] Rawle &c., all concur in the necessity that Congress should meet in Philadelphia, and vote their own adjournment. If it shall then be necessary to change the place, the question will be between New York and Lancaster [Pennsylvania]. The Pennsylvania members are very anxious for the latter, and will attend punctually to support it, as well as to support much for Muhlenburg [sic], and oppose

> the appointment of [William Loughton] Smith [1758-1812] (S.C.) speaker, which is intended by the Northern members.

The Vote

The House of Representatives was supposed to meet starting on 4 March 1789; however, because many of the representatives could not get to New York City on time, the body adjourned. Each day a roll was taken, and because so few members had arrived, the session was postponed and delayed until a quorum could be established. Finally, on 1 April, when James Schureman of New Jersey and Thomas Scott of Pennsylvania arrived, establishing a quorum, the House sat in session. Their first order of business: selecting a speaker. The journal of the House for that day notes:

> Resolved, That this House will proceed to the choice of a Speaker by ballot. The House accordingly proceeded to ballot for a Speaker, and upon examining the ballots, a majority of the votes of the whole House was found in favor of Frederick Augustus Muhlenberg, one of the Representatives for the State of Pennsylvania. Whereupon, the said Frederick Augustus Muhlenberg was conducted to the chair, from whence he made his acknowledgements to the House for so distinguished an honor.

Legacy as Speaker

The first duties of the new Congress were immense: there were no real national laws, and a new President, George Washington, had just been elected. The first duty was to count the electoral votes of the recently held election; Muhlenberg, as Speaker of the House, sat in a joint session with the U.S. Senate to count these tallies. Following that, a series of measures establishing executive departments, enacting revenue measures, creating a military for the nation, and drawing up a judicial system with a U.S. Supreme Court at its apex were all taken up in debate and voted on. In a letter to Richard Witty Peters, 18 June 1789, Muhlenberg complained about the massive growth of the federal government in such a short period:

> By Col. Delaney I have the Honour to transmit You a Sett [sic] of the Minutes of the House of Representatives, as far as they are at present

printed, and if you will be at the Trouble of having them filed I will transmit the preceeding [sic] Sheets as fast as they come from the press. I also inclose [sic] the Bill to establish the judicial Courts of the U. States as the same was reported to the Senate by a Comittee [sic] appointed for that purpose. A considerable Time I presume will elapse before the same is passed in the Senate & transmitted to our House, If your Time will permit to favour me with your Observations thereon you will lay me under particular Obligations. We have these two Days past had a very important and interesting Debate on a Motion to strike out the Words: "to be removeable by the president," in the bill for establ[ish]ing the Department of Foreign Affairs. The Question will probably be decided this Day, and I sincerely wish & hope the words may not be struck out, as without them I should consider the Act very imperfect indeed. The Anti's now begin to discover themselves, and they are on this Occasion bringing their whole force to a point, I think I see an antifederal [sic] Monster growing, which if it should gain Strength will I fear interrupt the Harmony with which we have hitherto proceeded.

At the same time, Muhlenberg complained about the low salary that was paid to members of that first Congress - just six dollars a day, which covered housing, meals, and transportation, especially in a city like New York even in that period: "This proves fully that the good of the United States requires a removal from this place, & whenever this happens I shall cheerfully vote to lessen the Salaries," he explained in a letter that showed his early support to move the Congress from New York City and to a "national" capital. He continued, "You have no conception at what extravagant rates every thing is paid for in this place, and the general principle seems to be this, That as the stay of Congress is doubtfull [sic] it is necessary to take time by the forelock."

A history of the House of Representatives, published by Congress in 1994, delved into the early history of the House and discussed the work of the first Congress under Muhlenberg's speakership:

The First Congress enacted many important and useful laws. It met for three sessions lasting a total of 519 days. It has not only to organize itself and to establish the basic institutions of the new government, but also to lay the foundations of the American economy. More than 60 major statutes were the legislative fruit of its efforts. It created the War, Treasury, and Foreign Affairs (State) Departments. It established the judicial courts of the United States, a Land Office, and a government for the Northwest Territory. It passed a tariff bill, an invalid pensions measure, and a bill for the regulation of the coastal trade. It established the permanent seat of the national government and fixed the compensation of executive and judicial officers and employees. It enacted the first annual appropriations acts, passed several relief bills, and legislated the first ten amendments to the Constitution. It considered scores of memorials and petitions as well as laws regulating patents and copyrights, bankruptcies, harbors, the punishment of crimes, naturalization, the importation of slaves, and intercourse with the Indian tribes. It also considered bills for the establishment of lighthouses and hospitals, the encouragement of commerce and navigation, the establishment of a uniform militia, conveyance of the mails, claims against the United States, the remission of fines, the encouragement of learning, progress of the useful arts, succession to the Presidency, reduction of the public debt, rates of foreign exchange, and the admission of Kentucky and Vermont into the Union.

Muhlenberg returned home in 1790, and was re-elected to a seat to serve in the Second Congress. Because the members of that body chose to not have one man serve more than one term as Speaker, those of that body selected Jonathan Trumbull, Jr., as the Speaker. During this Second Congress, a number of bills regarding the reform of the revenue collection system in the nation, which had become unpopular, came up for debate and passage. In the Third Congress, to which he was also elected, Muhlenberg became the candidate of the majority Federalist Party to serve as Speaker, and, after a vote against Anti-Federalist Theodore Sedgwick, Muhlenberg was again elected, despite the earlier agreement not to have any one man serve more than one term as Speaker. Reasons for the dissolution of the agreement are rarely delved upon in history books; however, it can be surmised that Muhlenberg was the most popular Federalist in the House, and, with his party in the majority, it was almost a foregone conclusion that he would be selected as the House leader. During this second tenure as Speaker, Muhlenberg oversaw discussions on taxation and revenue collection. Re-elected in 1794, he saw Jonathan Dayton selected as Speaker in the Fourth Congress. Muhlenberg never served again as Speaker.

After Leaving the Speakership
In the Fourth Congress (1795-97), perhaps the most contentious matter was the ratification of the Jay Treaty. Even though more than a decade had passed since the Revolutionary War had ended, Britain had not, as the treaty of peace had laid out, remunerated America for war reparations, and the English were also infringing on American territory and American sovereignty in the Caribbean; at the same time, British ships routinely stopped American ships on the high seas and seized, or "impressed," American sailors into duty into the British Navy. To end the disputes, President Washington sent former Chief Justice of the Supreme Court John Jay to London to negotiate an end to the diplomatic row. In 1795, Jay returned to the United States with what he believed was an amicable end to the problems between the former enemies; this agreement with Great Britain, however, was so divisive because it was seen as a capitulation to the British that Jay was burned in effigy in some American cities.

While the U.S. Senate ratified the treaty, several portions of it - including appropriating funds for the treaty to be implemented - had to be ratified as well by the House. Historian John Miller, in a history of the Federalists in power at the end of the eighteenth century, wrote,

> On April 29, 1796...the question of carrying the treaty into execution came before the House as a committee of the whole. The vote revealed that the representatives were evenly divided for and against implementing the treaty; whereupon Frederick Muhlenberg, the chairman of the House and a Republican, cast his vote in favor. This proved decisive: the next day, when a roll call vote was called for, the bill was passed by a vote of fifty-one to forty-eight. For this "base

> desertion of his party," Muhlenberg failed of re-election to the House in the next election. But a swifter and more dramatic retribution overtook him: a few days after he broke the deadlock in the House he was stabbed by his brother-in-law, a rabid Republican.

Returning home and out of politics for the first time in more than a decade, Muhlenberg nonetheless remained close to the debates in the political realm, becoming a member of the National Republican Party, led by Thomas Jefferson, and he supported Jefferson in print with the publication of several articles in English and German that were given wide circulation in Pennsylvania. In 1800, the Collector General of the Pennsylvania Land Office was removed by Governor Thomas McKean; the governor then asked Muhlenberg to take the vacant office. Muhlenberg agreed, and took office on 8 January 1800. But, at the time, he was seriously ill, but nevertheless moved to the-then capital, Lancaster, to do his work. Within a year, however, Muhlenberg was unable to continue. On 4 June 1801, just months after leaving his final political post, Muhlenberg died in Lancaster at the age of just 51. He was buried in Woodward Hill Cemetery in Lancaster. A plaque erected on his tomb years later reads, "Sacred to the Memory of Frederick Augustus Muhlenberg, Who was Born on the 1st Day of January, 1750, and Departed This Life on the 4th Day of June, 1801, aged 51 Years, 5 months, and 5 days." His time as a Lutheran minister is noted first; his service as the first Speaker of the U.S. House of Representatives is listed last among his accomplishments.

Further Reading:
Aldrich, John H., and Ruth W. Grant, "The Antifederalists, the First Congress, and the First Parties," *The Journal of Politics*, LV:2 (May 1993), 295-326.

Galloway, George B., "Precedents Established in the First Congress," *The Western Political Quarterly*, 11:3 (September 1958), 454-68.

Wilson, Rick K., "Transitional Governance in the United States: Lessons from the First Federal Congress," *Legislative Studies Quarterly*, XXIV:4 (November 1999), 543-68.

Jonathan Trumbull, Jr.

Served as Speaker:
October 24, 1791 - March 4, 1793

T he second Speaker of the House of Representatives, Jonathan Trumbull was, like his predecessor (and successor) in the Speaker's chair, Frederick A.C. Muhlenberg, the scion of a famed early American family. His incredibly successful political career, in which he served in the Treasury Department (1778-79), in the House of Representatives, in the Senate, and as Governor of Connecticut, is capped by his a single term as Speaker of the House, in which he was able, for the first time by a Speaker, to name the members of committees in the House, an expansion of the limited powers of that office.

Personal History

Trumbull was born in Lebanon, Connecticut, on 26 March 1740, the second son of Jonathan Trumbull, Sr., a longtime Connecticut politician, and his wife Faith (née Robinson), the daughter of a noted minister in Connecticut, the Rev. John Robinson, and a direct descendant of John and Priscilla Alden, two of the first colonists who sailed on the *Mayflower*. Historian I.W. Stuart's 1859 work on the elder Trumbull is the comprehensive work on the family's background, although some critics consider it un-

critical of Trumbull. He noted that the family originated in Scotland, "and owed its heraldic origin to the desperate gallantry of a young peasant, who when one of the kings of that country, being engaged in the chase, was attacked by a bull, and was in eminent danger," threw himself upon the bull and grabbed him by the horns, saving the king's life, he was graced by the king with the name *Turnbull* and given an estate in Scotland with the coat of arms showing three bulls' heads. Later members of this family moved to England, their name changing to *Trumble*. John Trumble of Cumberland County, England, came to America sometime in the seventeenth century and settled in Rowley, in Essex County, Massachusetts Colony.

A series of generations of farmers in and around the colonies of what is now the American northeast saw the name change from Trumble to Trumbull, and led to Jonathan Trumbull, Sr., born in Lebanon, Connecticut, on 12 October 1710. He rose to be elected Governor of Connecticut, serving from 1769 to 1784. Among his other five children was his son John Trumbull (1756-1843), who painted some of the most patriotic scenes of early America, including the surrenders of General John Burgoyne at Saratoga and Lord Cornwallis at Yorktown, as well as signing of the Declaration of Independence, while Joseph Trumbull served as a member of the Continental Congress (1774) and was Commissary General of the Continental Army (1775-77).

Jonathan Trumbull, Jr. received private tutoring from a local teacher, Nathan Tisdale, and in 1755, when only 15 years old, he was allowed to begin studies at Harvard College (now Harvard University). He was the salutatorian when he graduated in 1759, and remained at that school to earn his Master's degree in 1762. He returned to Lebanon, Connecticut, where he opened a small goods store to earn a living. In 1769, he married Eunice Backus.

Jonathan Trumbull's political career began in 1770, when he was elected to a seat on the Lebanon town Board of Selectmen. He remained in that position until 1775, when he was elected to a seat in the Connecticut General Assembly. On 28 July 1775, the Continental Congress, sitting in Philadelphia, unanimously named Trumbull as the "Pay master [sic] of the forces for the New York department," with the rank of Colonel. Trumbull's father, who served as Governor of Connecticut from 1769 to 1783, was an intimate of General George Washington, who referred to the elder Trumbull as "Brother Jonathan." Thus, to have the son of a close friend of Washington named to such a high position by the Continental Congress is not unheard of. Trumbull's brother, Joseph, died after a period of ill health on 23 July 1778, and Jonathan Trumbull resigned his office two days later, a move that was accepted by the Continental Congress four days after that. After working on his brother's affairs, Trumbull accepted the election to the Connecticut General Assembly again, serving as Speaker of that body that year. On 3 November 1778, the Continental Congress elected Trumbull as the first Comptroller, or supervisor of budgetary matters, of the U.S. Treasury. Trumbull served in this latter position until 8 June 1781, when he was named by the Continental Congress as General Washington's official secretary, succeeding Alexander Hamilton. A letter to the Board of Treasury, established under the Articles of Confederation to oversee budgetary matters in the weak national government (and which was supplanted by the Department of the Treasury following the pas-

sage of the Constitution in 1787), dated 23 June 1781, informed the Continental Congress that Trumbull was moving to work for General Washington, and that a blank space was left to show that there was no successor named to succeed him (misspellings have been left as they appeared in the original document):

Treasury Office June 23rd 1781

Whereas it appears by a letter to the Auditor General dated the 14th instant from Jonathan Trumbull Junr Commissioner appointed by Congress to settle the Acc^ts in the Depart^t of the late Comm^ry Genl of Purchases Joseph Trumbull, deceased, that he has at the request of his Excell^cy Genl Washington gone into his Family as his Secretary whereby a further prosecution of the settlement of the said Acc^ts is impeded; and it being necessary that the Acc^ts of the said Depart^t should be settled as speedily as possible, the following resolution is submitted -

Resolved, That _____ be and is hereby appointed a Commissioner in the room of Jonathan Trumbull J^r to prosecute in the settlement of the Acc^ts of the D^y purchasing and issuing Commisaries under the late Commisary Genl Joseph Trumbull Dec^d and in all other respects to perform the duties assigned to the said Jonathan Trumbull by the Act of Congress of the 5th of May 1779.

During his service to Washington, Trumbull held the rank of Lieutenant Colonel and held the official title of "military secretary." On 10 June 1783, Stephen Higginson of Massachusetts nominated Trumbull to serve as Secretary of Foreign Affairs - the equivalent of the Secretary of State - under the Articles of Confederation, but the post was given to John Jay.

Early Years in Congress

In late 1788, Trumbull was elected to a seat in the first Federal Congress, which opened in Philadelphia on 4 March 1789. He held this seat through the First (1789-91), Second (1791-93) and Third (1793-95) Congresses. In the First Congress, the members elected Frederick A.C. Muhlenberg of Pennsylvania as Speaker.

The Vote

In the Second Congress, there was a desire to elect a different member to hold that office so as not to have the power of the Speaker, however limited, in one member's hands for more than one Congress. When the Second Congress convened in Philadelphia on 24 October 1791, 69 members, with 39 "pro-administration" and 30 "anti-administration," held seats in the House, and they proceeded to the election of a Speaker. According to the *Journal of the House*, on the first ballot Trumbull won a majority of the votes, and was conducted to the chair to be sworn.

Acceptance Speech

After being sworn in as the new Speaker, he addressed the members:

> *Gentlemen: I find my self unable to express to you the full sense I have of the distinguished honor you have done me in the choice of your Speaker.*
>
> *The diffidence I feel in my abilities to discharge, with propriety, the duties of the Chair, is almost insuperable in my own mind. But, encouraged by the known candor of this Honorable body, and depending, as I think I may confidently do, on the kind assistance of each individual in it, I shall enter on its duties, with full assurances to you, Gentlemen, that I shall endeavor to conduct myself with that impartiality, integrity, and assiduity, which become the conspicuous station in which you have been pleased to place me.*

The reasons for Trumbull's selection over the more experienced Muhlenberg are clouded in the lack of records from the period; however, historian Mary Follett, in her 1902 work on the speakership and the role it played in the history of the nation up until that time, explained that loyalty to the Washington administration may have been the chief reason the Connecticut representative was named as Speaker:

> *The reason for the substitution of Trumbull in the [second] Congress may have been that suggested by Hildreth - the principle of rotation in office. Still Muhlenberg had shown signs of a leaning away from administration measures, and Trumbull may have been more trusted.*

Unfortunately, that is all Follett - or anyone else - can surmise for Trumbull's selection.

Legacy as Speaker

Trumbull served as Speaker from 24 October 1791 until the end of the Second Congress on 3 March 1793. Some histories mistakenly note that Trumbull served longer; one stated that "he served as Speaker from 1791 until his transfer to the Senate in 1795," clearly an error.

It was an age in which there were no established parties as we have today. Although listed as "pro-administration," Trumbull was, as was President Washington, a Federalist. Contemporary newspapers actually split the members of Congress into "Strict Constructionists" and "Loose Constructionists," with Trumbull being a member of the former group. Hubert Bruce Fuller, in his history of the House, explained, "Trumbull was an earnest Federalist whose orthodoxy was unquestioned, while Muhlenberg had wavered in his allegiance to certain administration measures. Still, sectional prejudice and the plea for rotation in the office - the American theory that every man fitted for office must have his turn - were probably more decisive factors in the displacement" of Muhlenberg. As Speaker, Trumbull was opposed by those opposed to the administration - the "anti-Federalists." The *American Whig Review*, the official magazine of the Whig Party in the middle of the nineteenth century, noted in October 1849,

> *A high degree of irritation prevailed during th[is] session [of Congress when Trumbull served as Speaker], and extended to the cabinet; Messrs. [Thomas] Jefferson and [Alexander] Hamilton, the acknowledged leaders of the parties, became irreconcilably hostile to each other. The object of the anti-Federalists, it had now become apparent, was the election of Mr. Jefferson to the presidency, when it should be vacated by Washington. At his insistence, they dropped their name, and substituted that if Republicans, but were called by the Federalists Democrats, a name to which they were not then partial.*

As with Speaker Muhlenberg in the First Congress, the speakership under Trumbull functioned merely as a moderator of debate. In January 1790, during the First Congress, the members had voted to allow the Speaker to choose the members of the respective committees. Originally, this power was to be given to all members by ballot, but this change in the rules, which was utilized first by Trumbull, was the first step in the evolution of the Speaker as the organizer of the House's functions and manager of its work.

On 28 October 1791, Trumbull addressed the House, aiming his remarks at President Washington:

> In receiving your address at the opening of the present session, the House of Representatives have taken an ample share in the feelings inspired by the actual prosperity, and flattering prospects of our country: and whilst, with becoming gratitude to heaven, we ascribe this happiness to the true source from which it flows, we behold with an animating pleasure, the degree in which the constitution and laws of the United States have been instrumental in dispensing it.
>
> It yields us particular satisfaction to learn the success with which the different important measures of the government have proceeded; as well as those specially provided for at the last session, as those of preceding date. The safety of our Western Frontiers, in which the lives and repose of our fellow citizens are involved, being peculiarly interesting, your communications on that subject are proportionally grateful to us. The gallantry and good conduct of the Militia, whose services were called for, are an honorable confirmation of the efficacy of that precious resource of a free State.

Historian De Alva Stanwood Alexander notes in his landmark 1916 work on the history and procedure of the House of Representatives that under Trumbull the committees of the House became more partisan, due to the change in rules allowing the Speaker to name committee members. In 1791, after a number of abolitionist societies sent memorials to the congress "for promoting the abolition of slavery, for the relief of free negroes, unlawfully held in bondage, and for improving the condition of the Africa race," Trumbull appointed members who Alexander noted "either opposed or [were] indifferent to the object of the investigation."

Because of the dearth of records from the early Congresses, few speeches or bills exist with Trumbull's name on them. Contemporary newspapers do report that he shepherded bills supporting "an act more effectually to provide for the National Defence, by establishing an [sic] Uniform Militia throughout the United States," as well as an act concerning the distilling of spirits in the country, but this appears to be all in the official record. As Speaker, Trumbull laid before the House a letter from the Library Company of Philadelphia offering its collection of books to the Congress. On 6 April 1792, he moderated when the House voted to apportion the next Congress based on the 1790 census, expanding that body to 120 members.

In the Third Congress (1793-95), those who had been "anti-administration" in the first two congresses and were now allied with Secretary of State Thomas Jefferson as "anti-Federalists" gained control of the House, and chose to elect former Speaker Muhlenberg to a second term despite his Federalist past; turned aside for a second term as speaker, Trumbull remained in the House.

After Leaving the Speakership

In 1794, Trumbull decided against running for a fourth term in the House, instead entering the race to succeed Senator Stephen Mix Mitchell, who had chosen not to run for re-election after serving the last two years of a vacancy in the Senate. Trumbull was elected to the seat by the Connecticut legislature, and took his seat in the U.S. Senate on 4 March 1795. He held that seat until his resignation on 10 June 1796, having been elected Lieutenant Governor of Connecticut. Working with Governor Oliver Wolcott, who had served in Washington's administration as Secretary of the Treasury, Trumbull succeeded Wolcott upon the latter's death on 1 December 1797, and, as his father had once served in that office, the son followed the father into the governorship of the state of Connecticut. Trumbull remained as Governor until his death, winning reelection every year for the next 11 years. He also served, at the same time, as the chief Judge of the Supreme Court of Errors, the court of appeals for the state.

In 1809, Trumbull became embroiled in the controversy over the Embargo Act and its successor enactment, the Non-Intercourse Act. In 1807, the Congress had enacted the Embargo Act to force bans on the shipment of goods to England and France, then fighting each other in a continental war in Europe that threatened to spread to the United States. This action was extremely unpopular, especially in New England, where most of the manufactured merchandise made there was shipped to England and France. Based on pressure from representatives from the region, on 1 March 1809, in the last days of the administration of Thomas Jefferson, Congress enacted the Non-Intercourse Act, which rescinded embargoes against all American shipping except those sent to England and France. Again, the Congress had misread the mood of the American people, particularly those in the New England region, and there were calls for its revocation as well. Trumbull, as Governor of Connecticut, sided with the manufacturers of his state and refused to comply, especially when President James Madison ordered that the Connecticut state militia be called out to enforce the embargo. A series of conventions were called in New England to resist the orders of the Madison administration, and Trumbull took the lead in calling the embargo unconstitutional.

On 7 August 1809, in the midst of the crisis over the actions of the federal and state governments, Trumbull succumbed to "dropsy of the heart" at his home in Lebanon, Connecticut, at the age of 69. He was laid to rest in the East Cemetery in Lebanon. The *Connecticut Courant* of Hartford noted in the paper's obituary of Trumbull that he left "behind him a character for worth unrivalled, and admired by all great and good men to whom he was known." His home, now known as the Jonathan Trumbull, Jr., House, is a national landmark in Lebanon, Connecticut. Lieutenant Governor John Treadwell succeeded Trumbull, and continued to fight against the embargo even after war with Britain began in 1812. Trumbull County, Ohio, was named in his honor. A history of that state noted in 1891, "If there is anything in a name to divert aspiration or give inspiration, it would have been difficult to find a more significant gift for a political division of territory. There are few names in American history possessing an equal range of meaning."

Excepting the dissertation by his biographer, John Ifkovic, few works that mention Jonathan Trumbull

have any serious discussion on his speakership, preferring instead to emphasize his service during the American Revolution or as Governor of Connecticut. As with many of the Speakers of the early period, Trumbull's tenure was based mainly on the model held by the British House of Commons, with the Speaker serving as a mere moderator of debate with few powers rather than the powerful Speaker that we have today who controls floor motions, committee and majority party agendas, and is one of the leading politicians in the nation. Trumbull's naming of committee members was a first for a Speaker, but that appears to have been the most important power that he wielded. It would not be until Henry Clay became Speaker two decades later that the power of the Speaker would be expanded.

Further Reading:
"Biographical Sketch of the Character of Governor Trumbull," *Connecticut Courant*, 1 November 1809, 2.

Journal of the House of Representatives of the United States, Being the First Session of the Second Congress: Begun and Held at the City of Philadelphia, October 24, 1791, and in the Sixteenth Year of the Independence of the Said States. Reprinted by Order of the House of Representatives (Washington: Printed by Gales & Seaton, 1826), 434.

Jonathan Dayton

Served as Speaker:
December 7, 1795 - March 4, 1799

He is the only signer of the Declaration of Independence to serve as Speaker of the U.S. House of Representatives; his lengthy political career included service in the New Jersey General Assembly, as a delegate to both the Constitutional Convention in 1787 as well as to the Continental Congress, as Speaker of the House in the Fourth (1795-97) and Fifth (1797-99) Congresses, and in the U.S. Senate (1799-1805). A veteran of the American Revolution, Jonathan Dayton was later implicated and arrested for being involved with the alleged conspiracy by former Vice President Aaron Burr to seize land in what is now the western United States, but he was never tried for treason. Despite this apparent "vindication," Dayton's name remains stained by his association with Burr, and many historians consider him one of the lesser occupants of the office of Speaker of the House.

Personal History

Dayton was born in Elizabethtown (now Elizabeth, New Jersey), formerly in Essex County, but now in Union County, on 16 October 1760, the eldest son of Elias Dayton, a wealthy merchant who later served in the American Revolution as a Brigadier General in the Continental Army, and his wife Hannah (née Rolfe) Dayton. Elias Dayton was a General of Brigade during the American Revolution, and although his name is not remembered now he was a distinguished officer in the conflict whose name was uttered with pride in his home state. The few sources that exist on the ancestry of the Dayton family show that the first member to come to America, Ralph Dayton, the Speaker's great-grandfather, emigrated from England and settled on Long Island in New York about 1650. His son, also named Jonathan Dayton, sailed from England and settled in Elizabethtown, in Essex County, New Jersey, around the period 1720-25. Elias Dayton (1737-1807), the father of the Speaker, served with distinction during the American Revolution, rising to the rank of Brigadier General. Historians Robert Wright, Jr., and Morris MacGregor, Jr., write of Dayton in a history of those men who fought in the American Revolution and signed the Declaration of Independence, "Dayton's father, Elias...was a militia officer in the French and Indian War who returned home to prosper as a merchant and colonial official. Dayton was clearly influenced by his family's position in the community and his father's ideas about government. Both men, like most Americans of their day, believed that the average citizen should defer to the views of his 'betters,' while prominent citizens, those with the largest stake in society, had an obligation to lead the community, sacrificing their own interests if necessary for the common good."

Jonathan Dayton's early education is merely guessed at by scholars: they believe that he probably attended the Elizabethtown Academy, and, about 1774, entered the College of New Jersey, now Princeton University. He graduated in 1776, but left to fight with the Continental Army and missed his commencement. (Dayton's official congressional biography mentions that prior to leaving college he "studied the law [and] was admitted to the bar." Other sources note that Princeton later bestowed on Dayton an honorary Doctor of Laws degree.) With the outset of the conflict, both Dayton and his father lent themselves in service to the colonial cause. Initially, they served together on the enforcement committee of Elizabethtown; in 1775, when a revolt arose against New Jersey's Royal Governor, William Franklin (the son of patriot Benjamin Franklin), a newly-formed Provincial Congress met to form a militia to fight the British and named the senior Dayton as the commander of the Third New Jersey Regiment. Elias Dayton, in turn, selected his 15-year-old son as an ensign in the unit.

During the American Revolution, Jonathan Dayton served as a member of the Third, and then later the Second, New Jersey Regiment of the Continental Army, rising to the rank of captain. He saw action in support of the American invasion of Canada, the construction and defense of Fort Schuyler (later Fort Stanwix in what is now Rome, New York), the battles of Brandywine Creek (1777), Germantown (1777), and Monmouth (1777). Both Daytons spent time with Washington's troops at Valley Forge during the winter of 1777. Jonathan Dayton was then named as an aide-de-camp to General John Sullivan, and with Sullivan's forces fought against the Iroquois in upstate New York (1779).

Returning to New Jersey, Dayton fought against the British at Springfield, New Jersey, from 7 to 23 June 1780. Four months later, on 5 October 1780, Dayton was captured by pro-British Tories at Herd's Tavern in Connecticut Farms (now Union, New Jersey), and handed over to the British. He was sent to what is now Staten Island, New York, where the British kept their prisoners of war. His time as a POW was short, however, when he was exchanged for a British prisoner held by the Americans. Assigned to the staff of General Benjamin Lincoln, Dayton was present at the siege of Yorktown (1782),

afterwards sent north to New York, where he served around New Windsor, New York. He was there when the war ended, and he was released from army service on 3 November 1783. According to every biography on Dayton, it was around this time, but with no exact date mentioned, that he married Susannah Williamson, also of Elizabethtown, and the brother of Matthias Williamson, a fellow student of Dayton's at the College of New Jersey. The two would eventually have one child.

According to the *American National Biography*, Dayton studied the law *after* the war and was admitted to the New Jersey bar in 1786 which, as previously noted, is in conflict with Dayton's congressional biography. Nevertheless, it is apparent that he never practiced the law for a lengthy period; in 1786, he was elected to a seat in the New Jersey Assembly, where he served for a single term until 1787. He also served for a single year, in 1790, in the same body. Historian Richard A. Harrison explained, "When the legislative session ended in May 1787, Dayton was already known as New Jersey's most industrious speculator in public debts and securities. His position in the assembly provided him with information to which other speculators were not privy, and he prospered. He also showed an interest in the settlement of the American West as early as November 1786, when he chaired a committee in the legislature that instructed New Jersey's congressional delegates to insist upon the country's right to navigate the Mississippi." Such speculation, particularly in the western expanses of the nation, would eventually lead to Dayton's political and economic downfall.

At the same time that Dayton was serving in the state legislature, he also served as one of the founders of the New Jersey chapter of the Society of the Cincinnati, a fraternal organization founded by Revolutionary veterans, and, with his father, formed "E. Dayton and Son," a mercantile business in Elizabethtown.

Early Years in Congress
In 1787, when notable public citizens were being named as delegates as a New Jersey delegate to the Federal Constitutional Convention, held in Philadelphia, to form a new government to replace the one run under the wholly ineffective Articles of

Confederation, Abraham Clark, a New Jerseyan who signed the Declaration of Independence, was named to his state's slate of delegates, but he demurred from the service. Due to his service during the American Revolution, Elias Dayton was requested to serve as a substitute to Clark. When the elder Dayton turned down the honor, Jonathan Dayton was named in his stead. Some of Dayton's correspondence from the convention has been preserved. For instance, on 28 June 1787, Dayton wrote to a friend regarding a speech delivered by fellow delegate Benjamin Franklin (whom he calls "Doctor Franklin") on the opening of future congressional sessions to be opened by a prayer:

The Doctor sat down; and never did I behold a countenance at once so dignified and delighted as was that of Washington at the close of the address; nor were the members of the convention generally less affected. The words of the venerable Franklin fell upon our ears with a weight an authority, even greater that we may suppose an oracle to have had in a Roman Senate!

Dayton was named to a group of delegates who would be responsible for the formation of the American government. Although he supported the initiatives of others who backed a tripartite form of government - forming Executive, Legislative, and Judicial branches - Dayton's real contribution to the convention was his idea for an "Electoral College" to decide who was elected President of the United States, instead of a system of direct voting for the presidency.

Returning home to New Jersey, Dayton found that his work at the convention had made him even more popular at home than even his service in the war had. The state legislature, in which he had served, quickly elected him to the closing session of the Continental Congress, then wrapping up business in Philadelphia. When his work there was concluded, Dayton returned to his seat in the lower house of the state legislature, serving as Speaker in 1790. That year, he was elected to a seat in the new federal House of Representatives, and took his seat in the Second Congress (1791-93). He would eventually serve a total of four terms in that body.

Taking his seat as a Federalist - the political party of President George Washington - he sided with the economic policies of Secretary of the Treasury Alexander Hamilton (with whom he had attended college). On 27 March 1794, Dayton recommended that the U.S. government take control of all debts owed by Americans to the British and "sequester" until the total value of the American assets seized by the British be totaled and counted against what was owed. Speaking on the floor of the House, he made extended remarks on the subject (which, like other remarks, were taken down in a third-person viewpoint by the congressional reporter):

The injuries and insults we have suffered from Great Britain, he conceived, need not be dwelt upon. They are well known, and it is universally acknowledged that we ought to adopt such measures as would screen us from a repetition of them, and secure to us reparation. The resolutions he had brought forward he intended as part of that system of defence and preservation, other portions of which had already received the sanction of the House. These resolutions, he conceived, would not be the least efficient part of that system.

During these early terms in Congress, Dayton worked to get congressional support for the Jay Treaty.

The Vote

On 7 December 1795, the first session of the Fourth Congress opened in Philadelphia. After the representatives were sworn in, the House then proceeded to the election of a Speaker. Frederick A.C. Muhlenberg of Pennsylvania had served as the Speaker in the First (1789-91) and Third (1793-95) Congresses, while Jonathan Trumbull had alternated with Muhlenberg by serving in the Second (1791-93) Congress. By 1795, however, the representatives were looking for a new occupant for the Speaker's chair. A vote was held, and Dayton was elected with no apparent opposition.

Acceptance Speech

He was conducted to the chair, and, before being sworn in, made a few comments to the assembled representatives:

Gentlemen: It is with real diffidence that I undertake the execution of the duties which you have done me the honor to assign to me. In dis-

charging them to the best of my abilities, I antic-
ipate, on your part, a liberal and indulgent
temper towards those decisions which may be
required from the Chair, and flatter myself that
I shall experience, upon all occasions, your
co-operation and support.

Dayton received congratulations from his close friend John Cleves Symmes (1742-1818), a fellow land speculator from New Jersey who served as a delegate to the Continental Congress (1785-86), who wrote, "I beg leave to congratulate you, Sir, on your appointment to the chair of the House of Representatives - this fact I have learned from report, not having seen any public paper for some weeks past; I hope you will find 'honor's easy chair' both agreeable and profitable, for $12 a day is very pretty [sic]: though I know not of what is expected, not how frequent the entertainments are which is usual for a Speaker of the House to give."

Legacy as Speaker

During his two terms as Speaker, which also coincided with his final two terms in the House, Dayton stood closely with the Federalist policies of the administration of President John Adams. When the Fifth Congress (1797-99) convened in Philadelphia on 15 May 1797, Dayton was re-elected Speaker, the first man to receive that honor in consecutive congresses. When a fight erupted on the floor of the House in 1798 between Reps. Matthew Lyon of Vermont and Roger Griswold of Connecticut, drawings of the incident show Dayton sitting in the Speaker's chair, the first time that a speaker was shown wielding any sort of power. In another historic move, Dayton presided over the first impeachment inquiry, involving Senator William Blount of Tennessee. Following a series of speculations in land in the western United States, as well as attempts to get Creek and Cherokee Indians to rise up against the Spanish and side with the British (and cause the lands to be sold eventually to the United States), Blount was impeached by the House on 3 July 1797. Blount had resigned (or had been expelled) on 8 July 1797, and the subsequent impeachment trial in the Senate ended because the body had no jurisdiction over his case any longer. Dayton continued to push the issue: on 3 January 1799, in a letter to Rep. James Ashton Bayard, Sr., chairman of the House manag-

ers who were administering the case of the House in the U.S. Senate, Dayton argued that

The House of Representatives of the United
States, prosecuting, on behalf of themselves and
the people of the United States, the Articles of
Impeachment exhibited by them to the Senate of
the United States against the said William
Blount, reply to the plea of the said William
Blount, and say, that the matters alleged in the
said plea are not sufficient to exempt the said
William Blount from answering the said Arti-
cles of Impeachment, because they say that, by
the Constitution of the United States, the
House of Representatives had power to prefer
the said Articles of Impeachment, and that the
Senate have the full and sole power to try the
same. Whereupon they demand that the plea
aforesaid, of the said William Blount, be not al-
lowed, but that the said William Blount be
compelled to answer the said Articles of Im-
peachment.

Unfortunately, other than some letters and records that make for rather dry reading, there is little record of what Dayton did as Speaker. This goes for nearly all of the early Speakers up to Henry Clay; at the time, the speakership was not seen in the same light of importance as it soon became and is now. William Henry Smith, whose 1928 history of the speakership and biographies of those who held the office was the first of its kind, stated,

[Dayton] was very active in debate, taking part
in almost every one. Even when Speaker he took
advantage of the House being in [the] Commit-
tee of the Whole to press his views on his col-
leagues...As Speaker he was always dignified. He
was a partisan Federalist, but the opposition
never charged him with being unduly partial in
his rulings. While in the Second and Third Con-
gresses he had been a frequent speaker, taking
part in all the major debates; in the Fourth and
Fifth Congresses he rarely addressed the House,
except when called upon for an interpretation of
some provision of the Constitution.

Ironically, at the same time that Dayton was presiding over charges against William Blount, he was speculating himself in land deals that would ultimately be his undoing. In the years since entering the House, and especially while serving as Speaker, Dayton was also engaging in extremely unethical land speculation, some of it done while using the power of the office of the Speaker as an imprimatur. In a letter to Secretary of the Treasury Oliver Wolcott, dated 15 September 1796, Dayton urged the Secretary to quickly allot funds for the survey of lands in the western areas of the United States, moneys that were supposed to be used for the discovery of potential military posts and other governmental sites but which Dayton wanted to have used so he and his friends could purchase them outright. In the letter, Dayton mentioned critics of the government's policy on finding such lands: "I hear some of them remark with pain, that the President and members have lands of their own to sell, or they would not be so neglectful in providing for the location of the military warrants, which then might come in competition with them." he penned. "The fact as to many of us holding such lands being undeniable, the imputation becomes from that circumstance more plausible, and enforces the necessity on the part of our government to defeat, as soon as possible, the charge of neglect."

After Leaving the Speakership

In 1798, Dayton was elected, as a Federalist, to a seat in the United States Senate. Serving from 4 March 1799 to 3 March 1805, he supported the Judiciary Act of 1801, which established the foundation of the American court system, the Louisiana Purchase of lands in the central United States that doubled the size of the nation, and voted for the acquittal of Justice Samuel Chase of the U.S. Supreme Court in Chase's impeachment trial.

Dayton's world began to come apart in 1800, when he sued two men, Francis Childs and William Denning, for debts they allegedly owed him. Childs and Denning then published "Public Speculation Unfolded" (1800), in which they charged that Dayton, while a public official as well as Speaker of the House had used his offices to enact legislation that aided him in land speculation, making him a rich man. Childs released numerous letters showing that "the said Jonathan Dayton was then Speaker of the House of Representatives in Congress, and resided, at that time, in the city of Philadelphia, and from his situation in public life, well knowing the advantages which would result from speculating in

land-office warrants, projected a speculation, and wrote to this defendant, in the city of New-York, to purchase a quantity of paper of that description." In one letter, Dayton wrote:

I transmit herewith Finlay's Commercial Register, which may be useful to you and L.D. & Co. as [a] matter of information. I hope to hear from you upon the subject of the warrants, when the mail which left New York yesterday arrives here. A large company is forming itself here, for the purchase of United States lands, and a part of their capital is to be 2000 military land warrants; but it will impossible for the company to procure them without paying a very high price.

Yours in haste,

Jona. Dayton.

P.S. You need not mention my name.

In later correspondence which Childs and Denning published, Dayton signed his name "Jona. D." and, much later, simply as "J.D."

When word of these allegations surfaced, a congressional investigation ensued. Historian Donald H. Stewart wrote in 1952 that while the Jeffersonians went after some Federalist officeholders, they aimed their greatest scorn at (and examination of) those Federalists who held important offices, especially in the national government. "Jonathan Dayton's earlier Ohio land speculations paled in significance, they insisted, beside his perfidy after becoming Speaker of the federal House of Representatives in 1795. At that time the Speaker's duties included paying out the salaries to the House members, and once again Dayton had an opportunity to benefit at public expense. In 1798 he drew from the Treasury $33,000 to pay less than one half that sum to the Representatives. Over a year later it was discovered that he had used $18,000 for speculative purposes. At the demand of Secretary of the Treasury [Oliver] Wolcott, Dayton finally returned the money, but paid no interest."

While the Childs/Denning scandal was ruinous to Dayton's reputation, it was his association with former Vice President Aaron Burr which destroyed him both physically and financially. Although little documentary evidence still exists, it is believed that Dayton used either private or public funds to aid Burr, the former Vice President, in his attempt to fund an uprising by Spanish forces against the British in what is now the western United States; Burr paid the moneys from Dayton to the Spanish plenipotentiary to the United States, Don Carlos Martinez de Yrujo y Tacón. Dayton allegedly met with the former Vice President in Philadelphia, agreeing to act with Burr to finance his capture of the western lands which would earn them and their associates a lot of money. In 1806, when Burr traveled to the West, Dayton desired to come along but came down with an illness and was forced to stay home. This may have been his saving grace. At the same time, Dayton was working with James Wilkinson, the American governor of the Louisiana Territory, to secure lands from the British. When President Thomas Jefferson sought to remove Wilkinson from his office, Dayton, who had received the news as a U.S. Senator, sent a private letter to Wilkinson, encrypted in a cipher, warning him of the move. "It is now well ascertained that you are to be displaced in [the] next session. Jefferson will affect to yield reluctantly to the public sentiment, but yield he will. Prepare yourself, therefore, for it. You know the rest." He concluded, "You are not a man to despair, or ever despond, especially when such prospects offer in another quarter. Are you ready? Are your numerous associates ready? Wealth and glory, Louisiana and Mexico! I shall have time to receive a letter from you before I set out for Ohio." Dayton even signed the letter "Ohio" to cover his own backside. An illness prevented Dayton from accompanying Burr's aborted 1806 expedition, but in 1807 Dayton was arrested for treason. He was released and never brought to trial but his national political career never recovered.

Burr's conspiracy was soon exposed, and he was indicted for treason. In 1807, Dayton was also arrested and charged with treason, an offense punishable by death. The indictment read:

> The grand inquest of the United States, for the district of Virginia, upon their oaths, present, that Jonathan Dayton, late a senator in the congress of the United States, from the state of New-Jersey; John Smith, a senator in the congress of the United States, from the state of Ohio; Comfort Tyler, late of the state of New-York; Israel Smith, later of the state of New-York; and David Floyd, late of the territory of Indiana, are guilty of treason against the United States, in levying war against the same; to wit, at Blannerhasset's Island, in the county of Wood, and state of Virginia, on the 13th day of December 1806.

When Burr was tried in August 1807, Luther Martin, the famed Federalist who was one of Burr's defense counsel, told the court that "Col. Burr and Gen. Dayton, he insisted, could not be convicted in this charge of misdemeanor, even if there had been one committed, because they were at a great distance. There must have been *an act committed*; and there must have been the presence of the parties to support the indictment." Despite pressure brought externally on the judge in the case - here, it being Chief Justice of the Supreme Court John Marshall - by President Jefferson for a conviction, Marshall eventually found, in Burr's case only, that there was not enough proof to sustain the indictment. Dayton, on the other hand, was never even brought to trial; in a sense, he remained in limbo for the remainder of his life, unable to clear his name or prove that he had not committed treason against the nation he had once led as Speaker of the lower house of its federal legislature.

Jefferson privately heaped scorn on Dayton, but when the latter wrote to him asking for the President to intervene in his case (of being "admitted to bail"), Jefferson wrote to him on 17 August 1807,

> I received your letter of the 6th inst. requesting my interference to have you admitted to bail, and I have considered it with a sincere disposition to administer every relief from unnecessary suffering, which lies within the limits of my regular authority. But when a person charged with an offence is placed in the possession of the judiciary authority, the laws commit to that solely the whole direction of the case; and any interference with it on the part of the Executive would be an encroachment on their independence, and open to just censure. And still more censurable would this be in a case originating, as yours does, not with the Executive, but an independent authority. I am persuaded therefore, that on reconsideration, you will be sensi-

ble that, in declining to interpose in the present case, I do but obey the vigorous prescriptions of duty. [I do it however with the less regret as I presume that the same provisions of the law which have given to the principal defendant the accommodation of common apartments, give the same right to yourself and every other defendant, in a country where the application of equal law to every condition of man is a fundamental principle.

Interestingly, a study of Burr's private journal, published in two volumes in 1903, shows no references whatsoever to or about Dayton or to the scandal that allegedly tied the men together.

In his final years, Dayton served a single two-year term in the New Jersey Assembly (1814-15), spending most of his time speculating - once again - in land in what is now Ohio, especially around the territory between the Great Miami and the Little Miami Rivers. His purchases of tracts of land eventually totaled some 250,000 acres; however, he never visited the area. Despite this, in his honor after his death, the city of Dayton, Ohio, was named for him. Dayton died in Elizabethtown on 9 October 1824, seven days shy of his 64th birthday. He was interred in a vault in St. John's Churchyard (now St. John's Episcopal Church) in that city. His nephew, William Lewis Dayton, was a noted U.S. Senator from New Jersey and Ambassador to France, and ran as the first Republican Vice President candidate in the 1856 election.

An enigma to historians, Jonathan Dayton remains one of the most obscure Speakers of the U.S. House, with no major biography written about him. Some of the remaining correspondence involving Dayton survives because of his letters to and from his friend John Cleves Symmes. A review of the number of sources on Dayton's life, as well as correspondence that has survived him, show one of the main reasons why he is as somewhat unknown. His congressional biography shows that of the fifteen institutions that contain letters to him and from him, only a few have any that he wrote, and of those there remain only a handful of letters with actual substance. Thus, Jonathan Dayton will remain to history the riddle and mystery that he was during his life.

Further Reading:
Harrison, Richard A., "Jonathan Dayton" in Richard A. Harrison, ed., *Princetonians, 1776-1783: A Biographical Dictionary* (Princeton, New Jersey: Princeton University Press; three volumes, 1976), III:31-42.

"Jonathan Dayton" in Robert K. Wright, Jr., and Morris J. MacGregor, Jr., *Soldier-Statesmen of the Constitution* (Washington, D.C.: Center of Military History, United States Army, 1987), 79-81.

Theodore Sedgwick

Served as Speaker:
December 2, 1799 - March 4, 1801

The chief biographer of Speaker Theodore Sedgwick, Richard Welch, wrote that his chief accomplishments were as "[Alexander] Hamilton's chief lieutenant in the House during the funding and assumption contents, the outstanding administration figure in the debate on the Jay Treaty resolution of Mr. [Edward] Livingston, and the senator most responsible for arming the nation in 1798 against the threat of war with France." As Speaker, from 1799 to 1801, Sedgwick oversaw the move of the nation's federal government from Philadelphia to the District of Columbia and the passage of the Judiciary Act of 1801, which established the first steps to having a federal judiciary.

Personal History
The scion of a famed New England family, Sedgwick was born in Hartford, Connecticut (his official congressional biography reports it being West Hartford), on 9 May 1746, the son of Benjamin Sedgwick, a merchant who owned his own store and farm, and his wife Ann (née Thompson) Sedgwick. The Sedgwick family originated in England; the first American ancestor, Robert Sedgwick, emigrated to the American colonies and settled in

Charleston, Massachusetts, in 1635, and two years later became the captain of artillery for the Massachusetts colonial Ancient and Honourable Artillery Company. According to a genealogical history of the Sedgwick family, Robert returned to England in 1654 to serve in the military employé of Sir Oliver Cromwell; he then saw action in the West Indies. After he returned to the colonies, he served with his sons William and Robert in the same military unit that he had joined when he first came to America. Benjamin Sedgwick, a direct descendant of Robert, died suddenly in 1757 when Theodore was 11, and he was raised by his mother and older brother John, the latter taking over the family business while running a local tavern.

Almost all biographies of Theodore Sedgwick fail to mention any semblance of early schooling; they universally state that he entered Yale College (now Yale University) in 1761. However, it appears that Sedgwick was "schooled in the divinity" and was sent to join the church when he abandoned it for the law. He did study theology at Yale, but he did not graduate. Instead, he moved to Great Barrington, Massachusetts, where Sedgwick studied the law under Colonel Mark Hopkins, who had served as the first Register of Deeds for Berkshire County, Massachusetts. He was admitted to the Massachusetts bar in 1766. He married Elizabeth Mason in 1768, but she died three years later of smallpox; Sedgwick then married Pamela Dwight, a member of a prestigious Massachusetts family, in 1774, and together they had 10 children, including Theodore Sedgwick, Jr. (1811-1859), an attorney in New York who served as the American attaché to Paris and District Attorney for the Southern District of New York, and Catherine Maria Sedgwick (1789-1861), one of the most important American female novelists of the nineteenth century. Although little on his law career is known other than his practices in Great Barrington and Sheffield, Massachusetts, Sedgwick was involved in a landmark legal case in 1772, in which he defended Elizabeth Freeman (also known as "Mum Bet"), a slave whose release had been ordered by the colony against their master, Colonel John Ashley. When Ashley refused the order to release Mum Bet and another black servant, identified only as Brom, he was taken to court, and Sedgwick defended the two black servants. In the case of *Brom and Bett v. Ashley*, the Supreme Judicial Court of Massachusetts ruled that the two were free, stating that "all men are born free and equal" and ending slavery in Massachusetts.

In the years that he served as an attorney, Sedgwick was deeply involved in the fight for the rights of the American colonies against Great Britain. In 1773, he was instrumental as the author of the "Sheffield Resolves" or "Sheffield Declaration," a list of grievances against the British government that highlighted abuses of the rights of the colonists. When the declaration received no notice from the English, a general assembly was established in Berkshire County, Massachusetts, and Sedgwick was elected as one of two representatives from Sheffield. There, he helped to draft the motions of the council objecting to the Intolerable Acts, a series of enactments passed by the British Parliament against the colonists for their role in the Boston Tea Party, a protest to exorbitant taxes levied on British tea. Sedgwick never advocated independence from Britain, but when the American Revolution began in 1776, Sedgwick volunteered for duty, and served, on the staff of General John Thomas during the failed American invasion of Canada in 1776; he also served at the Battle of White Plains, in New York, in 1776. He rose to the rank of Major. He was given a nonmilitary position, serving as Commissioner of Supply for the Northern Department of the Continental Army, purchasing and supplying good and supplies to the troops.

In 1780, as the war in the New England region began to end, Sedgwick returned home and was elected to a seat in the first session of the Massachusetts state House of Representatives, representing Sheffield. He was re-elected in 1781, 1782, and 1783, and, in 1784, he was elected to the Massachusetts state Senate, representing Berkshire County and serving until 1785, when he resigned when he was elected to the Continental Congress. He held that seat until 1786, and again in 1788. In 1787, he agreed to serve again in the Massachusetts state House, served as Speaker of that body in 1788 before he returned to the Continental Congress. That year, Sedgwick served as a delegate to the Massachusetts state convention that voted to adopt the Federal Constitution drawn up in Philadelphia the previous year.

Early Years in Congress
In 1788, following his service to the state constitutional convention, Sedgwick was elected as a Federalist to a seat in the first Federal Congress, which opened in New York City on 4 March 1789, and remained through the Fourth Congress (1797-99), resigning in June 1796. During the first two Congresses, great debates arose over the formation of the federal government and the functions they would perform. In the First Congress (1789-91), the organization of the executive departments was widely discussed. When a "Department of Foreign Affairs" (now the Department of State) was to be created, some believed that with the establishment of an entity to deal with foreign subjects, one should also be created that dealt with internal matters, to be designated the "Home Department" or "Department of Home Affairs." Introduced by Rep. John Vining of Maryland, it was opposed by Sedgwick, who argued that the office appeared to be unnecessary, with any functions of this "Home Department" easily fitting into the Department of Foreign Affairs. Vining's motion was defeated, and it was Sedgwick who introduced the bill that called for a committee

to be established to draft a bill to form a department as Vining requested. This motion was also defeated, and to find a resolution a committee was appointed, with Sedgwick, George Matthews of Georgia, and Henry Wynkoop of Pennsylvania as members. Four days later, on 31 July 1789, the committee reported on a resolution to create a sole Department of Foreign Affairs. After being approved by the whole House, it was sent to the Senate, and, upon passage there, to President Washington.

Another argument in the first two Congresses came with the introduction of a bill to establish post roads and grant a franking, or free mail, privilege to members of the House. The Constitutional provision that the government "establish post-offices and post-roads" was argued by the Federalists to be under governmental control, with the anti-Federalists demanding that the government delegate the business of the post office and post roads to the states. The chief debate lasted from 6 December 1791 to 3 February 1792, with Sedgwick becoming one of the most impassioned voices in the deliberations, calling for federal control of all post roads and their designation. When Rep. Nathaniel Niles, anti-Administration member from Vermont, introduced a motion to extend the post road in his home state to the towns of Windsor and Rutland, Sedgwick rose and introduced his own motion, "to strike out the clause which designates all the particular roads in the United States, in order to insert a clause vesting the power of designation them in the supreme executive [the President of the United States]." One newspaper noted that Sedgwick's motion "occasioned a debate, in which its constitutionality, and the reverse idea, were alternately advanced and denied - the committee rose without coming to a decision, and then the House adjourned." During his years in the House, Sedgwick was such a firm supporter of the policies of the Washington administration that when Secretary of the Treasury Alexander Hamilton resigned in 1795 the President offered the vacant cabinet position to Sedgwick, who declined. Sedgwick had been one of Hamilton's key men in the House in helping to establish the Department of the Treasury, and enact funding requests to help pay for much of the debt carried by the new federal government from the colonial governments and American Revolution.

Elected to the Senate

On 1 June 1796, Senator Caleb Strong of Massachusetts resigned his seat, and the General Court of Massachusetts - instead of the Governor - elected Sedgwick to fill the remainder of Strong's term, set to end on 3 March 1799. In a letter to President Washington, dated 26 June 1796, Sedgwick spoke about local Massachusetts politics and the role of anti-Federalists, and at the same time complained about having been elected to the U.S. Senate:

> *The views of the disorganizers of our government were never so well understood by the people here, as at the present moment, and yet I much fear that Mr. Skinner [Thomson Joseph Skinner (1752-1809)] will prevail in the election in this district. In politics he is exactly the counterpart of the Hon. Mr. [Joseph] Varnum, and yet he had had the address to make many good people believe him to be highly federal. Though, however, I do fear, my hopes preponderate. I need not say to you that the election of a Senator in the place of [Caleb] Strong [a strong supporter of the Washington administration], is very disagreeable to me. I had contemplated retirement with much pleasure, and when that event can now happen, consistently with my idea of duty, God only knows.*

In the Senate, Sedgwick was a strong supporter of Washington's successor, John Adams of Massachusetts. However, when Justice James Wilson of the U.S. Supreme Court died on 21 August 1798, Sedgwick requested that he be named to the open seat; instead, Adams passed him over for Bushrod Washington, a nephew of former President Washington, a personal insult that Sedgwick never forgave. However, he remained a staunch Federalist, and was an early author of the legislation that became the Alien and Sedition Acts of 1798, a series of enactments intended to suppress any political opposition to a potential war with France that nearly came about that year. Among these were the Alien Act, which empowered the President with the power to depot any alien who was "dangerous to the peace and safety of the United States" during wartime, and the Alien Enemies Act, which allowed for the arrest and deportation of a person working for an enemy power. The actions were so controversial that the reaction against them was explosive: when Virginia enacted the Virginia Resolution, protesting the acts, Sedgwick advocated sending troops to the border to force the state to rescind it. The backlash against the Federalists for passage of this act is considered by historians to have led to the election of anti-Federalist Thomas Jefferson as President in 1800.

Returning to the House

When his Senate term expired in 1799, Sedgwick returned home to Massachusetts, intending to retire from political; instead, he was elected to a seat in the Sixth Congress (1799-1801). As with his election to the Senate, Sedgwick saw his being sent back to the House as a matter of duty, even though he wrote to his friend Rufus King that "my evil destiny has conquered." The Sixth Congress convened in Washington on 2 December 1799. The Speaker in the Fifth Congress, Jonathan Dayton, had been elected to the U.S. Senate, precipitating the election of a new Speaker. This was the first order of business after the official seating of the members.

The Vote

The potential of having Sedgwick, a strong Federalist whose dislike of anti-Federalists was well known, united the opposition behind Nathaniel Macon of North Carolina, a political foe of Sedgwick's. The hatred between Sedgwick and Macon can be seen in a letter from Sedgwick to King just weeks before the vote: "It is said that the gentleman, they at present contemplate as the rival candidate, has agreed to be held up; but as I have ever thought of him with respect and indeed affection, I will not, at present, mention, even to you, his name." On the first ballot, with 85 votes in total and a majority needed for election, Sedgwick led with 42 votes to 27 for Macon and 13 for George Dent of Maryland. Without a majority, a second ballot was held, in which Sedgwick received 44 votes to 38 for Macon and 3 for Dent. Sedgwick was declared the elected Speaker, and he was conducted to the Speaker's chair to be sworn in.

Acceptance Speech

He then turned to the members of the Congress and gave some remarks:

> Although I am conscious of a deficiency of the talents which are desirable to discharge with usefulness and dignity the important duties of

> the high station to which I am raised, by the generous regard of the enlightened and virtuous representatives of my county, yet, reposing myself on the energy of their candid support, I will not shrink from the attempt.

> Accept, I pray you, gentlemen, my grateful acknowledgement of the honor you are pleased to confer; and, with it, an assurance, that no consideration shall seduce me to deviate, in the least degree, from a direct line of impartial integrity.

In 1967, historian Patrick Furlong discovered a series of letters from Rep. John Rutledge, Jr., Federalist of South Carolina, describing the behind-the- scenes fight for the speakership. Writing to his father-in-law, Bishop Robert Smith, Rutledge explained,

> Both houses of Congress met yesterday - Mr. Sedgwick is our Speaker, and we are to receive the Presidents [sic] speech this day at noon. The election of a Speaker puzzled and perplexed the federal part of the House more than any of the difficulties it has heretofore had to struggle with. The southern and middle States Delegates thought, that as the government was very much in eastern hands, and as there had been one Speaker from New England, and two from the middle States, it would be wise and proper to elect a southern gentleman to the chair, and they nominated me. The eastern Delegates acquiesced in the policy of the measure, but said they were pledged to support the election of Mr. Sedgwick by a variety of considerations which they mentioned, and which are too lengthy to enumerate to you at present.

Legacy as Speaker

As Speaker, Sedgwick fostered the increased buildup of the American military - most notably the Navy - for a potential war with France over economic depredations, oversaw the move of the federal government from Philadelphia to the new city of the District of Columbia in 1800. That year, he voted to break a tie to help enact the nation's first bankruptcy law. In 1801, he oversaw the enactment of the Judiciary Act of 1801, which reorganized the federal courts - first created in 1789 - into six judicial appeals courts just below the U.S. Supreme Court and expanded federal jurisdiction of these courts. The Congress also passed an act for the relief of persons imprisoned for debt. William Henry Smith, an historian of the Speakers, wrote, "As Speaker, Mr. Sedgwick was firm, and sometimes rather positive and aggressive in his rulings. There was little of the conciliatory element in his mental makeup. He had been born and reared in a puritanical atmosphere, and there was much of the puritanical intolerance in his administration."

Historians Randall Strahan, Matthew Gunning, and Richard L. Vining, Jr., wrote in 2006:

> The partisan rancor surrounding Sedgwick's speakership was not entirely due to his conduct of legislative matters. Sedgwick also was an active participant in a Federalist effort to engineer the selection of Republicans vice presidential candidate Aaron Burr over presidential candidate Thomas Jefferson when the 1800 presidential election was thrown into the House.

Sedgwick used the power of his office, and his career, to get the Federalists to deny the renomination of President Adams in 1800. After working behind the scenes to get Charles Cotesworth Pinckney of South Carolina the presidential nomination, which went to Adams, Sedgwick tried to get Pinckney put on state ballots as the vice presidential candidate of the Federalists, get him more electoral votes (presidential and vice presidential candidates received separate electoral vote totals at that time), throw the election into the House, and have the majority Federalists elect Pinckney as President. Instead, Vice President Thomas Jefferson, a political enemy of Sedgwick's, and former U.S. Senator Aaron Burr of New York received 73 electoral votes each, forcing a House vote on the election. With the Federalists in charge, it appeared that Burr would have enough votes to be elected President, but countering Sedgwick was his old friend Alexander Hamilton, who disliked Jefferson but hated Burr. Using his own influence through 36 ballots, Hamilton got enough Federalist support to get Jefferson the presidency and Burr, in second place, the vice presidency. Burr never forgave Hamilton for this slight, and during a duel in 1804 Burr shot and killed the former Treasury secretary. Sedgwick, as Speaker, was forced to announce the election of Jefferson as President.

Disgusted by the direction of the nation that was tipped off by his alienation from Adams, Sedgwick refused to run for re-election in 1800. On 3 March 1801, in his final day in office as Speaker, the House passed a resolution thanking Sedgwick for his service as Speaker, he then delivered a short address, his farewell to the House:

> Accept, gentlemen, my thanks for the respectful terms in which you have been pleased to express the opinion you entertain of the manner in which I have discharged the arduous duties of the station to which I was raised by your kind regard.
>
> Although I am conscious of having intended faithfully to execute the trust confided to this chair; yet I am sensible, that whatever success may have attended my endeavours, is justly attributable to the candid, and honorable, and firm support which you have constantly afforded: I cannot lay the least claim to any thing that I have done, because the generous which you had reposed in me, demanded, that I should devote all my feeble talents to your service.
>
> Being now about to retire from this house, and I hope, from the public councils forever, permit me, gentlemen, to bid you, collectively and individually, an affectionate farewell.

After Leaving the Speakership

Returning to Massachusetts, Sedgwick was named in 1802 as an associate justice of the Massachusetts Supreme Judicial Court, a position he held until his death. He attempted to reform that court through the institution of a court of equity, but his pleas for reform were dismissed. In 1806, when Chief Justice Richard Dana died, Sedgwick was passed over for the vacancy for Theophilus Parsons.

In 1807, Sedgwick's second wife died of insanity; the following year Sedgwick married one Penelope Russell. Theodore Sedgwick died in Boston on 24 January 1813 at the age of 66, and was buried in the Sedgwick family cemetery in Stockbridge, Massachusetts.

In 1888, an official portrait of Sedgwick was purchased by the U.S. House of Representatives and added to its collections. Rep. Francis W. Rockwell, Republican of Massachusetts, who in 1888 represented the area that Sedgwick lived in, officially accepted the portrait on behalf of the entire House:

Theodore Sedgwick won a high position in the Commonwealth of Massachusetts, in the councils of the Federal Party, and in Congress...A man of integrity, fidelity, and capacity, he leads a line of well-equipped Western Massachusetts men who have been honored, not alone by merited promotion at home, but who have been intrusted [sic] in the Congress of the United States with the high duty of framing, shaping, defending, maintaining the dignity, power, and humanity of a beloved country.

Further Reading:

Furlong, Patrick J., "John Rutledge, Jr., and the Election of a Speaker of the House in 1799," *William and Mary Quarterly*, 3rd Series, 24:3 (July 1967), 432-36.

Welch, Richard, *Theodore Sedgwick, Federalist: A Political Portrait* (Middletown, Connecticut: Wesleyan University Press, 1965).

See also pages 413, 415

Nathaniel Macon

Served as Speaker:
December 7, 1801 - March 4, 1807

The first man to hold the Speaker's chair for more than one term in a row, Nathaniel Macon was a longtime politician from North Carolina whose name became synonymous with respect and service to nation during his lifetime. Now forgotten, his tenure as Speaker (1801-07) was marked by his opposition to the Judiciary Act of 1798 and his break with President Thomas Jefferson, who he helped to get elected to the presidency and who aided in his rise to the speakership.

Personal History

Because so little has been written about Macon, the fact that a biography was penned in 1840 by Edward R. Cotten stands to reason that Macon would at least have had the facts behind his life investigated. Instead, Cotten's work is a mixture of religious tome and fictionalized account of Macon's life story. A biography written by Weldon Edwards in 1862 as *The Memoir of Nathaniel Macon* did lay out the facts of his life, but lasts for a mere 22 pages. It was left to historian William Dodd, whose 1903 work on Macon is considered the fundamental biography of the North Carolina politician and Speaker of the U.S. House of Representatives. According to Dodd,

the Macon family probably originated in the Saône-Loire Valley region of France. He discovered that a Jouserand de Mâcon was knighted there in 1321, with subsequent family members bearing the name "de Mâcon" as a sign of respect. When the family moved to the New World is not known, although Dodd believes that a French Huguenot with the name "Macon," spelled without the accent mark or the "de" settled in the Middle Plantation in Virginia in the seventeenth century. One of these Macon family members, Martha Macon, married one Orlando Jones; their granddaughter, Martha Dandridge, later married George Washington and became the first First Lady. Gideon Macon, Martha's brother, moved to North Carolina in the second or third decade of the eighteenth century and "took up lands" on the Shocco Creek near the Roanoke River, located near what is now Warrenton, North Carolina, establishing the estate known as "Macon Manor" and becoming a prosperous tobacco farmer. It was here that he married Priscilla Jones of Shocco. Nathaniel Macon, the sixth child of Gideon and Priscilla Macon, was born at "Macon Manor" on 17 December 1758. Gideon Macon died when his son was three, leaving his family some 3,000 acres of land and 25-30 slaves. The widowed Priscilla Mason raised her children on the family's estate, sending them to a small school-house nearby to earn the most rudimentary of an education. According to all sources on his life, Macon applied himself and became one of the best students in the area - so much so that he was given a scholarship to Princeton College (now Princeton University) in New Jersey.

Macon was at Princeton when the Revolutionary War exploded in 1775. The onset of this horrendous conflict forced the school to close, probably because of its proximity to New York City, where the war was heating up. Macon returned to North Carolina. His brother, John, had formed a company of volunteers to head north to fight the British, but Nathaniel Macon continued the study of the law to further his private career. It was not until 1779, however, when British troops threatened South Carolina, that he joined the militia as a soldier. Burning with the vigor of a patriot far too young to understand the realities of war, Macon nonetheless saw action against the British along the Delaware River.

Returning home, Macon was admitted to the state bar - although no records exist showing that he ever formally practiced the law. Instead, at least accord-ing to most biographies on Macon, in 1781, he be-gan what became a nearly life-long political career when he was elected to a seat in the North Carolina state Senate. This, however, is where history meets myth. William Dodd, in his 1903 biography of Macon, finds several differing accounts of when he was elected, why he was elected, and the terms of his service. Dodd explains, "[John Hill] Wheeler claims in one place that Macon was first elected, while a private soldier in the army, to a seat in the [state] Senate for the year 1781 and that without his knowledge or consent, and, in another, he states that Macon was a member of the [state] Senate from Warren county in 1780. [John W.] Moore [in his *History of North Carolina* (1880)], too, claims that he was first seen in a deliberative body in Newbern in 1780; and Cotton confidently declares that 'at the age of twenty-four years, whilst he was yet in the army his countrymen elected Mr. Macon a member of the legislature of his State without his solicitation or even his knowledge.' Unfortunately, the records of the Assembly for the year 1780 have

been lost and we are left to decide the subject for ourselves." Re-elected in 1782 and 1784, Macon opposed the enactment of the U.S. Constitution and advocated a weak national government. Macon so despised the idea of a central government over-seeing all of the states that in 1785 when he was elected to a seat in the Continental Congress he re-fused to serve, although Dodd says that Macon re-fused because of "insufficient or unsatisfactory remuneration." From 1782 until 1786, nothing of Macon's career remains to be researched. In 1782, he did marry Hannah Plummer of Virginia. She died in January 1790, and, although he was only 32 when widowed, Macon never remarried.

Early Years in Congress

In 1789, two different Constitutional conventions met, with the second, held at Fayetteville, adopting the Constitution, which had been drafted two years earlier. Although Macon was not a member of ei-ther of these meetings, when the Constitution was ratified, allowing for the election of representatives to the House of Representatives sitting in New York City, Macon was elected to a seat in that body in 1790, representing Hillsboro. Macon took his seat in the Second Congress, which met on 4 March 1791. He would eventually serve until 13 December 1815, when he resigned his seat in the House, hav-ing been elected to the U.S. Senate. One of his key moments during this portion of his tenure in the House came when he spoke up to oppose the Alien and Sedition Acts of 1798. "Let the States continue to punish when necessary licentiousness of the press; how is it come to pass that Congress should now conceive that they have the power to pass laws on this subject? This Government depends upon the State legislatures for existence. They have only to refuse to elect Senators to Congress and all is gone." He advocated a protective tariff for southern cotton, saying that such an important industry was key to American economical success; however, at the same time, when the North Carolina iron indus-try asked for such a tariff Macon said that such in-dustries needed to stand on the strength of their product.

When Congress convened for the Sixth Congress on 2 December 1799, the Federalists were divided into eastern and southern wings. In the vote for Speaker, Macon came close to winning the coveted seat but ultimately lost by six votes to Theodore Sedgwick of Massachusetts. Sedgwick, a Federalist, angered so-called Republicans, also known as Jeffersonian Republicans, by running the House with an iron hand.

The Vote and Acceptance Speech

On 7 December 1801, the first session of the Seventh Congress convened in Washington, D.C. Thomas Jefferson, the former Vice President, was elected President in 1800 and had been the leader of the nation since March 1801. The House organized with Republicans in the majority. The Journal of the House of Representatives notes:

> The House proceeded, by ballot, to the choice of a Speaker; and, upon examining the ballots, a majority of the votes of the Whole House was found in favor of Nathaniel Macon, one of the Representatives for the State of North Carolina: Whereupon, Mr. Macon was conducted to the chair, from whence he made his acknowledgments to the House, as followeth: "Gentlemen: Accept my sincere thanks for the honor you have conferred on me, in the choice just made. The duties of the Chair will be undertaken with great diffidence indeed; but it shall be my constant endeavor to discharge them with fidelity and impartiality."

Nathaniel Macon, who wished to advance President Jefferson's program, was now in command of the House, and in this role he could dole out patronage and assign his friends to plum committee assignments in order to get their votes for what he wanted to do.

Legacy as Speaker

In one of the most important statements in his entire House service, Macon took to the floor on 23 February 1802 to call for the repeal of the Judiciary Act, which established the U.S. Supreme Court and a series of lower courts that blanketed the country. After many debates about the question of the constitutionality of the act, Macon stated:

> The true question is, were there courts enough under the old system to do the business of the nation? In my opinion there was. We had no complaints that sits multiplied, or that business was generally delayed; and when gentlemen talk about Federal courts to do the business of the people, they seem to forget that there are State courts, and that the State courts have done, and will continue to do, almost the whole business of the people in every part of the Union; that but very few sits can be brought into the Federal courts, compared with those that may be brought into the State courts...I am sure the old system answered every purpose for the State I live in as well as the new.

Critics, at the time and historically, have pointed out that Macon consistently voted against military expenditures, especially for the Navy, even when war with France and England appeared imminent. It is believed that his perspective came about from his refusal to allow northern states, most notably Massachusetts and Connecticut, where many ships were built and where the best sailors came from, to control the nation's naval force. Macon also believed that northerners wanted to control the military so as to put an end to slavery.

At the same time that Jefferson and Macon were working to assist each other in the Executive Mansion and the House, Macon was in fact leaning away from Jefferson's foreign policy. This began in 1806, when Congress, to punish England, enacted the Non-Importation Act, forbidding the importation of specific British goods to end the British policy of kidnapping American sailors on the high seas, known as impressments. Macon opposed the act, in direct opposition to Jefferson. Macon was angered because he saw the tit-for-tat actions between Washington and London as something that could harm southern commerce. In fact, when the British reacted by restricting all shipping by countries that did not side with it against France, the Congress enacted the Embargo Act on 22 December 1807. These measures caused a breach between Jefferson and Macon, which forced Macon out of the speakership following the end of the Ninth Congress in 1807. Despite the fact that the Jeffersonian Republicans held the majority (in fact, the party gained two seats in the 1806 election, rising from 114 to 116 seats to 26 for the Federalists), those who still sided with President Jefferson helped push Macon out in favor of Joseph B. Varnum of Massachusetts.

After Leaving the Speakership

Macon remained in the House, and in 1809 rose to become the chairman of the House Foreign Relations Committee. He favored the War of 1812 against England, but he opposed the conscription of troops for a federal army as well as the levying of taxes to pay for such a force. He also opposed the rechartering of the United States Bank.

In December 1815, in the midst of his 13th term in the House, the North Carolina legislature elected Macon to the U.S. Senate, replacing Francis Locke, whose had resigned his seat. Macon ultimately sat in the Senate until 1828, serving during the Nineteenth Congress (1825-27) as the President Pro Tempore of that body. In the 1824 election, Macon was given 24 electoral votes for Vice President, coming in third behind John Calhoun's 182. Macon resigned his seat on 14 November 1828 due to ill health and returned to North Carolina. Forever associated with politics in his home state, Macon came out of retirement in 1835 to serve as President of the state Constitutional Convention, and, the following year, he was a presidential candidate on the Democratic ticket.

In his career in the Congress, Macon served for a total of 37 years in both houses, earning the title "Father of the House" for, up to that time, having served longer in that body that any other man (Representative John Dingell, Democrat of Michigan, currently holds the record of 53 years.) In 1828, Macon's native state named Macon County in his honor. He served in the North Carolina General Assembly, and in 1835 he served as President of the Constitutional Convention. Macon died suddenly at his residence, "Buck's Spring," near the city of Macon in Warren County on 29 June 1837, at the age of 79. He had been seriously ill for only a few hours, but in that short time he was able to ask a close neighbor to bury him in a simple and plain wooden coffin with a small pile of stones as a marker.

Charles Jared Ingersoll, who served with Macon in the U.S. House, opined of him in 1845,

> His system of government was to govern as little as possible. Extensive dissension, and little legislation, he held to be the policy and duty of Congress. Let alone, was his policy for nations, for parties, and for individuals; his strong preference in this respect, being probably strengthened by plantation life and property, which beget intractable independence, and embolden proprietors to claim a sort of Polish veto against whatever crosses their homestead, or requires their submission. Six years' service for a senator, were in his opinion five too many, and one enough for a representative in Congress. Tyranny begins where annual elections end, was one of his maxims. Nothing is more miserable than a splendid and expensive government, was another. He was a constant advocate of frequent elections, that all offices should be elective, and for short terms of office, not as the only democratic, but likewise as the most durable tenure.

Further Reading:

Cotten, Edward R., *Life of the Hon. Nathaniel Macon, of North Carolina; In Which There is Displayed Striking Instances of Virtue, Enterprise, Courage, Generosity and Patriotism. His Public Life: Illustrating the Blessing of Political Union, the Miseries of Faction, and the Mischiefs of Despotic Power in Any Government. His Private Life: Furnishing Lessons Upon the Science of Social Happiness and Religious Freedom, of Greater Value, Perhaps, Than are to be Fond in the Biography of any other Character, either Ancient or Modern, "Having Lived and Died Without an Enemy"* (Baltimore: Printed by Lucas & Deaver, 1840).

Dodd, William E., *The Life of Nathaniel Macon* (Raleigh, North Carolina: Edwards & Broughton, Printers and Binders, 1903).

Edwards, Weldon Nathaniel, *Memoir of Nathaniel Macon, of North Carolina* (Raleigh: Raleigh Register Steam Power Press, 1862).

See also page 418

Joseph Bradley Varnum

Served as Speaker:
October 26, 1807 - March 4, 1811

He was the last veteran of the American Revolution to serve as Speaker of the House, and the last in the line of Speakers who were mere figureheads in the office, which was changed by Joseph Varnum's successor, Henry Clay. A staunch anti-Federalist who was a leader of the Jeffersonian-Republican movement, Varnum was opposed to the construction of a national army and navy and direct taxation. His support for the Embargo Act of 1807 nearly cost him his political career, although he later served in the U.S. Senate.

Personal History

Varnum was born in Dracut (some sources spell it Dracutt), Massachusetts, on 9 February (29 January, Old Style), in either 1750 or 1751, the son of Major Samuel Varnum, a farmer, and his wife Hannah (née Mitchell) Varnum. Much of Varnum's early life is bathed in mystery, and for this reason the numerous sources on his life differ on several details. As to his exact date of birth, the "Vital Records of Dracut, Massachusetts, to the Year 1850" merely lists his date of death in 1821, although the Daughters of the American Revolution report his date of birth as being 1750. As well, his education - or lack thereof

- is misreported; his congressional biography, completed in 1878, reports that he had received "a public-school education," when Varnum had a limited education at best (modern biographies agree that he never attended school), and apparently taught himself to read and write. Federalists later charged in political campaigns that he was an illiterate. His brother, James Mitchell Varnum (1748-1789), was a lawyer who served as a general in the Continental Army during the American Revolution as well as representing Rhode Island in the Continental Congress (1780-81, 1787).

Joseph Varnum grew up on his family's farm; he never purchased a home, and lived on the farm for the entire time when he was not at war or in Congress. Many of the letters he wrote expressed a love of farming; Varnum explained that the farm, some 500 acres in size, had "more than ten miles of good stone fence upon it." In 1787, writing to his son while in Philadelphia, Varnum explained,

> *In order to Succeed in any profession or Occupation in life it is highly necessary and important to pay strict attention to the duties of it,*

and at all such times, as the nature thereof shall require. To be a Farmer, a consistent Farmer, happy in the Occupation, and respectable in Society, it is necessary to rise Early in the Morning, Pay Speedy attention to all necessary requirements, and take advantage of the Labours of the day, by performing the most arduous part, before the Sun arises to its Meridian Splendor. The strictest attention must be paid to the Buildings, Fences, Stock of Cattle, husbandry, tools, and every species of produce. All necessary repairs must be Early made. No part of the produce must be suffered to be wasted or lost for want of care. Thus the farmer becomes wealthy, respectable and happy.

When just 16, Varnum traveled to Boston, where he saw for the first time British troops marching to keep order in the city. The Boston Massacre, the shooting in 1770 by British soldiers of several colonial protesters including the free black Crispus Attucks, set off a frenzy of protest against the governing of the colonies by the English. In Dracut, two volunteer companies of troops were raised, with one of them electing Varnum as their leader with the rank of Captain. He used his viewing of the precision of the British troops in Boston to train the soldiers, and remained in this mode for the next several years. In 1774, when the need arose for colonists to fight the British, Varnum's soldiers were ready for action. They reorganized as a statewide militia, but retained Varnum as their official instructor, a position he held until the start of the American Revolution. Varnum saw action at Lexington, the first skirmish of that conflict. When the militia was reorganized in January 1776, Varnum was retained as its head. He held command of the militia, known as the Dracut Minute Men, until April 1787, when he was elected as a Colonel in the Seventh Regiment, Third Division of the Massachusetts state Militia. One of the soldiers in the militia, Joshua Pillsbury, wrote that while fighting under Varnum "our Armey that was on that Side [of] the River marched to Their ground and took posision [sic]. Genl. Burgoines [sic; should be Burgoyne's] Army Surrendred [sic] themselves Prisoners of War to the Amiricans [sic]." Varnum also saw action in Rhode Island in 1778.

In 1780, when the war in the area of Massachusetts was winding down, Varnum returned home and was elected to a seat in the Massachusetts state House, serving until 1785. He was then elected to the Massachusetts state Senate, representing Middlesex County, and held that position until 1795. Although he was an anti-Federalist, he was not a fiery orator on the major issues of the day, but he did adhere to the anti-Federalist program of opposition to a national army, a national navy, or direct taxation from the U.S. government. While in the state Senate, a rebellion against taxes by Daniel Shays and his followers in western Massachusetts threatened the stability of the entire federal government. Varnum left his seat and rejoined the state militia, giving General Benjamin Lincoln, fighting the Shays' Rebellion, additional support. Lincoln wrote to Varnum:

Sir: The business for which troops were ordered out seems to be pretty much over. Your services will be important, and are much needed in the General Court. It is, therefore, my wish that you assign your Company to ye next officer and meet the assembly as soon as possible. Your example in turning out on this occasion meets the esteem of your Country and entitles you to its thanks.

Varnum remained connected to the state militia for the remainder of his life: in 1802, he was named as a Brigadier-General, and in 1805 a Major-General, and was known throughout the remainder of his life as "General Varnum."

In 1788, Varnum was sent as a delegate to the Massachusetts state convention that ratified the Constitution. Following that gathering, he served as a Justice in the Massachusetts Court of Common Pleas, then as Chief Justice of the Court of General Sessions, the latter which considered matters relating to the state or local government or those involving the welfare of the community.

Early Years in Congress

In 1788, 1790, and 1792, Varnum was an unsuccessful candidate for a seat in the federal Congress. In 1794, he finally won the seat in an election decided against Federalist Samuel Dexter (later Secretary of the Treasury in the John Adams administration) by a mere 11 vote majority, and he entered the Fourth Congress (1795-97). Varnum soon became a leader of the anti-Federalists, opposing a national taxation system. In a speech during one of his early terms in Congress, he stated,

> I am clearly of the opinion that any sums needed for defraying the expenses of the Government or for the payment of its debts ought to be raised by duties on imposts and excises. That is the method of taxation with which we are acquainted and which experience has taught us the operation of under the Government. There are almost insuperable objections to a direct tax, and until all the objects of indirect taxation are exhausted, I presume the Government will never adopt one.

With the election of Thomas Jefferson as Vice President in 1797, then as President in 1801, Varnum became part of the movement of anti-Federalists into the loosely configured party known as the Jeffersonian-Republicans or National Republicans. And although he was a staunch supporter of Jefferson, he objected loudly when in 1803 the President conducted the Louisiana Purchase, the acquisition of some 530 million acres in what is now the middle section of the United States, from France. Jefferson proposed to split the Purchase into two territories, with a bill in Congress set to allow him to select the legislature and councils of government for these territories. Varnum stood as one of the loudest in denouncing this plan, demanding the direct election by the people of any legislature:

I am of the opinion that the bill provides such a kind of government as never has been known in the United States...Sound policy, no less than justice, dictates the propriety of making provision for the election of a legislature by the people. There is not only the common obligation of justice imposed on Congress to do this, but it is bound to do it by treaty. This treaty [with France] makes it obligatory to admit the inhabitants of Louisiana as soon as possible to the enjoyment of all the rights, privileges, advantages and immunities of citizens of the United States.

Varnum also was an early opponent of slavery and the slave trade.

In the Eighth (1803-05) and Ninth (1805-07) Congresses, the Jeffersonian-Republicans were split between those who backed Speaker Nathaniel Macon and a faction who opposed Macon's handling of the speakership. With the Federalists holding few seats in the House, such a split did not imperil Jeffersonian-Republican control of the body, but it did lead to the end of Macon's speakership.

The Vote
By the end of the Ninth Congress, the supporters of Macon were in the minority. The Tenth Congress met in Washington on 26 October 1807, with the first order of business electing a Speaker. The Jeffersonian-Republicans, also known as the National Republicans, controlled the House with 116 seats to 26 for the Federalists. On the first ballot, Varnum received 59 votes, to 17 for Rep. Charles Goldsborough, Federalist of Maryland, 17 for Rep. Burwell Bassett, Jeffersonian-Republican of Virginia, 8 for Rep. Josiah Masters, Jeffersonian-Republican of New York, and a scattering of the remainder of the votes for other candidates. The Clerk of the House declared Varnum to be elected, and he was conducted to the Speaker's chair by Rep. Philip Van Cortlandt, Jeffersonian-Republican of New York, and Rep. Willis Alston, Jeffersonian-Republican of North Carolina.

Acceptance Speech
After being sworn, Varnum addressed the House:

> You will please to accept my most grateful acknowledgments for the honor which by your suffrages on this occasion you have conferred upon me. I am sensible of my own inability to perform the important duties you have been pleased to assign me, in the most desirable manner; but relying on your candor and readiness to afford me your aid, I accept the trust. And be assured, gentlemen, that it will be my assiduous endeavor to discharge the duties of the office faithfully and impartially; and in a manner which in my opinion shall be best calculated to meet your wishes and afford me the consolation of an approving conscience.

Legacy as Speaker
Having opposed Macon and his selection for chairman of the House Committee on Ways and Means,

Rep. John Randolph of Virginia, one of Varnum's first acts as Speaker was to remove Randolph from the chairmanship of that committee and replacing him with Rep. George W. Campbell of Tennessee. Campbell was not supported by either faction of the Jeffersonian-Republicans, and the selection nearly cost Varnum critical support when he stood for re-election as Speaker in the Eleventh Congress (1809-11), which was the first contested speakership election ever. Sarah Binder, writing on the power of the Speakers before Henry Clay, explained,

Indeed, there was a vote in 1807 in the Tenth Congress that overturned a ruling by Speaker Varnum, who had held that approval of the previous question to cut off all debate and brought the House to an immediate vote on pending business. A bipartisan vote of 103-14 rejected the attempt to suppress minority rights of debate. However, near the close of the Eleventh Congress in February 1811, Speaker Varnum again was called on to interpret the effect of the previous question. This time, following the procedural precedent affirmed in the previous Congress, Varnum ruled that the right of debate could not be curtailed.

During the Eleventh Congress, one newspaper noted that "Mr. Varnum was opposed to giving the president the power to appoint the officers - he hoped the time had not yet come, when the constitution was to be violated in order to raise up an army. The constitution provided that the officers should be commissioned by the different state governments."

In one of his most controversial acts as Speaker, Varnum supported the passage of the Embargo Act, enacted on 22 December 1807, which answered the order by the British to seize or restrict all neutral shipping. This action prohibited all international trade to and from American ports in an effort to injure the economies of Britain and France, then at war. Instead of harming these two belligerents, however, American merchants, especially in New England, saw the act as a threat to their livelihood. Varnum's name being attached to it did not endear him to those in his home state, and in 1809, Varnum ran for Lieutenant Governor, with General Levi Lincoln, but his support for the embargo cost the ticket and they were defeated by Federalists

Christopher Gore and David Cobb. In 1810 Congress was forced to withdraw the Embargo Act.

In 1811, having finished his second term as Speaker, Varnum was elected to the U.S. Senate, replacing Timothy Pickering, and he resigned from the House on 29 June 1811. He was the last Speaker of the House to be a mere figurehead in that office; his successor, Henry Clay, transformed the speakership by involving himself in legislative deliberations, elevating the Speaker to a role he had not played in the tenures of those who came before him. Hubert Bruce Fuller, a historian of the speakership, said that Varnum's tenure in the office was "an epoch of commanding mediocrity."

After Leaving the Speakership

Varnum served in the Senate for the remainder of the term that ended on 3 March 1817, sitting as President *pro tempore* of the Senate during the Thirteenth Congress (1813-15). He also served as chairman of the Committee on [the] Militia in the Fourteenth Congress (1815-17). He ran for Governor of Massachusetts in 1813, but was defeated by Federalist Caleb Strong.

In 1817, Varnum attempted to win a second term in the Senate but was defeated because of his support for the War of 1812, which was widely unpopular in Massachusetts. Varnum left the Senate and returned to Massachusetts, where his neighbors, with who he had remained close, elected him to the state Senate, representing Middlesex County. In 1820, he served as a delegate to the state convention which revised the state's constitution. On 21 September 1821, Varnum suddenly became ill after riding his horse at his farm in Dracut; he returned home, told his family that the end was near, and gave directions for his funeral. He died at the age of either 70 or 71, and was buried in the family's private cemetery on the farm's grounds. His widow, Molly Butler Varnum, whom he had married in 1773, and for whom the Molly Butler Varnum chapter of the Daughters of the American Revolution is named, died in 1833, and was buried next to him.

The son of a farmer, who taught himself to read and write and learned how to train troops by mere observation, rose to become one of the most powerful officials in the American government. His two terms as Speaker were the last time that that office was run as a mere moderator of debate, the end of an age when the men who preside over the House of Representatives became not just a referee on the issues but a participant in the shaping of legislation. Joseph Varnum's speakership was the end of an era. Few histories of the office remember him despite his being a fair arbitrator in the House.

Further Reading:

Varnum, Joseph Bradley, *An Address Delivered to the Third Division of Massachusetts Militia, at a Review, on the Plains of Concord, 27th August, 1800. By Hon. Joseph B. Varnum Esq. Col. in the same Division* (Cambridge: Printed by William Hilliard, 1800).

Varnum, Joseph M., ed., "Autobiography of General Joseph B. Varnum," *Magazine of American History*, 20:5 (November 1888), 405-14.

HENRY CLAY.

Henry Clay

Served as Speaker:
November 4, 1811 - January 19, 1814
December 4, 1815 - October 28, 1820
December 1, 1823 - March 4, 1825

Henry Clay was perhaps one of the great giants of American politics in the first half of the nineteenth century, a fact confirmed by the U.S. Senate in 1955 when a committee of that body, chaired by then-Senator John F. Kennedy, named Clay among the five greatest Senators to serve in all of American history. Clay served seven terms in the U.S. House of Representatives, and except for one of them, he served as Speaker, including in his very first term - a remarkable achievement that will probably never be repeated or even closely copied. He served as Secretary of State (1825-29), and was integral to the formation of the "American System" of trade that became the basis of late twentieth century American foreign policy in the Western Hemisphere. He was thrice his party's nominee for President, and, in 1844, would have been elected had not he bungled the issue of slavery with which he wrestled for all of his political life. Known as "The Great Compromiser" for his fashioning of The Compromise of 1850, which attempted to settle the rights of states to enter the Union as either slave or free and head off disunion and civil war. Few politicians have had the historical impact as that of

Henry Clay: Speaker of the U.S. House, noted U.S. Senator from Kentucky, representative to the peace talks with Great Britain in 1814, Secretary of State, and three-time presidential candidate (1824, 1832, 1844) carrying the banner of three different parties. Yet Clay's name is mostly forgotten today save that of old books and periods of American history that have been glossed over, including Clay's support for slavery. Who this man was, who rose to be elected as Speaker of the House on his first day in office, remains an enigma more than a century and a half after his death. Charles M. Stewart, in a 1998 paper, stated, "Henry Clay is widely regarded to be the most significant personality in the antebellum House of Representatives. He is the only pre-Civil War Speaker to be subjected to major biographies, and the *only* Speaker whom each generation feels compelled to reexamine. To students of congressional history, Clay is most importantly remembered for transforming the office of Speaker into a partisan one."

Personal History

Despite having his name forever linked to his beloved Kentucky, Clay in fact was born on 12 April 1777 in Hanover, Virginia, in the area called at that time "The Slashes" because of its swamps, the son of the Rev. John Clay, a Baptist minister, and his wife Elizabeth (née Hudson) Clay. According to several sources, the Clays had a son named Henry earlier in their marriage, but he died in infancy and they named his later son with the same name. The Clay family originated in England, and Clay allegedly was related to Sir William Clay, who served in the British House of Commons. One of the earliest biographies of Clay, penned by George D. Prentice in 1831, was more of a campaign biography than anything else. In fact, the last three chapters of this work are believed to have been written by the poet John Greenleaf Whittier. The Rev. Clay died in 1781, leaving a widow and seven children, including his son Henry who was just four. Unable to finance an education for her youngest child, the widowed Elizabeth Clay committed her son to the charge of one Peter Deacon, an English schoolteacher who opened a small school in "The Slashes" section. In fact, Clay was later referred to as "The Mill-Boy of the Slashes." Elizabeth Clay married Capt. Henry Watkins, who raised Henry as his own son.

Clay finished his education and moved to Richmond, where he studied the law in the offices of Peter Tinsley, the Clerk of the Virginia High Court of Chancery. There, Clay came to the notice of two important Virginia politicians: Attorney General (and future Governor) Robert Brooke and Professor George Wythe (pronounced "with"), the former famed for his signing of the Declaration of Independence. Among those who had studied the law under Wythe included Thomas Jefferson, John Marshall, and St. George Tucker. As the Chancellor of Virginia, Clay served as his assistant. In 1797, Clay was admitted to the Virginia bar. However, instead of remaining in his home state, he moved south and west, to Lexington, Kentucky, where he opened a law practice. He would be associated with the Commonwealth of Kentucky for the remainder of his life. In Lexington, Clay became one of the most important legal minds of the city.

In 1803, at just 26 years of age, Clay's name was placed in election for a seat in the Kentucky state General Assembly, the lower house of the state legislature, without his knowledge. During the election, an open caucus of candidates, Clay was opposed by several well-known politicians of Fayette county, which the seat represented. He arrived at the caucus and told the crowd that, as his opposition had argued, he was young and inexperienced, and that he had not asked to have his name placed in nomination for the election. However, he added, as his name was now in the arena, he desired to win the election, after which he explained his political views. With the end of his remarks, the caucus continued, and Clay was elected by acclamation to the seat. He would remain a member of that body for three years.

Early Years in Congress

Following the resignation of Senator John Adair from the U.S. Senate, the Kentucky state legislature met to select a successor. Clay was the overwhelming favorite - despite the fact that the Constitution prescribes that all Senators must be at least 30 years old and Clay was four months short of that limitation. Nonetheless, the legislature elected him and sent him to Washington. When he arrived, the other Senators moved into a lengthy debate over whether Clay should be allowed to take his seat because he was constitutionality ineligible. After much deliberation, the Senate voted to seat him. Historians looking for a reason why this man with so little political experience was sent to occupy a vacant Senate seat need only look to a few months before his selection.

Earlier in 1806, when former Vice President Aaron Burr had been arrested in Kentucky on charges that he had been involved in attempts to section off a portion of the country and found his own nation, Clay appeared in court as his attorney of record. Burr had been wildly unpopular since an 1804 duel with former Secretary of the Treasury Alexander Hamilton that left Hamilton dead. Nonetheless, Clay, along with co-counsel John Allen, appeared in court on behalf of Burr and immediately charged that the district attorney had arrested the former Vice President in Kentucky because the DA had been a sympathizer of Hamilton's. Brought before a federal court, Clay challenged the entire arrest and had the indictment discharged. Clay became the focus of much respect for his firm deliberations in fighting for the freedom of this man so despised for his murder of Alexander Hamilton. It is for this reason, it is believed, that Clay was named to the Senate. Burr was later re-arrested and charged, but by that time Clay was in Washington and could not act as his attorney. At a later date, Clay was given the evidence that had been collected by the Jefferson administration for Burr's prosecution, including a letter written by Burr in a cipher to hide its true intentions, and Clay changed his mind about Burr's guilt. In 1815, when the two men accidentally met in New York City, Clay refused to shake Burr's hand.

Clay's appointment to the Senate was for a single session, until the end of Adair's term, and, when the session ended on 3 March 1807, he returned to Kentucky, where he again was elected to the Kentucky legislature. Ironically, it was during this session that Clay was selected as speaker of the body, a position he would later hold in the national legislature. He served in this body from 1808 until 1809.

In December 1809 (some sources report the date as 1810, which is in error), when U.S. Senator Buckner Thruston, Democratic Republican of Kentucky, was named to the U.S. Circuit Court for the District of Columbia, his seat became vacant, and again the legislature elected Clay to sit in the upper body of Congress. Clay only served the remaining time in Thruston's term, which lasted from 4 March 1810 to 3 March 1811. Clay did not accomplish much in this second Senate term; in fact, in his entire Senate service he spoke out on several subjects, mainly dealing with his support for internal improvements, such as the federally-funded construction of roads, bridges, and canals, as well as the protection of so-called "domestic manufactures," or industries native to one's state. In advocating national protection for both, he established what has been called by historians "The American System." However, we get a better glimpse of his work in the Senate from Washington Irving, in one of that author's famed letters of February 1811: "Clay, from Kentucky, spoke against the Bank [of the United States]. He is one of the finest fellows I have seen here, and one of the finest orators in the Senate, although I believe the youngest man in it. The galleries, however, were so much crowded with ladies and gentlemen, and such expectations had been expressed concerning his speech, that he was com-

pletely frightened, and acquitted himself very little to his own satisfaction. He is a man I have great personal regard for."

During Clay's second tenure in the Senate, he established precedents for actions that would occur long after he had passed into history. In 1841, Clay introduced a bank bill that the minority Democrats objected to. Instead of voting against it, the Democrats instituted a filibuster to halt its passage. The filibuster, coming from the Dutch word "vrijbuiter" meaning "pirate," is a long-standing tool of the minority in the Senate, since the beginning of the nation, to block and/or stymie the majority's ability to pass legislation out of that body. However, in this instance, Clay had had enough of the Democrats and their blocking of a bill he saw as important, and he moved to change the Senate rules to end debate at the majority's choosing. When even Clay's fellow Whigs refused to back his changes, he withdrew them and the ability of the minority to filibuster remained as it was. In 2005 and 2006, frustrated by the Democrat minority in the Senate to end filibusters on the president's judicial nominees, the Republicans threatened to do the same thing that Clay had tried - to limit debate at the majority's choosing. Those opposed the rule change called it "the nuclear option," and in the end the Democrats relented, allowing for up-or-down votes and the use of the filibuster only at certain times.

Clay did not like the Senate, in fact feeling distant from the people in this august body, and wished, if to serve in the Congress, to hold a seat in the so-called "people's branch," the U.S. House of Representatives. Telling the people of Kentucky that, "In presenting myself to your notice, I conform to the sentiments I have invariably felt, in favor of the station of an immediate representatives of the people," in November 1810 Clay won a seat in the U.S. House, and took his seat the following November.

The Vote
The Twelfth Congress convened in Washington on 4 November 1811 with 107 Jeffersonian Republicans (also known as National or Democratic-Republicans) to 36 Federalists. This Congress came together with the nation holding its breath over the impending and approaching war with Great Britain. It was here that Henry Clay, freshman congressman

to the House, was elected on the first ballot for the office of Speaker. Sources on Clay and on the Congress report that the vote was 79 votes for Clay to 48 votes for some unnamed opposition candidate; the *Journal of the House*, while not a verbatim account of the activities of the House but nonetheless an important source on speeches and actions of the body, does not give a vote tally nor is an opposition candidate to Clay named. What is important, perhaps, is that for the first time (and probably the last time) in American history, a representative sitting for his first term in the House was nominated by his party for the speakership, and his election came in a time when seniority and rank did not carry the weight that it does today was overcome.

Acceptance Speech

Clay was conducted to the Speaker's chair and given the oath of office. As was customary in those days, the new Speaker delivered some simple remarks to the assembled House members:

Gentlemen:

In coming to the station which you have done me the honor to assign me - an honor for which you will be pleased to accept my thanks - I obey rather your commands than my own inclination. I am sensible of the imperfections which I bring along with me, and a consciousness of these would deter me from attempting a discharge of the duties of the chair, did I not rely, confidently, upon your generous support.

Should the rare and delicate occasion present itself, when your Speaker shall be called upon to check or control the wanderings or intemperance in debate, your justice will, I hope, ascribed to his interposition the motives only of public good and a regard to the dignity of the House. And in all instances, be assured, gentlemen, that I shall, with infinite pleasure, afford every facility in my power to the despatch [sic] of public business, in the most agreeable manner.

Legacy as Speaker

As Speaker, especially in this first term, Clay battled with fiery debate those representatives who opposed conflict with England over numerous issues, most notably trade, borders, and the impressment or kidnapping of American sailors on the high seas, most notably John Randolph of Virginia and Josiah Quincy of Massachusetts. One member of Congress, witnessing the sparks brought forward by the arguments between the men, later wrote, "On this occasion Mr. Clay was a flame of fire. He had now brought Congress to the verge, of what he conceived to be, a war for liberty and honor; and his voice rang through the Capitol like a trumpet tone sounding for the onset. On the subject of the policy of the embargo, his eloquence, like a Roman phalanx, bore down all opposition; and he put to shame those of his opponents who flouted the Government as being unprepared for war."

With the speakership as his own bully pulpit, Clay pushed the administration of President James Madison towards war. When the House hesitated to rush into conflict, Clay went to the floor of the House to reassure its wavering members of the reasons why such hostilities were necessary. Quincy of Massachusetts continually attacked Clay and his supporters, declaring them to be "young politicians, with their pin-feathers yet unshed, the shell still sticking upon them; perfectly unfledged, though they fluttered and cackled on the floor." Clay hated England so much that he praised French general Napoleon Bonaparte, fighting the English on the European continent. In one speech in 1813, Clay heaped approval and even admiration onto Napoleon.

Bonaparte, has been called the scourge of mankind, the destroyer of Europe, the great robber, the infidel, the modern Attila, and Heaven knows by what other names. Really, gentlemen remind me of an obscure lady, in a city not very far off, who also took it into her head, in conversation with an accomplished French gentleman, to talk of the affairs of Europe. She, too, spoke of the destruction of the balance of power; stormed and raged about the insatiable ambition of the Emperor; called him the curse of mankind, the destroyer of Europe. The Frenchman listened to her with perfect patience, and when she had ceased said to her, with ineffable politeness, "Ma'am, it would give my master, the Emperor, infinite pain if he knew how hardly you thought of him".

On 30 July 1812, Rep. Langdon Cheves of South Carolina, later to become Speaker of the House himself, penned a note to Clay on Clay's influence as Speaker:

> Yours of the 15th July, inst., I received yesterday, at Philadelphia, at the very moment I was getting into the stage on my way to Carolina. You ask me, "What notice you ought to take of [John] Randolph's reply?" [C]ertainly none - none whatever. Were you to notice it he would reply again, and it would never terminate. He spoke with great truth in the beginning of the last session [of Congress], when he said the "Speaker of the House of Representatives was the second man in the nation"; and if this be true, as I think it is, it does not become the Speaker to enter into altercations with any member of the House, or even of the nation, in a public justification of his conduct, any more than it does to the first man in the nation - the President. I, therefore, thought you originally wrong. But if any notice of Mr. R.'s first publication was right, it was taken by you exactly in the manner, temperate and dignified, in which it ought to have been noticed. I think, as the question stands, you have entirely the advantage of the argument; and I think you would egregiously err, as the Speaker of the House of Representatives (it would be entirely different were it a question between Mr. Clay and Mr. R.) to point it on any other footing than that of argument.

In 1814, as the war between the United States and England drew to a close, President Madison named a number of influential men as commissioners to go to Belgium and iron out a peace treaty between the two nations. Among the group were John Quincy Adams, Albert Gallatin, James A. Bayard, Jonathan Russell, and Clay, who resigned from the speakership and the House on 19 January 1814 to almost unanimous applause from the members of the House.

The *Debates and Proceedings in the Congress of the United States* notes the machinations of Clay's resignation:

> The ordinary business of the day having been gone through - The Speaker addressed the House in the following terms: "Gentlemen: I have attended you today to announce my resignation of the distinguished station with which I have been honored by your kindness. In taking

> leave of you, gentlemen, I shall be excused for embracing the last occasion to express to you personally my thanks for the frank and liberal support the Chair has experience at your hands. Wherever I may go, in whatever situation I may be placed, I can never cease to cherish, with the fondest remembrance, the sentiments of esteem and respect with which you have inspired me."

Speaker Once Again - Returning to Congress

Clay served on the commission that signed the Treaty of Ghent that ended the War of 1812 between the United States and England. When Clay had completed his work for the treaty, he returned to Kentucky and was without opposition re-elected to his congressional seat after Langdon Cheves had held it following his resignation. Taking his seat in the Fourteenth Congress (1815-17), Clay was again elected Speaker, and held that office through the Fifteenth (1817-19) and Sixteenth (1819-21) Congresses. In 1819, as the bite of the economic panic of that year cascaded across the nation, Clay saw his own financial situation go downhill, and, facing financial ruin, resigned from the speakership and the House on 6 December 1819, replaced by Rep. John W. Taylor of New York. Clay did not serve in the Seventeenth Congress (1821-23); however, he returned to the House in 1823 for the Eighteenth Congress (1823-25) and was elected to the Nineteenth Congress (1825-27), although he never served in the 19th, and, again, he was elected Speaker of the House by the Democratic-Republicans, a record of service that will probably remain unchallenged by any future Speaker.

In 1820, Clay was the leading politician who helped to draft a compromise to end the threat of disunion and civil war over slavery. The state of Missouri was set to enter the Union as a slave state, and abolitionists rejected it, while those who stood for the rights of slaveholders argued for the enactment of the state's admittance to the Union. During a six-week period of the Seventeenth Congress, Clay debated the issue among House members, even arguing strenuously with John Randolph of Virginia. The Massachusetts author Samuel Griswold Goodrich wrote some 30 years later:

> I was in the House of Representatives but a single hour. While I was present there was no di-

rect discussion of the agitating subject which already filled everybody's mind, but still the excitement flared out occasionally in incidental allusions to it, like puffs of smoke and jets of flame which issue from a house that is on fire within. I recollect that Clay made a brief speech, thrilling the House by a single passage, in which he spoke of "poor, unheard Missouri," she being then without a representative in Congress. His tall, tossing form, his long, sweeping gestures, and, above all, his musical yet thrilling tones, made an impression upon me which I can never forget.

Clay helped to draft a compromise that allowed Missouri to be admitted as a slave state, but slavery would be made illegal north of the coordinates of 36° 30' latitude. It was Clay who pushed the relevant committee to hear arguments over the compromise, who ushered it to the House floor, and who ultimately argued for its passage. The Missouri Compromise allowed the country to delay the fight over slavery that would envelop it in just forty years. For his role in the debate, Clay became known as "The Great Compromiser."

Leaving the Speakership - Becoming Secretary of State

In 1824, having served in some capacity for more than 20 years in national politics, Clay decided to run for President to succeed James Monroe. Clay was one of four main candidates, a group that included General Andrew Jackson, the hero of the battle of New Orleans at the end of the War of 1812; John Quincy Adams of Massachusetts, Monroe's Secretary of State; and William Crawford, Monroe's Secretary of the Treasury, who suffered a stroke before the campaign began, leaving three main candidates. Following the vote in November 1824, no one candidate had a majority of popular or electoral votes, although Jackson led with 152,000 votes and 99 electoral votes, with Adams in second with 113,000 votes and 84 electoral votes, Crawford in third with 40,000 votes and 41 electoral votes, and Clay in fourth with 47,000 votes but only 36 electoral votes. As Speaker, Clay would have control over the House vote where the final count for President would take place. When the debate was over, the House declared Adams, and not Jackson, the winner. Jackson supporters claimed that Clay

made a "corrupt bargain" with Adams, a claim that was never supported with any firm truth but which was alleged even more when Clay resigned from the House on 6 March 1825 after President John Quincy Adams offered him the portfolio of Secretary of State. Adams later penned a letter explaining his reasons for choosing Clay:

As to my motives for tendering him the Department of State when I did, let that man who questions them come forward. Let him look around among statesman and legislators of this nation and of that day. Let him then select and name the man whom, by his preeminent talents, by his splendid services, by his ardent patriotism, by his all-embracing spirit...by his long experience in the affairs of the Union, foreign and domestic, a President of the United States, intent only upon the welfare and honor of the country, ought to have preferred to Henry Clay.

When now-Senator John Randolph of Virginia, Clay's political enemy, accused the Kentuckian of being an alcoholic, the two men dueled but neither was harmed in the fight.

At the end of all of this harangue over some alleged "bargain" was the fact that Henry Clay would never again be Speaker of the House. Historian Joseph Cooper wrote:

Henry Clay...wrought basic and permanent changes in the role of the speaker. Once he assumed the office in 1811 he transformed it from a weak and rather apolitical position into the focal point of leadership within the House. In contrast to his predecessors, he involved himself deeply and extensively in the decision-making process and employed his considerable talent and charm to assemble and maintain majority support for major policies that bore his stamp. Similarly, in the interests of his program he boldly began to exploit and even extend the various sorts of leverage the rules conferred on the speaker.

Added Mary Parker Follett, considered one of the best historians on the Speakers of the House and the institution of the office, "As a presiding officer, Clay from the first showed that he considered himself not the umpire, but the leader of the House: his object was clearly and expressly to govern the House as far as possible. In this he succeeded to an extent never before or since equalled [sic] by a Speaker of the House of Representatives. Clay was the boldest of Speakers. He made no attempt to disguise the fact that he was a political officer." In all, Clay was Speaker of the House throughout his House service, except for the second session of the 16th Congress. No American politician, past, present, or future, can claim such a mantle of leadership.

As America's top diplomat from 1825 to 1829, Clay tried to institute his "American System" of emphasizing trade in the Western Hemisphere over that with Europe. He tried to get the United States to participate in the Inter-American Congress in Panama in 1826, and updated the Adams-Onís Treaty of 1819, signed by President Adams when he was Secretary of State, which established the borders between the United States and Mexico. However, whereas as Speaker of the House he had control over the entire House, as Secretary of State he had little overall control over anything. In one yearly report, he complained that "there are too many and too incompatible duties devolved upon the Department...The necessary consequence of this variety and extent of business is, that it lessens responsibility, or renders the enforcement of it unjust." At the same time, he could not escape the charges of a "corrupt bargain" with Adams. He campaigned for the president in 1828, but Jackson got his revenge for the 1824 campaign and won in a landslide.

Re-elected to Congress - Senator Henry Clay
Out of Congress, out of power for the first time in many years, Clay returned home to Kentucky and his beloved estate, "Ashland." For the next two years he corresponded with many of his political allies and friends. In 1830, the Kentucky legislature nominated him as the state's favorite son candidate for the presidency in the 1832 election, and, in 1830, elected Clay to a seat in the U.S. Senate for the third time. He served in this tenure from 10 November 1831 until 31 March 1842, when he resigned the seat. He was a strong voice against the administration of his political enemy, President Andrew Jackson, and helped to override a presidential veto of the Bank of the United States act. He as now considered the head of the party; Daniel Webster wrote to him on May 29, 1830, "You are neces-

sarily at the head of one party, and General Jackson will be, if he is not already, identified with the other. The question will be put to the country. Let the country decide it." Nominated by the National Republicans at their national convention in Baltimore in December 1831, Clay and his running mate, John Sergeant of Pennsylvania, ran of a platform of Jackson's opposition to the Bank of the United States. But Jackson was widely popular in the country, and Clay was beaten in a landslide, 288 electoral votes to 49 and 687,502 votes to 530,189.

The 1832 election was the last for the National Republicans, and their members, including Clay, gradually moved into the Whig Party. In the Senate and in the nation as a whole, Clay became one of the party's leaders, speaking out against Jackson administration policies. When the president forced American Indians from their native lands in the South and Midwest to the west, Clay denounced the president. At the same time, as a slaveholder, he defended slavery. In 1833, he again faced the potential of disunion. South Carolina enacted an ordinance that nullified a protective tariff enacted by Congress. President Jackson threatened that if the state did not rescind the ordinance, a challenge to federal control of the nation, he would send troops to enforce it himself. Despite his opposition to Jackson, Clay helped broker a resolution between both sides that upheld the tariff but promised its repeal after seven years. Thus, it was Senator Henry Clay, and not President Andrew Jackson, who helped avoid a clash between the state of South Carolina and the federal government.

In 1839, during a speech in which he attacked those who would outlaw the practice of slavery, Clay made the famous statement that "I would rather be right than be President." he was considered the leading candidate for the Whig presidential nomination in 1840, but the Whigs, predominantly composed of antislavery elements, turned against him and nominated General William Henry Harrison for President instead, with Harrison winning the White House. Harrison died a month into his administration, and he was replaced by John Tyler, a Jacksonian Democrat added to the Whig ticket to earn cross-party support.

Leaving the Senate - A Run for President

Clay soundly opposed the new Tyler administration, and, deciding to devote himself to another presidential run, resigned his Senate seat on 31 March 1842. Despite not changing his views on slavery but calling for moderation on all sides to avoid disunion and civil war, Clay was nominated by the Whigs for President when they held their nominating convention in Baltimore in May 1844. Clay was opposed by Democrat James K. Polk who, like Clay, was a former Speaker of the House, the first time two Speakers faced each other in one campaign. Polk ran as a defender of the right to own slaves, calling for the admission of Texas as a slaveholding state.

Clay's numerous statements throughout his career on the issue of slavery, showing both a defense and a frowning upon it, confused many and hurt his chances. A published letter in which he called for the admission of Texas as a slave state while telling northern abolitionists that he would fight for the admission of Texas as a free state served to further injure his chances. The last harm to his campaign came in the form of the Liberty Party, a small group of northern abolitionists who saw both parties as defenders of slavery. This party nominated James G. Birney of Ohio for President and Senator Thomas Morris of Ohio for Vice President. Although this diminutive third party had no chance to win the election outright, it did have the power to throw the election to Polk. Although Polk won 275 electoral votes to Clay's 105, the popular vote count was 1,337,605 for Polk and 1,299,062 for Clay - a margin of just 38,000 out of 1.8 million total votes cast. Birney's 62,263 votes, had they gone to Clay, probably would have given him the presidency he so coveted, although it is impossible to say without a clear indication of where those votes would have come from. It was Clay's third defeat in a presidential election, and was to be his last. One writer noted the "cheers" "which his magic name evoked." He added, "Men shed tears at his defeat, and women went to bed sick from pure sympathy with his disappointment." One Rhode Island sea captain told the writer on the morning of the 1844 election, "Could my life insure the success of Henry Clay, I would freely lay it down this day."

Even to this day, Clay's defeat in the 1844 election, caused mainly over the subject of slavery, is a mystery to most historians. Clay had a longstanding abhorrence of slavery; he once called it "unsightly and revolting - an evil, and one of great magnitude." He described its power to keep the Union together, and to whip the U.S. government into a frenzy, noting "its baneful influences through the halls of legislation...twining its sable folds around the very pillars of government, contaminating and withering."

In 1836, he was elected as the President of the American Colonization Society, an organization established to send freed slaves back to Africa and freedom; at one meeting he stated:

> If I could be instrumental in eradicating the deepest stain upon the character of our country, and removing all cause of reproach on account of it, by foreign nations; if I could only be instrumental in ridding of this foul blot that revered State that gave me birth, or that not less beloved State which kindly adopted me as her son, I would not exchange the proud satisfaction which I should enjoy, for the honor of all the triumphs decreed to the most successful conqueror.

In fact, in his "letter of Emancipation," Clay wrote, "I am aware that there are respectable persons who believe that slavery is a blessing, that the institution ought to exist in every well organized society and that it is even favorable to the preservation of liberty. Happily the number who entertain these extravagant opinions is not very great and the time would be uselessly occupied in an elaborate refutation of them."

Clay earned the undying enmity of his fellow Kentuckians and southerners. One such critic, who published an 1851 pamphlet under the name of A Southern Clergyman, condemned Clay as one of those "traitors to the South, who love government office and national popularity more than their country."

Clay was now again out of the Congress, and despite his opposition to the war in Mexico his voice was not as important as it once had been. His son, Henry Clay, Jr., enlisted in the army and was killed in action in Mexico.

Re-elected as Senator - Clay's Final Years
In 1848, Clay tried to gain the Whig presidential nomination again, but he was beaten at the party's convention by war hero General Zachary Taylor. Clay instead accepted a fourth election to the U.S. Senate, and he took his seat on 4 March 1849. Again the nation confronted the evil of slavery, and Clay rose to draft an agreement, this time with Senator Stephen A. Douglas of Illinois, which allowed the New Mexico and Utah territories to enter the Union as slave states, while California entered as a free state. For the third time in his congressional career, Henry Clay had fashioned a remedy that was merely a bandage on a wound the nation would have to confront in a civil war that was now only a decade away. The *Daily National Intelligencer*, the main newspaper in Washington, stated, "The movement in the Senate yesterday by the distinguished Senator from Kentucky will not fail to attract the reader's attention. Coming from Mr. Clay, whether we regard his standing in the estimation of his countrymen, of the laudable motive which has induced him to bring forward his plan for reconciling the existing conflict of opinions concerning the new Territories, his proposition, as a whole, is entitled to the most respectful and the most grave consideration of all parties."

In 1849, Clay, whose health had begun to slowly deteriorate in 1844, came down with tuberculosis. He left Washington and went south to Cuba where he hoped the warm weather would be good for his health. He returned to the capital in December 1849, but his health continued to decline. On 29 June 1850, after a long fight, Clay succumbed to his illness at his residence in the National Hotel in Washington at the age of 75. Former Vice President John C. Calhoun, a political enemy of long standing, was quoted, "I don't like Clay...I wouldn't speak to him, but, by God! I love him."

An Enduring Legacy
It is perhaps owing to the power of the name and service of Henry Clay that when his correspondence and speeches were published in ten volumes just after the turn of the twentieth century, former Speaker Thomas B. Reed wrote the introduction. Reed wrote that Clay was "for more than forty years the most picturesque and remarkable figure in American politics." Even before his death, Clay's

eminence in the American political structure was realized by friend and foe alike. In an 1845 article in the *American Whig Review*, it was stated,

> From his birth in a farmhouse in Virginia amid the conflict of the Revolution, and his entrance, an unfriended youth, into the hardships of a professional life in the West, to his last exit from the chief counsel of the nation - whether lifting the hand of eloquence at the bar or in the senate-chamber...did Mr. Clay ever leave with one stain upon his public character, or without an addition to his honorable fame.

In 1955, more than a century after Clay's death, the Senate formed a committee, headed by then-Senator John F. Kennedy, to name the five greatest Senators and have their portraits be put on permanent display in the Senate Reception Room next to the Senate chamber. After much debate, Clay was named as one of the five, along with Daniel Webster of Massachusetts, John C. Calhoun of South Carolina, Robert M. La Follette, Sr., of Wisconsin, and Robert A. Taft, Sr., of Ohio. How ironic it is that this man of Virginia, adopted by Kentucky, who served for seven terms as Speaker of the House, was named one of the five greatest Senators in American history.

Further Reading:
Clay, Henry (Daniel Mallory, ed.), *The Life and Speeches of the Hon. Henry Clay* (New York: R.P. Bixby & Co.; two volumes, 1843).

———. *An Address of Henry Clay to the Public; Containing Certain Testimony in Refutation of the Charges Against Him Made by General Andrew Jackson, Touching the Last Presidential Election* (Washington, D.C.: Peter Force, 1827).

Colton, Calvin, *The Life and Times of Henry Clay* (New York: A.S. Barnes & Co.; two volumes, 1846).

———. ed., *The Private Correspondence of Henry Clay* (Boston: Published by Frederick Parker, 1856).

Follett, Mary Parker, "Henry Clay, as Speaker of the House," *New England Magazine*, 12:3 (May 1892), 344-49.

———. "Henry Clay as Speaker of the United States House of Representatives" in *Annual Report of the American Historical Association for the Year 1891* (Washington, D.C.: Government Printing Office, 1892), 257.

Hopkins, James F., ed., *Papers of Henry Clay* (Lexington: University of Kentucky Press; 10 volumes and 1 supplement, 1959-91).

Kennedy, John F., "Search for the Five Greatest Senators," *New York Times Magazine*, 14 April 1957, 14-16, 18.

Schurz, Carl, *Life of Henry Clay* (Boston: Houghton Mifflin Company; two volumes, 1891).

SPEECHES

OF THE

HON. HENRY CLAY,

OF THE

CONGRESS OF THE UNITED STATES.

BY

RICHARD CHAMBERS.

CINCINNATI:
STEREOTYPED BY SHEPARD & STEARNS.
West Third Street.
1842.

Langdon Cheves

Served as Speaker:
January 19, 1814 - March 4, 1815

Virtually forgotten by history, both for his rather short tenure as Speaker of the U.S. House (1813-14) but even for his longer and more controversial service as President of the Bank of the United States (1819-22), Langdon Cheves was an important figure in American financial circles in the early first quarter of the nineteenth century. Rising to become Speaker upon the resignation of Henry Clay, who was sent as an envoy to Europe to help end the War of 1812, Cheves' term was marked by his opposition to the recharter of the Bank of the United States - ironically an institution he would later head as its President.

Personal History

He rose from modest means from the backwoods of South Carolina, to become one of the most respected and more powerful men in America. Cheves (pronounced "Chev-is") was born in the village known as Bulltown Fort, in the Abbeville district in what is now known as Abbeville County, on the Rocky River, South Carolina, on 17 September 1776, the son and only child of Alexander Cheves, a Scotsman who emigrated to the American colonies and became a trader with the Indians, and

Mary (née Langdon) Cheves. (Historian Marion Brown, in her biography of Langdon Cheves that appears in *American National Biography*, reports that his father may in fact have been named Alexander Chivas or Chivis). What little is apparently known of Alexander Cheves is that he emigrated to America in 1762 and immediately began a thriving trading business in the Ninety Six district of South Carolina, just on the border of the Cherokee and Creek nations. In 1774 he married Mary Langdon, the daughter of a Virginia soldier who saw action in the American Revolution. The Cheves' moved to Bulltown Fort apparently to escape from several attacks on white settlers by Cherokee Indians, although Alexander Cheves did business with these and other Indian tribes in the area. The American Revolution did not treat the elder Cheves well, who was a Loyalist to the British. His sympathies for the British crown cost his business dearly. Bankrupt and forced to earn a living for his family, he moved to Charleston where he was able to obtain gainful employment. In 1779, however, Langdon Cheves' mother died, forcing his father to return to his old home to watch over his son. Alexander Cheves remarried, but his son and his new wife were never close, and he went to live with his father's brother's wife, Mrs. Thomas Cheves, where he remained until either 1785 or 1786.

At the age of 10, Langdon moved with his father and stepmother to Charleston, where he was apprenticed to a merchant in the city to learn the business trade. When he turned 16, he was promoted to the position of clerk. Thus, Langdon Cheves, who would rise to become one of the most powerful men in the American government, never received any formal schooling or education. In a long forgotten diary from the early nineteenth century that was published in 1897, it was noted, "F. tells me that Mr. Cheves, an eminent lawyer and legislator of Charleston (now about 30 years old) was never blest with advantages of education and only went to a woman's school for a few months, until when past 30 he went to somebody a little while to assist him in learning mathematics, but was a mere shop boy in his father's shop in King Street, but having got some taste for reading he resolved to study law and set in."

Cheves decided not to enter the business field, instead staying with the law, and he read the law in the offices of one Judge William Marshall, and, in 1797, Cheves was admitted to the South Carolina bar. (Cheves' congressional biography says that the date is 14 October 1797.) Cheves opened a law practice in Charleston, but his law career was cut short when he decided in 1802 to enter the political field. (Some sources note that Cheves' legal career lasted for a decade, when in fact it lasted less than 6 years.) In 1802 Cheves was elected as a city alderman for Charleston, and, that same year, he was also elected to a seat in the state House of Representatives, where he served from 1802 to 1804, and then again from 1806 to 1808. He refused a third term in the state House when he was elected as Attorney General for the state of South Carolina in 1808. Again, his time in this position was cut short by advancement to higher office.

Early Years in Congress

Following the resignation of Rep. Robert Marion, who had been elected to a seat in the Eleventh Congress (1809-11), Cheves ran to fill the vacancy and was elected on his own. Taking his seat in the Twelfth Congress for its second session on 31 De-

cember 1810, Cheves soon became part of the group of South Carolinians in the U.S. House and U.S. Senate known for their oratory: among them were John C. Calhoun, later to serve as Vice President, and William Lowndes, like Cheves a noted South Carolina attorney who served in the House (1811-22), becoming the chairman of the House Committee on Ways and Means. Cheves was named to the Committee on Naval Affairs, and became the chairman of the Committee on Ways and Means, both in his first term in Congress. In 1810 he was re-elected to the seat for the Thirteenth Congress (1811-13). In the first session of the Congress, Cheves remained a back-bench politician, gradually building himself up as a leading orator on current issues. Of one speech, delivered in March 1814 on the Loan Bill, the *Daily National Intelligencer* said that it was "one of the most impressive bursts of eloquent feeling that we ever witnessed." He joined with Calhoun, Lowndes, David Rogerson Williams, and Speaker of the House Henry Clay to become part of the group known as "The War Hawks" by supporting the War of 1812 and its prosecution against the British. Gradually, Cheves became Speaker Clay's trusted lieutenant, working with Clay to stand for the prosecution of the war against the British. As chairman of the Committee on Naval Affairs, he pushed for additional appropriations to strengthen and reinforce naval preparedness.

The Vote

The second session of the Thirteenth Congress began on 6 December 1813, and lasted until 18 April 1814. On 19 January 1814, Speaker of the House Clay, having been named as one of the commissioners to negotiate peace with Great Britain at talks in Belgium, resigned the speakership, setting off an election for that office that had not been held since Clay became Speaker on 4 November 1811. Cheves, in only his second term in Congress, was put forward as the candidate of those who opposed the administration of President James Madison, while Rep. Felix Grundy, Republican of Tennessee, was the nominee of those who supported the administration. The *Congressional Globe*, the official organ that printed the speeches of Congress, reported that:

"On the motion of Mr. [Elisha Reynolds] Potter [Federalist] of Rhode Island, the House proceeded to the choice of a Speaker. Messrs. Moore, Johnson, and Wheaton, were appointed tellers; and having counted the ballots, Mr. Moore reported, that the whole number of votes given in being one hundred and sixty five, eighty-three were necessary to a choice; that of these votes there were: for Langdon Cheves, 94; Felix Grundy, 59, Scattering, 12, and that Langdon Cheves, having a majority of votes, was duly elected Speaker of the House."

Acceptance Speech

Speaker Cheves' speech as reported in the *Congressional Globe* is as follows:

> *Gentlemen: I thank you for the flattering and distinguished honor you have conferred upon me. The best acknowledgment I can make of the gratitude which I profoundly feel, will be expressed in the exertion of every faculty I possess, to prove that your favor is not entirely unmerited. I am aware of the importance of the station to which you have elevated me, and of the difficult nature of the duties which it imposes; a difficulty to discharge them with reputation, not a little increased by the great ability with which they have been executed by the gentlemen who has just descended from the Chair; but with your support I shall not despair. Err, I undoubtedly often shall, and when my errors shall be calculated to effect, in the smallest degree, the interests of the House or the nation, I shall court your correction, and submit with cheerfulness and pleasure to your authority; but if they be immaterial, s frequent differences of opinion between the House and its presiding officer can add nothing to its dignity, and may diminish its usefulness, I shall ask, what I fear I shall too often need, your kind indulgence.*

Legacy as Speaker

Cheves' tenure as the ninth Speaker of the House lasted from 19 January 1814, when he was elected, until the end of the Thirteenth Congress on 4 March 1815, a period of only 14 months. All available sources on Cheves agree that his most notable accomplishment in that short period was the defeat of the bill to recharter the Bank of the United States on 2 January 1815. In fact, it was Cheves' vote - in a moment when he relinquished the Speaker's chair to both speak and vote on the mea-

sure - that helped to defeat the legislation. The bank, established in 1791 under a charter that lasted for 20 years, was created to help formulate all financial and economic matters of the newly formed United States, questions handled prior to the Constitution by the then-thirteen individual states. The institution that existed from 1791 to 1811, when its charter ran out, is called by historians the "First Bank of the United States." The bank was popular in the northern states, where commerce was handled by banking institutions, but not in the South, where the agricultural economy was not dominated by banks and where the bank was viewed with suspicion of a northern takeover of the South. The end of its charter in 1811 was hailed by southerners, and Cheves, from South Carolina, was one of the House leaders who opposed its recharter and restart in 1814. The *Journal of the House of Representatives* noted that:

> *The Speaker (Mr. Cheves, of South Carolina) rose. After adverting to the rule of the House, which makes it the right and duty of the Speaker to vote in two cases, of which this was one, he proceeded to assign briefly, the reasons which influenced him to vote against the bill. He noticed the opinions expressed on both sides of the House, for and against the measure; and declared his own conviction, that the bill proposed is dangerous, unexampled, and, he might almost say, a desperate resort. He cursorily examined the three views in which passage of the bill had been advocated, namely, as calculated to resuscitate the public credit; to establish a circulating medium; and to afford the ways and means for the support of Government. He delivered, with even more of his usual eloquence and impressiveness, his opinions on these several points, and concluded with expressing his solemn belief, that neither of these purposes would be answered by the bill. He denied that the passage of this bill was demanded by the safety of the nation; but intimated his opinion, that a national bank bill might be framed, by which the avowed objects of the present bill might be accomplished, which he had not doubt would unite a majority in its favor. Although the vote was painful for him to give, he was, therefore, obliged to vote in the negative.*

Cheves is also known for one other fact during his time as Speaker: on 23 December 1814, when Vice President Elbridge Gerry died in office, Cheves, as Speaker of the House, became the next in line for the Presidency, until Senator John Gaillard, Democratic-Republican of South Carolina, was named as the President *pro tempore* of the U.S. Senate.

The end of the war of 1812 in 1814, in part negotiated by former Speaker Henry Clay in Ghent, Belgium, led Cheves to refuse to run for re-election that year. Some historians believe that Cheves realized that Clay would return to the House and would want the speakership back, which would signal a demotion for Cheves, and he instead left the House altogether rather than suffer such an indignity. The *Journal of the House* noted Cheves' resignation from the speakership on his last day in office, 3 March 1815:

> *The ordinary business of the day having been gone through - The Speaker addressed the House in the following terms: "Gentlemen: I have attended you to-day to announce my resignation of the distinguished station with which I have been honored by your kindness. In taking leave of you, gentlemen, I shall be excused for embracing the last occasion to express to you personally my thanks for the frank and liberal support the Chair has experience at your hands. Wherever I may go, in whatever situation I may be placed, I can never cease to cherish, with the fondest remembrance, the sentiments of esteem and respect with which you have inspired me."*

President James Madison offered Cheves the portfolio of the Secretary of the Treasury, but Cheves refused the offer.

After the Speakership
Cheves returned to his native South Carolina, where returned to his law practice. In December 1816, he was elected an Associate Justice of Law and Appeal for the Superior Court of South Carolina. That same year, the U.S. Congress rechartered the Bank of the United States that Cheves had opposed, and President Madison signed the recharter into law before leaving office in 1817. However, the U.S. economy, marked by mismanagement by the James Monroe administration, slid into recession. By 1819, the Bank of the United States

was in dire financial condition, and its president, William Jones, resigned after a congressional committee condemned him in a report detailing his numerous failings in the position. In an effort to stabilize both the Bank and the American economy, the presidency of the Bank was offered by its board of directors to Cheves, who just a few years earlier had been voting against its creation. This "Second Bank of the United States" needed the stimulation and confidence brought on by one of its greatest critics. It is noted in the *American State Papers*, a collection of the papers of the U.S. Congress in the first 50 years of its existence, in the fourth volume on financial matters that arose during the first half century of the government, that "at a meeting of the Directors of the Bank of the United States, on Saturday, 6 March 1819, Langdon Cheves, Esq., was unanimously elected President, in the room of Samuel C. Fisher, Esq., resigned." Four weeks later, Cheves reported to Secretary of the Treasury William H. Crawford that the Bank of the United States was in terrible condition. "The very critical situation of the bank, which is becoming more so every hour, the great interests, both public and private, which are involved in its fate, and the intimate connexion [sic] it has with your Department, I hope will be a sufficient apology for the frequency of my communications," he explained on 6 April. A week later, on 13 April, he again wrote to Crawford on the urgency to assist the bank, which he saw as failing.

> *I have the honor to inclose you a copy of a resolve of the Board of the 12th instant.*
>
> *In the present straitened situation of the affairs of the bank, and the embarrassed state of commerce, it is utterly impossible for the bank to do more than meet its legal obligations to the Government. These, in their mildest shape, bear upon it with the most distressing weight. The Board has perceived in you a disposition to cherish and support the institution, and it therefore ventures to presume on your approbation of a measure which, on the maturest deliberation, it has unanimously deemed essential, not to its pecuniary advantage, but to its safety. I am authorized by the Board to make any general arrangements which may be agreeable to you in the mode of transferring the funds of the Gov-*

ernment, and the most prompt attention will be given to any particular directions which you from time to time be please to give.

Cheves served as the President of the Bank of the United States from March 1819 until his resignation in 1822. Cheves moved to the bank's headquarters in Philadelphia, and in his time as president helped to stabilize both the bank's financial situation as well as that of the nation as a whole. Historian Marion Brown noted that "Cheves instituted conservative policies, reining in the southern and western offices and insisting that each branch office balance its own accounts and cease issuing paper to be redeemed at other branches, particularly at those in the East. No longer could the branch offices depend on the total assets of the Bank of the United States to guarantee local paper. Cheves further insisted that state and local banks meet their loan commitments to the Bank through regular payments in specie or reliable notes." Edwin Perkins, in a 1984 article, explained,

> Langdon Cheves, when judged by his contemporaries for his performance as president of the Second Bank of the United States from 1819 to 1822, received only mixed reviews, but early twentieth-century historians significantly upgraded his rating and accorded his generally high marks for instituting sound management practices where they were allegedly lacking...Cheves' administration was free of scandal, but not totally exempt from criticism. Some charged that he was too conservative, even for a banker. The most serious accusation was that in his effort to build up the bank's reserves of specie, Cheves had precipitated a panic but then [had] done little to relieve the distress associated with the depression that lasted until 1823. His most vocal critic was William Gouge, an ally of President Andrew Jackson, who asserted that under Cheves' administration, "the bank was saved and the people were ruined."

In 1822, Cheves resigned as President of the Bank of the United States, to be replaced by Nicholas Biddle. Cheves was then named as the chief commissioner of claims under the Treaty of Ghent, signed by Henry Clay and others in 1814 to end the war; however, nearly a decade later, claims between the parties involved in the conflict were still being

ironed out and Cheves served as the commissioner to oversee the claims process. Cheves remained in Philadelphia during his tenure as commissioner, afterwards moving to Lancaster, Pennsylvania. However, in 1829, he returned home to South Carolina, where he stayed for the remainder of his life. For a number of years, he used his extensive agricultural holdings to cultivate rice in both South Carolina and Georgia.

In his later years, Cheves became an elder statesman, both of his party and for the South and its interests; in fact, Cheves was an early advocate of the secession of the southern states from the Union, but over the issue of tariff laws and the impact on southern agriculture rather than slavery. In 1832, when the southern states threatened to nullify, or disregard, federal laws regarding the collection of tariffs which hit their agricultural products hard, Cheves argued that an amalgamation of southern states could very well secede from the Union and make its own set of laws which would protect its industries. Pro-Cheves historians have argued that he was against secession, and that he allegedly wrote "three books" opposing any such move by the southern states, but none of these works has ever been found. In fact, editorials from South Carolina newspapers, including the pro-secessionist *Charleston Mercury*, show his intention to support secession. In one editorial, penned in 1844 and reprinted in the *Daily National Intelligencer* of Washington, D.C. (and which was found in the original publication in The British Library in London, England), Cheves wrote:

> The tariff I consider an act of insulting oppression, which ought to be borne only until it can be judiciously resisted...I do not think one state ought to resist alone...It might be different if the state were alone in the suffering; but standing in the midst of common sufferers, much more numerous than themselves, whose arms were folded, the presence of these could operate like a moral condemnation of their act, and chill the warm blood, though animated in so good a cause, and enfeeble the strong arm, just raised to strike. Resistance will be a very solemn act. If it be rashly attempted and fail, it will rivet our chains and bring on us new burdens and insults...Let associations be formed in every

southern and southwestern state and let them confer together and interchange views and information...and when ripe for it, and not before, let representatives from these states meet in convention and if circumstances promise success, let them then deliberate on the mode of resistance...Continue to enlighten the public mind - rouse the public feeling - excite the public shame for the degradation to which we have been brought.

Considered one of the "fire-eaters" (the name for those radicals in the South who stood for secession), Cheves gradually came to support secession for any interference in the slavery question. To these ends, a parley of those who desired secession met in Nashville, Tennessee, from 3 to 11 June 1850. Known as "The Nashville Convention," the meeting, attended by Cheves, was a response to growing pressures put on the South to end slavery, as well as the potential of the Congress to enact the Compromise of 1850, which allowed some new states to come into the Union as "free," or prohibiting slavery. The group eventually passed a resolution stating that southern states would secede if any restrictions were placed by the U.S. Congress on the right to own slaves, or to refuse to allow any of the new areas in the western United States just taken in the war with Mexico to limit the rights of slaveholders to settle and to own slaves there. Although nine southern states sent delegates, the convention was barely covered by the national media. Nevertheless, it was another step on the road to all-out civil war between the North and the South.

Following the death of U.S. Senator John C. Calhoun on 31 March 1850, South Carolina Governor Whitemarsh B. Seabrook offered the vacant seat to Cheves, who refused the honor. It would be his last shot at a political career, which had been, in all its facets, brief at best. In 1852, he attended the state convention at Columbia, South Carolina, which was held to again examine the issue of the secession of the state. Its formation came after a series of public letters from Cheves, as well as former Speaker of the House James L. Orr, calling for such a meeting, were issued. At the convention, Cheves was selected to chair a "Committee of 21" to issue a manifesto of the delegates. Their resolution read, "Resolved, by the people of South Carolina in Con-

vention assembled, That the frequent violations of the Constitution of the United States by the Federal government, and its encroachments upon the reserved rights of the sovereign states of this union, especially in relation to slavery, amply justify this state, so far as any duty or obligation to our confederates is involved, is dissolving at once all political connection with her co-States [sic], and that she forbears the exercise of this manifest right of self-government from consideration of expediency only." Despite this harsh threat against the U.S. government, historian Philip Hamer noted that "Cheves was very much afraid of the convention, which he called 'an infernal machine,' and was anxious to adjourn as quickly as possible." Cheves may have seen that while he and the South felt slighted in regard to the tariff issue, and wanted their right to own slaves left alone, the thought of actually moving forward with the secession of the southern states and what it would precipitate in reaction from the rest of the country, was something he was not willing to see happen to his beloved South.

Langdon Cheves died in Columbia, South Carolina, on 26 June 1857, two months shy of his 81st birthday, and was buried in the Magnolia Cemetery in Charleston, South Carolina. In his obituary, which appeared in the *Charleston Mercury*, it was noted that "one of the high features of Mr. Cheves' character was his public disinterestedness. He never sought office, and he never accepted it, save when he thought he could do the State some service. When he was selected by the Governor to fill the seat in the Senate, vacated by the death of our great [John C.] Calhoun, he only refused because he was an old man and unequal to the duties."

In her 1922 Master's thesis on Cheves, one of the few biographical works which exist on his life (and which, because of its age, is quite hard to get a copy of), Elizabeth Lindquist wrote about the former Speaker:

Langdon Cheves is a name which is today almost forgotten in American history. It is known to few people and loved by less, for Cheves had played the role of mediator - always an unpopular one - the target for the hatreds of all factions. At one time he was one of the most influential and well-known men in America, but he did not retain his important position for very long. As a private citizen he exerted great power over the thinking of the lower south, and especially of South Carolina, from 1830 to 1854. He sacrificed his popularity and his opportunities for public life upon the altar of his convictions for what he deemed the safety and honor of his state. He was aware of the fact that he could never again hold public office; but perhaps he found consolation in the thought that as a private citizen he could possess greater power over the sentiment of his state because his opinions would be considered more impartial.

Further Reading:

Cheves, Langdon, *Aristides; or, A Series of Papers on the Presidential Election* (Charleston, South Carolina: P. Freneau, 1808).

Huff, Archie Vernon, *Langdon Cheves of South Carolina* (Columbia: University of South Carolina Press, 1977).

Letter of the Hon. Langdon Cheves, to the Editors of the Charleston Mercury, Sept. 11, 1844 (Charleston, South Carolina: N.p., 1844).

Lindquist, Elizabeth K., "Langdon Cheves (South Carolina)" (Unpublished Master's thesis, the University of Chicago, 1922).

See also page 419

Dear Sir,   Philadelphia 8th May 1839

        Mrs Dulles (The Grand mother of my Boys) has
particularly desired that they should remain with her
till Monday, which I could not refuse. They will
on that day leave Philadª. for West Chester & be
with you in the Evening. They will go in the
Coach you recommended. —

                                    Very respectfully,
                                        Yr Obedt. Servt
                                        Langdon Cheves

Mr Bolmar
    West Chester,
            Pª

John W. Taylor

Served as Speaker:
November 15, 1820 - March 4, 1821
December 5, 1825 - March 4, 1827

He remains probably one of the most obscure of the 53 persons who have served as Speaker of the U.S. House of Representatives - so little known and remembered by history that his middle name remains, to this day, a mystery. His short service as Speaker of the House, for a single session in the 16th Congress (1820-21) and for both sessions of the 19th Congress (1825-27), is barely remembered in histories of that body. Taylor's short tenure saw him embroiled in the growing controversy over slavery and the admittance of the state of Missouri as either a slave state or a free one.

Personal History
He was born in the village of Charlton, in Saratoga County, New York, on 26 March 1784, the son of John Taylor, a farmer, and his wife Chloe (née Cox) Taylor. An extensive search of the censuses for New York State for 1790 and 1800 show no John Taylor or John W. Taylor in that area of the state. A further search for a birth certificate for a John W. Taylor again turned up no evidence of the family, although this could be explained because Taylor was born in a rural area in 1784, six years before the first national census, which may explain the lack of documenta-

tion. The family, as well, remains more myth than fact: all that is known of John Taylor, the father of John W. Taylor, was that he later became a judge. John W. Taylor received what is now called "home schooling," or an education at home from his parents based on their values.

In 1799, with this educational background in hand, Taylor attended the Union College in Schenectady, New York, which is still in existence under a 1795 charter. Taylor initially desired to enter the ministry, but while at Union College he became interested in legal studies and, following his graduation in 1803 he desired to enter into the study of the law. To earn a living while he studied the law, he taught school for a short time at the Ballston Centre Academy, which he helped to establish, in Ballston Spa, New York, while studying the law with one Samuel Cook. He was not admitted to the state bar until 1807, but once he did he began a law partnership with Cook in Ballston Spa. The following year Taylor was either named or elected as a justice of the peace, and then was appointed as the New York state loan commissioner. He also owned and ran a lumber mill in the town of Hadley, New York. He married Jane Hodge in 1806.

In December 1811, Taylor was elected to a seat in the New York state Assembly. A Republican - not the Republican Party of today, but a political movement known as the National Republican Party - who supported De Witt Clinton, a leading New York politician, Taylor benefited from backing Clinton. In the state legislature, Taylor was one of the leaders of the Republicans and served on a committee which debated the abolition of slavery. When a lottery that benefited his alma mater, Union College, was found to have been corrupt, Taylor served on an investigative panel examining the potential corruption.

Early Years in Congress

In November 1812, Taylor was elected to a seat in the U.S. House of Representatives, and he took his seat in the Thirteenth Congress (1813-15). A report by Taylor on the "admission of [the] Mississippi Territory into the Union" appears in the *American State Papers*, a collection of early documents by the U.S. Congress, but which appears with the date of 17 April 1812, describing Taylor as "from the committee," which would imply that he was sitting as a member of the House a year before the 1812 election. Strangely, this is not discussed in any of the few references on Taylor. In the report, the native New Yorker wrote:

> *Your committee are strongly impressed with the propriety and expediency of dividing the said Territory, so as to form of the same two States, whenever the population, within the limits of each section, shall render it just and proper; and they respectfully submit to the Senate the following divisional line, between the western and eastern sections of the said Territory, viz: up the Mobile river, to the point nearest it source, which falls on the eleventh degree of west longitude from the city of Washington; thence and course due north until the line intersects the waters of Bear creek; thence down the said creek to its confluence with the Tennessee river; thence down the said river to the northern boundary line of the said Territory.*

From the beginning of his service in the House, Taylor remained a stanch opponent of slavery: on 13 February 1819, when Rep. James Tallmadge, Jr. of New York introduced an amendment to the bill ad-

mitted Missouri as a slave state declaring all persons born in the state after the date of admission to be free, and allowing for the gradual emancipation of those who were slaves upon admission, Taylor was one of the amendment's most ardent supporters. In the debate, he said:

> *Our vote this day will determine whether the high destinies of this region, and, of those generations, shall be fulfilled or whether we shall defeat them by permitting slavery, with all its baleful consequences, to inherit the land. Let the magnitude of this question plead my apology, while I briefly address a few considerations to the sober judgment of patriots and statesmen.*
>
> *First: Has Congress power to require of Missouri a constitutional prohibition against the further introduction of slavery as a condition of her admission into the Union? Second: If the power exist[s], it is wise to exercise it?*

Taylor's speeches against slavery were the first to be heard in the Congress, and while he was castigated in the South as a madman he was widely respected for his views that were, at the time, not in the mainstream. His stand made him a leader of the group of House members who opposed slavery known as the "Restrictionists," based on their intent to restrict the expansion of slavery into new territories and states won through wars and the Louisiana Purchase.

The Vote

At the end of the first session of the 16th Congress on 15 May 1820, Speaker of the House Henry Clay resigned because of financial problems brought on by the financial Panic of 1819. As he gave up the prized office, Clay offered the name of John W. Taylor as his chosen successor. Admiration of Taylor for his stand against slavery led Clay to believe that he was a natural leader, and thus was the best potential Speaker for the second session of the 16th Congress. When that session convened on 13 November 1820, the battle to succeed Clay was based on sectional considerations, with Taylor being the "northern" candidate, although the *House Journal* shows the names of no other members who stood for the speakership. After 22 ballots, Taylor was named as the winner, and, in accordance with tradition, the winner was conducted to the Speaker's chair.

Acceptance Speech

At that time, Taylor made some brief comments:

Gentlemen: I approach the station to which your favor invites me, greatly distrusting my ability to fulfil [sic] your just expectations. Although the duties of the chair have become less arduous by improvements in its practice during the administration of my distinguished predecessor, I should not venture to assume their responsibilities without a firm reliance on your indulgent support. In all deliberative assemblies, the preservation of order must depend, in a greater degree, upon the members at large, than upon any efforts of a presiding officer. The forbearance and decorum which characterized this House in its former session, at a period of peculiar excitement, afford, of their continued exercise, a happy anticipation. For the confidence with which you have honored me, be pleased to accept my profound acknowledgements. In my best endeavors to merit your approbation, which shall not be intermitted, I can promise nothing more than diligence, and a constant aim at impartiality. I can hope for nothing greater than that these endeavors may not prove altogether unavailing.

Legacy as Speaker

Former Speaker Henry Clay, who supported the right to own slaves, apparently selected Taylor, a man from his own party, because Clay believed that the issue over the entrance of Missouri into the Union as either a free or slave state has passed, and that Taylor would bring stability to the House outside of that contentious issue. But Clay was wrong. Taylor served as the Speaker for only the second session of the 16th Congress (13 November 1820 to 3 March 1821), and little has been written about his duties during his short tenure. The one matter that was debated and discussed was slavery. In one of his first actions as Speaker, Taylor appointed a three-man committee to examine the Missouri Constitution once it was delivered to the House for ratification. Despite his background of opposing slavery at every turn, Taylor named two slaveowners' rights representatives, William Lowndes of South Carolina and Samuel Smith of Maryland, as well as one his "Restrictionist" ally John Sergeant of Pennsylvania, to the committee.

Their report, quickly delivered, merely dealt with the issue of whether free blacks could be moved into Missouri and remain free.

Ironically, Henry Clay returned to the House in late January 1821 and became embroiled in the deadlocking debate on Missouri. Clay counseled Taylor to name a select committee of 13 representatives to investigate the resolution admitting Missouri to the Union as a slave state further than Taylor's committee had. Again, it was an opportunity to pass the buck on the issue that had forced the entire House into a stalemate in which nothing was getting accomplished, but in an atmosphere of antislavery vs. proslavery it was the best that could be done. But once again the issue came to a head, and when this committee reported that southerners and proslavery advocates called for the introduction of Missouri into the Union as a slave state, moderates wanted an amendment allowing for free blacks to be allowed into the state and remain free, and Restrictionists demanded that the amendment to the constitution be rejected altogether. When the committee's report went to the floor of the House, the amendment allowing free blacks to remain free was defeated, with 82 for and 88 against. The impasse continued.

Next, Clay again called for the establishment of a committee, this time jointly with the U.S. Senate, which would be a "Committee on Compromise" and find a middle way. This committee once again recommended that Missouri be allowed to simply enter the Union as a slave state and, despite the previous action of the House, this time the bill passed, 87-81, as the strain of the entire session and the upcoming rush to adjourn pushed the House into action. Edward K. Spann, whose dissertation on Taylor is the only biographical examination of the man, gave a simple reason why the contentious Missouri constitution passed on this second vote: "The House was not ready to vote for almost anything and...rushed it through." Secessionists in the South warned that not allowing Missouri to be introduced as a slave state would force them to leave the Union, and a potential Civil War, which would happen in forty years, was averted with this vote. But the capitulation to the slaveowners' rights group in the House was not that body's most auspicious moment. And it marked the end of John W. Taylor's short tenure as Speaker not with a flourish but a vote against conscience and a rush for the doors towards adjournment.

On 3 March 1821, Taylor rose in the House chamber and addressed his colleagues:

> *Deeply penetrated with a sense of the kindness and liberality, which, in terms, and from a source the most flattering, have dictated the recent expression of your approbation, I shall ever esteem it the highest reward of any public services. If the duties of the Chair have been discharged in any degree to your satisfaction, it is attributable chiefly to those feelings of generosity which have covered my numerous errors, and which have rendered to purity of motive the deference due to superior merit. My inexperience has been compensated by your prudent counsels, and by a dignified deportment, which had seldom required the interposition of a presiding officer.*
>
> *Entertaining, gentlemen, for every member of this House no other sentiment than respect and friendship; endeared to many by recollections of united deliberation and effort, in a period of great national embarrassment; and grateful to all for the magnanimous support which constantly has been afforded to me, I shall never cease to rejoice in your individual welfare.*
>
> *Carry with you, gentlemen, to the bosom of your families and friends my best wishes for your prosperity, and, under the protecting care of a benign Providence, may each of you enjoy the continued confidence of the wise and good, and largely contribute to perpetuate the union and glory of our common country.*

In an abandonment of more of his allies, Taylor supported military budget cuts following the Panic of 1819. With less government expenditures, Taylor believed that the decline in tax revenues needed to be offset by budget cuts. But this angered Secretary of War John C. Calhoun and Secretary of the Navy Smith Thompson, as well as promilitary forces in New York.

Taylor paid for the submission to the slaveowners and their representatives in Congress, as well as his antagonizing of the Madison administration: when the

17th Congress convened on 3 December 1821, much of Taylor's support in the North vanished during the vote for Speaker. The contest took two days and 12 ballots in total, but Philip Pendleton Barbour of Virginia was elected as Speaker.

After Leaving the Speakership

Taylor remained in Congress, but took less of a leadership position. Instead, he became a close friend of John Quincy Adams of Massachusetts, one of the leading luminaries of the antislavery movement in the Congress. In 1824, Taylor became one of Adams' supporters in his presidential bid. In fact, in the close election that year, Taylor served, along with Philip P. Barbour, as the two representatives of the U.S. House in helping to count the electoral votes from the several states. Following the certification of Adams' election, Taylor received the new president's backing in succeeding Henry Clay - who had regained the speakership in the 17th Congress (1823-25) - for the second time as Speaker of the House. This time, Taylor was more supportive of the administration he represented in the House, but his enemies - among them future President Martin Van Buren - were working behind the scenes to undermine him. By the end of the 17th Congress, an amalgamation of the supporters of General Andrew Jackson - whom Adams had defeated in the 1824 election - and Senator William Crawford of Georgia, were opposing the Adams administration in the Congress. In the 1826 mid-term election, this group sent a majority to sit in the 18th Congress. When the members convened for the new Congress on 3 December 1827, Andrew Stevenson, Democrat of Virginia, was elected on the first ballot over Taylor by 10 votes. Once again, Taylor sat in a Congress that had rejected him as its Speaker.

Taylor remained in the House until 1833, defeated for re-election in 1832 when his political enemies spread unsubstantiated rumors of infidelity in his marriage. He returned to New York, where he settled in Saratoga County and practiced the law there for several years. In 1840 he was elected to the New York state Senate, but he suffered a stroke in 1842 and was forced to resign. He then moved to Cleveland, Ohio, to live with one of his daughters who cared for him. He remained at his daughter's home until his death on 18 September 1854 at the age of 70. His body was returned to his home state, and he was laid to rest in City Cemetery in Ballston Spa. Just six years after his death, the issue of slavery that he had dealt with in the 1820s exploded into the Civil War.

John W. Taylor, despite his near anonymity in American history, was an important politician at a time when the United States sought to get a grasp on the issue of the time - slavery - which could not be solved absent the secession of the slave states and/or a civil war. He worked to solve the impossible, and for that he deserves a better fate than the one history has dealt him.

Further Reading:

Alexander, DeAlva Stanwood, "John W. Taylor," *Quarterly Journal of the New York Historical Association*, 1 (January 1920); 14-37.

Spann, Edward K., "John W. Taylor, The Reluctant Partisan, 1784-1854" (Ph.D. dissertation, New York University, 1957).

————. "The Souring of Good Feelings: John W. Taylor and the Speakership Election of 1821," *New York History*, 41 (October 1960), 379-99.

104

Ballston May 6. 1833

Rev. W. B. Sprague

Dear Sir

In answer to your polite note of the 30ᵈ ult. I have to say, that although there are in my possession autographs of many distinguished individuals, they are principally of a character to render publication inexpedient. Some are letters from former Presidents, Vice Presidents, Senators, Representatives & Secretaries of Departments in relation to candidates for offices; others, expressive of free opinions in regard to political men & measures, perhaps not strictly confidential, but not designed for the public eye. If upon examination I shall meet with any, proper to communicate & worthy of your acceptance, I shall be happy to become a contributor to your interesting collection.

I have the honor to be
With great regards
your obidt servt
John W. Taylor

Philip Pendleton Barbour

Served as Speaker:
December 4, 1821 - March 4, 1823

He remains the only man to serve as Speaker of the U.S. House of Representatives and serve on the U.S. Supreme Court. His service in both offices was brief: he served just one term as Speaker, in the Seventeenth Congress (1821-23), and only five years on the high court (1836-41). His service as Speaker came more by accident, as it occurred when Henry Clay, who served as Speaker for nearly his entire tenure in the House, had left the body due to personal reasons, and the office became vacant due to the unpopularity of Clay's successor, Speaker John W. Taylor. The fifth of President Andrew Jackson's six U.S. Supreme Court nominations (the most by any nineteenth century President), Barbour is remembered more for his time on the Court than his speakership. Although his name is now largely forgotten, Philip P. Barbour, the scion of a famed Virginia family, was memorialized as one of the political giants of his time.

Personal History

Barbour was born in Orange County, Virginia, on 25 May 1783, the son of Thomas Barbour, a farmer and planter in rural Virginia and a member of the Virginia House of Burgesses, and his wife Isabella (née Thomas). Some sources note that Isabella Thomas Barbour may have been named Mary Thomas, but these are contemporary, while older sources give the first name. She was distantly related to Edmund Pendleton (1721-1803), who served in the Continental Congress. One of Philip Barbour's brothers, James Barbour (1775-1842), later served as the Governor of Virginia. Despite the closeness of the two brothers, their political leanings were quite different. In fact, explained Charles Peck in an 1899 work, "James was a verbose and ornate declaimer; Philip was a close, cogent reasoner [sic], without any attempt at elegance or display. He labored to convince the mind; James to control and direct the feelings." In fact, someone in the 19th century wrote sarcastically of differences between the two brothers, "Two Barbours to shave our Congress long did try; one shaves with froth, the other shaves dry."

According to Dr. Robert A. Brock and Virgil Lewis, it is claimed, without much documentation, that the Barbour family of Virginia is of Scottish origin, descended from John Barber or Barbar, a Scottish poet who served as the archdeacon of Aberdeen as early as 1357. One of his monumental and extant works, "The Bruce," is a chronicle of Robert the Bruce (1306-1329), a Scottish hero for the independence of his homeland. In land records for Virginia, the name of William Barber appears having purchased lands in York County in 1651. But because of the lack of a documented family history, these individuals may not be related to the Barbour family. The first Barbour whose relation to the family can be acknowledged is James Barbour, who purchased land in Spotsylvania County in 1731 and 1733. One of his sons, also named James Barbour, served in the Virginia House of Burgesses in 1764, and later served as the commander-in-chief of the militia for Culpeper County. James' son Thomas, the father of Philip Barbour, was, like other members of his family, a member of the Virginia House of Burgesses. According to Philip Barbour's official obituary in the official reports of the U.S. Supreme Court, written by Associate Justice Joseph Story, who sat on the high court with Barbour, Thomas Barbour "was one of those who, in 1769, signed the 'non-importation act' between this country and Great Britain." After the formation of the Union, he was elected to the legislature. Richard Henry Lee, in a letter to his brother, Arthur Lee, bore testimony to his worth, to the effect, "that he was glad that Thomas Barbour was in our state councils, for he was a truly intelligent and patriotic man." However, despite being a part of one of Virginia's great families, Thomas Barbour suffered a series of financial reverses, and he was unable to finance his son's education.

Nonetheless, Philip Barbour was aided by a local Episcopalian minister who taught him reading and began the study of the law. He entered the College of William and Mary in Williamsburg, Virginia, and graduated in 1799. The following year, after completing his law studies, he was admitted to the Virginia bar. However, desiring to capitalize on the incredible number of emigrants moving west, Barbour moved from his home state to Kentucky, and opened a law practice in the village of Bardstown. This lasted for little more than a year, however, and in 1801 he returned to Virginia and opened a law office in Gordonsville, Virginia.

It appeared for many years that Barbour would remain a country lawyer. He married Frances Todd Johnson, the daughter of a planter in Orange County, where Gordonsville was situated, and the couple had several children. In fact, he became a highly regarded attorney. In 1806, prospering from his career as an attorney, Barbour was able to buy, ironically from his father, a large parcel of land as well as a number of slaves. The land remained fallow until 1821, when Barbour had enough money to begin construction on a grand mansion called Frascati, designed by the architect John Perry, a friend of Thomas Jefferson who helped to design the University of Virginia.

In 1812, Barbour's brother was elected as the Governor of Virginia. At the same time, Philip Barbour was elected to a seat in the Virginia House of Delegates, the lower house of the state legislature. He sat for a single two-year term, serving on the finance and judiciary committees, and becoming a supporter of the war being waged against England, known to history as the War of 1812.

Early Years in Congress
In 1814, Barbour was elected as a Republican (not the modern Republican Party, but the Jeffersonian Republican Party) to the Thirteenth Congress, after the death of Rep. John Dawson left a vacancy. Barbour was eventually re-elected to the next five congresses, serving from 19 September 1814 until 3 March 1825 through the Eighteenth Congress (1823-25). There, he was a staunch advocate of states' rights over national power. At the same time that Philip Barbour sat in the House, his brother James, having left the Governor's mansion, served in the Senate - and, as previously noted, the brothers parted ways politically as well. While James supported the protectionist theory espoused by Representative (and Speaker of the House) Henry Clay, an agenda known as "The American System," Philip Barbour was a strict constitutionalist who railed against high tariffs and protection for American industries. Barbour's speech in 1820 against protectionism had earned him wide praise, and, as a member of the Committee on Manufactures, he voted against the protective tariff of 1816; he also voted against federally funded internal improvements, including the building of roads and canals, as well as the funding of a national bank, all policies he saw as infringing on the rights of states as denoted in the Tenth Amendment to the U.S. Constitution. Although not as important now, the fight over the federal funding of internal improvements

was a leading controversy in the nineteenth century. Most importantly, however, he argued against any restrictions on the right to own slaves.

Despite being a member of the National Republican Party, he challenged the party many times in numerous votes in the House, and he joined a group of Virginians, including John Randolph and Spencer Roane, among others, who backed a series of principles upholding states' rights. In 1816, the Congress, attempting to increase the pay of its members, enacted a law that became the focus of extreme controversy. Prior to the enactment of the "Compensation Act," which provided an increase in the salaries of congressmen to $1,500 a year, members of the House, particularly, were not well paid; in fact, some earned approximately $6 per day plus travel expenses per mile traveled. Although the passage of the law was wildly popular in the House, it was just as unpopular with the American people. Rep. Henry Clay, returning home to Kentucky, reported that he had not met with one constituent who supported the law. There is no record of whether or not Barbour supported the bill, but he did return to Virginia and found equal hatred and disgust for it. "Gentlemen mistake if they suppose that it was a storm raised only by a few factious printers," he told the House during a debate over the law after it became controversial. "They equally mistake if they suppose that it was merely a momentary ebullition of passion among the people." Then, describing the reaction across the nation, he added, "There was at first a violent excitement; gentlemen might call it, if they pleased, a storm. But that storm, even when its fury abated, subsided into a fixed and settled discontent at the measure; it met the disapprobation and excited the discontent of the grave, the reflecting, and the deliberate; and such he believed to be the case with an immense majority of the American people."

Barbour also argued for the constitutionality of the system of slavery. During the debate over the Missouri Compromise of 1820, he stated, "This is neither the time nor the occasion for the discussion of the abstract justice or injustice of slavery...we are the creatures of the Constitution, not its creators; we are called here to execute, not to make one. Let gentlemen, then, remember that it is not sufficient for them to show that slavery cannot be justified in

itself...they will yet fail to maintain their ground, unless they can also show that the Constitution gives us power over it." In another speech, he warned of the peril to the Union if slavery was challenged: "Let it not be supposed that I come here as the apostle of disunion...but, whilst I deprecate disunion as the most tremendous evil, I cannot shut my eyes against the light of experience." He counseled that admission of western states that barred slavery was also an evil as well, calling them "the theatre on which the title to itself may be decided, not by Constitutional debate...but by that force which always begins where constitutions end."

The Vote

The Seventeenth Congress convened in Washington on 3 December 1821. Whereas the Sixteenth Congress had been strongly in favor of protection of American industries, the Seventeenth leaned more towards free trade. In the Sixteenth Congress, Speaker of the House Henry Clay resigned for personal reasons, and Rep. John W. Taylor of New York was elected in his stead. But Taylor was an ardent abolitionist, and his political positions angered many of the southerners in the House. In this new Congress, the Jeffersonian Republicans held 155 seats to 32 for the Federalists. On 4 December, the second day of the new session, the House moved to elect a new Speaker. Although the *Journal of the House of Representatives* does not note the names of those nominated for the position or the votes taken, it does state that on the 12th ballot Philip P. Barbour was elected.

Acceptance Speech

Escorted to the Speaker's chair, he was sworn in by Rep. Robert Wright, Republican of Maryland. At that time, the new Speaker addressed his colleagues:

> *Gentlemen of the House of Representatives: I should do injustice to myself if I did not express to you the warm feelings of gratitude which have been excited in my bosom by the appointment which you have just conferred upon me. Those feelings are produced, not only by the consideration that this mark of your confidence is a distinguished one, but by the further consideration that it is as unexpected as it is distinguished. In accepting the office to which you have thus called me, I speak in the most perfect*

sincerity of heart when I assure you that I feel a fearful apprehension in relation to my ability to discharge its duties in a manner equal either to my own wishes or your expectations. I am sensible of the arduousness of the task; I am sensible too of my own it is, that, whatever can be done by diligent attention, and by an unceasing application of such capacity as I possess, shaft be done. As it respects myself, the only hope which I entertain that I shall, in any tolerable degree, acquit myself of the responsibility which I am about to assume, rests upon a consciousness that it will be my constant endeavor so to do; but my great reliance is on the support of this House, and its knowledge that the preservation of order is indispensably necessary to glove dignity to the proceedings of any deliberative body.

Legacy as Speaker

Despite his now occupying the most important position in the House, few biographies of Barbour go into detail on his work during the Seventeenth Congress. Even a search of the *Journal of the House* from the entire three sessions of that Congress show only several letters from others to Barbour relating merely to House business, including one from a representative who resigned to take a seat in the Senate and another from a man who accepted a medal based upon a House-passed resolution. William Henry Smith, an historian of the Speakers, explained Barbour's tenure as Speaker in one sentence: "A partisan in the strictest sense of the word, he presided with impartiality and materially strengthened his popularity with the members." Despite holding the most powerful position in the House of Representatives, the tenure of Philip Barbour in this capacity has been neatly wiped from the history books.

After Leaving the Speakership

In 1824, Barbour decided not to run for re-election to his House seat, desiring instead to return home to continue his law practice. Instead, he was named as a judge on the General Court for the Eastern District of Virginia. However, he did not sit on this court long, as his former constituents put his name up for election to the U.S. House again, and Barbour was elected to a seat in the Twentieth Congress (1827-29). Having been elected in opposition to the administration of President John Quincy Adams, Barbour fulfilled his constituents' desires as he railed against the policies of the Adams' administration in speech after speech in the House. Ironically, while Barbour was attacking the government, his brother James was serving in the Adams' cabinet as Secretary of War. Barbour earned such respect from southern supporters that in the Twenty-first Congress (1829-31) there was a short-lived move to elect him Speaker over the current Speaker, Andrew Stevenson, a Jacksonian Democrat. In 1828, moving from the Jeffersonian Republican Party to the Jacksonian Democratic Party, Barbour was one of the first to support General Andrew Jackson's 1828 presidential campaign, and worked to get the military hero of the Battle of New Orleans elected to the presidency. In 1829, Barbour was named as a delegate to the Virginia Constitutional Convention, and, when fellow delegate (and former President) James Monroe, the convention's president, took ill, Barbour was elected president in his place. Hugh Pleasants, writing in the *Southern Literary Messenger* in May 1851, offered his notice of Barbour at the convention:

No man could reason from premises to conclusions with more unerring certainty, or was less liable to be diverted from his path by the chicanery of an adversary. The view which he took of a subject was never very broad, but it was always strong, and he maintained it with an ability corresponding with its natural strength. He was a most formidable adversary in argument...if there was any fault to be found with the material of his public speeches, it may be said to be consisted in an inveterate habit of refining. The peculiar structure of his mind, and the skill which long habit had imparted, in handling the weapon of logic, no doubt led him into this error. From indulging in it too freely, he sometimes took what the law books call "a distinction without a difference," and wandered through all the mazes of metaphysics, lost himself and his hearers, in a cloud of abstractions.

Andrew Jackson's election, and Barbour's support of him, earned the Virginian high praise from the new administration, and consideration for high federal office once a vacancy could be found. In 1830, Jackson named Barbour as a judge on the Federal District Court for Eastern Virginia. Although the appeals courts system that now exists one step below the U.S. Supreme Court had not been established at that time, this appointment did place Barbour in one of the highest courts in the land. He sat on the court with Chief Justice John Marshall, who sat on that court as part of his circuit duties.

The Democrats, now the party of Jackson, convened for their national nominating convention in Baltimore on 21 May 1832, with delegates present from every state save Missouri. President Jackson was nominated for a second term to wild applause, but the real challenge was in the selection of his running mate, vacant due to the resignation on 12 December 1832 of Vice President John C. Calhoun. The names of several men were tossed into the ring, including Martin Van Buren, Barbour, and Richard M. Johnson of Kentucky, a hero of the wars against the Indians and, allegedly, the murderer of the Indian chieftain Tecumseh. On the first ballot, Van Buren had 208 votes, Barbour had 49, and Johnson had 26. Van Buren, having received the necessary (and, according to the new two-thirds rule instituted prior to this convention) votes, was declared the Vice Presidential candidate of the Democratic Party. Some of Barbour's supporters planned to place his name on state ballots for vice president and have the entire election thrown into the U.S. House, where they believed Barbour's popularity could get him elected over Van Buren, but the scheme failed.

Service on the Supreme Court

The resignation of Associate Justice of Supreme Court Gabriel Duvall on 15 January 1835 left a vacancy on the court that President Jackson needed to fill. From 1831, as Chief Justice Marshall aged and it became clear that his time come, President Jackson had considered many people for the high court's top position, including Barbour. The Virginian's political nemesis, former President John Quincy Adams, wrote in a letter that he feared for the court - and the nation - if Marshall retired and Jackson named Barbour to the chief justiceship. "If he [Marshall] should now be withdrawn, some shallow-pated wild-cat like Philip P. Barbour, fit for nothing but to tear the Union to rags and tatters, would be appointed in his place."

With Marshall's death on 6 July 1835, Jackson now had two vacancies to fill. On 28 December 1835 he named Attorney General Roger Brooke Taney to succeed Marshall, and, the same day, he nominated Barbour to fill Duvall's seat. Southerners were thrilled at Barbour's nomination; the *Richmond Enquirer* stated that he was "eminently fitted to adorn [the court] with his talents and enlighten with his inflexible and uncompromising states' rights principles." Barbour was confirmed by the U.S. Senate on 15 March 1836 by a vote of 30-11, and he took his seat on the high court.

Philip Barbour served for a mere five years on the Supreme Court, and all historians of the court agree that his service was too short to do much writing of opinions; Professor Frank Otto Gatell wrote that his short tenure did not allow him "to compile a distinctive and forceful judicial record." In fact, in those five years, Barbour only authored one opinion, that of *City of New York v. Miln* (11 Peters 102 [1837]), in which Barbour upheld a New York state law that called for ship captains docking their ships to provide information on all passengers on board, a law that Miln had fought as unconstitutional. Barbour, upholding his states' rights beliefs, wrote that the law provided for a state's general welfare. "Consequently, in relation to these, the authority of a state is complete, unqualified, and exclusive," he wrote. Barbour joined the majority opinions in *Charles River Bridge v. Warren Bridge* (11 Peters 420 [1837]) and *Briscoe v. Bank of Kentucky* (11 Peters 257 [1837]), the former a landmark legal finding. In all, he penned a dozen opinions in total, all of which upheld, in one way or another, the rights of states over that of the federal government. Daniel Webster, the famed orator and U.S. Senator, wrote in 1837, "Barbour I really think is honest & conscientious; & he is certainly intelligent; but his fear, or hatred, of the powers of this government is so great, his devotion to State rights so absolute, that perhaps [a case] could hardly arise, in which he would be willing to exercise the power of declaring a state law void."

In early February 1841, Barbour suddenly became ill with heart trouble. Near the end of the month he appeared to get better, and on the 24th he was attending a court conference and worked until 10 p.m. that evening. Early the next morning, however, possibly because of overwork and stress, he suffered a heart attack and died in his sleep. Barbour was just 57 years old. He was laid to rest not in his beloved Virginia but in the Congressional Cemetery in Washington, D.C.

Attorney General Henry D. Gilpin solemnly announced to the court as they convened for a session on 25 February that Barbour had died that same morning. Chief Justice Roger Brooke Taney then made a statement, echoing the feelings of the entire court towards their late colleague:

> I speak in the name of the Court, and by its authority, when I say that we have scarcely yet recovered from the unexpected blow which had fallen upon us. Our deceased brother, for weeks past, has been daily with us in the hall, listening to the animated and earnest discussions which the great subjects in controversy here naturally produce; and he has been with us, also, in the calmer scenes of the conference room, taking a full share in the deliberations of the Court, and always listened to with the most respectful attention. It was from one of these meetings, which had been protracted to a late hour of the night, that we all last parted from him apparently in his usual health; and in the morning we found that the associate whom we so highly respected, and the friend we so greatly esteemed, had been called away from us, and had passed to another, and we trust, a better world. The suddenness of the bereavement, the character of the Judge we have lost, and his worth as a man, made it proper to suspend the business of the Court until to-day. The time was necessary, not only to pay the honors due his memory, but to recollect and fit ourselves for renewed labors.

> Judge Barbour was a member of this Court but a few years; yet he had been long enough here to leave behind him, in the published proceedings of the Court, striking proofs of the clearness and vigor of his mind, and of his eminent learning and industry. But only those who have intimately associated with him as members of the same tribunal, can fully appreciate the frankness of his character, and the singleness and purity of purpose with which he endeavored to discharge his arduous duties. By those who have thus known him his memory will always

> be cherished with the most affectionate remembrance; and we will cordially unite with the bar in the honors they propose to pay his memory.

Further Reading:

Cynn, Paul P., "Philip Pendleton Barbour," *John P. Branch Historical Papers of Randolph-Macon College*, IV (1913), 67-77.

Gatell, Frank Otto, "Philip Pendleton Barbour" in Leon Friedman and Fred L. Israel, eds., *The Justices of the United States Supreme Court, 1789-1969: Their Lives and Major Opinions* (New York: Chelsea House Publishers; four volumes,1969), I:715-27.

Jacobsen, John Gregory, "Jackson's Judges: Six Appointments Who Shaped a Nation" (Ph.D. dissertation, the University of Nebraska, 2004).

Lowery, Charles D., "Barbour, Philip Pendleton" in John A. Garraty and Mark C. Carnes, gen. eds., *American National Biography* (New York: Oxford University Press; 24 volumes, 1999), 2:142-44.

Smith, William Henry, *Speakers of the House of Representatives of the United States with Personal Sketches of the Several Speakers* (Baltimore, Maryland: Simon J. Gaeng, 1928), 80-84.

Andrew Stevenson

Served as Speaker:
December 3, 1827 - June 2, 1834

Despite holding two of the most important posts during the nineteenth century - that of Speaker of the House of Representatives as well as Minister to the Court of St. James, now known as the American Ambassador to Great Britain, there are few mentions in American history of the name of Andrew Stevenson. The Virginian's service as Speaker from the start of the Twentieth Congress (1827-29) through the first session of the Twenty-third Congress (1833-35) has been brushed over by historians; further, his tenure as Minister to Britain has also been forgotten. Nonetheless, his service as Speaker came during a critical period when the question of the nullification of federal laws by individual states nearly led the country to a civil war.

Personal History

Stevenson was born in St. Mark's Parish, in Culpeper County, Virginia, on 23 March 1785, the son of the Rev. James Stevenson and his wife Frances Arnett (née Littlepage) Stevenson. Some controversy has enveloped around Stevenson's true birthdate; however, his tombstone, in the Enniscothy Cemetery, Albemarle County, Virginia, records his date of birth as 23 March 1785. Alas, like his birthdate, Stevenson's own family is mired in haziness and mystery more than true fact. His

only biographer, Francis Fry Wayland, in the landmark 1949 work on the Speaker's life, explained,

> Concerning the paternal forebears of Andrew Stevenson earlier than his father, the writer has been unable to obtain any information that seems to be dependable. He has found no original records of any sort bearing on the subject. According to one secondary account, James Stevenson, the father of Andrew, was the son of Francina Augustina Frisby and William Stevenson of Chestertown, Maryland, the son of William Stevenson of Lancashire, England. According to another account, however, this was not the case. James Stevenson was apparently of English and Scottish ancestry. His son Andrew, while American minister in London, stated on one occasion that his "Scotch feeling and pride" sprang from his partial Scottish lineage.

As to his maternal ancestors, Wayland - and other researchers - have found a tad more information:

> On his maternal side...Stevenson was descended from the Littlepages, who were of English origin. According to the genealogist Hayden, the first known Littlepage of Virginia was Richard, who received land in New Kent County in 1660. He was sheriff of New Kent

and vestryman of St. Peter's Parish. He was a large landowner in his county, as was his son Richard, also a vestryman at St. Peter's Parish.

Wayland notes that among the family was John Carter, who served as a member of the Virginia Convention of 1788, which ratified the U.S. Constitution, as well as serving as Attorney General for Virginia.

In the time when Andrew Stevenson was readied for his education, it was common for children of wealthy families not to attend schools, as they do now, but to study at home, or receive private tutoring. Stevenson's congressional biography merely states that he "pursued classical studies," which usually meant the study of math, science, and classical languages such as Greek and Latin. He was hired as an assistant to the clerk of the court in Henrico County in 1800, and in 1803 became the deputy clerk of the hustings court (defined as "a local court in parts of Virginia," particularly in the late eighteenth and early nineteenth century) in Richmond. Stevenson then attended the College of William and Mary in Williamsburg, Virginia, where he studied the law. In 1805, he was admitted to the state bar of Virginia. He opened a law office in Richmond.

Stevenson would have remained a country lawyer had he not entered the political field in 1809. In April of that year, he was elected to a seat in the Virginia House of Delegates, representing Richmond. He served for two separate tenures: 1809 to 1816, and then from 1819 to 1821, several times serving as Speaker of that body. There, he laid political markers for himself as a strict constructionist in his support of the rights of southerners to own slaves, and he became a devoted follower of Thomas Jefferson. But it appeared, at least by the end of 1811, that Stevenson, despite being a famed orator, was not going to advance very far in the political circles of Virginia.

That all changed on 26 December 1811, when, during a play, entitled *The Father, or Family Feuds*, at the Richmond Theatre, oil lights from the grand chandelier on the ceiling lit up the room, driving the crowd of more than 600 into a panic. Among these were Governor George W. Smith, who, after getting out, discovered that his child remained inside and went back in to rescue the rest of his family, as well

as Andrew Stevenson's own sister, Elizabeth, both of whom would perish in the flames. In all, 72 people were killed in the disaster, which also included A.B. Venable, president of the Bank of Virginia and many other prominent citizens of the state. James Barbour, the Speaker of the House of Delegates (and, later, a Speaker of the U.S. House of Representatives), was named as the new Governor. Replacing him as Speaker of the House of Delegates was Andrew Stevenson, still in mourning for his sister. He took the position, and led the body in continuing its work. When England cracked down on American trade and impressed, or kidnapped, sailors on American ships, Stevenson pushed for a resolution calling on the U.S. government "in all constitutional and legitimate measures which may be adopted in vindication of the rights and interests of the people of the United States and in support of the character and dignity of the government thereof." He continued his work in the House of Delegates, but, in 1813, he helped to raise a company of infantry, directing them in battle along the Potomac River, but he did not obtain a commission in the U.S. Army that he much desired and coveted.

Stevenson was married three times; his first wife, Mary Page White, died in 1812 only three years into their marriage while giving birth to the couple's first child, John White Stevenson (1812-1886), who, as a Democrat from Kentucky, served in the U.S. House of Representatives (1857-61), as Lieutenant Governor (1867) and Governor (1867-71) of Kentucky and in the U.S. Senate (1871-77). Stevenson four years later then married Sarah Coles, with whom he had one child. Coles, a cousin of Dolley Madison, the wife of Senator and President James Madison, gave Stevenson access to the power brokers in the circles of Virginia political power; Edward Coles, Sarah's brother, served as President Madison's personal secretary. His second wife died in 1848, and the following year he married Mary Schaaf of Washington, D.C.; they remained married until Stevenson's death in 1857.

In 1814, Stevenson ran for a seat in the U.S. House of Representatives. Opposed by fellow Democratic-Republican John Tyler - later to serve as Vice President and President of the United States - Stevenson lost in a close contest by less than 50 votes. Stevenson faced Tyler again in 1816, but again lost to him. Stevenson lost his seat in House of Delegates that year, but in 1818 he concentrated on that alone rather than run again against Tyler and was sent back to the lower body. In 1820, Tyler refused to be nominated for a fourth term, and he recommended to his constituents that Stevenson be elected in his place, although Stevenson turned down the honor that year. At the same time, Stevenson continued to stand for the rights of slaveowners and for the freedom to own slaves. Following the 1820 Missouri Compromise, which allowed the entrance of Missouri into the Union as a slave state, Stevenson introduced a resolution in the Virginia Assembly demanding that Virginia support Missouri's entrance, and that if any state stood against Missouri it would endanger the Union.

Early Years in Congress
In 1822, Stevenson was nominated and elected to a seat in the Eighteenth Congress (1823-25). Taking his seat, he fought vociferously against Henry Clay's "American System," which included the government funding of "internal improvements," or the construction of roads, schools, and other public accommodations. As a man who supported the rights of states to control their own affairs, Stevenson opposed any federal funding of such improvements. He also spoke out against a federal bankruptcy law and a federal tariff law. Stevenson remained in the minority during his first three terms in Congress.

In 1826, however, those allied with Stevenson - in support of former Presidential candidate General Andrew Jackson - won a majority of seats over those who backed President John Quincy Adams. In the Nineteenth Congress (1825-27), the pro-Adams - or pro-administration - forces held a narrow majority, with the pro-administration forces controlling the House by a slim 109-104 margin. In the 1826 election, the pro-Jackson members won 113 seats to 100 for those for Adams.

The Vote
The Twentieth Congress (1827-29) convened in Washington, D.C. on 3 December 1827, with the anti-Adams forces in control. Thus, a new Speaker would have to be elected, with the pro-Adams Speaker of the Nineteenth Congress, John W. Taylor of New York, now out of power. On the first ballot, Stevenson, in only his fourth term in the House, received 104 votes and was declared the elected Speaker. His opposition came from former Speaker Taylor, who received 94 votes, former Speaker Philip Pendleton Barbour (who had served as Speaker in the Seventeenth [1821-23] Congress) of Virginia with 4 votes, and three votes cast for differing candidates, none of who were named in the *Journal of the House of Representatives* or any other available document.

Acceptance Speech
Conducted to the Speaker's chair and given the oath of office by Rep. Thomas Newton, Jr., a pro-Adams (those who still supported former President Adams) congressman from Virginia, Stevenson then turned to the House that just elected him and gave some remarks, seen here in part:

> *Gentlemen: In accepting the distinguished honor which you have been please to confer upon me, I am penetrated with feelings of profound respect, and the deepest gratitude, and I receive it as the most flattering testimony of your confidence and favor. The office of Speaker of this House has been justly considered one of high and exalted character - arduous, in relation to the abilities necessary to its execution, and severely responsible and laborious. Its honor is to be measured by no ordinary standard of value. The individual, therefore, who shall fill this chair to his own reputation, and the advantage of the House, must be distinguished alike by knowledge, integrity, and diligence; he should possess an impartiality which secures confidence; a dignity that commands respect; and a temper and affability that disarm contention. From his general character and personal qualities, he must derive a power that will give force to his interpositions, and procure respect for his decisions. He must conciliate the esteem of the enlightened body over whom he presides.*

Rep. William Cabell Rives, Jacksonian of Virginia, wrote to his friend, fellow Jacksonian Rep. George Rockingham Gilmer of Georgia, "Many of us would have preferred Barbour to Stevenson, but we found the current had been setting too long in another direction, and had carried too many along with it to be changed; and in order to bring our whole force to bear upon Taylor...we all united in favor of Stevenson." Stevenson himself wrote to his close friend John Rutherfoord (1792-1866), later to serve as Governor of Virginia, "It was indeed a desperate struggle, and a scene of intense and awful interest. It was the severest trial of my life, and I had nigh sunk under it. How I ever got through, is more than I can tell." He added, "[The election] was wholly unexpected to them [supporters of President John Quincy Adams], and, strange to say, to us also." Speaking on the House floor later that year, 1826, Stevenson remarked,

> These, sir, are no times for great political experiments. Let us not shake the public confidence in the stability of our free institutions. Let us not especially attempt to swell the powers of this government, already too great, at the expense of the states. Let us guard the limits which divide the two Governments by a watchful and systematic jealousy, on the part of the rulers in both Governments.

Legacy as Speaker

Two major issues that Stevenson faced during his terms as Speaker were the fight between Congress and President Jackson over the re-chartering of the Bank of the United States and the imposition of tariffs on American industry. The First Bank of the United States, established as a federal institution in 1791 (it was closed in 1811, and a Second Bank was established in 1816, lasting until 1841), was despised and distrusted by states' rights advocates and by Jackson, who first removed its deposits and then refused to allow Congress to recharter the bank. As Speaker during the last two years of the administration of John Quincy Adams as well as the first five of that of President Andrew Jackson, Stevenson was uniquely in the middle of the controversy. Sometime after Jackson took office (the letter has no date), Representative Thomas Ritchie of Virginia warned Stevenson, now the Speaker of the House, of "the mischievous consequences of removing the Deposits." He added, "I fear we shall rue the precipitate step in sackcloth & ashes. But what is now to be done? It requires wiser heads and firmer hearts than mine to say." Writing to Virginia Governor John Floyd on 24 February 1834, the Speaker explained that he had taken delivery of resolutions enacted by the General Assembly of Virginia calling

the bank's existence unconstitutional, a stand that Floyd apparently disagreed with:

> I should have contented myself with the simple acknowledgment of the receipt of these resolutions but for the manner in which they have been communicated by you, and a wish to prevent my own opinions from being misunderstood...You are pleased to say in your letter addressed to me that the withdrawal of the public moneys from the Bank of the U. States has been the cause of inflicting deep and lasting injury upon the people of Virginia, and that the act by which it was done was a dangerous and alarming assumption of Power on the part of the President, manifesting a disposition to extend his official authority beyond its just and proper limit. In these opinions as well as those of as kindred character expressed in the Resolutions of the General Assembly, I not only do not concur, but entirely dissent from. I do not deem it needful, not would it be proper at this time and in this form to enter into the discussion of these grave and important questions; nor shall I attempt to trace out the causes which have produced the ruin and distress of which you speak, but of one thing I am quite sure, that the present state of things has neither been caused by the removal of the public monies from the Bank of the U. States nor by the course pursued by the Executive towards that Institution. They are probably more justly attributed to other causes connected with the transacting of the Bank itself, both before and since the removal took place.

In the second issue, in 1828, Stevenson came on board with President John Quincy Adams and helped to pass a tariff which "alter[ed]...the several sets imposing Duties on imports."

In opposition to President Adams, and then in support of President Jackson, Stevenson was a loyal - if not strict - Jacksonian. When Jackson ordered the removal of the tribes of Indians in the American South towards the west, despite the harshness and inhumanity of the policy, Stevenson as Speaker was there to support his President. When South Carolina and other southern states refused to adhere to a national tariff that they saw as imposing on their way of life, threatening a constitutional crisis, Stevenson, a states' rights advocate, nevertheless stood with Jackson and took a national and Unionist view. And, with the Bank of the United States issue, he once again stood as one of Jackson's firmest supporters in backing the removal of the federal deposits from that institution and closing the bank through the machinations first of the Executive and then with the support of Congress.

Even though Stevenson, as Speaker, controlled who sat on what committee, he could not get any of President Jackson's programs through the House Committee on Ways & Means until he replaced George McDuffie, Democrat of South Carolina, as chairman with James K. Polk of Tennessee, who was more accommodating. McDuffie, who had been chairman of Ways & Means since 1825, sided not with Jackson but with his home state during the nullification crisis in 1832, at the same time blocking legislation in his committee in defiance of his Speaker and his President. When McDuffie was delayed in returning to Washington at the start of the Twenty-second Congress (1833-35), Stevenson replaced him as chairman with Gulian Verplanck, Democrat of New York, on an *ad interim* basis. When McDuffie continued to be late, Stevenson saw the opportunity to get rid of a roadblock in enacting the President's legislative program and installed Polk as chairman, moving him from the Committee on Foreign Affairs to Ways & Means. When McDuffie finally did show up, he found his power gone; Stevenson worked with Polk and Verplanck to enact a reduction of tariffs on textiles, particularly those made in South Carolina, all in rebellion to McDuffie. The unpopularity of the action forced the Democrats and Jackson to get Henry Clay of Kentucky, now in the U.S. Senate, to fashion a conciliation to both sides known as the Compromise of 1833.

In *Hinds' Precedents of the House of Representatives of the United States*, a collection of parliamentary law and other motions that have become the foundation of how the House is run and named after its author, Asher Crosby Hinds, it is noted:

> In 1832, Andrew Stevenson being Speaker, Mr. Stanberry, of Ohio, in the course of debate, denounced the Speaker for his political course in severe language. The chair was then occupied temporarily by James K. Polk, who was afterwards Speaker. No notice was taken by the

> Speaker pro tempore or by any Member of that denunciation until after the speech of Mr. Stanberry had been concluded, when exceptions were taken to it. The next day a motion was made to censure the Member for denouncing the Speaker, which was regarded as contempt of the House. After a long debate that motion prevailed by a large majority. But in the course of the debate there was a question raised as to what were the exact words used by the Member in debate. There was then no Congressional Globe; nothing but Gales & Seaton's Register of the debates, which was not a verbatim report. To settle the question, however, Mr. Stanberry repeated and reaffirmed the language. The next day John Quincy Adams offered this rule, which was immediately laid on the table. Five years afterwards it was taken up and adopted, and has since formed a part of our parliamentary law.

Historian Bruce Fuller, whose 1909 work on the Speakers of the U.S. House remains one of the few histories of that office, did not give much coverage to Stevenson, despite the fact that the Virginian was the first man to ever be elected four times to the speakership, serving only a portion of that fourth term. He called Stevenson "a well disposed man of pleasing personality and easy habits" but barely covered his speakership as a whole, or its impact on the House and it history. He compares Stevenson to Clay, but only as - at that time - because both men had been the only Speakers to resign rather than be voted out of office.

A reason for Fuller's pessimistic coverage of Stevenson's three-plus terms as Speaker comes from Mary Parker Follett, considered one of the leading authorities on the speakership at the start of the twentieth century. In her landmark 1902 work *The Speaker of the House of Representatives*, she wrote of Stevenson:

> Of the strongly partisan character of Stevenson's speakership there is little doubt. Always anxious to help his party friends, he was restrained little by the traditional limitations of his office, and parliamentary law and precedent were violated when in conflict with Stevenson's aims. No Speaker, except perhaps [Nathaniel] Macon, has been so distinctly the President's

man as was Stevenson during Jackson's administration. For this reason General [Erastus] Root [Republican of New York] moved in 1832 that the investigating committee in regard to a national bank should be chosen by ballot. The vote was taken and stood 100 to 100. Stevenson then gave his casting-vote against the motion, thus deciding to appoint the committee himself. How active a part Stevenson took in the affairs of the House while Speaker, is shown by the fact that a majority of his constituents, differing from him on the subject of the removal and restoration of the public deposits [back into the Bank of the United States], demanded that he should either change is course of action or retire; either of these courses, Stevenson declared in a letter of May 9, 1834, he was willing to pursue.

In the letter, which appeared in *Niles' Register*, Stevenson tried to justify his almost slavish devotion to President Jackson. He wrote,

I may claim, I hope, at least, the virtue of never attempting to conceal my opinions and views upon political subjects. I have been in the habit, through my whole life, of speaking plainly, and openly, and undisguisedly, and meeting every question with boldness and decision. I shall continue to do so as long as I am in public life, and can assure you, that there has never been an occasion or moment, that I seize with more pleasure to state freely what I feel on this subject, and what I intend doing. I have not bee unapprised or the state of feeling and excitement in my district; nor of the attempts on the part of some of my political foes to wound me at home, whilst I was doing my duty here. To say that I have not been surprised and mortified, at the acrimony and bitterness with which I have been assailed, and at the unwarrantable attempts that have been made to misrepresent and injure me, would be uncandid; and especially, too, coming from those from whom I should least have expected it.

He added,

A representative is a public agent, who represents the wishes, interests, and sentiments of the people; and, though they may not choose to reg-

ulate his course by special instructions, in consequence of a presumption that he may often enjoy information that they do not possess, the real nature of their relation is not materially changed. "The virtue, spirit and essence of a house of representatives is their being the express image of the feelings of the nation."

On 30 May 1834, President Jackson, possibly as a reward for his faithful support, named Stevenson as the U.S. Minister to Great Britain, to replace Aaron Vail, who had been serving as the U.S. Chargé d'Affaires in London since 1832. On 13 June 1834, President Jackson sent to the Senate the following letter:

To the Senate:

I have this day received a resolution of the Senate of the 12th instant, requesting me to communicate to the Senate a copy of the first official communication which was made to Andrew Stevenson, of the intention of the president to nominate him as a minister plenipotentiary an envoy extraordinary to the United Kingdom of Great Britain and Ireland, and his answer thereto.

As a compliance with this resolution might be deemed an admission of the right of the Senate to call upon the president for confidential correspondence of this description, I consider it proper on this occasion to remark, that I do not acknowledge such a right. But, to avoid misrepresentation, I herewith transmit a copy of the paper in question, which was the only communication made to Mr. Stevenson on the subject.

This communication merely intimated the intention of the president, in the particular contingency, to offer to Mr. Stevenson to place of minister to the court of St. James; and to the negotiations to which it refers were commenced early in April, 1833, in this city, instead of London, and have been since conducted here, no further communication was made to him. I have no knowledge that an answer was received from Mr. Stevenson - none if to be found in the department of state, and none has been received by me.

Andrew Jackson

Stevenson, at the time was in ill health, and he quickly resigned not just the speakership but his House seat as well on 2 June 1834. When Stevenson resigned as Speaker, he was replaced on an *ad interim* basis by Rep. Henry Hubbard, Democrat of New Hampshire. Hubbard, whose "service" as Speaker lasted for only a short period, is rarely mentioned in histories of the U.S. House, as he was never formally elected as Speaker.

After Leaving the Speakership

What Jackson - and Stevenson - did not realize is that the former Speaker's support in the Senate, where he would face confirmation, was tenuous at best. A group of pro-bank supporters, as well as those who opposed Jackson's stand on nullification, decided to use Stevenson's nomination to injure the President. In those days, as opposed to now, there were no formal hearings for any presidential nominee; instead, the Senate merely argued the merits of a nomination and then voted. On 30 May 1834 the Senate Committee on Foreign Relations announced a negative report on the nomination, and, on 24 June, following a lengthy debate in the Senate, the nomination was rejected, 23-22. This was the second time in just four years the Senate rebuffed President Jackson; on 25 January 1832, it voted down his previous nominee for the ministership to London, Martin Van Buren.

Out of power for the first time in many years, Stevenson was again rewarded by President Jackson when he was named as the chairman of the Democratic Party convention, held in Baltimore from 20 to 22 May 1835 and which nominated, ironically, Martin Van Buren for President for the 1836 campaign. In March 1836, President Jackson again sent the name of Stevenson to the Senate for the position of U.S. Minister to the Court of St. James, and, despite once again having the Committee on Foreign Affairs recommend against the nomination, the Senate approved it on 16 March 1836, 26-19.

Stevenson served in London from 13 July 1836, when he presented his credentials to the British government, to 21 October 1841, when his recall was presented. Historian Sara B. Bearss wrote of his tenure:

> Stevenson's stint in London was a turbulent one. He negotiated most-favored nation status

> for American vessels trading with Singapore, aided in securing the Smithson legacy that led to the founding of the Smithsonian Institution, won indemnification for slaves seized from three American brigs and freed by British authorities in the Bahamas during the years 1831-35, sought reduction of British tariffs on American tobacco and rice, and worked toward a settlement of the dispute over the northeast boundary of the United States. Nevertheless, his successes were overshadowed by several political slips. He was chagrined when the New York Sunday Morning News reported that he hoped Britain would undergo a democratic revolution and repeal the act of union with Ireland in the wake of financial collapse.

While Minister, Stevenson got into an imbroglio with Daniel O'Connell, a member of the British House of Commons and an Irish nationalist known as "The Irish Liberator," first in the newspapers, and then when Stevenson challenged O'Connell to a duel. This followed O'Connell's statement that slavery in the U.S. was evil, and that Stevenson, as a defender of slavery, "traffics [sic] in blood, and...is a disgrace to human nature." In 1838, Rep. John Quincy Adams, the former President now sitting as a member of the U.S. House, submitted a report to the House to examine whether or not

> the said Andrew Stevenson, holding the privileged character of an ambassador, has, in concert with three other persons, citizens of the United States, one of whom, an officer in their navy, engaged in a conspiracy with intent to <u>stop the wind</u>, or, in the language of the laws of God and of man, to murder the said Daniel O'Connell in a duel, or by a premeditated provocation to a brawl.

Adams asked for Stevenson to be impeached and removed from office, but his motion was tabled, and Stevenson continued in London until the end of his tenure.

In 1840, when Whig William Henry Harrison won the presidency, Stevenson asked to be recalled from London. Harrison died only a month in office, but his successor, John Tyler, whom Stevenson had lost two congressional elections to, named famed orator Edward Everett to the post, and Stevenson returned home to Virginia. In 1842 he lost a close election for Governor of his home state, and he returned to the practice of the law. In 1846, he defended his close friend's son, Thomas Ritchie, Jr., when Ritchie stood trial for murdering a fellow newspaper editor in a duel. Still popular in his home state, in May 1848 Stevenson presided over the Democratic National Convention held in Baltimore. In 1852, when the Democrats, again meeting in Baltimore, nominated Senator Franklin Pierce for President, Stevenson was considered as a possible running mate to Pierce - who was from New Hampshire - as a balance to the ticket. Ultimately, however, Senator William Rufus De Vane King of Alabama was named instead.

In his final years, Stevenson served as the vice president of the Virginia Colonization Society, which sought to send slaves back to Africa for recolonization, and, in 1856, he was named as the rector of the University of Virginia. His second wife died in 1848, and he remarried in 1849; his third wife survived him. Andrew Stevenson died at his 895-acre estate, "Blenheim," located in Albemarle County, Virginia, on 18 January 1857 at the age of 71. He was laid to rest in Enniscothy Cemetery in Albemarle County. In 1908 and 1909, the *Century Illustrated Magazine*, in three separate issues, published letters from Stevenson's second wife, Sarah Coles Stevenson, which she wrote during Stevenson's tenure as Minister to London. These rare pieces of correspondence provide a rare insight into the daily life of an ambassador in a foreign land in the middle of the nineteenth century.

There are few instances of contemporary correspondence or diary entries showing any sort of likeability for Stevenson. John Quincy Adams, who served as President (1825-29) before his final service in the U.S. House of Representatives (1831-48), wrote of the Speaker, "Stevenson is one of those men whom troublous times always push into consequence and distinction - men of talents, of characters black with private infamy, detected, exposed, and yet maintaining their popularity and rising to power on the ruins of honor and virtue."

Further Reading:
Hizer, Trenton Eynon, "Virginia is Now Divided: Politics in the Old Dominion, 1820-1833" (Ph.D. dissertation, University of South Carolina, 1997).

Temperley, Howard, "The O'Connell-Stevenson Contretemps: A Reflection of the Anglo-American Slavery Issue," *Journal of Negro History*, 47:4 (October 1962), 217-33.

Wayland, Francis Fry, *Andrew Stevenson, Democrat and Diplomat, 1785-1857* (Philadelphia: University of Pennsylvania Press, 1949).

See also page 421

HON. JOHN BELL
SECRETARY OF WAR.

John Bell

Served as Speaker:
June 2, 1834 - March 4, 1835

Historians of the contentious national election of 1860 may remember the name of John Bell as candidate for President of the United States on the Constitutional Union ticket, an amalgamation of old-line Whigs and others who wanted to prevent the election of Abraham Lincoln as President, which would force the secession of the southern states and, thus, cause the outbreak of civil war between the North and South. Running with orator Edward Everett as his vice presidential nominee, their ticket got few votes and their "party," if one truly ever existed in any tangible form, died out soon after the election ended. But Bell should be remembered for his service as the Speaker of the House in the Twenty-third Congress (1833-35), as well as his short tenure as Secretary of War (1841) in the administrations of Presidents William Henry Harrison and John Tyler. An important Tennessee politician who battled General Andrew Jackson and his supporters for influence in that state, Bell was called "The Great Apostate" for moving from the Democratic Party and becoming a Whig despite being a major slaveholder in his native state.

Personal History

The son of Samuel and Margaret (née Edmiston) Bell, Bell was born on his family's farm at Mill Creek, a small settlement near Nashville, Tennessee, on 15 February 1797. Although he came from a family of itinerants, Bell was prepared by his father for a career, and he sent his son to local schools and then to Cumberland College (now Cumberland University) in Lebanon, Tennessee, from which he graduated in 1814 at the age of 17. Desiring a law career, Bell entered the law offices of a local Nashville attorney and was trained in the law. He was admitted to the bar in 1816, and opened a practice in the city of Franklin.

Early Years in Congress

In the second decade of the nineteenth century, Tennessee was dominated by the Democratic Party, and in 1817 Bell ran as a Democrat for a seat in the

Tennessee state Senate. Elected, he served a single term, but turned down a chance to run for re-election. Instead, he moved to Nashville, where he continued his law career. Yet he was constantly urged to run for office again, and, in 1826, nearly a decade after his first run for office, he agreed to campaign for a seat in the U.S. House of Representatives. His was opposed by Felix Grundy, a longtime Tennessee politician who was backed by the "father" of Tennessee politics, General Andrew Jackson, the hero of the Battle of New Orleans at the conclusion of the War of 1812 and, in 1824, a candidate for the presidency. Despite being opposed by Jackson, Bell won the seat, and became a member of the House starting in the Twentieth Congress (1827-29). That Congress was divided almost neatly down the middle, with 109 supporters of John Quincy Adams, who had beaten Jackson in the 1824 election, and 104 backing Jackson, who planned an 1828 run. In Congress, Bell sided with the Jacksonian wing of the Democratic Party over the pro-administration Adams Democrats, but he clashed with James K. Polk, another Tennessee politician who was backed by Jackson himself.

During his service in Congress, which lasted from the Twentieth Congress to the Twenty-sixth Congress (1827-41), Bell served as chairman of the Committee on Indian Affairs (Twenty-first through the Twenty-sixth Congresses) and chairman of the Committee on the Judiciary (Twenty-second and Twenty-third Congresses).

The Vote

On 2 June 1834, Speaker of the House Andrew Stevenson arose and addressed the members of the body, delivering a message that shocked the Legislature: he was resigning forthwith. Immediately, the members began a quick canvass of who would succeed Stevenson, a Virginian who had served two different tenures as Speaker of the House (1827-30, 1831-34). Although the records do not exist as to what other candidates were up for the balloting, the official *House Journal* - which, unfortunately, is not a verbatim record of the House but which was put together from various sources from the period - states that after 10 ballots, Bell was elected as Speaker and he was quickly sworn in. Mary Follett, in her 1902 history on the Speakers of the House, states that Bell was opposed by fellow Tennessean James K.

Polk, who later was elected Speaker and, in 1844, became the only Speaker to be elected President of the United States. According to Follett, Bell won 114 votes to 84 for Polk. The *House Journal* stated on the election of Bell:

> The House, on motion, proceeded by ballot to the choice of a Speaker in the place of Andrew Stevenson, resigned, and, upon an examination of the tenth ballot, it appeared that John Bell, one of the Representatives from the State of Tennessee, was duly elected; upon which, Mr. Bell was conducted to the Speaker's chair by Mr. John Quincy Adams and Mr. Richard M. Johnson, from whence he addressed the House.

Acceptance Speech

Speaker Bell's speech and oath of office as reported by the *House Journal* are as follows:

> Gentlemen of the House of Representatives:

> With the greatest sincerity I declare to you that, although I am duly and gratefully impressed with this mark of the partiality and confidence of the House, and by no means insensible to the distinction intended to be conferred on me, I am not without some distrust of the wisdom of my course in accepting the station which your choice has assigned me. Without the slightest experience in the chair, it may be justly apprehended that your selection of a presiding officer has been too much influenced by personal kindness and friendship; and I shall be quite happy if the public interest shall suffer no detriment through a defective administration of the duties of the chair. In ordinary times, and under ordinary circumstances, I could flatter myself that, by diligent application, I might be able, in a short time, to supply the want of experience, and to justify, in some degree, the confidence indicated by the House. That more than usual embarrassments must be encountered at this moment, by any incumbent of the chair, will be admitted by all. The impatience, not to say irritation, the natural result of a protracted session; the excitement growing out of those sharp conflicts of opinion upon questions of public policy, inherent in all free Governments - conflicts exasperated and embittered at the present moment in an extraordinary degree; all present them-

selves to increase the difficulties and call forth the exertions of a new and unpracticed incumbent of the chair. And I feel, gentlemen, that whatever exertions may be made on my part, must be vain without your forbearance; nay, that they must fail altogether, without your cordial support and co-operation. When I reflect how great are the interests connected with this House, its character and action - interests not of a day or of a party, but of all time, of posterity, and of all the parties which are or ever will be strayed against each other; and when I further reflect how much the character and action of this House depend upon a skilful, firm, and impartial administration of the duties of the chair, I confess I feel the deepest solicitude. It is not so generally, understood, I regret to believe, as it should be, in how great a degree the measures of a legislative assembly are modified and influenced by the manner of its deliberations. All will concede that if it shall ever happen that this body shall fall into disrepute, and fail to command the respect and confidence of the people, our institutions will be in the greatest peril. Not only the character of the House, the wisdom and efficiency of its action, but the existence of our admirable frame of polity itself, may be said to depend, in some degree, upon the order and dignity of the deliberations of this House. While, then, I entreat the indulgence of the House to my own defects, I earnestly invoke the assistance of every member of it in endeavoring to maintain and preserve, so far as depends upon the proceedings of this body, those great and primary interests of constitutional Government and freedom, in support of which, I am sure, whatever difference of opinion there may be upon points of construction, policy, or administration, there is not a heart here, nor an American heart any where, that does not beat high.*

The *House Journal* then concludes,

The oath of office to support the constitution of the United States was then administered to the Speaker elect, by Mr. Williams, one of the Representatives from the State of North Carolina...And then the House adjourned until to-morrow, 11 o'clock A.M.

Legacy as Speaker

Why was Bell elected Speaker of the House? The facts behind the decision seem clouded in history, but it appears that the issue of slavery may have been behind it. Up until his selection, Bell had been a firm supporter of slaveholders' rights, voting consistently with his party against any opportunity to reduce the rights of slaveowners and even with regularity against any chance to present petitions to Congress from antislavery activists demanding the end of the slave trade. Yet, at some point about 1833-34, Bell abandoned this wing of the Democratic Party and began what critics in 1860 called "consorting with the Abolitionists, Federalists, and disappointed Democrats, in order to reach the Speaker's chair." The evidence, presented in a campaign document issued by the Democratic National Committee in 1860 when Bell was a candidate for President, allegedly was that Bell made a deal to become Speaker in exchange for refusing to vote against several petitions demanding an end to slavery or the extension of it in any new states. But there is no evidence of such a deal, and Bell remained a slaveowner for many years after becoming and serving as Speaker.

Few sources exist on what Bell did as Speaker; what is stated in the historical record is that during his entire tenure in the Speaker's chair he argued against the programs of the Jackson administration, in its final year of power, and he opposed the candidacy of Vice President Martin Van Buren for president. John Quincy Adams, in his *Memoirs*, wrote of Bell, "He is on the whole a good Speaker, and impartial so far as he dares, though occasionally subservient from timidity."

When the Twenty-fourth Congress convened on 7 December 1835, Bell stood for re-election as Speaker. His political enemy, Martin Van Buren, was now President, and a majority of the Democrats in the House were Van Buren followers. Bell's opposition to Van Buren both in Tennessee and nationally was a sore point for those members. In a repeat of the fight for the speakership, which brought Bell to the Speaker's chair in 1834, he was opposed by Polk. James Schouler, in his *History of the United States*, states that Bell was defeated for a second term as Speaker because he was "read out" of the Democratic Party for opposing Van Buren and supporting Judge and Senator Hugh Lawson White of Tennessee for the presidency in 1836. Polk's victory in the speakership election was substantial, and Bell returned to the regular fold in the House. Two years later, at the start of the Twenty-fifth Congress, Polk was re-elected as Speaker, again over Bell, but this time only by 13 votes. Having paid with the speakership for his opposition to Van Buren, Bell exacerbated the situation by opposing every program of the Van Buren administration during the Twenty-fourth Congress. He attacked the patronage of the government, and with each speech mocked the President and his followers.

After Leaving the Speakership
In 1840, Bell threw his entire force behind General William Henry Harrison, the Whig candidate, for President, over Martin Van Buren, running for re-election. Harrison's electoral victory - the first for the Whig Party nationally - pleased Bell more than anything, as the "reign" of his political enemy Andrew Jackson had been forcibly ended. He wrote to a friend in Tennessee, "Have we not acheived [sic] a glorious triumph? What will Mr. Grundy say to this?" Bell believed that he could follow Harrison's victory up with re-election to the speakership. Instead, the new President offered Bell the post of Secretary of War in the new administration. Bell accepted, and took office on 5 March 1841.

Bell soon found himself in one of the most demanding challenges to face the country up to that point. The new president, after being sworn into office, spoke for several hours at his inauguration on 5 March 1841, and quickly caught a cold. On 4 April 1841 - a mere month into his administration - Harrison succumbed to his illness at the age of 68. The death of this military hero threw the entire government into turmoil; who would succeed him? Never before had this problem arose. Vice President John Tyler, a former Democrat who was a Whig in name only and had been placed on the Whig ticket to earn some Democratic votes, took control of the administration. Bell remained in the cabinet, probably to keep some semblance of order and to avoid having the government collapse. In this period, he quickly came to be at odds with President Tyler, who refused to sign any congressional legislation backed by Whigs, and instead instituted anti-Whig measures. On 12 September 1841, all but one cabi-

net member resigned in protest, including Bell. The Whig Party cut all ties to the President, and for the next two and a half years, the government was in full paralysis.

From the time he left the administration until 1847, Bell held no public office. He used this period to return to Tennessee and expand his investments in numerous industries, including coal and iron. He worked to stop his political rival, James K. Polk, from getting the Democratic nomination for President in 1844 and, when Polk won the party nod, fought to keep him from the presidency. In both cases, Bell failed, but Polk was a disaster as President, leading the country into war with Mexico, and only served one term.

In 1847, Bell was elected to a seat in the Tennessee state legislature, but, before he could take his seat, his fellow legislators elected him to a vacant seat in the U.S. Senate. Re-elected in 1853, he ultimately served two terms until leaving on 3 March 1859. During his tenure, Bell worked to try to head off a clash between the North and the South over the issue of slavery, which became more contentious with each passing year. In 1850, Bell initially dismissed Henry Clay's "Compromise of 1850," but he supported the entry of California and New Mexico into the Union and called for Texas to be split into proslavery and antislavery entities. Bell was a supporter of General Zachary Taylor for the Presidency in 1848 and General Winfield Scott for the same office in 1852. In his second Senate term, Bell was the only southerner in that body to vote against the repeal of the Missouri Compromise of 1820, which allowed one slave state to enter the Union at the same time one free state was admitted. In 1858, he opposed the introduction of Kansas into the Union as a slave state. That year, when Democrats won a majority of seats in the Tennessee legislature, he failed of re-election against Democrat Alfred Osborn Pope Nicholson.

The election of 1860 became more pivotal to the survival of the Union as the Republican Party, established in 1854 and running in only its second national campaign, nominated Abraham Lincoln, an abolitionist. Former Whigs and southern moderates who feared that Lincoln's election would force the secession of the southern slave states met in Baltimore, Maryland, in May 1860, formed the Constitutional Union Party, and named Bell for President and orator Edward Everett for Vice President. A study of the forces behind this blend of former Whigs, whose party had collapsed, southerners who feared civil war, and others who opposed Lincoln but could not stomach the proslavery Democrats, shows that the party had little chance of electoral victory. Their true goal, historians believe, was to deny any one candidate a majority of electoral votes, thus throwing the election into the House of Representatives where some agreement could be made and a moderate elected as President.

Bell's candidacy was a sectional one, trying to win small victories in states where Lincoln was strong and in others where the Democrats, split between southern and northern tickets, were winning. Bell did win his home state's electoral votes, along with those of Kentucky and Virginia. But the strategy failed because Lincoln swept the north with a total of 180 electoral votes. Bell and Everett garnered 13% of the vote, and a total of 39 electoral votes. In fact, the Constitutional Union ticket came in third of the four tickets, beating the "Northern Democrats" led by Senator Stephen A. Douglas, and behind that of the "Southern Democrats" of John C. Breckinridge. The secession of southern states started in December 1860, the month after the election of Lincoln. On 14 January 1861, one S.M. Strickler, a "citizen" from Junction City, Kansas, wrote to President-elect Lincoln, "Dear Sir - Will you permit an [sic] humble citizen to offer a suggestion in regard to the formation of your cabinet? Would not the appointment of John Bell of Tennessee have a tendency to allay the present excitement and to call to the support of your administration the American party and a large class of conservatives at the South? It seems to me that such would be the case. And as a Republican I would be much pleased, and have a much stronger faith in the settlement of our difficulties, if he could occupy a place in your Cabinet. There can be nothing wrong in consulting him with such a view. His appointment would convince the South at once that your administration would not be sectional." The new president passed on the suggestion from this citizen; instead, Lincoln selected Senator Simon Cameron of Pennsylvania for the position.

John Bell was not involved in the fighting of the Civil War; instead, he moved to Chattanooga, Tennessee, where he invested in the ironworks at Cumberland Furnace. In 1862, when Union forces invaded Tennessee, these facilities were damaged, and Bell's finances collapsed. Forced to sell his home, he became a refugee, spending time trying to reopen the ironworks as well as invest in other resources. After the war, he was able to recover financially, although his slaves were freed. Bell died at his home near Cumberland Furnace on 10 September 1869 at the age of 72; he was buried in Mount Olivet Cemetery near Nashville.

Despite a lifelong history of service to the United States, the name of John Bell appears to have slipped into obscurity. Even a recent examination of his life - in the multivolume *American National Biography*, published in 1999 - gave Bell's speakership one sentence in his entire biography, and except for Joseph Parks' 1950 biography of Bell there are no major works on his life. For a man who was the most powerful officer in the U.S. House for one term, and ran for President in 1860, it is a shameful legacy. Thomas Hart Benton, one of the nineteenth century's most important legislators, wrote of Bell, "[He] was a forcible speaker and always ready for debate. His resources seemed inexhaustible; he was a master of invective."

Further Reading:
Parks, Joseph H., *John Bell of Tennessee* (Baton Rouge: Louisiana State University Press, 1950).

Parks, Norman L., "The Career of John Bell of Tennessee in the United States House of Representatives" (Ph.D. dissertation, Vanderbilt University, 1942).

JOHN BELL OF TENNESSEE
From a photograph by Whitehurst Gallery, Washington, D.C.
(date unknown).

James Knox Polk

Served as Speaker:
December 7, 1835 - March 4, 1839

He is the only Speaker of the House of Representatives to rise to be elected and serve as President of the United States. In 1844, when he won his single term as President, he faced another Speaker in that campaign - Henry Clay - an occurrence that had not happened before and has not happened since. Although his service as Governor of Tennessee and President are remembered more than his tenure as Speaker, nonetheless James Polk's tenure as Speaker in the Twenty-fourth (1835-37) and Twenty-fifth (1837-39) Congresses are important for the institution of the "gag rule" of petitions against slavery, as well as the venom over slavery, which was to mark the next 20 years in the Congress, the two terms as Speaker coming during the last two years of the administration of Andrew Jackson and the first two of Martin Van Buren.

James Knox Polk was born in a clearing that was his family's farm near Little Sugar Creek, in Mecklenburg, North Carolina, on 2 November 1795. His parents, Samuel Polk and Jane (née Knox) Polk, were hardworking farmers who were followers of the religious doctrine of John Calvin. According to Eugene McCormac, one of Polk's bi-

ographers, the ancestry of the family can be traced back to 1075 and a man named Fulbert who lived in Scotland. His son, Petrius, took the name of Pollok from the estate he inherited. An ancestor, Sir Robert de Pollok, inherited an estate in Ireland and moved there in 1440, with his descendants eventually shortening the name to Polk. Sometime between 1680 and 1687 Robert Bruce Polk left Ireland with his eight children and moved to the American colonies, settling in Somerset County, Maryland. His grandson, William Polk, moved first to Pennsylvania and then to Mecklenburg County, North Carolina, where William's great-grandson, James K. Polk, would be born. Jane Knox was a great-grandniece of John Knox of Scotland; her father, James Knox of North Carolina, served in the American Revolution. James K. Polk's brother, William Hawkins Polk (1815-1862), would also later serve in Congress (1851-53) as an Independent Democrat.

When James, the eldest of 10 children, was 11, the family moved to Tennessee, the state with which Polk was to be identified for the rest of his life. Beset with poor health, he could not attend school and received little education during his early years. As he noted in his diary, one of the largest kept by a President of the United States, he explained, "I closed my education at a later period of life than is usual, in consequence of having been very much afflicted and enjoyed bad health in my youth. I did not commence the Latin Grammar until the 13th of July, 1813." Initially, his father placed him with a local merchant to earn a trade; only when Polk balked at the work did his father allow him to attend a small academy near Columbia, Tennessee. Polk's health continued to decline, until his parents took him to a doctor in Kentucky who performed abdominal surgery, a rarity at that time. It was discovered that Polk had a massive gallbladder stone, which was removed, and his health improved soon thereafter.

In 1815, at age 20, Polk entered the University of North Carolina. Three years later, he graduated first in his class, and proceeded to study the law under Felix Grundy, who would later serve as a U.S. Representative and U.S. Senator from Tennessee, as well as Attorney General (1838-39) in the Martin Van Buren administration. In 1820, Polk was admitted to the Tennessee bar and opened a practice in Columbia. The following year, he was selected as the captain of the local militia, but he quickly grew bored of serving in the military and, with Grundy's support, was named in 1821 as the chief clerk of the Tennessee state Senate, a position he held until 1823. In that latter year, he was elected on his own to a seat in the Tennessee state House of Representatives. In 1824 he married Sarah Childress, a member of a distinguished Tennessee family. The couple had no children. However, Sarah Polk became her husband's trusted aide, confidante, and advisor, and many historians believe that many of his speeches and debates were penned by her or with her advice. The year that he was married, Polk's grandfather Ezekiel Polk died, leaving an estate with thousands of acres of land in western Tennessee and 24 slaves. James Polk thus became a slaveowner, a role he would have difficulty with for years to come.

Early Years in Congress

Felix Grundy was a close associate of General Andrew Jackson, the hero of the Battle of New Orleans at the end of the War of 1812, and, with Grundy's and Jackson's support Polk ran for and won a seat in the U.S. House of Representatives in August 1825. Taking his place in the 19th Congress

(1825-27) that December as a Jacksonian, Polk opposed the policies of the administration of President John Quincy Adams, who had narrowly defeated Jackson in the 1824 presidential election. Polk supported a program of limited federal government, the rights of states, and the theory of "popular sovereignty," which held that the power of the people of states to control their own destinies was absolute over that of the federal government. This philosophy was utilized by those at the time who supported the rights of slaveowners. He also called for the abolishment of the Electoral College, demanding that there be a direct vote by the people for President and Vice President; he was named to a committee in April 1826 to look at amending the Constitution to do away with the Electoral College system, which eventually was retained.

At times, Polk's speeches were tinged with extremist rhetoric, designed to inflame his opposition. One of his *friends* wrote in a biography years after Polk's death:

> As a critic of the Adams administration, Polk did not rise above the political claptrap of the day. All that can be said in his favor in this respect is that he spoke less frequently than some of his colleagues. Even his private letters are tinctured with a bias and a bitterness that do him no credit.

Despite this view, when serving as Speaker Polk dealt with Adams who was elected to the House after his presidency had ended; Adams wrote that even with their differences that Polk extended to him "every kindness and courtesy imaginable." Re-elected overwhelmingly in 1827, Polk was named to the Committee on Foreign Relations, where he opposed a protective tariff for American industry.

In 1828, Polk returned to Tennessee to campaign for Andrew Jackson in his second run for the presidency against President John Quincy Adams. Polk, in horseback, rose across the state calling for Jackson's election. When Jackson won, Polk, as one of his close advisors, arranged to have the General travel from Nashville to Washington while thousands of well-wishers lined the roads to glimpse the President-elect. In the 20th Congress (1829-31), Polk was an enthusiastic supporter of President

Jackson's programs, including opposition to the Bank of the United States. When the state of South Carolina threatened to nullify the Tariff of 1828 in a direct warning to the President, Polk publicly opposed any sense of nullification by a state despite his support for states' rights. Polk also opposed the "American System" of Rep. Henry Clay, which called for increased federal spending for internal improvements such as roads and canals.

In June 1834, Speaker of the House Andrew Stevenson resigned his office to serve as the U.S. Minister to Great Britain, forcing the election of a new Speaker. At the time, those serving in the House were divided into pro-Jacksonians, known as Democratic-Republicans, and anti-Jacksonian, also known as National Republicans. In 1834, the two groups took the names of Democrats and Whigs. When the Twenty-third Congress met to elect Stevenson's successor, Polk was put up as a candidate for the office but lost in a close race to Rep. John Bell, also of Tennessee. Historian Powell Moore noted in a 1951 article that Polk was the candidate of the Jackson administration, but that Bell was elected with the votes of Jackson's opposition. While Polk did not get the coveted speakership, he was named as chairman of the Ways and Means Committee. As chairman, he opposed the re-funding of the Bank of the United States as a violation of the Constitution, a view supported by President Jackson. Polk delivered a speech on the floor denouncing the Bank for a lack of "self-discipline" in spending. Jackson told friends that "James Polk is the finest spokesman that this administration has." During that Congress, Speaker John Bell, a former supporter of Jackson's, came to oppose the President's policies and switched from being pro-administration to anti-administration. Polk saw Bell not just as a political enemy, but as a traitor; in numerous pieces of correspondence, Polk expressed bitterness at the defeat for the speakership and considered himself a martyr.

The Vote
Re-elected in 1835, Polk was put forward by the pro-administration side of the Jacksonians against Bell for Speaker. In a demonstration of the power of President Jackson, Polk was elected Speaker, 132 votes to 84, and was conducted to the Speaker's chair to take the oath.

Acceptance Speech
He then addressed the members of the House:

In accepting the high station to which I am called, by the voice of the assembled Representatives of the People, I am deeply impressed with the high distinction which is always conferred upon the presiding officer of this House, and with the weight of the responsibility which devolves upon him. Without experience in this place, called to preside over the deliberations of this House, I feel that I ought to invoke, in advance, the indulgent forbearance of its members, for any errors of judgment which may occur in the discharge of the new duties which will devolve upon me. It shall be my pleasure to endeavor to administer the laws which may be adopted for the government of the House, justly and impartially towards its members, and with a view to the preservation of that order which is indispensable to our character as a body, and to the promotion of the public interests. To preserve the dignity of this body, and its high character before the country, so far as shall depend upon its presiding officer, will be objects of my deepest solicitude; and I am sure I shall have the cooperation and support of all its members, in the discharge of my duty, with a view to these objects.

I return to you, gentlemen, my sincere acknowledgments for this manifestation of your confidence, in elevating me to this high station; and my ardent hope is, that our labors here may merit and receive the approbation of our constituents, and result in the advancement of the public good.

Legacy as Speaker
While Polk served as Speaker, the growing controversy over slavery continued to grow. On 18 December 1835, in one of the new Congress' first orders of business, Rep. William Jackson, Anti-Masonic member from Massachusetts, presented a petition from citizens of his own state asking Congress to abolish slavery in the District of Columbia. Rep. James Henry Hammond, Nullifier (supporting those who wanted to nullify the 1828 tariff) member from South Carolina, asked the Speaker that Jackson's petition not be accepted by the House, because

slavery was a right and no group could ask the Congress to make illegal what was backed by law. On 18 February 1836, Rep. Henry Laurens Pinckney, Nullifier from South Carolina, introduced a resolution calling on the House to accept no more petitions from abolitionist groups. These groups, all in the North, sent a persistent flow of appeals to the House asking that slavery be curtailed or abolished. Southerners saw the requests as a threat to the right to own slaves, and Hammond's resolution was designed to end that threat. Unable to pacify southerners who backed Hammond's resolution and northerners who wanted to see the right of free speech upheld, Polk appointed a committee to study the overall issue of slavery. This committee in turn recommended that Pinckney's resolution be accepted by the House. Denounced as a "gag rule," it called on all future petitions dealing with slavery be sent to a select committee for study, and that the Congress state that it had no power to halt the practice of slavery in any state, territory, or in the District of Columbia. With Polk serving as Speaker during the heated debate, the House passed the rule by a wide margin. Rep. Henry Alexander Wise, Whig of Virginia, was dejected from passage of the rule, calling on Congress to simply refuse to accept all petitions dealing with slavery. Wise also condemned Polk's handling of the matter, saying that the Speaker forced members to "vote like mules" without giving some of them the proper amount of time to debate.

Pinckney's resolution did not end the debate over slavery, or over the issue of petitions sent to Congress on the matter. Challenging the rule, Rep. George Nixon Briggs, anti-Jacksonian of Massachusetts, introduced another petition on February 15, 1836; Wise asked that the Speaker rule that the petition could not be received. Polk ruled that the Pinckney resolution referred only to previous petitions, and upheld Wise's motion. Polk's ruling was then overturned by a full vote of the House. Rep. Richard Irvine Manning, Jacksonian of South Carolina, despite being a supporter of slavery, criticized Polk's ruling in Wise's favor as a threat to the rules of the House. "If the Speaker," Manning said on the House floor, "can by his decision reverse this resolution...then he has the power to suspend, alter, change, any deliberate act of this House, intended as a rule for its governance." He added, "I know full

well the responsibility and delicacy of the Speaker's situation. I feel and acknowledge how important it is to the orderly management and proper deliberation of this body, that he should be sustained by all parties in his general efforts to preserve proper decorum." Congress would wrestle with the right to accept petitions and the "gag rule" until 1845, when it was annulled by abolitionists led by Rep. John Quincy Adams of Massachusetts.

Polk also used his power to push through legislation: he attempted to get Congress to enact the Independent Treasury Bill, but a coalition of Whigs and independent Democrats prevented its passage. Led by John Bell, a faction of Whigs challenged Polk and the Jacksonians at every turn, using every parliamentary motion they could to put a halt to his and the president's program, objecting with points of order and personally attacking Polk. One of the most ferocious in his attacks against Polk was Rep. Balie Peyton, of Tennessee, who alternated between Jacksonian and anti-Jacksonian and who was plainly in the Bell camp; friends of Polk feared that Peyton was goading the Speaker into a duel.

In 1836, Polk threw his support behind Vice President Martin Van Buren for the presidency. The Whigs threw their support behind three national candidates in a vain attempt to deny Van Buren a majority of electoral votes and throw the election into the House of Representatives. When Senator Hugh Lawson White of Tennessee was nominated by the Whigs as one of these candidates - the other two were Daniel Webster and General William Henry Harrison - Polk traveled across his state again in a stump for Van Buren. Although White carried Tennessee, the Whigs could not defeat Van Buren nationally. Polk himself was re-elected to the House - this time as a Democrat rather than as a Jacksonian - and won a second term as Speaker when the Democrats lost 15 seats to the Whigs but retained the majority. In the Twenty-fifth Congress (1837-39), Polk found it harder and harder to control the wildly varied factions of the Democratic Party in the House, which ran the gamut from antislavery northerners to proslavery southerners. William Henry Smith, an historian of the Speakers, wrote in 1928, "Mr. Polk was not by any means an admirable presiding officer. He lacked the thorough knowledge of parliamentary laws necessary for success in such a position. His old habit of endeavoring to evade direct decisions, and his ever-present fear of offending someone, all militated against his proving one of the great Speakers." However, because he had the full backing first of President Jackson and then of President Van Buren, Polk was able to cobble a coalition together that helped re-elect him as Speaker for the Twenty-fifth Congress (1837-39).

By the end of his second two-year term as Speaker, Polk realized that remaining as Speaker - and in the Congress - would not advance his career, and he made it a point to step down from both positions and run for a seat back home - the governorship of Tennessee. On 4 March 1839, he adjourned the House in his final day as Speaker. He told the members,

> The high office of Speaker, to which it has been twice the pleasure of the House to elevate me, has been at all times one of labor and high responsibility. It has been made my duty to decide more questions of parliamentary law and order, many of them of a complex and difficult character, arising often in the midst of high excitement, in the course of our proceedings, than had been decided, it is believed, by all my predecessors, from the foundation of the government. This House has uniformly sustained me, without distinction of the political parties of which it has been composed. I return them my thanks for their constant support in the discharge of the duties I have had to perform.

When Democrats introduced a resolution offering thanks to Polk for his service, a near riot among his opponents almost broke out. Rep. Seargent Smith Prentiss, Whig of Mississippi, denounced Polk on the House floor, stating, "A more perfect party Speaker, one who would be more disposed to bend the rules of the House to meet the purposes of his own side in politics, never had pressed the soft and ample cushions of that gorgeous chair." The resolution of thanks passed, but so many Democrats either voted against it or refused to vote that the small majority was embarrassing for a sitting Speaker.

After Leaving the Speakership
Despite being a Democrat in a year that the Whigs were slowly gaining control politically in the nation, Polk won the election in 1839 as Governor in a

close contest against Governor Newton Cannon, an ally of John Bell. Polk hoped that his service as Governor - rather than as Speaker - would lead to his gaining the Democrats' vice presidential nomination in 1840 or 1844, and, from there, he could reach for the presidency. But events served to interfere, at least in the short term, with Polk's plans: he lost his re-election bid in 1841 to James C. Jones, the Whig candidate, and, in a try to recapture the state house, lost again in 1843. It appeared, following this second electoral defeat that the political career of James K. Polk was over. Nonetheless, Polk wrote to a friend, "My sword is still unsheathed & I am still ready to do battle for our principles."

As the 1844 election drew closer, it appeared that the Whigs were prepared to nominate former Speaker Henry Clay for a third try at the White House, with former President Martin Van Buren as the Democratic nominee. Both men opposed the annexation of Texas and its entry into the Union as slave state, meaning that that issue would become moot in the election. Former President Jackson met with Polk in May 1844 and decided that Van Buren had destroyed his chances of winning southern votes with his anti-annexation statement and that the Democrats need to nominate a candidate who was pro-annexation and could capture the South; Jackson believed that Polk was that candidate and offered to back him for the presidential nomination. Polk later wrote to his close friend, fellow Tennessean Cave Johnson, that while he had "never aspired so high" he would accept the nomination if Van Buren did not get it.

At the 1844 Democratic National Convention in Baltimore, Van Buren led on the first seven ballots against Lewis Cass of Michigan but could not muster a majority. On the second day of the parley, historian George Bancroft, a delegate, nominated Polk as a compromise candidate to break the deadlock. The impasse appeared to grow on the eighth ballot as none of the three men could attain a majority, but on the ninth ballot, accusations of bribery and extortion by the Van Buren and Cass camps led delegates to swing to Polk, who was nominated by acclamation. George Mifflin Dallas of Pennsylvania, who was an advocate of a protective tariff in opposition to Polk, was nominated for Vice President. Polk called for the admission of Texas as a slave state, but assured northerners that he would call for the entrance of Oregon as a free state and as a balance to Texas' entry. At the same time, Henry Clay, the Whig candidate, did not oppose slavery and angered many Whigs who crossed over to support a fledgling abolitionist party, the Liberty Party, and their presidential candidate James G. Birney. Birney's siphoning of key antislavery votes from Clay threw New York State and its eight electoral votes to Polk and victory.

James K. Polk has been called the first "dark horse" candidate for the presidency, in that he had not been considered a leading candidate until his main opposition could not gain a majority and he won his party's nomination. It is because of Polk that the term "dark horse" has entered the American political lexicon.

Presidency of Polk

Having campaigned on the promise to only serve a single four-year term, Polk had only that time period in which to accomplish his goals. He set out to reduce protective tariffs, settle the Oregon boundary situation between the United States and Great Britain, and get California to enter the Union. Getting southern Democrats and northern Democrats to work together to lower the tariff in exchange for federal aid for internal improvements, Polk got the tariff through the bitterly divided Congress over Whig objections. In his inaugural address, Polk explained that he continued to oppose a national bank, stating, "The public money should not be mingled with the private funds of banks." His independent Treasury bill, which he tried to get passed as Speaker, was ushered through the House and Senate with ease. During the presidential campaign he had demanded that Britain acknowledge the border between Oregon and Canada be set at fifty-four degrees latitude and forty minutes longitude; the British wanted it further south. Thus, the slogan of Polk's campaign, "Fifty-four Forty or Fight!" became the key issue of his presidency. Through a series of negotiations, the Treaty of Oregon, signed in 1846, established 49 degrees, further south than even the United States was at first willing to go, as the border that officially delineates the boundary between the United States and Canada. The disposition was enormously unpopular in the country: Senator Edward A. Hannegan, Democrat

of Indiana, responded on the Senate floor to a colleague's defense of the pact:

> So long as one human eye remains to linger on the page of history the story of this abasement will be read, sending him and his name together to an infamy so profound, a damnation so deep, that the hand of resurrection will never drag him forth. So far as the whole tenor, spirit and meaning of the remarks of the Senator from North Carolina are concerned, if they speak the language of James K. Polk, then James K. Polk has spoken words of falsehood with the tongue of a serpent.

Perhaps the most controversy issue of Polk's presidency was over the annexation of Texas. John C. Calhoun, the Secretary of State in the John Tyler administration, sent a messenger to Texas 48 hours before Polk was inaugurated, asking the Texans to declare independence from Mexico. When the declaration was made, the threat from Mexico to go to war was carried out, leading to the Mexican-American War of 1846-48. The war was unpopular among the American people, and the Whigs dubbed it "Mr. Polk's War" and accused him of making gross errors in its prosecution despite voting for appropriations to pay for it. The first major war fought by the United States since the War of 1812, it resulted in the defeat of Mexico by the United States, with large swaths of land being annexed by America in the southwest. And while the territory of the nation was increased, the new lands opened up the slavery question again, with new states entering the Union as either slave or free. When Polk asked Congress for $2 million to buy a piece of land from Mexico, Rep. David Wilmot, Democrat of Pennsylvania, authored a resolution - called the Wilmot Proviso - that said that any land acquired from Mexico should be free from slavery. Polk denounced the decree as "mischievous and foolish," and while it passed the House it failed in the Senate.

The four years of his only term as President took an enormous physical toll on Polk, and by its conclusion he was in exceedingly ill health. When he left office in March 1849, his hair was pure white. Later that year, newspapers reported that he was seriously ill with diarrhea but not cholera as some newspapers had been reporting. His mother, still alive, took care of him, as did his wife and brother. On 15 June

1849, just four months since leaving the White House, Polk died at his residence in Nashville, probably of the diarrhea he had suffered from for many years. He was just 53 years old. On his coffin a plate was attached, which said simply, "J.K. Polk. Born November, 1795. Died June 15, 1849." In a eulogy, Levi Woodbury, who later served on the U.S. Supreme Court, stated, "It is only just to add that a nation laments his premature departure - a nation of proud of his name and fame - a nation will embalm his worth - a nation unites in paying the last sad honors to his memory." Polk was initially buried in the Felix Grundy family tomb in Nashville City Cemetery; later, his remains were removed to his home, Polk Place, by his widow, who outlived him by 43 years, the longest widowhood by any First Lady. In the last years of her life, the Polk mansion had become run down, and two years after her death it was demolished and the remains of her and her husband were removed to the grounds of the Tennessee state capitol in Nashville.

Historians remember James K. Polk for his one term as President of the United States rather than his two terms as Speaker of the House. Although he left few precedents as Speaker and may have been one of the weaker occupants of that office, nonetheless he moderated the House during a period of restlessness and growing intensity over the issue of slavery.

Further Reading:
Jenkins, John S., *The Life of James K. Polk, Late President of the United States* (Auburn, New York: James M. Alden, 1850).

McCormac, Eugene Irving, *James K. Polk: A Political Biography* (Berkeley, California: University of California Press, 1922).

George Eastman House

A RARE FIND: A RECENTLY DISCOVERED DAGUERREOTYPE taken about 1849, ten years after the invention of photography. President James K. Polk and his wife are in the center. The tall figure on the left with the smudged face is James Buchanan, Polk's Secretary of State. Next to him, his niece Harriet Lane.

The somewhat blurred figure on the right is none other than Dolley Madison, the vivacious widow of the fourth President—she could never hold still. At the time, she was 82 years old, but a man who saw her recounted that her arms and shoulders were as beautiful as those of a young woman. The remaining figures in the group escape positive identification.

Robert Mercer Taliaferro Hunter

Served as Speaker:
December 16, 1839 - March 4, 1841

Although he is barely remembered today, Robert M.T. Hunter was one of the most outspoken orators during his life for the rights of slaveowners and the institution of slavery. A powerful member of Congress from the time he entered the House in 1837 until he was expelled from the Senate in 1861, he rose to become Speaker in the Twenty-sixth Congress (1839-41). He later served in the Confederate government as that entity's Secretary of State (1861-62) and in the Confederate Senate.

Personal History

Hunter was born at the estate of his maternal grandfather, Muscoe Garnett, called "Mount Pleasant," near Loretto, in Essex County, Virginia, on 21 April 1809. The son of James Hunter and his wife Maria (née Garnett) Hunter, Robert Hunter was of Scottish heritage: a 1993 dissertation by Richard Randall Moore discovered that Hunter's great-grandfather was a Scottish merchant who came to the colonies to do business with the British. Hunter's daughter, Martha, who penned a 1903 biography of her father, reported that James Hunter, the great-great-great-grandfather of Robert Hunter, was born in Dunse, Scotland, in 1661, and that the

family eventually became rich on both sides of the Atlantic through commercial enterprises and property purchases. Hunter's paternal grandfather, William, married Sarah Garnett, making Richard Hunter's parents cousins to one another.

Robert Hunter received what is now referred to as home schooling, taught by one or both of his parents. His father, a wealthy planter, then hired a professional tutor to prepare his son for college. Hunter entered the University of Virginia at Charlottesville, graduating in 1828 as one of that institution's first graduate students. Hunter then studied the law under Judge Henry St. George Tucker of Winchester, Virginia, and was admitted to the state bar in 1830. He then opened a law practice in the village of Lloyds, Virginia.

Robert Hunter would have remained a country lawyer, but in 1835, when just 26 years old, he ran for and won a seat in the Virginia House of Delegates, and served in the sessions of that body in 1835-36 and 1836-37. Although he was elected as an independent with no connection to any political party, Hunter was a staunch Whig, who supported those elements who opposed the national administration of President Andrew Jackson. While in this body Hunter married Mary Evelina Dandridge, the niece of his law teacher, Judge Tucker.

Early Years in Congress

In 1836, Hunter was elected to a seat in the U.S. House of Representatives as a "States' Rights Whig," or someone who believed that state laws took precedence over national laws, most notably on the matter of slavery. Hunter, a firm backer of the right to own slaves, took his seat in the Twenty-fifth Congress (1837-39) and was one of that body's most ardent defenders of slaveowners' rights. Hunter eventually served in the Twenty-fifth, Twenty-sixth (1839-41), and Twenty-seventh (1841-43) Congresses.

The Twenty-sixth Congress convened in Washington, D.C. on 2 December 1839 with the Democrats holding a slim majority over the Whigs, 125 seats to 109. In addition, there were six anti-Masons and two Conservatives. However, on that first day, the Clerk of the House discovered that there were not enough members to make a quorum, and the House adjourned until the following day. A controversy immediately broke out: the Clerk had not recognized several members from New Jersey, all Democrats, whose election outcomes would be the subject of hearings later. When the House resumed business on 3 December 1839, the Clerk gave his reasons for not recognizing the members in a written statement. Objection broke out to the reading of the Clerk's statement, and when loud debate ensued the House again adjourned. When the House again convened, the Democrats tried to seat the five Democrats in question, but the Whigs resisted. A rancorous debate and days of voting on which set of candidates to seat as the official New Jersey delegation then proceeded, arguments which lasted for nearly two weeks and take up more than 50 pages of the *Journal of the House*. (The House finally decided not to seat either set of candidates; it was not until a resolution enacted on 10 March 1840 that the five Democrats were allowed to take their seats "without prejudice to the final rights of the claimants.")

The Vote

The House could not move to the election of a Speaker until this disagreement was settled. The election for the Speaker then proceeded; John W. Jones, Democrat of Virginia, led the balloting on the first vote with 113 votes over John Bell of Tennessee with 102. With 118 votes needed, the vote continued. On the second ballot, Jones continued to lead, 113 to 99, with Hunter getting 1 vote. Jones was unable to gain, and by the third ballot he was down to 110 votes; Hunter was up to 5. On the fourth ballot, Jones was at 101 votes, with William Dawson of Georgia at 77, and Hunter in third with 29. Dawson removed his name, and on the fifth ballot Jones remained on top, but with 71 votes, with Hunter in second with 68, and Dixon Lewis of Alabama with 49. Despite the Democrats being in control of the House, many elements of their party were from slaveholding states and sided with the Whigs on this issue. On the sixth vote, Dixon Lewis took the lead with 70 votes, with Hunter in second with 63, and Jones slipping to 39. The House then adjourned until the following day. It was not until the 11th ballot, taken on 16 December, that Hunter was finally selected as the Speaker, defeating John W. Jones, 119 votes to 55. (Jones himself would later serve as Speaker of the House in the Twenty-eighth Congress [1843-45]).

Acceptance Speech

Following his election, Hunter was conducted to the Speaker's chair by Rep. Linn Banks, Democrat of Virginia, and Rep. Abbott Lawrence, Whig of Massachusetts, and the new Speaker was given the oath of office by Rep. Lewis Williams, Whig of North Carolina. Before Hunter could make any remarks, the House adjourned until the next day. At noon on 17 December 1839, 30 year old Robert Hunter stood as the Speaker of the House of Representatives and addressed his fellow members:

The high and undeserved honor which you have conferred upon me has been so unexpected that even now I can scarcely find terms in which to express my grateful sense of your kindness. I trust, however, to be able to offer a better evidence of that sentiment in the earnest efforts which I shall make to discharge my duties justly and impartially. Called, as I have been, to this high station, not so much from any merits of my own as from the independence of my position, I shall feel it as especially due from me to you to preside as the Speaker, not of a party, but of the

House. While I shall deem it my duty, upon all proper occasions, to sustain the principles upon which I stand pledged before the country, I shall hold myself bound, at the same time, to afford every facility within my power to the full and fair expression of the wishes and sentiments of every section of this great Confederacy. You will doubtless deem it your duty, gentlemen, as the grand inquest of the nation, to investigate all matters of which the people ought to be informed; to retrench expenditures which are unnecessary or unconstitutional; to maintain the just relations between all of the great interests of the country, and to preserve inviolate the Constitution, which you will be sworn to support; while it will be mine to aid you in such labors with all of the means within my power. And although deeply impressed with a painful sense of my inexperience, and of the difficulties of a new and untried station, I am yet cheered by the hope that you will sustain me in my efforts to preserve the order of business and the decorum of debate. I am aware that party fervor is occasionally impatient of the restraint which it is the duty of the Chair to impose upon the asperities of debate, but at the same time I know that the just of all parties will sustain a Speaker who is honestly endeavoring to preserve the dignity of the House and the harmony of its members.

Permit me, in conclusion, gentlemen, to tender you the homage of my heartfelt thanks for the honor which you have conferred upon me, and to express the hope that your counsels may be so guided by wisdom as to redound to your own reputation and the welfare of our common country.

Legacy as Speaker

The Twenty-sixth Congress came into office just as the new President, Martin Van Buren, was inaugurated. These first two years of his administration dealt with two major issues: the northeast boundary of the United States, and the war in Florida with several Indian tribes. The border between what is now the state of Maine and the Canadian province of New Brunswick was, at that time, in doubt between the United States and Britain, the power that controlled Canada. The storm over the border intensified when several men from the Canadian side

allegedly trespassed across the border. The Governor of Maine sent an agent to the border, and he was seized by the trespassers and taken to the Canadian village of Fredericton. Diplomacy between the United States and England to settle the matter was backed by Congress, which provided the President with full power to do what he saw fit to defend American interests.

The war in Florida was a different matter. Having gone on for many years between Indians defending their lands and American troops, a treaty signed in 1832 and ratified by the Congress in 1836 seemed to end the matter. However, a series of massacres by Seminole Indians led to new hostilities, with General Thomas Jessup being backed by the President and Congress to defeat the tribes in the swamps of Florida. As Speaker, Hunter backed the President on both issues. Because he was more of a States' Rights Democrat than a Whig, however, he gradually became distanced from the party that elected him as Speaker. Although re-elected to his seat in 1840, the Whigs repudiated him and his leadership, and with that party gaining completed control over the House, elected Rep. John White, Whig of Kentucky, as the Speaker for the Twenty-seventh Congress (1841-43).

After Leaving the Speakership

In 1842, Willoughby Newton, a Whig, defeated Hunter in the general election (there was no Democratic candidate) by 150 votes. While out of Congress, Hunter worked to get former Vice President John C. Calhoun - who had resigned over differences with President Van Buren - elected President 1844. One of the controversies in Hunter's life deals not with himself, but with Calhoun, who was Hunter's close friend - both supported slavery - and mentor. In 1843 an autobiography of the former Vice President was published, and Hunter has been credited for the penmanship of the work. Calhoun himself stated that Hunter wrote the *entire* book; Hunter, however, including in a letter to his wife, took credit for only half of the biography. One historian, in discussing the numerous theories behind this story, believes that Hunter wrote the entire book, based on "previously published materials," while at the same time "receiving, to an undetermined degree, Calhoun's supervision and approval."

In 1844, Hunter won back his seat in the House, sitting in the Twenty-ninth Congress (1845-47). Before he could run for re-election, the Virginia legislature elected him to the U.S. Senate as a Democrat after Senator William Segar Archer could not win re-election. In the Senate, Hunter served as the chairman of the Senate Finance Committee, working on the Tariff of 1857. He continued to support slavery, and backed the Fugitive Slave Law, which forced the government to arrest those who aided in the fleeing of slaves to freedom, and spoke out against any compromise over the admittance of new states that did not allow slavery to remain legal. With two other giants in the U.S. Senate at that time, Robert Toombs of Georgia and Jefferson Davis of Mississippi, the three men were hailed as "The Southern Triumvirate" for their fiery and outspoken support for slavery.

At the 1860 Democratic National Convention in Baltimore, the party split between proslavery antislavery. Hunter was nominated for President by the proslavery wing of the party, but he never got enough support to win the nomination and he eventually threw his support behind former Vice President John C. Breckinridge. When the party broke into "northern" and "southern" wings, with the northern wing supporting Senator Stephen A. Douglas of Illinois and the southern wing backing Breckinridge, Hunter backed the southern or slave ticket. The election of antislavery advocate and Republican Abraham Lincoln threw the country into turmoil. In the Senate after the election, as the nation slid towards civil war, Hunter became one of a Committee of Thirteen that tried to mediate the crisis. When that move failed, Hunter called for a constitutional convention to rewrite the Constitution to solidify into that document the right to own slaves. Eventually, Hunter tried to get the Congress to enact a law calling for a "dual presidency," which would have one President of the United States representing the North, and another representing the South. Taking to the floor of the Senate on 11 January 1861, he gave his final address on the matter in the Congress:

> It is therefore now no more a question of saving or of preserving the old Union. We cannot recall the past; we cannot restore the dead; but the hope and the trust of those who desire a

> Union, are that we may be able to reconstruct a new government and a new Union, which perhaps may be more permanent and efficient than the old.

Unable to halt the rush of his state's secession, Hunter resigned from the Senate on 28 March 1861. A Senate panel investigated his actions, and, on 11 July 1861, expelled him from the body for "supporting the Confederate rebellion." His fellow Virginian, James M. Mason, was also expelled on that date, as well as eight others, all from the South. For additional Senators were expelled the following February.

Service to the Confederacy

Hunter returned to Virginia and served as a delegate to the Confederate Provisional Congress held in Montgomery, Alabama. On 24 July 1861, Confederate President Jefferson Davis named Hunter as the Confederate Secretary of State, replacing Robert Toombs, who had resigned. Hunter named his former fellow Senator, James M. Mason, to Britain to try to get European governments to recognize the Confederacy and give the southern regime aid. Hunter came to disagree wildly with Davis, who took over much of the responsibility of Hunter's position. Hunter believed that when Davis' term as President of the Confederate States ended in 1868, he himself would run and be elected President. He resigned his office on 1 February 1862 over continued arguments with Davis that threatened their friendship. Hunter was elected to a seat in the Confederate Senate, serving in the First and Second Confederate Congresses (1862-65).

By the beginning of 1865, Hunter realized that the Confederacy was going to lose the war to the North. Reaching out to the Lincoln administration, he arranged a meeting that included himself, Confederate Vice President Alexander H. Stephens, and former Supreme Court Justice John A. Campbell, with Lincoln and Secretary of State William H. Seward at Hampton Roads, Virginia. Despite the situation of the South, when Lincoln demanded an immediate ceasefire and surrender, Hunter angrily dismissed the suggestion, calling it "an absolute submission both as to rights and property...a submission as absolute as if we were passing through the Candine forks." Hunter returned to the Confederate Senate, where he tried to get a resolution passed calling for a surrender if the North allowed slaverholders in the South to keep their slaves. The motion, as with Hunter's motions in the U.S. Senate, went nowhere. Hunter was arrested by Union forces led by General Ulysses S. Grant, and imprisoned in Fort Pulaski, Tennessee. He was released in January 1866, and returned home to his estate, "Fonthill," in Essex County, Virginia.

His Final Years

Hunter later served as the delegate to the Virginia Underwood Convention (1867-68), which helped to write a new state constitution, and as State Treasurer for Virginia from 1874 to 1880. President Grover Cleveland named him as the collector for the port of Tappahannock, Virginia, in 1885. Hunter died at "Fonthill" on 18 July 1878 at the age 78. He was buried on the Hunter family burial ground, known as "Elmwood," near his birthplace of Loretto, Virginia.

Although his name is forgotten today - the well-studied *American National Biography* series does not even include his biography - Robert M.T. Hunter was a firebrand speaker for the rights of slaveowners in the middle of the nineteenth century. His speeches, cast from grandiose Latin and Roman oratory, are great examples of the debates that filled the halls of Congress during that time. His service to his country - and to his own country's enemy during a horrific civil war - is controversial but needs to be seen in the light of those times.

Further Reading:

Hunter, Martha T., *A Memoir of Robert M.T. Hunter, With An Address on His Life, by Col. L. Quinton Washington* (Washington, D.C.: The Neale Publishing Company, 1903).

Moore, Richard Randall, "In Search of a Safe Government: A Biography of R.M.T. Hunter of Virginia" (Ph.D. dissertation, University of South Carolina, 1993).

Simms, Henry Harrison, *Life of Robert M.T. Hunter: A Study in Sectionalism and Secession* (Richmond, Virginia: The William Byrd Press, 1935).

John White

Served as Speaker:
May 31, 1841 - March 4, 1843

He may be the most obscure Speaker of the U.S. House of Representatives, serving for a single two-year term in the Twenty-seventh Congress (1841-43), but it was his death at his own hands - a suicide that is still regarded as mysterious - which lends to White's obscurity and near mythology.

Personal History

What little is known about John White is that he was born near the village of Cumberland Gap (now Middlesboro), Kentucky, on 14 February 1802, the son of Hugh White and his wife Ann (née Lowrie) White, and a cousin of High Lawson White (1773-1840), one of the leading Jacksonian - and then anti-Jacksonian - U.S. Senators from Tennessee (1825-40), who contested the Democratic nomination for President with Martin Van Buren in 1840, as well as General Addison White (1824-1909), who served as a Whig in the Thirty-second Congress (1851-53) and in the Confederate army during the Civil War. Hugh White was the owner of the Goose Creek Salt Works in Clay County, Kentucky, and at a young age his son John gave up his educational pursuits to manage the

business. For this reason, it appears that White taught himself to read and write.

He attended Greenville College in western Kentucky, then studied the law with William Owsley (1782-1862), a noted Kentucky politician and jurist who served on the Kentucky Court of Appeals (1810) and was later was the Governor of Kentucky (1844-48). White was admitted to the state bar in 1823, and he opened a law practice in Richmond, in Madison County, Kentucky.

Early Years in Congress

In 1832, running as a Whig, White was elected to the Kentucky state House of Representatives, where he sat for a single 2-year term. Two years later, in 1834, he ran for the U.S. House of Representatives, and took his seat in the Twenty-fourth Congress (1835-37). He would serve in this capacity through the Twenty-eighth Congress (1843-45). A study of the official journal of the House during these congresses show little in the way of debate on major issues; for instance, in one day, 1 February 1836, White presented three official petitions from soldiers who served in the American Revolution, asking for funds to be paid to their estates. On 18

December 1837, he proposed that the Committee on the Post Office and Post Roads examine the potential of establishing several mail routes from points both inside Kentucky and to other states. White served on the Committee on the Territories (Twenty-fifth Congress) and the Committee on Roads and Canals (Twenty-fifth Congress).

The Vote

When the Twenty-seventh Congress assembled in Washington, D.C. on May 31, 1841, the House sat with 142 Whigs to 98 Democrats and 2 independents. One of the first orders of business was the election of a Speaker. White of Kentucky was nominated, as was John W. Jones of Virginia, Henry A. Wise of Virginia, and several others. With 111 votes needed for election, after one ballot White had 121 votes to 84 for Jones, and a smattering of votes scattered among the others. White was declared to be elected, and he was then conducted to the chair by Representatives Philip Triplett of Kentucky and George M. Keim of Pennsylvania.

Acceptance Speech

Once sworn, White gave an emphatic address to the assembled members of the House:

I cannot sufficiently express the obligations I feel for the distinguished honor conferred upon me. I undertake the discharge of the duties of this station with unfeigned distrust of my qualifications. I am sensible of the magnitude and difficulty of the task, of its arduous duties, of its high responsibilities. Six years' service in this body has taught me that this chair is no bed of down, especially in a time of great political excitement. Nothing but a conviction that the same generous confidence which placed me here would continue to support me in the faithful and impartial discharge of my duty could have induced me to accept this office. The duty of presiding over a numerous assembly like this, when even no party divisions exist - when no other than ordinary business is proposed to be considered and passed upon - is no easy task. But perhaps there has been no period in the history of this country when the duties of this Chair were more important, its responsibilities greater, its intrinsic difficulties more embarrassing. Independent of that excited party feeling - the natural result, in all free Governments, of per-

sonal rivalship [sic] - the consideration and discussion of those great questions which have caused the convention of this special Congress will no doubt give rise to high political excitement. Under these circumstances, I dare not hope I shall be able to give unqualified satisfaction, no matter how faithful, how zealous, how impartial I may be. It shall, however, be my constant purpose to discharge the functions of this station with a singleness of purpose and a fidelity of intention that will secure to me the approbation, I trust, of the just and liberal of all parties.

Candor, gentlemen, compels me to say I have never made the rules of this House or Parliamentary law my particular study. Experience in discharge of the duties of this Chair, I may say I have none. The qualifications necessary to a prompt and able discharge of the duties of Speaker are multifarious-some of them difficult. I will not detain you to enumerate them all; the mention of one, however, which I consider paramount to all others, I cannot omit; I need scarcely say I allude to that of impartiality-a rigid, an uncompromising impartiality towards every member; to the exercise of this qualification I pledge myself. The occupant of this Chair should neither lend the influence of his position to make this House subservient to Executive dictation, nor, on the other hand, to encourage a factious opposition to Executive recommendations. Passive obedience to Executive will is not less fatal to liberty than anarchy itself. The true spirit of a House of Representatives is to reflect faithfully the popular will. If it be true, as I hope and believe it is, that this House is the citadel of American freedom the great sheet-anchor of the Constitution the grand inquest of the nation-should not all its deliberations be characterized with order, with decorum, with dignity? I revoke you, gentlemen, let all our proceedings be marked with forbearance, moderation, courtesy, and patriotism. If, by any means, this body has impaired its high character as a dignified deliberative assembly, let us unite, one and all, to restore it to its former good standing. Nothing, in my humble judgement, would so effectually secure the perpetuity of our free institutions as a sacred observance of order in the deliberations of this House.

In conclusion, gentlemen, accept my grateful thanks for this high mark of confidence and respect. And I entreat you, let all our proceedings be such as to sustain the dignity of this House, maintain the honor of the country, promote the public good, and preserve, unimpaired, the integrity of this glorious Union.

Legacy as Speaker

A study of the contemporary records as well as later documents cannot show exactly why John White, with his meager record of speeches in the House, rose to be elected Speaker of that body. John Quincy Adams, in his diary detailing the times he lived in and the people he came to know, wrote of him:

White is a man of fine talents and an able debater, but his manner is so vehement and his articulation so rapid that it becomes altogether indistinct. He repeats the word "sir" every fifth word, and his discourse is one continued stream, without division into paragraphs or construction of sentences.

What makes White's election even more amazing is that he followed that of Robert M.T. Hunter, a Southern Democrat who is considered one of the better Speakers of the middle period of the nineteenth century. Nonetheless, at just 41 years old, John White was one of the highest elected officials in the United States. His tenure as Speaker lasted for just the two years of the Twenty-seventh Congress (1841-43). One of his most important rulings as Speaker came when the Committee on Rules deadlocked in reforming the rules of the House because it had to submit reports to the whole House all at the same time. White gave the committee new powers when he ruled that the committee could "make reports in part at different times." White also replaced the official wooden mace, or scepter used by the House as a symbol of the body's official authority, which had been used since 1814, with a silver one. Silvio Bedini, in a history of the mace and its use in the House, wrote that White ordered a new mace from William Adams, a dependable and honest silversmith in New York, writing to him, "You are authorized to have made a *Mace,* similar to the *one* destroyed by fire in the year 1814 - for the use of the House of Representatives."

In the 1844 election, Democrats won the White House and 49 seats in the House, taking majority control of that body. The Whigs, left with just 72 seats in the Twenty-eighth Congress, point White up for Speaker, but John W. Jones, Democrat of Virginia, won the speakership with 128 votes to 59 for White.

After Leaving the Speakership

On 4 December 1843, White left the Speaker's chair for the final time. He remained in the House until 8 February 1845, when he was appointed as a judge of the 19th Judicial district of Kentucky. He returned home to Richmond, Kentucky, and took his seat in the bench.

Just seven months later, on 22 September 1845, White took his own life by firing a pistol into his head. Two days later, on 24 September 1845, the *Lexington* [Kentucky] *Observer* reported on White's death at his own hands. The paper reported in words usually reserved for stories on horrific crimes and not for a former Speaker of the House:

Our city was thrown into great consternation yesterday morning by the intelligence from Richmond that the Hon. John White, of that place, had, on Monday evening, committed suicide by blowing his brains out with a pistol. The intelligence was the more startling from the character of the distinguished dead. He was cool, determined, self-poised, brave; and an act of this kind would have been expected as seen from any one in our State, as from John White...We have no further particulars than that some time in the forenoon of Monday [September 22], he told his family that he would retire to his room, and wished to be private - not to be interrupted. He did so, and about three o'clock the report of a pistol was heard, and upon going into the room it was found that he had put an end to his existence by placing a pistol against his right temple, and blowing a ball through his head. Pecuniary embarrassment is assigned as the cause, though nothing had been discovered, when our informant left, which indicated the reason.

The paper published a letter from a "Col. Irwin" - perhaps Rep. James Irvin, Whig of Pennsylvania, who served with White when the latter was the

Speaker on the Twenty-seventh Congress - which discussed White's suicide:

> *The manner of his death renders it doubly deplorable. For some months his health has been very feeble, accompanied by great depression of spirits. He returned yesterday, about 2 o'clock...from holding the Breathift Court, not, as his physician thought, any worse than when he left about a week previous. This morning he seemed to be somewhat worse in body and mind, but not to such an extent as to create any alarm in his family. He remained to-day mostly in one of the chambers of his house, until about 3 o'clock...when he shot himself with a pistol in the right temple, the ball coming out at the back part of the head, on the left side, and [he] expired immediately.*

White's body was buried in the State Cemetery in Frankfort, the Kentucky capital. His simple tombstone lists his name and dates of birth and death but nothing else about this man.

Few histories of the House mention John White except for his single term as Speaker, with few details on his tenure. He has been, as few people who have risen to his position, neatly erased from American history. Few letters from him exist: two could be found in the James K. Polk Papers in the Library of Congress, while a third is held by the Massachusetts Historical Society in the Leverett Saltonstall Papers. White is so little known that the standard biographical encyclopedias of famous Americans - the *Dictionary of American Biography* and the *American National Biography*, do not even list him or mention him. A third encyclopedia, *The National Cyclopædia of American Biography*, contains only a short reference to him with some of the facts, including the place of his birth, completely wrong - in total, a remarkable oversight that comes because White lived such a short life and died such a violent death at his own hand.

Further Reading:
Smith, William Henry, *Speakers of the House of Representatives of the United States with Personal Sketches of the Several Speakers* (Baltimore, Maryland: Simon J. Gaeng, 1928), 111-13.

John Winston Jones

Served as Speaker:
December 4, 1843 - March 4, 1845

He remains perhaps one of the most obscure and least known of the 53 Speakers of the U.S House of Representatives. Although he was a long-time political figure in his home state of Virginia, and served 10 terms in Congress during which he served a single term as Speaker, he is most forgotten except for the mere mention of his name in histories of the Congress or of the speakership.

Personal History

Jones was born on 22 November 1791 near Amelia Court House, in Amelia County, Virginia, the son of Alexander Jones and his wife Mary Ann (née Winston) Jones. Little is known of the family, and except for the few facts detailed here his genealogy and the sources of his family's roots are lost. Jones attended private schools, and, in 1813, graduated from the law department of the College of William and Mary in Williamsburg, Virginia. Jones was admitted to the Virginia bar that same year, and he began a law practice in Chesterfield County, Virginia. In 1818, he became the prosecuting attorney for the Fifth Judicial Circuit Court of Virginia, located in Chesterfield County. During this period, he married Harriet Bouisseau; among their children were Mary

Jones, who married George W. Towns, later the Governor of Georgia, and James Bouisseau Jones, who also became an attorney of some note in Virginia.

James Winston Jones served as a member of the Virginia State Constitutional Convention held in 1829 and 1830.

Early Years in Congress

Although he was a staunch Jacksonian who supported the policies of President Andrew Jackson, Jones ran as a Democrat for a seat in the U.S. House of Representatives in 1834. Elected, he took his seat in the Twenty-fourth Congress (1835-37), and eventually served until the end of the Twenty- eighth Congress (1843-45). Jones served as the chairman of the House Committee on Ways and Means - the main economic committee of the House - during the Twenty-sixth Congress (1839-41).

In 1842, Jones ran for re-election against John Minor Botts (1802-69), a Whig. Although Jones was re-elected, Botts contested the election. When the Twenty-eighth Congress opened in Washington on 4 December 1843, the issue over the Jones-Botts contest was still up in the air.

The Vote

The House, however, moved on that first day of business to elect Jones as Speaker of the House over Democrats John White of Kentucky and William Wilkins of Pennsylvania, 128 votes to 59 for White and 1 for Wilkins. On 21 May 1844, after a lengthy investigation, the House Committee on Elections voted to uphold Jones' right to the seat contested in 1842. A month later, on 8 June 1844, Botts withdrew his contest of the seat. Botts was eventually elected to the House, sitting in the Thirtieth Congress (1847-49).

Legacy as Speaker

A search of all available works on the Twenty-eighth Congress and its work shows only the name of John W. Jones as Speaker with no information as to anything he did. Histories of the speakership barely discuss his name, much less any major (or minor) legislation that he helped to move or debates that he participated in.

After Leaving the Speakership

In 1844, owing to ill health, John W. Jones refused to run for re-election to the House, and instead returned to Virginia. He spent considerable time recuperating at his estate, "Dellwood," located in Chesterfield County, northwest of Petersburg. When he did see his health improve, Jones returned to the practice of the law and, as one biography noted, "he was engaged in agricultural pursuits."

In 1846 he was elected to the Virginia House of Delegates, ironically serving as Speaker of that body in his single two-year term that ended in 1847. It was at this time that his ill health returned - his exact illness is not specified in any biography of him - and he returned to "Dellwood." It was there that Jones succumbed to his infirmity on 29 January 1848. He was interred in the family plot at the estate, one of three that he owned in the area. "Dellwood," as well as the Woodson Plantation and Clifton Hill (known today as Fort Clifton), were taken over by Jones' son John B. Jones. During the Civil War, "Dellwood" was used as a hospital by wounded soldiers from both sides of the conflict. The John Winston Jones Parkway in Chesterfield County is named in his honor.

John W. Jones has been completely forgotten by American history. Owing to Jones' obscurity is the fact that he delivered few speeches during his five terms in Congress. Of Jones' manuscript collections, few traces exist. The Library of Congress contained two letters from Jones in the papers of President Martin Van Buren, and the Virginia Historical Society holds an account book written by Jones and two letters from him in an unassociated collection of papers. Except for these, there does not appear to be any letters from Jones, which is one reason he has slipped into almost complete obscurity. His tenure as Speaker for a single two-year term of Congress, as well as his death at the age of 56 may be another reason for his status.

Further Reading:
Gordon, Armistead Churchill, Jr, "Jones, John Winston" in Allen Johnson and Dumas Malone, et al., eds., *Dictionary of American Biography* (New York: Charles Scribner's Sons; X volumes and 10 supplements, 1930-95), V:191-92.

See also page 423

John Wesley Davis

Served as Speaker:
December 1, 1845 - March 4, 1847

His service as Speaker of the House in the Twenty-ninth Congress (1845-47) was brief, uneventful, and, because of this, had rendered the name of John W. Davis almost completely lost in obscurity. In his life, Davis served as a medical doctor, a judge of a court in his adopted home state of Indiana, a state representative, and U.S. representative, and Speaker of the House. And yet he and his services are wholly forgotten.

Personal History

Davis was born in the village of New Holland, in Lancaster County, Pennsylvania, on 16 April 1799, the son of the Rev. John Davis and his wife, whose first name is unknown but whose maiden name appears to be Jones from all sources that exist on Davis. One of the few authors who has written on Davis' life, William Wesley Woollen, discovered a manuscript penned by Davis, as late as possibly right before Davis' death in 1859. In the manuscript, Davis explains,

> A portion of my childhood was spent with my maternal grandfather, Jones. When I was about ten years old my father purchased a farm one mile east of Shippensburg, in Cumberland county, Pennsylvania, and settled upon it. Until I was seventeen years of age most of my time was spent upon my father's farm; however, during that period I was bound an apprentice to a clockmaker by the name of Hendel M. Carlisle, but my health failed from confinement, and I quit that business and was next sent to learn storekeeping. Being changeful in my disposition, I did not long remain at it, and my father then sent me to a Latin school in Shippensburg, where I continued about a year, and then commenced the study of medicine in Carlisle, under the direction of Dr. George D. Foulke.

After his initial studies, Davis entered the Baltimore Medical College (now the University of Maryland at Baltimore), graduating in April 1821. He returned to Pennsylvania, having married one Ann Hoover.

Davis found work as a physician in Shippensburg discouraging, and in August 1821 he moved his family to the village of Old Town, in Allegheny County, Maryland. He practiced there for two years, afterwards once again picking up and moving - this time to Carlisle, Indiana, the state with which he would be identified for the remainder of his life. Davis noted in his manuscript that he arrived in Indiana with three cents in his pocket.

For the next three years, Davis built his reputation as an honest and successful country doctor in Carlisle. In 1826, he moved to the city of Terre Haute, where his entire family, including himself and his children, were stricken with bilious fever. (One source describes this malady as "typhoid, malaria, hepatitis or elevated temperature and bile emesis.") Once Davis himself had recovered - it does not appear that any of his family died from the illness - he returned to Carlisle and set up his practice again.

In 1828, at the age of 29, Davis was recruited by local Jacksonian Democrats to run for a seat in the Indiana state Senate, but he was defeated in a close race. Despite the loss, Davis decided to remain in the political arena, and he went to Indianapolis for the opening session of the state legislature and entered his name in the race for clerk of the state House. Davis was defeated for this position as well, but the victor pushed him to run for the post of sergeant-at-arms. Davis agreed, and was elected to this, his first elected office. The following year, under a new electoral law, Davis ran against Judge John H. Eaton for judge of the Probate Court of Sullivan County, Indiana. Victorious in this campaign, Davis served for two years. In 1831, Davis ran for a seat in the Indiana House of Representatives, elected to the first of six terms. In 1832 he was re-elected, and in that session, he was elected Speaker of the state House.

In 1832, President Jackson named Indiana Governor Jonathan Jennings to head a three-man commission to negotiate a treaty with Pottawatomie Indians to obtain Indian lands in what is now northern Indiana and southern Michigan. Jackson then named Davis, along with one Mark Crume (who is otherwise identified in documents and histories of the period), as the other commissioners. The group met the Indians at a fork of the Wabash River where the city of Huntington is now located. A witness, John H.B. Nowland, later wrote of what happened: "During the preliminary council, Dr. Davis, who was a pompous, big-feeling man, said something that gave offense to Obanoby, one of the head chiefs of the Pottawatomies. The chief addressed Governor Jennings [by] saying, 'Does our Great Fa-

ther intend to insult us by sending such men to treat with us? Why did he not send Generals [Lewis] Cass and [John] Tipton? You (pointing to the Governor) good man, and know how to treat us. (Pointing to Crume): He chipped beef for the squaws at Wabash...' Then, pointing to Dr. Davis, he said: 'Big man and damn fool.' The chief then spoke a few words to the Pottawatomies present, who gave one of their peculiar yells and left the council house, and could only be induced to return after several days, and then only through the great influence of Governor Jennings." The men remained, and, eventually, a treaty was signed at the forks of the Wabash, in which the Indians agreed to give up certain lands near what is now Lake Michigan in exchange for $15,000 cash each year for an unspecified period, relief from debts, and supplies.

Early Years in Congress

In 1832, Davis was nominated for a seat in the U.S. House of Representatives as a Jacksonian Democrat, but he was defeated by the anti-Jacksonian candidate, John Ewing (1789-1858). Two years later, Davis once again challenged Ewing, and this time was successful in his campaign and he took his seat in the Twenty-fourth Congress (1835-37). In 1836 Davis refused renomination to a second term due to ill health, although his particular illness is not apparent in any of the few existent biographies of him. Two years later, apparently having recovered, Davis once again ran for the House, and was elected, this time as a Democrat; Davis then served in the Twenty-sixth Congress (1839-41). In 1840, his long-time political enemy John Ewing challenged him again, and Davis was defeated in a year when Democrats lost 27 seats in the House and the Whigs took control of that body. Back in Indiana, Davis ran for his old seat in the state House of Representatives, and was elected for a single term.

In 1842, Davis ran for the U.S. House again, and again won back his old seat in an election that saw the Democrats win 49 seats and take back control of the House for the Twenty-eighth Congress (1843-45). During this Congress, Davis served as the chairman of the Committee on Public Lands.

The Vote

In the 1844 elections, Democrats lost five House seats but retained control of the body. However,

Speaker John W. Jones, Democrat of Virginia, did not run for re-election owing to poor health. Thus, when the Twenty-ninth Congress convened in Washington on 1 December 1845 with 142 Democrats, 79 Whigs, and six "American" or "Know-Nothing" members, a new Speaker had to be selected. Davis' name was placed in nomination, as was Samuel F. Vinton, Whig of Ohio, and Moses Norris, Jr., Democrat of New Hampshire. Other candidates, including Robert C. Winthrop, Whig of Massachusetts, were given some support, but the race was between Davis and Vinton. On the first ballot, Davis received 120 votes to 71 for Vinton. With a majority of the available votes received, Davis was declared by the clerk of the House to be duly elected as the Speaker. As was the custom, Vinton and Rep. James J. McKay, Democrat of North Carolina, were authorized to "conduct" Davis (bring him forth) to the Speaker's chair, where he was sworn in. Whereas newly-elected Speakers gave some sort of speech thanking the members for their support, the *Journal of the House* shows no such remarks from Davis, and the House quickly moved right after his swearing-in to important legislative business.

Legacy as Speaker
In this Congress, the two major issues were free trade and protectionism, and one of the former group, Davis, was elected Speaker, while a majority of the powerful Committee on Ways and Means stood for tariff reduction. Additional leading matters of the time included the annexation of Texas and the war with Mexico. Speaker Davis, although he made few published remarks, did give firm support to the administration of President James K. Polk, himself a former Speaker of the House. During this Congress, Davis was allegedly heckled for standing with the Polk administration no matter what the issue. Davis allegedly responded, "I will say now that I endorse everything the Democratic party has ever done, and everything that it ever will do."

After Leaving the Speakership
In 1846, despite holding one of the most powerful positions in the U.S. government, Davis decided that one term as Speaker was enough, and he refused to run for a second term as Speaker, and even for re-election to his House seat. He was out of of-

fice for just a year when President Polk rewarded him for his support as Speaker by naming him as a Commissioner to China. Whereas today diplomatic relations are conducted by ambassadors and ministers, the U.S. Commissioner to China was the President's main envoy to that country. Davis later wrote that the four-month-long voyage from the United States to China was most disagreeable, and that he disliked his time in China itself. Early in 1850, after less than a year into his assignment, Davis asked to be relieved of the office and sailed home.

Back in Indiana, Davis was elected again to the state House, and again he was elected as the Speaker of that body, although some minor disagreement - allegedly over legislation - angered him so that he resigned the office. In 1852, he was named as a delegate to the Democratic National Convention, held in Baltimore from 1 to 5 June 1852, and upon the election of officers to run the convention Davis was elected as chairman of the meeting. As chairman, Davis oversaw the nomination of Senator Franklin Pierce of New Hampshire for President and Senator William R. King of Alabama for Vice President.

Once he was inaugurated, President Pierce offered Davis in October 1853 the governorship of the Oregon Territory. Ironically, Abraham Lincoln had been offered the same position in the 1840s, but he had refused it. Davis, however, accepted. According to Hubert Howe Bancroft, Davis arrived in the territorial capital, Salem, on 2 December 1853 carrying $40,000 in cash, which Congress had appropriated for the construction of a capital building and a penitentiary. On 10 February 1854, he submitted to Congress - in a 2-page letter written to Speaker of the House Linn Boyd - a "statement of expenditures" dealing with the $40,000; one half was used to begin construction of a state penitentiary, with $14,400 remaining after initial costs had been paid out, with the other half being used for the erection of additional state buildings. In total, some $24,000 remained at the end of the first portion of consultation on the buildings to be built. Although he arrived prepared to work with all sides in the territory, Davis was doomed to failure almost from the start of his tenure. In 1850, President Zachary Taylor had named General John P. Gaines (1795-1858) of Kentucky, a fellow Whig and a member of the military staff of General Winfield Scott during the Mexican War, as the third territorial governor of the Oregon Territory, but Gaines was not accepted by the people in the territory and his administration was not a success. This appears to be what happened with Davis, whose appointment had come without any input from local politicians or others. Davis was seen as an easterner and an interloper who had been foisted upon them. When the new governor called for a constitutional convention to be held to establish Oregon as a state, a popular vote held on the question was defeated.

Only nine months into his tenure, and under fire from fellow Democrats and Whigs as well as the people of the territory, Davis resigned on 1 August 1854. Before leaving, he wrote a lengthy letter to the Democrats of the territory, denouncing them as indecisive on important issues and condemning their refusal to back his call for a state constitutional convention. Davis was so infuriated with the way he was treated that he refused to attend a farewell banquet given in his honor and quickly departed the territory to return to Indiana. As Hubert Bancroft stated, "There was no fault to be found with him, except that he was imported from the east. Although a good man, and a democrat, he was advised to resign, that [George Law] Curry [a former newspaperman from Missouri] might be appointed [to the] government, which was done in November following."

In his final years, Davis served a final term in the Indiana House of Representatives in 1856, and was a member of the Board of Visitors to the United States Military Academy at West Point in 1858. At just 60 years old, he returned to Indiana bankrupt and ill, and died at his home in Carlisle on 22 August 1859. He was buried in the City Cemetery in Carlisle.

John Wesley Davis has not just slipped into the obscurity of history; he has plunged into it and simply vanished from its annals. Even sources that should be places where his name exists, including the *Congressional Globe* and the journals of the U.S. House, particularly at the time of his election and service as Speaker, have few entries for him, and most of his speeches, of the few that he gave, are lost to us as well. According to his congressional biography, only two discourses on issues seem to exist in printed

form, *including Speech [of] June 27, 1840 on the Independent Treasury Bill*, published in 1840, and *Speech on Mr. Davis of Indiana, on an Appropriation for the Cumberland Road*, also published in 1840. Personal manuscript collections are few and far between; the largest of these appear to be a series of letters in the W.W. Corcoran Papers at the Library of Congress, and some individual letters in the Indiana Historical Society and the Indiana State Library, both in Indianapolis. Thus, except for these few sources and the aforementioned Master's thesis done in 1930, Davis' life is pretty much a blank. Nevertheless, his impact was felt during his congressional service, both as a congressman and as Speaker. William Henry Smith, an historian of the Speakers of the House, explains in his 1928 work on the office that one writer wrote of Davis, "Dr. Davis was a solid rather than a showy man. His imagination was small, but his perceptive faculties were large. He thoroughly understood parliamentary law, and was one of the best presiding officers in the country...Throughout Dr. Davis' long career no one ever doubted his honesty. He kept his hands clean. With opportunities for money-making possessed by few, he contented himself with his legitimate earnings, and died a poor man."

Further Reading:
Bedford, Hope, "John Wesley Davis" (Unpublished Master's thesis, Butler University [Indianapolis, Indiana], 1930).

————. "Davis, John Wesley" in Allen Johnson and Dumas Malone, et al., eds., *Dictionary of American Biography* (New York: Charles Scribner's Sons; X volumes and 10 supplements, 1930-95), V:136-37.

Robert Charles Winthrop

Served as Speaker:
December 6, 1847 - March 4, 1849

He is remembered for his flowing orations and lengthy speeches at enraptured audiences; less recalled is his service of six terms in the U.S. House of Representatives as well as one short term in the U.S. Senate, during which he spent a single two-year period as Speaker of the House during the Thirtieth Congress (1847-49). The last member of the Whig Party to hold that office, Robert Winthrop was the scion of a famed New England family, whose roots go back to the foundations of American history.

Personal History

He was born in Boston, Massachusetts, on 12 May 1809, the son and one of 14 children of Thomas Lindall Winthrop and his wife Elizabeth Bowdoin Temple Winthrop. In a eulogy delivered upon Winthrop's death in 1894, Daniel Goodwin stated:

Enumerating his American ancestry alone, our subject is descended from two Governors Winthrop; from Chief Justice Wait Winthrop; from both Governors Thomas and Joseph Dudley;

from Governor James Bowdoin, of Huguenot blood; from Hon. John Erving, one of the King's Council before the Revolution; from Hon. Edward Tyng, one of the King's Council in 1687; from Hon. Simon Lynde, the father and grandfather of two Chief Justices Benjamin Lynde; from Francis Browne, the ancestor also of Justice Joseph Story. His mother's father was Sir John Temple, the friend of Franklin, and son-in-law of Gov. Bowdoin. Temple was a kinsman and protégé of the great Chatham and the younger Pitt, and of the same family with Earl Temple and George Grenville, the late Lord Palmerston and Dukes of Buckingham and Chandos, a family distinguished in English history for nineteen generations.

Winthrop was a direct descendant of John Winthrop, one of the "founding fathers" of the American nation before there was an America, and who served as the first governor of the Massachusetts Bay Colony. Thomas Lindall Winthrop, the father of Robert, was a minor officeholder in Massachusetts, serving a term as Lieutenant Governor of the state (1826-33).

Privately tutored by his mother, and further educated at private schools, Winthrop entered Harvard College (now Harvard University) in 1823, when he was just 14 years old. He graduated in 1828, third in a class of 53, and then took up the study of law in the office of Daniel Webster, then an eminent attorney in Massachusetts, and later to rise to one of the most important U.S. Senators before his death in 1852. In 1831, Winthrop was admitted to the Massachusetts bar, and he opened a private law practice in Boston. However, he was interested, as members of his family had been before him, in politics, and he began to slowly leave behind the law and enter the political realm. He married Elizabeth Cabot Blanchard in 1832; on their honeymoon to Virginia and Washington, D.C., they were the guests of former President James Madison. (Elizabeth Winthrop would die in 1842 at age 29; Winthrop then married Mary Ann Cabot, with whom he had three children.)

In 1833, Winthrop delivered the first of his important orations, this one welcoming former Speaker of the House Henry Clay to Boston. Like Clay, Winthrop was a dedicated Whig, and during the decade he used his pen and his voice to oppose the administration of President Andrew Jackson, a Democrat. The main issue that led Winthrop to denounce the President was Jackson's attempts to remove the deposits of the Second Bank of the United States. In one oration condemning Jackson, Winthrop stated,

> There are some deposits more sacred than the public funds, deposits which money cannot pay for, which gold cannot redeem - certainly that gold which had been shorn of the badge of our liberty and the motto of our Union. Liberty and the Constitution which secures it, what are these but sacred, precious deposits, intrusted to our keeping by our fathers for our enjoyment and that of our posterity, and who that had an eye to the condition of his country can fail to see the vulture hand of Andrew Jackson hanging over and clutching at these deposits? His whole career has clearly manifested the tyrannous design to set up his arbitrary and despotic will as the sole standard of government and to make

> himself the master instead of the servant of the American people.

In 1834, Winthrop was elected to the state House of Representatives (some sources note it as the General Court of Massachusetts), where he served from 1835 until 1840; during his tenure, he served as Speaker of that body for his final term, 1838-40.

Early Years in Congress

Following the resignation of Rep. Abbott Lawrence from the U.S. House of Representatives on 18 September 1840, Winthrop ran for the open seat and was elected as a Whig; he immediately took his seat and served for the remainder of the Twenty-sixth Congress (1839-41). In November 1840, Winthrop ran for his own term for the House, and was elected; he then took his seat for a full term in the Twenty-seventh Congress (1841-43). Winthrop served in the House from 9 November 1840 until he resigned on 25 May 1842. During this early period of his tenure, Winthrop spoke in 1841 on behalf of the protection of American labor and manufacturing through the use of a high protective tariff. In 1843, he introduced a resolution in the Committee on Commerce calling for an end to the arrest and imprisonment of free black sailors whose ships stopped in southern ports.

It was during the 1840 campaign that Winthrop spoke out on what was the leading issue of the time: slavery. Winthrop took a "hands-off" attitude towards the matter, stating that while he abhorred slavery, he did not believe that Congress had the power to interfere with it where it existed at that time. He said of his personal views on slavery, "I have no hesitation in adding that my vote could never be withheld, if I had a vote to give in Congress or elsewhere, whenever I should see a just, practicable and constitutional mode of diminishing or mitigating so great an evil as slavery." Once elected to Congress, Winthrop joined the antislavery wing of the Whig Party to demand that petitions calling for the end of slavery be allowed to be introduced in Congress, a stand championed by Representative and former President John Quincy Adams of Massachusetts. Taking to the floor of the House in January 1844 and addressing Speaker John W. Jones, Winthrop told the members:

Mr. Speaker, we ask for these petitions only that you treat them as you treat other petitions. We set up for them no absurd or extravagant pretentions. We claim for tem no exclusive or engrossing attention. We desire only that you will adopt no prescriptive and passionate course toward them. We demand only that you will allow them to go through the same orderly round of reception, reference and report, with all other petitions. When they have gone through that round they will be just as much under your own control as they were before they entered on it. I heartily hope, sir, that this course is now about to be adopted. I hope it as an advocate of the right of petition. I hope it as a Northern man with Northern principles, if you please to term them so. But I hope it not less as an American citizen with American principles; as a friend of the Constitution and the Union; as one who is little disposed to interfere with any rights of other States as to surrender any rights of his own State; as one who, though he may see provisions of the Constitution which are odious in principle and unjust in practice - provisions which he would gladly have had omitted at the outset, and gladly see altered now if such alteration were practicable - is yet willing to stand by our Constitution as it is, our Union as it is, our Territory as it is!

Later, speaking before a crowd in Boston, he again demanded the right to introduce the petitions against slavery. He spoke in support of:

the inherent and inextinguishable elasticity of opinion, of conscience, of inquiry, which, like the great agent of modern art, gains only new force, fresh vigor, redoubled powers of progress and propulsion by every degree of compression and restraint; it is this to which the world owes all the liberty it has yet acquired, and to which it will owe all that is yet in store for it...Well, did John Milton exclaim in his noble defense of unlicensed printing, Give me liberty to know, to utter, and to argue freely above all liberties, for in securing that we secure the all sufficient instrument for achieving all other liberties.

At the same time, Winthrop clashed with the administration of President John Tyler, introducing a resolution - which was voted down overwhelmingly

- which declared that the U.S. government could not offer to annex Texas into the Union. The change of administrations to that of President James K. Polk in March 1845 did not change Winthrop's animosity towards the White House; when Polk offered the British arbitration to settle the question of the boundaries of what is now the state of Oregon, Winthrop joined with other critics of Polk and demanded that every inch of the Oregon Territory become part of the United States. Just days before Polk took office, but after his feelings for arbitration had become known, Winthrop denounced the new President:

No more negotiations! Why, Mr. Chairman, where is such a doctrine as this to lead us? Inevitably to war. To war with England now, to war with all the world hereafter, or certainly with all parts of the world with which we may have controversies of any sort, and even war never put an end to the necessity of negotiation.

In the midst of this session of Congress, on 25 May 1842, Winthrop resigned his seat and returned home to Massachusetts when he learned that his wife was dying. Following her death, he ran again for his old seat when his successor, Nathan Appleton, also resigned; Winthrop was again elected to the House, and he held this seat until his resignation on 30 July 1850 after being elected to the United States Senate. During his second tenure in the House, which lasted from 1843 until 1850, from the Twenty-seventh through to the Thirty-first Congresses, Winthrop remained a staunch Whig, backing the antislavery wing of the party in its attempt to head off the admittance to the Union of any new states that allowed slavery to flourish. He reserved some of his harshest comments towards opposition to the Fugitive Slave Law, enacted by the Congress in 1850 to end the practice of Northerners giving aid and comfort - and even aiding - in the escape of slaves from southern states. Winthrop took to the floor of the House to demand that the Fugitive Slave Law, if it must be enacted, include a provision that allowed for the writ of habeas corpus and fair trials for those accused of aiding slaves in their escape:

I hold it to be a just and reasonable provision, and one which ought to form a part of any bill which shall be passed for this purpose...There is a preliminary question, and that is whether he is

*a fugitive at all, whether he belongs or owes ser-
vice to anybody. It must always be a question
whether such a person be your slave or whether
he be our freeman a question which should be
tried where he is seized and when the immediate
liberty which he enjoys is about to be taken
away from him. I am in favor of recognizing the
right of trial by jury in all cases where a question of personal liberty is concerned.*

The Vote

The Thirtieth Congress convened in Washington
on 6 December 1847, with 115 Whigs and 108
Democrats. In the election for Speaker that began
and ended that same day, Winthrop was elected
Speaker over Democrat Linn Boyd (himself later to
serve as Speaker in the Thirty-second [1851-53]
and the Thirty-third [1853-55] Congresses), 108
votes to 61, with 19 votes being scattered amongst
other candidates. The "story" behind Winthrop's
election is scarcely known. When the Whigs, barely
in the majority, selected Winthrop as their candidate, several of the caucus wrote to Winthrop demanding to know his views on certain issues dear to
the party, most notably who he would promise to
name to certain committees. Winthrop responded
with a terse letter that he would not guarantee any
person any committee assignment before his election. For this impertinence and refusal to budge,
Winthrop did not receive the votes of all Whigs on
the first ballot, falling three short of a majority, with
six Whigs in total withholding their votes for him.
Pressure was put on the six, and on the next ballot
one moved his vote to the Massachusetts representative, with another refusing to vote, which left
Winthrop one vote shy of a majority. On the third
ballot, a Democrat who supported Linn Boyd left
the House chamber, giving Winthrop a "majority" of
those in attendance.

At just 38 years of age, Winthrop became the most
powerful officer in the U.S. House of Representatives.
However, historian Hubert Bruce Fuller, who wrote
about the Speakers in his 1909 work, stated that the
youthfulness of the Speakers during that period was
not unremarkable. "In recent years Congress has bestowed this honor upon older members apparently as
a crowing reward for long terms of honorable service," he explained. From the start of the nineteenth
century until the period spoken about by Fuller, the

Speakers were far younger. "Henry Clay when first
elected was but thirty-four, James K. Polk thirty-nine,
John Bell thirty-seven, Howell Cobb thirty-three, and
Robert M.T. Hunter, the youngest man ever elected
Speaker, was but thirty."

Legacy as Speaker

Why was Winthrop elected Speaker? Contemporary
accounts differ, although over the years historians
have injected various opinions. Rep. James G.
Blaine of Maine, later himself to serve as Speaker of
the House, wrote years later of Winthrop:

> *The chief reason for his selection as Speaker
> was his preeminent fitness for the important
> positive. He was but thirty-eight years of age,
> but he earned so valuable a reputation as a pre-
> siding officer that some of his decisions have
> been quoted as precedents in the National
> House and have been incorporated in perma-
> nent works on "Parliamentary Law."*

Mary Parker Follett, a noted historian of the office of
the Speaker as well as the speakership itself, wrote in
1902 how Winthrop's election as Speaker in 1847
was the first time since the start of the Twenty-seventh Congress in 1841, when John White of Kentucky was elected Speaker, that someone more than a
bland, unextraordinary representative was named to
head the House of Representatives; this period included the speakerships of White (1841-43), John W.
Jones of Virginia (1843-45), and John W. Davis
(1845-47) of Indiana, all of which are considered, in
one six year period, as little more than an interregnum in House history:

> *The succession of rather commonplace
> Speakers was broken by the election in 1847 of
> Mr. Winthrop, whose dignified incumbency is
> unlike that of any of his predecessors or succes-
> sors: he was the last man in the chair who tried
> to put into practice the elevated principles set
> forth by [Speaker Robert M.T.] Hunter. [Rep.
> James G.] Blaine says that Winthrop gained his
> nomination in the Whig caucus over Samuel F.
> Vinton, of Ohio, because he had voted for the
> Wilmot Proviso and Vinton against it. So far is
> this from true that Mr. Winthrop himself always
> stated that Mr. Vinton, his warm personal
> friend and twenty-five years older than Win-
> throp, might have had the nomination had he*

chosen. Instead [Vinton] came to him and said: "I cannot be Speaker. It is too hard work for me; I am too old for it. You must be Speaker." Winthrop was therefore nominated with Mr. Vinton's hearty support.

To demonstrate that Vinton was behind Winthrop's election, the Ohio representative was named as the chairman of the all-important Committee on Ways and Means.

Winthrop's election to Speaker, however, was not without intraparty fighting; in fact, it may be argued that the speakership election of 1847 was the first crack that eventually broke the Whig Party into proslavery and antislavery wings. Rep. Joshua Giddings of Ohio, a radical against slavery, refused to vote for the more moderate Winthrop; writing later to Horace Greeley, the-then editor of the *New York Tribune*, he explained:

[The Speaker] exerts more influence over the destinies of the nation than any other member of the government except the President. He arranges the committees to suit his own views. If a Whig is favor of prosecuting the war be elected Speaker, he will so arrange the committees as to secure reports approving of the continuance of our conquests in Mexico. If he be opposed to the war he will so arrange them as to have reports in favor of withdrawing our troops.

John Quincy Adams' vote for Winthrop - he even rose to administer the oath of office to the new Speaker - caused Adams' son, Charles Francis Adams, a so-called "Conscience" Whig in Massachusetts who opposed slavery at all costs, to fret that his father had sold out to the wing of the party less interested in destroying slavery altogether. "The news is that Mr. Winthrop is elected speaker of the House...by exactly the requisite majority. This was done by my father. I am afraid he has sacrificed us in the Commonwealth by it, but this is only making the labours which we have undertaken a little harder.

In a letter to fellow Whig John P. Kennedy, editor of the *American Whig Review* - who was scheduled to write a lengthy biography of the new Speaker in the next issue of the journal - Winthrop detailed the growing split between he and other Whig leaders in both the House and the Senate:

One word as to this thirty-day immortality I am to receive under your auspices. The Sumner-Giddings fraternity are trying hard to convince my Northern and Western friends that I am false to Northern principles, a truckler to Southern dictation, and a principal and constant supporter of this abominable war. Sumner is striking his lyre to this tune in the Boston Courier and Giddings has written verbose epistles to his constituents on the same subject. Meantime, certain Southern Whigs are defending their votes for me [for Speaker] by letters containing here and there unintentional inaccuracies. [Rep. Isaac Edward] Holmes [whom is listed as a Democrat from South Carolina, and not a Whig], for instance, unaccountably presents me as an anti-Wilmot Proviso man, while [Rep. Edward Carrington] Cabell [of Florida] (though his letter is generally excellent) has set down one or two matters in a way to do a little injustice to my views. The long and short of all this is that, as my votes are on record and my speeches in print, I am anxious to be presented by you in my real character; i.e., as an opponent of the war, as neither false to the North nor to the South, but as uniting with that sense of the evils of slavery which is common to the Free States, that respect for the Constitute and the Union which would infringe on no right of the Slave States. Sat verbum. You would be greatly edified by some of the newspapers I find in my mail. "This Winthrop," says as Western Loco-foco print, "is the fellow who sold himself to the South last year, by voting against the Wilmot Proviso." "The Wilmot Proviso," cries a Southern sheet, "call it not so, but rather the Winthrop Proviso, for Mr. Winthrop moved it two years before Mr. Wilmot thought of it!"

Winthrop found almost from the start of his speakership that the slavery issue was dogging him both within his party and from the opposition Democrats. He railed against those who opposed him on this difficult and troublesome issue; in a letter to a friend, he described the pressures of trying to run the House in the atmosphere that existed at the time:

Nobody can exaggerate the labor and anxiety to which I have been subjected. If I had been invested with the entire patronage of the presi-

dency, I could not have been teased and solicited more incessantly. Boys who want to be pages, women who want to sell apples, men who want to be clerks have surrounded me at every turn. Orphans and widows have clustered about me like bees, and where they could extract no honey they have left a sting. But the assignments of committees has been the hardest work I ever did in my life. In order to get through with it in season, I more than once locked myself into my study with a confidential clerk from noon till midnight, and now that I have fairly thrown off the mountain, I have the discomfort of knowing that I have dissatisfied not a few of my friends and probably all of my enemies. Indeed, there is no such thing as fully satisfying one's self in the solution of such a problem. Aside from the difficulty of reconciling geographical claims, there have been personal embarrassments. One of them was what to do with J.Q. Adams. Of late years he has declined to serve on committees; but this year, perhaps because his own party is again in power, he has signified no such purpose. The only place adequate to his dignity and experience was the Chairmanship of Foreign Affairs, but his views are so peculiar that, in the existing condition of the country, I was afraid to risk it.

This letter was written before 21 February 1848, when Adams collapsed on the floor of the House and died in the Speaker's office two days later. But Winthrop's complaints actually don't measure the bitterness and anger among some Whigs towards Winthrop and his role as Speaker. When Winthrop left the speaker's chair on 3 March 1849, he became the last member of the Whig Party to serve in that capacity. Democrats would control the speakership during the next three Congresses; in 1855, when the Democrats lost the majority, Republican Nathaniel P. Banks would be elected Speaker.

Little has been written about what Winthrop accomplished as Speaker. One biography, *The Twentieth Century Biographical Dictionary of Notable Americans*, notes only that Winthrop served as Speaker but was defeated after one term. Despite this lack of specifics, Winthrop is considered by historians as one of the better Speakers of the nineteenth century. Speaker historian Mary Follett wrote,

His mastery of parliamentary law combined with his firmness and prudence, and the vigor and promptness with which he administered his parliamentary duties, made him the able leader of the House in its most stormy crises: and with Giddings and the ardent abolitionists on one side, Toombs, Stephens, and the Southern extremists on the other, the unfailing presence of mind and power of command which Winthrop displayed in times of excitement and confusion were much needed in the Thirty-first Congress. His dignity won the respect as his grace and courtesy won the good-will of the House. Seldom has the Speaker's chair been filled with equal distinction.

Winthrop won re-election in 1848, and when the House convened on 3 December 1849 for the Thirty-first Congress, he was once again the Whig nominee for Speaker. The Democrats held a slim majority, 112 seats to 109 for the Whigs, but nine seats were held by Free Soil members, those who opposed slavery and felt that the Whigs were not fully against the practice. The Democrats nominated Howell Cobb of Georgia as their candidate for Speaker. Some Democrats, all from the North, refused to back Cobb's candidacy, leaving both potential Speakers short of a majority. Cobb led Winthrop, but on the fifteenth ballot Winthrop garnered 100 votes to Cobb's 66 to creep close to victory. On the twenty-fifth ballot, the Democrats removed Cobb's name from consideration and substituted him for Emery D. Potter of Ohio, but the deadlock could not be broken. In an effort to win Northern support, the Democrats then selected Rep. William J. Brown of Indiana on the thirty-second vote, and on the fortieth ballot he came within one vote of a majority. Then, a letter from Brown to the Free Soilers, promising them key committee assignments if they threw their backing to him, was leaked, and Brown was quickly removed from the deliberations. Finally, a resolution was agreed to that a roll call should be taken twice, and if there was still not a Speaker chosen the candidate who then received the highest number of votes would be elected. After the two ballots showed no winner, Howell Cobb, again the candidate of the Democrats, was elected with 102 votes, with Winthrop gaining 99 votes. The Free Soiler representatives refused to throw their votes to Winthrop, even though he was against slavery and Cobb was a proslavery advocate, mainly because Winthrop was not considered an abolitionist radical.

Winthrop was angered by the charge that he was not wholly against slavery. Later in the Thirty-first Congress, he confronted two men who voted against him - Rep. Andrew Jackson, Democrat of Tennessee, and Rep. Joshua Giddings of Ohio - for either being too much against slavery or not being against it enough. Taking to the floor, he railed,

> The honorable member from Tennessee (Johnson) coming next to the onslaught, and doing me the favor to rehearse before my face a speech which he had delivered behind my back at the last session, arraigned me in the most ferocious terms as having prostituted the prerogatives of the chair to sectional purposes, and as having framed all my committees in a manner and with a view to do injustice out the South. The honorable member from Ohio (Giddings) following him, after a due delay, denounced me with equal violence as having packed the most important of those committees for the purpose of betraying the North. The one proclaimed me to be the very author and originator of the Wilmot Proviso. The other reproached me as being a downright, or, at least, a disguised enemy to the Proviso. The one exclaimed, as the very climax of his condemnation: "I would sooner vote for Joshua R. Giddings himself than for Robert C. Winthrop." The other responded with an equally indignant emphasis: "I would sooner vote for Howell Cobb than for Robert C. Winthrop - he cannot be worse; he may do better."

After Leaving the Speakership

Winthrop remained in the House, an outspoken Whig on issues that he felt strongly about. On 8 May 1850, he spoke in the House Committee on the Whole to voice his opposition of the bill to admit California as a state:

> Sir, it is not to be denied that it is this spirit of annexation and conquest growing by what it feeds on, which has involved us all in our present troubles, and which threatens us with still greater troubles in the future...We are reaping the natural and just results of the annexation of Texas, and of the war which inevitably follow-
> ing that annexation. We have almost realized (as I believe I have somewhere else said) the fate of the greedy and ravenous bird in the old fable. Æsop tell us of an eagle, which, in one of its towering flights, seeing a bit of tempting flesh upon an altar, pounced upon it, and bore it away in triumph to its nest. But, by chance, he adds, a coal of fire from the altar was sticking to it at the time, which set fire to the nest and consumed it in a trice. And our American eagle, sir, has been seen stooping from its pride of place, and hovering over the altars of a weak neighboring power. It has at last pounced upon her provinces, and borne them away from her in triumph. But burning coals have clung to them! Discord and confusion have come with them! And our own American homestead is now threatened with conflagration!

Before Winthrop could decide whether or not to run again in 1850, events stepped in to make the issue moot: on 27 July 1850, following the resignation of his mentor Senator Daniel Webster, who had been named as Secretary of State in the cabinet of President Millard Fillmore, who had succeeded to the presidency following the death of President Zachary Taylor, Governor George N. Briggs of Massachusetts named Winthrop to the vacancy. Three days later, Winthrop was sworn in as a U.S. Senator, and he served until 1 February 1851, when Charles Sumner, noted for his firm support of the abolition of slavery, won the campaign as Webster's elected successor. Winthrop had been a candidate for the position in an unsuccessful effort. The following year, Winthrop was a candidate for Governor of Massachusetts, but he lost in a bitter race to Democrat George S. Boutwell. With this final setback, Winthrop's political career came to an end. Despite being offered various appointed offices, as well as diplomatic posts or other political prizes, he turned them all down, and spent the remainder of his life writing and speaking on history and literature. He also was occupied with a number of philanthropic interests, including serving as the President of the Massachusetts Historical Society (1855-85). He also penned numerous works, including *Memoir of Henry Clay* (Cambridge: J. Wilson & Son, 1880) and his own *Memoir of Robert Charles Winthrop* (Boston: Little, Brown and Co., 1897), which was published posthumously.

Robert C. Winthrop died in Boston, Massachusetts, on 16 November 1894 at the age of 85, and was buried in Mount Auburn Cemetery in Cambridge, Massachusetts. William Smith wrote about him in his history of the Speakers of the House, published in 1928:

> *As an orator entitled to take rank with Webster, Clay, and Calhoun, Robert Charles Winthrop was for many years an important figure in American political life. His place as [a] statesman will depend upon the angle of vision. His friends during his public life regarded him as a statesman of a very high order, but the careful student of history may not be willing to accept their estimate. He served six terms in the House of Representatives and a sort term in the United States Senate, but never formulated any great scheme of legislation, and although for a number of years classed among the leaders of his party, he never shaped the policy of his party.*

Further Reading:
Goodwin, Daniel, *In Memory of Robert C. Winthrop, by Daniel Goodwin, Before the Chicago Literary Club, November 26, 1888, and the Chicago Historical Society, November 20, 1894* (Chicago: Privately Printed, 1894).

Winthrop, Robert C., *An Address Delivered at the Music Hall, Boston, in Aid of the Fund for Ball's Equestrian Statue of Washington, on the Evening of 13 May 1859, by Robert C. Winthrop* (Boston: Little, Brown and Company, 1859).

————. *Memoir of Robert Charles Winthrop* (Boston: Little, Brown and Co., 1897).

See also page 458

WINTHROP, R.   ALS.   N. 74

1 Pemberton Square,
Wednesday Af'n

Dear Sir,
    If it is convenient
for you to stop at my house
tomorrow morning, at any
time between 9 & 11 o'
clock, it will give me pleas
-ure to see you on the
subject of your note.

Yours, very truly,

Robt C Winthrop.

Hon. Geo. Lunt,

WARREN,   289 Washington St.   BOSTON.

Howell Cobb

Served as Speaker:
December 22, 1849 - March 4, 1851

He rose to become the Speaker of the U.S. House of Representatives, Governor of Georgia, and Secretary of the Treasury in the James Buchanan administration. Yet the name of Howell Cobb is forgotten today. His lengthy career to state and nation ended when he sided with the Confederacy during the Civil War, which left his life in ruins just three years before his death.

Personal History

Born at his family's estate, "Cherry Hill," in Jefferson County, Georgia, on 7 September 1815, Cobb came from a distinguished Georgian family whose roots ran deep in American history. According to Lucian Knight, a famed Georgian historian, the Cobbs originated in Wales, although direct ancestors can be traced back to Bedford, Kent, and Norfolk counties in England. The first Cobb to come to the colonies, Joseph Cobb, settled along the James River near the early settlement of Jamestown, Virginia, about 1611. His colony, named Cobbham, gave birth to the later family members who later moved south and settled in what is now the state of Georgia. Among the better-known members of this family include Thomas Willis Cobb, who served in the U.S. House from 1817-20 and the U.S. Senate from 1823-28. Cobb County, in Georgia, is named for Thomas Willis Cobb. Howell Cobb's father, John Addison Cobb, was born in North Carolina but moved to Georgia as a young man. He married Sarah Rootes of Fredericksburg, Virginia. Howell Cobb's brother, Thomas R.R. Cobb, was a noted orator who penned "Cobb on Slavery," which defended the southern institution through legal means. In 1860, with the election of Abraham Lincoln to the presidency, Thomas Cobb was one of the fieriest of southern leaders who demanded that the entire region secede from the Union merely to protect the rights of slaveowners. He organized a band of troops in Georgia that became Cobb's Legion, and commanded the group until he was killed by a shell at Fredericksburg, Virginia, in 1862.

Howell Cobb and his family moved from Jefferson County to Athens, Georgia, when he was a child, and he received what was called "a classical education" at a local school in rural Georgia - simply put, it schooled students in math, science, and history - before he moved on to Franklin College (then a part of the University of Georgia) and graduated in

1834. He studied the law and became an attorney in 1836. The previous year, Cobb had married Mary Ann Lamar, the daughter of Col. Zachariah Lamar, and together they had 12 children.

Although he appeared to be headed for a career in the law, Cobb in fact was interested in politics as were other members of his family, and he became destined for a role in the political arena. In 1837, he was elected by the Georgia state legislature to serve as the solicitor general for the Western Judicial Circuit of the state. In this extremely important position, Cobb was given the responsibility of conducting criminal and civil trials on behalf of the state in that area of responsibility.

Early Years in Congress

In 1842, running on a platform that adhered to the tenets of the Jacksonian, or States' Rights, school of thinking, Cobb was elected to a seat in the U.S. House of Representatives. He took his seat when the 28th Congress began in December 1843. While he was a fervent advocate of the rights of slaveowners and states to set their own terms as to the boundaries of slavery, Cobb was also a Unionist, who desired to see the American nation remain as one entity, despite the growing and metastasizing cancer of slavery that was growing inside of it. In the House, Cobb quickly became a noted orator on behalf of the Democrats, and spoke out on such issues as the annexation of Texas, which he saw as a bulwark against the growing influence of radical abolitionists seeking to end slavery altogether.

The Mexican War became the leading issue in the Thirtieth Congress (1847-49). One biographical article on Cobb, written in 1858, stated, "In the Thirtieth Congress, Mr. Cobb took an active part in defending the administration of [President James K.] Polk from the attacks of the opposition, made upon him for his course relative to the Mexican War. His services on that occasion were highly appreciated by the administration, and especially by the War Department. The ability with which he defended the policy and the firmness exhibited in advocating the measures which led to hostility, placed him high in the confidence of Mr. Polk and his Cabinet, and secured for him the permanent and proud position, for so young a statesman, of being the leader of his party."

In one speech made on the floor of the House, Cobb noted the power of the party in controlling matters in the legislative body:

> What, Mr. Chairman, is party? Is it a mere catchword, used to delude, deceive, and impose upon the honest people of the land? Or is there something in that word, of principle, which commends it to the intelligence and integrity of the country? It is an association of men acting in concert with each other, to carry out great fundamental principles in the administration of government. Men of the same political faith agree to unite their efforts for the purpose of placing in the responsible offices of the government those of their fellow citizens whose opinions and principles accord with their own, in order that their government may be administered upon those principles which in their judgment will best promote the general interest and prosperity of the country.

In 1848, Cobb was elected to the Thirty-first Congress. The House at that time sat 233 representatives, with 113 Democrats, 108 Whigs, 9 Free Soilers (those Whigs who denounced slavery), one American, and 1 independent. The Whigs, who had had the majority in the Thirtieth Congress but had lost it in the 1848 election, turned over control of the House to the Democrats.

The Vote

On 4 December 1849, the House met to elect a Speaker. Within one roll call, it became obvious that the Democratic Party was deeply split over many issues, most notably the division over the Polk administration's mediations with England over the Oregon question and the matter of the boundary between Oregon and Canada, a move which was highly unpopular with Democrats. In vote after vote after vote, no one candidate for the speakership could gain a majority. Candidates such as Linn Boyd, Democrat of Kentucky, Robert C. Winthrop, Whig of Massachusetts (who had served as Speaker in the Thirtieth Congress), and Edward Stanly, Whig of North Carolina, were all given a number of votes, but none could get that cherished majority. After 42 votes, Boyd led with 51 votes, with Winthrop second with 36, Stanly in third with 30, and Cobb in fifth with 18.

This same result went on for days. Finally, on 22 December, Rep. Frederick P. Stanton, Democrat of Tennessee, introduced a resolution that if after three additional votes there was no winner, the member who received the most votes would be elected Speaker. Twice this resolution was voted down. Rep. Joshua Giddings, Free Soiler (and former Whig) of Ohio, offered a substitute to Stanton's resolution:

Whereas, the election of Speaker of this House is one of the highest and most important duties incumbent upon its members; and whereas, also, by common consent of every House of Representatives since the adoption of our constitution, a majority of all the votes given has been regarded as necessary to a choice of that officer; and whereas the freedom of debate has ever been regarded as one of the safeguards of American liberty; therefore, resolved, That a change in such election so as to elect a Speaker by a plurality of votes, while the minority are not permitted to discuss the propriety or constitutionality of such change, will be oppressive in operation, of dangerous tendency, and ought not to be adopted.

This resolution was narrowly passed, 113 votes to 106. A 60th vote was taken, and Cobb was ahead, 95 votes to Winthrop's 90. A scattering of candidates received the remainder of the votes. A 61st vote was taken: Cobb received 96 votes to Winthrop's 92. On the 62nd vote, Cobb and Winthrop were tied at 97 votes apiece. On the final vote, the 63rd, Cobb received 102 votes to Winthrop's 100. Rep. Stanly moved that Cobb be elected the Speaker, a resolution that passed 149 votes to 35. Thus, after nearly three weeks of bitter fighting and bargaining, Howell Cobb was elected as Speaker of the House, the first southerner to hold that position since John W. Jones who served as Speaker in the Twenty-eighth Congress (1843-45).

Legacy as Speaker

The same issues that led to the protracted vote to get a Speaker elected for the Thirty-first Congress also dogged that session. Despite having a majority, the Democrats were split into numerous factions. The session lasted until 30 September 1850, but little was done because of the raucous atmosphere.

Cobb tried to maneuver through the problems by calling for compromise on the issue of slavery, which dominated the Congress. Although he did not take part in the many debates on the issue, Cobb did realize that while he wished to defend slavery it could not be at the cost of the Union. It was for this stand that he was denounced in the South. It was for this viewpoint that while he seemed destined to become one of the most powerful Speakers, he could not break the logjam in the House and he decided at the end of the Thirty-first Congress to retire from the speakership and from his congressional seat.

After Leaving the Speakership

Cobb headed home to Georgia and ran for Governor of his home state. Although he had served the people of his state faithfully for many years, Cobb found himself under bitter attack from friend and foe alike. The Democrats in Georgia, as they were nationally, were divided into "Southern Rights" Democrats and "Union" Democrats. Cobb was nominated by the Union Democrats for Governor, and he spent the campaign defending the Compromise of 1850, which appeared to save the Union from the threat of secession and civil war. Cobb was able to gather together a combination of Union Democrats and Whigs to win the governorship. The success of the party in that 1850 election sealed the South's acceptance of the Compromise of 1850, but it earned Cobb the enmity of many who he had once counted as friends. In 1852, as the weaknesses of the Compromise of 1850 became apparent, and the nation slid closer to secession, Whigs and others in Cobb's coalition pulled out, leading to the collapse of the Union Democratic Party in Georgia. He campaigned for Democrat Franklin Pierce for the presidency in 1852. The following year, when his two-year gubernatorial term was over, Cobb returned to private life, his name permanently damaged in Democratic circles. That year, angry southern rights' Democrats in the Georgia state legislature blocked his election to the U.S. Senate. In reaction, Cobb decided to make a political comeback, and in 1854 he won his old congressional seat back. But now things had changed in Washington. When he had left at the end of the Thirty-first Congress, the Democrats held the majority. Now, in the Thirty-fourth Congress, the party was in a minority because of slavery, holding only 83 of 241 seats. Because the opposition could not muster a majority to elect a Speaker, Democrat Nathaniel P. Banks of Massachusetts, who opposed slavery, was serving in the Speaker's chair. Cobb made several speeches in this session of Congress, but he shied away from the slavery controversy.

In 1856, Cobb campaigned in the northern states on behalf of Secretary of State James Buchanan, the Democratic nominee for President. During the campaign Buchanan and Cobb became close friends. With Buchanan's election, he offered Cobb the portfolio of Secretary of State, which Cobb refused. Buchanan then offered the Secretary of the Treasury office, which Cobb accepted. During his nearly four years of service (1857-60), Cobb and the rest of the cabinet were overwhelmed with the onrushing secession crisis. In many instances, historians believe that Buchanan leaned on Cobb not for economic advice but for foreign policy guidance, despite Buchanan's own service as Secretary of State. The attempted introduction of Kansas as a slave state destroyed the Compromise of 1850, and forced Buchanan in December 1860 to remove Lewis Cass as Secretary of State and Cobb as Treasury Secretary. The secession of South Carolina came later that month, and the country moved closer to civil war.

Never a secessionist, who desired only a peaceful outcome to the slavery controversy, Cobb returned to Georgia, this time throwing his entire being into defending his home state and his beloved South. He became one of the state's leading spokesmen for secession, and historians believe that Georgia might not have followed South Carolina if not for Cobb. When the Civil War began, Cobb recruited a regiment of troops, and despite being 46 years old he led these troops into battle. Cobb saw action on the Peninsula against General George McClellan, and fought at Antietam in 1863. He rose to the rank of Major General, and continued to fight until the end of the war in 1865. He made his way back home to his family estate at Athens, Georgia, where he was arrested by Union troops and taken to Nashville, Tennessee, where he was to be removed back to Washington. Instead, the U.S. government released him, and Cobb returned home to Georgia.

The war had destroyed Cobb's life - his law practice was nonexistent, his estate ruined by war, his esti-

mated 1,000 slaves that he owned before the war were now free, his brother lay dead, and he was bankrupt. Thus, he began the slow, upward climb back to the privilege and respectability he had once known. In 1868, after three years of hard work, he had laid the groundwork to make a comeback, and to continue on this road he traveled to New York City. On 9 October 1868, while in the lobby of his hotel, he suffered an apparent stroke and died on the spot. Cobb was just 53 years old. His body was returned to Georgia, and he was laid to rest in the Oconee Cemetery in Athens, Georgia.

Julius Hillyer, who was a law partner of Cobb's, wrote upon his death, "In his political life, General Cobb arose far above the position of a mere party leader. His statesmanship reached a high nationality, and embraced within its compass all the interests of the country. Throughout the whole breadth of the realm, the views of General Cobb were understood and quoted as authority...He was eminently a national man, and his reputation constitutes a part of the rich treasures of the American people."

Further Reading:

Knight, Lucian Lamar, *Reminiscences of Famous Georgians, Embracing Episodes and Incidents in the Lives of the Great Men of the State. Also, an Appendix Devoted to Extracts from Speeches and Addresses* (Atlanta, Georgia: Franklin-Turner Company; two volumes, 1907), I:194-218.

Reid, Randy L., "Howell Cobb of Georgia, a Biography" (Ph.D. dissertation, Louisiana State University and Agricultural & Mechanical College; two volumes, 1995).

Simpson, John E., *Howell Cobb: The Politics of Ambition* (Chicago: Adams Press, 1973).

Linn Boyd

Served as Speaker:
December 1, 1851 - March 4, 1855

He served as the Speaker in the Thirty-second Congress (1851-53) and the Thirty-third (1853-55), but his name has slipped into complete obscurity. Histories of the House of Representatives mention his name only in passing, and, despite serving in the House for ten terms (1835-37, 1839-55), few initiatives that he was responsible for or involved in are mentioned. It would almost appear as if Linn Boyd existed not at all except for his name on the lists of men who served as Speaker of the House of Representatives. Perhaps this arises from the mystery behind much of his own life, as well.

Personal History
Born in Nashville, Tennessee, on 22 November 1800, he was the son of Abraham Boyd, a farmer, and his wife, whose name is unknown. Abraham Boyd was a veteran of the American Revolution, and after the war moved from his native South Carolina to Tennessee. In 1803, he moved again, this time taking his small family to a farm in Christian County, Kentucky, the state with which Linn Boyd would be identified for his entire political life. Abraham Boyd later served in the Kentucky legislature. His son, having received little education ex-

cept what he learned on the farm, became a firm supporter of Andrew Jackson, the former military officer and hero of the battle of New Orleans at the end of the War of 1812, who ran for President in 1824 before being elected in 1828 for the first of two terms. Linn Boyd, at the age of 26, was elected in November 1827 to the Kentucky House of Representatives, representing Calloway County in his first term and Trigg County in his second and third term. He ultimately served until 1831. The following year he married Alice C. Bennett; she died in 1845. Boyd married a second time, to one Ann Dixon, a widow, in 1850.

Early Years in Congress
In 1832, running as a Jacksonian Democrat, Boyd ran for a seat in the U.S. House of Representatives, but was defeated. Two years later, he ran a second campaign and won the election, taking his seat in the Twenty-fourth Congress (1835-37). (Some sources erroneously state that Boyd failed to win in 1833, and won his first term in some 1835 contest, when in fact the elections for the House are held every two years in even numbered years.) As Boyd was from Kentucky, whose native son Henry Clay

had served as Speaker and ran for President (and would so again in 1844 in a losing cause), and was a supporter of Clay's political enemy Andrew Jackson, Boyd's career seemed to be on a fast track to nowhere. In fact, instead of trying to negotiate with Clay, Boyd went headlong against him. In 1844, as Clay prepared to run another presidential campaign, Boyd took to the floor to once again dredge up the allegation that in the 1824 election, when Clay first ran for the presidency, he threw his support to the ultimate victor, John Quincy Adams, in exchange for being named as Adams' Secretary of State. This alleged arrangement was dubbed by Clay's enemies as "The Corrupt Bargain," despite there being no evidence of it or, if it did happen, any illegality having occurred. Henry Stuart Foote, who served as a U.S. Senator from Mississippi (1847-52) and as Governor of Mississippi (1852-54), later wrote:

> Linn Boyd, former speaker of the House of Representatives, called upon me one morning during the tempestuous session of 1850, and informed me that he had been for many years a bitter political adversary of Mr. Clay, and that he had, for a series of years, pressed with great earnestness the famous charge of _bargain and intrigue_ [Foote's italics] against him connected with the election of Mr. Adams; declared that he had been greatly struck with Mr. Clay's patriotic course in the advocacy of the compromise measures, and asked that I would call upon that gentleman and request on his behalf a face to face interview, that he might have an opportunity of making the _amende honorable_ [Foote's italics] as to past unkindness. I readily undertook the mission propounded, and very soon had the gratification of witnessing a thorough reconcilement between them.

In 1836, a nationwide Whig landslide cost Boyd his seat in Congress; however, in 1838, he ran for his former seat as a Democrat instead of as a Jacksonian Democrat and was elected to the Twenty-sixth Congress (1839-41). Boyd ultimately held the seat through the Thirty-third Congress (1853-55), during which he served as the chairman of the Committee on Territories in the Thirty-first Congress (1849-51). During his congressional career, Boyd served on the committee which prepared a plan for the annexation of what became the state of Texas.

Historian William Henry Smith claimed in a 1928 work on the Speakers of the House that others have stated that Boyd not only chaired the committee but authored the resolution that allowed Texas to enter the Union, although there is no evidence of this. He was a firm supporter of the Compromise of 1850, ironically authored by Henry Clay, which tried to find a middle road to avoid the issues of slavery and the admittance of states either as slave or free, a subject that eventually forced the break leading to the Civil War a decade later.

The Vote

When the Thirty-second Congress convened in Washington on 1 December 1851, the Democrats were in control of both houses. In the House, with 233 total seats and 4 delegates, Democrats dominated with 127 seats to 85 for the Whigs, with 10 Unionists, for Free Soilers, and a smattering of minor party members. Thus, on a motion by Rep. George Jones of Tennessee, the House quickly moved to a vote to elect a Speaker. In addition to Boyd, put forward as the Democrats' candidate, Rep. Edward Stanly of North Carolina, Rep. Joseph R. Chandler of Pennsylvania, Rep. Thaddeus Stevens of Pennsylvania, Rep. Thomas H. Bayly of Virginia, and several others, including Rep. Thomas S. Bocock of Virginia - later to serve as the Speaker of the Confederate House of Representatives during the Civil War - were also placed in nomination. On the first ballot, Boyd received 118 votes, with Stanly in second with 22 and Chandler in third with 21. Ten votes over the minimum needed for election, Boyd was declared the victor and he was "conducted to the chair" and sworn in as Speaker. Although new Speakers generally made some remarks to the House chamber at this point, the House Journal - not a verbatim compilation of remarks but an amalgamation of sources later put together by the House - show that Boyd made no such comments at that time.

Legacy as Speaker

But Linn Boyd was not just silent when he was elected as Speaker - there is scant evidence that he did more than that. While his name does appear in official documents and in the _House Journal_ as the Speaker, few sources on his life or of the Congress or of that period mention any substantial work he did or bills or resolutions that he authored or debates he participated in or speeches that he delivered. Historian Mary Parker Follett, whose 1902 work on the Speakers is still considered one of the finest on the subject despite being over a century old, wrote on Boyd, "[Speaker Howell] Cobb was succeeded in 1851 by Linn Boyd, a Kentuckian who carried on the work of his predecessor in as partisan a spirit, if not in as able a manner." But Parker gives no details, and that is the extent of her comments on Boyd. With Boyd having been elected as Speaker during the presidency of Millard Fillmore, one would expect that biographies of Fillmore would give some mention of his having worked with the Speaker of the House. But contemporary work after contemporary work on Fillmore from the nineteenth century show no mention of Boyd; even an examination of the biographies and papers of President Franklin Pierce, who served from 1853 until 1857, during the last of Boyd's terms as Speaker, shows no mention of him except for a letter from Pierce to Boyd regarding a report from the Secretary of the Interior, Robert McClelland. An obituary, printed the year following Boyd's death, which is wholly biased towards the former Speaker but nonetheless illustrates the lack of information on his tenure in that position, stated, "His election as Speaker of the House was a just tribute to the soundness of his judgment, to his impartiality of conduct, to the solid virtues of the man, and the integrity of his public life. The records of political biography may be safely challenged for a parallel to the life of Linn Boyd, in consistency, in moderation, avoiding all violent extremes, in firmness, in foresight as to results and consequences, and sagacity as to the permanent wishes and welfare of the people."

Although Boyd never achieved higher office, he did attempt it; in 1847, he pushed to get the Kentucky legislature to elect him to an open seat in the U.S. Senate, but he failed. In 1852, he published a now-forgotten pamphlet that he thought could get him the Democratic Party's presidential nomination that year, but he was passed over for Senator Franklin Pierce of New Hampshire.

After Leaving the Speakership

In 1854, although likely to continue as Speaker, he refused to run for a tenth term, and instead moved back to Kentucky, where he had established a home

in the city of Paducah in 1852. In 1856 his name was advanced as a "favorite son" of Kentucky to be the Vice Presidential running mate of Presidential candidate James Buchanan, the Secretary of State, but Boyd was passed over for John C. Breckinridge, a fellow Kentuckian.

In 1859, hoping to get elected as Governor of Kentucky in order to advance to the U.S. Senate, Boyd threw his name into contention but was defeated for the Democratic nomination by Beriah Magoffin (1815-1885), a state judge and longtime Democratic Party activist. Boyd was still popular in his home state, and, possibly to compensate him for leaving the House or to merely reward him with high office he was nominated for Lieutenant Governor. Magoffin and Boyd defeated the "opposition" candidate, Joshua Bell, and took office. However, when the state Senate convened with Boyd to serve as the President of that body, his health had quickly deteriorated from some unknown disease and he was too ill to serve. Just four months after being elected as lieutenant governor, Boyd died at his home in Paducah on 17 December 1859 at the age of just 59. He was laid to rest in Paducah's Oak Grove Cemetery. His grave, consisting of an obelisk with the dates of his birth and death as well as a plaque, reads, "Hon. Linn Boyd was [a] member of the KY. Legislature 1827-1829. He served in [the] U.S. House of Representatives 1835-1837 and again 1839-1855. With Henry Clay in the Senate He Successfully Pushed Through the Compromise of 1850 that Dealt with the Extension of Slavery and He Became Speaker of the House 1851-1855." Boyd was succeeded as lieutenant governor by Richard Taylor Jacob (1825-1903).

Henry G. Wheeler wrote of Boyd in 1848, "[He] was a gentleman whose usually quiescent course challenges but little of public observation, but whose influence over his party, in regard to some of the late and most important measures of its policy, has been exemplified in a manner not less signal than complimentary. He seems to possess an effective, but unpretending faculty of uniting discordant opinions, and concentrating them upon a general result, not surpassed by that of any member in the ranks of the Democratic Party."

Further Reading:

*Speech of Mr. Linn Boyd, of Kentucky, in Reply to the Hon.
John White, Relative to the Charge of Bargain Between Messrs.
Adams and Clay, in the Presidential Election of 1824-25*
(Washington: Privately published, 1844).

*Speeches and Proceedings Upon the Announcement of the
Death of the Hon. Linn Boyd, in the Senate and House of Representatives of Kentucky...1859* (Frankfort, Kentucky: Printed
at the Yeoman Office [by] J.B. Major, 1860).

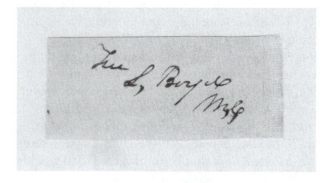

Nathaniel Prentiss Banks

Served as Speaker:
February 2, 1856 - March 4, 1857

His election as Speaker in the Thirty-fourth Congress (1855-57) came after the longest election to fill the office – a total of one hundred and thirty-three ballots taken over two full months – in the history of the U.S. House of Representatives. A Whig who moved first to the American, or "Know-Nothing," Party before he became a Republican, Banks was the only Speaker to be elected from a third party. His service in the Civil War has been criticized by historians, although at the time he was considered a hero.

Personal History

Banks was born in Waltham, Massachusetts, on 30 January 1816, the son and the eldest of nine children of Nathaniel Prentice Banks, Sr., a farmer and foreman of a cotton factory in Waltham, and Rebecca (née Greenwood) Banks. Although officially known as Nathaniel Banks, Jr., the younger Banks never used the "junior" as a part of his name. As well, although various biographies give his middle as either "Prentice" or "Prentiss," Banks apparently - and, according to one of his biographers - "preferred the -ce" form. Despite this, that same biographer, Fred Harvey Harrington, later wrote an article on Banks that uses the "Prentiss" version of the name.

The future Speaker has had two main biographers: Fred Harrington and James G. Hollandsworth. Harrington's study of Banks began in 1937, when his Ph.D. dissertation was presented to Columbia University for his degree in philosophy. He explained,

> The Banks name can be traced to the Norman conquest, the Massachusetts line to one Richard Banks' arrival in Boston in 1686, the year that saw the creation of the Dominion of New England, but neither in England nor in the Bay Colony did the family produce men of wealth or eminence. Their comparative obscurity prevents from following their movements and relationships, and though we know the family furnished more than twenty men to the Massachusetts Revolutionary forces, we cannot link there men directly with Nathaniel Prentice Banks...we find that a Henry Prentice, a great-great-grandfather of Banks' great-grandfather settled in Cambridge as a planter less than twenty years after the coming of the Pilgrims. The family prospered there, Henry's eldest son Solomon leaving an estate of nearly a thousand pounds. It was possible for Solomon's grandson (who bore his grandfather's name) to go to Harvard and become an ordained clergyman.

The younger Banks attended what are denoted by historians as "common schools" - usually small institutions of education where local children attended and received a well-rounded schooling in all types of subjects, including history, literature, and other matters. After this edition was completed, Banks went to work in the factory, the Boston Manufacturing Company, where his father was the foreman as a "bobbin boy," helping to weave cotton thread on the bobbins, or reels, of sewing machines. Journalist Charles Congdon wrote in 1880, "Mr. Banks' youth was passed in a position which is usually spoken of as humble: he was, I believe, a bobbin-boy in a Waltham cotton factory, and subsequently a good machinist. His peculiar success has been held up, in certain cheap biographies, as a stimulative example to other bobbin-boys, and to boys in general."

Although Banks was now a machinist by trade, he decided to branch out into other areas, editing a local newspaper before taking up the study of the law in the offices of Robert Rantoul, Jr., a Democrat who later served in both the U.S. House and Senate. Prior to the bar examinations that we have today, men became attorneys by studying the law in an office, usually of a local lawyer, and in a sense learning the law through real-life experience. Banks was admitted to the bar at the age of 23, but he only practiced for a short time in Boston. Speaking publicly on important local matters, most notably the prohibition of alcoholic beverages, Banks drew notice to himself as a gifted orator, and it was not long before he was being pushed to enter the political realm.

Despite the growing controversy over slavery in the United States, examinations of Banks' papers from this period show very little inclination to discuss the matter outside of a bland denunciation of the practice: in 1842, addressing the Neptune and Boyden fire companies, he made reference to "the national sin of slavery, that hangs like a cloud over the destinies of the land," but dealt more in his discourse with "the sweeping curse of intemperance." Perhaps Banks' hesitancy and timidity arose because he had decided to become a Democrat rather than a Whig, and the Democrats were part and parcel a proslavery entity. During the decade of the 1840s, however, Banks slowly moved toward a stance of firm opposition to slavery. In 1848, when the Demo-

crats recruited him to run for a seat in the lower house of the Massachusetts legislature, Banks put aside his hostility to slavery to run as a supporter of Lewis Cass, the former Secretary of State who was running for President on the Democratic ticket, whose backing of the theory of "popular sovereignty" - that each state must decide for itself whether to allow slavery or to ban it - would cost him the election that year to the Whig candidate, General Zachary Taylor. Banks, however, won his seat, despite the Democrats being in the minority in Waltham.

During his tenure in the Massachusetts state House (1849-52), Banks slowly moved away from his party concerning the slavery issue. He became the only Democrat in that body to oppose the Kansas-Nebraska bill, which would have allowed new states in the western United States to be opened up to slavery, a move that many historians believe paved the way for the horrific civil war that breached the nation a decade later. Although Banks served as speaker of the state House, he was out of step with his party on this important matter.

Early Years in Congress

In 1852, Banks was elected as a Democrat to a seat in the U.S. House of Representatives, serving in the Thirty-third Congress (1853-55). It was during this session that he formally left the Democrats to join the anti-immigrant American Party, also known as the "Know-Nothing" Party. (This epithet came about because, when asked about their stands on the issues, members were told to say that they "knew nothing.") The American Party had a limited following in Massachusetts; nevertheless, Banks was re-elected to his seat for the Thirty-fourth Congress (1855-57).

In 1854, a group of antislavery advocates from the Whig Party, which was slowly being torn apart by the slavery issue, met in Wisconsin and formed the Republican Party, an entity whose main platform goal was the ending of slavery and the granting of civil rights and the right to suffrage for black Americans, both free and slave. At the end of the Thirty-fourth Congress, Banks moved from the American Party to the Republican Party. This move was commensurate to Banks' own movement further and further against slavery. A vociferous opponent of the Kansas-Nebraska bill, which would allow the admission of Kansas as a slave state at the same time Nebraska would be allowed entrance to the Union as a free state, Banks took to the floor of the House on 18 May 1854 to maintain that wherever the U.S. government acquired territory, it had a right to control it as it saw fit, and that the government should allow people in both territories to decide whether or not to be slave or free. The North, he argued, stood foremost against southerners carrying their slaves into free territory.

> I desire to say, Mr. Chairman, in reference to my own political course, that I have not heretofore advocated this policy on the part of Congress. In the local politics of my own State, I have sustained the policy I thought best adapted to promote its welfare. In national politics, I have supported the policy of the Democratic Party. I advocated the annexation of Texas in 1844. I supported the doctrines of the 'Nicholson' letter in 1848, that Congressional legislation was unnecessary to exclude slavery from the Territories of New Mexico and California. I 'acquiesced' in the adjustment measures [the Compromise] of 1850. But I go no farther in that direction. I will stop where I am. I will begin no new crusade until I know where it is to end.

Banks was re-elected in 1854.

The first session of the Thirty-fourth Congress (1855-57) opened on 3 December 1855 with an amalgamation of antislavery members in the majority: this included 117 representatives broken down into "anti-Nebraska" seats, Republicans, antislavery Know-Nothings and even some northern Whigs who opposed slavery, opposed by 79 Democrats and 37 Whigs and Know-Nothings from southern states who supported slavery. The Republicans, with some assistance from the American or Know-Nothing Party, formed a powerful coalition against the proslavery administration of President Franklin Pierce, a Democrat.

The Vote

According to historians Jeffrey A. Jenkins and Timothy P. Nokken, who appear to be harsh critics of Banks, the chances of a quick election of a speaker quickly dissolved into a political game that wore on for days, then weeks:

> When the 34th House convened...four candidates for speaker had already emerged from the anti-administration assemblage. Two individuals, Nathaniel Banks...and Lewis D. Campbell [of Ohio], represented the anti-slavery contingent. Banks, a former Whig, Free Soiler, and Know-Nothing, was considered to be a "passionate anti-slavery man," but also a blatant opportunist who switched allegiances when opportunities for personal gain materialized. Campbell was a former Whig and Know-Nothing who the left Know-Nothing Party after the adoption of section twelve [which called for states that banned slavery to be admitted as free states to the Union under the Missouri Compromise of 1850]. Conceited and caustic, he was considered by many to be the most anti-slavery of all of the candidates. Two individuals also represented the Know-Nothing contingent: Humphrey Marshall (KY), a former Whig, and Henry M. Fuller (PA), a defender of the Kansas-Nebraska Act.

What appeared at first to be a stalled election of a Speaker broke down into factionalism and arguments over who was less against slavery or more against slavery. Over a period of two months, more than 21 different individuals placed their names into the vote for Speaker, encompassing 133 total ballots, the longest and most contentious speaker's election in U.S. House history. Finally, on 2 February, after an interlude of 60 days of wrangling and argument, Banks was elected Speaker of the House with 103 votes to 100 for Representative William Aiken of South Carolina; a further 11 votes were scattered among a number of candidates. The fight over slavery and a rising anger over the number of immigrants entering the United States were some of the factors owing to the growing tension in both the country and in the political realm. Banks, running not as a Republican but as a member of the American Party, was the only candidate who could win the Speaker's chair who was not a Democrat. With his election, he is the only third party member to ever win the speakership.

When the Clerk announced Banks' election, the House exploded into fits of joy, probably because the longest election in House history was finally over. Historian John Ford Rhodes later wrote, "The pent-up emotion of many weeks broke forth in wild tumult. The hall resounded with cheers. The vanquished tried to overpower the cheers with hisses.... The day after the election, [Horace] Greeley wrote [to journalist Charles A.] Dana, "Of course you understand that the election of Banks was 'fixed' before the House met yesterday morning. He would have had three votes more if necessary, perhaps five. There has been a great deal of science displayed in the premises, and all manner of negotiations. A genuine history of this election would beat any novel in interest." Banks biographer and historian Fred Harrington called Banks' election "The first Northern victory" in the Civil War that exploded in the country less than a decade later.

Acceptance Speech

Escorted to the Speaker's chair, Banks was sworn in, and then delivered some remarks to the members of the House:

> Before I proceed to complete my acceptance of the office to which I am elected, I will avail myself of your indulgence to express my acknowledgment for the honor conferred upon me. It would afford me far greater pleasure in taking the chair of the House were I supported even by the self-assurance that I could bring to the discharge of its duties, always arduous and delicate, and now environed with unusual difficulties, any capacity commensurate with their responsibility and dignity. I can only say that, in so far as I am able, I shall discharge any duty with fidelity to the Constitution, and with impartiality as it regards the rights of members. I have no personal objects to accomplish. I am animated by the single desire that I may in some degree aid in maintaining the well-established principles of our Government in their original and American signification; in developing the material interests of that portion of the continent we occupy, so far as we may do within the limited and legitimate powers conferred upon us; in enlarging and swelling the capacity of our Government for beneficent influences at home and abroad; and, above all, in preserving intact and in perpetuity the priceless privileges transmitted to us.

> I am, of course, aware that of my own strength I cannot hope to be equal to the perfect execution of the duties I now assume. I am, therefore, as every man must be who stands in such presence, a supplicant for your co-operation and indulgence; and, accepting your honors with this declaration, I again offer you my thanks.

Legacy as Speaker

The election of Banks, however, was seen around the country in various ways, from joy in the North in having an antislavery Republican as Speaker to denunciations from the South and from Democrats. The *New York Evening Post* said in an editorial, "the North has obtained...a victory which is principally valuable as the key and precursor to a perpetual supremacy over the national government." The *United States Democratic Review* called those who voted for Banks "Black Republicans" and denounced their choice for Speaker. "Sixty days of a congressional session, and half a million of the people's money wasted, to make Nathaniel P. Banks, Jr., Speaker at last!" the journal stated. "Who shall say we do not get the worth of our money? Let us put the vote on record for future reference. Probably one of these days *some* of the gentlemen who, happier than Dogberry, have had their wish, and are 'written down asses' to all time, will be glad to forget the act. We do not wish the people - the Democracy - to forget them." Writing in the *New York Weekly Tribune* on 5 July 1856, Horace Greeley, the paper's editor and a noted opponent of slavery, explained that Banks as Speaker and Rep. Galusha Grow of Pennsylvania were the "young chevaliers" of the Republican Party.

Banks would serve a single term as Speaker, during the growing furor over how the Congress should address the slavery issue. Almost from the start, the difficulties of his tenure were evident: Charles Francis Adams wrote to Senator Charles Sumner of Massachusetts, "Mr. Banks will have no bed of roses." He was forced to deal with a series of crises, most notably the fighting in Kansas between those who wished to have the state enter the Union as a free state, and those who wished to have slavery be legal there. A group of antislavery advocates formed a government that submitted a statehood resolution to the U.S. Congress; another group, composed of slaveowners from Missouri who had moved into

Kansas, organized a government under what was called the "Topeka Constitution." President Pierce had sent a special message to Congress on 24 January, before Banks was elected Speaker, condemning the northerners and insisting that Congress recognize the authority of the Topeka Constitution. To shore up his antislavery support, Banks wrote to Kansas Governor Charles Robinson an important letter, and also blamed southerners for the violence occurring in that state. Banks offered a compromise to the House, to send two attorneys to Kansas and then report back to the House; Democrats disagreed and voted instead for a substitution motion by Democrat George Grundy Dunn of Indiana. Banks later named the three members of the commission, which was eventually led by Rep. John Sherman of Ohio. Another important issue was the slowing American economy; John Savage wrote in 1860, "In the recess after the Thirty-fourth Congress, and during the financial crisis, Speaker Banks delivered a speech in Fanueil Hall [in Boston, Massachusetts] on the absorbing topic of the day, and, in view of the sufferings of working-people in consequence of being paid in paper money, advocated the reimbursement of labor with specie, and believe the time not far distant when the small notes given in competition for labor - and of which there were fifty millions of fives and under in circulation - would no longer exist; but gold and silver, in the hands of the working-classes, would give 'stability of a solid character to our currency.'"

Banks was one of the most powerful Speakers during the nineteenth century, if only for an accident of luck: Pierce's Vice President, William Rufus De Vane King, had died within months of taking office, and with no sitting Vice President, the Speaker became the most influential person in Congress. Mary Follett, an historian of the speakership, wrote in 1902,

> *Banks was one of the most popular as well as one of the most efficient Speakers. His prompt and impartial decisions, his courteous manner and ever-ready tact, won from him the admiration of the House. Yet, although he occupied the chair during a stirring time, he left no marked impress upon the development of the Speaker's office, and in later life he strenuously denied that the Speaker possessed great political power. In spite of this, however, he was one of our most*

> *famous Speakers, and his fitness for the position brought the House safely through some very delicate crises in the Kansas struggle.*

Despite Banks being ardently opposed to slavery, Rep. Alexander H. Stephens, Democrat from Georgia and later the Vice President of the Confederate States of America, said that Banks "was beyond doubt the most impartial Speaker I ever saw in the House of Representatives." Former Speaker Howell Cobb agreed, writing that "Mr. Banks was in all respects the best presiding officer he had ever seen in the [Speaker's] chair." Other Democrats, including those who were most in favor of slavery, slammed Banks for naming "antislavery extremists" to committee chairmanships. One newspaper denounced Banks' selections as "the most offensive and most reckless fanatics of the Free States."

In 1856, the Republicans prepared to run their first presidential ticket, and Banks delivered an address in New York calling for the nomination of explorer John C. Frémont for President, one of the first politicians to do so. Frémont was eventually named as the party's presidential candidate, with William Lewis Dayton as Vice President. Speaker Banks toured the country for Frémont, urging that the South remain in the Union but also denouncing the South's attempts to spread slavery to parts of the nation it had not been previously. "The South, having no literature of its own, having no science of its own, having no mechanical and manufacturing industry of its own, having but little or no commerce of its own, having no inventive power or genius or its own, having, in short, none of the elements of power that distinguish our civilization, has turned its attention chiefly, so far as its leading men are concerned, to the government of the country. Now, we of the North propose to divide this little matter with them," he told a crowd in New York on 25 September 1856. Frémont and Dayton lost the election, and the Democrats took control of the House. For the Thirty-fifth Congress (1857-59), Banks would be out of power as Speaker. When that Congress convened, Banks was nominated for Speaker, but the Democrats, in the majority, named Rep. James L. Orr of South Carolina as their candidate, and Orr was elected.

After Leaving the Speakership

In November 1857, Banks was elected as Governor of Massachusetts; he formally resigned his congressional seat on 24 December 1857. According to "Hinds' Precedents," a list of those standards and rules used during the history of the U.S. House, "On 4 January 1858 Mr. Speaker [James L.] Orr laid before the House, by unanimous consent, a letter from Mr. Nathaniel P. Banks, of Massachusetts, informing the House that he had transmitted his resignation to the governor of his State." Banks served as governor from January 1858 until January 1861, having been re-elected to a second one-year term in 1858, and a third in 1859. During his tenure, the Back Bay in Boston was given additional financial resources for education, one of the most important issues at the time. When the southern states seceded in December 1860, Banks, before leaving office, sent Massachusetts state troops to Washington, D.C. for the protection of the capital city.

In January 1861, Banks became the Vice President of the Illinois Central Railroad, succeeding George B. McClellan, who later served as the head of the Union army during the Civil War. Banks' term at the railroad was short; on 16 May 1861, following the outbreak of war between the North and the South, Banks enlisted in the U.S. Army and was given the rank of major general of Volunteers. His appointment as a general officer was one of the first made by President Abraham Lincoln. In his position, Banks raised recruits for the war effort. And while he appeared to be a good strategist, as a military fighter Banks was less than what was needed for such a massive undertaking; some historians call his military service "a disaster." During the campaign for the Shenandoah Valley, his tactical mistakes led to Union defeats; at the siege of Port Hudson, Louisiana (1863), Banks' sent troops into battle without proper planning that left thousands of Union soldiers dead. After overwhelming the Confederates for months, the southerners finally surrendered on 9 July 1863, giving the Union almost complete control over the Mississippi River. But Banks' mistakes had cost the Union dearly. The final straw came at the Red River campaign (1864) to seize the Confederate capital at Shreveport, Louisiana: Banks made the same blunders he had made previously, but this time following the victory of the Union Banks was left without a command. It was not until April 1865 when he did receive a new command, but by this time the war was over. Given control over the Department of the Gulf of Mexico, his tenure only lasted until he was mustered out of the army on 24 August 1865.

Despite the numerous errors that Banks had made during the war, he was nevertheless lauded as a hero by the press for helping to bring about a victory over the Confederacy. In December 1865, following the resignation of Rep. Daniel W. Gooch, Banks was elected again to the House of Representatives to fill the vacancy, and he remained in the House, this time as a Republican, until he declined re-election in 1872. Two years later, dissatisfied with the Republican Party, Banks ran for Congress as an Independent and was elected. During his tenure, which ended in 1879 at the end of the Forty-sixth Congress (1877-79), Banks returned to the Republican fold. After leaving Congress, he served as a U.S. Marshal. In 1888, at the age of 72, Banks ran a final time for a seat in Congress and was elected, again as a Republican, and he served during the Fifty-first Congress (1889-91), rising to chairman of the Committee on Expenditures in the Department of the Interior. Owing to declining physical health, he refused renomination in 1890 and retired from political life for the final time.

About 1892, Banks began to suffer from what one newspaper later called "the brain trouble" – which may have been the early onset of what we now call Alzheimer's disease, the slow wasting of the brain. In the summer of 1894, whatever was draining him of mental acuity "seemed to get a firmer grip on his intellect, and his family took him from his home in Waltham, Massachusetts, to Deer Isle, Maine, thinking that a change of scene and air might help him." Instead, Banks continued to waste away. On 1 September 1894, the *Washington Post* reported that Banks' family had gathered around him at his home in Boston, Massachusetts, anticipating his death. When that newspaper was printed, Banks had already succumbed to his illness early that same morning. Following a grand funeral at the Asbury Temple in Waltham, during which his body laid in state, Banks was laid to rest in the Grove Hill Cemetery in Waltham.

Further Reading:

Banks, Nathaniel P., *An Address, Delivered by Major-General N.P. Banks, at the Custom-House, New-Orleans, on the Fourth of July, 1865* (New York: Harper & Brothers, 1865).

Flinn, Frank M., *Campaigning with Banks in Louisiana, '63 and '64, and with Sheridan in the Shenandoah Valley in '64 and '65* (Lynn, Massachusetts: Thomas P. Nichols, 1887).

Harrington, Fred Harvey, "The Life of N.P. Banks to 1861" (Ph.D. dissertation, New York University, 1937).

————. *Fighting Politician: Major General N.P. Banks* (Philadelphia: University of Pennsylvania Press, 1948; reprint, Westport, Connecticut: Greenwood Press, 1970).

Hollandsworth, James G., *Pretense of Glory: The Life of General Nathaniel P. Banks* (Baton Rouge: Louisiana State University Press, 1998).

See also pages 437, 445, 447

The House of Representatives erupts in jubilation on 2 February 1856, as members celebrate the election of Speaker Nathaniel P. Banks. The election lasted two months, making it the longest Speaker's election in American history.

James Lawrence Orr

Served as Speaker:
December 7, 1857 - March 4, 1859

The career of southern politician James L. Orr spanned the period from a decade before the Civil War, when he served in the U.S. Congress and rose to become Speaker of the House in the Thirty-fifth Congress (1857-59), to service in the Confederate Senate and Confederate army during the war, to his service as Governor of South Carolina just after the war. He completed his service to his nation when he served as the U.S. Minister to Russia in his final year of life.

Personal History

Orr was born in the village of Craytonville, South Carolina, on 12 May 1822, the son of Christopher Orr and his wife Martha (née McCann) Orr. James Orr's great-grandfather, Robert Orr (some sources report his name as being John Orr), was born in Ireland and emigrated to America in 1730, settling in Bucks Court, Pennsylvania, later removing to Wake County, North Carolina. Despite his age, when the Revolutionary War broke out he volunteered to fight for his new country, and he fought alongside his six sons, including his youngest, Jehu Orr, who

settled near Pendleton, South Carolina, after the war had ended. His son, Christopher, the father of James Orr, was a successful merchant, and, in 1830, when his son was about eight, moved to the town of Anderson Courthouse, South Carolina, where he re-opened his business. His son James worked in the store as a bookkeeper while attending the nearby Anderson Academy. In 1839, at age 17, James Orr entered the University of Virginia, where he studied classical studies (including math and literature) and studied the law. In 1843, he returned home to South Carolina and was admitted to the bar, opening a practice in Anderson Courthouse. At the same time, he also worked as the editor of the local newspaper, the Anderson *Gazette*.

In 1844, when just 22 years old, Orr was elected to a seat in the South Carolina state legislature, serving until 1847 (a date Orr's congressional biography supports, while other sources report the end of his service coming in 1846, and others as 1848) and supporting internal improvements and the direct election of presidential electors.

Early Years in Congress

In 1848, he ran for and won a seat in the U.S. House of Representatives as a Democrat. But while Orr was a firm supporter of slavery - in fact, he was an owner of slaves - and would eventually throw his lot in with the Confederacy in the Civil War, he was not a secessionist or a radical when it came to the ultimate disposition of the nation, at least when his congressional career began. As Orr was growing up, South Carolina was the leading state in challenging the federal government in the area of states' rights - the right to own slaves, the right to nullify national laws that impeded on its textile industry, and other areas of concern. In the state legislature he had spoken out against any attempt at nullification as a threat to the Union. And despite being a southerner, he backed not the ideas of his fellow South Carolinian John C. Calhoun, who resigned the vice presidency over the nullification issue, but those of moderate Democrat Senator Stephen A. Douglas of Illinois. Orr was also a harsh critic of the American, or "Know-Nothing" Party, which stood on a platform of opposing the legal immigration of Irish Catholics; on 4 July 1854, Orr would deliver one of the first addresses by an American politician against the policies of the Know-Nothings, making his views known at Independence Hall in Philadelphia on that date. Taking his seat in the Thirty-first Congress (1849-51), Orr would sit until the conclusion of the Thirty-fifth Congress (1857-59), when he refused the nomination for an additional term. During his five terms, Orr was outspoken on the major issues of the day, including the annexation of Texas and the impact of the Wilmot Proviso, which guaranteed that any lands conquered in the war with Mexico not be allowed to enter the Union as slave territory, and his own support of the Fugitive Slave Act, which allowed for law enforcement to arrest escaping slaves and their supporters in free states. But Orr also backed the Compromise of 1850, a measure that admitted California as a free state. He served as the chairman of the Committee on Indian Affairs in the Thirty-fifth Congress. Historian William A. Foran, in discussing a letter from one of Orr's slaves named Alfred, which nearly led to a "conversion" of Orr, calls Orr "South Carolina's most powerful representative in the Congress of the United States." In the Thirty-third Congress (1853-55), he served as the chairman of the Committee of the Whole, in which he ably managed the debate over the Civil and Diplomatic Appropriations bill.

The issue of slavery, however, dominated not just Orr's speeches but the discourse and debate of the entire nation. Orr supported the Kansas-Nebraska Bill, which allowed Kansas to enter the Union as a slave state and Nebraska as a free one, and he worked with the Democrat leadership to get the enactment passed. In one speech that he delivered in December 1856 in support of the measure, he noted:

> The great object sought to be accomplished in the introduction and passage of that bill was this: the continual agitation of the Slavery question upon the floors of Congress had produced discord and dissension here; it had alienated the different parties of the Confederacy from each other, and was threatening the existence of the Government itself; and hence it was through best, but a majority of the members of Congress in 1854, to transfer, as far as possible, this agitation from the halls of Congress to the Territories themselves. Hence, the great and leading feature in that bill was to transfer the legislation and power of Congress on the Slavery and all other subjects to the Territorial Legislatures, and let the popular will there shape and form the laws for their own government without restriction, save the proviso that such legislation should be consistent with the Constitution and general laws of the United States.

In both 1856 and 1860, Orr was a delegate from South Carolina to the Democratic National Convention.

The Vote

The Congress that assembled in Washington on 7 December 1857 for the first session of the Thirty-fifth Congress was comprised of 132 Democrats and 90 Republicans, as well as 14 members of the American, or "Know-Nothing," Party, and one independent Democrat. After the clerk read the roll of members and discovered that a quorum was present, the House moved to the election of a Speaker. With the Democrats in full control of the House, the election of that party's nominee was assured. The Democrats named Orr as their candidate, and the minority Republicans named Rep. Galusha Grow of Pennsylvania as theirs. On the first ballot,

Orr received 128 votes to 84 for Grow. With 113 needed for a majority, Orr was acclaimed as the elected Speaker.

Acceptance Speech

He was then conducted to the Speaker's chair by Rep. Alexander Hamilton Stephens, Democrat of Georgia (who was later to serve as the first and only Vice President of the Confederate States of America), and Rep. Nathaniel Banks, Republican of Massachusetts. After Orr was sworn in, five delegates from territories out west, including New Mexico and Utah, were also sworn in. The new Speaker then addressed the House:

> Gentlemen of the House of Representatives: I thank you for the honor you have conferred in selected me to preside over your deliberations.
>
> The delicate and responsible duties of the Chair will be comparatively light if I shall be so fortunate as to secure, as doubtless I shall, your co-operation in maintaining the dignity and preserving the decorum of this body. The rules you may adopt to regulate your proceedings I shall seek most earnestly to administer firmly, faithfully, and impartially.
>
> The great interests confided to our charge by the people of this Confederacy admonish us to cultivate a patriotism as expansive as the Republic itself.
>
> I cherish the ardent hope that our public duties here may be discharged in such [a] manner as to uphold the Constitution, preserve the Union of these States, quicken their prosperity, and build up the greatness and glory of our common country.

The House quickly moved to its business, including offering a message to the President stating that the House had elected its leaders on both sides of the aisle and awaited his annual message.

Legacy as Speaker

Orr's election as Speaker was greeted in many quarters as a positive move for a Congress embroiled in the growing controversy over slavery and how it should be handled. The *National Era*, a Washington, D.C. newspaper, editorialized,

> Colonel Orr, the new Speaker, is one of the ablest men in Congress, and perhaps the most capable man for the Speaker's chair in the Democratic ranks. He has served three terms in the House, and is well fitted for his post by an extensive experience...Colonel Orr is a man about forty, of large frame, of a rotund stomach, and with a set of lungs of immense power. When he rises to catch the Speaker's attention, his shrill voice soars above the tumult of the House like the whistle of a locomotive. He is singularly prompt, quick-witted in argument and retort, and pays the closest attention to every detail of House business. The dullest and prosiest declaimer can boast of an attentive listener in Orr; and it is rather ominous to a new-comer in debate, when that flat-haired South Carolina, with a threadbare faded black coat, leans forward, puts one hand to his ear, cocks his eye rooster looking after clear weather, and asks whether he rightly understood the last remark of the honorable gentleman, and, if so, would like to inquire, &c., &c. It is quite an ordeal to go through.

Orr was one of the youngest men, up to that time, elected Speaker, at just 35 years old.

The Congress that Orr presided over was the second to last before the outbreak of the Civil War, and the last to have a Democratic Speaker until the Forty-fourth Congress (1875-77). Mary P. Follett, a noted historian of the speakership, explained, "Orr's administration...was one of the most trying in or history. Violent scenes took place in the House of Representatives, especially during the struggle over the Lecompton constitution. Orr's sympathies were manifestly with the South: the very year after his speakership he advocated a prompt secession from the Union in the event of the election of a Black Republican to the presidency." As the debate grew more extreme over slavery, Orr as Speaker became more and more unable to control the passions of the members.

After Leaving the Speakership

In 1858, while sitting as Speaker, Orr decided not to run for re-election, and he left Congress in March 1859. In 1860, as previously stated, he served as a delegate to the Democratic National Convention, held in Baltimore, which broke up when it was unable to name a presidential candidate due to the issue of slavery. When the party broke into northern and southern wings, Orr sided with the latter entity and backed its presidential nominee, General John C. Breckinridge. The election of Republican Abraham Lincoln led to the southern states seceding from the Union, with Orr's own South Carolina becoming the first to do so in February 1861. Orr had always fought for the Union; now he sided with his state in leaving the Union.

A convention on secession assembled in Columbia, South Carolina, on 17 November 1860, with 170 total delegates. For President of the convention, the candidates were Orr, General David F. Jamison, and James Chestnut, Jr., who had just resigned from the U.S. Senate. Jamison was elected on the fourth ballot. The convention ratified a secession measure which, as stated, led to the state leaving the Union in February 1861. Orr was then named as one of three commissioners sent to Washington to demand that the U.S. government peacefully hand over all forts held by the United States in South Carolina, including Fort Sumter in Charleston Harbor. When President Lincoln refused to agree to the demand, the new Confederacy fired on the fort and seized its occupants, setting off the Civil War.

Orr returned to South Carolina and organized "Orr's Regiment of Rifles," a regiment of South Carolina regular troops from the counties of Anderson, Abbeville, Pickens and Marion, and he became its leader. His service in the Confederate military was short; the South Carolina legislature elected Robert W. Barnwell and Orr to seats in the new Confederate Senate. Initially, Orr was favorable to Confederate President Jefferson Davis' emergency war powers and harsh measures to prosecute the conflict, but quickly backed away and assumed a states' rights stand and the right of the southern states to nullify Confederate government actions. Having argued against this stance while in the U.S. Congress, Orr had come, in effect, full circle in his thinking. By 1864, Orr came to the realization that the South could not win the war, and he warned President Davis to prepare for what would come when the conflict ended. He called for negotiations with the North to make the post-war peace as palatable as possible.

Unlike other Confederate politicians and military officers, at the end of the war Orr was not arrested or refused the right to vote. In fact, he was seen by the U.S. government as a stabilizing influence in his native state. The first post-war election for Governor was held in South Carolina on 18 October 1865, just five months after the end of the war. The vote was 9,928 for Orr and 9,185 for Wade Hampton. Orr took the oath of office on 27 November 1865. His first order of business was to get the legislature to enact the proposed federal amendment (later ratified as the Fourteenth Amendment to the Constitution) giving freedom to the slaves. Whereas freed slaves in South Carolina had, earlier that month, demanded the right of suffrage and full equality under the law, the legislature added a proviso to the amendment that did not allow the federal government to legislate the political or civil rights status of freed blacks.

As Governor, one of Orr's greatest challenges was the threat of the Ku Klux Klan. Formed just after the end of the war by whites angered at the freedom given to former slaves, the Klan used terror and intimidation and even murder as tactics in their continued war. Orr was called before the U.S. Senate committee investigating the outrages by the Klan. Asked to describe the Klan's actions, Orr seemed to blame their deeds on those who were at the other end of them, although he tempered his remarks to delineate between legal and illegal acts:

> It seems that in almost every single instance where they [the Klan] have given notice to persons in advance in these various counties, the persons notified have been those holding office in their respective county, such as auditors, treasurers, county commissioners, and so forth. In many instances I have no doubt such officials are incompetent. In some instances they are certainly sufficiently competent not to be disturbed in the performance of their duties. If they are incompetent there is a legal method of getting rid of them.

Asked by one congressman if those being attacked were black, Orr answered, "Most of them, though some whites have been waited upon, particularly in Fairfield, Union, and York counties. I think none in Newberry County have been waited upon."

The South Carolina legislature's refusal to enact full civil rights to freed blacks would be Orr's undoing. Orr offered the former slaves an amendment to the state constitution that would extend the right to vote to all blacks who could read and write and who owned $500 worth of land, conditions that few blacks could meet. The legislature refused even this modicum of reform, and to punish the state it came under the aegis of the Reconstruction Acts, which established military rule in the former Confederate states. Orr's position as Governor was abolished, and he left office.

Despite his record of siding with the South and resisting the passage of the Fourteenth Amendment, Orr was still seen as a moderating influence in South Carolina. Another constitutional convention was held in the state in January 1868, and Robert K. Scott was elected Governor and took office in July 1868. To reward Orr for his work to bring stability to the state after the war, Scott named him as a judge on the Eighth South Carolina Judicial Circuit, a post he held until 1870. Orr appeared before the Joint Select Committee to Inquire into the Condition of Affairs in the Late Insurrectionary States on 6 June 1871 to answer questions from the Congress on what he was doing to stem the tide of Ku Klux Klan violence in the state of South Carolina.

A Democrat for his entire political life, in 1870 Orr changed to the Republican Party, and in 1872 he served as a delegate to the party's national convention in Philadelphia. President Ulysses S. Grant further rewarded him by naming Orr as the U.S. Envoy Extraordinary and Minister Plenipotentiary of the United States to Russia, succeeding former Pennsylvania Governor Andrew G. Curtin, who served from 1869-72. Orr sailed to Russia, presenting his credentials to the Russian government on 18 March 1873. He arrived in St. Petersburg in the midst of a harsh winter, with seven feet of snow on the ground when he entered the city. The rigors of travel from the United States, matched with the brutal climate, took a toll on Orr's health. On 5 May 1873, less than two months after presenting his credentials as the U.S. Minister, Orr died in his hotel in St. Petersburg of pneumonia. He was just 51 years old. The *New-York Times* of 6 May 1873 merely mentioned his death in passing: "Hon. James L. Orr, the Ambassador of the United States, died in this city

to-night, of inflammation of the lungs. He had been ill from a cold for some time, but his death was wholly unexpected." His remains were sent to New York, where a Masonic funeral was held. Orr was then returned to South Carolina, and he was laid to rest in the Presbyterian Cemetery in Anderson, South Carolina. In a fitting tribute, Governor Franklin J. Moses of South Carolina issued an address to his state that announced the death of Orr, whom he said was one of the most eminent, useful, and devoted sons of South Carolina.

Further Reading:

Leemhuis, Roger P., *"James L. Orr and the Sectional Conflict.* (Washington, D.C.: University Press of America, 1979).

Savage, John, *Our Living Representative Men. From Official and Original Sources* (Philadelphia: Childs & Peterson, 1860), 382-96.

See also page 427

William Pennington

Served as Speaker:
February 1, 1860 - March 4, 1861

He was the first Republican Speaker of the House, serving in the Thirty-sixth Congress in his only term (1859-61) in that body; he later became the first sitting Speaker to be defeated for re-election. Nonetheless, William Pennington was a successful governor of his home state of New Jersey. He also played an important role in the last Congress to seat southern members before the outbreak of the Civil War. His death soon afterward has consigned his name to obscurity. He was born in Newark, New Jersey, on 4 May 1796. His father, William Sanford Pennington, served as governor of New Jersey (1813-15).

Personal History

William Pennington was given a classical education in the schools of Newark, after which he entered Princeton College (now Princeton University) and graduated in 1813, the same year his father took office as Governor. He studied the law in the office of Theodore Frelinghuysen, a noted New Jersey politician who served as Attorney General of New Jersey (1817-29), U.S. Senator from New Jersey

(1829-35), and the Vice Presidential nominee of the Whig Party (running with Henry Clay) in 1844. In 1817, Pennington was admitted to the New Jersey bar. Three years later, he was qualified as a counselor in the law, and he began the practice of the law in Newark that year. From 1817 until 1826, while his father served as a judge, Pennington served as a clerk of the federal district and circuit courts of the state of New Jersey.

Pennington would have probably remained an attorney, but he entered the political arena in 1828 when he was elected a member of the New York state Assembly. He had been a Jeffersonian Republican as his father had been, but by 1828 that party had fractured in the wake of the election of General Andrew Jackson to the presidency. Thus, in 1828, Pennington moved over to the National Republican Party, which had backed former President John Quincy Adams during his single term as President (1825-29). As one of the principals in this new movement in New Jersey, Pennington quickly rose to become an important state political leader. In 1834, with his backing, a fusion of National Republicans and other anti-Jacksonian elements in the state helped to form the Whig Party. The financial panic of 1837 was blamed on Jackson and his party, and it swept the Whigs into power in the state legislature. Now in control of state government, the Whigs elected Pennington as Governor; at the same time, he was also named as Chancellor of the state (the highest judicial office in the state at that time - comparable to the chief justice of the state supreme court), a dual role that has since been removed by law. Without direct election from the people, Pennington owed his elections to keeping his party in the majority in the legislature. Starting in 1838, he was re-elected to the governorship, and he held onto the position until 1843.

One of the most difficult periods in state electoral history occurred while Pennington was governor. In 1838, five separate congressional elections from New Jersey were contested; known to historians as "The Broad Seal War," it began when Pennington held that the Whig candidates won all five seats, basing his decision on an antiquated state law that did not allow him full access to electoral returns. The U.S. House of Representatives, however, in the hands of Democrats, overruled Pennington and after a year of investigation awarded all five seats to the Democrats. Pennington, while admitting that the House had the right to rule on the elections and their outcomes, nonetheless condemned the Democratic-controlled House for trampling on his state's right to elect candidates to the national body. Unable to undo what the House had decided, Pennington instead asked the legislature to draft a new law to allow for a greater examination of electoral returns in the state before the House heard such controversies. During his tenure, the Whigs also enacted a series of reformist legislation, including the construction of institutions for the blind, deaf, and insane. However, the Whigs failed to pass a law that allowed for the direct election of the governor, and, coupled with a failure to end the financial panic that had swept them into office, led to defeat for the party in 1843. Pennington paid in this election loss by being removed from office on 27 October 1843. He returned to his law practice in Newark, out of political office for the first time since 1828. He refused offers from President Millard Fillmore to serve as either the territorial governor of Minnesota or a Special Claims Adjuster examining claims against the United States following the Mexican-American War.

Early Years in Congress

Pennington did not re-enter the political arena until 1858, when he reluctantly ran for a seat in the U.S. House of Representatives. The Whig Party to which he had belonged had collapsed in the growing fight over the extension - or contraction - of slavery in the new states being added to the Union. Although the new Republican Party, formed from the ashes of the Whig Party in 1854, was growing more popular in the North, particularly in the northeast, in New Jersey the party's abolitionist platform was not popular, and it had to contend with the anti-immigrant and anti-Catholic American, or "Know-Nothing" Party for votes. Pennington was nominated by the Republicans for his moderate stand on slavery, which would not offend those Democrats disgusted with the proslavery element of their party or those Know-Nothings who were looking for a less controversial candidate for the House. In fact, while Pennington was a Republican, he did not oppose slavery and in fact was against abolitionist attempts to end the practice. Nonetheless, with this platform, Pennington won the election easily with 54% of the vote.

The Thirty-sixth Congress convened on 5 December 1859. Although the Republicans had a majority of seats in the House, having won 18 seats in the 1858 contest, there was no majority around any candidate for Speaker. Balloting - and negotiations behind the scenes - continued for eight full weeks. During this time, the House also erupted into angry debate over the predicament that slavery was bringing to the Union. A book recently published, titled *The Impending Crisis in the South*, predicted the end of slavery, and was denounced by proslavery Democrats in the House as they battled to try to win the speakership.

The Vote

The recent attack by abolitionists, led by John Brown, at Harper's Ferry, Virginia, also was injected into the choice of Speaker. The Democrats began by supporting Thomas S. Bocock of Virginia, a staunch defender of slavery, but by the final ballots the party was divided. On the final ballot, nine Democrats, all from the South, refused to vote for their compromise candidate, John A. McClernand of Illinois, who was an ally of Senator Stephen A. Douglas of that same state. The leading candidate to be Speaker appeared to be the Republican John Sherman, the brother of future General William Tecumseh Sherman; John Sherman later served as Secretary of the Treasury and Secretary of State. Sherman ran ahead of his opposition for numerous ballots, supported by Republicans and "anti-Lecompton Democrats," those who bucked their party and refused to support the admittance to the Union of the state of Kansas under the Lecompton Constitution, which was a proslavery charter. But, Sherman could not muster a majority needed for victory, and as ballot after ballot was taken, the frustration in the House continued to mount. Finally, on 1 February 1860, Sherman withdrew his name from the speakership race, and with his name removed Pennington received 117 votes on the 44th ballot and was duly declared as the new Speaker. McClernand came in second with 85 votes, and John Adams Gilmer of North Carolina, who did not belong to a party but is listed as "in opposition," was a distant third with 16 votes. The break in the deadlock came when John Bussing Haskin of New York, an anti-Lecompton Democrat, switched his vote from Sherman to Pennington; Henry Winter Davis, an American (also known as "The Know-Nothings") from Maryland, also changed his vote to Pennington, throwing the election to the former New Jersey governor. De Alva Stanwood Alexander, one of late nineteenth century and early twentieth century's greatest historians, gave perhaps the best reason why Pennington was selected in the midst of this chaos when he explained in 1916:

> Pennington was colorless. He had said nothing and done nothing which could in any wise involve him in controversy. Although a man of dignity and poise, who possessed Christian meekness and political integrity, with a desire to be fair and just, his ignorance of parliamentary practice and lack of political management emphasized his unfitness to direct the House at a time of such excitement. But his ability to organize the House in opposition to President Buchanan, who evinced the servility of Pierce, satisfied his party, while the absence of a public record commended him to anti-Lecompton

> Democrats and anti-slavery Americans, who recognized the gravity of the situation.

Just a little over five years in existence, the Republican Party had won a majority in the U.S. House and elected a Speaker. Rep. Thomas Carmichael Hindman, Democrat of Arkansas, stood up and denounced the selection as he was shouted down. "All I proposed to say was, that a Black Republican Speaker...has been elected by the votes of two members of the Know-Nothing Party."

Acceptance Speech
The clerk of the House appointed Reps. Bocock and Sherman to accompany the new Speaker to the chair to be sworn in. Once that was completed by Rep. John Smith Phelps of Missouri, the oldest serving member of the House, Pennington addressed the House:

> I return you my grateful acknowledgments for the distinguished honor you have been pleased to confer upon me in electing me Speaker of this House. Coming here, for the first time, at the present session, to be associated with you as a member, no event could have been more unlooked for than that I should be called on to preside over your deliberations. And my friends will do me the justice to say that I have not sought the position, as I certainly never desired it. I am, nevertheless, as conscious of the dignity and importance of this high office as any gentleman can be; but I should have been far better pleased had its duties been intrusted [sic] to abler and more experienced hands. After witnessing the almost insurmountable obstacles in the way of the organization of this House, I came to the conclusion that any gentleman, of any party, who could command a majority of the votes for Speaker, was bound, in deference to the public exigencies, to accept the responsibility as an act of patriotic duty, whether agreeable to his personal feelings or not. As that choice has unexpectedly fallen upon me, I have not hesitated to accept it. In the execution of this high trust, my object will be to do my duty with impartiality and justice to all. I shall have great necessity, gentlemen, for your indulgence in the new position in which I am placed, and I feel entire confidence I shall receive it at your hands.

A representative from the State of New Jersey, upon whose soil so many brilliant achievements were accomplished in the revolutionary war, and whose people have ever been distinguished for their devotion to the Constitution and the Union, I pray the Great Arbiter of our destinies that I may do no act to impair the integrity of either; that by wise and prudent counsels peace and order may yet reign in our midst, and our free institutions be perpetuated to our descendants. I feel I have a national heart, embracing all parts of our blessed Union.

Again thanking you for your kindness, I now enter upon the discharge of the arduous and complicated duties of my station.

Legacy as Speaker

As soon as Pennington's tenure as Speaker began he was already dealing with the innumerable troubles befalling the House. Immediately, numerous members called out "Mr. Speaker!" as they raised questions of order. Pennington then turned to mediate a fight between Reps. Horace F. Clark and John B. Haskin, both of New York, who had argued over the Lecompton Constitution, with Haskin threatening his fellow New Yorker with a pistol. After much discussion, the conflict was averted. Pennington also had to deal with his fellow Republican, Rep. Thaddeus Stevens, who, as he later said, "departed from the general rule of obeying party decrees, and voted for the honorable gentleman from North Carolina [Mr. Gilmer]." However, contemporaries and those historians who happen to mention Pennington note that he ran the House with humility, respect for all members, and with a sense of order during a period of chaos that was engulfing not just the House and the Senate but the nation as a whole. Pennington does come in for some harsh criticism for appointing only abolitionist Republicans and proslavery Democrats to the "Committee of 33," chaired by Rep. Thomas Corwin of Ohio, which sought to enact a plan to head off the secession of the southern states but to no avail. The "Corwin Amendment" to the U.S. Constitution would have endorsed the idea that slaves were property and that they could be moved into free territory and be retained, but it was defeated in the Senate.

Pennington ran for re-election in 1860 in the midst of perhaps the most contentious presidential election in American history. While the Republicans had nominated moderate abolitionist Abraham Lincoln for president, the Democrats - in two separate nominating conventions - had split into "Southern" and "Northern" wings, with the former demanding governmental protection for slavery and the latter calling for a "hands-off" approach to the entire matter. A fourth ticket, with former Speaker of the House John Bell and orator Edward Everett, was formed from former Whigs and others who wished to deny Lincoln a victory and avoid the secession of the southern slave states. Pennington, however, went down to defeat at the hands of Democrat Nehemiah Perry. At the same time, Republican Abraham Lincoln was losing the state to "Northern Democrat" Stephen A. Douglas, who won the state's 7 electoral votes. Pennington thus became the first - and one of only two - sitting Speakers to be defeated for re-election. (In 1994, Democrat Thomas S. Foley became the second.)

After Leaving the Speakership

Pennington apparently returned to the practice of law; however, on 16 February 1862, a little less than a year after leaving Congress, he died suddenly at the age of 65. According to New Jersey historian Lucius Q.C. Elmer, Pennington's death was "hastened, if not produced, by a large dose of morphine, administered through the mistake of an apothecary," although this cannot be confirmed. Pennington was buried in Mount Pleasant Cemetery in Newark.

Having served as Speaker of the House for the single term that he was seated in that body, William Pennington's name and service had slipped into obscurity. Few sources, contemporary or historical, mention his name except in relation to the drawn-out election in which he was elected as Speaker. Although he was not a radical Republican who desired to end slavery at all costs, Pennington's tenure is noted for the number of southern Democrats who vacated their seats in protest to the antislavery efforts of Pennington's supporters. He backed the controversial Covode Committee, headed by Rep. John Covode of Pennsylvania, which investigated corruption inside the Buchanan administration. In the end, for a single two-year term, William Pennington tried to hold the House together, a job he did about as well as anyone could under the circumstances.

Further Reading:

D'Alessio, Sister Serafina, "William Pennington" in Paul A. Stellhorn and Michael J. Birkner, eds., *The Governors of New Jersey, 1664-1974: Biographical Essays* (Trenton: New Jersey Historical Commission, 1982), 110-14.

Henig, Gerald S., "Henry Winter Davis and the Speakership Content of 1859-60," *Maryland Historical Magazine*, 68:1 (Spring 1973), 1-19.

See also page 450

Galusha Aaron Grow

Served as Speaker:
July 4, 1861 - March 4, 1863

For historians of agriculture in the United States, the name of Galusha Grow is best remembered for his authoring of the 1862 Homestead Act, which for the first time disposed the public lands for use in both settlement and agriculture. Grow's rise to serve as Speaker of the U.S. House in the Thirty-seventh Congress (1861-63), just as the Civil War was starting, is barely remembered if at all by historians of the House or of the massive conflict that was raging across the north and south; few history books mention his name in connection with the speakership except for those dedication to study of the office. Although Grow's initial congressional service was during the middle of the nineteenth century, he later returned to the House at the end of that century and served into the twentieth century before his death.

Personal History

Grow was born on 31 August 1823 in Ashford (now Eastford), in Windham County, Connecticut, the son of Joseph Grow and his wife Elizabeth (née Robbins), both farmers. According to several sources on his life, Grow was descended, at least on his father's

side, from a man named Grow of Ipswich, Massachusetts, who came from England in the seventeenth century. Biographers James Dubois and Gertrude Mathews state that when the infant Grow was being christened, his Aunt, visiting from Vermont, offered the name of the-then Vermont Governor, Jonas Galusha (1753-1834), and her own husband's name, Aaron, for the names of the new addition to the family. The child was named Aaron Galusha, but this was changed to Galusha Aaron. Joseph Grow, Galusha's father, died suddenly in 1837, leaving his widow to scatter the family; Galusha lived during this period with his maternal grandfather. In 1834, when Grow was 11, his mother was able to purchase a small farm near Glenwood, in Susquehanna County, Pennsylvania.

Helping to sustain his family's farm, Grow and his brothers and sisters aided their mother; for a time, Grow helped to cut logs and bring them down the Susquehanna River, leading to the Chesapeake River. It was during these trips that Grow became acquainted with the land system in America at the time, in which settlers struggled on land that they could never own because the government or localities controlled it. These experiences shaped his views, and turned him into an advocate for land reform, one of the measures he would promote and advance during his time in Congress.

Galusha Grow attended what was called a common, or rural, school in Glenwood, later going to the Franklin Academy in Susquehanna County. Completing his education, he went to Amherst College in Amherst, Massachusetts, from which he graduated in 1844. He was admitted to the Pennsylvania state bar three years later, and practiced law for a time near where he grew up. In the interregnum, however, Grow entered the political arena, campaigning for Democrat presidential candidate James Knox Polk in 1844. Here he met his eventual law partner, David Wilmot, the famed politician who penned the Wilmot Proviso, a declaration that stated that those future states in the American West shaped out of land won from Mexico in the war against that nation would not and could not be organized as slave states. In 1850, however, Wilmot was such a dividing influence among Pennsylvania Democrats, who feared that abolitionism or its advocacy would lead to diminished influence nationally, that he was asked to give up his House seat. While Wilmot acceded to the wishes of his party, he chose his law partner, Grow, to be the man he wanted to serve as the Democrat's candidate in the 1850 election.

Early Years in Congress
With Wilmot's backing and support, Grow was easily elected, and took his seat in the 32nd Congress (1851-53), which seated 127 Democrats, 85 Whigs, and a smattering of antislavery members. Grow was able to get himself re-elected to the seat in 1852, 1854, and 1856.

In 1856, the antislavery issue had torn the Democrats apart nationally, but particularly in the North. Grow, once a staunch Democrat, quickly departed his party for the new Republican Party, an entity formed that same year and comprised of antislavery Whigs and others formed into an amalgamation of members who agreed on that single issue. In 1856, Grow was elected as a Republican to the Thirty-fifth Congress (1857-59), and he remained in the Congress until the end of the Thirty-seventh Congress on 3 March 1863. In one of his key

speeches on the subject of slavery, Grow took to the floor of the House on 25 March 1858 to rail against the proslavery Lecompton Constitution being established for Kansas. This document came out of the fight for control of Kansas between antislavery advocates who were a majority in the state and proslavery masters who flooded into the state to keep it from declaring slavery illegal. The proslavery element took control of the machinery of state government, pushed out anyone who sided with the abolitionists, and proceeded to write their own constitution in the city of Lecompton, which was not even the state capitol but where the proslavery element had set up a new state government that had not been elected. The issue divided Democrats, some of whom wanted to accept the proslavery minority constitution, while others, who were leery of the slavery, decried the way the document was written and refused to vote for its acceptance, which would allow Kansas into the Union as a slave state in violation of the Compromise of 1850, fashioned to keep the country from fighting a deadly civil war. Grow, a former Democrat who now sided with the abolitionist Republican Party, spoke out against the Lecompton Constitution:

> *Peace among a brave people is not the fruit of injustice, not does agitation cease by the perpetration of wrong. For a third of a century, the advocates of slavery, while exercising unrestricted speech in its defense, have struggled to prevent all discussion against it - in the South, by penal statutes, mob law, and brute force; in the North, by dispersing assemblages of peaceable citizens, pelting their lecturers, burning their halls, and destroying their presses; in this forum of the people, by finality resolves all laws for the benefit of slavery, not, however, to affect those in behalf of freedom, and by attempts to stifle the great constitutional right of the people at all times to petition their government. Yet, despite threats, mob law, and finality resolves, the discussion goes on, and will continue to, so long as right and wrong, justice and injustice, humanity and inhumanity, shall struggle for supremacy in the affairs of men.*

On 6 February 1858, the issue over Lecompton hit home when Grow became involved in a fight on the House floor with Rep. Laurence Keitt, Democrat of

South Carolina. As the House debated the issue over the Lecompton constitution into the night, Keitt and Grow seemed to argue over a series of parliamentary procedures. When Rep. John Quitman, Democrat of Mississippi, rose to ask for time to speak on the matter in the early morning hours of 6 February, Grow stood and objected, railing against further debate and calling instead for a vote on the Lecompton issue. Keitt, a friend of Quitman's, rose, confronted Grow, who had crossed over to speak to another Democrat, and said to him, "If you want to object, go back to your side of the House, you black Republican puppy!" Grow yelled at him, "I will object when and where I please!" At that moment, Keitt went face-to-face with Grow, grabbing the Pennsylvanian by the throat, and, as the *Congressional Globe* noted, "At this moment a violent personal altercation commenced in the aisle at the right of the Speaker's chair, between Mr. Keitt and Mr. Grow. In an instant the House was in the greatest possible confusion. Members in every part of the Hall rushed over to the scene of the conflict, and several members seemed to participate in it." Speaker of the House James L. Orr, Democrat of South Carolina, ordered Sergeant-at-Arms Adam J. Glossbrenner to arrest any member refusing to stop the fighting. As the melee continued, two Republicans ripped the hairpiece from the head of Rep. William Barksdale, Democrat of Mississippi. One of two Republicans, Rep. John Potter of Wisconsin, yelled, "I've scalped him!' The House was able to adjourn for the night amid continued threats of violence, but reconvened two days later, when Republicans and Free Soilers combined to impede the referral of the Lecompton Constitution to the House Committee on Territories, blocking Kansas' entry into the Union until 1861, when it was admitted as a free state that outlawed slavery.

The Thirty-sixth Congress convened on 5 December 1859 with 109 Republicans, 101 Democrats, and 27 Americans or "Know-Nothings" who backed anti-immigrant measures. With no party having a firm majority of seats, it was feared that a lengthy and protracted fight to elect a Speaker, as had happened in 1855, when Nathaniel Banks was named after two months and 133 ballots, would ensue. John Sherman, later the Secretary of the Treasury (1877-81) and Secretary of State (1897-98) and brother of future Civil War General William

Tecumseh Sherman, wrote in his memoirs, "It was well understood that the Republican vote would be divided between Galusha A. Grow and myself, and it was agreed between us that whichever received a majority of the Republican vote would be considered as the nominee of that party." On the first vote, Sherman received 66 votes, with Grow getting 43. However, the Democrats were more solidly behind one candidate, and Thomas S. Bocock of Virginia got 86 votes. By the agreement, Grow withdrew his name. Sherman could not muster the necessary votes to win, and he withdrew later in the balloting. Republican William Pennington of New Jersey, in his first term in the House, was eventually selected as Speaker.

Grow continued to rail against slavery. In a letter to Kansas Governor Charles Robinson, he explained:

> *The Slavery men here are calculating to cheat Lecompton through either by directory voting or by fraudulent counting in the returns. And they pretend to believe that there is a majority on their side in the territory & say that this election on the Lecompton junior will show it. They are going to secure the passage of Lecompton by the vote if possible in order to fall back on that as a justification of their course. Unless they can do that they are utterly disgraced and must stand before the country as the supporters of the grosses frauds in trampling down the known will of the people. Let Lecompton be repudiated by an overwhelming majority at an election that the administration fixes and the dough faces will be exterminated next fall. We shall have the next Congress beyond a doubt & the Democrats even conceed [sic] it. Then Kansas will be admitted if not before for the condition in English bill about population will not bind a future Congress in their action.*

The Thirty-seventh Congress, chosen in the 1860 contest that saw Abraham Lincoln elected as the first Republican President, met in special session on 4 July 1861 following Lincoln's declaration for the Congress to meet which was delivered on 15 April. The House that met - the Senate had convened when Lincoln was inaugurated in March 1861 - was only a shell of what a Congress was supposed to be, with nearly all of its southern members missing due to the secession of the now-Confederate states.

Grow, having become more radical against slavery in the years since he ran as a Republican, was one of the most outspoken leaders against the evil practice.

The Vote

The first goal of the new Congress was to elect a Speaker. With most of the Democrats and proslavery members absent, there was no fighting for numerous candidates as previous Congresses had seen. On the first ballot, Grow won with 99 votes to 12 for John J. Crittenden of Kentucky (that state was still in the Union) and 11 for Francis P. Blair, Jr., of Missouri (which remained in the Union for the entire Civil War).

Acceptance Speech

With his election assured, Grow as taken to the Speaker's chair and sworn in. He then delivered comments to the assembled body; usually, these remarks were short, but Grow delivered a lengthy dialogue:

> *Gentlemen of the House of Representatives of the United States of America: Words of thanks for the honor conferred by the vote just announced would but feebly express the heart's gratitude. While appreciating this distinguished mark of your confidence, I am not unmindful of the trying duties incident to the position to which you have assigned me. Surrounded at all times by grave responsibility, it is doubly so in this hour of national disaster, when every consideration of gratitude to the past and obligation to the future tendrils around the present;*

> *Three score years ago fifty-six old merchants, farmers, lawyers, and mechanics, the representatives of a few feeble colonists, scattered along the Atlantic seaboard, met in convention to found a new empire, based on the inalienable rights of man. Seven years of bloody conflict ensued, and the 4th of July, 1776, is canonized in the hearts of the great and the good as the jubilee of oppressed nationalities, and in the calendar of heroic deeds it marks a new era in the history of the race. Three-quarters of a century have passed away, and those few feeble colonists, hemmed in by the ocean in front and the wilderness and the savage in the rear, have spanned a whole continent with a great empire*

> *of free States, rearing throughout its vast wilderness temples of science and of civilization upon the ruins of savage life. Happiness seldom if ever equalled [sic] has surrounded the domestic fireside, and prosperity unsurpassed has crowned the national energies. The liberties of the people have been secured at home and abroad, while the national ensign floated honored and respected in every commercial mart of the world.*

> *On the return of this glorious anniversary, after a period but little exceeding that of the allotted lifetime of man, the people's representatives are convened in the council chambers of the republic to deliberate upon the means for preserving the government under whose benign influence these grand results have been achieved.*

> *A rebellion - the most causeless in the history of the race - has developed a conspiracy of long standing to destroy the Constitution formed by the wisdom of our fathers, and the Union consecrated by their blood. This conspiracy, nurtured for long years in secret councils, first develops itself openly in acts of spoliation and plunder of public property, with the connivance or under the protection of treason enthroned in all the high places of the government, and at last in armed rebellion for the overthrow of the best government ever devised by man. Without an effort in the mode prescribed by the organic law for a redress of all grievances, the malcontents appeal only to the arbitrament of the sword, insult the nation's honor, trample upon its flag, and inaugurate a revolution which, if successful. would end in establishing petty, jarring confederacies, or despotism and anarchy, upon the ruins of the republic, and the destruction of its: liberties.*

> *The 19th of April, canonized in the first struggle for American nationality, has been re-consecrated in martyr blood. [Union General Gouverneur K.] Warren has his counterpart in Ellsworth, and the heroic deeds and patriotic sacrifices of the struggle for the establishment of the republic are being reproduced upon the battle field for its maintenance. Every race and tongue almost is represented in the grand legion of the Union, their standards proclaiming, in a*

language more impressive than words, that here indeed is the home of the emigrant and the asylum of the exile. No matter where was his birthplace, or in what clime his infancy was cradled, he devotes his life to the defense of his adopted land, the vindication of its honor, and the protection of its flag, with the same zeal with which he would guard his hearth-stone and his fireside. All parties, sects, and conditions of men, not corrupted by the institutions of human bondage, forgetting bygone rancors [sic] or prejudices, blend in one united phalanx for the integrity of the Union and the perpetuity of the republic.

Long years of peace, in the pursuit of sordid gain, instead of blunting the patriotic devotion of loyal citizens, seem but to have intensified its development when the existence of the government is threatened or its honor assailed. The merchant, the banker, and the tradesman, with an alacrity unparalleled, proffer their all at the altar of their country, while from the counter, the workshop, and the plough, brave hearts and stout arms, leaving their tasks unfinished, rush to the tented field. The air vibrates with martial strains, and the earth shakes with the tread of armed men.

In view of this grandest demonstration for self-preservation in the history of nationalities, desponding patriotism may be assured that the foundations of our national greatness still stand strong, and that the sentiment which to-day beats responsive in every loyal heart will for the future be realized. No flag alien to the sources of the Mississippi river will ever float permanently over its mouths till its waters are crimsoned in human gore, and not one foot of American soil can ever be wrenched from the jurisdiction of the Constitution of the United States until it is baptized in fire and blood.

Gentlemen, as your presiding officer, it becomes my duty to apprise you that any demonstrations of approval or disapproval of anything done or said during your sessions is a violation of parliamentary decorum; and the Chair would also inform the persons in the galleries that applause by them is a breach of the privileges of the House. The Chair hopes, therefore, that any demonstrations of applause will not be repeated.

"In God is our trust,

And the star-spangled banner forever shall wave

O'er the land of the free and the home of the brave."

Those who regard it as mere cloth bunting fail to comprehend its symbolical power. Wherever civilization dwells, or the name of Washington is known, it bears in its fold the concentrated power of armies and of navies, and surrounds its votaries with a defense more impregnable than battlement, wall, or tower. Wherever on the face of the earth an American citizen may wander, called by pleasure, business, or caprice, it is a shield secure against outrage and wrong-save on the soil of the land of his birth.

As the guardians of the rights and liberties of the people, it becomes your paramount duty to make it honored at home as it is respected abroad. A government that cannot command the loyalty of its own citizens is unworthy the respect of the world, and a government that will not protect its loyal citizens deserves the contempt of the world.

He who would tear down this grandest temple of constitutional liberty, thus blasting forever the hopes of crushed humanity, because its freeman, in the mode prescribed by the Constitution, select a Chief Magistrate not acceptable to him, is a parricide to his race, and should be regarded as a common enemy of mankind.

This Union once destroyed is a shattered vase that no human power can reconstruct in its original symmetry. "Coarse stones, when they are broken, may be cemented again - precious ones, never."

If the republic is to be dismembered, and the sun of its liberty must go out in endless night, let it set amid the roar of cannon and the din of battle, when there is no longer an arm to strike or a heart to bleed in its cause; so that coming generations may not reproach the present with *being too imbecile to preserve the priceless legacy bequeathed by our fathers, so as to transmit it unimpaired to future times.*

Again, gentlemen, thanking you for your confiding kindness, and invoking for our guidance wisdom from that Divine Power that led our fathers through the red sea of the revolution, I enter upon the discharge of the duties to which you assign me, relying upon your forbearance and co-operation, and trusting that your labors will contribute not a little to the greatness and glory of the republic.

Legacy as Speaker

In this Congress, the members who remained raised the first troops who were sent to Manassas to fight the Confederates, established that legal-tender notes be used by the population, and issued bonds to pay for the war. Just 17 days after Grow became the Speaker, the armies of the North and South clashed as what became known as the First Bull Run, resulting in a defeat for the Union. Grow wrote, "When the defeat at Bull Run occurred and the Union army was thrown into confusion and rout, Lincoln said to me one evening: 'My boys are green at the fighting business, but wait till they get licked enough to raise their dander! Then the cry will be 'On to Richmond' and no 'Stone-walls will stop them!'" When the Congress adjourned the special session, Grow, instead of going home, spent his time in Virginia military camps or hospitals. He worked to offer succor and relief to the Union soldiers he met with his sister-in-law, the wife of his brother Frederick.

When the Congress reconvened, such initiatives as the establishment of the Department of Agriculture and the enactment of the Pacific Railroad and Telegraph Law were passed. Now in charge of the House, Grow used his influence to enact a law based on the issue that was his greatest interest: homestead legislation. For years, Grow had tried to get the House to enact a law that allowed settlers to establish themselves on plots of unused public land and keep it after a period of clearing it and taking care of it. Grow saw this action as not only aiding those on the eastern coast, where he had lived his entire life, but assisting in the settling of the American West, which had been opening up to settlement

for more than 20 years. Because a Speaker cannot introduce legislation, Grow gave up the speakership temporarily - succeeded in an ad interim basis by Rep. Elihu Washburne of Illinois - to propose the bill. He told the House, "I want the Government to protect the rights of men, the hearthstones and firesides of those who have gone forth to people the wilderness and build up the great empires which to-day span the continent and have made this country the wonder and admiration of the world." Grow's legislation - written by him, but added to by others whose names and roles in its formation are lost to history - was eventually enacted by Congress in 1862, taking effect with President Lincoln's signature on 1 January 1863. The new law provided for the transfer of up to 160 acres of unoccupied public lands to any homesteader or settler for a fee of $1.25 an acre which would be paid after six months of residence. The settler would then promise to remain on and work the land for five years, after which it would become theirs. The law was a landmark in its breadth, allowing for the massive emigration westward by pioneering families who saw the ability to own their own plot of land as a godsend. The legislation remained on the books until 1976, when it expired in every American state except Alaska, where it ended in 1986.

While Galusha Grow was in the mainstream of the Republican Party, his radicalism against slavery brought opposition from home, and Democrats in control of the Pennsylvania legislature, who were far more moderate on the slavery issue, redrew his district to form a new district in which he was out of step with a majority of voters. Grow was defeated in the 1862 campaign, and after just a single two-year term as Speaker, he was forced to leave the speakership and the House. On 3 March 1863, the last day of the Thirty-seventh Congress, Rep. George H. Pendleton, Democrat of Ohio, introduced the following resolution:

Resolved, that the thanks of the House are due, and are hereby tendered, to the Hon. Galusha A. Grow, for the able, impartial, and courteous manner in which he has discharged the duties of Speaker during the present Congress.

The action passed unanimously. Few Congresses have thanked the outgoing Speaker in this manner.

After Leaving the Speakership

Despite being a Republican, Grow soon found himself at odds with the machine politics of the state run by Republican Simon Cameron (who served as Secretary of War in the Lincoln Administration), Cameron's son Donald, and Matthew Quay, all of whom hated Grow for not wanting to adhere to the party rather than to ideas. His opposition of the Camerons led to Grow's "bolting" the party to join the Liberal Republican movement in 1872, which nominated newspaper editor Horace Greeley for President in a losing campaign against Republican President Ulysses S. Grant. Although he was content not to belong to the Cameron machine, Grow's refusal to adhere to the party organization kept him out of any semblance of political power for the better part of three decades after the end of the Civil War. The Camerons, with their control of the state's political machinery, saw to it that Grow had no chance to get nominated for a House seat or win election in the legislature to the Senate. Instead, Grow turned to numerous business opportunities, such as investing in coal and railroad interests. In 1865, he was one of the leaders in establishing the Reno Oil and Land Company, serving as the establishment's first president. In the 1870s, Grow served as the president of the Houston and Great Northern Railway in Texas. In 1876 he was offered the post of U.S. Minister to Russia, but he declined it.

In 1894, when the power of the Camerons was all but gone, and more than three decades after he lost his House seat, Grow was elected as Pennsylvania's congressman-at-large to fill a vacancy caused by the death of William Lilly. Taking his seat in the Fifty-third Congress (1895-97), Grow was re-elected three times, serving until the end of the Fifty-seventh Congress on 3 March 1903. He was 72 years old when he entered Congress this second time, but he was accepted more as a party elder and wise man than as a senior citizen. He served as the chairman of the Committee on Education from the Fifty-fourth through the Fifty-seventh Congresses. In 1902, coming up on 79 years old, Grow refused a renomination to another term and retired to his home at Glenwood, near Scranton, Pennsylvania. Although he had been involved in many business pursuits over the years, by this time Grow was nearly bankrupt. It was Andrew Carnegie, the Scottish-American billionaire, who secretly paid him a private pension. In a letter to a friend, Carnegie explained his reasoning:

> He has done a great work for mankind, a work which will bless the ages, and he deserves to spend his remaining days in peace and comfort. By his statesmanship and intelligent efforts he saved our vast territory beyond the Mississippi River for the landless of our people and thus millions of free homes were made possible to the tillers of the soil. This work alone entitles him to the gratitude and homage of all Americans, and it is a distinct pleasure to feel that I have been able to befriend him in any way. It is vouchsafed to only a few men to do great things to bless mankind and Mr. Grow was one of the favored group.

Grow died at his home at Glenwood on 31 March 1907 at the age of 84. He was interred in the Harford Cemetery in Harford, Pennsylvania.

Ben: Perley Poore, who was a noted journalist and newspaper editor in the nineteenth century and came to know most of those who served in the Congress as intimates and lifelong friends, wrote in his 1886 work of reminiscences of those he met and knew in Congress, "He was a thorough politician and a good presiding officer, possessing the tact, the quickness of perception, and the decision acquired by editorial perception."

Further Reading:

Dubois, James T., and Gertrude Singleton Mathews, *Galusha A. Grow, Father of the Homestead Law* (Boston: Houghton Mifflin Company, 1917).

Free Homes for Free Men: Speech of Hon. G. A. Grow, of Pennsylvania, in the House of Representatives, February 29, 1860 (Detroit: Printed at the Detroit Tribune Office, 1860).

Ilisevich, Robert D., *Galusha A. Grow: The People's Candidate* (Pittsburgh: University of Pittsburgh Press, 1988).

Thomas Stanley Bocock

Served as Speaker:
February 18, 1862 - April 1865

Although wholly unknown today, Thomas S. Bocock holds a unique position in American history: he served as the one and only Speaker of the Confederate House of Representatives during the Civil War. He has slipped into such utter obscurity that the myriad of biographies, large and small, on Bocock list his middle name as either Stanley or "Salem." Even manuscript collections list the name alternatively. Despite his ignominious place in American history, Bocock was an important member of the U.S. Congress during his tenure (1847-61), speaking strongly on behalf of his native Virginia.

Personal History
He was born in Buckingham County (now Appomattox County), Virginia, on 16 May 1815, the son of John Thomas and Mary Bocock. Bocock's older brother, Willis P. Bocock (1807-1887), later served as Attorney General of Virginia. Thomas Bocock studied the law under his brother Willis (Bocock's congressional biography states that he was "educated by private tutors"), afterwards attending Hampden-Sidney College (now Hampden-Sydney

College) and graduating in 1838. He continued to read the law, and, in 1840, was admitted to the Virginia bar. He opened a practice in the town of Buckingham Court House.

Only two years into his practice, Bocock was elected to the State House of Delegates, where he served for a single two-year term. In 1844, he was elected as the prosecuting attorney (or, as some sources note, the Commonwealth attorney) for Buckingham County, serving from 1845 to 1846.

Early Years in Congress
A Democrat, Bocock was elected to the U.S. House of Representatives in 1846, and took his seat in the Thirtieth Congress (1847-49). During his tenure in the House, which lasted until 3 March 1861, Bocock rose to become the chairman of the Committee on Naval Affairs, serving during the Thirty-third (1853-55) and Thirty-fifth (1857-59) Congresses. It was as chairman of the Select Committee on Naval Contracts and Expenditures, a subcommittee of the Committee on Naval Affairs, that

Bocock ordered hearings in January 1859 concerning the Navy Department. An employee of that department, one D.B. Allen, alleged that certain officers were awarding contracts for the construction of ships based on ties to the involved companies, and that monies appropriated by the U.S. Congress for the upkeep of the navy yards and for the repair of vessels was being used for partisan political purposes. Following an investigation by the subcommittee, it issued a lengthy report, which found substance to the allegations. In his conclusion, Bocock wrote,

> [The committee finds] That the testimony taken in this investigation discloses the existence of glaring abuses in the Brooklyn navy yard, such as require the interposition of legislative reform; but justice requires us to say that these abuses have been slowly and gradually growing up during a long course of years, and that no particular administration should bear the entire blame therefor [sic]...that it is disclosed by the testimony in this case that the agency for the purchase of anthracite coal for the use of the Navy Department has been for some time past in the hands of a person wholly inefficient and grossly incompetent, and that reform is needed in the regulations which exist on that subject; but there is no proof which traces any knowledge of such incompetency and inefficiency to the responsible authorities in Washington, nor any which shows that the need of reform grows especially out of any act of theirs; on the contrary, it is expressly proven that the supply of coal for the navy service has been purchased during this administration upon terms relatively as favorable as ever before.

When the Thirty-sixth Congress (1859-61) convened in Washington, D.C. on 5 December 1859, the Republicans, in control of the House of Representatives, desired to elect Rep. John Sherman (brother of future General William Tecumseh Sherman) as the Speaker of the House. The Democrats - in the minority by a count of 116 Republicans, 83 Democrats, 19 in opposition to the James Buchanan administration, and a scattering of others belonging to third parties - worked to stop Sherman, who they considered an antislavery radical, from taking the Speaker's chair. Despite being in the mi-

nority by 33 seats, the Democrats bargained with the others in the House to form an "anti-Sherman majority" of 122. The election for a speaker dragged on for weeks, as both sides struggled to keep their troops in line. As long as Sherman was the issue, the Democrats had the votes to keep him from the speakership. Their candidate for Speaker, Bocock, in reality had no chance of winning; the coalition against Sherman held together because of the opposition specifically to Sherman.

Historian Ollinger Crenshaw wrote in 1942 on the impact of William Pennington's election as Speaker following one of the longest and most contentious elections for that post in the Thirty-sixth Congress, opening on 5 December 1859:

> That the speakership contest of 1859-60 exacerbated an already critical sectional conflict is a fact commonly known to historians. Long ago, the historian of the period, James Ford Rhodes, described the turbulent scenes which characterized the daily sessions of the House of Representatives, especially the initial eight weeks, from December 5, 1859, to February 1, 1860, of the Thirty-sixth Congress, during which the tug of war raged to gain control of the House by the election of a Speaker. The central point of the fight was the determination of the Republican membership to elect John Sherman and the equal determination of the Democrats and their allies that he should be defeated at all hazards.

In the end, Sherman realized that he could never be elected, and he gave way to first-term Rep. William Pennington of New Jersey, whose views on slavery were far less contentious. On 1 February 1860, Pennington received 117 votes on the 44th ballot, and was elected Speaker. The Democrats had long since abandoned the radical proslavery Bocock for more moderate candidates, but in the end they could not stop the Republicans from finally electing a Speaker.

At the 1860 Democratic National Convention held at Institute Hall in Charleston, South Carolina, Bocock won 1 vote - from Virginia - on the first ballot for President. Bocock sent a telegram to former Speaker and fellow Virginian Robert M.T. Hunter from the Charleston convention. "If Southern States remain in convention [Senator Stephan A.] Douglas['] nomination impossible. If they go out he is certain. Virginia goes for reasonable change in platform." The same day, Bocock sent a telegram to Rep. William Porcher Miles, Democrat from South Carolina: "If platform not satisfactory, Mississippi, Florida, and Texas will go out with the anti-Douglas men of Alabama aboard Arkansas. No nominations sooner than Saturday or Monday next." Senator Douglas of Illinois won the nomination on that ballot, causing radical proslavery Democrats to bolt from the convention. A parley was later held by these "Southern Democrats" in Baltimore, Maryland, and they nominated former Vice President John C. Breckinridge for President. Bocock cast his lot with the Southern wing of the party, which came in second in electoral votes in the 1860 campaign. The election of Republican Abraham Lincoln to the presidency in that campaign led to the secession from the Union of the Southern states and the onrush of the Civil War. As with the other Southern politicians who served in both the House and Senate, Bocock decided to cast his lot with his native Virginia and the South and resign their seats to return home. Owing to the controversy over the split in his party, Bocock had not run for re-election in 1860, and thus his departure from the House in March 1861 was expected.

A Confederate Government

The establishment of the Confederate States of America as a governmental entity to run the affairs of the seceded states forced the southerners to create a Congress and a Supreme Court very much like those in the United States government. To this end, elections for seats in a First Confederate Congress were held in late 1861, and Bocock was elected to a seat in this body. Historians have had to explain the myriad number of congresses held by the Confederacy. While the Provisional Confederate Congress met in Montgomery, Alabama - the initial capital of the Confederacy before Richmond, Virginia, was chosen as a permanent capital - from February to May 1861, a secondary Confederate Congress met in Richmond in three sessions from July 1861 to February 1862. These two parleys are not to be confused with the First Confederate Congress, elections for which were held on 6 November 1861 and which convened in Richmond. The Second Confederate Congress, elected in November 1863, held sessions for only a year before the fighting in the

war caused it to adjourn, and a final session was adjourned on 18 March 1865 as the Confederacy was collapsing.

The Vote

Thus, the First Confederate Congress met in February 1862 in Richmond, Virginia. One of the first acts of business of this body was the election of a Speaker, not unlike the business of the U.S. House of Representatives. As the *Journal of the Confederate Congress* noted:

> The Chair announced that the first business in order was the election of a Speaker. Mr. [Henry S.] Foote [of Tennessee] nominated the Hon. Thomas S. Bocock, a Representative from the State of Virginia. On motion of Mr. Foote, Mr. Bocock was declared unanimously elected Speaker of the House of Representatives for the First Congress. Mr. [William W.] Boyce [of South Carolina] moved that a committee of two be appointed to wait on the Speaker-elect and conduct him to the chair. The motion was agreed to; and the Chair appointed Messrs. Boyce and Foote. Mr. Bocock was then conducted to the chair, where the oath to support the Constitution of the Confederate States of America was administered by Mr. [Howell] Cobb [of Georgia], the presiding officer.

The *Journal* does not report that Bocock made any comments, so his thoughts on his election are lost to history.

Legacy as Speaker

There are only a few mentions in history books of Bocock's service as Speaker of the Confederate House. Histories of the Confederate Congress mention Bocock only in passing; his name mostly appears on laws and other business of the two Confederate Congresses merely as the Speaker. Bocock's biography in *The National Cyclopædia of American Biography* notes that "he served as chairman of a committee sent to President [Jefferson] Davis for the purpose of protesting against several features of his administration but he was a loyal upholder of the Confederacy throughout the war." In a *New York Times* article that appeared in November 1864, near the end of the Civil War, Bocock is merely identified as a member of the Confederate

House of Representatives, representing the Fifth District of Virginia. Perhaps the most that has been said of Bocock and his service comes from a nearly century old work: Henry William Elson wrote in 1914, "Under the permanent [Confederate] Constitution[,] two congresses were elected. The period of the first was from February 18, 1862, to February 18, 1864, four sessions being held. The second Congress began at the expiration of the first and continued till it was unceremoniously broken up, on March 18, 1865, by the proximity of General Grant's army. Thomas S. Bocock of Virginia was the Speaker of both Congresses."

The collapse of the Confederacy in late 1864 and early 1865 was sudden and led to the end of the Confederate Congress' ability to meet and pass laws. The fall of Richmond, Virginia, to Union troops ended that city's place as the capital of the southern government, and what remained of that entity fled south but never again had any measure of power. Soon after Richmond's fall, the war ended, and many of those who served in the Confederate government fled further south, left the country altogether, or were arrested by Union forces. It is unclear what happened to Bocock during this period although it appears that he surrendered to the Union and was almost immediately released to return to his old life. The end of the war impacted Bocock hard, both economically (the South's economic structure, based on agriculture, was almost completely destroyed) and politically, as it did many officials of the collapsing Confederate government.

Two surviving pieces of Bocock's correspondence from this time period illustrate this point. In a letter to an unknown woman merely referred to as "Sue," Bocock wrote, on 23 June 1865, that he foresaw hard times ahead for himself.

Confiscation, [and] Imprisonment all stare me in the face; and I trust very little clemency of our conquerors. They are bitter, intolerant, and exacting. He then explained, "The fate of a conquered people is always hard, and experience shows that ours will probably be harder than usual. If we could all get to some other country where we could make a comfortable living, and raise our children in peace and credit, I would be highly delighted. For the moment we can do

nothing but bear patiently and take what is put upon is with the best possible grace.

Continuing, Bocock slammed some of his former colleagues in the Confederate government.

I have a great aversion to the course of those who while the Confederacy lasted were very patriotic but who, since it fell, have shown an eagerness to help the rod that smites us...A great many men who if we had succeeded, would have claimed great credit for aiding our cause, are noisy now in declaring that they never were for secession. Our human nature!

In the second letter, dated 5 March 1869 and addressed to the editor of a Richmond newspaper, the *Examiner* - mostly probably Washington D. Coles, also known as W.D. Coles - Bocock explained,

I am of a retiring and modest disposition and under the 'new and <u>better</u>' government which has been provided for us, I am apprehensive of being recognized all too speedily, and being prized rather too highly...Liberty[,] liberty is gone, and the delusive idea of constitution popular government, is exploded for this age. Wounds in the Animal [sic] frame may...grow well, but such a wound as has been inflicted upon the vitals of our constitution will never heal. And they all go on in Washington and the North, as if nothing had happened...All is pomp & pageantry: the cry is 'ho! ho!' for the merry merry show, while the smoking lava flood is sweeping out to its work of desolation. The Constitute may have the name to live but it is dead, + the reign of an unrestrained mobocracy is established, to be followed in the not to distant future by civil convulsion & anarchy, which are ultimately in their force to crouch down beneath the rod of imperial power.

Explaining how the end of the war conflicted him in his love of Virginia, he penned,

My love for my old state, has been no ordinary feeling of attachment, it has been a controlling passion. Till a few days past I never contemplated seriously, under any circumstances, the idea of deserting her fortunes. Neither principalities nor power, neither life nor death, could have separated me from the love of her, while she was herself. I feel sure now that she will soon surrender her favor + glory upon the altar of supposed but elusive security, and then the strong cord that bound me to her will be sent in [unintelligible] - She will be Virginia no longer to me.

In the immediate aftermath of the war's conclusion, Bocock was again elected to the Virginia House of Delegates, serving from 1877 to 1879. In this capacity, he was a co-sponsor of the Bocock-Fowler Bill, which was a legislative attempt to alleviate the financial situation of Virginia during the period of Reconstruction. Bocock also tried to bring financial stability back into his life; during the last two decades of his life, he served as corporate attorney for the Atlantic, Mississippi, and Ohio Railroad as well as the Richmond and Alleghany Railroad. He also served as a delegate to the Democratic National Convention in 1868, 1876, and 1880. Married twice - the second time to the daughter of Charles James Faulkner, the U.S. Envoy to France under President James Buchanan - his second wife survived him.

Bocock was out of the public eye for the last several years of his life; in 1891, the *Atlanta Constitution* reported that "he has been an invalid for years." In July 1891, Bocock became seriously ill, and his health declined. He died at his home, "Wildway," located in Appomattox County, Virginia, on 5 August 1891 at the age of 76, and was buried in the Old Bocock Cemetery, a private burial ground, near Wildway, listed as both Bocock's home and the local town. In the obituary on his life, the *Washington Post* stated that "[he] was a gentleman of high character and attainments, and of universal popularity."

Despite the growing body of historical research into the people on both sides of the Civil War, specifically the politicians, Thomas Bocock seemed to have been lost in this resurgence of study. In a 1967 article while profiling members of the Confederate Congress, historian Richard E. Beringer never even mentioned Bocock's name, instead concentrating on far more obscure figures who served in both the U.S. and Confederate governments. Similarly, a 1936 article on enactments made during the last session of the Second Confederate Congress never mentions Bocock's name as Speaker of that body. Further works, including one on the Statutes of the Provisional Government of the Confederacy have an equal chance of mentioning the name of former

Speaker of the House Howell Cobb, serving as President of the Provisional Confederate Senate, than it would with the name of Bocock. Today, on Route 24 in Appomattox County, Virginia, a highway marker dedicated to Bocock as "the only Speaker of the Confederate House" is perhaps one of the only memorials to this man whose place in American history is secure but completely forgotten.

Further Reading:
Bocock, Thomas S., *Force Bill. Speech of the Hon. Thomas S. Bocock, of Virginia, Delivered in the House of Representatives, February 20 and 21, 1861* (Washington: W.H. Moore, Printer, 1861).

Schuyler Colfax

Served as Speaker:
December 7, 1863 - March 3, 1869

He is the first of two Speakers to be elected Vice President of the United States. The only Indianan to serve as Speaker, his service came during the crucial years during and just after the Civil War, when legislation dealing with the civil rights of freed slaves was enacted by Congress, including the Thirteenth, Fourteenth, and Fifteenth Amendments to the U.S. Constitution.

Personal History

He was born in New York City on 23 March 1823, the son of Schuyler Colfax, a bank clerk, and his wife, Hannah (née Stryker) Colfax. His grandfather, General William Colfax, was born in Connecticut in 1760, and served with the rank of Lieutenant in the Continental Army during the American Revolution, serving under George Washington as captain commandant of Washington's guards. When the war ended, he married Hester Schuyler, a cousin of famed Revolutionary war General Philip Schuyler. Schuyler Colfax, son of William and Hester and father of Speaker Schuyler Colfax, was the godson of George Washington. The elder Schuyler Colfax died of tuberculosis five months before his son's birth, leaving his widow to care for the child until she remarried in 1834 when he was 11. Schuyler Colfax

was raised by his stepfather, George W. Matthews. A sister of Schuyler Colfax also died before he was born, leaving him as his mother's only child. He received only a limited education, and by age 11 was working as a clerk in a store in New York City. Although his mother's marriage brought new income into the home, the family moved to Matthews' home in New Carlisle, in St. Joseph County, Indiana, where Colfax went to work at his stepfather's store as a clerk.

George Matthews was not just a storeowner but also served as village postmaster, a position that came due to political patronage. A Whig, in 1841 he was elected county auditor, and moved the family to the county seat, South Bend. He hired his stepson as his deputy, and Colfax got his first taste in politics, serving until 1849. Although his parents pushed him to return to school - he did read the law for a short time but dropped it - Colfax decided that his first love was politics and planned that as his career. By 1850, he was a prominent Whig in Indiana politics, and he began a lengthy correspondence with other Whigs around the country on political matters. He became a contributor of articles on politics to the *New York Tribune*, owned by Whig Horace

Greeley, and worked as a reporter for the *Indiana State Journal* in 1842 and 1843, reporting on the Indiana state Senate. In 1844, he played a prominent state role in campaigning for Henry Clay, the Whig candidate for President, in a losing effort. That year he married Evelyn Clark, and the two did not have any children. She would die in July 1863, just before Colfax became Speaker of the House. In 1845, Colfax became the half-owner and editor of the *St. Joseph Valley Register*, putting his journalistic talents and political beliefs on paper. He was just 22 years old.

Starting with just 250 subscribers to his paper, Colfax, over the next twenty years, built it into one of the most important and largest Whig - and then Republican - newspapers in Indiana. Conservative in flavor, it did not report on crime and supported temperance in the alcohol question. One unnamed editor, writing on the growing influence of the paper under Colfax's guidance, explained that the journal "always communicated to a daily political writer a valuable political impression." In 1848, and again in 1852, Colfax served as the secretary of the Whig National conventions.

By the 1850s, however, the one issue that Colfax, nor the owner or editor of any other journal or newspaper of the time, could ignore was that of slavery. Although a northern state, Indiana was controlled by Democrats who supported the right to own slaves. In 1850-51, Colfax served as a delegate to the Indiana constitutional convention as a member of the minority Whigs, where he called for the rights of freed slaves and other blacks in the state to be able to vote. When the convention ended, Colfax made his first, and only unsuccessful, run for a seat in the U.S. House. (Indiana at that time was the last state to hold congressional elections in odd-numbered years, a practice ended in 1852.) Colfax may have lost this race due to his (and his paper's) almost lukewarm and unenthusiastic support for the Compromise of 1850, a settlement between proslavery and antislavery forces that allowed Texas to enter the Union as a slave state and the territories of New Mexico, Nevada, Arizona, and Utah without the mention of slavery; as well, it included the Fugitive Slave Act, which forced local and state officials to assist in the capture and arrest of escaped slaves even in free states. The measure

was popular with Democrats, and it helped elect Colfax's opponent, Dr. Graham N. Fitch. The compromise, ironically, had been the brainchild of Colfax's political hero Henry Clay, who remained an idol to the Indianan. The losses of the Whigs in 1852 did not dim Colfax's support for the party; he wrote that his paper would "remain Whig to the backbone...We shall stand by the Whig banner to the last. We shall uphold and defend Whig principles..." That year, he was again nominated by the Whigs for a seat in the U.S. Congress, but he refused it on the grounds that the Democrats controlled the district by a 1,200 vote majority. Instead, Dr. Norman Eddy, a "Free Soil" or antislavery, Democrat, was elected.

In 1854, Democrats in Congress, among them Senator Stephen A. Douglas of Illinois, introduced the Kansas-Nebraska Bill, which allowed these two former territories to enter the Union and have the people vote for themselves as to whether they would be free or slave. This flew directly in the face of the Missouri Compromise of 1820, in which both areas were to remain free of slavery; an amendment was added to the 1854 act repealing that 1820 measure. Colfax editorialized in his paper: "It begins to be thought that if Douglas' Nebraska bill is pushed in its present shape it will blow all concerned sky high, and that those from the North who vote for it will have leave to stay at home and hoe cabbages." Dr. Eddy returned to the district and Colfax appealed to him to vote against the Kansas-Nebraska bill, but Eddy decided to vote for the bill. The bill passed the House, controlled by Democrats, 157 seats to 71 for the Whigs, and was signed into law by President Franklin Pierce.

The enactment of this law set off a firestorm that culminated in the explosion of the Civil War just 7 years later. Whigs and many "Free Soil" Democrats decided to form an antislavery party to counter the Democrats. Colfax called for Indiana Whigs to form "a union of Freemen for the sake of Freedom." Colfax became one of the leaders at a state convention of those opposed to the Kansas-Nebraska Act. Out of the convention was formed a new entity: the People's Party. It would soon be melded into a national entity formed in Wisconsin about the same time called the Republican Party. Colfax returned home to find that he had been nominated as the

People's Party candidate for a seat in the U.S. House. And while his main issue was slavery and the Kansas-Nebraska Act, Colfax also took some positions that earned him great enmity. At the time, the American, or "Know-Nothing," Party was running on an anti-Catholic and anti-immigrant (mostly against Germans and Irish) platform. Colfax made the mistake of attending a statewide convention of American Party members (who got their nickname from being asked what their party stood for and told people that they "know nothing" of its tenets). Colfax later said that he merely attended as a reporter rather than a delegate, but the damage was done, and he was verbally attacked by Germans in 1854 and physically attacked by Irish railroad workers in 1856. Despite this association, Colfax won the 1854 race over Eddy by 1,700 votes.

Early Years in Congress

Entering the Thirty-fourth Congress (1855-57), Colfax was part of a majority of those opposed to the Pierce administration, all of whom belonged to a mélange of political parties, including Republicans, anti-Nebraska Democrats, and Know- Nothings, all of whom disagreed with the President on slavery and the Kansas-Nebraska Act. Of the 241 seats, 100 were held by these members, with 83 Democrats and 51 Americans. But the opposition was divided over a candidate for Speaker, and this set off a battle for the speakership that lasted for two full months and 134 ballots - the most contentious fight over the Speaker's chair in the history of the U.S. Congress - and culminated in Rep. Nathaniel P. Banks, a Republican, being elected Speaker. Writing for his newspaper's editorial column, Colfax explained that "the protracted struggle for Speaker has resulted in a glorious victory for freedom." During his tenure in Congress, which ran from 1855 until the end of the Fortieth Congress on 3 March 1869, Colfax was nearly invisible, with no pieces of legislation enacted bearing his name; his official congressional biography does not even list any committees that he served on, although other sources show that as the chairman of the Post Offices and Post Roads Committee he tried to institute a system of improved overland mail service to California. Perhaps most importantly than any legislation, during his first session in Congress his speech on "the bogus laws of Kansas," where fighting be-

tween proslavery and antislavery forces for control of the state had left it with the sobriquet "Bloody Kansas," left him in good standing with abolitionist forces in the country. "In such a state of affairs as this, to talk of going to the polls and having the laws repealed is worse than a mockery," he said on the House floor, referring to a vote on whether Kansas should be free or slave. "It is an insult. It is like binding a man hand and foot, throwing him into the river, and telling him to swim to the shore and he will be saved. It is like loading a man with irons, and then telling him to run for his life. The only relief possible, if Kansas is not promptly admitted as a State, which I hope may be effected, is in a change of the administration and of the party that so recklessly misrules the land; and that will furnish an effectual relief."

Colfax was not an early backer of Abraham Lincoln for the presidency in 1860, but once Lincoln got the party's presidential nomination Colfax campaigned throughout Indiana for the Republican ticket. With Lincoln's election, Colfax was considered for a cabinet post, probably Postmaster General because of his work on the California mail issue, but in the end Montgomery Blair was selected for the position and Colfax remained in the House. He was re-elected in 1856, 1858, 1860, and 1862.

The Vote

The Thirty-eighth Congress assembled in Washington on 7 December 1863, in the middle of a civil war in which American was killing American over issues of slavery and disunion. The Democrats had won 28 seats in the 1862 mid-term elections, with their victories coming amongst those who viewed the war unfavorably and wished to end it as quickly as possible, but the Republicans retained the majority. Thus, the Thirty-eighth Congress would see 86 Republicans seated along with 72 Democrats, 16 so-called "Unconditional Unionists," 9 Unionists, and 2 independent Republicans. After initial business dealing with the credentials and seating of several members, the vote for Speaker proceeded. The previous Speaker, Galusha Grow, Republican of Pennsylvania, had been defeated in the 1862 campaign, opening the door to the election of a new Speaker. On the first ballot, Colfax, nominated by the Republicans, gained 101 votes to 42 for Rep. Samuel S. Cox, Democrat of New York, and 12 for

Rep. John Littleton Dawson, Democrat of Pennsylvania, with other votes going to a scattering of minor candidates. With the close of the vote, the Clerk of the House announced that Colfax was the duly elected Speaker.

Acceptance Speech

Conducted to the Speaker's chair by Reps. Dawson and Cox, Colfax then addressed the members of the House before he took the oath:

> To-day will be marked in American history as the opening of a Congress destined to face and settle the most important questions of the century: and during whose existence the rebellion, which has passed its culmination, will, beyond all question, thanks to our Army and Navy and Administration, die a deserved death. Not only will your constituents watch with the strictest scrutiny your deliberations here, but the friends of liberty, in the most distant lands, will be interested spectators of your acts in this greater than Roman forum. I invoke you to approach these grave questions with the calm thoughtfulness of statesmen, freeing your discussions from that acerbity which mars instead of advancing legislation, and with unshaken reliance on that divine Power which gave victory to those who formed this Union, and can give even greater victory to those who are seeking to save it from destruction by the hand of the parricide and traitor. I invoke you also to remember that sacred truth, which all history verifies, that "they who rule not in righteousness shall perish from the earth." Thank you with a grateful heart for this distinguished mark of your confidence and regard, and appealing to you all for that support and forbearance by the aid of which alone I can hope to succeed, I am now ready to take the oath of office, and enter upon the duties you have assigned me.

Colfax served as Speaker in the Thirty-eight, Thirty-ninth (1865-67), and Fortieth (1867-69) Congresses.

Legacy as Speaker

During his first term as Speaker, Colfax became involved in a major controversy that historians view as his greatest error in politics. On 8 April 1864, Rep. Alexander Long, Democrat of Ohio, went to the House floor and announced that he supported recognizing the independence of the Southern states formed into the Confederacy so that the Civil War could be ended quickly. Colfax was sitting as Speaker when this utterance was made; he immediately asked for a Speaker *pro tempore* to be selected so he could join the debate on the floor; Rep. Edward H. Rollins, Republican of New Hampshire, took the Speaker's chair, and Colfax introduced a resolution calling for Long to be expelled because of treason. The resolution was debated at length; those opposed argued that Long's words had not been "taken down" or officially entered into the record, with other saying that to expel a member for a speech was against the Constitution. Colfax continued to argue for Long's expulsion until he realized he did not have the votes for such a move, and, finally, agreed to have Long censured. The press denounced Colfax, but he remained stoic against the criticism, writing in a letter,

> The gentlemen on the other side, every one, indeed, who have referred to it at all, have been kind enough to speak of my impartiality as the Presiding Officer of the House. I thank them for this testimonial, which I have endeavored to deserve. But at the same time most of them have expressed "regret" that I left the Speaker's chair and came down upon the floor of the House. I have, however, no regret; not even denunciations of the press, nor the strictures of members upon this floor, to which I have listened in respectful silence without interrupting them, have caused me a moment's regret. I did it in the performance of what seemed to me an imperative duty, from conscientious conviction, and from no personal unkindness toward the gentleman from Ohio. I have no personal unkindness toward him or any human being who lives upon the earth...I stand upon this floor today by no condescension from that responsible position. No, sir, in that chair I am the servant of the House to administer its rules, but on the floor the equal of any other member - no more, no less. Duty is often unpleasant, sometimes distasteful and repulsive; but, sir, the man who will not fearlessly discharge his duty is not fit to be in public life.

In the Thirty-ninth Congress (1865-67), which began just weeks before President Lincoln was assassinated, the Congress dealt with some of the most important matters in the history of the nation, including the ways to deal with the former Confederate states, whether or not to impose harsh reconstruction measures on these states, what kind of rights to enact on behalf of the freed slaves, as well as how the Congress would confront political difficulties with Lincoln's successor, Andrew Johnson. With Colfax as Speaker, the Thirteenth Amendment to the U.S. Constitution, which banned slavery and involuntary servitude, was passed by both houses of Congress by January 1865 and was quickly ratified by the states; the Fourteenth Amendment, which naturalized as citizens all persons born in the United States, was proposed in the Thirty-ninth Congress in 1866 and ratified by 1868. In his last days as Speaker, on 25 February 1869, the House passed the Fifteenth Amendment, which declared that the "right of all citizens of the United States to vote shall not be denied or abridged...on account of race, color, or previous condition of servitude," with this final amendment becoming part of the Constitution in 1870.

On 14 April 1865, when the House began an adjournment for several weeks, Colfax decided to take a trip to the farthest western states in the Union. Stopping at the White House to speak with President Lincoln, he was urged to attend a theatre performance with the President and his wife that evening. Colfax, who was two years widowed (he would remarry in 1868), begged off; that evening, Lincoln was murdered by John Wilkes Booth, a Southern sympathizer.

As Speaker, Colfax asked that his vote in favor of these amendments be duly recorded by the Clerk. Ben: Perley Poore, a noted nineteenth century Washington journalist, said that Colfax presided over the House "in rather a slap-dash-knock-'em-down-auctioneer style, greatly in variance with the decorous dignity of his predecessors." Colfax modeled his speakership in the mold of his political hero, Henry Clay, who had been the longest-serving Speaker up to the twentieth century; however, because his only power was to appoint members to committees and preside over the House during debate, Colfax was more of a figurehead than a mod-

erator. Historians believe that the real "leader" of the House was Rep. Thaddeus Stevens, Republican of Pennsylvania, who served as the chairman of the House Appropriations Committee and as *de facto* House floor leader.

In 1868, as tensions with President Johnson came to a head, the Congress battled with him over the rights of freed slaves. Johnson's veto of the Freedman's Bureau Bill, as well as his attempts to lessen the impact of harsh reconstruction measures against the former Confederate states led many in the Congress to push for laws that impinged on presidential powers. Johnson's firing of Secretary of War Edwin M. Stanton, an official popular with Republicans in Congress, set off the move to impeach Johnson. Stanton's firing violated the Tenure of Office Act, which prohibited a President from firing any government official who had been confirmed by Congress. Colfax, who had shied away from advocating impeachment, saw Stanton's firing as a wholly illegal act, and he became the first Speaker to oversee an impeachment vote. The trial of the President, in the Senate, ended with acquittal when several Republicans switched sides and voted to keep Johnson in office just several months before he was to leave office anyway.

As the Johnson impeachment moved forward, Colfax was nominated for Vice President on the Republican ticket with General Ulysses S. Grant as the Republican Party convention in Chicago. The election of 1868 was a contest between Grant and Democrat Horatio Seymour, the Governor of New York State. Exceptionally popular for his service in the war (while Seymour was an unenthusiastic nominee who had not wanted to be a presidential candidate and was nominated against his wishes), Grant carried most of the North except New York and New Jersey, and most of the South save Georgia, Louisiana, and Kentucky, winning 214 electoral votes to Seymour's 80. Shortly after being elected Vice President, Colfax married Ellen Wade, the niece of Senator Benjamin Wade, Republican of Ohio, and the two had one child together, a son named Schuyler Colfax III.

On 3 March 1869, the last day of the second session of the Fortieth Congress, Colfax, as Vice President-elect, resigned his seat. As the *Congressional Globe*, the official journal of the Congress at the time, noted, Colfax stated that before proceeding to tender his resignation of the office of Speaker, to take effect at the election of his successor, he had asked Mr. James F. Wilson [of Iowa] to preside as Speaker *pro tempore* when he should leave the chair. He then addressed the House as follows:

The opening of the legislative day at the close of which I must enter upon another sphere of duty requires me to tender to you this resignation of the office by which your kindness and confidence I have held, to take effect on the election of a Speaker for the brief remainder of this session.

The parting word among friends about to separate is always a regretful one; but the farewell which takes me from this hall, in which so many years have been spent, excites in me emotions which it would be useless to attempt to conceal.

The fourteen years during which I have been associated with the representatives of the people here have been full of eventful legislation, of exciting issues, and of grave decisions, vitally affecting the entire republic. All these, with the accompanying scenes which so often reproduced in this arena of debate the warmth of feeling of our antagonizing constituencies, have passed into the domain of history. And I but refer to them to express the joy which apparently is shared by the mass of our countrymen that the storm-cloud of war which so long darkened out national horizon has at last passed away, leaving out imperilled [sic] Union saved; and that, by the decree of the people, more powerful than Presidents or Congresses, or armies, liberty was proclaimed throughout the land to all the inhabitants thereof.

But I cannot leave you without one word of rejoicing over the present position of our republic among the nations of the earth. With our military power and almost illimitable resources, exemplified by the wear that developed then; with our rapidly augmenting population and the welcome at our open gates to the oppressed of all other climes; with our vast and increasing agricultural, mechanical, manufacturing, and mineral capabilities; with our frontage on the two great oceans of the globe, and our almost completed Pacific railroad uniting these opposite

shores and becoming the highway of nations, the United States of America commands that respect among the powers of the world which insures the maintenance of all its national rights and the security of all its citizens from oppression or injustice abroad.

Nor is this all. The triumphant progress of free institutions here has had its potential influence beyond the sea. The right of the people to govern, based on the sacred principle of our Revolution, that all governments derive their just powers from the consent of the governed, is everywhere advancing, not with slow and measured steps, but with a rapidity that within a few years has been so signally illustrated in Great Britain, Spain, Italy, Prussia, Hungary, and other lands. May we not all hope that by the moral but powerful force of our example fetters may everywhere be broken, and that some of us may live to see that happy era when slavery and tyranny shall no more be known throughout the world from the rivers to the ends of the earth.

I cannot claim that in the share I have had in the deliberations and the legislation of this house, as a member and an officer, I have always done that which was wisest and best in word and act, for none of us are infallible. But that I have striven to perform faithfully every duty, and that, devoted as all know to principles that I have deemed correct, the honor and glory of our country have always been to me paramount and above all party ties, I can conscientiously assert; and that I have sought to mitigate rather than to intensify the asperities which the collisions of opposing parties so often evoke must be left to my fellow-members to verify.

After Leaving the Speakership
As Vice President, the first and last Speaker to hold that position, Colfax moved from presiding over the House as Speaker to presiding over the Senate as President. When he took control of the Senate floor on 4 March 1869, he became the first person in American history to preside over both Houses of Congress. However, finding little to do in the job, Colfax spent much of his free time writing and lecturing. He spoke almost not at all with President

Grant, and apparently had little if any impact on administration policy. Speculation arose that the President, who was a known alcoholic, would be replaced on the Republican ticket in 1872 by Colfax.

But the Indianan surprised the political world and his allies when, in September 1870, at just age 47, Colfax announced that he would retire at the end of his term as Vice President. "I will then have had eighteen years of continuous service at Washington, mostly on a stormy sea-long enough for any one; and my ambition is all gratified and satisfied," he told reporters. Secretly, however, he wanted to surprise his party and have them nominate him for President anyway. But at the 1872 Republican convention, Grant accepted another nomination as President, and he replaced Colfax with Senator Henry Wilson of Massachusetts. Although he accepted being removed from the ticket because of his prior statement, Colfax was inwardly bitter about being betrayed by Grant and Wilson.

Not even 50 years old, Colfax could have had additional political campaigns ahead of him, but a scandal arose that destroyed his career and his good name. In September 1872, after Colfax had been removed from the Republican ticket but before he left the vice presidency, the *New York Sun* reported that in 1868, before he had been nominated for Vice President, Colfax had taken bribes in the Crédit Mobilier affair. Named after the finance company that was established by Congress to help invest money in the construction of the transcontinental Union Pacific Railroad, it was alleged in the growing indignity tied to members of both parties that the company had used Rep. Oakes Ames, Republican of Massachusetts, to distribute company stock to members of Congress who voted for additional appropriations for the company. The paper got a copy of Ames' list, which showed stock being given to Colfax, Senator Henry Wilson, Rep. James A. Garfield of Ohio, and Rep. James G. Blaine of Maine, among others. Appearing before a congressional committee investigating the allegations, Colfax denied taking stocks or payoffs until a check endorsed in his own handwriting for $1,200, plus a deposit slip from his bank in that amount, implicated him in the corruption. A further allegation showed that a stationary manufacturer had paid Colfax $1,000 to get a government contract to produce envelopes for

the House Post Office Committee, which Colfax had served as chairman of at the time. An impeachment resolution in the House failed because Colfax was due to leave office in a few months, but he served this final period in office in disgrace.

After leaving office in March 1873, Colfax spent the remainder years of his life lecturing on the life of President Lincoln, speaking before large crowds about the martyred President while earning up to $2,500 per speech. Despite the scandal that ruined his name, he was still considered a potential candidate for a House or Senate seat from his home state, but he refused any such nomination. "You can't imagine the repugnance with which I now view the service of the many headed public," he wrote, "with all its toils, its innumerable exactions of all kinds, the never ending work and worry, the explanations about everything which the public think they have a right to, the lack of independence as to your goings and comings, the misunderstandings, the envyings, backbitings, etc., etc., etc."

On 13 January 1885, Colfax stopped in Mankato, Minnesota, on his way to a speaking engagement in Iowa. While waiting for a train in the extremely cold weather - it was perhaps 30 below zero -he suffered a massive heart attack on the train platform and died where he fell. Persons who came to his assistance only realized who he was - the former Vice President of the United States - when papers with his name and office were found in his pockets. Colfax was just 61 years old, but pictures taken of him shortly before his death show a much older man. His body was taken by train back to South Bend, Indiana, and he was laid to rest in City Cemetery.

Schuyler Colfax's congressional career, culminating in three terms as Speaker, was not highlighted by any major legislation introduced by him. The *Washington Post*, in an obituary on the former Vice President, stated, "He never developed the qualities of a great statesman, but that he was a capable legislator - popular with his constituents and, as a rule, faithful to their interests - has not been questioned. As Speaker of the House he exhibited, in their highest and best form, the qualities required for the successful administration of that arduous trust, but through all the unquestioned energies and resources of his nature there ran a strain of inherent weakness that

militated against their full development and finally
involved him in the meshes of the Crédit Mobilier
conspiracy. He went out of Congress under a cloud,
which he lacked the vigorous powers of self-asser-
tion and repulsion to ever entirely dissipate."

Further Reading:
Knight, Don R., "The Political Career of Schuyler Colfax
(Indiana)" (Master's thesis, Indiana University, 1929).

Smith, Willard H., "The Political Career of Schuyler Colfax
to His Election as Vice-President in 1868" (Ph.D. dissertation, Indiana University, 1939).

See also page 447

Theodore Medad Pomeroy

Served as Speaker:
March 3, 1869 - March 4, 1869

His service as Speaker of the House of Representatives is the among shortest on record - one day, 3 March 1869, in between the tenures of Speakers Schuyler Colfax, who had resigned the previous day to become the Vice President of the United States, and James G. Blaine, who could not take control of the speakership until 4 March. His single day as Speaker was undistinguished, and Pomeroy has become one of the most obscure men to "serve" as Speaker. His service came on his final day in the U.S. House, as he had not run for re-election in 1868. With an undistinguished congressional career, Pomeroy has slipped into the obscurity of history.

Personal History

He was born in Cayuga, in Cayuga County, New York, in between Auburn to the east and Rochester to the west, on 31 December 1824, the second son of Medad Pomeroy and his wife Lilly (née Maxwell), who herself was a native of Massachusetts. According to Rollin Hillyer Cooke, the family allegedly descended from one Sir Ralph de Pomeroy, "a knight of William the Conqueror, and received lands in Devon and Somerset. In Devon the ruins of the cas-

tle of Berry Pomeroy may still be seen," at least in 1906 when the book was written. One Eltweed Pomeroy came to the colonies in 1630 and settled in Dorchester, Massachusetts, later moving to Windsor, Connecticut. In 1672 he moved with his son, Medad, to Northampton, Massachusetts, and died there the following year. Theodore Pomeroy attended the common schools of Cayuga as well as the Munro Collegiate Institute in Elbridge, New York, before he entered Hamilton College in Clinton, New York, from which he graduated in 1842. He studied the law, and was admitted to the New York state bar in 1846. He proceeded to open a law practice in Auburn. In 1850, Pomeroy succeeded Ebenezer W. Arms as district attorney for Cayuga County, serving until 1856, when he was succeeded by Solomon Giles. In 1856, he was elected to a single one-year term in the New York State Assembly.

Early Years in Congress

In 1860, in the midst of perhaps the most contentious presidential election in American history, when the fate of the Union was the platform of the campaign, Pomeroy was nominated as a Republican for a seat in the U.S. House of Representatives. Elected, he took his seat in Thirty-seventh Congress (1861-63), and eventually served until leaving on 3 March 1869 at the end of Fortieth Congress (1867-69). He served as the chairman of the Committee on Expenditures in the Post Office Department in the Thirty-eight Congress (1863-65), as well as chairman of the Committee on Banking and Currency in the Thirty-ninth (1865-67) and Fortieth Congresses. In 1861, Pomeroy was admitted to the U.S. Supreme Court as an attorney able to argue before that court; his name appears in the lists of lawyers admitted to the court's bar in 66 U.S. Reports, also known as known as 1 Black after the court reporter of the time, former Attorney General Jeremiah Sullivan Black.

Much of Pomeroy's congressional career is a series of votes on the issues of the times; few if any of his speeches stand out to be remembered. In fact, in an age when important speeches by representatives and senators were published in pamphlet form and distributed for wide circulation, the only speech delivered by Pomeroy that could be found was one from 1862 in which he spoke about "Payment of Interest upon the Funded Debt in Coin Essential to Preserve the National Credit."

The Vote

In 1868, Pomeroy declined to run for re-election. On 3 March 1869, the last day of the Fortieth Congress, the House received a letter from Speaker of the House Schuyler Colfax, who had been elected Vice President the previous November and would be sworn in the following day, resigning the speakership. Even though the House had only minor work on this final day of the session, it needed an official Speaker to conduct business. Initially, Rep. James Wilson, Republican of Iowa, took the Speaker's chair as the Speaker *pro tempore*. However, Rep. Henry Laurens Dawes, Republican of Massachusetts, rose and moved that Theodore Pomeroy, on his final day in office, be elected as Speaker for "the remaining term of this Congress." Rep. Jon Van Schaick Lansing Pruyn, Democrat of New York, seconded the motion, and Rep. Wilson declared that Pomeroy had been elected. He appointed Dawes and Rep. George Washington Woodward of Pennsylvania to escort Pomeroy to the Speaker's chair to be sworn in. Dawes then swore the New Yorker in.

Acceptance Speech - A Short Tenure

On taking the chair, Pomeroy addressed the members of the House:

In assuming for the few remaining hours of the session the arduous duties of your Presiding Officer, I can simply thank you for the high compliment which you have conferred. It has been my pleasure for eight years to mingle humbly in the labors of this House; and in retiring, as I expect to within a brief period forever from all official connection with the American Congress, I carry with me at least this gratification, that in all those years I have never upon this floor received from a member of this House one word of unkindness nor one act of disrespect. The unanimity with which I have been chosen to preside for this brief period is evidence of itself that your choice carries with it no political significance. I can most cheerfully forego all the power and all the influence that attaches to the position of Speaker of the House; but there is a significance beyond which a man must be differently constituted from myself if he can ever forget, and which arises from the kind personal consideration which is involved in my unanimous election to this most honorable position.

The speech was met with unanimous applause. Pomeroy's single day as Speaker was short - the entire run of the debate officiated by Pomeroy as Speaker, published in the *Congressional Globe*, the official organ of the Congress, is only 33 pages in length.

After Leaving the Speakership

Returning to civilian life, Pomeroy entered the banking sector in Auburn, having served in his final year of Congress as the first Vice President and general counsel for the American Express Company. In 1875 and 1876 he served as the mayor of Auburn. Pomeroy attended the 1876 Republican National Convention, held in Cincinnati, Ohio, as a delegate for the nomination of Senator Roscoe Conkling of New York to be President. Governor Edwin D. Morgan of New York was the chairman of the Republican National Committee, and Pomeroy was named as temporary chairman of the convention. When Conkling could not gather enough delegates to capture the nomination, Pomeroy and the other New

York delegation members threw their support behind Ohio Governor Rutherford B. Hayes, who eventually captured the presidential nomination. New York was given the "consolation prize" by having William Wheeler of that state named as Hayes' running mate.

In his final years, Pomeroy served in the New York state Senate (1878-79), and, in 1891, he served on a committee in presenting a statue of his close friend, former Secretary of State William H. Seward, to the city of Auburn, New York. Pomeroy died in Auburn, New York, on 23 March 1905, and was buried in Fort Hill Cemetery in that city.

Completely forgotten and erased from the annals of American history - that is how we can describe this man who stepped into the limelight of congressional leadership for an ever so brief period of just one day. Only a few of his personal letters exist, including some 500 pieces of correspondence at the University of Rochester, New York, library. A biography by an unnamed (and alleged) relation, Robert Watson Pomeroy, entitled *A Sketch of the Life of Theodore Medad Pomeroy, 1824-1905*, was allegedly published in 1910 (the exact date remains a mystery) by the author but is almost impossible to find in any library anywhere. Except for these small bits of information, Pomeroy is invisible to American history.

Further Reading:
Barnes, William Horatio, *The Fortieth Congress of the United States: Historical and Biographical* (New York: Published by George E. Perine; two volumes, 1870), II:369.

Pomeroy, Theodore M., *Payment of Interest upon the Funded Debt in Coin Essential to Preserve the National Credit: Speech of Hon. Theodore M. Pomeroy, Delivered in the House of Representatives, February 19, 1862* (Washington: Scammel & Co., Printers, 1862).

JAMES G. BLAINE.

James Gillespie Blaine

Served as Speaker:
March 4, 1869 - March 4, 1875

But for the machinations of the candidacy of the Prohibition Party in New York State and his own political corruption, James G. Blaine would have been the twentieth President of the United States. Instead, he is consigned to disrepute and obscurity despite a life of service to the nation, including tenures in the U.S. House of Representatives, the U.S. Senate, and two tenures as Secretary of State. His service as Speaker of the House, in the 41st to the 43rd Congresses (1869-75), is likewise forgotten. Known as "The Plumed Knight" (named by orator Robert Ingersoll when he nominated Blaine for President in 1876), Blaine was perhaps one the best-known politicians in the United States in the late nineteenth century.

Personal History

He was born in the village of West Brownsville, Pennsylvania, on 31 January 1830, the son of Ephraim Lyon Blaine, a businessman, and his wife Maria (née Gillespie) Blaine. According to Edward Stanwood, one of the early twentieth century's biographers of Blaine, the family originated in Ireland. James Blaine, the great-great-grandfather of James Gillespie Blaine, emigrated from Londonderry, in

what is now Northern Ireland, in 1745, and settled first in Donegal, in Westmoreland County, Pennsylvania, moving to the village of Toboyne, where he built an estate on the banks of the Juniata River. James Blaine's great-grandfather, Ephraim Blaine, the eldest of nine children, was born in Ireland in 1741 and emigrated with his parents as an infant; he later took over his father's holdings and became a major landholder in Pennsylvania before he volunteered for service in the Continental Army during the American Revolution and served, with the rank of colonel, as the Commissary-General of the Continental Army. Ephraim's son, named James Gillespie Blaine, intended to become a politician in Pennsylvania but instead spent time in Europe, afterwards returning to his home state where he became an attorney. James Blaine received what is now called "home schooling," although he was sent to Lancaster, Ohio, at age 11 to live with his cousin, Thomas Ewing, who later served as the Secretary of the Treasury and the first Secretary of the Interior. Blaine received private tutoring from William Lyons, a British teacher who was a relation to Lord Lyons, the British Minister to the United States. Blaine completed his education at Washington College in Washington, Pennsylvania, in 1847 when he was just 17.

Blaine moved to Kentucky, where he became an instructor at the Western Military Institute, a boys' school in Blue Lick Springs, Kentucky. He married, and then returned to Pennsylvania where he studied the law in a move to become an attorney like his grandfather. Blaine's law studies did not go well, and he abandoned them after a period of time. Instead, he returned to teaching, going to work in 1852 at the Pennsylvania Institute for the Blind in Philadelphia. Two years later, for some unknown reason, Blaine quit his position and moved to Maine, a state with which he and his family had no prior relationship. There, he purchased, with a friend, the *Kennebec Journal* newspaper, and he became the editor of the paper. In the nineteenth century, newspapers became "organs" or mouthpieces of political parties, and Blaine turned the *Journal* into a Whig paper. In 1856, however, Blaine left the Whigs as that party dissolved over the issue of slavery, and he joined the new Republican Party, which had been formed two years earlier in opposition to slavery. In fact, in 1856, Blaine served as a delegate to the Republican Party's first national convention, held in Pittsburgh, and was elected as the convention's secretary. Returning to Maine, in 1857 Blaine sold his interest in the *Kennebec Journal* and purchased the *Portland Advertiser*, turning it into a Republican mouthpiece. In 1858, however, he was elected to a seat in the Maine state House of Representatives, and his career in journalism ended. Instead, his career as a politician began. He served in the state House from 1859 to 1862, with the last two years as Speaker of that body.

Early Years in Congress

In 1862, Blaine was elected to a seat in the U.S. House of Representatives. Taking his place in the Thirty-eighth Congress (1863-65), he supported the establishment of a National Bank system, somewhat along the lines of the Federal Reserve System in place today. Ultimately, Blaine saw service in the House through the Forty-fourth Congress (1875-77) until his resignation on 10 July 1876.

Rep. Schuyler Colfax of Indiana had served as the Speaker of the House in the first and second sessions of the Fortieth Congress (1867-69); however,

Rep. Theodore M. Pomeroy had served as Speaker in the single day of the third session of that Congress. Colfax had been elected as Vice President in 1868, leaving the speakership opened up for the first time since 1863.

The Vote

When the Forty-first Congress assembled in Washington on 4 March 1869, Blaine was the candidate of the Republicans, who carried the majority of the 252 seats in the House by a margin of 171 Republicans to 67 Democrats and five so-called "conservatives." The Democrats, badly outnumbered, placed forward the name of Rep. Michael C. Kerr of Indiana as their candidate for the speakership, but the conclusion to the election was inevitable, as Blaine was elected by a vote of 135 to 57. The *House Journal*, not a verbatim account of the activities of the House, merely states that Blaine was declared the duly elected Speaker of the House of Representatives, was conducted to the Speaker's chair by Reps. Henry L. Dawes of Massachusetts and Kerr, and, "after a brief address to the House" which has not survived, was given the oath of office. The House then began its business for that session of Congress.

Legacy as Speaker

Historians speculate as to the reasons for Blaine's rise, in only his third congressional term, to the speakership of the House. One reason put forward may be that Blaine lent strong support to the presidential candidacy of General Ulysses S. Grant in the 1868 election, which was won by Grant with Speaker Colfax as his running mate. During his tenure as Speaker, which lasted until the end of the Forty-third Congress (1873-75), Blaine became perhaps the most contentious occupant of the Speaker's chair at least during the nineteenth century and perhaps just behind that of Speaker Joseph G. Cannon overall. Blaine was, in his first two terms as Speaker, praised by many for his thoroughness in conducting House business and chairing debates. One journalist in Washington wrote in a private correspondence, "His quickness, his thorough knowledge of parliamentary law and of the rules, his firmness, clear voice, and impressive manner, his ready comprehension of subjects and situations, and his dash and brilliancy have been widely recognized, and really [have] made him a great presiding officer." Although many of the great issues involving the just-concluded Civil War were over, the main controversy was over Reconstruction. In 1871, Blaine broke with his party and called for an investigation into allegations of corruption and bad treatment by so-called "carpetbag" governments in the South against former Confederates. However, Blaine also helped to block legislation allowing these same former Confederates the right to vote again. Mary Parker Follett, one of the historians of the Speakership, called Blaine "a clever manipulator of the rules" of the House. Blaine would also serve as chairman of the Committee on Rules (Forty-third Congress).

When Blaine won re-election in 1872 and a third term as Speaker in the Forty-third Congress (1873-75), he told the House members who bestowed on him this great honor:

> The vote this moment announced by the Clerk is such an expression of your confidence as calls for my sincerest thanks. To be chosen Speaker of the American House of Representatives is always an honorable distinction; to be chosen a third time enhances the honor more than three-fold; to be chosen by the largest body that ever assembled in the Capitol imposes a burden of responsibility which only your indulgent kindness could embolden me to assume.

It was during the Forty-third Congress that allegations against Blaine being involved in rampant corruption began to surface. As the nation expanded westward in the years just after the Civil War, the main instrument in such growth and development were the railroads. In comparison with the modern controversy over "earmarks" that legislators slip into bills for pet projects and sops to contributors, in Congress in the mid-nineteenth century the railroads passed "gifts" and other contributions onto representatives and Senators in exchange for continued support for the expansion of railroad activity. Such payments were frowned upon, but were not illegal. In an investigation later conducted by the House Judiciary Committee, it was discovered that when the Little Rock and Fort Smith Railroad, an entity in which Blaine held bonds, went bankrupt, the receiver of the company, the Union Pacific Railroad, purchased the bonds from Blaine for an estimated $64,000. Blaine then supported legislation that gave the Union Pacific increased power in the

construction of railroads in the West. Accused of taking payoffs, Blaine went to the floor of the House on 24 April 1871 and denied the allegations wholly and with vigor. "I never had any business transactions whatever with the Union Pacific Railroad Company, or any of its officers or agents or representatives," he charged.

Evidence then arose showing that Blaine had written letters to Warren Fisher, Jr., of Boston, who sold the bonds to Blaine, thanking him for the sale. The letters were in the possession of Fisher's clerk, James Mulligan. In an action that only could be classified as being from the theater of the absurd, Blaine visited Mulligan in his Washington, D.C. hotel and asked to see the letters before Mulligan could hand them over to Congress. Mulligan complied, and the letters were never seen again. Blaine denied their existence; he even denied that he had visited Mulligan for anything but to get his side of the story. Under pressure from his colleagues over the burgeoning scandal, Blaine again took to the floor, this time with what he said were the now-famous "Mulligan Letters," and read selected portions into the record. No one was allowed to see what Blaine was referring to, and he later stated that these were notes that he destroyed. Although the Judiciary Committee investigation cleared Blaine of wrongdoing, the taint and smell of the scandal destroyed him and his ability to effectively act as Speaker.

In the 1874 mid-term elections, a political tidal wave swept the country, and, led by scandals in the Grant administration and in Congress, the Republicans lost 96 seats in the House, removed from the majority with Blaine losing the speakership. In his closing address to the House on 3 March 1875, the last day of the second session of the Forty-third Congress, Blaine spoke emotionally of his service as Speaker:

> Gentleman: I close with this hour a six years' service as Speaker of the House of Representatives — a period surpassed in length by but two of my predecessors, and equaled by only two others. The rapid mutations of personal and political fortune in this country have limited the great majority of those who have occupied this chair to shorter terms of service.

It would be the gravest insensibility to the honors and responsibilities of life not to be deeply touched by so signal a mark of public esteem as that I have thrice received at the hands of my political associates. I desire in this last moment to renew them, one and all, my thanks and my gratitude.

To those from whom I differ in my party relations - the minority of this House - I tender my acknowledgements for the generous courtesy with which they have treated me. By one of those sudden and decisive changes which distinguish popular institutions, and which conspicuously mark a free people, that minority is transformed in the ensuing Congress to the governing power of the House. However it might possibly have been under other circumstances, that event necessarily renders these words my farewell to the Chair.

The speakership of the American House of Representatives is a post of honor, of dignity, of power, of responsibility. Its duties are at once complex and continuous; they are both onerous and delicate; they are performed in the broad light of day, under the eyes of the whole people, subject at all times to the closest observation, and always attended with the sharpest criticism. I think no other official is held to such an instant and such rigid accountability. Parliamentary rulings in their very nature are peremptory; almost absolute in authority and instantaneous in effect. They cannot always be enforced in such as way as to win applause or secure popularity; but I am sure that no man of any party who is worthy to fill this chair will ever see a dividing line between duty and policy.

Thanking you once more, and thanking you cordially, for the honorable testimonial you have placed on record to my credit, I perform my only remaining duty in declaring that the Forty-third Congress has reached its constitutional limit, and that the House of Representatives stands adjourned for the day.

Ben: Perley Poore, a noted Washington journalist in the nineteenth century, wrote in his memoirs, "When by party changes it had become evident that a Democratic Speaker would succeed him, Mr.

Blaine made a near valedictory in adjourning the session, and as he declared the adjournment and dropped his gavel, a scene of tumultuous enthusiasm ensued. The crowed assemblage, floor and galleries, rose and greeted him with repeated salvos of applause, running in waves and side to side, with almost delirious cheering, clapping of hands, and waving of handkerchiefs. Fully five minutes, it seemed, he was detained, bowing and acknowledging with emotion, this tribute to the record he had made and for [a] full half hour afterward there poured toward his standing place, at the clerk's desk, a constant stream of members and citizens anxious to press his hand and express in words the admiration already shown in signs. None who were there can forget the impression made by this scene." Blaine was the candidate of the Republicans for the speakership in the Forty-fourth Congress, but he lost to Michael Kerr of Indiana by a vote of 173 to 106.

After Leaving the Speakership

By the end of his tenure as Speaker, Blaine had become the most popular Republican politician in the nation. Historians and even some contemporary commentators in Blaine's time noted that he had succeeded Henry Clay in the ranks of the politician who rose above party and station to become a probable presidential candidate. Thus, when the Republicans gathered in convention in Cincinnati on 14 June 1876 to nominate a presidential candidate, James Blaine, former Speaker of the House, was the leading aspirant. As the leader of the party faction known as the "Half Breeds," who were critical of the Grant administration, he was opposed by Senator Roscoe Conkling of New York, head of the group known as the "Stalwarts," or those who backed Grant completely and faithfully. Blaine led the party's apparatus, with approximately 300 votes out of 400 needed for the party nomination. Hanging over his head, however, was the charge of political corruption involving the railroads and bribes. This was forgotten, at least by the convention, when Robert G. Ingersoll, the noted nineteenth century orator, took to the podium to nominate Blaine. In his lengthy speech, he called Blaine "the Plumed Knight," a name which stuck to the former Speaker. Blaine led the balloting for President for six ballots before a dark horse candidate, Governor Rutherford B. Hayes, was nominated.

In June 1876, Secretary of the Treasury Benjamin Bristow resigned, and President Grant named Senator Lot Morrill of Maine as his successor. With a vacancy in the Senate, the Maine legislature elected Blaine to replace Morrill. Blaine resigned his House seat on 10 July 1876 to fill the remaining months of Morrill's term; later in 1876 the Maine legislature elected the former Speaker to a full term beginning in 1877 and lasting until 1883. In the Senate until 5 March 1881, when he resigned, Blaine became a noted statesman, rising to oppose increased Chinese immigration to the United States, supporting increased trade with nations in South America while also backing a protective tariff for American industries hurt by cheap foreign goods.

In 1880, Blaine was once again mentioned as a potential candidate for the presidency, but he lost to Rep. James A. Garfield. With Garfield's election, Blaine, still considered the leading statesman of his party, was offered the Secretary of State portfolio in the new administration. Blaine resigned his Senate seat on 5 March 1881 to take this office. As several Secretaries of State had risen to be elected President, Blaine saw this route as the one closest to getting him into the White House.

However, Blaine's tenure at the State Department was short. He clashed with the British over the issue of Canadian fisheries and their product being imported into the United States. Blaine also worked to forestall any attempt by the Europeans to build an isthmian canal across Central America. He used his experience in issues relating to trade in South America to push for increased business dealings with countries in the region.

On 2 July 1881, Blaine was accompanying President Garfield on a trip leaving the train station in Washington, D.C. when the President was approached by a lunatic, Charles Guiteau, who shot Garfield in the back. Garfield's health slowly went downhill until he ultimately succumbed to his wounds on 19 September 1881. Garfield was succeeded by Vice President Chester A. Arthur, and Blaine remained in the cabinet. He spent the remainder of his tenure at State formulating an international peace congress of the nations of Central and South America to meet in Washington. But Blaine soon found himself at odds with the more liberal Arthur over policy issues, and, on 19 December 1881, he resigned. His successor at State, Frederick Frelinghuysen, canceled the peace conference, although the idea remained a viable one, becoming the First Inter-American Conference held in Washington from October 1889 to April 1890.

For several years after leaving government, Blaine wrote articles on numerous national issues and became the elder statesman of the party. A former Speaker, Senator, and Secretary of State, the nomination of his party for President remained beyond his grasp. President Arthur's unpopularity in the party was his chance: at the 1884 Republican National Convention, held in Chicago in June, Blaine was one of three main contenders for the party's presidential nomination along with Senator Benjamin Harrison of Indiana and former Secretary of the Treasury Benjamin Bristow. Blaine was again nominated by Robert Ingersoll, who told the crowd, "The Republicans...want a man who knows that this government should protect every citizen at home and abroad; who knows that any government that will not defend its defenders, and protect its protectors, is a disgrace to the map of the world...the man who has, in full, heaped and rounded measure, all these splendid qualifications, is the present grand and gallant leader of the Republican party – James G. Blaine." Blaine led the balloting over Arthur for three ballots, and on the fourth he won an outright majority. The convention then selected Senator John Alexander Logan of Illinois as the Vice President nominee. The Democrats nominated Governor Grover Cleveland of New York as their presidential nominee.

The 1884 election is considered one of the dirtiest in American history. Charges that Cleveland fathered a child out of wedlock, coupled with the resurrection of the railroad bribery allegations against Blaine, filled the pages of the nation's newspapers. A group of liberal Republicans, styling themselves as reformers who could not support Blaine for President under any circumstances, called themselves "Mugwumps" (allegedly from the Algonquin Indian word *mugguomp*, meaning "war leader") and backed Cleveland - they included Charles Francis Adams, Jr., Henry Adams, the cartoonist Thomas Nast, the German-born politician Carl Schurz, and the writer Mark Twain, among others. The election, however, remained close between Blaine and Cleveland owing to Blaine's extensive congressional experience and Cleveland's thin resume as Sheriff of Buffalo and Governor of New York State. Then, on a visit to New York City, a Blaine supporter, the Rev. Samuel Burchard, a Presbyterian minister, told reporters that New York State would vote for Blaine because "we are Republicans and we don't propose to identify ourselves with the party whose antecedents have been rum, Romanism and rebellion." This referred to Irish Catholics, meant as a slur against their drinking habits, their religion - Roman Catholicism - and their fight against the British for freedom for Ireland. The Irish immigrants had voted for Democrats in large numbers, and it was unlikely that Blaine would get many of their votes anyway. Blaine either did not hear the statement or he agreed with it; most importantly, he never denounced it, and the slur uttered by Burchard backfired, as it was widely spread by Cleveland's supporters in the Irish-American community and fired up the voters in that group. Ironically, Blaine's own mother was a Roman Catholic, and he had a sister who was a Roman Catholic nun. Ultimately, the Burchard incident, mated with several other factors including the disillusionment of many Liberal Republicans with Blaine as their standard bearer, may have cost Blaine the presidency, as New York went to Cleveland by just 1,149 votes.

Historians cite at least three probable reasons for Blaine's defeat in 1884: first, Blaine's corruption was the most important factor that caused many in his party to shun him or cross over and cast their vote for Cleveland. Second, while historians refer to the episode with the Rev. Burchard as causing many Irish immigrants to vote for Cleveland, in fact it was the appearance on the New York electoral ticket of the Prohibition presidential candidates, led by former Republican Governor John P. St. John of Kansas for President and William Daniel for Vice President, which siphoned off critical votes from the Republicans (nationwide, the Prohibitionists won more than 150,000 votes, which were leaning Republican votes) and gave Cleveland his narrow victory in a state which, plainly as its sitting Governor, he should have won in a landslide. In total, Blaine lost to Cleveland by only 60,000 votes out of 10.1 million cast across the nation, with 182 electoral votes to Cleveland's 219. Perhaps the third, and most important, reason was that the nation was

tired of Republican rule, with the party having held the White House since 1860. Blaine wrote to newspaperman Murat Halstead soon after the election:

I feel quite serene over the result. As the Lord sent upon us an ass in the shape of a preacher, and a rainstorm, to lessen our vote in New York, I am disposed to feel resigned to the dispensation of defeat, which flowed directly from these agencies...in missing a great honor, I escaped a great and oppressive responsibility. You know - perhaps better than any one - how much I didn't want [Blaine's italics] the nomination; but perhaps, in view of all things, I have not made a loss by the canvass. At least I try to think not.

In the years after his ignominious defeat, Blaine spent some time overseas with his family. In 1887, as another election neared, he issued his "Paris Letter" from the French capital outlining his tariff platform. Many believed that Blaine's desire for the White House, coupled with President Cleveland's growing unpopularity, would make another run for the presidency a sure thing. Instead, in January 1888, Blaine wrote a lengthy letter stating that he did not want his name placed in nomination. When some supporters desired to nominate him anyway, he told reporters that he would not run even if nominated. His 1884 opponent, Senator Benjamin Harrison of Indiana, won the nomination, and won the election over Cleveland despite the Democrat getting more popular votes but fewer electoral votes. One of the new President-elect's moves was to offer Blaine the Secretary of State post. Blaine accepted, and on 5 March 1889 was sworn in for the second time as the leading American foreign policy officer. In this second tenure, which lasted until 4 June 1892, Blaine again worked on the issue of hemispheric cooperation, helping to foster the First Inter-American Conference, held in Washington from later 1889 to early 1890. Blaine also supported improved trade pacts with nations in Central and South America, an idea which was later put into practice by Presidents Franklin Delano Roosevelt, John F. Kennedy, and George W. Bush.

Always independent, Blaine found himself constrained by Harrison during his time at the State Department. In early 1892, his health began to fail, and he resigned on 4 June. He remained in Washington, where he died on 27 January 1893, four days before his 63rd birthday. Remembered as a giant of his times who just fell short of the presidency he so desired, his time as Speaker of the House was mentioned only in passing. He was buried in the Oak Hill Cemetery in Washington, D.C., but in 1920 his remains were removed to a crypt in Blaine Memorial Park in Augusta, Maine. In 1919, his Maine estate, known as "Blaine Estate," was presented by his daughter to the state, and now serves as the official residence of the Governor of the state.

Senator George F. Hoar of Massachusetts, who served with Blaine in the House, wrote of the former Speaker in his memoirs:

James G. Blaine was a man of many faults and many infirmities. But his life is a part of the history of his country. It will be better for his reputation that the chapter of that history which relates to him shall be written by a historian with a full and clear sense of those faults and infirmities, concealing nothing, and extenuating nothing. But also let him set nought [sic] down in malice. Mr. Blaine was a brilliant and able man, lovable, patriotic, far-seeing, kind. He acted in a great way under great responsibilities. He was wise and prudent when wisdom and prudence were demanded. If he had attained to the supreme object of his ambition and reached the goal of the presidency, if his life had been spared to complete his term, it would have been a most honorable period, in my opinion, in the history of the country. No man has lived in this country since Daniel Webster died, save [William] McKinley alone, who had so large a number of devoted friends and admirers in all parts of the country.

JAMES G. BLAINE.

Further Reading:
Blaine, James G., *Twenty Years of Congress: From Lincoln to Garfield* (Norwich, Connecticut: Henry Bill Publishing Co.; two volumes, 1884-86).

Crawford, Theron Clark, *James G. Blaine: A Study of His Life and Career* (Philadelphia: Edgewood Publishing Co., 1893).

Kitson, James T., "The Congressional Career of James G. Blaine, 1862-1876" (Ph.D. dissertation, Case Western Reserve University, 1971).

Stanwood, Edward, *James Gillespie Blaine* (Boston: Houghton, Mifflin and Company, 1905).

7

Department of State,
Washington, December 29, 1891.

To the

Diplomatic and Consular Officers
of the United States.

Gentlemen:

I herewith introduce to you
Mrs. A. R. Judd, wife of Norman B. Judd, Esq.
of Illinois, who was the diplomatic rep=
=resentative of the Government of the United
States in Germany from 1861 to 1865.

Mrs. Judd is travelling abroad, and
I bespeak for her your official cour=
=tesies.

I am, Gentlemen,
Your obedient servant,

James G. Blaine

Michael Crawford Kerr

Served as Speaker:
December 6, 1875 - August 19, 1876

His service as Speaker lasted from December 1875 until his death at age 49 from tuberculosis just eight months later, a period in which much of his work was done while he was recuperating from what would be his fatal illness, or by others serving as an interim Speaker. No major legislation bears his name, nor was any enacted during his short speakership, and he has slipped into obscurity since his death. Few history books mention him, and those that do relate to him only in passing.

Personal History

Kerr was born in or near the village of Titusville, in Crawford County, Pennsylvania, on 15 March 1827. Nothing is known of his family, or his ancestry; even his parents' names seemed to have escaped from historical memory. Historian Charles Lanman wrote in 1876 that Kerr was "chiefly self-educated." He received his primary education at the Erie Academy in Pennsylvania, and obtained his law degree from the Louisville University (now the University of Louisville in Kentucky) in 1851. He had married a "Miss Coover," a schoolmistress in Erie, after he graduated. The following year, after briefly living in Kentucky, Kerr relocated to New Albany, Indiana,

the state with which he would be associated for the remainder of his life, and opened a law practice there. In 1854 he served as the city attorney for New Albany, and in 1855 was the prosecuting attorney for Floyd County, Indiana. In 1856, Kerr was elected to the Indiana state legislature, serving in the sessions of that body in 1856 and 1857. When the Civil War broke out Kerr, a Democrat, sided with the Union - his wing of the party became known as "War Democrats" - but he did not join the army or see any fighting. In 1862, Kerr was named as the official reporter of the opinions of the Indiana state Supreme Court, a position he held until 1865. He eventually published five volumes of opinions of that body.

Early Years in Congress

In 1864 Kerr was elected to a seat in the U.S. House of Representatives, and he took his place in the Thirty-ninth Congress (1865-67), serving on the Committee on Private Land Claims and on Accounts. In the Fortieth Congress (1867-69), he served on the Committee on Elections and the Committee on Roads and Canals. In the Forty-first Congress (1869-71), the Democrats controlled only

67 seats to 171 for the Republicans, and because of their numbers were unable to do much to stop the tide of bills enacted by the majority party. In the election for Speaker, a foregone conclusion with the numbers being what they were, Rep. James G. Blaine of Maine was elected Speaker, with Kerr, the candidate of the minority Democrats, getting 57 votes to Blaine's 185. When first elected to Congress, Kerr, as a "War Democrat" who supported the prosecution of the Civil War by the administration of Abraham Lincoln, was opposed by "Copperhead" Democrats in his district who were against the conflict and wished to sue for peace with the Confederacy to end it as quickly as possible, whether or not slavery was ended or if the southern states remained out of the Union. However, after the end of the war, Kerr opposed the harsh Reconstruction policy imposed on the former Confederate states by Lincoln's successor, Andrew Johnson, also a "War Democrat," who had been the Governor of Tennessee.

During his time in the House, Kerr went against his party and against his constituents by backing the resumption of specie payments. During the Civil War, the government had issued some $450 million in currency to pay for the war; this money was not backed by gold or silver, known as "specie." After the war, those who held the currency wanted new notes to be issued that would keep the value of their currency at the same level; those who opposed the program feared the onset of inflation and pushed to have all further currency backed by gold. Many of Kerr's constituents held the old currency, and his support for new currency backed by gold made him unpopular. It was not until 1875 that Congress enacted the Specie Resumption Act, which allowed for the redemption of war currency for gold in 1879 to avoid a run on national gold resources. Kerr's stand, however, did not cost him his seat until 1872, when Democrat Godlove S. Orth defeated him in the primary for Indiana's congressman-at-large. Two years later, when Orth left his House seat to run for Governor of Indiana, Kerr ran for the seat again and was elected.

According to historian Albert House, in November 1870 Kerr was stricken with "typhoid pneumonia," and he suffered with the-then fatal lung disease for the rest of his life. Kerr spent much of the next six years visiting various clinics in the United States

and taking trips to Europe for his health, but his condition continued to deteriorate. By 1874, Kerr was in rapidly declining health.

The Democrats swept to victory in the 1874 midterm elections - a landslide electoral triumph so wide that the Democrats in the House picked up 100 seats and the majority for the Forty-fourth Congress. When the House met for a short extended session of the Forty-third Congress in December 1874, Democrats who knew they would control the next Congress decided to make sure that the Republicans did not enact any legislation whatsoever; some of the bills that were to be taken up included a civil rights bill, work on tariffs, and attempts to pass two bills that had previously failed that offered bond guarantees for the Texas & Pacific Railroad. Led by Samuel Randall of Pennsylvania, and including James B. Beck of Kentucky, William Niblack and William S. Holman of Indiana, and Fernando Wood of New York, the Democrats blocked the civil rights bill and bond action, but lost out on the tariff changes and the resumption of specie payments act.

Because of his work on stopping the Republican program, Randall appeared to be the leading candidate to serve as Speaker in the new Congress. However, when Democrats caucused prior to the Congress meeting, Randall was challenged by Kerr for the speakership. Considered to be an honest broker in debates who, because of his health, spoke with a low voice, almost a whisper, Kerr commanded a strong presence because of his leadership of the party in the Forty-first Congress, despite being frail and, in many cases, missing large chunks of congressional sessions. In opposition, Randall was a fiery speaker who was a specialist in parliamentary rulings but had spent the last several Congresses in the minority blocking the passage of legislation more than standing for any specific bill or action. In one area Randall was diametrically different than Kerr: he had a booming voice, almost shrill in sound, which could be heard during debates in all areas of the House. For months before the new Congress convened, Randall was writing to friends across the country and asking for assistance in winning the speakership. Kerr, on the other hand, spent the entire period from November 1874, when the election was held, until October 1875, when Congress would meet, resting and spending time nursing his fragile health. By November 1875, Kerr was in the best health he had been in years.

The Vote

When Congress re-convened in Washington on 6 December 1875, for the first session of the Forty-fourth Congress (the Senate had met in special session in March 1875), 173 Democrats and 105 Republicans were seated - including, for the first time, members from the new state of Colorado - and proceeded to elect a Speaker. The race for that position had been fierce and intense in the months leading up to the ultimate vote, and forced one of the four candidates - Democrat Fernando Wood of New York - to withdraw his name before balloting began because of a lack of support, and left a second, Democrat Samuel S. Cox of New York, to trail badly overall. Thus, the true contest was between two main leading candidates: Kerr and Randall. And although both of these men were from the North, they were on opposite sides of the debate over the enactment of civil rights legislation for the protection of freed and former slaves. What may have clinched the vote for Kerr over Randall were the defeats of several Democrats in Ohio and Pennsylvania over the issue of free trade and lower tariffs, with those Democrats taking Randall's side of the argument going down to defeat. The Democrats caucused prior to the first meeting of the new Congress; after three ballots of close voting, Kerr won 90 votes to 63 for Randall and 7 for Cox. Thus, when the Congress convened, Kerr was put forward as the Democrats' nominee for Speaker, a mere formality because their party controlled the majority. Republicans put up former Speaker James G. Blaine, but the vote quickly showed that Kerr was the elected Speaker.

Acceptance Speech

Once sworn in, Kerr was ushered to the podium and the Speaker's chair, then turned to the members of the House and delivered some remarks:

> I am truly gratified for the honor you have conferred in calling me to this exalted station. I profoundly appreciate the importance and delicacy of its duties. I shall doubtless many times need your patient indulgence. I pray that you will grant it, and with nothing but kindly feeling toward every member of the House, I promise

> that in all my official acts I will divest myself to the utmost of my ability of all personal bias, and observe complete fairness and impartiality towards all, and towards all the great and diversified interests of our country represented in this house.

Legacy as Speaker

Ironically, whereas the Democrats had blocked a tariff reduction and specie payments resumption bill in the Forty-third Congress when they were in the minority, Kerr now pushed these two issues forward, even naming to the Ways and Means Committee those supporters who would work to lower tariffs. Despite his personal support for them, Kerr's party was against them almost to a man, and even though Kerr controlled the machinations of the House neither bill was ever voted on in the House. Support from southern members led the new Speaker to named 21 of the 34 committee chairman from former slave states, giving Appropriations to Randall and Banking and Currency to Cox. Randall and Cox, along with Rep. Abram Hewitt of New York, worked to control the House when Kerr became too ill to do it himself. Historian Albert House believes that Kerr failed to advance his overall agenda because, as he notes, within a week of becoming Speaker his health failed, and his weakened state became clear to all who saw him. From February 1876, just two months into his tenure, until his death six months later, Kerr was in such debilitating and deteriorating condition that he was forced to miss large stretches of House sessions and debate, and Cox of New York sat in as Speaker *pro tempore*. House notes that Kerr, who had placed Randall as the chairman of the Appropriations Committee, "begged" the Pennsylvanian to take the Speaker's chair, but Randall resisted on the grounds that his work on the Appropriations Committee was unfinished and needed his full attention.

As the 1876 presidential campaign got underway, it was natural for some Democrats, particularly from Indiana, to talk about nominating Kerr for a spot on the party's national ticket. Perhaps Kerr knew that he was already so seriously ill that he would not live much longer; when J.H. Reall of Philadelphia, unknowing of Kerr's health, wrote an article in a newspaper calling for Kerr to be nominated for Vice

President, the Speaker penned him a letter of declination of the honor. He explained:

> *Several days ago I received by mail, accompanied with your card, an article over your name, published in the Delaware County Democrat of Dec. 30 last. I perused the article with much interest, and many of its views command my unqualified approval, but I have only time now to thank you for your very kind reference to me in that article, and to say that it is not my desire in any degree whatever that my name shall be used in connection with the national ticket of this year. The Indiana Democrats will present to our next National Convention another of her sons as a candidate for the Presidency - Gov. [Thomas] Hendricks - in whose advocacy for that high place I will stand with them in hearty co-operation. My judgment is that our friends this year cannot do better, if so well, than to nominate Gov. Hendricks.*

As Kerr was slowly dying, charges of corruption rose up against him. In either late March or early April 1876, allegations were brought to the attention of Reps. Lyman Kidder Bass of New York and Lorenzo Danford of Ohio, both Republicans sitting on the Committee on Expenditures in the War Department, that Kerr helped one Augustus H. Green gain an appointment in the U.S. Army as a 2nd Lieutenant in exchange for $600. Bass and Danford were hesitant to bring the charges forward because of Kerr's health, but in the end reported them to the chairman of their committee, Rep. Hiester Clymer, Democrat of Pennsylvania. In an investigation that lasted throughout the summer, the Committee on Expenditures in the War Department scrutinized the testimony and documents involved in the allegation. It was not until 13 June that the committee concluded that the claim was false and cleared Speaker Kerr of any wrongdoing.

Kerr Dies

In June 1876, gaunt and barely able to breathe, Kerr moved to Virginia, where he entered a sanitarium, the Rockbridge Alum Springs, in Alum Springs, Rockbridge County. There, on 19 August 1876, at just 49 years of age, Michael Kerr died from the illness that had plagued him for years. His passing came just four days after the Forty-fourth Congress had adjourned the first session. Kerr's body was returned to Indiana, and he was buried in Fairview Cemetery in New Albany. His tombstone, which appears to be fairly modern, mentions at its head that Kerr served as Speaker of the House of Representatives, albeit briefly, from 1875 to 1876. President Ulysses S Grant issued a proclamation on 21 August 1876, commemorating the deceased Speaker, writing that Kerr was "a man of great intellectual endowments, large culture, great probity and earnestness in his devotion to the public interests." William Henry Smith, an historian of the Speakers of the House, wrote in a history of the state of Indiana, "If not a great man, Michael Crawford Kerr was an honest, faithful and useful public servant. He was a man of pure conscience, strict integrity, and of large ability."

Kerr's speakership was brief, with few if any accomplishments made during its duration. His biography also appears to be of little interest: for instance, the important *Dictionary of American Biography* does not carry his biography. Few of his personal letters exist, and he appears to have no work on his life, of by him, ever published. Nonetheless, contemporary opinions of Kerr after his death were almost unanimous in their praise of him. The *Hartford Daily Courant* of Connecticut stated, "His integrity was never questioned, and his rulings as speaker were always fair and impartial." The *New York World* says of him, "In his manner he was simple and unpretentious, but the dignity of his character never failed to impress those with whom he came in contact."

Further Reading:

Lanman, Charles, *Biographical Annals of the Civil Government of the United States, During Its First Century. From Original and Official Sources* (Washington: James Anglim, Publisher, 1876), 239.

Smith, William Henry, *The History of the State of Indiana, from the Earliest Explorations by the French to the Present Time. Containing an Account of the Principal, Civil, Political, and Military Events, from 1763 to 1897* (Indianapolis, Indiana: The B.L. Blair Company; two volumes, 1897), II:798-800.

"Obituary. Michael C. Kerr," *New York Times*, 20 August 1876, 6.

See also page 462

M. C. Kerr
New Albany—
Ind—

Samuel Jackson Randall

Served as Speaker:
December 4, 1876 - March 4, 1881

He was perhaps the most powerful Speaker elected by Democrats from the end of the Civil War to the start of the twentieth century, but he has been forgotten entirely by history. Rising from his service as the powerful chairman of the House Appropriations Committee, Samuel J. Randall served as Speaker of the House from the Forty-fourth (1875-77) through the Forty-sixth (1879-81) Congresses. He rose to the speakership upon the death of Speaker Michael C. Kerr, and proved his worth through his great knowledge of tariff and business issues. Randall was born into two socially and politically prominent families, then rose through the ranks of first the Whig Party and then the Democratic Party to become one of the most powerful politicians in Pennsylvania.

Personal History

He was born in Philadelphia on 10 October 1828, the son of Josiah Randall, a Whig politician and attorney in Philadelphia, and his wife Ann (née Worrell) Randall, whose father was a noted member of the Jeffersonian Republican Party in Pennsylva-

nia. In a memorial to Samuel Randall in Congress following his death in 1890, fellow Pennsylvanian Charles O'Neill stated,

> *Josiah Randall, father of my colleague, stood abreast with the leaders of the bar of Philadelphia, and met in his professional life before judges and juries his contemporaries, Chauncey, Binney, Rawle, Sergeant, Brown, Dallas, the Ingersolls, Meredith, and others, who with him sustained the reputation of "the Philadelphia lawyer," that reputation having existed from the earliest days of the bar.*

Samuel Randall attended the common schools of Philadelphia before he entered the University Academy of Philadelphia. It does not appear that he earned a degree of any kind.

In 1849, when he was 21, Randall used his personal money to purchase a share in a coal business, as well as what his official congressional biography calls "mercantile pursuits," including selling surplus iron. In 1851, he married Fannie Agnes Ward, the daughter of Rep. Aaron Ward of New York, a Jacksonian who served in the U.S. House of Representatives from 1825 to 1843. Samuel Randall followed his father and father-in-law and entered the political field, running for a seat on the Philadelphia Common Council as a member of the American, or "Know-Nothing," Party, an entity based mostly on the hatred of foreigners immigrating to the United States. Randall gradually moved to the Whig wing of the American Party during his stint on the Common Council, which lasted from 1852 to 1856. With the disintegration of the American Party and the Whig Party in the mid-1850s, Randall and his father joined the Democratic Party. He then ran as a Democrat for a seat in the Pennsylvania state Senate, serving in that body in 1858 and 1859.

When the Civil War broke out in 1861, Randall put aside any political opportunities and volunteered for service in the Union army. He was appointed to the First Troop of Philadelphia that same year, seeing limited action for a period of three months in 1861. In 1863, he was commissioned as a captain in the same unit, again seeing limited if any action during that year. Following the massive battle at Gettysburg, Pennsylvania, in July 1863, he was promoted to the rank of provost marshal.

Early Years in Congress

In 1862, while waiting for a potential call-up to serve in the army, Randall was elected by Democrats in the First Pennsylvania district to a seat in the U.S. House of Representatives. He took his seat in the Thirty-eighth Congress that convened in December 1863, and he would hold the same seat continuously for the next 27 years, through the Fifty-first Congress (he later represented the Third district from 1875-90). In a move that still retains great controversy, Randall, along with 21 other Democrats, tried to negotiate an end to the Civil War in February 1864 if the South could retain the right to own slaves. Two months later, when two other "Peace Democrats" were censured by the House for their roles in also trying to negotiate a peace between the warring parties, Randall refused to vote for the measure. He also refused to vote for the conscription of soldiers needed to fight for the Union army and for the eventual emancipation of freed blacks. Randall went even further, arguing that free blacks - those who had been slaves before

the war but had been released, or those who had never been slaves at all - did not have the right to vote or use public accommodations. When the war ended, Randall denounced the three constitutional amendments that ended slavery forever and gave voting rights to the former slaves, as well as Reconstruction of the former Confederate states. In 1875, he led a filibuster for 72 hours in the House, which held up the passage of a bill that would have enforced the right of the President to suspend the writ of habeas corpus to bring the southern states into line over the rights of former slaves.

In 1875, when the Democrats took control of Congress, Randall moved to get elected as Speaker of the House. Although he had been what was called a "hard money" man - advocating the payment of Civil War debts as quickly as possible - he cultivated support from "soft money" members of Congress by calling for the issuance of $300 million to replace those Civil War banknotes. He also called for the delay of the 1879 specie payments of earlier debts to avoid deficit spending. However, he was opposed by Michael Crawford Kerr, the thin and sickly member from Indiana. Despite being in far better health, being applauded with leading the Democrats to victory in the 1874 elections, and being an expert in parliamentary rulings, Randall was in the fight of his life against Kerr. In the months following the election, from November 1874 until December 1875, when Congress would convene for the first session of the Forty-fourth Congress, Randall cultivated support from Democrats across the country. At the same time, Kerr, who was suffering the final stages of consumption, now called tuberculosis, was confined to his home trying to recover his failing health. Thus, when the new Congress opened on 6 December 1875, 173 Democrats sat as opposed to 105 Republicans. A dark horse for the speakership, Rep. Fernando Wood of New York, took his name out of contention, while a slightly more viable candidate, Rep. Samuel S. Cox, also of New York, had little and withering support behind Kerr and Randall. The Democrats caucused to select a Speaker candidate, and, on the third ballot, Kerr won with 90 votes to 90 for Randall and 7 for Cox. When the Congress met, Kerr's victory was decided because the Democrats had control over the House, and he won over former Speaker James G. Blaine. Randall's immediate chances to be Speaker were dashed, but he was given a conciliatory gift for finishing in second place when he succeeded Rep. James A. Garfield as chairman of the Committee on Appropriations. Here, he made his name by becoming an expert in the minutiae of tariff law.

The Vote

Usually, a candidate who comes in second in the race for the speakership has to wait until the next Congress to try again, if they get that chance at all. For Samuel Randall, that second chance came only a year in Michael Kerr's speakership. Kerr was a sickly man when he was elected Speaker, a fact which most if not all of those who chose him over Randall could not have avoided. In the following year, Kerr barely showed up for work as the consumptive disease continued to destroy his precarious health. Finally, on 19 August 1876, Kerr died in a sanitarium in Virginia at the age of 49. His death came just four days after the first session of the Forty-fourth Congress had adjourned. When that Congress reconvened for its second session on 4 December 1876, the task of choosing a Speaker for the second time in a year fell upon the Democrats. This time there was no contest or fight: Samuel Randall was elected over James Garfield, 161 votes to 82.

Acceptance Speech

The new Speaker was borne to the Speaker's chair to deliver some remarks and be sworn in. He spent some time remembering his deceased predecessor:

> Called to this position because of the death of the late Speaker, Mr. Kerr, of Indiana, I only express the universal sentiment in saying he was a good and great man, whose public and private life was characterized by purity, patriotism, and unswerving integrity. Nobody can more completely appreciate than I do, the high honor of presiding over the deliberations of the president of the American people, and for this mark of your esteem and confidence I return my profound and heartfelt acknowledgment.

Randall would serve as Speaker for the remainder of the Forty-fourth Congress, and be re-elected in the Forty-fifth Congress (1877-79) and the Forty-sixth Congress (1879-81).

Legacy as Speaker

Randall biographer Albert V. House completed both a 1935 dissertation as well as a major article on the impact of Randall on the rules and conduct of the House. He wrote,

> The hectic session which followed [Randall's election as Speaker] was occupied largely with the Electoral Count [from the 1876 election], yet Randall stamped his powerful personality on the House and the country by his course of action during the last few days of the session, when he forced the completion of the count over the protests of the filibusterers of his own party. However, his ruling of dilatory motions out of order during this session was not based on the rules of the House or on his own conception of the prerogative of his office, but on the mandatory provisions of the Electoral Act which had become law, largely through the efforts of Randall's own party.

Historian DeAlva Stanwood Alexander, in his landmark 1916 work on the history of procedure in the House of Representatives, compared Randall to one of the most powerful Speakers of the nineteenth century and perhaps in the history of the House, Thomas Brackett Reed:

> It is not easy to think of Samuel J. Randall and Thomas B. Reed serving elsewhere than in the House...They were leaders of men. They could brighten the driest details, inspire implicit confidence in their views, and arouse the admiration of the indifferent until their appeals divided members into two hostile camps; but they also hold their alignment without the loss of a vote and crush a less confident man who dared to offend. [Rep. William Ralls] Morrison, of Illinois, used to say in jest that no man "can be quite so wise as 'Sam' Randall looks."

When Randall became Speaker, the 1876 election was still undecided between Republican Rutherford B. Hayes and Democrat Samuel Tilden. Several state electoral counts were in dispute, throwing the election into the House of Representatives. Randall's job, as Speaker and as the leading Democrat in Washington, was to make sure that the electoral votes of those states still being challenged were given to Tilden to elect him as President. Because of the contentiousness - as well as the major disputes over each particular state, which were Florida, Louisiana, Oregon, and South Carolina - the Congress formed an Electoral Commission to decide each state's electoral votes. Initially Democrats controlled the commission, made up of 15 members (five representatives, five U.S. Senators, and five members of the U.S. Supreme Court), but a leading independent who Democrats expected would side with them, Justice David Davis, resigned his seat and was elected by the Illinois legislation to the U.S. Senate. His seat on the commission was taken by Justice Joseph P. Bradley, named to the Court by President Ulysses S. Grant. Bradley tipped the counting towards Hayes, and, in votes by the members, all 20 disputed electoral votes were awarded to Hayes, giving the Republican a 185-184 electoral count victory. Randall was incensed at the outcome, but to avoid a rupture in the House from Democrats who felt that they had been cheated out of the presidency, he exacted from Republicans a deal to end Reconstruction in the south, which did away with minority Republican governments in the former Confederate states as well as protections for the freed slaves. These states reverted back to prewar Democratic rule, ensuring that blacks would be disenfranchised and that the Democratic Party would continue to hold a majority of seats in the nation for the foreseeable future.

What Randall did do, in opposition to his introductory speech as Speaker, was conduct the House in ways that unified his opposition. Based on allegations of fraud by Republicans in the states awarded to Hayes, Randall established an investigation by Rep. Clarkson N. Potter, Democrat of New York, to look into whether votes were purchased. The Potter Committee later discovered - to Randall's embarrassment as well as the Democrats' - that Samuel Tilden's nephew had tried to buy votes for his uncle, while no vote-buying was tied to any Republicans. Randall also tried to cut the power of the voting rights portions of the Fourteenth and Fifteenth Amendments by attaching riders to appropriation bills ending election laws. President Hayes vetoed these bills, and Randall did not have enough votes in the House to override the vetoes. Mary Parker Follett, one of the chief historians of the Speakers of the House and its office, noted in 1902:

It is true that Randall made no more effort than his predecessor to change the political tone of the speakership. Like [James G.] Blaine, too, he was accused of an intimate acquaintance with the "gentlemen of the lobby." But while Blaine's first object was to make himself personally popular, and thus keep himself before the country, Randall aimed directly at increasing the influence of the speakership and making it a governing power. This purpose he carried out systematically; he first brought about a change in the rules, and then by his administration of these rules greatly increased the authority of the Chair.

In the 1880 election, while former Speaker candidate James A. Garfield was being elected to the presidency, the Republicans were picking up 19 seats to take a 151-128 majority (with 14 members of other parties or independents) in the House. Randall's time as Speaker, after two full terms and half of another, had ended. On 5 December 1881, J. Warren Keifer of Ohio defeated Randall for the speakership, 148 votes to 129, ending that era in House history. Even though the Democrats recaptured the majority in 1882 after only one term, the Democrats in the House chose John G. Carlisle of Kentucky over Randall to serve as Speaker, and the Pennsylvanian was relegated to the back benches. Noted congressional historian Robert V. Remini wrote:

With the Democrats in control of the House when the 48th Congress convened on 3 December 1883, they engaged in a bitter contest for the speakership between John G. Carlisle of Kentucky, a man who had led the fight against the demands by protectionists for higher tariff rates, and Samuel J. Randall of Pennsylvania, whose state demanded tariff protection and expected Randall to safeguard its interests. Carlisle set up his campaign headquarters in the Metropolitan Hotel, while Randall "surrounded by a group of Philadelphia business men," chose the Ebbitt House. Betting at the Willard Hotel was $500 to $300 that Randall would win because of the strong financial backing he received from business interests. When the Democratic Caucus convened on 1 December, it chose Carlisle, to the surprise of many. "The South and West elected

Carlisle tonight," *reported the Louisville Courier-Journal, "on a principle...It is the tariff." The party stands "for the reform of abuses, and for the rights of the people against monopolists of all kinds." It was the first time since the Civil War that protectionists had failed to elect one of their supporters to the office of Speaker. In the House election that followed, the vote for Speaker was 190 for Carlisle and 113 for [former Speaker] J. Warren Keifer.*

After Leaving the Speakership

As what happened when he lost the speakership to Michael C. Kerr, however, Randall was given the "concession" of serving as chairman of the all-important Committee on Appropriations, and here he once again showed his power by defeating tariff reduction bills, most notably those sponsored by fellow Democrat - and chief rival on the subject - William Ralls Morrison of Illinois. In 1888, Randall clashed with President Grover Cleveland, also a fellow Democrat, over patronage in Pennsylvania when Randall crossed the President over the Mills tariff bill that Cleveland pushed for and Randall helped to scuttle. As his power was being cut in the area of patronage, Randall learned that he had inoperable colon cancer. He spent the final years arguing against the reduction of tariff rates to preserve American business.

On 13 April 1890, Randall died at his home in Washington, D.C., at 120 C Street, Southeast. His passing was not unexpected, as his fellow Pennsylvanian, Republican Rep. Charles O'Neill, told the Congress days later during a period of official mourning for the former Speaker.

Despite his power and influence, little is remembered about Samuel Randall or his policies. His papers, in the Van Pelt Library of the University of Pennsylvania, should provide historians with the insights into this most mysterious man who served as the head of the U.S. House for nearly three terms.

In 1906, journalist Orlando Stealey, who covered Congress for the *Louisville* [Kentucky] *Courier-Journal*, wrote,

Randall was a natural and an ideal leader. His commanding presence attracted followers; his mastery of details, his boldness and unfaltering

courage, his mental alertness and resourcefulness...his industry was untiring, and when its fruition was presented to the House, as in the case of general appropriation bills, he was as firm as adamant. His work was performed intelligently, conscientiously, and in carrying it out he was alike indifferent to the persuasion of party associates and the attacks of political opponents. Randall's great success in his numerous contests in the House was based upon thorough knowledge of details and his wonderful tenacity in adhering to a settled purpose, born of conviction.

In his 1914 work on the life of Speaker Thomas B. Reed, historian Samuel W. McCall wrote about the service of Randall, particularly when fellow Democrat John G. Carlisle was selected to replace Randall as Minority Leader:

Thus Randall retired from the leadership of his party in the House. He had led it when in the minority. During three Congresses he had been Speaker. In the latter position he had rendered the country a signal service, and had possibly saved it from anarchy and civil war. When he was Speaker, in 1877, the great majority of his party in the House and in the country believed that [Samuel] Tilden had been elected to the presidency. Randall discarded the practice he himself had so often followed and refused to entertain dilatory motions, to the end that the count of the presidential vote might be consummated before the fourth of March, the day on which the new term was to begin. If Grant's terms had come to its constitutional end and his successor had not been determined upon, chaos itself would have intervened. The extent of the damage would have been incalculable with a weak or a small man in the Speaker's chair, and Randall reached a sublime height on that day when he put before himself the good of the country and, partisan as he usually was, and in defiance of many of his own party and of the precedents which he himself had helped to establish, he cleared the way for the completion of the count. Reed said of him, "Perhaps there may have been better parliamentarians, men of broader intellect and more learning, but there

have been few men with a will more like iron or
a courage more unfaltering."

Further Reading:
House, Albert V., "The Political Career of Samuel Jackson
Randall" (Ph.D. dissertation, University of Wisconsin,
1935).

————. "The Contributions of Samuel J. Randall to the
Rules of the National House of Representatives," *American
Political Science Review*, XXIX:5 (October 1935), 837-41.

"Samuel J. Randall Dead. Who Long Represented the
Pennsylvania Idea," *New-York Times*, 14 April 1890, 1.

See also page 462

Samuel J. Randall.

Joseph Warren Keifer

Served as Speaker:
December 5, 1881 - March 4, 1883

Despite his lengthy service in the U.S. House of Representatives, as well as his noted service during the Civil War, the name of Joseph Warren Keifer, better known as J. Warren Keifer, has slipped almost completely from the annals of American history, as well as that of the speakership of the House of Representatives, an office that he held during the Forty-seventh Congress (1881-83). Perhaps because his speakership is nudged - for a single term - between that of Democrats Samuel J. Randall and John G. Carlisle, because of the controversies that arose during his tenure, he has been completely forgotten. Despite living to nearly 100 years of age, even his death in 1932 gave few occasions to discuss his life.

Personal History

Born in his family's farm in Clark County, near Springfield, Ohio, on 30 January 1836, he was the son and apparently only child of Joseph Keifer, a farmer who also worked as a surveyor, and his wife Mary (née Smith). Almost nothing is known of the Keifer or Smith families except that Joseph Warren Smith's parents were hard-working and industrious farmers who self-taught their son, who completed

his education in a local school. He worked on his family's farm, later teaching for a single term (1852-53) in a school, although biographies on Keifer do not specify if it was the same school that he himself attended. In 1854, he entered Antioch College in Yellow Springs, Ohio, but he apparently left there the following year without a degree. In 1856, he began to study the law with a firm in Springfield, and, on 12 January 1858, was admitted to the Ohio bar.

Initially, it appears that Keifer sought to find a location for a law firm in a place other than his native Ohio: he spent two months traveling to numerous Midwestern cities to find the site for his practice, but, after this journey, he came home and decided to remain in Springfield. While practicing the law, according to one biographer, Philip VanderMeer, Keifer "joined a local fire company," although his congressional biography does not mention this fact at all. In 1860, Keifer married Eliza Stout, a local woman.

In 1861, attorney William H. Herndon, a close friend of Abraham Lincoln, wrote to Lincoln's secretary, John G. Nicolay, "Keifer is a very strong anti-secessionist - for the [U]nion and the Laws. He comes nearer to my doctrine than most democrats of the "Brackenridge [sic; should read 'Breckinridge'"] school.

The outbreak of the Civil War, precipitated by the election of Republican Abraham Lincoln to the presidency in 1860, followed by the secession of the southern slave states, gave Keifer his opportunity to serve his country in ways he probably would never have had the war not occurred. On 19 April 1861, he enlisted in the Union Army; eight days later, he was commissioned with the rank of Major in the Third Ohio Volunteer Infantry. On 12 February 1862 he was promoted to the rank of Lieutenant Colonel; on 30 September 1862 he was promoted to Colonel and commander of the One Hundred Tenth Ohio Volunteer Infantry. He was eventually promoted to brigadier general of Volunteers on 19 October 1864, and, finally, to the rank of Major General on 9 April 1865, just prior to the cessation of the conflict. He was finally mustered out of the service on 27 June 1865.

During his four years of service in the army of his country, Keifer participated and/or saw action in some of the most noted battles during the American Civil War, including at Petersburg, Richmond, and many others. In 1863, in his role as the commanding officer of the 110th Ohio Volunteer Infantry, Keifer was appointed by Brigadier General W.L. Elliott to report on the operations of his forces during a series of battles. The reports, which lasted until the end of the war in 1865, were published in 1866 as "Official Reports of Joseph Warren Keifer." They cover Keifer's accounts of the battles of Winchester, Brandy Station, the Wilderness, Spotsylvania, Cold Harbor, and Petersburg, among many others. Insightful and filled with detailed information on these now-infamous clashes of the Civil War, Keifer's reports are, even now, nearly a century and a half after their publication, some of the best sources for historians and Civil War enthusiasts. In his letter of farewell to the men under his command, published in the work as the last "report," Keifer wrote:

I mourn with you, and share in your sorrow, for the many brave comrades who have fallen in battle and have been stricken down with disease. Let us revere their memories and emulate their noble character and goodness. A proud and great nation will not neglect their afflicted families. The many disabled officers and soldiers will also be cared for by a grateful people and an affluent country...You have a proud name as soldiers; and I trust that, at your homes, you will so conduct yourselves that you will be honored and respected as good citizens.

On 5 May 1864, during the Battle of the Wilderness in what is now central Virginia, Keifer was severely wounded, which precipitated his leaving the service until he mended. In total during the war, Keifer was wounded four times. On 29 December 1864, President Lincoln assigned Keifer as a brigadier general; he was mustered out of the service on 27 June 1865 after having served four years and two months. On 1 July 1865 he was then promoted as a major general by brevet for, as his promotion stated, "gallant and distinguished services during the campaign ending in the surrender of the insurgent army under Gen. R.E. Lee." After leaving the service, he returned to his law practice.

Joseph Warren Keifer would have remained a local attorney in Ohio had he not entered the political field in 1868, when he was elected to a single one-year term in the Ohio state Senate. In addition to political work, he also rose to serve as a leader for the care of veterans from the Civil War; in this capacity, he served as the commander of the Department of Ohio for the Grand Army of the Republic (1868-70), perhaps the most important post-Civil War veterans' lobbying group. He raised money to help found the Soldiers' and Sailors' Orphans Home in Xenia, Ohio, and served as a trustee of the institution from 1870 to 1878 and again from 1903 to 1904. In 1876, he served as a delegate to the Republican National Convention, held in Cincinnati, which nominated Rutherford B. Hayes for President and William A. Wheeler for Vice President.

A staunch Republican who not only backed the program of the party but was an outspoken supporter of the passage of the Fourteenth and Fifteenth Amendments to the U.S. Constitution, both of which, with the Thirteenth Amendment, helped to end slavery at the end of the Civil War and try to give freed blacks equality in American social life as well as in voting.

Early Years in Congress

Following his return from the convention, Keifer was nominated by the Republicans for a seat in the U.S. House of Representatives after Rep. William Lawrence, the Republican who held the Eighth Ohio district seat, decided not to seek re-election. As his party's presidential candidate was winning an extremely close election (one that the Congress later had to make a final decision on), Keifer was winning the seat in the House. He entered that body for the Forty-fifth Congress (1877-79), and remained until the end of the Forty-seventh Congress (1881-83). Little has been written about Keifer's first two terms in Congress; even his official congressional biography does not even list the committees he sat on or what legislation, if any, that he tried to have enacted.

In the Forty-sixth Congress (1879-81), Democrats controlled the House by a 141-132 margin, with 20 independent members. Rep. Samuel J. Randall, Democrat of Pennsylvania, served as Speaker in that Congress. In the 1880 election, Republicans picked up 19 seats to control the House 151-128, with 14 independent members.

When the members of the Forty-seventh Congress (1881-83) assembled in Washington in early December 1881, no candidate for the speakership stood out. As the *Washington Post* noted on 1 December,

> At the hotels [where the members of the House and Senate usually stayed, rather than at their own homes as they do now] there was very little excitement last night. At the National the talk was in favor of [Frank] Hiscock [of New York] or Keifer. At the Arlington the claquers [from the French "to clap" - defined as "a group of people hired to applaud or heckle a performer"] all shouted for Hiscock. At the Riggs, [John Adam] Kasson [of Iowa] and [Thomas Brackett] Reed, of Maine, were the favorites. At the Ebbitt the cry was for Keifer, Kasson and [Godlove Stein] Orth [of Indiana], in the order named. At Willard's the current swept in favor of Hiscock, with [Mark Hill] Dunnell [of Minnesota] as the dark horse.

As Republicans began to arrive at the capital, the papers were reporting that three main candidates were in the mix: Hiscock, Keifer, and Kasson. How-

ever, within a single day, Hiscock's chances seemed to slide almost to nothingness, caused by opposition from some southern Republicans. As well, the *Washington Post* reported that the Pennsylvania delegation, backed by Senator Donald Cameron of that state, working in accord with Senator Roscoe Conkling of New York, were pushing their respective members to move from Hiscock to Keifer; two other California Republicans and one from Colorado also arrived in Washington and announced their support of Keifer. The only growing resistance to Keifer was coming, according to the paper, from the Massachusetts delegation, which was pushing for Rep. Thomas B. Reed of Maine. On 3 December, the Republicans met in caucus and selected Keifer as their candidate for Speaker.

The Vote

When the House convened on 5 December 1881, the entire country was in the midst of a mourning period following the death of President James A. Garfield, who had died in September after being shot by an assassin the previous July. Thus, this Congress that had been elected with Garfield's rise to the presidency in 1880 now came together to work with his successor, Chester Alan Arthur, in the Executive Mansion. In this Congress, in addition to the members of the two major parties, there were also 10 so-called "Nationals," as well as 2 "Readjuster" Democrats who caucused independently of their party, 1 Independent Democrat, and 1 Independent, making for 293 representatives and 8 delegates. The first order of business - the election of the Speaker -was a mere formality. The Democrats placed the name of Samuel J. Randall, who had served as Speaker in the Forty-fourth (1875-77), Forty-fifth (1877-79), and Forty-sixth (1879-81) Congresses as Speaker, as their candidate. Keifer won 148 votes to Randall's 129, with 8 additional votes scattered among several minority candidates.

Acceptance Speech

Conducted to the Speaker's chair and sworn in as Speaker, Keifer then turned to the House and delivered some comments. He noted that "with few grounds for party strife and bitterness...the present is an auspicious time to enact laws to guard against the incurrence of dangers to our institutions and to insure tranquility at perilous times in the future."

Legacy as Speaker

J. Warren Keifer served only this single two-year term as Speaker of the House. During this tenure, Keifer oversaw the passage of such landmark legislation as the Chinese Exclusion Act and the River and Harbors Act, both passed in 1882, and the ground-breaking Pendleton Civil Service Act of 1883, which changed civil service rules for the entire U.S. government for the first time. The Chinese Exclusion Act, ratified on 6 May 1882, restricted the influx of Chinese immigrants to the United States, seen at the time as a threat to native American labor, while also denying existing Chinese migrants already in the country from applying for American citizenship.

The Forty-seventh Congress also enacted the Tariff of 1883, denounced by its critics as the "Mongrel Tariff" for cutting only slightly monstrously high tariff rates on imported goods while at the same time leaving untouched protectionist barriers to free trade to protect American industry. In 1906, journalist Orlando O. Stealey, the Washington correspondent for the *Louisville* [Kentucky] *Courier-Journal*, discussed the Keifer speakership:

> *It fell to Speaker Keifer's lot to enforce new rules governing the proceedings of the House...These rules were as obnoxious to the Democrats as the famous Reed rules, so called, were to the minority a decade later, although they were less stringent in some respects. The Democrats assailed them with savage fury, but the grim veteran who had withstood a more dangerous fire on the battle-field courageously defended his rulings. The story had been told, and never controverted, that a cabal was conceived to throw him bodily out of the Speaker's chair and defy him to return to preside over the deliberations of that body. The conspirators included some of the most conspicuous Democrats on the floor...An intimation of the plot reached Keifer the night before it was to be executed. The next morning, undaunted, he made his appearance at the capitol, and at twelve o'clock mounted the dais and calmly called the House to order. He was prepared for emergencies, according to the tale as it has come down to the present generation, for in one of his pockets was a revolver.*

Because of the partisan way that he conducted business in the House, as well as allegations of political corruption, Keifer was an extremely polarizing figure, even among Republicans. In his 1914 work on the life of another Speaker, Thomas Brackett Reed, historian Samuel McCall wrote of the Congress that elected Keifer as its Speaker:

> *General Keifer of Ohio easily won the nomination for Speaker in the Republican caucus, and on account of the support of the so-called Readjuster members, aided by the absence of some of the Democrats, he was elected by a much larger plurality than he could have received on a straight party vote. Indeed, in his speech accepting the office he declared that no party in either House of Congress had an absolute majority over all the other parties. It was difficult to classify a few of the members, who might be called Greenbackers or Republicans, and there was a small group from Virginia known as Readjusters. There was, however, apparently a clear Republican majority of one over all other parties, which was sufficiently small to be responsible for plenty of excitement.*

Historian Mary Parker Follett, in her work on the history of the speakership, explained, "The marked feature of Keifer's administration was its partisan character; but his partisanship was rather that of weakness than of determined aggression. When he entered upon his office it was generally thought that he possessed moderate ability, impartiality, and the integrity of character; it was soon found out that he had neither the ability nor the fairness necessary for the speakership..." He was unable to properly staff the committees, the role of the Speaker, with men who knew what their specific responsibility was for, such as tax writing or tariff increase or decrease. Follett concluded,

> *But Keifer's inadequacy, already hinted at in his make-up of the committees, was emphasized ten-fold by his conduct in the chair. There he was weak and undignified, and his partisan rulings soon won him the contempt of Republicans as well as Democrats. Mr. Keifer had perhaps no different aim than other Speakers, to impose his own will on the House of Representatives; but he failed because he was not strong enough to carry out such a scheme, and because he was*

not keen enough to see the limits to which a Speaker can use political power without being denounced as a partisan.

When Keifer named one of his nephews as a "Clerk to the Speaker" and another as a "Clerk to the Speaker's table" as well as his son as the Speaker's "private secretary," newspapers denounced him. Keifer would serve but a single term as Speaker before even his supporters threw him overboard.

In the 1882 election, additional seats were added to the Congress following the results of the 1880 census. Thus, instead of 293 seats, the new Congress would have 325 members. The timing was right for the Democrats, as they picked up 68 total seats - both old and new - to turn a 151-128 minority in the Forty-seventh Congress to a 196-117 majority in the Forty-eighth Congress (1883-85). Keifer's unpopularity, coupled with the accusation of corruption that hung over his head, made any chance he would have of winning back the speakership a forgone conclusion. As the *New York Times* stated:

Mr. [George Washington] Geddes, [Democrat] of Ohio, named John G. Carlisle for the Democrats...Mr. Cannon, of Illinois, named Gen. Keifer for the Republicans, but [he] did not venture to make any complimentary allusions. All expectation of a strong opposition to Keifer had by this time been dissipated. Several of the leading Republicans had been exerting themselves in Keifer's behalf, urging their party associates not to begin the session by a fight on his account. Keifer himself stood in his place, evidently anxious and exhibiting his anxiety very plainly.

The vote was then taken, with 191 for Carlisle, 112 for Keifer, 2 for George Dexter Robinson, Republican of Massachusetts, 1 for John Sergeant Wise, Readjuster of Virginia, and 1 for James Wolcott Wadsworth, Republican of New York; these final votes were protest votes against the now-former Speaker. Keifer, along with former Speaker Randall, conducted Speaker-elect Carlisle to the podium to be sworn in. Keifer's career was effectively over.

After Leaving the Speakership
In this final congressional term, he served as a member of the Committee on Elections. In 1884,

Keifer failed to win the Republican nomination for his seat in Congress, and at the end of the Forty-eighth Congress in March 1885 he left Washington, returning to Ohio. Before leaving, however, Keifer leveled an accusation against Henry Van Ness Boynton (1835-1905), a decorated Union army officer during the American Civil War - he was awarded the Congressional Medal of Honor for bravery - who was working as the Washington, D.C., correspondent for the Cincinnati *Commercial Gazette*, accusing Boynton of "corrupt propositions intended to influence his official action" - in short, that Boynton approached Keifer and allegedly offered Keifer a bribe or some other financial remuneration in exchange for his support of a bill that Boynton was interested in. The Democrats, in the majority in the House, formed a panel and heard testimony in the case, but ultimately decided that the charges could not be sustained, and dismissed them.

Keifer's career appeared to be over, but, when the Spanish-American War began in 1898 Keifer, at 62 years of age, volunteered to once again serve his nation in a time of war. He was commissioned as a major general of Volunteers, serving from 9 June 1898 until 12 May 1899, although he never saw any action in either Cuba or the Philippines. In 1900, he was named as the first Commander-in-Chief of the Spanish War Veterans, an association dedicated to the welfare of veterans of that conflict; he served in that position until 1901.

In 1904, despite being nearly 70 years old, Keifer was nominated by the Republicans for a seat in the U.S. House of Representatives. Once again, his military exploits and service to his nation gave him high standing with the voters of his district, and they sent him back to Washington for a second stint in Congress. Keifer ultimately served during the Fifty-ninth (1905-07), Sixtieth (1907-09), and Sixty-first (1909-11) Congresses. In 1910, at 74 years old, he was passed over for renomination to a fourth consecutive term, and he retired at long last from politics, returning instead to his law practice in Ohio. In 1911, he wrote, *The Battle of Rich Mountain and Some Incidents*, which was privately published. On 22 April 1932, at the age of 96, Keifer died at his home in Springfield, Ohio. He was buried in Ferncliff Cemetery in that city.

There are few if any biographies of Keifer himself, although he is given short and abbreviated mentions in histories describing his service during the Civil War, or in histories of the Congress that he led as Speaker. His papers are split between the Clark County Historical Society in Springfield, Ohio, the Manuscript Division of the Library of Congress in Washington, D.C., and Syracuse University in New York; his papers in the Library of Congress, donated in 1958 by his son, William W. Keifer, consist mostly of letters from Keifer to his wife during the Civil War. He published numerous works, including *Slavery and Four Years of War: A Political History of Slavery in the United States* (two volumes, 1900) and his reports from the battlefield during the Civil War.

Further Reading:
Keifer, Joseph Warren, *Slavery and Four Years of War: A Political History of Slavery in the United States. Together with a Narrative of the Campaigns and Battles of the Civil War in Which the Author Took Part: 1861-1865* (New York: G.P. Putnam's Sons; two volumes, 1900).

John Griffin Carlisle

Served as Speaker:
December 3, 1883 - March 4, 1889

His service to his country includes time in the Kentucky state legislature, as Lieutenant Governor of Kentucky, as a U.S. Representative (1877-90), as a U.S. Senator (1890-93), and as Secretary of the Treasury (1893-97). Yet it is his tenure as Speaker of the House in the Forty-eighth, Forty-ninth, and Fiftieth Congresses which is barely mentioned in his biography. During his service as Speaker, he worked to reduce tariff rates and backed measures to issue bonds to help stimulate the American economy.

Personal History

Carlisle was born near the village of Covington, in Campbell (now Kenton) County, Kentucky, on 5 September 1835, the son of Lilbon Hardin Carlisle, a farmer, and his wife Mary (née Reynolds) Carlisle. Most biographies of Carlisle mention only the county he was born in, with little information on the place itself. Carlisle's only biographer, James A. Barnes, explained in his 1931 work on the Kentuckian, "The place was the extreme northeastern part of the Blue Grass section of Kentucky, near where the placid Licking [River] flows into the Ohio at Cincinnati. This western metropolis, already calling itself 'the queen city of the West' and boasting of numerous brick and limestone buildings, scattered among its wooden houses, had 30,000 people...Just across the river on the Kentucky side stood Covington, with fewer brick buildings, but according to Kentucky tradition just as many pretty faces and trim figures." The Carlisles were not wealthy, and their son attended local schools to earn an education. Afterward, he taught in the schools to earn a living, then studied the law under noted Kentucky attorney (and later Governor and U.S. Senator) John White Stevenson (whose father, Andrew, ironically served as Speaker of the House of Representatives), and the two men became close friends. In 1858, Carlisle was admitted to the Kentucky state bar, and joined Judge William B. Kinkead in forming a law firm in Covington.

Within a year of joining the firm, Carlisle was making political speeches against the American, or "Know-Nothing," Party, formed from the ashes of the Whig Party by those opposed to the immigration of Irish to the United States. In 1859, Carlisle was elected to a seat in the Kentucky state House of

Representatives, serving a two-year term until 1861. Although it was a slave state, Kentucky and its politicians were loathe to side with the Confederacy when the southern states seceded from the Union following the election of Republican Abraham Lincoln to the presidency in November 1860. Carlisle tried to broker a compromise between the sections in his limited capacity as a state legislator, but he also decried any attempt by the federal government to stop any state from seceding. Following the firing by southern radicals on Fort Sumter in South Carolina, which set off the Civil War, Carlisle voted to keep Kentucky neutral. But Carlisle was in a district that backed siding with the Union, and in 1861 these voters defeated him for a second term. Despite this loss, Carlisle remained neutral during the war and saw action with neither the Union nor the Confederacy. Following the end of the war, Carlisle firmly opposed the harsh Reconstruction imposed on the former Confederate states. In 1866, he was elected to a seat in the Kentucky state Senate, and was re-elected in 1869.

In 1867, Democrat John LaRue Helm was elected as the Governor of Kentucky, and, at the same time, Carlisle's close friend John W. Stevenson was elected Lieutenant Governor. Helm, however, was 65 when elected, and the campaign had taken a toll on his already precarious health. Sworn in as the 24th Governor of Kentucky on 3 September 1867, Helm died five days later. Stevenson succeeded him, but served for the entire term without a Lieutenant Governor. In 1871, however, when Stevenson ran for a second term, the Democrats in Kentucky nominated Carlisle as his running mate. With that party in control of the state's political machinery, such a nomination was in effect an election victory. Carlisle served until 1875. In 1872, while sitting as Lieutenant Governor, Carlisle served as the editor of the Louisville *Daily Ledger*.

Early Years in Congress
In 1876, after he left office, Carlisle was nominated for a seat in the U.S. House of Representatives, representing Kentucky's Sixth Congressional district. Carlisle ran on a platform of having silver serve as the financial support of the nation's currency; however, the main issue in the South was Reconstruction, which was wildly unpopular. The Democrats

had won control of the House in 1874; in 1876 the party lost 27 seats but retained the majority.

Carlisle served from the Forty-fifth through the Fifty-first Congresses, from 4 March 1877 until he resigned on 26 May 1890. In his first term in the House, Carlisle sided with the silver wing of the Democratic Party, supporting the repeal of the Special Payment Resumption Act of 1875 (18 Stat. 296), in which the government would honor the redemption of currency issued by the Union during the Civil War, but not until 1879 and only in gold, and that any paper money for amounts less than $1 would be issued now in silver coinage. Carlisle, and other Democrats, warned that those holding Civil War currency would rush to cash in their money if it were backed in gold rather than silver and that the financial crisis would impact farmers and workers. He also opposed any government land grants for the construction of railroad lines. In the Forty-sixth Congress (1879-81), Carlisle sat on the important Ways and Means Committee, the tax-writing committee of the House, where he called for the reduction in tariffs on imported goods. He also made a number of speeches calling for the repeal of civil rights laws enacted in the wake of the end of the Civil War, orations that earned him great respect among his fellow Democrats. In fact, at the 1880 Democratic National Convention in Cincinnati, Carlisle's name was mentioned as a potential presidential candidate, but he was eventually passed over for General Winfield S. Hancock. In 1884, the Democrats once again passed him over for Grover Cleveland. Historians speculate that the party was loath to nominate a southerner - albeit from a neutral state - for President so soon after the end of the Civil War.

The Democrats lost control of the House for the Forty-seventh Congress (1881-83), but two years later captured 68 seats to regain control of that body. In January 1883, the Congress convened for the second session of the Forty-seventh Congress to debate the tariff bill in front of the Congress that year. The bill came first before the Ways and Means Committee - and, on that committee were four Democrats who were deeply involved in the framing of the debate, including Carlisle, Samuel J. Randall of Pennsylvania, William Ralls Morrison of Illinois, and John Randolph Tucker of Virginia. Carlisle became the leader of the low-tariff wing of his party both on the committee and in the full House, with Randall, his fellow Democrat, demanding higher tariffs. This tariff bill, later dubbed the "Mongrel Tariff," called for the reduction in national tariffs by 1.5%. Those Democrats who supported the bill became known as "Carlisle Democrats." The opposition of the high-tariff Democrats led to a move to limit debate. Carlisle angrily took to the floor. "Such a proposition has never been heard of in the parliamentary history of the country, a proposition to destroy the freedom of debate on a bill to raise revenue." Dudley Chase Haskell, Republican of Kansas, retorted, "Stop your filibustering then." Carlisle answered, "Never under [the] gag rule."

The Vote

The Forty-eighth Congress was set to convene in Washington on 1 December 1883, but the jockeying for votes to elect the next Speaker had begun in the summer of that year. In November, the two leading candidates for the speakership - Carlisle and Randall - actually opened campaign offices in Washington, and Democrats in Congress soon became either "Carlisle men" or "Randall men." The *Washington Post* called the contest "a race for the swiftest." By 30 November, as the members of the new Congress streamed into Washington, D.C., newspapers were reporting that Randall did not have the votes necessary to win, but, if he threw his support behind Samuel S. Cox of New York, Carlisle would be forced out and another candidate selected who could garner a majority of the party's votes in the House. But Randall's forces remained loyal to him, and the day before the vote senior Democrats were admitting that Carlisle had the votes to win on the first ballot. On that first ballot, Carlisle had 106 votes, Randall had 52, and Cox trailed with 30.

Acceptance Speech

With such overwhelming support, far more than his rival Randall, Carlisle was the easy choice for Speaker. Rep. Andrew Curtin, a former Governor of Pennsylvania who now held a House seat, moved that the vote be made unanimous, and Carlisle was declared the Speaker. Escorted to the Speaker's chair, he was sworn in, and he then delivered some comments to the members of the House:

Mr. Chairman and Gentlemen of the Caucus: Your committee had just formally notified me of my unanimous nomination for the office of Speaker of the House of Representatives for the Forty-eighth Congress, and I am here to thank you very briefly and very earnestly for the confidence you have reposed in me. If this had been a mere personal contest between me and either of the three distinguished gentlemen whose names have been mentioned n connection with this nomination I should have had but little hope of success. They are all gentlemen of great ability, long experience and undoubted integrity, and I assure them and their friends that this contest closes so far as I am concerned without the slightest change in the friendly personal relations which have heretofore existed between us. Gentlemen, I trust that you may never have reason to regret your action this evening, and that when the labors of the Forty-eighth Congress are closed you may be able to congratulate yourselves that no material interest of your party or your country has been injuriously affected by my administration of the office for which you have nominated me. In fact I may go a step further and venture to express the confident hope that every substantial interest will be advanced and promoted by the united efforts of the presiding officer and the Democratic majority on the floor. Such a result will insure victory in the great contests yet to come and guarantee a long line of Democratic Executives, with an honest, economical and Constitutional administration of our public affairs. But, sir, you have yet much other labor to perform, and again thanking you for what you have already done, I shall say no more.

William Henry Smith, an historian of the Speakers of the House, wrote of him, "Mr. Carlisle's knowledge of parliamentary law was extensive and he was able to sustain precedents any of his rulings which were disputed. He was suave, courteous, and kindly to all, especially to new members. He has a right to be classed among the great Speakers. He was always dignified and patient." When the House opened its business on 3 December, Carlisle told the House, "The maintenance of order on the floor is essential - absolutely essential - to the intelligent and systematic transaction of public business, and I earnestly invoke your assistance in the enforcement of the rules adopted for the government of our proceedings."

Legacy as Speaker

Serving as both the Speaker and the chairman of the Committee on Rules in the Forty-eighth, Forty-ninth (1885-87) and Fiftieth (1887-89) Congresses, Carlisle was considered one of the better speakers of the period. As Speaker, he continued to support tariff reduction. In an 1884 work titled *Our Unjust Tariff Law. A Plain Statement about High Taxes,* Carlisle wrote a letter to the author that was included in the preface, in which he explained, "The question of revenue reform is now engaging the earnest attention of the people in every part of the country, and it is evident that the agitation must go on until the inequalities of or present system of taxation shall be removed, and the taxing power of the government restricted to its legitimate purposes." However, at the same time that he was calling for tariff reduction, Carlisle was also blocking any attempts at tax reform, which would lead to a lowering of taxes and increased growth in the economy. And while he was backed by President Cleveland in his attempts, he was blocked by Randall and the protectionist wing of the party that merged with Republicans who supported high tariffs.

In December 1887, Cleveland devoted his entire annual message - today delivered by the President as his State of the Union address - to the lowering of tariff rates as well as other matters to stimulate the economy. Working closely with fellow Democrat Roger Quarles Mills of Texas, Carlisle got the House to pass the Mills Bill in February 1888, a piece of legislation that authorized the Secretary of the Treasury to purchase bonds that were not yet due in order to reduce the massive surplus that had accumulated in the federal treasury and threatened the national economy. At the same time, Mills also introduced a bill to reduce the tariff. During the debate on the House floor, Carlisle followed Rep. Thomas B. Reed, Republican of Maine and the Minority Leader. Carlisle said,

> Although the question now presented is purely a practical one, it necessarily involves, to some extent, a discussion of the conflicting theories of taxation which have divided the people of this country ever since the organization of the Gov-

> ernment...The opposition to the bill has been directed mainly against that part of it which proposes to repeal or reduce the tax upon certain classes of imported goods; and, gentlemen, speaking for the interests which have long ago been relieved of all the burdens imposed on their industries, earnestly protest that the consumers of their products shall have no relief, or at least that they shall not have the full measure of relief contemplated by this bill.

In the 1888 election, Cleveland was narrowly defeated by Republican Benjamin Harrison, and the Democrats lost control of Congress as well, although Carlisle did hold his own seat. Following the electoral loss, President Cleveland summoned for Speaker Carlisle. George F. Parker, an historian of the Cleveland administration, explained, "When preparing his last annual message for the meeting of Congress in December 1888, he sent for the Speaker of the House, Mr. Carlisle, to consult with him concerning his attitude upon the tariff question. Mr. Carlisle told me, in 1890, that in opening the conversation the President said by way of preface: 'I have asked you to call and see me, Mr. Speaker, in order that I may get your views about that portion of my message which deals with the tariff question. You know that I have always been willing and anxious to consult the wishes of the leaders of my party on every public question; that I have tried to show that deference to their desires that their position demanded, and so far as it was consonant with the interest of the country, but I want to tell you now that if every other man in the country abandons this issue I shall stick to it.'" Carlisle also served as Minority Leader in the Fifty-first Congress (1889-91).

After Leaving the Speakership

On 26 May 1890, he resigned his House seat when he was named by Governor Simon Bolivar Buckner of Kentucky to fill the remainder of the term of Senator James Burnie Beck, who had died in office. Carlisle held the seat until his resignation on 4 February 1893. On 27 December 1891, the *Washington Post* published an interview with Carlisle and reporter Frank G. Carpenter, in which Carlisle was asked about his views of the speakership and how he conducted business during his tenure as Speaker. "When I was Speaker I tried to be fair and impartial in my decisions and I regarded my office as that of a judge rather than that of a politician," he told the newspaper. "This is, in my judgment, the true position of a Speaker. If I though the leaders of my party were at all in the wrong on questions of order, I decided against them, but if it was a matter of equal right, I of course gave the preference to the Democrats." Asked about his successor as Speaker, Charles Crisp, he noted, "Mr. Crisp is a cool, cautious, self-reliant, and able man. He never loses his temper and he had undoubted executive ability. I was in favor of Mr. Mills' election because he was a conspicuous representative of the Democratic party on tariff reform, and because his utterances during the last campaign were in accord with the attitude I think the party ought to take upon that subject during the coming Presidential campaign."

In his short stay of nearly three years in the U.S. Senate, Carlisle angrily denounced attempts by House Republicans to enact higher tariffs under the McKinley Tariff. In 1892, some Democrats desired to nominate Carlisle for President, but he asked that his name not be considered. Former President Cleveland was re-nominated, and, in a re-run of the 1888 campaign with a different ending, was elected over Harrison, the first time that a former President was re-elected to a nonconsecutive term. It is believed that when Carlisle asked not to be nominated for President that Cleveland would offer him a cabinet position if elected. After the election, Cleveland offered Carlisle the Treasury portfolio after Charles S. Fairchild, his Secretary of the Treasury in his first term, declined the offer. Nominated by Cleveland on 6 March 1893, Carlisle was approved by the Senate that same day and took office as the 41st Secretary of the Treasury.

During his tenure as Treasury Secretary, which lasted until the end of Cleveland's second term on 4 March 1897, Carlisle was forced to deal with the financial Panic of 1893, which came about due to a run on gold supplies in the United States. Carlisle ended the minting of silver coinage to stop the run. While this was unpopular in the farming community that was the backbone of the Democratic Party, Carlisle's opposition to the Wilson-Gorman Tariff Act of 1894, which imposed a 2% direct income tax on incomes over $3,000 per year, was denounced by those who saw him as protecting the rich over the poor. In 1895, in *Pollock v. Farmers' Loan and Trust Company* (157 US 429), the U.S. Supreme Court voided portions of the act, thus declaring that a federal income tax was unconstitutional. In an attempt to end the debate over gold vs. silver, Carlisle - with Cleveland's backing - pushed Congress to repeal the Sherman Silver Purchase Act of 1890. Although Congress eventually went along and rescinded the act, the move by Carlisle split the Democrats nationwide into gold and silver wings. However, the repeal of the act did not help the economy, and the McKinley Tariff Act exacerbated the already precarious import situation. The Democrats lost control of the House in 1894, and, in 1896, the party split in half over the monetary issue. Carlisle was pushed by the "Gold Democrat" wing to run for President, but he refused. Instead, a majority of the party nominated "Silver Democrat" William Jennings Bryan, and Carlisle left the party to support the "Gold Democrat" ticket of John McAuley Palmer for President and Carlisle's fellow Kentuckian Simon Bolivar Buckner for Vice President. The economy was the only issue of the campaign; during a speech in his hometown of Covington, Kentucky, Carlisle was pelted with rotten eggs by those who blamed him for the financial meltdown. The Gold Democratic ticket received only 134,000 votes, or 1% of the total cast. Ironically, Republican William McKinley, whose tariff bill helped to trigger the 1893 panic, was elected President over Bryan. The Gold Democrats ran in the 1900 campaign - again against Bryan - but received few votes and had little influence in the nation as a whole. Following the 1900 contest, the "Gold Democrats" either folded back into the Democratic Party or joined the Populist Party or even the Republican Party.

Carlisle left office in March 1897, but he continued to lend his name to the political debate in the nation. He penned an article for *Harper's Magazine* that appeared in an 1899 work, ironically by his former political opponent William Jennings Bryan, on "The Philippine Question," which discussed the U.S. invasion of that island nation during the Spanish-American War and our attempts to subdue an uprising against American rule. Carlisle explained, "Whether we shall enter upon a career of conquest and annexation in the islands of the seas adjacent to our shores and in distant parts of the world, or adhere to the peaceful continental policy which had heretofore characterized our national discourse, is by far the most important question yet presented for the consideration of our people in connection with the existing war with Spain."

Unpopular at home and in his own party, Carlisle settled in New York City, where he practiced law. In normal times he would be considered an elder statesman of his party, but few Democrats bothered with him. Carlisle was in New York when he fell ill while at the Hotel Wolcott. When his condition deteriorated, his family came to his side, and they were there when he died at 11 p.m. on 31 July 1910. He was 75 years old. His body was moved to Washington, D.C., where he retained a residence to be able to argue cases before the Supreme Court; afterwards his remains were taken home to Covington, Kentucky, where he was buried in the family plot in Linden Grove Cemetery.

Despite being completely forgotten today despite his extensive government service in both the legislative and executive branches, John Griffin Carlisle remains one of the most important politicians in the country during the last quarter of the nineteenth century. In the House, as he rose to a leadership position, and as Speaker, Carlisle was widely respected on both sides of the aisle. Rep. Abram Hewitt of New York said of him, "He is an intellectual slot machine. Drop a problem in and instantly, its solutions comes [sic] forth." President Cleveland, upon selecting him to serve in his cabinet, wrote of Carlisle,

> I believe that this is not only the very best selection that could be made for this office at such a vital time, but in this one instance I am willing to look ahead. You know me well enough to know that I care nothing for the perpetuation of personal power and do not often think of it; but our party has just come back with a striking victory, as the result of which to ought to maintain its hold for many years to come. It cannot do this if it enters upon its new duties in a haphazard sort of way. So, in thinking the matter over, I have reached the conclusion that it would be a wonderful thing if we could look forward to Mr. Carlisle as [a] successor to the Presidency in the term to follow mine. I realize how dangerous this is, and that both history and precedent are against its success, but as I look

at it now it seems to be a thing that ought to be kept in mind.

Further Reading:

Barnes, James, *John G. Carlisle, Financial Statesman* (New York: Dodd, Mead & Company, 1931; reprint, Gloucester, Massachusetts: Peter Smith, 1967).

Smith, William Henry, *Speakers of the House of Representatives of the United States with Personal Sketches of the Several Speakers* (Baltimore, Maryland: Simon J. Gaeng, 1928), 215-19.

Thomas Brackett Reed, Jr.

Served as Speaker:
December 4, 1889 - March 4, 1891
December 2, 1895 - March 4, 1899

The earliest biographer of Thomas Reed, Samuel McCall, wrote in 1914, just 12 years after the former Speaker's death, "Reed was the most powerful figure in either House of Congress during his time, or at least after he had opportunity to establish himself as he did in the first few years of service; and his contribution to the settlement of every great issue before the country was influential in a high degree." Known as "Czar" Reed for his almost mythical and powerful control over the House of Representatives during his service as Speaker (1889-91, 1895-99), he became one of its most experienced parliamentarians, writing the definitive works on the rule of legislative bodies in 1894, simply known as *Reed's Rules: A Manual of General Parliamentary Law.* His twelve terms in the House, including three as Speaker, came during some of the most momentous years in the period before the turn of the twentieth century. Despite his great power, his opposition to the Spanish-American War (1898) put an end to his career.

Personal History

Born in Portland, Maine, on 18 October 1839, Reed was the son of Thomas Brackett Reed, Sr., a fisher-

man, and his wife Mathilda Prince (née Mitchell) Reed. Reed became fascinated by his genealogy during his own life; when he heard a rumor that one of his great-grandmothers had lived to be 113 years old, he spent hours looking for confirmation of the report. In a letter from 1883 in which he referred to another great-grandmother, Lydia Ware Reed, he wrote, "I discovered that she lived in Eliot - but died in the prime of life at ninety-eight. I found that she was the great-granddaughter of Peter Ware, known as a stout citizen of York in the days when the Indians made the blockhouses much sought after by the judicious." In fact, he was descended directly from Sir Thomas and Mary Cornwall Reade of Hertfordshire; their son, Thomas Reade, came to America in 1630 with Governor John Winthrop (1587/8-1649) - the founder of the Massachusetts Colony who would be the ancestor of another Speaker of the House, Robert Charles Winthrop - purchased land in what is now Salem, Massachusetts, and became a prosperous land owner. His son changed the name to Reed, and subsequent generations kept the new spelling. Mathilda Mitchell, the second wife of Thomas Reed, Sr., was descended from Experience Mitchell, who landed at Plymouth in 1623 and married one of the women who sailed on the Mayflower. Thus, Thomas B. Reed, Jr. came from a distinguished line of ancestors with close ties to the foundation of the United States.

Reed received his early education in the local schools of Portland, Maine, including the Boys' High School. He entered Bowdoin College, in the coastal Maine village of Brunswick, and graduated in 1860, serving as a teacher and editing the college newspaper during his collegiate years to pay his bills. After graduation, he remained as a teacher, but after a year he tired of Maine and headed west, settling in California, where he taught and studied the law. He returned to Portland in 1863 where he joined the U.S. Navy in the midst of the Civil War to serve as an assistant paymaster on several ships that were on the Tennessee and Mississippi Rivers. After 18 months, he was discharged and returned to Maine, where he was admitted to the state bar. He opened a law practice in Portland and, in 1870, married a widow, Susan Jones, with whom he had two children.

In 1867, when he was just 28, Reed entered the political arena when he was elected as a Republican to the Maine state legislature. He was re-elected in 1868 but the following year ran for a seat in the state Senate. In 1870, he was elected as state Attorney General. He only served a single term in this office, and when he was refused renomination he returned to Portland, where he was named as the city solicitor (some sources call the office the city attorney), where he remained until 1877. In 1876, when Rep. James G. Blaine, who had served as Speaker of the House (1869-75), was elected to the U.S. Senate, his House seat became vacant and Reed was nominated as the Republican candidate to fill it. Reed was easily elected in a staunchly Republican state, and he took his seat in the Forty-fifth Congress (1877-79). Reed would eventually serve twelve consecutive terms until he resigned during the Fifty-sixth Congress (1897-99).

Early Years in Congress
As soon as he took his seat, Reed was named to the Potter Commission, established to examine the 1876 presidential election in which Democrat Samuel Tilden and his supporters believed that they had been cheated out of the presidency. Chaired by Rep.

Clarkson Nott Potter, Democrat of New York, the eleven-member commission instead uncovered a number of telegrams from the Tilden campaign to state election officials around the country that offered bribes to swing states from the Republican, Rutherford B. Hayes, to Tilden. The Potter Commission concluded that Hayes had not influenced the election in any way, and that Tilden had no idea that his supporters were using illegal means to win him the presidency. Reed personally questioned Tilden, and his skills at examining the witness earned him great respect from his colleagues. In the Forty-seventh Congress (1881-83), Reed was elevated to the chairmanship of the House Judiciary Committee; he also served as the chairman of the House Rules Committee in the Fifty-first, Fifty-fourth, and Fifty-fifth Congresses (1889-91, 1895-99), as well as sitting as a member of the Ways and Means Committee, the powerful tax-writing committee in the House. Democrats in Maine lambasted Reed for his challenges to Tilden as a member of the Potter Commission, but he nevertheless was able to win narrow victories for re-election in 1878 and 1880.

With the start of the Forty-ninth Congress (1885-87), when Democrats held a 182-141 majority in the U.S. House, Reed was the Republican candidate for Speaker of the House, which went to Rep. John G. Carlisle of Kentucky, 178 votes to 138. Now having risen to be the leader of his party in the House, Reed remained in this position until he retired from Congress 14 years later, whether the Republicans were in the majority or the minority. During this period, Reed was a loyal Republican, supporting the gold standard and even backing President Grover Cleveland's attempts to repeal the Silver Purchase Act of 1890. When Democrats in the House tried to enact measures that would deny blacks in the South the right to vote, he argued strenuously against them. He supported restrictions on immigration and protective tariffs. But his most important work came because of the House's arcane rules system. Under the rules, the minority could place a near veto on all legislation unless those times when the majority had an overwhelming number of votes for any one bill. Despite being in the minority during his first years in the House, Reed realized that this system allowed a near blockage of all work in the body. Writing in the *Century*

Magazine in March 1887, Reed argued that a firm hand, preferably from the Speaker, was needed to reign in the House and bring order and organization to the body after years of near anarchy and an inability to enact needed legislation:

> The system of avoiding action on important measures by means of these clogging rules has done much to demoralize the House...No man or set of men can often indulge in indirections without acquiring timid habits. Whether the House has timid habits or not it is not proper to say, for I have no desire to draw a railing indictment against so respectable a body. But there are times just prior to elections when the House seems to be but little inspired by the example of the Spartans at Thermopylae. Not only does courage seem to fail, but the sense of responsibility also. If the minority can dictate, the majority have no longer the responsibility for action, and become infirm of purpose.

The Vote

In 1888, the Republicans won 27 seats in the House and control of that body that they had not held since the 47th Congress (1881-83). It appeared that with Reed as the leader of the party, he was a shoe-in to be the next Speaker of the House. However, many Republicans desired Rep. William McKinley of Ohio to fill that office because he came from a key electoral state that had swung the 1888 election to the GOP and helped to win them back not only the House but the presidency as well. However, the party only held a twelve-seat majority, and any split could allow the minority Democrats to hold together and elect a minority Speaker. Arguing that he had led the party during its minority years, Reed's supporters, including Henry Cabot Lodge of Massachusetts, held a majority of the party's votes. On the first ballot in the Republican caucus to select their party candidate, Reed received 78 votes, or six short of a majority. On the second ballot he received 85 votes, or one more than was needed for election as party leader. On 2 December 1889, the full House validated the election of Reed as Speaker of the House, 166 votes to 154 for former Speaker Carlisle.

In hindsight, Reed's election to the speakership should come as no surprise, first because of his leadership of the party when it was in the minority, and second because McKinley did not have a firm hold on the members who backed his short-lived candidacy. Historian DeAlva Stanwood Alexander wrote in 1916 that,

> [M]en had already recognized him as a preeminently able leader, with Disraeli's gift for the pungent epigram, the vivid repartee and the rattling attack, and while he lacked the tact and perhaps the wisdom of Clay, evidenced by the disclosure of prejudices and provincial narrowness, he left the Chair a legacy of power which bunglers could easily misuse and make popular.

Ironically, had McKinley won the speakership, he would not have been elected President in 1896 and would not have been assassinated five years later.

Legacy as Speaker

As Speaker, Reed wielded terrific power - to name his members to specific committees, to dole out patronage, and the power of the control over legislation. But he found himself stymied by the same archaic rules that he had written about in 1887. In an article published in the *North American Review* in October 1889, Reed railed against "obstruction in the National House" by Democrats who refused to vote "present" that would allow a floor vote on needed legislation, a tactic employed by Republicans when they were in the minority. Pointing to the British House of Commons as a model that had instituted new rules which cut off debate from the minority trying to hold up needed legislation, Reed called for reform in the U.S. House. "What is a legislative body for?" he asked. "It is not merely to make laws. It is to decide on all questions of public grievance, to determine between the different views entertained by men of diverse interests, and to reconcile them both with justice. It must in some form hear the people." Unable to gather enough votes to pass needed legislation, Reed desired to do away with such rules as the use of repeated motions to adjourn the Congress to stop a vote on final passage of legislation. "Rules should not be barriers; they should be guides," he wrote.

Almost from the start of his speakership, Reed was faced with the Democrats blocking his operation of the House. The Democrats would announce that there was an absence of a quorum, or a necessary number of representatives in the House to allow for any business to go forward, and demand a roll call. But the rules allowed any member who did not answer the roll call to be considered not being present. Reed finally went to the Speaker's chair and ordered the clerk to list as "present" those members in the House, even if they did not answer when their name was called. When Reed first did this, those Democrats whose names were called rushed to the lectern to denounce the Speaker. There are few sources on all of those who were involved in this disagreement, but all agree that the first was Rep. James Bennett McCreary (1838-1918), Democrat of Kentucky. McCreary rushed to the Speaker's chair and said that Reed did not have the right, under the House's rules, to call him as present. Reed replied, "The Chair is making a statement of the fact that the gentleman from Kentucky is present. Does he deny it?" Another member, not identified, said to Reed, "You are a tyrant to rule over this House or the members of this House in any such way, and I denounce you as the worst tyrant that ever presided over a deliberative body." In another argument, Reed allowed the insults to be thrown at him for a full half hour before he stepped in and denigrated those speakers with his own argument:

> The House will not allow itself to be deceived by epithets. The facts which have transpired during the last few days have transpired in the presence of this House and of a very large auditory. No man can describe the action and judgment of the Chair in language which will endure unless that description be true...A man much more famous than any in this hall said, many years ago, that nobody could write him down but himself. Nobody can talk any member of this House down except himself. Whatever is done in the face of the world and is subject to its discriminating judgment. The proceedings of the House, so far as the Chair is concerned, have been orderly, suitable, in conformity to the rules of parliamentary laws, and the refusal of the Chair to entertain the motion to adjourn at this juncture is strictly in accordance therewith.

The Democrats tried every tactic to deny Reed the ability to conduct business, even hiding under desks and behind screens, before finally leaving the House

and boycotting all votes until Reed relented. He refused. In fact, as he later explained, if the Democrats had beaten him he would have resigned immediately. The new rule was used to great effect by the Republican majority. One unnamed Democrat, writing in the *North American Review* in 1890 under the *nom de plume* "X.M.C.," stated,

> The Speaker's success won great applause from his fellow-partisans in the House and in the country, as was entirely natural. But the correctness of his decision has not yet been demonstrated; and I venture the opinion that the ultimate and impartial judgment, both Parliamentary and popular, will be that, while the Speaker's design is praiseworthy, his method of carrying it into effect not only reverses all the safe precedents of the House, but violated the spirit and the letter of the Constitution of the United States.

Another unnamed Democrat, using the name "Judex," explained to readers of the same journal that while Democrats in the minority had their power lessened by Reed's new rule, when they would return the majority they could use it to their own advantage to stop Republican stoppage of Democratic legislation:

> The quorum should be counted by the House, and not by the clerk or by the Speaker...When it is apparent that a quorum is actually present, while less than a quorum has voted, it is entirely competent and proper for the House to direct that the members who abstain from voting should be placed at the bat, and that in the presence of the whole House their attendance be noted and they themselves counted as of the quorum.

Using the power of the majority, on strict party line votes Reed enacted the new rules that counted members based on their presence in the House. He also relaxed the rules in committees to allow them to work on legislation without interference from the minority, including the Rules Committee, which he chaired while serving as Speaker. Working in a triad with William McKinley, the chairman of the Ways and Means Committee, and Rep. Joseph Cannon, Republican of Illinois and the chairman of the House Appropriations Committee, he worked on what he called "legislation such as they [the American people] need." Thus, the Fifty-first Congress is called "The Billion Dollar Congress," as it enacted spending bills which totaled nearly $1 billion for the first time in the nation's history. The Congress also enacted a series of legislative edicts, including the Sherman Anti-Trust Act, the McKinley Tariff, a better system of pensions for military veterans and their relations, the establishment of the federal appeals court system, and increased rights for blacks in the South (this latter reform was killed in the Senate).

Democrats Control the House

In 1890 the Democrats won 86 seats and control of the House, and elected Charles Crisp of Georgia as Speaker in the Fifty-second Congress (1891-93). When the new Speaker refused to adhere to the rules that Reed had put into place to protect the majority, Reed showed them by instructing the minority Republicans to use the old rules to stymie any legislation that Democrats wanted to pass, including using the so-called "disappearing quorum" to avoid allowing any votes. Finally, after being obstructed by these old rules that they had defended most vociferously, the Democrats finally allowed Speaker Crisp to change them back to how Reed had instituted them when he was Speaker. Rep. James Beauchamp "Champ" Clark, later to serve as Speaker himself, called Reed "that masterful man" who "was far and away the most brilliant figure in American politics. He did much to bring order out of chaos and to expedite the transaction of business, and for this [he] deserves well." Reed later wrote of the Congress in which Crisp succeeded him as Speaker:

> When the House of Representatives of the Fifty-second Congress met, it met as a mob, and had kept up that interesting form of organization ever since. Of course, the Republican leaders could have driven the enemy into compact shape, covered them with reproaches, forced them to train, and otherwise have made an army of them. Then there would have been much glory won by the said leaders among the unthinking, but the exhibition would have been lost to the world of Democracy, as it really is a hopeless assortment of discordant differences, as

incapable of positive action as it is capable of infinite clamor.

Reed demanded that Congress take up additional reforms. In an article in the national magazine the *North American Review*, in May 1890, he explained:

> If the recent changes in the rules and practice of the House of Representatives were matters of mere party triumph or party policy, there would be little occasion ever again to mention the subject; for the acquiescence which has followed the full expression of public opinion would last through this Congress without other sanction. But the changes have been so beneficial that they ought not to be subject to any suspicion of being open to the charges of partisanship, of unfairness, or of destroying the liberty of the individual member.

Re-elected as Speaker

A financial depression in 1894 led to a landslide against the Democrats, with the Republicans winning 130 seats and control of the House in the Fifty-fourth Congress (1895-97). Despite the fact that Reed had overseen the loss of the majority in 1890, the Republicans in the House rewarded him with the speakership once again when the House convened on 2 December 1895, 240 votes to 95 for Crisp. Speaking to the House that had elected him Speaker for the second time, he said that it was very agreeable for him,

> To stand once more in...the place which I left four years ago...Nor shall I now speak of the future, for we are not now putting off the harness but putting it on. Yet I think I may venture to say of the future, in the light of the past, that if we do some things which for the moment seem inadequate, it may be that time, which has justified of us on many occasions, may do so again.

During this tenure as Speaker, Reed compiled his many rulings as Speaker - as well as those of previous speakers - into a volume titled, *Reed's Rules: A Manual of General Parliamentary Law*. In the preface, he explained the need for such a work:

> The object of this book is to present the rules of general parliamentary law in such a way that the system can be comprehended by persons

who may be called upon to preside over meetings of deliberative bodies, and by those who may desire to participate in the proceedings. The aim has been to so explain each notion that it may be understood by itself and also in its relations to other motion.

Since its initial publication in 1894, *Reed's Rules* has become a standard reference work for those making parliamentary decisions, and is still in use in the United States and around the world more than a century later.

With Democrat Grover Cleveland in the White House and a financial meltdown hitting in the nation's economy, the Republicans saw their chance to enact legislation as the key to winning the presidency in 1896. But the White House and the Congress were at loggerheads on many issues except for a few that Reed realized he could get passed. During this Congress, the most important foreign policy issue was that of the Venezuela Boundary. With Britain involved in the formation of the boundaries of that South American nation, President Cleveland called for the dispute to be decided by arbitration, which Britain refused. The President then sent a message to Congress in which he called British involvement in the area a violation of the Monroe Doctrine, and that "it is difficult to see why to that extent such European power does not thereby attempt to extend its system of government to that portion of the continent which is thus taken. This is precise action which President Monroe declared to be 'dangerous to our peace and safety.'" Almost warlike in tone, the resolution to back the President and demand arbitration was sent by Reed to the Committee on Foreign Affairs, which passed it out to the whole House, which then passed it without opposition. The nation appeared to be on the verge of war with England, but in the end the British accepted the arbitration demand and the controversy was diffused.

As the election of 1896 approached, Reed held himself out as a candidate for the Republican presidential nomination. But party leaders passed him over for his former rival for the speakership, William McKinley of Ohio, who was placed at the head of the ticket. Reed hoped to get second place with McKinley, but that slot went to Garrett Hobart of New Jersey. In 1896, the Republicans won control

of the White House and both houses of Congress, and Reed was once again elected as Speaker. Now with a Republican in the White House who would sign legislation he backed, Reed helped to move on the president's legislative priorities. One of these was the Tariff of 1897, sponsored by Rep. Nelson Dingley, Republican of Maine and the chairman of the House Ways & Means Committee, which became the highest protective tariff enacted in America up until that time, despite Republican opposition to it.

Reed remained a staunch supporter of President McKinley for the first year of the president's administration, but he parted ways with the president when the Spanish-American War broke out in 1898. Reed opposed the war, decrying any attempt to get involved in freeing the Cuban people from the yoke of Spanish oppression. But to avoid having a showdown with the president from his own party, Reed voted for the war. On 15 June 1898, the House voted 209 to 91 to approve Senate Joint Resolution 55, which provided for the annexation of Hawaii as an American territory. Reed had joined with Democrats and so-called "anti-imperialist" Republicans to block a vote on the resolution from even being debated on the House floor for nearly a month, but he was eventually forced by his fellow Republicans to allow a vote. Reed voted against the measure; his power as Speaker, however, was at an end. He was re-elected in 1898, but before the Fifty-sixth Congress could convene - when he would again be elected Speaker because he still was the Republican leader with barely any opposition to his holding of that position - he announced his resignation. Reed wrote to his old friend Asher C. Hinds, "I have tried, perhaps not always successfully, to make the acts of my public life accord with my conscience, and I cannot now do this thing." He publicly gave the reason that he needed to go into private business to make a living, but people who knew him saw that he could not continue in Congress supporting a war that he disagreed with.

After Leaving the Speakership
Moving to New York City, Reed became a member of the law firm of Simpson, Thatcher, and Barnum; at the same time, he wrote articles for numerous periodicals, including the *North American Review* and the *Century*, among others. On 29 November 1902,

he visited Washington, D.C. to conduct some legal business before the Supreme Court and to visit old friends in the House. There, he complained of feeling ill. It was discovered that he had Bright's Disease, a failure of the kidneys. Taken to a hospital, he labored for several days, until 7 December, when he succumbed to his illness at the age of 63. Reed died on the same day as the famed 19th century cartoonist Thomas Nast, so he had to "share" the honors and memories of the nation with Nast. Reed's body was returned to his native Maine, and he was buried in the Evergreen Cemetery in Portland. John Sharp Williams, who had served as the Democratic leader in the House when Reed was Speaker, referred to Reed as "that ever memorable genius, the ablest running debater the American people ever saw." In 1911, a statue was unveiled at Portland, Maine, in honor of Reed. Rep. Samuel Walker McCall, Republican of Massachusetts, spoke at the unveiling:

> But beyond his brilliance as a debater, his resplendent wit and his skill as a parliamentary leader, his title to remembrance rests upon his quality as a statesman...He had a great ambition, but it was not great enough to lead him to surrender any principle of government which he deemed vital. Like Webster, like Clay, and others of our most conspicuous statesmen, he was disappointed at not reaching the Presidency, but he could fitly aspire to the office, for he was of the fiber and nurture of which great Presidents are made.

Thomas B. Reed was known for his skill at parliamentary debate and rules, and he led the House with an iron hand with bitter wit. In one story which was remembered in all of the works about him, he listened to a speech on the floor of the House by Rep. William McKendree Springer (1836-1903), Democrat of Illinois, who remarked, "I would rather be right than be President," to which Reed interjected, referring to Springer as the denoted spokesman in the debate, "Mr. Speaker, don't let that worry you; you will never be either."

Further Reading:
McCall, Samuel Walker, *The Life of Thomas Brackett Reed* (Boston: Houghton Mifflin Company, 1914).

Offenberg, Richard Stanley, "The Political Career of Thomas Brackett Reed" (Ph.D. dissertation, New York University, 1963).

Tuchman, Barbara W., "Czar of the House," *American Heritage*, XIV:1 (December 1962), 32-35, 92-102.

Charles Frederick Crisp

Served as Speaker:
December 8, 1891 - March 4, 1895

espite the fact that America is the land of immigrants, it is strange that only two of the more than 50 persons who have served as Speaker of the U.S. House of Representatives were not born in the United States. While Frederick A.C. Muhlenberg, the first Speaker, was of German heritage, he was born in Pennsylvania. It is Charles F. Crisp, the Speaker for the Fifty-second and Fifty-third Congresses (1891-95), who is one of those two - the other is David Bremner Henderson, born in Scotland. A Civil War veteran, who was a longtime Georgia politician, Crisp was deeply involved in political matters and several controversies as Speaker.

Personal History

He was born in Sheffield, England, on 29 January 1845, the son of William Crisp and his wife Eliza. Both were English-born but naturalized American citizens, and at the time of their son's birth were visiting their native land. The Crisps were Shakespearean actors on the stage, and had spent the years before Charles' birth touring the United States. William Crisp returned to the United States sometime in 1845 on business matters, leaving his wife and infant son behind in England until the child was nine

months old. When the family returned as a whole to their new homeland, the touring continued until at least 1853 or 1854. For the sake of his son, who had spent his entire life on the road, or perhaps to find a degree of normalcy in their lives, the family settled in Georgia, where William Crisp became the manager of a theater in Savannah. Here, Charles Crisp received his earliest semblance of an education. In 1857, William Crisp transferred to the city of Macon, Georgia, and it was there that his son completed his schooling. Although Charles Crisp did some early acting in the theater, he did not follow in his parents' footsteps on the stage, although his brother William and sisters Cecilia and Jessica did.

Charles Crisp's life changed in 1861, when he was just 16 and the Civil War exploded over the issue of slavery and states' rights. Crisp and his brother Harry enlisted in the Confederate army, with Charles Crisp starting off as a 4th Corporal in Company K, known as the "Page Volunteers," of the 10th Virginia Infantry. He eventually rose to the rank of lieutenant (historian William Henry Smith reports that the rank was First Lieutenant) in Company K, of the 1oth Regiment of the Virginia Infantry, before he was captured on 12 May 1864 during the battle of the Wilderness and sent to Fort Delaware, located on Pea Patch Island in the Delaware River in Delaware. Crisp remained a prisoner until the South capitulated and the war ended. Released in June 1865, he returned home to Georgia, settling in the town of Ellaville in Schley County. He studied the law, and, in 1866, was admitted to the Georgia state bar. He opened a practice in Ellaville, marrying a local girl there in 1867. The couple had four children.

In 1872, Crisp moved his family to Americus, Georgia, after being appointed as Solicitor General for the Southwestern Judicial Circuit of Georgia; he was re-appointed to that position the following year. Four years later, in June 1877, he was named as a Superior Court judge for the same circuit, and elected by the Georgia General Assembly to that position in 1878 and again, for a four-year term, in 1880.

Early Years in Congress

In 1882, Crisp, a southern Democrat, was nominated for a seat in the U.S. Congress, representing the Third Georgia congressional district. Elected, he resigned his judgeship and took his seat in the Forty-eighth Congress (1883-85). Democrats were in control of the House, and John G. Carlisle of Kentucky was the Speaker of that body. Crisp would remain in that seat until his death, serving through to the Fifty-fourth Congress (1895-97). During his time in the House, Crisp served as chairman of the Committee on Elections (Fiftieth Congress) and chairman of the Committee on Rules (Fifty-second and Fifty-third Congresses). Crisp quickly made his name in the House, rising to support passage of the Interstate Commerce Act of 1887, which regulated railroad prices to aid farmers and business, and helping to pass that bill as well as the Sherman Silver Purchase Act of 1890.

The Vote

The Fifty-second Congress convened in Washington on 7 December 1891. The Republicans had been decimated in the 1890 mid-term election, and now the Democrats, who had captured 86 seats in that contest to control the House 238 seats to 86 for the Republicans, would elect the Speaker. This was the first Congress to sit members of a new political element in the nation: the Farmers' Alliance, a radical pro-farming group that had formed their own party and elected one Senator and 2 members of the House in the Fifty-second Congress. The Democrats quickly settled down to the election for Speaker. Among the candidates were Crisp, Roger Q. Mills of Texas, William M. Springer of Illinois, Benton McMillin of Tennessee, William H. Hatch of Missouri, and William D. Bynum of Indiana. The race, however, was between Crisp and Mills, with the balloting going on for the entire first day of the session. Crisp consistently led in votes, but Mills was a close second. Finally, after 29 ballots (some newspapers report 30 ballots), Crisp received 119 votes and the majority to 105 for Mills.

Acceptance Speech

Crisp was conducted from his seat to the Speaker's chair by Rep. Robert Patterson Clark Wilson, Democrat of Missouri, and Rep. Charles Triplett O'Ferrall, Democrat of Virginia, where he was given the oath of office. The new Speaker then addressed the House:

Representatives: Profoundly grateful for this mark of your confidence and esteem, I pledge myself here and now to devote whatever of industry and ability I possess to the advancement of the real interest of the Democratic Party. I beg to say to you now, when I speak the first words to you since I am your selection for Speaker, that my election means no step backward in tariff reform. I desire to say that there is in our party to-day no man who more earnestly believes in the Democratic doctrine of tariff reform than I do. After the long struggle through which we have passed, when Representatives are fatigued, and when other officers are to be nominated, it does not become me to consume your time. I wish to say, however, that during the progress of this canvass I have said no word respecting any individual or individuals which would at all justify him or them in having any feeling of unkindness against me. I have felt that it was a friendly struggle, I have felt that we were all Democrats, and that whatever might be the result of the contest, when this House shall meet and organize we will stand together as one body, working and laboring for the good of the party. I thank you again for your confidence and kindness, and beg to assure you that this whole contest had left in my bosom no unkind feeling toward any member of the House.

Crisp thus became the second Georgian to be elected Speaker - the first was Howell Cobb - and he would be the last from that state until Newt Gingrich was elected Speaker in 1995. In an editorial, the *Hartford Times* in Connecticut stated, "On tariff reform Mr. Crisp is not perhaps so extreme as some others. He is fair, conservative, and reasonable, and the country will have no cause of regret at his elevation to the speakership on account of his course in regard to that important matter. The House has certainly secured a capable and an excellent presiding officer." The *Washington Post* said of him, "He has been eight years in Congress, one of the foremost members of that body in usefulness, ability and leadership, and is an excellent parliamentarian. He is cool-headed and conservative, a safe man to trust with responsibilities, possessed of qualifications that peculiarly fit him for success in the honored and honorable chair that he will take today."

Legacy as Speaker

It appears that it was Crisp, as Speaker, who established the system of having a "floor leader" of his party - now known as either the Majority or Minority Leader - conduct business in place of the Speaker as party leader when he selected Rep. William Wilson of West Virginia as the chairman of the House Ways and Means Committee. James Beauchamp "Champ" Clark, who later rose to become Speaker in 1911, wrote in his memoirs, "As Crisp had no opposition among Democrats for his second term as Speaker, he was hands-free in making up his committee, and promptly appointed William L. Wilson of West Virginia, chairman of Ways and Means, thereby *ipso facto* making him the Democratic floor leader."

Although cast as reasonable, Crisp was wholly unreasonable when it came to the powers of the Speaker. Whereas Crisp had bitterly complained about the powers of his predecessor, Thomas B. Reed, and the refusal of the Republican majority to give any power to the Democratic minority when Crisp was the leader of his party in the minority, as Speaker Crisp quickly reinstated all of the powers

that had been stripped from Reed and in turn relegated the minority Republicans to powerlessness, waving away any protestations that they had. To be sure, these moves did not endear Crisp to the minority, and he was angrily confronted by Reed for his obvious hypocrisy. William Henry Smith, an historian of the speakership, penned that Reed "tormented" Crisp at every opportunity. But Crisp opened himself up to such trouble: He named himself as the chairman of the Committee on Rules, which controlled the legislation that came out of committee and to the floor of the House, and thus controlled the debate on the floor of the House as well as what legislation would be debated and passed. In 1892, the Democrats retained their majority despite losing 20 seats in the House, and Crisp was re-elected Speaker for the Fifty-third Congress (1893-95). His first term as Speaker came when Republican Benjamin Harrison was in the White House; the second came under Democrat Grover Cleveland during Cleveland's second non-consecutive term in the presidency.

The 1893 financial panic that swept the nation, and the blame that the American people put on the administration of President Cleveland as well as the Democrats in the House, led to a landslide for the Republicans in the 1894 mid-term election, with the Democrats losing 130 seats and the majority. When the Fifty-fifth Congress assembled in Washington on 4 March 1895, the House consisted of 254 Republicans, 93 Democrats, and nine Populists. In his memoirs, penned in 1920, future Speaker of the House Champ Clark, who served in the Fifty-fourth Congress, wrote of the despair and depression amongst Democrats who had lost the majority:

> *Ex-Speaker Crisp, having been the Democratic nominee for Speaker, was ipso facto minority leader; but his activities and energies were directed more to securing, over ex-Secretary of the Interior Hoke Smith, the Senatorship [from Georgia] than in performing the functions of the minority leadership. The truth is Crisp was thoroughly disgusted with his position as minority leader. It was a thankless task, and was at its worst in the Fifty-fourth Congress, for the Democrats had just been drubbed out of their boots, having lost everything at the preceding November election. They were sore - awfully*

sore - about everybody and everything, including themselves. Criminations and recriminations were the order of the day. All this so vexed Crisp that once he said to Joseph Weldon Bailey, of Texas, himself destined to the minority leadership: "Nobody can lead this wrangling, quarrelsome, factionalized Democratic minority. I do not intend to return to the House. I am going home to stand for the Senate. If I lose that, I will quit public life forever."

Following the death of Senator Alfred H. Colquitt of Georgia on 26 March 1894, the Governor of Georgia, William J. Northen, a Democrat, offered Crisp an *ad interim* appointment to the U.S. Senate to fill the remaining year of what was Colquitt's second Senate term. Crisp, sitting as Speaker of the House, declined the honor of being just another Senator.

After Leaving the Speakership

In 1896, when Crisp and the Democrats had lost the majority and Crisp was once again Minority Leader, another opportunity opened up for a Senate seat when the other sitting Senator from Georgia, John Brown Gordon, retired after only one term. Crisp declined to run for another term in the House of Representatives and instead announced his campaign for the Senate for a full term of his own. At that time, before the passage of the 17th Amendment to the Constitution, Senators were elected not by the people, as they are today, but by the legislatures of the states. Because the Georgia legislature was controlled entirely by the Democrats, Crisp was a shoo-in to be elected to the seat because he was the leading Democrat from that state in the House of Representatives, and because he had served as that body's speaker. Politics still played a role, however: that year the Democrats in Georgia split between "Gold Democrats" - those who supported the issuance of U.S. currency backed by gold - and "Silver Democrats," who wanted it backed by silver. Crisp was of the latter camp, and he campaigned across Georgia, debating Secretary of the Interior Hoke Smith, a fellow Georgian, over the issue. In the primary vote, Crisp won an overwhelming victory, and the state legislature, which would elect Gordon's replacement, seemed sure to elect Crisp to the U.S. Senate. In early October 1896 the general assembly, the lower house of the Georgia legislature,

was elected with a majority of Democrats, and prepared to meet to elect Crisp to the Senate.

But that honor would never be given. During the rough-and-tumble campaign in the hot summer of 1896, Crisp became seriously ill, and in September he checked into a sanitarium in Atlanta to try and improve his declining health. On 23 October 1896, shortly before the state legislature was set to convene, Crisp suffered what one newspaper merely called "an attack," which may have been a heart attack or a stroke, and died; he was just 51 years old, although in some photographs taken near the end of his life he appeared far older. His body was eventually buried in the Oak Grove Cemetery in Atlanta. His son, Charles Robert Crisp (1870-1937), was appointed by the Governor of Georgia to complete his father's congressional term, which ended in March 1897. He eventually won a seat on his own in 1912, sitting from the Sixty-third (1913-15) to the Seventy-second (1931-33) Congresses.

When Congress met for the first session of the Fifty-fourth Congress, the first meeting since Crisp's passing, memorials were given for this son of England who came to America as a small child and rose to become one of the most powerful politicians in America. Republican David B. Henderson of Iowa, who would serve as Speaker himself in the Fifty-sixth and Fifty-seventh Congresses and who differed with Crisp on many issues, nevertheless rose to reminisce about the deceased Georgian and he delivered remarks in his honor. "My relations with Mr. Crisp have been somewhat singular," Henderson said. "He was the first member of Congress with whom I held heated debate, and I believe I was the last with whom he had debate developing some of the feelings so often incident to our legislative life, but leaving no scar. Our relations always, saving our first experience, were of the most friendly character, and our first sharp encounter taught us, I believe, to respect each other." In an editorial, the *Washington Post* noted, "In the death of Hon. Charles Frederick Crisp, the State of Georgia loses its foremost statesman and the nation one of its most conscientious and useful legislators."

Charles Crisp was a strong southern Democrat who broke with the more conservative wing of his party, where he was situated politically, in supporting the Sherman Act of 1890 and becoming a "Silver Democrat." However, he does not appear to figure too highly in the history of the Grover Cleveland administration - Cleveland biographer Robert McElroy, whose two-volume 1923 work is considered the standard on the presidency of the 22nd and 24th President, does not even mention Crisp at all. Crisp has no articles, or major works done of his life, with the exception being a 1962 dissertation; future Speaker Champ Clark mentions him more than most histories of the period in which Crisp served as Speaker. It is a sad legacy for a man who rose so high in a land he was not even born in.

Further Reading:

Martin, S. Walter, "Charles F. Crisp: Speaker of the House," *Georgia Review*, VIII (Summer 1954), 167-77.

Malone, Preston St. Clair, "The Political Career of Charles Frederick Crisp" (Ph.D. dissertation, University of Georgia, 1962).

David Bremner Henderson

Served as Speaker:
December 4, 1899 - March 4, 1903

Aside from Charles F. Crisp, who was born in the United Kingdom, David B. Henderson is the only other Speaker of the House of Representatives to be foreign born. A Civil War veteran and Republican who served two terms as Speaker, Henderson was one of the most powerful Speakers in the last decade of the nineteenth century, expanding the power of the Speaker to recognize those who wished to speak on the House floor, and the power of the Speaker in the Rules Committee. Despite his two terms as Speaker, and his work to energize the power of that office, he has slipped into almost complete obscurity.

Personal History

The son and youngest of nine children of Thomas and Barbara (née Bremner) Henderson, both Scottish farmers, he was born in the village of Old Deer, in Aberdeenshire, Scotland, on 14 March 1840. Little is known of the family; however, an obituary of David Henderson noted that Thomas Henderson owned three stone houses in Old Deer, and was a poet and singer whose land dispute with the laird, or landed proprietor, of the town forced him and his family to leave the country for America. Although

the exact date of their emigration is unknown, all biographers of Henderson agree that by 1846 the family landed in Chicago with one gold English sovereign to their name, and then moved on to a farm in Rockwood, Winnebago County, Illinois. Three years later, they removed to Iowa, and settled on a farm in Fayette County. Henderson remained on his family's farm until the age of 21, receiving an education in rural Iowa schools. In 1856 he married Augusta Fox. He attended the Upper Iowa University in Fayette (one of Henderson's obituaries in 1906 reported that the school was in the city of Clermont, Iowa), although his time at the school as short, and it appears that he never received a degree from that institution.

The explosion of the Civil War in 1861 changed Henderson's life along with that of his adopted country: on 15 September 1861, he enlisted in the Union Army as a private in Company C of the Twelfth Regiment of the Iowa Volunteer Infantry. He was quickly commissioned as a First Lieutenant, and saw action at Fort Henry, Fort Donelson, and Shiloh; one of Henderson's obituaries states that one of his brothers was killed in the latter clash and was buried in an unmarked grave. On 15 February 1863, Henderson was severely wounded at the battle of Corinth, and, 10 days later, his left foot was amputated and he was discharged from the army. Biographies of Henderson claimed that his entire left leg was taken; however, Champ Clark, who later served as Speaker of the House, wrote in his memoirs that Henderson initially had his left foot, and not a leg, amputated, but that the stump gradually became infected and that the entire leg was later removed. Henderson was given of the position of the Commissioner of the Board of Enrollment for the third district of Iowa, serving from May 1863 until June 1864. Despite the loss of his leg, Henderson desired to serve in the Union army again, and he re-enlisted in June 1864, given the rank of colonel of the 46th Iowa Regiment and serving until the end of the war the following year. Although his highest rank was Colonel, Henderson was known as "General" throughout the remainder of his life.

Returning to Iowa at the end of the conflict, Henderson studied the law in the Dubuque, Iowa office of Bissel & Shiras, and was admitted to the Iowa state bar in 1865. He opened a practice in Dubuque. Shortly thereafter, however, he was appointed by the Governor of Iowa as the Collector of Internal Revenue for the third district of Iowa, serving in this office from November 1865 until June 1869, when he resigned to become a partner in the law firm of Shiras & Van Duzee. Later that year, he was named by President Ulysses S. Grant as the Assistant United States District Attorney for the northeastern district of Iowa, serving for two years until 1871. He then became a partner in the law firm of Henderson, Hurd, Lenehen & Kiesel, and remained with the firm for the remainder of the decade.

Early Years in Congress

In 1882, Henderson, a Republican, ran for a seat in the U.S. House of Representatives and was elected to the Forty-eighth Congress (1883-85). He was re-elected every two years, and served a total of nine terms until the end of the Fifty-seventh Congress (1901-03). During his congressional career, he served as chairman of the Committee on Militia (Fifty-first Congress), chairman of the Committee on the Judiciary (Fifty-fourth and Fifty-fifth Congresses), and the Committee on Rules (Fifty-sixth and Fifty-seventh Congresses). A member of the

Appropriations committee, he supported increased pensions for former Civil War soldiers. During one debate in which he denounced northerners who were part of the antiwar movement during the Civil War, a group known as "Copperheads," Henderson said, "I would rather spend an eternity in hell with a Confederate who tendered his life with his views, than be in heaven forever with a Northern Copperhead." Although he would later rise to become Speaker, Henderson spent nearly his entire congressional career in the shadows; of the biographies that exist of him, none mention any legislation that he supported or helped to get enacted in his first eight terms in Congress. In 1898, Henderson joined several other Republicans, including then-Speaker of the House Thomas B. Reed, in opposing the McKinley administration's move to start a war with Spain. During the debate on whether Congress would authorize the start of war, Henderson stated, "The truest patriot is he who keeps the peace of his people. It is easy to be an animal. It is easy to use claws and teeth and fight. He who can hold aloft in his country the white flag of peace, not of cowardice, comes nearest to his God."

In the 1898 mid-term election, Democrats won 37 seats in the House, but because they held only 124 seats in the Fifty-fifth Congress, it was not enough to capture the majority. Thus, in the Fifty-sixth Congress (1899-1901), the Republicans would control the House.

The Vote

The first session of that Congress did not convene until December 1899, and between the election and that period numerous House leaders jockeyed for support to win the speakership election; among these were Henderson and Thomas Reed, the Speaker in the two previous Congresses when Republicans held the majority. Without doubt, Reed, with his previous experience as Speaker as well as his position of seniority, was to be considered the leading candidate for the position. But in the Republican caucus held on 2 December, Henderson was the overwhelming favorite of the elected members, and won a majority of the Republican votes despite having opposed the war that was quickly won by the United States and was highly popular among the American people. Historian De Alva Stanwood Alexander wrote in 1916 that "to this day it remains an unsolved mystery why his party preferred Henderson for Speaker in 1899" over Reed. With his loss in the speakership race, Reed resigned his seat and left the Congress. Champ Clark, a Democrat and representative from Missouri, explained in his memoirs, "One reason why Colonel Henderson was elected Speaker was his uniform kindness to new members - which is gratefully remembered by many men to this day." Thus, when the House convened on 4 December, Henderson won on the first ballot, 177 votes to 153 votes for Democrat James Richardson of New York. Richardson, along with Rep. John C. Bell, Populist of Colorado, and Francis G. Newlands, "Silver" Democrat of Nevada, were called by the House Clerk to escort Henderson to the Speaker's chair, where he was sworn in.

Acceptance Speech
Turning to the assembled House members, Henderson told them:

> The voice of this House had called me to grave responsibilities. For that call I am most profoundly grateful, and I am keenly sensible of the weight of the responsibilities that attach to this great office. I am encouraged, however, by the thought that no member of this body can escape responsibility, either to his people or to his country. All of us are under bonds to do our best.

> The approval of the country; the approval of one's own conscience; the attainment of great results, are not secured by petty contests on narrow fields, but must be sought and won on broad, patriotic lines of thought and action.

> It is my duty, as it will be my aim and pleasure, to impartially administer the laws adopted for our Government, but no Speaker can be successful unless he had the co-operation of the members of this House.

> The generous partiality and kindness that have been shown to me by the entire membership here encourage me that such imperfections as I may have may be modified by the considerate and supporting disposition of those constituting this great body.

Henderson thus became the first man from west of the Mississippi River to be elected Speaker.

Legacy as Speaker
One of the issues he was forced to deal with almost immediately was the debate over the seating of Rep.-elect Brigham H. Roberts, Democrat of Utah, whose polygamous marriages made him extremely controversial. With Henderson overseeing the debate, Republicans voted along with Democrats to send the election of this man who admitted to marrying several women at once to a committee, which later ruled his election invalid.

Historians of the House tend to ignore the speakership of Henderson, viewing it more as an interregnum between that of Thomas Reed (1889-91, 1895-99) and Joseph Cannon (1903-08) than as a period for serious scholarship. However, a close study of Henderson and his two terms as Speaker show that his was an important period in that office's history, which established several significant precedents that became part of the power of the Speaker and the overall authority of the speakership. Prior to Henderson's tenure, a Speaker allowed anyone who desired to rise and talk about any issue of their choosing to speak on the House floor. Although it was under Speaker Thomas Reed that the Speaker first inquired, "For what purpose does the gentleman rise?" it became used commonly under Henderson. The controversial usage of this question became contested during the Fifty-sixth Congress when Rep. William Sulzer, Democrat of New York, rose to speak. Henderson, presiding in the Speaker's chair, asked the question that had begun to irritate many speakers who had never been forced to divulge the purpose of their remarks prior to their making them. Sulzer told Henderson that he wanted to introduce a resolution expressing sympathy for the Boers, the white farmers of what is now South Africa. Henderson would not allow Sulzer to speak, stating that "the Chair must recognize members upon which the Chair thinks should be considered." Whereas previous Speakers had acknowledged the right of members to appeal the power of the Chair to recognize members, Reed to a smaller extent, and then Henderson to a greater one, removed that power, making the Speaker more powerful in the process. Some historians believe that Henderson's successor as Speaker, Joseph Cannon of Illinois, consolidated power to become one of the most powerful speakers ever, but it was under Reed, and then Henderson, that this power was first established.

Legislation in the House during the nineteenth century was in the control of the chairman of the Committee on Rules and the two top majority members on that committee. Henderson, for the first time, sought to bring that power solely under the discretion of the Speaker, who before the 1910 revolt against Speaker Cannon was the chairman of that committee. While his efforts were met with resistance from his own party, especially those members whose authority would be curtailed, Henderson made the speakership stronger with this consolidation of power. But Henderson realized that there had to be a balance between a Speaker as virtual dictator and one who was too lame to control the House during debate.

He regarded Reed's speakership as being not a "servant" but a "master" of the Congress, and in an interview with Washington correspondent William Wolff Smith said that he wanted to govern with less than "a strong hand." Nonetheless, he remarked that because the House was prepared to "go in the other direction" and rapidly reduce the powers of the Speaker, which would create a House run by its then-350 members, he needed the powers to control the debate through the recognition of speakers and the legislation being introduced. This balance by Henderson is reflected by the comments of historian Donald Kennon, who, is his work of bibliographies of the Speakers, wrote of Henderson that when compared to "the brilliant and often imperious Thomas Brackett Reed, Henderson became known as a popular, though not brilliant, Speaker. Where Reed had ruled the House like a czar, Henderson managed affairs in a straightforward, businesslike manner."

A study of the works available on Henderson show that the opinions of this man - as well as his speakership - seem to differ between contemporary sources and those written long after he had left the House and died. Those written at the time portray him as a good Speaker who helped to officiate over the House with fairness and a lack of partisanship; later works that manage to mention him, with a few exceptions, seem to miss entirely his speakership as

some sort of space between that of Reed and Henderson's successor Joseph Cannon, call into question his true impact on the speakership, or just ignore home altogether in a shameful display of ignorance of this man.

On 16 September 1902, just after being nominated again for another term in the Congress, Henderson went to the House floor and told the stunned members of that body that he would refuse the nomination of his party and would leave the House at the end of the session the following March. In an editorial, the American *Review of Reviews*, the domestic version of the British magazine of the same name, noted:

> *It had been commonly supposed that Mr. Henderson would have no difficulty in carrying his district in November, and that, in case of continued Republican control of the House, he would be made Speaker of the Fifty-eighth Congress, as of the Fifty-sixth and the Fifty-seventh. The retirement of Speaker Henderson, therefore, was naturally dwelt upon by the press as an incident of striking significance. As Speaker, with power to make up the committees, Mr. Henderson would have been in position to exercise more influence than any other man in the United States upon the action of Congress in matters affecting industry, trade, and the public revenues. With the convictions which he entertains so strongly - and which do not seem to be different from those of the great majority of influential Republicans holding office - it was hard for the country to understand why he should declined a renomination which had already been tendered him by unanimous consent.*

Henderson's refusal to run for another term, which would most certainly have resulted in his re-election to his seat as well as his election to a third term as Speaker, has mystified historians for a century. In 1969, historians Nelson Polsby, Miriam Gallaher, and Barry Rundquist opened the controversy back up when they wrote in *American Political Science Review*, "[Joseph] Cannon became Speaker after Speaker Henderson, also a Republican, for somewhat mysterious reasons decided to retire from Congress." Appearing on page 799 of the journal, the investigation into why Henderson truly retired has come to be known as "The Page 799 Mystery." But an examination of contemporary sources, including newspapers, show that Henderson, who backed a high protective tariff in opposition to many in his own party as well as those back home, simply could not ask the voters of his district to support him when they were for free trade - it appears to be as simple as that. In a newspaper interview that appeared in the *Washington Post*, Henderson explained his reasoning:

I desire to say that after a careful study of conditions and political views in Iowa and in my own district, I am satisfied that I am not in harmony with a great many of the Republican voters who believe that free trade, in whole, or in part, will remedy the trust evil...I cannot part from a people that I have loved and that have honored me without leaving an expression of my earnest and sincere views on this and other vital public questions.

Henderson served for the remainder of the Fifty-seventh Congress. On 4 March 1903, he took to the House floor on his final day in office and addressed the members:

...An age spent under this Dome must give opportunity for forming many and strong ties. Constituted as I have been from childhood, friendship is an essential element of my life's food, and whether on the floor or in the Chair I have found a bountiful supply in this Hall. I have seen beautiful and instructive things on this floor - sharp, able, feeling debate; and debate, gentlemen, is the foundation and sustaining power of American liberty. But I have seen another beautiful thing. When the flag was raised in war I have seen both sides of this chamber, as one man, put $50,000,000 into the hands of the Chief Magistrate and say, "Lead on," without a dissenting voice. I say that from that hour I have believed that there was no future moment when disintegration could come to this Republic. And when I saw the young men from every State in the Union touching elbow to elbow and rushing into the ranks of war, there was absolute confirmation of that belief...I have no fears for the future of my country. Let no one be disturbed by the battles from this floor. As I said, they are guaranties of freedom,

and I approve of them. At times there may be scars left, but they are not scars that leave a permanent cripple, but scars that leave the soul and the manhood without a dangerous wound. For one, go where I may from this Hall, I shall carry with me in my heart an affectionate recollection of the friends that I have met here, and I do not know of one enemy.

When I took this chair I asked the support of this House to aid me in performing the duties of this office you conferred upon me. That gavel in my hand has never been defied by either side of this Chamber. It is a pleasure to say that. It has always secured obedience: recognition when order was demanded. Knowing how excited we are at times, that is a pleasant recollection for me.

After Leaving the Speakership

After leaving the House, Henderson followed two of his predecessors - John G. Carlisle and Thomas B. Reed - in moving to New York City to set up a law firm there. But unlike the other two men, Henderson did not meet with any success in this new venue, and after a year of discouragement he decided to return to Dubuque and re-establish his law career there.

In May 1905, Henderson contracted Paresis, a disease characterized by motor paralysis of the limbs, possibly brought on by a stroke. In September 1905 his condition worsened, and he was removed to Mercy Hospital in Dubuque, where he remained until his death. He suffered a massive stroke in early February 1906 that left him completely blind. On 25 February, Henderson succumbed to his illness, three weeks shy of his 66th birthday. After a funeral, which included having his body lie in state in the Capital building, he was laid to rest in Linwood Cemetery in Dubuque.

Few history books - including those about the House of Representatives - mention the name of David B. Henderson except in passing; a major 1957 article in the *Iowa Journal of History* relates as to his speakership, but the article itself is rarely cited in histories of the House of Representatives. Henderson has no official biography, and except for a few newspaper articles and the official debates in the House contained in the *Congressional Record* it is hard to find any mention of him. His official collection of papers, held by the University of Iowa Libraries in Iowa City hold only a few newspaper clippings and only a few letters, none of which go into any of his political activities. Other manuscript collections of Henderson's contemporaries have letters to and from Henderson, but again these are of a nature rarely relevant to an understanding of the man and his politics and his ideas. Yet Henderson's speakership was extremely important, as he was one in the line of the last strong Speakers in the period of the late nineteenth and early twentieth centuries, starting with Reed, and Charles Crisp, and on to Henderson and ending with Joseph Cannon, against whom the House revolted in 1910 and lessened the power of the office of the Speaker. David Henderson, a Scottish emigrant who came to America as a poor child, rose to the pinnacle of political power in America. He should be remembered better than history has treated him.

Further Reading:
Gates, Merrill E., ed.-in-chief, *Men of Mark in America: Ideals of American Life told in Biographies of Eminent Living Americans* (Washington, D.C.: Men of Mark Publishing Co.; two volumes, 1905), II:38-40.

Hoing, Willard L., "David B. Henderson: Speaker of the House," *Iowa Journal of History*, 55 (September 1957), 1-34.

See also page 463

HOUSE OF REPRESENTATIVES,
WASHINGTON.

Dubuque, Iowa.
April 30, 1899.

Very truly yours,

Joseph Gurney Cannon

Served as Speaker:
November 9, 1903 - March 4, 1911

In November 2003, the U.S. House of Representatives held a centenary conference to honor the one hundredth anniversary of Joseph Cannon becoming Speaker of the House. Ronald Peters, Jr., a noted American historian, said of this small man who wore a stovepipe hat, "Cannon was a colorful figure, earthy in appearance, demeanor, and sense of humor. He was the most prominent legislator of his day and perhaps, at that time, the only member of Congress to gain extensive public recognition." Historians who have studied the U.S. House of Representatives agree that Joseph Cannon was and will probably remain the most powerful Speaker of the House – and that during most of his tenure, which lasted only from the Fifty-eighth Congress (1903-05) through the Sixty-first Congress (1909-11), his power was unlimited and unchallenged until a group of disgruntled Republicans joined with Democrats in 1910 to bring down Cannon and limit the powers of the Speaker once and for all. Who this man was, and why "Cannonism" became part of the English language in the first de-

cade of the twentieth century, is a story that is part of the American body politic. But who Cannon was is as important.

Personal History

The son of Dr. Horace Franklin Cannon, a schoolteacher and self-taught physician, and his wife Gulielma (née Hollingsworth) Cannon, both Quakers, Joseph Gurney Cannon was born in New Garden, in Guildford County, North Carolina, on 7 May 1836. Although little is known about the family of Horace Cannon, except that his ancestors came from the Island of Man, it has been discovered that Gulielma Cannon was a direct descendant of George Fox (1624-1691), an English religious scholar who is called the father of the Religious Society of Friends, better known as the Quakers. Horace Cannon founded Guildford College, a Quaker school in North Carolina. Deeply religious and opposing slavery, the Cannons moved from North Carolina in 1840 and settled first in Parke County, near Bloomingdale, Indiana. Joseph Cannon was later to write, "Quaker and Huguenot, God-fearing and man-loving people, hunted from the haunts of Christian civilization, non-conformists in religion and non-combatants in war - these were my ancestors." The family was hit by tragedy in 1851 when Horace Cannon, attending to a patient in a heavy rain, got caught in a swollen creek and drowned. Joseph Cannon, at just 11, received what his congressional biography called "preparatory studies," then took a job at age 14 in a country store. With his savings he studied the law at the Cincinnati Law School in Ohio for six months, then returned to Indiana in 1858 and continued to study in the law offices of John P. Usher (who was later to serve as Secretary of the Interior in the administration of Abraham Lincoln) before being admitted to the state bar, after which he opened a law practice in Terre Haute that same year.

In 1859, after just a year in Terre Haute, Cannon moved to Tuscola, Illinois, east of Springfield, Illinois. He remained there until 1876, during which time he married a local girl, Mary Reed, a Methodist schoolteacher, who became his aide and assistant until her death in 1899. In 1861, Cannon was elected, as a Republican, as the state's attorney for the 27th Judicial District of Illinois, serving until December 1868. While sitting in the Fifty-sixth Congress (1899-1901), Cannon looked back on his service as the state's attorney, stating, "While there was much main strength and awkwardness in what I accomplished, I did occasionally win a verdict." For his entire political career, Cannon was condemned for not serving in the Union army during the Civil War. Although he never spoke about the subject, his biographers, including L. White Busbey, believe that Illinois Governor Richard Yates wanted to keep Cannon, a loyal Republican, in his judicial position to try and convict those Northerners deemed disloyal to the Union cause who were called "Copperheads."

As a Republican, one of Cannon's good friends was Abraham Lincoln, who in 1860 was elected President of the United States. The previous year, it was assumed that Cannon, and not Lincoln, would rise to a political career in Illinois. In 1906, A.R. Kanaga wrote in the *New York Times*, "In 1859, Joe Cannon was looked on in Illinois as a far bigger man intellectually than Abraham Lincoln. I will not discuss this question of intellect, but one thing is wor-

thy of mention, and that is this: Lincoln's greatest prototype is Cannon."

Early Years in Congress

In 1870, Cannon ran an unsuccessful campaign for a seat in the U.S. Congress. Two years later, he ran again, this time defeating Democrat James Pickrell, and he took his seat in the Forty-third Congress (1873-75). Republicans nationally had broken into two camps: those who backed President Ulysses S. Grant in his re-election campaign, and a group of reformist moderates who founded the Liberal Republican movement and backed journalist Horace Greeley for President that year. Cannon remained with the so-called "Regulars" in Illinois as Grant was easily winning the state, and as such received the plum appointment in his first term to the Committee on Post Offices and Post Roads that he had asked for. Cannon spent his time on this committee reforming the way postage had been paid in the postal service: until that time, the receiver of the mail would pay the postage at delivery; Cannon's reform changed this to having the sender pay for postage at the point of the package being sent. Other than this bill, Cannon never introduced another major piece of legislation, and none has his name on it. Perhaps his most famous quote on this matter was, "I will not help change existing law unless you put something better in its place." As chairman of the Committee on Appropriations, he aided the funding of the Spanish-American War (1898) with a $50 million emergency appropriation that he ushered through the House. But Cannon had done this without Speaker Reed's approval, and with Reed's opposition to the war the two men had an intense falling out. Cannon remained in the House until he was defeated in the 1890 election; he won the seat back two years later, and again sat in the House until 1912, when he was against defeated, only to win re-election two years later. Cannon's two electoral defeats came in years of heavy Republican losses in the House.

A staunch Republican, Cannon adhered strictly to his party's platform. A virulent opponent of civil service reform, he also voted for protectionist tariffs of American products. In 1901, he argued against reclamation measures for the western states, telling a member of Congress from Nevada that his state should instead be "a respectable county in the State of California." In 1902, as the chairman of the House Appropriations Committee, he helped to kill a bill that would have transferred control of lumber reserves in the American West from the Department of the Interior to the Department of Agriculture for their increased protection.

Before Joseph Cannon was elected the Speaker of the House in 1903, he was preceded in that office by two important men: Thomas Brackett Reed of Maine and David B. Henderson of Iowa. Known as "Czar Reed" for the almost-dictatorial way he ran the House as Speaker, Reed instituted a series of rules in the Fifty-first Congress (1889-91) that culminated in the Speaker running the House with little challenge to his power, including allowing the Speaker to name those who sat on important committees, including Rules and Ways and Means, as well as choosing the time when members of the minority party could speak on the floor during debate. In 1888, when Republicans re-captured control of the House, Cannon announced that he would run for Speaker, to be challenged by Reed and Rep. William McKinley of Ohio. Reed ultimately won the contest, but Cannon was given the consolation prize of being named as the chairman of the Committee on Rules, perhaps the most powerful committee in the House. From 1880, under Speaker Samuel J. Randall, through the end of the century under Speaker Reed, the Rules Committee controlled the way the Speaker could conduct and control debate in the entire House. Although the Democrats, then in the minority, argued loudly that Reed was becoming a dictator, Reed was supported by Cannon. "I say that a majority under the Constitution is entitled to legislate and that, if a contrary practice has grown up, such practice is unrepublican, undemocratic, against sound money policy, and contrary to the Constitution," he told the House. As chairman of the Rules Committee, Cannon helped to draft new rules for the Speaker. Because of his assistance to Reed to keep a firm hold on the Speaker's powers, one of Cannon's biographers, William Rea Gwinn, called him "Czar Reed's henchman."

The Vote
Speaker David Henderson of Iowa, who had succeeded Reed in the Fifty-seventh Congress (1901-03), retired from the House at the end of that congress, eliciting the election of a new Speaker. The Republican Party, which held 207 seats to 176 for the Democrats in the Fifty-eighth Congress (1903-05), met in caucus on 7 November 1903, to choose their candidate who would be elected Speaker when the House reconvened. Although Rep. William Peters Hepburn of Iowa was considered a leading contender for the position, he stepped aside because he felt that there should not be two successive Speakers from the same state, and because he wholly objected to his own party's stand on the rules for the Speaker. Cannon then won the unanimous consent of his own party. His slow rise to power, based on seniority, won him the office that was the pinnacle of a House career.

On 9 November 1903, the Fifty-eighth Congress opened in special session, called by President Theodore Roosevelt, in an effort to enact legislation making effective the Cuban Reciprocity Treaty, also known as the Treaty on Relations, signed on 22 May 1903. The first business of the House was to elect a Speaker: on the first ballot, Cannon received 198 votes to 165 for Rep. John Sharp Williams, Democrat of Mississippi.

Acceptance Speech
Williams and Rep. Charles Henry Grosvenor, Republican of Ohio, were then appointed by the House Clerk to accompany Cannon to the Speaker's chair to be sworn in. After a short address by Williams, Cannon told the members:

> Gentlemen, Members of the House, I appreciate the honor you confer in choosing me as the presiding officer of the house. After twenty-eight years' service in the house such expression of your confidence touches me profoundly. I thank you. In the performance of the duties of the office, I bring to the service a sincere desire to acquit myself with courtesy, efficiency and fairness. If I err, it will be an error of the head, not of the heart.

> The contests on the floor touching politics that abound in partisanship will be spirited and earnest. The majority determines. I am quite sure that in the consideration of the people's business, however sharp may be our differences, we will not forget that courtesy and demeanor should always obtain between manly opponents

who honestly differ. In the performance of the duties of the speaker I bespeak the kindly cooperation of each member of the house.

The *Washington Post* noted in its coverage of the first day of this Congress that "Speaker Cannon uses his left hand to wield the gavel, and points at members he recognizes with the forefinger of his right hand."

Legacy as Speaker

During his four terms as Speaker, through the Sixty-first Congress (1909-11), Cannon did little more than uphold the rules of the speakership and exerted those powers given the Speaker over the years. Historians who have examined his rulings as Speaker can find no dictatorial or mean-spirited actions against either political friend or foe that was not based in the rules of the way the Speaker was to run the House. Historians Keith Krehbiel and Alan Wiseman explained in 2001, "Thanks to the Republicans' solid 'procedural majority' in Congress - reinforced by 'Cannon's interpretation and use of his powers' - the Speaker 'could appoint committees - including the chairmen, determine the schedule of business, recognize members on the floor, appoint members to conference committees, [and] dispense favors of various kinds.'" Nonetheless, his style of leading the House came to be known as "Cannonism," which the *American Review of Reviews* defined in 1910 as "The present rules of the House of Representatives and the established customs under which the Speaker exercises the powers that the rules confer upon him." While Thomas B. Reed was "Czar" Reed, Cannon became known, quite dishonestly, as "the Tyrant from Illinois" despite following the same rules that his predecessors Charles Crisp and Davis Henderson had utilized. Working with Rep. Sereno Payne, Republican of New York, who served as the first Majority Leader from 1899 to 1911 (prior to Payne, the majority was run by the chairman of the House Ways and Means Committee), Cannon fashioned a machine in the House based on loyalty to the Speaker and seniority. Included in this group were Payne, who was also the chairman of the House Ways and Means Committee, John Dalzell of Pennsylvania, member of the Rules Committee, and James A. Tawney of Minnesota, chairman of the Appropriations Committee. If Cannon desired to have any legislation considered by the House, he had these three men manage it

through their powerful committees. Although Tawney was considered a maverick because he favored tariff reform, he was a steady supervisor of Cannon's program and was nicknamed "Cannon's favorite lieutenant."

Joseph Cannon came to the speakership at the same time that Theodore Roosevelt's program of progressivism was being implemented, which included attacks on large corporations known as trusts, the imposition of a tax on wealth, and better inspection of railroads and their rates for shipping. Cannon would have none of this. Roosevelt and Cannon were not just political enemies, but natural ones as well: in 1891, when Cannon, as chairman of the Committee on Appropriations, cut the budget of the Civil Service Commission, the commissioner, Theodore Roosevelt, appealed for the reinstatement of the funds and then came out and criticized Cannon. "We cannot escape from the fact that it was no credit to the Republican Party of the House that Mr. Cannon of Illinois should be one of its leaders," Roosevelt said. The enmity between the two men never lessened from that time, and now one was President and the other Speaker of the House - and both were from the same party. Cannon later wrote in his memoirs that he saw the relationship with Roosevelt in a light different than historians would make of it - as one between a leader and a legislator:

> *Roosevelt had the outlook of the executive and the ambition to do things; I had the more confined outlook of the legislator who had to consider ways of meeting the expenditures of new departments and expansions in Government...I think Mr. Roosevelt talked over with me virtually every serious recommendation to Congress before he made it, and requested me to sound out the leaders in the House, for he did want to recommend legislation simply to write messages. He wanted results and he wanted to know how to secure results with the least friction. He was a good sportsman and accepted what he could get so long as the legislation conformed even in part to his recommendations.*

The two men in fact worked together for the good of their party; in 1904, Roosevelt picked Cannon to serve as co-chairman of the Republican National Convention in Chicago, and Cannon campaigned for Roosevelt and the Republican slate in Illinois.

Following Roosevelt's landslide victory, he called together congressional leaders and asked that a tariff reduction be the emphasis of the next House session. All of the leaders except Cannon agreed, and, with the Speaker opposing the legislation, Roosevelt had to agree that such a matter would be put off "until the next presidential election." At the same time, Cannon continued to run the House with an iron hand. In 1905, when Rep. John Andrew Sullivan, Democrat of Massachusetts, raised a point of privilege on the floor, Cannon refused and berated Sullivan. Cannon later said that he did not attack Sullivan personally; if he had, he would have mentioned that Sullivan had been convicted of manslaughter at age 16 in 1885. However, Cannon was also friendly with many members of the Democratic minority, among them Rep. John Sharp Williams of Mississippi, who served as Minority Leader during Cannon's speakership. During an argument between the two men, Williams told a friend, "We are just reasoning together in brotherly love." During a floor debate in April 1904, Williams told Cannon, sitting as Speaker, "Mr. Speaker, I will always think you are as fair as I believe you will be," to which Cannon replied, "John, I'm going to be as fair as I can, consistent with the exigencies of American politics."

Cannon was not against all reform: in 1906, he helped guide the Pure Food bill through the House and to passage. But he was a target of organized labor that year during his re-election campaign because he had opposed a literacy test for immigrants, legislation which had been backed by the American Federation of Labor.

Following Roosevelt's election in 1904, it was assumed that he would not run for a third term in 1908. Many supporters of Cannon wanted to gain for him the presidential nomination, despite the fact that Cannon continually brushed them off. He did not, as he said, have "the Presidential bee" in his system, and resisted any attempts to form a campaign committee. At the Republican National Convention in Chicago in 1908, Cannon threw his support behind Roosevelt's hand-picked successor, Secretary of War William Howard Taft, although in the balloting for President, Cannon received 58 votes.

Starting about 1905, a wave of reform by Progressives, led by a group of Republicans from the Midwestern area of the country, challenged the power of the Speaker. In reality, most of these Republicans would have crossed over to the Democratic Party; however, *World's Work* magazine explained in 1909 that "in most of these states 'Democrat' still suggests rebel." This group was convinced that Cannon was out of touch with the times, and was using the almost-dictatorial power of the speakership to avoid any semblance of reform demanded by the country. Historian Kenneth Hechler wrote, "It was not so much that Cannon forced legislation through the protesting House as that he dried up the stream at its source and blocked those bills to which he and his associates were opposed." But these Progressive Republicans did not have one leader, and their numbers were small. It was not until Rep. George Norris, Republican of Nebraska, became the *de facto* organizer of a revolt against Cannon's power did the movement to lessen the authority of the Speaker gain any traction. Joining Norris was Rep. Victor Murdock of Kansas, Edmond H. Madison of Kansas, Miles Poindexter of Washington State, John M. Nelson of Wisconsin, and Charles A. Lindbergh - father of the aviator - of Minnesota. Eventually this group tagged "insurgents" who bucked their party and challenged the very power of the Speaker numbered about 40 out of 219 Republicans.

On 16 May 1908, the first challenged to Cannon came when Norris introduced a resolution calling on the members of all committees be chosen not by the Speaker but by the Committee on Rules. Cannon refused to let the resolution come to the floor. On 9 February 1909, Norris reintroduced the resolution which again was set aside. When the House convened in a special session of the 61st Congress to consider President Taft's tariff revision, 12 of the "insurgents" refused to vote for Cannon for Speaker; they then joined the Democrats to vote against ratifying the rules of the House. Cannon then pushed through a tariff bill - known as the Payne-Aldrich Tariff - that lowered some tariff rates but also raised some. Many Republicans who had been hesitant to support Norris and the "insurgents" came to believe, with passage of this single piece of legislation, that Cannon's power had to be challenged. The movement grew further when Cannon punished Norris and Murdock and several others by removing them from their committee assignments.

On 16 March 1910, during a debate on a resolution involving the census, Norris rose and asked that his amendment to the census resolution, regarding the rules of the House, be considered. Amazingly, Cannon agreed, and on the following day, 17 March, Norris again pushed to have the power of the Speaker to name members of committees removed. John Dalzell rose to raise a point of order against the Norris resolution. The Republicans then began a filibuster of the House debate to support Cannon. In the meantime, a compromise was worked on, to allow Cannon to give up naming members of committees in exchange for being allowed to remain on the Rules Committee. The "insurgents," backed by Democrats, refused. When the House reconvened after the filibuster, Cannon ruled for Dalzell's point of order that Norris was out of order; the House then voted 182 to 163 against Cannon's ruling. Then the Norris resolution was voted on; it passed, 191 to 156. Finally, on 19 March, after 29 grueling hours of debate over several days, Cannon realized that he had been beaten, and offered before the entire House to resign as Speaker. Rep. Albert S. Burleson, Democrat of Texas (later Postmaster General in the administration of Woodrow Wilson), offered a resolution asking for Cannon to step down on 20 March. Norris and Murdock, once on the same side, deviated in their support, with Norris now backing Cannon to remain as Speaker and Murdock pushing to have him removed. In the end, a majority of "insurgents" voted against the Burleson resolution, and it was defeated, 192-155. Cannon told the House that "I'll just keep on speaking and praying."

Although Cannon remained as Speaker, his grip on power was broken. Cannon himself denounced those Republicans who had helped to bring him down; in a speech before the Illinois Republican Association, he said, "There was a new majority made today. It consisted of the Democrats and a 15 per cent slough from the Republican Party. They destroyed the committee on rules. Then what did they do? A resolution was presented, declaring the office of the Speaker vacant. What did these men who have been denouncing my personality, these simon-pure followers of [Albert] Cummins [of Iowa]

and [Robert] La Follette [of Wisconsin] do then? Only nine of them had the courage of their convictions. The result was that while I was elected by a majority of 26 last March, they refused to turn me out by a majority of 36." He added, "May God bless and keep these men, for, so far as I am concerned, He can only bless them. Many so-called Republicans are, in fact, Populists, and are trying to outdo Bryanism."

Cannon's contempt for these men aside, in the end they had little further effect: none of them got back on the committees they had been kicked off of, and they never got a chance to control any of the legislation in the House. Cannon ran for re-election in the 1910 election, but the intra-party fight amongst Republicans had cost their party dearly: The Democrats picked up 58 seats and took the majority, 230 seats to 162 for the GOP. Ironically, the new Democratic Speaker, Champ Clark of Missouri, instituted the same brand of control over the House as did his predecessors, with the effect of shutting out the minority in the same ways that the Democrats had complained about for years.

After Leaving the Speakership

In 1912, as Democrat Woodrow Wilson was winning the White House and the Democrats were increasing their majority in the Congress to 291 seats against 134 for the Republicans, Cannon was losing his congressional seat to Democrat Frank Trimble O'Hair. He remained out of office for the two years of the Sixty-third Congress; in 1914, he ran against O'Hair and won back the seat he had held since 1873. During this final tenure in the House, which lasted through the Sixty-seventh Congress (1921-23), Cannon was considered the elder statesman of the party, given a level of respect and deference despite the fight that had lessened the Speaker's powers. On 7 May 1916, the House paused to recognize Cannon's 80th birthday. Rep. Frederick Gillett, Republican of Massachusetts, who later served as Speaker himself, rose to call Cannon "a sort of perpetual statesman emeritus" who was "an honor and a blessing to the American Congress."

In 1922, Cannon refused renomination, and at the end of the Sixty-seventh Congress retired to his home in Danville, Illinois. On 3 March 1923, on his last official day in office, Cannon was honored by being the first person to appear on the cover of *Time* magazine, in its first issue. Burdened in his final years with declining health, including heart trouble, Cannon died at his home in Danville on 12 November 1926, at the age of 90. He was buried in Spring Hill Cemetery in that city. In a mark of respect, one of his predecessors as Speaker, J. Warren Keifer, himself 90 years old at the time of Cannon's death, spoke with pride of Cannon. "From the first I was attracted to Mr. Cannon because of his straightforward way of dealing with people," Keifer stated. "He was honest and sincere. He served his country well."

Despite the revolution that broke the back of Cannon's speakership and changed the role of the Speaker of the House forever, Joseph Cannon is remembered rather well nearly a century after his own party brought him down. In 1962, the House of Representatives named the congressional office building just south of the Capitol Building, completed in 1908 as the House Office Building, as the Cannon House Office Building. He is now the second longest serving Republican Speaker in the history of the House, surpassed by fellow Illinoisan Dennis Hastert in 2006. And, with 48 years in the House during his career, he was the first member of that body to serve for four decades. He once said, "Sometimes in politics one must duel with skunks, but no one should be fool enough to allow skunks to choose the weapons."

Further Reading:

Cannon, Joseph Gurney, *Uncle Joe Cannon: The Story of a Pioneer American, as Told to L. White Busbey* (New York: Henry Holt, 1927).

Sarasohn, David, Baker, John D., "The Character of the Congressional Revolution of 1910," *Journal of American History*, 60:3 (December 1973), 679-91.

The Cannon Centenary Conference: The Changing Nature of the Speakership (House Document 108-204, 108th Congress, 2nd Session [2004].

United States Congress, House, *Joseph Gurney Cannon. Proceedings in the House of Representatives on the Eightieth Anniversary of his Birth. Saturday, May 6, 1916* (Washington, D.C.: Government Printing Office, 1916).

See also pages 466, 468

J. G. CANNON
18TH DIST. ILLINOIS

House of Representatives U. S.
Washington, D. C.

Sept. 20, 1919.

Charles B. Hubbell,

East Falmouth, Mass.

Dear Mr. Hubbell:

I have your favor of the 12th inst, and
thank you for your congratulations and good wishes.

If I should again visit Cape Cod I will pull the latch-
string of the Antlers Inn.

As ever with respect,

J. G. Cannon

James Beauchamp Clark

Served as Speaker:
April 4, 1911 - March 4, 1919

As Speaker of the House of Representatives, he shepherded Woodrow Wilson's economic and social program through the Congress; he also presided over the vote that sent American troops to fight in the First World War. Yet in 1912 Champ Clark nearly won the Democratic Presidential nomination, losing in a close race to Wilson at the party's nominating convention in Baltimore. One of those members of Congress who helped to bring down Speaker Joe Cannon in 1910, Clark rose to become one of the most powerful Speakers of the early twentieth century. His life story is along the lines of Horatio Alger.

Personal History

Born James Beauchamp (pronounced "Beecham") Clark in a log cabin on his family's farm near Lawrenceburg, in Anderson County, Kentucky, on 7 March 1850, he was the son of John Hampton Clark, a farmer, and his wife Aletha Jane (née Beauchamp) Clark. John Clark, a native of New Jersey, was a Quaker who moved west as a young man, where he married Aletha Beauchamp, a native of Kentucky whose roots were strong in that commonwealth. In his campaigns for the U.S. House of Representatives, Clark liked to brag that he was

able to remember his birthday because it fell on the same day that Daniel Webster made his famous "December 7th" speech in 1850, which supported the Fugitive Slave Act and effectively ended Webster's political career.

According to Clark, whose two volumes of memoirs, published in 1920, serve as perhaps the finest collection of sources, notes, and speeches of any of the Speakers who served in that office, his father was named for a much older half-brother who had been lost at sea before the second John Clark was born. The son of a family of Quakers, John Clark's great-great-grandfather settled in Connecticut in 1654. Clark's mother was a native of Kentucky, and, as he explained in his memoirs, "Her ancestors, the Beauchamps, Jetts, and Robertsons, were originally Virginians and were among the earliest pioneers in Kentucky. Her father, James T. Beauchamp, was, when quite a young man, a member of the Kentucky legislature." Aletha Clark died when her son was but three years old, and Clark wrote later that while he never remembered her, and never had a picture of her, her spirit remained with him throughout his life. John Clark made his living as a carriage and buggy maker, but when his wife died and his own health failed, he turned to working as the head of a singing school. An obituary for Champ Clark that appeared in 1921 stated, "His father feared he was frail because he had a large head and a small neck, and, at the age of 8, hired him out as a hand on a farm."

Just ten years old when the Civil War began, Clark later told stories of being a barefoot boy of twelve and witnessing firsthand the battle of Perryville, also known as the battle of Chaplin Hills (8 October 1862). Due to the necessity of growing up in a one-parent household whose lone parent was ill, Clark mostly educated himself through reading and writing. At 16, he was teaching in a small school, after which he entered Kentucky University (now Transylvania University in Lexington, Kentucky) in 1867. However, after three-and-a-half years and nearing graduation, he was expelled after a fight that led Clark to fire a pistol at the other student. Ironically, more than 30 years later, that same student who was nearly killed by Clark wrote to him as a congressman to get some assistance in getting a government claim fixed. Clark worked to make sure that, despite the history of antagonism between the two men, his constituent was assisted in his request.

After graduating, Clark returned to Kentucky, and worked again as a teacher in the village of Camden. A Campbellite, or follower of the religious order known as "The Disciples of Christ" founded by Alexander Campbell, Clark was urged by the son of Campbell to attend Bethany College in Bethany, West Virginia, a school established by the Campbellite order. He graduated from that institution in 1873. When Campbell asked Clark what he intended to do with his life, Clark answered, "Teach for a year and then go to the Cincinnati Law School." Instead, Campbell advised, he should apply to become the principal of the West Liberty State Normal School (now West Liberty State College in Liberty, West Virginia). In the application Clark sent, he explained, "I am twenty-two years old. My post office is Lawrenceburg, Kentucky. I am six feet, one inch tall, weigh 175 pounds, am a college graduate, a Democrat in politics, a Campbellite by religion, and a Master Mason. Yours truly, J.B. Clark." Clark was not hired for this position, but instead was accepted as president of Marshall College in Huntington, West Virginia, at a salary of $1,400 per

year. The job lasted but a year, with Clark resigning so that he could attend the Cincinnati Law School.

Clark graduated from the Cincinnati Law School in 1875, and was admitted to the Ohio bar that same year. Intending to move west, where he believed opportunities for him were best, he left for Wichita, Kansas. He did not do well in Wichita, and instead headed east and wound up in Missouri. He initially settled in Moberly, Missouri, then moved to Bowling Green, Missouri, where he opened a law practice in 1876. Two years later, he was elected the city attorney (although Clark's official congressional biography states that the offices were the deputy prosecuting attorney and prosecuting attorney for the whole of Pike County, Missouri) for both Bowling Green and Louisiana, Missouri. In 1888, he was elected to the Missouri state Assembly, or House of Representatives, serving from 1889 to 1891. In the latter year, Clark served as a delegate to the Trans-Mississippi Commercial Congress, which met in Denver, Colorado, in May 1891.

Early Years in Congress

In 1890, Clark ran for the Democratic nomination for a seat in the U.S. House of Representatives, but was defeated by fellow attorney Col. Richard H. Norton (1849-1918), who had held the seat since the 1888 election. In 1892, however, Clark battled Norton for a second time and defeated him in the primary, effectively winning an election in a district where Republicans were in the minority. Clark took his seat in the Fifty-third Congress (1893-95). However, in 1894, in the midst of a Republican landslide caused by the disastrous national economic panic of 1893, Clark lost his seat in the general election to Republican William M. Treloar. Treloar held the seat for a single term; in 1896, Clark challenged him a second time, and won back the seat to serve in the Fifty-fifth Congress (1897-99). Despite Clark's victory, the 1894 campaign had devastated the Democrats, and the Republicans retained control of the House under the command of Speaker of the House Thomas B. Reed. Clark, however, kept the seat he won back in 1896 for the remainder of his life. During this period he railed against the policy of the McKinley administration following the Spanish-American War (1898); in one of his better-known speeches, Clark spoke out against the annexation of Hawaii:

Why do we desire to expand our territory? It is too large already. You know, Mr. Speaker, with your long service here and your keen powers of observation, that from the beginning of things...the most perplexing questions of legislation, of government, and of politics, have grown out of our abnormal size. The largeness of our territory, our wide diversity of soil, climate, employment, and interest, have always been the stumbling-blocks to perfect unity...What shall it profit us even temporarily to do this thing? The annexationists draw a picture of these islands in rosy hues, and tell a dulcet [sweet] story of the free homesteads awaiting us in that tropical region. We are to get the crown lands in return for this four millions we are now appropriating and for the countless millions which we will expend in the future. As a matter of fact, the crown lands are absolutely worthless. Rest assured that the sugar barons have already secured titles to every foot of land of any value. The free homesteads to be carved out of the crown lands are a fake, pure and simple. All the crown lands which will ever be opened to homestead entry are too dry to till without irrigation, and so high up in the air that irrigation is impossible.

In 1903, in the Fifty-eighth Congress (1903-05), Clark ran for House Minority Leader, but he was defeated by Rep. John Sharp Williams of Mississippi. Williams held that important leadership position until 1908, when he ran for the U.S. Senate and was elected. With the position of Minority Leader now vacant, Clark placed his name in contention and was elected. He was now the leader of his party in the House, poised to become Speaker if the Democrats recaptured control of that body.

In 1910, the first sign that a Democratic takeover of the House, the first since the Fifty-third Congress (1893-95), was in the making. Under the rules of the House up until that time, the Speaker wielded extraordinary power - to name members of committees, to control the floor and the people who debated there (and how much time they had to speak), to recognize only those speakers during debate as he wished, and to manage the legislation coming out of committee, just a small part of his overall authority. Under Speaker Joseph G. Cannon,

who had served as Speaker since the Fifty-eighth Congress (1903-05), these powers became more pronounced and more restricting, although since the middle of the nineteenth century the Speaker as an officer had become one of the most powerful offices in the U.S. government outside of the presidency itself. Democrats, in the minority for nearly two decades, chafed in their powerlessness, unable to introduce legislation or control debate. However, siding with them in an attempt to break the power of the Speaker - any Speaker - were a block of liberal Republicans, dubbed "insurgents," who were also blocked from their agenda by the extremely conservative Cannon. These Republicans, a small group whose influence loomed large in a House split between 219 Republicans and 172 Democrats, endangered Cannon's speakership in ways no Speaker had ever been threatened. Working with Minority Leader Clark, these 30 Republicans banded together and joined in a motion to take away much of the power of the Speaker during a special session of the Sixty-first Congress in 1909. On the first vote to limit the Speaker's powers, 26 Republicans crossed the aisle to vote with the Democrats, but 23 conservative Democrats aided the regular Republicans to uphold Cannon's rule. Clark later wrote of this first defeat:

The next morning after our defeat all the papers announced, in great, black, flaring headlines, that the rules fight was over, and most of them congratulated Mr. Speaker Cannon and his "Regular Republicans" upon their crushing victory. They condemned the insurgent Republicans without mercy, and jeered at the Democrats with ghoulish glee. Henceforth, they declared, the demoralized and beaten Democrats would be a negligible quantity, and that "Uncle Joe," like Alexander Selkirk on his desert island, was "monarch of all he surveyed." His right there was none to dispute.

In a second move to limit the Speaker's power, one of the "insurgents," Rep. George Norris, Republican of Nebraska, presented a resolution to the House that called for a change in the House rules removing the Speaker's power to name the members of committees. When Speaker Cannon realized that he might not have the votes to stop Norris, Cannon began a one-man filibuster to halt the proceedings.

Clark, in his memoirs, claims that this is the only instance of a filibuster by a Speaker in the history of the House. When Cannon finished his lengthy remarks, he ruled the Norris resolution out of order, and the Democrats asked for an appeal. When the votes came in, the Democrats had held together all of their members, and some 30 Republicans had joined them to form a majority. The power of the Speaker had been broken. Regular Republicans turned on the members of the party who voted against the Speaker, forcing many of them from the party. In the 1910 election, the Democrats won 38 seats and formed a majority without any Republicans aiding them. The Democrats ran in that election on a national platform against "Cannonism" and pledging to elect Clark as Speaker if given a majority of seats.

The Vote

When the Sixty-second Congress convened on 4 April 1911, Clark was the leading - and, in simple terms, the only - contender to become Speaker of the House. Democrats placed his name in nomination, with Rep. James R. Mann of Illinois named by the Republicans. On the first ballot, Clark had 220 votes, Mann had 131, with 17 Republicans refusing to vote for Mann; their votes were scattered between Rep. Henry Allen Cooper of Wisconsin and Norris of Nebraska.

Acceptance Speech

After being introduced as the new Speaker by Mann, Clark addressed the House:

> My Democratic brethren, coupled with the joy of once more seeing a house, a large majority of which is of my own political faith, is a keen sense of our responsibility to our country and our kind. It is an old adage worthy of acceptation that where much is given, much is required.

> After sixteen years of exclusion from power in the House and fourteen years of exclusion from power in every department of Government, we are restored to power in the House of Representatives and in that alone. We are this day put upon trial, and the duty devolves upon us to demonstrate not so much the fine phrases as by good works that we are worthy of the confidence imposed in us by the voters of the land and that we are worthy of their wider confidence.

> We could not if we would and we would not if we could escape this severe test. We will not shirk our duty. We shrink not from the responsibility. That we will prove equal to the emergency in which we find ourselves placed through our own efforts and through our own desires, there can be no doubt, and the way to accomplish that is to fulfill with courage, intelligence, and patriotism the promises made before the election in order to win the election.

> By discharging our personal duty thoroughly and well, subordinating personal desires to principle and personal ambition to an exalted love of country, we will not only receive the indorsement [sic] of the people but what is far better - we will deserve their indorsement [sic].

Legacy as Speaker

Under an agreement between Clark and the other Democrats after their 1910 election victory, Clark would become Speaker while Rep. Oscar W. Underwood of Alabama would become the Majority Leader as well as the chairman of the powerful Ways and Means Committee - ironically, as Majority Leader, Underwood now had the power to name the members of committees, a power once given to the Speaker. The revolution that Clark had led a year earlier now left him as Speaker more as a figurehead than an officer with real power. Historians Charles Atkinson and Charles Beard warned about this, almost presciently, when they wrote in September 1911, "If the future can be read from the plainly written story of the past, the fate of the new system will depend, not upon its intrinsic merits, but upon its success in meeting the parliamentary situations that may arise in the House. Speaker Clark may find himself somewhat in the position of Speaker [Charles] Crisp in the Fifty-second and Fifty-third Congresses, and he may be forced to take measures quite as drastic." And despite winning the Congress, the legislative branch of the government was at war with the administration of President William Howard Taft, and for the final year of Taft's presidency little got done as far as legislation; the Democrats did not have a veto-proof majority, and Taft could not get the Congress to act on his legislative agenda. The talk turned from what would happen in the Congress to the upcoming presidential election.

The year 1912 became a key one in the life of Champ Clark. As the year began, he was the most powerful Democrat in Washington, having led his party to control of the U.S. House for the first time in nearly 20 years, and it appeared that he had a lock on the party's 1912 presidential nomination. At the same time, the Republicans were breaking into two camps: conservatives, who backed President Taft, and progressives, who wanted to renominate former President Theodore Roosevelt for the presidency. When Roosevelt won a series of primaries, party leaders, who never trusted the former President and refused on all grounds to allow his supporters to take over the party, maneuvered Taft into getting the party's nomination for a second term. Roosevelt and his backers walked out of the party's convention in Chicago, and formed the Progressive Party, also known as the "Bull Moose" Party. This schism in the Republican ranks gave the Democrats their first real chance to capture the White House since 1892.

To this end, when Democrats met in convention in Baltimore in June, with their chances to win the presidency improving, Clark was the leading candidate for the presidential nomination, but he was challenged by a number of important Democrats, including Governor Judson Harmon of Ohio, Rep. Underwood of Alabama, and Governor Woodrow Wilson of New Jersey. However, these other candidates were not as well-known nationally as Clark, hailed by rank-and-file Democrats for his ability to keep his caucus together in congressional votes. Although former Nebraska Representative and three-time presidential candidate William Jennings Bryan was not committed to any one candidate, a letter written years earlier by Wilson to a friend, highly uncomplimentary to Bryan, was thought to preclude any chance that he would get Bryan's backing. In fact, Clark, in his memoirs, states that he had an agreement with Bryan to support the Speaker for the nomination. Thus, when the convention opened, although Clark was slightly shy of the number of delegates needed for the nomination outright, newspapers labeled Clark as the presumptive nominee in a period when the nominee of a party was named at the convention.

And for the first 29 ballots, Clark led, with Wilson right behind him. On the key thirtieth ballot, in an effort to break the deadlock that could erode confidence in the party if it continued, Bryan threw his support not to Clark but to Wilson, and the New Jersey governor began to take control of the voting. Finally, on the 46th ballot, he won a majority of the delegates, and was declared the presidential nominee. In his memoirs, Clark addressed the betrayal he felt that Bryan perpetrated on him; he refers to the "vile and malicious slanders" of Bryan in getting the nomination for Wilson instead of himself. Clark ascribes Bryan's change to Wilson on two factors: Clark's denial of Bryan's "pull[ing] me around by the nose," and, more importantly, Bryan's alleged continued ambition to be President himself, a goal that had been lost in 1896, 1900, and 1908, and which he saw as having a better chance with Wilson as the nominee of the party than the Speaker. In the memoirs, Clark barely contains his contempt for Bryan as Clark explains how he led all candidates for the nomination after 29 ballots; Clark concluded by blasting Bryan's breach of "his instructions and by base and false insinuations - to use no uglier word - [that] robbed me of the nomination to which I was entitled by all the rules of decency, justice, honesty, common sense, and fair dealing." In this portion of his memoirs, simply titled "Baltimore," Clark's hatred of Bryan, even more than that of Wilson but including the New Jersey Governor, pours forth from the pages, and drips with venom and loathing of these men who had a hand in denying him the presidential nomination he felt strongly that he deserved.

But Champ Clark was a good soldier in his party, and with Wilson the nominee the Speaker went out to win the White House for the Democrats. Wilson's close election that November over Roosevelt, with President Taft running a distant third, gave the Democrats control of the White House and the House of Representatives for the first time since 1892. Despite continually feeling betrayed at losing the White House, Clark made it his work to help enact Wilson's "New Freedom" agenda of legislation in the House, and, as he had done with Taft as President, he held together the Democrat rank-and-file to get this done. However, as with all Presidents and all Congresses, there are times when differences arise: one of these came in February 1914, when

President Wilson asked the Congress to repeal the "free tolls" provision of the Panama Canal treaty between the United States and Panama. This specification stated that American ships could pass through the canal with tolls for those ships being exempt. All of the leaders in the House rejected the repeal - this included Clark, Majority Leader Underwood, Chairman of the House Appropriations Committee John J. Fitzgerald - whose committee would hear the legislation - and Minority Leader James Mann. Speaking on the matter, Clark went to the floor of the House and stated: "The amazing request of the President for the repeal, like the peace of God, passeth all understanding...We want war with no nation, but rather than surrender our right to complete our sovereignty over every square foot of our globe-encircling domain we will cheerfully face a world in arms."

Clark was elected to the Sixty-third (1913-15), the Sixty-fourth (1915-17), and Sixty-fifth Congresses (1917-19). In the Sixty-fifth Congress, the Republicans won a majority of seats, 215-214, but the addition of three Progressives, one Prohibitionist, and one Socialist (Victor Berger of Wisconsin) who voted with the Democrats helped to elect Clark again as the Speaker. In April 1917, just months after Wilson won a second term in which he pledged to keep the United States out of the war in Europe, he went to the Congress and asked for a declaration of war against Germany and her allies. The resolution passed Congress by a vote of 86-6 in the Senate and 373-50 in the House - but Speaker Champ Clark voted no on the resolution. A month later, in May 1917, Clark opposed the President again when he voted against the imposition of the Selective Service Act. Angered at the thought of sending American boys to fight in the European war, during debate over the resolution Clark chastised the audience in the House when they applauded a speech on preparation for combat. "The rules of the House forbid the people in the galleries to applaud or show dissent or assent regarding anything said on the floor," Clark said with a raised voice. "The men up there who applauded had better go downtown and enlist."

After Leaving the Speakership
In the 1918 mid-term elections, held just days before the war in Europe ended, the Democrats lost 36 seats in the House, and for the Sixty-sixth Congress (1919-21), the Republicans elected the Speaker, Rep. Frederick H. Gillett of Massachusetts. Clark retained the position of leadership when he was elected as Minority Leader. However, little is written of this final term that Clark served in the House. In 1920, the Republicans recaptured the White House and both houses of Congress in a landslide, including winning 62 seats in the House. In that election, in the ninth Missouri congressional district, Champ Clark, 70 years old, was defeated by nearly 5,000 votes by Republican Theodore Waldemar Hukreide, 42 years old. Clark conceded the election. It was the last time he stood before the voters.

In February 1921, just weeks before he would leave Congress for the final time, Clark's health took a turn for the worse, becoming critical in the last days of the month. Finally, during the afternoon of 2 March 1921, edema, or the buildup of water in the lungs, took his life. Clark was just five days shy of his 71st birthday. When the news of the former Speaker's passing was announced to the House, worked stopped for just thirty minutes. Although upon the death of a Speaker the House usually adjourns, Clark's family asked that the business of the body that Clark had served for 24 years continue. Respected by both sides, it was the Republican Majority Leader, Frank Mondell of Wyoming, who shook with emotion and sadness in asking the House for a thirty-minute recess in honor of Clark. Leading those in paying tribute to the former Speaker, ironically, was Rep. Joe Cannon, who Clark helped to bring down from the speakership in 1910:

Champ Clark died in harness as I believe he preferred to die. He was leader of his party in the House for many years and the popular Democratic leader of the country, although his party convention failed to recognize his leadership in the great contest of 1912. But, while that failure was, no doubt, a grievous disappointment, it did not swerve him in his loyalty to his party and in his devotion to the country. He was a real soldier who did not wear his heart on his sleeve, and he was a political antagonist worthy of any man's steel. Champ was my friend and colleague for more than a quarter of a century, and we engaged in many contests on the floor of the House without alienating our friendship or weakening our respect for each other.

Clark's funeral was held in the House chamber, one of the last times a deceased representative was given that high honor. Clark's son, Joel Bennett "Champ" Clark (1890-1954), followed in his father's footsteps and served in the U.S. Senate from Missouri (1933-45).

Clark died just as Woodrow Wilson was leaving office and Warren G. Harding was being inaugurated as the 29th President. Harding, despite being in the U.S. Senate, knew Clark, and Harding told reporters that he was friends with the Missourian. In fact, Harding stated that he was prepared to offer the former Speaker a position in his administration once he had taken office.

In writing about himself, Clark explained that his life was "nearly half a century of unremitting toil with no prospect of reaching a point this side [of] the grave when I can rest." He wrote, "There is so much to do in this world and such a brief space of years in which to do it. It really looks a pity that just about the time a man is best fitted to live, he usually dies. That this is a wise dispensation we cannot doubt, but I cannot understand it." He added, "I am as proud of my farm work as I am of my congressional service. I did my best for my employer on the farm. I do my best to make a faithful representative. A duty is a duty, whether performed on a rocky hill farm in an obscure portion of Kentucky or performed in the most splendid theater in the world, the house of representatives of the United States."

CHAMP CLARK,
LEADER.

WALLACE BASSFORD,
SECRETARY.

WARREN G. HATCHER,
HOWARD G. BUSCH,
ANNA M. CHASE,
CLERKS.

Minority Conference Rooms,

House of Representatives U. S.

Washington, D. C.

November 15, 1920.

Mr. Charles B. Hubbell,

c/o The Antlers,

East Falmouth, Massachusetts.

Dear Mr. Hubbell:

I received your cordial note of recent
date for which I thank you. It is pleasant indeed
to have such friends as you are.

Sincerely yours,

[signature: Champ Clark]

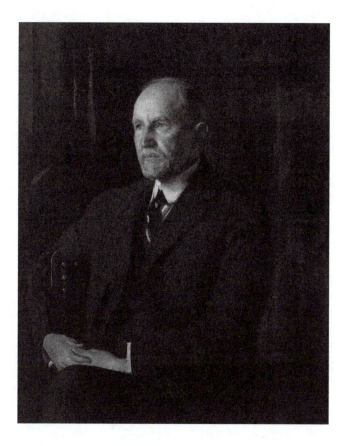

Frederick Huntington Gillett

Served as Speaker:
May 19, 1919 - March 3, 1925

He served as the Speaker of the House of Representatives for three full terms, from the Sixty-sixth (1919-21) through the Sixty-eighth (1923-25) Congresses, wedged between the tenures of Speakers Champ Clark and Nicholas Longworth. A noted Massachusetts politician whose service included stints as Assistant Attorney General of Massachusetts, as a member of that state's House of Representatives, as well as a U.S. Senator from Massachusetts (1925-31), nevertheless the name of Frederick H. Gillett has been neatly removed from American history; even in works on the speakership or on the House of Representatives itself, his name is barely mentioned.

Personal History

He was born in the city of Westfield, in Hampden County, Massachusetts, on 16 October 1851, the son of Edward Bates Gillett, a noted attorney in western Massachusetts, and his wife Lucy Douglass (née Fowler) Gillett. According to the 1915 work *Men of Mark in America*, Gillett's grandfather, Daniel Gillett, "was a merchant in South Hadley Falls. His mother was Lucy Douglass, daughter of James and Lucy (Douglass) Fowler of Westfield, [was] a

woman of superior mental and moral character impressing her characteristics on her son." Edward Bates Gillett (1818-1899) was a leading attorney in Massachusetts for most of his life, as well as serving in the Massachusetts state Senate (1852) and as District Attorney (1856-71). He was also a leading Republican in the state.

A son of privilege, Frederick Gillett spent only a short time in public schools before going abroad to study and vacation; during the trip, spent in Dresden, Germany, a private tutor educated him in the study of German, Greek, and Latin. On his return to the United States, he attended Amherst College in Amherst, Massachusetts, from which he earned a Bachelor's degree in 1874. He then entered the Harvard University Law School, and, in 1874, he graduated from that institution with an LL.B. or law degree. He began a law practice in Springfield, Massachusetts, with one Judge E.B. Maynard. A history of the state of Massachusetts, published in 1892, stated, "Mr. Gillett at once manifested a deep interest in political affairs, and during his residence in Springfield has been one of the most active workers in the ranks of his party." Although he would later enter the political field, Gillett retained his Springfield law office.

In 1878, after just a year of practicing the law, Gillett decided to enter the political field as a Republican. Elected that year as the Assistant Attorney General for the state of Massachusetts, he served from 1879 until 1882. Returning to his law practice, in 1890 he ran for and was elected to a seat in the Massachusetts state House of Representatives, where he served a single term until 1891.

Early Years in Congress
In 1892, Gillett ran for and was elected to a seat in the U.S. House of Representatives. Taking his seat in the Fifty-third (1893-95) Congress, he became a firm advocate of the rights of black Americans and a fierce critic of Democrats who were backed by the crooked Tammany Hall organization in New York State. Starting in the Fifty-sixth Congress (1899-1901), he served as the chairman of the House Committee on Reform in the Civil Service (now the Committee on the Post Office and Civil Service), a tenure that lasted until the end of the Sixty-second Congress (1909-11), when the Democrats took control of the House. During the administration of President Theodore Roosevelt, Gillett worked closely with the White House to initiate the government usage of merit-based reform in government hiring rather than based on political connections. As a member of the Committee on Appropriations from 1902 to 1919, he also pushed for the establishment of an independent Bureau of the Budget, a system that was implemented in the Budget Act of 1921.

In 1915, Gillett married Christine Rice Hoar, the widow of Rockwood Hoar, a fellow Massachusetts politician who was a close friend of Gillett's, and himself the son of U.S. Senator George Frisbie Hoar and the great-grandson of early American patriot Roger Sherman. In fact, Gillett became the official biographer of George Hoar, publishing his biography in 1934. Gillett and Christine Hoar remained married until Gillett's death in 1935.

When Democrat Champ Clark served as Speaker of the House during the period from the Sixty-first (1909-11) through the Sixty-fifth (1917-19) Congresses, Republican James R. Mann of Illinois served as Minority Leader. In the mid-term election of 1918,

the Republicans picked up 25 seats to retake the majority they had lost in 1910; as well, they recaptured the majority in the Senate, and thus for the first time since 1911 the GOP would run both houses of Congress. A new Speaker was to be selected. Mann naturally seemed to be the top candidate for the position, and a group of Republicans, mostly from the western United States, backed his candidacy. However, before the House could assemble for the Sixty-sixth Congress on 19 May 1919, called into special session by President Wilson over the negotiations held in Paris to end the First World War, Mann's hold on the speakership was whittled away by a coalition of more conservative Republicans in both the House and Senate, with the latter body's GOP members using their influence to fight against Mann.

The Vote
Historians believe that Mann's tenure as Minority Leader had been a period of lackluster accomplishment by the Republicans, and he was not seen as a leader who could serve as both Speaker and party leader at the same time. As historian George Rothwell Brown explained,

> Pressure was brought to bear upon Mann to induce him to withdraw as a candidate for the speakership, but he declined to do so. The choice of the faction which finally gained control fell upon Frederick H. Gillett, of Massachusetts, who had served in the House continuously since the Fifty-third Congress in 1893, and who ranked next in seniority to Mr. Cannon, the venerable "Father of the House." So well did Gillett's supporters conduct their campaign that his nomination became assured in advance of the meeting of the Republican congress at the beginning of the Sixty-sixth Congress, and they entered that caucus with enough votes to carry out their program, both with respect to the speakership, and the organization of the House.

When the House convened, Gillett defeated Clark for the speakership, 227 votes to 172.

Acceptance Speech
Ushered to the Speaker's chair, Gillett, before being sworn in, took some time before delivering some remarks.

Gentlemen: I thank you for this cordial demon-stration...I wish I could hope that this gavel will never be needed to check any less friendly and good-tempered disturbance. But I recognize this momentous session must bring periods of stress and excitement when it will be hard for us all to preserve that moderation and decorum benefit-ing the dignity of this body.

Legacy as Speaker

Despite being, at the time of his election as Speaker, one of the oldest and longest-serving members of the House, little has been written about Gillett's three terms as Speaker, during the Sixty-sixth (1919-21), Sixty-seventh (1921-23), and Sixty-eighth (1923-25) Congresses. In discussing Gillett, historian William Henry Smith, in his 1928 history of the speakership and the men who held the office up to that point in time, compared Gillett to Speaker Nathaniel Banks, who served a single term as Speaker during the Thirty-fourth Congress (1855-57). "When Mr. Banks was Speaker, the House consisted of two hundred and thirty-seven members. Under Speaker Gillett there were four hundred and thirty-five," Smith explained. He then contrasted the two eras in which both men served:

When Mr. Banks was Speaker the county was throbbing under the approaches of a great civil war. When Mr. Gillett assumed that high office the country was just emerging from a war that shook the world. It was the last Congress under the administration of President Wilson. The one great subject under consideration by Congress and by the people was the treaty of peace nego-tiated [by Wilson in Paris]. The House was di-vided in opinion on the subject, but all rejoiced that the war was over.

At the same time that Gillett was leading the House in the post-World War I period, he was also a friend to the Jewish people. In a letter he wrote in 1920, he explained why he felt that the area that is today called Israel, should become a homeland for Jews:

It seems to me most fitting that Palestine, to which nearly all the people in the civilized world turn with a sentiment of reverence, should again be under the control of her native people, whose dispersion had been the means of bring-ing home to all the nations among whom they

have been scattered their brilliant qualities of organization and thrift and indomitable energy and capacity for achievement...I hope the Zion-ist program will be successfully carried out, as it will gratify both the sentiment and sound judg-ment of the world.

Gillett was re-elected as Speaker for the Sixty-sev-enth and Sixty-eighth Congresses. In the Sixty-eighth Congress (1923-25), the Republicans ruled both houses with only slight majorities. Just four months before that Congress first convened, President Warren G. Harding died, and Vice Presi-dent Calvin Coolidge succeeded to the presidency. In the House, the GOP held a 225-207 majority over the Democrats, with 2 Farmer-Laborite mem-bers and 1 Socialist, all of whom voted with the Democrats. As well as, there were a group of Pro-gressive Republicans who sometimes voted with the Democrats; these seats cut the Republican vote to 208. In the Senate, the Republicans held 51 seats out of 100, but, as with the House, a number of Pro-gressive Republicans tipped the balance of power to the Democrats. As historian Lindsay Rogers ex-plained, "These shadow Republican majorities made improbable any effective leadership from the White House."

After Leaving the Speakership

In 1924, Gillett decided to forego a fourth term as Speaker, and instead was elected to the seat in the U.S. Senate held since 1892 by Henry Cabot Lodge, and he served in the seat for a single six-year term. During this tenure, he was a strong supporter of the American entry into the World Court at the Hague in the Netherlands. Historians Donald R. Kennon and Rebecca M. Rogers, in a history of the House Committee on Ways and Means, wrote, "The first congressional sponsor of birth control legislation was Senator Frederick H. Gillett (R-MA), who in 1930 was completing his first term in the Senate. Although he had served with distinction for 16 terms in the House, including three as Speaker, he was a lame duck Senator without power or influence."

In 1930, in the midst of the Depression, Gillett de-cided not to run for re-election to a second Senate term, telling reporters that "I resolved that I would not 'lag superfluous on the stage.'" When he de-parted Congress for the last time on 3 March 1931, he had served continuously for thirty-eight years. In the last decade of his life, Gillett divided his time between his home in Westfield, Massachusetts, in the summer, and one in Pasadena, California, in the winter. He wrote and published *The United States and the World Court* (New York: American Foundation, 1930).

In the last year of his life, Gillett was diagnosed with leukemia. In late 1934, he finished the last work on his biography of George Frisbie Hoar, and rushed to complete his own memoirs, but his increasing fragility prevented this. He returned from California to Massachusetts in early 1935 in rapidly declining health. Gillett entered the Springfield Hospital in Springfield, Massachusetts, on 10 July 1935, suffering from severe weakness from the disease. Three weeks later, on 31 July 1935, Gillett succumbed to the illness at the age of 83. He was laid to rest in Pine Hill Cemetery in Westfield.

Excepting for a few small biographical works, Gillett is almost universally forgotten by historians. Most of this can be attributed to the fact that Gillett destroyed nearly all of his personal papers and correspondence just prior to his death, leaving researchers with very little of his thoughts and ideas to study. As well, he is the only Speaker who served in the twentieth century who does not have his own separate biographical work. The only "major" collection of his writings appears to be thirteen notebooks, held by the archives of his alma mater, Amherst College, which contain notes taken by Gillett from 1871 to 1874 when he was at the institution being educated in Latin, religion, political science, and history. What remains besides these are dry obituaries in the nation's newspapers (most of which mentioned his death in passing; the *Washington Post* never even carried news of his death), or the volume of memorial addresses delivered by his fellow Senators that appeared in the *Congressional Record* for the 74th Congress, 1st Session (1935). Excepting for these, it almost appears as if Frederick Gillett never even existed at all, he left so little a mark on the speakership.

Further Reading:
Gates, Merrill E., Ed.-in-Chief, *Men of Mark in America: Ideals of American Life told in Biographies of Eminent Living Americans* (Washington, D.C.: Men of Mark Publishing Company; two volumes, 1905-06), I:374-75.

"Gillett Dies at 83; A Former Senator: Veteran of Long Service in Congress Succumbs at Springfield, Mass. Was Speaker of the House," *New York Times*, 31 July 1935, 17.

See also page 498

SIXTY-FOURTH CONGRESS.

JOHN J. FITZGERALD, N. Y., CHAIRMAN.
SWAGAR SHERLEY, KY.
ROBERT N. PAGE, N. C.
GEORGE W. RAUCH, IND.
JOSEPH W. BYRNS, TENN.
THOMAS UPTON SISSON, MISS.
WILLIAM P. BORLAND, MO.
JAMES MCANDREWS, ILL.
WILLIAM SCHLEY HOWARD, GA.
JOHN M. EVANS, MONT.
JOHN J. EAGAN, N. J.
JAMES P. BUCHANAN, TEX.
JAMES A. GALLIVAN, MASS.

FREDERICK H. GILLETT, MASS.
JAMES W. GOOD, IOWA.
FRANK W. MONDELL, WYO.
CHARLES R. DAVIS, MINN.
WILLIAM S. VARE, PA.
JOSEPH G. CANNON, ILL.
WILLIAM H. STAFFORD, WIS.
C. BASCOM SLEMP, VA.

FREDERICK H. GILLETT
2D DIST. MASSACHUSETTS

COMMITTEE ON APPROPRIATIONS

HOUSE OF REPRESENTATIVES

WASHINGTON, D. C.

April 25, 1917.

Elihu G. Loomis, Esq.,

15 State Street,

Boston, Mass.

My dear Loomis:

Your letter received and I note your suggestion, and will be glad to take it up with the committee.

Yours sincerely,

J H Gillett

Nicholas Longworth

Served as Speaker:
December 7, 1925 - March 4, 1931

He is remembered more for his marriage to Alice Roosevelt, the daughter of President Theodore Roosevelt, than for his service in the House of Representatives, which culminated in his tenure as Speaker (1925-31). Considered a strong Speaker, he was known by his political enemies as "Czar Nicholas." His death in April 1931, during a period when the GOP held a slim majority in the House following the 1930 mid-term election, concluded with a number of similar deaths of Republicans, which swung control to the Democrats and made John Nance Garner as Speaker in December 1931.

Personal History

He was born into wealth and privilege in Cincinnati, Ohio, on 5 November 1869, the son of Nicholas Longworth and his wife Susan (née Walker) Longworth. His paternal great-grandfather, Nicholas Longworth, studied to be a shoemaker in Cincinnati but became an attorney in the early part of the 19th century and invested heavily in real estate in the area - so much so, that by the time of his death in 1863, he was worth perhaps as much as $20 million. Under his guidance, Cincinnati, which came to be known as "The Queen City," grew from a sleepy backwater to a major American city. The role of the Longworth clan in English history is chronicled, although some of what has been told about the family is shrouded in mythology. According to Clara Longworth de Chambrun, Nicholas Longworth's sister and the family genealogist, "firm documentary ground is reached when the *Oxford Chronicle* says, "John Longworth, D.C., of New College, son of Lancelot Longworth of Kettelbury, Worcester, was installed prebendary [defined as 'an honorary canon'] in place of Richard Longworth deceased in 1590, and became later canon of Canterbury and archdeacon of Wells."

The child of one of Cincinnati's most wealthy families, Nicholas Longworth attended the prestigious Franklin School, a private institution, in that city, before entering Harvard College (now Harvard University) and graduating in 1891. He then spent a single year at the Harvard School of Law before transferring to the Cincinnati Law School, from which he graduated in 1894. Longworth was admitted to the Ohio bar that same year. Although he was armed with his law degree and stood poised, with his family's name and pedigree, to become a wealthy and influential attorney in his own right, Longworth sloughed off an attempt to gain a footing in the legal community of Cincinnati. Instead, he turned to the local political scene, becoming involved in civic affairs. He saw the Republican Party as the right movement to gain a toehold in the city's politics.

In 1897, Longworth ran for a seat in the Ohio state legislature, but in a year in which Democrats swept the elections in the state, Longworth was defeated. Instead, in 1898, he was elected to his first office, that as a member of the Cincinnati board of education. In 1899, he was again a candidate for the state House of Representatives, and he was elected, being one of only three Republicans elected that year, a group that included Lieutenant Governor Carl L. Nippert. It was a seat to which he was re-elected to a second one-year term in 1900. While he rose in Cincinnati politics, Longworth opposed the Republican machine of "Boss" George B. Cox, who controlled political patronage in the city. By challenging Cox's domination of the political realm, Longworth showed himself to be a reformer who did not adhere to strict party politics. In 1901, Longworth ran for and was elected to a seat in the Ohio state Senate, where he served until 1903. In that body, he became a close friend of Warren G. Harding, a newspaperman from Marion, Ohio, who eventually was elected to the U.S. Senate and then as President, serving from 1921 until 1923.

Early Years in Congress

Longworth's abilities to sway arguments in his direction - one source called him "a vote-getter" in the state legislature - led to his nomination in 1902 for a seat in the U.S. House of Representatives, taking his seat in the Fifty-eighth Congress (1903-05). Longworth would serve in the House from 1903 until his death in 1931, except for one two-year term. When he first entered the House, Longworth was only 33 years old.

In the House, he was first named to the Committee on Foreign Affairs; later, he was moved over to the Committee on Ways & Means. On that latter panel, Longworth became an expert in tax, revenue, and tariff legislation, all of which were dealt with by the committee. Longworth led the fight in the House to oppose the Underwood Tariff, introduced by Senator Oscar Underwood, Democrat of Alabama. Longworth was a supporter of the Fordney-McCumber Act of 1922, which raised tariff rates on imported goods into the United States and, some historians and economists believe, helped pave the way for the worldwide depression that followed a few years later.

While in Washington, Longworth courted and then married Alice Roosevelt, daughter of President Theodore Roosevelt. On 17 February 1906, the two were married in the East Room of the White House, one of the most dazzling weddings held in the Executive Mansion. Although the two had a close marriage and remained married until Longworth's death in 1931, Longworth told friends that he chafed under the weight of being known as "Theodore Roosevelt's son-in-law" or "the husband of Alice Roosevelt." His political enemies used the epithet of "Crown Prince Longworth" to try to portray him as out of touch with his constituents, but the Ohioan's likeability - he was a close friend of Texas Democrat John Nance Garner (who ironically succeeded Longworth as Speaker of the House in 1931), as well as other Democrats - enabled him to brush off the sobriquet.

In 1912, when the Republicans split into a conservative wing, led by President William Howard Taft, and the more liberal, or Progressive wing, with at its head former President Theodore Roosevelt, Longworth was pressured by forces inside his Ohio district to declare for Roosevelt and against Taft. Despite the fact that Longworth was married to Roosevelt's daughter - who told her husband to remain with the Republican Party - he put party ties over family ties. This choice, however, cost him re-election, as the Progressives fielded a congressional candidate, splitting the Republican vote and allowing Democrat Stanley E. Bowdle to win Longworth's seat by a mere 101 votes. Two years later, however, when the two wings of the party had calmed down their antagonistic views toward each other, Longworth ran against Bowdle and won back his seat easily. He entered the Sixty-fourth Congress on 4 March 1915, and remained in Congress until his death. As an expert in parliamentarian law, Longworth was elected as the assistant to the Minority Leader, Rep. James R. Mann, Republican of Illinois (there was no Minority Whip at that time). In 1919, he succeeded Mann as Republican Leader when Mann was defeated by Frederick H. Gillett for the speakership.

In the 1922 mid-term elections, Republicans captured organizational control of the House, winning 225 seats to the Democrats' 206, with the Farmer-Labor Party winning 2 seats and an additional one by a Socialist. However, because 17 Republicans were so-called "Progressives" who were moving away from the party to independence (and, in many cases, they voted with Democrats), the GOP was left with a "paper majority" of just 208 seats. It was because of these numbers that Congress convened on 3 December 1923 but could not elect a Speaker until two days later. Rep. Frederick Gillett, Republican of Massachusetts, was elected as Speaker for the second straight term, and Longworth was elected as Republican floor leader. Four months before the Sixty-eighth Congress (1923-25) convened, President Warren G. Harding died while on a trip to San Francisco, and was succeeded by Vice President Calvin Coolidge. During the Sixty-eighth Congress, the Republican majority had to compromise with the 17 Progressive Republicans to get legislation enacted.

In the 1924 election, Republicans retained control over the White House, while expanding their majority in the House to 247 to 183 for the Democrats, with the Farmer-Laborites capturing 3 seats, the Socialists one seat (Victor Berger of Wisconsin), and one Independent (Fiorello La Guardia of New York). Even with Progressive Republicans peeling away, the new numbers gave the Republicans an outright majority to control the House and organize the leadership as they saw fit.

The Vote
With Speaker Gillett having given up his seat to run - successfully - for a seat in the Senate - there would have to be an election for a new Speaker. On 27 February 1925, meeting in caucus to select their

slate of officers, Republicans elected Longworth as Speaker with 140 versus 85 for Rep. Martin B. Madden of Illinois. Rep. John Q. Tilson of Connecticut was named to succeed Longworth as Republican floor leader. On the same day, Speaker Frederick Gillett, who had been elected to the Senate and was wrapping up his last days in the House before moving on to the higher body, oversaw floor debate on a Senate bill that liberalized the Federal retirement act. A steering committee of House members to investigate the introduction of amendments to the Senate bill was named, to be led by Longworth.

On 7 December 1925, the Sixty-ninth Congress convened in Washington, D.C. Longworth was elected as Speaker, 229 votes to 186 for Rep. Finis J. Garrett, Democrat of Tennessee, with Rep. Henry A. Cooper, Republican of Wisconsin, gaining 13 votes from Progressive Republicans.

Acceptance Speech
Before taking the oath, Longworth spoke to the assembled members of the House:

> To you, members of my political party, who, by your voices, have with unanimity elected me to this office, I extend my heartfelt thanks. It is my highest hope that I may probe not unworthy of the trust you have imposed upon me...To you, members of the great minority party who have cast your votes,, as you were in honor to do for that scholarly statesman, that fine gentleman, that man who I am proud to call my friend, Finis Garrett, I extend my thanks for the clear evidence you have given me of your cordial good will.

When he took office as Speaker, Longworth sought to allay the fears of those who believed that he would become the second coming of Joseph Cannon; at the same time, he also laid down the marker that he would remake the image of the speakership into one that ruled the House with an iron, but temperamental, hand. He told the House members who had just elected him as Speaker:

> I propose to administer with the most rigid impartiality, with an eye single to the maintenance, to the fullest degree, of the dignity and the honor of the House and the rights and the privileges of its members. I promise you that

there will be no such thing as favoritism in the treatment by the chair of either parties or individuals. But on the other hand, the political side, to my mind, involves a question of party service. I believe it to be the duty of the speaker standing squarely on the platform of his party to assist in so far as he properly can the enactment of legislation in accordance with the declared principles and politics of his party. And by the same token, to resist the enactment of legislation in variance thereof. I believe in responsible party government.

Legacy as Speaker

In one of his first moves as Speaker, Longworth demonstrated the power of his office when he barred Republicans who had supported Senator Robert La Follette of Wisconsin when he ran for President in 1924 on the Progressive Party ticket. Despite his punishment of these members who bolted from the party, many conceded that Longworth was "a good fellow." But their apostasy had cost them dearly. When some Republicans opposed him on several issues, Longworth took to the Speaker's chair, where he noted to the insurgents: "Some of you won't be back here next year, and the roll call is going to show who some of them are.

Historian Donald C. Bacon wrote of him,

Longworth became Speaker of the House...in 1925, at a time when the office was weak and ineffectual. It had been so since 1910, when the House rebelled against the tyranny of Speaker Joseph Cannon and reduced the position to virtual insignificance. Longworth, with charm and canny maneuvering, reclaimed the speakership's lost power. From the moment he was elected [as Speaker], the Ohio Republican ruled with an iron firmness rivaling that of Cannon himself. The surprise was not that the House, despite its earlier experience under an autocratic leader, again trusted its fate to one man. Rather, it was that the individual who acquired such authority, seemingly without half trying, was the improbable Nick Longworth.

Bacon quoted Frank R. Kent, a writer for the *Baltimore Sun*, who wrote,

Without any revision of the rules he completely recovered the power of the speakership and was the undisputed leader of the House with as autocratic control as either Reed or Cannon. It is true he exercised this power with infinitely more tact and grace and gumption and without that touch of offensive arrogance that characterized former House Czars. But he was just as much a Czar. What Mr. Longworth clearly proved was this matter of leadership depends not so much on the rules but on the man.

During the decade of the 1920s and into that of the 1930s, Longworth was a consistent supporter of the Republican administrations of Presidents Harding, Coolidge, and Hoover, although he did oppose them on several matters, most notably his support for a "bonus" payment for American soldiers who served in the First World War, a measure that Coolidge vetoed. Longworth also opposed the Eighteenth Amendment to the Constitution, which outlawed the sale of alcoholic beverages. All in all, however, Longworth was a dyed-in-the-wool Republican. He was re-elected as Speaker in the Seventieth Congress (1927-29).

The crush of the financial and economic depression that struck the American economy in 1929 pressed down on the Republican Party because they were in power when it hit. President Herbert Hoover was unable to stem the flow of losses on Wall Street; in 1930, Republicans lost 52 seats in the mid-term elections to hold a slim majority. (However, Susan Stevens, in a 1980 dissertation, argues that the depression had little to do with the Republican losses, claiming that Prohibition, the Smoot-Hawley tariff and farm policy worked against the GOP nationwide.) Despite the worsening economic situation in the nation, it appeared that in the Seventy-first Congress (1931-33) that the GOP would retain the majority, with Longworth as Speaker.

Longworth Dies

In late March 1931, Longworth traveled south to rest after an arduous congressional session, spending time as a guest at the home of Dwight F. Davis (whose tennis career is honored with the Davis Cup) in Aiken, South Carolina. However, while there, the Speaker came down with a serious illness that seemed to overtake him as quickly as he caught it, and within days he was dead; Longworth suc-cumbed to pneumonia on 9 April 1931 at the age of 62. At his bedside were his wife and a Mrs. Curtis; Longworth's daughter, Paulina, was unable to reach him before he died. Longworth had gone to Aiken on 30 March to rest after the duties of serving as Speaker had sapped his strength. He had played some golf and did some light reading, but it ap-peared that his hectic schedule had worn down his immune system, allowing the pneumonia to over-take him.

With Longworth's death, which had been accompa-nied by the deaths of other Republicans since the 1930 mid-term election, the GOP majority was just one. In his last words to the House, which were de-livered when he gaveled close the last session of that body that he presided over as Speaker, Longworth looked forward to a time when he would be out of the House. In retrospect, however, his words are more than prophetic that he would not live to officiate over that body ever again. Taking to the podium on that final day of the third session of the Seventy-first Congress, on 5 January 1931, he told the House members,

> *Perhaps this is the last time I will address you from this rostrum. It is only an all-wise provi-dence who is going to determine which of the two major parties will organize the next house...With whatever providence may decree, I am abundantly satisfied. If I am to retire from this office I do so with profound gratitude to my colleagues, not so much for having elevated me to this, the greatest office in any legislature branch in any government of the world, but more for the evidence of the esteem and confi-dence you have had in me.*

Longworth's widow, Alice Roosevelt Longworth, de-clined the offer of a state funeral, instead taking her husband's body home to Cincinnati for burial. He was laid to rest in Spring Grove Cemetery in Cincinnati.

Little remains of Longworth's public papers. Most of these papers that were in his family's possession were destroyed when his home in Cincinnati, "Rookwood," was shuttered closed, although how this happened has never been adequately explained. According to the Library of Congress, which holds

the bulk of those Longworth papers not destroyed, "what remains consists of miscellaneous correspon-dence, newspaper clippings relating to political cam-paigns, scrapbooks from his student years at Harvard College, souvenir memorial books, and speeches." For the historian, other than these small pieces of the political and private life of Nicholas Longworth, only contemporary and historical exam-inations of the man and his record exist. Few of his speeches outside of the *Congressional Record* exist. Unfortunately, in addition, historians of the House, with only a few exceptions, have bypassed Longworth's six-year speakership, instead lumping him in with the post-Cannon years or circumvent-ing him altogether to concentrate instead on the short tenure as Speaker of John Nance Garner, who went on to the Vice Presidency under Franklin Delano Roosevelt.

In searching for memorials on Longworth's life and work by his fellow members of Congress, one note stood out - that from Fiorello LaGuardia, one of the Progressive Republicans who lost any control over the GOP when Longworth took over as Speaker. Remembering the Ohioan, La Guardia said, "He had the same domineering strength and control that Cannon exercised, although he exercised it without creating friction and protest. He left quite a record in the legislative history of the country."

Further Reading:
Bacon, Donald C., "Nicholas Longworth: The Genial Czar" in Roger H. Davidson, Susan Webb Hammond, and Ray-mond Smock, eds., *Masters of the House: Congressional Lead-ership over Two Centuries* (Boulder, Colorado: Westview Press, 1998), 119-44.

See also page 499

The Speaker's Rooms
House of Representatives U.S.
Washington, D.C.

January 28, 1930.

Miss Mary Louise Wolfenden,
Crum Creek Road,
Media, Pennsylvania.

My dear Miss Wolfenden:

Your letter of January 27th is received and in compliance with your request I am glad to give you my autograph. It is appended hereto.

Very truly yours,

Nicholas Longworth

John Nance Garner

Served as Speaker:
December 7, 1931 - March 4, 1933

Historians remember John Nance Garner for his nickname - "Cactus Jack" - and for his alleged remark that the vice presidency wasn't worth "a bucket of warm piss." Rising to become the 44th Speaker of the House due to an accident, when several Republicans died after the 1930 election, giving the House majority to the Democrats, Garner found himself wielding tremendous power in running the House. Putting that aside for higher office, he ran with Franklin Delano Roosevelt in 1932 as Vice President, hoping to succeed Roosevelt in 1940. Instead, Roosevelt betrayed Garner, ran for a third term, and unceremoniously dumped him from the Democratic ticket, leaving Garner without any power whatsoever. Garner's life - he lived until the age of 99 - is the stuff of history, although he has been neglected by that same history.

Personal History

He was born in his family's log cabin near Detroit, in Red River County, Texas, on 22 November 1868, the son and eldest of thirteen children of John Nance Garner III, and his wife Sarah (née Guest) Garner. According to historian Bascom Timmons, John Nance Garner's biographer, John Garner, grandfather of the future Speaker, originated in England:

The Garners and the Nances both came into Tennessee from Virginia. [John Garner II] was Scotch in the male line and Welsh in the other. Both lines went back into colonial times. The Garners and the Nances had done the things that good Americans did in those times. They had fought for the King against the French and for George Washington against the King. They had found the way to education and business success. They had moved west on the outer rim of advancing civilization.

John Nance Garner II married Rebecca Walpole, a direct descendant of Sir Robert Walpole (1676-1745), the first Prime Minister of England (1721-1742). Their son, John Nance Garner III, fought in the Confederate cavalry under General Joe Wheeler during the American Civil War. After the war ended, he married Rebecca Guest, a girl from Blossom Prairie, Texas. Building a home there, Garner and his wife began what became a large family. Their eldest, John Nance Garner IV (he never used the suffix), was born in that log cabin home. The younger Garner learned from his father, from an early age, the importance of politics; the future Speaker and Vice President remembered years later how his father took him to political rallies during the presidential election of 1876.

Garner attended local schools in nearby Blossom Prairie, the home where his grandmother had been born, as well as the town of Bogata. At the age of 18 he traveled to Nashville, Tennessee, where he enrolled in Vanderbilt University. However, he dropped out after a single semester. He returned to Texas, where he studied the law in the Clarksville office of the firm of Sims & Wright, and, in 1890, was admitted to the Texas bar. Garner ran for the position of city attorney of Clarksville, but he was defeated, and he then returned to the law. He opened a law practice with a friend, Tully Fuller, in the city of Uvalde, Texas, a city to which he was attached for the remainder of his life.

While practicing the law, Garner also entered the field of journalism, editing the Uvalde *Leader*, a weekly newspaper. From his law practice - which he eventually ended with Fuller and opened another with attorney W.D. Love - Garner became a wealthy man, and began a series of investments, including the purchase of the Zavalia County State Bank in Crystal City, Texas. But from the time of the 1876 election, Garner was interested in the political realm, and he entered it in 1894 when he was appointed to a vacancy as a Uvalde county judge. In 1895 he was elected for a full term on his own, but, in 1897, he was defeated for a third term. Instead of giving up, Garner ran for a seat in the Texas state House of Representatives, and in 1898 was elected to the first of two two-year terms in that body that ended in 1902. A staunch Democrat, Garner was best known for his authorship of a bill that would have cut the state of Texas into five different states, an action that was vetoed by Governor Joseph D. Sayers.

Another piece of legislation that Garner sponsored was the naming of Texas' state flower. Garner picked the prickly pear cactus, which was eventually adopted. Because of this one issue, Garner earned the nickname "Cactus Jack," which followed him for the remainder of his life. In another controversial move, Garner, as a member of the redistricting committee, helped to create what became the 15th Texas congressional district based on the 1900 census. Once the district was established, Garner declared his intention to run for the newly-created

seat. In an area where Democrats controlled every local and state office, Garner's securing of the Democratic nomination was akin to a victory in the general election. In November 1902, Garner was elected to a seat in the Fifty-eighth Congress (1903-05).

Early Years in Congress

Taking his seat on 9 November 1903, Garner served nearly thirty years in the House until his resignation on 4 March 1933. Named to the committees on rivers and canals as well as appropriations for the Department of State, Garner took a great interest in local Texas issues. One of these matters that Garner dealt with in his first term was the potential closure of Fort Brown, located near Brownsville, Texas, and the economic impact such a move would have for his district and beyond. James Haley wrote in 2006,

> It was left to...Garner...to importune the secretary of war and future president William Howard Taft to head off the calamity. "Mr. Secretary," he cajoled, "it's this way. We raise a lot of hay in my district. We have a lot of stores and we have the prettiest girls in the United States. The cavalry buys the hay for its horse, spends its pay in the stores, marries our girls, gets out of the army and helps us develop the country, and then more replacements come and do this same thing. It *is* economics, sir. It *is* economics." With such wheedling to keep federal troops and spending in the Valley, Cactus Jack Garner opened his fifteen terms in Congress which eventually led him to the speakership.

As he continued his service and his seniority rose, Garner soon became a member of the Democratic leadership. In the Seventy-first Congress (1929-31), he was elected as the Minority Floor Leader. In the 1930 mid-term elections, the Republicans held the majority in the House of Representatives, 236 to 198 seats, and it appeared that when the Congress met on 4 March 1931 they would re-elect Nicholas Longworth of Ohio as the Speaker of the House. However, before the House could meet, 19 representatives-elect died of various causes; Longworth himself died on 9 April 1931, leaving the House without proper leadership.

The Vote

From this time until December 1931, special elections were held for 14 of these open seats, changing control of the seats from Republican to Democrat, and, when the House reconvened on 7 December 1931, the House was tied at 217 votes for each party. The vote of the single Farmer-Labor representative, Paul John Kvale of Minnesota, threw control of the House to the Democrats, who, on 7 December 1931, elected Garner as Speaker. Henry T. Rainey, Democrat of Illinois, was elected Majority Leader, while Rep. Bertrand H. Snell, Republican of New York, was elected as the Minority Leader. Following his election as Speaker, Garner held a press conference in which he told reporters that "the Democrats will present a harmonious organization, never before equaled in the party's history."

Legacy as Speaker

John N. Garner only served as Speaker of the House from December 1931 until March 1933, a period of only 16 months. Despite being the first Democrat to serve as Speaker since Champ Clark (1911-19), little has been written of Garner's tenure in that position. *The National Cyclopædia of American Biography* noted that:

> *In that period...Garner fathered bills providing that the tariff commission make its reports to Congress instead of to the President, and initiated a joint Democratic steering committee for both [the] Senate and the House for the definition within the party of party policies. When a revolt occurred against a proposed sales tax, he made a dramatic appeal to the House, 29 March 1932, which resulted in a pledge of both parties to balance the budget.*

Historian Jordan Schwarz explained in 1964 that:

> *Garner's ability to compromise was well known. President [Herbert] Hoover considered him "a man of real statesmanship when he took off his political pistols." In Congress, Garner and his colleagues co-operated in the early part of the session in rubber-stamping administration proposals like the Reconstruction Finance Corporation, the debt moratorium, and the Glass-Steagall bill for extension of the Federal Reserve system. The last proved most abrasive to House Democrats when Garner, seeking*

> *quick passage, invoked limited debate. Despite accusations of "gag rule," the measure passed overwhelmingly; but Garner's expediency left many congressmen bitter, and they were not pacified when Hoover hailed their "fine spirit" of nonpartisanship.*

Unfortunately, few works on Garner's tenure as Speaker have been written; in histories of the House, his speakership earns him but a sentence or two at best.

When the Democrats met in convention in Chicago in June 1932, Garner served as a delegate from Texas. Along with the party's 1928 presidential candidate, former Governor Al Smith of New York, Garner was a leading candidate for the party's presidential nomination, even though he desired to remain as Speaker, especially when it appeared that the Democrats would pick up a tremendous number of seats in the 1932 election. His name was entered against his wishes in the Texas and California primaries, and he won landslides in both. It appeared that he would be a major force in the party's selection for President.

The stain of the Depression had settled onto the American economic system three years earlier, and now, with massive unemployment and a growing fear that the U.S. economy was in free fall, it was almost a given that whomever the Democrats nominated for President would be elected against Republican Herbert Hoover, renominated by his party. Publisher William Randolph Hearst, who did not want to see Smith nominated again, sent a letter to George Rothwell Brown, who had written a biography of Garner after he had been elected Speaker and who was Hearst's Washington correspondence for his newspapers:

> *Mr. Hearst is fearful that when Roosevelt's strength crumbles it will bring about either the election of Smith or [former Secretary of War Newton D.] Baker. Either would be disastrous. Tell Garner that the Chief [Hearst] believes that nothing can now save the country but for him to throw his votes to Governor Roosevelt.*

Handed the message, Garner read it and then penned a reply to Hearst: "Say to Mr. Hearst that I fully agree with him. He is right. Tell him I will carry out his suggestion and release my delegates to Roosevelt. At the convention, Democrats in several states changed their allegiance from Garner to Roosevelt. However, the New York Governor was unable to capture a majority of delegates until Garner ordered his floor manager, Rep. Sam Rayburn (who also later served as Speaker of the House), to have the Texas delegation swing their votes to Roosevelt. Rayburn was only able to get 54 of the 105 present delegates to vote for the New Yorker, but an additional 79 delegates - all of whom were unable to get to the floor to vote - held out for Garner and their votes, had they been cast, would have kept Roosevelt from the nomination. Texas put Roosevelt closer towards the nomination, but it was not until California's delegation also changed their votes from Garner to Roosevelt, and Illinois' votes swung to Roosevelt, that FDR was officially nominated for President. For his support, Garner was nominated for Vice President. On 8 November 1932, Garner, as Franklin Delano Roosevelt's running mate, was elected the 32nd Vice President of the United States, as the Democrats took 42 states and 472 electoral votes to Hoover's 59. Garner was also re-elected to the House; he resigned his seat on 4 March 1933 on the same day that he was sworn in as Vice President.

After Leaving the Speakership

Initially, Garner used his years of experience on Capitol Hill to cajole and push Democrats into supporting Roosevelt's massive economic program known as the New Deal, established to fight the Depression. Garner was the President's liaison with Congress; veteran Democrats who he had served with in the House respected and trusted him, while new Democrats credited Garner with helping Roosevelt, and by extension themselves, get elected to the House. As well, 19 Democrats that Garner had served with in the House had been elevated to the Senate, so he had additional pull in that body. Garner's close friend, Sam Rayburn, was advancing up the seniority ladder in the House, and in 1937 was elected as Majority Leader. Personally friendly, Garner would invite Democrats and Republicans to his home after lengthy congressional sessions to hold poker parties where the liquor flowed during Prohibition. The former Speaker called his parties his own "Board of Education" where he would continue

to work on congressmen to support the New Deal. Historians believe that during the first three months of the new administration, a period known as the "Hundred Days," Garner secretly aided in the passage of Roosevelt's economic program. During the later months and then years of his two terms as Vice President, Garner came to disagree with Roosevelt over deficit spending, but generally supported the administration.

As he came to discover following Roosevelt's re-election in 1936, Garner realized to his horror that while Speaker of the House, albeit only a short tenure, he nonetheless had more power over national policy than he did one heartbeat away from the presidency. Roosevelt slowly but surely edged him out of any decision making in the White House, and Garner found himself marginalized and then shut out even on Capitol Hill. The distancing was long in coming, however. As early as 1934, Garner had personally warned Roosevelt about advancing the New Deal too far; the following year he told friends that he was concerned that the President's programs had become "plain damn foolishness." Garner further distanced himself from the President when he saw Roosevelt's slavish attitude towards unions that Garner felt were destroying the American work ethic. When he confronted Roosevelt in private over the issue of protecting union workers' in sit-down strikes, the two men got into a shouting match, and from that time on Garner secretly opposed the President in his dealings with House and Senate members. Garner became so disenchanted with his position, and despondent that he had given up his true love as Speaker, that he said that the office of vice presidency was not worth "a bucket of warm piss."

The issue that broke the relationship between the two men - never close, but more of a business partnership - was Roosevelt's "court packing" plan in 1937. Stymied by a number of conservative Supreme Court justices who found many parts of the New Deal to be unconstitutional, Roosevelt presented a plan to Congress that those justices over the age of 70 would either be forced to retire or would be "supplemented" by another justice of the President's choosing, expanding the court from 9 members to upwards of 15. While the plan was clearly unconstitutional, Democrats who controlled the Congress embraced it and appeared ready to pass it. Garner, however, saw the scheme as an attack on the Constitution itself. Unable to get Democrats to block the plan, Garner left Washington and returned to his home in Uvalde, Texas - a sure sign that Garner was against the plan and at the same time was on the outs with the administration of which he was a part. Working behind the scenes through personal correspondence, Garner convinced a number of conservative Democrats and Republicans to oppose the plan. Many of these Democrats, realizing that Garner would be running for President in 1940 and that Roosevelt could not run for re-election, feared opposing Garner. Secretary of the Interior Harold Ickes, a Roosevelt partisan, said that the Vice President was "sticking his knife into the President's back." The Democratic party split into conservative and liberal wings, with Garner in control of that former and Roosevelt the latter. The two men did not speak, and Garner ordered his bloc of supporters in Congress to oppose the President at all turns.

In 1939, Garner set himself up to run for President, despite being 72 years old during the upcoming election year. Whereas he had thwarted Roosevelt's plan on Capitol Hill, Roosevelt now turned around and obstructed Garner's road to the party's presidential nomination. It was an unwritten agreement that Presidents would not seek third terms; however, in 1940, Roosevelt announced that because of the continuing economic crisis he would seek that unprecedented third term. Roosevelt controlled the party machinery, and Garner had no chance to dislodge him from the party's nomination. He was replaced on the party's ticket by Secretary of Commerce Henry Wallace. Roosevelt won that third term; on inauguration day, Garner barely attended the swearing in of his successor before catching a train home to Texas. He never returned to Washington.

In 1945, when Roosevelt died during his fourth term, reporters went to Garner's home to get a comment only to find that he and his wife had gone on a three-day fishing trip and did not intend to cut it short. When he returned, his secretary released a statement: "Mr. Garner will not have any comment, nor will I."

In the late 1940s, prior to his wife's death in 1948, the Garners burned all of his personal and public papers, preferring to leave only a collection of scrapbooks, which he donated to the Barker Texas History Center at the University of Texas at Austin. In 1952, Garner gave his home in Uvalde to the city, to be opened publicly as the Ettie Garner Public Library. That institution opened in 1973. In 1999, the John Nance Garner Museum became a part of the University of Texas's Center for American History.

In his last years, as he neared the century mark, Garner said that "I'll live to be 100 if it kills me." He nearly made it. He died in Uvalde on 7 November 1967 of a coronary occlusion, two weeks shy of his 99th birthday. He was buried in Uvalde Cemetery. President Lyndon Baines Johnson said of him, "Few have given so long a time and fewer still have used their years to such advantage. Few men in history have had more experience in government nor more respect from his colleagues."

Today, John Nance Garner is remembered in various ways, more for his irascible attitude and his terms as Vice President than his speakership. A man known for his cigars and whiskey and his ability to get legislation enacted, he was a giant in the area of rules and committee assignments.

Further Reading:
Romano, Michael J., "The Emergence of John Nance Garner as a Figure in American National Politics, 1924-1941" (Ph.D. dissertation, St. John's University, 1974).

Schwarz, Jordan A., *John Nance Garner and the Sales Tax Rebellion of 1932, Journal of Southern History*, XXX:2 (May 1964), 162-80.

Timmons, Bascom N., *Garner of Texas* (New York: Harper, 1948).

Henry Thomas Rainey

Served as Speaker:
March 9, 1933 - August 19, 1934

Speaker of the House (1933-34), Thomas Rainey was aged 73 when he became the 45th Speaker, and he served a little more than a year in that office until his death. A longtime Democratic politician who rose to become chairman of the House Ways and Means Committee, he was a staunch liberal who helped to usher in, unchallenged by any amendments, most of the first wave of legislation of Franklin Delano Roosevelt's New Deal economic program.

Personal History

Rainey was born in Carrollton, in Greene County, Illinois, on 20 August 1860, the son of John Rainey, a farmer who served as a Carrollton City councilman, and his wife Catherine (née Thomas) Rainey. According to one of his biographers, Marvin W. Block,

Rainey was the descendant of pioneer Greene County settlers. His grandfather, William C. Rainey, left Pennsylvania as a young man and emigrated to Kentucky, where he married. In

1832 he sold his holdings and moved to Greene County. There, in 1859, his son John married Miss Catherine ("Kate") Thomas, daughter of one of the first settlers to claim land north of Macoupin Creek. Catherine Thomas gave birth to three children, of whom Henry Thomas Rainey was the eldest.

Henry Rainey attended the local schools before going to the Knox Academy and then the Knox College in Galesburg, Illinois. Finishing his secondary education, Rainey moved to Massachusetts, where he attended Amherst College, earning a bachelor's degree in 1883. Heading west, he studied the law at the Union College of Law (now the Northwestern University Law School) in Chicago, Illinois, which bestowed on him a law degree in 1885. He was admitted to the Illinois bar that same year.

Returning to Carrollton, Rainey opened a law office, and the following year he was awarded a Master of Arts degree from Amherst, which was given by colleges at the time to graduating students who worked for two years in their given craft. During his period as an attorney, Rainey represented railroads and their interests. From 1887 until 1895 he served as Greene County's master in chancery, a position that is an assistant to the judge of a court, who works on such matters as paperwork, executing some powers of the court in the court, and computing damages in civil cases. It was during this period that Rainey became friends with William Jennings Bryan, a populist leader from Nebraska and Democrat who served in the U.S. House of Representatives (1891-94) and who later ran for President three times (1896, 1900, 1908) on a pro-agriculture populist platform, namely that of the free coinage of silver. Bryan's ideas rubbed off on Rainey, and by the end of the century the Illinois attorney was firmly committed as a registered Democrat.

Early Years in Congress

Rainey ran for and was elected to a seat in the U.S. House of Representatives, taking his seat on 4 March 1903 in the Fifty-eighth Congress. Although he was well known in Illinois' Twentieth congressional district for his work in the courts and as an attorney, he was denied its nomination for a House seat in 1898, 1900, and 1902, bypassed for better-known Democrats, before he finally won the backing of his party. At the time he took his seat, Democrats were in the minority in the House, with Representative Joseph G. Cannon, like Rainey from Illinois, serving as Speaker. The Minority leader was John Sharp Williams, Democrat of Mississippi. During his initial tenure, through the 66th Congress (1919-21), Rainey's wife, Ella, served as his legislative aide. In his time in the House, which lasted through 1934 (with two years out of office, 1921-23, following his only defeat), Rainey became a staunch advocate of a waterway from the Gulf Coast of the Mississippi River, which his district bordered, to the Great Lakes. Rainey was also a reliable and dependable supporter of organized labor, and he backed low tariffs on imported goods.

In 1904, in the midst of the wave that swept Democrats out of office in an election in which Theodore Roosevelt was elected President for his own term by a landslide, Rainey was one of only two Democrats to win re-election in Illinois. In 1911, he was named to the influential Ways and Means Committee, and five years later he helped to create the U.S. Tariff

Commission to establish a set rate of tariffs across the country. In 1912, the Democrats won control of the House, and Champ Clark of Missouri became the Speaker of the House. Rainey was an influential member of the House Ways and Means Committee; on this panel, he helped to institute the enactment of a federal income tax following the passage of the 16th Amendment to the U.S. Constitution in 1913. When Ways and Means Committee chairman Claude Kitchin became ill and could not serve for most of the period from 1917 to 1919, Rainey stepped in and served as Acting Chairman. Rainey was set to succeed the ailing Kitchin as permanent chairman (Kitchin was promoted to Majority Leader, but finally succumbed to his illness on 31 May 1923) when he was defeated in the 1920 election by Republican Guy L. Shaw. Shaw won, 33,375 votes to Rainey's 29,466 votes, but Rainey contested the election. The House held hearings, but ultimately held for Shaw, seating him in the Sixty-seventh Congress (1921-23). Ironically, Rainey was replaced on the Ways and Means Committee by John Nance Garner of Texas, who, like Rainey, would also serve as Speaker. Because the Republicans had recaptured control of the House, Rainey would have only served as ranking Democrat instead of chairman.

In 1922, Rainey again won the nomination of his party for the U.S. House, and in the general election he defeated Shaw and retook his seat in the Sixty-eighth Congress (1923-25), retaining his seat on the Ways and Means Committee. Although he had lost the advantages of seniority, he continued to advocate reform in agriculture, called for higher taxes for the rich, and was able to get government funds for levees for the Illinois River to limit flooding. In November 1930, when the Democrats took back the House in the midst of the Depression, Rainey was named as Majority Leader, an astounding advancement considering his 1920 defeat had cost him seniority in the party. Rainey had won the Majority Leader position in a tight race in which he defeated several better-known candidates - including Joseph W. Byrns of Tennessee. Nonetheless, Rainey used his new position during the 72nd Congress (1931-33) as a springboard to introduce several pieces of legislation he backed, including the plan for an international conference to lower tariffs worldwide, a bill that president Herbert Hoover vetoed.

Garner, who had replaced Rainey on the Ways and Means Committee, was now Speaker of the House, and the Texan was far more conservative than the liberal Rainey was. During an interview on NBC Radio on 4 January 1932, he said that he would push for an opening of trade with Soviet Russia and the passage of an emergency sales tax nationwide to help end the federal deficit. Rainey also challenged the administration of President Herbert Hoover, mired in the depths of the Depression. After the Democrats won control of the House, Hoover sent Republican Rep. Bertrand Snell of New York, a friend of Rainey's, to see what cooperation could be gotten from the new majority. When Snell asked for support for the welfare of the country, Rainey told Snell that he would not work to aid Hoover, but that "we intend to beat him." Although he was the second in charge in the House, Rainey could not get his fellow Democrats to vote for the sales tax increase that he desired. The issue split the party for months during the 1932 session. Rainey implored the House to vote for the tax increase, saying that "many of you do not seem to realize [that] we must balance the budget and we must balance it with real taxes and real money."

In November 1932, Rainey was re-elected to his seat, and Franklin Delano Roosevelt was elected as President - with Speaker John Nance Garner as his Vice President. With the speakership vacant, it was left to Rainey to fight for the position. Reporters asking Rainey if he would be Speaker were told that "I think I'm in line for that job."

The Vote
Despite his being Majority Leader, many Democrats were cautious about having the liberal Rainey as Speaker, and an intraparty feud developed between backers of Rainey and his opposition. Joseph W. Byrns of Tennessee, along with Thomas Henry Cullen of New York and John McDuffie of Alabama were the leading candidates; long-shots included William B. Bankhead of Alabama and Sam Rayburn of Texas - both of whom later served as Speaker. Although Garner backed McDuffie, President-elect Roosevelt threw his support behind Rainey. Many newly-elected Democrats owed their election in

1932 to Roosevelt's landslide election, and, in the party caucus on 2 March 1933, Rainey received 166 votes to McDuffie's 112. Seven days later, the whole Congress voted and Rainey was elected as the Speaker of the House. Joseph W. Byrns of Tennessee was elected Majority Leader.

Legacy as Speaker
The Seventy-third Congress convened in Washington on 9 March 1933, composed of 310 Democrats and 117 Republicans. Even with major defections from party votes, Speaker Rainey was able to carry out President Roosevelt's economic and other plans with barely any resistance from opponents. Rainey owed his election as Speaker to the more than 150 new Democrats who had been elected in 1932, and he did not forget them. As Pendleton Herring explained in 1934 in discussing this first session of the Thirty-fourth Congress:

> The creation of a Democratic steering committee was forecast by the election of Speaker Rainey. [Former Speaker] Garner had opposed a steering committee as an undesirable limitation on his powers. Disagreement on this point appeared in the last Congress. Rainey's advocacy of this committee was considered a leading factor in his election as speaker, particularly in view of the large number of Democrats coming from states previously Republican. The House was organized on an entirely new basis, in the opinion of the new speaker. The object of this innovation was to keep the party together and to ascertain the degree of party support for the Democratic program. "It is a long step forward," Rainey declared, "and it takes from the speaker power he has arbitrarily exercised and gives it back to the House. Failures in the last Congress have been due to the fact that the determination of policies has come directly from the speaker's chair; it will now come from the party. We will put over Mr. Roosevelt's program."

As the leading spokesman for the Roosevelt administration in the House, Rainey acceded to the President's call for a special session of Congress, the 25th time in the nation's history such an unusual session was called, to give the President emergency powers to fight the Depression. Biographer Robert Waller, in an article on Rainey's election as Speaker explained,

As Speaker of the House of Representatives during the era, Rainey played an important role, but one that is difficult to determine. Democratic control of the House meant largely the formal determination of the legislative procedures. For primary leadership in policy matters, Congress turned to the Chief Executive and his Brain Trusters [a number of advisors to the President on reform]. Rainey was in an ideal position to serve as middleman between executive wishes and legislative fulfillment. Unfortunately much of the intimate record of that relationship is lost forever because Franklin Roosevelt did not preserve memoranda of his personal conferences and phone conversations. Since most of the key legislative transactions were handled in this fashion, the record upon which to construct the climax of Rainey's career is severely limited at best. Nevertheless, Rainey's auxiliary role as publicist and interpreter of programs afford some insight into the legislative byplay which comprises a history of the early New Deal.

Rainey supported the Roosevelt plan without question, and in a series of lightning-quick votes over a period now dubbed "The 100 Days" (which lasted from 9 March to 16 June 1933), the Congress enacted laws such as the Agricultural Adjustment Act and Tennessee Valley Authority, and established the Civilian Conservation Corps and Public Works Administration, among other agencies. In total, 15 major pieces of legislation were passed and quickly signed into law by Roosevelt. These laws and government programs would affect all aspects of American life, from higher taxes, banking regulations, agricultural mandates, and other matters. When Republicans protested that these groundbreaking laws were being enacted with little if any debate, Rainey dismissed them out of hand: he told the *New York Times*:

The trouble with these Republicans for whom Snell and [Robert] Luce [of Massachusetts] and [Daniel Alden] Reed [of New York] and [Senator Frederic Collin] Walcott [of Connecticut] speak is that they are just about twenty or thirty years behind the times...They belong to a discredited school, and we are now busily engaged in trying to remedy the mistakes these

gentlemen and their followers have made in these last twelve years.

Rainey also turned his wrath to Democrats who did not support him, arguing that he would withhold patronage if they did not toe the party line. "You will be elected without any doubt," he told Democrats in their first term, "if you preach the Roosevelt philosophy and stand behind the President." During this special session, which ended on 16 June 1933, Rainey also traveled across the country, assuring worried audiences that Congress had given Roosevelt far too much power. "[We have not] created a dictatorship," he argued. Instead, Congress had established "a great machine with many throttles and levers, and we have said to the President: 'You are the engineer in charge of this machine.'" Roosevelt thanked Rainey for his "spirit of teamwork" and stated that the work between the Democratically controlled House and Senate and the President took "cognizance of a crisis in the affairs of our Nation and of the world...It has proved that our form of government can rise to an emergency and carry through a broad program in record time." Roosevelt's threat in his inaugural address that he would either get congressional backing for his program or do it himself was a major catalyst for the movement.

After the Congress adjourned, Rainey went on a national - and international - tour, going across America and even parts of Canada to speak about the New Deal reforms and their impact on the nation as a whole. He denounced those who called the New Deal dangerous as "unpatriotic" and said that he rejected any attempts "to create dissension and distrust."

Rainey Dies

In the summer of 1934, Rainey spent more time traveling. With Congress in recess after a December 1933 session, he eyed running for re-election in November 1934. However, just months shy of the election, while he was in St. Louis, Missouri, as part of his speaking tour, Rainey came down with pneumonia and was hospitalized. On 19 August 1934, he suffered a massive heart attack and died, just one day shy of his 74th birthday. His body was returned to Illinois, and, following a state funeral which was attended by President Roosevelt and 25 of Rainey's congressional colleagues, he was buried in Carrollton next to his parents. In their obituary of Rainey, the *Washington Post* wrote of the Illinoisan:

> He was a big man physically. Towering over most of his colleagues, his wide shoulders were topped by a neck like that of a circus strong man and a massive head, crowned with a mane of silvery hair that stuck out in all directions from his silk hat on formal occasions. His square jaws held a big black pipe rigidly, but when he spoke his tones were soft and amiable.

At his funeral, although only family, friends, and other associates were allowed into the actual service, more than 25,000 people stood outside Rainey's estate, Walnut Hall, to pay homage to the late Speaker.

One of the myriad of small but notable biographies of Rainey, composed in *The National Cyclopædia of American Biography*, stated, "Tall in stature, with powerful physique, full head of white hair and a venerable, though vigorous mien, Rainey was a striking figure while presiding over the house."

Unfortunately, more than seven decades after his passing, Rainey has slipped into the corridor of historical obscurity. His speakership, though brief, was important for its passage of major legislation dealing with the economic depression that was destroying the country. However, he is rarely mentioned or studied in histories of the House; as well as, few if any of Rainey's personal papers still exist. Two collections, one at the Library of Congress in Washington, D.C. and the other at the Herbert Hoover Library in West Branch, Iowa, contain little more than constituent letters and endorsements for his political career.

Further Reading:

Block, Marvin W., "Henry T. Rainey of Illinois," *Journal of the Illinois State Historical Society*, LXV:2 (Summer 1972): 142-57.

Waller, Robert A., *Rainey of Illinois: A Political Biography, 1903-34* (Urbana: University of Illinois Press, 1977).

The Speaker's Rooms
House of Representatives U.S.
Washington, D.C.

June 20, 1934

Mr. Frank H. Watt
Box 1179
Waco, Texas

My dear Mr. Watt:

I have autographed and am returning to you, under separate

cover, the very artistic little pencil sketch you made of me and,

I assure you, I am returning it with considerable reluctance. I

hate to part with it. It is one of the best sketches of myself

I have seen.

Very truly yours,

HENRY T. RAINEY

HTR/mst

Joseph Wellington Byrns, Sr.

Served as Speaker:
January 3, 1935 - June 4, 1936

A southern moderate who rose to become Speaker of the House in the Seventy-fourth Congress (1935-37), during the early years of the New Deal, Joseph W. Byrns was, for the portion of the single term that he served as Speaker, one of the foot soldiers for President Franklin Delano Roosevelt's program of economic revitalization for a country still battling the effects of the Great Depression. A respected Tennessee state legislator who served as the speaker of the lower house of the Tennessee House of Representatives, followed by 27 years in the U.S. House in which he became chairman of the House Appropriations Committee, his death from a heart attack after just a year as Speaker has consigned his name to obscurity.

Personal History

Born near Cedar Hill, in Robertson County, Tennessee, approximately 30 miles north of Nashville, on 20 July 1869, he was the son and eldest child of James Henry Byrns and his wife Mary Emily (née Jackson) Byrns, farmers who plowed the rough land of Tennessee. Byrns grew up on this farm until his family moved to Nashville when he was 15. His chief biographer, Ann Irish, noted in her 2001 work on Byrns' life:

The Byrns family, of Scots-Irish descent, had deep roots in Robertson County by Joe Byrns' time; his Byrns great-grandparents, counted among Robertson County pioneers, had settled in the countryside near the present-day town of Cedar Hill, the area where Byrns later grew up. Robertson County was on the frontier when the first Byrns arrived, but Congressman Byrns' time it was part of a well-established agricultural region. James, or 'Squire,' Byrns, Joe Byrns' great-grandfather, was born in South Carolina, but after James' father died in an 1801 yellow fever outbreak, the widowed mother moved her brood to Sumner County, Tennessee, just to the east of Robertson County.

James Byrns later served in the War of 1812, returning home to become a magistrate and landowner, as well as a slaveowner. Of Mary Jackson Byrns' family, nothing is known, except that she married James Henry Byrns in 1868, the year before Joseph Byrns was born, the first of seven children the couple had.

James Byrns received an education from what are called "common schools" - usually local schoolhouses that were attended by natives of the town or even the area where they were located. Until education became more centralized in the twentieth century, most people outside of large cities received their education in this manner. Byrns then went to Nashville High School, graduating in 1887. He then attended Vanderbilt University in Nashville, paying for his tuition by working in the tobacco fields of Robertson County. He graduated from Vanderbilt with an LL.B., or law, degree in 1890. The following year he established a law practice in Nashville. In 1898, he married Julia Woodward; they had one son, Joseph Wellington Byrns, Jr., who also became an attorney and was his father's law partner.

A Democrat, Byrns entered the political realm in 1894 when he ran for a seat in the Tennessee state House of Representatives, serving three two-year terms from 1895 to 1901. In 1899, he served as Speaker of that body. In 1900 he was elected to a seat in the state Senate. In 1902, he ran for the post of district attorney general for Davidson County, of which Nashville is a part, but he was defeated. This was the only political defeat in his career.

Early Years in Congress

In 1908, Byrns decided to run for a seat in the U.S. House of Representatives, but to get it he had to defeat fellow Democrat Rep. John Wesley Gaines, who had served in the House since the Fifty-fifth Congress (1897-99). Running on a platform of promising to fight for appropriations for a dam and a lock on the Cumberland River, Byrns beat Gaines in the Democrat primary, and, in that period when the Democrats controlled the state political machinery, was guaranteed victory in the general election. Entering the House in the Sixty-first Congress (1909-11), Byrns would serve in that body until his death on 4 June 1936. Historian and Byrns biographer Donald McCoy wrote, "After entering Congress, Byrns gained the promised appropriation, and he continued to cultivate his constituents over the years, working hard for their interests and impressing them with his gentleness, geniality, and folksiness. 'Call me Joe,' he often said. 'I don't like that 'Mister' stuff."

During his congressional career of 27 years, Byrns adhered to what was considered a standard liberal line. Initially elected as a supporter of Prohibition, he supported the party's platform plank in 1928, which called for the ending of the ban on the sale of alcoholic beverages. As a member of the House Appropriations Committee, he became an expert in budget matters; during the First World War, he was a key member in backing additional financial resources to help pay for the conflict. During the 1920s, as the U.S. economy grew and then retracted because of heavy tariffs passed by Republicans, Byrns was a critic of the taxes and spoke out vociferously about them. In 1928, he was named as the chairman of the Democratic National Congressional Committee, established to help elect Democrats to the House. In 1930, he was considered a leading candidate to run for an open Senate seat, but he withdrew his run for the place when increasing cardiac problems forced him to cut back on campaigning. A diligent and intense member of the House, he became known as "Work Horse Joe." But as his health problems – mostly heart trouble – grew, he was forced to curtail his work more and more. In 1933, when the Seventy-third Congress convened, Byrns reluctantly gave up his chairmanship of the Appropriations Committee and a newly-formed Economy Committee in exchange for being named as House Majority Leader. He was elected to this post by defeating Rep. John McDuffie of Alabama, who had served as the leader when John Nance Garner had served as Speaker. In this role, Byrns became one of the leaders in helping to usher through President Franklin Delano Roosevelt's plan for economic recovery from the Great Depression, known as The New Deal. Working with Speaker of the House Henry T. Rainey, Byrns pushed to have quick votes on the plans for expanded governmental intervention in the American economy. Byrns personally sponsored the legislation that eventually became the Civilian Conservation Corps (CCC), a government relief project for unemployed young men who would help to stop soil erosion and plant trees while earning a government stipend.

The Vote

When Speaker Rainey died suddenly on 19 August 1934, Byrns, as Majority Leader, seemed the natural candidate to succeed him. However, many Democrats who were not liberals, opposed having the Tennessean, once considered a conservative Democrat, as the new Speaker. As the *Washington Post* noted at the time, when Byrns was elected Majority Leader in the 1933 election, "Rainey and Byrns made their race on a liberal platform, while McDuffie was considered a conservative." Because of the politics behind the choice of Speaker, the election to fill the post did not happen until the mid-term elections were held in November 1934. Speaker historian Ronald M. Peters, Jr., explained that "'with his help,' it has been observed, 'the Democrats had actually increased their representation in the House in the off-year election of 1934,' with the result that many in his party who had been returned to their seats or were newcomers 'felt themselves indebted to him.'" Thus, when the Democrats met in Washington in December 1934 to choose their next leader, Byrns had a firm grasp on a majority of the party's rank-and-file. One of the key members lending support to Byrns was Rep. Joseph F. Guffey, Democrat of Pennsylvania, who had the previous month been elected to the U.S. Senate. As *Time* magazine noted in December 1934:

At the Capitol Boss Guffey herded them all together for a lesson in practical politics. As newcomers to Congress most of them could not expect much immediate preferment but Mr. Guffey pointed out that for them to get their due and perhaps a little more their best course was to stand and deliver their votes in a body. Twenty-three votes from Pennsylvania would put Representative Byrns into the speakership when Congress meets January 3 and for that each member of the delegation would undoubtedly get his reward in terms of good committee assignments. Senator-elect Guffey's men took one vote that pledged their 23 votes to Candidate Byrns. Beaming, "Joe" Byrns went into their caucus to thank them. "This," he asserted, "absolutely assures my election." He was not speaking in terms of political hyperbole. Two days later Representative [John Elliott] Rankin [of Mississippi] renounced his aspirations for the speakership. Later in the day Representative Rayburn did the same: "There are no alibis. Under the circumstances, I cannot be elected." And next morning Representative Bankhead dropped out of the contest.

With the necessary votes in his corner and the other candidates forced out of the race, Byrns' victory for the speakership was assured.

What few historians have discussed in relation to Byrns or the Speaker of the House, secretly President Roosevelt sent word that he did not want Byrns as Speaker. Although reported in a few media outlets at the time, the story went virtually unnoticed. The *Literary Digest*, one of the most influential news magazines of the time, noted,

While he made no open move to prevent the elevation of Joseph W. Byrns to that post, it was an open secret in Washington that Mr. Roosevelt had misgivings about the beetling-browed, lanky Tennessean. Toward the close of the previous session, the President had Mr. Byrns and the then-Speaker, Henry T. Rainey, now dead, on the carpet at the White House. He had been dissatisfied with the slowing down of the House organization after the rapid-fire action at the opening of the New Deal. Still fresh in his memory was Mr. Byrns' uncertainty in the House Democratic caucus which, within a week of the opening of Congress, had just barely rallied to the President's supporting his first tussle with the veterans' lobby. Joe Byrns, to the President, was just a big-hearted Southern politician who preferred the course of least resistance. Mr. Roosevelt, it is said, shuddered to think of committing the huge Democratic majority to such a leader.

Legacy as Speaker

Byrns was sworn in as Speaker on 3 January 1935 as the 47th Speaker of the House. Although he had the support of nearly all of the 319 Democrats, he desired to reach out to the party members to continue to earn their loyalty. He named fifteen "deputy whips," who were sent out to all the Democrats to keep in touch with them and see what he could do to continue to have their cooperation in running the House. As such, Byrns earned respect from even his most ardent critics in the party. In addition, he reached out to one of his early opponents for the speakership, William Bankhead of Alabama, to serve as Majority Leader. Despite his somewhat rocky relationship with President Roosevelt, Byrns was effective in getting New Deal legislation through the House as his predecessor, Henry T. Rainey, had done, in part by cajoling wavering Democrats on issues they might otherwise oppose. "Are you going to let them make a fool of your President? Are you going to let them wreck the Administration? Don't do it!" Byrns told his party's caucus. The Republican Minority Leader, Rep. Bertrand H. Snell of New York, said that Byrns' "intense loyalty to the chief executive and his adroit and skillful leadership that piloted administrative measures through the shoals and over the rocks of legislative processes."

Byrns Dies

In 1936, Byrns set about to run for re-election. The Congress was in the second session of the Seventy-fourth Congress on 3 June 1936 when the House adjourned out of respect for Rep. A. Piatt Andrew, Republican of Massachusetts, who had died the day before. Byrns left his office early that day and returned to his home, an apartment at the Mayflower Hotel in Washington, D.C. While there, he suffered a massive heart attack and fell into his chair where he usually relaxed after finishing his congressional work. His wife called for medical help, and he was rushed to a hospital. He appeared to be getting better until early the next morning, when he suffered a cerebral hemorrhage in his brain and died. Byrns was six weeks shy of 77 years old. The *Washington Post* noted in its coverage the next day that "although death had been unexpected, the Speaker had been under a severe strain in recent weeks as the second session of the Seventy-fourth Congress was speeded up in an effort to bring it to a close before the political conventions. Friends believe the tax upon the Speaker's vitality may have hastened the end and been partially responsible for his death."

The House met that morning in regular session, and, without a speaker, it was left to South Trimble, the Clerk of the House, to step forward as Speaker *ad interim* and inform the House of Byrns' death. "It is my painful duty," he told the shocked members, "to inform the House of the death of Speaker Byrns." For the second time in two short years, a Speaker of the House had died, forcing the election of a new Speaker. Meeting with leaders of his party, Majority Leader William Bankhead of Alabama decided that it would have to be necessary to elect a speaker for the remainder of the congressional session rather than have a Speaker *pro tempore* fill in during that period. Although it was customary for a new Speaker to deliver some remarks on his attaining the speakership, Bankhead passed on the occa-

sion, the first (and perhaps last) that such an event has occurred. Instead, Bankhead eulogized the deceased Speaker:

> *A thoughtful public must believe that, under the spirit of our democratic institutions, it is no small tribute of praise to be elected to this body for even one term of service...when such service is extended year by year and into decades as was the case of Joseph W. Byrns, it is indisputable evidence that he had by his character and ability gained such a high place in the esteem and affection of his constituency that no thought entered their minds of replacing by another this invaluable public servant.*

The only other remarks than those of Bankhead and John O'Connor were those of Rep. Samuel Davis McReynolds, Democrat of Tennessee, chairman of the House Foreign Affairs Committee, who told the House after Bankhead had been sworn in as the 48th Speaker:

> *I am about to offer the saddest resolution I have ever had to present: our beloved Joe Byrns has passed away. I have been with him in every fight in years. I was by his side when he died. Joe Byrns was a true and loyal friend. He loved the members of the House. They loved him. He tried always to be fair to both political parties and just in his rulings. He had gone through one of our most trying periods and, in my opinion, when history is written, he will go down in history as one of our greatest Speakers. He was the only Tennessean to grace the Speaker's bench in more than one hundred years. [As his voice broke, McReynolds told the House] I can say no more, Mr. Speaker.*

Byrns' body lay in state on 5 June 1936 in the Rotunda of the Capitol building, where so many state funerals were, and have since, been held. Byrns was the second-to-last Speaker to be afforded this honor; his successor, William Bankhead, received the same tribute in September 1940. The Congress then adjourned so that many of its members could travel by train to Nashville, Tennessee, where Byrns was laid to rest in Mount Olivet Cemetery in that city. His simple gravestone reads "Joseph W. Byrns. 1869-1936. Speaker of the 74th Congress."

Despite his early support for the New Deal programs of the Roosevelt administration, Byrns has slipped into obscurity. Most of his personal papers and letters were destroyed in a fire; the Springfield, Tennessee, Public Library has Byrns' personal scrapbooks of newspaper clippings and other correspondence; the Herbert Hoover Presidential Library in West Branch, Iowa, has only 45 pages of Byrns' papers. As well, only one major biography of Byrns has been written, with a Master's thesis adding to the story of his life. Although histories of the Roosevelt presidency do contain references to Byrns' role in the passage of the New Deal legislation, more space is devoted to Byrns' successors, namely William Bankhead and Sam Rayburn. Despite this consignment to historical insignificance, Byrns is remembered for being the man who helped to pass Franklin Roosevelt's program of recovery when the country was in the grips of financial and economic depression.

Further Reading:

Galloway, Jewell M., "The Public Life of Joseph W. Byrns," Master's thesis, University of Tennessee, 1962.

Irish, Ann B., *Joseph W. Byrns of Tennessee: A Political Biography* (Knoxville: University of Tennessee Press, 2001).

William Brockman Bankhead

Served as Speaker:
June 4, 1936 - September 15, 1940

The scion of a famed Alabama political family that also produced Senator John Hollis Bankhead, one of the most powerful Southern Democrats during the 1930s, William Bankhead rose to serve as Speaker of the U.S. House of Representatives, advancing many parts of Franklin Roosevelt's New Deal economic program in the House. With his death after just four short years as Speaker, he became the fourth of five Speakers to die in office.

Personal History

The son of John Hollis Bankhead (1842-1920) and his wife Tallulah (née Brockman) Bankhead, William Brockman Bankhead was born in Moscow, Alabama, on 12 April 1874. His father John Hollis Bankhead served in the Confederate Army during the Civil War; in the years after the conflict, he served in numerous political offices, including the Alabama state House (1865-67, 1880-81), the state Senate (1876-77), the U.S. House (1887-1907), and the U.S. Senate (1907-20), serving in the latter position until his death. The 1880 U.S. Census for the state of Alabama lists him as being born in Tennessee with the occupation of "commercial traveller" [sic], although his true vocation was as a farmer. He married Tallulah James Brockman, a member of the

famed Brockman family of South Carolina; her father, Thomas Patterson Brockman (1793?-1859), served in the South Carolina House and Senate in the 1840s and 1850s. Along with William Brockman Bankhead, the subject of this biography, his older brother, John Hollis Bankhead (1872-1946) also served in the U.S. Senate, rising to become one of the most powerful Southern Democrats during the 1920s and 1930s.

William Bankhead attended local schools in and around Moscow, before he attended the University of Alabama and graduated in 1892. He then went to the Georgetown University School of Law in Washington, D.C., from which graduated in 1895. In a mark of the vocation that his daughter, Tallulah, would later take up, William Bankhead became an actor on the stage in New York City. However, after a short period of this work he returned to Alabama and opened a law practice in Huntsville, later joining his brother, John, in a practice in the city of Jasper, Alabama. In 1900, Bankhead married Adelaide Eugenia (née Sledge), six years his junior, who would die only two years into their marriage. However, in that short period of time she bore three daughters with Bankhead, including Tallulah Brockman Bankhead (1902-1968), who became one of the better-known film actresses in the 1940s. Despite her family's incredible service in politics - with two U.S. Senators and one Speaker of the U.S. House - it is Tallulah Bankhead who is the best known of the clan.

John Hollis Bankhead's law firm in Jasper represented the railroads and the Alabama Power Company, and his son William was able to become a prosperous attorney in his own right. In 1902, Bankhead was elected to the Alabama state House of Representatives for a single two-year term, where he authored legislation making sure that blacks in the state did not have the right to vote. From 1910 to 1914, William Bankhead served as a local prosecutor in Jasper. He ran for a seat in the U.S. House in 1914, but was defeated. His father John Bankhead then reached out to his old friends in the state legislature, and a new congressional seat was created, which William Bankhead ran for in 1916 and was elected to.

Early Years in Congress

For his first two terms, in the 65th (1917-19) and 66th (1919-21) Congresses, Bankhead was a fervent supporter of President Woodrow Wilson. In the 1920s, while he was re-elected to his seat, the Democrats were in the minority and Bankhead made little progress in gaining a seniority position. However, he did work on such issues as agriculture, labor, and, specifically, of grants-in-aid, the giving of funds to the states for specific purposes, a concept which his father pioneered in the U.S. House and Senate.

For the 72nd Congress (1931-33), the Republicans won a slim margin of control of the House – 218 seats to 216 – but before Congress could convene a record 19 representatives died, with 14 of these throwing majority control to the Democrats for the first time in a decade. Rep. John Nance Garner of Texas was elected Speaker of the House. When the 73rd Congress convened on 4 March 1933, following the 1932 electoral landslide which placed the Democrats in firm control of the House – 313 seats to 117 Republicans and 5 Farmer-Labor representatives – the speakership was vacant, with former Speaker John Nance Garner having been elected Vice President of the United States. The House Majority Leader, Rep. Henry T. Rainey of Illinois,

was favored by President Franklin Delano Roosevelt, in his first day in the White House, to succeed Garner in the Speaker's chair. With Rainey moving higher on the seniority tree, Bankhead decided to try to win the Majority Leader's position, despite his lack of seniority and, most importantly, the fact that John McDuffie (1883-1950), also of Alabama, was in the running for the speakership. Bankhead quickly realized that he could not defeat McDuffie, and he bowed out of the race against his fellow Alabamian. The battle between the two men allowed a third candidate to win a majority of support from the Democratic caucus, and the Majority Leader position went to Rep. Joseph Byrns of Tennessee. Bankhead instead was given the *de facto* chair of the powerful Rules Committee, which had grown to become one of the most influential committees in the House. The chairmanship of that committee opened up because of the illness of Rep. Edward W. Pou of North Carolina; when Pou died on 1 April 1934 Bankhead was given the full chairmanship of the committee.

When Speaker Henry Rainey died after just 6 months in office, Bankhead emerged as the top candidate for Majority Leader because McDuffie had resigned in 1935 after President Franklin Delano Roosevelt appointed him as a judge for the U.S. District Court in Alabama. The two leading candidates for the speakership were Majority Leader Joseph Byrns and Rep. Sam Rayburn of Texas, who was prevented from moving into a senior position because the Texas delegation controlled a number of key House positions. When the balloting for the speakership began, Rayburn quickly realized that he could not defeat Byrns, stating that "I cannot be elected," and removed his name from contention. Byrns was without an opponent, and he was quickly elected as Speaker. To replace him as Majority Leader, the Democrats passed over Rayburn and elected Bankhead. At the same time, William's brother John had been elected to the U.S. Senate in 1930, making the two brothers in the years that followed the most powerful 1-2 combination in control of patronage and government aid for the state of Alabama. In the first years of the Depression, Bankhead changed his thinking from being against government spending to supporting it, although, in opposition to many southern Democrats he backed the Norris-La Guardia anti-Injunction Bill, a measure that labor unions sought to use to outlaw "yellow dog contracts" in which a worker agreed to not join a union as a condition for employment, and which prohibited federal courts from issuing injunctions against labor strikes against businesses.

With the election of Franklin Delano Roosevelt to the White House in 1932, the Bankhead brothers found themselves as supporters and advocates of the President's economic program, known as the New Deal, and with such backing came the power of the majority. The two brothers co-sponsored the Bankhead Cotton Control Act of 1934, the only piece of legislation to have William Bankhead's name on it. But for William Bankhead, the pressure of his leadership position became such that in early 1935 he suffered a serious heart attack, which, when he ran for and was elected as House Majority Leader, was not disclosed. In fact, Bankhead did not return to the House until January 1936. While in the hospital, he began a "diary" of sorts in which he told his life story; he explained, "I am of a politically minded family; my father served in the House and Senate consecutively for a third of a century. My older brother now sits in his seat in the Senate. I was raised on politics even from childhood. I have eaten of political pabulum [sic]; I have breathed the air of the conference, the hustings, the forum. I guess it might be said it is the breath of my nostrils."

The Vote

Just five months later, on 4 June 1936, Speaker Joseph Byrns died of heart failure after a meeting of the whole House, and, for the fourth time in just five years the House had to elect a new Speaker. Bankhead, as Majority Leader, was the only potential candidate to succeed Byrns, and he won election to head the House as its Speaker. The same day that Byrns died, the House met and quickly elected Bankhead as his successor. Rep. John J. O'Connor, Democrat of New York, told the hushed chamber that the quick election was "necessary in order that the House may function and that the machinery of Government may not stop." Although it was customary for a new Speaker to deliver some remarks, Bankhead passed on the occasion, the first (and perhaps last) that such an event has occurred. The only remarks other than those of O'Connor were those of Rep. Samuel Davis McReynolds, Democrat of Tennessee, the chairman of the House Foreign Affairs Committee, who waited until Bankhead had

been sworn in as the 48th Speaker to give a eulogy to the late Joseph Byrns. His voice breaking, the session was ended. The *Washington Post* editorialized, "The importance of the office of Speaker of the House is emphasized by the prompt election of Representative Bankhead to fill the vacancy caused by the sad and untimely death of Joseph W. Byrns. And it will perhaps be some consolation to Mr. Byrns' many friends and admirers that both the immediate replacement of House leadership and the choice for that post would unquestionably have been approved by him as eminently desirable for the smooth conduct of democratic institutions."

Legacy as Speaker

Bankhead's tenure as Speaker lasted throughout the remainder of the 74th Congress (1935-37), and through the 75th (1937-39) and 76th Congresses (1939-41). An expert parliamentarian, Bankhead was considered one of the better speakers of the period. *Time* magazine wrote upon Bankhead's death, "His way of rule was not the harsh Tsarism of Joe Cannon (1903-11), the rough-&-tumble domination of Nick Longworth (1925-31). Partly from natural bent, partly of necessity, he used the gentler arts of persuasion, parliamentary device, friendship. His pre-New Deal predecessors had special patronage to dispense, and patronage was power. Franklin Roosevelt took away most of the Speaker's patronage, leaving William Bankhead with no club to hold, no favors to give."

Although he had supported President Franklin Delano Roosevelt for the first years of the President's administration, as Speaker Bankhead came to loggerheads with Roosevelt over many of the President's initiatives. As a good political soldier for his party, however, he backed and supported Roosevelt despite deep misgivings back home in Alabama over some of these policies. One of these was the Court-Packing scheme. Following a series of defeats in the U.S. Supreme Court, which saw a number of his initiatives being struck down as unconstitutional, Roosevelt decided to "replace" several Justices on the court who were over the age of 70 with judges who would uphold his economic program. Many Democrats buckled at the idea of a President, even one as popular as Roosevelt, stacking the court with his own justices when he could not get the Court to do as he wanted, but Bankhead unenthusiastically defended the plan. After a lengthy debate in the Senate, the scheme went down to defeat even with a Democratic majority, and it never came back up for deliberation. Bankhead did support the President's increase in military spending, as well as an unsuccessful move to remove matériel sales to allies from the 1937 Neutrality Act.

In 1940, as Roosevelt's second term was coming to an end, it was supposed that he would honor tradition as other presidents had done and not seek a third term. Bankhead's supporters in Alabama pushed his name for President. Bankhead agreed to run, but only if he could continue Roosevelt's New Deal program. When Roosevelt announced that he would indeed run for a third term, Bankhead pushed ahead to get the Vice Presidential nomination with the backing of his brother, John. Roosevelt did not want Bankhead as his running mate; instead he selected Secretary of Agriculture Henry Wallace. The President then offered Bankhead the spot of keynote speaker at the Democratic National Convention. John Bankhead wrote to a friend in a letter that Roosevelt "is the most selfish men [sic] of all who have risen to the presidency." In a letter to a supporter dated 31 July 1940, William Bankhead expressed even deeper hatred of the man who he had defended even against Bankhead's interests and his supporters back home in Alabama, a loathing few history books speak about. "I don't think that it is necessary for me to tell you that I am deeply grieved over the results of the Chicago Convention [where Roosevelt was nominated for a third term]," he wrote. "You will agree, I am sure, that the Vice-Presidential nomination would have been mine had President Roosevelt not insisted on Secretary Wallace. The Convention was an ordeal that will not soon be forgotten. I venture to say that it was the most un-American and dictatorial meeting ever held by the great Democratic Party...President Roosevelt has double-crossed me for the last time. I shall never forgive him for the way he acted..." At the convention, many conservative Democrats who despised Wallace for his radical left-wing views did not listen to Roosevelt's explicit instructions and refused to vote for him for Vice President, instead pushing Bankhead in violation of the desires of the party hierarchy. Bankhead received 329 votes, but Wallace won the nomination with 627. Falling into line behind the party ticket, Bankhead agreed to open the party's campaign in Baltimore on September 10 with a rousing speech. Again, he put personal politics aside in favor of his party.

Bankhead Dies

On the morning of 10 September, Bankhead was found unconscious on the floor of his hotel room in Baltimore. Taken to the U.S. Naval Hospital at Bethesda, Maryland, Bankhead died there five days later of heart failure. With his death, Bankhead became the fourth of five Speakers to die in office. Following his death, Rep. John McCormack, Democrat of Massachusetts, later to serve as Speaker himself, introduced House Resolution 602 to name Rep. Sam Rayburn of Texas as the new Speaker. When there were no objections, Rayburn was taken to the Speaker's chair and given the oath of office. Almost following Bankhead's first move in office, Rayburn did not make any remarks on being sworn in as Speaker, and instead allowed the House to go into a period of memorializing his predecessor.

In 1932, in the midst of the Depression, the House voted that the funerals of sitting members would no longer be paid for from taxpayer funds. Bankhead's was the last funeral held in the House chamber. His body was taken back to Alabama, and laid to rest in the Oak Hill Cemetery in Jasper. Bankhead's nephew, Walter Will Bankhead (1897-1988), the son of John Hollis Bankhead, served in the U.S. House of Representatives for only a short time (1941) before resigning.

In his years in the House, Bankhead grew from a conservative Democrat to one who advocated the social spending for agriculture and labor, as well as increased government funds for highway construction. He also pushed Roosevelt's economic program, despite his misgivings about its expansion of the government; to a friend he wrote in 1937, "I am doing the best I can within my limitations to carry forward the duties of my office so as to bring no discredit upon its high traditions and the people of my state. There come times under the present situation when as leader of my Party I am compelled to assume so duties that are not always to my liking."

Further Reading:
Heacock, Walter J., "William Brockman Bankhead: A Biography" (Ph.D. dissertation, University of Wisconsin, 1953).

Heacock, Walter J., "William B. Bankhead and the New Deal," *Journal of Southern History*, 21 (August 1955), 347-59.

The Speaker's Rooms
House of Representatives H.S.
Washington, D.C.

April 12, 1938.

Hon. Charles A. Plumley,
House Office Building,
Washington, D. C.

My dear Charles:

You are always putting me in your debt.
I have just received the sample of Vermont maple sugar,
which I am sure is a perfect specimen and which I will
enjoy.

I also want to thank you most sincerely
for the cordial personal note which you sent me yesterday.
It is one of the gratifying compensations of my service
here to have the good will and good wishes of so many
of my true friends on the Republican side.

With best wishes, I am

Yours very sincerely,

W. B. Bankhead,

Samuel Taliaferro Rayburn

Served as Speaker:
September 16, 1940 - January 3, 1947
January 3, 1949 - January 3, 1953
January 3, 1955 - November 17, 1961

When Sam Rayburn died in November 1961, he was remembered for being the longest-serving Speaker of the U.S. House of Representatives in American history. Elected from a rural Texas district in 1912, he served nearly 50 years in the House, and, from 1940 to 1961, with only two periods of Republican control exempted (1947-49 and 1953-55), he served as Speaker. During those two terms not in the Speaker's chair, Rayburn served as the Minority Leader, returned to that post the second time by his party despite losing control of the House during the Eisenhower administration. With his death, an era marked by the strong control of the House by the Speaker passed, giving way to a more modern speakership dominated by a series of men (and now one woman) who have held the office since 1961.

Personal History

Although he was known as Sam Rayburn for his entire congressional career, as well as being identified with the state of Texas, he was in fact born Samuel Taliaferro Rayburn in a log cabin owned by his family near the village of Kingston, in rural Roane County in eastern Tennessee, on 6 January 1882, the eighth of his parents' eleven children. His par-

ents, William Marion Rayburn and Martha (née Waller) Rayburn, were cotton farmers who were struggling at the time of their son Samuel's birth just to survive. Both were descended from hardy stock: Historian Dwight Dorough, in his 1962 work *Mr. Sam*, noted Sam Rayburn's extensive genealogical chart from his mother, reaching back to one Richard Waller, knighted for his bravery in the battle of Agincourt in France in 1415. A descendant of Waller, George Waller, who was Rayburn's maternal great-great-grandfather, served as a colonel in the Continental Army and, according to Dorough, was a witness to the surrender of British General Lord Cornwallis at Yorktown in 1783. On his father's side, his grandfather, John Rayburn, traveled from Virginia to eastern Tennessee to start a new life in the burgeoning American frontier. William Marion Rayburn, Samuel's father, saw action in the Civil War as a soldier in the Confederate army.

By 1882, however, the Rayburn family was deep in the struggle just to survive on a farm that delivered little in the way of sustenance. Rayburn's sister Lucinda later stated, "It was all but impossible to wring a living from the small Tennessee farm for a family of nine." The Rayburns kept the farm alive for five more years, finally giving up in 1887 and moving to rural Fannin County, Texas, northeast of what is now Dallas, where William Rayburn used his life's savings to purchase forty acres of land. There, the entire family lived a bare existence farming cotton. Sam Rayburn worked picking cotton, eventually attending a local schoolhouse in the nearby town of Flag Springs.

When he turned 18, Rayburn left home with just $25 to his name, and entered what was then called E.L. Mayo's Normal School, now known as East Texas State College, located in Commerce, Texas. To pay for school, Rayburn worked odd jobs in the hours that he was not in class. In 1902 he finished three years of study in just two years, and was awarded a Bachelor of Science degree. He taught for an additional two years, leaving the vocation in 1904 to begin the study of the law at the University of Texas at Austin. He earned a law degree in 1908, and that same year he was admitted to the Texas state bar. He opened a law practice in Bonham, in Fannin County, Texas. Enticed to that town by a young attorney, Joseph Bailey, who ran for and won a seat in the U.S. House, Rayburn later wrote about his first time in what would become his home:

> I'd never been to Bonham since we bought the farm, and I was scared of all the rich townfolks in their store-bought clothes. But I found a flap in the canvas, and I stuck there like glue while old Joe Bailey made his speech. He went on for two solid hours, and I scarcely drew a breath the whole time. I can still feel the water dripping down my neck. I slopped around to the entrance again when he was through, saw him come out, and ran after him [for] five or six blocks until he got on a streetcar. Then I went home, wondering whether I'd ever be as big a man as Joe Bailey.

While studying for his law degree, Rayburn ran for and was elected as a Democrat to a seat in the Texas state House of Representatives in 1906. In 1911, during his final term in the state House, he was elected Speaker, and held that office for the final two years of his six-year tenure.

Early Years in Congress
In 1912, Rayburn ran for a seat in the U.S. House of Representatives, representing Texas' Fourth Con-

gressional district, when the incumbent, Rep. Choice B. Randell, decided to run for the Senate. Rayburn defeated a number of Democrats to win the party nomination, and easily defeated token Republican opposition in the general election; he took his seat in the Sixty-third Congress (1913-15). Rayburn would go on to serve more than 48 years in the House, until his death in November 1961. In that first Congress that he served, the Democrats held the majority, with Champ Clark of Missouri serving as Speaker. Rayburn became a certain vote for the economic and political programs of President Woodrow Wilson. Despite being considered a liberal, Rayburn was against rights for blacks, considering them inferior to whites. It was not until the 1950s that he disagreed with segregation.

Almost from the start of his congressional career, Rayburn became the protégé of John Nance Garner, a Democrat also from Texas. Elected to the House in 1902, Garner in 1913 was a member of the House Committee on Ways & Means, and he used his influence to get Rayburn a seat on the House Committee on Interstate and Foreign Commerce. From there, his rise in the leadership of the party in the House was rapid and, in many ways, unprecedented. Rayburn served as chairman of the Committee on Interstate and Foreign Commerce in the Seventy-second (1931-33), Seventy-third (1933-35), and Seventy-fourth (1935-37) Congresses. In 1932, when Garner ran for President, Rayburn served as his campaign manager.

In 1937, when the Seventy-fifth Congress (1937-39) convened, he was elected Majority Leader, to fill the vacancy created the previous June when then-Majority Leader William B. Bankhead was elected Speaker upon the death of Speaker Joseph W. Byrns. Rayburn would serve as Majority Leader through the remainder of the Seventy-fifth Congress and for a portion of the Seventy-sixth Congress (1939-41). When Bankhead died suddenly on 15 September 1940, leaving the Speaker's chair vacant for the fourth time in just nine years, Rayburn was the natural choice, as Majority Leader, to be advanced to the speakership. He had been considered a potential Speaker when Speaker Henry T. Rainey died in 1934, and, although Majority Leader Bankhead was given the speakership in 1935 when Speaker Joseph Byrns died, Bankhead's seriously ill health (he died just five years later) led Democrats to elect Rayburn as Majority Leader to succeed Bankhead should he die. Rayburn's service as second in the House leadership lasted less than four years.

The Vote

Rayburn's election as Speaker was quick and without much bandying about, as Speaker elections once held some surprise. A history of the House of Representatives noted that "with no objection or fanfare, the House agreed to the resolution and Rayburn received the oath of office. Without any remarks from the new Speaker, the House continued its business and presented memorials about Mr. Bankhead."

During this period that he rose to become Speaker, Rayburn was one of the key members who got President Franklin Delano Roosevelt's economic program, known as "The New Deal," enacted through Congress. In fact, Roosevelt wrote that he considered Rayburn "the most valuable man in Congress while the...programs of the New Deal were fighting for survival." John Nance Garner, who served as Franklin Delano Roosevelt's Vice President, later wrote that Rayburn authored several measures which Garner called "the Cornerstone of the New Deal." These included the Securities Act of 1933, the Securities Exchange Act of 1934, and the proposal that became the Federal Communications Commission (FCC). In 1936, he shepherded through Congress the Rural Electrification Act, which offered rural communities lower cost electric services, especially during the years of the depression. However, during the last years of the 1930s, as Vice President Garner became more and more dissatisfied with President Roosevelt, Rayburn also began to argue with the President and opposed him on a number of measures; when Roosevelt proposed expanding the U.S. Supreme Court for more liberals so that his New Deal initiatives would not be struck down, Garner labeled the action the "dictator bill." Still a loyal Democrat, Rayburn then ushered Roosevelt's wages and hours bill through the House.

Acceptance Speech

On 3 January 1941, when the Seventy-seventh Congress convened in Washington, Rayburn was elected Speaker for a term of his own. He told the members of the House,

> You have elevated me to a position, I must confess, that has been one of the ambitions of my lifetime. Today I will take the oath of office as a Representative from the Fourth Congressional District of the State of Texas for the fifteenth time. The House of Representatives has been my life and my love for this more than a quarter of a century. I love its traditions; I love its precedents; I love its dignity; I glory in the power of the House of Representatives. As your Speaker and presiding officer it shall be my highest hope and unswerving aim to preserve, protect, and defend the rights, prerogatives, and the power of the House of Representatives.

Legacy as Speaker

Sam Rayburn, known better as "Mr. Sam," would serve as Speaker of the House in every Congress controlled by Democrats from 1940 to 1961, from the Seventy-sixth through the Eighty-seventh Congresses. Only two times, in the Eightieth Congress (1947-49) and the Eighty-third Congress (1953-55), when the Republicans controlled the House, did he serve not as Speaker but as Minority Leader. His seventeen total years of service as Speaker makes him the longest serving Speaker in House history.

Rayburn was not just the Speaker, he was a dogged powerhouse who fashioned his imprint on the speakership. Using the power of the Speaker, Rayburn rewarded Democrats who supported him and the party, while punishing those who strayed from the party line as well as Republicans. In 1957 and 1960, he used his power against that of southern Democrats to get a floor vote - and ultimate passage - of important civil rights legislation. In 1956, when southern Democrats wanted to sign the so-called "Southern Manifesto" to protest the U.S. Supreme Court's decision to integrate the schools in the case of *Brown v. Board of Education of Topeka, Kansas*, Rayburn refused to sign it. Historian Tony Badger wrote,

> Rayburn, himself, regretted the <u>Brown</u> decision and hoped that Texas could "delay it coming into operation for as long a time as possible," but it was the law of the land. Like [Lyndon Baines] Johnson [also of Texas], he did not like

divisive sectional issues when raised in such a way that they could not be brokered into compromise within the Democratic Party. The Manifesto made such compromise difficult. In any case, he believed that "any congressman worth his sale can lead his district" and he thus encouraged his fellow Texans to avoid signing the Manifesto.

Sam Rayburn shaped the domestic legislation of three American Presidents - Woodrow Wilson, Franklin Delano Roosevelt, and Harry S. Truman - and has his name as either the author or backer of some of the most towering legislation of the twentieth century. Even when the President was of a different party, as it was during the 1950s with Republican Dwight D. Eisenhower in the White House, Rayburn worked closely to either support or oppose the President. Members across the aisle considered him a friend, and his honesty was legendary - in 48 years in the House, he went on only one political trip, and he paid for it himself out of his own pocket.

During the 1950s, with Eisenhower in the White House, Rayburn worked closely with Senate Majority Leader Lyndon Johnson, Democrat of Texas, and the two proved to be a potent political team in the Congress. In 1960, Johnson ran for President, but when he lost the party nomination to Senator John F. Kennedy, it was Rayburn who convinced Johnson to take Kennedy's offer of the vice presidency.

His Final Years

In late 1960, Rayburn's health began to fail; he lost weight and his appetite vanished. Examinations led to the discovery of inoperable colon cancer. Despite the diagnosis, Rayburn remained in the Speaker's chair, although twice in the middle of the 1961 he fainted in the chair. He told friends that he wanted to stay on the job to work on President Kennedy's program known as "The New Frontier."

By October 1961, however, it became impossible for Rayburn to work, and he left the Congress for his home on Texas. The cancer spread to his brain and then throughout his body. Finally, he died on 16 November 1961, just two months shy of his 80th birthday. He was buried in Willow Wild Cemetery in Bonham. His gravestone reads simply, "Mr. Sam Rayburn. Jan. 7, 1882-Nov. 16, 1961."

With seventeen total years as Speaker, Sam Rayburn holds a record that, in this day and age of term limits and potential majorities becoming minorities in the U.S. House of Representatives, looks like it will never be broken. On 30 January 1951, he broke Henry Clay's record in the Speaker's chair of four months 11 days, set between 1811 and 1825. On 12 June 1961, Rayburn had actually doubled Clay's record.

In 1949, Rayburn was awarded a $10,000 grant from Collier's Magazine for distinguished service to the nation. Rayburn took the money and started the Sam Rayburn Library in Bonham, Texas. His personal papers were initially housed there, until they were moved to the Center for American History at the University of Texas at Austin. The Library still remains as a center of study for American politics and government. In February 1965, more than three years after his death, the House of Representatives opened a third office building for its members, additions to the Cannon and Longworth Buildings. This third structure, named the Rayburn Building in his honor, was started in 1962 and completed in April 1965. Nine House committees and House support staff call the Rayburn Building their home. At the end of the century, *Roll Call* magazine, which monitors Congress, compiled their listing of the 10 most influential members of Congress of the 20th Century; in the listing, Speaker Joseph Cannon was first, with Newt Gingrich listed as third behind Senator Everett Dirksen of Illinois. Rayburn finished eighth overall, although the members he is in company with on this list are some of the giants of the House and Senate.

Near the end of his life, Rayburn spoke about his time in the House, both as a congressman and as Speaker. "The House of Representatives has been my life and it has been my love," he said. "I never had any ambition to be a governor or a senator. I wanted to come to this body and stay here as long as my people wanted me." He continued, "They have been as kind and fine to me as you have been." In October 1961, shortly before Rayburn's death, Majority Leader John McCormack wrote to historian Bascom Timmons, "I have felt for a long time that someone ought to write a book about the life of Sam Rayburn," he explained. "Such a book would be an inspiration to all persons who read the same, and it would certainly be an inspiration to future generations of Americans, particularly the youth in the molding of their character, because Speaker Rayburn's life is not only a Horatio Alger story, but it is a story of 'one of the great Americans of all time.'" McCormack had originally written "of our time" but had gone over the "our" with "all."

Further Reading:

Champagne, Anthony, *Congressman Sam Rayburn* (New Brunswick, New Jersey: Rutgers University Press, 1984).

Dorough, C. Dwight, *Mr. Sam* (New York: Random House, 1962).

Shanks, Alexander Graham, "Sam Rayburn and the New Deal, 1933-1936" (Ph.D. dissertation, The University of North Carolina at Chapel Hill, 1964).

HERBERT C. BONNER
1ST DISTRICT, N.C.

HENRY C. OGLESBY
SECRETARY

ASSISTANT SECRETARIES:
MARY ANDREWS WHICHARD
ANN KILBY

COMMITTEE:
CHAIRMAN, MERCHANT MARINE
AND FISHERIES

HOUSE OF REPRESENTATIVES, U. S.

WASHINGTON, D. C.

July 20, 1959

RECEIVED
JUL 21 1959

Mr. Paul M. Butler, Chairman
Democratic National Committee
1001 Connecticut Avenue, N.W.
Washington 6, D. C.

Dear Paul:

I have your letter of the 15th with enclosures.

You have done the Democratic Party a great disservice. I know of no other man who has labored with and for the Party any more than the Speaker of the House, Sam Rayburn. I have known Senator Johnson during the time he was a member of the House and of course have kept up my acquaintance with him since he moved to the Senate. He has my great admiration. In fact, they are a great team—Johnson and Rayburn.

It is easy for one to talk about what he would do here in Congress, and the ones I have known that talked the most on the outside did the least when they got here.

Sincerely,

Herbert C. Bonner

HCB:lb

SAM RAYBURN
4TH DISTRICT, TEXAS

The Speaker's Rooms
House of Representatives U.S.
Washington, D.C.

June 1, 1955

Mr. Lorimer Rich
35 West 53rd Street
New York 19, New York

Dear Mr. Rich:

I enjoyed my talk with you in the company
of Lowell Mellett, and if any move is made to change
the front of the Capitol, I am sure architects like
you, will be allowed to express themselves.

With every good wish to you, I am

Sincerely yours,

Sam Rayburn

Joseph William Martin, Jr.

Served as Speaker:
January 3, 1947 - January 3, 1949
January 3, 1953 - January 3, 1955

Although his name is forgotten today, Joseph Martin was the last Republican to serve as Speaker of the House, from 1953 to 1955, before Newt Gingrich took that station in 1995 in the 104th Congress. Martin, a moderate Republican from Massachusetts, traded the speakership with Sam Rayburn in Texas: the two men served as either Speaker or Minority Leader from 1939 until Martin was replaced as the Republican leader in 1959, with Rayburn dying of cancer in 1961. A man who many in his party considered a potential Presidential or Vice Presidential candidate, Martin worked closely with the administrations of Presidents Franklin Delano Roosevelt, Harry Truman, and Dwight D. Eisenhower to formulate foreign policy, although Martin vociferously fought against the domestic policies of Roosevelt and Truman.

Personal History
Born in North Attleboro, Massachusetts, on 3 November 1884, Martin was the son of Joseph William Martin, Sr., a blacksmith, and Catherine (née Keating) Martin, an emigrant from Ireland. Martin

detailed his family in his memoirs, *My First Fifty Years in Politics*, published in 1960. He wrote:

> *My father, Joseph William Martin, Sr., who had come from a farm near Plainfield, New Jersey, and established himself as a blacksmith in North Attleboro, was a Grover Cleveland Democrat. I was born November 3, 1884, the day before Cleveland was elected [as President] for the first time. [Cleveland lost the White House in 1888, but ran again in 1892 and was elected to a second non-consecutive term.] My father wanted to name me Grover Cleveland Martin. My mother, Catherine Keating Martin, an Irish immigrant, was a strong Republican and wouldn't hear of it. 'Grover's a dog's name,' she said. Our family of eight children, in which I was the eldest of six boys, finally took on a completely Republican coloration when my father deserted William Jennings Bryan on the gold issue in [1896].*

In 1890, the younger Martin, just six years old, went to work delivering newspapers to help support his family. At the same time, he continued his education, graduating from high school in 1902. Martin's work with newspapers elicited in him a love of journalism, and when he was offered a scholarship to Dartmouth College in Hanover, New Hampshire, he turned down the offer to instead go to work full time as a reporter for the North Attleboro *Sun*. A student of the politics of Republican Theodore Roosevelt, Martin moved towards the GOP and, in 1908, he and several friends pooled their money to buy the local Republican organ, the *Evening Chronicle*, and Martin was installed as the paper's editor. Martin pushed the Republican line even more than the previous owners, and was rewarded when the paper became a leading voice for the GOP in the state.

In 1911, Martin crossed from merely covering politics to participating in the field when he ran for a seat in the Massachusetts state House of Representatives. Because of the standards of the *Evening Chronicle* that Martin enunciated, namely that of independence, hard work, personal responsibility, and sobriety, friends and close associates believed that he would be a great candidate for office. He won in a close race, and eventually served six years in the state legislature: three one-year terms in the House, and three one-year terms in the state Senate. During his tenure in the lower body an election for U.S. Senator was held in 1912, the last time such an election took place before the passage and adoption of the Seventeenth Amendment to the U.S. Constitution in 1913 (which provided for the direct election of Senators by the people rather than by state legislatures). Because Republicans held control over the state House, a Republican would be elected to the seat; the selection was between Rep. Samuel W. McCall and Rep. John W. Weeks. Martin's backing of Weeks, which led Weeks to name Martin as his "floor leader" to pick up votes, proved to be an important stepping-stone for Martin. He would later become an ally of Weeks, as well as his son, Sinclair Weeks.

In 1914, after serving three terms in the state House, Martin ran for and was elected to a seat in the state Senate. There, he worked closely with the Republican Governor, Samuel W. McCall, whom he had worked against in the 1912 U.S. Senate election. In 1916, Martin served as a delegate to the Re-

publican National Convention, held that June in Chicago. The following year, he served as the chairman of the statewide legislative campaign for the 1918 elections. In 1922, he was named as the executive secretary of the Massachusetts state Republican Party. During this period of service, Martin became close friends - as well as a political ally - of Calvin Coolidge, the Massachusetts politician who rose from Governor of the state to Vice President in 1921 to President in 1923 when President Warren G. Harding died in office.

Early Years in Congress

In 1924, Martin decided to run for national office, and threw his hat in the ring for a seat in the U.S. House of Representatives. He would have to take on the incumbent, Rep. William S. Greene, who had a lengthy career in state and federal politics but at age 83 was vulnerable from charges of being too old. Martin appealed to voters to send a younger man to serve in the House, but Greene's record of service carried him, and the elder representative won the primary by nearly 3,000 votes. Only a week later, however, Greene fell and broke his hip; he died four days later from pneumonia. A group of political leaders from the 15th Congressional district came together in emergency session and decided to replace Greene on the ballot with Martin. At the same time, one Robert Leach of Taunton, Massachusetts, was named to finish the remainder of Greene's term while the election was held. Martin went on to defeat Democrat Arthur Jean Baptiste Cartier by nearly 10,000 votes. He took his seat in the Sixty-ninth Congress when it convened on 7 December 1925, and would remain in the U.S. House until his retirement at the end of the Eighty-ninth Congress (1965-67).

Although by today's political standards Martin would be considered a moderate Republican, in his day he was known as a rock-ribbed conservative who supported the administrations of Presidents Calvin Coolidge and Herbert Hoover during the 1920s and early 1930s. When Franklin Delano Roosevelt became President in 1933 and initiated the series of governmental programs, known as "The New Deal," to try to revive the depressed American economy, Martin saw the moves as a fascist attempt to take over the capitalist system in the United States. Despite the fact that Republicans had lost since 1930 a huge number of seats in both the House and Senate, and the Democrats were in charge of both bodies with huge majorities, Martin soon took center as one of the Republican leaders who argued forcefully against Roosevelt's policies. Martin voted consistently against such programs as the act that established the Tennessee Valley Authority (TVA) in 1933 and the Securities Exchange Act of 1934, among others. Working with fellow Reps. Bruce Barton and Hamilton Fish, both of New York, they maintained that Roosevelt was wrecking the economy with his policies, and was encouraging war when he sent packages of military aid to Britain at the end of the decade. In 1940, Roosevelt ran for a third term against these three men. Historian Ellsworth Barnard wrote about Roosevelt that "as for aid to Britain, he recalled Republican votes against the repeal of the arms embargo in the fall of 1939, and declared that the opposition in the House had been led by 'Martin, Barton and Fish.'" The phrase became so well-known that William Safire, the famed presidential speechwriter who later wrote for the *New York Times*, added it to his own work, *Safire's Political Dictionary*. Ironically, Martin and President Roosevelt were close friends, getting along quite well when they met to discuss policy matters; Martin later wrote that "Roosevelt's attack lent a new bond to our friendship. Afterward, whenever we three would meet one another here and there we used to refer to ourselves as 'members of the firm.'"

In 1939, Martin was elected Minority Leader. His goal - that of electing a Republican majority to the House - seemed to be an impossible task; at the time, in the Seventy-sixth Congress (1939-41), Democrats controlled 261 seats to 169 for the GOP, with 2 Progressives, 1 American Labor, and 1 Farmer-Labor members. However, he worked closely not only with Republicans, whom he held together to vote against the programs of the Democratic leadership, but also with disaffected Southern Democrats, many of whom disliked Roosevelt's plans for the economy. By 1939, the expansive New Deal programs that FDR had instituted six years earlier had shown little promise, with unemployment as high as it was when Roosevelt took over the White House. At the same time that Martin opposed Roosevelt's domestic policies, voting against TVA and the Securities Exchange Act (which established the

Securities and Exchange Commission), he also differed over the President's international strategy as well, taking a firm isolationist stand and denouncing Roosevelt's attempts to get the United States involved in what soon became the start of the Second World War in Europe and Asia. Martin opposed the lending of ships to Great Britain, a plan known as Lend-Lease, as well as the repeal of the Neutrality Act and the extension of the draft. But with his limited numbers in the House behind him, Martin knew he could offer only token opposition. As he wrote in his memoirs, "We could not stop the New Deal...when we tried it ran over us." He also wrote, "Through the violent years of Franklin Delano Roosevelt's New Deal my role of leader put me in the forefront of the opposition not only to many of Roosevelt's domestic spending programs, but also to measures, such as the lifting of the arms embargo, that threatened to drag us into war abroad long before Pearl Harbor did it for us."

A member of the Republican National Committee from 1936 to 1942, serving as chairman from 1940 to 1942, Martin also served as the chairman of five Republican National Conventions (1940, 1944, 1948, 1952, and 1956).

When the Japanese attacked Pearl Harbor in December 1941, Martin joined the other Republican members of the House and Senate and stood with President Roosevelt to support fighting Germany and Japan.

In 1946, after 16 years of Democratic control over the House, the GOP won 55 seats in the mid-term election and took over the majority in that body. That electoral tide against his party left President Harry S. Truman as the first Democrat since Woodrow Wilson in 1918 to have to rule with a Republican-led House. On 1 January 1947, the President wrote in his diary:

Called Joe Martin. He assured me that cooperation was at the top of his consideration. And that he wanted very much to help run the country for the general welfare. He told me that he would be most happy to talk to me at any time on any subject. I am inclined to believe that he meant what he said.

Nevertheless, Martin opposed Truman's "Fair Deal" policies for the American economy, which Martin labeled as "socialist."

The Vote

When the Eightieth Congress (1947-49) opened in Washington, D.C. on 3 January 1947, it was assured that Joseph Martin, already in the House for more than 21 years, would be elected Speaker of the House, the first Republican Speaker since Nicholas Longworth held the office in 1930. After he was elected, former Speaker Sam Rayburn made some comments about the new Speaker, calling him "your Speaker, my friend, your friend, the friend of mankind, a man of unquestioned character, of demonstrated ability, with a great, fine heart and with fairness."

Acceptance Speech

After being sworn in, Martin directed additional comments to the assembled members of the House, focusing mainly on the increased role of the United States in the affairs of the planet following the end of the Second World War:

In assuming the duties of the House of Representatives of the Eightieth Congress, in assuming the duties of Speaker of this House of Representatives, I am deeply grateful to my colleagues for having bestowed this signal honor upon me.

No man could fail to be deeply touched by the great honor and privilege of being the Speaker of this historic and august body. No man could fail to have a deep sense of responsibility in assuming the duties of the speakership because of the tremendous problems which beset our country and our times.

I pay warm tribute to the honorable and able gentleman from Texas [Sam Rayburn] whom I succeed to the chair, and who so generously and graciously presented me to the House.

Colleagues, the Eightieth Congress comes into existence in a time when most of the world lies crushed, broken, and in waste from the ravages of the most terrible war mankind has ever experienced.

Orderly government has, to a great extent, lost control in most countries.

Millions of men and women - and little children - are still displaced far from their native homes; they are still hungry; they are still dazed by the enormity of the horrible disaster which has wrecked their lives, laid waste their native lands, left them without homes, and, in many cases, bereft of loved ones.

Those millions of war-stricken peoples turn to the beacon of freedom and security, which, thank God, still burns brightly in the United States of America - sending its gleams of hope to the furthermost points of the world. If the torch of freedom and progress in the United States should flicker out, the world would be left in darkness. Therefore, for the sake of the world - of civilization - for the sake of those millions who have been crushed under the juggernaut of war - for the sake of our own future - we must keep the torch of freedom and progress alight in America.

So help us God, it is not going to flicker out.

Here at home we face grave and pressing problems. The debt into which this Nation has been plunged is of such magnitude it cannot be paid off in more than a century. Our people are bowed down under a burden of taxation which is well-nigh intolerable.

Strikes, industrial disagreements, scarcity of raw materials and machinery, and a large remnant of governmental controls still hamper production...

I say to you, my colleagues, with deep sincerity that, for the constructive accomplishment of good government, I hope to see a degree of cooperation between the Members on both sides of the aisle, and between this and the other branch of Congress, which will be unsurpassed in the history of our Nation.

When Martin was sworn in as Speaker, he made history: on that date, 3 January 1947, the first television broadcast of a House session was aired live to a local Washington, D.C. television station and then sent to stations in New York and Philadelphia. The program showed not only the opening day of the Eightieth Congress, but Speaker Martin's opening address to the House members.

Legacy as Speaker

James Joseph Kenneally wrote,

The Washington to which Martin came as Speaker in 1947 had changed considerably since his arrival as an untried congressman in 1925. The New Deal, World War II, and the onset of the Cold War had resulted in a population explosion, a construction boom, and the District's emergence as an international military, economic, and political center....Martin's management of the speakership was based on personal qualities that helped elevate him to that office and on his experience as minority leader. His integrity, loyalty, and good fellowship according to several witnesses left him without an enemy. Even further endearing him to his colleagues were his jumbling of words, such as recognizing "the gentleman from Rayburn, Mr. Texas" and announcing a committee to welcome Korean President Syngman Rhee as the president of India, which he corrected to Indiana. Martin attributed his success as leader to his affability and consensus building. "They like me; they know I try to be fair. We've got to stick together...But you can't drive them."

During his tenure as the Speaker of the Eightieth Congress, Martin spent more time in working with the administration of President Harry S. Truman than in opposing him; he supported Truman's requests for aid to Greece and Turkey as part of the European Recovery Program (ERP), known better as the Marshall Plan. However, Martin did lead the opposition in the House to much of Truman's domestic agenda, including his calls for national health insurance and assistance for public housing for the poor. One action that did occur during Martin's speakership was the move to make the Speaker of the House second in line, behind the Vice President, to succeed the President due to removal from office or death. Martin, in his memoirs, called it "a new dimension [that] was added to the office." He explained,

The original legislation on this question in 1792 provided that in such circumstances the first in line would be the President pro tempore of the Senate. The next after him would be the Speaker. This law remained in effect for ninety-four years until 1886 when, in the first administration of Grover Cleveland, Congress substituted a new system, designating the Secretary of State as first in line after the Vice-President. Following the Secretary of State, in the event he was available, the line of succession followed, in descending order of seniority, through the Cabinet. After the Secretary of State came the Secretary of the Treasury; after him the Secretary of War, and so on.

In his letter to the House asking for the Speaker to be designated as second in line behind the Vice President, Truman wrote,

A completely new House is elected every two years and always at the same time as the President and Vice-President. Usually, it is in agreement politically with the Chief Executive. Only one-third of the Senate, however, is elected with the President and Vice-President. The Senate might, therefore, have a majority hostile to the policies of the President and might conceivably fill the Presidential office with one not in sympathy with the will of the majority of the people.

When asked by reporters if he wished to be President, Martin told them that he wanted President Truman to live out his term. "I have no wish to be President," he said.

In 1948, as Truman was barely winning a first elected term - he had succeeded President Franklin Delano Roosevelt upon the latter's death in April 1945 - the Democrats were winning 83 seats to turn a 246-188 minority in the Eightieth Congress to a 263-171 majority in the Eighty-first. After just a single term as Speaker, Martin was relegated to the position of Minority Leader.

Minority Leader

He remained in that post during the Eighty-first and Eighty-second (1951-53) Congresses. During the latter Congress, Martin became entangled in a foreign policy mess that few politicians wish to find themselves in. In early April 1951, Martin received a letter from General Douglas MacArthur, the commander of United Nations forces fighting in South Korea against Communist North Korean and Chinese troops; in the correspondence, MacArthur criticized the failure of President Truman to utilize Nationalist Chinese soldiers from Taiwan to aid in the battle against the Communist Chinese. Martin inadvertently disclosed the contents of the letter on 5 April, which divulged the harsh criticism of the President by MacArthur, a breach of protocol in a nation where civilian rule of the military is paramount. On 11 April, following days of controversy over MacArthur's words, President Truman relieved him of the command of United Nations and United States forces, replacing him with General Mark Clark.

A Second Tenure as Speaker

In the 1952 election, as former General Dwight D. Eisenhower was winning the presidency, Republicans in the House captured 22 seats to take back the majority, 221 to 213. Again, Joseph Martin was elevated by his party to the speakership. His acceptance speech again touched on Martin's sincere hope that the two parties would work together for the betterment of the nation.

It was during Martin's second tenure as Speaker that for the first time in the history of the U.S. House gunfire was heard in the well of the House chamber. On 1 March 1954, several Puerto Rican terrorists entered what was then the Ladies Gallery, took up positions, and waited for an opportunity to attack the members. As historian Robert V. Remini explained:

> It was 2:20 p.m. and the House was in the midst of voting on a bill authorizing the continuation of a program for admitting Mexican farm laborers for temporary employment into this country. Lolita Lebron, a Harvard-educated radical, led a group of three followers: Rafael Cancel Miranda, Irvin Flores and Andrew Figueroa Cordero. They rose from the back row of the gallery as Lebron screamed, "Viva Puerto Rico libre," and waved a Puerto Rican flag. Then the three peppered the floor with twenty-nine shots from Lugers and an automatic pistol. One of the bullets struck the desk of Charles Halleck, the majority leader... Speaker Martin said he had just finished counting the ayes - there were 168 - and was about to call for the no votes "when I heard the first

> two or three cracks. I looked up to see what was going on and I moved back against the wall."

Two members, Ben F. Jensen, Republican of Iowa, and Alvin M. Bentley, Republican of Michigan, were gravely wounded, with three Democrats also hit. The men all recovered, but, as one witness noted, Bentley "was never really the same." Then in his first term, he did not run for re-election in 1960, running unsuccessfully for the U.S. Senate. He died in Arizona in 1969 at the age of 50; many believe that his early death was caused by the wounds he suffered during that attack.

During this second tenure as Speaker, Martin was involved in a rough intraparty squabble over taxes. The Revenue Act of 1951 had raised tax rates sharply to try to pay for the deficit incurred by the war in Korea. By the end of 1953, these measures were scheduled to end. Rep. Charles William Reed, Republican of Illinois and the chairman of the House Committee on Ways & Means, pushed to have these tax increases expire not at year's end but in the middle of 1953. Martin, along with Majority Leader Charles Halleck of Indiana, supported the plan of President Eisenhower to keep the tax increases going past their expiration date. Ignoring his party leaders and his President, Reed moved forward on his own plan, insisting that he would enact the cutoff of the raises, "no matter what Eisenhower, or Treasury Secretary [George M.] Humphrey, or anyone else had to say about it." The Committee on Ways & Means passed the bill out of committee 21-4 without any hearings. Martin then asked Committee on Rules chairman Leo Allen of Illinois to hold the bill in his own committee without bringing it to the floor for a vote. Reed could not get members of his own party to move the bill out of the Rules Committee, and it died there. He then turned to fighting the President's request to extend, for a period of six months into late 1953, an excess profits tax passed on business by Congress in 1950. When Reed refused to hold hearings in the Committee on Ways & Means, Martin threatened to move the legislation to the Rules Committee. Reed relented, and the committee, without his own approval, voted to send the bill to the floor on 8 July 1953. It then passed both houses of Congress, and was signed into law by President Eisenhower.

In the 1954 election, the Democrats picked up 19 seats and took back control of the House after just one term in the minority. In his memoirs, President Dwight D. Eisenhower wrote of the problems that came about among Republicans in handling their new minority status:

> When we lost control of the House in the 1954 elections, difficulties arose in the Republican leadership in the House. Having lost the speakership to Sam Rayburn, a Democrat, Joe Martin now elected to resume the post of party leader, a job that Charlie Halleck wanted to keep. Mr. Halleck is a high-tempered man and he wasted little time in making his dissatisfaction felt. He was a fighting leader and was valuable to me. Following our defeat, Mr. Martin had provided for Halleck no official place in the Republican leadership group, so I personally insisted that Halleck still attended the Legislative-leader meetings at the White House...Congressman Halleck grew restive and came to me for my "permission" to start a campaign to unseat Mr. Martin. I refused to endorse the idea, telling Mr. Halleck that such an action would cause a definite cleavage from top to bottom in the Republican delegation, and asking him to work, informally, to help get administration programs enacted into law. At the same time, I asked Mr. Martin to find some kind of official role for Halleck in the leadership group that would east the growing tension between the two. Martin refused, and the situation grew worse rather than better.

The tension between Martin and Halleck continued throughout the decade, culminating in the horrific loss of 49 seats in the mid-term election in 1958, leaving the GOP with just 153 seats to the Democrats' 283. When the Eighty-sixth Congress convened in Washington in January 1959, Martin, at 72 years of age, was replaced as Republican leader by his nemesis, Charles Halleck of Indiana, in the Republican caucus election. His leadership of the party, begun in 1939, ended after 20 years.

After Leaving the Speakership

During his last years in the House, Martin's power waned considerably. In 1966, he lost in the Republican primary to a newcomer, Margaret Heckler, who later served in the administration of President Ronald Reagan as Secretary of Health and Human Ser-

vices. Heckler was just 8 years old in 1939 when Joe Martin became the Republican leader. Now, at 82, he had been voted out of Congress altogether.

Joseph Martin, 83 years old, died less than a year and a half later, on 6 March 1968, in Fort Lauderdale, Florida, where he was vacationing. After his appendix ruptured, he was rushed to a local hospital, where he died of peritonitis. He had been in Florida living at the home of his nephew George Kelly since the previous October; his brother, Albert, the editor of the *North Attleboro Chronicle*, of which Joseph Martin was the publisher, told reporters that his brother had suffered from severe arthritis in recent years and was vacationing in the Sunshine State for his health.

In 40 years of service in the U.S. House of Representatives, Joseph Martin fought the good but unrewarding fight of the politician bucking the trends of the country he loved. Quiet in demeanor - the obituaries of him noted that his life was not exciting: "He never drank or smoked or played cards. He lived quietly in a Washington hotel, and would have a breakfast of melon, wholewheat [sic] toast and black coffee in the House restaurant, where as leader he would discuss legislation with other members" - he lived a solitary life in North Attleboro with his invalid mother, his widowed sister, and his brother. In lauding the man who opposed his party's politics during his entire congressional career, President Lyndon Baines Johnson said in a statement:

> Americans everywhere lament the death of Joseph W. Martin Jr. But we are joined also in enduring admiration and gratitude for the inspiring example of a friend, patriot and human being. For half a century Joe Martin demonstrated the finest qualities of legislator and statesman. He placed the Nation's trust first. Among those of who knew him well and worked long hours at his side, he will be missed but affectionately remembered.

Ray C. Bliss, chairman of the Republican National Committee, added, "He stood always on the side of the traditional American principles of representative government. Few men have contributed more to their party or their country." Rep. Gerald Ford, who replaced Charles Halleck as Minority Leader, said, "The country, the Republican Party, have lost a great statesman. Joe Martin's contribution to a better America will be indelibly written with his great record in the Congress of the United States." In honor of the former Speaker, the House adjourned from any further work for the remainder of that week. Following his funeral, Martin was laid to rest in Mount Hope Cemetery in Attleboro.

In his 2003 work on Martin's life, historian James Joseph Kenneally wrote that the Speaker never felt that he was a hyper-partisan, in the mold of the politicians that we see today, on any one issue. "In his own estimation Martin 'was never a fanatic on any issue,'" Kenneally explained,

> He was concerned more with the day-to-day running of the House than with the ideology - conservative or liberal. His approach to legislation was pragmatic, grounded in respect for the House's members of both parties, including even those Republicans who voted against him. At the conclusion of the Seventy-sixth Congress when paying tribute to the Democratic Speaker, his friend Sam Rayburn, Martin explicated his legislative philosophy: "We all come to Congress actuated by but a single purpose, and that is to promote the welfare of the common country...It is through honest differences of opinion and debate we reach the best conclusions. This is Americanism functioning in the American way. This must be continued if the people are to rule."

One Republican later said of Martin, "He was a victim of his belief that everybody was as nice a guy as he was. They weren't."

Further Reading:
Hasenfus, William Albert, "Managing Partner: Joseph W. Martin, Jr., Republican Leader of the United States House of Representatives, 1939-1959" (Ph.D. dissertation, Boston College [Massachusetts], 1986).

Kenneally, James Joseph, A Compassionate Conservative: A Political Biography of Joseph W. Martin, Jr., Speaker of the U.S. House of Representatives (Lanham, Maryland: Lexington Books, 2003).

Martin, Joseph W., My First Fifty Years in Politics: As Told to Robert J. Donovan (New York: McGraw-Hill Book Company, Inc., 1960).

JOSEPH W. MARTIN, JR.
14TH DIST. MASSACHUSETTS

Offices of Minority Leader
House of Representatives
Washington, D. C.

March 13, 1940

Mr. Dev. Miller
41 West 2nd St.
Maysville, Ky.

Dear Mr. Miller:

I have your letter and am very happy to add
my autograph to your collection.

Sincerely yours,

Joseph W. Martin Jr.

John William McCormack

Served as Speaker:
January 10, 1962 - January 3, 1971

A son of Irish immigrants who served 42 years in the U.S. House of Representatives, John McCormack rose to become Speaker of the House in 1961, serving for nearly nine years in that office during the period of the Vietnam War, the civil rights movement, and the institution of Lyndon Baines Johnson's "Great Society" of programs to aid the poor and uneducated. Rising to become speaker at age 70 - the second oldest person to ever hold the office - McCormack's tenure has been largely forgotten despite the work of the Congress over which he officiated.

Personal History
He was born in the poorest section of southern Boston, Massachusetts, populated mainly by Irish immigrants, on 21 December 1891, the son of Joseph H. McCormack, a stonemason, and his wife, Mary Ellen (née O'Brien) McCormack. The McCormacks were quintessential Irish migrants who found freedom in the new world of the United States. One of John McCormack's biographers, Lester Ira Gordon, wrote in 1976,

The story of McCormack's life properly begins in Ireland, where for centuries his ancestors labored in the soil to eke out a meager living. Surviving bad harvests and almost three hundred years of British rule, they remained in Ireland until the nineteenth century. McCormack's paternal grandparents immigrated to Canada around 1840 and his father Joseph H. McCormack came to the United States several years later. McCormack's maternal grandparents left Ireland in the late 1840s to escape the ravages of the great potato famine and eventually settled in Medford, Massachusetts, where John McCormack's mother, Mary Ellen O'Brien, was born.

The parents of John McCormack were to have 12 children, of which only three grew to adulthood. Nevertheless, McCormack's parents continued to display a love of their adopted country that they instilled in their son, who was to rise to become one of that adopted country's leading officials. In a 1973 interview, John McCormack said, "My mother kept telling me that America was a great land where there were no limits to a person's advancements if only he had ambition, courage, and determination, and she was right."

As opposed to families like the Kennedys, with whom he worked closely during his time in the House, John McCormack grew up in a part of Boston noted for its extreme poverty. When McCormack died in 1980, his obituary noted that:

> Most of the neighbors were poor, Irish and Catholic; the politics, flamboyant, personal and Democratic. He grew up in the "Last Hurrah" atmosphere of tenement wards where wakes, St. Patrick's Day parades and a florid oratorical style were important.

The family grew even poorer in 1904, when Joseph McCormack died, leaving his son John to take care of the family, which consisted of his widow and three sons (nine other children did not survive childhood). John McCormack quit school - at the time, he was in the eighth grade, attending the John A. Andrew School - to go to work as an errand boy for a Boston brokerage firm at $3 a week. When he took a better paying job ($.50 more a week) at a law firm, McCormack also began to study the law as a way of getting out of poverty. Working during the day and attending law school at night, McCormack passed the Massachusetts bar exam in 1913 and was admitted to the state bar. He had never even completed high school, but he was now an attorney. Unfortunately, his mother died two months before he passed the exam. A young man himself, McCormack was unable to keep custody of his two brothers, one of whom would serve in France during the First World War.

Rising quickly in the Massachusetts legal community, McCormack became respected for his hard work and legal acumen. In a 1970 interview, he said that "after I passed the bar, I could have obtained a position in a law office at $25 a week, which to me at that time was a great fortune, but I'd be sort of a super errand boy. I felt this would be inconsistent with the development of a mind of confidence in myself." He then worked to build up his own practice, a period that ended only when he was drafted for service in the U.S. military when the United States entered the First World War in 1917. A

Democrat, like his family and so many other immigrant families in his position, McCormack had been elected earlier that same year as a delegate to the Massachusetts Constitutional Convention, a seat he was forced to relinquish when he was drafted as a private. McCormack was never sent to France to fight, instead spending his time during the conflict either at Fort Devens in Massachusetts out Fort Lee in Virginia. He completed his enlistment in 1918 at Fort Devens, located in eastern Massachusetts. In 1920, McCormack married Harriet Joyce, a rising opera singer. Although the two remained married until Harriet's death in 1971, the couple did not have any children. Six years older than McCormack, she quietly acted as her husband's assistant and backer during his years in the U.S. House.

In 1919, released from the service, McCormack ran for a seat in the lower house of the Massachusetts legislature. He served three one-year terms in that body before running for and winning a seat in the state Senate, where he served from 1923 to 1926. In the final year of his tenure in the state Senate, 1925-26, McCormack served as the Minority Leader of the Democrats. In 1926, McCormack, desiring to advance in the political hierarchy, decided to challenge longtime Democratic Representative James Ambrose Gallivan, Born in Boston in 1866, Gallivan had served the voters of the 12th Massachusetts congressional district, comprising South Boston, Dorchester, and Roxbury, since taking the seat of popular - and corrupt - Boston politician James M. Curley in 1914; in 1926, Gallivan was seeking his sixth term in office. McCormack ran in the Democratic primary by emphasizing his support of the-then Governor of Massachusetts, David I. Walsh, running for the U.S. Senate, and the need for new leadership over experience. In the Democratic primary, however, Gallivan defeated McCormack by nearly 10,000 votes out of some 31,000 cast. Having given up his state Senate seat to run for Congress, McCormack was out of politics for the first time since 1917. He returned to the practice of law.

On 3 April 1928, Gallivan died, setting off a stampede of potential successors, all Democrats. Among them were state Senator William Hennessey, Boston School Board committeeman Edward Sullivan, and McCormack. McCormack ran on a platform of supporting the right of labor unions to collectively bargain, and backing the presidential campaign of New York Governor Alfred E. Smith. McCormack won the Democratic nomination on 18 September 1928, then defeated Republican Herbert Burr by over 40,000 votes out of some 80,000 cast. He was sworn into office on 3 December 1928, when the so-called "lame duck" session of Congress met, because he was filling the remainder of Gallivan's term. He was named to the Committee on Elections and the Committee on Territories. McCormack remained in the Congress until 1971, a period of more than 42 years.

Early Years in Congress

During his congressional service, McCormack rose in the ranks of seniority of his party, becoming Majority Leader three separate times (1940-47, 1949-53, and 1955-61). From the beginning of his career in the House, McCormack was a close friend and confidante of Rep. John Nance Garner of Texas, who in 1931 rose to become Speaker of the House. Despite Garner's more conservative voting record, as well as McCormack's liberal stands on issues, the two men were both supporters of President Franklin Delano Roosevelt's "New Deal" of government programs to try to end the depression in the early 1930s. McCormack's ties to Garner also paid off when Garner named the Massachusetts legislator to the all-important Committee on Ways & Means, which writes tax policy and deals with budgetary matters. In 1934, Congress established the Special Committee on Un-American Activities Authorized to Investigate Nazi Propaganda and Certain Other Activities, which is considered the precursor of the House Committee on Un-American Activities. The earlier committee is better known as the McCormack-Dickstein Committee, named after its chairman, John McCormack, and its vice chairman, Rep. Samuel Dickstein, Democrat of New York.

Following the departure of Speaker Garner to serve as Vice President in 1933, McCormack was involved in the tug of war to name his successor. Finally, in 1940, following the truncated speakerships of three Democrats, Henry T. Rainey, Joseph W. Byrns, and William B. Bankhead, all of whom died in office, McCormack threw his support for Speaker behind another Texan - this time, Rep. Sam Rayburn. Rayburn was in a tough fight with Rep. John J. O'Connor of New York for the Speaker's chair. O'Connor, a strong Irish Catholic from New York, was far closer in thinking, religion, and background to McCormack, but McCormack saw the Democratic Party as being unable to grow past the urban immigrant vote if it stuck with O'Connor instead of Rayburn, a more conservative and compromising Democrat from Texas. In exchange for his backing, McCormack was elected as the Democrat Floor Leader, which meant that he would serve as Majority Leader or Minority Leader, depending on who controlled the House.

In the latter years of the 1930s, McCormack, working with Rayburn and other Democrats, was able to help push through much of President Roosevelt's economic program, even as the Depression continued unabated. McCormack remained in the shadow of Rayburn for all of the 1940s and 1950s as the Texan served as Speaker and, during two terms when the Republicans were in the majority, as Minority Leader. During this period, he remains, at least in domestic affairs, the classic liberal, embracing increased appropriations for the unemployed and housing and social programs, and standing for the establishment of a national health care system run by the government. In foreign relations, however, McCormack backed President Harry S. Truman's strong stand against the Soviet Union, and supported Truman's call for an aid package of some $400 million to Greece and Turkey in 1947. In a July 1956 letter to Rep. Emanuel Celler, Democrat of New York, and chairman at the time of the House Judiciary Committee, Paul Butler, chairman of the Democratic National Committee, wrote that he believed that the party should nominate McCormack for Vice President at the 1956 Democratic National Convention:

> *After some good hard thought on the subject, I have concluded that an excellent candidate for the Vice Presidency would be Representative John W. McCormack, our Majority Leader...He is very highly regarded by the members of the House and Senate; he comes from a populous state in the East; and his religious affiliation would help the ticket. There is added strength in his candidacy because he is associated in the people's minds with the New and Fair Deals and he has been a vocal supporter of*

civil rights. His record should thus be triply significant in metropolitan areas.

Ironically, it was at this period of time that another Massachusetts politician, John F. Kennedy, was rising in the ranks of the party, first in the U.S. House, then the U.S .Senate and, in 1960, to become the party's presidential nomination. Despite both being liberals from Massachusetts, McCormack and Kennedy had even less in common than McCormack had with Rayburn: Kennedy, from a wealthy family, was far younger than McCormack and the two men never had much of a relationship, if one ever did exist. In 1956, when Kennedy was considered for the vice presidential nomination with the party's presidential nominee, Adlai Stevenson (a nomination that eventually went to Senator Estes Kefauver of Tennessee), McCormack only reluctantly backed Kennedy and waited until the last minute to endorse the Senator once he won the party's presidential nod in 1960. In 1962, relations between the two men went from cold to nasty when McCormack's nephew, John McCormack, ran an ultimately unsuccessful campaign for John F. Kennedy's open Senate seat, defeated by the President's younger brother, Edward M. "Ted" Kennedy.

The Vote

On 16 November 1961, following a lengthy bout with cancer, Speaker Rayburn died, leaving a vacuum of power in the House not seen since the overthrow of Speaker Joe Cannon in 1910. Although there was a sudden rush to fill the empty speakership, it was apparent that McCormack, the Majority Leader, would have the speakership if he wanted it. President Kennedy, in office less than a year, did not and could not oppose a fellow Massachusetts politician for the position. Having served as the second-in-command to Sam Rayburn since 1940, few were willing to fight the stalwart Democrat. On 21 December 1962, McCormack turned 70, making him the oldest man ever to be elected as Speaker for his first term. That election came on 9 January 1962, when the Democratic caucus selected him as their leader, a technicality since the Democrats controlled the majority. The following day, McCormack was elected Speaker over Republican Charles Halleck to become the 45th Speaker of the House.

Acceptance Speech

As *Time* magazine noted:

> *When McCormack mounted the rostrum to voice his thanks and to take the oath of office (administered by Georgia's Carl Vinson, the dean of the House), his smile flickered. It was a supreme moment for John McCormack - one he had dreamed of for half his life. Yet McCormack could sense a melancholy and a reserve in the House mood.*
>
> *The House was haunted. McCormack evoked the spirit in the opening words of his acceptance speech: "Speaker Rayburn was not only a great man. He was a good man." For all of McCormack's days as Speaker, he will be pursued by the memory of his predecessor and dear friend, the little Texan who had presided over the House more than twice as long as any other man. The House had rarely given a Speaker such wholehearted trust and respect.*
>
> *There was no Democratic challenge to Majority Leader McCormack's more or less automatic succession to Rayburn's chair - nor was there any marked enthusiasm about it. Some liberal columnists and editorial writers grumbled, but the young liberals of the House, much closer in "style" to their President than to their new Speaker, were too prudent to voice their misgivings publicly.*

McCormack thus became the first Roman Catholic to ever be elected as Speaker.

Legacy as Speaker

In 1947, the Congress changed the line of succession that made the Speaker of the House second in line to the presidency behind the Vice President, replacing the Secretary of State. On 22 November 1963, when President Kennedy was assassinated and, with Vice President Lyndon Baines Johnson's ascension to the presidency, there was no vice president, making McCormack second in line to the presidency. In an agreement between Johnson and McCormack, signed on 23 December 1963, the President agreed that if for any reason Johnson was unable to carry out the duties of his office he would immediately turn the reins of power over the Speaker McCormack. Because Johnson was not in the best of health - he had suffered a serious heart attack in 1955 - for the remainder of Kennedy's term McCormack literally sat one heartbeat from the presidency. Because of this status, the Speaker was given unprecedented access to the White House, and he sat in on national security and other meetings; McCormack also served as a member of the National Security Council, the top-secret group that helps form national security policy for the president. Because McCormack acted in effect as the "Acting Vice President," in 1967 Congress enacted the agreement into law as the 25th Amendment to the U.S. Constitution.

In 1964, during his second term as Speaker, McCormack pushed through the House two pieces of legislation that were embraced by President Kennedy: a civil rights bill and economic aid to the poor. In the civil rights bill, which became the Civil Rights Act of 1964, racial discrimination in nearly all areas of public accommodation, including housing, restaurants, hotels and motels, and other areas, was outlawed. A month before the legislation passed the House by a vote of 290 to 130 on 10 February 1964, McCormack told a reporter that the action was "one of the most important measures from a moral viewpoint to be considered by the Congress in many years." The bill was sent to the U.S. Senate, where it also passed and was signed into law by President Johnson in July 1964. McCormack's support of President Johnson's "war on poverty," much like his own backing for President Roosevelt's "New Deal" of economic programs in the 1930s, was in keeping with his political bent. The first piece of Johnson's plan was the enactment of the Economic Opportunity Act, which created training and other programs for poor youth, while also establishing a group known as Volunteers in Service to America, or VISTA. As Speaker, McCormack helped to shelter this legislation through the House despite Republican opposition.

Although in his first years as Speaker McCormack saw numerous legislative successes, he soon became a target of younger, more liberal, members of the Democratic Party. While many in this group felt that diplomacy with the USSR was in the nation's interest, McCormack saw Russia as a continuing threat and argued against compromise and diplomacy. Hearing that McCormack faced growing op-

position from inside his own party, President Johnson told reporters:

> *From the first time I entered the House of Representatives as a young Congressman to this very hour, I have known few men whose courage and compassion, decency of character and honorable objectives match that of Speaker McCormack. He is my friend and counselor. I feel better being President knowing that Speaker McCormack is by my side.*

Although Johnson was far more conservative than McCormack, in 1964 the Speaker, serving as permanent chairman of the Democratic National Convention, stood as Johnson was unanimously nominated as the party's presidential nominee that year in Atlantic City, New Jersey. McCormack campaigned for Johnson, and in November the Democrats won 36 seats to extend their majority from 259 seats to 295 seats (the Republicans went from 176 seats to 140) in the Eighty-ninth Congress (1965-67). With this increased power, McCormack was able to push through the House large sections of Johnson's Great Society program.

At the same time, however, McCormack was consolidating power for himself and the small group of men around him in controlling the House. In 1964, McCormack pushed to have the Rules Committee - the same committee that was involved in the revolt over Speaker Joe Cannon - expanded. Despite widespread opposition to his plan, McCormack won a bloody fight. The 1964 election, while giving the Democrats more seats in the House, also brought more liberals to the body. These new members formed the Democratic Study Group (DSG), which outlined a series of rules changes which would remove power from the more conservative and more southern members of the party and place it in the hands of the Northeastern liberal faction. McCormack warned the group that he would not be a "slave" to the liberal in the party. A change to the rule that allowed the Speaker to "force" the Rules Committee to report on measures that failed in committee but were supported by a majority of the party, known as the "21 day rule," passed in January 1965 by a slim 23 vote margin. In 1967, however, after the Democrats lost 48 seats in the House and liberals no longer commanded a majority inside the party, the rule was quietly done away with.

Critics of McCormack - and even some unbiased historians - disparage his tenure as Speaker as one in which the "old rules" that made reform of the House so hard to come by were reinforced, specifically by McCormack and the leaders around him. To this end, historian Roger Davidson wrote in 1988 that "Speaker John McCormack (1962-1971) resisted most of the changes; his successor, Carl Albert (1971-1777), who mediated between the barons and the reformers, was a transitional figure who hesitated to use the tools newly granted to him by the rules changes. Thomas P. O'Neill (1977-1986), a moderate reformer in his earlier years, moved cautiously into the brave new world." In 1965, the first major voice against McCormack was heard when Rep. Richard Bolling, Democrat of Missouri, published "House Out of Order," in which he slammed McCormack's leadership. Three years later, Bolling once again indicted McCormack in "Power in the House," which once again trod new ground in having a Speaker condemned not only while he was still in office, but by a member of his own caucus and party. Bolling wrote that McCormack opposed the Legislative Reorganization Act of 1946. He explained, "Behind the scenes, Speaker McCormack has exerted every effort to prevent enactment of any version of the bill designed to provide a limited measure of modernization of the antiquated machinery and antiquated ways of doing business in both House and Senate." Historian David Rohde, explaining that McCormack utilized the existing system of power in the House, wrote in 1991,

> *Speaker McCormack employed the whip organization more frequently than Rayburn, particularly for discovering members' vote intentions, but the organization remained the same. The whip and his deputy were appointed by the Speaker and majority leader, but the assistant whips were selected by their zones. The method of selection varied. Sometimes assistants were just appointed by the senior Democrat in the zone; in other cases they were elected. Thus assistant whips were not necessarily loyal to the leadership or supportive of party policy.*

In another move that angered the liberal members of his party, McCormack refused to allow Rep. Adam Clayton Powell, Democrat of New York, to be seated after Powell became caught up in a number of scandals. When Powell sued to be able to take his seat, he named McCormack as the defendant. When the U.S. Supreme Court decided the case in 1965 - in Powell's favor - the case was concluded as *Powell v. McCormack* (395 US 486).

What made McCormack wholly unacceptable to Democrats was his stand in support of the Vietnam War. Matthew Green, in a 2004 dissertation on House leadership, explained,

> *Working with the chairman of the Armed Services Committee, L. Mendel Rivers (D-SC), [McCormack] scheduled an "avalanche of loyal votes" to keep legislators on record in support of the war, and "held the Democrats in line" on the issue. To be sure, only a minority of Democrats at first expressed opposition to the war, or even uncertainty of its direction and progress; but McCormack's goal was not to ensure passage of pro-Vietnam legislation, but to minimize any open dissent, particularly by legislators from his party.*

Rep. Morris Udall of Arizona, one of the liberals who did not support the Speaker, was highly critical of McCormack, stating that "he's standoffish, highhanded, not warm at all. He's blunt and brusque, doesn't mix with the boys or go out and get drunk with them." But, Udall noted, the "main thing people have against him is his total lack of tact and finesse. Just about everybody I have talked with, especially among the younger men, said they'd have voted for anybody running against McCormack." Historian Robert Remini then wrote,

> *Actually, the Speaker was generally liked "but rarely feared." He lacked effective and forceful leadership, especially in regard to liberal legislation, and seemed to represent the old order of conducting House business. Several times in the past there had been calls for McCormack to withdraw, both by members and the press... Udall begged McCormack to resign and urged Majority Leader Carl Albert to take his place. This revolt by some members was given greater urgency when the Washington Post printed an editorial on January 17, 1967, in which it suggested that the Speaker "step down gracefully before further disarray within the House detracts from his long record of legislative service."*

Despite the intraparty fight, a majority of Democrats re-elected McCormack as Speaker in the Ninetieth Congress (1967-69).

Two years later, however, as the House was poised to elect McCormack as Speaker for the Ninety-first Congress (1969-71), Udall challenged McCormack for the speakership, questioning his commitment to the party and arguing that the 78-year-old McCormack was too old for the post. Udall fell short of his goal, but while McCormack won election to another term he was privately warned by leading Democrats that he needed to step down to avoid a break in the party. One Democrat, Jerome R. Waldie of California, wanted to hold a vote of no confidence in the Speaker, a ground-breaking move. Waldie's move for a vote was defeated, 192-23. For McCormack, however, the handwriting was on the wall. During the first session of the Ninety-first Congress, it was revealed that an aide to the Speaker, Martin Sweig, as well as one of his close friends, Nathan Voloshen, had used the name of the Speaker's office to lobby a government agency on behalf of a private client. Although McCormack denied any personal wrongdoing in the matter, it illustrated his continued distance from the speakership and from the Democratic rank-and-file. (Sweig and Voloshen were later indicted for their role in the scandal.) But McCormack was a fighter, and did not like being pushed out of an office he had wanted all of his life. What may have convinced him in the end, however, was the rapidly declining health of his wife, Harriet. It was stated with some certainty that since their marriage in 1920, they two had never spent a night apart. Finally, on 20 May 1970, he announced that he would not stand for re-election at the end of the Ninety-first Congress. Asked why he was announcing the move in May rather than waiting until later in the year, McCormack said, "I didn't want to hold off and let some nincompoop get the nomination."

After Leaving the Speakership

In his final years, McCormack weathered the death of his wife in December 1971. The following month, he returned to Boston, and never went back to Washington. There he remained until his health failed in early 1980. On 22 November 1980, McCormack died of pneumonia in a nursing home in Dedham, Massachusetts, at the age of 88. He was buried in Saint Joseph Cemetery in West Roxbury, Massachusetts, just outside of Boston. The then Speaker, Thomas P. "Tip" O'Neill, also of Massachusetts, told reporters, "We have lost a great American. I have lost a close friend and political mentor of 40 years." The McCormack Graduate School of Policy Studies at the University of Massachusetts at Boston was named in his honor.

Further Reading:
Bolling, Richard Walker, *House Out of Order* (New York: E.P. Dutton & Co., 1965).

Memorial Addresses and other Tributes in the Congress of the United States on the Life and Contributions of John W. McCormack (House Document 97-33, 97th Congress, 1st Session [1981]).

Nelson, Garrison, "Irish Identity Politics: The Reinvention of Speaker John W. McCormack of Boston," *New England Journal of Public Policy*, 15 (Fall/Winter 1999/2000), 7-34.

JOHN W. McCORMACK
12TH DIST., MASSACHUSETTS

EUGENE T. KINNALY
ADMINISTRATIVE ASSISTANT

BOSTON OFFICE:
JAMES V. HARTREY
SECRETARY

WASHINGTON OFFICE:
MARTIN SWEIG
SECRETARY

Congress of the United States
House of Representatives
Office of the Majority Leader
Washington, D. C.
October 20, 1961

Mr. Bascom N. Timmons
Senate Press Gallery
The Capitol
Washington, D. C.

Dear Bascom:

A friend of mine has sent me the recent article you
have written about our dear and valued friend; -- the Speaker,
and I want to convey to you my feelings of thanks on the excellent
informative and human interest article you wrote about our dear
friend, as well as the story of one of the great Americans of our
time.

I have felt for a long time that someone ought to
write a book about the life of Sam Rayburn. Such a book would
be an inspiration to all persons who read the same, and it would
certainly be an inspiration to future generations of Americans,
particularly the youth in the molding of their character, because
Speaker Rayburn's life is not only a Horatio Alger story, but is
Americans of all time."

d I feel most keenly the serious
d friend. We pray and hope for his
be with us for a long, long time to

l regards, I am

Sincerely yours,

[signature: John W. McCormack]

EIGHTY-FOURTH CONGRESS

EMANUEL CELLER, N. Y., CHAIRMAN

FRANCIS E. WALTER, PA.
THOMAS J. LANE, MASS.
MICHAEL A. FEIGHAN, OHIO
FRANK CHELF, KY.
EDWIN E. WILLIS, LA.
JAMES B. FRAZIER, JR., TENN.
PETER W. RODINO, JR., N. J.
WOODROW W. JONES, N. C.
E. L. FORRESTER, GA.
BYRON G. ROGERS, COLO.
HAROLD D. DONOHUE, MASS.
JACK B. BROOKS, TEX.
WILLIAM M. TUCK, VA.
ROBERT T. ASHMORE, S. C.
JAMES M. QUIGLEY, PA.
CHARLES A. BOYLE, ILL.
IRWIN D. DAVIDSON, N. Y.

KENNETH B. KEATING, N. Y.
WILLIAM M. McCULLOCH, OHIO
RUTH THOMPSON, MICH.
PATRICK J. HILLINGS, CALIF.
SHEPARD J. CRUMPACKER, JR., IND.
WILLIAM E. MILLER, N. Y.
DEAN P. TAYLOR, N. Y.
USHER L. BURDICK, N. DAK.
LAURENCE CURTIS, MASS.
JOHN M. ROBSION, JR., KY.
DE WITT S. HYDE, MD.
RICHARD H. POFF, VA.
HUGH SCOTT, PA.

STAFF DIRECTOR:
BESS E. DICK

GENERAL COUNSEL:
WILLIAM R. FOLEY

LEGISLATIVE ASSISTANTS:
WALTER M. BESTERMAN
WALTER R. LEE

LAW REVISION COUNSEL:
CHARLES J. ZINN

ADMINISTRATIVE ASSISTANT:
BESSIE M. ORCUTT

HOUSE OF REPRESENTATIVES, U. S.
COMMITTEE ON THE JUDICIARY
WASHINGTON, D. C.

July 26, 1956

PERSONAL AND
CONFIDENTIAL

Mr. Paul Butler, Chairman
Democratic National Committee
1001 Connecticut Avenue, NW
Washington 6, D. C.

Dear Paul:

After some good hard thought on the subject, I
have concluded that an excellent candidate for the Vice
Presidency would be Representative John W. McCormack, our
majority leader. He is very highly regarded by the members of the House and Senate; he comes from a populous
state in the East; and his religious affiliation would help
the ticket. There is added strength in his candidacy because he is associated in the people's minds with the New
and Fair Deals and he has also been a vocal supporter of
civil rights. His record should be thus triply significant
in metropolitan areas.

I would like to talk more about this when we meet
in Chicago. With warmest greetings, I am

Sincerely yours,

[signature: Manny]

EMANUEL CELLER

EC:db

[stamp: RECEIVED JUL 27 1956 DEMOCRATIC NATIONAL COMMITTEE]

Carl Bert Albert

Served as Speaker:
January 21, 1971 - January 3, 1977

The only Oklahoman to serve as Speaker of the House, as well as being the highest-ranking Oklahoman in American political history, Carl Albert's career in the House spanned the period from 1947 to 1977, the last six years in service as Speaker, during which he oversaw the last years of the Vietnam War, the passage of the 26th Amendment to the U.S. Constitution, and the impeachment inquiry into President Richard M. Nixon, becoming the second Speaker to serve during such an investigation (Schuyler Colfax was the first in 1868). A man of short stature - he was just 5 feet 4 inches tall - he was known as "The Little Giant from Little Dixie."

Personal History

Albert was born on 10 May 1908, in a mining camp near North McAlester, Oklahoma, the son and eldest of five children of Ernest Homer Albert, a coal miner and farmer, and his wife Leona (née Scott) Albert. Despite there being a dearth of sources on the life of Albert, the one major biographical examination of him outside his 1990 autobiography is a 1974 article that appeared in *Chronicles of*

Oklahoma. In it, Albert, recalling *Recollections of My Early Life,* explained the poverty of his family into which he was born:

> *I have some recollections about my father starting the Little Bolen Mine...For instance, I remember him bringing the engine for the new mine in a wagon by our house. The wagon was pulled by a team of mules, called Mack and Kit, who were my father's pride and joy. They were later to be our principal farm animals and were kept until they died...My great-grandfather, Eli Albert, also gave my father a beautiful black horse, called Nick, which lived to be quite old. This had to be before June 9, 1906, when my great-grandfather died at Wilburton, Indian Territory.*

Although Carl Albert's father Ernest Albert barely earned a living as he worked a hardscrabble existence to support his family, in 1911 he was able to purchase a small farm in the village called Flowery Mound, Oklahoma, which was also known by locals as "Bug Tussle."

Carl Albert attended local schools before studying political science at the University of Oklahoma and, after graduating Phi Beta Kappa in 1931, he earned a prestigious Rhodes scholarship to Oxford University in England, where he studied law before he earned a degree in that field from that school in 1934, as well as a Bachelor of Civil Laws from St. Peter's College in Oxford. In 1935, after he returned to the United States, Albert was admitted to the Oklahoma bar and he subsequently opened a law practice in Oklahoma City. At the same time, he also worked as a leasing agent for several petroleum companies doing business in Oklahoma, and for a period of three years worked for the Federal Housing Administration. During his time in school, he won several awards for public speeches and oratory.

When the United States entered the Second World War in December 1941, Albert volunteered for service and was commissioned a private in the U.S. Army Air Force and was sent to the Pacific Theatre of Operations. Although later transferred to Third Armored Division for a short period, he eventually wound up in the Judge Advocate General (JAG) Corps. In 1942, he married Mary Harmon. For his service in action during the conflict, Albert was awarded a Bronze Star for heroism in battle.

In 1946, with the rank of Lt. Colonel, Albert left the JAG Corps and returned to Oklahoma, intending to remain a county lawyer. Instead, when Rep. Paul Stewart (1892-1950), a Democrat who had sat in the Seventy-eighth (1943-45) and Seventy-ninth (1945-47) Congresses, decided not to seek re-election due to ill health, Albert entered the race to succeed him. In a primary in which there were several Democrats vying for the seat, Albert came in second, some 2,700 votes behind Democrat Bill Steger. A runoff was forced because no candidate got the required 50%. Three weeks after Albert came in second, he won the primary, beating Steger by 330 votes out of some 58,000 cast. Albert easily beat Republican John Fuller to win the seat for Oklahoma's Third district.

Early Years in Congress
On 3 January 1947, Albert took his seat as a representative in the Eightieth Congress (1947-49). According to stories repeated in nearly all of his biographies, on that day, as Albert arrived to take

his seat, he was mistaken by a veteran Representative not for an incoming congressman, but for a House page, owing to his extremely short (five feet, four inches) stature. The representative - unnamed by all but Albert - called him over and said, "Son, take these papers over to my office."

During his tenure in Congress, through to the end of the Ninety-fourth Congress (1975-77), Albert demonstrated a strict liberal voting record, supporting massive government spending for social welfare and other programs for the poor and those of his area, including farm price supports, although he was also a hawk on defense matters; in the latter arena, he backed President Harry S. Truman's policy of funding the rebuilding of western Europe with "Marshall Aid," as well as the containment of the USSR. He was an ally of oil companies that did business in Oklahoma, working to pass legislation favorable to them. One area that remains controversial in his record is his objection to civil rights legislation; he voted against the Civil Rights Act of 1957, supported by President Dwight D. Eisenhower, as well as the first civil rights legislation of the Kennedy and Johnson administrations. He eventually voted for these actions only when they were tied to antipoverty measures.

When Albert came to Congress, the Republicans held the majority, although in the 1948 elections the Democrats re-took control of the House; Albert came under the influence of Democratic leader Rep. Sam Rayburn of Texas, who served as Speaker continuously except for two terms from 1940 to 1961. In 1955, when Minority Whip John W. McCormack was advanced to Majority Leader (Rayburn was elevated to Speaker), Albert was promoted to Majority Whip, the third-highest ranking office in the House. Speaker Rayburn actually favored Albert as his successor, not the more liberal McCormack. From this grand position of leadership a mere eight years into his congressional service, Albert quickly moved up the ladder of responsibility. Just seven years after becoming whip, the 1961 death of Rayburn and the elevation of Majority Leader McCormack to the speakership in 1962 opened the Majority Leader position for Albert, and he was elected to it by his fellow Democrats. 14 years after entering the House of Representatives, Carl Albert stood just one step away from the highest elective office in the House. As Majority Leader (1962-71), Albert took the role of "chief cheerleader" of the policies of the administration of President John F. Kennedy, making sure that the President's legislative priorities were given immediate attention by the House; in the area of health care, Albert helped shuttle through the initial Kennedy proposal - later enacted under his successor, Lyndon Baines Johnson, after Kennedy's assassination - for an extensive program of health insurance for the elderly, which later became Medicare. When Albert encountered resistance in the House from a coalition of Republicans and Democrats, Albert tried to do an end-run and have the legislation passed first by the Senate as an amendment to a welfare bill. Albert's initial move failed, and he stirred up a hornet's nest of controversy when he pushed for new rules in the House giving the majority Democrats more control over what kind of legislation would be passed, without input from the minority. He accomplished this by naming more hard-line liberals to the Rules Committee, and they in turn backed Albert's new plan. Utilizing these new rules, Albert was able to get the legislation - enacted as the Social Security Act of 1965 - passed and signed into law. Albert also used these rules to push President Johnson's social programs for the poor and disadvantaged known as "The Great Society."

The Vietnam War began while the Democrats controlled both the presidency and the Congress, and Albert backed the war for many years. In fact, in 1968, when he served as chairman of the Democratic National Convention in Chicago, Illinois, he was harshly disparaged by antiwar Democrats who he helped to shut out of the convention's proceedings. The party was deeply split over the war, and the assassinations of the Rev. Dr. Martin Luther King, Jr., and Senator Robert F. Kennedy of New York further sent the party into disorder and tumult. When Richard Nixon was elected President in 1968, Albert stood not as the cheerleader of the President's policies but as the manager of the opposition in the House.

Elected as Speaker
In 1969, after seven years as Speaker, John McCormack came under withering criticism from inside his own party as to his handling of the speakership. Nearly 80 years old and part of the "old

school" of pre-World War II politics, McCormack's style and ability to recognize only those members he supported left many liberals inside the party frustrated and angling to remove him from the speakership. In fact, when the Ninety-first Congress (1969-71) convened, Democrats in opposition to McCormack's tenure for another term as Speaker coalesced around Rep. Morris Udall of Arizona, who mounted a challenge to McCormack. Albert, ever the good soldier, stayed out of the fight, which in the end went to McCormack. Albert had to keep his caucus together, as another Democrat, Jerome R. Waldie of California, pushed for a no-confidence vote against the Speaker, an unheard-of parliamentary measure. The ability to hold that vote was defeated, but McCormack came to realize that he could no longer continue to run for Speaker. A financial scandal tied to one of McCormack's aides and a close friend ended any support McCormack may have had. On 20 May 1970 he announced that he would not run for another term, either as Speaker or for his congressional seat. This opened the way for Albert to run for Speaker in the Ninety-second Congress (1971-73). When that Congress convened with Democrats in the majority 255-180, Albert's election as Speaker was assured despite his long tenure of service (which, after McCormack, was seen as a negative and not a positive) and his close ties to former Speaker McCormack. As one of the leaders of the House majority, Albert was unpopular among the newcomers to the House; however, because he was the Majority Leader, it would have been impossible to deny him the speakership, as persons in that role, since the early twentieth century, have always been elevated to the Speaker's chair.

Legacy as Speaker
Although considered, especially by historians of the House, to be a classical late twentieth century liberal, Albert's overall record was much more moderate than it was advertised. In addition to supporting the 26th Amendment to the U.S. Constitution and tax reform, he also backed the enactment of giving police the right to enter homes with a warrant of not informing those inside that they were coming, known as "no knock" legislation. It was not until 1973 that he opposed any further fighting in Vietnam, and, because of his ties to the oil drilling in-

dustry in Oklahoma, he backed initiatives to assist the petroleum companies. On domestic matters Albert did side with the more liberal side of his party, including support for assistance to families, the Equal Rights Amendment (ERA) for women, and legislation to aid consumers.

Albert served as Speaker from the start of the Ninety-second Congress (1971-73) to the end of the Ninety-fourth Congress (1975-77). By the last term of his speakership, his unpopularity had risen to record levels among younger Democrats, who desired to see a more liberal and reformist representative sitting in the Speaker's chair. However, a closer look - and a span of years since he stepped down - at Albert's tenure shows that he was more of a reformist than he has been credited for. Historian Ronald M. Peters, Jr., during the Cannon Centenary Conference on the speakership in 2003, noted that the era of reform that we are currently in began, he believes, with the Albert speakership:

> In the 30 years since the reform movement of the early seventies, the speakership has undergone substantial change. The evolving character of the office has demonstrated two tendencies: a shift in emphasis from the parliamentary role of presiding officer to the political role of party leader, and a shift in attention from legislation to events external to the legislative process...Albert bridged the transition from the pre-reform to the post-reform eras. He straddled the transition from the old order to the new, but his orientation toward the speakership was distinctly traditional. Albert was well known for a punctilious attendance on his duties as presiding officer, recognizing Members to speak, ruling on points of order, and so forth. He was often to be found in the chair, and felt that it was the best place to be if one wanted to feel the pulse of the institution, as Members knew where to find him and would frequently come to visit with him. When not presiding, Albert was typically to be found in his office, arriving at 7 each morning and usually not leaving the building until the early evening. His attendance at political functions was intermittent, and participation in fundraising events was rare. Albert did initiate some changes consistent with the new order. He proposed a legislative agenda, was the first to

> use an ad hoc committee to process legislation, the first to utilize a party task force to define a party position, and the first to hire a full-time press secretary.

One of the key moments during Albert's speakership was the impeachment inquiry of, and House vote to impeach, President Richard M. Nixon. While Albert did not chair the inquiry in the Committee on the Judiciary, he did oversee the House vote which lodged three articles of impeachment against the President for his role in the corruption affair known as Watergate.

In a letter to a man in Maryland in April 1973 regarding the-then burgeoning scandal that would consume the nation, the Congress, and, ultimately, the Nixon presidency, Albert wrote:

> The separation of Constitutional powers between the Executive and Legislative branches is a matter of paramount interest at this time. Several official and non-official groups are looking into the question of impoundment of funds, executive privilege and reorganization, and war powers, the four principal areas where questions have been raised with respect to the Executive Department's overstepping its Constitutional prerogatives. While we recognize generally that the President has the authority to control the flow of funds on a limited basis, when it comes to completely voiding Congressionally-endorsed programs there is reason to believe he has virtually changed Congressional policy and overstepped Constitutional bounds by impoundment of funds. This and other problems involving [the] separation of powers will be seriously examined with remedial action in mind during the next year.

In 1973, as Watergate was rising as a political story, Vice President Spiro T. Agnew was indicted by a federal grand jury for tax evasion relating to money he accepted as Governor of Maryland. With his indictment, Agnew resigned, leaving the vice presidency vacant and Speaker Carl Albert first in line to the Presidency should anything happen to force President Nixon from power. This is the closest the Speaker has come to becoming President since the rule making the Speaker in line of succession for the presidency behind the Vice President was instituted in the Presidential Succession Act of 1947. Nixon moved quickly to replace Agnew; under the 25th Amendment, he nominated House Minority Leader Gerald R. Ford, Republican of Michigan, to be Vice President in October 1973. However, Albert realized that he, as the Speaker officiating over the possible impeachment and removal of the President, could move in such a way to make himself President, an action that Albert realized would be politically damaging. He announced that as a Democrat, he could not in good conscience succeed a Republican President, and would, if Nixon were removed and Albert became the Acting President, he would resign as soon as the Congress confirmed a Republican as the new President. This entire question became moot when Congress ratified Gerald Ford as the Vice President in December 1973.

The following year saw Carl Albert become the second Speaker in American history to oversee the impeachment vote against a President of the United States. (Speaker Schuyler Colfax oversaw the vote against President Andrew Johnson in 1868; Speaker Newt Gingrich would officiate over the vote to impeach President Bill Clinton in 1998.) After the Committee on the Judiciary approved three articles of impeachment, Albert managed the debate in the House that endorsed the articles to send the matter to the Senate for a trial. Nixon, who faced certain conviction in the upper body, resigned the presidency on 8 August 1974. Once again, the vice presidency was made vacant, as Vice President Ford became President, again leaving Speaker Albert as a potential President, a situation that was fixed when Ford nominated Governor Nelson Rockefeller of New York as Vice President and he was confirmed.

For many years, people realized that Carl Albert had a serious problem with alcoholism. In 1972, he was involved in a serious car accident in which he hit two cars; although it was suspected that he had been drinking and driving, no charges were ever brought against him.

When Albert was first elected Speaker, he already realized that his time in the position would be short, owing to the unpopularity of Speaker McCormack. As such, Albert promised at that time that he would serve as Speaker until 1978, when he would turn 70. In 1976, however, scandal turned any support he had in the House against him: he was

caught up in the Tongsun Park scandal, named after a South Korean lobbyist who paid bribes to numerous congressional members to gain favor for him and his government; the scandal became huge news when it was discovered that Park was a member of South Korean intelligence. Due to this and other issues, opposition had grown to such an extent among Democratic newcomers in the House that Albert announced that he would not seek re-election to his House seat that year. He left the House at the end of the Ninety-fourth Congress on 4 January 1977.

After Leaving the Speakership

Instead of becoming a wealthy lobbyist or a paid speaker, Albert returned home to McAlester, Oklahoma, even refusing to serve on corporate boards. In 1979, he established the Carl Albert Center at the University of Oklahoma in Norman, where congressional policy as well as the life and career of Carl Albert are studied. His personal papers are housed there, as are those of other congressional members. In 1990, he published, with the aid of Professor Danney Goebel, his memoirs, *Little Giant: The Life and Times of Speaker Carl Albert*.

In his final years, Albert suffered from a series of health-related ailments, including undergoing triple-bypass heart surgery in 1985 after having suffered heart attacks in 1966 and 1981, and, during the 1980s, a bout with cancer. On 4 February 2000, Albert died at the McAlester Regional Health Center in McAlester, Oklahoma. Survived by his wife and his two children, Albert was buried in Oak Hill Memorial Park in McAlester. His tombstone reads simply "Carl Bert Albert, May 10, 1908-Feb. 4, 2000. Speaker, U.S. House of Representatives, Jan. 1971-Jan. 1977."

Despite serving as Speaker for six years, and nearly rising to the vice presidency or the presidency twice, little has been written of the life and services of Carl Bert Albert, at least until recently. However, excepting for his 1990 memoir and a few magazine articles, his service and speakership are nearly forgotten three decades after he left the office, a strange event considering that he served during the end of the Vietnam War and during the Watergate scandal that became the second impeachment of a President and eventually ended with his resignation, the first in

American history. In reviewing Albert's memoir, Joseph Cooper of Johns Hopkins University wrote,

> In sum...there can be little doubt that Carl Albert deeply understood the politics of the House of his era. Otherwise he would not have risen to the speakership. What is far more rare is that he also deeply understood the House as an institution and used his speakership to defend and strengthen it.

Further Reading:

Albert, Carl Bert, "Recollections of My Early Life," *Chronicles of Oklahoma*, LII:1 (Spring 1974), 30-37.

———. with Danney Goble, *Little Giant: The Life and Times of Speaker Carl Albert* (Norman, Oklahoma: University of Oklahoma Press, 1990).

Kling, William, "Carl Albert is Sworn in as Speaker of the House", *Chicago Tribune*, 22 January 1971, 2.

CARL ALBERT, M. C.
3D DISTRICT, OKLAHOMA

Congress of the United States

House of Representatives

Office of the Democratic Whip

Washington, D. C.

McAlester, Oklahoma
November 17, 1958

RECEIVED
NOV 19 1958

Honorable Paul M. Butler, Chairman
Democratic National Committee
1001 Connecticut Avenue, N.W.
Washington 6, D. C.

Dear Paul:

Thanks for your very kind letter of
congratulations. I certainly appreciated hearing from you, and I am
deeply grateful for your words of
encouragement.

I hope everything is going well with
you, and with every good wish, I am

Sincerely,

Carl

CARL ALBERT, M. C.

CA:nm

The Speaker's Rooms
U.S. House of Representatives
Washington, D. C. 20515
April 18, 1973

Mr. Saul Zalesch
6229 Woodcrest Avenue
Baltimore, Maryland 21209

Dear Saul:

Thank you for your letter. The separation of Constitutional
powers between the Executive and the Legislative branches is
a matter of paramount interest at this time. Several official
and non-official groups are looking into the question of
impoundment of funds, executive privilege and re-organization,
and war powers, the four principal areas where questions have
been raised with respect to the Executive Department's over-
stepping its Constitutional prerogatives. While we recognize
generally that the President has authority to control the flow
of funds on a limited basis, when it comes to completely voiding
Congressionally-endorsed programs there is reason to believe he
has virtually changed Congressional policy and overstepped
Constitutional bounds by impoundment of funds. This and other
problems involving separation of powers will be seriously
examined with remedial action in mind during the next year.

With every good wish, I am

                              Sincerely,

                              Carl Albert

                              The Speaker

CA/ptk

Thomas Phillip O'Neill, Jr.

Served as Speaker:
January 4, 1977 - January 3, 1987

He is remembered for his axiom that "all politics are local." From the time when he was first elected to the U.S. House of Representatives in 1953, until he was elevated to the speakership in 1977, he rose through his party's leadership, serving as Majority Whip and Majority Leader. During his ten years as Speaker, he clashed with Presidents Jimmy Carter and Ronald Reagan over domestic spending and social programs. Mary Russell, writing in the *Washington Post* in 1977, said of him, "Tip O'Neill at all times has one great political weapon at his disposal. He understands so well that all political, power is primarily an illusion. If people think you have power, then you have power. Power is an illusion. Illusion, mirrors and blue smoke..."

Personal History

O'Neill was born in Cambridge, in Middlesex County, Massachusetts, on 9 December 1912, the son and one of four children of Thomas O'Neill, Jr., a bricklayer and superintendent of sewers in Cambridge who at the time of his son's birth was a member of the Cambridge City Counsel, and his wife

Rose Ann (née Tolan) O'Neill. The younger O'Neill earned the name "Tip" from his friends, who gave him the nickname "Foul Tip" in honor of a baseball player, James Edward O'Neill (no relation), who played for the St. Louis Browns in the late nineteenth century and had a propensity of hitting foul tips into the stands. "Tip"O'Neill was a lifelong baseball fan, particularly of his hometown Boston Red Sox. John A. Ferrell, who wrote a major work on O'Neill in 2001, wrote,

> In the early part of the nineteenth century, an intrepid couple named Daniel and Catherine Quinlan O'Connell took their brood of children from Ireland to North America. They settled in Portland, Maine, for a time, then made their way to Massachusetts. They were blessed with hardy sons who worked as laborers and on the railroads. They came from Mallow, a small market town in the county of Cork. They were Tip O'Neill's great-great-grandparents.

Having married in 1797, Ferrell explained, the O'Connells were part of the massive wave of immigration from Ireland to America that changed the face of the United States. When they settled in Massachusetts, they established a family residence that continues to this day. Eventually, the O'Connells merged with other families, and Daniel and Catherine O'Connell's great-grandson, Thomas O'Neill, married Rose Ann Tolan. Rose Ann O'Neill died of tuberculosis when her son Thomas was just nine months old, and he was taken care of, as was the rest of the family, by nuns at the family's parish church, as well as a French-Canadian maid. In 1920, Thomas O'Neill, Sr., married one Mary Cain, who helped bring the junior O'Neill up.

Attending parochial schools, O'Neill graduated from St. John's High School in 1931. He was interested in politics from the age of 15, when he campaigned for Democrat Al Smith for President in 1928. O'Neill later wrote how he sympathized with Smith, a fellow Roman Catholic. "All I knew was that Al Smith was an Irish Catholic and we had been suppressed all our lives," he remembered. After high school, O'Neill attended Boston College in Chestnut Hill, Massachusetts, from which he graduated with a bachelor's degree in 1936.

The Great Depression and the consistent bigotry against those of an Irish background in Massachusetts impacted O'Neill and shaped him into the man and the politician that he later became. When he worked an odd job of cutting grass at Harvard University, he was laughed at by richer students, and O'Neill hated them for it. He also hated these students because he saw them drinking alcohol during Prohibition. As he later wrote, "Who the hell do these people think they are, I said to myself, that the law means nothing to them?" The election of Democrat Franklin Delano Roosevelt, and his imposition of government economic programs known as the New Deal, persuaded O'Neill that ultimately government itself could change injustice and intolerance. He continued to work in odd jobs, including as an insurance agent.

Before earning his bachelor's degree, O'Neill entered the field of politics, running for a seat on the Cambridge City Council. Although O'Neill was well known in his neighborhood, he took the votes of friends and neighbors for granted, and in the end he lost by 150 votes and came in ninth, at a time when the top eight winners were elected to the council. Realizing that he

relied on his reputation instead of actively campaigning, O'Neill earned a valuable lesson that he never forgot for the remainder of his career.

In 1936, after he had completed his college courses, O'Neill once again entered politics, this time running for a seat in the Massachusetts House of Representatives. Elected at a time when Democrats came to dominate the state, O'Neill won re-election in 1938 and continued in that body until 1952. In 1948, he rose to become Speaker of the state House when the Democrats won an outright majority for the first time since the Civil War. A dyed-in-the-wool liberal, O'Neill believed that government was the solution to the problems in the lives of the people, advocating increased teachers' salaries and, at a time before the civil rights movement, helping to outlaw discrimination based on race or age.

Early Years in Congress
In 1952, O'Neill decided to move to the national stage, running for a seat in the U.S. House of Representatives, which had been held from 1947 by John F. Kennedy, who was vacating it to run for the U.S. Senate. O'Neill defeated Republican Michael LoPresti in a close race, and, on 3 January 1953, he took his seat in the Eighty-third Congress (1953-55). O'Neill would serve in this seat until the end of the Ninety-ninth Congress (1985-87).

Thomas P. "Tip" O'Neill came from the old school of American politics, and, when he first entered Congress, that body was run that way, with control of legislation in the hands of committee chairmen and the Speaker of the House. O'Neill's philosophy was symbolized in the sign that he placed on his desk during his time in Congress: "It's nice to be important, but it's more important to be nice." In his second term, he was named to the prestigious Committee on Rules, and became a confidante of the-then Democratic whip, John W. McCormack, also of Massachusetts. As McCormack rose in the leadership of the Democratic Party, O'Neill followed him, especially when McCormack became Speaker in 1962. On 21 January 1971, when McCormack stepped down from the speakership and from his seat in the House, and Majority Leader Carl Albert was elected Speaker, O'Neill was elected as the Democratic whip and, the following year, when then-Majority Leader Hale Boggs of Louisiana disappeared on a plane trip to Alaska, he was named to the vacancy. Thus, on 3 January 1973, after 20 years in the House, "Tip" O'Neill had advanced to become the second most powerful Democrat in the House, second only to the Speaker, Carl Albert of Oklahoma.

As a member of the Rules Committee, O'Neill participated in a number of important legislative actions, most notably the writing of the several civil rights bills of the late 1950s and early 1960s. He clashed repeatedly with the chairman of the committee, Howard W. Smith, Democrat of Virginia, who opposed all civil rights action. In 1961, when newly elected President John F. Kennedy pushed a new civil rights bill in the House, O'Neill, working with Speaker of the House Sam Rayburn, enlarged the committee membership to circumvent Smith and cut off any chance that the Virginian had to stymie the bill's passage. And while O'Neill was close with President Kennedy - O'Neill held Kennedy's old House seat - he was excluded from the President's inner circle by many of the President's aides, who were dubbed "the Irish mafia." These included Lawrence O'Brien and Kenny O'Donnell, and even the President's brother, Robert Kennedy, who called O'Neill "That big fat Irish bastard."

The issue that dominated the House during the latter years of the 1960s was the American involvement in the Vietnam War. In March 1971, O'Neill became the first Republican or Democrat leader who called for the withdrawal of American troops from Vietnam by the end of that year. O'Neill earned great enmity from the Nixon administration for his stand, as during the 1960s O'Neill had fought for, and won, a Department of Defense promise not to close the Boston Naval Yard. In fact, whereas O'Neill had supported the Johnson administration during its years in power (1963-69), he took a strong stand against the Nixon administration and its Republican policies. In 1972, when Nixon was re-elected in a landslide, O'Neill nevertheless opposed the President, particularly angering Speaker Carl Albert and chairman of the House Judiciary Committee Peter Rodino, Democrat of New Jersey, whom O'Neill saw as too hesitant to fight Nixon. When Nixon got into ethical trouble over what would become the Watergate scandal, O'Neill

became one of the first House leaders to call for the President's impeachment. It was during these years, from the Eighty-ninth (1965-67) through the Ninety-second (1971-73) Congresses, that O'Neill served as the chairman of the Select Committee on Campaign Expenditures.

It was during this period, when he served as Majority Leader, that O'Neill got into ethical trouble, although few biographies of him mention the episodes. Starting in 1973, O'Neill became close to South Korean lobbyist Tongsun Park, allowing Park to pay for two large birthday bashes in O'Neill's honor. When Park was exposed in the so-called "Koreagate" scandal, O'Neill's name was largely kept out of the stories by the media. Ironically, it was Speaker Carl Albert, whose own dealings with Park became front-page news, who suffered, being forced to relinquish his House seat in the 1976 election. In another ethical lapse, in 1975, O'Neill contacted Secretary of Housing and Urban Development Carla A. Hills to try to intervene in a federal loan application for James P. Wilmot, who had served as the chairman of the Finance Committee of the Democratic Party. O'Neill asked Secretary Hills to green light the loan of some $2 million for a housing project for Wilmot, evading the lengthy investigative process such loans go through. Due to O'Neill's intervention, the money was speeded up for Wilmot. Once again, the incident was barely reported in the media if at all, and no ethics investigation was ever launched against O'Neill.

The Vote
O'Neill heralded the election in 1976 of Democrat Jimmy Carter to the presidency. The retirement of Speaker Albert that same year also opened the speakership for only the second time since 1962. When the Ninety-fifth Congress convened in Washington on 4 January 1977, O'Neill, who had been elected as the choice of the Democrats for Speaker the previous month, won election to the position without opposition in his party; he defeated Republican Minority Leader John J. Rhodes of Arizona, 290 votes to 142. Thomas P. O'Neill, Jr., who had grown up in poverty in Massachusetts, rose to become one of the most powerful men in the American government at the age of 64. As he explained in his memoirs,

Some politicians have a yearning to be president, but from the time I first came to Washington in 1953, my private ambition was to become Speaker of the House. I had done the job successfully in the Massachusetts legislature, and I was confidant that I could do just as well in the House of Representatives... During my years as majority leader, Carl Albert had assured me half a dozen times that I'd take over as Speaker when he stepped down. But in June 1976, when Carl announced that he was going to run for another term in the House, I was caught by surprise. I was out in California, helping to raise funds for the congressional campaigns of [Democrats] Charles Wilson and Norman Mineta. A group of us were sitting around the pool at the hotel when Norm came over and said, "Tip, I just heard on the radio that Carl Albert is retiring. Let me be the first to support you for Speaker." I started to round out commitments, but it soon became clear that I had no opposition.

Legacy as Speaker

Although O'Neill and the new President, Jimmy Carter, came from the same party, both viewed each other suspiciously, and for this reason they had a rocky relationship for Carter's entire term of office. Carter, from Georgia, saw O'Neill as part of the "old crowd" of Democrats who had run the House with only two two-year interruptions since the days of Franklin Delano Roosevelt; O'Neill, on the other hand, reacted to the former Governor of Georgia the same as one of the Boston Brahmins he had come to hate at Harvard, who looked down on the poor and treated them with contempt. Carter felt that he had come to the presidency with a mandate to change the country following the Watergate scandal, and he was not in the mood to compromise in any way, even if it meant compromise with Democrats from his own party. He had run the state government in Georgia that way, and he intended to do the same in Washington. He sent legislation to Capitol Hill without consulting any of the House or Senate leadership, particularly Speaker O'Neill, and he did not meet regularly with any congressional members to get their input on important legislative matters. Of White House Chief of Staff Hamilton Jordan, O'Neill later wrote in his memoirs, *Man of*

the House (1987), "As far as Jordan was concerned, a House speaker was something you bought on sale at Radio Shack." When O'Neill and Carter first met at the White House, the President told the Speaker that as Governor, he had fought the wishes of the Georgia state legislators when they opposed him, and he would not hesitate to do the same if the House or Senate Democrats tried to fight him. Feeling that he was popular enough with the American people, he warned O'Neill that if the Speaker tried to fight him, the Democrats would run against O'Neill in the 1978 mid-term elections.

In the end, O'Neill did compromise, helping Carter to enact some of his legislative priorities into law, including welfare reform and an energy policy that included the establishment of a cabinet-level Department of Energy. Yet the two men continued to clash, particularly over the precedence of a balanced budget, which Carter had promised when he ran for President. As O'Neill biographer John Farrell explained, Carter was determined to slow down government spending. "And across the table is Tip O'Neill, the quintessential New Deal Democrat - unrepentant, un-reconstructed, and determined to follow the Roosevelt philosophy of tax and tax, spend and spend, elect and elect...and basically standing for much of what Jimmy Carter had come to Washington to change." Despite the increasing animosity between the men, O'Neill remained the loyal Democrat. When fellow Massachusetts Senator Ted Kennedy challenged Carter for the 1980 Democratic Party presidential nomination, O'Neill remained neutral and did not side with Kennedy, who lost to Carter. But four years of bad economic news and an administration seen as weak against the nation's enemies took a toll on Democrats, and on election night Carter lost the president in a landslide to former California Governor Ronald Reagan. As the night wore on, Carter's defeat became more and more obvious. The President went on television and conceded to Reagan, even as polls remained open in California. O'Neill had personally pleaded with Carter to wait until the polls had closed, but Carter had ignored him, and many Democrats on the west coast of the United States went down to defeat as their supporters walked away from voting because the presidential race had already been called. O'Neill was furious; in a last jab at Carter, he told one of the President's aides, "You guys came in like a bunch of pricks, and you're going out the same way." The Republicans in the House picked up 33 seats, the largest pickup by the party in a presidential election since 1920. When the Ninety-seventh Congress (1981-83) convened, Democrats held the majority, but by a 243-192 advantage. Republicans were 26 seats shy of a majority, and O'Neill had to work with the opposition in a substantial way for the first time in decades.

One of O'Neill's greatest challenges, specifically after the 1980 election that brought more Republicans to the House, GOP control over the U.S. Senate, and Reagan to the White House, was that a substantial portion of O'Neill's own party was dominated by conservative Democrats. In 1980, these Democrats, feeling left out by the increasingly liberal Democrat leadership, formed the Conservative Democratic Forum (CDF). In 1981, when Reagan submitted his FY 1982 budget, these conservative Democrats bucked their own party and joined Republicans to pass a budget aimed less at social programs and more at national defense and tax cuts to stimulate the economy. Although O'Neill personally got along with Reagan - both were of Irish heritage - the Speaker detested the President and made sometimes snide comments about him, calling Reagan "Herbert Hoover with a smile." Reagan had equally biting comments about O'Neill; the President wrote that O'Neill was "an old-fashioned pol" who could "turn off his charm and friendship like a light switch and become as blood thirsty as a piranha. Until six o'clock, I was the enemy and he never let me forget it."

Even when the economy improved and "Reaganomics" proved to be the engine that rebuilt the American economy in the 1980s, O'Neill continued to deride the President and his economic program as being harsh towards the poor and the social programs that O'Neill trumpeted. Gradually, even the media portrayed O'Neill as out of step with the American people; *Time* magazine (18 May 1981) derided him when he voted against the Gramm-Latta budget resolution, which sought to cut government spending and reduce the deficit. "At that moment," wrote journalist Robert Ajemian, "it was clear that the nation's most powerful Democrat had been badly, perhaps even fatally, wounded." He added, "O'Neill is beginning to show

an uncharacteristic passivity, as if events are already intimidating him...It was obvious that he still had an emotional hold on the House. But the hold is loosening now, and it looks very much as if the job Tip O'Neill has worked a lifetime for is offering challenges he cannot meet." Whispers began to be heard that some anti-O'Neill Democrats were working behind the scenes to find one candidate to support who could challenge O'Neill for the speakership following the 1982 elections. O'Neill told reporters that "For a while, I was a solitary voice crying in the wilderness." The Speaker and his party were "blessed" with a recession that struck in mid-1981 and which was blamed on Reagan and the GOP. In 1982, the Democrats picked up 26 seats to increase their majority to 269 to 165. When the Ninety-eighth Congress (1983-85) convened on 3 January 1983, O'Neill was once again elected Speaker. He had held the majority and even increased it, and disarmed his critics.

On 17 March 1983, O'Neill hosted the first St. Patrick's Day lunch on Capitol Hill. Joining the Speaker and other House and Senate members was President Reagan. To foster a spirit of "Irishness," O'Neill kept reporters out of the lunch. "I'm going to cook you some Boston corned beef and I'm going to have an Irish storyteller there," O'Neill told the President. Reagan shot back with a laugh, "I'll have to polish up some new Irish jokes." Reagan and O'Neill eventually came to a personal truce, especially when the President invited O'Neill to the presidential residence in the White House to celebrate his 70th birthday. Secretly, the men worked together to try to bring peace to Northern Ireland, then in the grips of a homicidal religious civil war.

In his final two terms as Speaker, in the Ninety-eighth and Ninety-ninth (1985-87) Congresses, O'Neill was unable to keep his party together. At the time, the Democrats were composed of southern conservatives who strayed from the party leadership and crossed the aisle to vote with Republicans on issues backed by the Reagan administration, and northern liberals who wanted to resist Reagan at every turn, even if it meant defeat. In 1986, during his seventeenth term in Congress, O'Neill announced that he would not stand for re-election that year. Few knew at the time that he was in the beginning stages of colon cancer, a disease he would fight for the remainder of his life. In summing up his congressional career, most notably his tenure as Speaker, historian Robert V. Remini wrote:

> [T]he record Tip left was impressive. The years O'Neill presided over the House were years in which an efficient legislative operation slowly evolved. But it required strong leadership. Take, for example, the 99th Congress (1985-87). It revised the tax code more completely than at any time since World War II; it enacted stiffer environmental regulations; it raised student aid; and it revised immigration law. To a large extent the success resulting from the fact that bills were brought to the floor with limitations on the amendments that could be proposed. In the past bills were amended to death and took months to debate. Together with the Rules Committee, the Speaker made sure both debate and amendments were kept under tight control. Debate was reduced to a few days, leaving members with a sense of pride that the House, unlike the Senate, functioned intelligently and swiftly.

O'Neill was asked about the role of the Speaker, and he noted,

> You know, you ask me what are my powers and my authority around here. The power to recognize on the floor; little odds and ends - like men get pride out of the prestige of handling the Committee of the Whole, being named the Speaker for the day; those little trips that come along - like those trips to China, trips to Russia, things of that nature; or other ad hoc committees or special committees, which I have assignments to; plus the fact that there is a certain aura and respect that goes with the Speaker's office.

In 1996, in discussing O'Neill's role in the advancement of the speakership, Walter Oleszek wrote,

> O'Neill's ten-year tenure as Speaker transformed the post in an important respect. He elevated the national visibility of the speakership and thus the office's potential in articulate and establish the House's agenda. "[Speaker] Sam Rayburn could have walked down the street of Spokane without anybody noticing him," said

then-Majority Leader [Tom] Foley. "Tip O'Neill couldn't do that, and it is very unlikely that any future Speaker will be anonymous to the country. In short, O'Neill ushered 'in a new age in the House without ever being a new age politician.'"

After Leaving the Speakership

In 1990, after leaving office, O'Neill had a major operation to remove the cancer that was continuing to grow in his colon. At the same time, the former Speaker spoke out about the disease and went on television on the subject, becoming the national face of the fight against colon cancer. On 18 November 1991, President George H.W. Bush awarded O'Neill the Presidential Medal of Freedom, the highest award bestowed on a non-military citizen of the United States. Bush, a Republican, said of O'Neill, a Democrat:

> In his 50 years of public service, Thomas P. O'Neill, Jr. was not just a man of the House of Representatives; he was a man for the American people. Inheriting the public service tradition from his father, Tip O'Neill had an uncanny ability to understand people and politics. He won 25 consecutive elections, rising to become Speaker of both the Massachusetts and United States House of Representatives while always maintaining his humor, humility, and touch with the people he served. He said, "All politics is local," but he demonstrated that faithful service to the people also well serves the Nation. The United States honors this distinguished legislator for his leadership, amity, good humor, and commitment to service and freedom.

In his final years, O'Neill lived in his old apartment in Washington, D.C., a condo in Florida, or his home in Harwich Port, Massachusetts. On 5 January 1994, O'Neill died of cardiac arrest at Brigham and Women's Hospital in Boston, Massachusetts, a month past his 81st birthday. Following a tribute from Democrats and Republicans alike, he was buried in Mt. Pleasant Cemetery in Harwich Port.

Tributes to O'Neill, both from political friends and foes, poured in. The-then Speaker of the House, Thomas S. Foley, Democrat of Washington State, called him "the model of what a representative and a leader of the American people should be." Rep. Robert H. Michel, Republican of Illinois, who at the time was the House Minority Leader, said, "Partisanship was put aside, and we could be the best of friends." Senator Bob Dole, Republican of Kansas, said of him, "He was the Congressman's Congressman." He added that O'Neill "certainly will go down in history as one of the great political leaders of our time."

Thomas "Tip" O'Neill was considered "the last liberal" from the era of Franklin Delano Roosevelt and the New Deal, when government was involved heavily in the lives of the American people. And, he was proud to remain a liberal of that period even when it was no longer fashionable, or even politically expedient. However, O'Neill was not a classic liberal; when he went on NBC News' *Meet the Press* on 11 December 1977, he announced for the first time that he was "strongly against" abortion, because it was "an issue of high morals." Asking how he could oppose his own party on the issue, he answered, "How can I be a leader in the United States Congress?" In an era when one's television appearance was paramount, O'Neill also went against the grain; in his obituary, Bart Barnes wrote that "he was a large, joyous, generous-spirited man with a bulbous nose, yellowed white hair that flopped over his forehead and an ever-present cigar." During the 1980s, he became the stereotypical liberal, too concerned with government than with the people it was trying to help. When the Republicans ran a commercial showing a heavy-set old man who looked like O'Neill, the announcer said that "the Democrats have run out of gas."

For students of O'Neill, the "Tip" O'Neill Papers are located at the Boston College Library in Massachusetts. In addition to his memoirs, *Man of the House*, O'Neill also penned, with Gary Hymel, *All Politics Is Local: And Other Rules of the Game*, which appeared after his death.

Further Reading:
Brandt, Karl Gerard, "Deficit Politics and Democratic Unity: The Saga of Tip O'Neill, Jim Wright, and the Conservative Democrats in the House of Representatives during the Reagan Era" (Ph.D. dissertation, The University of Texas at Austin, 2003).

Farrell, John A., *Tip O'Neill and the Democratic Century* (Boston: Little, Brown, 2001).

O'Neill, Thomas P., Jr., with William Novak, *Man of the House: The Life and Political Memoirs of Speaker Tip O'Neill* (New York: Random House, 1987).

James Claude Wright, Jr.

Served as Speaker:
January 6, 1987 - June 6, 1989

In 1987, Jim Wright of Texas, whose career in the House had already spanned 32 years, became the 48th Speaker of the House, succeeded Thomas P. "Tip" O'Neill. Like O'Neill, Wright was an expert in the rules of the House and his accession to the speakership seemed almost natural. Unlike O'Neill, however, Wright's combative style, combined with a seeming arrogance that shut out not only Republicans from House business but also Democrats who did not toe the leadership's line, made him few friends. Within two years of his becoming Speaker, amidst increased turmoil among even the Democratic caucus and allegations of rampant corruption, Wright resigned first the speakership and then his House seat. His rise to the pinnacle of power was slow, but his fall from that high station in the federal legislative branch was rapid and painful to watch. A Texas politician in the fashion of fellow Texans and Speakers John Nance Garner and Sam Rayburn, who in fact was a protégé of Rayburn, Wright's style of leadership made enemies both in his own party and the opposition, which may have been one of the chief reasons why he had so little support when ethics charges were lodged against him.

Personal History

Born in Fort Worth, Texas, on 22 December 1922, Wright was the son and first child of James Claude Wright, Sr., and his wife Marie (née Lyster) Wright. Excepting for Wright himself, few sources document his ancestry and family. According to Mark William Beasley, author of a 1978 dissertation on Wright's early years, the future Speaker could trace his mother's roots to Irish and Australian emigrants to America:

> His mother's paternal grandparents traced their heritage to Dungannon in County Tyrone, Ireland. Her grandmother descended from the Caulfields and the Hayningtons, notable members of the landed gentry; preserved remnants of a manor house owned by that family still stand in Dungannon. Wright's maternal grandfather, Harry Haynington Lyster, born in Australia, received a degree in civil engineering from Heidelberg University in Germany before joining a great uncle, Charles Ligar (a retired surveyor-general of Australia), late in the 1880s on a rugged 640-acre Texas ranch, located

twenty-five miles west of Fort Worth. In 1891 he met and wed nineteen-year-old Lena Crowder (a local school teacher). He father, William Monroe Crowder, a former Confederate cavalry bugler, had migrated from Tennessee to Parker County, Texas, in 1882, where he farmed and taught school.

The Lysters moved to New Mexico, where their daughter, Marie, the mother of Jim Wright, was born in 1894. She met her future husband, James Wright, Sr., at a fair in Texas sometime after 1910. Wright's family is less documented; it is believed that they originated, as well, in County Tyrone, Ireland, afterwards moving to America and then emigrating from western Virginia and eastern Tennessee to Texas sometime in the late nineteenth century. James Claude Wright, Sr., was born in Shady Grove, Texas, in 1890. His father died when he was an infant, and his mother suffered from polio and was confined to a wheelchair; the elder Wright worked his way through a series of positions, including as a clerk and making bricks. After the turn of the century he became a boxer; while traveling to earn some money he met Marie Lyster, and the two later moved to Texas, where Wright served in the U.S. Army with General "Black Jack" Pershing in hunting for Mexican bandit and murderer Pancho Villa in Mexico. In 1916 the two were married; Wright later served in Europe during the First World War. Their first child, James Wright, Jr., was born for years after the end of that conflict.

The younger Wright attended local schools in Fort Worth and Dallas, then attended Weatherford (Texas) College from 1939 to 1940, and then the University of Texas from 1940 to 1941. Following the Japanese attack on Pearl Harbor, Hawaii, on 7 December 1941, which led to American entry into the Second World War, Wright enlisted in the U.S. Army Air Force that same month and, in early 1942, was commissioned with the rank of 2nd Lieutenant. Serving with the 380th Bomb Group (Heavy) in the South Pacific as a bombardier, he was awarded a Distinguished Flying Cross for his service during the conflict. Wright later wrote about his service in the war in his 2005 work, *The Flying Circus: Pacific War - 1943 - As Seen through a Bombsight.* At war's end, Wright returned to Weatherford, Texas, where he became a partner

with his father in the National Trades Day Association, a company that was involved in national trade extension and advertising.

A Democrat, Wright ran for his first office shortly after returning from the war. In 1946, he was elected to a seat in the Texas state House of Representatives, serving a single term until 1949. Defeated for re-election in a bitter campaign, he rebounded and in 1950 he was elected the mayor of Weatherford, serving until 1954. He served as the president of the League of Texas Municipalities in 1953, and was a delegate to Democratic National Conventions starting in 1956. In 1988, his first and only convention when he was Speaker, he served as the chairman of the Democratic National Convention held in Atlanta, Georgia.

Early Years in Congress

In 1954, Wright ran for and was elected to a seat in the U.S. House of Representatives representing Texas's twelfth district, after he challenged the incumbent, Democrat Rep. Wingate H. Lucas, who had held the seat since 1947 but who many in the district saw as too conservative. With the state dominated by the Democrats, Wright easily won the seat in November against token Republican opposition. Taking his seat in January 1955 in the Eighty-fourth Congress (1955-57), Wright would hold the 12th district seat for the next 34 years, a total of 17 terms and part of an 18th term, until his resignation on 30 June 1989. In 1961, he ran for a U.S. Senate seat from Texas, but he was defeated in the Democratic primary, but he retained his House seat and remained in the lower body of the Congress. As events would later bear out, Wright was a highly partisan Democrat who used the power of his office to force the issues he believed in whether or not they were popular; in one instance, he sponsored a revision of the law - now known with derision in Dallas-Fort Worth as the Wright Amendment - which limited and controlled the amount of air traffic out of Love Field, one of the city's then two major airports, so that the Dallas-Fort Worth International Airport, now known as DFW, could grow into the major transportation hub that it is now. Many in the area blame Wright for the concentration of air traffic and noise around DFW to Wright's action that would have allowed

Love Field to spread the noise and traffic around to the other part of the city.

During his tenure through eighteen terms, Wright slowly rose up the ladder of the party's seniority system. In 1977, when Majority Leader Thomas P. "Tip" O'Neill was promoted to the Speaker's chair, Wright was elected as his successor in the Majority Leader position, but only by one vote, demonstrating the bitterness many even in his own party felt for him. In this capacity, the second most powerful leadership position in the House, Wright served as the leader of the Democrats from the Ninety-fifth (1977-79) through the Ninety-ninth (1985-87) Congresses. When Speaker O'Neill decided in 1986 not to seek re-election to his House seat and, thus, to another term as Speaker, his announcement set off a firestorm in the fight to succeed him as Speaker.

The Vote

The election of a new Speaker for the 100th Congress (1987-89) would be the first in 10 years, and only the third since 1962. The Democrats won five seats in that new Congress to give them a 258-177 majority, and, in the party caucus, Majority Leader Wright easily won a majority of his party's votes to advance to the speakership. When the 100th Congress convened in Washington on 3 January 1987, Wright was elected as the 49th Speaker of the House.

Acceptance Speech

Escorted to the Speaker's chair, he was sworn in and then delivered remarks to the House members:

To stand here in this place at this time, by your choice, is a treasure more precious than any material possession and an honor more sublime than royalty. To be Speaker of the U.S. House of Representatives is the highest responsibility that can come to a lawmaker anywhere in the world. It is a gift which only the Members of this House can give. Aware of the greatness of your gift, I offer you the abounding thanks of a full and grateful heart. Aware of the responsibilities it entails, I pledge to do my very best to the end that all of us together may achieve the grand expectations of those who wrote the Constitution 200 years ago, and the contemporary

hopes of our fellow Americans who last November elected us and sent us here to attend to the unfinished business of our Nation.

Legacy as Speaker

Wright ultimately served the whole of the 100th Congress, and part of the 101st (1989-91). Scholars Lawrence C. Dodd and Bruce I. Oppenheimer wrote:

As Speaker, [Wright] moved quickly to establish himself as a hands-on leader who would pursue an ambitious legislative agenda and act as "micromanager" of the legislative process. In doing so, he used the Steering and Policy Committee as a central policy committee, made aggressive use of the Rules Committee to restrict debate and to speed action on bills he considered top priority, and took a particularly powerful role in foreign policy, particularly on U.S. support for the Nicaraguan contras. During his speakership, in short, he transformed the office from consensus builder to agenda setter, from power broker to power wielder, and from congressional and national force into an international presence.

In a biography of Wright that appeared in *The Encyclopedia of the United States Congress* in 1995, it was said of the Speaker,

Wright's one full Congress as Speaker, the 100th, was one of the most legislatively productive terms in a generation. Wright himself was at the center of it all. He began by calling for higher taxes to cut the deficit; by the end of the year President Ronald Reagan had dropped his opposition and signed a modest tax increase into law. Wright's lone-wolf drive for conciliation in Nicaragua, many Democrats believed, contributed as much to the eventual downfall of an anti-American leftist regime as did the Reagan administration's support of armed rebellion.

Almost from the start of his speakership, Wright exhibited a partisanship unlike that of "Tip" O'Neill, as well as any previous Speaker in more than 50 years who desired to serve more than one term in that office. In July 1988, he chaired the Democratic National Convention in Atlanta, Georgia, that nominated fellow Texan Senator Lloyd Bentsen for

Vice President. Wright is remembered best during that parley for introducing a young John F. Kennedy, Jr., who was later killed in a 1999 plane crash. At the same time, Wright was more than willing to win votes on the House floor while sacrificing good relations with the minority Republicans, an effort that led to increased activism among the Republican base and aggressive efforts by the Republicans in the House to resist Wright at every turn. In a history of *The American Congress*, published in 2007, it was explained,

> Upon gaining the speakership, Wright bullied committees to act quickly on a range of domestic legislation, leading Republicans to complain about a new House dictatorship. In the foreign policy arena, Wright broke through unwritten limits on congressional involvement by negotiating directly with representatives of the contending governments and factions in Central America.

Historian Robert V. Remini, in an examination of the period of Wright's speakership, wrote in 2006:

> [A]s Speaker he worsened the relationship between the two parties. He excluded Republicans from any involvement in House business, intensifying the angry exchanges on the floor over appropriations, taxes, housing, health and sundry other issues. It was even known that Democrats on a particular committee "went into a back room and approved a bill that hadn't even been written - they approved it 'in concept'. I'd never heard of such a thing," complained [Republican Don] Sundquist of Tennessee, a member of that committee. "Not only did they not consult with us, we had no paperwork. They approved a bill that they described to us but hadn't yet written!"

In one incident that Republicans cited even years later as one of the moments where Wright turned the House into a cauldron of divisiveness, he utilized a rarely-used parliamentary procedure to keep open a vote to allow Democrats to pass a budget reconciliation bill, even though it appeared during the allotted time for the vote that they did not have enough support. Remini, examining the role these actions had in Wright's eventual fall from power, added:

> Then Wright did something that really infuriated the Republicans. On October 29, 1987, he delayed a vote on a reconciliation bill that raised taxes in order to reduce the budget deficit by $40 billion over two years. Under normal circumstances, announcement of the results of the balloting was delayed fifteen minutes to give stragglers an opportunity to cast their votes. When the fifteen minutes expired on the reconciliation bill, the measure had lost, 205 to 206. Republicans reveled. They shouted at Wright to declare the bill defeated. But he stood silently on the dais. Minutes passed. Finally, a voice rang out, "Hold the vote!" Democrat Jim Chapman of Texas rushed down the aisle and switched his vote by asking for a green card. At that moment, Wright shouted at [Representative David] Bonior [Democrat of Michigan], "Take back that damn red card." Then, in what seemed to some as a triumphant voice, he cried, "if there are no other members in the chamber who desire to vote..." Republicans booed. Trent Lott [Republican of Mississippi] slammed his fist against a lectern and nearly shattered it. But Wright continued, "Or if there are no other members who desire to change their vote, on this vote the yeas are 206, [and the neas are] 205."

Rep. Dick Cheney of Wyoming, who later served as Secretary of Defense (1989-93) and Vice President of the United States (2001-09), wrote an op-ed in the *Washington Post* denouncing the Speaker for his bullying of the minority.

What may have truly started Wright's fall as Speaker, aside from the corruption that eventually cost him his place in Congress, were his attempts to craft a separate foreign policy from that of the Reagan administration. As well, he turned the House into not just a partisan place but one in which he derided the minority Republicans and made them less important than they were, a sure road to anger and incitement. Previous Speakers who served during times that the White House was held by the opposition party held that foreign policy, and how it was conducted, was to be the domain of the executive branch. With Wright, and with the Democrats in the 100th and 101st Congresses, this all changed: with many Democrats in opposition to the Reagan administration's anti-Communist policies in Central

America, particularly in regards to aid to the anti-Communist rebels known as the Contras fighting the Soviet-backed Sandinista government of President Daniel Ortega in Nicaragua, Wright took a firm stand in resisting any aid to these rebels and in lending support to the pro-Soviet government in Nicaragua. Historian Robert Williams wrote,

In the vacuum of U.S. foreign policy in central America which followed the revelations of the Reagan administration's involvement in the Iran-Contra scandal, it was Speaker Jim Wright who took it upon himself to try to fill the void by attempting to broker his own Nicaraguan peace plan by having discussions with leaders of foreign governments. This unprecedented initiative was not well received by the Reagan White House or by the Republicans in Congress who regarded his action as improper, as a usurpation of power.

But what got Wright into real difficulty was his flagrant abuse of House rules. His good friend, Texas real estate developer George Mallick, allowed Wright to use his personal condo, and Wright paid Mallick thousands of dollars for the use of the living area, in violation of House rules that banned gifts in excess of $100 or more. There were other allegations of abuse of House rules and improper use of his office to aid and assist campaign contributors.

But the worst of the allegations lodged against Wright concerned his memoirs. Published in 1984, *Reflections of a Public Man* was a book that Wright sold to lobbyists, who bought the book in bulk just before doing business with the Speaker. Wright had gotten the little-read memoir published by Carlos Moore, whose printing company had worked for Wright's campaigns for years in Texas. Finally, Wright received 55% of the royalties from the sale of the book, while most authors received anywhere from 10% to 15%. In May 1988, a congressional watchdog group, Common Cause, called on Congress to investigate the allegations. Just days later, one of Wright's greatest nemeses in the House, Rep. Newt Gingrich, Republican of Georgia, sent a letter signed by he and 72 other Republicans in the House to the House Committee on Standards and Official Conduct, better known as the House Ethics Committee, echoing Common Cause's call for an investigation. The Democrat-led committee voted

unanimously on 9 June 1988 to conduct a preliminary inquiry; later, a full-blown investigation was ordered, and a special outside counsel, Chicago attorney Richard J. Phelan, was retained. Wright testified for more than five hours before the committee, and on 22 February 1989, Phelan gave his 279-page report to the Committee. It alleged that on 69 separate occasions, Wright had broken congressional rules - specifically regarding the cozy book deal he had profited from, and taking more than $145,000 in gifts from his friend George Mallick. An allegation that Wright was illegally involved in an oil-well deal that resulted in huge profits for Wright was never investigated, and, in the end, the House committee dropped more than half of the allegations Phelan disclosed. Wright's attorneys claimed that the committee and Phelan were "misinterpreting" House rules so as to make Wright look guilty, and asked for the Speaker to be exonerated. He was not.

The Democrats in the House, as well as the House leadership, were stunned by the allegations and the findings by the House Ethics Committee. No matter how much they could call the charges "politically instigated," a panel of Wright's fellow Democrats had found him to be in violation of House rules. In May 1989, the crisis over Wright got worse, when Rep. Tony Coelho, Democrat of California, resigned his post as Majority Whip and his House seat rather than face an investigation of his own financial problems. Republicans, sensing blood in the water, called for hearings to be held on the charges against Wright. Democrats in the House could not envision allowing such hearings to go forward if they wished to retain their majority in the 1990 midterm elections. Pressure was put upon Speaker Wright to step down.

Resignation of the Speaker

On 31 May 1989, Wright took to the floor of the House to deliver his resignation speech, and to direct a stinging rebuke at the "mindless cannibalism" of ethics investigations. As his voice quivered with emotion, Wright said, "Let me give you back this job you gave to me as a propitiation for all of this season of bad will that has grown up among us...I don't want to be a party to tearing up this institution. I love it." Wright thus became the first sitting Speaker of the House to resign his post because of scandal. Less than a month later, on 30 June 1989,

Wright resigned from the House altogether, ending a 44-year congressional career. He and his wife returned to Texas, where he still lives to this day.

Dennis F. Thompson, writing on institutional corruption in American politics, explained in 1995:

> *The charges against Wright combine in the same case the individual and institutional corruption found, respectively, in the cases of [Senator David] Durenberger and the Keating Five...The presence of both kinds of corruption in the same case offer an opportunity for a direct comparison. Confronted with a case of both kinds of corruption, the House ethics committee took seriously only the allegations of individual corruption, even though they were arguably less serious than those of institutional corruption.*

As of this writing, Wright lives in Dallas, Texas. In addition to the aforementioned work that were published in 1984 as his memoirs, Wright is the author of other books on public policy and Congress, including *The Coming Water Famine* (1966), *Congress and Conscience: Essays by Jim Wright* (1970), *Worth it All: My War for Peace* (1993), and *Balance of Power: Presidents and Congress from the Era of McCarthy to the Age of Gingrich* (1996).

Further Reading:
Beasley, Mark William "Prelude to Leadership: Jim Wright, 1922-1963" (Ph.D. dissertation, Pepperdine University, 1978).

Report of the Special Counsel in the Matter of Speaker James C. Wright, Jr. Committee on Standards of Official Conduct, U.S. House of Representatives, One Hundred First Congress (Washington, D.C.: Government Printing Office, 1989).

See also pages 502, 509

For Jeffrey Washburn
with best wishes —

Thomas Stephen Foley

Served as Speaker:
June 6, 1989 - January 3, 1995

When elected as Speaker in 1989 to succeed Speaker Jim Wright, who resigned under an ethical cloud, Thomas S. Foley of Washington State became the first Speaker from a state west of the Rocky Mountains. Five years later, when he was defeated during the electoral landslide that ended forty years of Democratic control of the House, Foley became the first sitting Speaker since William Pennington in 1860 to lose his seat. During his short tenure as Speaker, Foley was criticized for his opposition to term limits and his support of a ban on assault rifles, with both issues being used against him in the 1994 campaign. In 1997, he was named as the U.S. Ambassador to Japan by President Bill Clinton, a position he served in until 2001. His speakership, rarely examined by historians, may be seen in the future as part of an interregnum from the end of that of Tip O'Neill in 1987 to the speakership of Newt Gingrich in 1995.

Personal History

Foley was born in Spokane, Washington State, on 6 March 1929, the only son of Ralph Foley, an attorney, and Helen Marie (née Higgins) Foley, a teacher. On both sides of his family, Foley could trace their beginnings to Ireland. His paternal grandfather, Cornelius Foley, came to America at age 16; he wrote back to his girlfriend and future wife, Elizabeth, to come to America; the two initially settled into Minnesota but then moved to Spokane. On the maternal side of the family, Stephen and Anne Higgins, Irish emigrants, settled near Spokane. Ralph Foley served as the prosecutor of Spokane County during the 1930s, eventually rising to serve as a judge on the county superior court for 35 years, one of the longest in state history. Although Thomas Foley and his parents lived in the exclusive South Hill area of Spokane, the home of many Republicans, the family moved politically to the left and supported, during the 1930s, the administrations of President Franklin Delano Roosevelt. Thomas Foley remembered years later, "My family didn't have a lot of money. But in the 1930s, with a steady income [from his father] and the little income that my mother had, we lived very comfortably. We were surrounded by people who lived much more comfortably."

Thomas Foley did not do well in high school, flunking many subjects, although he was known as a skilled debater, despite a pronounced lisp. He worked summer jobs that continued after he graduated from the Jesuit-run Gonzaga Preparatory School in 1946 and he entered Gonzaga University in Spokane in 1947. Unable to change his academic career from the poor start that he got in high school, Foley transferred to the University of Washington at Seattle when he was threatened with dismissal from Gonzaga. At the University of Washington, however, Foley improved his grades and graduated with a bachelor's degree in 1951. He initially intended to follow his father's career by studying the law at the University of Washington's Law School, but he quickly realized that the law was not for him and instead he enrolled at that same university's Graduate School of Far Eastern and Russian Studies, intending to become a professor in history. When studies there did not work out, Foley returned to the law school and earned his LL.B. degree in 1957. Foley joined his cousin Hank Higgins in a law practice in Spokane, but this only lasted for less than a year.

In 1958, Foley gave up a private law practice and instead was named that year as the deputy prosecutor for Spokane County. In 1960, Washington State Attorney General John O'Connell named him as Assistant State Attorney General for Eastern Washington, with offices in Spokane. The following year, Senate Henry M. "Scoop" Jackson of Washington State, a friend of Ralph Foley who had worked with him since the 1930s when Jackson had served as the prosecutor for Snohomish County, named his son Tom Foley as the assistant chief clerk and special counsel for the U.S. Senate Committee on the Interior and Insular Affairs. The job may have been a political stepping-stone for Foley; Jackson soon convinced him to return to Washington State and run, as a Democrat, against Rep. Walt Horan, the Republican representative who held the state's Fifth Congressional district seat in the U.S. House. Horan, who had held the seat since 1942, looked vulnerable in 1964, when President Lyndon Baines Johnson was running for his own elected term as President following the assassination of John F. Kennedy. Foley was the only Democrat to run against Horan that year, and he ran as an expert in agricultural affairs in a district, located in the eastern-most

part of the state and one that was more rural than urban. With the backing of Jackson as well as the other Washington State Senator, Warren G. Magnuson, and the support of organized labor, Foley was able to win a narrow victory by more than 11,000 votes as President Johnson was winning a landslide against Republican Barry Goldwater. He took his seat when the Eighty-ninth Congress convened in Washington on 4 January 1965.

Early Years in Congress

Thomas Foley would hold the Fifth district seat for the next 14 elections, winning each one with more ease with only two exceptions: in 1978 he eked out a victory against conservative activist Rick James; in 1980, Dr. John Sonneland came within four percentage points of beating Foley. The Fifth district became more conservative as the years passed. In the meantime, he was working his way up through the ranks of the Democratic Party seniority ladder, rising to become the chairman of the House Committee on Agriculture in 1974. In 1980, he was elected by his party's caucus as Majority Whip; seven years later he was elected as Majority Leader, one step below the Speaker, when James C. Wright of Texas succeeded Tip O'Neill as Speaker of the House.

During the remainder of the 1960s and into the 1970s and 1980s, Foley became known for his more liberal views; even after he rose to become Speaker in 1989, he continued this outlook even as the nation grew more conservative. Although he had won his seat due to the landside of Lyndon Johnson in 1964, and he supported Johnson's programs of aid to the poor and indigent known as The Great Society, Foley came to differ with the President over the war in Vietnam. A member of the House Committee on Agriculture, he authored the Meat Inspection Act of 1967, which gave to states aid to insure greater inspections of meat packing facilities. In a controversial move, he voted against a 1968 anticrime bill, enacted following the assassinations of the Rev. Dr. Martin Luther King, Jr., and Senator Robert F. Kennedy of New York, because Foley disagreed with a provision giving the government more authority to wiretap the phones of criminals. However, he was also known for injecting some bitter reality into his party's dealings with Republicans in Congress as well as the administration of President Ronald Reagan. In 1982, when Reagan agreed to call for a hike in taxes to try to cut the budget deficit, Foley was selected to give the Democrats' response. Instead of blasting Reagan or pushing his or his party's plans, Foley welcomed the President's call, at the same time castigating Democrats who he said needed to face "economic reality" and try to assist Reagan in improving the economy, then in recession. It was the first time many in the country had seen Foley, and he received high marks for his candor.

Following the close of the Ninety-ninth Congress (1985-87), Speaker of the House Tip O'Neill resigned his office and left the House, making the way for the election of a new Speaker. Jim Wright of Texas, the Majority Leader under O'Neill, was assured of rising to the vacant speakership. With Foley holding the Majority Whip position, number three in the House leadership, he also moved up and succeeded Wright as Majority Leader, and Rep. Tony Coelho of California was elected Majority Whip. During his 2 1/2 years as Majority Leader, Foley served as a member of the Permanent Select Committee on Intelligence, as well as the Select Committee to Investigate Covert Arms Transactions with Iran, known as the Iran-Contra Committee.

Re-elected in 1988, Foley soon discovered that Speaker Jim Wright was deeply involved in political corruption surrounding sales of a book as well as other financial matters; an investigation by the House Committee on Ethics led to a report, released on 17 April 1989, that Wright had violated House rules in 69 different circumstances. Pressure was soon brought to bear on Wright to step down; on 31 May 1989, the Speaker went to the House floor and announced not only that he was stepping down as Speaker but would leave his House seat as well. In an emotional speech, the soon-to-be retiring Speaker told the House that he wanted the entire episode to end. "Let me give you back this job you gave to me as a propitiation for all of this season of bad will that has grown among us," he said. "Let that be a total payment for the anger and hostility we feel toward each other."

The Vote

On 6 June, just seven days later, the House voted, on straight party lines, 251 to 164, to elevate Foley to the speakership, selecting him over the Minority Leader, Republican Robert Michel of Illinois. He thus became the first Speaker from a state west of the Rocky Mountains. Some Democrats, who chose Foley in a closed-door caucus meeting, were hesitant about the Washington State Democrat because, as the *Washington Post* stated, "he has no instinct for the jugular." Rep. Tony Coelho, Democrat of California (who would later himself have to resign from the House under an ethical cloud), told his fellow Democrats in opposing Foley, "Tom has a reserved reputation for being a statesman, a velvet glove. You must be the iron fist."

Acceptance Speech

Foley was escorted to the Speaker's chair, and then delivered some remarks in an attempt to soothe feelings between Democrats, who were angry over the "overthrow" of Speaker Wright, and Republicans, who had been shut out of House deliberations and other measures during Wright's speakership and felt emboldened after bringing him down. The new Speaker tried to set a more conciliatory tone:

> We need to debate and decide with reason and without rancor. After 25 years in the House, there should be no doubt that I am proud to be a Democrat...I am deeply conscious, however, of the obligation I bear as speaker of the House. I am speaker of the whole House, not of one party, but to each and every member of the House, undivided by the center aisle. I pledge to protect the rights and privileges of all members.

Legacy as Speaker

Foley served as Speaker for the remainder of the 101st Congress (1989-91), as well as all of the 102nd (1991-93) and 103rd (1993-95). Although he served in a period of great political division, many of Foley's political opponents do agree that he often promoted compromise with Republicans, a stand that sometimes cost him the support of his own party. Many Democrats desired a more confrontational approach to the minority, at the same time also desiring to challenge not only the congressional Republicans but the administration of President George H.W. Bush (1989-93). Foley worked better with President Bill Clinton during Clinton's first two years in office, from 1993 to 1995. One of Foley's key legislative accomplishments with Clinton as President came when the Speaker bucked his own party and helped Clinton to pass in the House the North American Free Trade Agreement (NAFTA) with Canada and Mexico, a treaty that brought down trade barriers between the three countries that make up North America. Foley got the approval in the House mainly from Republicans, with more than three-fifths of Democrats opposing it.

Foley got into trouble starting in 1992. When revelations of financial and other irregularities in the operations of the House Bank and the House Post Office came to light, Foley was blamed even though he was never accused of actually being involved in the corruption. The scandals did bring down several big-name Democrats, including Rep. Dan Rostenkowski, Democrat of Illinois, who served as chairman of the powerful House Committee on Ways & Means. But because the Speaker of the House controlled the House Bank and the House Post Office, Foley ultimately took the blame for their failures. Lurid stories of overdrawn checks - especially by members who knew that House rules prohibited such conduct - and bank drafts, and stamps being doled out to congressmen and then resold, kept the story alive in the national media for much of 1992 and 1993. At the same time that Foley was battling to keep his own caucus together under the strain of the allegations, he was also deeply involved in a political controversy back in his home state. He opposed any efforts to enact a term limitation law on Washington State's officials, and in 1991 he backed a state referendum to reject the limits that passed. Those who wanted term limits continued their drive, and, in 1992, another ballot initiative was on the ballot, this time being approved. Foley took the law to court, arguing that voters had no constitutional right to impose any eligibility requirements on federal offices or the officers who held the positions. Foley won in federal court, and his victory was upheld. However, Foley won a pyrrhic victory, one in which a small battle is won but the war itself is lost.

In 1994, events came together that swept the Democrats from the majority in the House for the first time since the GOP controlled the Eighty-third Congress (1953-55). President Bill Clinton's personal unpopularity contributed to the atmosphere: in the first two years of his first term, Clinton's attempts to roll back the rights of people to own guns, coupled with a

grandiose plan to nationalize the entire health care system, which ultimately went down to defeat in the Congress, put the Democrats on the defensive. The two previously named scandals in the House also added to the unpopularity of the Democratic Party overall. Lastly, Foley's "victory" over term limits in his home state made him look like he was out of touch with his own constituents. Thus, in 1994, in Foley's bid for a 16th term in the House, his Republican opponent, George Nethercutt, used the issue against him, using in commercials and speeches "Foley against the People of the State of Washington," the name of his case that overturned the term limits ballot initiative. Nethercutt was part of the program by Rep. Newt Gingrich, Republican of Georgia and the Minority Whip in the House, called "A Contract with America."

Gathering incumbent Republicans as well as Republican candidates for office on the Capitol steps, Gingrich had them sign their names to this "contract," a series of promises that the GOP would institute if they were elected to a majority. Republicans went into the 1994 mid-term elections looking like a fresh and bold party, while Foley's Democrats appeared to be tired, out of ideas, and mired in corruption. In the end, every negative connotation was used against Foley, and it led to his losing, 110,057 votes to 106,074 votes, a difference of less than 4,000 votes out of some 216,000 cast. Foley thus became the first sitting Speaker of the House to lose his seat since William Pennington lost in 1860.

In his 1999 memoirs, Foley explained his defeat, blaming it in many ways on the atmosphere around he and the Congress:

> ...We were overwhelmed by a whole series of problems fighting off attacks by the term limits people, the National Rifle Association, and other groups such as anti-D.C. statehood. There was the unpopularity of the President in eastern Washington. Between 1994 and 1996 when he was re-elected, the President's numbers doubled. The nadir was 1994. I've never, and don't, blame any loss on the President, but it was not a good climate for Democrats...

> ...The speakership, which in other circumstances and geographies would be considered an impregnable advantage, was ironically a disad-

vantage in 1994 in eastern Washington. The approach of the opposition was: If there is any problem in the district, why hasn't it been corrected if the Speaker is so powerful? Why does the rain not fall on our crops, why do our children rebel against their parents, why is there trouble in the land? And, if he does good things, are you really comfortable with this long self-indulgence by Congress? Isn't it time for some new Puritanism and self restraint? There was also the wonderful argument that you here in the Fifth District are empowered more than any other people in the country. If you're sick and tired of what's going on in the federal government and Washington, D.C., you have a voice amplified beyond imagination in other parts of the country. They can only fire a member of Congress: You can fire the Speaker. It was a rather clever approach.

After Leaving the Speakership

Out of office for the first time since 1964, Foley remained in government service, when President Clinton named him as the chairman of the President's Foreign Intelligence Advisory Board, which advised the President on foreign intelligence matters. When he left the position, he went to work as a lobbyist for the Washington, D.C. law and lobbying firm of Akin, Gump, Strauss, Hauer, & Feld. In 1997, Clinton appointed Foley as the U.S. Ambassador to Japan, where he served until the end of the Clinton administration in 2001. When he returned to the United States, he went back to work for Akin, Gump, Strauss, Hauer, & Feld. In 2003, Governor Gary Locke, Democrat of Washington State, awarded Foley the Medal of Merit, the highest award given by that state. He has since served as the North American Chairman of the Trilateral Commission, a group of more than 300 citizens around the world formed in 1973 to study international problems.

Further Reading:

Biggs, Jeffrey R., and Thomas S. Foley, *Honor in the House: Speaker Tom Foley* (Pullman, Washington: Washington State University Press, 1999).

Bird, Robert Kenton, "The Speaker from Spokane: The Rise and Fall of Tom Foley as a Congressional Leader" (Ph.D. dissertation, Washington State University, 1999).

Mason, John Lyman, "Majority Party Leadership in the United States House of Representatives, 1977-1996: Sanction, Inclusion, and Protection" (Ph.D. dissertation, The University of Texas at Austin, 1998).

See also page 519

Newton Leroy Gingrich

Served as Speaker:
January 4, 1995 - January 3, 1999

When Bill Clinton assumed the presidency in 1993, Newt Gingrich, as the House Minority Leader, helped to unify his party in opposition to nearly all of the new president's congressional initiatives. One of these key moments was the firm resistance by Republicans in the House and Senate to Clinton's national health care initiative, tagged by critics as a massive and bloated bureaucratic scheme designed to take control of the entire American health care system and make it similar to the government-run approach in the United Kingdom and Canada. Although the minority in the House of Representatives has few powers to halt the legislative agenda of the majority, Gingrich used every power at his and his party's disposal to label the health care plan as a prescription for disaster for the American economy. The following year, embracing a package of reforms and legislative initiatives called "A Contract with America," Gingrich led the Republicans into the majority for the first time in half a century. One of the most powerful Speakers of the twentieth century - and one of the most polarizing - he was the first Republican to serve more than one consecutive term as Speaker since Nicholas Longworth did it from the Sixty-ninth (1925-27) through the Seventy-first (1929-31) Congresses.

Personal History

Born in Harrisburg, Pennsylvania, on 17 June 1943, as Newton Leroy McPherson, he was the son of Newton Searles McPherson and Kathleen (née Daugherty) McPherson. Although the two were later married, Newton McPherson did not see his son much and the two were divorced. Kathleen Daugherty then met and married Robert Bruce Gingrich, a career army officer, and he in turn adopted her son, giving him his last name. Gingrich rarely discusses his family, and the issue of his birth father remains blurry at best. Robert Gingrich was assigned to a number of military bases during the 1940s and 1950s, and as such Newt Gingrich received much of his schooling in France and what was then West Germany. When Robert Gingrich took his new family to meet a close friend in France who had served in the Second World War, Newt Gingrich listened to the man's stories about the war he fought in as well as the First World War - the man lived near the battlefield of Verdun, a massive World War I clash between Britain, France, and Germany - and became almost instantly a student of history. In school in West Germany, the young Gingrich wrote of the balance of power in the world and confidently told his teacher that one day he would run for a seat in the U.S. House of Representatives.

In 1959, when he was 16, Gingrich returned to the United States, this time to live with his family in Columbus, Georgia. He attended Baker high school there; in 1961, when he graduated, he entered Emory University in Atlanta, Georgia, earning a Bachelor's degree in 1965. He later earned a Master's degree from Tulane University in New Orleans, Louisiana, in 1968, and, from that latter institution, his Ph.D. in modern European history in 1971. At the same time, Gingrich became close to a teacher at Baker High, Jacquleine Battley, who was seven years his senior. Nevertheless, in 1962, Gingrich and Battley married when he was 19 and she was 26.

While at Emory and Tulane, Gingrich was slowly shaped by world events, melding into the conservative politician that he was later to become. Initially, he was given draft deferments from fighting in the Vietnam War, and for a time he experimented with marijuana. However, by 1968 he had swung to the right side of the political aisle, campaigning for Governor Nelson A. Rockefeller for President, mainly because Rockefeller stood for civil rights for black Americans. In 1970, while Gingrich was finishing his doctorate degree at Tulane, he accepted a teaching position at West Georgia College in Carrollton, Georgia. After earning his Ph.D., he desired to head the history department at West Georgia College, but he was turned down, instead remaining as a faculty member.

By 1974, Gingrich had tired of teaching and aspired to run for a political seat. He told his students that he wanted to run for a seat in the U.S. House of Representatives, and that, even though he was now a firm Republican, he would one day serve as Speaker of that body. He entered the race for the Sixth Congressional district seat held by Rep. John J. Flynt, Jr. Although a virtually unknown and a political neophyte, Gingrich ran an effective campaign and came within less than 3,000 votes of winning the election against a popular Democrat. Two years later, Gingrich again ran against Flynt, but once again lost a close race.

In 1978, Flynt announced his retirement, setting off a battle to succeed him. For the third time, Gingrich threw his hat into the ring and won the Republican nomination. Calling for lower taxes to aid economic growth, he defeated Democrat Virginia Shapard, a Georgia state Senator, by nearly 8,000 votes.

Early Years in Congress

On 15 January 1979, he took his seat in the Ninety-sixth Congress (1979-81). Almost from the start of his congressional career, Gingrich became known as a bomb-thrower, who challenged not only the Democrats but his own party's leadership in the House, who he blasted as being too timid to take on the majority Democrats and fight for what they believed in. Encircling himself within a group of like-minded Republicans, he called for a slow capture of seats for the Republicans until, he believed, the party could control the majority by the end of the 1980s. It would be a daunting task: the last time the party held the majority and elected a Speaker was in the Eighty-third Congress (1953-55), when Joseph Martin of Massachusetts held the speakership.

In the 1980s, it appeared that Gingrich would simply remain as a back bencher in the Republican ranks, although he had taken a strong stand against the speakership of Democrat Tip O'Neill. But it was during the tenure of Jim Wright as Speaker that Gingrich rose above the others and used the House rules to his benefit. One such rule is known as "special orders," which allow any member of the House to speak on any topic for up to one hour after the business of the House is completed. Gingrich and other Republicans would sometimes debate issues long after the House had adjourned; more importantly, however, they would be seen and heard on C-Span, the Cable-Satellite Public Affairs Network, an all-access channel (which later expanded into C-Span 1 for the House, C-Span 2 for the Senate, and C-Span 3 for other governmental programming) and carried nationwide, disseminated in ways newspapers or other forms of communication could never accomplish. Gingrich saw the new channel as a way to bring his party's message to the people without the filter of the liberal media. Calling for tax cuts and spending priorities that gave the U.S. military more funding, Gingrich and his group of renegade Republicans sometimes spoke for hours at a time on issues before the cameras. Even though nearly all of the sessions took place before an empty House - Speaker of the House Tip O'Neill criticized the action as somehow fraudulent - Gingrich realized that the speeches were highly effective.

But Gingrich also went for the jugular when it came to political corruption. In 1979, when Rep. Charles Diggs, Democrat of Michigan, was convicted of embezzlement, Gingrich was one of the first to call for Diggs' expulsion from the House. Instead, the Democratic majority merely censured Diggs, who resigned from the House nearly a year after that action. (He eventually served 14 months in prison.) Again, when Rep. Gerry Studds, Democrat of Massachusetts, was caught having sex with a male page, Gingrich made an issue of the case and demanded Studds' removal; to his chagrin, the Democrats once again merely censured Studds and allowed the case to go away. This apparent cover-up of corruption as well as a general antithesis to anything the minority Republicans wanted in the House led Gingrich to call attention to the way the Democrats ran the Congress. In 1989, he wrote in the *Conservative Digest*, a right-wing magazine:

> *The Democratic Party is now controlled by a coalition of liberal activists, corrupt big city machines, labor bosses and House incumbents who use gerrymandering, rigged election rules, and a million dollars from the taxpayers per election cycle to buy invulnerability. When Republicans have the courage to point out just how unrepresentative, and even weird, liberal values are, we gain votes...Fear and corruption now stalk the House of Representatives in a way we've never witnessed before in our history.*

When Gingrich wrote these words, he was in a battle to help bring down Speaker of the House James C. "Jim" Wright. Elected Speaker in 1987, Wright angered many Republicans by nearly shutting them out of the budget process as well as other deliberations on matters before the House. When allegations of corruption and violations of House rules by Wright came to light, Gingrich was the loudest voice, starting soon after Wright took office, demanding investigations. Gingrich wrote, "Jim Wright as speaker of the House is the personification of this sick system in which rules are violated, pockets are filled with improper money. America's secrets are leaked - and nothing is done about it. That a man with so corrupt a record as Jim Wright is second in line to be President should frighten

even decent American." Democrats denounced Gingrich's tactics, and some mainstream Republicans even recoiled at his tactics. Gingrich was blasted in the media: in 1989, *Time* magazine wrote, "One view is that Newt Gingrich is a bomb thrower. A fire-breathing Republican Congressman from Georgia, he is more interested in right-wing grandstanding than in fostering bipartisanship...Another view is that Newt Gingrich is a visionary. An impassioned reformer...[who] brings innovative thinking and respect for deeply felt American values to the House."

In 1988, Gingrich won re-election to his House seat, and, when 101st Congress (1989-91) convened, he was elected as the Minority Whip, the number three elected position in the leadership of the party in the House. When he had begun his crusade against Speaker Wright in 1987, few believed that anything would happen to the Speaker, who was widely protected by his party. In early 1989, however, as the House Committee on Standards and Official Conduct looked into the allegations against Wright, it was discovered that he had violated more than 60 rules of the House, including earning highly irregular royalties from the sale of his 1984 memoirs. As rumors of the report of the committee started to circulate, Gingrich drove home his disparagement of Wright. He told the *New York Times* in June 1988, "I am so deeply frightened by the nature of the corrupt left-wing machine in the House that it would have been worse to do nothing...Jim Wright has reached a point psychologically, in his ego, where there are no boundaries left." Two months after the committee released its scathing report, Speaker Wright resigned both the Speaker's chair and his own House seat on 6 June 1989.

From 1989, when Gingrich's work to bring down Speaker Wright paid off, until 1994, the Georgian continued to work to highlight what he saw as rampant corruption amongst the Democratic leadership in the House. In 1993, after Democrat Bill Clinton became President and tried to push through the Congress a disliked health care initiative, as well as attempts to ban certain types of guns, the unpopularity of the Democrats grew when two scandals arose in the House: the House Bank scandal and the House Post Office scandal. In each, it was discovered that years of gross mismanagement allowed rules to be broken, leading to theft and misconduct by leading Democrats and some Republicans. However, the public blamed the Democrats, who had controlled the House since 1955, and the Clinton administration. In the wake of this disapproval of the Democrats, Gingrich and other Republicans formulated the "Contract with America," a series of initiatives that the party promised would be enacted if the Republicans were given the majority in the next Congress. In another move in which he used the media to effect, Gingrich had incumbent Republicans and those wishing to be elected assemble on the steps of the U.S. House to "sign" the contract.

The Vote

In the election in November 1994, Republicans won 54 seats to capture their first majority in half a century, changing a 258-176 minority in the 103rd Congress (1993-95) to a 230-204 majority in the 104th Congress (1995-97). The shock of the loss of the majority for the Democrats was heard around the country and the world. On 4 January 1995, when the One Hundred Fourth Congress opened, Gingrich was elected Speaker over Democrat Richard Gephardt, who handed the gavel of the Speaker over to Gingrich.

Acceptance Speech

The new Speaker then delivered his opening remarks to the new Congress:

I have two gavels, actually. Dick happened to use one that - maybe this was appropriate. This is a Georgia gavel I just got this morning, done by Dorsey Newman of Tallapoosa, who decided that the gavels he saw on TV weren't big enough or strong enough, so he cut down a walnut tree in his backyard, made a gavel, put a commemorative item and sent it up here. So this is a genuine Georgia gavel. I'm the first Georgia Speaker in over a hundred years. The last one, by the way, had a weird accent, too. Speaker Crisp was born in Britain. His parents were actors and they came to the U.S. - a good word, by the way, for the value we get from immigration.

And secondly, this is the gavel that Speaker Martin used. Now I'm not sure what it says about the inflation of Government, if you put them side by side, but this was the gavel used by

the last Republican Speaker. And - And I want to comment for a minute on two men who served as my leader, and from whom I learned so much and who are here today...

Instantly, the Republicans put into order a series of initiatives that they wished to have implemented in the House to make it run better. They enacted a rule that it would take a three-fifths vote, rather than a simple majority, to impose an income tax increase; Democrats called it dangerous and unconstitutional. The new majority also approved a new rule limiting the term of any Speaker to eight years or four terms, and committee chairmanships to six years or three terms. Democrats strongly opposed a rule that subjected the Congress to civil rights, work safety, and fair-employment laws that people outside of Congress must obey by law.

At the same time that the Republicans were taking control of both houses of Congress - the GOP also took over the majority in the U.S. Senate as well - the media began to write off President Bill Clinton as a lame duck who was the first Democrat to lose the majority in Congress since the Republicans won control of the House in the Sixty-sixth Congress in 1919 with Woodrow Wilson in the White House. Historians Norman Thomas and Joseph Pika wrote in 1996, "Gingrich's sudden ability to eclipse President Clinton seemed to usher in a new era - the 'preempted presidency.'" It prompted an unexpected question: Had the era of presidential preeminence come to an end? For the first four months of 1995, at least, this seemed to be the case as Clinton appeared irrelevant to the debates swirling in Washington and throughout the nation. Thus, from January 1995 until the end of his term, Clinton's tenure was a 'presidency by veto.' Realizing that he could not stop the bills coming out of the Republican-controlled House of Representatives, or even have the Democrats in the Senate stop everything or alter much that was being passed in that upper body, Clinton was able to halt the Republican onslaught merely by vetoing as many bills as he could, realizing that the Republicans did not have a veto-proof majority in either house of Congress.

Clinton began to fight Republicans on a number of issues, including a balanced budget and foreign policy, that ultimately led to a showdown between the President and Congress that culminated in the government shutdown that lasted for 27 days at the end of 1995 and into 1996. Clinton, using the bully pulpit of the presidency, blamed the Republicans in Congress, and Gingrich in particular, for the shutdown; the media happily went along, tagging Gingrich as "The Gingrich Who Stole Christmas," who was indifferent to the wants and needs of the American people. When the Republicans tried to cut spending to balance the budget, again they were portrayed as injuring old people; some media outlets even stated that "Gingrich wanted to throw Grandma into the street." Clinton used the media and Gingrich's mistakes in formulating policy to his advantage; he ran a nasty re-election campaign, utilizing images of Gingrich and Senate Majority Leader Bob Dole, Republican of Kansas, who was the 1996 Republican Presidential candidate, in black and white to make them appear dark and ominous. The trick worked, and Clinton, who just two years earlier looked like a dead duck, sailed to re-election. The Republicans, however, held onto the majority, and Clinton was saddled for six years of his eight years in the White House with the Republicans in control of at least one house of Congress. Behind the scenes, however, were rumbles of discontent, with many conservatives secretly blaming Gingrich for Clinton's re-election.

In January 1998, a year into his second term, it was discovered that Clinton had been having a long-term relationship with a White House worker, Monica Lewinsky. When he was asked under oath during a deposition involving an Arkansas state worker's allegations of sexual harassment about the alleged affair, Clinton lied under oath. The allegations of lying under oath and obstruction of justice set off an inquiry in the House Committee on the Judiciary of the impeachment of the President, only the third in American history. The investigation by Kenneth Starr, an independent counsel hired to look into several other Clinton scandals, coincided with the House inquiry. Starr finally reported to the House that he felt Clinton had committed impeachable offenses, and the House voted out three articles of impeachment, charging perjury, obstruction of justice, and abuse of power. Democrats in both the House and Senate denounced the impeachment inquiry and vote.

The 1998 mid-term election came during this entire sordid affair, and many Americans, despite believing that Clinton was guilty, felt that impeachment was too far, and Republicans lost seats in the election in November 1998. The prevailing story of the 1998 elections, as far as common history is perceived, is that that mid-term campaign ultimately turned out to be a disaster for the Republicans. In fact, as statistics show, only four incumbent Republicans were defeated, and the Democrats picked up a total of five seats in a year when the party in opposition to the President gains seats. However, as Phillip B. Bridgmon wrote in an examination of the 1998 and 2000 House elections:

> When we consider all factors together, 1998 was both remarkable yet predictable. Historical patterns suggested Republicans would make major gains in the second midterm election of a two-term presidency. However, issues such as expenditures, quality of candidates, seats at risk, [and] district partisan leanings all pointed to a much more competitive balance between the parties.

During this same period, Gingrich came under the scrutiny of the same ethics charges he had thrown at Democrats for years. Democrats filed some 84 ethics charges at Gingrich, including that he had not paid taxes on a college course in which he taught political subjects. The House Committee on Ethics ruled that Gingrich should pay some $300,000 in taxes for this course. (In 1999, the IRS held that Gingrich had not violated any tax laws and declined to prosecute him or any group involved in the courses.) Gingrich also faced charges that he had profited from a book he had written that was a best seller.

Although the Republicans maintained the majority in the 1998 election, for the first time in three consecutive elections since Nicholas Longworth presided as Speaker over the Sixty-ninth (1925-27), Seventieth (1927-29), and Seventy-first (1929-31) Congresses, a majority of Republicans blamed Gingrich for the party's problems. From the time of the election until the convening of the 106th Congress in January 1999, Gingrich realized that he would be challenged again by a number of Republicans for the speakership, and that he did not have the votes to sustain his own election. On 6 November 1999, just days after winning re-election, Gingrich announced that he would step down as Speaker. "Today I have reached a difficult personal decision. I will not be a candidate for Speaker of the 106th Congress," he said in a written statement. The decision came just hours after House Committee on Appropriations chairman Bob Livingston, Republican of Louisiana, announced that he would challenge Gingrich for the Speaker's post, which followed several others. Forced to choose between the man who had brought them up to the mountain of the majority and continued unpopularity, the Republicans blinked and threw Gingrich aside. Ultimately, Livingston won the election to succeed Gingrich; however, Livingston had had an affair years earlier, and, in the midst of the Clinton impeachment, he was forced to step down as Speaker-elect, making way for the election of Rep. John Dennis Hastert, Republican of Illinois, to be the Speaker in 106th Congress. Gingrich never took his seat in that Congress, and he resigned soon after.

After Leaving the Speakership
In the years since leaving the speakership, Gingrich had remained one of the most vocal voices of the Republican Party. He delivers speeches, writes books (including works of history on the Civil War that have become best sellers), and writes for the American Enterprise Institute and the Hoover Institute, both conservative think tanks. He also appears on television, most notably as an analyst on the Fox News Channel. He considered a possible run for President in the 2008 election, but ultimately he did not run.

At the end of the century, *Roll Call* magazine, which monitors Congress, compiled their listing of the 10 most influential members of Congress of the 20th Century; in the listing, Speaker Joseph Cannon was first, with Newt Gingrich listed as third behind Senator Everett Dirksen of Illinois. Gingrich finished way ahead of Speaker Sam Rayburn, who finished eighth. Although he served for only two full terms as Speaker, he may have done more to shape that office than any man since Cannon or Rayburn.

Further Reading:
Gillespie, Ed, and Bob Schellhas, *Contract with America: The Bold Plan by Rep. Newt Gingrich, Rep. Dick Armey and the House Republicans to Change the Nation* (New York: Times Books, 1994).

Steely, Mel, *The Gentleman from Georgia: The Biography of Newt Gingrich* (Macon, Georgia: Mercer University Press, 2000).

See also page 524

Robert Linlithgow Livingston, Jr.

Served as Speaker:
December 19, 1998
Stepped down as speaker-elect.

He is remembered as "The Speaker that Wasn't": elected by the Republicans in late 1998 to succeed Speaker Newt Gingrich, in the midst of the House impeachment hearings over the Monica Lewinsky scandal and President Bill Clinton, Rep. Robert Livingston suddenly told the House that he was resigning both the speakership and his House seat because of extramarital affairs he had been conducting. The shock of having the newly elected Speaker give up his position even before he could be sworn in stunned the political establishment and the American people. Little known before his selection and resignation, Livingston is the scion of a famed American family who were some of the most important members of the formation of the early American nation.

Personal History
Livingston, born in Colorado Springs, Colorado, on 30 April 1943, is the son of Robert Lithgow Livingston, a salesman and World War II veteran, and his wife Dorothy (née Godwin) Livingston. Although born in Colorado, Livingston is considered a Louisianan because he grew up in New Orleans and served as a Representative from Louisiana.

Robert Livingston is the scion of a famed American family. The first American ancestor of the Livingstons was Robert Livingston (1654-1728), better known as "Robert the Elder," born in Ancrum, Roxburghshire, Scotland, the son of a Scottish Presbyterian minister who emigrated first to Rotterdam, Holland, in 1663, then to what is now New England ten years later, finally settling in what was then the village of Albany, New York, in 1674. He and his wife, Alida Schuyler Livingston, had nine children, including Philip Livingston (1686-1749). Philip, in turn, had two sons who made a great impact on American history: Philip Livingston (1716-1778), who signed the Declaration of Independence, and William Livingston (1723-1790), who signed the U.S. Constitution. Other family members include Henry Brockholst Livingston (1757-1813), who served on the United States Supreme Court (1806-23); Stephen Van Rensselaer III (1764-1839), who served as Lieutenant Governor of New York (1795-1801); and Edward Livingston (1764-1836), a member of the U.S. House of Representatives (1823-29) and U.S. Senate (1829-31), as well as Secretary of State (1831-33) in the administration of President Martin Van Buren. In all, the Livingstons can trace their heritage to an incredible number of important Americans, including Presidents George H.W. Bush and George W. Bush; First Lady Eleanor Roosevelt; Hamilton Fish (1808-1893), who served as Governor of New York State (1849-50), a member of the House of Representatives (1843-45) and the Senate (1851-57), and Secretary of State (1869-77) in the administration of President Ulysses S. Grant; the Astor family (through marriage); and even actor Montgomery Clift.

After attending and graduating from St. Martin's Episcopal High School in New Orleans in 1960, Livingston joined the U.S. Navy and served from 1961 to 1963. He then entered the Naval Reserve, where he remained until being declared inactive in 1967. He attended Tulane University in New Orleans and earned a Bachelor's degree in economics in 1967. He then earned a Juris Doctor, or law, degree, from Tulane's School of Law in 1968. That same year he was admitted to the Louisiana bar. He would earn a Master's degree from the Loyola Institute of Politics in Chicago, Illinois, in 1973.

Entering private practice, Livingston joined the law firm of David C. Treen, who would later be elected as the first Republican Governor of Louisiana since Reconstruction. Having Treen as his law partner opened new political doors for Livingston. In 1970 he was named as the Assistant United States Attorney and deputy chief for the criminal division of the U.S. Attorney's Office in New Orleans, remaining there until 1973. He also went to work as the Chief special prosecutor and chief, armed robbery division, in the Orleans Parish district attorney's office (1974-75). He also served as the Chief prosecutor of the organized crime unit of the office of Louisiana Attorney General William J. "Billy" Guste from 1975-76.

Early Years in Congress

Despite working for Guste, a Democrat, Livingston in 1976 decided to run for a seat in the U.S. House of Representatives, which opened up when Rep. F. Edward Hébert, chairman of the House Committee

on Armed Services, decided to retire after 36 years in the House. Livingston won the Republican nomination, but lost in the general election to state representative Richard Tonry. As soon as Tonry was elected, however, allegations of illegal campaign contributions and so-called "tombstone voting" (in which dead people somehow vote) came up against him. Democrats in Congress did not want Tonry to resign or to be investigated, but pressure from Republicans and the media forced him to announce his resignation on 4 May 1977, after just three months in the House. Immediately, Tonry declared that he would run the special election to succeed himself. Livingston jumped again into the race and won the Republican nomination; Tonry lost the Democrat nomination to a little-known state legislator, and Livingston won the seat. (In 1978, Tonry was convicted on 11 counts of campaign finance violations and sentenced to one year in prison, but he never spent any time in jail for his crimes.) He took his seat in the Ninety-fifth Congress on 27 August 1977. He would remain in the House until his resignation on 1 March 1999, rising to become the powerful chairman of the House Committee on Appropriations (One Hundred Fourth and One Hundred Fifth Congresses), where he became known as a budget cutter and one who desired to have a balanced budget without massive government spending.

In 1994, Republicans captured control of the majority in the House of Representatives for the first time since 1955. Newt Gingrich, of Georgia, became the Speaker of the House, with Livingston one of his key allies. However, over the next three years the relationship between the two men crumbled; so much so, that by 1998 Livingston decided to challenge Gingrich for the speakership, particularly when the impeachment inquiry into President Bill Clinton backfired on the party and Democrats won five seats in the 1998 mid-term election. Livingston's decision to challenge Gingrich for the speakership was an uncommon occurrence in the House, where the Speaker remains as Speaker until their party loses the majority or they die. It was only the second time in nearly forty years that a party's leadership post was contested by another member. Historians Steven S. Smith, Jason M. Roberts and Ryan J. Vander Wielen explained,

In the mid-1960s, Gerald Ford (R-Michigan) successfully challenged incumbent House minority leader Charles Halleck (R-Indiana), but not until 1998 was another top party leader challenged. In 1998, Speaker Newt Gingrich was challenged by Bob Livingston and became the first speaker to retire under threat of a challenge from within his own party. Livingston was then elected speaker.

Resigning the Speakership

As the 106th Congress was poised to open in January 1999, it appeared that Robert Livingston would be elected Speaker. However, events out of his control would force him to resign that coveted position. On 17 December 1998, amid rumors that sleazy internet investigators working for pornography publisher Larry Flynt, who owned *Hustler* magazine, were looking into his past to try to get revenge for the investigation against President Clinton, Livingston took to the floor of the House to denounce the attacks and to admit to what the rumors were claiming: that Livingston had affairs during his marriage:

> *When I did an early interview with the media after announcing my candidacy for Speaker, I told a reporter that I was running for Speaker, NOT Sainthood. There was a reason for those words...Because of the tremendous trust and responsibility my colleagues have placed in me, and because of forces outside of this institution seeking to influence the upcoming events and/or media coverage of these events, I have decided to inform my colleagues and my constituents that during my 33 year marriage to my wife, Bonnie, I have on occasion strayed from my marriage and doing so nearly cost me my marriage and my family. I sought marriage and spiritual counseling, and have received forgiveness from my wife and family, for which I am eternally grateful.*

The House, as well as the nation, was shocked and saddened by Livingston's admitted affair and his intention to resign an office that few people have the chance to rise to. On 1 March 1999, Livingston resigned from the House altogether.

After Leaving Congress

In the years since his shocking revelation, Livingston has returned to become an important voice in Washington, D.C. He founded The Livingston Group, a lobbying form in Washington; one of his clients, the government of Turkey, hired him because Livingston does not believe that Turkish troops massacred Armenian civilians during the First World War. Livingston lobbied House members not to support a resolution condemning Turkey for these alleged atrocities. In 2003, he was inducted into the Louisiana Political Museum and Hall of Fame in Winnfield, Louisiana.

Further Reading:

Dangerfield, George, *Chancellor Robert R. Livingston of New York, 1746-1813* (New York: Harcourt, Brace, 1960).

Leder, Lawrence H., *Robert Livingston, 1654-1728, and the Politics of Colonial New York* (Chapel Hill: University of North Carolina Press for the Institute of Early American Culture at Williamsburg, Virginia, 1961).

See also page 532

John Dennis Hastert

Served as Speaker:
January 6, 1999 - January 3, 2007

Few spectators of the goings-on on Capitol Hill in Washington, D.C., in 1999 could have foretold that a mild-mannered and soft-speaking Dennis Hastert, one-time high school wrestling coach, would be elected to a seat in the U.S. House of Representatives and then rise to become Speaker of the House - and in the midst of a scandal that cost a long-term congressman from Louisiana, Robert Livingston, the speakership. Hastert has become the longest-serving Republican speaker since Nicholas Longworth, who served from 1926 to 1932, and the longest-serving Republican Speaker overall, surpassing Joseph Cannon in June 2006.

Personal History

Hastert was born in Aurora, Illinois, on 2 January 1942, the eldest of three sons of Jack and Naomi Hastert. In his autobiography, *Speaker* (2004), Hastert wrote of his family history:

> *Their ancestors, the first Hasterts in America, had emigrated from Osweiler, Luxembourg, in the 1860s, fearing that the tiny nation was about to get gobbled up by one of its hungry European neighbors, and they settled in an immigrant neighborhood in Aurora's northeast*

side called Pigeon Hill. Those ancestors, my great-grandfather Christian Hastert and his brother Matteus, were blacksmiths, wheelwrights, and wagonbuilders. They soon found jobs, probably building rail cars, in the Chicago-Burlington Railroad's yards and shops...On my mother's side, my grandparents were of German descent. They had come to Illinois from an industrial section of Philadelphia called Bridesburg. My grandfather John, who was tall and graceful, had played semi-professional basketball for an ammunition company in or near Wilkes-Barre. His playing name was Jack Russell; he and his teammates traveled with drop-net cages - that's how basketball players got to be called cagers - and they used old military armories for games.

Hastert, known as Dennis or Denny, attended local schools in Aurora; he then went to Wheaton College in Wheaton, Illinois, west of Chicago, where he earned a bachelor's degree in economics in 1964. He then attended graduate school at Northern Illinois University in DeKalb, Illinois, from which he earned a Master's degree in the philosophy of education in 1967. After he earned his bachelor's degree, Hastert got a job as a high school teacher in Yorkville, Illinois, later becoming the school's wrestling coach. From all outward appearances, at least until 1980, it appeared that Dennis Hastert would remain a small-town American teacher, who worked in his family's restaurant business for a short period of time.

In 1980, however, Hastert entered the political field when he ran, as a Republican, for a seat in the Illinois state House of Representatives. He served then for six years, becoming a close friend and aide to Illinois state Senator John Grotberg. In a 1999 *Washington Post* story on Hastert's rise to power, it was noted that,

> Hastert developed a reputation as an effective dealmaker in the state House, asking his colleagues to write their spending requests on a notepad so he could carry them into negotiating sessions. He also proved to be a strong party leader, according to former state representative John Countryman (R), who served with Hastert on the Appropriations Committee. "We had pre-meetings at 7 in the morning. He would say, 'Okay, Countryman, here's your point. This is where we don't want you to go. So you know, you were coached,' he said. 'Most legislators at that point were waking up, drinking coffee and eating their bagels.'"

Early Years in Congress

In 1984, Grotberg, Hastert's mentor and friend, was elected to a seat in the U.S. House of Representatives. However, when he went to run for re-election in 1986 he fell ill with colon cancer, and had to step aside. (He would succumb to the cancer that November at the age of 61.) The Republicans in the district nominated Hastert to fill the vacancy, and he defeated Democrat Mary Lou Keams, a local coroner, with 52% of the vote. Taking his seat in the 100th Congress (1987-89), Hastert was a staunch Republican, supporting the party's minority on numerous issues, including opposition to abortion. In 1994, when the Republicans captured the majority in the House for the first time since 1955, Newt Gingrich was elected as Speaker, and Hastert was named as the Majority Whip, the third-highest office in the leadership. As Whip, he brought Republicans to the floor for crucial votes and counting

votes on important legislation. Although a Gingrich loyalist, many Democrats saw Hastert as a man who had a reputation as working with the other side of the political aisle.

In 1998, when the Democrats won five seats in the midst of the impeachment of President Bill Clinton, Speaker Gingrich, facing a conservative revolt in the House, resigned the speakership and opening the way for a number of powerful Republicans to rise to the Speaker's chair. One of these was Rep. Bob Livingston of Louisiana, the scion of a famed American family and himself the chairman of the House Committee on Appropriations. In November 1998 Livingston won the majority of Republican votes to become Speaker. Before he could be sworn in, though, a secret from Livingston's past rose up and struck him down: he had had an affair during his marriage, and it forced him to step aside.

The Vote

For the second time in just a few months, the Republicans needed to elect a Speaker designate. One of the leading candidates for the post was Rep. Christopher Cox of California. Having been involved in a threatened coup against Speaker Gingrich in 1997 and aided in his resignation in 1998, Cox was seen by many conservatives as too brash for the speakership. Excepting for Majority Leader Tom DeLay of Texas, there was no one else for the empty speakership. Republicans then reached over DeLay to the party's number three, the Whip, and selected Hastert as the Speaker on 6 January 1999.

Acceptance Speech

After he was sworn in and accepted the gavel from Minority Leader Richard Gephardt, Hastert made some remarks to the House:

> Those of you here in this House know me. But Hastert is not exactly a household name across America. So our fellow citizens deserve to know who I am and what I am going to do. What I am is a former high school teacher, a wrestling and football coach, a small businessman and a state legislator. And for the last 12 years I've been a member of this House. I am indebted to the people of the 14th Congressional District of

Illinois who continue to send me here to represent them.

I believe in limited government. But when government does act it must be for the good of the people. And serving in this body is a privilege - it is not a right - and each of us was sent here to conduct the people's business. And I intend to get down to business. That means formulating, debating and voting on legislation that addresses the problems that the American people want solved.

In the turbulent days behind us, debate on merits often gave way to personal attacks. Some have felt slighted, insulted or ignored. That is wrong, and that will change. Solutions to problems cannot be found in a pool of bitterness. They can be found in an environment which we trust one another's word, where we generate heat and passion, but where we recognize that each member is equally important to our overall mission of improving life for the American people. In short, I believe all of us, regardless of party, can respect one another, and even as fiercely as we disagree on particular issues.

Ceci Connolly and Juleit Eilperin of the *Washington Post* noted upon Hastert's election:

While Hastert has mastered the nuts and bolts of legislating, helping pass key elements of the House GOP's "Contract with America" and securing government projects for constituents, he has never articulated the kind of grand vision offered by his predecessor. In an era where the speaker of the House has become a national party spokesman, the incoming speaker is not known for the pithy sound bites that modern politics demands. But supporters say Hastert is the right leader for these tumultuous times. A lumbering man with an easy smile, Hastert has a great talent for coaxing votes out of recalcitrant lawmakers. Republicans describe him as a firm but fair chief deputy whip without a hint of scandal, no small qualification during a time when other politicians have been beset by questions about their marital fidelity.

However, Richard Cohen of the *Washington Post*, wrote in *National Journal* in 1999:

Expectations were low...when Rep. J. Dennis Hastert, R-Ill., was elevated from obscurity to the House leadership. At the time, House Republicans were reeling from four bruising years in the majority, years marred by frequent intraparty blowups and two net-loss elections...Judging by two dozen interviews with House Republicans and senior aides, Hastert has met these decidedly low expectations, and may have exceeded them. Republicans not only survived in Hastert's first year as their Speaker, they believed that they scored a few political points along the way.

Dennis Hastert would become the longest-serving Republican Speaker in the history of the U.S. House of Representatives. During his time in that office, which ended on 4 January 2007 at the start of the 109th Congress (2007-09), Hastert worked on such problems as fixing Social Security and Medicare, improving education with the passage of the No Child Left Behind Act (NCLBA) in 2001, and voting for the use of American forces in two land wars in Afghanistan and Iraq, which came following the devastating terrorist attacks of 11 September 2001 on New York, Washington, D.C., and Pennsylvania. Although he was the Speaker, Hastert was the leader of the GOP on health care reform, which he saw as a vital foundation of the American economy without placing the system in the hands of the U.S. government. Before becoming Speaker, he had been one of those who worked to pass the Patient Protection Act, enacted on 24 July 1998 and which expanded the choices of Americans to affordable health care without, as stated before, any government mandates or dictates. In 2001, however, during the first year of the administration of President George W. Bush, Hastert was unable to hold the Republican side of the House together when campaign finance reform - championed by Bush's 2000 primary opponent Senator John S. McCain of Arizona - was enacted by the House despite Bush's reservations about the legislation. David Broder wrote in the *Washington Post*:

House Speaker J. Dennis Hastert (R-Ill.), until last week a wizard at keeping his narrow majority unified, saw 19 of his moderate colleagues rebel on a key procedural vote and hand him the most embarrassing defeat in his 30 months in office - rejection of the rules of debate for the campaign finance bill. Both moderates and conservatives in the House Republican Conference complained bitterly about Hastert's handling of the issue, leaving unanswered questions about the speaker's ability to restore order in the ranks...The blowup is notably ill-timed, with the House scheduled to deal with critically important pieces of the Bush legislative agenda between now and the August recess. Battle lines are drawn with the Democrats on the patients' bill of rights, federal aid to church-based social programs and a series of appropriations bills testing the limits of Bush's budget. Any defections on the Republican side could spell political disaster for the president. A Republican lawmaker with close ties to the White House said Saturday, "Denny [Hastert] is the only one of our top leadership who can keep a train wreck from happening...This is the first time we've had a real fissure on our side."

Later in his tenure, Hastert was able to enact important Trade Promotion Authority, also known as "fast track," which allows a President to negotiate trade treaties with countries and then have the Congress either pass them or reject them without adding deal-killing amendments. Most importantly, however, Hastert and other GOP leaders pushed through a bitterly divided Congress massive tax cuts by President Bush which many credit for heading off a national recession that hit in the months before President Clinton left office in 2001 and which was exacerbated by the terrorist attacks of 11 September 2001. Hastert further oversaw the passage of the Provide Appropriate Tools Required to Intercept and Obstruct Terrorism Act of 2001, also known as the USA Patriot Act, utilized to crack down on potential terrorist activity inside the United States, legislation which critics labeled as an assault on the civil liberties of American citizens. This legislation, however, passed 337-79 in the House and 98-1 in the Senate, giving bipartisan support to its controversial measures.

On 7 October 2002, as the House debated giving President Bush the authority to go to war against Iraq, Hastert gave up the Speaker's chair for a short period so that he could speak to the House with his thoughts on the measure:

This resolution authorizes the President to use necessary and appropriate military force against Saddam Hussein's regime in Iraq to defend the national security interests of the United States and to enforce the United Nations Security Council resolutions that Hussein has routinely ignored over the last decade. We take this step knowing that Saddam Hussein is a threat to the American people, to Iraq's neighbors, and to the civilized world at large.

We have a sacred duty to do all that we can to insure that what happened on September 11th never happens to America again. On September 11, 2001, this nation changed utterly. On that fateful morning, Americans woke up with the usual expectations. Go to work, provide for the family, feed the children, live the American dream. Firemen, stockbrokers, custodians, police officers, office workers, all started their day, perhaps with a cup of coffee, perhaps hurrying to get to work on time. But those plans were shattered when those planes hit the World Trade Towers and the Pentagon. All of us lost our innocence that day. Before September 11th, we all believed that the troubles that infected the rest of the world couldn't impact us. We lived in splendid isolation, protected by two vast oceans. Before, war and disorder were distant rumblings from a far land. But on September 11th, that distant rumbling hit New York and Virginia.

Some may question the connection between Iraq and those terrorists who hijacked those planes. There is no doubt that Iraq supports and harbors those terrorists who wish harm to the United States. Is there a direct connection between Iraq and Al Qaeda? The President thinks so.

Should we wait until we are attacked again before finding out for sure, or should we do all that we can to disarm Saddam Hussein's regime before they provide Al Qaeda weapons of mass destruction?

Last year, this Capitol Building was attacked, when someone mailed anthrax-laden letters to members of the Senate. We have never found the perpetrator. Was that a terrorist attack? Undoubtedly. Was it connected to Al Qaeda or

Saddam Hussein? We don't know, but it served as a wake up call to all Americans. Why don't we take the biological and chemical weapons away from his regime before we find out for sure?

For those you who are worried about the doctrine of preemption, let me say that this is not a new conflict with Iraq. Our planes, which have been patrolling the no-fly zone since the end of the Persian Gulf War have been fired upon by the Iraqi military hundreds of times. This conflict is ongoing. Only now, it has become critical that we take the next step.

We know Saddam Hussein is a bad actor. We know what he did to the people of Kuwait when he invaded there. We know what he did to his neighbors in Iran when he used chemical weapons in the Iran-Iraq war. We know that he gassed his own people - including women and children - to put down a rebellion.

For those who argue that we must build a consensus with the United Nations, let me say that we are taking effective action to save the United Nations.

Earlier this century, fascist regimes in Italy and Germany routinely ignored the dictates of the League of Nations. Both Mussolini and Hitler built up their armies, invaded their neighbors and oppressed their citizens, all in the face of an ineffective League of Nations.

We must not allow the United Nations go the way of the League of Nations. We must give the U.N. the backbone it needs to enforce its own resolutions. But if the U.N. refuses to save itself, we must take all appropriate action to protect our citizens.

Edmund Burke once said that that the only thing necessary for the triumph of evil is for good men to do nothing. We must not let evil triumph. We must do something. We must pass this resolution and support the President as he works to disarm Saddam Hussein and win the war against terrorists.

When American troops incurred massive casualties in Iraq and President Bush became more unpopular, Republicans suffered at the ballot box: in the One

108th Congress (2003-05), they controlled 229 seats to 204 for the Democrats, with 1 independent. The party picked up three seats in the 109th Congress (2005-07) for a total of 232, but, in the 2006 mid-term election, the GOP lost 30 seats and the majority, giving the Democrats a 233-202 margin. On 4 January 2007, Hastert handed the Speaker's gavel to Nancy Pelosi, the first female Speaker of the House.

After Leaving the Speakership

Normally, a defeated Speaker becomes the Minority Leader; in this case, however, Hastert refused any leadership post and merely became another Republican representative. On 15 November 2007, he went to the House floor and announced that as of 26 November 2007 he would resign from the House.

Remembered as a common man who rose to one of the highest offices in the land, on 1 June 2006 Dennis Hastert surpassed Joseph Cannon as the longest serving Republican Speaker of the House; Cannon had served 7 years and 5 months from 1903 to 1911.

Further Reading:
"Hastert, Dennis" in *Current Biography 1999* (New York: H.W. Wilson, 2000).

Hastert, John Dennis, *Speaker: Lessons from Forty Years in Coaching and Politics* (Washington, D.C.: Regnery Publishing, Inc., 2004).

See also pages 535, 541

Nancy D'Alesandro Pelosi

Served as Speaker:
January 4, 2007 Incumbent

On 4 January 2007, when the 110th Congress (2007-09) convened in Washington, D.C., Nancy Pelosi, the first woman to serve as the head of a party in the U.S. House of Representatives, was sworn in as the Speaker of the House, the first woman to hold that eminent office. With a background in a political family on the East Coast, her rise to become a political leader on the West Coast made her one of the most important female leaders in the Democratic Party in the history of that entity. She was quite vocal about her liberal voting record of being against the U.S. war in Iraq and for government spending over tax cuts. In 2008, her party added additional seats to their majority, giving her another term as Speaker.

Personal History

Born Annunciata Patricia D'Alesandro on 26 March 1940 in the Little Italy section of Baltimore, Maryland, she is the daughter of Thomas D'Alesandro, Jr. and his wife Annunciata (née Lombardi) D'Alesandro. A family with a lengthy political pedigree, it began when Thomas D'Alesandro, Jr. (1903-1987), served as a U.S. Representative from Baltimore, Maryland (1939-47), then as Mayor of that city (1947-59). During this time he was a close friend - known as "Tommy" - to Presidents from Franklin Delano Roosevelt to Harry S. Truman and John F. Kennedy. He

ended his career with an unsuccessful run for the Senate in 1958 and a stint as a member of the Federal Renegotiation Board, appointed by President Kennedy, from 1961-69. Pelosi's mother, Annunciata D'Alesandro, an immigrant from Italy, dropped out of law school to raise her children. Her son, Thomas D'Alesandro, III, also served as the Mayor of Baltimore. Her daughter, Nancy, attended local schools, including the Institute of Notre Dame, a Catholic high school for girls in Baltimore, then graduated from Trinity College (now Trinity Washington University) in Washington, D.C. in 1962. While attending school, she interned as an aide to Senator Daniel Brewster, Democrat of Maryland; one of her co-workers was Steny Hoyer, who would eventually serve under Pelosi as Majority Leader. While attending Trinity, she met Paul Frank Pelosi, a businessman and an investor, and the two were married in September 1963. For the next 18 years, Nancy Pelosi was involved in bringing up her family in her husband's native city, San Francisco, and it did not appear that she would become involved in politics like her father and brother.

In 1977, Pelosi was elected as the party chairwoman for Northern California for the California state Democratic Party. She became a close friend and ally of Rep. Philip Burton, Democrat of California, who was a powerhouse congressman from San Francisco. In 1981, upon Burton's urging, Pelosi ran for and was elected as the chairman of the California state Democratic Party, where she served until 1983. That same year, Burton died, and his widow Sala Burton was named to his vacant seat. Pelosi, at this time, served as Finance chairman of the Democratic Senatorial Campaign Committee, which assists Democrats in getting elected to the U.S. Senate, from 1985-86. She also used her influence to get the Democrats to hold their 1984 presidential nominating convention in San Francisco.

In late 1986, Sala Burton became ill with cancer, and decided not to run for re-election to her congressional seat in 1988. She stated quite clearly that she wanted Pelosi to run for the open seat. Events, however, soon intervened; on 1 February 1987, just after being sworn in to her third term in Congress, Sala Burton succumbed to her cancer, leaving the seat open. In a special election, held on 7 April 1987, Pelosi defeated San Francisco Supervisor Harry Britt in the Democratic primary, then Republican Harriet Ross in the general election on 2 June 1987.

Early Years in Congress
She took her seat in the 100th Congress on 9 June 1987. She would serve on the House Committee on Appropriations and the House Committee on Intelligence, becoming the ranking Democrat on the latter committee just before her election as Speaker in 2007. She also served on the House Committee on Banking, Finance and Urban Affairs, as well as the Committee on Government Operations. She was the sponsor of legislation such as increasing government funds for AIDS research and subsidizing housing for low- and moderate-income people.

In 1994, the Democrats lost their majority, and from the start of the 104th Congress (1995-97) until the 110th (2007-09), Nancy Pelosi was situated in the minority. Nevertheless, she continued an upward climb into the party's leadership. In 2001, when Minority Whip David E. Bonior of Michigan stepped down from his seat, Pelosi was elected in his place, the first woman to hold the Whip position, which is the second highest in the minority and third highest in the majority. Working with Minority Leader Richard Gephardt of Missouri, she opposed the tax cuts of President George W. Bush, and voted against

U.S. participation in the war in Iraq. She also took a strong stand against Social Security reform, as that government program faced a future of potential bankruptcy. In 2002, Gephardt resigned his Minority Leader position to run for President in 2004, and Pelosi was elected in his place, making her the first woman to ever lead a party in the U.S. House of Representatives. Her service would last until the end of the 109th Congress (2005-07). As Minority Leader, Pelosi disagreed with many in her party that President Bush's policies warranted an impeachment inquiry, although she strongly rebuked the President and Republicans for allegedly "lying" about the presence of weapons of mass destruction in Iraq before the war started. In early 2006, as polls showed that the Democrats could pick up enough seats to win back the majority, Pelosi told colleagues that any impeachment inquiry was "off the table."

First Female Speaker-Acceptance Speech
In the 2006 mid-term elections, Democrats picked up 31 seats to turn a 232-202 (with one independent) minority in the 109th Congress into a 233-202 majority in the 110th. On 4 January 2007, Pelosi was sworn in as the first female Speaker of the House. She told the members of the House:

> *This is an historic moment, for Congress, and for the women of this country. It is a moment for which we have waited more than 200 years. Never losing faith, we waited through the many years of struggle to achieve our rights. But women weren't just waiting; women were working. Never losing faith, we worked to redeem the promise of America, that all men and women are created equal...For our daughters and granddaughters, today we have broken the marble ceiling. To our daughters and our granddaughters, the sky is the limit.*

Legacy as Speaker
Many blamed the war in Iraq for President Bush's unpopularity and the resurgence of the Democrats. When the President suggested in early January 2007 that he would increase the number of American troops in that country in a "surge" to win the war, Pelosi, along with Senate Majority Leader Harry Reid, Democrat of Nevada, sent a letter to the President asking him not to send additional forces to

Iraq. "[T]here is no purely military solution in Iraq," they wrote:

There is only a political solution. Adding more combat troops will only endanger more Americans and stretch our military to the breaking point for no strategic gain...Rather than deploy additional forces to Iraq, we believe the way forward is to begin the phased redeployment of our forces in the next four to six months, while shifting the principal mission of our forces there from combat to training, logistics, force protection and counter-terror.

Bush refused to listen to Pelosi or Reid, and dispatched an additional 30,000 troops to Iraq. Pelosi and Reid attempted to cut off funding for the troops, but this move backfired and support for the war rose as Iraq stabilized and the number of troop deaths fell to some of their lowest levels. On 12 December 2007, she blasted Republicans for opposing her party's attempts to cut off funding for the troops in Iraq. "They like this war. They want this war to continue," she told reporters at her weekly news conference in the Capitol. "We thought that they shared the view of so many people in our country that we needed a new direction in Iraq. But the Republicans have made it very clear that this is not just George Bush's war. This is the war of the Republicans in Congress." When asked if she believed that Republicans "like war," she backed off. "I shouldn't say they like the war," she said. "They support the war, the course of action that the president is on." She called the conflict in Iraq "a catastrophic mistake." House Minority Leader John Boehner of Ohio dismissed Pelosi's remarks. "Republicans have stood on principle to protect current and future generations of Americans, whether it polled well or not. The success our troops are having in Iraq today is proof positive that our stance was the right one."

Pelosi involved herself in American foreign relations and affairs, and was roundly criticized for it. In May 2007, when Colombian President Álvaro Uribe visted the United States, Pelosi publicly lambasted him for not cracking down hard enough on "paramilitary groups" that she felt were intimidating labor organizations. In 2008, to punish Colombia, she refused to hold hearings or schedule a vote on the Colombia Free Trade Agreement (CAFTA).

Despite her sense that any impeachment inquiry of the Bush administration would backfire in the faces of the Democrats, Pelosi decided to allow hearings to go forward. Responding to the introduction of an article of impeachment by Rep. Dennis Kucinich of Ohio, she said,

This is a Judiciary Committee matter, and I believe we will see some attention being paid to it by the Judiciary Committee. Not necessarily taking up the Articles of Impeachment because that would have to be approved on the floor, but to have some hearings on the subject. My expectation is that there will be some review of that in the Committee.

As the war in Iraq changed for the better, Pelosi and the Democrats were seen more and more as the party involved in the status quo rather than as reformers. Polls across the country in the middle of 2008 showed that the Democrats' unpopularity rose to 85-90%, endangering their majority. In October 2007, Pelosi admitted that the Democrats were unpopular, but she blamed the Bush administration for all of her party's problems. "I know that Congress has low approval ratings," Pelosi said at her weekly news conference. "I don't approve of Congress, because we haven't done anything that - we haven't been effective in ending the war in Iraq. And if you asked me in a phone call, as ardent a Democrat as I am, I would disapprove of Congress as well." In the 2008 election, however, Democrats picked up 21 seats to make their majority in 111th Congress (2009-11) 257 seats to 178 for the GOP. On 6 January 2009, Pelosi was sworn in for a second 2-year term as Speaker of the House.

In 2008, after Republicans brought procedural matters before the House and Pelosi was unable to stop the counts, the Speaker decided, in the 111th Congress to change House rules that disallowed any such motions by the minority. In the first change of these rules since 1822, the right of the minority to make a motion to recommit would be taken away, a rule that the Republicans strengthened when they took the majority in 1995. Outraged, Republicans announced that they would call procedural motions every half hour if Pelosi went through with her plans to change the rules. Pelosi also turned on Democrats who she felt were not 100% behind her plans for the House. When she disagreed with Rep.

John Dingell of Michigan or Rep. Jane Harman of California, she stripped both of them of their committee assignments, including Dingell, who was replaced as the chairman of the House Committee on Energy and Commerce by Rep. Henry Waxman of California, a Pelosi ally.

Further Reading:
Petre, Elizabeth A., "Rhetoric, Identification, and Personae: Comparing Condoleezza Rice and Nancy Pelosi" (Master of Science thesis, Department of Speech Communication, the Graduate School, Southern Illinois University at Carbondale, 2006).

See also page 539

Historical Essays

The Speaker of the House of Commons in England: Formation of the Office

The Speaker of the U.S. House of Representatives owes its existence to the office that exists in the British Parliament. Although the two offices are now quite different, with differing powers and other distinctions, when the U.S. House was begun after independence it was based on the office that had already existed for half a millennium in England.

In his 1843 two-volume composition on the early history of the British House of Commons, Charles Townsend began by starting with a discussion of the speakership of that body. "The first speakers of the House of Commons were chosen from belted knights and commoners of distinction, the choice being made by the House, but in accordance with the previous nomination of the king," he wrote. Almost from the start of its formation, the Speaker has had duties laid out before him in a methodical fashion. James Alexander Manning, the British historian who documented the lives of the Speakers of the Commons in his noted 1851 work, laid out in the preface of the "duties of [the] Speaker of the House of Commons." He explained, "This great officer must have anciently, as at present, the organ or mouth-piece of the Commons, although in modern times he is more occupied in presiding over the deliberations of the House, than in delivering speeches on their behalf." Manning then went into a lengthy conversation on the role of the Speaker, some of which, to the American ear, seems quite different than anything the original, or even modern, Speaker of the House has as part of their responsibilities. He explained:

> Amongst the duties of the Speaker, are the following: To read to the Sovereign petitions or addresses from the Commons, and to deliver, in the royal presence, whether at the Palace [of Westminster] or in the House of Lords, such speeches as are usually made on behalf of the Commons; to manage in the name of the House, where counsel, witnesses, or prisoners, are at the bar; to reprimand persons who have incurred the displeasure of the House; to issues warrants of committal or release for breaches of privilege; to communicate in writing with any parties, when so instructed by the House; to exercise vigilance in reference to private bills, especially with a view to protect property in general, or the rights of individuals, from undue encroachment or injury; to express the thanks or approbation of the Commons to distinguished personages; to control and regulate the subordinate officers of the House; to entertain the members at dinner, in due succession, and at stated periods; to adjourn the House at four o'clock, if forty members be not present; [and] to appoint tellers on divisions [in the number of members who wish to vote on a particular bill or action].

In essence, the Speaker of the British House of Commons is a nonpartisan officer, not chosen or selected for their party affiliation but their demeanor and character, as well as their ability to handle the above-mentioned duties, while at the same time, being the face and voice of the Commons itself.

Early History of the Speakership (1258-1366)

The true history of the speakership of the House of Commons in England begins in the mists of history: what is known is that in 1258, Peter de Montfort was named as the head of the Parliamentary session that met that year in Oxford and has become known as "The Mad Parliament." But de Montfort's rise to become a "speaker" for the House of Commons was short-lived, and while he is considered the first "speaker," the office did not continue after him and it remained unused for more than a century afterwards. In his 1914 work on the history of the men who had served up until that time as Speaker of the House of Commons, historian Michael MacDonagh explained that the office's origins began in the Parliament of 1376, known to history as "The Good Parliament" for its numerous reforms of royal and other abuses. At the time that this body assembled, King Edward I was dying; his son, also named Edward (but nicknamed "The Black Prince") was the Prince of Wales and heir to the English throne, was also dying from an unknown disease. Another son of Edward I, John of Gaunt, the Duke of Lancaster, appeared to take the throne of England in the name of his family. Despite the fact that Richard, the son of Edward the Black Prince, was next in line to the throne, John of Gaunt's machinations to seize power left him in bad standing with the parliamentarians who assembled at Westminster on 28 April 1376 for the first session of the House of Commons.

With many members missing - they did not show up, or had been delayed on the many roads leading into London - the House adjourned until the following day. When that time came, with many more members in attendance, John of Gaunt presided over the session. Immediate action was needed for the passage of increased funds for supplies for English troops fighting the war in France, a conflict that had been underway for nearly 40 years, and would continue for 77 additional years - a struggle known as The Hundred Years' War. After hearing the arguments for the increased supplies, the Commons members moved to the Chapter House down the street at Westminster Abbey. Built in 1250 by Masons, the structure was used by Benedictine monks for their religious meetings. Here, the members argued over their opposition to the additional supplies as well as the thought of having John of Gaunt as the royal standard. The members then elected Sir Peter de la Mere, a knight of the shire for Herefordshire who was also a bitter opponent of John of Gaunt, as their official spokesman to air the Commons' grievances before the sovereign. In a sense, the "Speaker" was created out of necessity rather than a ploy to elevate one Commoner over another, or to grab power.

When the Commons assembled again the following day, John of Gaunt was sitting again in the place of the King. According to historian MacDonagh, de la Mere then stood up and,

> Stated the demands of the Commons in a vigorous and independent speech. They were grievously oppressed by taxation. This, however, they would take in good part, nor grieve at it, if the money were properly spent, but it was evident that neither the King nor the Realm has any profit thereby. They therefore insisted upon an inquiry into expenditure, and removal from office or from the Court of certain close advisors of the King, to whose misdemeanours they attributed the existing public abuses.

From this demand, it was discovered numerous aides and others were involved in gross thievery: Lord Latimer, a close friend of John of Gaunt, lost his chance to rise to the office of Chamberlain, the official title of the man in charge of running and administering the affairs of the royal household; Richard Lions (also Lyons), a banker who lent money to the King at usurious rates, was arrested and sent to the Tower of London; Alice Perrers, the mistress of King Edward I, who had taken untold riches and purchased jewels and land, was also arrested and eventually banished from the royal household. Latimer was impeached - one of the first uses of that legal penalty to be used by the lower house of Parliament - tried before the House of Commons in 1376, and found guilty; however, King Edward III later pardoned Latimer, and in 1377 he was named a member of Richard II's royal council, a move that outraged members of Parliament. Despite the lax sentences for these criminals, the standard had been set: one man would "speak" for the concerns of the House of Commons, and the King would have to listen to this "speaker." Thus, in the fire of the times, was born the office of the speakership. William Cobbett, the chronicler of the Parliament at Westminster whose multivolume series has documented the actions and speeches in the Commons much the same way that *The Congressional Globe* and *The Congressional Record* would one day cover in the United States Congress, discussed de la Mere's selection, although he moved quickly to de la Mere's first speech as Speaker rather than on his selection.

The "office" of the Speaker, if one could say that such an office did exist, did not have the trappings of one with official duties, and as such its position did not remain for long. In the next Parliament, known as the "Bad Parliament" of 1377, John of Gaunt dissolved the Commons and the House of Lords and imprisoned Sir Peter de la Mere, installing in his place Sir Thomas Hungerford, John of Gaunt's personal steward, to be a more compliant "Speaker." This new Parliament undid many of the reforms of the previous Parliament and even instituted new taxes, including a poll tax. De la Mere was imprisoned without trial at Nottingham Castle, and, ironically, it was through the maneuverings of Alice Perrers that de la Mere was released. In exchange, the "Bad Parliament" reversed Perrers' conviction and sentence.

De la Mere and other knights who presided as the official spokesmen - not so much as a Speaker as we consider the holder of the office today in the United Kingdom, but more as an official presenter of the Commons' arguments - of the lower house of Parliament were known in those early periods as the Prolocutor (defined as "1. a chairperson of the lower house of convocation in a province of the Church of England, or 2. a spokesman [archaic]," from the Latin *prolocut*, "to speak out.") In the intervening years, for the next century, several unidentified men held the title of Prolocutor instead of Speaker.

The Reigns of Richard II to Henry VII (1367-1624)

It was not until the reign of Richard II (1367-1400; reigned 1377-1400) that the "Speaker" of the Parliament became an identified office. Thomas Curson Hansard, later to become the publisher of the official speeches and transcripts of the House of Commons, wrote a comprehensive history of that deliberative body, which was published in 24 volumes in 1762. He explained, "The Speaker in the time of Richard II was a minion of the King...and greatly the occasion of the misfortunes of those times." James Alexander Manning, whose mid-nineteenth century work documented the lives of the Speakers of the House of Commons, wrote on the first man considered as a real "Speaker:"

> *Sir Thomas Hungerford, one of the Knights of the Shire for Wilts, styled in the Parliament rolls [as]* Monsieur Thomas de Hungerford, chevalier, qui avoid les paroles pur les communes d'Angleterre en cet Parliament...*is the first speaker of the House of Commons on record, although little doubt can be entertained that all previous Parliaments, from the earliest period of their being called together, must have chosen one among their body for the purposes of regulating the order of their proceedings, the presentation of their petitions to the King, which, if assented to, were the only laws they had the power of proposing at that early stage of legislative authority, and generally to act as the organ or mouth-piece of the whole.*

Hansard's history of the English Parliament states that Hungerford was selected as the Speaker in the first Parliament of Richard II, the so-called "Bad Parliament" (as opposed to the "Good Parliament," which came right before it), held at Westminster 15 days after Michaelmas, or St. Michael's Mass, in 1377.

The first years of the speakership showed that the men who held sway over the affairs of the Parliament were not "independent" politicians. In 1381, Sir Richard Waldegrave opposed taking the speakership because he did not want to become an agent of the King in the House. Nonetheless, he did serve, as did Sir John Bussy, elected in 1394. Bussy presided over - but had little to do with - a petition by the whole House condemning the spending profligacy of King Richard II on his personal residence. Angered beyond reason at this challenge to his authority, even if it did come from the people's representatives in the House of Commons, the King himself went to the House and demanded from Bussy the name of the man who had authored the petition; Bussy named Sir Thomas Haxey, who was arrested, tried for treason, and sentenced to death, although the sentence was never carried out. (In fact, in 1399, after he deposed Richard, King Henry IV asked Parliament to reinstate Haxey's possessions and reverse the treason verdict as "against the law and custom which has been before in Parliament.") Ironically, after war broke out between Richard II and Henry IV in 1399 for control of the English crown, and Richard II surrendered at Bristol, Bussy was found hiding with Richard. William Shakespeare wrote that Harry Hereford, known as Bolingbroke, said that Bussy was "a caterpillar of this commonwealth I have sworn to weed and pluck away." Hereford had Bussy quickly tried on treason and beheaded in Bristol. At the same time, however, Henry IV realized the limits of the speakership. In 1410, he admonished Speaker Geoffrey Chaucer - son of the famed writer - to see that there were no "unbecoming words from the Commons," and that they did not attempt "anything inconsistent with decency." In fact, until the seventeenth century, the Speaker was considered the spokesman for the Crown in the House of Commons rather than the official who spoke for the Parliament itself.

The makeup of the House of Commons was unique in many ways. In a 1983 dissertation about the Commons that met in 1491, Dale Casper explained,

> The Chapter House of Westminster Abbey was the locus [a center or source of power, a place and/or locality] in October of 1491 for the gathering of 296 men who had been elected to give counsel to the king in his high court of parliament. A great blend of fifteenth-century professions and occupations came together that early fall. Lawyers, squires, farmers, tradesmen, local government officials, royal office holders, and other interested parties had sought and obtained seats in parliament.

Casper then noted that despite having many members of that parliament who had years of experience, either politically or militarily in some of King Henry VII's conflicts, they were all bypassed in the selection of a new Speaker. "The Speaker of this parliament was not, however, chosen from those men possessing several years of parliamentary experience," Casper wrote. "The man selected by the king and chosen by the membership of the Commons to express their opinions before the king and lords of the realm was Sir Richard Empson, who was elected from Northamptonshire, and was sitting in only his second parliament." Empson, born about 1450, rose in the years after serving as Speaker to become Chancellor of the Duchy of Lancaster; however, he fell out of favor with Henry VII's son, Henry VIII, and, in a case that historians conclude was trumped up, was arrested with Edmund Dudley and, in August 1510, was beheaded on Tower Hill, near what is now the Tower of London.

Charles I to Charles II (1625-1685)

Through the sixteenth and into the seventeenth centuries, the Speaker remained a close confidante to the King. Even in 1625, when the first signs of angst among the members of the Commons were beginning to rise, the King's choice of Speaker, Thomas Crewe, who had been the Speaker in the previous Parliament, was elected easily. In 1640, Charles' choice, William Lenthall, who had served in the "Short Parliament" (1640), was selected as Speaker of the "Long Parliament" (which lasted, because it could not be adjourned without the agreement of all of its members, until 1660). Lenthall was

considered, at least for the first years of his speakership, a weak Speaker who could not contain debate in the Commons.

Perhaps the turning point in the development of the Speaker as an independent office from the Crown came in 1642, when King Charles I himself came into the House chambers to search for five members facing charges of high treason. When Speaker Lenthall, was asked by the King if he knew the location of these five members, Lenthall stated, "May it please your Majesty, I have neither eyes nor tongue to speak in this place by as the House is pleased to direct me, whose servant I am here." This incident marked the beginning not only of the independence of the Speaker from the Crown, but to this day the King or Queen of England, in a mostly ceremonial move, must be "invited" to enter the House of Commons chambers to deliver their annual address to the Parliament. It was during this period that the House of Commons, and the Speaker, became not agents of the government but agents *against* the government, and the reign of Charles I. Lenthall went against the King and led the Parliament in its rebellion against the Crown. In some instances, he sided with the rebels, and in others with Charles; in a letter to Sir Thomas Fairfax, commander of the rebel forces, he called the general the "Saviour of the Parliament and people's libertie." When the King was captured in 1649 and put on trial, Lenthall sat as Speaker throughout the proceedings. In 1653, when Oliver Cromwell expelled the Long Parliament from London, and Lenthall refused to give up the Speaker's chair, he was removed by force. He was succeeded by the Rev. Francis Rous or Rouse, who served as Speaker during the "Barebones Parliament" (named for the London preacher Praise-God Barebon, also known as known as Barebone).

Following the restoration of the Stuart family to the throne of England through Charles I's son, Charles II, the Commons saw the development of the party system and the establishment of the Whig and Tory parties. In a history of the House of Commons during the early seventeenth century, Gertrude Amspoker wrote:

> The Speaker's position in the Elizabethan House of Commons had been a remarkably influential one. In large measure, he determined the order of business and could stop proceedings

which had incurred the Crown's displeasure. To a notable degree, he could push or retard bills through his power to determine when they were to read, committed, or put to the question for passage. He gave the House an epitome of a bill's content. A modern historian has pointed out that the Speaker frequently "had private interviews with members of the Commons, nominally to seek their opinions, actually in many cases to impress his will upon them." He participated in debate, could interrupt it when he chose, and decided which member was to have the floor. He worded questions for voting and decided when votes were to be taken. He decided the result of an oral vote; divisions, which might contradict him, were rare. He decided the moment of adjournment at the end of a day's business.

Seventeenth Century to Modern Times

The seventeenth and eighteenth centuries saw major changes in the way the King reacted to having a Speaker in the House of Commons, with these changes becoming permanent after the Glorious Revolution (1688). Under William III (reigned 1689-1702), the Speaker was seen not as a member of a body in opposition to the King, but a part of his regime. In fact, Robert Harley served both as Speaker of the House of Commons and as Secretary of State in the King's cabinet from 1704 to 1705. The Speakers during this period remained close to the King; it was not until the speakership of Arthur Onslow, who served as Speaker from 1728 to 1761, that a reduction in the relationship between the monarch and the Speaker came about.

During the nineteenth and twentieth centuries, the Speaker became once again an extension of the King or Queen; Henry Addington (served 1801), and Sir Arthur Wellesley-Peel (served 1884-95) were just two of the Speakers who were spokesmen not just for the majority party in the Commons but for the sovereign. One difference between the British Speaker and his American counterpart is that the Commons Speaker must resign from his (or her) respective party upon election as Speaker. A factsheet on the Commons notes that,

the Speaker must, of course, be above party political controversy and must be seen to be com-

pletely impartial in all public matters. All sides in the House rely on the Speaker's disinterest and respect that he or she must stand aside from controversy. Accordingly, on election the Speaker resigns from his or her political party. Even after retirement, a former Speaker will take no part in political issues, and if appointed to the House of Lords will sit as a Cross-Bencher. Assuming the office of Speaker will, to a great extent, mean shedding old loyalties and friendships within the House. The Speaker must keep apart from old party colleagues or any one group or interest and does not, for instance, frequent the Commons dining rooms or bars.

In 1841, when this rule was instituted to stop the speakership from becoming a political wedge to be used by one side or another, Robert Peel, the Prime Minister and leader of the Conservatives, saw to it that Charles Shaw-Lefevre, the Liberal Speaker, was re-elected. The end of the twentieth century saw a distinct change in the Commons speakership: In 1992, Betty Boothroyd, representing West Bromwich West in the House of Commons, was named as the first female Speaker, serving for eight years until she became Baroness Boothroyd of Sandwell and was created a Life Peer in the House of Lords. She was succeeded by Michael John Martin, who became the first Scottish Speaker to preside over the British House of Commons; in 2005, he was re-elected, and, as of this writing, continues to hold that seat. Martin is also the first Roman Catholic to serve as the Commons Speaker since Mary I was Queen (1553-58).

As with its American counterpart, the British House of Commons has endured several controversial elections, most notably that of 1895, when William Court Gully was elected Speaker despite the considerable support behind Sir Matthew White Ridley, a widely respected MP. When Speaker Douglas Clifton Brown retired before the 1951 general election, it was considered good form to elect his deputy, James Milner, the First Baron Milner of Leeds, as Speaker, but the Conservatives, who won that election, instead elected William Shepherd Morrison (later the Viscount Dunrossil), who won and served until 1959, when he was given a peerage and named to succeed Sir William Slim as the Governor-General of Australia. Selwyn Lloyd, a Conservative, was elected in 1971 despite being perceived by the Liberals as a weak politician.

As with the U.S. House of Representatives, the Speakers of the British House of Commons are heralded in their respective office. There have been more than 150 Speakers since record-keeping started, and their names and dates of service are listed, inscribed in gold leaf on the walls of Room C of the new House of Commons Library, which, along with rooms A and B, overlook the Thames River. The old library, later called the Lower Library, was obliterated in the fire of 1834 that destroyed nearly the entire structure of Westminster where the House of Commons and House of Lords meet.

In 1890, James Bryce, the noted British historian, author of *The American Commonwealth*, was asked by the *North American Review* to pen an article which was "a word as to the speakership" in the United States and its relation to the British model. He explained,

> In [the American] Congress the Speaker is for many purposes the leader of the majority. The majority is often advised by him, and usually reckons on him to help it to carry out his will. The hare might as well hope that the huntsman would call off the hounds as the minority expect the Speaker to restrain an impatient majority. But in Parliament the Speaker and the chairman of committees...are and have always been non-partisan officials. Each, no doubt, has be-

> longed to a party and has always been chosen on the proposition of a party leader. But the Speaker is deemed, once he has assumed the wig and gown of office, to have so distinctly renounced and divested himself of all party trappings that, if he is willing to go on serving in a new Parliament in which the party to which he belonged is in the minority, the majority is, nevertheless, expected to elect him anew.

Bryce used as an example, Speaker Sir Henry Brand, a member of the Liberal Party, who was elected by the Tories in 1874, and served until 1883. Such a move in the American Congress is impossible, as the two parties that battle for control of the House every two years install their party leader as Speaker when they achieve or keep the majority. Ten years later, British writer Sydney Brooks also assessed the differences and similarities between the two Speakers in an article in the same magazine.

As opposed to the British House of Commons, no Speaker in the U.S. House has ever met a violent death, although several have left office due to scandal and one - Michael C. Kerr (served 1875-76) - died of tuberculosis soon after leaving office. Nine Speakers of the House of Commons have been either murdered, beheaded by the Crown, or died in battle. This includes Sir John Wenlock (served 1455-56), killed at the Battle of Tewkesbury (1471), and Sir Thomas More (served 1523), beheaded by King Henry VIII for opposing his divorce from Catherine of Aragon.

The Speaker in the Earliest Legislative Bodies in American History

The Speaker of the U.S. House of Representatives was based, at least in part, on the Speaker of the British House of Commons. However, before the House of Representatives was established as a body, the American colonies had their own legislatures, and it was here that the first Speakers served in what was to become the United States and demonstrated their power. This essay focuses specifically on the role of the Speaker in these early legislative bodies.

Early Colonial Assemblies

In pre-Constitutional America - the years before 1787 - power was held by the individual colonies, and, during and after the American Revolution, by the weak Continental Congress. The men, who led the legislative bodies of the colonies, as well as the Continental Congress, were designated as "Speaker," although their powers and offices differ greatly from what we consider to be a Speaker today. In 1909, Asher C. Hinds (1863-1919), the-then U.S. Representative from Maine (1895-1911) who would later achieve greatness from his compilation of the rules of the House now known as *Hinds Precedents*, wrote in an article on the history of the speakership on the office's foundation in the men who served as Speaker of the colonial assemblies during the years before the formation of the United States of America:

> When the Constitution was framed the members of the convention spent very little time over the House of Representatives. The reason of this is that the house was an existing political institution, each colony having had under its own peculiar name a house of representatives for many years...The Constitution, therefore, did not create a speaker, but adopted an existing officer; and a careful examination of the proceedings of the convention in relation to this fact, makes it plain that the speaker they adopted was the speaker of the colonial house of representatives, of whom they had intimate personal knowledge, rather than the speaker of the house of commons, whom they knew of it a theoretical way only.

Unfortunately, there is little to investigate when it comes to these early "Speakers" - as House historian Mary Parker Follett wrote in 1902, "Cobbett's and Hansard's "Debates" afford material for a study of the speakership of the House of Commons, but in the case of the colonies there is little besides the meagre [sic] records of assemblies; the ground has as yet hardly been broken for a study of colonial political institutions." More than a century after Follett wrote these words, the situation is nearly the same: for the historian who wishes to either view the records of the earliest colonial legislative bodies or, to even a further extent, the accounts of the work or of the lives of the men who served as "Speaker" of these bodies, there is a virtual wasteland.

Asher Crosby's assertion that the Constitutional Convention's approval of a Speaker was based more on the speakers of the early colonial legislatures rather than the Speaker of the House of Commons is a misnomer: the early colonial speakers *were* based on the Speaker of the House of Commons. Because the first legislative bodies in the colonies were in effect extensions of the British government in America, that each colony had its own "mini" House of Commons was not an uncommon event. The only difference that could exist was whether or not the royal governor, in his role as executive, could overrule the legislature or even ignore their work altogether.

House of Burgesses

The first legislative assembly in the colonies was the House of Burgesses in Virginia. While the House of Burgesses was a form of "self-rule" for the colonists, in fact the body was a mere extension of the British Parliament, designed to follow London's rules and regulations. One of the best sources for the early history of the legislatures is a 1983 dissertation by Sanford William Peterson. In discussing the formation of the Virginia House of Burgesses, he explained that historian William Wirt Henry, in an 1894 article that appeared in the *Virginia Historical Magazine*, "reasoned [that] the first House of Burgesses succeeded because John Pory sat as its first Speaker. Pory was the only member of the first assembly with Parliamentary experience, 'having served in parliament he was able to give order to their proceedings, and proper form to their acts.'" Henry notes in his 1894 article that "having served in Parliament he was able to give order to their proceedings, and proper form to their acts." As Peterson relates, Pory served for six years in the British House of Commons, from 1605 to 1611; however, he discovered that Pory had a serious drinking problem and probably was not the "experienced parliamentarian" he was thought to be. Nevertheless, he is remembered - unlike nearly all of the men who served as Speaker in colonial legislatures - in a biography, which was written by William S. Powell in 1977 as *John Pory, the Life and Letters of a Man of Many Parts*.

It appears, at least from the record, that the two most important legislative bodies during the colonial period were those in Virginia and Massachusetts, with Pennsylvania a close third. In the former, the House of Burgesses, a number of men who held the speakership have come down to history for their work in all areas of political study. In a collection of the papers and correspondence of famed patriot Patrick Henry, his grandson, William Wirt Henry, noted that,

> *John Robinson, the Speaker of the [Virginia] House [of Burgesses], had filled the chair for twenty-five years with great dignity. He was possessed of a strong mind, which was enlarged by great experience, and of a benevolence of spirit and courtesy of manner which rendered him exceedingly popular...As Speaker of the House he was also Treasurer of the colony, and was altogether the most influential member of that body. The high offices he held caused him to be warmly attached to the royal government, and he was very averse to taking any step which would be censured by the Ministry.*

One of the leading speakers of the Virginia House of Burgesses was Sir John Randolph, ancestor of the famed Randolph family that sent several members to the U.S. Congress. A biography of Speaker Randolph noted that,

> *...the progenitor of the Randolphs of Virginia was William of Yorkshire, England, who settled at Turkey Island, on the James River. He was a nephew of Thomas Randolph, the poet...Several*

of his son were men of distinction: William was a member of the Council and Treasurer of the Colony. Isham was a member of the House of Burgesses, from Goochland, 1740, and Adjutant General of the Colony. Richard was a member of the House of Burgesses, 1740, for Henrico, and succeeded his brother as treasurer. Sir John was Speaker of the House of Burgesses and Attorney General.

Other Colonial Legislatures

It appears that Thomas Hutchinson served as Speaker of the Massachusetts House from 1746 to 1748, starting in the position when he was just 35. In Pennsylvania, the Assembly noted in 1767 that,

> *The Speaker [shall] have the Power to nominate Persons for Committees, and that none who are nominated refuse the Service; not that any of the Members shall be hereby debarred of their Privilege of nominating Persons, if they think fit, or rejecting such as are nominated by the Speaker; in which case the opinion of the House shall govern...*

Patrick Henry's grandson, William Wirt Henry, noted that at the Continental Congress "Pennsylvania had at the head of her delegation John Galloway, the clever Speaker of her legislature, who proved to be a Tory in disguise."

In New York, Governor William Burnet complained to the Lord of Trade in 1727 about the actions of Speaker Adolphe Philips, which led to the governor dissolving the state Assembly. He explained that,

> *...[the] Assembly had passed some Extraordinary Resolves about the Court of Chancery which was all done at the suggestion of the Speaker, who had lately lost a cause in Chancery, and against whom I had signed a Decree only two days before. The evident partiality of the House in being thus Directed by one that was a Party, and entering into his Resentment, made me think it necessary to dissolve them, and to publish an Answer to their Resolves made by the Council.*

Historian William Browne related in 1883 that "There were, of course, other variations in the rules of order for these colonial legislatures. In Maryland, the presiding officer was called 'the Lieuten^t grall.' In Virginia, South Carolina, and Pennsylvania, he was 'Mr. Speaker.'" Historian A.S. Salley, Jr., found that in South Carolina, a rule enacted in 1692 mandated that "he shall not make any further Discourse on ye Same day wthout [sic] Leave of the Speaker."

In the colony of Georgia, Noble Wimberly Jones refused the speakership of the General Assembly, then refused an offer by Governor James Wright to hold the office, setting off a power struggle. Eventually the House of Lords in London held, in the case of *Campbell v. Hall* (1774), that the King's decision making did not include altering the laws of colonies or the dismissal of colonial governmental officials.

The Continental Congress
The formation of the Continental Congress in 1774 led to the first national legislature in what would become the United States. That body, in laying out a governmental structure, initially proposed to form a "Grand Council," which would run the projected United States, with a Speaker, like that of the British House of Commons, to be at the head of this council. The proposal that was first laid out, stated:

> *That the Grand Council shall meet once in every year if they shall think it necessary, and oftener, if occasions shall require, at such time and place as they shall adjourn to at the last preceding meeting, or as they shall be called to meet at, by the President General on any emergency. That the Grand Council shall have power to choose their Speaker, and shall hold and exercise all the like rights, liberties, and privileges as are held and exercised by and in the House of Commons of Great Britain.*

Ironically, in 1787, when the Constitution was drawn up and approved, the section that established the Speaker of the House used almost this precise language. It would become the only statement of the Constitution on the speakership. One of the men who served as "President of the Continental Congress," in effect the Speaker of that body, was Peyton Randolph, whose relation Sir John Randolph had served, as previously noted, as Speaker of the Virginia House of Burgesses.

In the vein of Peyton Randolph, other men who served in that somewhat mysterious office of "Presi-

dent of the Continental Congress" included Henry Middleton (served 22-26 October 1774), John Hancock (served 2 July 1776-29 October 1777), who later was the first signer of the Declaration of Independence, and John Jay (served 10 December 1778-28 September 1779), who later served as the first Chief Justice of the U.S. Supreme Court. In 1781, this vaunted office became "President of the United States in Congress Assembled," again perhaps more of a Speaker than a "President." Several men served in this capacity right up until 4 March 1789, when George Washington was inaugurated as President under the new U.S. Constitution. At the same time, the new Federal House of Representatives was given the right to "chuse" a Speaker; in the First Congress (1789-91), it was Frederick Augustus Conrad Muhlenberg of Pennsylvania. Muhlenberg had served as the Speaker of the General Assembly of Pennsylvania as well as the President of the Council of Censors of that Commonwealth. However, the break between state and federal was not complete; of the Speakers who served in the House of Representatives between 1789 and 1841, five (Muhlenberg, Trumbull, Sedgwick, Clay, and Andrew Stevenson) had served previously as the presiding officer in state legislative bodies.

Joseph Story, the noted legal expert and judge who rose to serve as an Associate Justice on the Supreme Court, wrote of his time as the Speaker of the Massachusetts House of Representatives:

> *Cheered, indeed, by your kindness, I have been able, in controversies, marked with peculiar political zeal, to appreciate the excellence of those established rules which invite liberal discussions, but define the boundary of right, and check the intemperance of debate. I have learned that rigid enforcement of these rules, while it enables the majority to mature their measures with wisdom and dignity, is the only barrier of the rights of the minority against the encroachments of power and ambition. If anything can restrain the impetuosity of triumph, or the vehemence of opposition - if anything can awaken the glow of oratory, and the spirit of virtue - if anything can preserve the courtesy of generous minds amidst the rivalries and jealousies of contending parties, it will be found in the protection with*

which these rules encircle and shield every member of the legislative body.

Luther Stearns Cushing compiled the duties of legislative speakers in his 1856 work, *Lex Parliamentaria Americana*. In part, he explained that the Speaker was, like his or her counterpart in the U.S. House, the chief of debate and deliberation. He wrote:

As a committee of the whole can only sit while the house is sitting - being in fact the house itself sitting in committee - it is necessary that the speaker should be constantly present in the committee, and take official notice of its proceedings, in order to resume the chair of the house, whenever the committee shall see fit to rise and report; or, to resume it without any direction of the committee, when any public business shall arise in which the house is concerned, or when notice is taken, and it appears, that a quorum of the committee is not present; or in case any sudden disorder should occur, which the committee as such, would have no power to suppress.

If such "disorder" shall occur, Cushing noted, "It is thus in the power of the speaker, whenever the exigency requires it, to take the chair at once, and resume the house."

Difficulty in Studying Early Speakers Using Historical Documents

Despite being some of the most powerful politicians in American history, a vast majority of the Speakers have slipped into a realm of obscurity from which few can be dislodged. Writing on their lives and their service, even from contemporary sources, proved to be an incredible task for people so well known during their time. Even recent Speakers - including Carl Albert, Tom Foley, Dennis Hastert, and Nancy Pelosi - were not as easy to discover who they were or what made or makes them tick; finding the earlier Speakers demonstrated just how hard this task had become.

For instance, let us focus on one Speaker in particular: John White (1802-1845), who served for a single two-year term as Speaker during the Twenty-seventh Congress (1841-43). His official biography in the *The Biographical Directory of the United States Congress*, now completely online, runs for only eight lines - that's it. The vaunted in *Dictionary of American Biography* does not include his biography; the more recent (and billed as more inclusive) *American National Biography* also lacks his life story. Despite the fact that White served for ten years in the House - from 1835 to 1845 - he apparently did not give many speeches, as only three printed discourses could be found, all of which are nearly impossible to find unless one gets lucky with an obscure collection at some library somewhere. As well, only three letters *in total* could be found bearing White's signature: two in the James K. Polk Papers in the Library of Congress, and one other in the Leverett Saltonstall Papers at the Massachusetts Historical Society in Boston. Thus arises the question: how does one try to find information on the thoughts and words of John White, who rose to serve as Speaker of the House?

The Annals of Congress
Until recently, this is a problem shared by all who study Congress. The first thought is: speeches, speeches! There must be a publication that contains all of the speeches of the House and Senate, where so many orators blessed the pages of the nation's newspapers and printed pamphlets with their words. Yet, until 1873, there is nothing like that. The first

attempt to "capture" the words of lawmakers came in *The Annals of Congress*, a publication that first appeared in 1834 and lasted until 1856. It was an amalgamation of printed and unprinted papers collected by Joseph Gales, Sr., who founded the famed printing house of Gales and Seaton and published many of the nation's earliest congressional documents. Officially titled *The Debates and Proceedings in the Congress of the United States; with an Appendix, Containing Important State Papers and Public Documents, and All the Laws of a Public Nature; with a Copious Index*, *The Annals* began the coverage of Congress from its very first session in New York on 4 March 1789, when President George Washington was sworn in for his first term.

Now also online courtesy of the Library of Congress, which admits that the 42 volumes are compiled "using the best records available, primarily newspaper accounts…[s]peeches are paraphrased rather than presented verbatim, but the record of debate is nonetheless fuller than that available from the House and Senate journals." Despite the fact that the Constitution mandated that "Each House shall keep a Journal of its proceedings," the speeches and debates of the first congresses were not collected until most of the men who served in them were long dead. And even then these orations were riddled with errors that could not be rectified because, again, those who had heard them had long since passed away.

Newspapers and Journals
For historians of the House, however, the task to find some semblance of what the early Speakers said or did is far easier than historians of the Senate; while newspapers were allowed to cover the House - newspapers such as the *Gazette of the United States* and the *Aurora* in Philadelphia, for instance - and sometimes printed their accounts daily of the sessions, the Senate closed its doors to all but the official *Senate Journal*, which, like the *House Journal*, was not a verbatim account but a collected version. Other sources, including journals of persons who served or others at the time, as well as manuscript collections and other personal correspondence, try

to fill the vacuum, but in most cases fail dismally. At the same time that this lack of contemporary reporting gives those studying the early Speakers fits, further missing sources aid in the confusion. Historian William Lee Miller, whose 1996 work on the history of the debates about slavery in the House is a landmark of its kind, explained, in some detail, as to the dilemma modern historians have in finding the *exact* words of the members of Congress of the years before 1873:

> *The Congressional Record of today did not yet exist in the 1830s and 1840s. The Congressional Globe and its sometime competitor the Register of Debates were records of the debates in the House and the Senate kept by private printing firms - Blair and Rives, Gales and Seaton - that competed for selection as official printer. They had partisan and factional alliances, and sometimes these would show through the record. They would send a reporter to the chamber to copy down what he could; if his attention wandered, some solon's great flight of oratory might be lost to history. Congressmen would often hand a full copy of their remarks to the reporter, or carry it around to the printer's office the next morning, and in that case the full speech would spread itself on the page. The reporter making his own effort to get down what was said might scramble to reproduce it all as best he could, in the congressman's voice, or he might shift without warning into the third person: "He said..." Or he might just give a swift reporter's summary: "the congressman spoke at great length on the petition question, mentioning the Magna Carta." Long speeches would receive short summary; short exchanges would be captured in full. A sleepy reporter would confuse one congressman from Massachusetts with another, and the printer's office, in haste, would get the date wrong. Sometimes the reporter would simply characterize what was happening on the floor, without trying to record its substance: "After a long and noisy discussion"; "interrupted by deafening cries to order"; "great agitation in the House"; "Great confusion here prevailed, so that it was impossible to hear with distinction." The confession that the reporter could not hear was spread upon the record, apparently without embarrassment, fairly often: "Some remarks*

> *were here made by the Speaker not heard by the Reporter"; "Mr. Everett offered some remarks which were not sufficiently understood by the Reporter to enable him to give them"; "Mr. Weller and Mr. Holmes conversed across each other, but of what passed the Reporter has no idea." Paradoxically, the limitations and errors and personal touches reassure the reader of the essential value of the record, by reminding him that the reporter, an actual human being, was really there, trying to record what he heard and saw.*

Yet Miller, who dissected the inner works of this period of American history, barely mentions the Speakers who played the greatest role in the formation, notably Speakers James K. Polk and John White. As for the latter, he merely calls him a "slaveholder" and then moves on.

Letters, Papers, and Biographies

But Miller is not an exception, but the rule. Of these early Speakers, except for Macon and Clay, there is sometimes a blank and empty slate. Few of their manuscripts exist, if any ever did; and for some their only letters to other people, such as George Washington or Thomas Jefferson or John Adams, are the only pieces of correspondence to be found. In fact, even up to Speaker Joseph Cannon, in the first years of the twentieth century, there appears to stand out not one major Speaker, save that of Henry Clay and Polk, with the former being a giant in the U.S. Senate (and three-time presidential candidate), and the latter being the only Speaker elected President, in 1844. Clay's name was resurrected recently with a 1991 biography by historian Robert V. Remini. But when one wants to seek information about John W. Jones, or Philip Pendleton Barbour (who later served on the U.S. Supreme Court, making his ignominy all the more disheartening), or John W. Davis, there is nothing. Of Speaker John W. Taylor, even a search of the record of his birth shows that his middle name is unknown and will probably remain a mystery. Speaker Robert Mercer Taliaferro Hunter, perhaps one of the most important southern figures in the secessionist movement that led to the Civil War, has become a nameless, faceless mark on history.

Yet the amateur historian or layman could reasonably argue that some of the earliest Presidents were given coverage through biographies, and other works. This is true, but for a different reason. Let us take the papers of some of the Presidents, for instance. Even those who served whose names are not remembered well - Zachary Taylor, or Millard Fillmore, or even John Tyler - have their official papers and manuscript collections lodged in major institutions such as the Library of Congress, and have had lengthy biographies written about them, despite their obscurity. But for such Speakers as Jonathan Trumbull, or Joseph B. Varnum or even Nathaniel Macon - the latter considered one of the greatest of the pre-Henry Clay era Speakers - there is little or nothing. Macon does have three of his own biographies, but they were written in 1840, 1862, and 1903, and none are extensive.

The Role of the Speaker

Why is this? Because, to put it simply, the Constitution built the presidency into an office with some power, while the speakership, mentioned in only one sentence, is what the members of the House made it to be. And those early Speakers were mere figureheads than any semblance of a national leader, unlike the Speakers since Joseph Cannon, who served in the first two decades of the twentieth century, or a Sam Rayburn, or a Newt Gingrich. But even these more recent Speakers have only become known as their profile in the growing forms of media - radio, then television, then satellite, and now the Internet) - grew.

Could the obscurity of the Speakers be because of their overall role? In a 2006 article, scholars Randal Strahan, Matthew Gunning, and Richard L. Vining, Jr., wrote of tracing the role of the Speaker "from Moderator to Leader" from 1789 to 1841. They explained,

One feature of the early "moderator" or "parliamentary" Speakership was an understanding that Speakers should refrain from active involvement in debates on policy issues before the House. House rules proscribed the Speaker's participation from the chair in debates on policy matters, and early Speakers are said also to have honored an informal prohibition on participation in debates in the Committee of the

Whole as well. In turn, the defining characteristics of the more political speakership that developed later included active, public leadership on policy and party matters.

In a speech given before the Cannon Centenary Conference in Washington, D.C. in 2003 to commemorate the 100th anniversary of the election of Joseph Cannon as Speaker, Professor Ronald M. Peters, Jr., noted:

The speakership of the House had not always been so powerful an office nor such a pure expression of party interest as Cannon made it. During the formative years of the Republic, the political party system was in flux, and House Speakers were not usually cast in the role of national party leaders. Henry Clay of Kentucky, the most important Speaker of the antebellum period, was indeed a partisan figure, but his influence extended beyond the circle of his partisan supporters and as a national figure he, in effect, transcended the offices that he held. Other antebellum Speakers were less noteworthy. It was not until the Civil War, with the rise of the stable, two-party system that we have known since, that the speakership became defined as a position of party responsibility...Several Speakers during this period became powerful political leaders. These included Republicans James G. Blaine of Maine, Thomas B. Reed of Maine, and Cannon himself, and Democrats such as Samuel J. Randall of Pennsylvania, John G. Carlisle of Kentucky, and Charles F. Crisp of Georgia.

At the same time that the speakership has been getting more attention, still the men (and now woman) who have served in the office continue to be hidden in the shadows. When Newt Gingrich of Georgia rose to become Speaker in 104th Congress (1995-97), it was noted that he was the first Republican Speaker "in fifty years." Many commentators had to dig out collections of historical facts to find the name of that last Republican Speaker: Joseph W. Martin, Jr., who served in the Eightieth Congress (1947-49) and the Eighty-third Congress (1953-55).

However, a counter-argument to the dispute over why the study of the Speakers and their lives and services has fallen into obscurity can be made, based on three names: Henry Clay, Daniel Webster, and John C. Calhoun. These three giants of the Senate - in 1957, a Senate committee listed them all among the 10 greatest Senators who ever served - are all remembered today, even more amazing considering that each died before 1860. Why are they remembered as mere Senators when men who sat in the chair of the Speaker of the House of Representatives are forgotten? Because these three, and others like them - the list is not exhaustive, but is far longer for them than any of the Speakers - were leaders of national movements, most notably in the proslavery (Calhoun) and unionist factions in the Senate. Clay was responsible for the compromises of 1820 and 1850, both of which averted, at least for a time, the onrushing Civil War. Webster was also involved in brokering the 1850 settlement, while Calhoun, who did sit as Secretary of War (1817-25) and Vice President (1824-32), was a firm advocate of the rights of slaveowners who warned of the breakup of the Union if the Congress attempted to outlaw slavery.

In Britain, as opposed to the United States, there has been a tendency to try to document the lives of the men who served as Speaker: in 1808 appeared *Characteristic Sketches of Some of the Most Distinguished Speakers in the House of Commons*, which, even 200 years later, is far better about the British Speakers than anything that appeared during that first century of the American Speaker. In the United States, this chore has become more difficult with each passing year, despite the historical importance of the work and services of these men.

When former Speaker John White committed suicide in his home in September 1845, few newspapers even covered it. Imagine the coverage if such an event occurred in today's 24/7 world of news everywhere, on all the time. Perhaps history has changed - but, for many of these figures, it is too late. We can only try to undo the damage done.

The Role of the Speaker in the Impeachments of Three Presidents

Although the role of the Speaker of the House of Representatives is only tangentially mentioned in the U.S. Constitution, and the role and powers of the office are not outlined at all in that founding document, it has become the duty of the Speaker to oversee the hearing of impeachment inquiries, which originate in the House, and supervise the floor voting over whether or not, once an impeachment is voted in the positive by the full House, to send the indictment to the U.S. Senate for a trial. If the inquiry gets a majority of votes, the Speaker also designates "floor managers" who control the arguments of the House during the Senate trial. Thus, arises the examination of the impeachment inquiries of three U.S. Presidents - Andrew Johnson in 1868, Richard M. Nixon in 1973-74, and William Jefferson Clinton in 1998-99, with two of those inquiries going forward to trials in the Senate. In the two that went forward, Speaker Schuyler Colfax presided over the 1868 impeachment inquiry over President Andrew Johnson for his violation of the Tenure of Office Act of 1867, while Speaker Newt Gingrich presided over the 1998 impeachment of President Bill Clinton for committing perjury under oath. In the third inquiry, Speaker Carl Albert presided over the impeachment hearings for President Richard M. Nixon and his role in the Watergate scandal. This third inquiry was near to completion when Nixon resigned the presidency on 8 August 1974, thus leaving no reason for a trial to be held in the Senate. In this essay, we examine the roles of these three Speakers in perhaps one of the most important checks on the power of the President by the legislative branch: the right to impeach and remove a President for "high crimes and misdemeanors."

Although the role of the Speaker in the U.S. House is barely discussed in the U.S. Constitution, save for one sentence, the act of the impeachment and removal of officers of the government is specifically laid out. Article II, Section 4 of the Constitution states:

The President, Vice President and all civil Officers of the United States, shall be removed from Office on Impeachment for, and Conviction of, Treason, Bribery, or other high Crimes and Misdemeanors.

The impeachment of a President was widely argued about in the years before 1868, most notably in the case of John Tyler, who rose to the presidency upon the death of President William Henry Harrison after just a month in office in 1841. But the moves to impeach Tyler were more for his political leanings - he had been elected on the Whig ticket but was more of a proslavery Democrat, and he stymied the activities of the Whig-led Twenty-seventh Congress (1841-43). It was not until 1868, when another occupant of the White House by accident rather than election, Andrew Johnson, incurred the wrath of the Congress and forced their impeachment and near conviction of him.

Impeachment of Andrew Johnson (1868)

In 1903, historian David Miller De Witt, having been given rare access (even now) to the papers of Andrew Johnson by Johnson's daughter, wrote:

The impeachment of President Johnson was the culmination of a struggle between the executive and legislative branches of the government of the United States over the problem of what came to be called Reconstruction, a struggle which, ante-dating Johnson's own administration, troubled the administration of his lamented predecessor [Abraham Lincoln].

At the same time, Republicans in Congress, many of whom have been labeled by historians as "radicals" because they desired to change the Constitution to protect the rights of freed slaves and guarantee that slavery or even involuntary servitude would never again exist under law, were using the office of Secretary of War Edwin M. Stanton to undermine the Johnson administration. Johnson, a former Governor of Tennessee, was a "War Democrat" who supported Lincoln in his first term and kept his state in the Union when nearly every other southern slaveholding state seceded; in exchange for his support, in 1864 Lincoln, desperately needing the support of Democrats who favored the war to save his own chances of re-election, ditched Vice President Hannibal Hamlin and replaced him on the ticket with Johnson. Running not as the Republican Party but as the "Union Party," Lincoln and Johnson won a narrow but stunning victory that came about because of several victories on the battlefield for the Union forces, which precipitated the end of the horrific conflict of the Civil War.

Just a month into his second term, Lincoln was assassinated, and Johnson, who had little in common with the vast majority of Republicans in the House and Senate, tried to end the Reconstruction of the former Confederate states while also impairing the Republican agenda. According to Senator Henry Wilson, Republican of Massachusetts, who later served as Vice President, Stanton, who sympathized with the Republicans, was aiding them with secret messages on Johnson and his inner circle; that "he put himself in communication with the Republicans in Congress, and kept them well informed of what was going on in the councils of the administration." The House and Senate leadership, led by Speaker Schuyler Colfax, established a "committee of vigilance" to keep tabs on Johnson, with Wilson and Colfax serving as members. Colfax is considered one of the House moderates on the issues separating the President and Congress; however, as Johnson continued to force the Congress to override veto after veto, even moderates such as Colfax realized that Johnson and the Congress were headed for a constitutional showdown.

Johnson answered each charge with a charge of his own, in many ways exacerbating the situation. He vetoed the Freedman's Bureau bill, a veto that was easily overridden, as well as other legislation such as the District [of Columbia] Suffrage Bill and the Military Reconstruction Bill, all intended to aid former slaves or to further the cause of the rehabilitation of the southern states. Thus, the move to impeach Johnson had been underway for some time; on 7 January 1867, Rep. James M. Ashley, Republican of Ohio, introduced articles of impeachment, charging the President with "a usurpation of power and violation of law," among other matters. The House Committee on the Judiciary investigated the subject, but found that going forward was deemed "inexpedient." And there, it appeared, the issue had died. Johnson, however, wanted to continue to pick at

the fresh wound growing between he and the House, and, finally, the pus of the sore burst into the open.

When rumors surfaced that he wanted to remove from office Secretary Stanton, the Congress enacted - over Johnson's veto - the Tenure of Office Act of 1867, which specifically stated that any cabinet officer who had been confirmed by Congress could only be removed by a similar vote of Congress. When Johnson realized that Stanton was an enemy inside his own camp, he dismissed the Lincoln-appointed official, and the President set up a clash with Congress that had been lurking since he had taken office in a drunken state.

On 21 February 1868, Johnson sent the following letter to Stanton:

Executive Mansion

Sir:- By virtue of power and authority vested in me, as President, by the Constitution and laws of the United States, you are hereby removed from office, as Secretary of the Department of War, and your functions as such will terminate upon receipt of this communication. You will transfer to Brevet Major-General

Lorenzo Thomas, Adjutant-General of the Army, who has this day been authorized and empowered to act as Secretary of War ad interim, all records, papers, and other public properly now in your custody and charge.

Respectfully, yours,

(Signed) Andrew Johnson,

President of the United States

Stanton immediately sent a letter to Speaker Colfax:

Sir:- General Thomas has just delivered to me a copy of the inclosed order, which you will please communicate to the House of Representatives.

Your obedient servant,

Edwin M. Stanton, Secretary of War

Colfax was able to bring together the diverse members of his caucus to once and for all oppose the President and to initiate an impeachment inquiry.

He referred the action of the President to the House Committee on Reconstruction to hold a hearing as to what to do next. In one day, the committee found that the President had violated the Tenure of Office Act, a violation it deemed to be an impeachable offense.

On 22 February, Rep. Thaddeus Stevens, Republican of Pennsylvania, rose in the House to report on the committee's findings; Speaker Colfax sat in the Speaker's chair as the report was read aloud, cautioning the members and any persons in the gallery to preserve order and to listen carefully. A history of the Fortieth Congress (1867-69), published in 1869, noted:

> An earnest debate ensued, which was closed with a speech written by Mr. Stevens, but read by the Clerk of the House. The veteran Chairman of the Committee and former leader of the House, with a mind still vigorous, found his physical strength insufficient for personal participation in debate. After two days' discussion, on the 24th of February, the Resolution to impeach the President passed the House by a vote of one hundred and twenty-six to forty-seven.

As with other matters involving the speakership in the nineteenth century, there is little in the record regarding Colfax's further actions in the area of the impeachment. A standard work on the subject, *The Great Impeachment and Trial of Andrew Johnson: President of the United States* (1868), mentions Colfax only in passing, noting that after the House approved articles of impeachment against the President that "Speaker Colfax announced as managers of the impeachment trial on the part of the House, Messrs. Thaddeus Stevens, B.F. Butler, John A. Bingham, George S. Boutwell, J.F. Wilson, T. Williams, and John A. Logan." The inquiry had begun on 21 February; the House approved 11 separate articles of impeachment on 2 March. Two days later, the House managers, assigned by Speaker Colfax, presented these articles to the Senate; John Armor Bingham, Republican of Ohio, read the articles to the Senate.

Ironically, in one of the only major biographies of Colfax, done by the Rev. A.Y. Moore in 1868, there is barely any mention of the Johnson impeachment or even Colfax's role in the inquiry. As well, most histories of Johnson's impeachment skip over the House proceedings and move straight to the Senate trial; however, for purposes involving the subject of the Speakers of the House, Speaker Colfax was not a House manager in the Senate trial and thus we do not discuss that portion of the history here, leaving it for other venues.

Impeachment of Richard M. Nixon (1973-74)

The House waited more than a century before a second impeachment inquiry into a President of the United States moved further than some minor hearings or even the threat of a full-blown investigation. In 1972, while running for a second term in the White House, President Richard Nixon ordered the bugging of the headquarters of the Democratic National Convention in the Watergate Hotel. When the men involved in the burglary, members of Nixon's own Committee to Re-elect the President, were caught by the police, Nixon and his aides conspired to cobble together funds to pay the men to keep quiet about their ties to the White House. While all of this was wholly illegal, what nailed the President and his administration were the tapes the President made of the goings-on in the Oval Office, recordings that captured the President and his aides obstructing justice and covering up the entire affair, which came to be known as Watergate.

Nixon defeated Democrat George McGovern in that 1972 election by a landslide, but soon after he was sworn in for a second term the President and his administration found itself being investigated on all fronts, from the media to the halls of Congress. In February 1973, the U.S. Senate established the Select Committee on Presidential Campaign Activities. Chaired by Senator Sam Ervin, Democrat of North Carolina, the committee was set up more to examine the ways that alleged "dirty tricks" were played by Nixon and his committee than any provable crime.

However, the following months proved to be a bonanza, as one of the Watergate burglars told the judge hearing his case, John J. Sirica, that he had been pressured by the White House to remain silent about the administration's role in the burglary. The acting Director of the FBI, L. Patrick Gray, resigned after admitting that he had destroyed evidence in the Watergate probe. On 30 April, just ten days after Gray resigned, four high Nixon administration officials, including Chief of Staff H.R. Haldeman and Attorney General Richard Kleindienst, resigned. On 17 May, the Senate committee began televised hearings into what was becoming a growing scandal that was consuming the White House as the war in Vietnam was being fought. In June 1973, former counsel to the President John Dean admitted that the President had been warned about "a cancer on the presidency" in the form of a cover-up of the entire Watergate affair. In July, presidential aide Alexander Butterworth reported to a shocked committee - and an equally shocked nation - that President Nixon had had an expansive taping system installed in the Oval Office to record all of his telephone and other conversations, probably for historical reasons. But the tapes probably had on them evidence of the President's role in the Watergate cover-up. Special Prosecutor Archibald Cox, who had been investigating the scandal for some time, was now emboldened: he demanded that tapes for certain dates be turned over to his office. When the President refused, and Cox pressed, on 20 October 1973 Nixon ordered the new Attorney General, Eliot Richardson, to fire Cox. When Richardson refused and resigned, the President charged his second-in-command, Deputy Attorney General William Ruckelshaus, to fire Cox. When Ruckelshaus refused and, like Richardson, resigned, it was left to Solicitor General Robert H. Bork to rescue the Department of Justice and fire Cox. The entire episode, coming during a weekend when Nixon figured that few would be watching or paying attention, was called in the media "the Saturday Night Massacre."

Within days, the U.S. House ordered hearings in the Committee on the Judiciary. Committee chairman Peter Rodino, Democrat of New Jersey, began the inquiry into the possible impeachment of the President of the United States on 30 October. Rodino had risen to become chairman of the committee in 1973 when the sitting chairman, Emanuel Celler of New York, had lost his bid for re-election. That same month, Vice President Spiro Agnew resigned following allegations that as Governor of Maryland, prior to being elected Vice President, he had taken bribes from milk producers. Ironically, for a period until a new Vice President could be selected, Speaker of the House Carl Albert was first in line

for the presidency. Nixon and Albert had known each other for many years: both had entered the House in the Eightieth Congress (1947-49). But other than this, they had little in common politically by 1973. For Albert to have injected himself into the administration as it was slowly being eaten away by Watergate would have been more detrimental to Albert's career than even he desired. At the same time, he could have slowed down hearings held in both houses of Congress to confirm Nixon's choice to succeed Agnew as Vice President, former Minority Leader Gerald R. Ford, Republican of Michigan. When Democrats in the House demanded Nixon's immediate impeachment, a move that would make Albert the President, he cautioned them against undoing an election unless crimes committed by the President could be shown to have occurred.

Unlike Speaker Schuyler Colfax more than a century earlier, Albert took a hands-off attitude towards the Nixon impeachment inquiry, allowing Rodino, as well as others in his caucus, to handle the day-to-day affairs of the investigation. In his obituary from the year 2000, it was noted about Albert that "[c]lose associates credit the handling of the impeachment issue to Mr. Albert's insistence that the hearings be conducted in a fair manner." In another obituary, it said:

> Some Democrats had urged him to accelerate the Nixon impeachment and slow the confirmation of Ford as vice president so that he might be able to seize the presidency. But Albert resisted, although he did have a blueprint for a presidential transition prepared secretly. "I didn't even tell the leadership of the House what I was doing," he recalled in 1982. "If I had indicated that I wanted it, it would have been a national scandal because the press then would really have clobbered us for anything we did that indicated any rush to get Nixon."

Whatever his politics, Albert conducted himself in a way that historians believe did the speakership proud.

Remaining behind the scenes of the impeachment inquiry, Albert nevertheless gave indications as to his ultimate decision on the President. In May 1973 he wrote to a constituent in Oklahoma:

It appears that some of the President's top aides have done irreparable damage to the Presidency and to the nation and I am saddened and sickened by their actions. At this time I know of no evidence direct or hearsay that the President approved the flagrant abuse of power and the abbrogation [sic] of the law by the people on his staff. I believe, however, that this matter must have a full and thorough investigation by an independent prosecutor.

When Rep. Robert Drinan (D-MA) introduced a resolution to impeach the President in the summer of 1973, Albert wrote to another constituent, "Since I, as Speaker of the House, could conceivably preside over impeachment proceedings and am second in the line of succession to the presidency, I think it would be unwise for me to make any public comment at this time concerning the Watergate affair." Amazingly, reading some of the correspondence from Albert makes it appear that he was protecting the President's rights more than his own party could or would. To another constituent he wrote after the tapes of White House conversations were demanded of the White House, "Although the tape recordings could throw some light on specific issues, it is unlikely that they will provide conclusive proof of wrong doing..." When Nixon fought the release of the tapes, even up to the U.S. Supreme Court, Albert changed his thinking. "The President responded to a congressional subpoena by going before the public on television," he wrote. "I think this is very serious business and so far as I am concerned evidence would have to be really convincing before I would vote to impeach a president. Impeachment should be taken only for the most serious reasons but [for Congress] not to take action when the integrity of government is at stake would be a bigger mistake."

On 24 July 1974, in a unanimous 8-0 decision (*United States v. Nixon*), the Supreme Court held that the President could not use executive privilege to withhold the tapes from a legal investigation, and ordered him to turn them over to the new independent counsel, Leon Jaworski. The House Committee on the Judiciary adopted three articles of impeachment, and sent them for a full vote to the House floor. On 5 August, the President revealed in released transcripts of the tapes that, on one of these tapes, Nixon could clearly be heard ordering the impediment to the initial investigation of the Watergate break-in. On 6 August 1974, the House prepared to vote on articles of impeachment against President Nixon. Speaker Albert told NBC News, "We've decided that it won't take as much time probably as we had originally thought. Hopefully, we can finish the entire proceedings in a week. This is one of the most important things we've ever done in this House, and we are not going to have any summary operation."

But, even as the House prepared to vote on the three articles, a number of high-ranking congressional Republicans went to the White House to tell the President that he would be impeached in the House and faced almost certain conviction in the Senate following a trial in that body, and that he would only prolong the nation's agony by holding out until the bitter end. On 8 August 1974, Nixon went on national television to announce that he would resign the presidency the following day. Speaker Albert later said that he told the President prior to his announcement, "I have not once pushed anybody to accept any kind of evidence. I have nothing to do with recommending that you be impeached." Following Nixon's resignation on 9 August and the installment of Vice President Gerald Ford as the 38th President, Albert told reporters:

All of you who have talked to me everyday...know that I never made a judgment on the President of the United States and said I never would until the case was in. You didn't have to be a counter. I think I know how to count Congressmen. I think I know when there were enough members in the House to give a small margin for impeachment but the margin grew by yesterday to astounding proportions and they grew because the President had not come clean about a certain conversation that took place about ten months before he said he knew anything about it.

Albert completed the impeachment process by allowing the House to vote to approve the articles on 20 August and, two days later, officially published them. With no trial to be held in the Senate, the impeachment process ended with that action on 22 August 1974.

Despite the lack of an actual impeachment vote, the process to impeach President Richard Nixon nevertheless must be considered as an impeachment process, and the work of Speaker Carl Albert in the process must be examined as well. Albert discusses it in his memoirs, but few histories of the Nixon impeachment discuss Albert or his role.

Impeachment of William Jefferson Clinton (1998-99)

The last presidential impeachment inquiry is still in the memories of people young enough to remember it; after all, it was just a decade ago, in 1999. It was the first time many in the nation saw what an impeachment looked like, as it was televised from start to finish. Like the 1868 impeachment of Andrew Johnson, the 1999 trial ended in an acquittal. However, unlike the 1868 trial, the 1999 tribunal was based not on political differences, but on a President who lied and obstructed justice to cover up an affair he was having.

In 1997, Bill Clinton stood tall. He had just become the first Democrat since Lyndon Baines Johnson to win a second term in office, and the first since Franklin Delano Roosevelt to win it having been elected to a first term. However, his party still did not control the House or the Senate, making the possibilities of legislation with the Republicans, many of whom despised Clinton, near high impossible. But, that was just the beginning. Because, as Clinton was at the White House celebrating his second term victory, he went into the crowd to shake the hands of supporters; one of these was a young girl, in a beret, who hugged the President. No one watching the tape knew who the girl was, but in just a few months her name would become the most well known in the world. The girl, Monica Lewinsky, a low-level White House aide, was having a long-term sexual affair with the President, in the Oval Office, at times when no one was looking, including the First Lady.

We need to back up here, though. In 1992, when Clinton first ran for President, numerous sexual harassment allegations arose against him, although no names ever came forward to support the charges. Clinton won the presidency despite having what one aide called "a bimbo eruption" and his problem with continuing to have affairs outside of his marriage.

In 1994, however, before the statute of limitations could end, a former Arkansas employee, Paula Corbin Jones, filed a lawsuit against Clinton, claiming that in 1991 he got her into a hotel room in Arkansas and then exposed himself in an effort to get sex. When she refused his advances, she alleged that he punished her by withholding promotions. The story was kept quiet for years, mainly rumors among the tabloid crowd, until a reporter for *American Spectator*, a conservative magazine, went down to Arkansas, found Jones, and printed a story about the alleged encounter. Jones' lawsuit opened the door to the allegations that had surfaced, again without proof, from 1992.

When Jones filed her lawsuit, Clinton and his supporters called Jones every name in the book (including a liar); his legal defense claimed in court that one could not sue a sitting President. A number of courts heard the challenge; finally, it reached the U.S. Supreme Court, which ruled, unanimously, on 27 May 1997 that Clinton could not use the office of the President to hide from the lawsuit. Jones' lawyers were allowed to depose the President in the White House. During the deposition, they asked him, point blank, if he had had "sexual relations" with a White House intern named Monica Lewinsky. Clinton, caught off guard, said that he had not, despite being under oath. The assertion was clearly a lie - and, a lie under oath is perjury. The President of the United States had just committed a "high crime and misdemeanor."

What Clinton and his team had no knowledge of was that Lewinsky had divulged her affair to a friend, Linda Tripp, a former Department of Defense employee, who, as an opponent of Clinton, fed the information back to Jones' lawyers. Realizing that he had just committed a crime, Clinton told his secretary, Betty Currie, to retrieve gifts he had given to Lewinsky, which now made the crime obstruction of justice. To keep Lewinsky quiet about the affair, Clinton ordered his friend Vernon Jordan, the former head of the National Urban League, to get Lewinsky a job in New York City, away from cameras and reporters in the District of Columbia.

When rumors of the affair with Lewinsky, as well as his denial in the Jones' lawsuit, came to light, reporters confronted Clinton at the White House on

26 January 1998. Standing before them, he issued a strong denial:

> But I want to say one thing to the American people. I want you to listen to me. I'm going to say this again. I did not have sexual relations with that woman, Miss Lewinsky. I never told anybody to lie, not a single time - never. These allegations are false. And I need to go back to work for the American people.

The denial sounded solid. In fact, Clinton was lying. What he did not know was that on 15 January, just 11 days earlier, Attorney General Janet Reno had approached Special Counsel Kenneth W. Starr, named to investigate several other Clinton administration scandals, to look into the Jones/Lewinsky allegations. His investigators worked with Lewinsky, who supplied to Starr's office materials that proved that she had had an affair, and a long-running one at that, with Clinton. One of these pieces of evidence was a blue dress that Clinton had left sexual material on. When DNA testing of the dress showed that Clinton had indeed had an affair with Lewinsky, he realized that he had to own up to the affair and his lies surrounding it. On 17 August 1998, Clinton testified before a grand jury, by closed-circuit from the White House to the courthouse, where he admitted that he indeed had a "relationship" with Lewinsky but said that he told the truth when he denied the affair in the Jones deposition. That night, Clinton went on national television to repeat his admission that he had had an affair, but that he had not lied under oath or committed any other crimes. He called his time with Lewinsky "an inappropriate relationship."

On 9 September 1998, in the midst of an election campaign, Starr presented his findings to the House Committee on the Judiciary, which had opened an impeachment inquiry. Starr told the committee that there was "substantial and credible information that President William Jefferson Clinton committed acts that may constitute grounds for an impeachment," and that he had obstructed justice when he ordered Lewinsky to file in the Jones case an affidavit that the President knew would be false."

Working behind the scenes, Speaker of the House Newt Gingrich nervously awaited the outcome of the committee hearings for two reasons: one, his party was in the midst of a tough re-election battle while impeaching a politically popular President; and two, Gingrich himself was in the middle of an affair with an aide. Mirroring Speaker Schuyler Colfax in 1868 more than Speaker Carl Albert in 1973-74, Gingrich played a tremendously small role in the impeachment of Bill Clinton. In fact, in histories of the Clinton impeachment, Gingrich's name is rarely found.

On 8 October 1998, the House voted 258 to 163 to authorize a full-blown impeachment hearing in the Committee on the Judiciary. The hearings were delayed until after the 1998 mid-term elections; on 19 November, the hearings opened with a strong statement from committee chairman Henry Hyde of Illinois. Democrats who wished to merely "censure" the President failed on 8 December to get enough votes in the House. Finally, on 11 and 12 December 1998, the Committee on the Judiciary voted to approve four articles of impeachment against Clinton and sent them to the House floor for a vote. In a show of how divided the House was over this issue, two of the articles were voted down by the House; two others, alleging perjury by the President and obstruction of justice, were approved on 19 December by votes of 228-206 (article 1) and 221-212 (article 2). While Speaker Gingrich officiated over this solemn vote, again he spoke little about it, instead remaining behind the scenes. House managers for the impeachment trial were selected, and these members then went to the Senate to present the two articles for trial. Opening on 7 January 1999 with Chief Justice of the Supreme Court William H. Rehnquist in the chair overseeing the events, the trial lasted until 12 February with no witnesses being called. Although many Democrats admitted that Clinton was guilty of the crimes of which he was charged, they could not vote to convict without opening a rupture in their party. Moving quickly to a vote on 12 February, with a two-thirds vote needed for conviction, the Senate voted 45-55 on article 1 and 50-50 on article 2. Clinton remained in office until 20 January 2001; during the last years of his second term he settled with Jones in an out-of-court settlement of $800,000.

The three impeachment inquiries held by the House regarding Presidents of the United States only - many other officials have been impeached - is one of the rare parts of the office of the Speaker rarely discussed by historians or by the Speakers themselves. Former Speaker Gingrich rarely talks about the Clinton impeachment despite being an acclaimed author and lecturer in the years since leaving the speakership and the House of Representatives; Speaker Albert wrote about it only in passing in his memoirs; Speaker Colfax never discussed it, and biographies of his life barely speaker on the matter. Perhaps it is the lack of specificity that the Founders gave to the Speaker's role, or conceivably it is the small number of impeachments that actually occur that have left this vital role out of the histories of the speakership. Whatever the reason, the function and responsibility of the Speaker to conduct an impeachment inquiry and to preside over House votes on impeachment articles remains one of the Speakers' most powerful weapons.

The Office of the Speaker from Frederick Muhlenberg to David Henderson (1789-1903)

The speakership of the U.S. House of Representatives can be easily categorized as having many eras, but for the sake of this essay and the next we will break down the history of that office into two epochs: first, from the first Speaker, Frederick Augustus Conrad Muhlenberg, to the 35th, David Bremner Henderson, and, in the next essay, from the 36th, Joseph Gurney Cannon, to the 53rd, Nancy Pelosi. We make the split between Henderson and Cannon not in a chronological fashion because of the dates when one speakership ended and another began, in 1903, but because Henderson represented the "old" speakership of the mere moderator, while Cannon embodied the "new" speakership which dominated not just the office of the Speaker, but became a party leader, a spokesman for the party in which the Speaker was a member, and a consolidator of patronage on committees and in other venues in the House. Cannon, even a century after he first became Speaker, is considered the founder of that modern speakership. In that vein, we will end here with Cannon's immediate predecessor and begin the next essay with him.

Frederick Muhlenberg to Joseph Varnum (1789-1811)

Thus, we start at the beginning of that first epoch. When the First Congress assembled in the old city hall in New York on 4 March 1789, 59 members of the House of Representatives were set to appear to represent those states in the Union at the time. Because of travel and other delays, only 13 representatives had appeared, forcing an adjournment. North Carolina and Rhode Island had not even ratified the U.S. Constitution, so their members could not yet take their seats. It was not until 1 April, nearly a month into that first heady session of that first Congress, that a quorum was seated, and Frederick Augustus Conrad Muhlenberg of Pennsylvania was elected as Speaker. The last member, Benjamin Bourn, the only representative from Rhode Island, did not take his seat until 17 December 1790. In summing up Muhlenberg's work in that first Congress, William Henry Smith explained in 1928, "Mr. Muhlenberg presided over the three sessions of that Congress with great dignity, taking but little part in

the open debates, but wielding a wide influence as to the shaping of legislation."

He was replaced in the Second Congress (1791-93) by Jonathan Trumbull of Connecticut, for no other reason, as many historians agree, than the members of the House did not want one man to serve in that office too long in a ploy to gather too much control for himself. However, as other historians note, Muhlenberg was not as loyal to the administration of President George Washington as he had been upon his election as Speaker, and it is believed that the President pushed to have a more trustworthy and faithful man sitting in the Speaker's chair to push the administration's program in the House. When the Third Congress (1793-95) convened, however, a two-party system - or, at least, the earliest semblance of one - was forming into Federalist and anti-Federalist factions; those in the latter camp helped elect Muhlenberg as Speaker for a second time, defeating the Federalist nominee (and candidate of the Washington administration) Theodore Sedgwick of Massachusetts. Little has been written of Muhlenberg's second stint as Speaker, although, as historian Smith noted above, it can be assumed that he conducted himself in much the same way; however, now it may be further assumed that he was now firmly in the opposition to the President rather than one who promoted his program.

The Fourth Congress (1795-97) saw a small majority for those in the anti-Federalist camp, but the Federalists were able to elect their own man, Jonathan Dayton of New Jersey. It is noted that this is the first and last time in House history that a member of the minority party - combined with some votes from the majority - was elected Speaker. Historian Richard Hildreth, in his *History of the United States*, wrote:

All of the Federalists voted for Dayton, as the only person at all connected with their part who had the slightest chance of success; while Dayton's personal influence, his former zeal for the sequestration of British debts, and the belief that he would hardly sustain a treaty, one of the articles of which seemed leveled at his motion on that subject, secured him the votes of many opponents of the administration.

Dayton's speakership - again, of which little is known because of a combination of the rules of the time and the dearth of contemporary sources - must have been successful, because, even though in the Fifth Congress (1797-99), William Loughton Smith (1758-1812) of South Carolina became the leader of the Federalists in the House, the party re-elected Dayton as the Speaker. Nevertheless, more modern historians find much to be desired in Dayton's speakership. Asher C. Hinds, whose manual of House rules is known as *Hind's Precedents*, stated in 1909, "Dayton...conducted himself so violently in partisan debate on the floor that he was called to order by the temporary occupant of the chair."

Dayton's successors, from Theodore Sedgwick (served 1799-1801) to Joseph Varnum (served 1807-11), were cut in the mold of what the founding fathers probably wanted the Speaker to be: a mere moderator of debate and nothing more. But with the election of Nathaniel Macon in 1801, a change occurred. Macon was the first Speaker to be elected to three successive Congresses, doing away forever with the concept of not letting on man try to acquire so much power in the Speaker's chair. Macon was also the first Southerner to sit as Speaker. Most importantly, however, he was not a "Speaker" in the mold of his predecessors, but was an extension of the administration of President Thomas Jefferson, although DeAlva Stanwood Alexander, in his 1916 work on the *History and Procedure in the House*, wrote that "The choice of Speaker Macon...rendered the House completely subservient to the Chief Executive. Even the appointment of chairmen of important committees, especially those which act as organs of communication with the President, were consented to, if not...suggested by, the Administration." Henry Adams, in his massive multivolume *History of the United States*, wrote of Macon that the North Carolinian was "a typical homespun planter, honest and simple, erring more often in his grammar and spelling than in his moral principles, but knowing little of the world beyond the borders of Carolina. No man in history has left a better name than Macon, but the name was all he left." Macon did oversee the controversial 1800 election, split between Jefferson and Aaron Burr

(and which left Jefferson as President and Burr as Vice President), and he pushed for a Constitutional amendment to allow for the President and Vice President to be elected on one ticket rather than as individuals. When Macon saw that the amendment would fail because of one vote, he stepped down from the Speaker's chair and, in a rare move, voted aye on the matter and helped it pass. For the first time, a Speaker had voted on legislation on the House floor. By the end of his three-term tenure, Macon was extremely unpopular, and he was easily defeated for a fourth term in the Tenth Congress (1807-09) by Joseph B. Varnum of Massachusetts. Varnum, a Federalist, was an interregnum between the strong speakerships of Macon and Henry Clay.

Henry Clay to John W. Davis (1811-1847)

Clay, who was elected As Speaker on his first day in the House on 4 November 1811, took the reins of the Twelfth Congress (1811-13) and, through five terms as Speaker, broken up by his resignation in 1814 and the speakership of Langdon Cheves, made the Speaker one of the most powerful offices in the government, almost a secondary President. Clay was elected in the midst of a national crisis over the threat of war with Great Britain; he was a member among other House members known as "The War Hawks" who wanted war and were prepared to vote for it in the Congress. Clay as Speaker, at least by the "old rules" of the House, was not supposed to inject himself into the debate over the war, but he was changing the office and he became not just a moderator, as previous Speakers had been, but an actual participant.

In 1847, when Robert C. Winthrop was elected Speaker, Clay, then a U.S. Senator, wrote to him with advice on how to conduct himself: "Decide promptly and never give the reasons for your decisions. The House will sustain your decisions, but there will always be men to cavil and quarrel over your reasons." Mary Parker Follett, one of the preeminent historians of the Speakers and the speakership, wrote in 1902:

Clay's success in ruling the House was not due simply to the fact that he realized the parliamentary power of his office, but even more to his quickness in so using his position as to influence the mind of the House. Thus the duty of stating the question from the confusion of debate was one particularly suited to Clay's gifts. His ability as a parliamentarian is justly summed up in Mr. Winthrop's criticism when he says: "He was no painstaking student of parliamentary law, but more frequently found the rules of governance in his own instinctive sense of what was practicable and proper in 'Hatsell's Precedents,' or 'Jefferson's Manual.'"

Clay would later run three times for President - in 1824, 1832, and 1844, all unsuccessfully - but he became a giant in the U.S. Senate for his role in brokering the Compromise of 1850, which headed off the Civil War for another decade.

In between Clay's tenure was, as mentioned, Langdon Cheves, but even he appears to be more in the mold of the early Speakers than Clay. After Clay returned from serving as a delegate to the peace talks between the United States and England and once again served as Speaker, a number of men held that office without much impact on the office. John W. Taylor of New York, Philip P. Barbour of Virginia, Andrew Stevenson of Virginia (who served four terms as Speaker before being named as the U.S. Minister to Great Britain), John Bell of Tennessee, James K. Polk of Tennessee, Robert Mercer Taliaferro Hunter of Virginia, John White of Kentucky, John W. Jones of Virginia, and John W. Davis of Indiana were all highly forgettable during their respective tenures as Speaker. The constant thread running through their service is that they tamped down active opposition to slavery, although in 1844 former Speaker Polk, who had left Congress after he was elected Governor of Tennessee, was elected President, the only Speaker to advance to the White House. John Quincy Adams, who served in the U.S. House after his presidential term had ended, wrote of Davis, from a state where slavery was outlawed, "The Speaker, a pro-slavery Republican from the free State of Indiana, buckled close to the slave-mongers."

Robert C. Winthrop to William Pennington (1847-1863)

Robert C. Winthrop, the scion of a famed Massachusetts family, won the Whig nomination for Speaker in the Thirtieth Congress (1847-49) by defeating Rep. Samuel F. Vinton of Ohio, who was widely expected to get the party nod and, in a Congress with a mere six seat majority for the Whigs, win the speakership. Although some historians speculate that Vinton lost because he was not sufficiently against slavery - he had voted against the Wilmot Proviso - it actually came about because Vinton, at 55 years old, went to Winthrop and told him, "I cannot be Speaker. It is too hard work for me; I am too old for it. You must be Speaker." Vinton was given the chairmanship of the Committee on Ways and Means as a concession. In the election for Speaker, some abolitionist Whigs felt that even Winthrop had not been against the war with Mexico, and voted against him; Winthrop won on the third ballot by defeating Democrat Linn Boyd. One of these members who went against Winthrop, Joshua Giddings of Indiana, wrote to Horace Greeley, the famed Whig newspaper editor who later founded the *New York Tribune*, prior to Winthrop's election,

The Whig party has never ceased to condemn the war. Their disgust for it was never stronger than at present, and it is gaining strength every day. With these circumstances surrounding them, the Whig members of Congress will assemble. The first duty that will devolve upon them will be the election of a Speaker. That officer exerts more influence over the destinies of the nation than any other member of the government except the President. He arranges the committees to suit his own views. If a Whig in favor of prosecuting the war be elected Speaker, he will so arrange the committees as to secure reports approving of the continuance of our conquests in Mexico. If he be opposed to the war he will so arrange them as to have reports in favor of withdrawing our troops. Which course will the Whig party in the House of Representatives pursue? A more momentous question was never presented to the Whig party. Should they elect an anti-war candidate, and the Committee of Ways and Means should be so constituted as to report against the further conquest of Mexico, it is quite possible that Whigs enough would vote with the Democrats to reverse the reports of committees, and to make the necessary appropriations to carry on hostilities. But such an act of a few individuals would not involve the party, and we may escape the odium and responsibility of such act.

Winthrop tried to separate the politics of his party from the speakership, but in doing so incurred the wrath of many in his own party; in 1849, he was narrowly defeated for a second term as Speaker, succeeded by Howell Cobb of Georgia. Cobb, who later served as a member of the Confederate Congress, used his speakership to preserve the rights of southern slavery, again earning enmity from his political enemies who saw him as politicizing the Speaker's chair. In 1851, Cobb lost the chair to Linn Boyd, of Kentucky, who served for two Congresses, the Thirty-second (1851-53) and the Thirty-third (1853-55).

Following the 1854 election, the House met in December 1855 but could not agree on a Speaker. Through December, into the new year of 1856, and into February, no one candidate could muster a majority of the vote. In a tussle between the protectors of slavery and those who wished to abolish it, the election swung for 133 ballots, a record, when Nathaniel P. Banks, of Massachusetts, was elected over Democrat William Aiken of South Carolina. Thomas Brackett Reed, who himself later served as Speaker, wrote, "Banks that day was in the prime of vigor and personal comeliness. Dressed in blue, with [a] closely buttoned coat, his well-chosen language, his graceful figure and gesture, and his aggressive way carried with him the whole audience." Although Banks was as nonpartisan as he could be, the slavery issue dominated the Congress and continued to eat away at the fabric of the nation. John W. Forney, who served as Clerk of the House during Banks' speakership, wrote years later:

General Banks has just been defeated for Congress in Massachusetts, after a long career, but cannot forget the manner in which he pronounced his inaugural address as Speaker of the House sixteen years ago. His deportment during the succeeding session, his impartiality, his courtesy, and his uniform integrity, privileged him to be an unrivaled statesman, and I am not without hope that we shall hear of him honorably in the future. [John Anthony] Quitman [Democrat of Mississippi], [William] Barksdale [Democrat of Mississippi], [Albert] Rust [Democrat of Arkansas], [Lawrence] Keitt

[Democrat of South Carolina], [George] Eustis [American of Louisiana], and other Southern fire-eaters [those who would rather "eat fire" than give up the right of slavery] have gone to their last account. They were men of varied and distinguished abilities, and yet not one of them, if he could speak from his grave, but would say that Nathaniel P. Banks was a just and honest presiding officer.

Ironically, Banks' speakership lasted but one Congress; he was succeeded in the Thirty-seventh Congress (1857-59) by James Lawrence Orr of South Carolina. Orr oversaw the raucous debate on the admittance of Kansas over the Lecompton Constitution, which would have allowed that state to be run by slaveholders rather than being a free state as the Compromise of 1850 had promised. Orr also served for a single term as Speaker; in 1860, after he had left the Speaker's chair, he called for "the prompt secession from the Union [of the southern states] in the event of the election of a Black Republican to the presidency." In 1858, the new Republican Party, created just four years earlier in Wisconsin from the ashes of the Whig Party and including antislavery elements of the Free Soil and abolitionist wing of the Democratic Party, elected a majority in the U.S. House, and, in a move mirroring that of Henry Clay in November 1811, they elected William Pennington of New Jersey as Speaker in his first term in the House. Their first choice for the Speaker's chair, John Sherman of Ohio, had been torpedoed by Democrats who denounced his allegedly "radical" stands against slavery, and a lengthy battle to get a majority of votes for an "acceptable" candidate ensued, not unlike the 1855-56 fight. Upon election, Northerners found no fault with Pennington, except for Clement L. Vallandigham, who later, as a so-called "Copperhead Democrat," tried to broker an end to the Civil War by making sure slavery was enshrined in the U.S. Constitution. On Pennington, he stated in a letter, "Your Speaker, whatever his national disposition may be is, by the necessities of his office, a despot." Although he had had prior legislative experience - he had served a single term in the lower in the New Jersey legislature - Pennington was unfortunately out of his element when it came to handling the rigors of the speakership. Samuel S. Cox of New York later wrote in 1885 that Pennington was "the most thoroughly unaccomplished man in parliamentary law who ever wielded the gavel."

Pennington's tenure lasted for the single term of the Thirty-sixth Congress (1859-61), during which the Civil War broke out among the southern states in reaction to the November 1860 election of Republican Abraham Lincoln to the presidency. In July 1861, when the House organized, many Democrats had walked out to side with the seceding southern states, allowing for the election of a Republican Speaker. After he had a fight with Democrat Lawrence M. Keitt of South Carolina, Galusha Grow of Pennsylvania was elected Speaker in the Thirty-seventh Congress because, as James G. Blaine wrote in his memoirs, "of his activity in the anti-slavery struggles." William Holman of Indiana wrote of Grow that "no man who was ever Speaker more largely or more beneficially influenced the general course of our legislation. He was a born leader among men." Despite this praise, Grow served only a single term as Speaker; in 1863, he was defeated for re-election. In 1994, when Speaker Thomas S. Foley was defeated, commentators noted the name of Speaker Galusha Grow, the last sitting Speaker to be defeated for re-election.

Schuyler Colfax to Michael C. Kerr (1863-1875)

In the midst of the war that would define America's course as a nation, Schuyler Colfax was elected Speaker in the Thirty-eighth Congress (1863-65), and would serve three terms through the end of the Fortieth Congress (1867-69). House Clerk John Forney wrote of Colfax, "He has been the embodiment of the war policy of the government." A close ally of Abraham Lincoln who aided the President in the prosecution of the war through congressional legislation, Colfax quickly turned against Lincoln's successor, Andrew Johnson, who took office after Lincoln was assassinated in April 1865. When the Thirty-ninth Congress (1865-67) convened, Colfax spoke about the new President's policy on the reconstruction of the now-defeated southern states; Johnson took issue with the Speaker's remarks. The Rev. Ambrose Y. Moore, who authored an 1868 biography of Colfax, wrote in that work,

This was the first speech of any Congressman taking issue with the President's "policy," and Mr.

Johnson has always denounced it as the initiation of the Congressional policy which antagonized his...The next day Mr. Colfax called upon President Johnson; the President was not at all pleased with the speech, and was sorry that Mr. Colfax had not consulted with him before speaking to the assembling Congress and the country upon the important subject of reconstruction.

Colfax has been both denounced and praised for his tenure as Speaker: Biographer Moore relates that one unnamed member of Congress said of Colfax, "He sometimes announces the passage of a bill as if it were merely reading the record of the House." However, James G. Blaine of Maine, who later served as Speaker, wrote of Colfax's remarks at the opening of the Fortieth Congress (1867-69):

The address of the Speaker on taking the chair is usually confined to thanks for his election and courteous assurance of the impartiality and good intentions. But Mr. Colfax, instinctively quick, as he always was, to discern the current of popular thought, incorporated in his ceremonial address some very decisive political declarations. Referring to the fact that the Thirty-eighth Congress had closed nine months before, with the "storm cloud of war still lowering over us," and rejoicing that "today from shore to shore of our land there is peace," he proceeded to indicate the line of policy which the people expected. "The duties of Congress," said he, "are as obvious as the sun's pathway in the heavens. Its first and highest obligation is to guarantee to every States a republican form of government, to establish the rebellious States anew on such basis of enduring justice as will guarantee all safeguards to the people and protection to all men in their inalienable rights."

It was during this session that Colfax oversaw the impeachment inquiry against President Johnson that led to the Senate trial in which Johnson was acquitted by one vote. Although many historians have denounced that impeachment as political rather than criminal in nature, Colfax appears to have dodged any overall criticism for his role in the action.

Colfax was elected Vice President with Ulysses S. Grant in 1868, and he left office on 3 March 1869, paving the way for Theodore Medad Pomeroy of New York to serve for a single day as Speaker until the new Congress convened on 4 March 1869. Most histories of the speakership mention Pomeroy, mainly because they consider him not to have been elected Speaker, but to have been named as Speaker *pro tempore*, or a "temporary Speaker." A check of the records show that Pomeroy was indeed elected for that single day's tenure, but, alas, he had no policy to advocate or rules to uphold; strangely, though, his impact was possibly as weak as some of the Speakers who served for an entire two-year term.

After Colfax departed the Speaker's chair, the speakership itself came under a period of continuity rather than the upheaval it had suffered for more than 30 years. James G. Blaine of Maine was elected Speaker of the Forty-first Congress (1869-71), and held the chair until the end of the Forty-third Congress (1873-75). When he became embroiled in a controversial debate with Benjamin Butler of Massachusetts, chairman of the Committee on Reconstruction, Blaine went to the floor of the House to denounce a letter Butler had written on Blaine's attempts to bury a report he did not like in committee. Blaine was incensed,

> *Nobody regrets more sincerely than I do...any occurrence which calls me to take the floor...Mr. Speaker, in old times it was the ordinary habit of the Speaker of the House of Representatives to take part in debate. That custom has fallen into disuse. For one, I am glad that it had. For one I approve of the conclusion that forbids it. The Speaker should, with consistent fidelity to his own party, be the impartial administrator of the rules of the House, and a constant participation in the discussion of members would take him from that appearance of impartiality which is so important to maintain in the rulings of the Chair. But at the same time I despise and denounce the insolence of the gentleman from Massachusetts when he attempts to say that the Representative from the third district of the State of Maine has no right to frame a resolution; has no right to seek that under the rules that resolution shall be adopted; has no right to ask the judgment of the House upon that resolution. Why, even the insolence of the gentleman himself never reached that sublime height*

> *before, and that is the extent of my offending, that I wrote a resolution - that I took it to various gentlemen on this side of the House - that I said to the gentlemen on the other side of the House, "This is a resolution on which you cannot afford to filibuster; it is a resolution demanding a fair, impartial investigation, and under the rules I desire that this resolution may be offered, and my colleague (Mr. Peters) will offer it."*

But Blaine, like Colfax before him, became caught up in the scandal known as the Crédit Mobilier, in which stock for a transcontinental railroad was sold to members of Congress in exchange for support for more appropriations for the railroad, and while his ties to the company did not ruin his speakership or his congressional career - he later went on to serve with some distinction in the Senate - it did come back to haunt him in 1884 when he was the Republican presidential nominee, costing him the votes of reformers who bolted the party in favor of Democrat Grover Cleveland, who won a narrow victory.

Samuel Jackson Randall to John G. Carlisle (1875-1889)

Blaine's successor, Michael C. Kerr, the first Democrat to hold the Speaker's chair since 1859, was dying of tuberculosis when elected Speaker and lived but a year. He was succeeded by the powerful chairman of the House Committee on Ways and Means, Samuel Jackson Randall, Democrat of Pennsylvania, who served three terms from the Forty-fourth Congress (1875-77) through the Forty-sixth Congress (1879-81). In 1877, Randall oversaw the congressional investigation of the close presidential election between Republican Rutherford B. Hayes and Democrat Samuel Tilden. Tilden, who on election day was short of electoral victory, was denied the presidency outright because three southern states could not accurately report their votes. An Electoral Commission, composed of members of the House, Senate, and justices on the Supreme Court, examined the disputed ballots and finally concluded that Hayes would receive those states' electoral votes and, ultimately, the presidency.

Randall, a staunch and partisan Democrat who hated Hayes, concluded that if he stood in the way of the Republican's election he could well initiate a civil war, and negotiated a clean transition in return for Hayes' promise to remove federal troops from the former Confederate states and end Reconstruction, allowing Democrats to retake control of those states by denying blacks the right to vote. His predecessor Blaine wrote of him, "He never neglects his public duties and never forgets the interests of the Democratic Party." One of the duties of the Speaker is the right to recognize members to speak on the floor of the House. Speaker after Speaker have admitted this right, making sure to preserve it no matter the subject of the speech about to be made. However, in 1881, Randall refused to follow this precedent, telling the House that "the right of recognition just as absolutely in the Chair as the judgment of the Supreme Court is absolute in its interpretation of the law." In 1883, Speaker J. Warren Keifer upheld Randall's ruling, stating that "no appeal of the kind had ever been entertained."

Although the Republicans appeared to have the majority of the House in their grasp after the Civil War, as noted the Democrats won back control in 1874 and held it through the speakerships of Michael C. Kerr and Samuel J. Randall. In 1880 the Republicans took back the House, but lost it two years later, and, except for Thomas B. Reed serving as Speaker for two terms, they would not hold it again in the nineteenth century. In 1882, the Democrats won back the House after a short two years out of power and elected John G. Carlisle of Kentucky as Speaker - he would hold the Speaker's chair from the Forty-eighth Congress (1883-85) through the Fiftieth Congress (1887-89). In her 1902 work on the Speakers, Mary Parker Follett explained:

> Carlisle's term is of the greatest interest because he boldly laid down in regard to the speakership a principle which, if already gaining ground, had never been asserted so openly as it was throughout his administration. It was the principle that the powers of the Chair should be used, not in a spirit of balancing favors to majority and minority, not even in a spirit of obedience to the dictates of the majority, but in accordance with the Speaker's individual judgment. He considered it the Speaker's duty to be the leader of Congress, to have a definite legislative policy, and to take every means in his power to secure the accomplishment of that policy. He

> himself shirked neither the duty nor the responsibility: again and again he opposed the will of a large majority of the House by refusing recognition to members who wished to take up important business; his committees also, while fair and able, represented Carlisle's views more closely than any one's else. By every other means which his office afford, he sought, entirely regardless of his position as chairman, to impose his will on the House and to be the real source of the legislation of the United States.

Historian Robert V. Remini, in his 2006 history of the House, adds,

> As Speaker, Carlisle expanded the power of the Rules Committee by initiating the practice of appointing the chairmen of Ways and Means and Appropriations to sit as regular members of this committee. Indeed, his committee appointments and his control of recognition on the floor furthered his ability to impose his will on the House. He frequently turned to a member and asked, "For what purpose does the gentleman rise?" and then refused recognition if he disagreed with whatever the member had in mind. He could be tough and autocratic when it came to floor recognition.

Carlisle would later serve as the Secretary of the Treasury in the second nonconsecutive administration of President Grover Cleveland.

Thomas B. Reed to David B. Henderson (1889-1903)

In 1888, the Republicans won back control of the House (and, for the first time since 1875, that party controlled both houses of Congress as well as the presidency), and elected as Speaker Thomas Brackett Reed of Maine. Reed would become, second to Henry Clay, the most important nineteenth century Speaker. Congressional Quarterly, in a history of the Congress, wrote in 1988:

> The House over which Reed took control was plagued by filibusters that slowed the conduct of business. Democratic representatives refused to answer quorum calls (even though present and visible on the House floor) and introduced a flurry of dilatory motions to harry their opponents and delay the passage of legislation.

Reed's insistence that all members present - whether answering or not - be counted towards a quorum caused pandemonium on the floor. Members tried to hide and were prevented from leaving by the Sergeant-at-arms, who was ordered to lock the door. Reed ruled further that the chair would not entertain motions whose purpose was to delay business. These and other "Reed Rules" were formally incorporated into the rules of the House in 1890.

Reed, through the process of naming the chairmen of committees, appointed Rep. William McKinley of Ohio as the chairman of the Committee on Ways and Means, and McKinley steered through the tariff of 1890, which led to an economic downturn.

But under Reed, the House changed in ways that would be blamed by Democrats and historians not on Reed, but on his successor, Joseph G. Cannon, leading to a revolt in 1910. In the Fifty-first Congress (1889-91), Reed used the powers of the Speaker to the utmost. In previous Congresses, the Democrats used the lack of a quorum to keep the House from conducting business they did not like. Under these old rules, if a member did not call out to his name but was on the House floor, he would not be counted, and thus could deny the majority a quorum. Reed charged that if a member were merely present, he would be counted; a quorum would exist, and legislation would go forward. In one of the first uses of this new rule, he confronted Rep. James Bennett McCreary, Democrat of Kentucky, who, when his name was called and he was pronounced as present, sprang to his feet to denounce the Speaker and refuse to allow his presence to be certified. Reed refused to back down, demanding to know if the member was present or not. When McCreary had no answer, he sneered, "You are a tyrant to rule over this House or the members of this House in any such way, and I denounce you as the worst tyrant that every presided over a deliberative body." Reed did not back down, stating that "The House will not allow itself to be deceived by epithets." The Democrats, in the minority, could no longer use that tactic to stall the legislative process.

In 1890, the Democrats won back the House, and elected British-born Charles Frederick Crisp of Georgia as the Speaker. In an ironic twist, Reed, now the Minority Leader, tried to use the same measures Democrats had used in the minority to block the new majority's legislative agenda. Crisp and the Democrats, who had once denounced the "Reed Rules," now embraced them. Speaker Charles Crisp noted that he, at times when he was Minority Leader, was unable to control his own party in the House. He wrote to a friend, "Nobody can lead this wrangling, quarrelsome, factionalized Democratic minority." In the majority, however, during two terms during the Fifty-second (1891-93) and Fifty-third (1893-95) Congresses, he is considered one of the more substantial Speakers.

However, one more piece of evidence as to the lack of scholarship on the Speakers - although it is just one instance - comes in a 1976 article by Carl V. Harris on the splits between Southern Democrats in the House from 1873 to 1897; there is not one single mention of the men who served as Speaker during this period, which included Democrats Michael C. Kerr, Samuel J. Randall, John G. Carlisle, and Charles F. Crisp.

In 1894, the Republicans won back the House, and Reed was installed again as Speaker. He would serve during the Fifty-fourth (1895-97) and Fifty-fifth (1897-99) Congresses, expanding on his rulings that have become important as precedents for the use of later Speakers in parliamentary control over the House. Differing with his own party and his own President because of the onset of the war with Spain in 1898, Reed broke with the GOP and left Congress in 1899.

He was replaced as Speaker by David Bremner Henderson, a Scottish-born veteran of the Civil War who lost part of a leg during battle. O.O. Stealey, a Washington correspondent, wrote in 1906:

An innovation that made a stir at the time, and which gave weight to the charge that he was attempting to "out-Czar" Reed, has a simple explanation and the fact that it remains engrafted on the procedure of the House justifies the assumption that his action was correct. Reed maintained the fiction of recognizing members on the floor as they demanded recognition under the rule requiring them to arise and address the chair. Thus his desk in the "morning hour" would be surrounded by a circle of members clamoring "Mr. Speaker!" in the hope of catch-

ing his eye. Reed would calmly survey the crowd and then recognize first one on one side, then one on the other, the whole proceedings having the semblance of being real. As a matter of fact, Mr. Reed had been privately sought beforehand and recognized only those with whom previous arrangements had been made. When he came in, Mr. Henderson saw no reason for maintaining this pleasantly and calmly notified the members that in the future they would arrange with him for recognition and he would grant it according to the schedule, after the proposed bills had been scanned and approved. The result was, the members remained in their seats and were decorously recognized in turn. While the effect was the same, yet the absence of the crowd around the desk ostensibly seeking recognition, unpleasantly emphasized the control of the House by the Speaker through the power of recognition.

It was Henderson who installed Rep. Joseph Cannon of Illinois on the Committee on Ways and Means, a move that would lead, many believe, to the overthrow of the Speaker's powers in 1910.

But that story will have to wait for the right time and place - and, for the next essay. Because, as the nineteenth century ended and the twentieth century began, David Henderson, a veteran of the Civil War, was the Speaker. He would remain so through the rest of the Fifty-sixth Congress (1899-1901), as well as the Fifty-seventh Congress (1901-03). In 1903, however, Republicans, who kept control over the House, changed direction and elected Joseph Cannon, known colloquially as "Uncle Joe," as Speaker. Cannon was a mix of Henry Clay, Thomas Reed, and Samuel Randall. He was an expert parliamentarian, a stern conservative Republican who did not like anyone who did not share his politics and his values, and he prized loyalty above most anything else. Joseph Cannon was very; very far from what the Founding Fathers had probably envisioned as a Speaker of the U.S. House. He was certainly different than the first Speaker, Frederick A.C. Muhlenberg, elected just 114 years earlier. Cannon would be the basis for which the speakership would evolve in the twentieth and twenty-first centuries.

The Office of the Speaker from Joseph Cannon to
Nancy Pelosi (1903-2009)

"It is all very well for the President of the United States to suggest to Congress a forward-looking legislative program. That is one of the duties of the President. It is a horse of another color to get such a program accepted by even the President's own party in either House or Senate...To accomplish this result it was necessary for the President and the Speaker to work in close harmony."
- *Joseph G. Cannon, Speaker of the House, 1903-11*

The name of Joseph Cannon evokes the misuse of power, of "czarism," and other inferences of dictatorial leadership in the U.S. House by its leading officer, the Speaker. Unfortunately, those images are only part of the story, as Cannon was only using the tools that his predecessors had used and which he followed. Historians sometimes get the story wrong; here, they get the facts wrong as well. Another part of the story is that under Cannon's successors, including Sam Rayburn, the same domineering rules were implemented, leading to the increase of power in the speakership from the middle of the twentieth century onward. At the end of the first decade of the twenty-first century, Speaker Nancy Pelosi executed rules that nearly shut out, if not completely dismissed, the Republican minority. But, alas, that remains for the end of our story, because here we examine the speakership from Cannon, in 1903, to Pelosi, in 2009.

Speaker Joseph G. Cannon

When elected as Speaker of the House in the Fifty-eighth Congress (1903-05), Cannon merely followed the rules as they had been carried out by the several speakers before him, all but one Republican. In fact, a strict analysis of the usage of rules by the Speakers of the late nineteenth and the early twentieth centuries shows that Cannon's speakership was no more of a "dictatorship" than any of these others, however it may be portrayed in the media or by historians. Cannon had gotten a bad rap, and it is time that the truth of his tenure was told, *accurately.*

From the year 1903 and on, hearing that a Speaker named members of the committees as well as being

a member of the Rules Committee sounds ominous and lends a foreboding sense to that slow creep of tyranny feared by the Nation's founders. Nevertheless, the image remains unchallenged. In 2001, historians Keith Krehbiel and Alan Wiseman examined the empirical evidence and found that many of the "facts" behind Cannon were in fact unsupported stories, promoted in most cases by his political enemies. They wrote:

While the view of Cannon as tyrant is plausible and widely accepted, the supporting evidence consists predominantly of anecdotes, newspaper editorials, and personal interviews. Such sources are obviously important in journalistic and historical research...It is possible, for instance, that many conclusions about Cannon's speakership in particular, and this period in legislative history in general, are generalizations based on atypical cases. Nearly any congressional scholar can provide evidence of Cannon's fixation with party control by citing the case in which a progressive Republican, Irvine Lenroot of Wisconsin, was exiled to the House Committee on Ventilation and Acoustics. It does not follow, however, that isolated incidents of so-called tyranny justify sweeping generalizations about the height of partisanship in Congress.

Historian Charles Jones, writing, ironically, on the "limits" of the speakership in 1968, explained:

Since his election in 1903, Speaker Joseph G. Cannon had enjoyed rather substantial procedural majorities and due to the growth of the speakership and Cannon's interpretation and use of his powers, a procedural majority carried with it awesome authority. He could appoint committees - including the chairmen, determine the schedule of business, recognize members on the floor, appoint members to conference committees, dispense favors of various kinds.

In 1910, following years in which Cannon marginalized a number of left-leaning Republicans, known then as Progressives, through their committee assignments (or lack thereof) and their ability to speak on the floor, these members allied with the Democrats in the minority and challenged Speaker Cannon's power structure. Historian David Sarasohn examined the attitudes and stories of these "insurgents" who brought Cannon down: many of them refused to join the Democrat Party because, as one member noted, that entity was still tied, in name and belief system, to the same Democrats who bolted the nation and drove the country to civil war over slavery five decades before. Led by Rep. George Norris of Nebraska, these Progressives, mostly from the Midwestern portion of the country and labeled as "insurgents," voted to reject the rules of the Speaker and refused to allow him to continue unless he withdrew as a member of the House Committee on Rules and allowed reform of the rules for all members. The battle, pitched over several days, saw the nearly complete refutation of Cannon's speakership, save for a vote to have him removed, which failed. In Norris' papers in the Library of Congress is a Western Union telegram from one J.M. Grace of Mascot, Nebraska, who cabled to Norris on 22 March 1910: "Congratulations, all of the fifth district will take their hats off for you, always thought you were a good fellow keep on insurging."

Cannon's "fall" from power was portrayed in the media - and by historians - as widespread as could have been possible. However, history is usually written by the victors and not the defeated, and as such Cannon's "overthrow" by his political enemies and opponents in 1910 is characterized as such. John D. Baker, writing in 1973, saw a different side to the story: he believes that the Progressives were in fact limited in their fight against Cannon, who remained as Speaker with his power nearly intact. Baker explained:

> If the Insurgents were unwilling to remove Cannon from office, they were also unwilling to seek membership on the newly organized Rules Committee and, thereby, implement their attempt by effectively weakening Cannon. Although Norris was offered support for a bid for Rules Committee membership, he refused it and permitted Cannon's lieutenant, John Dalzell [Republican of Pennsylvania], to secure the balance of power for the speaker.

In a celebration of Cannon's 80th birthday in 1916, his fellow representatives went to the House floor and paid homage to this son of Illinois who had served as Speaker. One of them, Republican Frederick H. Gillett of Massachusetts, would himself later serve as Speaker of the House. Gillett said of Cannon:

> I am the only person who ever served on the Appropriations Committee when Mr. Cannon was its chairman. To my mind that was the most glorious and useful part of his career...To see him in his glory, you should have seen him as chairman of Appropriations, in the thick of the fray, without manuscript or notes, but all ablaze with energy, now entertaining the House with his quaint conceits and now convincing them with his powerful and ingenious arguments...That, to my mind, was the sphere where his abilities shone the best advantage. He is by nature a floor leader. He has the courage, the fearlessness, and that quickness of mind and of tongue accelerating under fire, which a man effective on this floor.

As historian Robert Lopez, in a 1998 dissertation, noted, until Cannon's fall from power, "the structure of leadership [in the House]...was very centralized and coordinated. Essentially, the Speaker controlled all aspects of the legislative process, including the right of floor recognition, committee appointments, and the [membership of] the Rules Committee." Lopez adds that "with Cannon's fall, leadership power of the Speaker was significantly curtailed." It was not until the 1970s, when liberal Democrats in the House believed that they had established permanent control of the majority in that body for their party, that they could afford to allow the Speaker to become powerful again, granting the Speaker effective power over the House as a whole.

Speaker James Beauchamp Clark

The Republicans lost control of the House in 1910, leading to the election of the first Democratic Speaker in 16 years, James Beauchamp "Champ" Clark of Missouri. A hard-nosed politician who had battled Speaker Cannon for years, he would serve from the start of the Sixty-second Congress (1911-13) to the end of the Sixty-fifth Congress (1917-19). Clark was apt to make glorious speaking blunders: as Speaker, when debate centered around a reciprocity agreement with Canada, Clark noted that "I look forward to the time when the American flag will fly over every square foot of British North

America up to the North Pole." Because of this one statement, the Canadian government of Sir Wilfrid Laurier collapsed, and, in new elections in 1911, was voted out of office. Nevertheless, Clark was an effective Speaker for the four terms that he held that office. Lewis L. Gould, in a biography of Clark, wrote:

> As Speaker in the 1911 session of Congress, Clark continued to hold the Democrats together and to make issues regarding tariff reduction and antitrust policy that shaped the party's agenda for the 1912 presidential election. He found that the fight against Cannon had reduced the Speaker's power, and he served not as the sole leader of his party but as a kind of co-equal with the majority leader [Oscar Wilder Underwood of Alabama] and the powerful chairmen of committees...He had the support of western Democrats who had long followed William Jennings Bryan, he won the endorsement of William Randolph Hearst and his newspapers, and his record as Speaker had been better than observers had expected. His backers depicted him "as a rock of safety."

But while Clark could be bombastic, he was remembered fondly by his critics as well. In an article in *The Outlook* magazine that appeared following Clark's death in 1921, it was noted that:

> As Speaker of the House....until the Democratic reverse [in 1918] came he was a National figure. Speaker [Frederick] Gillett paid him the compliment of saying that, as Speaker, Champ Clark always set aside partisanship, while Mr. [James R.] Mann, who fought with Clark on the floor as a parliamentary enemy, declared that he not only respected but loved his former adversary.

Speaker Frederick H. Gillett
In 1918, just after the First World War ended in an armistice, Democrats lost control of the House, and Frederick H. Gillett of Massachusetts was elected as Speaker. Gillett, who was chosen by his party by having the long-time Minority Leader, James R. Mann of Illinois, passed over, would serve from the start of the Sixty-sixth Congress (1919-21) to the end of the Sixty-eighth Congress (1923-25). One contemporary source believes that Gillett beat out

Mann because the latter had been uniformly against "preparedness" for the onset of American participation in the First World War. This article in *World's Work* magazine in 1919 stated:

> Mr. Gillett's record on the one question which, in these days, overtops all others in importance, is completely satisfactory. He had always stood for preparedness, he has always voted in the right side in all the questions that rose prior to our entrance into the War, and he was anti-German and pro-American long before our official declaration against Germany.

Speaker Nicholas Longworth
Gillett's speakership, alas, is rarely considered in the gist of House history; his successor, Nicholas Longworth, is mentioned, albeit barely. As with all cases of studying the House, contemporary sources are best: in a magazine interview just after being elected Speaker, Longworth noted about Congress:

> I have been a member of the House of Representatives [for] ten terms. That is twenty years. During the whole of that time we have been attacked, denounced, despised, hunted, harried, blamed, looked down upon, excoriated, and flayed. I refuse to take it personally. I have looked into history. I find that we did not start being unpopular when I became a Congressman. We were unpopular even when Lincoln was a Congressman. We were unpopular even when John Quincy Adams was a Congressman. We were unpopular even when Henry Clay was a Congressman. We have always been unpopular.

In another interview, he noted,

> I promise you at the next session there will be an effective majority to take responsibility. If we fail, you have an opportunity to turn us out two years from now. We are united thoroughly on the basic principles of government. We are glad of the responsibility and think we are going to make good.

Longworth would serve from the start of the Sixty-ninth Congress (1925-27) until his death on 9 April 1931, after the Seventy-first Congress (1929-31) had been completed. In the 1930 elections, Republicans won a majority, but between that time and the meeting of the Seventy-second Congress (1931-33) on 7 December 1931, 19 representatives-elect died, including Longworth; in 14 of these cases, party control of the seats switched in special elections, giving the Democrats a slight majority when the House convened that December.

Speaker John Nance Garner

Longworth, deceased, was replaced not by a Republican but by Democrat John Nance Garner. Garner, a long-time Texas politician, instantly took control of the House by pushing for a tax increase on the rich in the middle of the Depression. One source noted that while Speaker, "Garner fathered bills providing that the tariff commission make its reports to Congress instead of to the president, and initiated a joint Democratic steering committee for both [the] Senate and [the] House for the definition within the party of party policies." Although Democrats went along with his support for an income tax raise, when Garner advocated a sale tax increase he feared a revolt on both sides of the aisle; he then took to the floor in his capacity not as Speaker but as party leader - again, a role changed by Speaker Cannon from previous speakers - and, on 29 March 1932, asked for bipartisanship in balancing the budget through the sales tax, a move which was successful. Garner served as Speaker for that single Congress - in 1932, he ran for President but settled for second on the party ticket with Governor Franklin Delano Roosevelt of New York.

Speaker Henry Thomas Rainey

On 9 March 1933, five days after Garner was sworn in as Vice President, the House elected Henry Thomas Rainey as the Speaker in the Seventy-third Congress (1933-35). At 72, Rainey was one of the oldest persons to ever be elected Speaker for the first time.

Of the bulk of the period that Speaker Rainey served during that Congress, both houses of that body, dominated by large majorities of Democrats, enacted every spending bill that the administration of President Franklin Delano Roosevelt wanted. Historian James T. Patterson explained in 1967:

Significantly, Roosevelt received not only almost everything he wanted from a willing Congress,

but he received it easily. The passage of eleven key bills in the House consumed only forty hours of debate. "Legislation," said one experienced Democratic congressman, "was coming in and being passed like grist from a mill, most of the time, with very little debate..." Most spectacularly, the emergency banking bill passed in the House after forty minutes' debate, before printed copies had reached the hands of the representatives, and with a din a voices shouting, "Vote, Vote, Vote."

Ironically, when the Democrats took control of the White House and both houses of Congress following the 2008 elections, some bills were enacted by the Speaker of the House, Nancy Pelosi, in much the same way: with little debate and little scrutiny of the massive amounts of spending placed into the legislation.

Speakers Joseph W. Byrns, William B. Bankhead, Sam Rayburn, and Joseph W. Martin

But while Speakers Henry Rainey, Joseph W. Byrns, and William B. Bankhead were running the House like the personal political machinery of President Franklin Roosevelt, they were pushing themselves - and their health - to the brink of collapse. In quick succession, Rainey and Byrns died within 22 months of each other, and the third of the Speakers to serve under Roosevelt, William Bankhead, served until 1940 before dying of the strain brought on by the speakership. In all, Roosevelt served with a total of four Speakers - the last being Sam Rayburn, who survived him - a record that seems solid in standing untouched.

When the aforementioned Rayburn was elected Speaker on 16 September 1940, it marked the start of an era in which this one man, save for two two-year congressional sessions, would serve as Speaker, until his death in 1961 - a total of more than 17 years in the Speaker's chair. With the rapid turnover of Congress seen today, aside from the bitter partisanship and intra party feuds, it seems unlikely that we will ever see one person, man or woman, hold onto the Speaker's position or, in the case of Rayburn (known as "Mr. Sam"), as head of his party for that entire period (for the two terms when the Republicans were in the majority, Rayburn served as Minority Leader).

To examine the record of Sam Rayburn as Speaker is to write a book on that alone; to summarize, it is nearly impossible. Known for his folksy Texas manner, bitter honesty, and beloved ability to cajole even his deepest opponent to his side of the argument, Rayburn was able to shepherd majority legislation through the House from the New Deal to the New Frontier - from Presidents Franklin Delano Roosevelt to Harry S. Truman to John F. Kennedy, and even from President Dwight D. Eisenhower, whom he worked with both as Speaker and Minority Leader. His axiom - "You cannot lead people by trying to drive them. Persuasion and reason are the only ways to lead them" - was used by him in all of his negotiations to pass legislation. In an obituary written in 1961, Richard Lyons wrote in the *Washington Post and Times Herald*, "

Mr. Sam looked tough and he could twist arms when necessary. But he didn't like it and he didn't do it often. His power and effectiveness was based more on respect and affection and personal loyalty...He held a unique position in the House or anywhere else in Government. Members of Congress traditionally refer to each other during debate in such phony terms as "distinguished." But when members referred to Mr. Rayburn as "our beloved Speaker," and everyone did, they meant it.

As noted, in two congressional sessions - in the Eightieth Congress (1947-49) and the Eighty-third Congress (1953-55) - the Republicans captured control of the House and elected Joseph W. Martin, Jr., as Speaker, with Rayburn serving as Minority Leader. In fact, from 1939, two years after Rayburn became House Leader of the Democrats, until 1959, when Martin was dislodged as the House Leader of the Republicans and two years before Rayburn's death, both men served continually together in their respective roles - again, a position that probably will never be seen again. In his two terms as Speaker, Martin opposed the policies of President Harry S. Truman, and then guided the programs of President Dwight D. Eisenhower through the House.

Speaker John W. McCormack

Rayburn's death on 16 November 1961 opened the speakership for the first time in many years; Majority Leader John W. McCormack was elected as Rayburn's successor on 9 January 1962, and he had

mighty large shoes to fill. In his three-plus terms as Speaker, for the remainder of the Eighty-seventh Congress (1961-63), and through the Eighty-eighth (1963-65), Eighty-ninth (1965-67), Ninetieth (1967-69) and Ninety-first (1969-71) Congresses, McCormack was one of the leaders enacting much of John F. Kennedy's and Lyndon Baines Johnson's legislative agenda, most notably Johnson's economic program know as "The Great Society," a complete reworking of the US economic system which saw tens of billions of dollars spent to aid the poor and disadvantaged.

Historian Mark Gelfand, who wrote of McCormack on the series *American National Biography*, explained,

> McCormack's ascension to the speakership in January 1962...created additional tensions with President Kennedy. Rayburn had had little success in getting southern Democrats to back the president's more expansive liberal agenda, including a cabinet-level Department of Urban Affairs and Housing, health insurance for the elderly, and federal aid to education, and McCormack, despite his long ties with southern congressmen, fared no better. Also, McCormack, the first Roman Catholic to be Speaker, helped defeat Kennedy's aid to education bill because it contained no assistance for parochial schools.

McCormack worked much easier and closer with President Lyndon Baines Johnson, who succeeded to the presidency upon Kennedy's assassination in November 1963. During this period, he supported Johnson's fighting of the war in Vietnam, as well as the President's economic and domestic policy known as "The Great Society."

In 1969, at the start of the Ninety-first Congress, many liberal Democrats who had chafed under McCormack's old style of leadership desired a change in the Speaker's chair. Initially, Rep. Morris Udall of Utah claimed to be a candidate for Speaker, but, with no sitting Speaker ever challenged for his seat, Udall's trial balloon went nowhere. In 1970, another liberal Democrat, Jerome R. Waldie of California, called for a vote of "no confidence" against Speaker McCormack. While this second test was dodged, McCormack's days as Speaker were numbered. A financial scandal involving the Speaker's own office and an aide, tied to bribery and payoffs, led to McCormack announcing in May 1970 that he would not seek the speakership in the Ninety-second Congress (1971-73). This led to the election as Speaker of Carl Albert, the first Oklahoman to serve in that position.

Speaker Carl Albert

A moderate Democrat who also backed the war in Vietnam throughout the 1960s and into the 1970s, Albert was faced almost immediately with the same challenges from liberals who brought down Speaker McCormack: they rejected Albert as part of the "old school" of House leadership; as well, they also opposed Albert's working with the Nixon administration from 1969 on. Although considered a weak Speaker who had few legislative accomplishments, Albert is best known for having officiated over the impeachment inquiry over President Nixon.

Historians of recent House history label the period prior to the 1970s as the "pre-reform" period, while anything after that is considered the "post-reform" period. Historian Matthew Green explained the line in the sand that separated these epochs when he wrote:

> Politics in the House underwent a gradual but significant shift in the 1970s. Young, activist, liberal, and independent Democrats, consisting of an ever-larger proportion of the party caucus, were willing to challenge internal status quo procedures and power structures. Together with reform-minded House Republicans and younger legislators from both parties, these Democrats pressed for significant institutional changes that dispersed influence over the agenda, committee assignments, and policy-making in several directions: toward individual legislators; toward subcommittees, where junior Democrats could play a greater role in shaping policy; towards the party caucus, where individual Democrats could exert more influence; and towards the party leadership, particularly the Speaker.

Green notes that in 1975, Speaker Carl Albert became the first Speaker since Joseph Cannon in 1910 to possess the power to appoint all of his party's seats on the Rules Committee.

Speaker Thomas P. "Tip" O'Neill

After only three terms as Speaker, Albert stood down, and was succeeded by Thomas P. "Tip" O'Neill, who was elected at the start of the Ninety-fifth Congress (1977-79). Serving for five full terms until the end of the Ninety-ninth Congress (1985-87), O'Neill was a staunch liberal who fought with two Presidents: Democrat Jimmy Carter and Republican Ronald Reagan. Angered at Carter's standoffish attitude and refusal to allow congressional Democrats to shape the party's agenda in the House, and by Reagan's tax cuts and slashing of domestic programs, O'Neill clashed frequently with the White House and became the face of Democrats who were slowly being tagged as out of touch with the ideals of average Americans. Despite this, O'Neill invigorated Democrats, who retained control of the House for the third consecutive decade.

Speakers James C. Wright and Thomas Foley

O'Neill's successor, James C. "Jim" Wright, Jr., a moderate Texan, came from a different school than his predecessors. While they had been protégés of former Speaker Sam Rayburn, Wright, who had come to Congress in 1954 and had served with Rayburn, nevertheless was a more confrontational figure who desired to enact legislation, whether he could get bipartisan consensus on it or not. At the same time, Wright went behind the back of the administration of Presidents Ronald Reagan and George H.W. Bush during his term and a half as Speaker, during the 100th (1987-89) and 101st (1989-91) Congresses. One area where Wright made enemies was in foreign policy, usually left to the Executive Branch to conduct with little interference from the Congress. Opposing the policy of the administration of funding anti-Communist guerrillas, known as the Contras, in Nicaragua, as well as supporting other anti-Communist movements in Central and South America, liberal Democrats in the House held hearings and then cut off funding, first in the early 1980s under Speaker O'Neill and then under Speaker Wright, to the contras. The defeat of this last funding request - instead, in its place, Democrats enacted an aid package for the pro-Moscow Sandinista government in Nicaragua - in March 1988, led President Reagan to allegedly pound his desk and yell, "This is the same old thing by Congress. Look at all the countries that went down the tubes right after Vietnam because of congressional interference in foreign policy!"

Perhaps Wright's biggest mistake was making an enemy of a little-known Republican firecracker named Newt Gingrich of Georgia. Desiring to break the stranglehold of Democratic control of the House of more than three decades, Gingrich used every congressional rule to harass Democrats; Gingrich also used the institution of television cameras into the House chamber to spread the Republican message of growth through tax cuts and military strength for the nation. While Gingrich was a thorn in the side of Speaker O'Neill, he became a mortal enemy of Speaker Wright. So when rumors of financial impropriety arose against Wright, Gingrich and other Republicans joined outside watchdog groups and demanded an ethics investigation of the Speaker. Democrats initially chalked up Gingrich's call for such an inquiry with a wave of their hand; but when the House Ethics Committee found nearly 70 instances where Wright had violated House rules, including selling his memoirs to lobbyists in exchange for campaign donations, and using the home of a lobbyist contributor and then not reporting the usage as a gift, Wright tumbled and then fell from his perch of power. On 1 June 1989, Wright went to the well of the House and resigned the speakership, the first sitting Speaker to resign under an ethical cloud. Democrats, shell-shocked at the events before them, quickly named Majority Leader Thomas S. Foley as the Speaker.

Foley, the first member from Washington State to rise to the speakership, consolidated his party into a cohesive unit again, opposing the policies of President George H.W. Bush. But during his two-plus terms as Speaker, Foley, who never got into ethical trouble of his own, presided over two major scandals, the House Banking Scandal and the House Post Office Scandal - both of which showed that years of Democratic control had led to mismanagement. In 1993, when President Bill Clinton's administration began, Democrats in the Congress helped to pass his budget and seem poised to enact Clinton's major campaign promise: universal health care. But the Clinton proposal became bogged down over massive administration details of the plan, and it never passed either House of Congress.

Speaker Newt Gingrich

The following year, Republicans, in the minority in the House since 1955, ran against Clinton, the health care debacle, and forty years of Democratic control by portraying them all as out of touch with the concerns of ordinary Americans. Signing a series of promises known as "A Contract with America," conceived by Gingrich and other Republicans, the GOP picked up 54 seats - including that of Speaker Thomas Foley - to take control of the House for the first time since the Eighty-third Congress. Gingrich was elected Speaker, the second Georgian to hold that coveted office. In quick succession, the new Republican majority enacted a series of reforms, bringing the House of Representatives into the twentieth century by forcing the House to observe laws that other segments of American society had to comply with. During his service in the 104th (1995-97) and 105th (1997-99) Congresses, Gingrich changed the face of the speakership by instituting strong leadership over the House.

At the same time, however, Gingrich made enemies of his own; President Bill Clinton, realizing that the 1994 GOP takeover of the House effectively ended his enactment of health-care reform, ran in 1996 against the alleged excesses of the Gingrich-led House and won a second term, the first since Franklin Delano Roosevelt to do so. Clinton served for the last two years of his first term and for the entire four years of his second term by vetoing Republican-enacted bills. A clash between the two strong leaders was bound to come - and come it did.

In early 1998, allegations that Clinton had had an elicit affair with a White House intern, covered it up, lied about it before a federal judge, and obstructed justice, led to the third impeachment inquiry in the House of a President of the United States. A special prosecutor, Kenneth W. Starr, a former Solicitor General, reported to the House Committee on the Judiciary that Clinton had committed impeachable offenses, and the House enacted three articles of impeachment. Following a trial in the Senate, however, Clinton was acquitted when a three-fourths vote against him could not be mustered. In the midst of this fight over impeachment, the 1998 mid-term elections were held, and Democrats picked up five seats while the GOP retained the majority. Realizing that his effectiveness as Speaker was ended, Gingrich resigned first the speakership and then his House seat. Initially, he was replaced by Bob Livingston of Louisiana; however, before Livingston could be formally elected, he disclosed that he had had an elicit affair while married, and resigned the speakership.

Speaker John Dennis "Denny" Hastert

Republicans then turned to a former wrestling coach, John Dennis "Denny" Hastert of Illinois to serve as Speaker. Sworn in on 6 January 1999, Hastert would become the longest-serving Republican Speaker in House history.

During his four terms as Speaker, from the start of the 104th Congress (1999-2001) through to the end of the 109th Congress (2005-07), Hastert worked with the Clinton administration in its last two years, and with the administration of President George W. Bush in its first six. In 2001, terrorists hijacked several aircraft and crashed them into buildings in New York City and Washington, D.C. and a field in Pennsylvania, killing nearly 3,000 Americans. The U.S. Congress enacted a war resolution that authorized the United States to go to war against the Islamic terrorists known as al-Qa'ida, or "The Base," in Afghanistan, as well as the USA PATRIOT Act, which gave the government additional tools to monitor and arrest terrorist suspects. In 2003, Hastert oversaw the congressional debate over the United States going to war in Iraq and dislodging its leader, Saddam Hussein, over the use of weapons of mass destruction Saddam had been building. As American casualties mounted in both conflicts, the wars became increasingly unpopular. As well, under Hastert and the GOP, spending in the Congress exploded, leading to massive deficits.

Speaker Nancy Pelosi

In 2006, public dissatisfaction with President George W. Bush and the Republican Congress led to massive losses for the GOP in the mid-term elections, and the rise of Nancy Pelosi - elected Democrat Majority Leader in 2004 - to become the first female Speaker of the U.S. House. Sworn in on 4 January 2007, Pelosi has served through the 110th Congress (2007-09) and, as of this writing, through the 111th Congress (2009-11). Pelosi, like Speakers Wright, Foley, and Gingrich before her, is a highly polarizing figure. Using language that most politicians shy away from, she repeatedly called President George W. Bush "a total failure" and, when Republicans blocked the Democrats attempts to cut off funding for the war in Iraq, that "Republicans love war." In the 111th Congress, Pelosi used the speakership to enact rules to cut Republicans out of any chance of debating or stopping the Democrats from enacting their economic and domestic programs. At the same time, in the first weeks of this Congress, Pelosi worked with President Barack Obama to enact an economic stimulus bill valued at nearly $800 billion, one which every Republican in the House voted against. In February 2009, Pelosi visited Pope Benedict XVI at the Vatican and was harshly rebuked for her support of the right to have an abortion.

And, so, we reach the end of the story that is the speakership since Joseph Cannon was harshly condemned as "Uncle Joe" and "Czar Cannon." We have seen Speakers from all walks of life, one rising to become Vice President, one once being a wrestling coach, and another being the first female Speaker. Historians can view the speakership as having changed drastically since Joseph Cannon served as Speaker, but when Nancy Pelosi forced two Democrats out of their committee chairmanships and replaced them with her own candidates, and when she serves as the head of her party in the House, and when she shuts the minority out of participation in House debates, it all brings back the specter that Democrats criticized Cannon for so long ago. Perhaps the wheel had come around; perhaps, as well, as George Santayana warned about, that those who ignore history are doomed to repeat it. Is history repeating itself now, as it did when Joseph Cannon was Speaker? Only the reader - and the historian - can decide for themselves.

The Four "Missing" Speakers Who Served Less Than a Day

One of the "lost" stories of the history of the office of the Speaker of the House of Representatives is the number of men who served in that capacity for an extremely brief period - in short, one day. Theodore Pomeroy, who served but a single day as Speaker at the end of the 40th Congress on 3 March 1869, is given his own biography in the main text of this work; however, Pomeroy was one of five different men who served but a single day, or a period of several short days, as Speaker. The other four men are universally forgotten; few sources exist on their lives, and their brief service as Speaker rarely appears even in histories of the House of Representatives. Despite this dearth of information, let us at least examine who these men were. We do owe them that, even if their place in the history of the U.S. House is minute, obscure, and little discussed.

Speaker George Dent (1756-1813)

The first of these four men to be examined is George Dent. Born on his father's estate (his exact date of birth appears to be lost, lending to his obscurity), known as "Windsor Castle," on the Mattowoman River in Charles County, Maryland, he served during the Revolutionary War as a first lieutenant in the militia of Charles and St. Mary's Counties under the direction of Capt. Thomas H. Marshall. After the conclusion of the war, Dent served as a member of the Maryland House of Assembly (1782-90), during which he served as Speaker *pro tempore* in 1788 and as the elected Speaker of that body in 1789 and 1790. After serving as a justice of the Charles County Court (1791-92), he was a member of the Maryland state Senate, rising to the office of president of that body before he resigned on 21 December 1792, having been elected, as a candidate who sided with the administration of President George Washington, to a seat in the U.S. House of Representatives. Dent took his seat in the Third Congress on 4 March 1793, joining the Federalist Party and winning re-election to the Fourth (1795-97), Fifth (1797-99), and Sixth (1799-1801) Congresses.

Although Dent's official congressional biography mentions that he was the "Speaker *pro tempore* of the House at various times from 1797 to 1799,"

other sources note that the first time was in 1798: "Dent, of Maryland, [was] elected Speaker on 20 April 1798, owing to the illness of Speaker Jonathan Dayton. He was again elected Speaker on 28 May 1798 when Dayton again became ill." These two dates in 1798 match what other reference sources - and they are few and far between - have to say on the matter. In a 1967 article on the election of the Speaker in 1799, historian Patrick J. Furlong wrote,

> The available evidence reveals nothing to explain the Republican support for George Dent, a Maryland member of somewhat uncertain party loyalty but clear Federalist tendencies at this time. Dent had served frequently as chairman of the Committee of the Whole during the preceding sessions, having been appointed to this responsible and politically delicate position by a Federalist Speaker. (In the Sixth Congress [1799-1801]) he was again appointed to preside (over the full House) by Speaker Sedgwick, succeeding Rutledge as chairman. Macon, from North Carolina, was one of the leading Republican members, and in 1801 he was elected Speaker.

As for Dent, he returned seamlessly back into the shadow of anonymity from whence he came. On 4 April 1801, he was appointed by President Thomas Jefferson to serve as the U.S. marshal for the District Court for the Potomac District in Washington, D.C., then near the start of its existence as the "federal city" and the capitol of the nation. Dent apparently stayed on the job only a short time, as in 1802 he "moved to Georgia" and settled near what is now the city of Augusta. Dent died there on 2 December 1813, presumably aged 57; his body was laid to rest on the estate he had established there.

Speaker Henry Hubbard (1784-1857)

The second man to serve for a short period, as Speaker was Henry Hubbard of New Hampshire. Born in Charlestown, in Sullivan County, New Hampshire, on 3 May 1784, he received an education studded with what historians call "classical studies" - in short, Latin, math, classical literature, etc. - under private tutors. Hubbard entered Dartmouth College in Hanover, New Hampshire, and graduated from there in 1803. He studied the law in Portsmouth in that same state, and, in 1806, was admitted to the state bar, opening a practice in his native Charlestown. It appears from this period that Hubbard served as a "town moderator" some 16 times, starting in 1810. He served as a selectman three times, and, from 1812-15, 1819-20, and 1823-27 as a member of the New Hampshire state House of Representatives. In that latter body, he served three times as Speaker. In 1823 he began a five year stint as the state Solicitor for Cheshire County, New Hampshire, and, in 1827, a two year term as a probate judge for Sullivan County.

In 1828, Hubbard was elected, as a Jacksonian, to a seat in the Twenty-first Congress (1829-31), holding the seat through the Twenty-second (1831-33) and Twenty-third (1833-35) Congresses. In the Twenty-second Congress, he served as the chairman of the Committee on Revolutionary Pensions.

According to the few works that mention his name, even in passing, Hubbard served as the Speaker *pro tempore* on 19 May 1834, during the Twenty-third Congress, when the speakership of Andrew Stevenson was coming to an end - he had been nominated to be the U.S. Minister to Great Britain, and his nomination had been held up in the Senate - and that of John Bell was almost ready to begin the following month. However, research has shown that even in this small exercise, the date of the action is wholly wrong: Hubbard was allowed to serve as Speaker on 16 May, not 19 May. As the *House Journal* noted (with swiftness and speed):

> The Speaker having withdrawn, Mr. Hubbard was substituted to act as Speaker, and continued to officiate as such for the remainder of the day.

There is no further record as to anything Hubbard may have done as Speaker, other than to, as the journal stated, "officiate."

In 1834, Hubbard was elected, as a Jacksonian Democrat, to the U.S. Senate, where he served from 4 March 1835 until 3 March 1841. He was not a candidate for re-election in 1840; instead, he returned home, where he was elected as the Governor of New Hampshire. He served in that office for a single two year term (1841-43). Finally, he served as a U.S subtreasurer in Boston, Massachusetts, from 1846 until 1849. Hubbard died in Charleston, New

Hampshire, on 5 June 1857, one month past his 73rd birthday, and he was buried in Forest Hill Cemetery.

Henry Hubbard is so forgotten, and has slipped so far into obscurity, that he appears to have no sources on his life, save for a single article that appeared in the *United States Democratic Review* in August 1841. Other than that, none of his manuscripts, if any ever did exist, no longer are extant, and any speeches he made in Congress are buried in the *Congressional Globe* or some other encapsulation of congressional discourses and debates.

Speaker George Washington Hopkins (1804-1861)

Our next filler of the Speaker's chair for a short period is George Washington Hopkins of Virginia. Born near the Goochland Court House in Goochland County, Virginia, on 22 February 1804, Hopkins attended what were called "common schools," which, at a time when most people lived in a rural setting, were mostly local one-room schoolhouses for local children. He studied the law, and was admitted to the state bar in 1834, opening a practice in Lebanon, Virginia. Entering the political realm, he was elected to the State House of Delegates and served a single two-year term, 1833-35.

In 1834, Hopkins was elected, as a Jacksonian - a follower of President Andrew Jackson - to a seat in the U.S. House of Representatives, taking his seat in the Twenty-fourth Congress (1835-37). In 1836, he ran for re-election, this time as a Jacksonian Democrat, and won the seat in the Twenty-fifth Congress (1837-39). In 1838, he ran on a minor party ticket, the Conservative Party, which advocated the protection of slavery in the United States, and won a seat in the Twenty-sixth Congress (1839-41). In 1840, he ran again as a Democrat, and again was elected, this time to the Twenty-seventh (1841-43), Twenty-eighth (1843-45), and Twenty-ninth (1845-47) Congresses. In the final two congresses, he served as the chairman of the Committee on the Post Office and Post Roads.

According to all available sources, Hopkins was "elected Speaker on 28 February 1845" when Speaker John W. Jones stepped aside for a day for some reason. According to the *House Journal*, following a debate in which Rep. John Quincy Adams presented a report "of a special joint committee of the house of representatives of the State of Massachusetts, to which was referred so much of the annual message of the governor of said State as relates to the annexation of Texas," it was noted that:

> *The Speaker having withdrawn, Mr. Hopkins was substituted to act as Speaker, and continued to officiate as such for the remainder of the day.*

No other note or mention of Hopkins as Speaker was made for the rest of that day's session.

In 1846, Hopkins refused to run for re-election, instead accepting an appointment from President James K. Polk to serve as the Chargé d'Affaires to Portugal, where he served from 3 March 1847 until 18 October 1849, when, according to the Department of State, he presented his recall, to be succeeded by James Brown Clay of Kentucky. Back in the United States, Hopkins served as a member of the state House of Delegates in 1850 and 1851, and as a member of the state constitutional convention held in this same two years. He also was a judge of the circuit court of Washington and surrounding counties. In 1856, Hopkins ran for, and was elected, as a Democrat to the U.S. House, taking his seat in the Thirty-fifth Congress (1857-59), during which he served as the chairman of the Committee on Foreign Affairs. In 1858, with the potential of civil war rapidly descending on all portions of the nation, Hopkins did not run for re-election. Instead, he returned home, where he resumed the practice of law in Abingdon, Virginia, although in 1859 he was elected to the state House of Delegates, were he served until his death on 1 March 1861 in Richmond, the state capitol, just days after his 57th birthday. Hopkins was buried in the Sinking Springs Cemetery in Abingdon.

Speaker Armistead Burt (1802-1883)

The last of the four men who served those short, short periods as Speaker without much due or recognition is Armistead Burt (1802-1883), who served for two days - 19 and 20 June 1848 - when Speaker Robert C. Winthrop became ill. Amazingly, Burt is not as obscure one would expect of the men profiled in this essay; his congressional biography details some manuscripts, most notably at Duke University in Durham, North Carolina. Nevertheless, his "speakership" is barely mentioned in histo-

ries of the House. Born at Clouds Creek, a settlement near Edgefield, in the Edgefield District, South Carolina, on 13 November 1802, Burt relocated with his parents to Pendleton, South Carolina, at an early age. At his new home, he was schooled in preparatory studies for university; however, he studied the law, was admitted to the state bar in 1823, and opened a practice in Pendleton. In 1828, he moved the practice to Abbeville, South Carolina, where he also was involved in what his official congressional biography calls "agricultural pursuits," usually a codeword for investing in crops such as tobacco, corn, etc.

Entering politics, Burt was elected to the South Carolina House of Representatives, serving five single one-year terms (1834-35, 1838-41). In 1842, as a Democrat, he was elected to the U.S. House of Representatives, taking his seat in the Twenty-eighth Congress (1843-45) and remaining in the House until the conclusion of the Thirty-third Congress (1853-55). He served as chairman of the Committee on Military Affairs in the Thirty-first (1849-51) and Thirty-second (1851-53) Congresses.

All sources on the sessions of the Thirtieth Congress (1847-49) agree that, on two occasions, on two days back-to-back, Speaker Robert C. Winthrop left the Speaker's chair "when ill" and handed over the duties of the Speaker to Armistead Burt, selected in his place. The journal of the House reports that on 19 June 1848:

> *The regular hour of meeting having arrived, the Clerk called the House to order, and stated, that in consequence of the indisposition of the Speaker, he could not attend the session of the House today; and that, therefore, it became necessary that the House should choose a presiding officer pro tempore.*

> *Thereupon, on motion of Mr. [George] Ashmun [of Massachusetts], Resolved, That Mr. Burt, of South Carolina, should preside as Speaker of the House for this day; and Mr. Burt accordingly took the chair.*

The journal then related what occurred the following day, 20 June 1848:

The Clerk called the House to order, and stated that the Speaker was still so much indisposed as to prevent him from resuming the duties of the chair;

And, thereupon, On motion of Mr. Daniel P. King [Whig of Massachusetts], it was unanimously Resolved, That Mr. Armistead Burt, of South Carolina, be appointed Speaker pro tempore to discharge the duties of the chair during the present week, if the Speaker shall remain so long unable to give his attendance.

On motion of Mr. Ashmun, by leave, it was Resolved, That the Clerk inform the Senate, that in the absence of the Speaker, by reason of illness, the House has made choice of the honorable Armistead Burt, one of the Representatives from the State of South Carolina, as Speaker pro tempore.

And that was it. Winthrop recovered, retook the Speaker's chair, and Armistead Burt returned to the shadows of anonymity, at least in the eyes of the historical record. Calvin Townsend, an historian whose 1873 work is the best "contemporary" source we can rely on regarding the subject of this essay, states that Burt was "first appointed, on account of the sickness of the Speaker, for one day; then for the remainder of the session." However, Townsend is the only source to claim this amount of service in the Speaker's chair for Burt.

Burt did not run for re-election in 1852, instead returning to his native South Carolina and reopening his law practice in the city of Abbeville. He survived the Civil War (although his role in that conflict is not clear), serving as a delegate to the Democratic National Convention held at Tammany Hall in New York City. Burt remained out of politics, instead keeping his law office thriving. He died in Abbeville on 30 October 1883, one month shy of his 81st birthday. He was buried in the Episcopal Cemetery in that city. As mentioned, some of his private correspondence does remain, although most of the letters deal with secession; after 1860, Duke University reports, the letters relate chiefly with Burt's law practice, most notably with the management of the estates of Confederate soldiers.

As we stated at the beginning of this essay, Theodore Pomeroy, who, like these men, served for a day or only a bit longer as Speaker, has been given his own place among the Speakers who appear in all of the history books. The layman or historian or critic may ask why: the answer is, plainly, because in nearly every list of Speakers that the author came across in the six years of writing this work, he found the name of Pomeroy, even if his term of service was a fill-in between that of Schuyler Colfax, who left office on 3 March 1869, before the last day of his term as Speaker, to prepare to become Vice President, and James G. Blaine, who took over on 4 March 1869 at the start of the Fortieth Congress. Pomeroy is remembered by historians; the men profiled in this essay are not. It is just that simple.

Five Controversial Elections for Speaker -
1839, 1849, 1855, 1859, and 1923

The elections held every two years for the U.S. Congress usually settle who will be the majority and minority party status for the next congressional session long before that particular session begins. With that certainty, of course, comes the assurance that the majority's leader will be chosen as the Speaker when that vote is taken when the new Congress convenes the following January. But, in five distinct occasions in congressional history, the Congress struggled to elect a Speaker, leading to days - and, in some cases weeks, even months - of debate and argument and, finally, in all five cases, led to dark horse candidates who were eventually elected through compromise. This essay focuses on these five contentious elections, held in 1839, 1849, 1855, 1859, and 1923. The first four came about because of slavery; the last arose due to the ascendancy of the Progressive Party in American politics.

Speaker Robert M.T. Hunter - 1839

Through the early years of the decade of the 1830s, the issue of slavery slowly, but ever so majestically, reared its ugly head into the swirls of the cauldron that was the floor of the U.S. House of Representatives. Southerners blasted, cajoled, and in many ways threatened those who dared even whisper any hint of trying to stop slavery, much less actually trying to curtail it or even outlaw it altogether. The elections of Andrew Stevenson of Virginia as Speaker in the Twenty-third Congress (1833-35), of John Bell of Tennessee as Speaker to succeed Stevenson in that Congress when Stevenson was named as the U.S. Minister to Great Britain, of James K. Polk of Tennessee as Speaker in the Twenty-fourth (1835-37) and Twenty-fifth (1837-39) Congresses, all led to a growing unease among many Northerners that the South was running the Congress through an atmosphere of intimidation, fear, and threats of breaking up the Union if the right of slavery was encroached upon. Worse, yet, the Democrats in the House had instituted a rule that put an end to the admission of petitions from concerned citizens calling for the ending of slavery in the District of Columbia, which took place just steps away from representatives of the people who walked to work each day as human be-

ings were being sold into bondage. Called by its opponents as "the gag rule," an effort was led by its greatest antagonist, former President and Representative John Quincy Adams of Massachusetts, to do everything he could to shake up the southerners who pushed for the rule and embarrass them each day with his entreaties to preserve the fundamental right of the people to petition their government. In the Twenty-fifth Congress, Speaker Polk had done his utmost to preserve the rights of proslavery representatives to speak on the House floor while making sure that those who stood for the abolition of slavery, or even those who did not comport with the entire right to own slaves, were not allowed to make any comments on the floor. At the end of that Congress, on 3 March 1839, there was great consternation as nearly 60 representatives refused to offer a vote of thanks to the outgoing Speaker, a rare slap in the face to a man who had just been elected Governor of Tennessee and who would, in six short years, be inaugurated as President of the United States.

The Twenty-sixth Congress convened on 2 December 1839. The Democrats were barely in control of the House (119 seats to 118), with a small majority owing to Whig victories in the 1838 elections that came about because of the economic panic of 1837, blamed on the administration of President Martin Van Buren, a Democrat. This majority was confirmed when the Democrats, in a controversial move, fought that seating of the entire New Jersey delegation, whose election certificates had been held up because Whigs in that state won the seats. At that time, members of Congress were elected in what was called the "general ticket system," in which states would seat blocks of representatives rather than by congressional district as they are elected now. Thus, as a party controlled the machinery of a state, it could elect a block of representatives to Congress rather than have a split among those who won. The Whigs, controlling the party machinery, sent six Whigs to Congress. The Democrats, in no mood to hand over that state to the Whigs, protested. Their seating or, in this case, their nonseating, led to a split in the House that gave no party a firm majority, setting up a fight for the speakership.

The issue over the seating of the New Jersey delegation, however, was not settled for three months after the Congress met; in the meantime, when the House finally assembled and moved to seat a Speaker, there was no consensus as to a potential candidate. For the first three days of the session, there was no presiding officer; John Quincy Adams, a Whig and the former President of the United States who now sat in the House, was elected on 5 December as the chairman *pro tempore* of the House with the task of sitting as a "Speaker" in name only. For the next fifteen days, the House argued over who could be an acceptable candidate for the speakership. Aiding in that turmoil was the Clerk of the House, Hugh A. Garland of Virginia, a Democrat who desired to see his party control the House again; and, in that vein, he used every tactic in his power to minimize the Whig debate and advance the Democrats' arguments. As Mary Parker Follett, a noted historian of the Speakers of the U.S. House, wrote in 1902, upon Garland's moves against the Whigs, particularly in making sure that the New Jersey Whigs were not seated:

> *Tumult and disorder reigned. The Clerk stubbornly refused to put any question to the House, declaring that he had no right to do so. After four days of disorganization John Quincy Adams arose from his seat and made an earnest appeal to the House to discharge its solemn and immediate duty of organization by proceeding with the roll-call, calling those members from New Jersey who held certificates signed by the Governor of the State. "But who put the question?" still urged a timid member. "I will put the question myself," replied John Quincy Adams. The Clerk attempted to make an explanation, but was cried down.*

As the journal of the House noted, on 5 December, the representatives, unable to elect a Speaker, moved to elect a "chairman of the House" to serve *until* the election of the Speaker. But, in a move that was as hilarious as ironic, this effort broke down along sectional lines because of...you know the answer...slavery. Robert Barnwell Rhett, Democrat of South Carolina, a fiery advocate of slavery known as a "fire eater" (so called because, allegedly, they

would rather "eat fire" than allow slavery to be abolished), moved a resolution that Lewis Williams, Whig of North Carolina, who was the oldest member of the House at 57 years of age, be appointed as chairman. Williams objected to serving, and that ended that. Then, in some strange attempt either at levity or brevity or something else lost to history, Rhett called on Adams, perhaps one of the greatest foes of slavery, to serve as chairman. Despite Adams' controversial attempts at trying to abolish slavery, including introducing petitions to end the practice in the District of Columbia even after Democrats had instituted the "gag" against the introduction of such petitions, Rhett's motion "passed in the affirmative" (there is no breakdown of the vote, so we do not know how many objected), and "Adams was conducted to the chair by two members of the House, and proceeded to the discharge of the duties of the chair."

So, with Adams now sitting as the "Chairman of the House" rather than as the "Speaker of the House," the House proceeded to vote to exclude any and all members of the New Jersey delegation, because the Democrats did not want the Whigs tilting the count in the House to help elect a Whig Speaker, and the Whigs had to sit and accept the outcome because without the New Jersey delegation they were in the minority, even if it was a minority of one. But the Democrats held together on this all-important vote, and, thus, without the New Jersey members, the Democrats now had a shot of electing one of their own as Speaker, even if it meant a Whig-majority House when the New Jersey members were seated. For the layman, or even the historian, it appears to be a comedy of errors that only grew in size as each day passed.

Days of arguing over the seating of other members, and continued anger over the decision over the New Jersey delegation led the House to do nothing but argue until 14 December. It was on that day, again with Adams sitting in the Speaker's chair, that the first vote (finally!) for Speaker was held. And on that first ballot John W. Jones, Democrat of Virginia (who would serve as Speaker in the Twenty-eighth Congress [1843-45]), received 113 votes to 102 for John Bell, Whig of Tennessee, who had already served as Speaker in the Twenty-third Congress (1833-35). William C. Dawson of Georgia received 11 votes, and three others received a combined total of 9 votes. With 118 votes needed to constitute a majority, neither Jones nor Bell were elected. On the second vote, Jones received 113 votes to 99 for Bell, and Dawson still far back in third place with 11. With Jones just five votes shy of a majority, it appeared that he would be elected Speaker once again. Yet, on the fourth vote, he dropped to 101 votes; Bell *really* dropped, to sixth place, with just 2 votes; William C. Dawson was now second with 77, and a newcomer, Robert Mercer Taliaferro Hunter, Democrat of Virginia, was third with 29. On the fifth vote, Jones was now down to 71 votes - still in the lead, but shrinking - with Hunter now in second with 68 votes, and Dixon Hall Lewis, Democrat of Alabama, in third with 49. But wait...can you notice the theme running through all of the leading candidates at this precise moment? *All of them were Southerners, and all of them supported slavery.* On the sixth vote, Lewis took the lead with 79 votes, Hunter remained in second with 63, and Jones, formerly in the lead, now dropped to fourth with 39. John Bell rose to fifth with 21 votes.

Saturday, 14 December, made way to Monday, 16 December, and more tallies. A seventh vote brought Dixon Lewis of Alabama 110 votes, eight shy of victory, while Bell rose to 64 and Hunter dropped to 22. With several members not appearing (a majority of members voting, not of the total House, were necessary), a candidate needed only 115 votes to win the speakership on this vote. On the eighth vote, with 117 votes needed for victory, Lewis got 113 - four shy - with Bell in second with 80. On the ninth vote, Bell's support evaporated; Lewis received 110 votes, Hunter was now in second with 59, and Bell plummeted to third with 33 votes. In total, eleven ballots over that fifteen-day period were taken, and in each ballot the split between the Northern and Southern sections became more and more pronounced.

Robert M.T. Hunter had shown his growing strength on the tenth ballot, securing 85 votes to 73 for Lewis and only 14 for John W. Jones. It was on the eleventh, and final, canvass, that Hunter got more than the 117 votes needed to capture the majority, winning 119 votes to 55 for John W. Jones of Virginia. George May Keim, Democrat of Pennsyl-

vania, was a distant third with 24. As D.R Anderson wrote in 1906, "It would appear from [his ultimate] showing that Hunter had no original strength - was the choice of no party, was hardly thought of, but that in the course of balloting he was found to be the available man."

The Speaker-elect was conducted to the Speaker's chair by Linn Banks, Democrat of Virginia, and Abbott Lawrence, Whig of Massachusetts, and given the oath of office. The members were so numb at the finality of Hunter's election that where a new Speaker usually delivers some comments after being sworn, the House instead adjourned, coming back into session at 12 o'clock noon the following day, 17 December 1839. Hunter then proceeded to deliver some comments and observations; he noted that he was "deeply impressed with a painful sense of my inexperience, and of the difficulties of a new and untried station," yet he was "cheered by the hope that you will sustain me in my efforts to preserve the order of business and the decorum of debate."

And so closed the first major contest for the speakership; it would not be the last. Strangely, little about this particular election has been written, at least to any great degree that such a struggle for the Speaker's chair would entail or invite serious scrutiny. A study of the few available works on Hunter, an obscure politician on his own despite serving as Speaker, shows that the 1839 election, whether considered contentious or not, and his rise to the speakership of the House, and his tenure as Speaker, and his service in that Congress, is all mentioned only in passing. Why this is so, about a man who played an important, albeit minor, role in the secession movement in the two decades before the Civil War exploded in 1860-61, remains a mystery. His service in the Senate, from 1847 to 1862, is remembered more. In his memoirs, John Quincy Adams noted that Hunter was "a good-hearted, weak-headed young man." Perhaps this is why, as I noted in the essay on the difficulty in studying the early Speakers using historical documents, that many of the Speakers who served before Joseph Cannon in the first years of the twentieth century have slipped into unrecoverable obscurity.

Speaker Howell Cobb - 1849

The same arguments that exacerbated and extended the 1839 contest and led to Robert Hunter's ultimate election arose again with a vengeance just ten years later, when once more the issue of slavery drove a wedge right through the heart of the U.S. House. The new Free Soil Party, formed from disenchanted Whigs who detested slavery - and, to a greater degree, their own party's refusal to tackle the issue - had elected several members to the House; their numbers, joined by some northern Democrats who also wanted to be rid of slavery, forced both the Democrats and the Whigs to reach out to these independent members in order to gain a majority and elect the Speaker. The Democrats chose as their candidate Howell Cobb of Georgia, considered by historians to have been a moderate on the slavery issue but, in fact, was a staunch supporter of the right to own slaves and would, when the Civil War broke out, stand with the Confederacy in both military and political service. However, we pan back to 1849, 11 years before that horrific conflict struck. The Whigs nominated Robert C. Winthrop, considered by southerners to be a radical abolitionist who was a threat to their way of life of owning slaves. Winthrop was an abolitionist, but he was not "enough" of an abolitionist to please the Free Soilers, mainly because he was prepared to name to important committees, such as the Committee on the District of Columbia, where the Free Soilers wanted slavery made extinct, those who did not support their program. Members of the Free Soil Party in the House, led by Rep. Joshua Giddings of Indiana, considered Winthrop a heretic on the issue of abolitionism and would not support him for Speaker. This would prove to be Winthrop's Achilles' Heel, and he would pay for it in the end.

Some Whigs, fearing that Winthrop's election was slipping away, tried to get reassurances that if he won the Democrats would not resist his naming of certain people to important committees. One Democrat, William J. Brown of Indiana, who supported the right to own slaves, promised to name Whigs as the chairmen of committees if he were the compromise candidate for Speaker; however, when the letters between the Whigs and Brown were leaked, southerners denounced Brown and their overall effort, and Brown had to withdraw any consideration for the speakership.

The Thirty-first Congress (1849-51) convened on 3 December 1849, and the first vote for Speaker was held on that first day. Howell Cobb received 103 votes to 96 for Robert C. Winthrop, with a scattering of 22 additional votes spread among a number of candidates, most of whom had no chance of being elected. One of these was James L. Orr of South Carolina, who would later serve as Speaker in the Thirty-fifth Congress (1857-59). A second vote was quickly held, showing that Cobb had 102 votes to 96 for Winthrop. Those numbers stayed the same through the third, fourth, and fifth votes. On the sixth vote, Cobb dropped to 101 votes and Winthrop rose to 97 votes. On the seventh tally, Cobb declined to 100. On the twelfth vote, held on 5 December, the two men were tied at 97 votes apiece; on the thirteenth vote, Winthrop took the lead, 98 votes to 93.

After fifty-nine ballots had been taken, the main candidates had fallen by the wayside; on that count, Edward Stanly, Whig of North Carolina, led with 75 votes, with John Alexander McClernand, Democrat of Illinois, second with 50. Finally, the assembled representatives had begun to tire quickly. It had become clear that, unlike 1839, when two weeks of fighting had produced a Speaker, this fight was different and that the rules had to be changed. Finally, a resolution was introduced that stated that "if after the roll shall have been called three times no member shall have received a majority of the whole number of votes, the roll shall again be called, and the member who shall receive the largest number of votes, provided it be a majority of a quorum, shall be declared chosen Speaker."

On the next tally, the sixtieth, held on 22 December 1849, Cobb, back in the running, led with 95 votes to 90 for Winthrop, also back as the candidate of his party. On the sixty-first vote, Cobb led, 96 to 92 for Winthrop. Incredibly, on the sixty-second vote, the two men were tied with 97 votes apiece, leading to the contentious sixty-third, and, as it turned out, final, vote: Cobb received 102 votes to 100 for Winthrop. Stanly of North Carolina offered a resolution that Cobb be elected as Speaker, a declaration that passed 149-35. Cobb was ushered to the Speaker's chair by Winthrop and Rep. James McDowell, Democrat of Virginia, and, after he delivered his remarks, was sworn in.

The 1849 election, from the view of 160 years of history, was in fact a turning point in the American political scene. Mary Parker Follett explained in 1902:

Southern suspense was now relieved. If the Whigs had elected their candidate in 1849 the Civil War might have been delayed, for the committees of this Congress affected the Compromise of 1850. It is probable that Mr. Winthrop's prestige would have carried him into the Senate and eventually have affected the make-up of the Republican Party. The choice of a very pronounced pro-slavery and Southern man at this crisis undoubtedly aggravated the struggles of the following decade.

But there is an argument to be made with Follett's hypothesis; after all, the movement toward abolition continued with Cobb as Speaker, and would have continued with Winthrop in that chair; it is also plausible to believe that Winthrop as Speaker would have overseen the prohibition of slavery in the District of Columbia, a move which, like the election of Abraham Lincoln to the presidency in 1860, would probably have precipitated the southern states to walk out of the Union. So, perhaps the election of Howell Cobb, or the failure of the election of Robert C. Winthrop, in 1849 was not so much a turning point as just one more stone in the road that this country had to travel down that would come with the fight to end slavery. Nothing would have stopped the abolitionists in the North, and nothing would have stopped the slaveholders in the South. 1849 would become 1860 soon enough, whoever was elected.

Speaker Nathaniel Prentiss Banks - 1855

Just a few short years after the fight over Howell Cobb, the Congress elected in 1854 met the following year and failed to elect a Speaker, and set off a prolonged crisis that led to nineteen separate candidates for the Speaker's chair and balloting that went on for two months, from December 1855 until February 1856. Thus, when a Speaker was finally chosen, he sat in that office only until the end of the Thirty-fourth Congress (1855-57).

The 1854 elections, coming in the middle of the first - and only - term of President Franklin Pierce, a northerner who supported slavery, confirmed the growing strength in the North of the abolitionist movement. George H. Mayer wrote, in a history of the Republican Party in 1967, "When the votes were counted...the Democrats knew that they had lost, but nobody knew who had won." The vote gave a coalition of Republicans, a year after that party was formed, and American Party members, a majority. The American Party was better known as the "Know-Nothing" Party (a name which arose when, asked by people what their party stood for, said that they "knew nothing"). The American Party was composed mainly of former Whigs, many of whom were nativists, opposed to the ever-growing influx of immigrants from Ireland (predominantly Catholic) and Germany, although the party did split between northern Know-Nothings, who were more abolitionist, and southern Know-Nothings, who supported the right to own slaves. Fred Harvey Harrington, Banks' biographer, noted in a 1936 article:

The election over...Banks went to Washington to plunge into a contest more severe than any he had known in Massachusetts. This, the celebrated speakership contest of the Thirty-fourth Congress, lasted nine full weeks and ended with Banks' elevation to the chair as the candidate of the anti-slavery forces. The elections of 1854 had gone against [President] Pierce, and there was an anti-slavery majority in the House in December 1855. This was, however, anything but a unified majority, for it included anti-Nebraska Democrats, Free Soilers, and Whigs, as well as Know Nothings of all kinds - "North Americans," "South Americans," Whig, Democrat, and Free Soil Americans. It is no wonder that the printers of the [Congressional] Globe, despairing of cataloguing the members properly, omitted party designations altogether and that no less than twenty-one members received votes on the opening ballot.

In the months that transpired after the election, Democrats, Republicans, and Know-Nothings jockeyed to find a suitable candidate to put forward for the speakership. When the House convened on 3 December 1855, four members stood as the candidates of their respective caucuses in the House. Know-Nothings, who backed slavery chose Humphrey Marshall of Kentucky, a former Whig, and Henry M. Fuller of Pennsylvania, trying to get either elected as Speaker. Republicans offered Lewis D. Campbell of Ohio, a rabid antislavery advocate and former Whig and Know-Nothing who left the American Party over the issue of immigration. Finally, northern Know-Nothings submitted the name of Nathaniel Prentiss Banks of Massachusetts, a former Whig who had also belonged to the Free Soil Party, an entity which was the forerunner of the Republican Party with its main platform stand of the abolition of slavery. Of the candidates, Campbell was considered the further against slavery, while Marshall was the polar opposite. In a House split so badly over slavery that parties broke up into northern and southern wings, the possibility was that Banks or Fuller, or perhaps another as yet unnamed representative would eventually be elected to the Speaker's chair. Of course, at the start of the Thirty-fourth Congress, that appeared to be the way it was. But that was not how it was, or how it would be.

A study by historians of the journals of the U.S. House will find, at least prior to that Thirty-fourth Congress, that the journal opens with a roll call of the elected members, moving quickly to the election of the Speaker, which was usually accomplished in one or two ballots, or, in the case of the 1839 contest, previously discussed, which elected Robert Mercer Taliaferro Hunter to the speakership, two weeks of balloting; however, that journal for the Thirty-fourth Congress opens with the ballots taken for Speaker and then lasts and lasts and lasts...ballot after ballot after ballot, all deadlocked and all for naught. Remember that the House first convened on 3 December 1855 - through that cold winter in Washington, the members of the House could find no candidate who could garner the necessary number of votes to win a majority as required by the House rules. Days turned into weeks, and 1855 turned into 1856, and January 1856 turned into February 1856. In the meantime, no business of the House could get done until the first act of the Congress, naming a Speaker who could moderate debates and decide on committee assignments and so forth, was accomplished. One hundred and thirty-three tallies would go by until a candidate was finally elected. But more on that later.

For the first 450 pages of the House Journal for that first session of the Thirty-fourth Congress, the floor fights over who would emerge as Speaker went on

and on. It would be impossible, short of publishing a book solely on this single election for Speaker, to fully illustrate each vote that pushed the members closer and closer to full-blown exhaustion over those cold winter months in December 1855 and into January and February 1856. Historians Jeffery A. Jenkins and Timothy P. Nokken, in a 2000 article, stated,

> *After the initial deadlock on the first ballot, voting continued over the course of the week without producing a majority winner...On December 5, Marshall took his name out of consideration, which left the Southern Know Nothings, after scattering their votes for several ballots, to coalesce around Fuller, the only major Know Nothing candidate left in the race. On the evening of December 6, the anti-slavery contingent organized a caucus and agreed to settle on Banks as their sole candidate, leaving Campbell to withdraw from the race the following day. Thus, four days into the contest, only three viable candidates remained in the field: Richardson, Banks, and Fuller.*

Needless to say that it is not only the printed words of the journal of the House, but contemporary correspondence, that best illustrate the day-to-day horse trading and dealing and voting that categorized those attempts at electing a Speaker. One rich source of contemporary materials are the letters of Rep. Edwin Barber Morgan, a Whig elected to the Thirty-fourth Congress who wrote home to his family about the failure to elect a Speaker. His original letters are laid out as a primary document; on 12 December 1855, he predicted that "I am certain we can elect no man but Banks & ought not to. His principles are right & true & he would make a splendid officer & organize the Committees right & upon a Northern platform, & I had rather the whole thing should go by the board than have a half & half fellow in that seat."

Finally, fatigue got the better of the representatives: on the 130th ballot, again with no candidate having a majority, it was decided that the person with the highest number should win. Of course, in a House that had gone this long fighting over one candidate or another, this could not be accomplished right away. Finally, on 2 February 1856, on, as previously stated, the 133rd ballot, Banks of Massachusetts leapt over that impenetrable barrier of the most votes out of 214 total, winning 103 ballots to 100 for William Aiken, Democrat of South Carolina, with Henry M. Fuller in third with 6, Lewis D. Campbell with 4, and Daniel Wells, Jr., Democrat of Wisconsin, with a single vote. Banks was ushered to the Speaker's chair and he delivered some remarks, brief though they were, never once mentioning the issue that had caused all of the controversy - slavery - and one which in four short years would lead to the worst conflict on American soil, the Civil War. Before that war would break out, however, would come the Thirty-sixth Congress (1859-61), and, for the fourth time in just twenty years, another fight for the speakership.

Speaker William Pennington - 1859

In the 1858 election, the last one before that contentious 1860 campaign that sent Abraham Lincoln to the White House and led to the secession of the southern slaveholding states and the onset of the Civil War, the Republican Party won a majority of seats and the U.S. House continued its march towards the eventual move to abolish slavery. Ollinger Crenshaw, writing about the divisive speakership contest in the Congress that followed, stated in a 1942 article,

> That the speakership contest of 1859-1860 exacerbated an already critical sectional conflict is a fact commonly known to historians. Long ago, the historian of the period, James Ford Rhodes, described the turbulent scenes which characterized the daily sessions of the House of Representatives, especially the initial eight weeks, from December 5, 1859, to February 1, 1860, of the Thirty-sixth Congress, during which the tug of war raged to gain control of the House by the election of a Speaker.

Republicans, who controlled the lower chamber of the Congress, 109 to 101, intended to nominate and elect John Sherman, a noted Ohio politician (and the brother of the eventual Civil War General William Tecumseh Sherman) who would eventually serve in two future administrations as Secretary of State and Secretary of the Treasury. In the portion of this story, however, Sherman was a highly respected member of the House; at least, he was highly respected by those who were in his party.

Among Democrats, most notably those who supported the rights of slaveowners, Sherman was an anathema whose rise to the speakership had to be opposed no matter what. The urgency to oppose the Ohioan became even more pronounced among southerners because of the recent execution of John Brown, the abolitionist radical who used force to try to free slaves in Virginia and whose capture, trial, and hanging split the country even more into proslave and antislave camps. The House, like the nation it was supposed to represent, was as split as the general populace.

On the first ballot, despite having an antislavery majority in the House, the members sided more with the choice of the Democrats, Thomas S. Bocock of Virginia, who received 86 votes, several votes shy of a majority. Sherman was second with 66, with Republican Galusha A. Grow of Pennsylvania third with 43. A member of the American, or Know-Nothing, Party, Alexander R. Boteler of Virginia, was last with 14 tallies. (Histories of the Congress call Boteler, among 20 others in the House in that session, a "South American," referring to the section of his party rather than his being from south of the border.)

The threat of Sherman's possible rise to the Speaker's chair caused mayhem to rise among the southern slaveholders and their protectors. Rep. John B. Clark, Democrat of Missouri, introduced a resolution condemning the publication of Hinton R. Helper's *The Impending Crisis of the South - How to Meet It*, an 1857 work, by a southerner, who condemned slavery and stated that allowing it to continue would be the undoing of the Union. The book was injected into the debate over the speakership because Sherman had written a blurb for the book's jacket praising it - before he had ever read it. Clark's resolution used the controversy over the book and Sherman's tenuous ties to it to try to derail the Ohioan's candidacy for the Speaker's chair:

> *Resolved, That the doctrine and sentiments of a certain book, called "The Impending Crisis of the South - How to Meet It," purporting to have been written by one Hinton R. Helper, are insurrectionary and hostile to the domestic peace and tranquility of the country, and that no Member of this House who has indorsed and*

recommended it, or the compend from it, is fit to be speaker of this House.

Unable to win the speakership outright, the Democrats decided to tar Sherman with the broad brush of alleged scandal and force the Republicans to name another - and more palatable - nominee. Ironically, potential speaker Galusha A. Grow had also signed the jacket for Helper, but because his chances were considered too low to win the election, the Democrats never aimed their fire at him.

Unable to elect a Speaker, the chaotic House then settled down to a massive debate - on Helper, on those who had supported Helper (either accidentally or by design), the right of people to own slaves, and the rights of those to protest slavery under the Constitution. One Republican, William Pennington of New Jersey, said that the deliberations included "all things on the earth and under the earth." At one point, Sherman took to the floor not only to dissuade the Democrats that he was siding with Helper, but also that he would not do anything to interfere with the right of owning slaves. "Allow me to say, once and for all (and I have said it five times on this floor), that I am opposed to any interference whatever by the people of the free States with the relations of master and slave in the slave States." He also tried to argue that his support for Helper's book was inadvertent at best. "I do not recollect signing that paper referred to; but I presume, from my name appearing in the printed list, that I did sign it," he told the members on the floor. "I have never read Mr. Helper's book, or the compendium founded upon it. I never have seen a copy of either." But the attacks from Democrats upon Sherman's character were withering, and over a period of days he considered bowing out of the speaker's election.

One W.C. Allen wrote to Sherman on 7 January 1860, "It is generally conceeded [sic] that should you be called to fill the Chair - that the South would at once cool down as they did at the time that Banks was elected," referring, of course, to the previously discussed Speaker's election of Nathaniel Prentiss Banks in the Thirty-fourth Congress in 1856. With Sherman continuing his candidacy, and his party supporting him, the move to elect him persisted. Bocock, unable to win a majority of votes, threw in the towel on the 11th ballot (he would later side with his home state of Virginia and the

Confederacy in the Civil War, and ironically serve as Speaker of the Confederate House of Representatives during that conflict), and, with the realization that no Democrat would be elected, was replaced by a series of members of the American or Know-Nothing Party who tried but failed to gain a majority, including John A. McClernand of Illinois, Charles L. Scott of California, and John S. Millson of Virginia. One of these, William N.H. Smith of North Carolina, won 112 votes on the 39th ballot, three shy of victory. Democrats were angry at their inability to elect even a minority Speaker; Robert Toombs of Georgia, one of the most radical of the so-called "fire eaters" who stood for either full rights for slaveholders or the end of the Union, wrote on 26 December 1859 to Alexander H. Stephens of Georgia, who later served as Vice President of the Confederate States of America, "We are all at sea here; [there is] no organization of the House and no appreciation of the real state of the times by our friends in either house." But the Republicans could not elect a Speaker, either, and when they pushed in mid-January 1860 to elect a speaker by a plurality vote rather than a majority vote, a move which failed, the crisis deepened. In a vain attempt to elect a more moderate figure instead of a radical abolitionist, Rep. Roger Atkinson Pryor, Democrat of Virginia, recommended that the House select either Thomas Corwin of Ohio or a newcomer to the body - then in his first term - such as William Pennington of New Jersey. But Pryor chastised Republicans as being unable to support these candidates because they didn't want to just win, but to beat the Democrats:

> *Your purpose is not only to vanquish us, but to degrade us...Your purpose is to impart the sting of personal insult to our defeat...No, gentlemen of the Opposition; if you are lovers of the Union, you must take down this candidate of yours [Sherman]; for I tell you, in all candor, that the election of the honorable member from Ohio will intensify and inflame and propagate that extraordinary state of agitation and resentment that now prevails everywhere through the slaveholding States.*

At the time Pryor said this, it was assumed that Senator William Henry Seward of New York, considered - at least in the South - as a radical abolitionist - would win the Republican presidential nomination in 1860 and, if he won, southerners were threatening to storm out of the Union. Pryor likened Sherman's victory with a potential Seward presidency; that a Speaker John Sherman would be "a dismal vaticination ["a prophesy, or the act of prophesying"] of the ultimate catastrophe in the election of William H. Seward."

Fearing that Sherman's election would set off a series of events that could well destroy the Union, the Republicans in the House lost their nerve and began to distance themselves from the Ohioan, although on the 39th ballot he still remained in the race. Historian Victor Hicken, writing in 1960, explained, "After Smith's failure to carry the House, both parties lay almost exhausted; the Democrats were divided as well. The Republicans were the first to pull themselves off the floor, throwing their support to another old-long Whig from New Jersey, William Pennington."

In quick order, the party turned to freshman Pennington of New Jersey. Pennington, 63 years old, had served as Governor of New Jersey (1837-42), and had been tapped by Republicans to run for the House seat in 1858 because he was considered a moderate on the issue of slavery who would not intimidate Democrats and others in the opposing camp. In fact, Pennington actively opposed the Republican plank of trying to outlaw the interstate slave trade as well as the selling of slaves in the District of Columbia. Now, however, Pennington was selected as the "compromise" candidate for the speakership - in effect, the only man either party could get through the appalling election crisis. On the 44th and final ballot, Pennington received 117 votes and the majority, and was declared the Speaker-elect. One vote for the New Jerseyan came from Rep. Henry Winter Davis, a member of the American Party from Maryland; he had wanted to vote for his fellow Know-Nothing, William Smith of North Carolina, but realized that Smith could not win and held out until Smith withdrew. Once this was done, Davis sided with Pennington, a vote that put the Republican into the Speaker's chair. Davis was hailed as a hero in the North - the Chicago *Press & Tribune* said that "his boldness and his elevation above mere partisan considerations are worthy of all praise" - and denounced as a villain in the South - the *Baltimore Sun* called his vote for Pen-

nington "a foul calumny, a reckless libel." Pennington's speakership is considered a failure by historians; Rep. Martin Jenkins Crawford, Democrat of Georgia, wrote to Alexander H. Stephens on the new Speaker, mocking him "old Miss Pennington."

Democrats feared the election of any Republican - historians believed that it would unleash a series of investigations into the administration of President James Buchanan. However, as historian Mary Parker Follett explained, "It is interesting to notice, in the account of the proceedings of that day, that as soon as Mr. Pennington was really elected the demeanor of the Democrats changed, and they became at once respectful and civil in order to gain what little they could from a hostile Speaker." She added, in a side note, that

...it was noted during the swearing-in of members that such fire-eaters as [Lucius Quintus Cincinnatus] Lamar [Democrat of Mississippi], [John Jones] McRae [Democrat of Mississippi], [Martin Jenkins] Crawford, [George Smith] Houston [Democrat of Alabama], and [Laurence Massillon] Keitt [Democrat of South Carolina] were especially respectful in their greetings of the Speaker, as they advanced to take the constitutional oath, the warm pressure of the hand and the profound bow seeming to say, "Governor, we hope to have conspicuous places on your committees."

For the fourth time in just twenty years, the fight for the speakership had been long, prolonged, protracted, and measured the split in the Congress that mirrored the divide in the country that was quickly becoming a huge gash in the fabric of the Union. Less than a year after William Pennington won election as Speaker, the southern states would begin a proceeding of secession from the Union, leading to Civil War and hundreds of thousands of deaths. For the House of Representatives, however, the fights for the Speaker's chair would never again come down to who supported slavery and who did not. In fact, only one more time, in 1923, would a speakership election be anything more than a mere formality. Next, we examine that election, the last time the mystery over who would serve as Speaker at the start of a new Congress would ever arise.

Speaker Frederick H. Gillett - 1923

Just months before the death of President Warren G. Harding, the House met for the first session of the Sixty-eighth Congress (1923-25). As opposed to the other Speaker elections discussed in this essay, when that Congress convened there already was a sitting Speaker - Frederick H. Gillett, of Massachusetts, had first been elected to the chair in the Sixty-sixth Congress (1919-21), and, when the Sixty-eighth Congress opened, he was prepared to sit for his third two-year term as Speaker. From all outward appearances, this election should have gone off as a mere formality: Republicans held a 225-207 majority, with two members from the Farmer-Labor Party (the Democrats in Minnesota are now elected under this label rather than the Democratic Party) and 1 Socialist. The Democrats had won a huge number of seats in the 1922 mid-term election, gaining 76 seats that cut a 302-131 GOP majority in the Sixty-seventh Congress (1921-23). Still, the Republicans would be able to organize the House with Gillett as the Speaker. At least, on paper, that is the way things would have been.

But one has to remember that from 1910 until nearly the end of the 1920s, the Republican Party split between old-time conservatives and Progressives, with the latter group sometimes siding with Democrats in their moves to push legislation. In 1910, these Progressives helped to overthrow Speaker of the House Joseph G. Cannon; in 1912, they split the Republican Party's presidential campaign and allowed Democrat Woodrow Wilson to win the White House, which, in 1916, he was able to retain. In 1920, many Progressives returned to the party fold, allowing Senator Warren G. Harding to be elected President.

In 1924, however, the same liberal Republicans who now considered themselves as Progressives desired to help elect Senator Robert LaFollette of Wisconsin to the White House. Harding's death in 1923 - and allegations of massive fraud and corruption in his administration - led these Progressives to try to remove Harding's successor, Calvin Coolidge, from the party ticket and replace him with LaFollette. When that move failed, LaFollette ran as a Progressive on a third-party ticket. But, we are getting ahead of ourselves here, because to understand

1924 we have to look at 1922, and the mid-term elections held that year, and examine why a Republican Party that lost 76 seats in the House but retained a majority could not re-elect the sitting Speaker. And that leads us to our story, which starts when that Sixty-eighth Congress convened in Washington, D.C. on 3 December 1923.

In the Senate, the Progressives challenged the power of Albert Cummins of Iowa, the Senate President *pro tem* and chairman of the Committee on Interstate Commerce. When they could not remove Cummins, the Progressives sided with Democrats to elect as the committee chairman "Cotton Ed" Smith of South Carolina, who thus became the only Democrat in U.S. Senate history to chair a committee in a Republican-controlled Senate. The House situation was, in many ways, worse for the GOP: some 60 Progressives held the balance of power, including nearly the entire Wisconsin delegation. This group met on 30 November 1923 and selected Rep. John Mandt Nelson of Wisconsin as their leader. Nelson told the group that they had to stick together to get their program enacted, even if it meant halting the election of Gillett as Speaker. "We are not going to walk on a pathway of roses," Nelson thundered in what was called a "stirring address." He continued, "We are going to be sifted as wheat. We are going to be tried as gold in a furnace. All real progressives will be put to the acid test."

When the voting got underway for Speaker, Gillett, the nominated candidate of the GOP, received 190 votes and the majority; Henry Allen Cooper of Wisconsin, the candidate of the Progressives, received only 15 votes. However, other Republicans, including Edward John King, Magne Fred Michaelson, and Frank R. Reid, all of Illinois, and William Francis James and Roy Orchard Woodruff of Michigan, all put their names into contention as opposed to Gillett. However, the fight over the speakership was more an exercise in getting prizes for the Progressives than in electing their own Speaker; in total, over two days and eight ballots, they held out until the majority of Republicans acceded to their demands. This finally happened when several Progressives met with the new Majority Leader, Nicholas Longworth (who would be elected Speaker in the Sixty-ninth Congress) - these included John Mandt Nelson, Roy O. Woodruff of Michigan, and Fiorello

La Guardia of New York - and got an agreement to debate a revision of the rules of the House while, at the same time, getting a seat on the Rules Committee for Nelson. When the deal had been hammered out, Henry T. Rainey of Illinois - also, to be elected Speaker in the Seventy-third Congress (1933-35) - praised Longworth for maneuvering the House debate over Gillett "between the Scylla of progressive Republicanism...and the Charybdis of conservative Republicanism...There is not a scratch on the ship. The paint is absolutely intact."

Historian Robert R. Lopez, in a 1998 dissertation, agreed that the split inside the GOP came about because of a lack of reform rather than differences over policy. As he explained,

> The most famous attempt at structural reform occurred during the first session of the 68th Congress. In the opening days, Republican Progressive members joined Democrats in threatening to delay the re-election of Mr. Gillett as Speaker unless several rules changes were instituted. The leadership, realizing [that] it did not have the votes to overrule the Progressives, agreed to a revision of the rules to be reported in the House in a month. On January 14, 1924, the House agreed to the following changes[:] the discharge petition, a motion to force a committee to report a bill to the floor, now only required a majority vote (as opposed to a two-thirds vote). Reports from the Committee on Rules could be called up by any member designated by the Committee, with or without the approval of the chairman. Lastly, non-germane amendments were allowed on the floor. All of these rules changes were designed to weaken the leadership structure and permit a more open legislative environment.

In an afternote, when Gillett stepped down from the Speaker's chair for the final time at the end of that controversial Sixty-eighth Congress, he told the members, "I would rather be speaker of the House than hold any other position in the world."

As with the aforementioned elections that we discussed in this essay, the 1923 vote, despite being the most recent of the group, is as blurred out of history as the others. No matter what work is referred to, no matter the few sources on Congress that are consulted, all appear to either mention Gillett's 1923 re-election in passing or not at all. A 1988 work on the history of Congress mentions Gillett's successor, Nicholas Longworth, who served as Speaker from 1925 to 1931, but again neglects Gillett and the 1923 contest. A 1981 article by historians Joseph Cooper and David W. Brady on the U.S. House from Cannon to Rayburn is just one example. Although it mentions the period after Cannon (and ignores the speakership of Champ Clark, but that is an argument for another day and another essay), the "1920s" are lumped into one paragraph, after which the text switches first to the "1930s" and the rise of the Democrats, right to the speakership of Sam Rayburn. It is almost as if there was an unidentifiable interregnum between Cannon and Rayburn, from 1911 to 1940. Of course no such thing happened, but you wouldn't know it from this source and others. It is why finding information on the Speakers and even the elections that made them the Speaker is extremely challenging.

Since the controversial 1923 contest in which Gillett was selected as Speaker, the House has been able to elect a Speaker from the majority party without any debate or discussion.

Speaker pro tempore Samuel Sullivan Cox

The register of those who served as Speaker of the House do not usually list the name of Samuel S. Cox, only because he was never elected Speaker and served during several periods as Speaker *pro tempore*. Known as "Sunset" Cox because of an editorial he wrote as a newspaperman, he represented Columbus, Ohio, in the U.S. House in the 1850s before losing the seat in 1864 and moving to New York, where he was elected by Tammany Hall to the House and served in that body for nearly the remainder of his life in two separate tenures. Although not noted for any specific major legislation bearing his name, he was remembered by his colleagues in the House for his fairness as Speaker and his handling of debate.

Cox was born in Zanesville, Ohio, on September 30, 1824, the son of Ezekiel Taylor Cox, who served as the Clerk of Supreme Court of Ohio, and his wife Maria Matilda (née Sullivan). Samuel Cox was educated at Ohio University and at Brown University in Providence, Rhode Island, graduating from the latter institution in 1846. He then studied the law, and was admitted to the Ohio bar in 1849 and opened a practice in Zanesville. In 1853, Cox left the law and entered the field of journalism when he purchased the *Columbus Statesman*, a newspaper in Columbus, Ohio, and served as the journal's editor until 1854. He had married Julia Buckingham in 1849; the couple had no children. While writing for the paper, he wrote a column about a sunset and its effect on him; the piece won him the sobriquet "Sunset" Cox.

Years in Congress
In 1855, Cox left Ohio when he was appointed as the Secretary to the American diplomatic legation to Peru, but he returned within a year. In 1856, Cox was elected to a seat in the U.S. House of Representatives, entering the Thirty-fifth Congress (1857-59) and remaining in that body until March 3, 1865, during which he served as the chairman of the Committee on Revolutionary Claims (Thirty-fifth Congress). During Cox's first term in the House, the most important matter facing the Congress and its members, as well as the entire nation, was that of slavery. At the time, Kansas was

tearing itself apart over the issue of entering the Union as a free or slave state; Cox, a Democrat, broke with his party and his president, James Buchanan, over the issue.

Taking to the House on December 10, 1857, the first speech in the renovated House chamber, Cox argued that the people of Kansas alone must decide what kind of state constitution they wanted. "I propose now to nail against the door, at the threshold of this Congress, my theses," Cox spoke, almost taking the role of the reformer in the mold of Martin Luther and the church door at Wittenberg. "When the proper time comes I will defend them, whether from the assaults of political friend or foe. I would fain be silent, sir, here and now. But silence, which is said to be as 'harmless as a rose's breath,' may be perilous as a pestilence." He then went on to call for a "hands-off" policy by Congress on the decision-making process in Kansas. "I maintain...that domestic institutions mean all which are local, not national - State, not Federal. It means that and only - that always. [I maintain] that the people were to be left perfectly free to establish or abolish slavery, as well as to form and regulate their other institutions." In 1864, at the height of the Civil War and in a year when Abraham Lincoln was winning re-election to a second term in the White House, Cox, a Democrat, was defeated in his own campaign for a fourth term in the House. Moving to New York City after he left the Congress, Cox opened a law practice there and appeared to be finished with a political career.

However, in 1868, Cox ran for and was elected to a seat in the U.S. House of Representatives from New York - becoming one of only a handful of members of Congress to be elected from more than one state - and he took his seat in the Forty-first Congress (1869-71). He was re-elected to the Forty-second Congress (1871-73). In 1872, attempting to run for a third term in this seat, Cox received the nominations of both the Democrats in New York and the Liberal Republicans, a breakaway faction of the Republican Party opposed in 1872 to a second presidential term for President Ulysses S. Grant, whose administration had been mired in corruption. Despite having these two nominations, Cox was defeated, although he did run well ahead of the Liberal Republican national ticket in votes. During this second tenure in the House, Cox served on the committee which investigated the reign of terror of the Ku Klux Klan in the American South, then under harsh Reconstruction measures.

Following the death of Rep. James Brooks of New York on April 30, 1873, a special election was held to fill the vacancy for the remainder of the Forty-third Congress (1873-75). Cox was nominated as the Democrat for that seat, and he was elected, taking his seat in the Congress he would have been elected to had he won in 1872. Cox remained in the House during this third tenure through the Forty-ninth Congress (1883-85), until his resignation on May 20, 1885. He served as the chairman of the Committee on Banking and Currency (Forty-fourth Congress), the Committee on the Census (Forty-sixth Congress), the Committee on Foreign Affairs (Forty-sixth Congress), and the Committee on Naval Affairs (Forty-eighth Congress). While in Congress during these three tenures, Cox penned several works, including a collection of his thoughts and speeches on different subjects he debated in the House, titled *Eight Years in Congress, from 1857 to 1865* (1865), *Puritanism in Politics* (1868), and a two-volume work on *Union, Disunion, and Reunion: Three Decades of Federal Legislation, 1855-1885* (1885). He also authored *The Buckeye Abroad* (1851).

Legacy as Speaker pro tempore

In the speakership contest in the Forty-fourth Congress (1875-77) in December 1875, Cox received 31 votes on the first ballot, 21 on the second, and 7 on the third before fellow Democrat Michael C. Kerr of Indiana was finally elected as Speaker. But Kerr was seriously ill with a form of tuberculosis, which would take his life after less than a year as Speaker. For most of the Forty-fourth Congress, Kerr was absent for long stretches of time due to the deterioration of his health, and Cox served as Speaker *pro tempore*,

from the Latin "for the time being" - a person who sits in an office in a temporary position. Thus, Cox was never formally elected as Speaker, but an examination of the records of the Forty-fourth Congress, including debates and legislation, show the name of the Speaker more often to be that of Samuel S. Cox and not Michael C. Kerr.

Although Cox, during his entire congressional career, attached himself to no particular piece of legislation, some biographies mention that he "framed the new census law, and was the author of the plan of apportionment adopted in that session (1877-78)." Cox was considered by his political allies and opponents a fair arbiter as Speaker *pro tempore* and a competent debater. Historian De Alva Stanwood Alexander noted that Speaker James G. Blaine liked to hand the Speaker's gavel to Cox when Blaine served as Speaker in the Forty-first (1869-71), Forty-second (1871-73), and Forty-third (1873-75) Congresses; and that Cox often presided over and conducted lively and entertaining debates on the House floor.

Rep. Thomas B. Reed of Maine, later to serve as Speaker, called Cox "a whole skirmish line." Criticizing Republicans in Maine, who represented a state with a stern prohibition law, Cox stated that they drank "a great deal of whiskey clandestinely." Reed, from Maine, replied, "When my friend from New York takes it, it does not remain clandestine very long." However, aside from his name being listed as Speaker during that session, little can be found on any accomplishment of Cox as Speaker.

Further Reading:

Cox, Samuel Sullivan, *Eight Years in Congress, from 1857 to 1865* (New York: D. Appleton and Company, 1865).

Lindsey, David, *"Sunset" Cox: Irrepressible Democrat* (Detroit: Wayne State University Press, 1959).

Primary Documents: Articles, Letters, and Speeches

John Rutledge Writes of the Election of
Theodore Sedgwick as Speaker, 1799

The following letter was penned by John Rutledge, Jr. (1766-1819), Federalist representative from South Carolina, who was a chief contender for Speaker of the House of Representatives in the Sixth Congress (1799-1801), but lost on the second ballot to Theodore Sedgwick, Federalist of Massachusetts. Written to "The Right Reverend Bishop Smith" of Charleston, South Carolina (referring to Robert Smith, who was Rutledge's father-in-law), the letter discussed the backroom party politics that gave the Speaker's chair to Sedgwick and denied it to Rutledge. Dated 3 December 1799, just days after Sedgwick's election, it was mailed to Bishop Smith on 5 December. The text, with all of its typographical and spelling errors, is hereby reproduced exactly as it was written by Rutledge.

❧

Philadelphia
3 December, 1799

My dear Sir

Both houses of Congress met yesterday - Mr Sedgwick is our Speaker, and we are to receive the Presidents speech this day at noon. The election of a Speaker puzzled and perplexed the federal part of the House more than any of the difficulties it has heretofore had to struggle with. The southern and middle States Delegates thought, that as the government was very much in eastern hands, and as there had been one Speaker from New England[1], and two from the middle States[2], it would be wise and proper to elect a southern gentleman to the chair, and they nominated me. The eastern Delegates acquiesced in the policy of the measure, but said they were pledged to support the election of Mr Sedgwick by a variety of considerations which they mentioned, and which are too lengthy to enumerate to you at present. The opposition, finding a division among us, hoped it would enable them to elect a Mr

Macon[3] and laid their plans accordingly. The friends of government had three meetings on this subject without coming to any determination - the eastern men were very tenacious of Mr Sedgwick, and the southern of myself - but as all the delegates from the east were present, and not two thirds of the southern representation, I found I could not obtain the election without having two more votes than my friends could calculate upon, and rather than hazard having Mr Macon Speaker, I requested General Marshall, who called on me in his way to the fourth meeting of our party, (and which took place but an hour before the meeting of Congress) to say - that if our eastern friends had not the same view he and others had of the political expediency of taking a Speaker from the representation of the southern section of the union, and persisted in their wishes and endeavours to have Mr Sedgwick elected, it was my desire (as far as it was a question about myself) that my friends should unite his, and have him elected handsomely. To mention, at the same time, that several of the opposition members despairing of being able to elect Mr Macon, and (on account of his irritating habits) disliking Mr Sedgwick more than myself, had signified their desire of voting for me under the idea that with the southern suffrages and theirs I should be elected by a great majority, but that I had resisted this proposition, because in my opinion a station of honor could not be honorable to me unless honorably obtained, and that I would not accept public favors *unless proferred by my friends*. This communication, as you will readily believed, delighted the Yankeys - it dispelled at once all their difficulties - they were loud in my praises, and offered to pledge themselves to place me in the Chair when Sedgwick should leave it - but General Marshall insisted that nothing of the sort might be understood, for Mr. Rutledge and his friends would not have it supposed he had *made a bargain* for the chair. This arrangement was concluded so late in the day that the two Georgia Delegates, who came

Source: John Rutledge, Jr., to Bishop Robert Smith, 3 December 1799, Box 1, Folder 8, *The John Rutledge Papers*, Collection #948, Southern Historical Collection, The Wilson Library, University of North Carolina at Chapel Hill.

See also page 21

into the House after it was formed, did not notified of it, voted for me, which presented Sedgwicks
being elected at the first ballot. We have nothing
very late from Europe, and I can not yet tell you
what kind of a session we shall have - our prospects
are much brightened by the new Members we have
among us - some of them are men of talents and
most of them governmental - Finding in the eastern
States a great confusion of ideas respecting the
Pinckney family - that some people supposed the essays published under the signature of the "So
Carolina Planter" were written by General
Pinckney, and that many believed him to be the
brother of Charles, I though it expedient to give the
publ[ic] some biographical sketches of that family
and did so in the Newport gazette - they will be re-
published here this evening I expect, and you shall
receive a copy of them by this or the succeeding
post. I have not yet seen Mr Stoddert[4] but will to-
morrow, and speak to him about John Smiths going
to Sea. Pray give my love to the Boys - good God my
dear friend how lucky, truly lucky, they were in not
going with Hamilton[5]! They had a very narrow escape from a dreadful sort of passage, and you from a
great deal of anxiety and uneasiness it would have
occasioned you. I request you will remember me to
all our friends and believe me to be

Your affectionate Son
and sincere friend
J. Rutledge Junior

Footnotes:

[1] Rutledge refers to Speaker Jonathan Trumbull, who served as
Speaker in the Second Congress (1791-93).

[2] This refers to Frederick A.C. Muhlenberg of Pennsylvania, who
served as Speaker in the First (1789-91) and Third (1793-95) Congresses, and Jonathan Dayton of New Jersey, who served as Speaker in
the Fourth (1795-97) and Fifth (1797-99) Congresses.

[3] Referring to Nathaniel Macon, Democratic-Republican (later moving to become a Jacksonian, then returning to become a Democratic-Republican) of North Carolina, who would serve as Speaker
from the Seventh (1801-03) through the Ninth (1805-07) Congresses.

[4] Referring to Benjamin Stoddert, who served as the first Secretary of
the Navy, 1798-1801.

[5] Alexander Hamilton (1755-1801), the first Secretary of the Treasury
(1789-95).

Theodore Sedgwick's Letter:
"To the Electors of the First Western District," 1800

On June 4, 1800, Speaker of the House Theodore Sedgwick wrote the following letter to his constituents, after it had been announced that he would not seek re-election to his seat in Congress and was retiring from public life. All of the original spellings containing in the letter have been retained.

◈

Fellow-Citizens!

When, by the solicitation of my friends, at the last election, I was indicted, once more to devote my feeble services to my Country; it was known that retirement was my wish, and I, then, declared a hope that, thereafter, confidence with which you have so long honored me, might be reposed in some one else. To repeat this hope, and to take of you, as a public man, a final and affectionate leave, are the objects of this address.

I have long at the unsolicited, and frequently, by me, undesired appointment of my Fellow-Citizens devoted myself to their service. The honors which I have received, as the testimony of their regard, have been dear to my heart; for they have never been the result of flattery or processions on my part. The former is always an evidence of a man or dishonest mind - the latter, in my opinion, should also, be carefully avoided, by public men, expecting public favors - They may, however, without blemish, be made by one who seeks the shade of private life, and especially, if done with an honest intention, of promoting the welfare of his country.

The former part of my life was, in union with my countrymen, devoted to effect a revolution most singular, and the most important, which, probably, the world has ever known; the latter to render that revolution truly beneficial.

To men enlightened, as are the Inhabitants of New-England, it need not be observed, that inestimably precious as is liberty, it can, in no way, be secured,

but by the protection of government - a government of sufficient energy to control the inordinate exercise of passions directed to self-gratification. This energy must be the result either of actual force, or of public confidence. The latter is the basis of our government. It is the only foundation on which it rests. Remove that foundation and it inevitably, tumbles into ruins. The principle is, that the men elected to rule, in the manner proscribed by the Constitution, combined as their interest is, and inseparably united, with that of the people, will, in the public conduct, intend to promote the general welfare; and that they will not wantonly violate their duty, and thereby destroy, with their own, the public happiness. It implies not perfection of wisdom, but honesty of intention. That liberty which is valuable to a virtuous mind, is security in the use and enjoyment of our property, and in the performance of all actions, not injurious to others; and it is obvious, that a community which could command the whole physical force of the nation, for the security of every individual of which it is composed, from an entire affection and confidence in rulers of their own choice, would possess prodigious advantages over all others.

In many ages and countries, experiments have been made, under various modifications, to establish, on this principle, institutions honorable and beneficial to mankind. But, alas! the attempts of the wise and virtuous to perpetrate them, have been defeated, by the wicked arts of the profligate and ambitious. Misrepresentation and falshood [sic], processions of ardent attachment to popular pretentions, gross adulation, mean cringing to unprincipled demagogues, flattering turbulent passions, taking advantage of ignorance and inflaming prejudice, have been the means, while power, dominion and tyranny were the ends. Hence it is that governments of confidence have given place to those of force. And unless our countrymen shall be inspired with wisdom, the predictions that our republican projects will, also vanish, will be verified; and we shall add an-

Source: "From the Western Star. To the Electors of the first Western District," *Connecticut Courant*, June 23, 1800, 1.
See also page 21.

other sad example to those which delusion has plunged in ruin.

It is now eleven years since the present government has commenced its operations. During this time I will not say that all of its measures have been perfect, for it has been conducted by human agents - I will, however, declare it has not erred from intention - it has committed no acts of injustice or oppression - it has never wantonly imposed any public burden. On the contrary, in the imposition of those it deemed indispensable, it has fought every alleviation in its power. It received the charge of our public affairs, at a time when, by the imbecility of our former system, the reputation which our nation had acquired, by its glorious and successful struggle for freedom and independence, was almost annihilated; when confidence public and private was almost destroyed; when states had become the rivals of each other; and legislative hostility was not only declared, but vigorously prosecuted by them; when our federative importance was derided and insulted, and we were, soft becoming, not indeed in name, but in fact, the colonies of the maritime nations of Europe; and when loaded as the people were with taxes, and universally complaining of their weight and burden, instead of a diminution of the debt, the interest accumulated, and unpaid was nearly the amount of one half of the principal.

Receiving the charge of our national interests under these circumstances - having a new and untried system to put into motion - having provision to make for a large debt, the price of our freedom and independence; for which the former government had been found inadequate - and having by its own wisdom, without the aid of precedent by which to regulate its course, to devise the means of executing a continuation, which was intended "to form a more perfect union, establish justice, ensure domestic tranquility, provide for the common defence [sic], promote the general welfare, and secure the blessings of liberty to ourselves and our posterity" - surely the men on whom this mighty task was devolved, had a right to expect, of a generous people, a candid construction of their honest intentions. A just review of the effects which have been produced, by the progress of their labors, will determine how far they are entitled to indulgence or approbation.

The government has had to contend with difficulties which were neither foreseen nor expected; for who could have believed, that in less than ten years, we should have had to defray the expence [sic] of suppression two insurrections, raised by the artful misrepresentations of wicked men? Yet this to the disgrace of our country, has been the case; we have been obliged to sacrifice treasure to purchase peace with the powers of Barbary, and to redeem our citizens, there from slavery we have been at great charge in sustaining a long and expensive Indian war and in the protection of our frontiers; we have suffered immensely, by the plunder of our commerce; we have fortified our ports and harbors; we have created a very considerable navy. Credit, public and private, is restored. Our navigation is infinitely extended - our tonnage now, exceeding that of Great-Britain; at the commencement of the present reign. Yet our debt at the beginning of the present year was nearly four millions less than at that of 1791, when we first began the payment of the interest. But what is infinitely more dear to humanity, under circumstances of extreme irritation, such has been the temper, the moderation and the magnanimity of the government, that peace has been preserved, and we have kept ourselves separated, from the fences of horror which are desolating Europe. It is, too, soothing to the honest pride of an American, that all men, our own degenerate citizens, and jacobin [sic] renegades from other countries among us excepting, speak in terms of respect and honor of the conduct of our government. Is not this, my Fellow-Citizens, when it can with truth be added, that it all has been effected without one act of tyranny of oppression, a glorious reverse of our situation in 1789? Yet have not all these things secured to the government the affections of the people, or itself against the malignant enterprizes [sic] of its enemies. I speak now of New-England; that is, I trust, essentially, found. But at this moment it is a doubt, whether, throughout the nation, the friends or enemies of the government, are the most numerous. How has this been effected?

To give a full answer to that question would require an history [sic], in detail, of the opposition, with all its windings and turnings, from the meeting of the federal convention, to the present day. Suffice it to say, that the party, unsteady in all things else, in their attention to two objects, have been, undeviatingly, pertinacious[1] - in their malignant slander of the characters of those whom they believed possessed the public confidence; and in their misrepresentation of the measures of the government. As an instance of the first, we cannot but remember, the great, the glorious WASHINGTON, the pride of our country - the ornament of human nature. Him they represented as ambitious, altho' he never fought, but always shunned public office - as the tool of Great-Britain, altho' he had severed America from her empire - As a man of no religion, altho' no one was more respectfully observant of religious duties. In short for his most eminent virtues they charged against him, the opposite vices. At the same time they have directed the most gross and slanderous abuse against all his friends, and those whom they deemed the influential supporters of his administration. With regard to the measures of the Government, if its enemies may be credited, it has performed no one meritorious act; but its whole conduct has been mischievous. Endless would be the talk to expose and correct all the vile slanders which have been wantonly lavished on it; nor is the attempt necessary - instances enough will occur, to the recollection of every man, who feels for the honor of his country, or perceives his own interest to be connected with the preservation of the Constitution. It will be sufficient to say, that the government has been charged with conduct, faithless as it respected our foreign connections - insidious and traiterous [sic] as it related to the domestic administration. By these means alarms and suspicions have been created; a Government, I will not say perfect, but honest and patriotic, has been slandered, and the effects, for why should not the truth be de-

clared? have become extensive and alarming. Your danger, which is great, tho' not desperate, I have thought it my duty, among the last acts of my public life, to proclaim to you. God grant that I may be mistaken in the magnitude of this danger; but I do most solemnly declare, that my conviction is perfect, that it cannot be averted, but by more extensively, than at present, known in this part of the United States.

In returning to the scenes of private life, after more than twenty years constant employment in public ones, I will cheerfully submit to, and, as my feeble means may enable me support those systems of government which I have advanced.

As a private man, I indulge the hope of enjoying the delights of free and local intercourse - and if in the pursuit of political objects, which I have deemed important, I have said or done aught, to the injury of the feelings of any honest man, it will, I hope, be forgiven, with the same facility, that any supposed wrong, which I may have received, will be forgotten.

That you, my friends, may be served with as much fidelity and more success than has fallen to my lot; and that our Country may be happy, prosperous and free, is my sincere and ardent prayer.

THEODORE SEDGWICK,
Stockbridge, June 4, 1800

Footnotes:

[1] Stubborn.

Excerpt from 1903 Biography of Nathaniel Macon on being Elected Speaker, 1801

Few sources document the speakership of Nathaniel Macon of North Carolina, who served as Speaker in the Seventh (1801-03), Eighth (1803-05), and Ninth (1805-07) Congresses. Even the few biographies of Macon that were written, all in the nineteenth century, cover his speakership within one single page. The only work that appears to have gone into any depth whatsoever on this period is William E. Dodd's 1903 biography, *The Life of Nathaniel Macon.* The following, a small excerpt from that work, documents the start of Macon's speakership, starting with his initial election to the chair on December 1801.

❧

Congress assembled promptly that December, and on the first day of their session and on the first ballot Nathaniel Macon was elected Speaker. Schouler[1], in his history of the United States, says Macon "was a man of independent views and upright character, of frugal tendencies in public and private, not always in full sympathy with his party, but differing dispassionately when he differed at all; and so constantly re-elected, as in later years to be called the Father of the House." These characteristics were in the main the cause of his election to the speakership. He had developed in Congress more of the character of a judge than of a party leader and a wise judge, too, and as has been noted in a former chapter, he knew the history of the House, its precedents in all important measures; he had served ten years, had seldom been absent from his seat and had taken a decided stand in every debate which had come up during those years; he had done good work on various committees and had but once in his ten years in Congress been called to order by the Speaker; besides, he had the confidence of the President and consequently the support of the great Virginia delegation, especially that of the tall, sallow youth from up the Roanoke, John Randolph. On the following day the new Speaker appointed young Randolph chairman of the Committee on Ways and Means. With Jefferson as President, Macon as Speaker of the House and Randolph at the head of the most important committee in Congress, genuine Republican measures and manners were sure to have the right of and Randolph at the head of the most important committee in Congress, genuine Republican measures and manners were sure to have the right of way in Washington; and the Republican political machine was in fine order, well oiled and ready for the fierce onslaughts, which every one expected. One head, one mind dominated that Congress and several succeeding ones, and for the time being there was smooth sailing for the ship of state.

Footnotes:

[1] See James Schouler, *History of the United States, Under the Constitution* (Washington, D.C.: W.H. & O.H. Morrison; two volumes, 1880), II:20.

Source: Dodd, William E., *The Life of Nathaniel Macon* (Raleigh, North Carolina: Edwards & Broughton, Printers and Binders, 1903), 172-73.

See also page 27

Langdon Cheves's Remarks on being Elected Speaker
upon Resignation of Henry Clay, 19 January 1814

After being named as one of the negotiators of a truce with Great Britain over the War of 1812 - a conflict which he staunchly supported - Speaker of the House Henry Clay resigned as Speaker, allowing for the first speakership change since the start of the Twelfth Congress in 1811. The House then moved to elect his successor: Langdon Cheves of South Carolina. The following, from *The Debates and Proceedings in the Congress of the United States*, contains not only remarks regarding Clay's resignation but the election for his successor and comments by Cheves upon his election.

๛

RESIGNATION OF THE SPEAKER, &c.

The ordinary business of the day having been gone through -

The Speaker addressed the House in the following terms:

'Gentlemen: I have attended you to-day to announce my resignation of the distinguished station in the House with which I have been honored by your kindness. In taking leave of you, gentlemen, I shall be excused for embracing the last occasion to express to you personally my thanks for the frank and liberal support the Chair has experienced at your hands. Wherever I may go, in whatever situation I may be placed, I can never cease to cherish, with the fondest remembrance, the sentiments of esteem and respect with which you have inspired me.'

The Speaker having left the Chair, and it remaining vacant -

Mr. [William] Findlay of Pennsylvania moved that the House come to the following resolution:

Resolved, That the thanks of this House be presented to Henry Clay, in testimony of their approbation of his conduct in arduous and important duties assigned to him as Speaker of the House.

The question having been put on this resolution by the Clerk, it was decided in the affirmative - for the resolution, 144, against it, 9.

A motion was then made to adjourn, and negatived - for adjournment, 70, against it, 90.

On motion of Mr. [Elisha Reynolds] Potter of Rhode Island, the House proceeded to the choice of a Speaker.

Messrs. [Nicholas Ruxton] Moore [Republican of Maryland], [Richard Menton] Johnson [Democrat-Republican of Kentucky], and [Laban] Wheaton [Federalist of Massachusetts], were appointed tellers; and having counted the ballots, Mr. Moore reported, that the whole number of votes given in being one hundred and sixty-five, eighty-three were necessary to a choice; that of these votes there were -

For Langdon Cheves	94
Felix Grundy	59
Scattering	12

and that Langdon Cheves, having a majority of votes, was duly elected Speaker of the House.

Mr. Cheves was accordingly conducted to the Chair, and made his acknowledgments to the House in the following words:

'Gentlemen: I thank you for the flattering and distinguished honor you have conferred upon me. The best acknowledgment I can make of the gratitude which I profoundly feel, will be expressed in the exertion of every faculty I posses, to prove that your favor is not entirely unmerited. I am aware of the

Source: *The Debates and Proceedings in the Congress of the United States; with an Appendix, Containing Important State Papers and Public Documents, and All the Laws of a Public Nature; with a Copious Index. Thirteenth Congress - First Session. Comprising the Period from May 24, 1813, to August 2, 1814, Inclusive. Compiled from Authentic Materials* (Washington: Printed and Published at Gales and Seaton, 1854), 1057-58.

See also page 47

importance of the station to which you have elevated
me, and of the difficult nature of the duties which it
imposes; a difficulty to discharge them with reputation, not a little increased by the great ability with
which they have been executed by the gentleman
who has just descended from the Chair; but with
your support I shall not despair. Err, I undoubtedly often shall; and when my errors shall be calculated to
affect, in the smallest degree, the interests of the
House or the nation, I shall court your correction,
and submit with cheerfulness and pleasure to your
authority; but if they be immaterial, as frequent differences of opinion between the House and its presiding officers can add nothing to its dignity, and may
diminish its usefulness, I shall ask, what I fear I shall
too often need, your kind indulgence.'

The oath to support the Constitution of the United
States was then administered to him by Mr. Findley,
one of the Representatives from the State of Pennsylvania; and then the House adjourned.

Andrew Stevenson Addresses the House of Representatives on his Election as Speaker, 1827

When the Twentieth Congress (1827-29) convened in Washington, D.C. on 3 December 1827, the forces who backed President Andrew Jackson controlled the House, 113 seats to 100 for those who supported former President John Quincy Adams, defeated for re-election by Jackson in the contentious 1828 presidential election. On the first ballot, Rep. Andrew Stevenson of Virginia received 104 votes and was declared the elected Speaker; former Speaker John W. Taylor (who served as Speaker in the Nineteenth Congress) received 94 votes, and former Speaker Philip P. Barbour (who served as Speaker in the Seventeenth [1821-23]) Congress received four votes. Three additional votes were spread among differing candidates. Conducted to the Speaker's chair and given the oath, Stevenson delivered the customary remarks to the members of the full House:

≈

"Gentlemen: In accepting the distinguished honor which you have been please to confer upon me, I am penetrated with feelings of profound respect, and the deepest gratitude, and I receive it as the most flattering testimony of your confidence and favor. The office of Speaker of this House has been justly considered one of high and exalted character - arduous, in relation to the abilities necessary to its execution, and severely responsible and laborious. Its honor is to be measured by no ordinary standard of value. The individual, therefore, who shall fill this chair to his own reputation, and the advantage of the House, must be distinguished alike by knowledge, integrity, and diligence; he should possess an impartiality which secures confidence; a dignity that commands respect; and a temper and affability that disarm contention. From his general character and personal qualities, he must derive a power that will give force to his interpositions, and procure respect for his decisions. He must conciliate the esteem of the enlightened body over whom he presides.

"These, gentlemen, are some of the leading qualifications necessary for this arduous station. I certainly do not possess them. I know my own inability too well to believe that I shall be enabled to meet the expectations of my friends, or discharge the high trust reposed in me, in a matter suitable to its dignity and importance. Bringing with me but little knowledge or experience, I shall, no doubt, often err, and stand in need of your utmost forbearance. Let me hope that, on such occasions, you will scan my conduct with candor and liberality, and extend towards me the same kind indulgence which has heretofore characterized your conduct to the Chair. All that I can promise, will be a devotion of my time to your service, and an independent discharge of my duties in a plain and manly way. My gratitude for a distinction so little merited, shall stimulate me to supply, by diligence and application, what I want in knowledge and ability; and, however I may fail in other respects, I shall endeavor, at least, to entitle myself to the real suffrages of zeal and impartiality.

"I need not admonish you, gentlemen, of the magnitude of your trust, nor to say any thing as to the manner in which it ought to be discharged. We must all be sensible, that, in the deliberations and proceedings of this House, the character and permanent interests of our common country are deeply involved. It was in the organization and purity of this branch of the National Government (endeared to the warmest affections), that our fathers believed they had provided the best security for the principles of free government, and the liberty and happiness of the People. Virtuous, enlightened, and patriotic, this House may justly be regarded as the citadel of American Liberty."

Source: *Journal of the House of Representatives of the United States, Being the First Session of the Twentieth Congress: Begun and Held at the City of Washington, December 3, 1827, and in the Fifty-Second Year of the Independence of the United States* (Washington: Printed at Gales & Seaton, 1827), 8.

See also page 67

"Animated, then, by a virtuous and enlightened zeal, let us endeavor to realize the just expectations of our constituents; and let our proceedings be characterized by a cool and deliberate exertion of the talents, fortitude, and patriotism, of the House, as the surest and best means of sustaining the honor, and promoting the welfare and happiness of our beloved country."

Representative John W. Jones of Virginia
Speaks on Slavery, 1835

On 22 December 1835, the House of Representatives resumed debate over a petition, presented by Rep. George Nixon Briggs, anti-Jacksonian of Massachusetts, to abolish slavery in the District of Columbia. A number of congressmen debated the subject, including John W. Jones, Democrat of Virginia, who later served as Speaker of the House in the Twenty-eighth Congress (1843-45). After Rep. Henry Alexander Wise, Whig of Virginia, stated that the Congress "had no power to legislate on the subject," Jones took to the floor to make his remarks, in which he addressed not just the subject of the petitions being sent to Congress from abolitionists praying for an end to slavery, but the sending by these same abolitionists of pamphlets from northern cities to the South to spread the word and demand the abolition of slavery. Jones, in some of the harshest language ever used to defend slavery, said that "the people of the South held their slaves by a title as secure, by an authority as high and as sacred, as that by which that gentleman held title to his horse, his house, or, to use his own language, 'his place upon that floor.'"

The following, while not a verbatim transcript of his speech, is an encapsulation of his remarks. Because this is a summary and not the actual speech, Jones is sometimes referred to as "Mr. J."

❧

"Mr. JONES, of Virginia, said he did not rise to discuss the merits of the proposition which would be necessarily presented by the petition now offered to the Housel that was what he not only did not desire to do, but it was what he dare not do. He designed briefly to assign the reasons which would induce him to reconsider the vote by which, in a moment of inadvertence, the petition had been sent to the Committee for the District of Columbia; and also to reply to the objections urged by gentlemen to the course now proposed to be adopted in reference to

that, and he hoped all other petitions of the same character. He expressed himself grateful to the gentleman from Pennsylvania [Mr. Ingersoll [1]] for the remarks he had made this morning. But while he rendered this tribute to the good feelings and sympathies of the gentleman, he hoped his own motives would be duly appreciated by him when he said he could never consent to entertain or discuss here the right by which the people of the South held title to their slaves. The great object he desired was, to obtain a direct vote upon these petitions, which continued daily to come in; and that the solicitude he felt on the subject arose from a conviction upon his own mind, that nothing but a direct vote would satisfy the members from the South, or quiet the apprehensions of their constituents; and deeply as he lamented the necessity which rendered it proper, in the opinion of the honorable gentleman, to go into this debate - unwilling as he had always been, so far, to countenance the views of these misguided, deluded, and infatuated men, who for years past had been scattering firebrands among the people of the South, and who, to accomplish their base purposes, were willing not only to aim a deadly blow at their prosperity as a people, but to peril the lives of millions, and endanger the perpetuity of the Union - he felt as though he should be unfaithful to the high trust confided to him if he did not contribute his aid in obtaining a direct vote upon this all-absorbing question.

But a few days ago there seemed to exist a unanimity of sentiment upon this deeply interesting subject which had very seldom manifested itself upon any important question which had come up for consideration before the Representatives of the people; there was then heard from all sides of the House a wish expressed, not only to put down the Abolitionists, but to do it in the most effectual possible manner; and the great point of difficulty was, to determine upon the mode by which it could be most effectually done.

Source: *Register of Debates in Congress, Comprising the Leading Debates and Incidents of the First Session of the Twenty-fouth Congress. Volume XII* (Washington: printed and published by Gales and Seaton, 1836), 2034-38

See also page 99

With one of the modes (Mr. J. said) he should be satisfied. Promptly to reject these petitions as they were presented, he believed, would meet the opprobation [2] of southern gentlemen; and if they, who were more deeply interested than all others, regarded that mode of disposing of them as effectual to the accomplishment of the great object they had in view, and the people of the East and of the North really intended, in good faith, to cooperate with them (as he believed they did), he could perceive no good reason why the proposition to reject should not be sustained.

It had been said, that gentlemen from the South were over sensitive, and disposed to act with too much precipitation on this subject. It had also been contended, that this course of proceeding was calculated to abridge the great right of petition; and others there were who thought the only proper course was to refer them to a committee. The intimation that this was a subject upon which the people of the South were sensitive, was just. The fact could not be disguised, that there existed throughout the slaveholding States an excitement which had been witnessed at any former period of their history; and strangely indeed must he be constituted who could look upon the conduct of the Abolitionists, and witness the scenes to which it had given rise in the South, and not have his sensibility wrought up to the very highest pitch. Was it not known to every gentleman upon this floor that numerous abolition societies had been formed in the eastern and northern States - frowned upon, indignantly frowned upon, he believed, by the intelligent, the well-informed, and respectable portions of these communities - but could they shut their eyes to the fact, that these societies existed; that they had gone on to collect large sums of money, and had put into operation large printing-presses which were worked by steam? Yes, sir, worked by steam, with the open and avowed object of effecting the immediate abolition of slavery in the southern States. That by means of these two great revolutionizers [sic] of the world - he meant steam power and the press - they had caused to be printed, and, by means of the public mails, circulated throughout the slaveholding States, large numbers of newspapers, pamphlets, tracts, and pictures, calculated, in an eminent degree, to rouse and inflame the passions of the slaves against their masters, to urge them on to deeds of death, and to involve them in all the horrors of a servile war - productions which (Mr. J. said) he would take upon himself to say, were as foul libels upon the people of the South as were ever printed. And, if to add insult to injury, there were those here who had the charity to believe that they were influenced in their conduct by humane and religious motives. If, indeed (said Mr. J.), this most uncalled-for, officious, and dangerous intermeddling with the rights of others be dictated by religion, he would say it was not the religion which was inculcated by the Savior of the world, or taught by his disciples.

Mr. JONES said he hoped it would not be understood by anything he had said, that he was in favor of abridging either the freedom of the press or the freedom of speech; far from it; he regarded them as the great safeguards to our republican institutions. There was, however, a difference between the freedom and the licentiousness of the press; and what he objected to was, the right of these misguided and deluded men to propagate slander, to instigate murder, to disturb the peace of States, and to endanger the Union; and, if persisted in by them, he called upon the Representatives of the people to interpose, and stamp their conduct with the seal of their disapprobation.

But (said Mr. J.) we have been told by the gentlemen from New York and Massachusetts [Mr. Beardsley and Mr. Adams [3]] that to vote to reject this petition would be to abridge the right of the people to petition Congress. He admitted that to be a right, the free exercise of which was secured to the people by the Constitution, and he would be among the last, he hoped the very last, to lay violent hands upon that sacred instrument; he had sworn to support it, and, as a Representative of the people, support it he would, at every hazard, for upon it depended the last hope of freedom throughout the world; and if he could be satisfied that any constitutional right of the people was to be invaded by the course he proposed in disposing of that petition, he would be the first to abandon the position he then occupied. But (said Mr. J.) in what consists the right of petition, if it be not to set forth, in written form, the grievances complained of, with a view to procure upon them the action of Congress; and had not these petitioners already enjoyed that right? Did not the proceedings which had taken place upon this petition furnish the affirmative answer to the inquiry? Had they not petitioned, had not their petitions been presented by a member in his place, received by the House, read by the Clerk? And was Congress not then engaged in endeavoring to dispose of it in conformity with rules which had been made and adopted for the government of the House; and if it should ever be disposed of, would not this petition have been so fully considered, as it could have been, had any other form of proceeding been adopted? Mr. J. said, that when a petition had been presented to the House, received, and read by the Clerk (unless it should be afterwards withdrawn by the consent of the House), it became the property of the Representatives of the people; they might refuse to consider it, lay it on the table, postpone it to a day certain, refer it to the committee, or, what they had in vain attempted here, they might reject it. Here, then, were five several ways in which this petition might legally and properly be disposed of; and how it was that the disposition of it in one of these modes, in preference to another (all of which were prescribed by the rules of the House), was, in any possible way, to affect the right of the people to petition Congress, he was wholly at a loss to comprehend.

But they were told by the gentleman from Massachusetts [Mr. Adams], that, if these petitions were sent to a committee, they would there be allowed to 'sleep the sleep of death'; and that thereafter we should be troubled with no others of like character. Would to God that this assurance of the honorable gentleman could be realized; but they had only look to the past history of their legislation upon that subject to be satisfied that the expected consummation, to which he looked forward, had existence nowhere except in the fertile imagination of him who conceived it. It would then be seen that that course had been tried again and again; still these petitions continued to flow in upon them, and would continue to do so so long as they were received and referred to committees. What (he inquired) was the object in referring subjects to a committee? It was to collect information which, in the ordinary course of legislation, could not conveniently be collected in any other way. But did this House stand in need of information upon the subject sought to be brought to its notice by that petition? Certainly not. It was well

understood that it was a subject to which public attention had been long turned with the most intense interest; that from the river St. Lawrence to the Gulf of Mexico the best talents of the country had been almost everywhere engaged in its consideration, and in communication information to the people. So soon as the excitement over the country commenced, meeting after meeting was called in the southern States in almost every town and county; discussion after discussion was had before the people; resolution after resolution adopted, until, like a wave from the ocean, it swept over the whole southern country. It resulted in strong appeals to our brethren of the North to step forth and aid us in putting down these base attempts upon our rights, our property, and our lives. And it was with mingled emotions of pride and pleasure he referred to the fact that these appeals were not made in vain; they, too, called the people together; meetings were held throughout the whole eastern and northern countries; and the measures adopted by those meetings for a time gave quiet, and, to some extent, allayed the excitement in the South, and it was for gentlemen from the North to say whether we may still rely upon their assurances by heartily cooperating with us in putting this subject to rest by a direct and decisive vote upon the question.

Mr. J. said it must be obvious, that there could be no need of further information upon the subject to enable gentlemen to vote understandingly upon it. Why, then, send it to a committee? Was it believed that the report of a committee was to produce any effect upon the Abolitionists? Did gentlemen flatter themselves that the spirit of fanaticism could be checked by a calm, dispassionate, and logical argument? To such he would recommend to read the reports of committees which have already made on like petitions, and he doubted not but that gentlemen would be satisfied that no benefit was likely to result from the adoption of the same course in reference to the petition before them. So far from that course of proceeding having had a tendency to check the wild spirit of fanaticism now abroad in the land, the reverse was true; for the tables of gentlemen were now groaning under the weight of similar petitions.

The gentleman from Massachusetts [Mr. Adams] has referred to his own course on a former occasion, in reference to this subject; this was commenced in a tone and in a spirit which seemed to Mr. J. to bespeak the deep anxiety which he felt to allay the very unpleasant excitement which had begun to show itself in the House; and to reconcile, if he could, the causes of discontent which continued to agitate and disturb the people of the South; he viewed the remarks of that gentleman as oil poured out upon the troubled waters. It was, however, but the calm which precedes the storm. At length, lashing himself up to a state of high excitement, he asked what it was the South desired? Was it (said he) to discuss the 'sublime merits of slavery'? That was a subject which Mr. J. could not discuss with that gentleman; and taint them as he might with their slaves, whose condition they had no agency in producing, and no means of changing, he would take that occasion to say to him, that the people of the South held their slaves by a title as secure, by an authority as high and as sacred, as that by which that gentleman held title to his horse, his house, or, to use his own language, 'his place upon that floor.' They held them under the Constitution and laws of the land.

That gentleman [Mr. Adams] had also taken occasion to refer the members from the South to Mason and Dixon's line, warning them that every member to the north of that line, who should discuss this subject, would send forth to the world an incendiary pamphlet; and although that general seemed to speak as one 'having authority,' he had seen too many evidences not to be satisfied of the error into which he had fallen. He saw assembled here, from every quarter of this widely extended Union, patriots prepared to make every sacrifice upon the altar of their country's good. He lamented to hear what had fallen from the gentleman from Massachusetts upon that subject; he believed that gentleman himself, in his calmer moments, would lament it. The people had cause to lament it. But, if that be the course determined upon by [the] gentleman, the sooner we had it acted out the better. This he would take occasion to say to him: let those threatened pamphlets come when they might, they would be received by the people of the South as it became freemen who knew their rights, and knowing, dared maintain them.

Mr. J. remarked, in conclusion, that he had felt himself called upon to say this much in explanation of his own views, with an earnest desire that a direct vote on the subject might be obtained."

Footnotes:

[1] Referring to Rep. Joseph Reed Ingersoll, anti-Jacksonian of Pennsylvania.

[2] Sic; should be "approbation."

[3] Rep. Samuel Beardsley, Jacksonian of New York, and John Quincy Adams, Whig of Massachusetts.

Honorable James L. Orr's Speech
on Slavery, 8 May 1850

James Lawrence Orr, Democrat of South Carolina, took to the floor of the US House of Representatives on 8 May 1850 to denounce those abolitionists in the North who were arguing that slavery should be outlawed by Congress. Using statistics and other devices, Orr - who later served as Speaker of the House in the Thirty-fifth Congress (1857-59) - called those who opposed slavery "fanatics" and told the House that in his estimation any attempt to do away with slavery would end in "disunion." The following, from a published version of the speech which was printed that same year, is the complete speech by Orr.

❧

The House being in Committee of the Whole on the state of the Union, on the President's Message transmitting the Constitution of California -

Mr. Orr said: Mr. Chairman: I propose, in the brief hour allotted to me, to examine and present what I conceive to be Northern sentiment upon the subject of slavery, and the inevitable results of that sentiment. I believe, sir, there is much misunderstanding, both at the North and the South, as to the extent and character of that feeling. I know the misapprehension that exists in that part of the country which I have the honor to represent, and I desire to lay before my constituents and the people of the South the result of my observations since I have been a member of this House, so that they may be prepared to judge of the proper means of meeting, counteracting, and repelling that sentiment.

The first evidence of abolition sentiment in the Northern States to which I refer, is to be found in the numerous abolition societies organized in every part of that section of the Union, composed of large numbers of individuals of all classes and sexes. These societies meet at stated periods, for the avowed purpose of advancing their political and moral tenets; they appoint their emissaries, who traverse the country, and who, by their slanders, poison the minds of the masses of their people as to the true character of the institution of slavery. They have established newspapers and periodicals, which are circulated in great profusion, not only in the non-slaveholding States, but are thrown broadcast over the South, through the mails, for the purpose of planting the thorn of discontent in the bosoms of our now happy slaves, and inciting them to the perpetration of the bloody scenes of St. Domingo. These auxiliaries of the American Anti-slavery Society, not content with a general combination against the institutions of the South, form a component part of the American and Foreign Anti-slavery Society, in which they unite with the zealots of foreign countries in an unjust crusade against their brethren of the South. Most of the avowed abolitionists have, however, the merit of frankness at least. They seek to emancipate our slaves, it is true, but concede that it cannot be done consistently with the Constitution; they therefore declare an uncompromising war against the Constitution and the Union; while others, who intend to effect the same end, have not the candor to own it, and hypocritically profess an attachment to the Constitution which they are really seeking to destroy.

Another evidence of the extent of abolition sentiment in the Northern States is, the promotion of certain gentlemen to seats in the other wing of this Capitol. I allude, sir, first to the election of Wm. H. Seward. It might be that this "faction," as the Abolitionists have been denominated, could, through their societies and conventions, create some attention, and excite the contempt of sensible, moderate men, for their fanaticism; but I would inquire, how comes it to pass that, insignificant as it is said to be, it is enabled to elect from the great State of New York - the Empire State - a man to represent it in the Senate of the United States, whose greatest distinction has been his untiring advocacy of the doctrines of abolition? Does it not show that the major part of the people of that State sympathize deeply

Source: *Speech of the Hon. James L. Orr, of South Carolina, on the Slavery Question. Delivered in the House of Representatives, May 8, 1850* (Washington: Printed by J.&O. T. Towers, 1850).

See also page 133

with their Senator in his nefarious principles? Look at the recent election, by the Legislature of Ohio - a State in numbers second only to New York - of S. P. Chase[1], to represent that State in the Senate of the United States. He has been amongst the most zealous of all his infatuated compeers: even Wm. H. Seward[2] was not more so, in the advocacy of radical abolition, and the Legislature of Ohio, knowing his sentiments, and representing the people of that State, have honored him with one of the highest official stations on earth. Others, too, have been elected to that body, who owe their promotion to pledges given their constituents, that they would oppose the admission of any more slave States or slave territory into the Union, and favor the application of the Wilmot proviso - that true scion from an abolition stock - to the territories acquired from Mexico. One would suppose that when a Senator avowed that, acting as a Senator, he recognized a higher obligation than his oath to support the Constitution of the United States - an obligation which requires him to violate and set aside the provisions of that sacred instrument - the Legislature of his State, then in session, would have promptly branded such a declaration with the infamy it deserves. Such a declaration, it is known to the country, was recently made in the Senate by the Senator from New York to whom I have alluded - but the Legislature of that State adopted no resolutions condemnatory of this sentiment.

They did, however, pass resolutions, with great unanimity, sustaining fully the utra[3] positions of their distinguished - no, their notorious Senator. Resolutions have been adopted in every non- slaveholding State, instructing their Senators and requesting their Representatives in Congress to vote in favor of the adoption of the Wilmot proviso, and in opposition, in many cases, to the admission of any other slave States.

Mr. McLanahan[4] asked if the gentleman from South Carolina had observed that the Legislature of Pennsylvania had recently laid upon the table resolutions in favor of the Wilmot proviso?

Mr. Orr: I have; and I honor the patriotism of your constituents in coming to the rescue of the Constitution in these perilous times. Instructions, such as I have spoken of, did pass the Legislature of Pennsylvania two years ago. I repeat the assertion, that every non-slaveholding State has passed resolutions of an unmistakable abolition character. Yet the unceasing efforts of the press here, and of newspaper correspondents, are directed to induce the people of the South to believe that this hostility to our institutions is confined to a few fanatics, and that abolition is not the general sentiment of the country.

Another evidence of the progress of abolition sentiment is the legislation of the non-slaveholding States obstructing the delivering up of fugitive slaves. What is the constitutional provision upon that subject? "No person held to service or labor in one State, under the laws thereof, escaping into another, shall, in consequence of any law or regulation therein, be discharged from such service or labor, but shall be delivered up on claim of the party to whom such service or labor may be due." Some of the Northern States have passed laws imposing heavy penalties on any State officer who may aid the owner in recovering his runaway slave. The State officers of all the States swear to support the Constitution of the United States as well as the Constitution of the State in which the officer resides. Now, if the Constitution of the United States requires that a person held to service shall be delivered up, and a State officer refuses to obey that provision, does he prove faithful to his oath? And is not the penalty imposed by the particular State a compulsion upon the officer to commit perjury? This legislation reflects truly the feeling of the Northern States upon this subject. When a slave escapes, friends receive him with open arms, and. clandestinely convey him beyond the reach of his lawful owner. If the slave, perchance, is overtaken, or hunted out of his secret hiding place, the owner perils his life, through the lawless violence of the mob, in reclaiming his property and in asserting rights solemnly guarantied to him by the Constitution. The laws and popular tumults against the master, to which I have adverted, clearly indicates the settled, deliberate purpose of the Northern States to deprive us of our rights in that species of property.

Northern sentiment on the subject of abolition speaks trumpet-tongued in the political privileges conferred on free negroes in some of the Northern States. Maine, New Hampshire, Vermont, Massachusetts, Rhode Island, and New York, all extend the right of suffrage to the African. At the last State election in New York the free negroes held the balance of power between the two political parties. Representatives upon this floor receive the votes of this degraded class, and the success of republican institutions is made to depend upon the judgment and intelligence of the free negro sovereigns. The aim of the abolitionists looks first to the emancipation of our slaves throughout the South, and then is to follow their elevation to all the social and political privileges of the white man. The thick-lipped African is to march up to the same ballot-box, eat at the same table, and sit in the same parlor with the white man. This, the Abolitionists would say, "is a consummation devoutly to be wished for."

Another evidence, sir, of the progress and intolerance of this sentiment is to be found in the separation of two of the most numerous and respectable Christian denominations in this country (the Baptist and the Methodist). They assembled in convention and conference, year after year, to advance that holy cause in which they had mutually embarked. But, sir, the demon of fanatical discord stalked into their associations; Christian charity and brotherly love were impotent in resisting its encroachment upon their peace and union; Northern members demanded that their Southern brethren should surrender and eschew the institutions of the country in which they lived - that they should become traitors to the State to which their allegiance was due, and prove recreant to their obligations to the community in which they resided. They were too holy to commune at the same altar with their Southern brethren, until the latter should pronounce slavery a sin, and agree to enlist in an effort for its extinction. The terms were too ignominious for Christians or patriots. With a manly independence, the Southern wing of both denominations rejected the offer, and the separation of their churches ensued. These two, sir, were heavy blows against our political union, from the shocks of which we have not yet recovered.

Another evidence of the extent of this sentiment is exhibited in the popularity, the universal popularity, of the doctrine of free soil - the legitimate scion, as I before remarked, of the abolition stock. The popularity of that doctrine is not to be judged by the independent free-soil party organization. Those who candidly avow the opinion are few in number; they refuse to co-operate with either of the other parties, and hence a separate organization; but the mass of the Northern people comprising the two great political parties sympathize in sentiment and feeling with the free-soilers. It is idle to disguise the fact. The speeches delivered by Northern Representatives since the commencement of this discussion is a thorough vindication of the truth of this assertion. They may be well arranged in two classes, one of which broadly asserts that the North has been guilty of no aggression upon the South - that the South has no just cause of complaint against them - that our demand to share equally in the common property of all the States is an aggression upon the North - that our fugitive slaves are always promptly surrendered upon the demand of the owner. This is the language addressed by them to Northern constituencies; they do not appeal to them to quiet this infamous agitation - they do not remind them of their constitutional obligations; and thus their course can have no other effect than to fan the flames of fanaticism until they shall burn out the vitals of the Constitution and Union.

The other class show equally, in their speeches, their attachment to the doctrines of free soil. Every Northern man of this class who has addressed the committee on this subject, except my friend from Indiana [Mr. Gorman][5], and my friend from Pennsylvania [Mr. Ross][6], is in the same category. Their speeches open, generally, with a violent philippic against the South. They charge us with arrogance, and some of them are in hot haste in volunteering their services to march troops into our midst to force us to continue in the Union if we should choose to secede from it. They tell us that they are in favor of non-intervention. What does this non-intervention amount to? If it were a bona fide non-interference with our rights, it would be all that the South could ask - all that she has a right to demand under the Constitution. But this much she does demand; and, depend upon it, she will be appeased by nothing less. Some of the Northern non-interventionists deny that Congress has the power to pass the Wilmot proviso; others maintain the position that Congress has the power, but should not exercise it, and straightway offer the excuse to their constituents that it is not necessary to pass it - that the Mexican laws are in force, and they exclude slavery. This is the opinion entertained by General Cass and all the non-intervention northern Democrats in this House. Is not this a heavy tribute which non-intervention pays to free-soil? It is tantamount to saying, we are in favor of the end which the proviso aims to accomplish, viz: the exclusion of the slave States from all the territory acquired from Mexico - we oppose its adoption only because we regard it as unnecessary, and because we believe the course we propose to pursue will most effectually subserve the end without giving offence and producing irritation in the South. I repeat it, sir, such non-intervention pays a heavy tribute to abolitionism.

Another, and perhaps, Mr. Chairman, the most pregnant indication of the progress of abolition sentiment, is the remarkable condition of things that now exists throughout the country in relation to the admission of California into the Union. I venture to say that never in the history of this Government has any important question been presented for the consideration of Congress where party lines were all broken down as they have been on this question. It is an Administration measure - one which certainly reflects but little credit upon its wisdom or patriotism. Parties have but recently emerged from the heat of a presidential struggle, and upon all other questions, save this alone, which have been introduced into this House at the present session, partisan gladiators have waged as fierce a contest as in days of yore. Irregular and objectionable as all the California proceedings have been, but one solitary Representative (I refer again to my friend Mr. Ross) from the free States has avowed himself opposed to its admission into the Union; parties are broken down - the North is making it a sectional question. Northern Whigs and Northern Democrats, Whig Free-Soilers and Democratic Free-Soilers all rally upon this common platform, and the emulation between them is great who shall be foremost in introducing this embryo State into the Union. Some of the objections to its admission into the Union I will briefly notice. No census had been taken either by the authority of the pretended State or by the authority of Congress. We have no official information which would authorize us to determine whether the population was ten thousand or one hundred thousand. The number of votes said to have been polled in the ratification of the constitution was about thirteen thousand. This number of voters, where the population is an average one, would indicate a population of seventy thousand souls. The proportion of the adult male population in California is

greater by far than in the States, comparatively few women or children having emigrated thither. If the number of votes polled be adopted as the criterion by which the population is to be adjudged, it could not have exceeded, at the date of the ratification of the constitution, forty thousand; and, with these facts. Congress is importuned to admit California with two Representatives, with a less population of American citizens than each member on this floor represents.

Then as to its boundaries, they contain sufficient territory to make five large States, and embrace a sea-coast of more than eight hundred miles.

The convention which framed the constitution was not called by authority of Congress, but by a military officer, who, by virtue of the commission he held under the Government of the United States, exercised the functions of civil governor. His ukase[7] directed that the convention should consist of thirty-seven members. After the convention was elected, it assembled, and, by a vote for which it had no authority, not even from the military dictator, it increased the number of delegates from thirty-seven to seventy-nine, and allowed the additional number, without referring it to the people, to take their seats, they being the defeated candidates at the election. In my judgment it was the duty of the President to have censured the officer who thus exercised the high prerogative of military dictator. If the President had desired to carry out the will of Congress according to his pledges, that officer could not have escaped punishment, for Congress at its last session positively refused to allow the people of California to do that which the military governor, by a military order or proclamation, bearing striking analogies to an order, instructed them to do.

Who are the people of California? A world in miniature - the four quarters of the globe are represented there. No naturalization laws having been passed, there was no legal impediment to their exercising the right of suffrage. The whole proceeding - not having the consent of Congress, the rightful legislature of the territory - was illegal and revolutionary. I repeat, Mr. Chairman, that with all these irregularities we find every party in Congress from the Northern States in favor of the admission of California into the Union - and why? For no other reason than that slavery has been excluded by her constitution. If her people had assembled under lawful authority, with an ascertained population equal to the present ratio of representation, they alone would have had the power to determine the question whether slavery should or should not exist within her limits. If that decision had been to exclude slavery, no murmur of complaint would have been heard from any Southern man; but I undertake to say here, if slavery had been tolerated, we should have found just as unanimous a sentiment in the Northern States against her admission into the Union as we now find in favor of that proposition; and I do not make this assertion without good foundation. When Florida applied for admission into the Union, a large minority in Congress voted against it, when every initiatory step had been regular, on the isolated ground that she was a slaveholding State.

I have other evidences, Mr. Chairman, of Northern sentiment upon the subject of slavery. The speech recently delivered by the distinguished Senator from Massachusetts (Mr. Webster)[8], and the action of the House in laying upon the table the resolution of the gentleman from Ohio, in the early part of the session, has induced the belief in the South that a sense of justice had returned to their Northern brethren. These appearances are deceptive. It is an illusion which I deeply deplore. The Senator from Massachusetts made a truly patriotic speech; but what did he propose? All that he offered was, to give to the South her clearly-defined constitutional rights. This gratified us. It gratified us to know that a distinguished Northern man would frankly and ingenuously concede our rights, and enforce their execution by his vote and voice. How has that speech been received in the State of Massachusetts, of which he is the proudest ornament? Her legislature was in session; and fearing lest that speech might contain the balm to heal the divisions of the country, straightway new poison was poured into the wound. Resolutions were passed, taking the strongest and most offensive ground. They did not instruct him, it is true, for the dominant party do not assume the right to instruct; but that Senator has not been sustained by his immediate constituents. A few have endorsed his sentiments, but a large majority of the people and of the press of Massachusetts have condemned him. He has not been more fortunate here - one after another of the Massachusetts delegation has addressed the committee, all as-

suming positions adverse to those taken by Mr. Webster. The only hope of aid in this House took its departure to-day, when the honorable gentleman who preceded me (Mr. Winthrop)[9] announced himself in favor of General Taylor's[10] unstatesmanlike plan of settling the existing difficulties. Daniel Webster once spoke and could speak for New England. The waves of fanaticism have broken over the land of the Pilgrim Fathers, and are sweeping off the influence and power of her best and brightest men. When his genius has proved itself impotent to stay this onward wave in the minds of those whose service he has so much honored, upon what ground can the South rest her hopes of peace and safety in this Government?

The action of the House in laying Root's resolution upon the table promised fruits which will never be gathered. If the proviso is not pressed at the present session, it will not be because the North have abated one tittle[11] in their devotion to it. The advocates of that measure are satisfied they will accomplish their purpose quite as effectually, and much more adroitly, in another way. But, sir, there is still further evidence of Northern sentiment. We have been told by one gentleman, in this debate, "that the only way in which the abolition of slavery in the States can be constitutionally effected, is to confine it within its present limits"; another said "that no more slave States or slave Territory should come into this Union - sooner civil war," &c.; another, "the Wilmot proviso was an abiding principle in the hearts of the people of the free States"; and still another, who is a moderate Northern man, "that slavery was a national shame and a national disgrace." I quote these sentiments that they may be contrasted with the oft-reiterated assertion, that it is not the purpose of the Northern States to abolish slavery where it now exists. They tell us plainly they can effect abolition in the States, through the legislation of this Government, without violating the Constitution; and they admit, further, that they will do it by indirect means, but their constitutional scruples forbid direct legislation in abolishing slavery.

Now, sir, I have a great contempt for the morality or honesty of that sort of reasoning which would make an act unconstitutional if executed directly, but satisfies the conscience that it is constitutional if done indirectly.

The institution of slavery being a "national shame and a national disgrace" in the opinion of the North, and having the power to abolish it by indirect means, the legislation of this Government (for the North have the majority) is to be hostile to our institutions. We then present this anomaly, that a Government established by wise and patriotic men for the security and safety of the persons and property of all its parts - a Government which derives its sustenance by taxation upon all its parts, is to depart so far from the purposes of its creation as to destroy, by its hostile legislation, the property of one-half of the States composing that Government; and that, too, when the States thus threatened are in such a hopeless minority in Congress that they are unable to protect themselves against that hostile, unconstitutional legislation. The value of our slave property is some sixteen hundred millions of dollars: this is to be destroyed through a majority. The rule for construing the Constitution, which is fast being established, is, that the majority have the right to rule, and whatever construction they give is the true construction. Such, Mr. Chairman, is not our reading or construction of that instrument. The Constitution is to protect the rights of minorities; majorities have always the ability to protect themselves. If they have the absolute right of making and construing, then there is no necessity for a written Constitution. If the will of the majority is absolute, it is the strong against the weak - the law of force which existed between individuals before Governments was instituted. If the power now claimed for the Northern States is persevered in, it requires no spirit of prophecy to foresee that it must end in disunion. The institution of slavery is so intimately interwoven with society and is so indispensable to our social, political, and national prosperity, that it will not be surrendered so long as there is a Southern hand to strike in its defence. We intend to preserve and perpetuate it. We have another demand, and that is, that we shall be allowed to enjoy our property in peace, quiet, and security. I tell Northern gentlemen to-day, that five years will not elapse before they will be required to make their choice between non-intervention and non-agitation through Congress on the one hand, and a dissolution of this Government on the other; and I tell Southern people, if this agitation is continued during that time, their peace and personal security will require them

to choose between secession and negro emancipation. Sir, I do not desire to be considered an alarmist; but if gentlemen will recur to the history of the country, they will learn that the anti-slavery party was contemptible and insignificant, but it has now grown to be a great colossal power, overshadowing almost the entire North, and has enlisted under its banner all the political parties there. If its progress is as rapid in the next five years as for the last ten, you will find no Northern Representative who will so far outrage the sentiment of his constituents as to oppose even the abolition of slavery in the States.

I will here digress, Mr. Chairman, to reply to a complaint which has been urged by several Northern gentlemen, charging that the South has for a series of years occupied the Federal offices. On reference to the past, it will be found to be true that the South has held a larger share of the prominent offices of the Government than those of the North. I am able to give a satisfactory reason for this fact, and to show whence it arises. When a Southern man enters into public life, he is brought in by the party to which he is attached, and he is continued in office, if he be a faithful representative, so long as his party continues in the ascendancy, or until he chooses voluntarily to retire. In the North a different rule prevails - rotation in office is the recognised system with all parties. The rule may be a correct one in offices of profit merely, but when applied to representatives, either State or Federal, the constituent can never be so well represented. Southern men remain longer in Congress; they have therefore better opportunities for the development of their genius and talent, and their experience gives them the advantage over abler men who are without experience; their services become more conspicuous; and when individuals are selected for prominent stations in the Government, they are placed there because they have more national reputation. But Northern gentlemen, whilst they have observed this fact, with some manifestations of jealousy, forget that nearly three-fourths of the public expenditures of this Government fall into the Northern lap. The gentleman from Illinois [Mr. Harris][12] denied, for the first time, as I believe, this statement, and went into a minute examination for the purpose of showing that the South had received more than her proportiate share of those expenditures. He obtained the services of an experienced clerk in making the calculation, and he reports that in a period of ten years, out of nineteen millions for local appropriations, nine millions have been given to the South, while only ten millions have gone to the North. The clerk has committed a palpable blunder, and I wonder that he has not been guillotined ere this for incompetency or infidelity. Only nineteen millions of dollars expended on local objects during a period of ten years! The gentleman from Illinois hurries to the census of 1840, to learn there that this appropriation gives to every white person in the North $102, and at the South $190. I propose to advert to a few items only, which I suppose the clerk did not embrace in his calculations. They will show which section of the Union has foraged most liberally from the public treasury. The expenditure for pensions up to 1838 amounted in the Northern States to $28,000,000; in the Southern States to $7,000,000. New York contributed to the support of the revolutionary war $7,179,983, and had received in 1838, in pensions, $7,850,054.[13]

The public lands donated by Congress to the Northern States have been worth $7,584,899; the same in the South $4,025,000. Since the establishment of the Government, the cost of collecting the customs has been $53,000,000; $43,000,000 expended in the North, and $10,000,000 in the South. Bounties on pickled fish, &c., in the North, exclusively, $10,000,000. The forts on the Northern coast have cost, on each mile, $838; on the Southern coast $535 per mile. In 1846 there was one light-house to every fifty miles of Northern coast; whilst in the South there was one for every two hundred and seventy-six miles. The expenditures for internal improvements from 1824 to 1833, in the North, was $5,194,441; in the South $957,000. From 1834 to 1845, for the same purpose, in the North, $7,231,639; and in the South $1,171,.500.

This much, sir, with reference to what the gentleman said about appropriations. I propose now to examine so much of the same gentleman's speech as to the relative number of troops furnished by the North and the South in the late war with Mexico. I adopt his figures, and assume them to be correct. The South furnished 47,649 volunteers; the North 24,712. The gentleman says that this is not the fair way of making the calculation - that the amount of

service rendered in months is "the fairest way of making the calculation." His figures show that the South furnished service in months 365,500 months; the North 309,400. This still gives the South a preponderance. Not contented, however, with this result, he sets out upon a third series of figures, that he may give the North the superiority. This calculation includes all the enlistments made during the war, as also for the ten new regiments; and assumes that two-thirds of these enlistments were from the North; and when his calculation is footed up, the North furnished service equal to 813,648 months, and the South equal to 627,625 months. Well, I go back to the census of 1840, and he, at least, can make no objection to the authority, having appealed to this source in the first branch of his argument. I therefore take his figures, and reply with his authority. If the South furnished 47,049 volunteers, according to population the North should have furnished 98,148. They furnished 24,712 - deficit of their just proportion 73,436.

The South furnished service of volunteers in months equal to 365,500 months. The North should have furnished service in months equal to 754,020 months; they furnished 309,400 - deficit of their just proportion 444,620. But if the enlistments are superadded to the above, it will be seen that the North furnished in months equal to 813,648; the South 627,625. The North should have furnished service in months 1,294,780 months - deficit of her just proportion 481,132. I enter into these calculations for the purpose, of vindicating the truth of the Southern Address - for the purpose of vindicating the truth of the allegations which have been made by Southern members on this floor, that the South contributed more than her just proportion of troops in making the acquisitions from Mexico which the North mean to exclude us from, either through the Wilmot proviso or the "non-intervention" policy, in connection with the pretence that the Mexican laws are in force. He went a little further, and introduced an estimate of the service by the North and the South in the Revolutionary war. He says, for the continental line of the Revolution, the North furnished 172,436 men, and the South 59,335.

It is known, Mr. Chairman, to every one who is familiar with the history of the Revolution, that a very large proportion of the troops that were engaged in that protracted and perilous contest were not connected with the continental army. If the gentleman had made an accurate examination of the number of troops furnished by each of the States, he would have found that Virginia alone furnished 66,721. Pennsylvania, with a population equal to Virginia, furnished 34,965; New York 29,836; South Carolina 31,131. South Carolina sent thirty-seven out of every forty-two of her citizens capable of bearing arms, Massachusetts thirty-two, Connecticut thirty. New Hampshire eighteen.

I will answer with statistical facts the delusion existing in the minds of some who believe that the pecuniary and social condition is more elevated in the North than in the South. We have heard that Virginia was sinking - was falling fast into decay; that her sisters have advanced in prosperity and wealth whilst she has been retrograding - all of which is attributed to her system of domestic servitude. Why, sir, this is but an assumption - a most unwarrantable assumption - because it has no foundation in fact. The abolitionists make their proselytes believe that Virginia is in a most dilapidated state - that her forests have all been destroyed - the face of her fields furrowed with deep gullies - and that her low grounds have been exhausted by unskillful husbandry. Virginia has more wealth according to population than any one of the Northern States. The average wealth of each inhabitant, free and slave, is $471; or free alone, $741. In Kentucky the average wealth of each inhabitant, free and slave, is $319; whilst that of Ohio is but $227; Pennsylvania $219; New York $228. And, sir, the productions of the slaveholding States will compare favorably with the non-slaveholding. The advantage will be found to be largely on the side of the former in the value of those productions. The South produces more Indian corn, and the North more wheat; but the South has a complete monopoly, by soil and climate, in the production of cotton, sugar, rice, and tobacco.

The value of these four crops the last year exceeds $125,000,000. But compare the productions of individual States. Michigan and Arkansas were admitted into the Union about the same time: Michigan is one of the most flourishing of the northwestern States, washed on three sides by navigable waters, and enjoying an extensive system of internal improvements; and her crops last year yielded to each

inhabitant $31.50. The crop of Arkansas yielded to each white inhabitant $101; and if the slaves are counted as persons, the value of the crop was $81.50 for each inhabitant : so that the production of Arkansas, with a fertile soil, though not a genial climate, nearly trebles that of Michigan.

Mr. Chairman, I am admonished that my hour is drawing rapidly to its close; I therefore return to the subject from which I digressed longer than I intended. Whether slavery be a sin or not, is a question with which this Government has nothing to do. It is recognised by the Constitution, and protected to the fullest extent. He who believes it sinful, therefore, and feels a moral duty devolving upon him to extirpate it, should candidly avow himself a disunionist, and seek to dissolve this supposed sinful alliance. If, on the contrary, he is ready to abide by the Constitution, in letter and spirit, then his warfare against slavery is ended - he must ground his arms, and cease to agitate. It is a matter of indifference to us whether you consider slavery right or wrong; we alone must be the judges of its blessings and its curses. We do not complain of your abstract opinions upon that subject; but it becomes a question of the profoundest interest to us, when you make your abstract opinions on the morality of the institution the basis of your political action.

The abolition feeling in the North is founded in religious fanaticism - its votaries, like fanatics in every age of the world, are guided neither by religion, morality, nor justice. The Scripture argument in favor of slavery is unanswerable; but still argument never reaches the understanding or conscience of the fanatic. The history of the Crusades, which involved Europe in blood and carnage, well illustrates its folly and madness, when kings and nations vied with each other in their benevolent and Christian purpose of expelling the Infidels from the city of Jerusalem. When the phrensy[14] of madness sears the brain, reason, the great helm of human action, fails to control its motions; and here is the great danger of abolition. The masses may be sincere; but when they attempt to enforce, as they are now doing, a supposed moral obligation through political channels, without regard to the rights of others, or the supreme law of the land, cool-headed and discreet men must rise up in the majesty of their strength and crush it, or consent to give up our institutions, and be crushed by it. Fanaticism is not often sated until it has gorged itself with blood or ruin.

The dangers to the Republic every patriot desires may be averted, and the union of these States preserved in its pristine purity. It is endeared to us by a thousand ties hallowed by the memories of the past, and excites in the mind emotions little short of veneration. I desire it to be preserved, but it must be preserved in its purity, if it is worth preserving at all. That man is the disunionist who will trample down the Constitution and destroy the rights of the States. I have spoken plainly, sir, of the perils to which we are exposed. I know that my section of the Union is deceived and deluded as to the true situation of this controversy. They have cherished with abiding confidence the hope that their Northern brethren would cease their aggressions and do them justice. The events which have transpired here, and to which I have adverted (Webster's speech, and the laying of Root's resolution[15] on the table,) have added to the delusion. I warn them to rise from the lethargy into which they have been betrayed. I tell them now, in all candor, that I see no returning sense of justice in the North. They should appoint their delegates to the Nashville Convention[16]: let them assemble there, and deliberate upon the grave issues which abolition has presented - let them concentrate the sentiment of the South, and lay such plans as will defeat the ends of abolitionists. Every Southern State should be fully represented there by her ablest Constitution-loving sons. That convention, sir, will meet, although it is probable that the confident expectation of a compromise will prevent its being as numerously attended as it would have been some months back, the people believing that the necessity of its convening has passed away. I fear, sir, they have been deluded into the hope of compromise, so industriously instilled into their minds for the purpose of defeating the Nashville Convention. That effort has been partially successful; but the convention will nevertheless assemble, and the South will not readily forget those by whom they have been deceived. Sir, it has been fashionable to denounce that convention, and to disparage the purposes of those who called it. For one, I am not ashamed of that convention - nothing could make me ashamed of it, but the failure of the South, or of those with whom my honor is more immediately bound up, to attend

it. The ends of that convention were high and holy; it was called to protect the Constitution, to save the Union, by taking such steps as might prevent, if possible, the consummation of measures which would probably lead to the destruction of both. Had the purpose been disunion, those who called that convention would have waited until the irretrievable step had been taken, and nothing left to the South but submission or secession. The present is a critical conjuncture of political affairs; there is a propriety, nay, almost a necessity, for Southern men to commune with each other. I, for one, wish that harmony may mark their deliberations, and that the result of those deliberations may be worthy of the occasion and of the cause for which they will convene.

Footnotes:

[1] Referring to Salmon Portland Chase (1808-1873), who served as a US Senator from Ohio (1849-62), then as Secretary of the Treasury in the Lincoln administration (1862-64), then as Chief Justice of the US Supreme Court (1864-73).

[2] William Henry Seward (1801-1872), US Senator from New York (1849-60) and a firm opponent of slavery, who later served as Secretary of State under Abraham Lincoln and Andrew Johnson.

[3] This is a typographical error, and could be "ultra." There is no such word as "utra."

[4] James Xavier McLanahan (1809-1861), Democrat of Pennsylvania, who served in the US House of Representatives in the Thirty-first (1849-51) and Thirty-second (1851-53) Congresses.

[5] Willis Arnold Gorman (1816-1876), Democrat from Indiana.

[6] Thomas Ross (1806-1865), Democrat from Pennsylvania.

[7] A *ukase* is defined as any order or proclamation by an absolute or arbitrary authority.

[8] Daniel Webster (1782-1852), Federalist, pro-Adams, anti-Jacksonian, and Whig Representative (1813-29) and Senator (1829-50) from Massachusetts.

[9] Robert Charles Winthrop (1809-1894), Whig Representative (1839-49) and Senator (1849-51) from Massachusetts. He served as Speaker of the US House of Representatives in the Thirtieth Congress (1847-49).

[10] General Zachary Taylor (1784-1850), hero of the Mexican War of 1848, was elected President of the United States in 1848 but died, mid-way into his term, on 4 July 1850, just two months after this speech was delivered.

[11] A *tittle* is defined as a very small part or quantity; a particle, jot, or whit.

[12] Isham Green Harris (1818-1897), Democrat Representative (1849-53) and Senator (1877-99) from Tennessee.

[13] In the published version of this speech, Orr noted, "I am indebted to the author of a pamphlet entitled 'The Union, past and future - how it works, and how to save it,' for many of these statistics."

[14] "Phrensy," which is probably an old form of the more modern "frenzy," is defined as violent and irrational excitement; delirium.

[15] Referring to the antislavery motion by Joseph Mosley Root (1807-1879), Whig and then a Free Soiler from Ohio.

[16] From 3-12 June 1850, delegates from nine slave states met in convention in Nashville, Tennessee, to plot their response to a series of abolitionist moves in the US Congress. While many so-called "fire eaters" (pro-slavery advocates who stood for slavery or disunion) attended the meeting, it was a more moderate faction that controlled the gathering and ironed out a manifesto calling for the protection of slavery in the states south of the border line established in the Missouri Compromise of 1820, which they believed extended west to the Pacific Ocean. This set up allowing California and other states formed from territory received from Mexico in the 1848 war to become slave states, an action that precipitated the Civil War a decade later.

Letters of Representative Edwin Barber Morgan on Speakership Contest of 1855-56

Rep. Edwin Barber Morgan (1806-1881) was elected as a Whig in the Thirty-third Congress (1853-55), but in the Thirty-fourth Congress, and until he declined renomination in 1858, Morgan changed his party affiliation to that of a Republican. In the following letters, penned from Washington, D.C. during the fight to elect a Speaker of the House of Representatives that lasted from 3 December 1855 until 2 February 1856, Morgan outlines to his family, including his mother and brothers, the machinations and numerous ballots that swung the election back and forth until Nathaniel P. Banks, Republican of Massachusetts, was finally elected on the record 103rd ballot. They appear here with all of the original spellings and/or typographical errors left intact; some words were truncated or redacted from the original because of the usage of foul language.

ॐ

November 28 1855

I arriv[d] last night. A large majority of the members will be here tonight. Cullom[1] will probably be Clerk. As to Speaker, it is all in the wind. No one can tell anything about it. He can guess only. I cant do better than yourself.

I am in my old rooms[2] & no doubt shall remain, but shall talk it up this evening or in the morning. The prices here are *awful*. Every one says he will not stand it & then comes the other question, where shall I go and do better. Everything here is about as we left it, neither better or worse.

The Southern & K.N.[3] members are giving the lullaby notes of give us a good National[4] man, not an ultra one for Speaker, & my fear is not from what I see or hear, but from the fact that they always succeed & that dough faces[5] will still be found. God grant that the race, if not now, may soon become extinct. I had rather vote today for the most bitter & decided Locofoco-Nebraska man[6] at the South

than for one of your *National* c___d dough faces of the North who is neither hot or cold, fish or fowl. Let us have a bold out & out man. I hope however not to be compelled to meet under either the one or the other.

11 1/2 P.M. We have just had a meeting in my rooms of some 20 members, to canvass matters.

———

November 30, 1855.

We have done nothing today but caucus & endeavor to concentrate opinion upon Speaker, &c. All is harmony, & we hope to have little trouble in the organization, yet we cant guess at results. You will get them faster & sooner than I can write them.

Seward[7] and Weed[8] will be here tonight.

———

December 1, 1855.

We have been caucusing all the morning & have decided not to have a nominating caucus. Banks, I think, will be the Speaker, so it looks, so *I hope*, though I may not vote for him at first, out of policy, which he himself advises, for he had just left my room where we have had an hours free talk with Sage[9] and Pringle[10]. He is all right. Our friends are in fine spirits, & all will be well, or I am no prophet.

Weed & daughter are at our hotel. Seward came last night.

Cullom will be Clerk.

———

December 2, 1855.

Banks stock looks well today, yet some other man, perhaps Pennington[11], may be taken up. We decided *not to have a caucus*. We did not want one. You will see the proceedings of the Loco caucus last evening.

Source: *The Register of the Edwin Barber Morgan Papers*, MS Series Morgan papers, VI [Political], Wells College Archives, Long Library, Wells College, Aurora, New York.

See also page 125

It is just what we wanted. Could not fix it any better.[12]

———

December 3, 1855.

We go to the House in an hour or two to commence the battle. The wires will tell all about it faster than my pen.

We loose [sic] one vote in our State in Mr. Childs[13] of N. York who is sick & probably will never reach here. Out fire will be scatter[d], but it will come out all right. I have very little fear of results.

———

December 6, 1855.

We have as you will learn balloted six times more today making 24 [ballots in total], & are about as when we began. I am certain we shall succeed in the end, but when that is to come I cant tell. We endeavor to keep cool & step on no mans toes but that will not work much longer.

Banks and Campbells[14] friends can get together on either or some other man in 10 minutes, but we have off sided crooked timber to work upon & we hope by their own better judgment or the public indignation they will be made to *feel & act* right.

An half dozen would be great men think they may be struck by lightning, & after balloting again & again all will be drop[d] and they may become *the man*. Poor d___s. Their votes however in this close time are vital. I go at 10 this evening to a private caucus of a dozen to settle upon some policy that *we* will pursue.

———

December 9, 1855.

We expect to elect Banks as Speaker tomorrow without failure. He will be a glorious fellow.

———

December 10, 1855.

We have had another feverish day. Strained Banks up to 107 [votes], as you will have observed before this reaches you, but we are much afraid the *breeching* will give way in the morning & spill us out upon the way.

We are much excited at the course of the K.N.[s] of our State who have had & now hold the power to elect a free Northern man for Speaker over Slave masters of the South. Clark[15], Valk[16], Whitney[17], Haven[18], Wheeler[19] have had it in their own hands on Saturday & today & yet the rascals refuse. What can be said of them at home & what can the *free soil & honest K.N.[s]* say of them? I regret the necessity of becoming so much excited thus[20] early in the session.

Brooks[21] of the Express is here laboring to distract & keep his men out of the ring & prevent an organization.

John Wheeler, poor dunce, has the maggot in his head that he can be Speaker. Of course no other man ever dreamed of it, & it makes an ass of him.

We have had 30 men in my rooms for an hour & laid our plans for tomorrow. How well we shall succeed the Lord only knows, but we shall do our best & that is all we promise. Pennington & Campbell are sour, yet vote with us, but will be glad to drop out when they can. At present, they dare not.

It has been proposed today to elect by plurality. That can never be by my vote, if we sit here till 4 March, [18]57, without doing one thing. We cannot afford to take the risk for it is my opinion if it were done every Southern & some Northern K.N.[s] would drop at once on to Richardson[22] & elect him.

Every card is being drawn this evening for the morrow.

The feeling at home I know must be feverish, & I beg the true free soil K.N.[s] will watch their men & see what they are doing & then say whether they approve of their brethren here & decide whether they are not truly the proslavery party in disguise.

I am working a *little* harder than I wish but at present see no other way. Remember me to our good friends.

———

December 12, 1855.

The Speakership is all by the ears this morning & no man knows when there will be one. Pennington is acting bad. I am certain we can elect no man but Banks & ought not to. His principles are right & true & he would make a splendid officer & organize the Committees right & upon a Northern platform,

& I had rather the whole thing should go by the board than have a half & half fellow in that seat. Brooks, Haven & that class of K.N.ˢ are at work night & day to prevent an organization & put it finally in the dough face hands. Brooks is all over the house whispering to one, calling out another, & debauching every weak sister, or brother as you will have it. Yet these infernal rascals at home talk about being opposed to slavery. Oh, the c___d scamps. If our free soil & honest K.N.ˢ at home could look at these, their leaders, they would leave them & drop off like the foliage after a severe frost.

———

December 13, 1855.

We are just as before in regard to Speaker. Our Spartan band expect to camp down on Banks & go for no one else until the end of our term & let the responsibility rest where it belongs, in the "*Fillmore K.N.ˢ.*" The free soil K.N.ˢ of the west and east go with us to a man & we act in concert. We expect some of our 105 or 106 will leave us today.

Pennington is nowhere now. It is ascertained that many of the Southern National K.N.ˢ have only been waiting for us to run him up, that they might jump on & elect him. A man is judgᵈ by the company he keeps.

———

December 22, 1855.

We have a band of good & true men who stand shoulder to shoulder in this fight for Speaker, but as ever, we have dough faces enough to block the wheels for the time, but we shall triumph over the scamps. These dough faces are being smoked out day after day.

We believe we can on Monday adopt the plurality rule & then Banks will certainly be elected. We can hardly realize the immense difference it will make for freedom if we can place such a man in the Chair as Banks, rather than a Richardson or a Fuller.[23] We can then get reports & bring all of the rascality which for many years has been buried up by the Southern Speakers & Committees. I have never been more constantly engaged than since I came here, in counselling [sic] with the *true men* & sus-

taining the weak kneed & those who want more backbone.

It is one of the most singular facts that some of our new members, when they hear the old Southern croakers talk about the dissolution of the Union, really believe them in earnest. We have adopted a rule that when one of them talks of dissolution in the House, we make our side of the House ring with laughter, sing out, "Goodby [sic] John," & other things of the kind, which always turns their remarks & threats into ridicule.

———

December 26, 1855.

I am in tip top condition, notwithstanding you may not have heard from me. By a note from me to Mother you will see that I have been to N. York, brot [sic, should be "brought"] Charl [Morgan's wife Charlotte] to Pha [sic, should read "Philadelphia"] & that she will be here this evening.

We are now doing the same thing over & over again without any prospect of a better result. I learn by those who remained here yesterday that nothing new occurred, so that nothing new is to be expected.

———

December 27, 1855.

Charl and Louise [Morgan's daughter] came to Baltimore last evening & arrived at 11 this morning. It is a great comfort to get her here & have us together once more.

We are at this moment quite excited. Banks lacks but three votes of an election. Where they are to come from, I cant tell.

———

December 30, 1855.

Four weeks have gone by & here we are as we were. The Administration are becoming excessively tired of this business. Pierce is very anxious to get out his message & is wanting some legislation without delay. Our friends are immovable, except the dough faces who have voted with us, from 6 to 10 who not unlikely will go over to Pennington or some other man who cant be trusted. Our boys will not move from Banks & will march out with our true Northern banners flying, or sink with it like Phario's army in the Red Sea of Slavery and dough faceism.

It has become a matter of honor to stand by our guns, & stand we will. It is nothing but the Fillmore K.N.[s] that keep us in this condition. Haven has said that he will vote for Orr[24] if necessary to keep out any one suspected of Republicanism. He carried Edwards[25] of Chatauqua Co. with him, Whitney, Valk & Wheeler of our State.

We have offered to take the plurality rule three times & shall not again offer it, nor shall we, as heretofore, press the election, but at the usual hour shall vote to adjourn & wait until the Administration members are willing we shall organize, & we will try & wait as long as they are willing to wait, if it is 4 March 57.

If such is to be the cause of K.N.[s], God save us from their embrace. But I am certain that our K.N.[s] at least a great majority of them, will never sanction such rascality.

If we ever get so that I can leave, shall come & spend a day with you.

December 31, 1855.

We are in a terrible uproar at this moment in regard to the Message[26] just sent in which *we* are resolved not to receive, although it is being read in the Senate at this time. Every man is upon his feet crying, Mr. Clerk, Mr. Clerk, Mr. Clerk. It is a hot time. You will see it all by the papers. It is a rascally proceeding.

January 2, 1856.

The New Year is upon us & it gives us no new light in regard to Speaker. We are as we were. It is daily expected that a few men, half a dozen or less, who have voted with us rather under protest may leave us. Yet we rather think that they cant muster sufficient courage to perpetrate so great an outrage. *Time* will give us our members & that will only be when the Administration must have legislation. I think we have backbone enough to keep out of the House the President's infamous message until we are organiz[d]. We are at this moment, as we have been during the morning, contending against it &

such will probably be the daily employment for some time.

January 4, 1856.

Not a word of news. We are doing as heretofore. Have 90 ballotings and it looks as though we were further from an election than at any time for a month. We cant move and dont intend doing so. Let the Administration back down when they please.

January 5, 1856.

There are no new developments in regard to Speaker. Of course we are to go on in the old way. I was delighted to learn that Banks was elected Speaker by the Auburn Daily rec[d] [should be "Record"] this morning. It seems easier to elect him there than here.

January 8, 1856.

We are adjourn[d] over today by the votes of the Locos, South Americans[27], & the straglers [sic]. Last night the Locos had a caucus & agreed not to adjourn tomorrow until a Speaker is elected. We shall join heartily with them & stand up like men, I trust, & bring this long defer[d] matter to a close. We say Banks or Richardson shall be the man & if the outsiders and Fillmore K.N.[s] are resolved upon having Richardson, the sooner the better. Yet we have no fears of that result. The next news now looks as though you could expect the organization of the House, yet I promise nothing.

Seward has a party this evening. All of the N.Y. delegates & families are invited. The sleighing was never better in any country than here. Nearly a foot deep & beautiful weather. We have had no mail from New York in 48 hours & more. This is the third day.

We are constantly hunting up the weak kneed & weak back[d] fellows in our ranks. Many of them require as much attention as the sheep with the foot rot. For what particular *good* purpose the Almighty ever made dough faces for, I am yet to learn.

January 9, 1856.

We have enter[d] the Hall this morning with a determination not to adjourn until a Speaker is elected. With what success time must determine & the telegraph will advise you. I know if our men will stand up to the rack, we can elect Banks before we adjourn.

The truth is, we could elect as one were it not for the war between the South Americans & Southern Democrats. They are vieing [sic; should be "vying"] with each other in their devotion to the Slave power & our Fillmore K.N.[s] to join their South American allies.

January 10, 1856.

We came to the House yesterday at 12 M. It is not 8 1/4 A.M. We have not slept or eat[en] since yesterday & we are constantly voting against adjournment. The roll is being call[d]. The Locos agreed to stay with us, but they are backing down & it is probable we shall soon get away, but not by the votes of our friends.

Not less than a dozen of our opponents have been & are still as drunk as owls. Thanks to our good friends *not one* of them is in the least intoxicated.

Of course we are feeling fine without a minutes sleep but we have done our best to organize & shall continue to do so.

January 15, 1856.

For four days we have had no western mail, for three days, none from N. York. The R.R. [railroads] have been block[d] up.

Yesterday we had a day of platforms. Richardson, Banks & Fuller laid them down. When you see them, you will learn how proud a one we stand upon, the dignified & elegant manner that Banks bore himself brot [sic; should be "brought"] down the House & galeries [sic]. The others were a mere effort to see who could be the greatest dough face. Fuller, the K.N., succeeded best & was consider[d] the most consummate one that had taken the stand in years. He went to the very verge. Yes, a Pennsylva-

nia K.N. does all this. What in God's name will our K.N.[s] say to this infernal doctrine. If they dont approve, & I know they will not, they should see where their leaders, Brooks, Haven & Co., are leading them & the name & influence of their party.

January 22, 1856.

We are plowing along as usual, crying out Banks, Banks, Banks, yes & no, as other questions come up, & there we are to stand till our political doomsday, never to yield to our opponents who know nigger in the morning, nigger at noon, nigger at night, & until broad daylight. Not a vote or thought with them that is not directly connected with slavery & its aggressions. To such a clan we can never, *no never*, yield.

Weed arriv[d] last night to remain two or three days. Seward will probably make a great speech sustaining the position of our Country in regard to Central America. This will set the South to howling & they in turn will have to become the *Union savers* & peace makers.

January 24, 1856.

At this moment we are in great excitement in regard to the President's Message. Every man is upon his feet & a terrible uproar exists. it will be recd, no doubt, but not with my vote. The papers will tell you first about it. Great times, these, & quite as much excitement as is good for most constituents. We are all as usual. Our friends stand up to Banks & no warning of closure. Cant write in this *hubbub*.

January 26, 1856.

I believe from developments that we *certainly shall elect Banks* on Monday or Tuesday at the furthest, *possibly* today. There is no mistake about it. The Administration cannot stand it longer. They must have an organization. Having found the bottom of dough faceism, & satisfied they cannot make further inroads upon our ranks, they are to *cave in* & give us the organization.

Thank God there is at last a North, but He only knows how long it will last. We have, after the election of a Speaker, much labor & severe labor to per-form, yet our boys will enter upon the work with full purpose to do their whole duty. Whatever is done will be done over the heads of the few Fillmore K.N.[s] with whom we are cursed. I cannot speak of those poor d___s who are here & who have violated every pretence they have had for freedom & given all the aid & comfort to the Slave breeders, either directly or indirectly, & yet after this exhibition that same man is securing Silver Gray[28] delegates from our State to the National K.N. Convention.

Well, there is *one* man that will never bow down to the Slave power & I am certain there is a noble band of his neighbors who are just as decided. It is wonderful, yet not singular, that a man who is open, defiant & above board at Washington in opposition to those parties who are constantly encroaching upon our rights, is respected & treated in the most kind manner & applauded for his independence by the men who are opposed, while they *detest the trim-mer*. Toombs[29] and Stephens[30] said to me the other day, "they respected me for the open and undis-guised opposition to the Nebraska Bill & for finally calling for the *last vote* given upon the bill when I *knew* it was all over." "Yes," said Toombs, "You call[d] out to your friends to give the d___d thing its last kick." I mention this merely to show you how they feel when men act like men.

———

January 28, 1856.

We hoped to have accomplished the election of a Speaker about three days [ago] within a day or two, yet we are afloat & the Lord only knows when we shall approach it.

At this moment Dunn[31] of Ind[a] is making a wicked & corrupt speech, doing all in his power to defeat our candidate. We have more trouble, a vast deal more, with the few traitors in our own camp who vote with us, yet are constantly in communication with our open enemies.

The Lord only knows when we shall get through, but time brings an end to all things, & probably will to this. It is enough to make a poor d___l sick, yet we shall labor to the end & never give up the ship.

———

January 30, 1856.

We are now in an excitement in regard to plurality rule offer[d] by Clingman.[32] We are voting upon it. *Very close.* If carried, Banks will be Speaker at once. The wires will tell you.

The excitement last night was intense in regard to the attack on Greeley[33]. It was the most cowardly thing possible. G___ is in his seat today watching the *rascals*.

———

January 31, 1856.

We are at this moment again voting for the plurality rule. What it will amount to, cant say. Close vote anyhow. We think it certain Banks will be elected & in all probability, this week, but the Lord or the d___l, dont know which, can tell.

We have traitors in our camp *who vote with us* yet give aid & comfort to our enemies in all other man-ner of ways. They are to be found principally in the districts bordering upon the Slave states & have Sil-ver Gray proclivities.

———

February 1, 1856.

We have just had a vote on the plurality rule & a change of 2 votes would have carried it. Those we shall get today or tomorrow I have no doubt & then just as little that Banks will be elected. We are quiet, yet there is as much excitement in the House, *deep & still*, as I ever saw. Each vote is expected to be the last or final one, & every vote is watched with intense interest.

We have got the *rascals*, I verily believe.

———

February 2, 1856.

We have just obtain the plurality rule & now com-mences the fillibustering [sic] for adjournment & all manners of things. I dont think we shall elect before Monday & the contest is between Banks and Aiken[34]. The latter owns about 1000 negroes, is a nullifier, cant see across the House, is so near sighted, but he is nigger for breakfast, dinner, supper & lodging. That, in short, is the only issue.

God grant that the friends of freedom for once shall triumph.

———

February 3, 1856.

Long before the recpt [receipt] of this you will have learned the glorious result of last night in the election Banks over Aiken, 103 to 100. Never was there such a triumph gained by freemen for freedom over the Slave breeders & Slave power in this country. When the result was declared, it seemed as though the pent up feelings & the breathless anxiety of nine long weeks could not be satisfied with the prolong[d] & vociferous cheers that went up from the members & the intensely crowded galeries [sic], while the Coalition upon the opposite side of the House of Americans (God forgive them for stealing so sacred a name) & the Democrats, united almost to man for Aiken, the nullifier & one of the largest slave holders in the Union, they, I say, look[d] daggers & swore like pirates.

For once there had been found a North, & that North will never know the labor & intense anxiety of that band of true men who have spent their days & nights in coaxing, threatening & persuading the limber backed & the dough faces to stand up to the rack. A band of 25 men have had almost every night a private meeting to report upon lame ducks & to apportion each mans duty. Most faithfully & truly has it been executed & we have the results. No efforts have been spared by our opponents to make further inroads upon is. What shall be said of the K.N.[s]? They, poor souls, could not vote for Banks because he was not American enough for them, but could vote for Aiken, one of the most bitter opponents of them, because he owned 1000 negroes & was one of the most odious Slave breeders of the South.

And such men lead them, our free soil friends of the K.N. Party. Even in that good old County of Cayuga, there is no escape for them. The Silver Grays & proslavery men are their leaders & will control their conventions, for the whole thing is a mere piece of machinery, & these leaders (look at them, Fillmore, Haven, Brooks, Ullman & Co.) care no more about Catholics & placing the Bible in the Schools, ect. [sic] than the Devil did about his promise when he stood upon the mount & pledg[d]

the vast plains below, for which he had no title. And what makes it more provoking is that these men, when you talk to them about it here, laugh outright & own up that it is all humbug, but that it is good for votes. They are (I speak of the leaders) as great a pack of hipocrites [sic] as ever sung a lip.

When, I have fill[d] up the sheet & only intended saying a word or two.

———

February 5, 1856.

Yesterday we elected Cullom Clerk at Short notice & last evening we had a caucus for other officers. I have fears that we shall encounter the "isms" when we attempt to elect today & may not be successful. The wires will tell you.

Since the election of Banks, I am persuaded that we shall have a working majority in our House. Now the straglers [sic] & weak kneed are very clever & as chivalrous as you could desire. They have done it all. We hope & expect to work them in, as you do the sweepings of a woolen mill into a comfortable fabric. It makes a mighty difference in Washington who is in power. The knee bends easily & the mind is governed instinctively by the almighty dollar.

———

February 6, 1856.

It is funny to see what a clever set of fellows these Locos are now, including the S. Americans, ect. [sic] All wants places for their friends, for Pages, &c. & all want a place on important Com [should read "Committees"] & think Banks & the Republicans very clever fellows. Never was there such a change & for *such evident purposes*.

———

February 7, 1856.

We adjourn[d] over yesterday until Monday to give the Speaker time to make his Committees. Banks is presiding so like a man fully conscious of his ability, taking the reigns in his hands & driving through, that he commands the admiration of all parties.

Dough faceism is at a discount. K.N. is here defunct, or rather it is merged (I mean the free soil part) with us, while the Fillmore wing goes substantially with the Slave breeders.

———

February 15, 1856.

We are full of business now & shall have lots more of it. No peace for the wicked.

Footnotes:

[1] Referring to Rep. William Cullom, Whig from Tennessee. Cullom, first elected to Congress in the Thirty-second Congress (1851-53), was, as Morgan predicted, elected Clerk of the House on 4 February 1856.

[2] Morgan had a room at the famous Willard Hotel in Washington, D.C.

[3] Referring to the "Know-Nothing" members, part of the anti-immigrant American Party.

[4] Know-Nothings were sometimes called "Nationals."

[5] "Dough faces" refers to those Northerners who were wishy-washy on the slavery issue and thus not members of the Whig Party. Morgan appears to have complete contempt for these members.

[6] The name "Locofocos," coined after a small match used for political meetings held in New York State, was given to pro-slavery Democrats in that state; the name, used by Whigs in the 1850s before the advent of the Republican Party, soon became an epithet for all pro-slavery Democrats. In this portion, Morgan shows less hatred for pro-Nebraska constitution slavery members than for Know-Nothings who did not take a firm stand on slavery. Morgan also refers to them in later letters as "Loco" or "Locos."

[7] Senator William Henry Seward, later to run for President in 1860 and to serve as Secretary of State in the Abraham Lincoln and Andrew Johnson administrations, was one of the leaders of the New York delegation in Congress.

[8] Thurlow Weed (1797-1882) was the political boss for New York State.

[9] Referring to Rep. Russell Sage, Whig from New York.

[10] Referring to Rep. Benjamin Pringle, Whig from New York.

[11] Referring to Rep. Alexander C.M. Pennington, Know-Nothing from New Jersey. He is not to be confused with Rep. William Pennington, also from New Jersey but a Republican, who ironically was elected after a protracted debate as Speaker in the Thirty-sixth Congress (1859-61).

[12] Morgan refers to a caucus of Democrats held the previous night that condemned the American, or Know-Nothing, Party members in the House.

[13] Referring to Rep. Thomas Child, Jr., Whig from New York and anti-slavery, anti-Nebraska representative, who became seriously ill before the Congress convened and he never took his seat during the Thirty-fourth Congress.

[14] Referring to Rep. Lewis D. Campbell, Whig of Ohio, who was a leading candidate for Speaker during the first early balloting.

[15] Referring to Rep. Bayard Clark, American from New York.

[16] Referring to Rep. William W. Valk, American from New York.

[17] Referring to Rep. Thomas R. Whitney, American from New York.

[18] Referring to Rep. Solomon G. Haven, American from New York.

[19] Referring to Rep. John Wheeler, American from New York.

[20] Probably should read "this early in the session."

[21] Referring to former Rep. James Brooks, Whig from New York, who during the Thirty-fourth Congress returned to Washington as the congressional correspondent for the New York *Evening Express*, which he also owned and edited.

[22] Referring to Rep. William A. Richardson, Democrat of Illinois, his party's candidate for the speakership.

[23] Referring to Rep. Henry M. Fuller, a former Whig and American from Pennsylvania in the Thirty-fourth Congress, who was the leading Know-Nothing candidate for the speakership.

[24] Referring to Rep. James L. Orr, Democrat and pro-administration member from South Carolina, who was to be elected Speaker of the Thirty-fifth Congress (1857-59).

[25] Referring to Rep. Francis S. Edwards, American from New York.

[26] This is in reference to President Franklin Pierce's annual message, now known as the State of the Union. After Thomas Jefferson, presidents delivered their annual messages to Congress in a report, rather than reading it as is now done.

[27] This refers to southern members of the American, or "Know-Nothing," Party.

[28] "Silver Gray" was the name given to conservative Whigs who left the party in 1850 over the Whig Party's movement against slavery. By 1855-56, the name was an epithet used against all former Whigs in the North who joined the American or "Know-Nothing" Party merely over the issue of slavery. Former President Millard Fillmore, running for President in 1856 as a "Know-Nothing," was gathering the support of these "Silver Grays" in his campaign for the White House.

[29] Former Rep. Robert Toombs, Democrat of Georgia, was elected to the US Senate in 1852.

[30] Referring to Rep. Alexander H. Stephens, Democrat of Georgia, one of the leaders of his party in the House and a staunch advocate of the right to own slaves. When his state seceded from the Union, Stephens was elected as Vice President of the Confederate States of America.

[31] Referring to former Rep. George G. Dunn, Whig from Indiana, who switched to the Republican Party and was elected to a seat in the Thirty-fourth Congress.

[32] Referring to Rep. Thomas L. Clingman, Democrat of North Carolina.

[33] Horace Greeley (1811-72) of New York was a noted newspaperman who served a single four month period in the US House during the Thirtieth Congress (from 4 December 1848 to 3 March 1849) because the sitting congressman had been ultimately refused his seat. The "attack" described by Barber is in reference to a verbal, and not physical, assault.

[34] Rep. William Aiken, Democrat of South Carolina, was the candidate of the pro-administration Democrats after the name of Rep. William Richardson was withdrawn.

Speaker Nathaniel Banks Attempts to Win Free Soil Votes for Presidential Nominee John C. Frémont, 1856

In 1856, Speaker Nathaniel Banks worked to get Free Soilers, those former Whigs who fought for the end of slavery, to cross over from their third party - known simply as the Free Soil Party - to the Republican Party, founded in 1854 in Ripon, Wisconsin, and establish one entity as the anti-slavery party, instead of having anti-slavery votes being spread between several national tickets. In the following two pieces of correspondence, Banks relates how he worked during the presidential campaign that year to get Free Soilers to support and vote for John C. Frémont, the Republican's first presidential candidate.

☙

New York, March 17, 1856
176 Second Avenue

My Dear Sir,

Your letter of February reached me in Washington some time since. I read it with much satisfaction. It was a great pleasure to me to find that you retained so lively a recollection of our intercourse in California. But, my own experience is that permanent & valuable friendships are most formed in contests and struggles. If a man has good points then they become salient & we know each other suddenly.

I had both been thinking and speaking of you latterly. The Banks balloting in the House and your movements in Kansas had naturally carried my mind back to our hundred and forty odd in California and your letter came seasonably and fitly to complete the connection. We were defeated then, but that contest was only an incident in a great struggle, and the victory was deferred not lost. You have carried to another field the same principle with courage and ability to maintain it, and I make you my sincere congratulations on your success - incomplete so far but destined in the end to triumph absolutely.

I have been waiting to see what shape the Kansas question would take in Congress, that I might be enabled to give you some views in relation to the probable result. Nothing yet has been accomplished, but I am satisfied that in the end Congress will take effectual measures to lay before the American people the exact truth concerning your affairs. Neither you nor I can have any doubt what verdict the people will pronounce upon a truthful exposition. It has to be feared from the proclamation of the President that he intends to recognize the usurpation in Kansas as the legitimate government, and that its sedition law, the test oath and the means to be taken to expel its people as aliens, will all directly or indirectly be supported by the army of the United States. Your position will undoubtedly be difficult, but you know I have great confidence in your firmness and prudence. When the critical moment arrives you must act for yourself - no man can give you counsel. A true man will always find the best counsel in that inspiration which a good cause never fails to give him at the instant of trial. All history teaches us that great results are ruled by a wise Providence & we are but units in the great plan. Your action will be determined by events as they present themselves and at this distance I can only say that I sympathize cordially with you, and that as you stood by me firmly and generously when we were defeated by the nullifiers in California, I have every disposition to stand by you in the same way in your battle with them in Kansas.

You see that what I have been saying is more a reply to the suggestions which your condition makes to me than any answer to your letter, which more particularly regards myself. The notices which you had seen of me in connection with the Presidency come from a partial disposition of friends who thing of me more flatteringly than I do of myself, and do not therefore call for any action from us.

Source: Malin, James C., "Speaker Banks Courts the Free-Soilers: The Frémont-Robinson Letter of 1856," *New England Quarterly*, XII:1 (March 1939), 103-12.

See also page 125

Repeating that I am really and sincerely gratified in the renewal of our old friendship, or rather in the expression of it, which I hope will not hereafter have so long an interval I am,

Yours very truly,
J.C. Frémont

———

Gov. Charles Robinson
Lawrence, Kansas

Attention, however, should be directed to Banks's [sic] covering letter:

Washington, March 19.

My Dear Sir:

I enclose to you by request of Col. Frémont, a letter left by him previous to his departure from this city. If it embodies such sentiment as I have heard him express favorable to the interests of your friends in Kansas, and the Free State cause, I think it would be expedient that it should have immediate publication among your people. Of that you can very safely judge for yourself. We are in expectation of being able to do something in Congress that will [be] an effectual aid to Kansas. Our difficulties are numerous, and those we have to contend with are able

and resolute. I think our friends, however, are their equals, and shall be disappointed if we are not able to accomplish much that will aid you. We are in good spirits and hopeful. The Kansas question will meet its first decision in the House this week, and I think it will not be against us.

You will of course have seen that the name of Col. Frémont is freely used in connection with the Presidency. We think he is a safe man, and that he can be elected. Opinion however is not yet fully formed, but his prospects are improving daily. The sentiments of our friends in Kansas will be well considered in the States, and weigh heavily in favor of anyone who shall be supported by them.

We trust you will stand in the great fight for Freedom with unfailing steadfastness. Be assured our people will carry your cause through triumphantly.

Very truly yours,

N.P. Banks, Sp.[1]
Gov. Robinson
Kansas.

Footnote:

[1] Banks signs his name with "Sp." denoting that he is the sitting Speaker of the House.

Schuyler Colfax's Letter on the Election of Nathaniel Banks as Speaker, 1856

Rep. Schuyler Colfax, Republican of Indiana, who himself was later to serve as Speaker of the House, penned this letter in February 1856 on the election of Nathaniel Banks of Massachusetts to the speakership:

❧

WASHINGTON, February 6, 1856.

The electric wires have long since flashed the news over our whole Union that the protracted struggle for Speaker has resulted in a glorious victory for freedom, and that Nathaniel P. Banks, of Massachusetts, presides over the House of Representatives. But though this letter will be old news, so far as that event is concerned, it may be expected of me that I should give some of the closing scenes of this unprecedented contest.

During the latter part of last week, it was evident that the wall of partition between the Democrats and the South Americans[1] was to be broken down, that a fusion of Administration and Southern Know-Nothing members was to take place on some candidate acceptable to both parties, and that this combined array was to elect a Speaker, if possible. On Thursday, therefore, when a proposition was read by Mr. Trippe[2], of Georgia, (Know-Nothing,) to elect Mr. Smith[3], of Virginia, it was rejected by but ten majority ayes, one hundred; noes, one hundred and ten; and on Friday, when Mr. Jones[4], of Tennessee, the chairman of the Democratic caucus, ignored both the party nomination and the platform by offering Mordecai Oliver, of Missouri, an old-line Whig, who had voted for Richardson[5] and Orr[6] on pro-slavery grounds, but had never participated in their caucuses, the nomination polled one hundred and one votes. A subsequent resolution to elect Mr. Banks polled one hundred and three votes, when W. E. W. Cobb[7], of Alabama, proposed for Speaker Governor Aiken[8], of South Carolina, the largest slaveholder in the House, said to own one thousand three hundred negroes, and to be worth a million of dollars. He had never participated in any Democratic caucus, did not stand on their platform, and was understood not to be hostile to Southern Know-Nothings. Mr. Orr, the Democratic nominee, rose and gave in his adhesion to the proposition, earnestly urging Governor Aiken's election. The vote being taken, the two parties opposed to the Republicans, combined nearly their entire vote upon him, and he polled one hundred and three votes, lacking but four of an election. The House immediately adjourned, and all felt that the struggle was to end the next day.

That night Washington city was full of excitement. Some of Mr. Banks' friends felt dispirited, and feared defeat, as Governor Aiken's vote had risen one vote higher than theirs; but the great bulk stood firm, and by ten o'clock it was unanimously decided that the colors should be nailed to the mast.

Saturday morning the galleries and all the passages to the Representative hall were crowded long before the hour of meeting. As soon as the journal was read, the plurality rule was adopted, and the three ballots, which were to precede the final and decisive vote, were taken. Then the Clerk commenced slowly calling the roll of names for the one hundred and thirty-fourth vote for Speaker, on which the candidate receiving the highest number of votes was to be declared elected. The opposition were [sic] sanguine of electing Governor Aiken; but the Republicans knew that Mr. Banks would be chosen. The response of every anti-Banks member was listened to with manifest interest, as well as anxiety, on all sides; and many, as they voted, took occasion to explain the reasons for their support of Aiken.

At last the roll-call was completed. When all the names had been called through, Banks had one hundred and three votes, and Aiken ninety-three; but the rules allow members to change their votes or record their names at any time before the result

Source: Moore, Rev. A.Y., *The Life of Schuyler Colfax* (Philadelphia: T.B. Peterson & Brothers, 1868), 80-84.

See also page 125

is announced; and amid considerable excitement, member after member, who had voted for Fuller, rose, and changed to Aiken.

His vote ran up to ninety-four, ninety-five, ninety-six, ninety-seven, ninety-eight, ninety-nine, one hundred, and there it stopped, exactly where we supposed it would, while there were three more votes that Mr. Banks could have obtained, if necessary, to defeat the South Carolina candidate.

Before the result could be announced, Mr. Cox[9], an Aiken man, moved to adjourn, which was not in order; but Mr. Benson[10], of Maine, one of the tellers, instantly rose, and, with a loud voice, declared the number of votes cast for each candidate, and announced that, in conformity with the resolution adopted by the House, authorizing a plurality to elect on this ballot, N. P. Banks, Jr., a Representative from Massachusetts, was elected Speaker of the Thirty-fourth Congress. The scene that followed this defies description. Not a Representative remained in his seat. The ladies, who had been sitting in the gallery for seven long hours, exultingly waved their handkerchiefs, and from hall and gallery rang forth most enthusiastic applause, mingled with hisses from those who did not approve of the result. When order was restored, Mr. Rust[11] and Mr. A.K. Marshall[12] insisted that Mr. Banks was not yet elected; that a majority vote was necessary to confirm it. But Governor Aiken promptly rose, and asked permission to conduct the Speaker elect to the chair, and Messrs. Cobb, Clingman[13] and Jones, and other Democrats, insisted that the election was legal, and it was confirmed by a vote of one hundred and fifty-five to forty. Mr. Banks was then conducted to the chair; delivered a brief and happily conceived inaugural; was sworn in by Mr. Giddings[14], the oldest member; and the House adjourned.

The scattering votes were six for Mr. Fuller[15], four for Mr. Campbell[16], cast by Messrs. Dunn, Scott, Moore, and Harrison, and one cast by Mr. Wells[17], of Wisconsin, for Mr. Hickman[18] of Pennsylvania. Two members who were present did not vote. The vote for Mr. Aiken showed the following singular compound: Orr and Humphrey Marshall[19], who made an elaborate anti-Catholic speech last winter, and John Kelly[20], a member of the Catholic church, Howell Cobb[21] and Percy Walker[22], Glancy Jones[23] and Trippe, A. H. Stephens[24] and Zollicoffer[25]; and

so on through. But the coalition, though a strong one, did not win.

I have but little room for any extended comment on this result, so auspicious to the cause of freedom. Six years ago, when the Fugitive Slave Law first came into this House, there was a decided majority opposed to it; but one after another, during the two months it was pending, 'conquered their prejudices,' and it finally passed. So also two years ago, when the Nebraska bill was first reported to the House, a majority were opposed to it; but in a month or so it was carried. Now, I rejoice to say, the aspect of affairs is far different. For two months the Republicans have stood fast by their cause and their candidate, and have come out of this protracted contest as strong and united as they went in, and what is better still, victorious besides. We have heard for weeks that the Union would be dissolved if Banks was elected; but he is sitting in the Speaker's chair as I write, presiding over the House, as if it had been the business of his life, and the Union yet survives.

Southern men acknowledge frankly that when a Speaker is elected without a solitary Southern vote, and over the opposition of three parties in the North, it is indeed a victory won by inflexible persistence and unyielding backbone.

Footnotes:

[1] Colfax is not referring to those in South America, but those Know-Nothing members from the American South.

[2] Rep. Robert Pleasant Trippe (1819-1900), American of Georgia.

[3] Rep. William Smith (1797-1887), Democrat of Virginia.

[4] Rep. George Washington Jones (1806-1884), Democrat of Tennessee.

[5] Rep. William Alexander Richardson (1811-1875), Democrat of Illinois.

[6] James Lawrence Orr (1822-1873), Democrat of South Carolina.

[7] Rep. Williamson Robert Winfield Cobb (1807-1864), Democrat of Alabama.

[8] Rep. William Aiken (1806-1887), Democrat of South Carolina.

[9] Rep. Leander Martin Cox (1812-1865), American of Kentucky.

[10] Rep. Samuel Page Benson (1804-1876), Opposition Member of Maine.

[11] Rep. Albert Rust (?-1870), Democrat of Arkansas.

[12] Rep. Alexander Keith Marshall (1808-1884), American of Kentucky.

[13] Rep. Thomas Lanier Clingman (1812-1897), Whig of North Carolina.

[14] Rep. Joshua Reed Giddings (1795-1864), Opposition Member of Ohio.

[15] Unknown - could be either Rep. Henry Mills Fuller (1820-1860), Opposition Member of Pennsylvania, or Rep. Thomas James Duncan Fuller (1808-1876), Democrat of Maine.

[16] Unknown - could be either Rep. James Hepburn Campbell (1820-1895), Opposition Member of Pennsylvania, Rep. John Pierce Campbell, Jr. (1820-1888), American of Kentucky, or Rep. Lewis Davis Campbell (1811-1882), Opposition Member of Ohio.

[17] Rep. Daniel Wells, Jr. (1808-1902), Democrat of Wisconsin.

[18] Rep. John Hickman (1810-1875), Democrat of Pennsylvania.

[19] Rep. Humphrey Marshall (1812-1872), American of Kentucky.

[20] Rep. John Kelly (1822-1886), Democrat of New York.

[21] Rep. Howell Cobb (1815-1868), Democrat of Georgia.

[22] Rep. Percy Walker (1812-1880), American of Alabama.

[23] Rep. Jehu Glancy Jones (1811-1878), Democrat of Pennsylvania.

[24] Rep. Alexander Hamilton Stephens (1812-1883), Democrat of Georgia.

[25] Rep. Felix Kirk Zollicoffer (1812-1862), Whig of Tennessee.

Excerpts from John Sherman's 1895 Autobiography: the Controversial Speakership Election of 1859

Following the disastrous assault by abolitionist John Brown on the federal armory at Harper's Ferry, Virginia (now in West Virginia), which led to Brown's capture - along with several of his compatriots - and subsequent execution, the US House met to open the second session for the Thirty-fifth Congress on 5 December 1859 to choose a Speaker. What followed was a lengthy debate which lasted until 1 February 1860, nearly two full months of haggling in which various candidates, including Rep. John Sherman, Republican of Ohio, were candidates for the speakership. During the debate over who would be finally elected Speaker, Sherman's alleged endorsement of a controversial book by a southerner denouncing slavery became one of the most contentious issues surrounding the election. In this excerpt from Sherman's memoirs, published in 1895 in two volumes, the Ohioan describes the issues surrounding that landmark 1859 speakership election, as well as the matters and concerns of the members of the House, nearly divided in two between Republicans and Democrats with a small group of anti-immigrant Americans, or "Know-Nothings," representatives taking up the remaining seats, issues that included slavery and the powderkeg that divisive question would ignite less than a year later with the election of Republican Abraham Lincoln to the presidency.

❧

"Under such exciting conditions Congress convened on the 5th day of December, 1859, divided politically into 109 Republicans, 101 Democrats, and 27 Americans. No party having a majority, it was feared by some that the scenes of 1855, when Banks[1] was elected speaker only after a long struggle, would be repeated. That contest was ended by the adoption of the plurality rule, but in this case a majority could not agree upon such a rule, and the only possible way of electing a speaker was by fusing of Members until a majority voted for one person.

It was well understood that the Republican vote would be divided between Galusha A. Grow and myself, and it was agreed between us that whichever received a majority of the Republican vote should be considered as the nominee of that party. On the first vote for speaker, Thomas S. Bocock[2], of Virginia, the Democratic candidate, received 86 votes, I received 66, Galusha A. Grow 43, and 21 scattering. Mr. Grow then withdrew his name. On the same day John B. Clark, of Missouri, offered this resolution:

'Whereas certain Members of this House, now in nomination for speaker, did indorse and recommend the book herein mentioned,

'Resolved, That the doctrine and sentiments of a certain book, called *The Impending Crisis of the South - How to Meet It*, purporting to have been written by one Hinton R. Helper, are insurrectionary and hostile to the domestic peace and tranquility of the country, and that no Member of this House who has indorsed and recommended it, or the compend from it, is fit to be speaker of this House.'

In the absence of rules, Mr. Clark was allowed to speak without limit and he continued that day and the next, reading and speaking about the Helper book. John A. Gilmer, of North Carolina, offered as a substitute for the resolution of Mr. Clark a long preamble closing with this resolution:

'*Therefore resolved*, That, fully indorsing these national sentiments, it is the duty of every good citizen of this Union to resist all attempts at renewing, in Congress or out of it, the slavery agitation, under whatever shape and color this attempt may be made.'

A motion was made to lay both resolutions on the table, and was lost by a tie vote of 116 yeas and 116 nays. In the absence of rules a general debate followed, in which southern Members threatened that

Source: Sherman, John, *John Sherman's Recollections of Forty Years in the House, Senate and Cabinet: An Autobiography* (Chicago: The Werner Company; two volumes, 1895), I:168-80.

See also page 139

their constituents would go out of the Union. The excitement over the proposition to compile a political pamphlet, by F.P. Blair[3], an eminent Democrat and slaveholder, from a book called *The Impending Crisis,* written and printed by a southern man, seemed so ludicrous that we regarded it as manufactured frenzy. After John S. Millson, of Virginia, a conservative Democrat, who was opposed to the introduction of the Clark resolution, had exhibited unusual feeling, I said:

'I have until this moment regarded this debate with indifference, because I presumed it was indulged in for the purpose of prevented an organization. But the manner of the gentleman from Virginia, my respect for his long experience in the House, my respect for his character, and the serious impression which this matter seems to have made upon his mind, induce me to say a few words. I ask that the letter which I send up may be read.'

————

The following letter was thereupon read from the clerk's desk:

Washington City, December 6, 1859.

Dear Sir: - I perceive that a debate has arisen in Congress in which Mr. Helper's book, *The Impending Crisis,* is brought up as an exponent of Republican principles. As the names of many leading Republicans are presented as recommending a compendium of the volume, it is proper that I should explain how those names were obtained in advance of the publication. Mr. Helper brought his book to me at Silver Spring to examine and recommend, if I thought well of it, as a work to be encouraged by Republicans. I had never seen it before. After its perusal, I either wrote to Mr. Helper, or told him that it was objectionable in many particulars, to which I adverted; and he promised me, in writing, that he would obviate the objections by omitting entirely or altering the matter objected to. I understand that it was in consequence of his assurance to me that the obnoxious matter in the original publication would be expurgated, that Members of Congress and other influential men among the Republicans were induced to give their countenance to the circulation of the edition so to be expurgated.

F.P. Blair
Silver Spring
Hon. John Sherman

I then continued:

"I do not recollect signing the paper referred to; but I promise, from my name appearing in the printed list, that I did sign it. I therefore make no excuse of that kind. I never read Mr. Helper's book, or the compendium founded upon it. I have never a copy of either. And here, Mr. Clerk, I might leave the matter; but as many harsh things have been said about me, I desire to say that since I have been a Member of this House, I have always endeavored to cultivate the courtesies and kind relations that are due from one gentleman to another. I never addressed to any Member such language as I have heard to-day. I never desire such language to be addressed to me, if I can avoid it. I appeal to my public record, during a period of four years, in this body; and I say now that there is not a single question agitating the public mind, not a single topic on which there can be sectional jealousy or sectional controversy, unless gentlemen on the other side of the House thrust such subjects upon us. I repeat, not a single question. We have pursued a course of studied silence. It is our intention to organize the House quietly, decently, in order, without vituperations; and we trust to show the Members on all sides of the House that the party with which have the honor to act can administer this House and administer this government without trespassing on the rights of any."

Soon after, in answer to an inquiry from Shelton F. Leake, of Virginia, I said:

"Allow me to say, once and for all, and I have said it five times on this floor, that I am opposed to any interference whatever of the people of the free states, with the relation of master and slave in the slave states."

This was following by a heated debate, the manifest purpose of which was to excite sectional animosity, and to compel southern Americans to cooperate with the Democratic Members in the election of a Democrat for speaker. The second ballot, taken on the close of the session on December 8, exhibited no material change except that the Republican vote concentrated on me. I received 107 votes, Mr. Bocock 88, Mr. Gilmer 22, and 14 scattering.

The debate continued and was participated in by my colleague, S.S. Cox[4], who asked me about the fugitive slave law. I declined, as I had before, to answer any interrogatories and said: 'I will state to him, and to gentlemen on the other side of the House, that I stand upon my public record. I do not expect the support of gentlemen on that side of the House, who have, for the last four years, been engaged in a series of measures - none of which I approve. I have no answers to give to them.'

The third ballot produced no material change. I received 110, Bocock 88, Gilmer 20, and 13 scattering.

In the meantime, the invasion of Harper's Ferry was debated in the Senate at great length and with extreme violence, producing in both Houses intense irritation and excitement. Keitt[5], of South Carolina, charged upon the Republicans the responsibility of Helper's book and John Brown's foray, exclaiming: 'The south here asks nothing but its rights...I would have no more; but, as God is my judge, as one of its Representatives, I would shatter this republic from turret to foundation-stone before I would take one tittle less.' Lamar[6], of Mississippi, declared that the Republicans were not 'guilt-less of the blood of John Brown and his co-conspirators, and the innocent men, the victims of his ruthless vengeance.' Pryor[7], of Virginia, said Helper's book riots 'in rebellion, treason, and insurrection, and is precisely in the spirit of this act which startled us a few weeks since at Harper's Ferry.' Crawford[8], of Georgia, declared, 'We will never submit to the inauguration of a black Republican President.'

The Republicans generally remained silent and demanded a vote.

Mr. Corwin[9], then a Representative from Ohio, elected after a long absence from public life, endeavored to quiet the storm. Frequent threats of violence were uttered. Angry controversies sprang up between Members and personal collisions were repeatedly threatened by Members, armed and ready for conflict. No such scenes had ever before occurred in the Congress of the United States. It appeared many times that the threatened war would commence on the floor of the House of Representa-

tives. The House remains in session the week between Christmas and New Year's Day. During this excitement my vote steadily increased until on the 4th day of January, 1860, on the 25th ballot, I came within three votes of election; the whole number of votes cast being 207; necessary to a choice 104, of which I received 101. John A. McClernand, of Illinois, received 33, Gilmer 14, Clement L. Vallandigham, of Ohio, 12, and the remainder were scattering.

At this time, Henry Winter David, of Maryland, an American, said to me, and to others, that whenever his vote would elect me it should be cast for me. J. Morrison Harris, also an American from the same state, was understood to occupy the same position. [Of] Garnett B. Adrain, of New Jersey, an anti-Lecompton Democrat[10], who had been elected by Republicans, it was hoped would do the same. Horace F. Clark, of New York, also an anti-Lecompton Democrat who had been elected by Republicans, could at any moment have settled the controversy in my favor. It was well known that I stood ready to withdraw whenever the requisite number of votes could be concentrated upon any Republican Members. The deadlock continued.

On the 20th of January, 1860, Mr. Clark, who had introduced the Helper resolution, said:

'I wish to make a personal explanation with regard to my personal feelings in the matter of this resolution. I never read the letter of which the gentleman from Georgia speaks, and do not take to myself articles that appear in newspapers, unless they make imputations against my moral integrity. That resolution was introduced by me, as I have frequently remarked, with no personal ill-feeling towards Mr. Sherman, the Republican candidate for speaker, apart from what I considered to be an improper act of his - namely, the recommendation of that book. So far as that affects his political or social character, he must of course bear it.'

I replied as follows:

'The gentleman from Missouri, for the first time, I believe, has announced that it was his purpose, in introducing this resolution, to give gentlemen an opportunity to explain their relations to the Helper book. I ask him now whether he is willing to withdraw the resolution for the purpose he has indicated, temporarily, or for any time?'

Mr. Clark said:

'I will endeavor to answer the gentleman. I avowed my purpose frankly at the time I introduced the resolution, in the remarks with which I accompanied its introduction. The gentleman from Ohio propounds the question more directly whether I am willing to withdraw the resolution for the purpose which I avow? Sir, at the very instant it was offered, I gave the gentleman that opportunity and I have given it to him since. I say to the gentleman that he has had two opportunities to make that explanation; but he has failed to relieve himself of the responsibility he took when he signed that book and recommended its circulation.'

I replied:

'I will say that that opportunity has never been rendered to me. When the gentleman introduced his resolution, offensive in its character, at an improper time, in an improper manner, he cut off - what he says now he desires to give - an opportunity for explanation. It is true that three days afterwards, when the gentleman from Virginia (Mr. Millson) appealed to me, I stated to him frankly how my name became connected with that paper. I did not sign the paper; but it seems that the Hon. E.D. Morgan[11], a member of the last Congress, and a friend of mine, came to me when I was in my place, and asked me to sign a recommendation for the circulation of a political pamphlet, to be compiled by a committee, of which Mr. Blair, slaveholder of Missouri, was one, from a large book by Helper, a North Carolinian. I said to him that I had not the time to examine the book; thereupon the gentleman attached my name to that paper. This information I did not have at the time the gentleman from Virginia addressed me; but I said to him I had no recollection of having signed the paper, but presumed that I had, from my name appearing in the printed list. I subsequently acquired it from Mr. Morgan, whose letter was published. That I believe was sufficient under the circumstances. I know there are Members on that side of the House who have considered it as satisfactory; and my friends so regard it. At the time I stated that I had not read the book, that I did not know what was in it.

'The gentleman alludes to another time. The other day, when this subject was again brought before the House by him, in language which, although he claims to be courteous, I could not regard as such, when I was, by implication, but with a disclaimer of personal offense, charged with disseminating treason, with lighting the torch in the dwelling of my southern brethren, and of crimes of which, if I were guilty, I should not be entitled to a seat upon this floor, I then rose in my place, and told the gentleman from Missouri that if he would withdraw that resolution I would answer this book page by page, or those extracts one by one, and tell him whether I approved them or not. The gentleman refused to withdraw the resolution. Long ago he was notified by me, and my friend from Pennsylvania (Mr. Morris) announced on the floor, that this resolution was regarded by me as a menace, and, if withdrawn, would lead to a frank avowal, or disavowal.

'I say not that I do not believe it is the desire of the gentleman to give me that opportunity. If he does desire it, I am willing to do now what I said I would have done then. And I say, with equal emphasis, that never, so help me God, whether or not the speaker's chair is to be occupied by me, will I do so while that resolution is before this body, undisposed of. I regard it as offensive in its tone, unprecedented, unparliamentary, and an invasion of the rights of representation. Under the menace clearly contained in it, I never will explain a single word contained in those extracts.

'If the gentleman will withdraw his resolution, even for a moment, to relieve me from the menace - he may reinstate it afterwards if he chooses - I will then say what I have to say in regard to those extracts. But while it stands before the House, intended as a stigma upon me, and sustained by an argument without precedent in parliamentary history, he cannot expect me to say more than I have done. I believe not only my friends, but the gentlemen on the other side of the House, who have a sense of honor, believe that my position is correct. I know that some of them regard my statement made on the third day of the session as full and satisfactory, and all that, under the circumstances, it was proper for me to indicate.

'For the gentleman now to press this matter; to agitate the country; to spread these extracts over the south, and to charge the sentiments of this book upon me, and my associates here; to proclaim, day after day, that the Republicans entertain these sentiments and indorse them, is not that ingenuous, candid and manly course which a great party like the Democratic party ought to pursue. While we may conduct our political quarrels with heat, and discuss matters with zeal and determination, it ought to be done with fairness and frankness. The mode in which this resolution has been pressed before the country, and I, with my hands tied and my lips sealed as a candidate, have been arraigned day by day, is without a precedent, not only in history but in party caucuses, in state legislatures, in state conventions or anywhere else.

'I said when I rose the other day that my public opinions were on record. I say so now. Gentlemen upon the other side have said that they have examined that record to ascertain what my political opinions were. They will look in vain for anything to excite insurrection, to disturb the peace, to invade the rights of the states, to alienate the north and south from each other, or to loosen the ties of fraternal fellowship by which our people have been and should be bound together. I am for the Union and the constitution, with all the compromises under which it was formed, and all the obligations which it imposes. This has always been my position; and those opinions have been avowed by me on this floor and stand now upon your records. Who has brought anything from that record against me that is worthy of answer?

'I have never sought to invade the rights of the southern states. I have never sought to trample upon the rights of citizens of the southern states. I have my ideas about slavery in the territories, and at the proper time and in the proper way I am willing to discuss the question. I never made but one speech on the subject of slavery, and that was in reference to what I regarded as an improper remark made by President Pierce in 1856. I then spread upon the record my opinions on the subject; and I have found no man to call them into question. They are the opinions of the body of the Republicans. They are the opinions which I now entertain. Gentlemen are at liberty to discuss these questions as much as they choose, and I will bear my share of

the responsibility for entertaining those opinions. But I now speak to my personal record...

'Again these gentlemen, while publishing in their speeches all over the country that I am in effect a traitor, etc., by implication, it is true, disavowing, as I am glad to say each of them have done, any design to be personally offensive, but in a way that answers the same purpose; yet when called upon to show proofs or specifications, they fail to do so; and the only act for which I have been arraigned before the American people is that, in a moment when I was sitting here, busy at my desk, and one of my friends, and late a Member of this House, came to me and asked me to sign a paper recommending the publication of a political tract; that, when I authorized my name to be put to that recommendation, by that very act I became a traitor and would place the torch in the hands of the incendiary. I say this is not fair argument. And I again repeat that if the Member from Missouri (Mr. Clark) desires to know what my sentiments are in regard to the extracts read at the clerk's table, the only portion of the Helper book I have ever seen or read, I will give them if he will remove a menace from me. I never did do anything under menace. I never will. It is not in my blood and these gentlemen cannot put it there.'

Mr. Clark rose to speak, but I continued:

'The gentleman will excuse me, I have, so far as I am concerned in this contest, been quiet and patient. I desire an organization of the House opposed to the administration. I think it is our highest duty to investigate, to examine and analyze the mode in which the executive powers of this government have been administered for a few years past. That is my desire. Yes sir, I said here, in the first remark I made, that I did not believe the slavery question would come up at all during this session. I came here with the expectation that we would have a business session, that we would examine into the business affairs of this government, and that we would analyze the causes of the increased expenditures of the government and the proper measures of redress and retrenchment. I did not believe that the slavery question would come up, and but for the unfortunate affair of Brown at Harper's Ferry, I did not believe there by any feeling on the subject. Northern Members came here with kindly feelings, no man approving of the foray of John Brown and every man willing to say so; every man willing to admit it as an act of lawless violence. We came here hoping that, at this time of peace and quiet, we might examine, inquire into, and pass upon, practical measures of legislation tending to harmonize the conflicting elements of the government and strengthen the bonds of Union. The interests of a great and growing people present practical questions enough to tax the ability and patriotism of us all.

'Such was our duty; but the moment we arrived here - before, sir, we had even a formal vote, - this question of slavery was raised by the introduction of the resolution of the gentleman from Missouri. It has had the effect of exciting the public mind with an irritating controversy. It has impaired the public credit and retarded the public business. The debate founded upon it has been unjust, offensive, wrong, not only to the Republicans here, not only to those with whom I act, but to all our common constituents, north and south. The gentlemen who have advocated that resolution have stirred up bad blood, and all because certain gentlemen have recommended that a compilation be made of a book. Even yet we may retrieve the loss of valuable time. We could now go to work, organize this House and administer the powers of this House with fairness and impartiality.

'In conclusion, let me say that by no act or effort have I sought the position I now occupy before the House. The honor was tendered me by the generous confidence and partiality of those with whom it has been my pride to act, politically. Their conduct in this irritating controversy has justified my attachment.

'If I shall ever reach the speaker's chair, it will be with untrammeled hands and with an honest purpose to discharge every duty in the spirit which the oath of office enjoins; and to organize the House with reference to the rights and interests of every section, the peace and prosperity of the whole Union, and the efficient discharge of all the business of the government. And whenever friends who have so gallantly and liberally sustained me this far believe that my name in any way presents an obstacle to success, it is my sincere wish that they should adopt some other. Whenever any one of my political friends can combine a greater number of votes than I have honored with, or sufficient to elect him by a majority or plurality rule, I will not stand in this po-

sition one hour; I will retire from the field, and yield to any other general with whom I set, the barren honors of the speaker's chair; and I promise my friends a grateful recognition of the unsolicited honor conferred upon me, and a zealous and earnest cooperation.'

Pending the vote on the 39th ballot and before it was announced, Robert Mallory, of Kentucky, an American, appealed to the Democrats to vote for William N.H. Smith, of North Carolina, also an American, which would elect him. The Democrats thereupon changed their votes to Mr. Smith, making many speeches in explanation of their action. Perceiving that this would elect Mr. Smith I arose and for the first time cast my ballot for speaker, voting for Mr. Corwin. Three other Members who had voted for Mr. Smith changed their votes, which defeated the election on that ballot.

After this vote I conferred with Davis and George Briggs, of New York, Americans, and Adrain[12]. I had the positive assurance of these three gentlemen that if I withdraw they would vote for William Pennington, of New Jersey, and thus secure a Republican organization of the House. I referred this proposition to my Republican associates, and a majority of them were opposed to any change. Francis E. Spinner, of New York, said he never would change his vote from me, and Thaddeus Stevens said he never would do so until the crack of doom. When afterwards reminded of this Mr. Stevens said he thought he 'heard it cracking.'

I felt the responsibility, but on the 30th of January, 1860, I determined to withdraw. In doing so I made the following remarks, as printed in the *Congressional Globe*:

'Mr. Clerk - [Loud cries of "Down," "Down," "Order," "Order," "Let us have the question," etc.] Eight weeks ago, I was honored by the votes of a large plurality of my fellow Members for the high office of speaker of this House. Since that time they have adhered to their choice with a fidelity that has won my devotion and respect; and, as I believe, the approbation of their constituents. They have stood undismayed amidst threats of disunion and disorganization; conscious of the rectitude of their purposes; warm in their attachment to the constitution and Union, and obedient to the rules of order and the laws. They have been silent, firm, manly. On the other hand, they have seen their ancient adversary and their natural adversary reviving anew the firs of sectional discord, and broken in fragments. They have seen some of them shielding themselves behind a written combination to prevent the majority of the House from prescribing rules for its organization. They have heard others openly pronounce threats of disunion; and proclaim that if a Republican be duly elected President of the United States, they would tear down this fair fabric of our rights and liberties, and break up the union of these states. And now we have seen our ancient adversary, broken, dispersed and disorganized, unite in supporting a gentleman who was elected to Congress as an American, in open, avowed opposition to the Democratic organization.

'I should regret exceedingly, and believe it would be a national calamity, to have anyone who is a supporter, directly or indirectly, of this administration, or who owes it any allegiance, favor or affection, occupying a position of importance or prominence in the House. I would regard it as a public calamity to have the power of this House placed, directly or indirectly, under the control of this administration. It would be, it seems to me, a fatal policy to trust the power of this House to the control of the gentlemen who have proclaimed that under any circumstances, or in any event, they would dissolve the union of these states. For this reason we would be wanting in our duty to our God and our country, if we did not avert such a result of this contest. I regard it as the highest duty of patriotism to submerge personal feelings, to sacrifice all personal preferences and all private interests, to the good of our common country. I said here a few days ago, and I always stood in the position, that when I became convinced that any of my political friends or associates could receive further support outside of the Republican organization, I would retire from the field and yield to him the honor of the position that the partiality of friends has assigned to me. I believe that time has now arrived. I believe that a greater concentration can now be made on another gentleman, who, from the beginning, has acted with me.

'Therefore, I respectfully withdraw my name as a candidate. And in doing so, allow me to return my heartfelt thanks for the generous and hearty thanks for the generous and hearty support of all my political friends, and especially to those gentlemen with whom I have not the tie of a party name, but the higher one of a common purpose and sympathy. And if I can ask of them one more favor, it would be that in an unbroken column, with an unfaltering front and unwavering line, each of them will cast his vote in favor of any one of our number who can command the highest vote, or who can be elected speaker of this House.'

A ballot was immediately taken, but, much to my chagrin, the gentlemen named did not change their votes, and Mr. Pennington still lacked three votes of an election. I again appealed to Davis and Briggs, and finally, on the 1st of February, Mr. Pennington received their votes. The result was announced: Pennington, 117 votes, McClernand, 85; Gilmer, 16; 15 scattering; giving Pennington a majority of one, and thus, after a long and violent contest, a Republican was elected speaker of the House of Representatives.

[...]

I had voted for Mr. Pennington during the contest, had a high respect for him as a gentleman of character and influence, long a chancellor of his state, and a good Republican."

Footnotes:

[1] Rep. Nathaniel P. Banks, Republican of Massachusetts, served as Speaker in the Thirty-fourth Congress (1855-57), when he was a member of the American, or "Know-Nothing," Party.

[2] Rep. Thomas S. Bocock, Democrat of Virginia, later served as the Speaker of the Confederate House of Representatives during the US Civil War (1861-65).

[3] Rep. Francis Preston Blair (1821-75), also known as Frank Blair, was the scion of a famed family of Maryland politicians, including his father Francis P. Blair, Sr., and his brother Montgomery Blair, who would later serve in the Lincoln administration as Postmaster General.

[4] Referring to Rep. Samuel Sullivan Cox, Democrat of New York.

[5] Referring to Rep. Laurence M. Keitt, Democrat of South Carolina.

[6] Referring to Rep. Lucius Quintus Cincinnatus Lamar, Democrat of Mississippi, who later served in the US Senate (1877-87) and served as the Secretary of the Interior (1885-88) in the Grover Cleveland administration, and on the US Supreme Court (1888-93)

[7] Referring to Rep. Roger A. Pryor, Democrat of Virginia.

[8] Referring to Rep. Martin J. Crawford, Democrat of Georgia.

[9] Referring to Rep. Thomas Corwin, Republican of Ohio.

[10] Being an "anti-Lecompton Democrat" refers to those who opposed to a pro-slavery constitution being pushed for the state of Kansas. This constitution, enacted by the minority slaveholders in the state, was

drafted at the city of Lecompton. It was one of the reasons for a series of brutal attacks between the two sides of the slavery issue which gave rise to the period of "Bloody Kansas."

[11] Referring to US Senator Edwin D. Morgan, Republican of New York, who served from the Thirty-fifth Congress (1857-59) until the Fortieth Congress (1867-69).

[12] Referring to Rep. Garnett Bowditch Adrain (1815-78), Democrat of New Jersey.

Letters from Robert C. Winthrop, 1872 & 1883

In 1872 and 1883, years after he had left the service of the US Congress, where he had served as Speaker (1847-49), former Rep. Robert Charles Winthrop of Massachusetts wrote two separate and important letters to his close friend Charles Deane, a merchant in Massachusetts. Discussing events - and men - who by that time had passed into history, Winthrop conversed in the first correspondence about the intrigues inside Congress, mainly between himself and former Rep. Joshua Giddings of Indiana; in the second, 11 years later, he discusses a book by Henry Stuart Foote, a political contemporary of Winthrop in the US Senate, who penned a book in 1874 that Winthrop discovered years later was filled with what he felt were gross inaccuracies of his own record. Winthrop also delves into the speakership in these two pieces of correspondence, writing on the office as a whole - and the difficulties in handling it - as well as his own political problems, which led to the shortening of his career in Washington.

❧

Brookline, 27 August, 1872

Dear Mr. Deane,

I return the *History of the Rebellion - Its Authors & Causes* by the late Joshua R. Giddings[1]. In reading this, & some other works on the same subject, of recent publication, I am continually reminded of the old fable of the Forester & the Lion. It is one of Aesop's I believe. At any rate, it is very familiar. The forester, you remember pointed to a statue of a man striding over a vanquished lion, as proof positive of the inferiority of the lion. 'But let me be the carver, said the lion, & I will make the lion striding over the man.' These *ex-parte* accounts are very untrustworthy. I have no wish to say anything harsh of Giddings, more especially since he is dead. He had many good qualities, but a scrupulous utterance of the truth was not one of them. His book is a mere attempt to justify a rash public career, & to make himself out the Hero of the whole Antislavery

struggle. He paints or carves himself as *the* Man striding the vanquished lion. But has a good many competitors for this place in the picture now-a-days, & they may be safely left to fight it out among themselves.

Giddings always coveted martyrdom, & lost no opportunity, as his book shows, to magnify & intensify every indignity which he could succeed in provoking the Hotspurs of the South to offer him. He insisted on exaggerating a Censure into an Expulsion, & rushed out of the House in the most dramatic style.[2] John Quincy Adams never resigned because resolutions of censure were hurled at him. He stood up all the stronger. But Giddings could not be satisfied without throwing up his Commission, & thus really giving a triumph to his adversaries, in order to signalize himself as a martyr.

Yet his book, so far as I have gone, is much freer from personal abuse than I had expected to find it.

His allusions to myself are quite temperate. His omissions in regard to my course are more extraordinary than his expressions. He no where mentions my arguments on the Right of Petition, which so many experts told me at the time was the first presentation of the true Parliamentary doctrine. He no where mentions my original Resolution against Texas[3], or the Anti Slavery proviso I offered to the Oregon Bill before Wilmot had been heard of in that relation. He makes but slight reference to my Resolutions & none at all to my Report, on the Imprisonment of Colored Seamen on page 212; while as to the contest I had in the Senate on the same subject in 1850, he is wholly mute. Nor does he allude to my vote against the Fugitive Slave Law.

I am glad to see, too, that he forbore from renewing in this work the charge which was a main element in the vindication of himself for not voting for me as Speaker - viz - that I had attended a meeting on the morning of the day on which the Mexican War Bill was passed, & had asked all the Whigs to vote for it.

Source: Winthrop to Charles Deane, 27 August 1872, and Winthrop to Deane, 10 August 1883, *The Robert C. Winthrop Papers,* Massachusetts Historical Society, Boston, Massachusetts.

See also page 105

He insisted on this charge till it was proved false by his own witnesses; & he seems to have finally abandoned it. So far, so good.

His footnote on the 262[d]. page is remarkable. It says that I, 'feeling aggrieved, replied to the writer, & a most unpleasant personal & political controversy arose between them, which continued for some four or five years.' What an exaggeration! I never took the slightest notice of Gidding's [sic; should read Giddings'] vote against me in 1847, as Speaker, or of anything said by him on the subject, until the 21st. of February 1850, & then only in a public speech, in which I noticed Root[4], & Andrew Johnson, & other assailants from different parties & sections, as much as I did him. Soon afterwards, I was transferred to the Senate, & I never saw him, (unless passing in the corridors) again, or had the slightest conversation or correspondence or controversy with him.

But the footnote on the next page (263), with the text & caption of the page itself, are still more remarkable. 'Official intrigue of the Speaker'!!! 'The Committees were all arranged by him in such a manner as to effect the political objectives which had in view.'! 'The first of these was the election of Gen[l] Taylor'! This last point is funny. Taylor was not nominated for nearly six months after my Comm[ers].[5] were appointed; & his election did not come round for nearly a year. And what possible influence the appointment of Comm[ers]. in Congress should have on a Presidential Election is beyond my comprehension.

As to the 'intrigue,' the only overture I had was from Dr. Palfrey[6], who I know well had no corrupt or sinister intentions. But no approach was ever made to me except that, either before or after my election to the Chair. I literally locked myself up in my own room at Gadsby's for three days, while the House had a recess, & made the Committees without consultation with any one. It was the hardest work I ever did in my life. To parcel out so many men, with so many claims, personal, political, & geographical, among so many different Committees, giving a fair proportion to different sections & parties, was to me a puzzle beyond all Chinese intricacy.

The result, as I anticipated, did not fully satisfy either friend or foe - nor even myself. There is no such thing as satisfying one's self in the solution of such a problem.

But the complaints came from the South at the first moment. Toombs[7] was indignant at my putting Vinton[8] first, & himself second, on the 'Ways and Means.' Stephens[9] expected a higher preferment than he received. The whole North Carolina Delegation turned the cold shoulder upon me for not having made them more prominent. Meantime the Democrats, having had the speakership so long, & with it the control of all the Committees were clamorous against me. It was almost always so, at first; - but the feeling soon passed away.

Nothing remained by the absolutely *false* charges contained on this page of Mr. Giddings's book. There is not one scintilla of truth in the allegations there made. The Committees were neither arranged for any such purposes as he describes, nor did they accomplish the results, so far as Slavery was concerned, which he attributes to them. The records of Congress will show the injustice of these charges.

Even the National Era, the great Free Soil Organ at Washington, vindicated at least one of my Comm[ers] (on Territories, the most important of all in this relation) from Mr. Giddings's censures.

The truth is, that there were but half a dozen of these extreme men in the House, & unless I had packed them all into one Comm[ee].[10], & had anything relating to Slavery to that one Committee, they would never have been content. It is rather striking, however, that Mr. Tuck[11] of N.H., who united with Dr. Palfrey & Giddings in voting against me when I was elected (in spite of the example & remonstrances [sic] of John Quincy Adams) - *voted for me* at last, in company with Horace Mann[12] & others, when I was a Candidate for a second term, & after my Committees & the result of them had been fully manifested. Horace Mann declared openly that he had considered it hardly less than Providential, for the interests of free soil, that I had been Speaker when I was!

Now I do not profess to have been an Abolitionist, or a Free-Soiler, in any technical sense. I can claim no part or lot in that great agitation & strife which resulted in Civil War, & through Civil War, in the extinction of Slavery. I always opposed the extension of Slavery, & did what I could do to keep the peace between the North & South, hoping that a way would be opened one of these days, in the good providence of God, for the gradual emancipation, on some basis which would be safe both for the blacks & the whites. I make no pretension to have been infallible, & I doubt not I made as many mistakes as my neighbors. But this whole imputation of Mr. Giddings, - page, caption & footnote - is flagrantly false.

I dare say he had persuaded himself that there was some foundation for it, & I make all allowances for his prejudiced and passionate nature. It is enough to say that he was as much mistaken in these assertions, as he was in regard to that meeting about the War Bill, which had no foundation except his own heated imagination or confused remembrance of things.

There is nothing else in the book with which I am personally concerned, though I see, at every turn of the leaf, abundant evidences of careless or one-sided statement. But I have written more than I thought of doing. I hope you will preserve my letter, as I keep no copy of it.

There is a Newspaper of which I have but one. I wish I could procure half a dozen. It is the Boston Journal of Friday Evening, 8th of February, 1850. It was published while my canvass for Senator must have been going on. I was in Washington, & knew nothing about it. But it goes through my whole career, so far as Slavery is concerned, vote by vote, in eleven articles, covering the whole of the first page, & part of the last. The record is very full, & I should be willing to be judged by it.

Thanking you for the loan of the volume, which I return herewith, I am, as ever,

Faithfully Yours,
/a/ Rob$^{t.}$ C. Winthrop.

❧

Charles Deane Esq.

Brookline, 10 August, 1883

Dear Mr. Deane, I return the *Casket of Reminiscences* of Henry S. Foote, & thank you for sending it to me.[13] Foote was a man of some cleverness & of a good deal of desultory leading. But his *Reminiscences* betray, at every page, his carelessness & inaccuracy. On page 5, he speaks of John Quincy Adams having

fallen "while in the act of delivering an eloquent & powerful Speech upon a question which involved his feelings very deeply," &c. &c. Now, Mr. Adams fell while in the act of addressing me & with a paper in his hand of which he had not announced the nature. I can hear, to this day, his ringing cry "Mr. Speaker, Mr. Speaker," & see him sinking to the floor without another word. He was forthwith carried into my Speaker's room, & I was with him when he died two days afterwards. I described the scene, as a fit subject for an Historical picture, in my Address on Luxury & the Fine Arts, & the description may be read in my 2^{d}. vol. of Addressed & Speeches, p. 483. - It furnishes a sufficient illustration of the *exactness* of Foote's *Reminiscences!* He was a slip-shod person, a great busybody, always ready to supply pistols for a duel, or to play second in any affair of what used to be called honor. He often figured as a buffoon in the Senate Chamber, & gave occasions to all sorts of dramatic scenes. Still, he had many attractive & amiable traits, & we all likes to conciliate his good will. His book contains a few noteworthy facts, *if they are facts*. Dr. Green should get a copy for our Rebellion Collection, as he should, also, a copy of the *Life of Genl Dix*, & of the *Life of Buchanan*.

I am sorry to have escaped any notice of Foote's *Reminiscences*. I had a little brush with him in the Senate in 1850. You will find it in the accompanying pamphlet, of which I have just hunted up a copy to refresh my own memory. I have been reading over the whole pamphlet, & though 33 years have elapsed since the Debate occurred, I was almost as much roused as I was in 1850. This little pamphlet contains an account of the most stirring controversy in which I was ever engaged. I had Jefferson Davis[14], & Judge Butler[15], & Berrien[16], & Foote, & Soulé[17], all upon me successively, &, though I say it who should not, I did not come off second best. I have always considered this scene as among the Memorabilia of my public life. I remember that such men as Theodore Parker[18], Anson Burlingame[19], R.H. Dana[20], - as well as Everett[21] & Appleton[22], - wrote to congratulate me on my triumph! But the Free Soilers all persisted in their Coalition with the Democrats, & refused to vote for me as Senator, while Webster & some of the old Whigs turned a cold shoulder upon me because I refused to vote for the Fugitive Slave Law. And so ended my official life, after 17 years service in State & Nation. I do not regret it, I never did, though I may regret the way in which it was done. I had had enough of party strife, & enough of public honor, as Speaker & Senator. As I look back on the whole matter now, I rejoice that a good Providence gave me the opportunity of doing some good in the world in other ways, & that I was not destined to remain in political service. Historical Societies & Peabody Trusts & Provident Associations & other such things have afforded me more congenial occupation. If I had been chosen Senator again, or Governor, I should have lost them all.

I was always on good terms with Foote. I saw him last in Washington after this book must have been published. He started up aghast at seeing me. He must have thought I had died during the War. But he hailed me with rapture, said I was "the man of men," & proposed to write an article at once nominating me as a Candidate for President!! I believe he is dead himself now, & I would say nothing but good of him.

Pardon my prolixity, & believe me always,

Yours Sincerely,
/s/ Robᵗ. C. Winthrop.
Charles Deane Esq., LLD.

Footnotes:

1 Giddings (1795-1864) was an ardent and radical abolitionist who preached the demise of slavery for his entire congressional career, 1839-42, and 1843-59.

2 In 1842, Giddings demanded the House of Representatives enact a resolution that said that any assertion by slaves of their right to liberty was not a violation of the laws of the United States. The House, led by the pro-slavery Democrats, censured Giddings for his comment, with that motion being approved 125-69. In protest, Giddings resigned his seat on 22 March 1842 and returned home to Indiana, where he asked his constituents to vote him in the special election to fill the seat and send him right back to Washington. Giddings won the election and returned to the House just five weeks after he had been censured.

3 Referring to the opposition in Congress to the annexation of Texas by the United States.

4 Referring to Rep. Joseph Mosley Root, Whig and, later, a Free Soiler, from Ohio.

5 Should be read as "Commissioners."

6 Referring to Rep. John Gorham Palfrey, Whig of Massachusetts.

7 Referring to Rep. Robert A. Toombs, Whig of South Carolina.

8 Referring to Rep. Samuel Finley Vinton, Whig of Ohio.

9 Referring to Rep. Alexander H. Stephens, Whig, then Unionist, then Democrat of Georgia (who later served as Vice President of the Confederacy during the US Civil War).

10 To be read as "Committee."

11 Referring to Rep. Amos Tuck, Whig of New Hampshire.

12 Horace Mann, noted 19th century educator, served in the US House of Representatives from Massachusetts (1849-53) as a Whig and then as a Free Soiler.

13 Henry S. Foote, *Casket of Reminiscences* (Washington, D.C.: Chronicle Publishing Company, 1874). Henry Stuart Foote (1804-1880), Democrat of Mississippi, served as a US Senator (1847-52) and Governor (1852-54) of that state.

14 Jefferson Davis, Democrat from Mississippi, was one of the leading advocates for the rights of slaveowners during his tenure in the US House (1845-47) and the US Senate (1847-60); he later served as the first and only President of the Confederate States of America during the Civil War.

15 Andrew Pickens Butler (1797-1856), Democrat from South Carolina (1846-57), was one of the most emphatic pro-slavery members of the US Senate.

16 John Mcpherson Berrien (1781-1856), Jacksonian and later a Whig from Georgia, was a hard-line supporter of the rights of slaveowners, and opposed the Compromise of 1850 as well as the Wilmot Proviso.

17 Pierre Soulé (1801-1870), Democrat from Louisiana, was against the secession of the southern states, but supported his home state once it had left the Union. He fled the United States at the end of the war to settle for a time in Cuba, only returning to his homeland years later.

18 Theodore Parker (1810-1860) was a noted Minister in the Unitarian Church who was a fierce advocate of abolitionism and the end of slavery

19 Anson Burlingame (1820-1870) was an attorney from Boston, Massachusetts, who was an early supporter of the antislavery Free Soil Party. Elected to a seat in the US House of Representatives (1855-61), he furiously opposed slavery. Following the assault on Senator Charles Sumner by Rep. Preston Brooks of South Carolina for Sumner's alleged demeaning of slavery, Burlingame denounced Brooks as "the vilest sort of coward." Brooks challenged Burlingame to a duel, but never showed up when he became aware that Burlingame was an excellent marksman.

20 Richard Henry Dana, Jr. (1815-1882), an attorney and author, is known for his writings, most notably *Two Years Before the Mast* (1840) and *To Cuba and Back* (1859).

21 Edward Everett (1794-1865), Whig US Representative (1825-35) from and Governor of Massachusetts (1836-39), US Minister to England (1841-45), president of Harvard University (1846-49), US Secretary of State (1852-53), and US Senator (1853-54) from Massachusetts, was one of the most outspoken orators of his generation. In 1860, he ran as Vice President on the doomed Constitutional Union Party ticket with former Speaker of the House John Bell in a vain attempt to head off the election of Republican Abraham Lincoln and initiate the secession of southern states and civil war. In 1863, Everett preceded Lincoln in speaking at the dedication of the military cemetery at Gettysburg, Pennsylvania, following the horrific battle there.

22 Nathan Appleton (1779-1861), a noted manufacturer from the New England region, filled the vacancy in the US House created when Winthrop resigned in 1842 to care for his dying wife; Appleton himself served for only a short period in the US House, resigning before the end of that term, which occurred in March 1843.

Samuel Randall Accepts the Speakership Following the
Death of Speaker Michael Kerr, 1876

Following the death of Speaker Michael C. Kerr, the members of the Forty-fourth Congress re-convened in Washington on 4 December 1876 and elected Samuel J. Randall, Democrat of Pennsylvania, as the Speaker. The following are Randall's remarks to the House after his election:

❧

"Gentlemen of the House of Representatives: Called to this position because of the death of the late Speaker, Mr. Kerr, of Indiana, I only express the universal sentiment in saying he was a good and great man, whose public and private life was characterized by purity, patriotism, and unswerving integrity. Nobody can more completely appreciate than I do, the high honor of presiding over the deliberations of the president of the American people, and for this mark of your esteem and confidence I return my profound and heartfelt acknowledgment. In the discharge of the important duties confided in me I shall endeavor to be absolutely fair and impartial. While enforcing the rules and upholding the constitutional prerogatives of the body, I shall, at the same time, protect each and every member in the rights and privileges to which he may justly be entitled. In the exercise of the parliamentary powers of the chair, it will be my duty and my pleasure to give true expression, in the appointment of committees, to the opinions and wishes of the House upon every question presented - believing myself, as I really am, no more than the voice of the House itself. We stand in the presence of events which strain and test in the last degree our form of government. Our liberties, consecrated by so many sacrifices in the past, and preserved amid the rejoicings of an exultant people to our centennial anniversary as one among the nations of the earth, must be maintained at every hazard.

The people look confidently to your moderation, to your patient, calm, firm judgment and wisdom, at this time fraught with so many perils. Let us not, I beseech of you, disappoint their just expectation and their keen sense of right; but, by vigilance, prevent even the slightest departure from the Constitution and laws, forgetting in the moment of difficulty that we are the adherents of a party, and only remembering that we are American citizens, with a country to save, which will be lost if unauthorized and unconstitutional acts on the part of Executive officers be not frowned upon at once with relentless and unsparing condemnation."

Source: "[The] House of Representatives," *New York Times*, 5 December 1876, 2.

See also pages 179, 185

"The New Speaker:" A Look at Speaker David Henderson, *Munsey's Magazine*, 1899

Following the election in November 1899 of Rep. David Bremner Henderson of Iowa to be Speaker of the House, succeeding the retiring Speaker Thomas Brackett Reed, Rep. Charles A. Boutelle, Republican of Maine, penned a biography of the new Speaker which appeared in *Munsey's Magazine*, at the time one of the most influential journals of news and opinion. The following is the complete article that appeared in that magazine:

శ

Next to the Presidency of the United States the office of Speaker of the National House of Representatives has long been recognized as the most powerful and important post in out popular form of government, and the character and attainments of the men who have held it have reflected the high estimate placed upon its dignity and influence. In the one hundred and ten years of Congress, the speakership has been occupied by Representatives from fourteen States, of which Kentucky furnished the incumbent for twenty two years, ten of which were served by Henry Clay*; Virginia and Maine come next with twelve years each; then Pennsylvania with eleven, Massachusetts with ten, Indiana with nine, New Jersey, North Carolina, Tennessee, and Georgia each with six years, New York and South Carolina with three years each, and Connecticut and Ohio with two years each. On the list of Speakers are such distinguished names as those of Henry Clay, James K. Polk, John Bell, Galusha A. Grow, Schuyler Colfax, Samuel J. Randall, Michael C. Kerr, James G. Blaine, John G. Carlisle, and Thomas B. Reed.

Upon Mr. Reed's announcement, last spring, that he intended to withdraw from Congressional life, the choice of his successor became a most important matter of political interest, with a strong inclination to seek the next Speaker in the West, which had so steadily and generously supported Mr. Reed. There being two prominent aspirants from New York and

two from Illinois, the choice, as voiced by public sentiment, rapidly and strongly centered upon the candidate unanimously and enthusiastically presented by Iowa, in the person of its gallant soldier-statesman, Col. David Bremner Henderson, of Dubuque.

This was no accidental result, as it brought to the front one who had won his spurs in battle and forum, and who had been for years closely identified with the leadership in the House, which we entered together in the Forty Eighth Congress. Colonel Henderson has served on the important committees of banking and currency, the militia, and the census, for many years on the appropriations committee, and throughout the Fifty Fourth and Fifty Fifth Congresses as chairman of the judiciary committee and Speaker Reed's principal lieutenant on the committee on rules, which has had to deal directly with the disposition of the most important public business. In point of experience and judgment, he enjoys to a remarkable degree the confidence and esteem of those who have served with him during his long career at Washington, and in all that goes to make up the best elements of popularity he is held in especially warm personal regard alike by young and old members on both sides of the House.

The next Speaker's public record on all the great questions of legislation furnishes ample hostage for confidence in his wisdom and firmness. His stand on the currency question has been unequivocally for sound money, and no abler champion of the development of American industries can be found on the stump or in Congress. He has the courage of his convictions, and expresses them with utmost force and effect whenever occasion arises. No more striking illustration of his independence and vigor could be desired than his ringing plea for peace, delivered at a time when excitement was threatening to run away with Congress. On March 8, 1898, in the debate on the bill putting fifty millions of dollars at the disposal of the President to provide in his discretion

Source: Boutelle, Charles A., "The New Speaker," *Munsey's Magazine*, XXII:3 (December 1899), 384-86.

See also page 217

for any needed preparations for the national defense, Colonel Henderson electrified the House by these words:

Mr. Speaker, I have read of the elder days of the republic. I live in the better days of the republic. The lesson of this afternoon is a beautiful one for our country. In the elder days there were Tories. I fear a Tory would be thrown out of this hall this afternoon. But, Mr. Speaker, there will be no war. That is my judgment. I do not believe that war is hanging over the American people. In this republic our great aim should be for peace.

The truest patriot is he who secures and keeps peace for his people. It is easy to be an animal. It is easy to use claws and teeth, and to fight. He who can hold aloft in his country the white flag of peace, not of cowardice, rises nearest to his God. No country on earth seeks to avoid war as this country does. No country on earth need fear war less than America. With our boundless resources, with our great credit, with a people who, no matter what their past, are absolutely united in standing as one man, I say that no country is so well armed for war as the United States of America. I do not speak as an Iowan; I speak as a citizen of the United States, and I believe that today we are heart and hand together for what is best for this republic.

The young man who today pledges "all the vigor of his early manhood for his country" commands my respect, but I do not believe he will have to use it.

I have had letters from my people who wanted us to take Cuba, to punish Spain. I simply write back that no international law makes the United States the regulator of the wrongs of earth. God has written no motto on the banner of our country that demands of us the regulating of the wrongs of other countries to their people. We all sympathize with the liberty loving and fighting Cubans, but they are citizens of another government. So long as that question is before us, I follow the advice of Washington, recommending that we mind strictly our own business.

But if they touch the rights of this country, or dare to lay unholy hands upon our territory or our rights, then I, too, become "a fighting Quaker," and will join the vigorous manhood of my young friend who spoke. But let us not lose our heads while our hearts are beating. He can fight best who keeps his blood the coolest. He can serve his people best who thinks most before striking.

This administration, President and Cabinet, are as loyal as many men on this floor, and I claim no more for it. This administration will look before it leaps. This day's work and tomorrow's will teach the administration that when a leap is needed they will have this country back of them, and to a man.

This was at a time when President McKinley was striving to secure a just settlement of the Cuban troubles without war with Spain, and was appealing to those of us in Congress who agreed with him to hold the excitable elements in check. A little more than a month later, when events had unmistakably swept the country to the very brink of war, the one legged veteran of Iowa arose again and forcibly declared himself for action as follows:

The resolution reported but a brief time ago from the committee on foreign affairs by the gentleman from Pennsylvania (Mr. Adams[1]) is stamped with the unanimous judgment of the Republican members of that committee. The time has come, in the opinion of this country, for action on this great question. It has been discussed by the public press; it has been discussed in the pulpit; it has been discussed in the House and in the Senate; it has been discussed at every fireside in the American republic, and we believe, Mr. Speaker, that the time has come, sad as it is, that I must express it, when this country can no longer delay acting in the Cuban situation. Everything has been done by our Chief Executive to secure peace on that island without arms, but in vain; and the time has come when arms, the last resort, must be appealed to by our country. I have been and am for peace, but not at the expense of my country's peace and honor. Spain must leave the western seas, and forever.

The two extracts present a graphic and truthful picture of the strong, generous, patriotic, earnest man, who is to direct the deliberations of the popular branch of the next Congress. While of the Reed school of parliamentary doctrine, and one of the late Speaker's most confidential and trusted supporters, Speaker Henderson has an individuality that will stand on its own merit and a conception of the responsibilities and dignities of his great office that will not permit the loss of a jot or tittle of its prestige in his hands. The gavel material perhaps seem at times to be wielded somewhat more gently, but it will be held by the hand of a master, and the great office of the presiding officer of the United States House of Representatives will lose none of its vitality of influence, and none of the power in promoting the business of a great people, while it shall be administered by David Bremner Henderson of Iowa.

*Mr. Clay served as Speaker during the first sessions of the Thirteenth and Sixteenth Congresses, Langdon Cheves, of South Carolina, being chosen Speaker for the second of the Thirteenth, and John W. Taylor, of New York, for the second session of the Sixteenth, Mr. Clay having resigned in both instances.

Footnote:

[1] Adams, of Pennsylvania.

On the Insurgency Against Speaker Joseph G. Cannon: *The Sun* of New York, 16-20 March 1910

Following a vote by the House of Representatives on a motion by Rep. George Norris, Republican of Nebraska, that the Speaker be stripped of the power to name members of House committees, Speaker Joseph G. Cannon took to the Speaker's chair and offered his resignation to the full House. The following are his remarks which came after the Norris resolution was passed:

✌

"Gentlemen of the House of Representatives: Actions, not words, determine the conduct and the sincerity of men in the affairs of life. This is a government by the people, acting through the representatives of a majority of the people. Results cannot be had except by a majority, and in the House of Representatives, a majority, being responsible, should have full power, and should exercise that power; otherwise the majority is inefficient and does not perform its function. The office of the minority is to put the majority on its good behavior, advocating in good faith the policies which it professes, every ready to take advantage of the mistakes of the majority party, and appeal to the country for its vindication.

"From time to time heretofore the majority has become the minority, as in the present case, and from time to time hereafter the majority will become the minority. The country believes that the Republican Party has a majority of 44 in the House of Representatives at this time, yet such is not the case.

"The present Speaker of the House has, to the best of his ability, and judgment, cooperated with the Republican Party, and, so far in the history of this Congress, the Republican Party in the House has been enabled, by a very small majority, when the test came, to legislate in conformity with the policies and the platform of the Republican Party. Such action, of course, begot criticism - which the Speaker does not deprecate - on the part of the minority party.

"The Speaker cannot be unmindful of the fact, as evidenced by three previous elections to the speakership, that in the past he has enjoyed the confidence of the Republican Party of the country and of the Republican members of the House; but the assault upon the Speaker of the House by the minority, supplanted by the efforts of the so-called insurgents, shows that the Democratic minority, aided by a number of so-called insurgents, constituting 15 per cent of the majority party in the House, is now in the majority, and that the Speaker of the House is not in harmony with the actual majority of the House, as evidenced by the vote just taken.

"There are two courses open for the Speaker to pursue, One is to resign and permit the new combination of Democrats and insurgents to choose a Speaker in harmony with its acts and purposes. The other is for that combination to declare a vacancy in the office of Speaker, and proceed to the election of a new Speaker.

"After consideration, at this state of the session of the House, with much of important legislation pending, involving the pledges of the Republican platform and their crystallization into law, believing that his resignation might consume weeks of time in the reorganization of the House, the Speaker, being in harmony with the Republican policies and desirous of carrying them out, declines by his own motion to precipitate a contest upon the House in the election of a new Speaker, a contest that might greatly endanger the final passage of all legislation necessary to redeem Republican pledges and fulfill Republican promises.

"This is one reason why the Speaker does not resign at once, and another is this: In the judgment of the present Speaker, a resignation is in and of itself a confession of weakness or a mistake, or an apology for past actions. The Speaker is not conscious of having done any political wrong.

Source: "Speaker Cannon's Address After Powers of His Office Were Curtailed," *Washington Times*, March 20, 1910, 3.

See also page 225

"The same rules are in force in this House that have been in force for two decades. The Speaker has construed the rules as he found them, and as they have been construed by previous Speakers, from Thomas B. Reed's incumbency down to the present time.

"Heretofore the Speaker has been a member of the committee on rules, covering a period of 60 years, and the present Speaker has neither sought new power nor has he unjustly used that already conferred upon him.

"There has been much talk on the part of the minority and of the insurgents of the 'czarism' of the Speaker, culminating in the action taken today. The real truth is that there is no coherent Republican majority in the House of Representatives. Therefore, the real majority ought to have the courage of its convictions and logically meet the situation that confronts it.

"The Speaker does now believe, and always has believed, that this is a government through parties, and that parties can act only through majorities. The Speaker has always believed in and bowed to the will of the majority in convention, in caucus, and in the legislative hall, and today profoundly believes that to act otherwise is to disorganize parties, is to prevent coherent action in any legislative body, is to make impossible the reflection of the wishes of the people in statutes and in laws.

"The Speaker has always said that under the Constitution it is a question of the highest privilege for an actual majority of the House at any time to choose a new Speaker, and again notifies the House that the Speaker will at this moment, or at any time while he remains Speaker, entertain, in conformity with the highest constitutional privilege, a motion by any member to vacate the office of the speakership and choose a new Speaker, and, under existing conditions, would welcome such action upon the part of the actual majority of the House, so that power and responsibility may rest with the Democratic and insurgent members, who by the last vote evidently constitute a majority of this House. The Chair is now ready to entertain such a motion."

Speaker Joseph G. Cannon's Speech Following the Victory of the "Insurgents," 1910

By 1910, Speaker Joseph G. Cannon ruled the House with an iron hand. Working on the rules established by his predecessors, Republicans and Democrats, Cannon only allowed those representatives who he wished to recognize to speak on the floor of the House. By March of that year, Democrats, in the minority, as well as a large bloc of Republicans, desired to break Cannon's hold on the power of the speakership. However, these disparate parties were unsure as to how to challenge Cannon. The rupture came on 15 March 1910, when a simple argument over an appropriation for an automobile for Speaker Cannon and for Vice President James Schoolcraft Sherman was voted down against Cannon's wishes. Seeing an opening, the forces arrayed against Cannon then began to challenge him at every turn, and for the next several days they were able to hold together to eventually bring down Cannon and, as many historians believe, permanently alter the power of the speaker that was only restored by Sam Rayburn, Thomas P. "Tip" O'Neill, and Newt Gingrich from the mid- to late-twentieth century. In these accounts, rarely-seen but fascinating, which appeared in *The Sun* newspaper of New York, the slow move against Cannon, which lasted until the House voted on 19 March to strip Cannon of his seat on the Rules Committee as well as his power to name members of the House committees, is told.

❧

16 March 1910, 1:

INSURGENTS ROUT REGULARS

Three Votes in the House End in Victory

Sharp Contest Over the Legislation Bill Involving Payment of Chauffeurs for the Vice-President and the Speaker - Corporation Tax Rider Beaten

Washington, March 15 - That the insurgent Republicans in the House are merely resting on the arms ready to strike at the leaders when the opportunity presents itself was shown to-day. Things had been running along smoothly and members were getting ready for adjournment at 5 o'clock when word was brought to the leaders that the insurgents were holding a war dance to perfect plans for an onslaught on a certain provision of the legislative bill which was up for consideration.

The insurgents, combining with the Democrats, gave the signal for the rally against the House organization a few minutes after 5 o'clock. A flight then followed that was continued for more than two hours, the insurgent-Democratic alliance routing the organization at every turn.

The section of the bill selected for attack was that making appropriations for automobiles for use of the Vice-President and the Speaker. The amendment proposing to strike out this appropriation was presented by Representative [Martin David] Foster, a Democrat from Illinois. To it was attached a rider reducing the appropriation to enable the Secretary of the Treasury to administer the publicity feature of the corporation tax law by $100,000, the amount asked by the President, to $75,000.

The insurgents and their Democratic colleagues got into action just at the moment the legislative bill was about to be put on its passage. Representative [Joseph Bentley] Bennet[1] of New York and two other members jumped to their feet with motions, but Bennet[1] was recognized by Speaker Cannon. He moved to recommit the measure without instruction. Half a dozen other members were clamoring for recognition so that they could move to recommit with instructions to eliminate the obnoxious paragraph.

Sources: *The Sun* of New York, issues for 16-20 March 1910; see also the coverage in *Washington Times*, 20 March 1910, as well as "Cannon Downed by the Insurgents[,] Defies the Democrats and Wins," *The Call* [San Francisco, California], 20 March 1910, 21; *The Biographical Directory of the United States Congress* (online) was used to find the actual, and not printed, names of some of those involved in the debate.

See also page 225

At this point Representative [Frederick Huntington] Gillett cut off the hubbub by moving the previous question on the Bennet[1] motion. Owing to the number of unpaired Republican absentees[,] this was defeated, 110 to 97.

Then Representative Foster of Illinois amended the Bennet[1] motion by moving to recommit with instructions to eliminate the automobiles. This carried, 113 to 94.

When the bill was taken up for passage that part of it relating to the corporation tax law was defeated and the appropriation enabling the Secretary of the Treasury to enforce the law therefore stands at $100,000.

At the last session Congress authorized the purchase of automobiles for the use of the Vice-President and the Speaker. The provision of the legislative bill continuing appropriations for this purpose was covered into contingent accounts of the House and the Senate. It was the aim of Representative Foster at the outset merely to knock out of the bill an item providing compensation for the chauffeurs employed by the Vice-President and the Speaker.

As adopted the Foster amendment provides that no funds shall be set apart for the maintenance of the automobiles used by Mr. Sherman and Mr. Cannon. If this provision becomes a law Messrs. Sherman and Cannon will each have a Government automobile on his hands with no Government funds to make the wheels go round.

———

17 March 1910, 1:

SPEAKER CANNON OVERRULED

———

THE DEMOCRATIC-INSURGENT COMBINE WINS AGAIN

Uncle Joe Said He Would Be Gratified if He was Overruled, as It Would Show That the Majority of the House and Not an Oligarchy Controlled

Washington, March 16 - Speaker Cannon was subjected to the humiliation of having one of his decisions from the chair overruled to-day by a

combination of insurgent Republicans, near insurgents and Democrats. A dent was made in the House organization, but Uncle Joe says he is content. The fact that he was overruled, he announced, was the best of evidence that instead of the House being in the control of one man it is really dominated by the majority, as he has always contended. That the insurgents will take advantage of every opportunity to embarrass Mr. Cannon and his organization is now evident to the leaders.

The insurgent band has been quiescent lately, but only because its members did not want to be placed in the attitude of obstructing the legislation recommended by President Taft. Yesterday the insurgents ran amuck and knocked out an appropriation for the maintenance of Uncle Joe Cannon's Vice-President Sherman's Government automobiles. They did that to 'even up' with Uncle Joe, and their rally to-day was prompted by the same motive.

The demonstration against the House organization to-day came as a surprise to the leaders. They had hardly recovered from the rout of yesterday. The measure attacked was a joint resolution reported by Representative [Edgar Dean] Crumpacker, chairman of the Committee on the Census, providing for the segregation of the Slavonic minorities in the coming census enumeration. Chairman Crumpacker called up this resolution immediately upon the approval of the journal of yesterday's proceedings.

Representative [Joseph John] Fitzgerald of New York made the point that under the rules Wednesday of each week is set aside for the consideration of bills on the House and union calendars and no measure could replace this order of business except by a two-third vote of the House. Mr. Crumpacker replied that the resolution had the right of way under a privilege conferred by the Constitution, which transcended the rules of the House.

The Speaker upheld Mr. Crumpacker's contention, whereupon Mr. Fitzgerald appealed from the decision of the Chair.

In the course of the debate Mr. Crumpacker received word that while he undoubtedly had all the argument on his side a canvass disclosed that he did not have the votes. Then Mr. Crumpacker tried to beat a retreat by moving that the bill be laid aside until to-morrow.

The leaders rallied their forces, but the insurgents and the Democrats were too much for them and the Crumpacker motion was lost by a vote of 153 to 121, thirty-eight Republicans siding with the minority. The Republicans who joined with the Democrats were [Hamilton] Fish and [Herbert] Parsons of New York, [Joseph Bentley] Bennett of Kentucky, [Charles Russell] Davis, [Andrew John] Volstead, [Charles August] Lindbergh, [Clarence Benjamin] Miller, [Halvor] Steenerson and [Frederick Clement] Stevens of Minnesota, [William Joseph] Carey[1], [Henry Allen] Cooper, [James Henry] Davidson, [Irvine] Lenroot, [Elmer Addison] Morse, [Arthur William] Kopp and [John Mandt] Nelson of Wisconsin, [Frank Plowman] Woods, [Albert Foster] Dawson, [James William] Good, [Gilbert Nelson] Haugen, [Nathan Edward] Kendall and [Charles Edgar] Pickett of Iowa, [Augustus Peabody] Gardner of Massachusetts, [Asle] Gronna of North Dakota, [Even Wever] Martin of South Dakota, [Everis Anson] Hayes of California, [Edwin Werter] Higgins of Connecticut, [Edmund Howard] Hinshaw, [Moses Pierce] Kinkaid and [George William] Norris of Nebraska, [Leonard Paul] Howland, [David Adams] Hollingsworth and [Adna Romulus] Johnson of Ohio, [Edmond Haggard] Madison and [Victor] Murdock of Kansas, [Campbell Bascom] Slemp of Virginia, [Miles] Poindexter of Washington and [Charles Elroy] Townsend of Michigan.

The motion of Mr. Fitzgerald (Dem) appealing from the decision of the Speaker was then again taken up. Before the motion was put Mr. Cannon made an address in which he outlined the issue. He had no pride of opinion in his ruling, he said. The pending resolution was clearly entailed to the constitutional privilege. No rule in the House empowered the Speaker to overlook that fact. Speaker Cannon added that it would gratify him if he were overruled as it would be notice to the country that the House was controlled by a majority and not by an oligarchy as claimed. Uncle Joe had his wish. His ruling was overturned by a vote of 163 to 111. On this occasion forty-two Republicans joined with their Democratic brethren. The Republicans who "insurged" against the Speaker on this vote were [Butler]

Ames of Massachusetts, [John Wesley] Langley of Kentucky, [Charles Nelson] Pray of Montana and [William Henry] Stafford of Wisconsin and those who voted against the resolution in the previous ballot.

Differences of opinion are advanced by the parliamentarians of the House as to the precedent established to-day. Some take the position that under no circumstances in the future can any business no matter how important, displace the business allotted to calendar Wednesday. Representative Fitzgerald, a close student of the rules, contends that by a two-thirds vote, the House may at will set aside the prescribed order of business and take up any measure that suits its fancy. This holds true of calendar Wednesday, or any other day, according to Mr. Fitzgerald.

Calendar Wednesday was created by the Fitzgerald resolution, which was adopted as an incident to the insurgent fight on the rules early in the special session last April. It was intended to afford a means of considering bills that the insurgents claimed were denied a hearing at the whim or will of the Speaker.

The House leaders had a roundup to-night to talk over the situation. Things have been running smoothly in the House of late and it was thought the insurgents would keep quiet for the rest of the session. It now develops that every time the insurgents have a chance to punch a hole in the organization without placing an obstacle in the way of the Administration programme they will be busy.

Yesterday's defeat is directly chargeable to the absence of regulars. That wasn't true of the outcome to-day. Early in the day, on motion of Republican Whip [John Wilbur] Dwight [of New York], there was a call of the House. Members were brought in and told that they had to stay. With a pretty good attendance, however, the organization was bested.

---

18 March 1910, 1 & 2:

CANNON BATTLES FOR HIS POWER

Insurgents and Democrats in All Night Fight for Control of House

———

No Quorum There at 3:15 A.M.

———

The Regular Republican Organization Defeated on Five Test Roll Calls

———

Caught Off His Guard, Speaker Cannon Entertains a Motion That Results in a Bitter Fight Over the Rules - It Put Before the House the Norris Resolution to Increase the Membership of the Committee on Rules to Fifteen and Making the Speaker Ineligible for Member of the New Committee - The Fight Then Began and Was One of the Most Stubborn Ever Witnessed in the House - The Speaker Attacked by Several Insurgents and Takes the Floor in His Own Defense.

Washington, March 18, 3:15 A.M. - The Republican organization is engaged in a fight for existence, which at this hour has tailed off into an endurance struggle. A combination of insurgent Republicans and Democrats has won out on five roll calls, designed to effect either adjournment or recess.

So many regulars have withdrawn that a quorum is lacking and the sergeant-at-arms and his men are out now searching for the absent ones with orders to arrest any who won't come in. The departed Representatives have locked themselves in at home and the chances are that not for eight hours yet will there be a quorum.

It was a day of dramatic situations in the House. Caught off guard by Representative Norris of Nebraska, one of the insurgent leaders, Speaker Cannon entertained a motion that resulted in precipitating a rough and tumble fight over the rules, a situation that the leaders have been trying to stave off all sessions and one for which the insurgents had been waiting patiently.

Seldom in the history of the House has there been witnessed such exciting incidents as marked the day's proceedings. The insurgents and Democrats, flushed with the victories attained Tuesday and Wednesday, went into the fray with confidence, and after once rebuking the Speaker they returned to the attack by unexpectedly throwing into the House

a resolution proposing the creation of a new Committee on Rules and making the Speaker ineligible for appointment to the new committee.

HOW THE FIGHT BEGAN

The innocent cause of all the excitement of the day was the census resolution that kicked up so much excitement on Wednesday. The House passed this resolution in due season, after a little flurry, during which the House rebuked the Speaker by refusing to entertain a motion that he put. A sufficient number of insurgents joined with the Democrats to bring about this result.

In passing the census resolution, however, the House indorsed the proposition that this measure was under consideration as a matter of constitutional privilege. This principle once recognized, the insurgents took advantage of the opening. Representative Norris led the attack. Rising in his place, he addressed the Speaker. He was at once recognized.

"I desire to present a resolution which is entitled to recognition under the constitutional privilege," said Mr. Norris.

Speaker Cannon, unsuspecting the trap into which he was about to be led, caused the resolution to be read. It provided for a new Committee on Rules to be elected by the House and to go into effect at once. The fight began at once and it will go down into the history of the House as one of the most stubborn partisan struggles ever witnessed in that body.

Arrayed on one side were thirty or more Republicans and the Democratic minority and on the other the responsible Republican leadership.

DEFEATED EFFORTS TO ADJOURN

Twice the leaders tried to adjourn the House and once, at 11:15 to-night, to take a recess until morning, but they were voted down. Every effort was made by the leader to bring in absentees. Telegrams were despatched to New York, Philadelphia, and other cities to bring in seventeen members whom they hope will help out their cause.

At midnight four of these members, [Joel] Cook of Pennsylvania, [George Deardorff] McCreary of Pennsylvania, Alcott of New York[3], and [John

Philip] Swasey of Maine, reached the House. The first two had rushed to Washington from Philadelphia and Alcott[3] and Swasey hurried over from New York. Others of the regular supporters are expected before daylight. The appearance of the four Cannon men revived hope that an all night session might be avoided.

The spirits of the organization men soon fell through, when the Democrats, [William] Richardson of Alabama, [Joseph Taylor] Robinson of Arkansas and [Benjamin Grubb] Humphreys of Mississippi, arrived in the chamber. They also had made quick dashes to the national Capital from New York in response to telegrams. Three sick men had been pulled out of their beds earlier in the night to reinforce the regulars, but without avail.

The Norris resolution creating a new Committee on Rules was patterned after one introduced in the House in the Fifty-second Congress by Representative Tom Watson, the Georgia Populist. The Democrats controlled the House then. Crisp was Speaker then, and no consideration was given the Watson resolution.

The Norris resolution provides for a committee of fifteen, to be representative of the various sections, it being specifically provided that the Speaker shall not be a member of this organization. If this resolution goes through it will mean the end of the present organization rules in the House.

The insurgents and Democrats contended at midnight that they had a majority of five for the resolution. The House leaders say that with the seventeen absentees they will be able to defeat the resolution and that they will not put the resolution to vote until they are certain of their ground. Here is the text of the resolution:

Resolved, That the rules of the House be amended as follows: The Committee on Rules shall consist of fifteen members, nine of whom shall be members of the majority party and six of whom shall be members of the minority party, to be selected as follows: The States of Union shall have been divided, by a committee of three, elected to the House for that purpose into nine groups; each group containing, as near as may be, an equal number of members belonging to the majority party. The States of the Un-

ion shall likewise be divided into six groups, such group containing, as near as may be, an equal number of members belonging to the minority party.

At 10:00 o'clock A.M. of the day following the adoption of the report of said committee, each of said groups shall meet and select one of its number, a member of the Committee on Rules. The place of meeting for each of said groups shall be designated by the said committee of three, in its report. Each of said groups shall report to the House the name of the member selected for membership on the Committee on Rules.

The Committee on Rules shall select its own chairman. The Speaker shall not be eligible to membership on said Committee. All rules of parts thereof inconsistent with the foregoing resolution are hereby repealed.

LEADERS HOLD COUNCIL OF WAR

The trouble began early in the day. Apprehending another insurgent demonstration, the leaders held a council of war in Mr. Cannon's room just before the House met at noon. It was decided then that the regular forces should be rallied for an emergency, and accordingly Republican whip Dwight made the point as soon as Speaker Cannon rapped for order that a quorum was not present. A call of the House was authorized, and in half an hour Mr. Cannon announced that a majority was present, and that the House was ready to proceed to business.

Representative Crumpacker of Indiana, whose census resolution reported by the House Committee on Census caused the flareup on Wednesday, took the floor. He asked that the resolution be considered, repeating his argument that it was privileged under the Constitution in as much as that instrument made it mandatory on Congress to take a census at regular intervals. This privilege, he declared, transcended the rules of the House. Representative [Thomas Stalker] Butler of Pennsylvania made a point of order against the motion.

On Wednesday the House refused to acknowledge the constitutional privilege claimed for the resolution on the ground that such recognition would permit of an invasion of the rights attaching to calendar Wednesday. After a short debate the question was again put to the House by the Speaker in this form: "Is the resolution in order as a matter of constitutional privilege, the House rules prescribing other business to the contrary notwithstanding."

ORGANIZATION DEFEATED

The insurgents, combining with the Democrats, voted down this proposition, taking the position that if carried it would in effect be a reversal of the action of Wednesday. On this issue, the House organization was defeated by a vote of 142 to 137.

The question was then put in a new form by Representative [Oscar] Underwood of Alabama, as follows: "Is the joint resolution called up by the gentleman from Indiana in order now?" This was carried by an overwhelming majority. According to the insurgents, the adoption of the Crumpacker resolution under the form of the motion put by Mr. Underwood admitted the constitutional privilege of their resolution without requiring the House to pass on that question direct, but this argument, the regulars say, is a mere quibble.

The Crumpacker resolution, whose merits have not been the subject of controversy at any time in the storm of the last few days, was then passed by a viva voce vote[4]. Then it was that the real fight of the day began. For weeks the insurgents had been waiting for an opportunity to precipitate a row on the rules.

NORRIS RESOLUTION CALLED UP

The Norris resolution was sprung on an unsuspecting organization when the organization was about to proceed with the business of the day. Representative Norris of Nebraska, one of the simon-pure[5] insurgents, rose in his place.

"For what purpose does the gentleman rise?" queried the Speaker.

"I rise," said Mr. Norris, "to call up a resolution of constitutional privilege."

Mr. Cannon hesitated a moment and then directed that the resolution be read. The leaders realized at once that the organization was face to face with a fight for its existence.

Few members were present, when the Norris resolution was reported from the desk. Apparently the regulars thought that the trouble was over for the

day after the Crumpacker resolution had been disposed of. The Norris resolution, however, had hardly been read when messengers were speeding out to the corridors and committee rooms summoning the organization forces back to the firing line. Some of the regulars themselves joined in this recruiting work. There was every evidence that the Cannon forces appreciated from the start that they were confronted with a mighty serious situation.

DALZELL RAISES A POINT

Representative [John] Dalzell of Pennsylvania, a member of the Rules Committee, made the point that the resolution was not in order under the rules. Mr. Norris replied that he did not ask recognition for the measure under the rules but in accordance with the terms of a mandate clearly set forth in the Constitution.

"The House has voted here to-day for a resolution admitted to consideration on a question of constitutional privilege," said Mr. Norris. "It was argued for the resolution that it was privileged under the constitutional question that a census shall be taken. The Constitution provides that the House may formulate rules to govern its own conduct. A resolution, therefore, that pertains to the rules has a constitutional privilege and this privilege cannot be abridged by the dictum of the Speaker or the written rules of the House."

Representatives Dalzell and Olmstead[6] of Pennsylvania, [Sereno] Payne and [Jacob Sloat] Fassett of New York, and other regulars combated this proposition. A number of insurgents, including Representatives Poindexter of Washington [State] and Madison of Kansas and Nelson of Wisconsin upheld it.

POINDEXTER ATTACKS UNCLE JOE

Representative Poindexter's speech was extremely bitter. He denounced the Speaker as a tyrant, declared that the rules were tyrannical in their operations and asserted that under them the House had ceased to be a representative body. Mr. Poindexter was repeatedly interrupted by regulars. Representative [James Albertus] Tawney remarked that the present Committee on Rules was named by the Republican caucus and not by the Speaker, as charged by the member from Washington [State].

"It was on my motion made in caucus," shouted Mr. Tawney, "under which the Republican members of the Rules Committee were designated."

"That means," interjected Mr. Norris, "that the Rules were selected in advance by the Speaker and that the caucus merely confirmed his selections. Any man who knows how things are conducted here is well aware that any motion made by the gentleman from Minnesota originates not far from the Speaker."

This sally brought forth applause from insurgents and Democrats.

Continuing his remarks, Mr. Poindexter declared that the time had arrived when the sheep would be separated from the goats.

"We must all show our hands now," he shouted. "Those who pose as insurgents at home and as stalwarts in the House must stand up and be counted."

Representatives Madison, Nelson, Fish and the other insurgents spoke in a similar vein. Mr. Fish was in a happy frame of mind. He said that his experience with the Committee on Rules had been a most unhappy one. It had convinced him that there should be many changes. He had introduced a resolution relating to the parcels post that had been ignored by the committee, although he had urged the committee individually and collectively to take action.

SENATORS HURRY IN TO SEE THE FUN

By this time the news of what was going on in the House had reached the Senate side of the Capitol and many of the Senators left their committee rooms and hurried over to see the fun. To some of the Senators, however, the situation seemed to be far from amusing. One or two of the organization leaders in the Senate called members of the Cannon forces out into the lobbies and asked them just how serious the situation was. The Senators seemed to think that if the insurgents and Democrats were successful it would raise hob with this session's legislative programme, even though the insurgents contend that they have no disposition to impede the President's programme.

While these conferences were going on out in the lobby, the House chamber itself presented a scene of great excitement. The insurgents and the Democrats applauded vigorously every point made by their speakers, and the Administration forces when they had an opportunity apparently tried to outdo the opposition in the noise-making line. Many of the Representatives were so excited that they made no attempt to keep their seats, but danced around in the aisle and in front of the Speaker's desk.

UNCLE JOE BANGS HIS GAVEL

Every little while Uncle Joe's gavel would descend with a bang, but he would hardly get the call for order out before one of his excited lieutenants would be tapping his arms and asking for further orders. The House galleries also were crowded by this time and the common people seemed to be enjoying the discomfiture of the regular organization immensely.

The regulars argued in substance that a resolution relating to the rules could not be considered under the constitutional privilege. In the case of the census, it was pointed out, the direction of the Constitution was mandatory, while in the case of the rules it was argued that the Constitution merely said that the House "may" formulate rules. Mr. Dalzell pointed out that the House could proceed without rules, doing business under general parliamentary laws, as was the case in the Fifty-first Congress, when a controversy over the subject made it impossible to adopt a code of procedure.

All of the regulars contended that the rules could be revised only by means provided in the rules themselves, namely by the introduction of a resolution and its reference to a committee on rules. The insurgents jeered this proposition. They replied that a rule resolution referred to the Committee on Rules would meet the fate of all measures that did not coincide with the views of that body, of which the Speaker was the dominating spirit.

PAYNE WARNS INSURGENTS

Representative Payne of New York brought the name of President Taft into the debate. If the pending resolution were passed, he declared with emphasis, chaos would result and the legislative programme of the Administration would be endangered. He warned the Republican insurgents that they were treading on dangerous ground and that they should think well before they took the leap. Addressing the Republican side and pointing to the Democrats he shouted, "Beware of Greeks bearing gifts!"

Then there was a great uproar from both sides and up jumped about half a dozen insurgents who wanted to give Representative Payne a verbal trimming.

Representatives Poindexter and Madison and Ham Fish of New York had their innings. The scored Mr. Payne for bringing the name of the President into the discussion. Mr. Fish said that the proposed reform was not menacing to the Administration programme and that the President was not concerned in the fight.

"If there is any man here who can say that the President is opposed to a change in the rules let him rise in his place now," shouted Mr. Fish. New York's big Representative paused for reply. No one accepted the invitation. Then he waved his hand significantly and the insurgent warwhoop sounded again.

FASSETT ORATES FOR THE REGULARS

A speech in behalf of the organization was made by Representative Fassett, and the regulars applauded wildly. Mr. Fassett's plea was that every Republican ought to be regular. He dubbed the insurgents "assistant Democrats" and read a letter written by Theodore Roosevelt in 1906 in which Mr. Roosevelt eulogized the work of the Fifty-ninth Congress and spoke of Mr. Cannon in the most complimentary terms.

While all this orating was going on the leaders were bending every energy to get their forces into line. Two or three members were called from sick beds. Representative [Charles Luman] Knapp of New York came walking in looking very pale. He was one of the sick ones who had been routed out.

INSURGENTS WIN FIRST ROUND

About 6:35 the leaders thought they had the situation well in hand and accordingly Representative Tawney of Minnesota moved that the House take a recess until this morning at 11 o'clock. But the regulars had not reckoned with the host. The motion was lost by a vote of 142 to 147, seven members voting present. Twenty-six Republicans sided with the Democrats in opposing adjournment, as follows: Cary and Davidson of Wisconsin, Davis of Minne-

sota, Fish of New York, [Otto Godfrey] Foelker of New York, Fowler of New Jersey, Gardner of Massachusetts, Gronna of South Dakota, Haugen of Iowa, Hayes of California, Hinshaw of Nebraska, Kopp of Wisconsin, Lenroot of Wisconsin, [Elbert Hamilton] Hubbard and Kendall of Iowa, Kinkaid of Nebraska, Lindbergh of Minnesota, Murdock and Madison of Kansas, Miller of Minnesota, Morse of Wisconsin, Nelson of Wisconsin, Norris of Nebraska, Pickett of Iowa, Poindexter of Washington [State] and Volstead of Minnesota.

The debate was then resumed, Representative [George Roland] Malby of New York taking the floor to oppose the House resolution. After the vote against the motion to adjourn members quickly dispersed for dinner. Representative [Ernest William] Roberts of Massachusetts made a point of no quorum. Representative Crumpacker, then demanded a roll call on the question as to whether there should be a call of the House to determine whether a quorum was present. The Republican regulars in this manner embarked upon a filibuster to stave off a vote on the Norris resolution.

FOWLER ATTACKS THE RULES AND THE SPEAKER

Representative Fowler of New Jersey made an impassioned attack on the present rules. Since he was removed from the chairmanship of the Committee on Banking and Currency by Speaker Cannon he has been one of the Speaker's most active and bitter enemies. His remarks were heard with close attention and he was frequently interrupted by loud and prolonged applause from the Democrats and insurgents. Referring to his deposition as chairman of the Committee on Banking and Currency after he had fallen out with Speaker Cannon, Mr. Fowler said that he had "been up against" the influence of the Speaker and thanked God he had the courage to resist it.

"The power of the Speaker to make and unmake men," he declared, "is the most corrupting thing in American political life."

If the House adopted the Norris amendment to make a rules committee of fifteen members, elective by the House, Mr. Fowler declared he would go into the Republican caucus and help to elect the nine Republican members of that committee.

REEDER OF KANSAS JEERED

Mr. Fowler was followed by Representative Reeder of Kansas, who defended the rules. The Democrats didn't want to hear Mr. Reeder, and his remarks were greeted by catcalls and jeers. "Sit down," shouted a Democrat, "we don't want to hear you." Mr. Reeder demanded order on the Democratic side and proceeded.

Representative Cooper of Wisconsin, an insurgent, then addressed the House. He attacked the rules and the Speaker and urged a change in the House procedure. Mr. Cooper also took a shot at the unfortunate and abused Mr. Reeder.

"I smiled only once during his speech," said Mr. Cooper, "and that was when he said he was inclined to think. The gentleman's remarks up to that point had given no evidence of it."

Mr. Cooper referred to the fact that Speaker Cannon had called him a demagogue and a populist.

"If I wanted to call names," said Mr. Cooper, "I might say that Mr. Cannon voted for free silver, greenbacks and the resumption act."

CANNON JUMPS TO HIS FEET

Mr. Cooper's personal references to Speaker Cannon were very severe. Uncle Joe twirled his gavel nervously and finally jumped to his feet to speak. The appearance of the Speaker in the discussion was followed by one of the most interesting scenes witnessed in the House since the Speaker became intrenched behind the Reed rules.

Mr. Cooper had made the charge that the Speaker had meted out punishment to the insurgents against the rules by retiring them from committees or by reducing them in rank. Mr. Cooper cited the case of Representative Gardner of Massachusetts. He charged that the chairmanship of the Committee on Industrial Arts was taken from Mr. Gardner because of his activity in the insurgent ranks. Mr. Cannon had long since left the chair and was standing with a group of members on the steps of the Speaker's rostrum.

"May I interrupt the general there?" inquired Mr. Cannon.

"You may, sir," replied Mr. Cooper.

"Is Mr. Gardner here?" exclaimed the Speaker. "I wish him to tell the exact facts."

GARDNER WASN'T PUNISHED

Mr. Gardner responded, saying in substance that prior to the organization of the committees at the beginning of Congress he was told that he could retain his chairmanship. He had a conversation with the Speaker on the subject. Mr. Cannon told him that he would be reappointed chairman of the Industrial Arts Committee, but that if he took it he would have to continue his activities with the insurgent band or lay himself open to the charge that he had tied up with the organization in exchange for continued service at the head of his committee. At that time Mr. Gardner contemplated quitting the insurgent band. Mr. Gardner then told the Speaker that he would not take the chairmanship.

"Are those the facts, Mr. Speaker?" asked Mr. Gardner.

"They are," replied Mr. Cannon.

Mr. Cooper's version of the story was that in the conference between the Speaker and Mr. Gardner the latter was told that the other insurgents were to be punished and Mr. Gardner said he wanted to go with the others, that an exception in his case might excite suspicion as to the integrity of his activities with the insurgents.

INSURGENTS WHO WERE PUNISHED

Mr. Cooper then called upon Norris of Nebraska to rise. In reply to questions Norris said he had been removed from active committees and put on dead ones.

The next "witness" brought forward by Mr. Cooper in an effort to prove his case against the Speaker was Murdock of Kansas, he of the red hair and eruptive disposition.

"What were your committee assignments in the last Congress?" queried inquisitor Cooper.

"Was a member of the Committee on Post Offices and Post Roads," replied Mr. Murdock.

"What is your rank now as compared with that of a year ago?" questioned Mr. Cooper.

"I stand tenth on the committee now," replied Mr. Murdock. "If I had not been shoved down by the Speaker, I would have stood fourth on that committee to-day."

Mr. Murdock added that he was thrown down because he did not yield his judgment to that of the chairman of the committee and the Speaker.

Exit Murdock from the "witness stand."

Fowler, of New Jersey, who was relieved of the chairmanship of the Committee on Banking and Currency at the beginning of this Congress, was the next in line. He testified that this assignment was taken from him because of his opposition to the Speaker and the organization.

THE SPEAKER EXPLAINS

"May I say a word at this point?" said Speaker Cannon, who had been stroking his whiskers meditatively. Mr. Cooper yielded, and the Speaker went on to say that under the rules of the House it was the duty of the Speaker to appoint the committees. In exercising that function, Mr. Cannon said that he was responsible to the House and the country. He then explained why Mr. Fowler was taken off the Committee on Banking and Currency. In the last Congress the Republicans, in party caucus, had declared in favor of the passage of the Vreeland emergency currency bill. The committee, headed by Mr. Fowler, refused to report that measure. It became necessary then through a motion, made from the floor, to discharge the committee from further consideration of the measure. This motion was passed, and Mr. Fowler, having gone counter to the wishes of the party as expressed in the caucus, was, in Mr. Cannon's opinion, no longer entitled to consideration at the hands of the Republican leadership. For that reason he was deposed. Punishment was meted out to Norris, Murdock and Cooper for like reasons, he said. This remarkable question and answer proceeding was listened to intently by the crowded house and Cooper received an ovation from the insurgent wing.

CANNON URGES ADJOURNMENT

Speaker Cannon by this time had resumed the chair. Pounding for order, the Speaker made a statement from the chair. He suggested that the Speaker and the members were weary and urged that adjournment be taken in order that further consideration might be given to the Norris amendment and all that it involved. He pleaded against hasty and ill-considered action.

"The Speaker will be glad," said Mr. Cannon, "if the House in its wisdom sees fit to adjourn."

At this the Democrats and insurgents looked at one another and shook their heads emphatically. There were whispers, low but emphatic, from all over the House of "No" and "Let's finish it now."

Chairman Tawney of the Appropriations Committee jumped to his feet.

"Mr. Speaker," he said, "I move the House do now adjourn."

The regulars voted solidly and vociferously in the affirmative, but they were outhowled by the allies. And on motion of Representative [Joseph Holt] Gaines of West Virginia the yeas and nays were ordered on the motion to adjourn.

INSURGENTS WIN SECOND AND THIRD ROUND

 Excitement in the House while the roll was being called was intense. When Speaker Cannon finally announced the vote as 142 and only 137 for adjournment the insurgents applauded loudly. This was a gain of four votes from the first vote on adjournment which had been taken about five hours earlier.

The defeat of the regulars on the second attempt to shut off the debate and lay the entire question over until to-morrow was no sooner announced than Representative Tawney was again on his feet with a motion that the House take a recess until to-morrow morning. Mr. Tawney rightly was under the impression that the insurgents feared that if they consented to an adjournment they might have difficulty in getting their question before the House again under such favorable circumstances. Mr. Tawney therefore explained that the recess would not effect the status of the debate on the Crumpacker resolution in any way and that it would be taken up again to-morrow.

The insurgents, however, were not disposed to take any chances and many of them shook their heads against the proposition. Again the ayes and noes were ordered on the motion for a recess and this time the insurgents showed that they were in control of the situation by a vote of 142 to 139.

It was 11:15 o'clock when this third defeat of the House organization was announced and members were beginning to settle themselves down for a session that might last all night.

REINFORCEMENTS ARRIVE

At about midnight Representatives Olcott of New York, Cook and McCreary of Pennsylvania and Swayze[7] of Maine, who had been out of town, reached Washington, and the leaders then decided to make another effort to recess.

At 12:15 Representative Tawney moved that the House take a recess until 11:55 this morning.

Minority Leader [Champ] Clark [of Missouri] insisted that the Speaker should rule on the pending question, which was as to the admissibility under the rules of the Norris resolution. Mr. Clark insisted that it was the duty of the Speaker to rule, and he charged the Speaker with responsibility for the filibuster that had delayed action. The refusal of the Speaker to rule, Mr. Clark contended, was a striking instance of the Speaker's control. The whole performance was "indecent," Mr. Clark averred. Mr. Clark concluded by moving that the Speaker be required to rule.

Representative [James Robert] Mann of Illinois took the floor to discuss the motion made by Mr. Clark. "It is a remarkable thing," cried Mr. Mann, "that every time the Democratic side gets in partial control of the House it attempts to stifle debate." Catcalls and jeers greeted the remark.

With some heat Mr. Mann announced that he would discuss the point of order. The Democrats, being in the most hilarious mood, applauded this statement vigorously.

Mr. Mann then claimed that the insurgents and Democrats displayed the most remarkable inconsistency in claiming constitutional privilege for the Norris amendment while refusing the same thing to the Crumpacker resolution.

CANNON TAKES ACTIVE PART IN THE FIGHT

Never did the personality of Speaker Cannon stand out more prominently than in the long and bitter fight of to-day and to-night. With his lieutenants in a state of panic, with even the usually imperturbable John Dalzell of Pennsylvania very much up in the air, Mr. Cannon never more deserving of the title of the "Iron Duke of Illinois," has kept his forces together and has fought the good fight. Every moment of the day he was either in the chair presiding or on the floor taking an active and at times audible part in the proceedings. With hands in pockets and unlighted cigar in his mouth he listened, grim and unsmiling, to the bitter and at times vigorous attacks on himself.

At 1 A.M. Representative Mann of Illinois was addressing the House. The Cannon forces showed no intention at that hour of putting the Norris resolution to a vote and the insurgents were still determined not to assent to an adjournment.

By actual count at 1:20 o'clock twelve Representatives were asleep in their seats, but Representative Mann was still going strong. Representative Crumpacker, whose census resolution started the trouble, was one of those slumbering.

At 1:30 o'clock Representative Tawney again moved that the House take a recess until 11:30. He based his appeal on justice to the House employees. The insurgents insisted on a yea and nay vote. The Cannon lieutenants hustled around to wake up some of their supporters.

Butler Ames of Massachusetts, who had been voting with the organization all day, went over to the side of allies, thereby causing consternation among the regulars.

At 1:50 Representative Dalzell, who was presiding, announced the vote as 134 ayes and 135 nays. This was the fifth time the regulars had been voted down in the course of the day but the vote was closest of all.

Representative Dwight, the Republican whip, as a last resort began to send the Cannon regulars home with a view to raising the point that a quorum was not present.

At 2:05 o'clock Speaker Cannon pronounced that the clerk had made a mistake in counting the votes in the last recess moving and that it stood 134 votes to 141 against the recess instead of 134 to 135.

By this time nearly all the regulars had left the chamber and Representative Tawney, a Cannon man, raised the point of order that there was no quorum. Representative Underwood, Democrat, threatened to block this game by having a call of the House, which would mean that the sergeant-at-arms and his assistants would be sent out to bring the regular Republicans back.

When the Republican regulars left the House under guard of Whip Dwight they intended to lock the doors of their houses, so as not to let themselves be found by the sergeant-at-arms and his lieutenants.

At 2:30 a call of the House established the lack of a quorum and the Speaker, because of the insistence of the insurgents, ordered the sergeant-at-arms to arrest the absentees and to bring them into the House.

If the sergeant-at-arms gets some of them he will have to batter down their front doors or jimmy the windows. Speaker Cannon under the rules of the House was obliged to give the order to the police officers of the House.

This order means that the House will have to remain in session at least until a quorum is obtained. Many of the insurgents were preparing to take a snooze pending the results of the sergeant-at-arms's efforts. He and his lieutenants left the Capitol in automobiles on their hunt for absentee members at 2:35 A.M.

Nobody expects to see a quorum present before 11 in the morning. Speaker Cannon at 2:40 o'clock still was in the chair and the insurgents were orating at each other. The quorum was lacking by forty-one members.

Representative Underwood asked for the arrest of the absent members and it was ordered.

Representative [Ollie Murray] James (Dem.) of Kentucky arose at 2:50 o'clock and suggested that Speaker Cannon send the minority's deputies out after the absentees. He was willing to guarantee that these deputies would do a good deal better work at rousing the Republican regulars out of bed than would the Cannon deputies.

Mr. James charged the Cannon organization deputies with having no intention of bringing the absentees in. The Speaker declined to accept Mr. James's suggestion.

The Republican leaders admit that the situation at 3 o'clock amounts to a recess and that there is no chance of getting a quorum before 11 o'clock.

Col. [Henry A.] Casson, sergeant-at-arms, resented Mr. James's remarks and suggested that Mr. James himself select Democratic deputies. This James did and these deputies left the Capitol at 3 o'clock with orders to get the Republican members out of their beds, put them under arrest, and hand them before the bar of the House.

———

19 March 1910, 1 & 2:

CANNON MAY GO DOWN TO DEFEAT

———

His Close Friends Admit That His Opponents Control the Situation

———

Rumor That He May Resign

———

Three Conferences of the Opposing Forces Result in Disagreement

———

The Cannon Forces Consent to an Enlargement of the Committee on Rules From Five to Ten and to Have the Committeemen Elected by the House, but Will Not Consent to Eliminate the Speaker - This the Insurgents Refuse to Accept - Another Proposed Compromise Is to Allow the Speaker to Serve

Until March 5 and Then Retire - Another Is to Allow the New Rules Committee to Select Its Own Chairman - This May Be Moved To-day. House Takes a Recess Until Morning.

Washington, March 18. - Speaker Cannon's close friends acknowledged to-night that the combination of insurgents and Democrats had control of the situation in the House and that unless some compromise can be effected or there is a break in the Democratic ranks the Speaker is likely to go down to defeat. This admission was made with noticeable sadness by the men who have stood shoulder to shoulder with Speaker Cannon for many years in dominating the affairs of the House.

Mr. Cannon's friends believe further that he may resign from the speakership if he is beaten in the present fight.

Speaker Cannon's supporters themselves, after an all night struggle on the floor of the House, made overtures to the insurgents in the hope of reaching a common ground on which both can stand. Three conferences were held by representatives of the two Republican factions in the course of the day, but when the House voted a recess at 4 o'clock this afternoon until to-morrow morning, the deadlock was still on.

The Cannon forces have consented to an enlargement of the Committee on Rules from five to ten members, six to be selected from the majority and four from the minority party. They have further consented to have these ten committeemen nominated by a party caucus and elected by the House instead of being appointed by the Speaker.

The Norris resolution, which has brought the trouble in the House to a head, provides for the election of fifteen members to the Rules Committee by the House. The compromise proposition as submitted by the Cannon forces is acceptable to the near insurgents, except in one additional feature. The near insurgents, to say nothing of the real radicals, will not listen to any proposition which does not include the elimination of the Speaker from the membership of the committee. This is the point in which the two Republican factions in the House are immediately at issue.

Speaker Cannon's friends have told the near insurgents that they will not stand for any proposition that humiliates the Speaker through such an elimination provision. The insurgent conferees have found it impossible thus far to accept any compromise that does not contain this feature, and members of the insurgent band were emphatic to-night in declaring that they will not alter their attitude.

Efforts are being made to-night and probably will be continued in the morning to get the Speaker himself to solve this embarrassing question. Several of Mr. Cannon's closest friends are urging him to go into a party conference and volunteer the assurance that he will not serve on a new Rules Committee.

ANOTHER GROUND OF COMPROMISE

Another ground for compromise that is being suggested by the Cannon forces is that the Speaker be allowed to serve out his term on the present Rules Committee until March 4 under a gentlemen's agreement that he will not serve after that date. In the hope that some such understanding can be reached a resolution was drafted in to-day's conference which while providing for the enlargement of the Rules Committee and its selection by the House contains nothing derogatory to the Speaker. Here is the resolution that has been proposed for substitution in place of the Norris resolution:

The Committee on Rules shall consist of ten members, six of whom shall be members of the majority party and four of whom shall be members of the minority party, all of whom shall be elected by the House by majority vote.

The Committee on Rules shall select its own chairman.

All rules of parts thereof inconsistent with this resolution are hereby repealed.

It is understood that the plan of the organization leaders to-night, if a compromise along these lines can be reached, is that this resolution or one similar to it shall be introduced in the House by Mr. Cannon's own Rules Committee at to-morrow's session and pushed through without debate. Speaker Cannon himself, it is understood, has taken the stand that he will go down fighting rather than consent to the humiliation that would attend the passage of a resolution specifically eliminating him from the Rules Committee. The Speaker's close friends also said that they will fall with him if necessary rather than acquiesce in any such action.

INSURGENTS INSIST ON SPEAKER'S ELIMINATION

The Speaker's friends admit that the course which they advised of a gentlemen's agreement is merely a quibble that is intended to save the Speaker personal feelings in the event of things going against them. It is not at all certain that a voluntary withdrawal by the Speaker from the Rules Committee after March 4 next year would be satisfactory to the real insurgents. Men like Cooper of Wisconsin, Murdock of Kansas, Poindexter of Washington [State], and one or two others insist that they will be satisfied with nothing less than a definite statement of elimination in the resolution.

Representative Dalzell of Pennsylvania was in conference for a long time with Speaker Cannon to-night and there were further conferences between the committees of the two factions, but it was said that nothing definite would be determined until the joint meeting of the committees at 9 o'clock tomorrow.

It was the general impression here to-night that if Speaker Cannon consented to give his word that he will retire from the Rules Committee after March 4 next and a compromise plan is carried through on this basis it will mean his elimination also from the speakership and possibly from active politics.

TO RULE ON NORRIS RESOLUTION

It is the intention of the insurgents to-night, if no agreement is reached at the conference to-morrow morning, to insist upon a ruling by the Speaker immediately after the House reconvenes on the point of order raised on the Norris resolution. It is under this point of order that the fight of more than twenty-four hours has been carried on. The Norris resolution, providing for the reorganization of the Rules Committee, was introduced under the plea of a constitutional privilege. Representative Dalzell made the point of order that constitutional privilege did not apply, and Speaker Cannon, holding his ruling back on this point, has let the debate run on for more than twenty-four hours in the hope finally of

finding himself in a position where he will be able to defeat the resolution.

That the Speaker will deliver his ruling on the point of order to-morrow morning is pretty certain. Mr. Cannon was on the point of delivering his decision just before the House took a recess at 4 o'clock this afternoon. The Speaker seemed to be in a pretty angry mood and it was said that he was resenting the suggestions that were being made by his friends to compromise.

"The Chair is prepared to rule," said the Speaker as he banged his desk with his gavel.

CANNON SURPRISES HIS SUPPORTERS

In a moment the House was in silence, but before the Speaker had begun Representative Tawney jumped up and moved that a recess be taken until to-morrow morning. Representative [Charles Lafayette] Bartlett of Georgia said that this motion was out of order and he was sustained by the Speaker. This action of Mr. Cannon occasioned almost as much surprise among his supporters as the announcement that he was ready to rule on the point of order. It was evident that something had gone wrong between the Speaker and his friends.

Representative Gaines of West Virginia was on his feet in a second with a motion that the Speaker's ruling be postponed until to-morrow morning. This motion was carried by a vote of 161 to 151, many of the insurgents thus voting for a delay that they had already condemned in previous votes. One of the most interesting features about this ballot was the voting of Representative Mann of Illinois, one of Speaker Cannon's closest friends. He cast his ballot against a postponement of the ruling.

Said Mr. Mann later, "I voted against postponement because I was not willing to continue the fight. I am not willing to agree to any proposition thus far suggested by the so-called insurgents. If they want to take the responsibility of disrupting the organization of the House that is their right, and I would not undertake to criticise them. If they win they will have the responsibility of legislation and I will have the fun of being in a minority."

INSURGENTS IN A MORE CONCILIATORY MOOD

This vote wasn't the first one of the day in which insurgents had shown that they were in a more conciliatory mood than they had been in last night's session. They had broken away from their Democratic allies for the first time in two days in a vote at 2 o'clock in the afternoon providing for a recess until 4 o'clock. On that vote Representatives Miller, [James Breck] Perkins [of New York], Fish, Volstead, Foelker, Woods, Kendall, Kinkaid, and Pickett separated from the Democrats and the real radicals and cast their votes with the regular organization. They explained that they had done this because they believed the national interest of the party demanded a satisfactory compromise if it could be reached.

In the vote taken at 4 o'clock for a postponement of the Speaker's ruling until to-morrow morning, the regular Republicans gained four more votes from the ranks of the insurgents, Gardner, Hinshaw, Steenerson and Hayes. Besides these Davidson, who had not voted on the previous recess vote, cast his ballot with the regulars, while Foelker, who had voted on the first recess motion, failed to vote this time. All told, the regulars had taken twelve insurgent votes on this ballot.

The near insurgents declared, however, that there was no significance in this change; that they would be found lined up firmly with the Democrats to-morrow morning if the compromise did not go through. The insurgents say that they will have thirty-three Republican votes against the Speaker's point of order ruling and that there will be fully that number voting against the regular organization on the question of reorganizing the House rules.

Some of the insurgents figured that they would be able to defeat the Speaker on his point of order ruling by at least four votes and they hoped to be able to make the margin still wider on the question of the rules.

DEMOCRATS UNCERTAIN

There is, however, one feature of the situation that leads many to refrain from counting Uncle Joe as down and out, and that is the uncertainty of the Democrats. It is true that they have held together thus far, but it is recalled that they went to pieces on a previous question when the insurgents thought they had the Speaker cornered on this same question. It is known that the Speaker's friends are pulling every wire possible to break into the Democratic line. Representative Fitzgerald, who introduced the resolution that blocked the insurgents' efforts a year ago, arrived in town to-day.

The day's session of the House was not as stormy as that of last night, but it was replete with spectacular features. A sight of Uncle Joe in action was itself worth going a long distance to see. The old veteran, his jaw firmly set with the customary cigar tilted upward and with a red carnation in his buttonhole - the same carnation that has been there through twenty-four hours of strenuous fighting - paced the corridors with perfect self-composure and with a pleasing word for friend and enemy alike. If he was going down to defeat he was carrying with him the admiration of his enemies.

REPUBLICANS BREAK A QUORUM

It was a sorry looking lot of insurgents and Democrats who saw the darn light break through the glass roof of the House chamber. The Republican regulars, acting under orders from whip Dwight, had deserted the chamber at about 3 o'clock in the morn for the purpose of breaking a quorum. This method of discouraging the allies and holding in check their activities had been adopted by the Cannon forces after they had been routed on every attempt to get an adjournment or a recess. They figured that the insurgents and Democrats would soon tire of holding the fort alone, or at least that they would wear the edge off their enthusiasm if they remained in the chamber.

The allies, however, were too fearful of what might happen if they absented themselves from the chamber and so they stuck it out bravely from 3 o'clock in the morning until 7:30, the latter hour being the first time that there had been a quorum in the House since whip Dwight had passed out his order to the Republican regulars to make themselves scarce. In the tedious hours that had intervened the allies tried to keep awake by carrying on an attack from the floor of the House upon the meek looking sergeant-at-arms and calling upon Speaker Cannon and Representative Dalzell, who now and then relieved the Speaker, to explain why the aforesaid sergeant-at-arms and his faithful assistants had not been able to produce the Republican organization members on the warrants that had been issued for their arrest by order of the House. There is no doubt that Uncle Joe could have thrown considerable light on this question if he had wanted to, but he contented himself with informing the inquirers that the deputies, armed with warrants, were out scurrying around in automobiles trying to lay hands on the absent members.

HOLLINGSWORTH LANDED HOPPING MAD

The hardworking deputies succeeded in landing just one Republican organization member before daylight and he was Representative Hollingsworth of Ohio, an elderly gentleman with a walruslike mustache who obtained some notoriety not long ago by demanding that the name and face of Jefferson Davis be removed from the silver service presented by the State of Mississippi to the battleship of that name. It was 7 o'clock in the morning when Mr. Hollingsworth entered the chamber in tow of a deputy. The Ohio member wore his tie under one ear and showed other evidences of a hurried toilet. He was hopping mad, and he didn't care who knew it. He placed his hat and gloves on a convenient desk and waved his arms wildly in the air.

"A parliamentary inquiry, Mr. Speaker!" he shouted. "Who was it who came to my room in the Willard Hotel at 4 o'clock in the morning and arrested me? I want to know who made the motion that I be arrested! I had retired like a decent gentleman. I did not think Joe Cannon would do such small business as this."

Mr. Hollingsworth's wrath was so real and his appearance so ludicrous that the House laughed until it choked and then laughed some more. It turned out, to the further amusement of the house as Mr. Hollingsworth proceeded with his complaint that he had left the chamber at midnight, after having taken the precaution to make a pair with a Democrat, and that he had the permission of whip Dwight to leave.

"I want to know," demanded Mr. Hollingsworth, gurgling with rage, "if I have been imposed upon! Have I been singled out to be arrested?"

"Where does the gentleman live?" asked Representative Ollie James of Kentucky.

"At the Willard Hotel," replied Mr. Hollingsworth.

"Then," said Mr. James, as the members laughed some more, "I would suggest that no Republican who lives at the Willard has any right to be paired with a Democrat."

"I decline to yield any further," shrieked Mr. Hollingsworth, who was convinced by this time that the whole world was against him. "I demand to know from the Speaker why I was arrested when I was properly paired and had the permission of the whip to leave."

"Oh," said Mr. Dalzell, who was in the chair, "the gentleman was not arrested."

"Then," cried Hollingsworth with a despairing gesture, "who came to my room at 4 o'clock on St. Patrick's Day with a warrant for me?"

Representative James and some of the other Democrats continued to pick at Mr. Hollingsworth until he nearly exploded.

NICK LONGWORTH NABBED

Along about 6 o'clock Nick Longworth appeared in one of the lobby doors. He was the second organization man that the deputies had nabbed. They had routed Nick out of his bed, and waiting on the front porch until he had dressed marched him up to the Capitol. Nick looked sleepy, but happy. He dropped into his seat and pretty soon his chin was reclining on his shirt bosom and the soft dawn light had soothed him to sleep.

The allies before Mr. Longworth had arrived had, however, become so peevish over the failure of the sergeant-at-arms to yank some of the absentees out of bed that they had passed a resolution over the ruling of Mr. Dalzell, who was in the chair, calling on the sergeant-at-arms to explain what he had done and why he didn't do more.

John Cannon, a fine old gray haired Republican who is only about five feet tall, came into the chamber, looking scared almost to death. He told the House he had sent four deputies out in automobiles, and although they had visited all the leading hotels in Washington and many private residences they had been unable to rout out anybody but the indignant Mr. Hollingsworth. They had succeeded, however, in booking five careless Democrats.

"As far as I can see," cried Representative Ollie James of Kentucky, "the deputies have been taking an early morning joy ride. They have been so signally unsuccessful in rounding up absentees by automobile that I suggest they use camels now."

Representative Norris of Nebraska, author of the resolution that has caused the big fight over the House rules, said that he believed that the sergeant-at-arms has been negligent in his duty in this instance and he proposed to introduce a resolution calling for an investigation and if necessary the election of a new sergeant-at-arms.

TWENTY DEPUTIES TO HUNT ABSENTEES

The allies became so impatient about 5 o'clock over the idea that the regulars were home snoozing in their beds while they were sentenced to the hard House seats, that they overruled the decision by Representative Dalzell and voted to appoint twenty deputies of their own to go out and arrest those Cannon representatives. That was all right so far as it went. They had the blank warrants and they quickly recruited the twenty deputies from clerks in the committee rooms, but the trouble was that Uncle Joe refused to sign the warrants. There was such an uproar over this that one Democrat who had been snoring over in one corner of the chamber for more than an hour was interrupted. Uncle Joe was defiant. Banging his gavel he declared that the only warrants authorized by the House were those which he had signed and placed in the hands of Sergeant-at-Arms Casson. He added that there was not a quorum present when the subsequent action was taken and he would not assume the responsibility of issuing warrants on that questionable authority.

About 7 o'clock some of the sergeant-at-arms's deputies appeared with a few more Republicans and then the Cannon men began to dribble in, looking mighty fresh and comfortable compared with the disheveled appearance of those who had remained all night on the floor. After 7:20 one of the insurgents made a point of no quorum, which necessitated a

roll call. The roll call showed 198 present while only 195 were needed for a quorum.

QUORUM DISAPPEARS

The allies seemed to be more hopeful then that they would get action of some sort or other on the point of order before the House. They hadn't reckoned though with the parliamentary schemes of the Cannon forces, for a moment later when the roll call on the question of a quorum was brought up again it was found that several members of the Cannon organization had disappeared. That's the way the proceedings dragged along all the early part of the morning. Speaker Cannon's quorum was pretty much like the Irishman's flea - now it was there and now it wasn't. It was apparent to the insurgents that the Speaker and his friends were merely baiting them, that the Speaker wanted to create the impression that the sergeant-at-arms had done something toward rounding up the Republican organization men, but at the same time he had no immediate intention of having enough of them in the chamber at any one time to enable the allies to proceed with business. It was evident that Speaker Cannon was playing a waiting game while compromise was being urged by some of his followers.

INSURGENTS OPPOSE RECESS

The extreme suspicion of the insurgents toward the regulars was well illustrated when some of the regulars suggested along about 2 o'clock that they take an hour's recess so that the cleaners could enter the chamber and sweep the floor. Goodness knows there was need enough for a sweeping. The aisles were cluttered with a twenty-four hour collection of scraps of paper and other debris and the chamber looked generally as if it had been mixed up with a hurricane. The insurgents, however, rejected this cleaning up suggestion, fearing that it might involve some change in the parliamentary situation of advantage to the regulars. The cleaners had to be content with walking down the aisles and picking up what they could.

By this time the galleries had filled again and long lines were standing in the corridors waiting for admission. Among those in the gallery were the wives of many of the members, who seemed to enjoy the disheveled appearance of their husbands as they moved about the floor.

RUMORS OF POSSIBLE COMPROMISE

Rumors of a possible compromise were current in the chamber from shortly after daylight and occasioned considerable concern on the part of the Democrats. It was not, however, until about 10 o'clock that the word came from the regulars that they would like to meet representatives of the insurgents at 11:30 o'clock with a view of finding a common ground, if possible, upon which they could consider plans for saving the party. This was the conference held in Representative Gardner's room and which failed to yield any definite results.

While the conference between the two factions was on the House practically went into a state of coma again. Some of the insurgents and Democrats who had remained on duty all night were so badly used up that they could hardly keep their eyes open, while some of them made no pretence of fighting nature any longer and moved over to a corner or out into the cloakroom where they could snooze without attracting much attention.

Uncle Joe himself, however, seemed to be little affected by his all night vigil and the intense strain under which he had labored. With the butt of a cigar in his mouth, tilted at the usual Cannon angle, he wandered about the corridors, self-possessed and apparently ready to fight to the end. Even his enemies were ready to concede that Uncle Joe hasn't a peer as a fighter.

NO AGREEMENT - ANOTHER CONFERENCE

The insurgents filed back into the House at 11:47, after their conference, and it immediately became known that no agreement had been reached, but that there was a possibility of a recess being taken. The insurgents returned from their conference in a sullen and determined frame of mind. It was shortly after this that the insurgents selected Messrs. Gardner of Massachusetts, Hayes of California, Lenroot of Wisconsin and Norris of Nebraska to meet a representation from the Cannon forces in another conference in an attempt to find a basis of agreement in the concessions which the regulars were willing to make.

Every little while the resentment felt by the Democrats against the sergeant-at-arms would flare up. A motion was prepared by one of the Democratic members providing for the removal of the sergeant-at-arms for willful negligence, but this member finally relented when it became known that until the Speaker had ruled on the point of order raised on the Norris resolution such a motion could not be entertained.

Representative [Dorsey William] Shackleford of Missouri afforded the gallery a few minutes of pleasure when he declared that the Speaker had privately instructed the sergeant-at-arms not to arrest absentees because he was unable to command a majority vote.

"The Speaker of this House is maintaining a state of anarchy!" shouted Mr. Shackleford.

QUARTET SINGS RAGTIME SONGS

About this time a quartet of very sleepy Representatives started up the song "There'll Be a Hot Time in the Old Town To-night." The singers were over in one corner of the chamber. Representative [Joseph Hamilton] Moore of Pennsylvania, who was in the chair, nearly broke the gavel banging for order.

"The sergeant-at-arms sits there," shouted Mr. Shackleford above the din of the ragtime chorus, "and makes no effort to perform his duty because the Speaker may have privately directed him to pursue that course of non-action. But the sergeant-at-arms is bound to arrest absentees and bring them in here. When he refuses to do that he is bringing anarchy upon us."

Representative Payne of New York happened in at this time. He characterized Mr. Shackleford's remarks as a harangue.

"I hope the winds of the caves will cease for a few minutes," shouted Mr. Payne across the aisle toward the Missouri member.

SPEAKER GETS A NEW GAVEL

The Speaker's gavel had been so badly used up by the banging of the last twenty-four hours that Mr. Cannon brought in a new one. The appearance of the Speaker with his new "weapon" was greeted with applause. There were plenty of evidences of the intense earnestness which marked the struggle on both sides. For instance, Representative [John William] Boehne, Democrat, Indiana, who has been very ill, insisted on coming to the House to-day to support his party colleagues. The Ballinger-Pinchot committee[8], which was scheduled to hold a hearing to-day, went by the board because Representative Madison, of Kansas, one of the surge leaders, had to be in his seat on the floor. He staggered into the room of the Ballinger-Pinchot committee this morning, explaining, "Gentlemen, I will do my best to keep up, but I am utterly exhausted." Out of consideration for Mr. Madison the committee adjourned and he expressed his thanks.

BOTH SIDES GET REINFORCEMENTS

By noon seventeen members who were out of town when the bitter fight began yesterday had returned to Washington in response to the urgent summons of the leaders and were in their seats. The regular Republicans who had come back were [Samuel Walker] McCall of Massachusetts, [James Samuel] Simmons of New York, [Michael Edward] Driscoll of New York, [Reuben Osborne] Moon of Pennsylvania, [John Kinley] Tener of Pennsylvania, [Philip Pitt] Campbell of Kansas, [Edwin] Denby of Michigan, [Frank Mellen] Nye of Minnesota, [James Francis] Burke of Pennsylvania and Foelker of New York.

The insurgents also had been reinforced by Representatives [Herbert] Parsons of New York, [Joseph Lafayette] Rhinock of Ohio, [Joshua Willis] Alexander of Missouri, and [Joseph Frderick Cockey] Talbot of Maryland. Three Democrats, Boehne of Indiana, [Richmond Pearson] Hobson of Alabama, and [Edward William] Pou of North Carolina also had put in an appearance. The arrival of the absentees, however, made no material difference in the lineup.

BREAK IN INSURGENT RANKS - RECESS VOTED

There was a vast amount of orating between 12 and 2 o'clock, and then the first definite indication of a more compromising spirit between the Republican factions became evident. Representative Martin of South Dakota, a near insurgent, moved that the House take a recess until 4 o'clock. This motion

was carried by a vote of 161 to 154. It was the first break in the insurgent ranks in the long fight, nine of them switching over and voting with the regular Cannon Republicans. The insurgents who voted were Parsons and Fish of New York, Miller and Volstead of Minnesota, Kinkaid of Nebraska, Foelker of New York and Woods, Kendall and Pickett of Iowa. The result of the vote occasioned a great uproar in the House, the insurgents who thus had broken away from the conference with their Democratic brothers for the first time in two days explained that they were for recess on the theory that a better opportunity thus would be afforded to consider the compromise proposal. The same men had voted against a recess once or twice in the early hours this morning and their change of vote was at once taken as an indication that the insurgents were beginning to realize the seriousness of the situation from a party standpoint, and that they were willing to try to settle their family quarrels in private.

ANOTHER CONFERENCE HELD

It was rumored immediately after this vote that President Taft had interceded with some of the insurgents by way of impressing them with the serious consequences that must come to the party from a continuance of the present struggle. This rumor was revived at other times in the day, but it was not verified. The same committees that had a conference earlier in the day got together again during the two hour recess period. In the interval members of the House seized upon the opportunity to eat and to get a wink or two of sleep on the committee room lounges.

When the House met again at 4 o'clock it was known that the committees had again failed to reach any conclusion on which a compromise could be based. Then it was that the vote was taken which resulted in a recess until to-morrow morning. The announcement of this vote was received with a big demonstration on the floor and in the gallery.

———

20 March 1910, 1 & 2:

CANNON SHORN OF HIS POWER

———

He Is Eliminated From Committee on Rules by a Vote of 191 to 155

————

House Refuses to Oust Him

————

Resolution Declaring the Speaker's Chair Vacant Defeated by 36 Majority

————

The Speaker Had Previously Announced That He Would Entertain Such a Motion, and His Challenge Was Accepted - Only Seven Insurgents Vote With the Democrats to Depose Uncle Joe - Under the Insurgent Victory the Rules Committee Will Be Enlarged to Ten Members and the Cannon Organization Will Be Deprived of Its Former Absolute Control.

Washington, March 19 - Speaker Cannon went down to defeat to-day, but when his enemies believed him to be in utter rout he turned and forced from them what practically amounts to a vote of confidence. It was the last play of a veteran fighter and of a parliamentarian whose hand has been trained by years of practical experience.

The Speaker was forced from the Committee on Rules by a vote of 191 to 155, forty Republican insurgents siding with the solid Democratic vote. The trick that the Speaker turned on his enemies was in the form of a resolution presented by Representative [Albert Sidney] Burleson of Texas, a Democrat, declaring the Speaker's chair vacant, and ordering an election of Mr. Cannon's successor. The Speaker already had announced from the chair amid an impressive silence that he would entertain such a motion. It was promptly voted down by 191 to 155 amid a scene that is probably without parallel in the history of the House of Representatives. Only seven insurgents sided with the Democrats in voting to depose Uncle Joe from the post that he had held for seven years. As a matter of fact, the proposition to oust him from the speakership was rejected by a majority of thirty-six, which is ten more than the majority that the Speaker had when he was first elected to the office.

By paving the way for this vote on the speakership question, which never has been directly involved in

the present fight, Mr. Cannon adroitly drew a line of cleavage between the issue presented in his eventual defeat and that shown as Cannonism. The vote will go before the country as the best of evidence that Cannon the individual was not the issue in the present struggle, but that it was the system which he had inherited from his predecessor. It was a mighty clever move on the Speaker's part and it also was the child of his own brain, as his advisors had been urging him to throw down his gavel and resign.

REGULARS SHORN OF POWER

The Committee on Rules under the insurgent victory to-day will be changed from the form which it has had for half a century and the Cannon organization will be shorn of the power which it has exercised under it for the last seven years. The committee will be enlarged, probably on Monday, from five to ten members, all of whom shall be elected by the House itself instead of being appointed by the Speaker. Of the ten, six are to be Republicans and four Democrats. In the selection of the members of this committee will be found the possibility of another big row in the House, although it is conceded that the insurgents and the Democrats will be able to carry out their will in the matter if they stick together. On this point, however, there is a much greater chance of a split. The resolution adopted by the insurgents and Democratic vote specifically eliminates the Speaker from the committee.

From the very beginning of the fight in the House to-day it was apparent to everybody that the Cannon organization would be humbled and the control of the House, temporarily at least, transferred from the Republican normal majority to the actual majority composed of the insurgents and the Democrats. The first test vote foreshadowed defeat for the regulars and each succeeding vote demonstrated as the day wore on that the insurgents were gathering strength.

NEVER SUCH A SESSION

Never in the history of the House, according to old timers here, has there been such a session. It was simply one scene of disorder after another. The House at times was utterly beyond the control of the presiding officer, and members - regulars, insurgents, and Democrats, all acted at times like wild men. While there were no fist fights among the factionists, there were disputes that led almost to personal encounters, and it seemed on one or two occasions as if the House was going to turn itself into a crazy mob.

Uncle Joe, the most vitally concerned of them all, was apparently the coolest. He never lost his head, and also kept a close guard brake on his temper, which was irritated to the extreme on several occasions. Also his rulings on points made by both insurgents and Democrats never were more impartial and free from bias. He stood like a rock against his enemies and his conduct elicited only words of commendation from both friend and foe.

There was a fine old war dance by the insurgents and Democrats when the announcement was made by the Speaker that the Norris resolution had been adopted. The insurgents whooped with joy, the Democrats, many of then, voiced their satisfaction with rebel yells, while the regulars hooted in derision.

THE WILDEST SCENE

The most impressive scene and also the wildest came, however, when the Burleson resolution was introduced, just after Speaker Cannon had announced that he would entertain a resolution declaring the Speaker's chair vacant.

"Mr. Speaker," roared the Texas member, brandishing his resolution above his head and stepping out into the aisle. "I have a motion to vacate the Speaker's chair which I wish to present to the House."

The words were hardly out of Burleson's mouth when Shirley[9] of Kentucky, a Democrat, who is lame, limped down the aisle and began to plead with Burleson. He put his arms on Burleson's shoulders and tried to force him back into his seat, shook his finger under the Texan's nose and finally brandished his arms above Burleson's head, trying in wild excitement to make him see that he was doing the very thing that the Speaker and the regular Republicans had hoped that somebody on the minority side would be idiotic enough to do.

Mr. Shirley punched Burleson in the ribs and waved his arm over toward the Republican side of the chamber. He was evidently trying to demonstrate to Mr. Burleson that only a glance over there was necessary to show how joyously the Republicans received the Democratic proposition. They were grinning like Cheshire cats, every one of the old guard, and slapping one another on the back and whispering the good tidings from ear to ear.

BURLESON WOULDN'T SEE

But Mr. Burleson would not see. He shook the Kentuckian off, waved his arms defiantly to scatter the score or more of Democrats who had crowded around him to endeavor to induce him to withdraw his motion to vacate the chair and continued to bawl for recognition and for action on his proposition.

The Democrats who were opposed to the introduction of the Burleson resolution feared that its passage would mean the elimination of the Cannon campaign issue in the present fight next fall. There were more Democrats, however, who favored the introduction of the resolution than were opposed to it.

It was with a joyous abandon, far different from the feeling they had displayed earlier in the day, when defeat after defeat had been their portion, that the regulars, with the help of a few near insurgents and Democrats, voted down the proposition to adjourn. A demand for the yeas and nays was flatly refused.

INSURGENTS IN A FIX

It was mighty apparent by this time that the insurgents appreciated the beautiful fix they were in. If they stood by their violent criticisms of "Czar" Cannon and voted accordingly the minority would be able, perhaps within the next hour or so, to elect a Democratic Speaker of a Republican House. On the other hand, if the insurgents declined to support the Burleson motion and voted to retain Uncle Joe in the chair they were put in the unbelievable position of being inconsistent and two-faced.

"Start up the music; let the dance go on," cried Chairman Tawney of the Appropriations Committee in an exceedingly unparliamentary tone. And the dance went on.

Mr. Burleson, who had never paused for a moment in his arm waving, document brandishing performance, got the eye of the Chair again and in a flash, his resolution had been carried to the desk and was being read. While Democrats all over the House continued to shout at him, to sit down and shut up, Mr. Burleson, paying no attention, demanded the previous question to choke off all debate.

He got it. Republican regulars and snorting Democrats jumped to their feet all over the House. Again the insurgents were noticeable from the fact that they remained in their chairs, apparently afflicted with acute melancholia. No record vote was demanded on this proposition, as it was merely a preliminary to the main question of whether the House should then and there depose the Speaker, Without another word on either side Mr. Burleson demanded a yea and nay vote on the resolution itself, and again the solid strength of the body, excepting only the insurgents backed him up.

ACUTE INTERESTS IN THE VOTE

The vote was on. The acute interest in it may be understood from the fact that a majority of the members on both sides had official roll calls in front of them and checked off the for and against votes as the reading clerk called name after name. Of course what they wanted to know was how the insurgents were going to vote - whether they split all to pieces on this mighty ticklish question or whether they would vote solidly one way or another.

The first insurgent named on the list was Representative Cary of Wisconsin, a short, fat, red faced gentleman, who had been trying to raise Ned with the local gaslight company and who prides himself on the fact that his knife is out at all hours of the day and night for all varieties of predatory wealth and all forms of grinding and oppressive monopoly.

"Aye!" yelled Cary when his name was called, indicating that he wanted to see Uncle Joe thrown out of the window in a figurative sense. And of course the insurgents and the Cemeteries cheered, the minority taking heart for a moment and believing that perhaps the whole insurgent strength would be thrown that way.

But they did not hold this idea long. As name after name was called it became very apparent that only

the most radical of the insurgents were voting to depose Uncle Joe and that the substantial members of the "outlaw" band, like Gardner of Massachusetts, Norris of Nebraska, and others had declined to, as far as that.

As each insurgent registered his vote he was cheered and jeered, depending on whether he stuck by the allied combination or whether he jumped back to his own party's parlor and sat down again. If he stuck the Democrats were for him. If he voted against the Burleson motion the regular Republicans welcomed him with loud applause.

HOUSE VOTES NOT TO DEPOSE UNCLE JOE

At last - and it seemed a long time, considering the nerve tension in the House at the time - the second call on this roll came to an end and the House grew as still as death awaiting the announcement of the vote by Sereno E. Payne of New York who when the members started to vote on the proposition to depose Mr. Cannon had been called in to take the chair.

The journal clerk with a smile on his face - he is a Republican appointee and a great admirer of Mr. Cannon - passed the vote slip up to Mr. Payne.

The Speaker pro tem adjusted his glasses. "On this vote," he said as everybody within hearing distance leaned forward to catch the result, "the ayes are 135 and the noes are 191, and the motion is lost."

SCENE OF NOISY TUMULT

Mr. Payne started to say something else, but what it was nobody will ever know. For in a fleeting second the old guard was on its feet yelling like mad. One member tossed his hat in the air and when it came down he put his foot in it and laughed like a child. Another grabbed a colleague around the neck and hugged him in a regular frenzy of joy. And the slaps as staid Republicans, old and young, clapped one another on the back sounded like a new sort of rapid fire artillery. Louder and louder swelled the volume of the tumult and just then two members unfurled a big American flag and marched with it up the centre aisle.

The galleries had gone crazy too. Among the spectators were the wives, sons and daughters of members who had reason to be vitally interested in the result. And, too, there were many people from out of town drawn from the cosmopolitan crowd that throngs the national Capitol during sessions of Congress and local residents by the hundreds. No convention cheering records were broken, but it is doubtful if much more noise ever came from an equal number of throats.

CANNON RECEIVES CONGRATULATIONS

The House soon adjourned and then came the most interesting scene of the entire afternoon. The Democrats and the insurgents filed out of the chamber almost immediately, some of them quiet, some of them glum, some of them profane. But the old guard stayed behind, and as Speaker Cannon, who had been watching the proceedings from a seat on the floor, started out he was surrounded and forced up two steps on the rostrum. There, leaning against one of the marble supports of the Speaker's desk, his mouth, that had been grim for days, relaxed in a smile, he stood to receive the congratulations of his friends.

Way in the back of the chamber the regulars formed [a] line and marched up the centre aisle to the Speaker's desk.

"Dear Uncle Joe," was the song they sang to a popular air as they advanced on their old friend, colleague and political chief. Dalzell of Pennsylvania headed the line. As he came up to where the Speaker stood he put out his hand. The Speaker grasped it. Then they just stood there, the two old cronies; they looked at each other and smiled.

"We're a little shot up, John," said the Speaker. "But we're still on top, Joe," said Dalzell.

It was like that for half an hour. Tawney of Minnesota and Mr. Cannon hugged each other and everybody in the line had something nice to say to the Speaker and he had something nice to say to them.

After this it was soon over. "Dear Uncle Joe" was sung a couple of times more and the old guard, glad that it was all over, happy to have got off so easily, quickly scattered.

INSURGENTS WHO VOTED TO DEPOSE UNCLE JOE

The nine men who voted for Mr. Cannon's deposition as Speaker were all simon pure radicals: Perry[11],

Cooper, Lenroot of Wisconsin, Nelson, Lindbergh and Davis of Minnesota; Gronna of North Dakota, Murdock of Kansas and Poindexter of Washington [State].

Many of the insurgents who did not vote against Speaker Cannon have been making redhot speeches against him in their districts. They are in a pretty pickle now and will be busy for weeks explaining why they did not kick Uncle Joe out when they had the opportunity.

Shirley[9], white-lipped and earnest, hobbled down into the well of the House where amid the uproar he contended that Burleson's motion to fire the Speaker was out of order inasmuch as a motion to adjourn, made by Norris, was pending. In his contention he was supported by most of the insurgents.

Finally, after a lot of argument, Speaker Cannon ruled that although he would be happy to entertain the Burleson motion to relieve him of his job, on precedent and practice he was forced to hold that the motion to adjourn was before the House and had to be acted upon.

He are the 39 insurgents who voted against the regulars for a change in the Rules Committee:

[William Oscar] Barnard of Indiana, Cary of Wisconsin, Dawson of Iowa, Davidson of Wisconsin, Fish of New York, Fowler of New Jersey, Gronna of North Dakota, Hayes of California, Hollingsworth of Ohio, Howland of Ohio, Kopp of Wisconsin, Johnson of Ohio, Cooper of Wisconsin, Davis of Minnesota, Foelker of New York, Gardner of Massachusetts, Haugen of Iowa, Hinshaw of Nebraska, Hubbard of Iowa, Kinkaid of Nebraska, [Gustav] Küstermann of Wisconsin, Lenroot of Wisconsin, Lindbergh of Minnesota, Madison of Kansas, Miller of Minnesota, Martin of South Dakota, Morse of Wisconsin, Murdock of Kansas, Parsons of New York, Pickett of Iowa, [Frank] Plumley of Vermont, Poindexter of Washington [State], Steenerson of Minnesota, [Edward Livingston] Taylor of Ohio, Townsend of Michigan, Volstead of Minnesota and Woods of Iowa.

COMPROMISE CONFERENCE

The crowd began to gather at the Capitol shortly after daylight. The excitement over the great fight in the House of Representatives has been running high for several days and it seemed as if all Washington, official and otherwise, wanted to be present at what it believed would be the culmination of the struggle. The corridors were jammed with people when the members of the compromise committee from the two factions arrived at the Capitol at 9 o'clock in the morning. It was realized by both sides that this 9 o'clock conference would represent absolutely the last effort that would be made to reach a settlement of the differences and that in failing in this the fight immediately would be taken up on the floor of the House, to be waged to a finish.

The only point involved in the compromise conference was whether or not the Speaker should be eliminated from the Committee on Rules. The Cannon forces realized that the insurgents controlled the situation and their request that Uncle Joe be spared this humiliation was more in the nature of a final appearance then as a suggestion.

INSURGENTS INSIST ON ELIMINATING CANNON

The insurgents were willing to accept the regulars' concession of enlarging the Rules Committee from five to ten, instead of to fifteen, and to have it elected by the House but the insurgents refused absolutely to enter into any compromise which did not provide for the elimination of the Speaker from the committee. The insurgents on the conference committee were willing to accept a compromise which would postpone the operation of the elimination provision until after Uncle Joe's term had expired, but this proposition was not acceptable to the radical wing of the insurgent band, to such men as Murdock of Kansas, Cooper of Wisconsin, Poindexter of Washington [State], and others.

The insurgents were represented at this final compromise conference by Norris of Nebraska, Hayes of California, Gardner of Massachusetts and Lenroot of Wisconsin. The Cannon forces were represented by Tawney of Minnesota, [Walter Inglewood] Smith of Iowa, Mann of Illinois, Payne of New York and Dalzell of Pennsylvania.

The early morning crowd, always seeking the centre of activity, had gathered down in the corridor at the door of the Ways and Means Committee room, where the conference was being held. The Cannon conferees were the first to file out and it was apparent from their gloomy appearance that the attempt to reach an agreement had failed. The insurgents, on the other hand, emerged from the committee room smiling and confident.

CANNON TOLD OF HIS DOOM

It was then 11 o'clock. The Cannon conference committee proceeded immediately to the Speaker's room, where they reported to him the result of their efforts. The report amounted practically to the signing of Uncle Joe's political death warrant, but the old man accepted it with a smile and said:

"Well, gentlemen, I am ready to take the question before the House."

The insurgent committee in the meantime had called a conference of the Republican insurgents. They submitted the question there whether the insurgents as a whole would be willing to accept a proposition which would allow Uncle Joe to serve out his term as a member of the Rules Committee and then retire. The more radical of the insurgents declined to entertain this suggestion, and the negotiations were formally declared off, when word was sent to the Cannon forces that the fight would be taken up on the floor of the House.

It wasn't long after the failure of the compromise effort that Uncle Joe emerged from his committee room. He showed no signs of anxiety and had a cheery good morning for employees and others who greeted him.

By 11:55, the hour set for the reconvening of the House, the galleries of the House and the corridor on that side of the Capitol were crowded. The plaza in front of the Capitol was cluttered with automobiles and even Representatives themselves had hard work in working their way through the well nigh impassible ham inside the building.

UNCLE JOE GREETED WITH APPLAUSE

At five minutes of noon practically every Representative was in his seat and members and spectators were eagerly awaiting the entry of Speaker Cannon. The appearance of the veteran when he finally appeared in the doorway and stepped toward the rostrum was the signal for a loud outburst of applause from the regular Republicans and the galleries. For several minutes the House was in an uproar. Mr. Cannon looked as grim and determined as on the first day of the struggle, when he ruled the disorderly body with an iron hand. Down came the gavel with a bang and he called sharply for order.

"The chaplain will offer the daily prayer," said the Speaker, in measured tones, and silence fell over the chamber.

While the journal of yesterday's proceedings was being read, insurgents and regulars were scurrying about drawing their lines closer for the coming battle.

Several members had corrections to suggest to the record of the twenty-nine hour session that terminated yesterday afternoon. The last correction had hardly been recorded when Representative Gaines of West Virginia jumped to his feet and moved that the House adjourn "in order that the Republicans might have an opportunity to confer."

WOULDN'T ENTERTAIN MOTION TO ADJOURN

The Speaker's determination to bring the fight to a conclusion was apparent when he refused to entertain the motion made by Mr. Gaines. Thereupon Mr. Cannon caused to be reported the Norris resolution providing for a reorganization of the Rules Committee. It was the introduction of this resolution which brought the fight to a head two days ago. The resolution read, the Speaker proceeded to deliver his ruling on the point of order made against it by Representative Dalzell when the fight had first started. It was under this point of order that the bitter debates of the last two days have been waged.

Mr. Norris, when he introduced his resolution, had contended that it was entitled to consideration as a matter of constitutional privilege. Mr. Dalzell's point against it had been that if given consideration at all it would be under the rules and not under constitutional privilege.

The Speaker's long delayed ruling sustained Dalzell's point of order and opened the way for the fight on the Norris resolution. The Speaker read his ruling - it took him about ten minutes and every word rang out clear and firm in the tense silence.

THE FIGHT BEGINS

The galleries and the members on the floor greeted this ruling with a great demonstration. When order had been restored Mr. Norris moved an appeal from the decision of the Chair. Dalzell was on his feet shouting for recognition. He moved a counter motion that the Norris resolution be laid on the table.

At that point Representative Gaines of West Virginia, a Republican regular, interrupted again with a motion for adjournment. The Speaker and the most of the Republican regulars again showed that they were opposed to any further postponement of the inevitable, and by an overwhelming viva voce vote, the Gaines motion was defeated.

The question then returned to the Dalzell motion that the appeal from the Speaker's decision on the Norris resolution should be laid on the table. The ayes and nays were demanded and the roll call was followed with the closest attention by the House and the galleries. Everybody realized, that it would disclose the relative lineup of the two forces and would indicate pretty early whether Uncle Joe was to go down to defeat or whether he had succeeded in breaking into the Democratic forces.

REGULARS BEATEN, 181 TO 164

It was apparent early in the roll call that the insurgents were standing together in their full strength. As Taylor and Johnson of Ohio deserted the organization there were groans from the regulars and applause on the Democratic side. Before the roll call was half through it was certain that the organization was beaten and that a new deal in the House was about to be declared. Uncle Joe's face during the roll call showed not a single sign of nervousness. Standing erect, with jaws set and the gavel clutched in his hand, he looked the picture of determination and defiance. With a clear, steady voice he announced that the Dalzell motion was lost by a vote of 181 to 164.

The announcement of the vote was received with shouts of joy by the insurgents and the Democrats, who jumped up from their seats, danced around in the aisles and waved their arms frantically. The crowd in the galleries contributed its full share to the uproar. In the meantime Uncle Joe had been banging away his gavel and shouting for order. It was fully five minutes before the tumult had died down.

REPUBLICANS WHO VOTED AGAINST CANNON

Thirty-five Republican Representatives voted with the solid Democratic representation on this motion. The insurgents even had exceeded their own estimate of their strength by two votes. Those who thus voted against the organization were Ames of Massachusetts, Cooper of Wisconsin, Davidson of Wisconsin, Cary of Wisconsin, Davis of Minnesota, Fish of New York, Foelker of New York, Fowler of New Jersey, Gardner of Massachusetts, Good of Iowa, Gronna of North Dakota, Haugen of Iowa, Hayes of California, Hinshaw of Nebraska, Hubbard of Iowa, Howland of Ohio, Johnson of Ohio, Kendall of Iowa, Kopp of Wisconsin, Kinkaid of Nebraska, Lindbergh of Minnesota, Lenroot of Wisconsin, Madison of Kansas, Martin of South Dakota, Miller of Minnesota, Morse of Wisconsin, Murdock of Kansas, Nelson of Wisconsin, Norris of Nebraska, Pickett of Iowa, Poindexter of Washington [State], Steenerson of Minnesota, Taylor of Ohio, Volstead of Minnesota and Woods of Iowa.

The Speaker then put the issue: "Shall the ruling of the Chair sustaining the Dalzell point of order by the judgment of the House?"

On this report Mr. Morris moved the previous question and again a vote was taken. For a second time the insurgents drew blood and there was absolutely no doubt that they were in complete control of the situation. The vote was 182 to 160, showing a gain in point of majority from 17 to 22.

After this vote the insurgents again snowed the regulars under to the tune of 182 to 160 on the question as to whether the ruling of the Chair declaring the Norris resolution out of order should stand as the judgment of the House.

The House was now face to face with the issue of whether a new Committee on Rules should be organized along the lines suggested in the Norris resolution. This resolution provided in substance for a Committee on Rules to be composed of nine Republicans and six Democrats, the committee to be elected by the House.

FACING THE REAL ISSUE

It was at this point in the proceedings that the responsible leadership of the House officially acknowledged that it was no longer in control.

Representative Norris, the Republican insurgent, held the floor. It was true, of course, that the presiding officer was friendly to the regulars, but the insurgent-Democratic combination had shown on three votes that it was in command. For the first time within the memory of man Representative Dalzell of the Committee on Rules and the leader in all Republican fights over the rules was compelled to seek terms with the insurgent leader.

An effort was made to reach an agreement for a debate on the merits of the resolution, Representative Norris suggesting that each side have an hour and a half. To this the regulars objected, Representative [William August] Rodenberg of Illinois insisting that five hours should be allowed for each side. The regulars, however, were in the attitude of asking their enemies' consent on this question of House procedure. The squabble ended, however, without any understanding being reached and the debate proceeded under the ordinary rules of the House.

CHAMP CLARK OPENS THE DEBATE

Representative Champ Clark, leader of the Democratic minority, was the first speaker.

"This is not a personal fight against Joseph G. Cannon," said he. "I can lay my hand on my heart and say that relations with that distinguished personage always have been pleasant. This is not a fight against the system. It does not make any difference if the system had been sanctified by time. No other proposition, in my mind, is pending before us to-day. I have always believed that the Speaker's position as chairman of the Committee on Rules gives him more power than any one man ought to have over the destinies of this republic. We need not mince words: this is a revolution."

Representative Lenroot of Wisconsin, an insurgent, urged all Republicans to vote to change the rules and take away the Speaker's power. This was the only means, he said, of serving the Republican party in the campaign about to be begun or of insuring the election of a Republican House.

Representative Nye of Minute delivered a stirring appeal to the Republicans to stand by the regular organization.

"I have not always been in accord with the desires of the Republican Party," said he, "nor have I been close to the present Speaker of the House, but for forty years this country has done Joseph G. Cannon honor, and now you seek to sacrifice him to make a Roman holiday."

Mr. Nye quoted from "Old Ironsides," urging the Republicans "to sever every threadbare sail and give her to the god of the storms," referring, of course, to the regular organization. Prolonged applause greeted his speech.

NORRIS RESOLUTION PRESENTED

Representative Norris of Nebraska then presented his substitute resolution providing for the reorganization or the Committee on Rules.

Representative Martin of South Dakota wanted to offer a substitute resolution providing that the Speaker should not be eliminated as a member of the Committee on Rules till the end of the present Congress, but Representative Norris would not consent. There was another wrangle between the regulars and the insurgents as to the amount of time that should be consumed in debate.

Representative [Henry De Lamar] Clayton of Alabama jumped up and shouted, "The Speaker and his kitchen cabinet, the Committee on Rules, has throttled the desire of the real majority of this House too often."

"If this proposed amendment to the rules is adopted," said Representative Underwood of Alabama, the Democratic whip, "we will have reached an era of parliamentary practice in this body. Speaker Reed in securing the adoption of rules to enable a majority of the House to do business at any time vested more power in the Speaker than any one man should have. There the power has remained until to-day. After this resolution passes the real leader of the majority party in this House will be the chairman of the enlarged Committee on Rules, and not the Speaker."

When Victor Murdock, red-headed insurgent from Kansas, jumped to his feet to talk for three minutes he was cheered by the Democrats and his fellow insurgents. He predicted Republican defeat in the next campaign unless some change was made.

Representative Hayes of California arose to declare that in giving the Norris resolution his support he was acting only from a patriotic desire to make the House procedure what is should be. He wanted to go on the record as having said that he had received only fair treatment from the Speaker of the House and from the members of the present rules committee.

EFFORT TO SUBMIT A SUBSTITUTE FAILS

Representative Olmstead of Pennsylvania tried to obtain permission to submit a substitute resolution which provided for the election of a committee to revise the House rules. Mr. Norris, however, declined to yield and the Olmstead resolution fell by the wayside.

Representative Tawney and one or two others of the Cannon forces declared that they would support the Olmsted resolution if it was brought to a vote. This Olmsted resolution obviously was offered for the purpose of affording an opportunity for several of the regulars who live in insurgent sections of the country to put themselves on record as favoring a reorganization of the Rules Committee, this to offset for political purposes the vote which they intended to cast later against the Norris resolution and in support of the Speaker.

"The resolution offered by Mr. Norris of Nebraska," declared Mr. McCall of Massachusetts, "is aimed at the Speaker of the House. The same is true of the substitute offered by Representative Martin of South Dakota. I do not propose to vote for either of them. The purpose of this movement is to hand the Speaker over to the minority, bound hand and foot. The present Speaker will go, however, with his head erect, in the simple majesty of American manhood. You are doing the bidding of a band of literary highwaymen who have been able to smirch the reputation of public men."

It was apparent by this time that a good many of the insurgents were seeking to draw a line of cleavage between Mr. Cannon as a personal factor in the fight and the system which he represents.

"I deny absolutely," said Representative Norris of Nebraska, "that this effort to amend the rules is intended as a personal slap at the Speaker. We are fighting for a principle. I deny also that this is an anti-Republican movement. From every hamlet, from every village, from every fireside of every farm, prayers are going up to-day for the success of this movement."

This was too much for the regulars. Jeers and cat-calls and shrieks greeted the statement. When this derisive demonstration had died away the Democrats, wishing to show what they thought of Mr. Norris and his statement, applauded and cheered loudly.

CANNON BEATEN, 191 TO 155

Everybody had got impatient over the speechmaking before an hour had elapsed and there was a sigh of relief when Representative Norris arose and moved the previous question on his substitute resolution. The motion on the previous question was carried by a vote of 178 to 159, only one insurgent, Martin of South Dakota, voting with the organization Republicans. This vote foreshadowed with absolutely certainty the defeat of the House organization on the resolution itself, which was adopted a few minutes later by a vote of 191 to 155. The galleries received the announcement of the vote with a hum of excitement while the insurgents and the Democrats danced around on the floor in joy of this successful conclusion of a fight that has been running on sporadically for more than a year. The Speaker himself took the vote like a real fighter, so far as it was apparent, it made no impression upon him. He pounded away with his gavel in the same old way and shouted for order in a voice that had lost none of its firmness. After the cheers of the allies which followed the passage of the Norris resolution had died away, Norris with a smile of triumph in his face raised his right hand, high above his head, and shouted:

"Mr. Speaker, I move the House do now adjourn."

The Speaker paused a moment, rustling several typewritten sheets in his hands, looked around the chamber and laid down his gavel.

"The Speaker," he said, "begs the indulgencies of the House for a few remarks."

Instantly an uproar which had followed the motion to adjourn died away. Every one realized that the real crisis of the day had been reached. A great majority of the members on the floor believed that the Speaker intended then and there to present his resignation to the body. In the galleries, the spectators leaned forward breathlessly. On the floor the members sought their seats.

UNCLE JOE ADDRESSED THE HOUSE

The Speaker looked out over the House, adjusted his steel-bowed spectacles and began to read. This is what he said:

GENTLEMEN OF THE HOUSE OF REPRESENTATIVES: Actions, not words, determine the conduct and sincerity of men in the affairs of life. This is a government by the people, acting through the representatives of a majority of the people. Results cannot be had except by a majority, and in the House of Representatives a majority, being responsible, shall have full power and should exercise that power; otherwise the majority is inefficient and does not perform its function. The office of the minority is to put the majority on its good behavior, advocating in good faith the policies which it professes, ever ready to take advantage of the mistakes of the majority party and appeal to the country for its vindication.

From time to time heretofore the majority had become the minority, as in the present case, and from time to time hereafter the majority will become the minority. The country believes that the Republican party has a majority of 47 in the House of Representatives at this time[10], but such is not the case.

The present Speaker of the House had to the best of his ability and judgment cooperated with the Republican party, and so far in the history of this Congress the Republican party in the House has been enabled by a very small majority when the test came to legislate in conformity with the policies and the platform of the Republican party. Such action of course begot criticism, which the Speaker does not deprecate on the part of the minority party.

The Speaker cannot be unmindful of the fact, as evidenced by three previous elections to the speakership, that in the past he has enjoyed the confidence of the Republican party of the country and of the

Republican members of the House, but the assault upon the Speaker of the House by the minority, supplemented by the efforts of the so-called insurgents, constituting 15 percent of the majority, and that the Speaker of the House is not in harmony with the actual majority of the House as evidenced by the vote just taken.

There are two courses open for the Speaker to pursue. One is to resign and permit the new combination of Democrats and insurgents to choose a Speaker in harmony with its aims and purposes. The other is for that combination to declare a vacancy in the office of the Speaker and proceed to the election of a new Speaker. After consideration at this stage of the session of the House, with much of important legislation pending involving the pledges of the Republican platform and their crystallization into law, believing that his resignation might consume weeks of time in the reorganization of the House, the Speaker being in harmony with Republican policies and desirous of carrying them out, declines by his own motion to precipitate a contest upon the House in the election of a new Speaker, a contest that might greatly endanger the final passage of all legislation necessary to redeem Republican promises. This is one reason why the Speaker does not resign at once, and another reason is this: in the judgment of the present Speaker a resignation is in and of itself a confession of weakness or mistake, or an apology for past actions. The Speaker is not conscious of having done any political wrong. The same rules are in force in this House that have been in force for two decades. The Speaker has construed the rules as he found them and as they have been construed by previous Speakers from Thomas B. Reed's incumbency down to the present time.

Heretofore the Speaker has been a member of the Committee on Rules covering a period of fifty years, and the present Speaker has neither sought new power nor has he unjustly used that already conferred upon him.

There has been much talk on the part of the minority and the insurgents of the "czarism" if the Speaker, culminating in the action taken to-day. The real truth is that there is no coherent Republican majority in the House of Representatives. Therefore the real majority ought to have the cour-

age of its convictions and logically meet the situation that confronts it.

The Speaker does not believe and always has that this is a Government through parties, and that parties can act only through majorities. The Speaker has always believed in and bowed to the will of the majority in convention, in caucus and in the legislative hall, and to-day profoundly believes that to act otherwise is to disorganize parties, is to prevent coherent action in any legislative body, is to make impossible the reflection of the wishes of the people in statutes and in laws.

The Speaker has always said that under the Constitution it is a question of the highest privilege for an actual majority of the House at any time to choose a new Speaker, and again notifies the House that the Speaker will at this moment, or at any other time while he remains Speaker, entertain in conformity with the highest constitutional privilege a motion by any member to vacate the office of the speakership and choose a new Speaker, and under existing conditions would welcome such action upon the part of the actual majority of the House, so that power and responsibility may rest with the Democratic and insurgent members, who by the last vote evidently constitute a majority of this House. The chairman is now ready to entertain such [a] motion.

EVERY REPUBLICAN CHEERS

Uncle Joe's announcement that he was more than willing to entertain a motion that the Speaker's chair be vacated, aye, that he would welcome such a motion, brought the Republican side to its feet as one man. And how they howled. Their efforts in this direction put everything else in the way of uproar that had been attempted that day to shame. Here and there, sitting quietly in their seats on the Republican side, were the insurgents, the balance of power throughout the day. Their apathetic attitude was particularly noticeable as they sat among their cheering colleagues. The only member on his feet on the Democratic side was Burleson of Texas. He was standing on his feet waving a paper above his head and shouting something that was indistinguishable in the uproar. He was red in the fact and very much in earnest.

It was then that the remarkable scene over the Burleson resolution and the Speaker's vote of confidence occurred. The members remained on the floor for an hour or so after the fight was over, chatting and laughing over the incidents of the strenuous two days that have just ended.

Footnotes:

[1] An error - this should read "Bennett" and not "Bennet."

[2] An error - this should read "Cary" and not "Carey."

[3] This is a typographical error - the member is Jacob Van Vechten Olcott (1856-1940) of New York, not Alcott.

[4] Literally, "a vote by word of mouth; a voice vote."

[5] Defined as "one who is genuinely and thoroughly pure."

[6] This is a typographical error - the member is Martin Edgar Olmsted (1847-1913) of Pennsylvania, not Olmstead.

[7] This is a typographical error - the member is John Philip Swasey (1839-1928) of Maine, not Swayze.

[8] The Ballinger-Pinchot Committee, better known as the Joint Committee to Investigate [the] Interior Department and Forestry Service and chaired by Rep. Knute Nelson, Republican of Minnesota, investigated allegations by Gifford Pinchot, the Chief Forester of the US government, that Richard Ballinger, the Secretary of the Interior under President William Howard Taft, allegedly approved land claims based on alleged ties to those making the claims. Although no evidence was ever shown that Ballinger did anything wrong - this congressional committee backed up Ballinger's innocence - he was forced to resign in March 1911 and the episode split the Republican Party into pro-conservation and anti-conservation wings, a schism that led to the 1912 presidential election of Democrat Woodrow Wilson.

[9] This is a typographical error - the member is Joseph Swagar Sherley (1871-1941) of Kentucky, not Shirley.

[10] With 398 members of the House (which included four delegates and 3 "resident commissioners"), the Republicans had a 219-171 majority in that Sixty-first Congress (1909-11).

[11] Once again, the name of Rep. William Joseph Cary (1865-1934) of Wisconsin is printed wrong. In fact, other newspapers got his name wrong: for instance, see "Cannonism Is Overthrown," *New-York Tribune*, 20 March 1910, 1.

Speaker-elect Frederick H. Gillett's Remarks to the House of Representatives: *Congressional Record,* 19 May 1919

Following his election as Speaker, Rep. Frederick Gillett of Massachusetts took to the podium near the Speaker's chair and, before being sworn in, delivered some remarks to the assembled members of Congress. The following, from the *Congressional Record,* are the totality of his remarks on his election:

❧

"Gentlemen of the House of Representatives, I thank you for this cordial demonstration. I wish I could hope that this gavel will never be needed to check any less friendly and good-tempered disturbance. But I recognize this momentous session must bring periods of stress and excitement when it will be hard for us all to preserve that moderation and decorum benefiting the dignity of this body.

I hope that the good feeling and mutual respect which exists today, although it may at times be clouded and dimmed, will, at the end of this Congress, be no less general and genuine.

To you who have conferred upon this high office I feel the deepest gratitude. Both my training and my taste have made it attractive to me. There is no

other in the world for which I would exchange it. Perhaps I ought to throw a ring into the sea to propitiate the goals. I have served under five Speakers, Crisp, Reed, Henderson, Cannon, and Clark, all men of high character and great ability, some of them men of extraordinary ability, and I have now no ambition except by an honorable and acceptable performance of my duty to prove myself not unworthy of that exalted company and of your partiality. To achieve that I ask your aid and cooperation.

There are facing this Congress problems so grave and so difficult as to demand our most industrious application and combined wisdom. Upon our success in solving them hangs the immediate prosperity and the future development of the Nation. They are so momentous that that they may well sober partisanship and disarm prejudice. I am sure you will enter upon your task with high purpose, and I pledge you it will be my aim to exercise the power you have conferred upon me fairly, impartially, judicially, and with scrupulous regard for the rights and for the feelings of every Member of the House."

Source: *Congressional Record. Proceedings and Debates of the First Session of the Sixty-sixth Congress of the United States. Volume LVIII, Parts 1-2, 19 May 1919* (Washington: Government Printing Office, 1919), 8.

See also page 241

Speaker Nicholas Longworth's Remarks to the House of Representatives: *Congressional Record,* 7 December 1925

On 7 December 1925, Nicholas Longworth, Republican of Massachusetts, was elected Speaker of the House to succeed Frederick H. Gillett, who had been elected to a seat in the US Senate. Longworth was elected, 229 votes to 186 for Democrat Finis J. Garrett of Tennessee, with Progressive Republicans giving 13 votes to Rep. Henry A. Cooper, Republican of Wisconsin. Longworth then delivered the following remarks to the assembled members:

❧

"To you, members of my political party, who, by your voices, have with unanimity elected me to this office, I extend my heartfelt thanks. It is my highest hope that I may prove not unworthy of the trust you have imposed upon me." He then added, "To you, members of the great minority party who have cast your votes, as you were in honor to do for that scholarly statesman, that fine gentleman, that man who I am proud to call my friend, Finis Garrett, I extend my thanks for the clear evidence you have given me of your cordial good will."

Source: Longworth remarks on being elected Speaker in the *Congressional Record. Proceedings and Debates of the First Session of the Sixty-ninth Congress of the United States of America (Including the Special Session of the Senate). Volume LVIII, Part 12, 7 December 1925* (Washington: Government Printing Office, 1925), 380-82.

See also page 247

Excerpts from a US House History: Collection of Portraits of the Speaker in the US House of Representatives, 1927

In 1927, Charles Fairman, a famed art curator and historian, collected a history of the art in the Capitol Building in Washington, D.C. and an examination of the lives of the artists who made that art. In Chapter XV, "Speakers of the House of Representatives Collection of Their Portraits Commenced," Fairman examined the collection held at the time of portraits of just a few of the men who had served as Speaker of the House until that time. In the following excerpts from that specific portion of the work, the collection and its history is discussed:

☙

In that section of the House wing of the Capitol usually referred to as the Speaker's lobby a collection of 37 portraits of former Speakers is to be found. Definite information concerning the reasons for this collection is not readily obtainable, if possible. It seems, however, that it had its origin in a collection of engravings and photographs of former Speakers once contained in the room occupied by the Speaker as an office. In Keim's *Illustrated Handbook of Washington* (1875), we find the following, which perhaps will explain something of the conditions existing at the time of the publication of that book:

On the left of the south corridor is the member's retiring room now used by the official reporters...On the right the doors open into the hall and on the left is the Sergeant at Arms room, in which the mace is kept when the House of Representatives is not in session. The Speaker's room, next on the left, is entirely furnished in iron enriched with gilt. The furniture and fittings are extremely fine. On the walls are engravings or photographs of the Speakers.

It is probably from this small collection of pictures, which were of quite a small size and contained in oval frames, that the present collection of 37 portraits had its origin. It will be remembered that in 1852 there was presented to the Nation and accepted to be placed in the Library of Congress a

portrait of Henry Clay, by Giuseppe Fagnani. This portrait is now in the collection in the Speaker's lobby and is probably one of the earliest painted portraits in that collection. It presumably, however, was retained in the Library of Congress until a businesslike method of collecting portraits of former Speakers had been inaugurated. Just when this movement commenced is not at this time known, but it probably followed soon after the three rooms described in Keim's guidebook as the room occupied by the Official Reporters, the Sergeant at Arms' room, and the Speaker's room were converted into one large room now used as the Member's retiring room. This change in the original plan arose from a desire on the part of the Members of the House of Representatives for an improved condition of ventilation, a question which was constantly recurring in the history of the proceedings of the House. It did not even seem to be confined to regular cycles, but was liable to be introduced upon almost any occasion...

It is safe to conclude that with the changes made the small photographs and engravings of the Speakers seemed out of place in the retiring room and were finally placed in the Speaker's lobby. In fact, the writer was informed by a former employee of the House, John Chancey, whose period of service extended over a time antedating the changes made by which the retiring room was formed, that these small oval pictures referred to were at one time all of the portraits representing the Speakers hanging in the Speaker's lobby. It is very easy to assume that with the introduction of some full-sized portraits in oil the smaller portraits seemed out of place, and the collection of portraits in oil naturally followed. During the past 15 years nearly two-thirds of the present number of portraits have been placed in the Speaker's lobby. It should not be understood that all of this number (two-thirds) are original or newly acquired portraits, for the reason that prior to 1911 there were hanging in the Speaker's lobby a large number of portraits in crayon, in highly orna-

---

Source: Fairman, Charles, *Art and Artists of the Capitol of The United States of America, Senate Document 95, 69th Congress, 1st Session* (Washington, D.C.: Government Printing Office, 1927), 277-90.

mented gilt frames, which were properly considered as being out of harmony with some of the really fine portraits in oil then in the lobby, so that by the resolution of March 3, 1911, which provided for 19 portraits for the Speaker's lobby, it was the intention to replace all of the crayon portraits by portraits in oil. Previous to this time, however, there had been several notable portraits in oil furnished by the States or individuals for the Speaker's lobby, the most celebrated of which was probably the portrait of Thomas B. Reed, by John S. Sargent. This was presented by several Members of the Fifty-first Congress to the National House of Representatives. The presence in such a collection of a portrait by Sargent is sufficient to give a certain distinction to the entire collection. There were, however, other portraits of note. Massachusetts, about 1885, had presented to this collection the portrait of Robert C. Winthrop, painted by Daniel Huntington, one of the most celebrated portrait painters of his period, and, in April 1886, the Legislature of Massachusetts authorized the funding for the National Capitol at Washington of "worthy portraits" of former Speakers Sedgwick, Varnum, and Banks. These portraits were by the following artists: Theodore Sedgwick was painted by Edgar Parker and a copy from a work by Gilbert Stuart; Joseph B. Varnum was painted by Charles L. Elliott; and Nathaniel P. Banks was painted by Robert W. Vonnoh. These portraits were presented January 19, 1888, at which time public exercises were held in the House of Representatives and speeches were made by Mr. Long, Mr. Rockwell, Mr. Allen, Mr. Collins, Mr. Hayden, and Mr. Lodge, all of Massachusetts...

Other portraits in the collection to be found in the Speaker's lobby, placed there prior to 1911, were those of Frederick Muhlenberg, Jonathan Trumbull, John W. Taylor, Samuel J. Randall, James G. Blaine, Charles F. Crisp, Galusha A. Grow, and David B. Henderson, of Iowa. The last-named portrait is by Freeman Thorp, who also painted the portrait of

James G. Blaine...Mr. Thorp is also represented in the Speaker's lobby by the portrait of Schuyler Colfax and in the room of the House Committee on Appropriations by portraits of Joseph G. Cannon and James A. Tawney; in the room of the House Committee on Ways and Means by the portraits of William McKinley and Claude Kitchin; and in the Senate main corridor by the portrait of President Lincoln, the last work executed by Mr. Thorp for the Capitol...

The portrait of Frederick Muhlenberg, by Samuel B. Waugh, is one of the most interesting of the early portraits in the collection in the Speaker's lobby. It is a copy of an earlier portrait by Joseph Wright, painted at a period prior to 1800 by that celebrated artist...

The portraits of Galusha A. Grow and Samuel J. Randall are the work of W.A. Greaves...The portrait of John W. Taylor is the work of Miss Caroline L. Ormes Ransom...The portrait of Jonathan Trumbull is by Harry I. Thompson...

This concludes the list of the portraits contained in the Speaker's lobby at the time of the passage of the resolution of March 3, 1911, which provided for 19 portraits in oil to be added to this collection....

There are some portraits in the House wing of the Capitol other than in the Speaker's lobby which should be referred to at this time. In 1871 there was purchased a notable portrait of Henry Clay, the work of John Neagle. This portrait now hangs facing the east staircase of the House wing and it is of such a large size that it would be conspicuous in any collection. Before being hung in its present location it was exhibited in Statuary Hall and probably remained there for some years after its purchase. The price paid was $1,500, and the purchase was made of Garrett C. Neagle, a son of John Neagle and a grandson of Thomas Scully.

Excerpts from Congressional Report of Ethical
Charges Against Speaker Jim Wright, 1989

On 17 April 1989, the House Committee on Standards and Official Conduct released its report which charged that then-Speaker Jim Wright of Texas had been involved in numerous violations of House rules. The following, which are excerpts from the report of the committee and its chairman, Rep. Julian Dixon, Democrat of California, lay out five specific counts against Wright, as well as excerpts of the defense laid out by Wright and his lawyers to the committee before it released its report. At the head of the report is the official statement by chairman Dixon:

❧

SPECIAL TO THE *NEW YORK TIMES*

Published: April 18, 1989, A11

Here are the five counts of the report of the House Committee on Standards of Official Conduct charging Speaker Jim Wright with violations of House rules, and excerpts of the particulars for each count. Along with the charges are excerpts from the defense prepared by Mr. Wright's lawyers, given when the Speaker responded on March 7 to the committee's inquiry. Representative Julian C. Dixon, the California Democrat who is chairman of the committee, issued a statement at a news conference this morning announcing the panel's action.

[Statement of Committee chairman Julian Dixon:]

The Committee on Standards of Official Conduct has unanimously approved a statement of alleged violation regarding House Speaker James C. Wright Jr. The statement of alleged violation was formally delivered yesterday.

A statement of alleged violation signals the commencement of an adjudicatory proceeding. Under the committee's rules of procedure, the committee will determine, in a trial-like setting, whether the facts of each alleged violation have been proved by clear and convincing evidence. At this point, we have only determined there is reason to believe that violations occurred.

The statement of alleged violation emanates from the six-count preliminary inquiry resolution adopted June 9, 1988. It represents a determination by the committee that in 69 instances, there is reason to believe that Representative Wright violated the code of official conduct, and other House rules which apply to him as a member of Congress.

A statement of alleged violation is the name given by the committee's rules to charges filed on completion of a preliminary inquiry. This preliminary inquiry was voted last June. The special outside counsel's report was filed on Feb. 21, 1989.

Filing of the counsel's report triggered a three-phase decision-making process. First, one full week was designated as a reading period. All committee members were able to examine the report and supporting materials.

In the second phase, the committee received an extensive oral presentation by the special counsel and by counsel for Representative Wright. Immediately afterwards, the committee commenced phase three, its deliberations.

After nine days of oral presentations, the committee deliberated an additional eight days. We had before us not only the counsel's report, but the sworn testimony of over 70 witnesses and thousands of documents. Approximately three dozen roll-call votes were taken.

Violations Are Seen[:]

The committee concluded that there was reason to believe that violations of controlling standards of conduct occurred in the following instances:

See also page 317

- In the committee's view, seven bulk sales of the Representative Wright's book, *Reflections of a Public Man,* demonstrated an overall scheme to evade the House outside earned income limit (Rule 47) because honorarium payments were recharacterized as royalties. One sale also appeared to violate the statute limiting the amount that can be accepted for one appearance. In an eighth instance, the committee found that Representative Wright received an undisclosed gift because not all books paid for by a private individual were delivered.

- From 1979 to 1988, Representative Wright appears to have accepted nearly $145,000 in gifts from George Mallick, as follows:

- Free housing, 1979-1984: $31,698;

- Reduced housing costs, 1985-1988: $21,790;

- Salary to Mrs. Wright, 1981-1984: $72,000; and

- Use and maintenance of an automobile, 1983-1988: $19,391.

These were not reported on Representative Wright's financial disclosure statements. In addition, the committee determined that there was reason to believe that Mr. Mallick was a person with a direct interest in legislation.

Members of Congress do not exist in a "vacuum" and should be expected to have personal friends with whom gifts can be exchanged. However, the nature and extent of the apparent gifts from Mr. Mallick indicates that Representative Wright did not exercise reasonable care to avoid even the appearance of impropriety, which is the hallmark of the House gift rule.

Points Panel Discounted

Much attention will be given to the fact that a statement of alleged violations has been issued. Fairness dictates, however, that the record reflect that the majority of the assertions of improper conduct raised against Representative Wright did not warrant further action. Specifically, the committee did not find reason to believe that violations occurred with respect to the following transactions:

- Representative Wright's alleged lobbying on behalf of a constituent with whom he had interests in private gas ventures, of his acquisition of those interests.

- The alleged use of campaign funds to pay for publication of Representative Wright's book, *Reflections of a Public Man.*

- The alleged misuse of Congressional staff or official resources to prepare *Reflections of a Public Man,* and

- Allegedly improper loan transactions involving Mrs. Marlene Mallick and Representative Wright's wife.

- Finally, while the Congressman's dealings with representatives of the Federal Home Loan Bank Board may have been intemperate, the committee was not persuaded that there is reason to believe that he exercised undue influence in his dealings with that agency.

In addition to the issuance of a statement of alleged violation and the dismissal of the other charges, one further matter remains unresolved. That concerns the circumstances surrounding the acquisition by Mallightco of a 4 percent interest in an oil and gas well in Orange County, Tex., known as the North Sabine Lake Prospect. While approximately $9,000 was paid for this interest, currently available evidence suggests that Mallightco entered into a loan transaction in which the interest was valued at $440,000. It appears that at the time of the loan transaction, the well was clearly not a successful venture. The committee has issued a series of subpoenas to obtain the information necessary to resolve the remaining questions.

The committee has decided to release the complete text of the report of the special outside counsel at the same time as the statement of alleged violation. The committee has also decided to explain why no further action was taken on other matters addressed in the special outside counsel's report. This should avoid any claim that an allegation was ignored or did not receive full committee consideration.

Accordingly, the committee is today releasing both the special outside counsel's report and a statement of the committee in the matter of Representative

Wright. Copies of the statement of alleged violation are also being made available.

By agreement, no members of the committee will have any comment on the votes taken during the committee's deliberations. In addition, the committee will have no further disclosures of information or documents in this matter except in accordance with committee and House rules.

Allegations

Count 1

The committee has reason to believe that, during calendar years 1984-1987, Representative Wright violated House Rules...in connection with the marketing and sale of his book, *Reflections of a Public Man*. The record indicates that in each of seven instances, Representative Wright received income denominated as royalty (based on a royalty of 55 percent of book price) from the sales of books, such sales having been arranged in lieu of traditional honoraria compensation for speeches. The committee has reason to believe that the subject book sales were intended to avoid the limitations of law and House rules on the reporting and receipt of outside earned income, honoraria, and gifts. Accordingly, the committee believes that, notwithstanding that the Congressman's income was nominally a royalty derived from the sale of books, because each "sale" was arranged as compensation for a speech, the result is that the income was, in fact, the honorarium for the speech. The seven instances, amount of income, and resultant alleged violations are described below. An eighth instance alleging an undisclosed gift is also described.

March 11, 1986, Speech to the Fertilizer Institute[:]

The record indicates that in conjunction with Representative Wright's speech, the institute had expressed its desire "to do something" for him, such as present the Congressman with a suitable memento, "such as a plaque, or small gift, et cetera." It was suggested that the institute purchase copies of the Congressman's book, *Reflections of a Public Man*. Accordingly, prior to Representative Wright's appearance, the Fertilizer Institute purchased $2,023 worth of the book.

The committee has reason to believe that the $1,112.65 Representative Wright received as royalty income from this sale of books was, in fact, the honorarium for his speech to the Fertilizer Institute and constituted unreported outside earned income in violation of the limitation of House Rule XLVII and House Rule XLIV regarding financial disclosure.

Wright's Earlier Response

House Rule XLVII limiting the amount of outside earned income specifically exempts from the definition of outside earned income "copyright royalties." The rationale for exempting royalties stems from the underlying purpose of the limitation on outside earned income, i.e., that a member should devote essentially full time to his Congressional duties...

Thus, Congress exempted copyright royalties because authorship of works and the subsequent receipt of royalties from the sales of those works were generally viewed as not interfering with a member's performance of official duties.

The Speaker's appearance at an event or a speech was never conditioned on a purchase of books.

Outside counsel's central argument is that the bulk purchases were all made in payment for a speech or appearance. Outside counsel apparently deposed or received affidavits from 19 of the alleged 76 bulk purchasers. Of those 19, the Speaker made an appearance before 11. In 8 cases at least, there was no appearance at all. There is no evidence that the 11 appearances were in any way contingent upon the purchase of books. In fact, they were not. These appearances were over a period of at least a year, during which the Speaker made approximately 200 appearances. Outside counsel made it sound as though the staff specifically arranged these events and the purchase of books in a deliberate scheme to convert honoraria into royalties. On the contrary, the evidence shows no such plan.

The method in which the book was marketed does not alter the fact that the proceeds from the sales were royalties.

Despite outside counsel's argument, there is nothing improper or indeed, uncommon about bulk purchase of books. The Committee on Standards has heard ample testimony that many of the bulk purchasers of Mr. Wright's book frequently purchase multiple copies of books to distribute them as gifts, etc....The book buyers had no knowledge of the royalty agreement and specifically, no knowledge of amounts paid to Jim Wright, but instead purchased the book on its own merits...

No evidence suggests that the Speaker ever communicated, either orally or in writing, his desire that a particular individual purchase books.

Count 2

The alleged violations described below arise as a result of Representative and Mrs. Wright's relationship with Mr. and Mrs. George Mallick, the two couples' joint ownership of an investment corporation known as Mallightco Inc., and Mrs. Wright's purported employment association with the corporation.

The record indicates that during the period 1979 through 1984, Representative and Mrs. Wright were provided free housing in two apartments located in Fort Worth, Tex. Particularly with respect to the Wrights' free use of an apartment during 1980 through 1984, such free use was arranged by Mr. George Mallick but not as part of Mrs. Wright's compensation from Mallightco Inc. The committee has reason to believe that Mr. Mallick is an individual with a direct interest in legislation.

While the alleged gifts of free housing involved were assertedly provided to Mrs. Wright, the benefits derived therefrom are imputed to the Congressman because of the circumstance indicating that the free housing was not provided to Mrs. Wright wholly independent of her spousal relationship. Notably, Representative Wright and Mr. Mallick maintained a close social relationship for a period of years prior to the time Mr. Mallick arranged the free housing. Finally, Representative Wright shared the benefits of Mr. Mallick's gift of free housing to the same extent as did his wife.

The record indicates that in calendar year 1984, Representative Wright received a gift of free housing valued at $7,800 arising out of his free use of an apartment located at 1067 Roaring Springs Road, Fort Worth, Tex., and controlled by George Mallick, an individual the committee has reason to believe had a direct interest in legislation.

Because this gift to Representative Wright was not reported on his Financial Disclosure Statement for calendar year 1984 as required by House Rule XLIV, the committee has reason to believe Representative Wright violated House Rule XLIV and House Rule XLIII, clause 4, the latter of which imposes a limit of $100 on gifts received from persons with a direct interest in legislation.

Count 3

The alleged violations described below arise as a result of Representative and Mrs. Wright's relationship with Mr. and Mrs. George Mallick. The record indicates that during the period 1985 through 1988, Representative and Mrs. Wright were provided reduced-rate housing in an apartment/townhouse located in Fort Worth, Tex., During this period and notwithstanding the fact that Representative and Mrs. Wright had exclusive use and control of the apartment/townhouse which included the placement of their personal belongings and furnishings, payment for their use was based upon a per diem rate reflecting only those days for which the Congressman and/or his wife were physically present in the apartment/townhouse.

Accordingly, the committee has reason to believe that the per diem arrangement represented a gift to Representative Wright and his wife because it did not take into account the fact that the Wrights had totally relocated their personal effects in the apartment/townhouse in conjunction with their exclusive use of the facility. The committee also has reason to believe that Mr. Mallick is an individual with a direct interest in legislation.

The record indicates that in calendar year 1985, Representative Wright received a gift of reduced housing cost valued at $6,918 arising out of his use of an apartment/townhouse located at 1067 Roaring Springs Road, Fort Worth, Tex., and controlled by George Mallick, an individual the committee has reason to believe had a direct interest in legislation.

Because this gift to Representative Wright was not reported on his Financial Disclosure Statement for calendar year 1985 as required by House Rule XLIV, the committee has reason to believe that Representative Wright violated House Rule XLIV and House Rule XLIII, clause 4, the latter of which imposes a limit of $100 on gifts received from persons with a direct interest in legislation.

The Wright's use of the condominium between 1979 and 1984 was in connection with Betty Wright's employment and was not a gift.

Outside counsel has argued that the provision to the Wrights of an apartment owned by Marlene Mallick and, subsequently, a condominium owned by Steven Mallick resulted in a gift to the Wrights. Outside counsel's argument is based on the unsupported assertion that the living arrangements which were made available to Betty Wright as part of her employment by Mallick Properties and then by Mallightco were a gift, because Betty Wright's employment was a sham. This suggestion is without basis in fact or in law.

From 1979-1981, when Betty Wright worked for Mallick Properties, she used an apartment owned by Marlene Mallick. From 1981-1984, while Mrs. Wright was employed by Mallightco, the condominium owned by Stephen Mallick was made available for her use. In both instances, Betty Wright was provided the use of the apartment or condominium because, in George Mallick's business judgment, it was a convenience to him to have his employees, including Betty Wright, close at hand to the working premises...Thus, he specifically did not view any of the living arrangements provided for employees as gifts. Particularly in Mrs. Wright's situation, he knew that with her busy schedule, he was more likely to meet with her if she was close by when in Forth Worth. Therefore, he allowed her to use the condo.

The Wrights paid a reasonable daily rate for the use of the condominium from 1985 to 1988 and therefore, it was not a gift.

Outside counsel has further suggested that after 1984, when the Wrights began paying a per diem rental, the condominium resulted in a gift to the Wrights because the rental paid was insufficient. This suggestion is without merit.

After Betty Wright's employment ended in 1984, the Wrights paid for the condominium on a per diem basis, calculated from the market rental rate. The Wrights insisted upon this arrangement to be absolutely sure a gift would not occur.... The parties

believed that the per diem rate was a fair rental value for the Wrights' usage. The fact is that the apartment would not have been rented to anyone or used at all had the Wrights not used it...The payment of rent means no gift was made.

Outside counsel ignored the fact that in 1985, the per diem arrangement was described to the chief counsel to the Committee or Standards by a reporter...It was reported that this arrangement "does not appear improper." The Mallicks relied on this approval to continue with the arrangement.

Count 4

The alleged violations described below arise as a result of Representative and Mrs. Wright's relationship with Mr. and Mrs. George Mallick, the two couples' joint ownership of an investment corporation known as Mallightco Inc., and Mrs. Wright's purported employment association with the corporation. The record indicates that during the period 1981 through 1984, Mrs. Wright received a total of $72,000 ($18,000 a year) in compensation as an employee of Mallightco Inc. During this four-year period, there was no evidence either supporting or establishing that the money paid to Mrs. Wright was in return for identifiable services or work products that she provided to Mallightco Inc. Accordingly, the committee has reason to believe that the compensation paid to Mrs. Wright was a gift from Mr. George Mallick who was in charge of the corporation's activities including those of its employees. The committee also has reason to believe that Mr. Mallick is an individual with a direct interest in legislation.

While the alleged gifts of salary involved were assertedly provided to Mrs. Wright, the benefits derived therefrom are imputed to the Congressman because of the circumstance indicating that such gifts were not provided to Mrs. Wright wholly independent of her spousal relationship. Notably, Representative Wright and Mr. Mallick maintained a close social relationship for a period of years prior to the time Mrs. Wright was placed on Mallightco Inc.'s payroll.

The record indicates that in calendar year 1984, Mrs. Wright received compensation in the amount of $18,000 from Mallightco Inc. Because there is no evidence supporting or establishing that the money paid to Mrs. Wright was in return for identifiable services or work products that she provided to Mallightco Inc., the $18,000 paid to her was, therefore, an apparent gift.

Moreover, because this gift was not reported on Representative Wright's Financial Disclosure Statement for calendar year 1984 as required by House Rule XLIV, the committee has reason to believe that Representative Wright violated House Rule XLIV and House Rule XLIII, clause 4, the latter of which imposes a limit of $100 on gifts received from persons having a direct interest in legislation.

Betty Wright is a highly qualified individual who was paid for her services to Mallightco.

Outside counsel has argued that Betty Wright was not a legitimate employee of Mallightco. That claim blatantly disregards the evidence before the committee, specifically the sworn testimony of three individuals.

Betty Wright was qualified through her background and experience, having worked previously for a real estate developer and a major hotel...For Mallightco, she performed a variety of services for her salary. She studied and analyzed specific investments in Fort Worth, Washington, D.C. and elsewhere and rendered advice for Mallightco...Not only did she recommend investments to take advantage of but she also recommended which opportunities to avoid. . . . Certainly, her services were worth the $18,000 she received annually.

In this investigation, outside counsel received testimony from at least three individuals concerning specific investments and general subjects researched by Mrs. Wright. There is not a shred of evidence contradicting this testimony. There is specific testimony that from 1981-87, Mrs. Wright worked for Mallightco from 5 to 7 days per month...In fact, there is no basis in the record for him to distinguish between the validity of her employment by Mallick Properties as compared to the employment by Mallightco, yet he found her employment by Mallick Properties valid.

The uncontroverted evidence before the Committee on Standards is that Mrs. Wright engaged in services commensurate with her salary. Innuendo and

speculation may not be the basis for this committee choosing to believe the opposite of the uncontradicted evidence. Outside counsel has failed to produce clear and convincing evidence that Betty Wright did not perform services for Mallightco. In the absence of that proof, no gift resulted from Betty Wright's employment.

Count 5

The alleged violations described below arise as a result of Representative and Mrs. Wright's relationship with Mr. and Mrs. George Mallick, the two couples' joint ownership of an investment corporation known as Mallightco Inc., and Mrs. Wright's purported employment association with the corporation. The record indicates that during the period 1983 through 1988, Mrs. Wright was provided the free use of a 1979 Cadillac Seville, including maintenance and operation costs (e.g., insurance, registration and repair) of the vehicle, assertedly by virtue of her employment association with Mallightco Inc. The record further indicates that Mrs. Wright's employment association with Mallightco Inc. terminated on Dec. 31, 1984, and that her use of the vehicle subsequent to 1984 could not be predicated upon an employment association with the corporation.

Finally, the record indicates that the automobile was located in Washington beginning in 1983 and that the records of Mallightco Inc. began referring to the Cadillac as Mrs. Wright's car. There is no evidence indicating that Mrs. Wright's use of the vehicle in Washington, D.C., was necessary since the corporation's business headquarters were located in Fort Worth, Tex., and there is no record supporting or establishing that she performed any duties for Mallightco in the District of Columbia. Mrs. Wright's use of the vehicle was arranged by Mr. Mallick, an individual whom the committee believes has a direct interest in legislation.

While the alleged gifts of the free use of an automobile and associated operation and maintenance costs were assertedly provided to Mrs. Wright, the benefits derived therefrom are imputed to the Congressman because of the circumstance indicating that such gifts were not provided to Mrs. Wright wholly independent of her spousal relationship. Notably, Representative Wright and Mr. Mallick maintained a close social relationship for a period of years prior to the time Mr. Mallick arranged the free use of the automobile and associated maintenance and operation costs.

Since the gift of automobile usage was not reported on Representative Wright's Financial Disclosure Statement for calendar year 1984 as required by House Rule XLIV, the committee has reason to believe that Representative Wright violated House Rule XLIV and House Rule XLIII, clause 4, the latter of which imposes a limit of $100 on gifts received from persons having a direct interest in legislation.

The record indicates that in calendar year 1987, Mrs. Wright was provided free use of a 1979 Cadillac Seville which was an asset of Mallightco, Inc. and under the control of George Mallick, an individual the committee has reason to believe had a direct interest in legislation. Because there is no evidence that Mrs. Wright required the use of this automobile after her employment association with that organization was terminated, the free use of the automobile was a gift to Representative Wright and his wife valued at $1,416.

Since the gift of automobile usage was not reported on Representative Wright's Financial Disclosure Statement for calendar year 1987 as required by House Rule XLIV, the committee has reason to believe that Representative Wright violated House Rule XLIV and House Rule XLIII, clause 4, the latter of which imposes a limit of $100 on gifts received from persons having a direct interest in legislation.

In addition to the foregoing, the record indicates that in calendar year 1987, Representative Wright and his wife received a gift of $2,849.02 represent-

ing the costs to maintain and insure the 1979 Cadillac Seville provided by George Mallick, as described above.

Because this gift of the costs of automobile maintenance and operation was not reported on Representative Wright's Financial Disclosure Statement for calendar year 1987 as required by House Rule XLIV, the committee has reason to believe that Representative Wright violated House Rule XLIV and House Rule XLIII, clause 4, the latter of which imposes a limit of $100 on gifts received from persons having a direct interest in legislation.

Outside counsel has additionally suggested that a car provided to Betty Wright by Mallightco resulted in a gift to her.

This matter was inadvertently overlooked by the Blind Trustee at the formation of the Jim Wright Blind Trust. Again, Outside counsel chooses to ignore the evidence that the matter was simply overlooked even though there is no evidence to support his contrary conclusion. Although Mrs. Wright was permitted the use of an idle company car, it was always intended when the car was moved to Washington, D.C., that it would be paid for, and it was never intended to be a gift. While the Blind Trustee was supposed to have accounted for the car at the trust's formation, he failed to do so.

Outside counsel asserts that when Mrs. Wright used the car in 1985-1987, she had no relationship with Mallightco...That is incorrect. She was an owner and officer of Mallightco during that time. The car lent to Betty Wright in 1983, has since been purchased by the Trust for its 1983 value plus interest. Thus, there is no issue remaining as to the car, despite Outside Counsel's argument to the contrary.

Speaker Jim Wright Resigns from Speakership and
Congress, 31 May 1989

In 1987, House Majority Leader James Wright, Democrat of Texas, was elected Speaker, succeeding Thomas P. "Tip" O'Neill, who had not run for re-election to the 100th Congress (1987-89). Almost from the start of his speakership, Wright deviated from O'Neill's cautious leadership, pushing through legislation without input from the minority Republicans, and leading a charge against the foreign policy of the Reagan administration in areas that Speakers usually did not venture into. The atmosphere created by Wright's tenure led to calls from Republicans, most notably a then unknown representative from Georgia named Newt Gingrich, for ethics investigations into Wright's business and personal dealings. When several of these matters led to further investigation - leading, in the end, to the House Ethics Committee report showed that Wright had violated the rules of conduct of the House some 69 times, including accepting housing and other improper gifts from a constituent to making undeclared income from a book deal that should have been cleared with the House - Wright realized that the increased media speculation and the continuance of a House investigation that would have probably led to further steps being taken against him meant the end of his speakership. On 31 May 1989, Wright took to the floor of the House, with its seats and galleries packed, and, in a lengthy speech, first defended himself against all of the allegations lodged against him, then announced that he would be stepping down as Speaker, followed by his resignation from the House seat he had held since 1954. Unable to convince his detractors that he was trying to save the House from further ruin, he lashed out at those who had targeted him, mocking their "frenzy of feeding on other people's reputation." He said, "It is grievously hurtful to our society when vilification becomes an accepted form of political debate, when negative campaigning becomes a full-time occupation, when members of each party become self-appointed vigilantes." The following is

the text of Wright's speech to the House, taken from the *Congressional Record:*

House Chair: The Chair recognizes the distinguished Speaker of the House.

Wright: Mr. Speaker, I ask unanimous consent that I may be heard on point of personal privilege.

House Chair: The distinguished speaker is recognized for one hour.

Wright: Mr. Speaker, I ask unanimous consent that I may provide and extend my remarks and that I may include extraneous matter.

House Chair: Without objection, so ordered.

Wright: Mr. Speaker, for thirty-four years I have had the great privilege to be a member of this institution, the people's House, and I shall forever be grateful for that wondrous privilege. I never cease to be thankful to the people of the Twelfth District of Texas for their friendship and their understanding and their partiality toward me. Eighteen times they have voted to permit me the grand privilege of representing them here in this repository of the democratic principles. Only a few days ago, even in face of harsh news accounts and bitter criticisms, they indicated in a poll taken by the leading newspaper in the district that 78 percent of them approved of my services and that includes 73 percent of the Republicans in my district, and I'm very proud of that.

And you, my colleagues, Democrats and Republicans, I owe a great deal to you. You have given me the greatest gift within your power to give. To be the Speaker of the United States House of Representatives is the grandest opportunity that can come to any lawmaker anywhere in the Western world. And I would be deeply remiss if I didn't express my sincere appreciation to you for that opportunity. I hope that I have reflected credit upon the people of my

Source: Wright's Resignation Speech in the *Congressional Record. Procedings and Debates of the 101st Congress, First Session.* (Washington, DC: Goverment Printing Office, 1989), H2238-H2248

See also page 317

district who know me best, perhaps, and upon the people of this House who, next to them, who know me best.

I am...I am proud of a number of the things that we've done together while you have let me be your Speaker. I am proud of the record of the 100th Congress. Many people feel that it is the most responsive and most productive Congress in perhaps twenty-five years. And all of you who were here in that Congress had a part in that. Many of the things we did were truly bipartisan in character.

Together, we made it possible for great leaps forward to be made in such things as our competitiveness in the world. Together, we fashioned the beginnings of a truly effective war on drugs, to stamp out that menace to the streets and schools and homes of our nation. We began the effort to help the homeless. We still have work to do to make housing affordable to low income Americans so that there won't be any homeless in this country. We did things to help abate catastrophic illness, and to provide welfare reform legislation, clean water legislation, and a great many other things that I shall not detail. For your help, your great work, and for permitting me to be a part of this institution while that was happening, I thank you. And I shall forever be grateful for your cooperation.

And I love this institution. I want to assure each of you that under no circumstances - having spent more than half of my life here, this House being my home - would I ever knowingly or intentionally do or say anything to violate its rules or detract from its standards.

Now all of us are prone to human error. The Speaker of the House is, in fact, the chief enforcer of the rules of the House and it's really a wonderful thing that any member of the House may at his will bring question against any other member - and under our rules that has to be looked into - and I have no quarrel with that, nor any criticism of people who serve on the committee on Standards. It's a thankless job, and we have to have such a committee.

For over a year, well, just about a year, I have ached to tell my side of the story. That to which I have to respond keeps changing. But today, silence is no longer tolerable; nor for the good of the House is it

even desirable. And so without any rancor and without any bitterness or any hard feelings toward anybody, I thank you for indulging me as I answer to you and to the American people for my honor, my reputation, and all the things I've tried to stand for all these years.

For the past year, while the committee on standards has had these matters under advisement, I have ached for the opportunity to speak. Almost daily I besought them to let me come and answer whatever questions they had on their minds. Finally, on the 14th of September, they gave me one day in which to do that. I gratefully went and spent the whole morning and the whole afternoon answering as candidly and as freely as possibly I could any question that anyone would ask and I believe when I left everyone was reasonably well satisfied.

Suffice to say that the five original charges that had been lodged were dropped, dismissed. In their place, however, came three additional charges. Well, some said 69. Well, the 69 are merely a matter of multiple counting of the three. And in April, the committee said, well, they thought there was some reason to believe that rules may have been violated in these three basic areas. I owe it to you and to the American people to give a straightforward answer on those three areas. I'm convinced that I'm right; maybe I'm wrong.

I know that each of us, as Benjamin Franklin suggested, should be careful to "doubt a little of his own infallibility," but before those charges were issued as fast leaks, filtered out almost daily, tarnishing my reputation and by inference spilling over on the reputation of this institution, I pleaded for the privilege to come and answer those questions before charges were made. Under the rules that was not permitted to me and they were formally made.

And so let's - let's look at them, one by one, dispassionately. The committee has raised these three basic questions. It doesn't say that there is "clear and convincing proof" that I violated the rules. It doesn't say that they know I violated them. It just says they have some reason to believe I may have. And for these last few weeks I've been trying to find that and get an opportunity to address it. Now is the day - I'm going to do it now.

The three questions are these:

Did my wife Betty's employment, at 18,000 dollars a year for some four years, by a small investment corporation which she and I formed with friends of ours, George and Marlene Mallick, and the attendant benefits of that employment - the use of an apartment when she was in Fort Worth on company business and the use of the company-owned car - constitute merely a sham and a subterfuge and a gift from our friend, Mr. Mallick? Was Betty's employment and those things related to it a gift?

You've read in papers the suggestion made by committee counsel that I may have received up to 145,000 dollars in gifts from my friend, Mr. Mallick. Half of it, 72,000, was Betty's income, Betty's salary. The other half involved the use of a car and the use of an apartment on a per diem basis. Now, whether it's right or wrong, let's look at it. Betty's employment. Was that a gift?

First question I should like to - I suppose you might be asking, Why - why was Betty working for the corporation? Why - why did we put her to work at 18,000 dollars a year? The answer is really very simple. She was the only one of the four of us who had the time and the inclination to look into the investment opportunities that our investment corporation was created to explore. George Mallick, my partner, was too busy looking after his own interests; he had business interests of his own. Marlene Mallick was raising a family. I was busy being a member of Congress and majority leader. I didn't have any time to spend on it. Betty alone, among all others, had the time and the opportunity and the experience and the desire to give effort and energy to exploring and promoting investment opportunities.

She did indeed perform work, and it paid off for the little corporation. She did it well. She studied and followed the stock market on regional stocks - buying and selling - some of them I have brought into the corporation that I'd owned personally - my personal estate. She advised us of when was a good time to sell and when was a good time to buy. And the corporation made some money on those regional stocks, not a lot of money by some people's standards, but we made some money.

Betty paid for her salary several times over. She maintained very frequent contact with a drilling company, that was drilling a series of gas wells, exploratory gas wells in West Texas in which each of the four partners had an interest, having borrowed money from the corporation in order to do that. She visited the site of drilling and maintained contact with the company for us in that instance. She went to New York and studied the gem stone business and the corporation made an investment in gem stones - made some money on that. She looked into the possibility of the corporation [undecipherable] building apartment complexes for young people, but concluded that the interest rates were unfavorable. Betty spent a considerable amount of time studying the wine culture industry, which was then just getting started in Texas, and she made an economic study that concluded it was too speculative for a little corporation of our type. She looked into other prospective investments such as a small, limited partnership in the movie *Annie* and the prospective venture in sulfur extraction, but advised against both of those investments and it's lucky for us that she did because people invested in it and lost money.

Now I want to include for printing in the record affidavits from several business people who know from their personal experience and attest to the work that Betty did in this regard, and it will appear in the record at this point an affidavit by Pamela L. Smith, one by K. F. Schnider, one by John Freeman, one by Luis A. Ferris Jr., and one by J.D. Williams - all attesting to their personal knowledge of these things that Betty did in working for the corporation for 18,000 dollars a year.

The outside counsel employed by the committee that suggested that Mrs. Wright's employment somehow amounted to a gift - I don't know why but he assumed that the services she rendered couldn't have been worth 18,000 dollars a year. How he concludes that she didn't perform duties is to me a mystery. On page 20 of the statement of alleged violations, you'll find a very strange suggestion based on a statement that, quote, "There was no evidence either supporting or establishing that the money paid to Mrs. Wright was in return for identifiable services or work products." Now, frankly, I don't know exactly what Mr. Phelan means by "work product."

You want so many pages of cancelled short-hand notes? So many pages of typed manuscript? She wasn't a carpenter. Is a woman's mental study and her time and her advice not to be counted as a work product? How the committee could conclude that there was no evidence that Betty performed duties is very puzzling to me. They don't offer any evidence that she did not. When I was before the committee that wasn't one of the things that were being considered. They didn't ask me to go into any elaborate detail, as I have just done, to tell of the things that she did. They assumed, assumed that there was no evidence.

Ah, but there was evidence! The two people of whom questions were asked aside from myself, Mr. Mallick himself, and Pamela Smith, both testified that she did work. Mr. Phelan's report says that they couldn't identify but maybe twelve days in the whole four-year period in which she worked. That's an inaccurate representation of what they said. Pamela Smith, both in this affidavit and in her testimony before the committee, clearly said she saw Betty there from five to seven days every month, and on weekends. And she spoke of her knowledge of her doing work in Washington and New York and elsewhere. So, there's evidence.

Well, is one to conclude that my wife's services to our little corporation were worth less than 18,000 dollars a year? It's not worth it? For most of her adult life, Mrs. Wright has been a business person. She's been an officer in a large hotel, an officer in a successful real estate and construction firm, a professional staff person on a congressional committee. She was making more than 18,000 dollars when she worked at the congressional committee.

And here's the irony, the supreme irony. In nineteen hundred and seventy six, when I was elected majority leader, Betty voluntarily left her job as a professional staff person on the committee, so as to avoid any criticism of this institution or of her husband on the grounds that we both were on the public payroll. How many colleagues in the House and the Senate do you know whose wives are on the public payroll doing good work? And you know, Betty didn't want to be the cause for even unfounded criticism. She was legally entitled to continue. She had not [undecipherable] that job before our marriage, but she chose to leave to save the institution and

her husband from unwarranted criticism. That's the kind of person she is.

Now, it just seems to me that there isn't any justification at all for anybody's even raising a question about whether she earned 18,000 dollars a year. Should a member of Congress have to prove that his wife earned that much money? Bear in mind, this money was not paid by Mr. Mallick; the money was paid by the corporation of which Betty and I were half owners - half ours, anyway.

Now, in addition to her salary as a gift, outside counsel contends, in his summing up 145,000 dollars worth of "gifts," that Betty had the use of a company car. That's...that's true - she did. For the first three years, it was used largely by Mr. and Mrs. Mallick. It wasn't Mr. Mallick's car. It was the company car. The company bought and paid for it. We owned half of it. The next four years Betty had most of the use of it.

Now, I've done what I can to resolve any doubt. I want to do the right thing, the honorable thing. I bought and paid for that car out of my personal funds. The trustee of my blind trust, at my instruction, paid the corporation full book value for the car on the day Betty first started driving it on company business, through the whole time she had it in her possession, plus interest! The interest amounted to about 9,000 dollars. What more can I do? Does that make it right?

[undecipherable]

Now concerning the apartment, Betty and I have been more than anxious to do what's right and honorable about that. We didn't think there was anything wrong with paying a per diem rate. The apartment was not held out for rent to anybody else. It wasn't owned for rental purposes. The Mallick family didn't want anybody else in the apartment. They owned about five apartments in this apartment unit—complex—area. They held them out for their employees, for their family. Wouldn't have been anybody in the apartment paying any amount of money at all if they hadn't permitted us when we were in town - and Betty was doing company business - to occupy the apartment. We paid on a daily basis for our use of that apartment.

Meanwhile, in an effort to resolve any doubt, last year I told Mr. Mallick that I didn't like the situation being criticized. He said, well, Ralph Lotkin, the committee counsel, said that it was all right. It was in the paper - printed in the paper four years ago, the Fort Worth newspaper - a statement quoting the chief counsel of the committee on standards, Mr. Lotkin, saying he didn't see anything improper with it. I relied on that.

Nevertheless, last year I said to George Mallick, I said, "I want to buy the apartment, George. I'll pay you for it." I did. I paid the amount suggested and appraised by two real estate persons in Fort Worth, 58,000 dollars. Now if anybody thinks that's too low a price I'll sell it to you today for 58,000 dollars.

Well, I just wanted to clear the air, and remove doubts, and say, if we made a mistake, we've done what we can to set things right. I - I don't think we violated any rules. I think you're entitled to know that. My respect for you leads me to want to tell you that.

The second alleged violation continues on the assumption that Betty's employment and these little benefits that she had were gifts. And then it further assumes that George Mallick, our friend and business partner, had a direct interest in influencing legislation, which would make it illegal for us to accept gifts from him.

Now how do they arrive at that suggestion? I've known this man for more than 25 years. He's been my friend, good, decent, hardworking man of Lebanese extraction. His father had a wholesale grocery store there. His grandfather came with a wagon, a cart to Georgia. He's been successful, moderately so. Never once in all the years I've known this man has he ever asked me to vote for or against any piece of legislation. Not once. That's not the basis of our friendship - not how our relationship goes. You have friends like that. They don't ask for anything. All they want is to be a friend. Not one time has he ever asked me to intercede with any administrative agency of government in behalf of him, or of any institution in which he has interest. Not once, not once.

So how do they say that he had a direct interest in influencing legislation? Well, on page 58 of the committee report, it is suggested that simply because he was in the real estate business, that he had some oil and gas investments, the committee might

"infer," - that's the word - the committee might infer that he could be deemed a person with an interest of a direct nature in legislation. The committee suggests he might have an interest in the tax code. Well, who doesn't? You know, I mean every taxpayer's got an interest in the tax code. Everybody who ever expects to receive social security has an interest in the social security code. All people have an interest of some kind in the results of legislation, don't they? That's not were talking about. We're talking about whether or not they have a direct interest in trying to influence the course of legislation.

Now where would you go to find out what that means - if somebody wanted to associate with you some way and be in business with you some way back home in a legal, perfectly legal way - whether he had an interest in the legislation or not? Who would you consult if you were in doubt about it? I wasn't in doubt, but suppose you were. Wouldn't you think you'd consult the publication of the committee? Or consult the people that wrote the rules?

Well, the people who wrote the rules don't think George Mallick had an interest in legislation. David Obey was the chairman of the committee that drafted those rules. He asserts clearly, unequivocally, emphatically, unambiguously, both in an affidavit that he wrote and a report he wrote for the *Washington Post* that [the rule] doesn't fit George Mallick's case. He doesn't have an interest in legislation as defined under the rules, the rules that David and his committee wrote.

Harold Sawyer, former Republican member from Michigan, who served on that committee along with David Obey, says the same thing. I have here an affidavit from Mr. Sawyer in which he states exactly that same conclusion. And there's an affidavit of Donald F. Terry, who was currently - is employed now by the committee on small business, but was a staff member on the commission on administrative review, which was charged in 1976 with the responsibility for drafting new rules for the official conduct for the House. Most of what he refers to has to do with the question of book royalties. Now I shall come to that next, but in these matters these three people, who had a great deal to do with writing the rule, say that's not what they intended when they wrote the rule. I offer these for printing in the record.

Where else might you turn if you were in doubt? Might you not possibly go to the commitee itself and see what advisory opinions it has given? Here is the publication the committee sends to all of us to tell us what is and is not legal. Each year we receive this as instructions for filling out our financial disclosure statement. Appendix E is an advisory opinion number 10, which defines who has a direct interest in legislation under the law. It says that "If the member does not believe that the donor of the gift has a distinct or special interest in the congressional legislative process which sets him clearly apart from the general public," well, "then the member should feel free to accept such gifts." That's the official advice from the committee given to every member. And then it defines in the summary who has an interest in legislation as prohibited under the rule.

Four classes, that's all: registered lobbyists - George Mallick's not a registered lobbyist; somebody who employs a registered lobbyist - George Mallick never did that; somebody who directs or operates a political action committee - George Mallick has never done that; or, finally, any other individual which the member knows - not should know or ought to suspect or ought to infer - but which the member knows has a distinct and special interest in influencing or affecting the legislative process. Not just somebody who's got an interest financially in the outcome of legislation - not at all! Somebody that you know has a direct or special interest in influencing the outcome of the legislative process, which sets that individual apart from the general public. Well, that was just simply not the case with George Mallick. And so he had no direct interest in legislation, any type that anybody could define.

Now we have motions before the committee - to set that aside, set aside that presumption of a man's having a direct interest in legislation if you haven't got a reason to believe he has. The only thing that they have suggested is that in 1986 his son borrowed money from a savings and loan to build a little shopping center of his own, wholly apart and foreign to any investments that Betty and I had - nothing to do with them, at all - his son, and that in 1987 the lending institution had to foreclose.

You know, but the period when Betty was employed, presumably as a gift, was 1981 to 1984. Now, he couldn't have known in '81 and '84 that his son was going to borrow money in '86, and the thing go bad in '87, and economic decline make it impossible to pay off his note on time. He couldn't have known that. And anyway, would you stretch the thing to the point of saying that just anybody who has a member of his family that owes money to a bank or a savings and loan is forbidden? Of course you wouldn't. That covers more than half the citizens in the country.

The people who wrote the rules don't believe that he's covered. The people who have been interpreting the rules don't believe he's covered. And, so I think under all reasonable circumstances that motion ought to be agreed to, ought to be agreed to - if rules mean anything, if we're not just going to turn the whole thing on its head and change the rules by whim every time we turn around.

Now the only other basic question - just one that remains in the statement of alleged violations - concerns the sale of a book, a little book now you'll recall, *Reflections of a Public Man*, which I wrote and which was sold sometimes in bulk quantities. The people who took it and gave it away to other people - students, newspapers, public officials, and members of their organizations. And I wanted them to. You know, I wanted to get the widest possible distribution of the - of the book. A book that you write is kind of part of you. You think of it as a child almost. It's probably not great literature, but I like it. Marty Toulch [sp?] in the *New York Times*, John Silber, President of Boston University, Jim Lehrer of *McNeil/Lehrer Report*, and Dr. Tucker, Chancellor of TCU, all said nice things about it, and I appreciate that.

Now, the contention of the committee, as I understand it, is that this book project, to publish that book - on which I got three dollars and a quarter for every book that sold - was a kind of a sham and a subterfuge itself and an overall scheme for me to exceed and violate the outside earning limitations of a member of Congress.

Do - I mean, do you think that I'd do something like that? The purpose of the book - three dollars and a quarter is what I got out of it and I didn't get any advance - the purpose of the book was to publish something that could be sold at a small price and get wide distribution. If - If monetary gain had been my primary interest, don't you think I would have gone to one of the big Madison Avenue publications, the houses there that give you a big advance? Hey, I know people who received advances before a single book sells from those big companies - twice and three times as much as I got in total sales of those books.

If there had been a scheme to get around outside earning limits, that's what I might have done. I hear that a woman author of a book called *Mayflower Madam* got 750,000 dollars in advance royalties. I don't know that to be true. Our former speaker, Mr. [Thomas P.] O'Neill [Jr., (D-Mass.)], is said to have received a million dollars for his excellent and readable book in advance before any of them were sold. I have read that a woman named Kitty Kelly has received as much as two million dollars in advance royalties for a book she's written on Nancy Reagan, which, as I understand it, is not even an authorized biography. Well so much for that.

It is true, I think, that people on my staff were eager to sell these books. They knew I wanted them sold. I've got to accept some responsibility for that if it was wrong, but the rule doesn't say it was wrong. It couldn't have been an overall scheme to avoid outside earning limits because the rules are clear. They're not equivocal. The rules expressly exempt royalty income. And that too is attested to by David Obey. And it's attested to by Donald Terry, who gives the rational and the expression. There wasn't any exception; book royalties were exempted. Now maybe they shouldn't have been. You know, maybe - maybe somebody got the impression that buying a book was the price of getting me to make a speech. I never intended that impression. I never suggested that. I hope that friends of mine did not.

Of all the books that were sold, the outside counsel suggests that seven cases involved instances where individuals associated with organizations to which I made speeches bought multiple copies of the books and distributed them among members of the organization or others. Now I have not been permitted to see the copy of their testimony, so I don't know what exactly they said. I've asked people on my staff, did you tell these folks that they had to buy these books or I wouldn't make a speech? They said no, they didn't.

The total amount, as I figure, from all of those sales that it involved is about 7,700 dollars - that's what I received. You know, I would do whatever would be necessary, whatever was right. If those people were under the impression that I wasn't going to make a speech to them unless they bought a bunch of books, if they wanted their money, I'd give them that money. I don't want the money. That's not important. What's important is a person's honor and his integrity.

During that three-year period when the counsel says there are seven instances where I made speeches to groups and they bought copies of these books, seven groups, seven instances, I made at least 700 speeches for which I didn't get any honorarium. Didn't offer to sell anybody a book. Nobody had the chance to buy a book. Do you suppose if I'd done an overall scheme, it wouldn't have been a wider kind of an experience than that - I - I don't know. I'm just saying to you that I didn't intend to try to violate the outside earning limitations and I don't believe legally that I did. Some of the rest of you make a lot of speeches. How many speeches do you suppose you make that you don't get anything for? Most of us do.

Well, what can I do? One other thing about the book that I suppose needs elaboration. It involves the allegation in the statement of alleged violations that a man named S. Gene Payte - P-A-Y-T-E, Gene Payte - a reputable businessman in Fort Worth, paid for more books that he got from the publisher - that they didn't deliver enough books to him. Now that's - that's what was said in the report of the outside counsel. S. Gene Payte, upon reading that report, issued an affidavit that is not ambiguous at all. Here's what Mr. Payte says. I'll read, in part, this affidavit and put the whole thing in the record.

He says, "I have read the report of special outside counsel Richard J. Phelan on the preliminary inquiry conducted pursuant to the committee's U9 resolution as it relates to my testimony. I also have reviewed the transcript of my deposition testimony. The report and also the conclusions reached by the special counsel ignores much of the most pertinent testimony in the transcript, takes certain statements out of context, distorts clear statements of fact, and in general fails fairly inaccurately to summarize the matters as to which I testified.

The conclusion reached by the special counsel that quote - I quote from the outside counsel's report - that violated the rule' so and so 'calls for was based upon a category assertion that (quote) 'Gene Payte did not receive the books' (close quote).

The special counsel asserts Payte testified - and I'm quoting - that only he 'received between 300 and 500 copies of the whole book for 600,000 - for 6,000 dollars' and makes the flat statement (quote) 'Gene Payte did not receive the books' - citing as authority Payte's transcript."

Now, here's what Payte says: "On the contrary, I did not so testify. I stated not once, but three times that I believe 1,000 books were delivered to me (transcript 27, 40, 41). The special counsel ignores this testimony. Instead, he cites transcript 77 and that citation does not support the special counsel's assertion. Transcript 77 shows that congressman Myers, not I, made the comment. I believe you said you received 3 to 500 books. I did not confirm that recollection - my reply being I would like to have all the books; in fact I never so testified."

So this is a copy of that affidavit, which I should like to submit for the record - together with a copy of a letter that was sent by the committee to Mr. Payte after he issued this affidavit, telling him he ought not to comment.

What do you think of that? A private citizen, a reputable citizen of my community, misquoted in a document published at public expense, sent widely to newspapers throughout the country, widely cited as authority, uncritically, assumed to be accurate. The citizen being misquoted issues an affidavit to straighten it out, so that he is not misquoted in the public record. And then he's warned by the committee that he might be held in violation and in contempt of Congress if he doesn't shut up. First Amendment rights supersede any rules of any committee. And any citizen of the United States ought to have the right to have him - his own testimony correctly characterized and not be threatened or silenced by a House committee. Any House committee owes to the citizen of the United States that right and that privilege.

Well, those are basically the matters that pend before the committee and our motion to dismiss. Those mo-

tions could clear the air. Rules are important - just like the - the constancy of what a law means is important to a citizen, if they can resolve these particular legal issues as to what constitutes "direct interest in legislation" and whether or not book royalties are exempt, as the rules say they are. I think it's important for the motions to be ruled upon, and I earnestly hope that the committee will look at it from that standpoint and grant our motions.

Members are entitled to know what the rules mean and if they still mean what they meant when they were written and promulgated. Now maybe the rules need to be changed. If so, let's change them in a legal, orderly way. Let's vote on it. Let's vote to change them. Maybe the whole process needs some change and clarification. You know, we - we may want to consider - the House may want to consider - establishing a House counsel to whom members can look for official advice and then rely on that advice. The rules of the committee itself might need some reconsideration. Having gone through this agonizing experience for about a year now - I mean, almost every day there's a news story in a newspaper leaked, without any chance for me to know what's coming next and no chance for me to go to the committee and answer it and say, "Hey, wait a minute, that - that's not correct; that's not right."

Maybe the committee - as it's currently required to sit as kind of a grand jury and petit jury both - ought to have a different composition, rather than those who issue the statement of alleged violations being the same people who have to judge them. I think it clearly is difficult to expect members who've publicly announced a reason to believe there's a violation to reverse their position at a hearing stage and dismiss charges against a member. Maybe once a report of alleged violations is issued, the committee rules ought to allow the member to respond expeditiously. You know, to deny a member the opportunity to reply quickly can cause serious political injury. It's unfair. Once alleged violations are announced, the committee ought to just immediately release to the member all the evidence that it could have to indicate that that's happened. In my case, for example, the committee has yet to release any witness testimony or documents that it obtained during the investigation.

Why hide the evidence? What's there to hide? This ought not to be the kind of proceeding in which strategic maneuvering be allowed to override fundamental relations of fair play. Now, I kind of - I urge the abolition of the gag order too, which the committee said it forbids any witnesses who comes and makes a deposition from discussing publicly or telling his side of the thing. And I just suppose the charges which the committee concludes are unfounded should not be published and widely disseminated, as though they were true and bore the imprimatur of the committee's approval.

Well, there are other things you want to consider. I - I'm not trying to give you a [sic] exhaustive list of what might happen. I - I know there are others who have views that are equally relevant. You know, perhaps we want to consider a [sic] outright abolition of all honoraria and speaking fees altogether. Maybe we want to do that - I don't know; it's up to the House - in exchange for a straightforward, honest increase in the salary for members of all three branches of the government. It is intolerably hurtful to our government that qualified members of the executive and legislative branches are resigning because of the ambiguities and the confusion surrounding the ethics laws and because of their own consequent vulnerability to personal attack. That's a shame. It's happening.

And it is grievously hurtful to our society when vilification becomes an accepted form of political debate and negative campaigning becomes a full-time occupation; when members of each party become self-appointed vigilantes carrying out personal vendettas against members of the other party. In God's name, that's not what this institution is supposed to be all about. When vengeance becomes more desirable than vindication and harsh personal attacks upon one another's motives and one another's character drown out the quiet logic of serious debate on important issues, things that we ought to be involved in. Surely that's unworthy of our institution and unworthy of our American political process. All of us in both political parties must resolve to bring this period of mindless cannibalism to an end!! We've done enough of it!

I...I...I pray to God that we will do that and restore the spirit that always existed in this House. When I first came here, all those years ago, 1955, this was a

place where a man's word was his bond, and his honor and truth of what he said to you were assumed. He didn't have to prove it. I remember one time Cleve Bailey of West Virginia, in a moment of impassioned concern over a tariff bill, jumped up and made an objection to the fact that Chet Holliefield had voted - in those days we - we shouted our answers to the votes, and Holliefield was back there in the back and Bailey said, "I object to the gentleman from California's vote being counted. He came down and voted late. He said he was not in the chamber when his name was called and therefore he's not entitled to vote."

It was a close vote. Speaker Rayburn grew red as a tomato and I thought he was gonna break the gavel when he hammered. He said, "The chair always takes the word of a member." And then because I was sitting over here behind Cleve Bailey, I heard other members come and say, "Cleve, you're wrong. Chet was back there behind the rail and I was standing by him when he answered; his answer just wasn't heard." And others said you shouldn't have said that. And Cleve Bailey, crusty old West Virginian, came down here and abjectly, literally with tears in his eyes, apologized, for having questioned the word of a member. Now we need that.

Have I made mistakes? Oh, boy, how many? I - I made a lot of mistakes. Mistakes in judgment, oh yeah, a lot of 'em. I'll make some more. Recently, let me just comment on this briefly, because it's such a sensational thing and injury's been done to me in this particular moment because of it. John, John Mack; many of you remember him, know him; I think a lot of you like him, respect him. I helped John one time in his life when he was about 19 years old, 20, I didn't know him, never had met him.

I didn't know the nature of the crime that he had been convicted of. I knew only that John Mack was a young man who my daughter had known in high school and my daughter was married to his brother, incidentally; that's how she knew about John. And she mentioned it to me. All I knew was that he'd been convicted of assault and that he'd served 27 months in a Fairfax County jail. Contrary to what's been published, I did not interfere with the court. I didn't suggest anything to the court. I didn't have anything to do with his sentencing. I really didn't under - didn't know and didn't inquire. Maybe that's bad judgment. I didn't inquire as to the exact nature of the crime.

The sheriff's office in Fairfax County called and asked me if I would know of any job that I could help this young man get. They wanted to parole him. They said he said he'd been a model rehabilitative prisoner. And I gave him a job as a file clerk. You know, 9,000 dollars a year. After that he - he really blossomed and grew and developed and those of you who know him can't conceive - as I never could conceive when finally just two years ago I read in the newspaper - the precise nature of that crime. It just didn't fit his character. Married and had two beautiful children, wonderfully responsible, and I think become a very fine person.

Now, was that bad judgment? Yeah, maybe so. It doesn't have anything to do with the rules but it's got all mixed up with it, and I don't think, though, that it's bad judgment to try to give a young man a second chance. Maybe I should have known more about it, but in this case I...I...I...I think...I think he has turned out well and I...I don't believe that America really stands for the idea that a person should ever...forever be condemned. But I think maybe he ought to have a second chance. And that's what I thought in the case of John Mack, and good judgment or bad, I mean, that's...that's it. And I...I believe in giving somebody a second chance.

Have I contributed unwittingly to this manic idea of frenzy of feeding on other people's reputations? Have I...have I caused a lot of this? So maybe I have. God I hope I haven't. But maybe I have. Have I been too partisan? Too insistent? Too abrasive? Too determined to have my way? Perhaps. [I] think so. If I've offended anybody in the other party, I'm sorry. I never meant to. Would not have done so intentionally. Always tried to treat all of our colleagues - Democrats and Republicans - with respect. Are there things I'd do differently if I had 'em to do over again? Oh boy. How many may I name for you?

Well, I tell you what. I'm going to make you a proposition. Let me give you back this job you gave to me as a propitiation for all of this season of bad will that has grown among us. Give it back to you. I will resign as Speaker of the House effective upon the election of my successor. And I'll ask that we call a caucus on the Democratic side for next Tuesday to choose a successor. I don't want to be a party to tearing up the institution: I love it.

To tell you the truth, this year it has been very difficult for me to offer the kind of moral leadership that our organization needs, because every time I've tried to talk about the needs of the country, about the needs for affordable homes - both Jack Kemp's idea and the idea we're developing here - every time I've tried to talk about the need for minimum wage, tried to talk about the need for daycare centers, embracing ideas on both sides of the aisle, the media have not been interested in that. They wanted to ask me about petty personal finances.

You need...you need somebody else. So I want to give you that back. And we'll have a caucus on Tuesday. And then I will offer to resign from the House some time before the end of June. Let that be a total payment for the anger and hostility we feel toward each other. Let's not try to get even with each other. Republicans please don't get it in your heads you need to get somebody else because of John Tower. Democrats, please don't feel that you need to get somebody on the other side because of me. We ought to be more mature than that.

Let's restore to this institution the rightful priorities of what's good for this country. And let's all work together and try to achieve them. The nation has important business and it can't afford these distractions. And that's why I offer to resign.

I've enjoyed these years in the Congress. I am grateful for all of you who have taught me things and been patient with me. Horace Greeley had a quote that Harry Truman used to like: "Fame is a vapor, popularity an accident. Riches take wings; those who cheer today may curse tomorrow; only one thing endures -character." I'm not a bitter man. I'm not going to be. I'm a lucky man. God has given me the privilege of serving in this greatest institution on earth for a great many years, and I'm grateful to the people of my district in Texas. I'm grateful to you my colleagues - all of you. And God bless this institution. And God bless the United States.

"Tom Foley and the Changing of the Guard,"
Washington Post, 1 June 1989

The resignation of Speaker James Wright following allegations of massive fraud and corruption led to the rise of Thomas S. Foley, Democrat of Washington State, to the speakership, the first to hold that position who came from west of the Rocky Mountains. As Foley assumed the Speaker's chair, the *Washington Post* examined "the changing of the guard," which looked at the new Speaker's past as well as what he would bring to the speakership:

◈

Tom Foley and the Changing of the Guard
The Gentleman From Washington, True to Form

———

By Jacqueline Trescott
Washington Post Staff Writer

———

As Jim Wright was saying "let me give you back this job," Thomas Foley watched the historic announcement from the grand brown leather chair of the speaker. He looked stoic, somber in a gray suit and ready to applaud, as he had all these months, the explanations and defense of his embattled colleague.

Next Tuesday, a new speaker of the House of Representatives will be elected, and by all scenarios, that man will be Foley. Then the chair will be officially his. Right after Wright announced his resignation yesterday, making possible the Foley succession, the majority leader walked around the floor of the House, kibitzing with colleagues, sitting somberly with Rep. Tony Coelho (D-Calif.) for a few minutes. He was not fielding congratulations; he was plotting strategy.

True to the Foley form, the majority leader took another opportunity yesterday afternoon to praise the departing speaker. Waving to the reports assembled in his office, Foley declined all television, radio and print interviews and instead released a statement: "For 40 years in public service, Jim Wright has been a symbol of constancy, courage and commitment to principle...History will remember him as a great member and a great speaker."

This is not the first time Foley has downplayed his own ambitions and turned a moment of political awkwardness into an hour of generosity.

During his first congressional campaign in 1964, he repeatedly cited the "distinguished service" his opponent had given the state of Washington for 22 years. Foley didn't miss a chance to praise incumbent Republican Rep. Walt Horan's effectiveness, his service, his generosity.

"So many people would ask me: 'Why are you running against Walt Horan?' recalls Foley, his booming voice ripe with mock dismay and amazement. If I had said, 'Because he is a dirty, no-good son-of-a-gun,' I would have been booed off every stage in eastern Washington. It was not what I thought; it was not what the voters thought."

Foley acknowledges that conventional "political judgment might tell you it's better to [make generous statements] after the polls close," but Horan praised "the gentlemanly way" of his 35-year-old opponent a week before the election anyway. Foley, a former prosecuting attorney and assistant state attorney general who had already spent two years as a Capitol Hill lawyer, won with 53 percent of the vote. On the day of his swearing-in, Horan introduced him to the other members in the House cloakrooms. One of the new congressman's first acts was to give a reception for the man he succeeded.

For the last few weeks that same spirit of fatalistic cordiality has marked Foley's life in the House and his defense of Wright. Even with the sudden resig-

See also page 325.

nation last weekend of Coelho, the third member of the Democratic leadership, Foley has brushed off any suggestion of "crisis" in the party or Congress.

"Foley's selection would be by acclamation," says one veteran congressional aide. Another senior staffer on the Senate side said the House's comfort level with Foley is palpable. "This is not Nixon-Agnew - you lose Nixon, you've got Agnew. This is not the case where they are praying for Bush's health. Everyone trusts him; everyone knows he can do the job."

However, aware of Foley's reputation as an interfactional bridgebuilder, some Republicans are already nostalgic for Wright's more partisan style. "We can get the [GOP] blood churning with Jim Wright there...but not with Tom. Tom's a gentleman, a class article," said Rep. Phil Crane (R-Ill.) recently.

"He is uncomfortable in discussing it...He considers Mr. Wright's problems another problem for the institution he loves," says Rep. Sid Morrison (R-Wash.). Adds another Foley friend in Congress, a Democrat: "This is not the way he wanted to become speaker."

"There isn't a vacancy or about to be a vacancy," Foley has insisted for weeks, when asked about his possible elevation to Wright's job. In February, after Wright angered many in Congress by backing off the push for a congressional pay raise, Foley had to quash a "Foley for Speaker" button campaign. But he slips easily into an institutional description of the odds involved in being No. 2. There is, he says, "a heavy tradition of majority leaders succeeding. But I am not running for speaker, and nobody is running for speaker, and the speaker is the speaker. Whenever the time comes when he leaves that office, and I think it will be many years in the future, and if I am in the Congress, I would probably like to be considered for speaker. I think it would be strange if someone didn't."

But Foley is clearly annoyed at what he sees as the current mean-spiritedness of the political world. He had taken personally the questions raised recently about the employment of congressional wives and other possible conflicts of interest. Since shortly after their marriage in 1968, Heather Strachan Foley, an experienced Hill staffer and lawyer, has worked

as an unpaid administrative assistant in his office. She declined to be interviewed for this story.

"There is almost a Roman games spirit abroad. You pick up the front page and see who has been devoured by the lions today," says Foley. Usually the tall and broad legislator has a bemused look on his houndlike face, but now his features are tense, even stony. He deplores what he terms a national appetite for "politics by ethics inquiry." "If it continues much longer," he says, "the impression - I don't say the reality - but the impression many of the people in the country may get is this is a sort of gladiatorial Congress and that the public's business...[is] taking at least second place to the bloodstained sands of the congressional arena."

So, while loyally supporting the speaker, Foley also met with the House whips, negotiated a budget compromise and tends to his district's concerns. The day after the House ethics committee said Wright had violated rules in 69 instances, Foley had a meeting with members of the Washington delegation over the fate of the spotted owl.

――――――

In January 1975 a number of reform-minded politicians decided some of the senior (and some thought recalcitrant) committee chairmen should be removed. One target was W.R. Poage (D-Tex.), the 75-year-old chairman of the powerful Agriculture Committee. Foley, the second-ranking Democrat on the committee, refused to have anything to do with the ouster strategy even though he was chairman of the liberal Democratic Study Group, which had suggested the reforms. Instead Foley became Poage's primary defender, praising him to a closed caucus on the House floor and lecturing the freshman members on Poage's fairness. "He had the grace to strongly defend Poage when it was apparent he would be beneficiary" of Poage's removal, recalled former representative Don Bonker of Washington state. "It was an extraordinary moment in House history." When Poage lost by three votes, Foley's name was submitted for chairman. Poage received a standing ovation for a speech in support of Foley, and Foley became chairman and Poage vice chairman.

"I guess one of the things one thinks about here is that people who have very different conclusions about public policy can recognize that someone who doesn't share their view is also motivated well. There is a terrible tendency to demonize the opposition," says Foley.

Such understanding, extended to political opponents, is one of the facets of Foley's complex reputation. His caution, his knack at consensus building, his skill with the most arcane House rules, his joy at legislative scenarios, his respect for the process and his ability to listen with what a friend calls a "Jesuit mind" permit him to hear all sides and then synthesize a strategy for the vote and a thoughtful interpretation for the media. These traits have inspired some of his colleagues twice to float his name for vice president, and a survey of senior Hill staffers last year named him the most effective House member.

"With Foley 'knowledge is power' is a truism," says Rep. Dan Glickman (D-Kan.), who served on the Agriculture Committee for 10 years with Foley. "He had this incredible repository of knowledge of the department and the programs. He would make mincemeat of witnesses from time to time...To succeed in his job does not require one to be terribly smart on an intellectual level, but Foley has been able to combine his high personal character with being an intellectual."

Foley himself pleads guilty to the Jesuit approach. He was trained at a Jesuit college before finishing at the University of Washington. "I joke sometimes that the word 'Jesuit' in the dictionary is defined as a member of the Society of Jesus, a Roman Catholic religious order for men established by Ignatius Loyola.' The next word in some dictionaries is 'jesuitical: sly, crafty, deceitful to some length,'" he says. His laugh echoes in the majority leader's vaulted, dark blue office. He adds quickly, as if the shadow of some cleric is looking over his shoulder: "The pride of Jesuit teaching was to teach people to think, to analyze and to question."

While many congressmen are aggressive Type A personalities, Foley says, and focus on a particular issue with great intensity, he sees himself as the Type B mediator who tries "to reconcile the clash of ideas." That professional push for compromise triggers the critics who fault him for being too cautious. "I do have some ability to look at things from different perspectives...Tip O'Neill used to say that Tom

Foley can see three sides of every issue. I probably plead guilty once in a while.

Of course the hazard of this can be a certain literalism.

One day Floyd Hicks, then a congressman from Washington, rushed out to the floor with about one minute to vote. He asked Foley why people were voting against a bill. Foley told him. "So he went up and voted no," Foley remembers. "A few minutes later he looked up and saw me voting aye. He came back and said, 'I thought you said this was a bad bill.' I said, 'No, you asked me why people were voting no.'"

———

Though Foley earned the nickname "Senator" in high school, this son of a well-known judge and grandson of a homesteader had to be persuaded by Scoop Jackson to run against Horan. He filed at the last minute and had to borrow the money.

Early on he received a memorable baptism into the political spotlight. During his first term he was at Dulles Airport waiting to take an afternoon flight home when an airline agent came to the mobile lounge and told him, very loudly, that he had a call from President Lyndon Johnson. "I was sort of impressed; everyone else seemed impressed," recalls Foley. When they got though the phone, the agent cleared the room and Foley identified himself to the White House operator. "A familiar Texas voice comes on and says 'John'? I said, 'No, Mr. President, Tom Foley' '[Plenty of expletives.] I wanted John Fogarty of Rhode Island.' Bam." When the president slammed down the phone, says Foley, the newly minted congressman experienced "the single most deflating moment of my political career." But, he thought, "Wait! Who knows?" He smoked a cigarette, walked outside, and when the agent asked him if he had finished his conversation with the president, Foley said yes. When he got back to the plane, his ticket had been upgraded to first class.

The slice of eastern Washington that has sent Foley here for 25 years is a conservative region where the people routinely vote Republican. It is so conservative that at least three of his opponents were members of the John Birch Society. Even so, in 25 years Foley has had only a couple of squeaker elections. Rich in farms, forests and rivers, Washington is a strong environmental state, but Foley's position on some issues has disappointed some environmental groups. Neither Foley, Wright nor Coelho, the House majority whip, signed the Vento-Green letter last year calling for park protection and reduction of acid rain. "It was an important signal. We would hope he would assert himself more," said Paul Pritchard, executive director of the National Parks and Conservation Association. The League of Conservation Voters gave him a 50 rating, while the House average is 54; the average for Democratic members is 66 and the average for the Washington delegation is 68. "We would like to see these scores higher, but compared to Jim Wright they are high," says a league spokesman.

In 1979 a coalition of farmers brought their tractorcade protest here. Foley, whose district had suffered a drought, and Bob Bergland, then agriculture secretary and a former member of the Agriculture Committee, were focal points of the protest.

When he later arranged for a subcommittee under Poage to have a hearing in Washington state, feeling against the federal government was so high that patrol cars had to escort Foley and the other representatives to the meeting at the Washington State University gym. About 1,600 farmers showed up with 150 testifying. Every time Foley would get up to do a press interview or take a bathroom break, remembers Eugene Moos, a wheat farmer recruited by Foley to be a member of the Agriculture Committee staff, the farmers would shout, "Where's Foley? Where's Foley?"

The hearing, however, turned out to be a turning point in Foley's relationship with the farmers, previously some of his most conservative constituents. In addition to appreciating his chairmanship of the Agriculture Committee - only one farm bill was vetoed during his tenure - they were won over, Foley watchers say, by his broadening mandate and responsibilities. Often cited as evidence of his building power are an impassioned speech about the expanding food stamp program, his nationally televised address urging bipartisan support of Reagan's tax hike plan in 1982 - which reportedly won him more than 60 Democratic votes - his negotiation of the $4.6 billion jobs bill, which Reagan signed in 1983, and his chairmanship of bipartisan committees to work on the budget since 1985.

When the Gramm-Rudman deficit reduction plan was first passed by the Senate, it was seen by legislative types as bad legislation and by the political types as bad politics. Foley got what one congressional aide called "the thankless task" of putting together the House response. "He kept everybody talking and worked out the differences," recalled Rep. Bill Gray (D-Pa.), then chairman of the House Budget Committee and an opponent of Gramm-Rudman. At the end of Foley's negotiations, another Hill veteran said, "he was seen as someone who could be a leader, wasn't just a number two guy and not just a go-along, get-along guy."

In the mid-1970s Foley began to feel what he called "the restrictions" of a committee chairmanship. "It is both deepening and somewhat narrowing," says Foley. While he was anxious to speak up on a variety of issues, Foley didn't want to trample on anyone else's turf. But, he says, "I was interested in other areas other than agriculture."

His move up the leadership ranks began in 1977 when he defeated then-representative Shirley Chisholm for chairman of the Democratic Caucus by a 194-96 vote. In 1981 O'Neill selected Foley as whip because of his parliamentary skills. When O'Neill announced his retirement in 1986 Foley called every single Democrat in the House to announce that he wanted the majority leader post Wright would vacate.

With Wright as speaker, Foley has been the quietest, most predictable of the Wright-Coelho-Foley triad. He's been called a good navigator and brakeman, but even some supporters wonder privately if he could be partisan enough to be effective as speaker. Lobbyist Frank Vacca says Foley represents "the epitome of a Jesuit education. He's sensible, pragmatic, fair. And he's a great one with dialogue." Vacca, vice president for government relations with MidAmerica Dairymen, remembers Foley once, when suffering from a bad back, reclining on his office couch to hear the lobbyist's views about a farm bill.

Parts of the Foley folklore are literally underfoot. Alice, a 16-year-old Belgian shepherd dog, starred in last fall's campaign ad for the congressman. She got more air time than Foley, who refers to her as the "publicity hound." Roger, a cat who adopted the

Foleys on a Caribbean vacation, is occasionally brought to the Capitol to be a mousebuster. The congressman himself, however, is more than a dog and cat man. His nonpolitical interests range widely from Bach to Mozart to electronic gadgetry and the Japanese language and culture.

In the early 1970s Foley agreed to be the grand marshal at the annual Omak Stampede and thought he was going to ride slowly around the ring with the Culville Indian Reservation princess and the Omak Stampede queen. The first thing that went awry was that both women were trick riders and galloped around doing fancy acrobatics. Then he joined a procession of 50 mounted sheriff posses carrying American flags, who he thought would do a slow trot but instead executed a cavalry charge.

Then, all hell broke loose. "A flag dipped in front of my horse's head, shied the horse and he started going counterclockwise. The rest were going clockwise. I lost the stirrup. I lost the rein. I was trying to control a very balky horse in the middle of a cloud of dust. The announcer's voice came booming over," recalls Foley, and here he does his best John Wayne drawl: "'Well, folks, I guess you can see that our good congressman Tom Foley hasn't been wasting his time and money back in Washington taking riding lessons."

Speaker Newt Gingrich's Opening Remarks to the 104th Congress, 4 January 1995

In 1994, the Republicans took control of the US House of Representatives for the first time in 50 years. Rep. Newt Gingrich, who guided the party to its stunning electoral victory, was elected Speaker, the first Republican to hold that post since Joseph Martin, Jr., who held it in the Eighty-third Congress (1953-55). The following, from the *Congressional Record*, is the complete text of Gingrich's remarks to the House on his first day as Speaker:

∾

"Let me say first of all that I am deeply grateful to my good friend, Dick Gephardt. When my side maybe overreacted to your statement about ending 40 years of Democratic rule, I could not help but look over at Bob Michel, who has often been up here and who knows that everything Dick said was true. This is difficult and painful to lose, and on my side of the aisle, we have for 20 elections been on the losing side.

Yet there is something so wonderful about the process by which a free people decides things. In my own case, I lost two elections, and with the good help of my friend Vic Fazio came close to losing two others. I am sorry, guys, it just did not quite work out. Yet I can tell you that every time when the polls closed and I waited for the votes to come in, I felt good, because win or lose, we have been part of this process. In a little while, I am going to ask the dean of the House, John Dingell, to swear me in, to insist on the bipartisan nature of the way in which we together work in this House. John's father was one of the great stalwarts of the New Deal, a man who, as an FDR Democrat, created modern America. I think that John and his father represent a tradition that we all have to recognize and respect, and recognize that the America we are now going to try to lead grew from that tradition and is part of that great heritage.

I also want to take just a moment to thank Speaker Foley, who was extraordinarily generous, both in his public utterances and in everything that he and Mrs. Foley did to help Marianne and me, and to help our staff make the transition. I think that he worked very hard to reestablish the dignity of the House. We can all be proud of the reputation that he takes and of the spirit with which he led the speakership. Our best wishes go to Speaker and Mrs. Foley.

I also want to thank the various House officers, who have been just extraordinary. I want to say for the public record that faced with a result none of them wanted, in a situation I suspect none of them expected, that within 48 hours every officer of this House reacted as a patriot, worked overtime, bent over backwards, and in every way helped us. I am very grateful, and this House I think owes a debt of gratitude to every officer that the Democrats elected 2 years ago.

This is a historic moment. I was asked over and over, how did it feel, and the only word that comes close to adequate is overwhelming. I feel overwhelmed in every way, overwhelmed by all the Georgians who came up, overwhelmed by my extended family that is here, overwhelmed by the historic moment. I walked out and stood on the balcony just outside of the Speaker's office, looking down the Mall this morning, very early. I was just overwhelmed by the view, with two men I will introduce and know very, very well. Just the sense of being part of America, being part of this great tradition, is truly overwhelming.

I have two gavels. Actually, Dick happened to use one. Maybe this was appropriate. This was a Georgia gavel I just got this morning, done by Dorsey Newman of Tallapoosa. He decided that the gavels he saw on TV weren't big enough or strong enough, so he cut down a walnut tree in his backyard, made a gavel, put a commemorative item on it, and sent it

---

Source: "Election of the Speaker" in *Congressional Record. Proceedings and Debates of the 104th Congress, First Session. Vol. 141, No. 1* (Washington, D.C.: Government Printing Office, 2005), H2-H7.

See also page 331

up here. So this is a genuine Georgia gavel, and I am the first Georgia Speaker in over 100 years. The last one, by the way, had a weird accent, too. Speaker Crisp was born in Britain. His parents were actors and they came to the United States - a good word, by the way, for the value we get from immigration.

Second, this is the gavel that Speaker Martin used. I am not sure what it says about the inflation of Government, to put them side by side, but this was the gavel used by the last Republican Speaker. I want to comment for a minute on two men who served as my leaders, from whom I learned so much and who are here today.

When I arrived as a freshman, the Republican Party, deeply dispirited by Watergate and by the loss of the Presidency, banded together and worked with a leader who helped pave the way for our great party victory of 1980, a man who just did a marvelous job. I cannot speak too highly of what I learned about integrity and leadership and courage from serving with him in my freshman term. He is here with us again today. I hope all of you will recognize Congressman John Rhodes of Arizona. I want to say also that at our request, the second person was not sure he should be here at all, then he thought he was going to hide in the back of the room. I insisted that he come on down front, someone whom I regard as a mentor. I think virtually every Democrat in the House would say he is a man who genuinely cares about, loves the House, and represents the best spirit of the House. He is a man who I studied under and, on whom I hope as Speaker I can always rely for advice. I hope frankly I can emulate his commitment to this institution and his willingness to try to reach beyond his personal interest and partisanship. I hope all of you will join me in thanking for his years of service, Congressman Bob Michel of Illinois.

I am very fortunate today. My Mom and my Dad are here, they are right up there in the gallery. Bob and Kit Gingrich. I am so delighted that they were both able to be here. Sometimes when you get to my age, you cannot have everyone near you that you would like to have. I cannot say how much I learned from my Dad and his years of serving in the U.S. Army and how much I learned from my Mother, who is clearly my most enthusiastic cheerleader. My daughters are here up in the gallery, too. They are Kathy Lovewith and her husband Paul, and Jackie and her

husband Mark Zyler. Of course, the person who clearly is my closest friend and my best adviser and whom if I listened to about 20 percent more, I would get in less trouble, my wife Marianne, is in the gallery as well.

I have a very large extended family between Marianne and me. They are virtually all in town, and we have done our part for the Washington tourist season. But I could not help, when I first came on the floor earlier, I saw a number of the young people who are here. I met a number of the children who are on the floor and the young adults, who are close to 12 years of age. I could not help but think that sitting in the back rail near the center of the House is one of my nephews, Kevin McPherson, who is 5. My nieces Susan Brown, who is 6, and Emily Brown, who is 8, and Laura McPherson, who is 9, are all back there, too. That is probably more than I was allowed to bring in, but they are my nieces and my nephews. I have two other nephews a little older who are sitting in the gallery. I could not help but think as a way I wanted to start the speakership and to talk to every Member, that in a sense these young people around us are what this institution is really all about. Much more than the negative advertising and the interest groups and all the different things that make politics all too often cynical, nasty, and sometimes frankly just plain miserable, what makes politics worthwhile is the choice, as Dick Gephardt said, between what we see so tragically on the evening news and the way we try to work very hard to make this system of free, representative self-government work.

The ultimate reason for doing that is these children, the country they will inherit, and the world they will live in. We are starting the 104th Congress. I do not know if you have ever thought about this, but for 208 years, we bring together the most diverse country in the history of the world. We send all sorts of people here. Each of us could find at least one Member we thought was weird. I will tell you, if you went around the room the person chosen to be weird would be different for virtually every one of us. Because we do allow and insist upon the right of a free people to send an extraordinary diversity of people here. Brian Lamb of C-SPAN read to me Friday a phrase from de Tocqueville that was so central to the House. I have been reading Remini's biography of Henry Clay and Clay, as the first strong Speaker, always preferred the House. He preferred the House to the Senate although he served in both. He said the House is more vital, more active, more dynamic, and more common.

This is what de Tocqueville wrote: 'Often there is not a distinguished man in the whole number. Its members are almost all obscure individuals whose names bring no associations to mind. They are mostly village lawyers, men in trade, or even persons belonging to the lower classes of society.' If we include women, I do not know that we would change much. But the word 'vulgar' in de Tocqueville's time had a very particular meaning. It is a meaning the world would do well to study in this room. You see, de Tocqueville was an aristocrat. He lived in a world of kings and princes. The folks who come here do so by the one single act that their citizens freely chose them. I do not care what your ethnic background is, or your ideology. I do not care if you are younger or older. I do not care if you are born in America of if you are a naturalized citizen. Everyone of the 435 people have equal standing because their citizens freely sent them. Their voice should be heard and they should have a right to participate. It is the most marvelous act of a complex giant country trying to argue and talk. And, as Dick Gephardt said, to have a great debate, to reach great decisions, not through a civil war, not by bombing one of our regional capitals, not by killing a half million people, and not by having snipers.

Let me say unequivocally, I condemn all acts of violence against the law by all people for all reasons. This is a society of law and a society of civil behavior. Here we are as commoners together, to some extent Democrats and Republicans, to some extent liberals and conservatives, but Americans all. Steve Gunderson today gave me a copy of the *Portable Abraham Lincoln*. He suggested there is much for me to learn about our party, but I would also say that it does not hurt to have a copy of the portable F.D.R. This is a great country of great people. If there is any one factor or act of my life that strikes me as I stand up here as the first Republican in 40 years to do so. When I first became whip in 1989, Russia was beginning to change, the Soviet Union as it was then. Into my whip's office one day came eight Russians and a Lithuanian, members of the Communist

Party, newspaper editors. They asked me, 'What does a whip do?' They said, 'In Russia we have never had a free parliament since 1917 and that was only for a few months, so what do you do?' I tried to explain, as Dave Bonior or Tom DeLay might now. It is a little strange if you are from a dictatorship to explain you are called the whip but you do not really have a whip, you are elected by the people you are supposed to pressure - other members. If you pressure them too much they will not reelect you. On the other hand If you do not pressure them enough they will not reelect you.

Democracy is hard. It is frustrating. So our group came into the Chamber. The Lithuanian was a man in his late sixties, and I allowed him to come up here and sit and be Speaker, something many of us have done with constituents. Remember, this is the very beginning of perestroika and glasnost. When he came out of the chair, he was physically trembling. He was almost in tears. He said, 'Ever since World War II, I have remembered what the Americans did and I have never believed the propaganda. But I have to tell you, I did not think in my life that I would be able to sit at the center of freedom.' It was one of the most overwhelming, compelling moments of my life. It struck me that something I could not help but think of when we were here with President [Nelson] Mandela [of South Africa]. I went over and saw Ron Dellums and thought of the great work Ron had done to extend freedom across the planet. You get that sense of emotion when you see something so totally different than you had expected. Here was a man who reminded me first of all that while presidents are important, they are in effect an elected kingship, that this and the other body across the way are where freedom has to be fought out. That is the tradition I hope that we will take with us as we go to work.

Today we had a bipartisan prayer service. Frank Wolf made some very important points. He said, 'We have to recognize that many of our most painful problems as a country are moral problems, problems of dealing with ourselves and with life.' He said character is the key to leadership and we have to deal with that. He preached a little bit. I do not think he thought he was preaching, but he was. It was about a spirit of reconciliation. He talked about caring about our spouses and our children and our families. If we are not prepared to model our own family life beyond just having them here for 1 day, if we are not prepared to care about our children and we are not prepared to care about our families, then by what arrogance do we think we will transcend our behavior to care about others?

That is why with Congressman Gephardt's help we have established a bipartisan task force on the family. We have established the principle that we are going to set schedules we stick to so families can count on time to be together, built around school schedules so that families can get to know each other, and not just by seeing us on C-SPAN. I will also say that means one of the strongest recommendations of the bipartisan committee, is that we have 17 minutes to vote. This is the bipartisan committee's recommendations, not just mine. They pointed out that if we take the time we spent in the last Congress where we waited for one more Member, and one more, and one more, that we literally can shorten the business and get people home if we will be strict and firm. At one point this year we had a 45-minute vote. I hope all of my colleagues are paying attention because we are in fact going to work very hard to have 17 minute votes and it is over.

So, leave on the first bell, not the second bell. Okay?

This may seem particularly inappropriate to say on the first day because this will be the busiest day on opening day in congressional history. I want to read just a part of the Contract with America. I don't mean this as a partisan act, but rather to remind all of us what we are about to go through and why. Those of us who ended up in the majority stood on these steps and signed a contract, and here is part of what it says: On the first day of the 104ᵗʰ Congress the new Republican majority will immediately pass the following reforms aimed at restoring the faith and trust of the American people in their government:

First, require all laws that apply to the rest of the country also to apply equally to the Congress.

Second, select a major, independent auditing firm to conduct a comprehensive audit of the Congress for waste, fraud or abuse.

Third, cut the number of House committees and cut committee staffs by a third.

Fourth, limit the terms of all committee chairs.

Fifth, ban the casting of proxy votes in committees.

Sixth, require committee meetings to be open to the public.

Seven, require a three-fifths majority vote to pass a tax increase.

Eight, guarantee an honest accounting of our federal budget by implementing zero baseline budgeting.

Now, I told Dick Gephardt last night that if I had to do it over again we would have pledged within 3 days that we will do these things, but that is not what we said. So we have ourselves in a little bit of a box here.

Then we go a step further. I carry the *T.V. Guide* version of the contract with me at all times. We then say that within the first 100 days of the 104th Congress we shall bring to the House floor the following bills, each to be given full and open debate, each to be given a full and clear vote, and each to be immediately available for inspection. We made it available that day. We listed 10 items.

A balanced budget amendment and line-item veto, a bill to stop violent criminals, emphasizing among other things an effective and enforceable death penalty.

Third was welfare reform.

Fourth, legislation protecting our kids.

Fifth was to provide tax cuts for families.

Sixth was a bill to strengthen our national defense.

Seventh was a bill to raise the senior citizens' earning limit.

Eighth was legislation rolling back Government regulations.

Ninth was a commonsense legal reform bill, and tenth was congressional term limits legislation.

Our commitment on our side, and this is an absolute obligation, is first of all to work today until we are done. I know that is going to inconvenience people who have families and supporters. But we were hired to do a job, and we have to start today to prove we will do it. Second, I would say to our friends in the Democratic Party that we are going to work with you, and we are really laying out a schedule working with the minority leader to make sure that we can set dates certain to go home. That does mean that if 2 or 3 weeks out we are running short we will, frankly, have longer sessions on Tuesday, Wednesday, and Thursday. We will try to work this out on a bipartisan basis to, in a workmanlike way, get it done. It is going to mean the busiest early months since 1933.

Beyond the Contract I think there are two giant challenges. I know I am a partisan figure. But I really hope today that I can speak for a minute to my friends in the Democratic Party as well as my own colleagues, and speak to the country about these two challenges so that I hope we can have a real dialog.

One challenge is to achieve a balanced budget by 2002. I think both Democratic and Republican Governors will say we can do that but it is hard. I do not think we can do it in a year or two. I do not think we ought to lie to the American people. This is a huge, complicated job.

The second challenge is to find a way to truly replace the current welfare state with an opportunity society. Let me talk very briefly about both challenges. First, on the balanced budget I think we can get it done. I think the baby boomers are now old enough that we can have an honest dialog about priorities, about resources, about what works, and what does not work. Let me say I have already told Vice President Gore that we are going to invite him to address a Republican conference. We would have invited him in December but he had to go to Moscow, I believe there are grounds for us to talk together and to work together, to have hearings together, and to have task forces together.

If we set priorities, if we apply the principles of Edwards, Deming and of Peter Drucker we can build on the Vice President's reinventing government effort and we can focus on transforming, not just cutting. The choice becomes not just do you want more or do you want less, but are there ways to do it better? Can we learn from the private sector, can we learn from Ford, IBM, from Microsoft, from what General Motors has had to go through? I think on a bipartisan basis we owe it to our children and grandchildren to get this Government in order and

to be able to actually pay our way. I think 2002 is a reasonable time frame. I would hope that together we could open a dialog with the American people.

I have said that I think Social Security ought to be off limits, at least for the first 4 to 6 years of the process, because I think it will just destroy us if we try to bring it into the game. But let me say about everything else, whether it is Medicare, or it is agricultural subsidies, or it is defense or anything that I think the greatest Democratic President of the 20th century, and in my judgment the greatest President of the 20th century, said it right.

On March 4, 1933, he stood in braces as a man who had polio at a time when nobody who had that kind of disability could be anything in public life. He was President of the United States, and he stood in front of this Capitol on a rainy March day and he said, 'We have nothing to fear but fear itself.' I want every one of us to reach out in that spirit and pledge to live up to that spirit, and I think frankly on a bipartisan basis. I would say to Members of the Black and Hispanic Caucuses that I would hope we could arrange by late spring to genuinely share districts.

You could have a Republican who frankly may not know a thing about your district agree to come for a long weekend with you, and you will agree to go for a long weekend with them. We begin a dialog and an openness that is totally different than people are used to seeing in politics in America. I believe if we do that we can then create a dialog that can lead to a balanced budget. But I think we have a greater challenge. I do want to pick up directly on what Dick Gephardt said, because he said it right. No Republican here should kid themselves about it. The greatest leaders in fighting for an integrated America in the 20th century were in the Democratic Party. The fact is, it was the liberal wing of the Democratic Party that ended segregation. The fact is that it was Franklin Delano Roosevelt who gave hope to a Nation that was in distress and could have slid into dictatorship. Every Republican has much to learn from studying what the Democrats did right.

But I would say to my friends in the Democratic Party that there is much to what Ronald Reagan was trying to get done. There's much to what is being done today by Republicans like Bill Weld, and

John Engler, and Tommy Thompson, and George Allen, and Christy Whitman, and Pete Wilson. There is much we can share with each other.

We must replace the welfare state with an opportunity society. The balanced budget is the right thing to do. But it does not in my mind have the moral urgency of coming to grips with what is happening to the poorest Americans. I commend to all Marvin Olasky's *The Tragedy of American Compassion.* Olasky goes back for 300 years and looked at what has worked in America, how we have helped people rise beyond poverty, and how we have reached out to save people. He may not have the answers, but he has the right sense of where we have to go as Americans. I do not believe that there is a single American who can see a news report of a 4-year-old thrown off of a public housing project in Chicago by other children and killed and not feel that a part of your heart went, too.

I think of my nephew in the back, Kevin, and how all of us feel about our children. How can any American read about an 11-year-old buried with his Teddy bear because he killed a 14-year-old, and then another 14-year-old killed him, and not have some sense of 'My God, where has this country gone?' How can we not decide that this is a moral crisis equal to segregation, equal to slavery? How can we not insist that every day we take steps to do something? I have seldom been more shaken than I was after the election when I had breakfast with two members of the Black Caucus. One of them said to me, 'Can you imagine what it is like to visit a first-grade class and realize that every fourth or fifth young boy in that class may be dead or in jail within 15 years? And they are your constituents and you are helpless to change it?'

For some reason, I do not know why, maybe because I visit a lot of schools, that got through. I mean, that personalized it. That made it real, not just statistics, but real people. Then I tried to explain part of my thoughts by talking about the need for alternatives to the bureaucracy, and we got into what I think frankly has been a pretty distorted and cheap debate over orphanages. Let me say, first of all, my father, who is here today, was a foster child. He was adopted as a teenager. I am adopted. We have relatives who were adopted. We are not talking out of some vague impersonal Dickens *Bleak House* mid-

dle-class intellectual model. We have lived the alternatives. I believe when we are told that children are so lost in the city bureaucracies that there are children who end up in dumpsters, when we are told that there are children doomed to go to schools where 70 or 80 percent of them will not graduate, when we are told of public housing projects that are so dangerous that if any private sector ran them they would be put in jail, and the only solution we are given is, 'Well, we will study it, we will get around to it,' my only point is that this is unacceptable.

We can find ways immediately to do things better, to reach out, break through the bureaucracy and give every young American child a better chance. Let me suggest to you Morris Schectman's new book. I do not agree with all of it, but it is fascinating. It is entitled *Working Without a Net.* It is an effort to argue that in the 21st century we have to create our own safety nets. He draws a distinction between caring and caretaking. It is worth every American reading. He said caretaking is when you bother me a little bit, and I do enough, I feel better because I think I took care of you. That is not any good to you at all. You may be in fact an alcoholic and I just gave you the money to buy the bottle that kills you, but I feel better and go home. He said caring is actually stopping and dealing with the human being, trying to understand enough about them to genuinely make sure you improve their life, even if you have to start with a conversation like, 'If you will quit drinking, I will help you get a job.' This is a lot harder conversation than, 'I feel better. I gave him a buck or 5 bucks.'

I want to commend every Member on both sides to look carefully. I say to those Republicans who believe in total privatization, you cannot believe in the Good Samaritan and explain that as long as business is making money we can walk by a fellow American who is hurt and not do something. I would say to my friends on the left who believe there has never been a government program that was not worth keeping, you cannot look at some of the results we now have and not want to reach out to the humans and forget the bureaucracies. If we could build that attitude on both sides of this aisle, we would be an amazingly different place, and the country would begin to be a different place. We have to create a partnership. We have to reach out to the American people. We are going to do a lot of important things.

Thanks to the House Information System and Congressman Vern Ehlers, as of today we are going to be on line for the whole country, every amendment, every conference report. We are working with C-SPAN and others, and Congressman Gephardt has agreed to help on a bipartisan basis to make the building more open to television, more accessible to the American people. We have talk radio hosts here today for the first time. I hope to have a bipartisan effort to make the place accessible for all talk radio hosts of all backgrounds, no matter their ideology. The House Historian's office is going to be more aggressively run on a bipartisan basis to reach out to Close Up, and to other groups to teach what the legislative struggle is about. I think over time we can and will this Spring rethink campaign reform and lobbying reform and review all ethics, including the gift rule.

But that isn't enough. Our challenge shouldn't be just to balance the budget or to pass the Contract. Our challenge should not be anything that is just legislative. We are supposed to, each one of us, be leaders. I think our challenge has to be to set as our goal, and maybe we are not going to get there in 2 years. This ought to be the goal that we go home and we tell people we believe in: that there will be a Monday morning when for the entire weekend not a single child was killed anywhere in America; that there will be a Monday morning when every child in the country went to a school that they and their parents thought prepared them as citizens and prepared them to compete in the world market; that there will be a Monday morning where it was easy to find a job or create a job, and your own Government did not punish you if you tried. We should not be happy just with the language of politicians and the language of legislation.

We should insist that our success for America is felt in the neighborhoods, in the communities, is felt by real people living real lives who can say, 'Yes, we are safer, we are healthier, we are better educated, America succeeds.' This morning's closing hymn at the prayer service was the 'Battle Hymn of the Republic.' It is hard to be in this building, look down past Grant to the Lincoln Memorial and not realize how painful and how difficult that battle hymn is.

The key phrase is, 'As he died to make men holy, let us live to make men free.'

It is not just political freedom, although I agree with everything Congressman Gephardt said earlier. If you cannot afford to leave the public housing project, you are not free. If you do not know how to find a job and do not know how to create a job, you are not free. If you cannot find a place that will educate you, you are not free. If you are afraid to walk to the store because you could get killed, you are not free. So as all of us over the coming months sing that song, 'As he died to make men holy, let us live to make men free.'

I want us to dedicate ourselves to reach out in a genuinely nonpartisan way to be honest with each other. I promise each of you that without regard to party my door is going to be open. I will listen to each of you. I will try to work with each of you. I will put in long hours, and I will guarantee that I will listen to you first. I will let you get it all out before I give you my version, because you have been patient with me today, and you have given me a chance to set the stage. But I want to close by reminding all of us of how much bigger this is than us. Because beyond talking with the American people, beyond working together, I think we can only be successful if we start with our limits.

I was very struck this morning with something Bill Emerson used, a very famous quote of Benjamin Franklin, at the point where the Constitutional Convention was deadlocked. People were tired, and there was a real possibility that the Convention was going to break up. Franklin, who was quite old and had been relatively quiet for the entire Convention, suddenly stood up and was angry, and he said : I have lived, sir, a long time, and the longer I live the more convincing proofs I see of this truth, that God governs in the affairs of men, and if a sparrow cannot fall to the ground without His notice, is it possible that an empire can rise without His aid? At that point the Constitutional Convention stopped. They took a day off for fasting and prayer. Then, having stopped and come together, they went back, and they solved the great question of large and small States. They wrote the Constitution, and the United States was created.

All I can do is pledge to you that, if each of us will reach out prayerfully and try to genuinely understand each other, if we will recognize that in this building we symbolize America, and that we have an obligation to talk with each other, then I think a year from now we can look on the 104th Congress as a truly amazing institution without regard to party, without regard to ideology. We can say, 'Here America comes to work, and here we are preparing for those children a better future.' Thank you. Good luck and God bless you.

Speaker-elect Bob Livingston's Resignation Speech,
19 December 1998

Following the resignation of Speaker of the House Newt Gingrich, Republicans who held the majority in the House elected Bob Livingston of Louisiana as the next Speaker. This came at the height of the impeachment inquiry against President Bill Clinton, who had perjured himself in a federal lawsuit in which he was sued for sexual harassment by a former Arkansas worker. Before he could be sworn in as Speaker, however, allegations that Livingston had been involved in several extramarital affairs led the Louisianan to take the House floor, resign the speakership, and call for President Clinton's resignation as well. On the same day that Livingston made his announcement, the House voted affirmatively on two counts of impeachment against the President. Stunned by Livingston's action, the Republicans then were forced to vote on a new Speaker, and Rep. Dennis Hastert of Illinois was elected in his stead. The following are Livingston's remarks on the floor of the House, 19 December 1998:

೭

"Mr. Speaker, I rise with the fondest hopes that the bitterness engendered in this debate will at its conclusion be put aside and that all members will return to their families for the holidays mindful of what has been done here by we as agents of principle. We have fulfilled our duty to our magnificent Constitution.

"Yes, our young men and women in the uniformed armed services have in these last few days, set about the task of ridding the earth of the threat of weapons of mass destruction in the hands of an enemy of civilization, Saddam Hussein. And they have performed their tasks with valor and fortitude and that we may freely engage in this most unpleasant aspect of self-government, as was envisioned by our forefathers. I very much regret the enmity and the hostility that has been bred in the halls of Congress for the last months and year. I want so very much to pacify and cool our raging tempers and return to an era when differences were confined to the debate; to not a personal attack or assassination of character.

"I am proud to serve in this institution. And I respect every member of this body. Each of us stands here because a majority of roughly 600,000 people had the confidence to vest us with this authority to act as their agents in a representative democracy.

"When given the chance, we often find that aside from political and partisan differences, we have much in common with one another. But we never discover what that common ground may be with the gulf between the sides of this narrow aisle.

"The debate has done nothing to bring us together, and I greatly regret that it has become quite literally the opening gambit of the intended Livingston speakership. I most certainly would have written a different scenario, had I had the chance.

"But we are all pawns from the chess board and we're playing our parts in a drama that is neither fiction nor unimportant. Indeed, it is of utmost significance in the course of American history. And my desire to create an environment for healing must take lesser precedence then must the search for responsibility, duty and justice within the format provided by the U.S. Constitution.

"I believe we are in active pursuit of these goals. And I give great credit to the gentleman from Illinois [Mr. Hyde[1]] and the gentleman from Michigan [Mr. Conyers[2]], and Mr. Tom Mooney and all the members and staff, majority and minority, of the judiciary committee for their deliberate and conscientious effort on this most difficult task.

"We are nearing completion and however the vote turns out, no one may say that we did not own up to our constitutional responsibility, as members of

Sources: Livingston remarks in *Congressional Record: Proceedings and Debates of the 105th Congress, Second Session*, 144:155 (19 December 1998), H11969-70

See also page 339

Congress in a careful, respectful, and insightful debate. Much credit is due our presiding officer, the gentleman from Illinois [Rep. Ray LaHood], who's done an outstanding job.

"Ladies and gentlemen, we differ on process. The minority believes that we acted too hastily in view of the troops in the field, and that we omitted an alternative from the options available for consideration. We in the majority believe we have properly begun the debate, after setting aside a whole day to honor and praise our troops in the effort that they are extending on our behalf. General Schwarzkopf, the commander of the troops in Iraq several years ago, agreed with us on the Brian Williams show on MSNBC just two nights ago. We believe, we believe that the constitution envisioned that censure not be a part of the debate on whether or not to impeach the president. And we are supported there by comments by then majority leader Tip O'Neill during the Nixon impeachment proceedings.

"So there are differences in process. What about substance? The minority has maintained that the president has not perjured himself, and that even if he did, such perjury was not intended within the term high crimes and misdemeanors delineated in Article II, Section 4 our Constitution.

"Surely, no president has been impeached for perjury, but at least three federal judges have been impeached and convicted under the perjury statutes. And so, perjury, a felony punishable by up to five years in the penitentiary, is a crime for which the president may be held accountable, no matter the circumstances.

"Perjury is a felony, as I've said, and fully 116 people are serving time in federal prison, as we speak, for perjury today. And yes, there have been several instances of people going to prison following convictions for perjury involving lies under oath under sexual circumstances.

"The average citizen knows that he or she must not lie under oath. Ms. Christine Simms of Rockville, Maryland, wrote to the Judiciary Committee just two weeks ago and said, and I quote:

'I, too, was called upon to give answers under oath in interrogatories during a civil proceeding. Truthful answers to those questions would be embarrassing to me and what I knew exposed me to criticism and had a potential to ruin my life, particularly as it related to my children, whom I love very much. In short, I was scared to tell the truth. However, I did just that. I could not lie when I was sworn to tell the truth, no matter what the risks, nor the degree of temptation to take the easy way out. Parts of my life have been difficult since that time because elements of that testimony have been used to scorn me. But, I, as a common citizen was compelled by my conscience to tell the truth.' End quote.

"Yes, our nation is founded on law, and not on the whim of man. We are not ruled by kings or emperors, and there is no divine right of presidents. A president is an ordinary citizen vested with the power to govern and sworn to preserve, protect and defend the Constitution of the United States. Inherit in that oath is a responsibility to live within its laws, with no higher or lower expectations than the average citizen, just like Ms. Simms.

"When the president appeared at the deposition of Ms. Jones and secondly before the federal grand jury, he was sworn to a second oath - to tell the truth, the whole truth, and nothing but the truth so help you God. This, according to witnesses, to the Judiciary Committee and before the special counsel, he did not do. For this I will vote to impeach the president of the United States and ask this case be considered by the United States Senate and that other body of this great Congress uphold their responsibility to render justice on these most serious charges.

"But to the President, I would say:

'Sir you have done great damage to this nation over this past year and while your defenders are contending that further impeachment proceedings would only protract and exacerbate the damage to this country, I say that you have the power to terminate that damage and heal the wounds that you have created. You sir, may resign your post.'

"I can only challenge you in such fashion that I am willing to heed my own words.

"To my colleagues, my friends and most especially my wife and family, I have hurt you all deeply and I beg your forgiveness.

"I was prepared to lead our narrow majority as speaker, and I believe I had it in me to do a fine job. But I cannot do that job or be the kind of leader that I would like to be under current circumstances, so I must set the example that I hope President Clinton will follow. I will not stand for Speaker of the House on January 6, but rather I shall remain as a back bencher in this Congress that I so dearly love for approximately six months into the 106th Congress, whereupon I shall vacate my seat and ask my governor to call a special election to take my place.

"I thank my constituents for the opportunity to serve them. I hope they will not think badly of me for leaving. I thank Alan Martin, my chief of staff, and all of my staff for their tireless work on my behalf. And I thank my wife most especially for standing by me. I love her very much.

"God bless America."

Footnotes:

[1] Referring to Rep. Henry Hyde, Republican of Illinois, who at the time served as chairman of the House Judiciary Committee.

[2] Referring to Rep. John Conyers, Democrat of Michigan, who at the time served as the ranking minority member of the House Judiciary Committee.

Dennis Hastert Becomes Speaker, 6 January 1999

After Speaker Newt Gingrich resigned his office, and his successor Rep. Bob Livingston stepped aside after allegations of an extramarital affair came to light, the Republicans in the House voted to make their Whip, Rep. J. Dennis Hastert of Illinois, to serve as Speaker. Hastert won 220 votes to 205 for Rep. Richard Gephardt, Democrat of Missouri. Hastert was then ushered to the Speaker's chair and sworn in to office. The following, from the *Congressional Record*, are Hastert's remarks following his swearing in:

❧

Gephardt: Mr. Speaker and members of the House, before I hand the gavel over to our new speaker, let me say to him simply let's bury the hatchet. First, I want to say to the new speaker that Jane Gephardt and I would like to invite him and his wife Jean to our congressional district in Missouri, and I hope that in the days ahead Jane and I can come to your congressional district in Illinois. The only problem I have with this new speaker is that as I understand it he's a Chicago Cubs fan and...

Speaker Hastert: But my wife's a Cardinals fan.

Gephardt: And all of you know that I'm a St. Louis Cardinals fan - and he tells me his wife is a St. Louis Cardinals fan, which gives me real hope. But if Sammy Sosa and Mark McGwire can figure it out, so can we.

Now, Mr. Speaker, you know that over the next two years I am going to work hard to win a majority back for democratic values and ideas. But I want to shift the focus today away from politics to other ideas, to other efforts that we can make together to do us all proud. Let's put to rest finally the poisonous politics that has infected this place.

Let's join together, not only in words but in deeds, to do right by the people to live up to our oaths, and to move our nation forward into a new century of prosperity. This is hallowed ground. This is a precious place where we have nurtured and protected for generations our democracy. We have a burden - all of us - and we have a responsibility to live up to those who have gone before us, and today and in the future to reach toward the sky and to listen to our better angels. It is in this spirit that I am proud to hand the gavel to the new speaker of the House, the gentleman from Illinois, Dennis Hastert.

Speaker Hastert: Thank you, Mr. Speak - Mr. Leader - for your kind and thoughtful remarks. I'm going to break tradition, and at this point I am going to ask you to hold the gavel so that I may go down to the floor.

Customarily a new speaker gives his first remarks from the speaker's chair. And while I have great respect for the traditions of this House and this institution, I am breaking tradition this once because my legislative home is here on the floor with you, and so is my heart.

To you, the members of the 106th Congress, to my family and friends and constituents, I say thank you. This is not a job that I sought, but one that I embrace with determination and enthusiasm. In the next few minutes I will share with you how I plan to carry out the job that you have given me.

But first I think we need to take a moment - and I want to say goodbye to a member of this House who made history. Newt, this institution has been forever transformed by your presence, and for years to come all Americans will benefit from the changes that you've championed - a balanced budget, welfare reform, tax relief. And in fact this week families all over America are beginning to calculate their taxes. And to help them they'll find a child tax credit made possible by the Congress that you led. Thank you, Newt, good luck, and God bless you in your new endeavors.

Source: "Election of Speaker" in *Congressional Record: Proceedings and Debates of the 105th Congress, First Session* (Washington, D.C.: Government Printing Office, 1999), 42-45.

See also page 343

Those of you here in this House know me. But Hastert is not exactly a household name across America. So our fellow citizens deserve to know who I am and what I am going to do. What I am is a former high school teacher, a wrestling and football coach, a small businessman and a state legislator. And for the last 12 years I've been a member of this House. I am indebted to the people of the 14th Congressional District of Illinois who continue to send me here to represent them.

I believe in limited government. But when government does act it must be for the good of the people. And serving in this body is a privilege - it is not a right - and each of us was sent here to conduct the people's business. And I intend to get down to business. That means formulating, debating and voting on legislation that addresses the problems that the American people want solved.

In the turbulent days behind us, debate on merits often gave way to personal attacks. Some have felt slighted, insulted or ignored. That is wrong, and that will change. Solutions to problems cannot be found in a pool of bitterness. They can be found in an environment which we trust one another's word, where we generate heat and passion, but where we recognize that each member is equally important to our overall mission of improving life for the American people. In short, I believe all of us, regardless of party, can respect one another, and even as fiercely as we disagree on particular issues.

And speaking of people who find ways to work together across the political fence, let me bring an analogy to a personal level. Two good Illinois friends of mine - George Ryan, the Republican governor-elect and Richard Daley, the Democratic mayor of Chicago, are in the visitors' gallery side by side, and I will ask them to stand to be recognized.

Those who know me well will tell you that I am true to my word. To me a commitment is a commitment, and what you see and hear today is what you will see and hear tomorrow.

Nobody knows me better than my family. My wife Jean and our sons Josh and Ethan are here today. They are my reason for being, and Jean, she keeps me - helps me keep my feet on the ground. And she and the boys are my daily reminder that home is on the Fox River and not the Potomac River. To Jean, Josh and Ethan, thank you for everything, and I love you.

As a teacher I explained the story of America year after year, and I soon came to realize that it was a story, but a story that keeps changing, for we Americans are restless people and we like to tackle and solve problems. And we are constantly renewing our nation, experimenting and creating new ways of doing things. And I like to work against the backdrop of American basics - freedom, liberty, responsibility and opportunity. You can count on me to be a work horse.

My experience as a football and wrestling coach taught me some other lessons that apply here. A good coach knows when to step back and let others shine in the spotlight.

President Reagan for years had a plaque in his office that said it all: There is no limit to what can be accomplished if you don't mind who gets the credit. A good coach doesn't rely on only a few star players, and everyone on the squad has something to offer. And you never get to the finals without a well-rounded team, and above all a coach worth his salt will instill in his team a sense of fair play, camaraderie, respect for the game, and for the opposition. Without those victory is hollow and defeat represents opportunities lost. I found that to be true around here too.

So where do we go from here? Some media pundits say that we'll have two years of stalemate because the Republican majority is too small. And some say that the White House bent on revenge will not give us a moment's peace. And some say the minority in this House will prevent passage of serious legislation so that they can later claim this was a do-nothing Congress. Washington is a town of rumors and guesses and speculation. So none of this comes as a surprise. But none of it needs to come true - that is, if we really respect the voters that sent us here.

To my Republican colleagues I say it's time to put forward the major elements of our legislative program. We will succeed or fail, depending upon how sensible a program we offer. And to my Democratic colleagues I will say I will meet you halfway - maybe more so on occasion. But cooperation is a two-way street, and I expect you to meet me halfway too. The president and a number of Democrats here in the House have been saying it is time to address several issues head-on. I'll buy that. But I think we should agree that stalemate is not an option; solutions are.

And to all my colleagues I say we must get our job done, and done now. And we have an obligation to pass all the appropriations bills by this summer, and we will not leave this chamber until we do.

I intend to be a good listener, but I want to hear ideas and the debate that flows from them. And I will have a low tolerance for campaign speeches masquerading as debate, whatever the source.

Our country faces four big challenges which we must address. And next - but not next month or next year or the year after that, but now. And each challenge involves an element of our security. And first is retirement and health security. Both our Social Security and Medicare programs will run into brick walls in a few years if we don't do something about them now. And we must make sure that Social Security is there for those who depend on it and those who expect to. We also must consider options for younger workers, so that they can look forward to an even brighter retirement.

Nearly a year ago President Clinton came here to give his State of the Union address. He called for reform of Social Security. This year I invite him to return to give us his reform plan. And he has my assurance that it will be taken seriously.

Second, we must ensure a secure future for America's children by insisting that every child has a good school and a safe, drug-free environment. In my 16 years as a teacher I learned that most of the decisions having to do with education are best left to the people closest to the situation - parents, teachers, school board members. What should the federal government's role be? It should be to see that as many education dollars go directly to the classroom where they will do the most good.

And the next is economic security. In the early '80s we adopted policies that lay the foundations for long-term growth. And except for one brief period that growth has continued ever since. And we want our economy to keep on growing. Well, toward that

end it's time for us in Congress to put a microscope to the ways that government takes money from our fellow citizens and how it spends it.

There is a culture here in Washington that has grown unchallenged for too long. It combines three notions: one is that government has prior claim to the earnings of all Americans, as if they work for the government and not the other way around. Another notion is that a government program once it's begun will never end. And a third notion is that every program must grow each passing year. Well, to borrow a musical line, it just ain't necessarily so - at least it won't be as long as I am around here and have something to say about it.

We must measure every dollar we spend by this criterion: Is it really necessary? This is important. For most Americans money doesn't come easy. When I was a kid, to make ends meet my dad had a feed business and he worked nights in a restaurant. My mom raised chickens and sold the eggs. And I still remember when tax time came around our family really felt it. What we need is a leaner, more efficient government, along with tax policies that spur and sustain growth by giving tax relief to all working Americans.

And finally there's the challenge of America's security in a world of danger and uncertainty. Without it other elements of our security won't be possible. And we no longer worry about Soviet nuclear bombs raining down on us. And today there are different worries. The sudden violence of a terrorist bomb, the silent threat of biological weapons, or the rogue state that aims a deadly missile at one of our cities. We need a defense capability that matches these turn-of-the-century threats. And we have asked the men and women of our armed forces to take on assignments in many corners of the earth; yet we have not given them the best equipment or preparation that they need to match those assignments. That must be corrected.

These are not Democratic or Republican issues. They are American issues. We should be able to reach agreement quickly on the goals. And, yes, we are going to argue about the means. But if we are in earnest about our responsibilities we will find common ground to get the job done. In the process we will build the people's faith in this great United States Congress.

As a classroom teacher and a coach I learned the value of brevity. I learned that it's work, not talk, that wins championships. In closing I want you to know just how proud I am to be chosen to be your speaker. And there's a big job ahead for all of us. And so I ask that God bless this House as we move forward together. Thank you very much."

Nancy Pelosi's Remarks on Becoming
First Female Speaker, 4 January 2007

On 4 January 2007, Nancy Pelosi, Democrat of California, was sworn in as the Speaker of the House, the first female to hold that position. The following, her remarks to the members of the House following her swearing in, come from the *Congressional Record* of 4 January 2007:

֎

"Thank you my colleagues, thank you leader (John) Boehner (R-Ohio). I accept this gavel in the spirit of partnership, not partisanship, and I look forward to working with you Mr. Boehner and the Republicans in the Congress on behalf of the American people.

After giving away this gavel in the last two Congresses, I'm glad someone else had the honor today. In this House, we may belong to different parties, but we serve one country. We stand united in our pride and prayers for our men and women in the armed forces. They are working together to protect America, and we, in this House, must also work together to build a future worthy of their sacrifice.

In this hour, we need and pray for the character, courage, and civility of a former member of this House - President Ford. He healed the country when it needed healing. This is another time, another war, and another trial of our American will, imagination, and spirit. Let us honor his memory, not just in eulogy, but in dialogue and trust across the aisle. Let us express our condolences and appreciation to Mrs. Ford and the entire Ford family for their decades of service to our country.

With today's convening of the 110th Congress, we begin anew. I congratulate all members of Congress on your election; I especially want to congratulate our new members of Congress. The genius of our Founders was that every two years, new members bring to this House their spirit of renewal and hope for the American people. This Congress is reinvigo-

rated new members by your optimism, your idealism, and your commitment to our country. Let us acknowledge your families, whose support has made your leadership possible.

Each of us brings to this new Congress our shared values, our commitment to the Constitution, and our personal experience. My path to Congress and the speakership began in Baltimore where my father was mayor. I was raised in a large family that was devoutly Catholic, deeply patriotic, very proud of our Italian American heritage, and staunchly Democratic. My parents taught us that public service was a noble calling, and that we had a responsibility to help those in need. I viewed them as working on the side of the angels and now they are with them. I am so proud that my brother Tommy D'Alesandro, who was also a mayor of Baltimore, is here leading my D'Alesandro family today. Forty-three years ago, Paul Pelosi and I were married. We raised our five children in San Francisco, where Paul was born and raised. I want to thank Paul and our children Nancy Corinne, Christine, Jacqueline, Paul, and Alexandra and our six magnificent grandchildren for giving me their love, support and the confidence to go from the kitchen to the Congress. And I thank my constituents in San Francisco and to the state of California for the privilege of representing them in Congress. Saint Francis of Assisi is our city's patron saint, and his song of St. Francis is our city's anthem: 'Lord, make me a channel of thy peace; where there is darkness may we bring light, where there is hatred, may we bring love, and where there is despair, may we bring hope.' Hope, hope, that is what America is about and it is in that spirit that I was sent to Congress.

And today, I thank my colleagues. By electing me speaker, you have brought us closer to the ideal of equality that is America's heritage and America's hope. This is an historic moment - and I thank the leader for acknowledging it. I think you Leader

---

Source: "Election of the Speaker" in *Congressional Record. Proceedings and Debates of the 110th Congress, First Session. Vol. 153, No. 1* (Washington, D.C.: Government Printing Office, 2007), H2-H5.

See also page 349

Boehner. It is an historic moment for the Congress, and an historic moment for the women of this country. It is a moment for which we have waited over 200 years. Never losing faith, we waited through the many years of struggle to achieve our rights. But women weren't just waiting; women were working. Never losing faith, we worked to redeem the promise of America, that all men and women are created equal. For our daughters and grand-daughters, today we have broken the marble ceiling. For our daughters and our granddaughters, the sky is the limit, anything is possible for them. The election of 2006 was a call to change - not merely to change the control of Congress, but for a new direction for our country. Nowhere were the American people more clear about the need for a new direction than in the war in Iraq. The American people rejected an open-ended obligation to a war without end. Shortly, President Bush will address the nation on the subject of Iraq. It is the responsibility of the president to articulate a new plan for Iraq that makes it clear to the Iraqis that they must defend their own streets and their own security, a plan that promotes stability in the region, and a plan that allows us to responsibly redeploy our troops. Let us work together to be the Congress that rebuilds our military to meet the national security challenges of the 21st century. Let us be the Congress that strongly honors our responsibility to protect the American people from terrorism. Let us be the Congress that never forgets our commitment to our veterans and our first responders, always honoring them as the heroes that they are.

The American people also spoke clearly for a new direction here at home - they desire a new vision, a new America, built on the values that have made our country great. Our founders envisioned a new America driven by optimism, opportunity, and strength. So confident were they in the America they were advancing, they put on the seal, the great seal of the United States, 'novus ordo seclorum' - a new order for the centuries. Centuries, they spoke of the centuries. They envisioned America as a just and good place, as a fair and efficient society, as a source of opportunity for all. This vision has sustained us for over 200 years, and it accounts for what is best in our great nation: liberty, opportunity, and justice.

Now it is our responsibility to carry forth that vision of a new America into the 21st century. A new America that seizes the future and forges 21st Century solutions through discovery, creativity, and innovation, sustaining our economic leadership and ensuring our national security. A new America with a vibrant and strengthened middle class for whom college is affordable, health care is accessible, and retirement reliable. A new America that declares our energy independence, promotes domestic sources of renewable energy, and combats climate change. A new America that is strong, secure, and a respected leader among the community of nations. And the American people told us they expected us to work together for fiscal responsibility, with the highest ethical standards and with civility and bipartisanship.

After years of historic deficits, this 110th Congress will commit itself to a higher standard: pay as you go, no new deficit spending. Our new America will provide unlimited opportunity for future generations, not burden them with mountains of debt. In order to achieve our new America for the 21st century, we must return this House to the American people. So our first order of business is passing the toughest congressional ethics reform in history. This new Congress doesn't have two years or 200 days. Let us join together in the first 100 hours to make this Congress the most honest and open Congress in history - 100 hours.

This openness requires respect for every voice in the Congress. As Thomas Jefferson said, 'Every difference of opinion is not a difference of principle.' My colleagues elected me to be Speaker of the House - the entire House. Respectful of the vision of our Founders, the expectations of our people, and the great challenges that we face, we have an obligation to reach beyond partisanship to work for all Americans. Let us all stand together to move our country forward, seeking common ground for the common good. We have made history, now let us make progress for the America people. May God bless our work, and may God bless America."

Dennis Hastert Announces his Resignation from the US House of Representatives, 15 November 2007

Having lost the speakership earlier in the year, at the start of the 110th Congress (2007-09), Rep. Dennis Hastert, Republican of Illinois, went to the floor of the US House on 15 November 2007 and announced that effective on 26 November 2007 he would resign his seat and return home to Illinois. The representative, first elected to the House in 1986 who rose to the speakership in 1999, spoke for 16 minutes and was hugged by his successor in the Speaker's chair, Nancy Pelosi of California. The following, courtesy of *American Rhetoric*, is a complete transcript of Hastert's remarks:

❧

"Madam Speaker, as members of Congress, we are not here just to vote, but to speak - to give voice on this floor to the aspirations of our constituents. So, this place where we speak, the well of the House, is very special to me. When I was a freshman congressman in 1987, I delivered my first remarks from this podium.

12 years later on January 6th, 1999, when I was first sworn in as speaker, I made my acceptance speech from here, as well. I explained at the time that I was breaking the tradition of the speaker by making acceptance remarks from the - not from the speaker's chair, because my legislative home is here on the floor, with you, and so is my heart.

Well, my heart is still here; it always will be. But the Bible reminds us, in the book of Ecclesiastes, through everything, there's a season and a time for every purpose under heaven. And I think that pretty much sums up our existence in this place.

So now, after 21 years in serving the people of Illinois in this House, the time has come for me to make my last speech from this podium.

Our founding fathers envisioned a citizen legislature. And it's time for this legislator to return to being a private citizen.

And, Madam Speaker, when I was re-elected as speaker of this House in January of 2003, I was able to congratulate you on being the first woman to be nominated as speaker. And just four short years later, you surpassed that achievement, and became the first woman elected as speaker.

And I have to admit that as we went into that 2006 election, I was hoping that you would put off that achievement just a little bit longer.

I think all of us in this House, regardless of party or our affiliation, were proud to be serving when that last ceiling was shattered.

And I would also like to thank you, Madam Speaker, for the many courtesies that you have shown me as a former speaker of this House during the past year, including the opportunity to formally say good-bye to all of my colleagues here today.

I will get myself into trouble if I start singling out members in these remarks. I owe so much to so many of you for your friendship, for the many things that you've taught me and for your support during some very difficult days, such as the aftermath of 9/11 when I became a wartime speaker that I would be remiss if I did not extend a heartfelt thank you to my colleagues and former colleagues in the Illinois congressional delegation and my freshman class of 1986. We've accomplished much, working together.

And I also want to thank my leader, the gentleman from Ohio, Mr. Boehner, and his fellow Republican leaders, who head a vibrant minority, the largest Republican minority since 1955, a minority that is demonstrating to the country that it should, and I think will, lead this House again yet someday.

I also want to thank the chairman of the Energy and Commerce Committee, the dean of this House, the gentleman from Michigan, Mr. Dingell, who for four times administered to me the oath of office as speaker.

Source: "Farewell to Congress Address," delivered 15 November 2007, courtesy of *American Rhetoric*, online at http://www.americanrhetoric.com/speeches/dennishastertfarewellotcongress.htm. Michael E. Eidenmuller, transcriber.

See also page 343

You, Chairman Dingell, and our Republican leader on the committee, Mr. Barton, welcomed me home to the committee, and I've enjoyed working this past year, and we've tried to tackle some of the most important issues that face our nation, such as energy security and health care and telecommunications. And for that I thank both of you gentlemen.

More than 25 years ago, when I entered politics, I never envisioned that this former teacher and wrestling coach from Kendall County, Illinois, would have the opportunity to lead the United States House of Representatives. It was you, the members of this house, who gave me that opportunity longer than any other member of my party in history, and I'm grateful to you.

Becoming Speaker was a very humbling experience, an opportunity that only 51 men and one woman have ever had since 1789. I suspect that sitting here in this chamber are several men and women who will someday have the honor to be speaker of this house.

But whether that honor comes your way or not, you're already the trustee of one of the most wonderful jobs that anyone wanting to serve their country can have. You are a member of the United States House of Representatives, entrusted by more than 700,000 people, citizens, to represent them.

Eleven times the voters of the 14th district of Illinois hired me as their representative. It's been a journey that we've traveled together, and every year brought new challenges.

I am proud of so many of the things that I was able to work on over those years: working to make health care more affordable and accessible by creating tax-free health savings accounts; delivering on long-awaited prescription drug coverage for seniors, while, at the same time, modernizing Medicare for the 21st century; passing two of the largest tax relief packages for working Americans in our nation's history, which encouraged Americans to invest and small businesses to grow and to create new jobs; and reducing the unfair Social Security earnings limit on our senior citizens that needed to work.

And back home in Illinois, I was proud to work on environmental issues, like the removal of the dangerous thorium tailings from West Chicago, Illinois, and preserving the vital drinking water supply of the people of the Fox Valley.

But ultimately, the most important responsibility for any of us who serve this House is to provide for the defense of this nation. It's our most solemn obligation.

On September 11, 2001, I became a wartime speaker. And together, we became a wartime Congress. On that dark day, our Congress was united. We were not Republicans or Democrats. We were just Americans.

We stood shoulder to shoulder on the steps of this Capitol and vowed to do whatever was necessary. And in the following days and weeks and months, President Bush, Leader Gephardt and I worked together.

We tried to bind the wounds of those victimized by the attacks, and then made sure that it would never happen again.

We demanded that our intelligence agencies do a better job of sharing information, that we gave law enforcement more effective tools and resources to guard against attack.

And we made an unprecedented investment in homeland security. And did we get it all right? Of course not. Only hindsight is 20/20. But through those efforts and the grace of God, we have avoided additional attacks on American soil.

There's no doubt in my mind that the American people are safer today because of the heroic actions of our men and women who serve our armed services and intelligence agencies, and because of the actions taken here by our Congress.

It's popular these days to ask political figures what mistakes they've made, where they've failed. As a former history teacher, I know such analysis is best tempered by time and reflection, and that is probably best left to others.

But I will say this: I continue to worry about the breakdown of civility in our political discourse. I tried my best, but I wish I had been more successful.

When I addressed this chamber for the first time as your speaker, I noted that solutions to problems cannot be found in a pool of bitterness. Those words are as true today as they were then.

We each have a responsibility to be passionate about the beliefs. That is healthy government. But we also have a responsibility to be civil, to be open-minded and to be fair - to listen to one another.

To listen to one another, to work in good faith to find solutions to the challenges facing this nation - that is why the American people sent us here. They did not send us here just to get re-elected.

As speaker, I served with two presidents. President Clinton and I worked together to fight the flow of drugs from Colombia - drugs that destroy the lives of our children. And despite our differences on some issues, we were able to find common ground on others.

For most of my years as speaker, President Bush has been our war- time president. I believe history will judge him as a man of courage and foresight, as well as resolve. And I must say, I was proud to serve by his side and honored to call him a friend.

No member of Congress could succeed in serving his or her constituents without the help of a dedicated staff. They often worked long hours and hard days. Many of them gave some of their most productive years to this institution.

And I want to thank all of them and each of them for their service. And I also want to thank all of the people who make and have made this great body function on a daily basis - the officers of the House, the Capitol Police, the chaplain, the permanent staff. They are dedicated professionals who I came to appreciate even more during my years as speaker.

I am also blessed to have a family that helped me every day over these 21 years. My two sons, Josh and Ethan, my daughter-in-law, Heidi, and our newest addition, my grandson, Jack Hastert, and, most importantly, I want to thank my wife, Jean, who is here in the gallery today.

And thank you, Jean, for the love and the help that you've given me.

In 2003, during the Cannon Centenary Conference on the changing nature of the speakership, I said that at the end of the day, the speaker of the House is really just the person who stands up for the American people. That is the same role that every man and woman who serves here should play.

Our founders dreamed of a nation, a nation empowered by freedom, where citizens would find justice, where hard working men and women would find economic opportunity.

Each of us who comes to this place has different ideas of how to preserve and enhance that dream. It's on the floor of this House where those ideas clash peacefully. And through that struggle, our democracy is renewed.

Never lose sight of the fact that you participate in the greatest ongoing democratic ritual in the world. We are, as President Reagan often remind us, a shining city on a hill. Always be mindful of your duties to your constituents and be respectful of the traditions of this institution.

I pray that God will guide you and all that you do in these halls, that he gives you the knowledge to do the people's work, the strength to persevere and the wisdom to know when to listen to what others have to say.

Madam Speaker, there's a tradition among Olympic wrestlers that you leave your shoes on the mat after your last match. Well, don't be alarmed, Madam Speaker.

I won't be challenging the rules of decorum by removing my shoes on the House floor. But I do hope that I have left a few footprints behind that may be of value to those who come after me, just as I have benefited from the footprints of those who I followed to this most wonderful of institutions, the people's House.

May God bless each of you. May God bless this House. May God bless the United States of America.

Goodbye, friends."

Timeline: 1789 - 2009

4 March 1789: The US House of Representatives meets for the first time in Federal Hall in New York City. With many members unable to reach the city in time, the session adjourns until there is a quorum.

1 April 1789: The US House is able to attain its first quorum. Frederick Augustus Conrad Muhlenberg of Pennsylvania is elected as the first Speaker of the House.

4 May 1789 - In a speech on the floor of the House, Rep. James Madison of Virginia says that he will introduce a resolution on 25 May to create additional rights that are not listed in the US Constitution, but that date comes and goes with no word from Madison.

18 May 1789 - The US House enacts its first legislation, the Oath of Office Bill. The oath, utilized to this day in the House with some minor changes, reads, "I, ____, a Representative of the United States in the Congress thereof, do solemnly swear in the presence of Almighty God, that I will support the Constitution of the United States. So help me God." President George Washington signed it into law on 1 June 1789.

8 June 1789: After a month of work, Rep. James Madison of Virginia proposes the first of several amendments to the US Constitution. He tells the US House, "It appears to me that this House is bound by every native of prudence, not to let the first session pass over without proposing to the State Legislatures some things to be incorporated into the constitution, that will render it as acceptable to the whole people of the United States, as it has been found acceptable." Eventually, twelve amendments would be submitted to the States in September 1789, with 10 being ratified (as the Bill of Rights); the final amendment comes into operation on 15 December 1791.

15 June 1789: James Madison writes to Edmund Randolph on the ongoing debate to add a Bill of Rights to the US Constitution. "The inclosed paper contains the proposition made on Monday last on the subject of amendments," he explained. "It is limited to points which are important in the eyes of many and can be objectionable in those of none. The structure & stamina of the Govt. are as little touched as possible. Nothing of a controvertible na-

ture can be expected to make its way thro' the caprice & discord of opinions which would encounter it in Congs. when 2/3 must concur in each House, & in the State Legislatures 3/4 of which will be requisite to its final success. The article which I fear most for is that which respects the representation. The small States betray already a coolness towards it. And I am not sure that another local policy may not mingle its poison in the healing experiment."

9 July 1790 - The House enacts the Permanent Seat of Government Act, 32 to 29, which makes the new District of Columbia in Virginia as the new location of the federal government. After years of sitting in temporary quarters first in New York City and then Philadelphia, the government would have its own home in the District of Columbia, defined in the legislation as "not exceeding ten miles square...be located as hereafter directed on the river Potomac, at some place between the mouths of the Eastern Branch and Connogochegue." President George Washington signs the legislation into law on 16 July.

24 July 1789 - The House establishes the Committee on Ways & Means with the jurisdiction over all budgetary, finance, and taxation matters. The oldest standing committee in the House, it was created on this date as a select committee, becoming a standing committee in the Fourth Congress (1795-97).

17 September 1789 - The House votes to establish the US Supreme Court under the Judiciary Act of 1789. Following the dictates of the US Constitution, which, in Article III, Section 1, states that "the judicial Power of the United States, shall be vested in one supreme Court," the legislation calls for five associate justices and 1 Chief Justice, as well as instituting 13 judicial districts across the country. Whereas today the justices of the Supreme Court sit in Washington to hear cases, the early justices had to "ride circuit" and hear cases in the specific circuit that they had jurisdiction over. President George Washington signs the legislation into law on 24 September 1789, and names John Jay, a member of the Continental Congress, as the first Chief Justice.

25 September 1789 - The House votes to submit the first twelve amendments to the US Constitution to the states. Authored by Rep. James Madison, they cover matters not originally included in the

Constitution, including the right of free speech, the right to petition the government for a redress of grievances, the right to bear arms, and the rights of states to have powers not enumerated in the Constitution.

6 December 1790 - The First Congress (1789-91) convenes in Philadelphia, Pennsylvania, for the first time, in Congress Hall in that city, after moving from its first quarters in New York City. The members who sat in that session of the First Congress knew that their stay in Philadelphia would be short, as a new Federal Capitol was then being constructed in a section of Virginia to be known as the District of Columbia. Philadelphia would remain the "national capital" until 1800, when the Congress moved permanently to the District of Columbia.

27 January 1791: The US House passes the Excise Whiskey Tax by a vote of 32-21, an action which set off the so-called "Whiskey Rebellion," where farmers who were taxed on domestic and imported alcoholic beverages rioted against the federal government. Three years later, after farmers in Pennsylvania attacked federal agents, President George Washington sent some 13,000 militia troops to put down the uprising.

27 January 1791 - Anger at the inability for the US Congress to find a permanent home is aired in an editorial in the New York Daily Advertiser. The paper states, "Where will Congress find a resting place? They have led a kind of vagrant life ever since 1774...Every place they have taken to reside has been too hot to hold them; We pity the poor congress-men, thus kicked around and cuffed about from post to pillar - Where can they find a home?"

24 October 1791 - Jonathan Trumbull, Jr., of Connecticut, is elected Speaker of the House for the Second Congress. The son of a respected Governor of his state, Trumbull served as an aide to General George Washington during the American Revolution. The House turned to Trumbull after agreeing that the Speaker in the First Congress (1789-91), Frederick A.C. Muhlenberg, should not be re-elected so as to not allow any one Speaker to have too much power. Once he was sworn in, Trumbull told the House, "Gentlemen: I find myself unable to express to you the full sense I have of

the distinguished honor you have done me in the choice of your Speaker...I shall enter on its duties, with full assurances...that I shall endeavor to conduct myself with that impartiality, integrity, and assiduity, which become the conspicuous station in which you have been pleased to place me." Trumbull was not re-elected Speaker in the Third Congress (1793-95); instead, the House turned back to former Speaker Muhlenberg, making Trumbull the first Speaker to succeed and be succeeded by the same person.

27 March 1792: The US House votes to authorize a congressional committee to investigate the defeat of US military forces under Maj. Gen. Arthur St. Clair by Indian tribes in the Northwest Territory. This begins the first congressional investigation in House history.

18 September 1793: President George Washington lays the cornerstone for what will become the US Capitol Building in the new District of Columbia. Because there is no building, the Congress will not move to the district until 1800.

7 July 1797: The US House votes to impeach Senator William Blount of Tennessee for conspiring to provoke Indian tribes to fight with the British against the Spanish in what is now western Florida. The US Senate, on 8 July, votes to dismiss the impeachment after it expels him from that body.

15 February 1798 - The first fight in the US House breaks out between Matthew Lyon of Vermont and Roger Griswold of Connecticut. In images drawn of the fight, Speaker Jonathan Dayton is shown watching the exchange of blows.

10 July 1798 - The House enacts the Sedition Act, punishing any person for publishing "false, scandalous, or malicious writing" against the United States.

17 November 1800 - The US House meets for the first time in the North Wing of the US Capitol Building in the Senate's quarters, because the South Wing, where it will be located, is not yet completed.

22 November 1800 - President John Adams delivers his fourth annual message - now known as the State of the Union - to the US Congress, meeting in a joint session of the Fourth Congress (1799-1801). The Congress received the message for the first time in the Capitol Building in the District of Columbia, where the federal government had moved from Philadelphia. In his message, President Adams congratulated both houses of Congress for the move. "I congratulate the People of the United States on the assembling of Congress at the permanent seat of their Government; and I congratulate you, gentlemen, on the prospect of a residence not to be changed: Although there is cause to apprehend that accommodations are not now so complete as might be wished, yet there is great reason to believe that this inconvenience will cease with the present session," he wrote. Adams was the last President to deliver the message in person to the Congress until Woodrow Wilson did it in 1913.

17 February 1801 - The US House elects Thomas Jefferson as President and Aaron Burr as Vice President when it decides the election of 1800. In response, the Twelfth Amendment to the US Constitution is enacted, allowing for the election of separate tickets rather than the first and second finishers in the election.

25 October 1803 - The House votes, 90 to 25, to approve the payment of $11 million dollars to France for the Louisiana Purchase. President Thomas Jefferson had settled on the sum during negotiations with France without any congressional input. Opponents of the legislation in the House believed that it was unconstitutional for a President to agree to any deal with a foreign power that was not agreed to by Congress. One of the challengers to the deal, Rep. John Randolph, the chairman of the House Committee on Ways & Means, said during the debate over the payment, "Does not the President...submit this subject to Congress for their sanction? Does he not recognize the principle...that no treaty is binding until we pass the laws for executing it?" Once Congress passed the legislation, Jefferson paid France on 10 November 1803. The del added some 828,000 square miles to the borders of the United States, from Louisiana to where Montana is now located.

17 December 1805 - The House votes to establish the Committee on Public Lands, to oversee all matters relating to the new territory that was just purchased from France as part of the Louisiana Purchase. Sponsored by Rep. William Findley, Republican of Pennsylvania, the resolution called for the creation of "a committee respecting the lands of the United States." The committee was charged with considering "all such petitions, and matters or things, respecting the lands of the United States, as shall be presented, or shall or may come into question, and be referred to them by the House; and to report their opinion thereupon, together with such propositions for relief therein, as to them shall seem expedient."

26 October 1807 - The House convenes for the first time in its official section of the US Capitol Building, as the opening session of the Tenth Congress (1807-09) began.

4 November 1811 - On his first day in the US House, Rep. Henry Clay is elected Speaker of the House, the first - and perhaps last - time this will happen. Clay would go on to become one of the most important Speakers in House history.

4 June 1812 - The House voted, 79 to 49, to adopt a resolution of war against Great Britain and Ireland, the first time the House used the constitutional power to declare war. Led by Speaker Henry Clay, who belonged to the pro-war faction in the House known as "The War Hawks," the House splits sectionally, with members from southern and western states voting for the resolution but northeastern representatives voting against it.

24 August 1814 - British troops march on Washington, D.C., destroying the White House and nearly demolishing the Capitol Building.

26 January 1820 - Rep. John W. Taylor, Republican of New York, introduces a resolution calling for the admission of Missouri into the Union as a slave state. This came following the December 1819 entry of Alabama as a slave state; Missouri's admission would make one more slave state than free and shifting the balance of power to the slave states. A compromise allowed Maine to enter the Union at the same time; brokered by Speaker of the House Henry Clay, and known as the Missouri Compromise, it barred slavery in any state north of 36°30' north latitude. The settlement allowed the stability of free states and slave states to remain unchallenged.

3 March 1820 - Congress enacts the legislation known as The Missouri Compromise. To head off a constitutional crisis over the admission of states that outlawed slavery, Southerners demanded that for each "free" state admitted one slave state had to come into the Union at the same time to keep the balance between the sections. The compromise specified a border of 36'30 - all states north of this line would be free, and all state south of it would allow slavery. Although unwieldy and controversial, the compromise held off the bitter and divisive subject of slavery from becoming one endangering the Union for three decades.

10 December 1824 - Marie-Joseph Paul Yves Roch Gilbert du Motier, the Marquis de Lafayette, a French general who aided the colonists in their fight against the British in the Revolutionary War, becomes the first foreign personage to address the US House of Representatives.

9 February 1825 - In the only election of its kind, the US House elects Secretary of State John Quincy Adams as President. None of the four major candidates in the 1824 election could muster a majority of the electoral vote, throwing the election into the House. Although former General Andrew Jackson had won more electoral votes than any other candidate, Speaker of the House Henry Clay threw his 37 electoral votes to Adams, giving him the majority and the election. Jackson's supporters denounced Clay's "Corrupt Bargain," especially after Clay resigned from the House when he was named as Adams' Secretary of State.

22 April 1828 - The House enacts a large protective tariff, called by its opponents the "Tariff of Abominations," 105 to 94, which protects the manufacturing and textile industries of New England and western agricultural goods, while at the same time leading to a tax on foreign imports that hurt the southern cotton industry. Angered at the law, officials in South Carolina threaten to disobey the law. The conflict splits the nation into those supporting the federal government's right to levy tariffs and nullifiers who way to defy federal law. One of those in the latter camp is Vice President John C. Calhoun. Following Calhoun's lead in denouncing the tariff, in November 1832 the South Carolina state legislature nullifies the tariff in a direct challenge to the federal government. The crisis is averted in January 1833 when a compromise tariff is enacted and South Carolina backs down.

1 February 1836 - Rep. James Henry Hammond, Nullifier (one who supported the nullification by states of federal laws) of South Carolina, takes to the floor of the US House and delivers a defense of slavery, the first time a member of the House has made such comments. In demanding that those who wished to outlaw slavery not be allowed to deliver petitions for its abolition, he called those who wised to do so part of a "systematic plan of operation, intended to subvert the institutions of the South." He added, "I believe it [slavery] to be the greatest of all the great blessings which a kind Providence has bestowed upon our glorious region."

1 May 1836 - Refusing to accept any petitions from abolitionists asking to outlaw slavery in the United States, the US House votes to institute a rule disallowing any further introduction of such petitions. Dubbed the "gag rule" by its detractors, the action was the first time that Congress refused to allow the right of petition to be carried out. Rep. John Quincy Adams, one of the leaders in introducing such petitions, called out, "I hold the resolution to be a direct violation of the Constitution of the United States." On 25 May, as Adams persisted in introducing antislavery petitions, he angrily asked, "Am I gagged or am I not?" Adams would work for the next several years to overcome the suppressive rule; the House finally voted to repeal it on 3 December 1844.

13 March 1845 - The US House votes, 173 to 14, to declare war against Mexico. The vote comes two days after President James K. Polk - a former Speaker of the House - asked for the declaration due to the invasion of the United States by Mexican forces that left 11 American soldiers dead in what has become known as the Thornton Affair. One of the 14 to vote against the war resolution is former President John Quincy Adams, who decried the war as being conducted to get additional territory to expand slavery.

8 August 1846 - Rep. David Wilmot, Democrat of Pennsylvania, introduces a rider to an appropriations bill calling for the exclusion of slavery from any territory captured from Mexico in the Spanish-American War. Known as the Wilmot Proviso, the clause read: "Provided, That, as an express and fundamental condition to the acquisition of any territory from the Republic of Mexico by the United

States, by virtue of any treaty which may be negotiated between them, and to the use by the Executive of the moneys herein appropriated, neither slavery nor involuntary servitude shall ever exist in any part of said territory, except for crime, whereof the party shall first be duly convicted." The House passes the bill, 85-80, on the same day as it was introduced. Southerners, led by Senator John C. Calhoun, Democrat of South Carolina, defeat the measure in the US Senate.

21 February 1848 - While speaking at his desk, former President John Quincy Adams, sitting as a member of the US House, suffers a stroke and collapses to the floor. The attack occurs during a debate on whether or not to refer a specific resolution to the House Committee on Military Affairs. Rising to vote against the resolution, Adams suffered the stroke while Rep. Washington Hunt, Whig of New York, interrupted the proceedings to give attention to Adams. Several members carried Adams to the Rotunda for fresh air, then, seeing that he was in serious condition, took him to the Speaker's Lobby (now the Lindy Claiborne Boggs Congressional Women's Reading Room). Adams was able to thank his fellow members for attending to him. He then lapsed into a coma and died two days later, on 23 February, at the age of 80. The spot where Adams falls is now marked in Statuary Hall in what used to be the Old House Chamber.

22 May 1854 - The House approved the Kansas-Nebraska Act, 113 to 100, repealing the Missouri Compromise of 1820 and allowing states to vote whether or not to accept slavery in their respective territories, a theory known as "popular sovereignty." After the passage of the act, Rep. Alexander H. Stevens, Democrat of South Carolina, who later served as Vice President of the Confederate States of America, wrote, "I feel as if the Mission of my life was performed." Instead of quieting the dispute over slavery, the action led to increased violence in Kansas before that state entered the Union as a free state.

2 February 1856 - Following 133 ballots spread over two months, the House finally elects a Speaker: Nathaniel Banks, American (also known as "Know Nothings") of Massachusetts, wins the contest over William Aiken, Democrat of South

Carolina, 103 votes to 100. The issue of slavery rises further to split the House despite Banks' victory.

22 May 1856 - Senator Charles Sumner is nearly beaten to death by two proslavery representatives in response to a speech Sumner made against slavery. On 19 and 20 May, Sumner denounced so-called "border ruffians" who were entering Kansas and terrorizing those people who desired to have a state free of slavery. He then denounced the authors of the Kansas-Nebraska Act, Senator Stephen A. Douglas of Illinois and Senator Andrew Butler of South Carolina, comparing Douglas to Don Quixote and Butler to Sancho Panza. Sumner also mocked Butler, who had suffered a stroke earlier in the year, by making fun of his inability to speak properly. On 22 May, Rep. Preston Brooks, Democrat of South Carolina and Butler's nephew, approached Sumner in the empty US Senate chamber and struck him repeatedly with a heavy cane. Brooks was aided in holding Sumner down by Rep. Laurence M. Keitt, also of South Carolina, and Rep. Henry A. Edmundson of Virginia. Brooks hit Sumner until the cane broke, and Sumner, blinded by the blood pouring from his head, stumbled off and collapsed. Infuriated by the attack, William Cullen Bryant wrote in the *New York Evening Post*, "The South cannot tolerate free speech anywhere, and would stifle it in Washington with the bludgeon and the bowie-knife, as they are now trying to stifle it in Kansas by massacre, rapine, and murder. Has it come to this, that we must speak with bated breath in the presence of our Southern masters? Are we to be chastised as they chastise their slaves? Are we too, slaves, slaves for life, a target for their brutal blows, when we do not comport ourselves to please them?" Sumner took three years to recover from his wounds; Brooks died in 1857 at age 37, while Keitt served in the Confederate Army and was killed in action in 1864.

26 June 1857 - Former Speaker Langdon Cheves, the eighth Speaker who served during the Twelfth Congress following the resignation of Speaker Henry Clay, dies in Columbia, South Carolina, two months shy of his 81st birthday. In his last years, Cheves had become an advocate of the secession of the southern states to protect the right to own slaves.

16 December 1857 - The House convenes for the opening of the Thirty-fifth Congress (1857-59) in its new chamber after moving from the original House Chamber, now known as Statuary Hall. Designed by Thomas U. Walter, the Architect of the Capitol, massive expansion of both houses began on 4 July 1851. By this time the House, which had been meeting in the Old House Chamber since 1819, needed additional space for the growing number of members from western states. Jacob Collamer of Vermont, who served in both the House and the Senate, wrote that the new House Chamber was "entirely overburdened...by the great variety of colors [in it]...I think it sort of [like] Joseph's coat."

6 February 1858: The US House endures a lengthy argument over whether the so-called proslavery "Lecompton Constitution" will be adopted by the Congress, allowing Kansas to enter the Union. Initially, Galusha A. Grow, Republican of Pennsylvania, later to serve as Speaker of the House, traded insults with Laurence Keitt, Democrat of South Carolina, which led to actual fighting between the men. When others came forward to break up the struggle, they, too, became involved in the exchange of blows. While Speaker of the House James L. Orr begged for an end to the fighting and ordered the Sergeant-at-Arms to arrest the men, William Barksdale, Democrat of Mississippi, had his toupee ripped from his head. This led to an end to the fisticuffs. Two days later, the full House voted not to adopt the Lecompton Constitution, instead sending it to the House Committee on Territories. Kansas would enter the Union as a free state instead of a proslavery state.

5 December 1859 - The House convenes the Thirty-sixth Congress, two days after abolitionist John Brown was hanged in Virginia for his raid on the armory in Harper's Ferry, Virginia. The issue of slavery and the potential secession of the slave states dominates the election of a Speaker, leading to a prolonged period lasting for 44 total ballots that culminated on 1 February 1860 with the election of Republican William Pennington of New Jersey over Democrat John A. McClernand of Illinois finishing second.

24 December 1860 - The House received a letter from the representatives of the state of South Carolina announcing that that state had seceded from the Union. Signed by Reps. John Ashmore, Milledge Bonham, William Boyce, and John McQueen, the message declared that "the people of their State of South Carolina, in their sovereign capacity, have resumed the powers...delegated by the Federal Government of the United States, and have thereby dissolved our connection with the House of Representatives." Less than two months later, in February 1861, South Carolina troops would fire on the federal garrison at Fort Sumter in Charleston Harbor, setting off the Civil War.

28 February 1862 - The House enacts the Homestead Act, granting to prospective buyers up to 160 acres of public lands if they occupy it and take care of it for five years.

11 April 1862 - Led by Thaddeus Stevens of Pennsylvania, Republicans enact a law, 92 to 38, that abolishes slavery in the District of Columbia while offering compensation for slave owners. With nearly all southern members absent after the southern states seceded from the Union, the measure passed with only token opposition.

4 May 1864 - The US House passed the Wade-Davis Reconstruction Bill, 73 to 49, instituting a program for the reconstruction of the southern states that composed the Confederacy in the US Civil War. Named for its sponsors, Rep. Henry Winter Davis, Republican of Maryland, and Senator Benjamin Wade, Republican of Ohio, the law established Congress authority over the matter of reconstruction, both economic and political. Davis stated that until Congress recognized that the former Confederate states had been reformed and blacks given their civil rights, "a state government organized under its auspices, there is no government in the rebel states except the authority of Congress." President Abraham Lincoln, seeking to impose a less harsh program of bringing the southern states back into the Union, pocket vetoed the bill; the Congress was unable to override the veto, but later enacted provisions of the bill in future legislation.

31 January 1865 - The House enacts the Thirteenth Amendment to the US Constitution, which abolishes slavery, by a vote of 119 to 56. The amendment was sponsored by Rep. James Ashley, Republican of Ohio, after it failed to gain the required two-thirds vote in June 1864. Calling on his fellow representatives, he stated that "the genius of history with iron pen is waiting to record our verdict...which shall declare America is free." When its passage was assured, the House broke into a celebration at the historical moment. The *Chicago Tribune* noted that "The final announcement of the vote was the sequel for a whirlwind of applause wholly unprecedented in Congressional annals... The galleries led off, giving cheer after cheer. The members on the floor then joined in the shouting, throwing up their hats and clapping their hands." The amendment became effective on 6 December 1865 when Georgia ratified it.

4 December 1865 - The Thirty-ninth Congress (1865-67) convenes, with Rep. Thaddeus Stevens, Republican of Pennsylvania, introducing a resolution establishing the Joint Committee on Reconstruction. Formed with nine members from the House and six from the Senate, the committee would oversee all matters relating to the reconstruction of the former Confederate states, and their re-entry back into the Union. Speaking on the House floor, Stevens told the body, "[The Southerners] have torn their constitutional states into atoms and built on their foundations fabrics of a totally different character." He added, "Dead states cannot restore their own existence...[Congress] is the only power that can act in that matter." The House approved Stevens' resolution, 133 to 36.

13 June 1866 - The House enacts the Fourteenth Amendment to the US Constitution, granting freed slaves and free men the rights of all citizens.

3 June 1867 - Following an inquiry in the House Committee on the Judiciary, the committee votes, 5 to 4, not to send articles of impeachment against President Andrew Johnson to the full House.

21 November 1867 - The House Committee on the Judiciary voted, 5 to 4, to send one article of impeachment against President Andrew Johnson to the full House, but the House votes to reject the recommendation.

24 February 1868 - The House voted, 126 to 47, to impeach President Andrew Johnson for violating the Office of Tenure Act. Following a Senate trial, Johnson is acquitted on 26 May 1868.

25 June 1868 - President Andrew Johnson vetoes the Omnibus Southern States Admission Bill, which established strict guidelines for the former Confederate states to re-enter the Union. The main portion of the bill forced the states to ratify the Fourteenth Amendment to the US Constitution. Angered by Johnson's rejection of the act, the House voted on the same day that it received his veto message to override the veto, 108 to 32, with 54 representatives abstaining. The Senate also quickly took up the veto, overriding it by the required two-thirds vote. This was one of 29 pieces of Reconstruction legislation enacted by Congress that Johnson vetoed; the Congress was able to override 15 of those vetoes.

27 February 1869: Rep. John Willis Menard, Republican of Louisiana, becomes the first black man to address the US House of Representatives. Menard's 1868 election is eventually ruled as invalid; it would not be until the following year, in 1870, that a black, Joseph Rainey of South Carolina, would officially be elected and take his seat in the House.

3 March 1869 - On the last day of the Fortieth Congress (1867-69), Speaker Schuyler Colfax resigns his position to prepare to be sworn in as Vice President the following day. For the last day of the congressional session, Theodore Pomeroy, Republican of New York, is sworn in as Speaker for the single 24 hour period - the shortest official "speakership" in House history. Pomeroy thanked the assembled members "for the kind personal consideration which is involved in my unanimous election to this most honorable position."

10 September 1869 - Speaker John Bell dies at his home at Cumberland Furnace, Tennessee, on the banks of the Cumberland River, at the age of 73, nine years after running on a third party ticket, the Constitutional Union Party, to try to head off the approaching Civil War. Former President Andrew Johnson, a fellow Tennessean, said of him, "I always found him to be a man of decided talent, a patriot and lover of his country."

4 September 1872 - The New York *Sun* newspaper exposes the so-called Crédit Mobilier scandal. When the US government looked for bids to construct a railway across the continental United

States, a sham company was established and took government funds for this purpose. One of the members of the "company," Rep. Oakes Ames, Republican of Massachusetts, sold shares to representatives in Congress, including Vice President and former Speaker Schuyler Colfax and James Brooks, Democrat of New York. When the *Sun* unearthed the truth behind the sale of the bonds, Speaker James G. Blaine ordered an investigation; in December 1872 he charged Rep. Luke Potter Poland, Republican of Vermont, to chair a special committee. In his letter to Poland, Blaine noted that the "charge of the bribery of members is one of the gravest any legislative body is called upon to answer, and demands a prompt, thorough, and impartial investigation." The Poland Committee reported its findings on 18 February 1873, leading to the censure of Ames and Brooks for the role in the scandal.

6 January 1874 - For the first time, a black member of Congress, Rep. Robert Elliott, Republican of South Carolina, and one of seven blacks in the Forty-third Congress (1873-75), delivered a major speech on slavery and race. Taking to the floor of the House, Elliott delivered a defense of the civil rights of black Americans and asked for the passage of Senator Charles Sumner's Civil Rights Bill, then under consideration in the Congress, which would prohibit racial segregation in schools, housing, and public transportation. Addressing Rep. Alexander H. Stephens, Democrat of Georgia, who had served as the Vice President of the Confederacy during the Civil War and who had just delivered - from a wheelchair - a stern speech opposing Sumner's bill, Elliott stated, "I regret, sir, that the dark hue of my skin may lend a color to the imputation that I am controlled by motives personal to myself in my advocacy of this great measure of national justice." He then added, "The motive that impels me is restricted to no such boundary, but is as broad as your Constitution. I advocate it because it is right." Although Democrats weakened the bill, it was enacted by the House on 4 February 1875.

4 February 1875 - The House enacts the Civil Rights Act of 1875, 162 to 99. Originally introduced in the US Senate by Senator Charles Sumner, Republican of Massachusetts, in 1870, the bill engendered opposition from Democrats who saw the granting of the right to vote to freed slaves as the

end of Democratic rule in the former Confederate states. Although the original legislation outlawed racial segregation and discrimination in nearly all areas of American society, Republicans were forced to scale back the bill's provisions under public pressure not to give full civil rights to black Americans. The seven black representatives sitting in the House passionately called for the passage of the legislation. James Rapier, Republican of Alabama, stated on the House floor, "Every day my life and property are exposed, are left to the mercy of others, and will be so long as every hotel-keeper, railroad conductor, and steamboat captain can refuse me with impunity...After all, this question resolves itself into this: either I am a man or I am not a man." Because the bill had been so weakened, it did not do much to stem the tide of racial segregation. In 1883, the US Supreme Court struck the act down as unconstitutional, holding that the Congress could not legislate the conduct of private businesses.

1 February 1877 - The House convenes in a joint session with the Senate in the Forty-fifth Congress (1877-79) to count the electoral votes of the controversial 1876 election between Republican Rutherford B. Hayes and Democrat Samuel Tilden. Tilden had 184 electoral votes, one shy of victory, with three southern states and one western state - Florida, Louisiana, Oregon, and South Carolina - not being able to accurately report their votes. Both campaigns submitted electoral slates from these states, and with the Electoral Commission established by Congress, the votes would be counted and a decision on the election made. *The New-York Times* reported that "there was a great desire to witness a fair count, and curiosity was increased by the expectation that the new law would afford some new diversion to the formality of the counting." The Commission decided to award all of the disputed electoral votes to Hayes, giving him 185 electoral votes to Tilden's 184, and the presidency.

13 January 1885 - While standing on a train platform in a snow storm waiting for a train, former Speaker of the House and Vice President Schuyler Colfax collapses and dies. None of those who come to his aid realize who he is; he is only identified from papers in his possession.

29 January 1890: Speaker Thomas B. Reed rules that members in the House who did not call "present" when called were still to be counted in forming a quorum. Until this ruling, members who did not wish to be counted could avoid this by not acknowledging that they were present, causing an inability for the majority to get legislation enacted. Democrats, outraged over the change, called Reed a "tyrant." Ironically, when Democrats took control of the House, Reed, as Minority Leader, used the same tactic to deny Speaker Charles Crisp a quorum, until Crisp adopted Reed's rule on the so-called "disappearing quorum."

1 October 1890 - The House approves, 164 to 142, the Tariff of 1890, known as the McKinley Tariff after its author, Rep. William McKinley of Ohio. The legislation raised tariff rates for a wide range of manufactured products, some up to 50% of their value. During the debate on the House floor, when Rep. Richard W. Townshend, Democrat of Illinois, stood to oppose the measure, Speaker Thomas B. Reed, acknowledging the heckling from Republicans, said to Townshend, "It is not the speech we complain of so much as the monotony of the thing; we want a change." Republicans paid at the polls for the enactment; the following month, Democrats won 93 seats in the House and took control of the majority.

13 April 1898 - The House passed House Resolution 233, 325 to 19, recognizing Cuban independence from Spain. President William McKinley signs the bill into law on 20 April; that same day, Spain broke off diplomatic relations with the United States. Four days later, Spain declared war on the United States, and, on 25 April, the House voted for a war resolution against the Spanish crown, setting off the Spanish-American War.

15 June 1898 - The House votes 209 to 91 to approve Senate Joint Resolution 55, which annexes the territory of Hawaii to the United States. Despite the lopsided vote, the resolution gave rise to an odd allegiance of opponents to the annexation, most notably Democrats who were voting against the administration of President William McKinley and Republicans who wee considered "anti-imperialist," most notably Speaker of the House Thomas Brackett Reed. Reed in fact used his powers as Speaker to block consideration of the bill for a month before its adherents forced him to bring it to the floor for debate and a vote. Reed was so in-

censed by the vote that he would refuse to run for re-election that year.

4 September 1899 - Speaker Thomas B. Reed, a harsh opponent of the Spanish-American War, resigns from the House. First elected in 1876, Reed, from Maine, rose to be elected Speaker in the Fifty-first Congress (1889-91), and serving in that same position in the Fifty-fourth (1895-97) and Fifty-fifth (1897-99) Congresses. Known for his reformist rules that earned him the sobriquet "Czar Reed" by his political enemies, Reed opposed the war aims of fellow Republican President William McKinley. Unable to reconcile his position as the Speaker with opposition to the President, he resigned the speakership and his own congressional seat.

4 December 1899 - As David B. Henderson, a Civil War veteran, is sworn in as Speaker of the House, Sereno Payne of New York becomes the Floor Leader for the Republicans and James Richardson of Tennessee becomes the Floor Leader for the Democrats. This is the first time that the two parties have specific leaders controlling their respective members.

7 December 1902 - Former Speaker Thomas Brackett Reed, who had resigned from the House just three years earlier, dies in Washington, D.C. of Bright's Disease, a malady of the kidneys. Having entered the practice of the law after leaving the House, Reed was in Washington when he collapsed on 29 November 1902 and died in a hospital days later.

9 November 1903 - Joseph G. Cannon of Illinois is elected Speaker; until he leaves the position in 1911, Cannon will become one of the most powerful Speakers in House history.

12 December 1908 - The first House Office Building (HOB) opens in Washington, D.C. Intended as an area for office space for the burgeoning members of Congress and for 14 different House committees, it would be named for Speaker Joseph G. Cannon.

19 March 1910 - In a fight that leaves the House broken and split, progressive Republicans join Democrats in voting to strip Speaker Joseph G. Cannon of the power to name committee chairmen, as well as his ability to serve on the Committee on Rules.

2 April 1917 - Rep. Jeannette Rankin of Montana becomes the first woman to become a member of Congress when she is sworn in to the Sixty-fifth Congress (1917-19). Introduced into the House by her colleague from Montana, John M. Evans, it was observed that Rankin looked like a mature bride rather than a strong-minded female." This observer noted, "When her name was called the House cheered and rose, so that she had to rise and bow twice, which she did with entire self-possession."

6 April 1917 - The US House, hearing the call of President Woodrow Wilson, adopts a resolution of war, 373 to 50, against Imperial Germany, entering the United States in the First World War. Democrats and Republicans alike were among those who opposed the resolution; among them was the first female in the House, Rep. Jeannette Rankin of Montana. When she refused to say out loud how she would vote, former Speaker Joseph G. Cannon went to her and said, "Little woman, you cannot afford not to vote. You represent the womanhood of the country in the American Congress" Rankin then voted no, stating "I want to stand by my country - but I cannot vote for war."

21 May 1919 - The House votes, 304 to 89, to approve the Nineteenth Amendment to the US Constitution, granting females the right to vote. Introduced by Rep. James R. Mann, Republican of Illinois, as "The Susan B. Anthony Amendment," it was opposed by Democrats and Republicans alike. Rep. Benjamin Focht, Republican of Pennsylvania, said during the debate, "no man from New York, Pennsylvania, or Ohio, down in his heart, favors this thing." Nevertheless, it passed the House and Senate and, on 26 August 1920, Secretary of State Bainbridge Colby declared it to be ratified. This came just in time for women to participate in the 1920 presidential and congressional elections.

28 October 1919 - The House votes to override President Woodrow Wilson's veto of the National Prohibition Act. Also known as the Volstead Act, after its author, Rep. Andrew Volstead, Republican of Minnesota, who was the chairman of the House Committee on the Judiciary, it prohibited the manufacture and sale of alcoholic beverages. During debate on the legislation, Volstead told the House, "The American people have said that they do not want any liquor sold, and they have said it emphati-

cally by passing almost unanimously the constitutional amendment." Wilson's veto was also overridden in the US Senate. The law remained on the books until the passage of the Twenty-First Amendment to the US Constitution, which ended Prohibition in 1933.

19 December 1922 - The first live radio broadcast of a US House session is transmitted by a local radio station in Washington, D.C. Rep. Vincent Morrison Brennan, Republican of Michigan, in his only term in the US House of Representatives, had pushed for the radio broadcasts. "It is my purpose to enable all members of Congress as well as the country at large, to 'listen in' on the doings on the floor of the House," he said during a debate on the use of radio in the House. Members opposed to live broadcasts of House business stopped any additional airings for more than 50 years until the late 1970s.

12 April 1924 - The House passes the Immigration Act of 1924, 322 to 71, establishing a system of quotas for immigrants, limiting them to two percent of their numbers already in the United States in 1890; as well, it banned all Japanese immigrants from the country. In all, only 150,000 migrants per year would be allowed into the United States. Rep. Albert Johnson, Republican of Washington State, who authored the act, stated during the floor debate, "It has become necessary that the United States cease to function as an asylum." The ban on Japanese emigration would not be lifted until 1952.

11 June 1929 - The House enacts the Permanent Apportionment Act, which establishes the set number of seats in the US House at 435. Starting with the 1930 census, states will apportion the number of members of the House based on this specific law.

14 June 1930 - In an attempt to fight the depression, the House enacts the Smoot-Hawley Tariff, which raised tariff rates on all imported goods in an effort to protect American industry. Instead of helping end the economic downturn, it exacerbates it, as other nations protect their industries and causing a halt to foreign trade. The nation sinks deeper into the depression.

15 June 1932 - The House voted 211 to 176 to approve a bonus bill for veterans of the First World War worth some $2.4 billion dollars. Sponsored by

Rep. Wright Patman, Democrat of Texas, the enactment was the culmination of a long struggle to approve the bonus, or payment, to the soldiers of that conflict, an effort which included a so-called "Bonus March" and a sit-in of veterans outside of Washington, D.C. During this debate over the bonus, on 14 June, Rep. Edward Eslick, Democrat of Tennessee, suffered a heart attack and died on the House floor. With the passage of the legislation in the midst of the depression, each veteran received approximately $1,000.

16 June 1933 - The first session of the Seventy-third Congress (1933-35) is adjourned. Dubbed as "The 100 days," the session began on 9 March and saw the enactment of 15 major pieces of legislation which created the foundation for President Franklin Delano Roosevelt's "New Deal" to try to rescue the nation from the depths of the depression. Among these actions, established were the Agricultural Adjustment Act, the Civilian Conservation Corps, the Public Works Administration, and the Tennessee Valley Authority Act. President Roosevelt thanked the Congress, controlled in large numbers by Democrats, for taking "cognizance of a crisis in the affairs of our Nation and of the world...It has proved that our form of government can rise to an emergency and carry through a broad program in record time." The President credited Speaker Henry T. Rainey with "a spirit of teamwork."

29 March 1934 - The House enacts the Reciprocal Trade Agreement Act, 274-11, granting the President the power, lodged with the Congress, to levy and collect tariffs. Republicans objected to the legislation; Rep. Allen Treadway of Massachusetts, the ranking Republican on the House Committee on Ways & Means, said that the enactment would "surrender the taxing power of Congress to the President and his subordinates in violation of both the letter and spirit of the Constitution."

19 August 1934 - Speaker Henry T. Rainey dies suddenly of a heart attack while campaigning in St. Louis, Missouri, one day shy of his 74th birthday. Rainey, who had succeeded Speaker John Nance Garner when Garner had become Vice President under President Franklin Delano Roosevelt, had served just a year and a half in the Speaker's chair before his death.

3 January 1935 - The House convenes for the Seventy-fourth Congress (1935-37) for the first time under the Twentieth Amendment to the US Constitution, which stipulated that congressional sessions open not on 4 March but in January. Calling the House into order, Clerk of the House South Trimble stated, "This is the first time in 146 years that an old Congress dies and a new one is born on the 3rd day of January...today we inaugurate the first session of the Seventy-fourth Congress."

5 April 1935 - The House enacts the Social Security Act of 1935, 372 to 73, which for the first time established a federal program of relief for the elderly after they retired and for those who could not work due to illness or injury. Because of arguments between this legislation and that enacted in the US Senate, it took months of negotiations in conference between the two houses, and it was not until 14 August 1935 that President Franklin Delano Roosevelt was able to sign the bill into law.

4 June 1936 - Speaker Joseph W. Byrns, Sr., dies suddenly after suffering a heart attack at his home in the Mayflower Hotel in Washington, D.C. Byrns, 76 years old, had served less than a year and half as Speaker, having succeeded Henry T. Rainey, who had died after just a year and a half in the Speakership. William B. Bankhead of Alabama is quickly elected as Byrns' successor. He tells the House members, "A thoughtful public must believe that, under the spirit of our democratic institutions, it is no small tribute of praise to be elected to this body for even one term of service." He adds, "...when such service is extended year by year and into decades as was the case of Joseph W. Byrns, it is indisputable evidence that he had by his character and ability gained such a high place in the esteem and affection of his constituency that no thought entered their minds of replacing by another this invaluable public servant."

25 June 1938 - The House passes the Fair Labor Standards Act, the last piece of legislation involved in the program of economic stimulus enacted by Congress for President Franklin Delano Roosevelt known as "The New Deal." The legislation laid down a number of standards in the conduct of labor rights, setting a maximum 40 hour workweek, with a minimum wage of 25 cents per hour. The act also set into stone the prohibition on child labor in the United States.

15 September 1940 - Speaker William B. Bankhead dies in a hospital in Baltimore, Maryland, just four days after he was found unconscious in his hotel room while campaigning for President Franklin Delano Roosevelt's unprecedented third term. Bankhead, who had served as Speaker since 1936, had succeeded Speaker Joseph W. Byrns, Sr. Bankhead became the third Speaker to die of heart failure while Franklin Roosevelt served as President, and the fourth overall to die in office.

16 September 1940 - With the death of Speaker William B. Bankhead, the House elects Rep. Sam Rayburn of Texas as Speaker. Until his death in November 1961, Rayburn would serve as Speaker for 17 years and as leader of the Democrats in the minority for four years, a record that will probably never be broken.

8 December 1941 - The US Congress meets in joint session to hear President Franklin Delano Roosevelt call for the United States to declare war on Japan and Germany. The appeal came one day after Japanese forces attacked the US base at Pearl Harbor, Hawaii, sinking much of America's Pacific Fleet and killing more than 3,000 American sailors and civilians. "With confidence in our armed forces, with the unbounding determination of our people, we will gain the inevitable triumph. So help us God," Roosevelt told the members, still shocked as news of the attack continued to trickle in from Hawaii. Rep. Jeannette Rankin of Montana votes against US entry in the Second World War. With this vote, tied with her vote against American entry in the First World War, Rankin becomes the only representative to vote against both conflicts.

3 January 1945 - The House votes to make the Select Committee on Un-American Activities (SCUAA), established in 1938, a standing committee known as the House Committee on Un-American Activities (HUAC). As a select committee, the members investigated fascist and pro-German groups working in the United States before the Second World War; with its establishment as a standing committee, under the guidance of John E. Rankin, Democrat of Mississippi, the focus changed to investigating Communist and Communist-front

groups in the United States working for the Soviet Union. Rankin used the wide investigative powers of the committee to search for Communists across the spectrum of American society. He stated that the committee was collecting "a wealth of information that has gone far toward protecting this Nation from saboteurs of all kinds." In the 1950s and into the 1960s, HUAC was utilized to strip areas of American life such as the entertainment industry and even government of those sympathizing with the Soviet Union.

2 August 1946 - The House enacts the first Legislative Reorganization Act, which cuts the number of committees in the House and requires that lobbyists register with the US government.

3 January 1947: The first television broadcast from the US House of Representatives shows the first session of the Eightieth Congress, presided over by Speaker Joseph W. Martin, Jr.

19 April 1951 - In a joint session of Congress, General Douglas MacArthur delivers his farewell address to the American people. Only a week before, President Harry S Truman had relieved MacArthur of the commander of American forces fighting in Korea against Communist North Korean and Chinese forces. Truman had removed MacArthur after the general openly advocated an attack on mainland China to try to stop the Chinese advance in the conflict. MacArthur ended his speech to Congress with a now-famous phrase: "Old soldiers never die, they just fade away...I now close my military career and just fade away, an old soldier who tried to do his duty as God gave him the light to see that duty."

1 March 1954: Four Puerto Rican terrorists attack the US House of Representatives from the gallery, wounding several congressmen. While Speaker Joseph W. Martin, Jr., is calling the roll call, the terrorists, wielding handguns, open fire on the members of the House assembled below the gallery. Five representatives - Alvin Bentley of Michigan, Ben Jensen of Iowa, Clifford Davis of Tennessee, George Fallon of Maryland, and Kenneth Roberts of Alabama - are all wounded; all survive, although Bentley was critically wounded which probably leads to his early death.

16 November 1961: Speaker Sam Rayburn dies of cancer at his home in Bonham, Texas, ending the tenure of the longest-serving Speaker in US House history. Having loved serving in the House since 1913, Rayburn noted late in his career, "The House of Representatives has been my life and it has been my love. I never had any ambition to be a governor or a senator. I wanted to come to this body and stay here as long as my people wanted me." He added, "They have been as kind and fine to me as you have been."

21 May 1962: The two House office buildings are renamed in honor of two former Speakers, Joseph G. Cannon and Nicholas Longworth. A third House building is under construction, to be completed by 1965.

27 August 1962 - The House votes, 295 to 86, to pass the Twenty-Fourth Amendment to the US Constitution, which outlawed the poll tax as a requirement for voting. Utilized in five southern states - Alabama, Arkansas, Mississippi, Texas, and Virginia - as a tool to keep blacks from voting, it was castigated by some as not being protective enough of the right to vote. One critic, Rep. John V. Lindsay, Republican of New York, said, "If we're going to have a constitutional amendment, let's have a meaningful one." Nevertheless, it passed by houses by the required two-thirds vote, and, on 23 January 1964, it became part of the Constitution when South Dakota ratified it.

27 November 1963 - President Lyndon Baines Johnson addresses a joint session of the US Congress for the first time as President, just five days after President John F. Kennedy was assassinated in Dallas, Texas. During the address, the President called for "the earliest possible passage of the civil rights bill and a tax cut as the best way of honoring" his slain predecessor.

2 July 1964 - The House enacts the Civil Rights Act of 1964, giving widespread protection to the rights of black Americans, including voting rights, and paving the way for the end of school segregation in any state of the Union.

23 February 1965: The third US House office building opens; it is named the Rayburn House Of-fice Building in honor of former Speaker Sam Rayburn.

3 August 1965 - The House approves, 328 to 74, the Voting Rights Act, one of the most sweeping pieces of legislation enacted in the 20th century dealing with voting rights. Aimed at making sure that black Americans were protected from state officials who sought to diminish their right to vote, the legislation also prohibited the use of literacy tests and poll taxes to keep anyone from voting. With the Senate approving the action, President Lyndon Baines Johnson signed the act into law on 6 August.

10 January 1967 - The House votes 363 to 65 to refuse to seat Rep. Adam Clayton Powell, Jr., Democrat of New York. Powell, who had won the seat in the Ninetieth Congress (1967-69), was accused of financial improprieties which led the House leadership to refuse to seat him. Powell went to the House floor and pled his case to his fellow congressmen. "My conscience is clear," he stated. "I am in God's hands and your hands. All I hope is that you have a good sleep tonight." On 1 March 1967, a special House committee looking into Powell's case recommended that he be seated but censured. Instead, the House voted 307 to 116 to continue to refuse to seat him. In a special election in April 1967, Powell was elected to the vacant seat. In the meantime, Powell had sued Speaker of the House John W. McCormack for refusing to allow him to take his seat. In June 1969, in the landmark ruling *Powell v. McCormack*, the US Supreme Court held that the House could not exclude a member as long as they met the requirements outlined in the US Constitution, namely reaching the required age, being a citizen of the United States, and living in the district they were representing.

23 March 1971 - The US House passes the Twenty-Sixth Amendment to the US Constitution, 400 to 19, which lowered the voting age to 18 from 21. Enacted in response to protests during the Vietnam War that men being sent to fight in that conflict were too young to vote, the amendment was ratified by the necessary 2/3rds of the states on 30 June 1971 when Ohio ratified it. Those covered by the amendment were able to vote in the 1972 presidential and congressional elections.

23 January 1973 - Under the Legislative Reorganization Act of 1970, the House mandated that an electronic voting system would be installed in the House to make the voting and roll call process easier. This is the first day that the new system is used.

20 December 1973 - The House passes the Endangered Species Act, the first major piece of environmental legislation enacted by Congress to protect imperiled animals and plants in the United States, by a vote of 355 to 4. Introduced in January 1973, both houses of Congress debated the action and then sent a strong House bill and a weaker Senate bill to conference. When signed into law by President Richard M. Nixon on 28 December, the act replaced the Endangered Species Act of 1969, which did not have any consequences for the destruction or killing of endangered species. The 1973 act gave the Secretary of the Interior new powers to enforce environmental laws and establish an Endangered Species List. The first animal placed on the list becomes the American bald eagle, the symbol of the nation since its founding. It was finally removed from that list in 2007.

12 July 1974 - The Congressional Budget and Impoundment Control Act of 1974 is signed into law by President Richard M. Nixon, which reformed the Budget and Accounting Act of 1921, established a House Committee on the Budget, and changed the date of the start of the budgetary fiscal year (FY) from 1 July to 1 October of each year. Democrat Albert Ullman, Democrat of Oregon, would be named as the first chairman of the new Budget Committee.

27 July 1974 - The House Committee on the Judiciary approves the first of three articles of impeachment against President Richard M. Nixon. Facing impeachment when the full House voted, and a certain conviction in the US Senate on charges of obstruction of justice, abuse of presidential power, and contempt of Congress, Nixon will resign the presidency on 9 August 1974.

15 March 1977 - The US House of Representatives begins a three-month trial of utilizing closed-circuit television of House proceedings. The House would approve further televised measures in 1978, and, on 19 March 1979, would go forward with permanent televised proceedings.

19 March 1979 - The US House begins permanent live telecasts of its sessions and floor proceedings. The Cable-Satellite Public Affairs Network (C-SPAN) centers nearly all of its initial programming around these broadcasts.

17 March 1983 - Speaker Thomas P. "Tip" O'Neill hosts the first St. Patrick's Day lunch. Despite being a political opponent of President Ronald Reagan, O'Neill and the President are both of Irish ancestry and share their love of Ireland and family together. O'Neill tells Reagan, "I'm going to cook you some Boston corned beef and I'm going to have an Irish storyteller there," to which the President replies, "I'll have to polish up some new Irish jokes."

21 August 1994 - The House enacts the Violent Crime Control and Law Enforcement Act of 1994, 235 to 195, which amended the Omnibus Crime Control and Safe Streets Act of 1968. Pushed by the administration of President William Jefferson "Bill" Clinton, the legislation granted funds to local law enforcement for additional police, and to make better cooperation between federal and state officials and agencies. One of the most controversial aspects of the bill are a number of prohibitions on certain guns, leading to vast opposition from gun rights groups and conservatives in both parties. The legislation, intended to showcase the Democrats as a law-and-order party, instead was used by opponents of gun control as evidence of the expansive reach of government against the Second Amendment by the Clinton administration, and led to Republicans picking up 54 seats in the 1994 midterm election and control of the US House of Representatives.

4 January 1995 - For he first time in 40 years, Republicans take control of the majority in the US House of Representatives. Newt Gingrich of Georgia, who had served as Minority Whip in the previous Congress, rises to become the first Republican Speaker since Joseph W. Martin, Jr., in 1955.

19 December 1998 - The full House votes two articles of impeachment against President William Jefferson "Bill" Clinton, charging him with obstruction of justice and perjury. Following a Senate trial, Clinton will be acquitted on 12 February 1999.

4 February 2000 - Speaker of the House Carl Bert Albert died at his home in McAlester, Oklahoma at the age of 91. Albert had been in retirement since leaving the House at the end of the Ninety-fourth Congress (1975-77) after three terms as Speaker. Recalling later his reaction to leaving the House for the final time on 3 January 1977, he said, "I was tired when I left," adding that "I wanted to go home."

19 June 2002 - Following the terrorist attacks on the United States on 11 September 2001, the House adopts House Resolution 449 to create the Select Committee on Homeland Security, the first new standing committee established in the House since 1974. The move came in a response to a call from President George W. Bush to establish a cabinet-level agency to handle domestic homeland security affairs. Rep. Christopher Cox, Republican of California, is named as the first chairman of the Select Committee.

10 October 2002 - The US House votes 296-133 to authorize President George W. Bush to go to war against Iraq and end the regime of Iraq President Saddam Hussein. The US Senate enacts the authorization the following day, and it is signed into law on 16 October. The US waited until 19 March 2003 to finally launch an air attack on Saddam's government.

4 January 2005 - On the first day of the One Hundred Ninth Congress, the US House establishes the House Committee on Homeland Security, to oversee all House matters dealing with the security of the nation that came about following the 11 September 2001 terror attacks on New York City, Washington, D.C., and Pennsylvania. This full committee replaces the Select Committee on Homeland Security which had been established after the attacks.

4 January 2007 - Nancy Pelosi becomes the first female Speaker of the US House of Representatives when she is sworn in to officiate over the One Hundred Tenth Congress.

13 February 2009 - The US House – as well as the US Senate – passes the American Recovery and Reinvestment Act, known as the Stimulus Bill, sending it to the President for his signature. The bill, enacted in the House with no Republican votes, spends nearly $900 billion to try to revive the slowing US economy, in its 14th month of recession.

Sources: No one source was used to form this timeline; some information came during research for the rest of the book from sources too numerous to list here, while other information was gathered courtesy of the US House of Representatives Office of the Historian.

Appendices

Appendix A

Years Served in Congress before Election as Speaker

Frederick A.C Muhlenberg, Henry Clay and William Pennington were elected as Speaker on their first day in Congress. In the modern era, however, with the exception of Dennis Hastert, those elected as Speaker have had a long tenure in the House of Representatives while rising in their respective parties' leadership. The following illustrates the number of years that each Speaker served in Congress prior to their election as Speaker.

Speaker	Years Served Before Election as Speaker	Date of Election
Frederick A.C. Muhlenberg	Less than one year	1789
Jonathan Trumbull	Three years	1791
Jonathan Dayton	Four years	1795
Theodore Sedgwick	Eleven years	1799
Nathaniel Macon	Ten years	1801
Joseph B. Varnum	Twelve years	1807
Henry Clay	Less than one year	1811
Langdon Cheves	Five years	1814
John W. Taylor	Seven years	1820
James Barbour	Six years	1821
Andrew Stevenson	Six years	1827
John Bell	Seven years	1834
James K. Polk	Ten years	1835
Robert M.T. Hunter	Two years	1839
John White	Six years	1841
John W. Jones	Eight years	1843
John W. Davis	Six years	1845
Robert C. Winthrop	Eight years	1847
Howell Cobb	Six years	1849
Linn Boyd	Fourteen years	1851
Nathaniel Banks	Two years	1855
James L. Orr	Seven years	1857
William Pennington	Less than one year	1859
Galusha Grow	Ten years	1861
Schuyler Colfax	Eight years	1863
Theodore Pomeroy	Eight years	1869
James G. Blaine	Six years	1869
Michael C. Kerr	Eight years	1875
Samuel Randall	Thirteen years	1876
J. Warren Keifer	Four years	1881
John Carlisle	Six years	1883
Thomas B. Reed	Twelve years	1889
Charles Crisp	Eight years	1891
David Henderson	Sixteen years	1899
Joseph G. Cannon	Twenty-eight years	1903
Champ Clark	Twenty-six years	1911
Frederick Gillett	Twenty-six years	1919

Speaker	Years Served Before Election as Speaker	Date of Election
Nicholas Longworth	Twenty-two years	1925
John Nance Garner	Twenty-six years	1931
Henry T. Rainey	Twenty-eight years	1933
Joseph Byrns	Twenty-five years	1935
William Bankhead	Fifteen years	1936
Sam Rayburn	Twenty-seven years	1940
Joseph Martin	Twenty-two years	1946
William Mccormack	Thirty-four years	1962
Carl Albert	Twenty-four years	1971
Thomas P. O'neill	Twenty-four years	1977
James C. Wright, Jr.	Thirty-two years	1987
Thomas S. Foley	Twenty-four years	1989
Newt Gingrich	Sixteen years	1995
Dennis Hastert	Twelve years	1999
Nancy Pelosi	Twenty-one years	2007

Appendix B

Individuals Receiving Votes for Speaker, 1863-2009

The following shows the votes in the elections for Speaker from the Thirty-eighth Congress (1863-65) through to the One Hundred Eleventh Congress (2009-11). The winning candidate's name is in bold. The number of votes received by a particular candidate may not necessarily reflect the numbers for the majority and minority in the House, as some members did not vote or voted for other candidates rather than the main party leaders.

Year	Republican Nominee	Votes	Democratic Nominee	Votes	Others Receiving Votes
1863	**Schuyler Colfax** (IN)	86	None	72	
1865	**Schuyler Colfax** (IN)	136	James Brooks (NY)	38	
1867	**Schuyler Colfax** (IN)	173	Samuel S. Marshall (IL)	47	
1869	**James G. Blaine** (ME)	171	Michael C. Kerr (IN)	67	
1871	**James G. Blaine** (ME)	136	George W. Morgan (OH)	104	
1873	**James G. Blaine** (ME)	199	Fernando Wood (NY)	88	
1875	James G. Blaine (ME)	103	**Michael C. Kerr** (IN)	182	
1876[1]	James A. Garfield (OH)	82	**Samuel J. Randall** (PA)	161	
1877	James A. Garfield (OH)	136	**Samuel J. Randall** (PA)	155	
1879	James A. Garfield (OH)	132	**Samuel J. Randall** (PA)	142	
1881	**J. Warren Keifer** (OH)	151	Samuel J. Randall (PA)	128	
1883	J. Warren Keifer (OH)	117	**John G. Carlisle** (KY)	196	
1885	Thomas B. Reed (ME)	141	**John G. Carlisle** (KY)	182	
1887	Thomas B. Reed (ME)	152	**John G. Carlisle** (KY)	167	
1889	**Thomas B. Reed** (ME)	179	John G. Carlisle (KY)	152	
1891	Thomas B. Reed (ME)	86	**Charles F. Crisp** (GA)	238	
1893	Thomas B. Reed (ME)	124	**Charles F. Crisp** (GA)	218	
1895	**Thomas B. Reed** (ME)	254	Charles F. Crisp (GA)	93	
1897	**Thomas B. Reed** (ME)	206	Joseph W. Bailey (TX)	124	
1899	**David B. Henderson** (IO)	187	James D. Richardson (TN)	161	
1901	**David B. Henderson** (IO)	200	James D. Richardson (TN)	151	
1903	**Joseph G. Cannon** (IL)	207	John B. Williams (MS)	176	
1905	**Joseph G. Cannon** (IL)	251	John B. Williams (MS)	135	
1907	**Joseph G. Cannon** (IL)	223	John B. Williams (MS)	167	
1909	**Joseph G. Cannon** (IL)	219	James "Champ" Clark (MO)	172	
1911	James R. Mann (NY)	162	**James "Champ" Clark** (MO)	230	
1913	James R. Mann (NY)	134	**James "Champ" Clark** (MO)	291	Victor Murdock (P-KS)* Henry A. Cooper (R-WI) John M. Nelson (R-WI)
1915	James R. Mann (NY)	196	**James "Champ" Clark** (MO)	230	
1917	James R. Mann (NY)	214	**James "Champ" Clark** (MO)	215	Irvine L. Lenroot (R-WI) Frederick H. Gillett (R-MA)
1919	**Frederick H. Gillett** (MA)	240	James "Champ" Clark	192	
1921	**Frederick H. Gillett** (MA)	302	Claude Kitchin (NC)	131	
1923	**Frederick H. Gillett** (MA)	225	Finis J. Garrett (TN)	207	Henry A. Cooper (R-WI)* Martin B. Madden (R-IL)*
1925	**Frederick H. Gillett** (MA)	247	Finis J. Garrett (TN)	183	Henry A. Cooper (R-WI)*
1927	**Nicholas Longworth** (OH)	238	Finis J. Garrett (TN)	194	
1929	**Nicholas Longworth** (OH)	270	John Nance Garner (TX)	164	
1931	Bertrand H. Snell (NY)	216	**John Nance Garner** (TX)	218	George J. Schneider (R-WI)
1933	Bertrand H. Snell (NY)	117	**Henry T. Rainey** (IL)[2]	313	
1935	Bertrand H. Snell (NY)	103	**Joseph W. Byrns** (TN)[3]	322	
1936[1,4]			**William B. Bankhead** (AL)		
1937	Bertrand H. Snell (NY)	88	**William B. Bankhead** (AL)	334	

Year	Republican Nominee	Votes	Democratic Nominee	Votes	Others Receiving Votes
1939	Joseph W. Martin (MA)	169	**William B. Bankhead** (AL)[5]	262	
1940[1,6]			Sam Rayburn (TX)		
1941	Joseph W. Martin (MA)	162	**Sam Rayburn** (TX)	267	
1943	Joseph W. Martin (MA)	209	**Sam Rayburn** (TX)	222	
1945	Joseph W. Martin (MA)	191	**Sam Rayburn** (TX)	242	
1947	**Joseph W. Martin** (MA)	246	Sam Rayburn (TX)	188	
1949	Joseph W. Martin (MA)	171	**Sam Rayburn** (TX)	263	
1951	Joseph W. Martin (MA)	199	**Sam Rayburn** (TX)	235	
1953	**Joseph W. Martin** (MA)	221	Sam Rayburn (TX)	213	
1955	Joseph W. Martin (MA)	203	**Sam Rayburn** (TX)	232	
1957	Joseph W. Martin (MA)	201	**Sam Rayburn** (TX)	234	
1959	Charles S. Halleck (IN)	153	**Sam Rayburn** (TX)	283	
1961	Charles S. Halleck (IN)	174	**Sam Rayburn** (TX)[7]	263	
1961[1,8]			**John W. McCormack** (MA)		
1963	Charles S. Halleck (IN)	176	**John W. McCormack** (MA)	259	
1965	Gerald R. Ford (MI)	40	**John W. McCormack** (MA)	295	
1967	Gerald R. Ford (MI)	187	**John W. McCormack** (MA)	247	
1969	Gerald R. Ford (MI)	192	**John W. McCormack** (MA)	243	
1971	Gerald R. Ford (MI)	180	**Carl B. Albert** (OK)	255	
1973	Gerald R. Ford (MI)	192	**Carl B. Albert** (OK)	242	
1975	John Rhodes (AZ)	144	**Carl B. Albert** (OK)	291	
1977	John Rhodes (AZ)	143	**Thomas P. O'Neill** (MA)	292	
1979	John Rhodes (AZ)	158	**Thomas P. O'Neill** (MA)	277	
1981	Robert H. Michel (IL)	192	**Thomas P. O'Neill** (MA)	242	
1983	Robert H. Michel (IL)	166	**Thomas P. O'Neill** (MA)	269	
1985	Robert H. Michel (IL)	182	**Thomas O. O'Neill** (MA)	253	
1987	Robert H. Michel (IL)	177	**James C. Wright** (TX)	258	
1989	Robert H. Michel (IL)	175	**James C. Wright** (TX)[9]	260	
1989[1]			**Thomas S. Foley** (WA)		
1991	Robert H. Michel (IL)	167	**Thomas S. Foley** (WA)	267	
1993	Robert H. Michel (IL)	176	**Thomas S. Foley** (WA)	258	
1995	**Newt Gingrich** (GA)	230	Richard A. Gephardt (MO)	204	
1997	**Newt Gingrich** (GA)	228	Richard A. Gephardt (MO)	206	
1999	**Robert Livingston** (LA)[10]	223	Richard A. Gephardt (MO)	211	
1999	**J. Dennis Hastert** (IL)	223	Richard A. Gephardt (MO)	211	
2001	**J. Dennis Hastert** (IL)	221	Richard A. Gephardt (MO)	212	
2003	**J. Dennis Hastert** (IL)	229	Nancy Pelosi (CA)	204	
2005	**J. Dennis Hastert** (IL)	232	Nancy Pelosi (CA)	202	
2007	John A. Boehner (OH)	202	**Nancy Pelosi** (CA)	233	
2009	John A. Boehner (OH)	178	**Nancy Pelosi** (CA)	257	

Key:
* Other candidate(s) formally placed in nomination.

Footnotes:
[1] Special election to fill a vacancy caused by the death or resignation of the sitting Speaker.
[2] Died 19 August 1934 after just six months in the Speaker's chair.
[3] Died 4 June 1936 after just five months in the Speaker's chair.
[4] Succeeded to the Speakership on 4 June 1936 with no formal election being held.
[5] Died 15 September 1940.
[6] No formal election was held; Rayburn simply succeeded to the Speakership.
[7] Died 16 November 1961.
[8] McCormack was elected to the Speakership without a formal election being held.
[9] Caught in an ethics scandal, Wright resigned the Speakership on 31 May 1989, and formally left the House on 30 June 1989.
[10] Livingston was nominated by the Republican caucus to be the Speaker, but he resigned on 19 December 1998 before he could be formally elected because it was revealed that he had cheated in his marriage. He formally resigned his seat on 1 March 1999.

Sources: Jenkins, Jeffery A., and Charles Stewart III, "Speakership Elections since 1860: The Rise of the Organizational Caucus," Paper presented at the Seventh Annual Meeting of the Congress and History Conference, George Washington University, Washington, D.C., 2008, 70-72, as well as information provided by numerous other sources.

Appendix C

The Presidents of the Continental Congress

Although the Continental Congress, the precursor of the modern US Congress, did not have a Speaker who deliberated and moderated debate, some historians consider the office of the President of the Continental Congress to be a "speakership" that controlled its activities. Below are the dates of service of those of served as presidents of the Continental Congress from its inception in 1774 until 1778 when it was abolished, making way for the First Federal Congress.

September 5, 1774 - October 22, 1774	Peyton Randolph	Virginia
October 22, 1774 - October 26, 1774	Henry Middleton	South Carolina
May 10, 1775 - May 19, 1775	Peyton Randolph	Virginia
May 19, 1775 - October 31, 1777	John Hancock	Massachusetts
November 1, 1777 - December 9, 1778	Henry Laurens	South Carolina
December 10, 1778 - September 28, 1779	John Jay	New York
September 28, 1779 - July 10, 1781	Samuel Huntington	Connecticut
July 10, 1781 - October 23, 1781	Thomas McKean	Delaware
November 3, 1781 - November 2, 1782	John Hanson	Maryland
November 4, 1782 - November 1, 1783	Elias Boudinot	New Jersey
November 3, 1783 - June 3, 1784	Thomas Mifflin	Pennsylvania
November 30, 1784 - November 4, 1785	Richard Henry Lee	Virginia
November 23, 1785 - June 6, 1786	John Hancock	Massachusetts[1]
June 6, 1786 - November 3, 1786	Nathaniel Gorham	Massachusetts
February 2, 1786 - October 30, 1787	Arthur St. Clair	Pennsylvania
January 22, 1787 - November 1, 1788	Cyrus Griffin	Virginia

Footnote:
[1] Hancock was ill when elected, and never served during this period of tenure.

Appendix D

Gains or Losses by the President's Party in Midterm Elections, 1862-2008

The following table shows the results of the President's party during mid-term elections. A main goal of political parties, since the first Congress in 1789, has been to gain control of a majority of seats in the House — the key to electing a Speaker.

Year	President	Party Holding the Presidency	Gains/Losses in the House by the President's Party	Gains/Losses in the Senate by the President's Party
1862	Lincoln	Republican	-3	+8
1866	Johnson	Republican[1]	-2	0
1870	Grant	Republican	-31	-4
1874	Grant	Republican	-96	-8
1878	Hayes	Republican	-9	-6
1882	Arthur	Republican	-33	+3
1886	Cleveland	Democrat	-12	+3
1890	Harrison	Republican	-85	0
1894	Cleveland	Democrat	-116	-5
1898	McKinley	Republican	-21	+7
1902	Roosevelt	Republican	+9[2]	+2
1906	Roosevelt	Republican	-28	+3
1910	Taft	Republican	-57	-10
1914	Wilson	Democrat	-59	+5
1918	Wilson	Democrat	-19	-6
1922	Harding	Republican	-75	-8
1926	Coolidge	Republican	-10	-6
1930	Hoover	Republican	-49	-8
1934	Roosevelt	Democrat	+9	+10
1938	Roosevelt	Democrat	-71	-6
1942	Roosevelt	Democrat	-55	-9
1946	Truman	Democrat	-55	-12
1950	Truman	Democrat	-29	-6
1954	Eisenhower	Republican	-18	-1
1958	Eisenhower	Republican	-48	-13
1962	Kennedy	Democrat	-4	+3
1966	Johnson	Democrat	-47	-4
1970	Nixon	Republican	-12	+2
1974	Ford	Republican	-48	-5
1978	Carter	Democrat	-15	-3
1982	Reagan	Republican	-26	+1
1986	Reagan	Republican	-5	-8
1990	Bush	Republican	-8	+1
1994	Clinton	Democrat	-54	-3
1998	Clinton	Democrat	+5	0
2002	Bush	Republican	+8	+1
2006	Bush	Republican	-30	-6

Footnotes:

[1] Andrew Johnson is listed here as a Republican, although he had been a "War Democrat" when Governor of Tennessee, and was selected as Lincoln's running mate in 1864 to create not a Republican ticket but a "Union" ticket. For reasons of technicality only, 1866 is given as having the Republicans control the White House.

[2] Although the GOP gained nine seats in the 1902 election, in fact they lost seats overall; the 1900 census expanded the House from the 357 representatives, 4 delegates, and 1 Resident Commissioner who sat in the Fifty-seventh Congress (1901-03) t0 386 representatives, 4 delegates, and 1 Resident Commissioner who sat in the Fifty-eighth Congress (1903-05). Thus, the Republicans' 200-151 advantage (with 5 Populists and 1 Silver Republican) in the Fifty-seventh Congress was "reduced" to a 207-176 (with three Independent Republicans) in the Fifty-eighth Congress.

Sources: Stanley, Harold W., and Richard G. Niemi, "Vital Statistics on American Politics" (Washington, D.C.: CQ Press, 1992), 203; as well as additional information from newspaper and other sources.

Appendix E

Speakers by State, with Date of Election

The following denotes the Speaker and the Session in which he or she served. It also gives the state that they represented, as well as the exact date of their election to the Speaker's chair during that particular Congress.

Congress	Speaker	State Represented	Date Elected
1st	Frederick A.C. Muhlenberg	Pennsylvania	1 April 1789
2nd	Jonathan Trumbull	Connecticut	24 October 1791
3rd	Frederick A.C. Muhlenberg	Pennsylvania	2 December 1793
4th	Jonathan Dayton	New Jersey	7 December 1795[1]
5th	Jonathan Dayton	New Jersey	15 May 1797
6th	Theodore Sedgwick	Massachusetts	2 December 1799
7th	Nathaniel Macon	North Carolina	7 December 1801
8th	Nathaniel Macon	North Carolina	17 October 1803
9th	Nathaniel Macon	North Carolina	2 December 1805
10th	Joseph B. Varnum	Massachusetts	26 October 1807
11th	Joseph B. Varnum	Massachusetts	22 May 1809
12th	Henry Clay	Kentucky	4 November 1811[2]
13th	Henry Clay	Kentucky	24 May 1813
13th	Langdon Cheves	South Carolina	19 January 1814
14th	Henry Clay	Kentucky	4 December 1815[3]
15th	Henry Clay	Kentucky	1 December 1817
16th	Henry Clay	Kentucky	6 December 1819
16th	John W. Taylor	New York	15 November 1820
17th	Philip P. Barbour	Virginia	4 December 1821
18th	Henry Clay	Kentucky	1 December 1823
19th	John W. Taylor	New York	5 December 1825
20th	Andrew Stevenson	Virginia	3 December 1827
21st	Andrew Stevenson	Virginia	7 December 1829
22nd	Andrew Stevenson	Virginia	5 December 1831
23rd	Andrew Stevenson	Virginia	2 December 1833
23rd	John Bell	Tennessee	2 June 1834
24th	James K. Polk	Tennessee	7 December 1835
25th	James K. Polk	Tennessee	4 September 1837
26th	Robert M.T. Hunter	Virginia	16 December 1839
27th	John White	Kentucky	31 May 1841
28th	John W. Jones	Virginia	4 December 1843
29th	John W. Davis	Indiana	1 December 1845
30th	Robert C. Winthrop	Massachusetts	6 December 1847
31st	Howell Cobb	Georgia	22 December 1849
32nd	Linn Boyd	Kentucky	1 December 1851
33rd	Linn Boyd	Kentucky	5 December 1853
34th	Nathaniel P. Banks	Massachusetts	2 February 1856
35th	James L. Orr	South Carolina	7 December 1857
36th	William Pennington	New Jersey	1 February 1860
37th	Galusha A. Grow	Pennsylvania	4 July 1861

Congress	Speaker	State Represented	Date Elected
38th	Schuyler Colfax	Indiana	7 December 1863
39th	Schuyler Colfax	Indiana	4 December 1865
40th	Schuyler Colfax	Indiana	4 March 1867
40th	Theodore M. Pomeroy	New York	3 March 1869[4]
41st	James G. Blaine	Maine	4 March 1869
42nd	James G. Blaine	Maine	4 March 1871
43rd	James G. Blaine	Maine	1 December 1873
44th	Michael C. Kerr	Indiana	6 December 1875[5]
44th	Samuel J. Randall	Pennsylvania	4 December 1876
45th	Samuel J. Randall	Pennsylvania	15 October 1877
46th	Samuel J. Randall	Pennsylvania	18 March 1879
47th	J. Warren Keifer	Ohio	5 December 1881
48th	John G. Carlisle	Kentucky	3 December 1883
49th	John G. Carlisle	Kentucky	7 December 1885
50th	John G. Carlisle	Kentucky	5 December 1887
51st	Thomas B. Reed	Maine	2 December 1889
52nd	Charles F. Crisp	Georgia	8 December 1891
53rd	Charles F. Crisp	Georgia	7 August 1893
54th	Thomas B. Reed	Maine	2 December 1895
55th	Thomas B. Reed	Maine	15 March 1897
56th	David B. Henderson	Iowa	4 December 1899
57th	David B. Henderson	Iowa	2 December 1901
58th	Joseph G. Cannon	Illinois	9 November 1903
59th	Joseph G. Cannon	Illinois	4 December 1905
60th	Joseph G. Cannon	Illinois	2 December 1907
61st	Joseph G. Cannon	Illinois	15 March 1909
62nd	Champ Clark	Missouri	4 April 1911
63rd	Champ Clark	Missouri	7 April 1913
64th	Champ Clark	Missouri	6 December 1915
65th	Champ Clark	Missouri	2 April 1917
66th	Frederick H. Gillett	Massachusetts	19 May 1919
67th	Frederick H. Gillett	Massachusetts	11 April 1921
68th	Frederick H. Gillett	Massachusetts	3 December 1923
69th	Nicholas Longworth	Ohio	7 December 1925
70th	Nicholas Longworth	Ohio	5 December 1927
71st	Nicholas Longworth	Ohio	15 April 1929
72nd	John N. Garner	Texas	7 December 1931
73rd	Henry T. Rainey	Illinois	9 March 1933[6]
74th	Joseph W. Byrns	Tennessee	3 January 1935[7]
74th	William B. Bankhead	Alabama	4 June 1936[8]
75th	William B. Bankhead	Alabama	5 January 1937
76th	William B. Bankhead	Alabama	3 January 1939
76th	Sam T. Rayburn	Texas	16 September 1940
77th	Sam T. Rayburn	Texas	3 January 1941
78th	Sam T. Rayburn	Texas	6 January 1943
79th	Sam T. Rayburn	Texas	3 January 1945
80th	Joseph W. Martin	Massachusetts	3 January 1947
81st	Sam T. Rayburn	Texas	3 January 1949

Congress	Speaker	State Represented	Date Elected
82nd	Sam T. Rayburn	Texas	3 January 1951
83rd	Joseph W. Martin	Massachusetts	3 January 1953
84th	Sam T. Rayburn	Texas	3 January 1955
85th	Sam T. Rayburn	Texas	3 January 1957
86th	Sam T. Rayburn	Texas	7 January 1959
87th	Sam T. Rayburn	Texas	3 January 1961[9]
88th	John W. McCormack	Massachusetts	9 January 1962
89th	John W. McCormack	Massachusetts	4 January 1965
90th	John W. McCormack	Massachusetts	10 January 1967
91st	John W. McCormack	Massachusetts	3 January 1969
92nd	Carl Albert	Oklahoma	21 January 1971
93rd	Carl Albert	Oklahoma	3 January 1973
94th	Carl Albert	Oklahoma	14 January 1975
95th	Thomas P. O'Neill, Jr.	Massachusetts	4 January 1977
96th	Thomas P. O'Neill, Jr.	Massachusetts	15 January 1979
97th	Thomas P. O'Neill, Jr.	Massachusetts	5 January 1981
98th	Thomas P. O'Neill, Jr.	Massachusetts	3 January 1983
99th	Thomas P. O'Neill, Jr.	Massachusetts	3 January 1985
100th	James C. Wright, Jr.	Texas	6 January 1987
101st	James C. Wright, Jr.	Texas	3 January 1989[10]
101st	Thomas S. Foley	Washington State	6 June 1989
102nd	Thomas S. Foley	Washington State	3 January 1991
103rd	Thomas S. Foley	Washington State	5 January 1993
104th	Newt Gingrich	Georgia	4 January 1995
105th	Newt Gingrich	Georgia	7 January 1997
106th	John Dennis Hastert	Illinois	6 January 1999
107th	John Dennis Hastert	Illinois	3 January 2001
108th	John Dennis Hastert	Illinois	7 January 2003
109th	John Dennis Hastert	Illinois	4 January 2005
110th	Nancy Pelosi	California	4 January 2007
111th	Nancy Pelosi	California	6 January 2009

Footnotes:
[1] Resigned from the House of Representatives, 19 January 1814.
[2] Resigned on 28 October 1820.
[3] Resigned from the House of Representatives, 6 March 1825.
[4] Elected Speaker on 3 March 1869, and served one just day.
[5] Died in office, 19 August 1876.
[6] Died in office, 19 August 1934.
[7] Died in office, 4 June 1936.
[8] Died in office, 15 September 1940.
[9] Died, 16 November 1961.
[10] Resigned from the House of Representatives, 6 June 1989.

Source: Biographical Directory of the U.S. Congress, Congressional Research Service.

Appendix F

Majority & Minority Leaders (1899 to the Present)

The following is a list of party leaders in each specific Congress. These leaders usually have been elected Speaker when their party recaptured control of the House.

Congress	Years	Majority Leader	Minority Leader
56th	1899-1901	Sereno E. Payne (R-NY)	James D. Richardson (D-TN)
57th	1901-03	Sereno E. Payne (R-NY)	James D. Richardson (D-TN)
58th	1903-05	Sereno E. Payne (R-NY)	John Sharp Williams (D-MS)
59th	1905-07	Sereno E. Payne (R-NY)	John Sharp Williams (D-MS)
60th	1907-09[1]	Sereno E. Payne (R-NY)	John Sharp Williams (D-MS)
60th	1907-09[2]	Sereno E. Payne (R-NY)	James Beauchamp Clark (D-MO)
61st	1909-11	Sereno E. Payne (R-NY)	James Beauchamp Clark (D-MO)
62nd	1911-13	Oscar W. Underwood (D-AL)	James R. Mann (R-IL)
63rd	1913-15	Oscar W. Underwood (D-AL)	James R. Mann (R-IL)
64th	1915-17	Claude Kitchin (D-NC)	James R. Mann (R-IL)
65th	1917-19	Claude Kitchin (D-NC)	James R. Mann (R-IL)
66th	1918-21	Frank W. Mondell (R-WY)	James Beauchamp Clark (D-MO)
67th	1921-23	Frank W. Mondell (R-WY)	Claude Kitchin (D-NC)
68th	1923-25	Nicholas Longworth (R-OH)	Finis J. Garrett (D-TN)
69th	1925-27	John Q. Tilson (R-CT)	Finis J. Garrett (D-TN)
70th	1927-29	John Q. Tilson (R-CT)	Finis J. Garrett (D-TN)
71st	1929-31	John Q. Tilson (R-CT)	John N. Garner (D-TX)
72nd	1931-33	Henry T. Rainey (D-IL)	Bertrand H. Snell (R-NY)
73rd	1933-35	Joseph W. Byrns (D-TN)[3]	Bertrand H. Snell (R-NY)
74th	1935-37	William B. Bankhead (D-AL)[4]	Bertrand H. Snell (R-NY)
75th	1937-39	Sam Rayburn (D-TX)	Bertrand H. Snell (R-NY)
76th	1939-41	Sam Rayburn (D-TX)[5]	Joseph W. Martin, Jr. (R-MA)
76th	1939-41	John W. McCormack (D-MA)[6]	Joseph W. Martin, Jr. (R-MA)
77th	1941-43	John W. McCormack (D-MA)	Joseph W. Martin, Jr. (R-MA)
78th	1943-45	John W. McCormack (D-MA)	Joseph W. Martin, Jr. (R-MA)
79th	1945-47	John W. McCormack (D-MA)	Joseph W. Martin, Jr. (R-MA)
80th	1947-49	Charles A. Halleck (R-IN)	Sam Rayburn (D-TX)
81st	1949-51	John W. McCormack (D-MA)	Joseph W. Martin, Jr. (R-MA)
82nd	1951-53	John W. McCormack (D-MA)	Joseph W. Martin, Jr. (R-MA)
83rd	1953-55	Charles A. Halleck (R-IN)	Sam Rayburn (D-TX)
84th	1955-57	John W. McCormack (D-MA)	Joseph W. Martin, Jr. (R-MA)
85th	1957-59	John W. McCormack (D-MA)	Joseph W. Martin, Jr. (R-MA)
86th	1959-61	John W. McCormack (D-MA)	Charles A. Halleck (R-IN)
87th	1961-63	John W. McCormack (D-MA)[7]	Charles A. Halleck (R-IN)
87th	1961-63	Carl B. Albert (D-OK)[8]	Charles A. Halleck (R-IN)
88th	1963-65	Carl B. Albert (D-OK)	Charles A. Halleck (R-IN)
89th	1965-67	Carl B. Albert (D-OK)	Gerald R. Ford (R-MI)
90th	1967-69	Carl B. Albert (D-OK)	Gerald R. Ford (R-MI)
91st	1969-71	Carl B. Albert (D-OK)	Gerald R. Ford (R-MI)
92nd	1971-73	Hale Boggs (D-LA)[9]	Gerald R. Ford (R-MI)

Congress	Years	Majority Leader	Minority Leader
93rd	1973-75	Thomas P. O'Neill Jr. (D-MA)	Gerald R. Ford (R-MI)[10]
93rd	1973-75	Thomas P. O'Neill Jr. (D-MA)	John J. Rhodes (R-AZ)
94th	1975-77	Thomas P. O'Neill Jr. (D-MA)	John J. Rhodes (R-AZ)
95th	1977-79	James C. Wright, Jr. (D-TX)	John J. Rhodes (R-AZ)
96th	1979-81	James C. Wright, Jr. (D-TX)	John J. Rhodes (R-AZ)
97th	1981-83	James C. Wright, Jr. (D-TX)	Robert H. Michel (R-IL)
98th	1983-85	James C. Wright, Jr. (D-TX)	Robert H. Michel (R-IL)
99th	1985-87	James C. Wright, Jr. (D-TX)	Robert H. Michel (R-IL)
100th	1987-89	Thomas S. Foley (D-WA)	Robert H. Michel (R-IL)
101st	1989-91	Thomas S. Foley (D-WA)[11]	Robert H. Michel (R-IL)
101st	1989-91	Richard A. Gephardt (D-MO)[12]	Robert H. Michel (R-IL)
102nd	1991-93	Richard A. Gephardt (D-MO)	Robert H. Michel (R-IL)
103rd	1993-95	Richard A. Gephardt (D-MO)	Robert H. Michel (R-IL)
104th	1995-97	Richard K. Armey (R-TX)	Richard A. Gephardt (D-MO)
105th	1997-99	Richard K. Armey (R-TX)	Richard A. Gephardt (D-MO)
106th	1999-2001	Richard K. Armey (R-TX)	Richard A. Gephardt (D-MO)
107th	2001-03	Richard K. Armey (R-TX)	Richard A. Gephardt (D-MO)
108th	2003-05	Tom DeLay (R-TX)	Nancy Pelosi (D-CA)
109th	2005-07	Tom DeLay (R-TX)[13]	Nancy Pelosi (D-CA)
109th	2005-07	Roy Blunt (R-MO)[14]	Nancy Pelosi (D-CA)
109th	2005-07	John Boehner (R-OH)[15]	Nancy Pelosi (D-CA)
110th	2007-09	Steny Hoyer (D-MD)	John Boehner (R-OH)
111th	2009-11	Steny Hoyer (D-MD)	John Boehner (R-OH)

Footnotes:

[1] John Sharp Williams served for only the first session of the Sixtieth Congress.

[2] James Beauchamp "Champ" Clark served for only the second session of the Sixtieth Congress.

[3] Elected Speaker; died in office, 4 June 1936.

[4] Elected Speaker; died in office, 15 September 1940.

[5] Elected Speaker on 16 September 1940, following the death of Speaker William Bankhead.

[6] Elected Majority Leader on 26 September 1940, after that office was vacated by Sam Rayburn, who was elected Speaker. Rep. Lindsay Warren, Democrat of North Carolina, served as Acting Majority Leader from 19 to 26 September 1940 until McCormack's election.

[7] Elected Speaker on 10 January 1962, at the start of the second session of the Eighty-second Congress, to fill the vacancy caused by the 16 November 1961 death of Speaker Sam Rayburn.

[8] Elected Majority Leader on 10 January 1962, to fill the vacancy caused by the election of Majority Leader John McCormack to the Speakership.

[9] Disappeared while flying from Anchorage, to Juneau, Alaska, on 16 October 1972. His body was never found, and he was later officially ruled as deceased.

[10] Resigned from the House, 6 December 1973, after he was confirmed by the US Senate to become the Vice President of the United States, filling the vacancy caused by the resignation of Vice President Spiro T. Agnew.

[11] Elected Speaker on 6 June 1989, following the resignation that same day of Speaker James C. Wright.

[12] Elected Majority leader on 14 June 1989, to fill he vacancy caused by the election of Majority Leader Thomas S. Foley to the speakership on 6 June 1989.

[13] On 28 September 2005, after he was indicted by a Texas grand jury for conspiracy in a campaign finance corruption case, DeLay stepped down as Majority Leader. DeLay later resigned his seat in Congress on 9 June 2006. Charges were eventually thrown out, and he was never tried.

[14] Elected as Interim Majority Leader when Rep. DeLay stepped down on 28 September 2005.

[15] Elected as permanent Majority Leader by the Republican Conference on 2 February 2006.

Appendix G

Party Distribution in Congress, 1789-2009

The following shows the party distribution of the House of Representatives from the First Congress (1789-91) to the One Hundred Eleventh Congress (2009-11). A key for the parties is at the end of the listing.

Congress	Years	Party Distribution
1st	1789-91	37 Pro-Administration, 28 Anti-Administration
2nd	1791-93	39 Pro-Administration, 30 Anti-Administration
3rd	1793-95	53 Anti-Administration, 51 Pro-Administration
4th	1795-97	59 JfR, 47 Fed
5th	1797-99	57 Fed, 49 JfR
6th	1799-1801	60 Fed, 46 JfR
7th	1801-03	68 JfR, 38 Fed
8th	1803-05	103 JfR, 39 Fed
9th	1805-07	114 JfR, 28 Fed
10th	1807-09	116 JfR, 26 Fed
11th	1809-11	92 JfR, 50 Fed
12th	1811-13	107 JfR, 36 Fed
13th	1813-15	114 JfR, 68 Fed
14th	1815-17	119 JfR, 64 Fed
15th	1817-19	146 JfR, 39 Fed
16th	1819-21	160 JfR, 26 Fed
17th	1821-23	155 JfR, 32 Fed
18th	1823-25	72 ACR, 64 JkR, 53 CR, 15 ACF, 7 JkF, 2 CF
19th	1825-27	109 Pro-Adams, 104 Pro-Jackson
20th	1827-29	113 Pro-Jackson, 100 Pro-Adams
21st	1829-31	136 Pro-Jackson, 82 Anti-Jackson, 5 AM
22nd	1831-33	136 Pro-Jackson, 66 Anti-Jackson, 17 AM, 4 Null
23rd	1833-35	143 Pro-Jackson, 63 Anti-Jackson, 25 AM, 9 Null
24th	1835-37	143 Pro-Jackson, 75 Anti-Jackson, 16 AM, 8 Null
25th	1837-39	128 D, 100 W, 7 AM, 6 Null, 1 I
26th	1839-41	125 D, 109 W, 6 AM, 2 Con
27th	1841-43	142 W, 98 D, 1 I, 1 ID
28th	1843-45	147 D, 72 W, 2 L&O, 1 ID, 1 IW
29th	1845-47	142 D, 79 W, 6 Amer
30th	1847-49	116 W, 110 D, 2 ID, 1 Amer, 1 I
31st	1849-51	113 D, 108 W, 9 FS, 1 Amer, 1 I
32nd	1851-53	127 D, 85 W, 10 U, 4 FS, 3 ID, 3 S-R, 1 IW
33rd	1853-55	157 D, 71 W, 4 FS, 1 I, 1 ID
34th	1855-57	100 O, 85 D, 51 Amer
35th	1857-59	132 D, 90 R, 14 Amer, 1 ID
36th	1859-61	116 R, 83 D, 19 O, 8 ALD, 7 ID, 5 Amer
37th	1861-63	108 R, 44 D, 26 UN, 2 CU, 2 U, 1 ID
38th	1863-65	86 R, 72 D, 16 CU, 9 UN, 2 IR
39th	1865-67	136 R, 38 D, 13 CU, 5 UN, 1 IR
40th	1867-69	173 R, 47 D, 4 I
41st	1869-71	171 R, 67 D, 5 I
42nd	1871-73	136 R, 104 D, 2 LR, 1 IR

Congress	Years	Party Distribution
43rd	1873-75	199 R, 88 D, 4 LR, 1 ID
44th	1875-77	182 D, 103 R, 4 IR, 1 ID, 1 IR
45th	1877-79	155 D, 136 R, 2 ID
46th	1879-81	141 D, 132 R, 13 Nat, 7 ID
47th	1881-83	151 R, 128 D, 10 Nat, 2 RD, 1 I, 1 ID
48th	1883-85	196 D, 117 R, 4 Radj, 3 ID, 2 Nat, 1 IR, 2 I
49th	1885-87	182 D, 141 R, 1 ID, 1 Nat
50th	1887-89	167 D, 152 R, 2 IR, 1 Lab, 1 I, 1 Nat
51st	1889-91	179 R, 152 D, 1 Lab
52nd	1891-93	238 D, 86 R, 8 Pop
53rd	1893-95	218 D, 124 R, 11 Pop, 2 ID, 1 Silv
54th	1895-97	254 R, 93 D, 9 Pop, 1 Silv
55th	1897-99	206 R, 124 D, 22 Pop, 3 SR, 1 IR, 1 Silv
56th	1899-1901	187 R, 161 D, 5 Pop, 2 SR, 1 IP, 1 Silv
57th	1901-03	200 R, 151 D, 5 Pop, 1 SR
58th	1903-05	207 R, 176 D, 3 IR
59th	1905-07	251 R, 135 D
60th	1907-09	223 R, 167 D, 1 IR
61st	1909-11	219 R, 172 D
62nd	1911-13	230 D, 162 R, 1 ProgR, 1 Soc
63rd	1913-15	291 D, 134 R, 9 Prog, 1 I
64th	1915-17	230 D, 196 R, 6 Prog, 1 I, 1 Proh, 1 Soc
65th	1917-19	215 R, 214 D, 3 Prog, 1 IR, 1 Proh, 1 Soc
66th	1919-21	240 R, 192 D, 1 Proh, 1 UL
67th	1921-23	302 R, 131 D, 1 IR, 1 Soc
68th	1923-25	225 R, 207 D, 2 F-L, 1 Soc
69th	1925-27	247 R, 183 D, 3 F-L, 1 A-L, 1 Soc
70th	1927-29	238 R, 194 D, 2 F-L, 1 Soc
71st	1929-31	270 R, 164 D, 1 F-L
72nd	1931-33	218 R, 216 D, 1 F-L
73rd	1933-35	313 D, 117, 5 F-L
74th	1935-37	322 D, 103 R, 7 Prog, 3 F-L
75th	1937-39	334 D, 88 R, 8 Prog, 5 F-L
76th	1939-41	262 D, 169 R, 2 Prog, 1 A-L, 1 F-L
77th	1941-43	267 D, 162 R, 3 Prog, 1 A-L, 1 F-L, 1 ID
78th	1943-45	222 D, 209 R, 2 Prog, 1 A-L, 1 F-L
79th	1945-47	242 D, 191 R, 1 A-L, 1 Prog
80th	1947-49	246 R, 188 D, 1 A-L
81st	1949-51	263 D, 171 R, 1 A-L
82nd	1951-53	235 D, 199 R, 1 I
83rd	1953-55	221 R, 213 D
84th	1955-57	232 D, 203 R
85th	1957-59	234 D, 201 R
86th	1959-61	283 D, 153 R
87th	1961-63	263 D, 174 R
88th	1963-65	259 D, 176 R
89th	1965-67	295 D, 140 R
90th	1967-69	247 D, 187 R
91st	1969-71	243 D, 192 R
92nd	1971-73	255 D, 180 R

Congress	Years	Party Distribution
93rd	1973-75	242 D, 192 R, 1 ID
94th	1975-77	291 D, 144 R
95th	1977-79	292 D, 143 R
96th	1979-81	277 D, 158 R
97th	1981-83	242 D, 192 R, 1 I
98th	1983-85	269 D, 166 R
99th	1985-87	253 D, 182 R
100th	1987-89	258 D, 177 R
101st	1989-91	260 D, 175 R
102nd	1991-93	267 D, 167 R, 1 I
103rd	1993-95	258 D, 176 R, 1 I
104th	1995-97	230 R, 204 D, 1 I
105th	1997-99	228 R, 206 D, 1 I
106th	1999-2001	223 R, 211 D, 1 I
107th	2001-03	221 R, 212 D, 2 I
108th	2003-05	229 R, 204 D, 1 I
109th	2005-06	232 R, 202 D, 1 I
110th	2007-09	236 D, 199 R
111th	2009-11	257 D, 178 R

Note: the number of seats changed due to the addition of new districts caused by the censuses that had been conducted in 1800, 1810, etc. For example, in the 7th Congress (1801-03), which still reflected the 1790 census, there were 107 Representatives and 2 Delegates. In the 8th Congress (1803-05), however, the number of seats increased to 142, with only 1 Delegate.

Party Key:
ACF: Adams/Clay Federalist
ACR: Adams/Clay Republican
A-L: American-Labor
ALD: Anti-Lecompton Democrat
AM: Anti-Masonic
Amer: American
CF: Crawford Federalist
CR: Crawford Republican
CU: Constitutional Unionist
D: Democrat
Fed: Federalist
F-L: Farmer-Labor
FS: Free Soiler
I: Independent (not caucusing with any party)
ID: Independent Democrat
IP: Independent Populist
IR: Independent Republican
IW: Independent Whig
JkF: Jacksonian-Federalist
JfR: Jeffersonian-Republican
JkR: Jacksonian-Republican
L&O: Law and Order
Lab: Laborite
LR: Liberal Republican
Nat: Nationalist
Null: Nullifiers
O: Opposition [to the President]
Pop: Populist
Prog: Progressive
ProgR: Progressive Republican
Proh: Prohibition
R: Republican
Radj: Readjuster
RD: Readjuster Democrat
Silv: Silverite
Soc: Socialist
SR: Silver Republican
S-R: States' Rights
U: Union/Unionist
UL: Union Labor
W: Whig

Photo and Illustration Credits

1. Carl Albert - Collection of the U.S. House of Representatives
2. William Bankhead - Collection of the U.S. House of Representatives
3. Nathaniel P. Banks - Courtesy of the Library of Congress, LC-USZ62-11942
4. Philip P. Barbour - Architect of the Capital
5. John Bell - Courtesy of the Library of Congress, LC-USZ62-58464
6. James G. Blaine - Courtesy of the Library of Congress, LC-DIG-pga-02168
7. Thomas Bocock - Reprinted with permission from The Library of Virginia
8. Linn Boyd - Collection of the U.S. House of Representatives
9. Joseph Byrns - Architect of the Capital
10. Joseph G. Cannon - Courtesy of the Library of Congress, LC-USZ62-132251
11. John G. Carlisle - Courtesy of the Library of Congress, LC-DIG-cwpbh-04037
12. Langdon Cheves - Architect of the Capital
13. James Beauchamp Clark - Architect of the Capital
14. Henry Clay - Courtesy of the Library of Congress, LC-USZ62-71348
15. Howell Cobb - Courtesy of the Library of Congress, LC-USZ62-110081
16. Schuyler Colfax - Courtesy of the Library of Congress, LC-DIG-cwpbh-01935
17. Charles F. Crisp - Collection of the U.S. House of Representatives
18. John W. Davis - Architect of the Capital
19. Jonathan Dayton - Courtesy of the Library of Congress, LC-USZ62-20465
20. Thomas Foley - Collection of the U.S. House of Representatives
21. John Nance Garner - Collection of the U.S. House of Representatives
22. Frederick Gillett - Collection of the U.S. House of Representatives
23. Newt Gingrich - Collection of the U.S. House of Representatives
24. Galusha A. Grow - Courtesy of the Library of Congress, LC-DIG-cwpbh-04054
25. Dennis Hastert - Image Courtesy of the Office of the Clerk
26. David B. Henderson - Architect of the Capital
27. Robert M.T. Hunter - Architect of the Capital
28. John W. Jones - Architect of the Capital
29. J. Warren Keifer - Courtesy of the Library of Congress, LC-DIG-npcc-03896
30. Michael C. Kerr - Courtesy of the Library of Congress, LC-DIG-cwpbh-04462
31. Robert Livingston - Collection of the U.S. House of Representatives
32. Nicholas Longworth - Courtesy of the Library of Congress, LC-USZ62-1824
33. Nathaniel Macon - Architect of the Capital
34. Joseph Martin - Collection of the U.S. House of Representatives
35. John W. McCormack - Collection of the U.S. House of Representatives
36. Frederick Muhlenberg - Architect of the Capital
37. Thomas P. O'Neill Jr. - Collection of the U.S. House of Representatives
38. James L. Orr - Courtesy of the Library of Congress, LC-DIG-cwpbh-02854
39. Nancy Pelosi - U.S. House of Representatives
40. William Pennington - Courtesy of the Library of Congress, LC-USZ62-107178
41. James K. Polk - Courtesy of the Library of Congress, LC-USZ62-24806
42. Theodore M. Pomeroy - Architect of the Capital
43. Henry T. Rainey - Collection of the U.S. House of Representatives
44. Samuel J. Randall - Courtesy of the Library of Congress, LC-DIG-cwpbh-00799
45. Sam Rayburn - Collection of the U.S. House of Representatives
46. Thomas B. Reed - Courtesy of the Library of Congress, LC-USZ62-89505
47. Theodore Sedgwick - Architect of the Capital
48. Andrew Stevenson - Collection of the U.S. House of Representatives
49. John W. Taylor - Architect of the Capital
50. Jonathan Trumbull - Architect of the Capital
51. Joseph Varnum - Architect of the Capital
52. John White - Architect of the Capital
53. Robert C. Winthrop - Collection of the U.S. House of Representatives
54. James C. Wright - Collection of the U.S. House of Representatives

Note: Credits are for image that appears on the first page of each Speaker biography. All other images in this edition are courtesy of Mark Grossman

Bibliography

Books

Adams, George Burton and H.M. Stevens, "Select Documents of English Constitutional History" (London: Macmillan, 1935).

Adams, Charles Francis, ed., "The Works of John Adams" (Boston: Little, Brown and Company; ten volumes, 1850-56).

Adams, John Quincy (Charles Francis Adams, ed.), "Memoirs of John Quincy Adams, Comprising Portions of His Diary from 1795 to 1848" (Philadelphia: J.B. Lippincott & Co.; twelve volumes, 1874-77).

Adams, Henry, "History of the United States of America During the Administrations of Thomas Jefferson and James Madison, 1801-1816" (New York: Charles Scribner's Sons; nine volumes, 1889-91).

Agricola [pseud.], "The Virginia Doctrines, Not Nullification" (Richmond, Virginia: Samuel Shepherd & Co., 1832).

Albert, Carl Bert, and Danney Goebel, "Little Giant: The Life and Times of Speaker Carl Albert" (Norman: University of Oklahoma Press, 1990).

Aldrich, John H., "Why Parties? The Origin and Transformation of Party Politics in America" (Chicago: The University of Chicago Press, 1995).

Alexander, De Alva Stanwood, "History and Procedure of the House of Representatives" (Boston: Houghton Mifflin Company, 1916).

Alexander, Holmes Moss, "The Famous Five" (New York: Bookmailer, 1958).

Ambler, Charles Henry, "Thomas Ritchie: A Study in Virginia Politics" (Richmond, Virginia: Bell Book & Stationary Co., 1913).

Anbinder, Tyler, "Nativism and Slavery: The Northern Know-Nothings & the Politics of the 1850s" (New York: Oxford University Press, 1992).

Anderson, Charles, "A Funeral Oration of Henry Clay" (Cincinnati: Ben Franklin Office Print, 1852).

Appleton, John (Wayne Cutler, ed.), "North for Union: John Appleton's Journal of a Tour to New England Made by President Polk in June and July 1847" (Nashville, Tennessee: Vanderbilt University Press, 1986).

Aspinal, Arthur, et al., "Parliament Through Seven Centuries" (London: The Hansard Society for Parliamentary Government, 1962).

Bancroft, Frederic, "The Life of William H. Seward" (New York: Harper & Brothers; two volumes, 1900).

_____. ed., "Speeches, Correspondence, and Political Papers of Carl Schurz" (New York: G.P. Putnam's Sons; six volumes, 1913).

Bates, Ernest Sutherland, "The Story of the Supreme Court" (New York: The Bobbs-Merrill Company, 1938).

Baxter, Maurice G., "Henry Clay and the American System" (Lexington: University Press of Kentucky, 1995).

_____. "Henry Clay: The Lawyer" (Lexington: University Press of Kentucky, 2000).

Beale, Howard K., ed., "The Diary of Edward Bates, 1859-1866" in "Annual Report of the American Historical Association for the Year 1930" (Washington, D.C.: Government Printing Office; four volumes, 1933), IV only.

Bell, Rudolph, "Party and Faction in American Politics: The House of Representatives, 1789-1801" (Westport, Connecticut: Greenwood Press, 1973).

Benton, Thomas Hart, "'Thirty Years' View; or, a History of the Working of the American Government for Thirty Years, from 1820 to 1850" (New York: D. Appleton and Company; two volumes, 1858).

Bergeron, Paul H., "The Presidency of James K. Polk" (Lawrence: University Press of Kansas, 1987).

Biggs, Jeffrey R., "Honor in the House: Speaker Tom Foley" (Pullman: Washington State University Press, 1999).

Binder, Sarah A., "Minority Rights, Majority Rule: Partisanship and the Development of Congress" (Cambridge: Cambridge University Press, 1997).

Binney, Charles James Fox, "The History and Genealogy of the Prentice, or Prentiss, Family, in New England, Etc., from 1631 to 1883" (Boston: Published by the Editor, 1883).

Blaine, James G., "Twenty Years of Congress: From Lincoln to Garfield" (Norwich, Connecticut: The Henry Bill Publishing Company; two volumes, 1884-86).

Boddie, John Bennett, "Southside Virginia Families" (Baltimore, Maryland: Genealogical Publishing Company; two volumes, 1966).

Bolles, Blair, "Tyrant From Illinois: Uncle Joe Cannon's Experiment With Personal Power" (New York: Norton, 1951).

Bolling, Richard, "Power in the House: A History of the Leadership of the House of Representatives" (New York: Capricorn Books, 1974).

Bond, Beverley W., Jr., ed., "The Correspondence of John Cleves Symmes, Founder of the Miami Purchase" (New York: The Macmillan Co., 1926).

Bowles, Samuel, "Across the Continent: A Summer's Journey to the Rocky Mountains, the Mormons, the Pacific

States, with Speaker Colfax" (Springfield, Massachusetts: Samuel Bowles & Company, 1865).

Bradlaugh, Charles, "The Rules, Customs, and Procedure of the House of Commons" (London: S. Sonnenschein & Co., 1889).

Brady, David W., "Critical Elections and Congressional Policy Making" (Stanford, California: Stanford University Press, 1988).

Brant, Irving, "James Madison" (Indianapolis: The Bobbs-Merrill Company; six volumes, 1941-61).

Brooks, Robert Preston, "Howell Cobb and the Crisis of 1850" (Athens, Georgia: no publisher, 1918).

Brown, Everett S., and Ruth C. Silva, ed., "The Missouri Compromises and Presidential Politics, 1820-1825" (St. Louis: St. Louis Historical Society, 1926).

Brown, Everit, and Albert Strauss, "A Dictionary of American Politics, etc." (New York: A.L. Burt, 1892).

Brown, George R., "The Leadership of Congress" (Indianapolis, Indiana: The Bobbs-Merrill Company, 1922).

Busbey, L. White, "Uncle Joe Cannon: The Story of a Pioneer American" (New York: Henry Holt, 1927).

Cannon, Clarence A., "Cannon's Precedents of the House of Representatives of the United States" (Washington, DC: U.S. Government Printing Office, 1936).

Carson, Hampton L., "The History of the Supreme Court of the United States" (Philadelphia: P.W. Ziegler and Company; two volumes, 1902).

Catterall, Ralph C.H., "The Second Bank of the United States" (Chicago: The University of Chicago Press, 1903).

Cheves, Langdon, "Aristides; or, A Series of Papers on the Presidential Election" (Charleston, South Carolina: P. Freneau, 1808).

_____. "Letter of the Hon. Langdon Cheves, to the Charleston Mercury, on Southern Wrongs, Sept. 1844" (Charleston, South Carolina: no publisher, 1844).

_____. "Speech of Hon. Langdon Cheves, in the Southern Convention, at Nashville, Tennessee, November 14, 1850" ([Tennessee]: Southern Rights Association, 1850).

Chiu, Chang-Wei, "The Speaker of the House of Representatives Since 1896" (New York: Columbia University Press, 1928).

Chrimes, Stanley Baldwin, "English Constitutional Ideas in the Fifteenth Century" (Cambridge: Cambridge University Press, 1936).

Clark, Champ, "My Quarter Century of American Politics" (New York: Harper and Brothers; two volumes, 1920).

Clay, Thomas Hart, "Henry Clay" (Philadelphia: G.W. Jacobs Co., 1910).

Clift, G. Glenn, "Governors of Kentucky, 1792-1942" (Cynthiana, Kentucky: The Hobson Press, 1942).

Cobbett, William (Thomas Curson Hansard, ed.), "Cobbett's Parliamentary History of England" (London: Printed by T. Curson Hansard, Peterborough-Court, Fleet-Street; thirty-six volumes, 1806-20).

Cole, Donald B., "The President of Andrew Jackson" (Lawrence: University Press of Kansas, 1993).

Colton, Calvin, "The Last Seven Years of the Life of Henry Clay" (New York: A.S. Barnes Co., 1856).

_____. ed. "The Private Correspondence of Henry Clay" (New York: A.S. Barnes & Co., 1855).

_____. ed., "The Works of Henry Clay" (New York: A.S. Barnes & Co.; six volumes, 1855-57).

_____. ed., "The Speeches of Henry Clay" (New York: A.S. Barnes Co.; two volumes, 1857).

_____. ed., "The Works of Henry Clay, Comprising His Life, Correspondence, and Speeches" (New York: G.P. Putnam's Sons; ten volumes, 1904).

Congdon, Charles T., "Reminiscences of a Journalist" (Boston: James R. Osgood and Company, 1880).

Congressional Quarterly, "Congress A to Z: CQ's Ready Reference Encyclopedia" (Washington, D.C.: Congressional Quarterly Inc., 1988).

Cooper, Joseph, "The Origins of the Standing Committees and the Development of the Modern House" (Houston, Texas: Rice University Press, 1970)

Cooper, William Ross, "The Ancestral Family Lineage of James Knox Polk, President of the United States of America" (Hickman Mills, Missouri: no publisher, 1941).

Cox, Samuel S., "Union, Disunion, Reunion: Three Decades of Federal Legislation" (Providence, Rhode Island: J.A. & R.A. Reid, 1885).

Crandall, Andrew Wallace, "The Early History of the Republican Party" (Boston: R.G. Badger, 1930).

Cotten, Edward R., "Life of the Hon. Nathaniel Macon, of North Carolina, etc." (Baltimore: Printed by Lucas & Deaver, 1840).

Cunningham, Noble E., Jr., "The Jeffersonian Republicans: The Formation of Party Organization, 1789-1801" (Chapel Hill: University of North Carolina Press, 1957).

_____. "The Jefferson-Republicans in Power, 1801-1809" (Chapel Hill: Institute of Early American Culture and History, University of North Carolina Press, 1963).

_____. "The Presidency of James Monroe" (Lawrence: University Press of Kansas, 1996).

_____. ed., "Circular Letters of Congressmen to Their Constituents, 1789-1829" (Chapel Hill, North Carolina: Published for the Institute of Early American History and Culture by the University of North Carolina Press; three volumes, 1978).

Currie, David P., "The Constitution in Congress: Descent into the Maelstrom, 1829-1861" (Chicago: University of Chicago Press, 2005).

Curtis, James C., "The Fox at Bay: Martin Van Buren and the Presidency" (Lexington, Kentucky: University of Kentucky Press, 1970).

Cushing, Luther Stearns, "Lex Parliamentaria Americana. Elements of the Law and Practice of Legislative Assemblies in the United States of America" (Boston: Little, Brown and Company, 1856).

Dallas, George Mifflin, "The Life and Public Services of James Knox Polk. With a Compendium of His Speeches on Various Public Measures. Also, a Sketch of the Life of the Hon. George Mifflin Dallas" (Baltimore: Published by Nathaniel Hickman, 1844).

Dasent, Arthur Irwin, "The Speakers of the House of Commons, from the Earliest Times to the Present Day, etc." (New York: John Lane Company, 1911).

Davidson, Roger H., Susan Webb Hammond and Raymond W. Smock, eds., "Masters of the House: Congressional Leadership Over Two Centuries" (Boulder, Colorado: Westview Press, 1998).

Davies, Godfrey, "Bibliography of British History. Stuart Period, 1603-1714" (Oxford: At the Clarendon Press, 1928).

De Chambrun, Clara Longworth, "The Making of Nicholas Longworth: Annals of an American Family" (New York: Ray Long & Richard R. Smith, Inc., 1933).

Democratic National Committee, "The Public Record and Past History of John Bell and Edw'd Everett" (Washington, D.C.: Democratic National Committee, 1860).

Desmond, Humphrey J., "The Know Nothing Party" (Washington: The New Century Press, 1904).

Devens, Richard Miller [Frazar Kirkland, pseud.], "Cyclopædia of Commercial and Business Anecdotes, etc." (New York: D. Appleton & Company; two volumes, 1864-65).

D'Ewes, Sir Simonds, ed., "The Journals of All the Parliaments During the Reign of Queen Elizabeth" (London: Printed for John Starkey at the Mitre in Fleetstreet near Temple-Bar, 1682).

Dodd, Lawrence C., and Bruce I. Oppenheimer, eds., "Congress Reconsidered" (Washington, D.C.: CQ Press, 2001).

Dodd, William E., "The Life of Nathaniel Macon" (Raleigh, North Carolina: Edwards & Broughton, Printers and Binders, 1903).

Doenecke, Justus D., "The Presidencies of James A. Garfield and Chester A. Arthur" (Lawrence: University Press of Kansas, 1981).

Dorough, C. Dwight, "Mr. Sam" (New York: Random House, 1962).

Dubin, Michael J., "United States Congressional Elections, 1788-1997" (Jefferson, North Carolina: McFarland & Company, 1998).

Duisberre, William, "Slavemaster President: The Double Career of James Polk" (New York: Oxford University Press, 2003).

Eaton, Clement, "Henry Clay and the Art of American Politics" (Boston: Little, Brown, 1957).

Edwards, Weldon Nathaniel, "Memoir of Nathaniel Macon, of North Carolina" (Raleigh, North Carolina: Raleigh Register Steam Power Press, 1862).

Ellis, Richard E., "The Union at Risk: Jacksonian Democracy, States' Rights, and the Nullification Crisis" (New York: Oxford University Press, 1987).

Elsynge, Henry, "The Ancient Method and Manner of Holding Parliaments in England" (London: Printed for S[amuel] S[peed], and to be Sold by Tho[mas] Dring, over against the Inner Temple-gate in Fleet-street, 1675).

Ewing, Cortez A.M., "The Judges of the Supreme Court, 1789-1947" (Minneapolis: The University of Minnesota Press, 1938).

Farmer, John, "A Genealogical Register of the First Settlers of New-England, etc." (Lancaster, Massachusetts: Published by Carter, Andrews, & Co.: Sold by Hilliard, Gray, & Co. and Carter & Hendee, Boston, 1829).

Farrell, John J., ed., "James K. Polk, 1795-1849: Chronology, Documents, Bibliographical Aids" (Dobbs Ferry, New York: Oceana Publications, 1970).

Faulkner, Harold Underwood, "Politics, Reform and Expansion, 1890-1900" (New York: Harper & Brothers, 1959).

Fite, Emerson David, "The Presidential Campaign of 1860" (New York: The Macmillan Company, 1911).

Fitzpatrick, John C., ed., "The Diaries of George Washington, 1748-1799" (New York: Houghton Mifflin Company; four volumes, 1925).

Flinn, Frank M., "Campaigning with Banks in Louisiana, '63 and '64, and with Sheridan in the Shenandoah Valley in '64 and '65" (Lynn, Massachusetts: Thomas P. Nichols, 1887).

Follett, Mary Parker, "The Speaker of the House of Representatives" (New York: Longmans, Green, and Co., 1902).

Foote, Henry Stuart, "Eulogy Upon the Life and Character of James K. Polk" (Washington: T. Ritchie, Printer, 1849).

Ford, Paul Leicester, ed., "The Writings of Thomas Jefferson" (New York: G.P. Putnam's Sons; ten volumes, 1892-99).

Ford, Worthington C., ed., "The Writings of John Quincy Adams" (New York: The Macmillan Company; seven volumes, 1913-17).

Freehling, William W., "The Road to Disunion: Secessionists at Bay, 1776-1854" (New York: Oxford University Press, 1990).

Frothingham, Paul Revere, "Edward Everett, Orator and Statesman" (Boston: Houghton Mifflin Company, 1925).

Fuller, Hubert Bruce, "The Speakers of the House" (Boston: Little, Brown & Company, 1909).

Fuller, T[homas], ed., "Ephemeris Parliamentaria; or, A Faithful Register of the Transactions in Parliament, in the Third and Fourth Years of the Reign of King Charles, etc." (London: Printed for John Williams and Francis Eglesfield, 1654).

_____. "History of the House of Representatives" (New York: Thomas Crowell, 1961).

Garraty, John A., and Mark C. Carnes, gen. eds., "American National Biography" (New York: Oxford University Press; 24 volumes, 1999).

Garrett, Samuel B., "An Oration on the Life, Character and Public Services of the Late President James K. Polk" (Lawrenceburg, Tennessee: Printed at the "Middle Tennessean" Office, 1849).

Gatell, Frank Otto, "Jacksonian America, 1815-1840" (Englewood Cliffs, New Jersey: Prentice-Hall, 1970).

Giddings, Joshua R., "History of the Rebellion. Its Authors and Causes" (New York: Follet, Foster & Co., 1864).

Gienapp, William E., "The Origins of the Republican Party, 1852-1856" (New York: Oxford University Press, 1987).

Gold, Lewis L., "The Presidency of William McKinley" (Lawrence: University of Kansas Press, 1980).

Graber, Mark, "The Jacksonian Makings of the Taney Court," University of Maryland Legal Studies Research Paper, No. 2005-63 (2005).

Greeley, Horace, "Recollections of a Busy Life: Including Reminiscences of American Politics and Politicians, etc." (New York: J.B. Ford & Co., Printing-House Square, 1869).

Gross, Charles, "The Sources and Literature of English History, from the Earliest Times to About 1485" (London: Longmans, Green, and Co., 1900).

Haines, Lynn, "Law Making in America: The Story of the 1911-12 Session of the Sixty-Second Congress" (Bethesda, Maryland: Privately Published, 1912).

Hamilton, John C., ed., "The Works of Alexander Hamilton" (New York: C.S. Francis and Company; seven volumes, 1851).

Hamilton, Stanislaus, ed., "The Writings of James Monroe" (New York: G.P. Putnam's Sons; seven volumes, 1898-1903).

Hansard, Thomas Curson, ed., "The Parliamentary Debates, Begun by W[illiam]. Cobbett, and Continued Under the Superintendence of T.C. Hansard" (London: [The British Parliament]; 211 volumes [in three series: 1st Series, 41 volumes; 2nd Series, 25 vol

Hardeman, D.B., and Donald C. Bacon, "Rayburn: A Biography" (Austin: Texas Monthly Press, 1987).

_____. "Fighting Politician: Major General N.P. Banks" (Philadelphia: University of Pennsylvania Press, 1948; report, Westport, Connecticut: Greenwood Press, 1970).

Hasbrouck, Paul DeWitt, "Party Government in the House of Representatives" (New York: Macmillan, 1927).

Haskell, Louisa Porter, "Langdon Cheves and the United States Bank" (Washington: Government Printing Office, 1897).

Hatsell, John, "Precedents of Proceedings in the House of Commons; With Observations" (London: Printed for E. Lynch and P. Byrne; two volumes, 1818).

Hechler, Kenneth W., "Insurgency-Personalities and Politics of the Taft Era" (New York: Columbia University Press, 1940).

Henry, William Wirt, "Patrick Henry: Life, Correspondence and Speeches" (New York: Charles Scribner's Sons; two volumes, 1891).

Hickman, George H., "The Life and Public Services of the Hon. James Knox Polk, etc." (Baltimore, Maryland: N. Hickman, 1844).

Hollandsworth, James G., "Pretense of Glory: The Life of General Nathaniel P. Banks" (Baton Rouge: Louisiana State University Press, 1998).

Hollister, Ovando James, "Life of Schuyler Colfax" (New York: Funk & Wagnalls, 1886).

Hollister, Wilfred R., and Harry Norman, "Five Famous Missourians: Authentic Biographical Sketches of Samuel L. Clemens, Richard P. Bland, Champ Clark, James M. Greenwood, and Joseph O. Shelby" (Kansas City, Missouri: Hudson-Kimberly Publishing Co.,

Holt, James, "Congressional Insurgents and the Party System, 1900-1916" (Cambridge, Massachusetts: Harvard University Press, 1967).

Holt, Michael F., "The Rise and Fall of the American Whig Party: Jacksonian Politics and the Onset of the Civil War" (New York: Oxford University Press, 1999).

Hopkins, James, Mary Hargreaves, Robert Seager II, Melba Porter Hay, eds. et al., "The Papers of Henry Clay, 1797-1852" (Lexington: University Press of Kentucky; 11 volumes, 1959-92).

Howe, George F., "Chester A. Arthur" (New York: Dodd, Mead and Co., 1934).

Hunt, Gaillard, ed., "The Writings of James Madison" (New York: G.P. Putnam's Sons; nine volumes, 1900-10).

Ingersoll, Charles J., "Historical Sketch of the Second War Between the United States of America, and Great Britain, etc." (Philadelphia: Lea and Blanchard; three volumes, 1845).

Jeffers, H. Paul, "An Honest President: The Life and Presidencies of Grover Cleveland" (New York: William Morrow, 2000).

Jenkins, John Stilwell, "James Knox Polk, and a History of his Administration" (Auburn and Buffalo, New York: J. E. Beardsley, 1850; reprint, Auburn, New York: James M. Alden, 1851).

_____. "The Life of James K. Polk, Late President of the United States" (Auburn, New York: James M. Alden, 1850).

Jennings, Walter Wilson, "The American Embargo, 1807-1809," University of Iowa Studies: Studies in the Social Sciences, VIII:1 (1 December 1921).

Jillson, Calvin, and Rick K. Wilson, "Congressional Dynamics: Structure, Coordination, & Choice in the First American Congress, 1884-1789" (Stanford: Stanford University Press, 1994).

Johnson, Allen, and Dumas Malone, et al., eds., "Dictionary of American Biography" (New York: Charles Scribner's Sons; X volumes and 10 supplements, 1930-95).

Johnson, Zachary T., "Political Policies of Howell Cobb" (Nashville, Tennessee: George Peabody College for Teachers, 1929).

Josephy, Alvin M., Jr., "On the Hill: A History of the American Congress" (New York: Touchstone, 1979).

Kass, Alvin, "Politics in New York State, 1800-1830" (Syracuse, New York: Syracuse University Press, 1965).

Keifer, Joseph Warren, "Official reports of J. Warren Keifer, Brevet Major General of Volunteers, U. S. A., etc." (Springfield: Ohio: Daily Republic Steam Job Office, 1866).

_____. "Slavery and Four Years of War: A Political History of Slavery in the United States, Together with a Narrative of the Campaigns and Battles of the Civil War in which the Author Took Part, 1861-1865" (New York: George Putnam, 1900).

Kennon, Donald R., ed., "The Speakers of the U.S. House of Representatives: A Bibliography, 1789-1984" (Baltimore: Johns Hopkins University Press, 1986).

King, Charles R., ed., "The Life and Correspondence of Rufus King: Comprising His Letters, Private and Official, His Public Documents and His Speeches" (New York: G.P. Putnam's Sons;; six volumes, 1894-1900).

Knox, Thomas W., "The Republican Party and Its Leaders. A History of the Party from Its Beginning to the Present Time, etc." (New York: P.F. Collier, Publisher, 1892).

Lanman, Charles, "Dictionary of the United States Congress, Containing Biographical Sketches of Its Members from the Foundation of the Government, etc." (Philadelphia: J.B. Lippincott & Co., 1859).

_____. "Biographical Annals of the Civil Government of the United States, During Its First Century. From Original and Official Sources" (Washington: James Anglim, Publisher, 1876).

_____. "Biographical Annals of the Civil Government of the United States, During Its First Century. From Original and Official Sources" (New York: J.M. Morrison, Publisher, 1887).

"Legislative and Documentary History of the Bank of the United States: Including the Original Bank of North America. Compiled by M. St. Clair Clarke and D.A. Hall" (Washington: Printed by Gales and Seaton, 1832).

Lieber, Francis, "On Civil Liberty and Self-Government" (Philadelphia: J.B. Lippincott & Co., 1859).

Lowery, Charles D., "James Barbour, a Jeffersonian Republican" (University, Alabama: The University of Alabama Press, 1984).

Mann, William J., "Life and Times of Henry Melchior Mühlenberg" (Philadelphia: G.W. Frederick, 1887).

Manning, James Alexander, "The Lives of the Speakers of the House of Commons, From the Time of King Edward III to Queen Victoria, etc." (London: George Willis, 1851).

Marcham, Frederick G., "A Constitutional History of Modern England: 1485 to the Present" (New York: Harper and Bros., 1960).

Margulies, Herbert F., "Reconciliation and Revival: James R. Mann and the House Republicans in the Wilson Era" (Westport, Connecticut: Greenwood Books, 1996).

Martin, Joseph William, Jr., "My First Fifty Years in Politics, as told to Robert J. Donovon" (New York: McGraw-Hill, 1960).

Mayer, George H., "The Republican Party, 1854-1966" (New York: Oxford University Press, 1967).

Mayo, Bernard, "Henry Clay: Spokesman of the Old West" (Boston: Houghton Mifflin, 1937).

Mays, David J., "Edmund Pendleton, 1721-1803: A Biography" (Cambridge: Harvard University Press, 1952).

McCall, Samuel W., "The Life of Thomas Brackett Reed" (Boston: Houghton Mifflin Company, 1914).

McCormac, Eugene Irving. James K. Polk: A Political Biography" (Berkeley, California: University of California Press; two volumes, 1922).

Merli, Frank J., and Theodore Wilson, eds., "Makers of American Diplomacy" (New York: Scribner's, 1974).

Merrill, Horace Samuel, "Bourbon Leader: Grover Cleveland and the Democratic Party" (Boston: Houghton Mifflin, 1957).

Miller, John C., "The Federalist Era, 1789-1801" (New York: Harper Torchbooks, 1963).

Miller, William Lee, "Arguments about Slavery: The Great Battle in the United States Congress" (New York: Alfred A. Knopf, 1996).

"Minutes of the Provincial Council of Pennsylvania, From the Organization to the Termination of the Proprietary Government" (Harrisburg, Pennsylvania: Printed by Theo. Fenn & Co.; ten volumes, 1851-52).

"Minutes of the Supreme Executive Council of Pennsylvania, From its Organization to the Termination of the Revolution" (Harrisburg, Pennsylvania: Printed by Theo. Fenn & Co.; six volumes, 1853).

Montgomery, Horace, "Howell Cobb's Confederate Career" (Tuscaloosa, Alabama: Confederate Publishing, 1959).

Moore, The Rev. Ambrose Yoemans, "The Life of Schuyler Colfax. By [the] Rev. A.Y. Moore" (Philadelphia: T.B. Peterson & Brothers, 1868).

Moore, Frank, ed., "The Rebellion Record: A Diary of American Events. With Documents, Narratives, Illustrative Incidents, Poetry, Etc." (New York: D. Van Nostrand; 11 volumes and one supplement, 1867).

Moore, John Bassett, ed., "The Works of James Buchanan, Comprising Speeches, State Papers, and Private Correspondence" (Philadelphia: J.B. Lippincott Company; twelve volumes, 1908-11).

Morison, Samuel Eliot, "The Growth of the American Republic" (New York: Oxford University Press, 1930).

Muhlenberg, Rev. Dr. Henry, "English-German & German-English Dictionary, with a German Grammar, and Principles of Pronunciation for Both Languages." (Lancaster, Pennsylvania: Printed by William Hamilton; two volumes, 1812).

Nevins, Allan, "Grover Cleveland: A Study in Courage" (New York: Dodd, Mead & Co., 1932).

Newmyer, R. Kent, "The Supreme Court under Marshall and Taney" (New York: Thomas Y. Crowell Company, 1968).

Oleszek, Walter J., "Congressional Procedures and the Policy Process" (Washington, D.C.: CQ Press, 1996).

Palgrave, Reginald F.D., "The House of Commons: Illustrations of its History and Practice, etc." (London: Macmillan, 1869).

Parks, Joseph H., "John Bell of Tennessee" (Baton Rouge: Louisiana State University Press, 1950).

"The Parliamentary or Constitutional History of England; From the Earliest Times, to the Restoration of King Charles II, etc." (London: Printed for J. and R. Tonson, and R. Millar, in the Strand; and W. Sandby, in Fleet-Street; 24 volumes, 1762).

Patterson, James T., "Congressional Conservatism and the New Deal: The Growth of the Conservative Coalition in Congress, 1933-1939" (Lexington, Kentucky: University of Kentucky Press, 1967).

Pauli, Reinhold, "Simon De Montfort, Earl of Leicester, The Creator of the House of Commons" (London: Trübner & Co., Ludgate Hill, 1876).

Peters, Ronald M., "The American Speakership: The Office in Historical Perspective" (Baltimore: Johns Hopkins University Press, 1997).

Peterson, Merrill D., "The Great Triumvirate: Webster, Clay, and Calhoun" (New York: Oxford University Press, 1987).

Pletcher, David M., "The Awkward Years: Diplomacy under Garfield and Arthur" (Columbia: University of Missouri Press, 1962).

Poage, George Rawlings, "Henry Clay and the Whig Party" (Chapel Hill: The University of North Carolina Press, 1936).

Polk, James Knox (Milo Milton Quaife, ed.), "The Diary of James K. Polk During his Presidency, 1845 to 1849" (Chicago: Published for the Chicago Historical Society by A. C. McClurg and Company, 1910).

_____ (Herbert Weaver, ed.), "Correspondence of James K. Polk" (Nashville, Tennessee: Vanderbilt University Press; nine volumes, 1969).

Pollard, Albert Frederick, "The Evolution of Parliament" (London: Longmans, Green, 1920).

Poore, Ben Perley, "Perley's Reminiscences of Sixty Years in the National Metropolis, etc." (Philadelphia: Hubbard Brothers, Publishers; two volumes, 1886).

Pope, Thomas E., "The Weary Boys: Colonel J. Warren Keifer and the 110th Ohio Volunteer Infantry" (Kent, Ohio: Kent State University Press, 2002).

Randolph, John, "The Speech of Sir John Randolph, upon his being Elected Speaker of the House of Burgesses, of Virginia" (Williamsburg [Va.]: Printed by William Parks, 1734).

Reagan, John H. (Walter Flavius McCaleb, ed.), "Memoirs, with Special Reference to Secession and the Civil War" (New York: The Neale Publishing Company, 1906).

Remini, Robert V., "Henry Clay: Statesman for the Union" (New York: W.W. Norton & Company, 1991).

_____. "The House: The History of the House of Representatives" (New York: HarperCollins, 2006).

Rhodes, James Ford, "History of the United States from the Compromise of 1850" (New York: Harper & Brothers, Publishers; eight volumes, 1892-1919).

Richardson, Leon Burr, "William E. Chandler, Republican" (New York: Dodd, Mead & Co., 1940).

_____. "The Old Republicans: Southern Conservatism in the Age of Jefferson" (New York: Columbia University Press, 1965).

Robinson, William A., "Thomas B. Reed: Parliamentarian" (New York: Dodd, Mead, and Company, 1930).

Rodell, Fred, "Nine Men: A Political History of the Supreme Court from 1790 to 1955" (New York: Random House, 1955).

Rogers, Joseph Morgan, "The True Henry Clay" (Philadelphia: J.B. Lippincott Co., 1904).

Roskell, John Smith, "The Commons and Their Speakers in English Parliaments, 1376-1523" (Manchester, United Kingdom: Manchester University Press, 1965).

Ross, Thomas Richard, "Jonathon Prentiss Dolliver: A Study in Political Integrity and Independence" (Iowa City: State Historical Society of Iowa, 1958).

Rowell, Chester H., "A Historical and Legal Digest of all the Contested Election Cases in the House of Representatives of the United States, from the First to the Fifty-sixth Congress, 1789-1901" (Washington, D.C.: Government Printing Office, 1901).

Rutland, Robert Allen, "The Presidency of James Madison" (Lawrence: University of Kansas, 1990).

Savage, John, "Our Living Representative Men: From Official and Original Sources" (Philadelphia: Childs & Peterson, 1860).

Schmucker, Samuel M., "The Life and Times of Henry Clay" (Philadelphia: J.E. Potter Co., 1860).

Schott, Thomas E., "Alexander H. Stephens of Georgia" (Baton Rouge: Louisiana State University Press, 1988).

Schouler, James, "History of the United States of America under the Constitution" (Washington, D.C.: W.H. Morrison; five volumes, 1880-91).

Schurz, Carl, "Life of Henry Clay" (Boston: Houghton, Mifflin; two volumes, 1898).

Sellers, Charles Grier, Jr., "James K. Polk, Jacksonian: 1795-1843" (Princeton: Princeton University Press, 1957).

Sewell, Richard, "Ballots for Freedom: Antislavery Politics in the United States, 1837-1860" (New York: Norton, 1976).

Shankman, Kimberly Christner, "Compromise and the Constitution: The Political Thought of Henry Clay" (Lanham, Maryland: Lexington Books, 1999).

Sherman, John, "Recollections of Forty Years in the House, Senate and Cabinet: An Autobiography" (Chicago: Werner; two volumes, 1895).

Shryock, Richard Harrison, "Georgia and the Union in 1850" (Durham, North Carolina: Duke University Press, 1926).

Sievers, Harry J., "Benjamin Harrison: Hoosier President" (Indianapolis: The Bobbs-Merrill Co., 1968).

Simpson, John Eddins, "Howell Cobb: The Politics of Ambition" (Chicago: Adams Press, 1973).

Smith, James Morton, "Freedom's Fetters: The Alien and Sedition Laws and Civil Liberties" (Ithaca, New York: Cornell University Press, 1956).

Smith, Theodore Clarke, "The Life and Letters of James Abram Garfield" (New Haven, Connecticut: Yale University Press, 1925).

Smith, Sir Thomas (Leonard Alston, ed.), "De Republica Anglorum. A Discourse on the Commonwealth of England" (Cambridge: The University Press, 1906).

Smith, William Ernest, "The Francis Preston Blair Family in Politics" (New York: The Macmillan Company, 1933).

Sparks, Jared, ed., "The Writings of George Washington" (Boston: J.B. Russell; twelve volumes, 1833-37).

Stealey, Orlando Oscar, "Twenty Years in the Press Gallery. A Concise History of Important Legislation, from the 48th to the 58th Congress, etc." (New York: Publishers Printing Company, Printers, 1906).

Story, William W., ed., "Life and Letters of Joseph Story, Associate Justice of the Supreme Court of the United States, and Dane Professor of Harvard University. Edited by His Son, William W. Story" (London: John Chapman; two volumes, 1851).

Stuart, I.W., "Life of Jonathan Trumbull, Sen., Governor of Connecticut" (Boston: Crocker & Brewster, 1859).

Sumner, Charles, "His Complete Works. With [an] Introduction by Hon. George Frisbie Hoar" (Boston: Lee & Shepard; twenty volumes, 1900).

"'The Union Edition.' Bell and Everett. The Regular Campaign Edition, known as 'The Union Edition' of The Life, Speeches, and Public Services of Hon. John Bell, Together with a Life of Hon. Edward Everett, Union Candidates for the Offices of Presiden

"The Virginia and Kentucky Resolutions of 1798 and '99; with Jefferson's Original Draught Thereof. Also Madison's Report, Calhoun's Address, Resolutions of the Several States in Relation to State Rights" (Washington: Jonathan Elliot, 1832).

Thomas, Benjamin Franklin, "Speeches in the Second and Third Sessions of the Thirty-seventh Congress, and the Vacation" (Boston: Printed by John Wilson and Son, 1863).

Townsend, W. Charles, "History of the House of Commons, From the Convention Parliament of 1688-9 to the Passing of the Reform Bill, in 1832" (London: Henry Colburn, Publisher; 2 volumes, 1843).

Tyler, Alice Felt, "The Foreign Policy of James G. Blaine" (Minneapolis: The University of Minnesota Press, 1927).

Van Deusen, Glyndon G., "The Life of Henry Clay" (Boston: Little, Brown, 1937).

_____. "The Jacksonian Era, 1828-1848" (New York: Harper & Row, 1959).

Varnum, John Marshall, "The Varnums of Dracutt (in Massachusetts). A History of George Varnum, etc." (Boston: David Clapp & Son, Printers, 1967).

Varnum, Joseph, "An Address, Delivered to the Third Division of Massachusetts Militia, at a Review, on the Plains of Concord, 27th August, 1800" (Cambridge, Massachusetts: Printed by William Hilliard, 1800).

"Vital Records of Waltham, Massachusetts, to the Year 1850" (Boston: Published by the New England Historic Genealogical Society, at the Charge of the Eddy Town-Record Fund, 1904).

Waller, Robert A., "Rainey of Illinois: A Political Biography, 1903-34" (Urbana: University of Illinois Press, 1977).

Warner, Ezra J., and W. Buck Yearns, "Biographical Register of the Confederate Congress" (Baton Rouge: Louisiana State University Press, 1975).

Watson, Harry L., "Andrew Jackson vs. Henry Clay: Democracy and Development in Antebellum America" (Boston: Bedford, 1998).

Webb, William Larkin, "Champ Clark" (New York: The Neale Publishing Co., 1912).

Wheeler, John Hill, "Historical Sketches of North Carolina: from 1584 to 1851, etc." (Philadelphia: Lippincott, Grambo and Co.; eleven volumes, 1851).

White, Leonard D., "The Federalists: A Study in Administrative History" (New York: Macmillan, 1948).

_____. "The Jeffersonians: A Study in Administrative History, 1801-1829" (New York: Macmillan, 1951).

_____. "The Jacksonians: A Study in Administrative History, 1829-1861" (New York: Macmillan, 1954).

_____. with Jean Schneider, "The Republican Era, 1869-1901: A Study in Administrative History" (New York: Macmillan, 1958).

Wilkinson, Bertie, "Constitutional History of England in the Fifteenth Century" (London: Longmans, 1914).

Winthrop, Robert C., "Memoir of Henry Clay" (Cambridge, Massachusetts: J. Wilson and Son, 1880).

Young, James Sterling, "The Washington Community: 1800-1828" (New York: Columbia University Press, 1966).

Articles

Abram, Michael, and Joseph Cooper, "The Rise of Seniority in the House of Representatives," *Polity*, 1 (Fall 1968), 52-85.

Adams, Charles Francis, "John Quincy Adams and Speaker Andrew Stevenson of Virginia: An Episode of the Twenty-Second Congress (1832)," *Proceedings of the Massachusetts Historical Society*, 2nd Series, XIX (December 1906), 504-53.

"Advice from Michael C. Kerr to a Reconstructed Rebel Congressman," *Indiana Magazine of History*, XXXVII:3 (September 1941), 257-61.

_____. and Ruth W. Grant, "The Antifederalists, the First Congress, and the First Parties," *The Journal of Politics*, LV:2 (May 1993), 295-326.

"A Letter of General James Wilkinson, 1806," *The American Historical Review*, IX:3 (April 1904), 533-37.

Andres, Gary J., "Observations on a Post-Gingrich House," *PS: Political Science and Politics*, XXXII:3 (September 1999), 571-74.

Archbold, W.A.J., "A Diary of the Parliament of 1626," *English Historical Review*, XVII (October 1902), 730-37.

Armour, Alexander W., "Revolutionary War Discharges," *The William and Mary Quarterly*, 2nd Series, XXI:4 (October 1941), 344-60.

Atkinson, C.R., and Charles A. Beard, "The Syndication of the Speakership," *Political Science Quarterly*, XXVI:3 (September 1911), 381-414.

Bachelor, Stanley, "Suspension of the Rules, the Order of Business, and the Development of Congressional Procedure," *Legislative Studies Quarterly*, XV:1. (February 1990), 49-63.

Badger, Tony, "Southerners Who Refused to Sign the Southern Manifesto," *The Historical Journal*, XXXXII:2 (June 1999), 517-34.

Baker, John D., "The Character of the Congressional Revolution of 1910," *Journal of American History*, LX:3 (December 1973), 679-91.

Bassett, John Spencer, ed., "James K. Polk and His Constituents, 1831-1832," *The American Historical Review*, XVIII:1 (October 1922), 69-77.

Baylen, Joseph O., ed., "A Letter of James L. Orr, Minister to Russia, 1873," *South Carolina Historical Magazine*, LXI (October 1960), 225-31.

Bearss, Sara B., "Henry Clay and the American Claims against Portugal, 1850," *Journal of the Early Republic*, 7 (Summer 1987), 167-80.

Bedini, Silvio A., "The Mace and the Gavel: Symbols of Government in America," *Transactions of the American Philosophical Society*, New Series, 87:4 (1997), i-xi, 1-84.

Benedict, Michael Les, "Southern Democrats in the Crisis of 1876-1877: A Reconsideration of Reunion and Reaction," *The Journal of Southern History*, XXXXVI:4 (November 1980), 489-524.

Bennett, Susan Smythe, "The Cheves Family of South Carolina," *South Carolina Historical and Genealogical Magazine*, XXXV (July-October 1934), 79-95, 130-52.

Bergeron, Paul H., "James K. Polk and the Jacksonian Press in Tennessee," *Tennessee Historical Quarterly*, XXXXI (Fall 1982), 257-77.

Beringer, Richard E., "A Profile of the Members of the Confederate Congress," *The Journal of Southern History*, 33:4 (November 1967), 518-41.

"Biographical Sketches: Hon. Howell Cobb," *The United States Democratic Review*, XXXXI:2 (February 1858), 131-40.

Blakey, George T., "Rendezvous with Republicanism: John Pope vs. Henry Clay in 1816," *Indiana Magazine of History*, LXII (September 1966), 233-50.

Block, Marvin W., "Henry T. Rainey of Illinois," *Journal of the Illinois State Historical Society*, LXV:2 (Summer 1972): 142-57.

Bogue, Allan G., and Mark Paul Marlaire, "Of Mess and Men: The Boardinghouse and Congressional Voting, 1821-1842," *American Journal of Political Science*, 19 (May 1975), 207-30.

Borome, Joseph, "Two Letters of Robert Charles Winthrop," *The Mississippi Valley Historical Review*, XXXVIII:2 (September 1951), 289-96.

Breese, Donald H., "James L. Orr, Calhoun, and the Co-operationist Tradition in South Carolina," *South Carolina Historical Magazine*, LXXX (October 1979), 273-85.

Brent, Robert A., "Between Calhoun and Webster: Clay in 1850," *Southern Quarterly*, VIII (April 1970), 293-308.

Brewer, Mark D., and Jeffrey M. Stonecash, "Class, Race Issues, and Declining White Support for the Democratic Party in the South," *Political Behavior*, 23:2. (June 2001), 131-55.

Brooks, Robert Preston, "Howell Cobb and the Crisis of 1850," *The Mississippi Valley Historical Review*, IV:3 (December 1917), 279-98.

Brooks, Sydney, "Congress and Parliament: A Contrast," *The North American Review*, CLXX:518 (January 1900), 78-85.

Brown, Everett S., and Ruth C. Silva, "Presidential Succession and Inability," *The Journal of Politics*, XI:1 (February 1949), 236-56.

Bryce, James, "A Word as to the Speakership," *The North American Review*, CL:CCCVII (October 1890), 385-98.

Burch, Samuel, "On the Journals of the House of Representatives, 1836," *The American Historical Review*, XXIX:3 (April 1924), 510-12.

Caldwell, Joshua W. "John Bell of Tennessee: A Chapter of Political History," *American Historical Review*, 4 (July 1899), 652-64.

Carson, David A., "That Ground called Quiddism: John Randolph's War with the Jefferson Administration," *Journal of American Studies*, 20 (1986), 71-92.

Chrimes, Stanley Baldwin, "House of Lords and House of Commons in the Fifteenth Century," *English Historical Review*, 49:195 (July 1934), 494-97.

Clark, Champ, "The Work of the Democratic House," *The North American Review*, 194 (September 1911), 337-43.

Cogan, Jacob Katz, "The Reynolds Affair and the Politics of Character," *Journal of the Early Republic*, XVI:3 (Autumn 1996), 389-417.

Cometti, Elizabeth, "John Rutledge, Jr., Federalist," *The Journal of Southern History*, XIII:2 (May 1947), 186-219.

Cooper, John Milton, Jr., "The Command of Gold Reversed: American Loans to Britain, 1915-1917," *The Pacific Historical Review*, XXXXV:2 (May 1976), 209-30.

Cooper, Joseph, "Jeffersonian Attitudes toward Executive Leadership and Committee Development in the House of Representatives, 1789-1829," *The Western Political Quarterly*, XVIII:1 (March 1965), 45-63.

_____. and David W. Brady, "Institutional Context and Leadership Style: The House from Cannon to Rayburn," *The American Political Science Review*, LXXV:2 (June 1981), 411-25.

Crenshaw, Ollinger, "The Speakership Contest of 1859-1860: John Sherman's Election a Cause of Disruption?" *The Mississippi Valley Historical Review*, XXIX:3 (December 1942), 323-38.

Cunningham, Noble E., Jr., "Nathaniel Macon and the Southern Protest against National Consolidation," *North Carolina Historical Review*, XXXII (July 1955), 376-84.

_____. "Who Were the Quids?," *The Mississippi Valley Historical Review*, L:2 (September 1963), 252-63.

Currie, David P., "The Constitution in Congress: The Third Congress, 1793-1795," *The University of Chicago Law Review*, LXIII:1 (Winter 1996), 1-48.

Davidson, Roger H., "The New Centralization on Capitol Hill," *Review of Politics*, L (Summer 1988), 346-64.

Dimmig, Jeffrey S., "Palatine Liberty: Pennsylvania German Opposition to the Direct Tax of 1798," *The American Journal of Legal History*, XXXXV:4 (October 2001), 371-90.

Dodd, William E., "The Place of Nathaniel Macon in Southern History," *American Historical Review*, VII (July 1902), 663-75.

Eichert, Magdalen, "Henry Clay's Policy of Distribution of the Proceeds from Public Land Sales," *Register of the Kentucky Historical Society*, LII (January 1954), 25-32.

Field, Walter T. "The Amherst Illustrious: Speaker Rainey," *Amherst Graduates' Quarterly*, 24 (November 1934), 22-24.

"The First Judges of the Federal Courts," *The American Journal of Legal History*, I:1 (January 1957), 76-78.

Follett, Mary Parker, "Henry Clay as Speaker of the United States House of Representatives" *Annual Report of the American Historical Association for the Year 1891* (Washington: Government Printing Office; two volumes, 1892).

Foran, William A., "Attempted Conversion of James L. Orr," *Journal of Negro History*, XXXIX (April 1954), 137-39.

Fritz, Harry W., "The War Hawks of 1812: Party Leadership in the Twelfth Congress," *Capitol Studies*, 5 (1977), 25-42.

Furlong, Patrick J., "John Rutledge, Jr., and the Election of a Speaker of the House in 1799," *The William and Mary Quarterly*, 3rd Series, XXIV:3 (July 1967), 432-36.

_____. "The Origins of the House Committee of Ways and Means," *The William and Mary Quarterly*, 3rd Series, XXV:4 (October 1968), 587-604.

Galloway, George B., "Precedents Established in the First Congress," *The Western Political Quarterly*, XI:3 (September 1958), 454-68.

Gatell, Frank Otto, "Palfrey's Vote, the Conscience Whigs, and the Election of Speaker Winthrop," *The New England Quarterly*, XXXI: 2 (June 1958), 218-31.

Gilliam, Will D., Jr., "Party Regularity in Three Kentucky Elections and Union Volunteering," *The Journal of Southern History*, XVI:4 (November 1950), 511-18.

Greely, A.W., "The Speaker and the Committees of the House of Representatives," *The North American Review*, CLXVI:CCCXCIV (January 1898), 24-31.

Grossman, Joel B., and Stephen L. Wasby, "The Senate and Supreme Court Nominations: Some Reflections," *Duke Law Journal*, 1972:3 (August 1972), 557-91.

Hamilton, Holman, "'The Cave of the Winds' and the Compromise of 1850," *The Journal of Southern History*, XXIII:3 (August 1957), 331-53.

Hammond, Bray, "The Second Bank of the United States," *Transactions of the American Philosophical Society*, New Series, XXXXIII:1 (1953), 80-85.

Harrington, Fred Harvey, "Nathaniel Prentiss Banks: A Study in Anti-Slavery Politics," *The New England Quarterly*, 9:4 (December 1936), 626-54.

_____. "The First Northern Victory," *The Journal of Southern History*, V:2 (May 1939), 186-205.

Harris, Carl V., "Right Fork or Left Fork? The Section-Party Alignments of Southern Democrats in Congress, 1873-1897," *The Journal of Southern History*, 42:4. (November 1976), 471-506.

Harrison, Joseph Hobson, Jr., "Martin Van Buren and His Southern Supporters." *The Journal of Southern History*, XXII:4 (November 1956), 438-58.

Hatzenbuehler, Ronald L., "Party Unity and the Decision for War in the House of Representatives, 1812," *William and Mary Quarterly*, 29 (July 1972), 367-90.

_____. "The War Hawks and the Question of Congressional Leadership in 1812," *The Pacific Historical Review*, XXXXV:1 (February 1976), 1-22.

Heacock, Walter J., "William B. Bankhead and the New Deal," *The Journal of Southern History*, 21 (August 1955), 347-59.

Hening, Gerald S., "Henry Winter Davis and the Speakership Contest of 1859-1860," *Maryland Historical Magazine*, LXVIII:1 (Spring 1973), 1-19.

Herring, E. Pendleton, "First Session of the Seventy-third Congress, March 3, 1933, to June 16, 1933," *The American Political Science Review*, 28:1 (February 1934), 65-83.

_____. "Second Session of the Seventy-third Congress, January 3, 1934, to June 18, 1934," *The American Political Science Review*, 28:5 (October 1934), 852-66.

Hicken, Victor, "John A. McClernand and the House Speakership Struggle of 1859," *Journal of the Illinois State Historical Society*, LIII:2 (Summer 1960), 163-78.

Hinds, Asher Crosby, "The Speaker of the House of Representatives," *The American Political Science Review*, III:2 (May 1909), 155-66.

Hoadley, John F., "The Emergence of Political Parties in Congress, 1789-1803," *The American Political Science Review*, LXXIV:3 (September 1980), 757-79.

Hollcroft, Temple R., "A Congressman's Letters on the Speaker Election in the Thirty-fourth Congress," *The Mississippi Valley Historical Review*, XXXXIII:3 (December 1956), 444-58.

Holmes, William F., "The Southern Farmers' Alliance and the Georgia Senatorial Election of 1890," *The Journal of Southern History*, L:2 (May 1984), 197-224.

House, Albert V., Jr., "The Contributions of Samuel J. Randall to the Rules of the National House of Representatives," *The American Political Science Review*, XXIX:5 (October 1935), 837-41.

_____. "The Speakership Contest of 1875: Democratic Response to Power, *The Journal of American History*, 52:2 (September 1965), 252-74.

Hubbell, John T. "Three Georgia Unionists and the Compromise of 1850," *Georgia Historical Quarterly*, LI (September 1967), 307-23.

Jenkins, Jeffery A., and Timothy P. Nokken, "The Institutional Origins of the Republican Party: Spatial Voting and the House Speakership Election of 1855-56," *Legislative Studies Quarterly*, XXV:1 (February 2000), 101-30.

Jones, Charles O., "Joseph G. Cannon and Howard W. Smith: An Essay on the Limits of Leadership in the House of Representatives," *Journal of Politics*, 30:3 (August 1968), 617-46.

Judex, "The Speaker and His Critics," *The North American Review*, CCCCV (August 1890), 237-50.

Kengor, Paul, "The Vice President, Secretary of State, and Foreign Policy," *Political Science Quarterly*, CXV:2 (Summer 2000), 175-99.

Kenneally, James J., "Black Republicans During the New Deal: The Role of Joseph W. Martin, Jr.," *Review of Politics*, LV:1 (Winter 1993), 117-39.

Krehbiel, Keith, and Alan Wiseman, "Joseph G. Cannon: Majoritarian from Illinois," *Legislative Studies Quarterly*, XXVI: (August 2001), 357-89.

Krueger, David W., "The Clay-Tyler Feud, 1841-1842" *Filson Club History Quarterly*, XXXXII (April 1968), 162-77.

Latimer, Margaret Kinard, "South Carolina: A Protagonist of the War of 1812," *The American Historical Review*, LXI:4 (July 1956), 914-29.

"Letters to Caleb Strong, 1786, 1800," *The American Historical Review*, IV:2 (January 1899), 328-30.

Lientz, Gerald R., "House Speaker Elections and Congressional Parties, 1789-1860," *Capitol Studies*, VI (Spring 1978), 63-89.

Link, Arthur S., "The Underwood Presidential Movement of 1912," *The Journal of Southern History*, XI:2 (May 1945), 230-45.

_____. "The Baltimore Convention of 1912," *The American Historical Review*, L:4 (July 1945), 691-713.

Ludlum, Robert P., "Joshua Giddings, Radical," *The Mississippi Valley Historical Review*, XXIII:1 (June 1936), 49-60.

MacEacheren, Elaine, "Emancipation of Slavery in Massachusetts: A Reexamination 1770-1790," *The Journal of Negro History*, LV:4 (October 1970), 289-306.

Macmahon, Arthur W., "American Government and Politics: First Session of the Sixty-Ninth Congress, December 7, 1925, to July 3, 1926," *The American Political Science Review*, XX:3 (August 1926), 604-22.

_____. "First Session of the Seventy-First Congress," *The American Political Science Review*, XXIV:1 (February 1930), 38-59.

"[The] Macon Family," *The William and Mary Quarterly*, VI:1 (July 1897), 33-36.

Malin, James C., "Speaker Banks Courts the Free-Soilers: The Frémont-Robinson Letter of 1856," *The New England Quarterly*, XII:1 (March 1939), 103-12.

Maltzman, Forrest and Eric Lawrence, "Why Did Speaker Henderson Resign? The Page 799 Mystery is Solved," *Public Affairs Report*, XXXXI:4 (2000), 7-8.

Martin, S. Walter, "Charles F. Crisp, Speaker of the House," *The Georgia Review*, VIII:1 (Summer 1954), 167-77.

McCormick, Richard P., "New Jersey's First Congressional Election, 1789: A Case Study in Political Skullduggery," *The William and Mary Quarterly*, 3rd Series, VI:2 (April 1949), 237-50.

_____. "Was There a 'Whig Strategy' in 1836?" *Journal of the Early Republic*, IV:1 (Spring 1984), 47-70.

Mering, John V., "The Slave-State Constitutional Unionists and the Politics of Consensus," *The Journal of Southern History*, XXXXIII:3 (August 1977), 395-410.

"Missouri Compromise: Letters to James Barbour, Senator of Virginia in the Congress of the United States," *William & Mary Quarterly*, Series 1, X (July 1901), 5-24.

Moger, Allen W., "The Origin of the Democratic Machine in Virginia," *The Journal of Southern History*, VIII:2 (May 1942), 183-209.

Moore, Frederick W., "Representation in the National Congress from the Seceding States, 1861-65," *The American Historical Review*, II:2 (January 1897), 279-93.

_____. "Representation in the National Congress from the Seceding States, 1861-65," *The American Historical Review*, II:3 (April 1897), 461-71.

Moore, Powell, "James K. Polk: Tennessee Politician," *Journal of Southern History*, XVII (November 1951), 493-516.

Morris, William A., "The Beginnings of the House of Commons," *The Pacific Historical Review*, II:2 (June 1933), 141-57.

Morrison, Geoffrey Fahy, "Champ Clark and the Rules Revolution of 1910," *Capitol Studies*, II (Winter 1974), 43-56.

"Mr. Clay - the Texas Question," *The American Review: A Whig Journal of Politics, Literature, Art and Science*, I (January 1845), 75-81.

"Nathaniel Macon," *The United States Democratic Review*, 1:1 (October 1837), 17-27.

Nelson, Garrison, "Irish Identity Politics: The Reinvention of Speaker John W. McCormack of Boston," *New England Journal of Public Policy*, XV (Fall/Winter 1999/2000), 7-34.

Oleszek, Walter J., "Party Whips in the United States Senate," *The Journal of Politics*, XXXIII:4 (November 1971), 955-79.

Ornstein, Norman J., and Amy L. Schenkenberg, "The 1995 Congress: The First Hundred Days and Beyond," *Political Science Quarterly*, CX:2 (Summer 1995), 183-206.

"Panic of 1893," *The Quarterly Journal of Economics*, VIII:2 (January 1894), 252-56.

Parks, Norman L., "The Career of John Bell as Congressman from Tennessee, 1827-1841," *Tennessee Historical Quarterly*, I (September 1942), 229-49.

Patterson, Samuel C., "Party Leadership in the U. S. Senate," *Legislative Studies Quarterly*, XIIII:3. (August 1989), 393-413.

Perkins, Edwin J., "Langdon Cheves and the Panic of 1819: A Reassessment," *The Journal of Economic History*, XXXXIV:2 (June 1984), 455-61.

Pettengill, Ray W., "To Saratoga and Back 1777," *The New England Quarterly*, X:4 (December 1937), 785-89.

Phelips, Edward, and F.G. Marcham, "The Speaker's Claim for Freedom of Speech, 1604," *The English Historical Review*, XXXXIV:175 (July 1929), 453-54.

Phillips, Ulrich B., ed., "The Correspondence of Robert Toombs, Alexander H. Stephens, and Howell Cobb" in *Annual Report of the American Historical Association for the Year*

1911 (Washington, D.C.: Government Printing Office; two volumes, 1913).

Pittman, R. Carter, "Jasper Yeates's Notes on the Pennsylvania Ratifying Convention, 1787," *The William and Mary Quarterly*, 3rd Series, XXII:2 (April 1965), 301-18.

Phelips, Edward, and F.G. Marcham, "The Speaker's Claim for Freedom of Speech, 1604," *The English Historical Review*, XLIV:175 (July 1929), 453-54.

Pleasants, Hugh R., "Sketches of the Virginia Convention of 1829-30," *The Southern Literary Messenger*, XVII:5 (May 1851), 297-304.

Press, O.C., "The Prediction of Midterm Elections," *The Western Political Quarterly*, IX:3 (September 1956), 691-98.

Reed, Thomas B., "Democracy at St. Louis," *The North American Review*, CCCLXXX (July 1888), 37-44.

_____. "Obstruction in the National House," *The North American Review*, 149:395 (October 1889), 421-29;

_____. "The Limitations of the Speakership," *The North American Review*, CL:400 (March 1890), 382-90.

_____. "Reforms Needed in the House," *The North American Review*, 150:402 (May 1890), 537-47.

"Reports of the American Convention of Abolition Societies on Negroes and on Slavery, their Appeals to Congress, and their Addresses to the Citizens of the United States," *The Journal of Negro History*, VI:3 (July 1921), 335-59.

Risjord, Norman K., "1812: Conservatives, War Hawks and the Nation's Honor," *The William and Mary Quarterly*, 3rd Series, XVIII:2 (April 1961), 196-210.

_____. "Partisanship and Power: House Committees and the Powers of the Speaker, 1789-1801," *The William and Mary Quarterly*, 3rd Series, IL:4 (October 1992), 628-51.

Rogers, Lindsay, "American Government and Politics: The Second, Third and Fourth Sessions of the Sixty-Seventh Congress," *The American Political Science Review*, XVIII:1 (February 1924), 79-95.

_____. "First and Second Sessions of the Sixty-Eighth Congress," *The American Political Science Review*, XIX:4 (November 1925), 761-72.

Round, J.H., "John Doreward, Speaker (1399, 1413)," *The English Historical Review*, 29:116 (October 1914), 717-19.

Ryan, Mary P., "Party Formation in the United States Congress, 1789 to 1796: A Quantitative Analysis," *William & Mary Quarterly*, XXVIII (1971), 523-42.

Sarasohn, David, "The Insurgent Republicans: Insurgent Image and Republican Reality," *Social Science History*, III:3/4 (1979), 245-61.

Schickler, Eric, "Institutional Change in the House of Representatives, 1867-1998: A Test of Partisan and Ideological Power Balance Models," *The American Political Science Review*, 94:2 (June 2000), 269-88.

Schwarz, Jordan A., "John Nance Garner and the Sales Tax Rebellion of 1932," *The Journal of Southern History*, XXX:2 (May 1964), 162-80.

Silbey, Joel H., "John C. Calhoun and the Limits of Southern Congressional Unity, 1841-1850," *Historian*, XXX (November 1967), 58-71.

Simpson, John E., "Prelude to Compromise: Howell Cobb and the House Speakership Battle of 1849," *Georgia Historical Quarterly*, LVIII (Winter 1974), 389-99.

_____. "After 'The First Northern Victory': The Republican Party Comes to Congress, 1855-1856," *Journal of Interdisciplinary History*, X (1989), 1-24.

Sims, C.S., "The Speaker of the House of Commons in the Early Seventeenth Century," *The American Historical Review*, XLV (October 1939), 90-95.

_____, ed., " The Moderne Forme of the Parliaments of England," *The American Historical Review*, LIII:2 (January 1948), 288-305.

Sinclair, Barbara, "The Speaker's Task Force in the Post-Reform House of Representatives," *The American Political Science Review*, LXXV:2 (June 1981), 397-410.

_____. "The Emergence of Strong Leadership in the 1980s House of Representatives," *The Journal of Politics*, LIV:3 (August 1992), 657-84.

Smelser, Marshall, "The Passage of the Naval Act of 1794," *Military Affairs*, XXII:1 (Spring 1958), 1-12.

Spann, Edward K., "The Souring of Good Feelings: John W. Taylor and the Speakership Election of 1821," *New York History*, XXXXI (1960), 379-99.

Sparlin, Estal E., "Bryan and the 1912 Democratic Convention," *The Mississippi Valley Historical Review*, XXII:4 (March 1936), 537-46.

Stephenson, N.W., "Southern Nationalism in South Carolina in 1851," *The American Historical Review*, XXXVI:2 (January 1931), 314-35.

Stevens, Harry R., "Henry Clay, the Bank, and the West in 1824," *The American Historical Review*, LX:4 (July 1955), 843-48.

Stewart, Donald H., "The Press and Political Corruption During the Federalist Administrations," *Political Science Quarterly*, LXVII:3 (September 1952), 426-46.

Stonecash, Jeffrey M., and Mack D. Mariani, "Republican Gains in the House in the 1994 Elections: Class Polarization in American Politics," *Political Science Quarterly*, CXV:1 (Spring 2000), 93-113.

Strahan, Randall, Vincent G. Moscardelli; Moshe Haspel; and Richard S. Wike, The Clay Speakership Revisited," *Polity*, XXXII:4 (Summer 2000), 561-93.

_____. Matthew Gunning, and Richard L. Vining, "From Moderator to Leader: Floor Participation by U.S. House Speakers, 1789-1841," *Social Science History*, XXX:1 (Spring 2006), 51-74.

Strateman, Catherine, "*Expedicio Billarum Antiquitus*: An Unpublished Chapter of Elsynge's Treatise on Parliament," *The American Historical Review*, XXXXII:2, (January 1937), 225-43.

Surrency, Edwin C., "The Judiciary Act of 1801," *The American Journal of Legal History*, II:1 (January 1958), 53-65.

Teiser, Sidney, "The Genesis of the Supreme Court," *Virginia Law Review*, XXV:4 (February 1939), 398-421.

"The Progress of the World: Speaker Henderson's Retirement," *The American Monthly Review of Reviews*, XXVI:4 (October 1902), 387-89.

"The Speaker of the House of Commons," *The American Historical Review*, XXXXV:1 (October 1939), 90-95.

"The Twenty-Eighth Congress," *The American Whig Review*, 1:3 (March 1845), 221-31.

Turberville, Arthur Stanely, "The House of Lords under Charles II," *The English Historical Review*, XXXXV:177 (January 1930), 58-77.

Turner, Kathryn, "The Appointment of Chief Justice Marshall," *The William and Mary Quarterly*, 3rd Series, XVII:2 (April 1960), 143-63.

_____. "Federalist Policy and the Judiciary Act of 1801," *The William and Mary Quarterly*, 3rd Series, XXII:1 (January 1965), 3-32.

Walters, Raymond, Jr., "The Origins of the Second Bank of the United States," *The Journal of Political Economy*, LIII:2 (June 1945), 115-31.

Walton, Brian G., "The Elections for the Thirtieth Congress and the Presidential Candidacy of Zachary Taylor," *The Journal of Southern History*, XXXV:2 (May 1969), 186-202.

Ward, Norman, "The Formative Years of the House of Commons, 1867-91," *The Canadian Journal of Economics and Political Science / Revue Canadienne d'Economique et de Science Politique*, XVIII:4 (November 1952), 431-51.

Wiecek, William M., "Slavery and Abolition Before the United States Supreme Court, 1820-1860," *The Journal of American History*, LXV:1 (June 1978), 34-59.

Williams, T. Harry, "General Banks and the Radical Republicans in the Civil War," *The New England Quarterly*, XII:2 (June 1939), 268-80.

Wilson, Keith, "Education as a Vehicle of Racial Control: Major General N. P. Banks in Louisiana, 1863-64," *The Journal of Negro Education*, L:2 (Spring 1981), 156-70.

Wilson, Rick K., "Transitional Governance in the United States: Lessons from the First Federal Congress," *Legislative Studies Quarterly*, XXIV:4 (November 1999), 543-68.

_____. and Calvin Jillson, "Leadership Patterns in the Continental Congress: 1774-1789," *Legislative Studies Quarterly*, XIV:1 (February 1989), 5-37.

Wiltse, Charles M., "The Authorship of the War Report of 1812," *American Historical Review*, XXXXIX:2 (January 1944), 253-59.

Winkler, James R. "Henry Clay: A Current Assessment," *Register of the Kentucky Historical Society*, LXX (July 1972), 179-86.

Wolff, Gerald, "The Slavocracy and the Homestead Problem of 1854," *Agricultural History*, XXXX:2 (April 1966), 101-12.

Wright, David McCord, "Langdon Cheves and Nicholas Biddle: New Data for a New Interpretation," *The Journal of Economic History*, XIII:3 (Summer 1953), 305-19.

X.M.C., "Speaker Reed's Error," *The North American Review*, CLI (July 1890), 90-111.

Zilversmit, Arthur, "Quok Walker, Mumbet, and the Abolition of Slavery in Massachusetts," *The William and Mary Quarterly*, 3rd Series, XXV:4 (October 1968), 614-24.

Unpublished Master's Theses, Dissertations and Other Papers

Amspoker, Gertrude Joanne, "The Development of Procedure in the House of Commons in the Early Stuart Period (1603-1629)" (Ph.D. dissertation, University of Minnesota, 1959).

Arnold, David R., "The Leadership behaviors of America's First Darkhorse: James Knox Polk" (Ed.D. dissertation, University of La Verne [California], 1999).

Atkinson, Charles R., "The Committee on Rules and the Overthrow of Speaker Cannon" (unpublished Ph.D. dissertation, Columbia University, 1911).

Baker, William E. "The Political Career of Henry T. Rainey, 1903-1934" (Master's thesis, University of Maryland, 1953).

Barlow, William R., "Congress During the War of 1812" (Ph.D. dissertation, Ohio State University, 1961).

Barry, Stephen John, "Nathaniel Macon: The Prophet of Pure Republicanism, 1758-1837" (Ph.D. dissertation, State University of New York at Buffalo, 1996).

Beasley, Mark William, "Prelude to Leadership: Jim Wright, 1922-1963" (Ph.D. dissertation, Texas Christian University, 1997).

Bell, Rudolph, "Politics and Factions, 1789-1801" (Ph.D. dissertation, City University of New York, 1969).

Binkley, Robert W., Jr., "The American System; An Example of Nineteenth-Century Economic Thinking-It's Definition by Its Author, Henry Clay" (Ph.D. dissertation, Columbia University, 1950).

Bird, Robert Kenton, "The Speaker from Spokane: The Rise and Fall of Tom Foley as a Congressional Leader" (Ph.D. dissertation, Washington State University, 1999).

Block, Marvin W., "Henry Thomas Rainey: Some Major Aspects of His Legislative Career" (Master's thesis, Illinois State Normal University, 1960).

Brandt, Karl Gerard, "Deficit Politics and Democratic Unity: The Saga of Tip O'Neill, Jim Wright, and the Conservative Democrats in the House of Representatives during the Reagan Era" (Ph.D. dissertation, Louisiana State University and Agricultural & Mechanical College, 2003).

Brannen, Ralph Neal, "John McDuffie: State Legislator, Congressman, Federal Judge, 1883-1950" (Ph.D. dissertation, Auburn University, 1975).

Casper, Dale Edward, "The King's Good Servants: The Commons House in 1491" (Ph.D. dissertation, the University of Minnesota, 1980).

Champagne, Raymond W., Jr., "The House of Representatives and American Foreign Policy during the Washington Administration, 1789-1797" (Ph.D. dissertation, Loyola University of Chicago, 1973).

Chiu, Chang-Wei, "The Speaker of the House of Representatives Since 1896" (Ph.D. dissertation, Columbia University, 1928).

Cooper, Joseph, "Congress and Its Committees" (Ph.D. dissertation, Harvard University, 1961).

Devoti, John, "The Patriotic Business of Seeking Office: James K. Polk and the Patronage" (Ph.D. dissertation, Temple University, 2005).

Eichert, Magdalen, "A Consideration of the Interests Which Lay Behind the Attitudes of Benton, Clay, Webster, and Calhoun in the Development of Public Land Policy, 1830-1841" (Ph.D. dissertation, New York University, 1950).

Fowler, Harold, "Edward Seymour, Speaker of the House of Commons, 1673-1678" (Ph.D. dissertation, Harvard University, 1934).

Furlong, Patrick J., "The Evolution of Political Organization in the House of Representatives, 1789-1801" (Ph.D. dissertation, Northwestern University, 1966).

Galloway, Jewell Morrell, "The Public Life of Joseph W. Byrns" (Master's thesis, University of Tennessee, 1962).

Gannon, Nell W., "Howell Cobb: A Political Biography" (Ph.D. dissertation, University of California at Berkeley, 1933).

Gantz, Richard Alan, "Henry Clay and the Harvest of Bitter Fruit: The Struggle with John Tyler, 1841-1842" (Ph.D. dissertation, Indiana University, 1986).

Goldman, Perry Myron, "The Republic of Virtue and Other Essays on the Politics of the Early National Period" (Ph.D. dissertation, Columbia University, 1970).

Gordon, Lester Ira, "John McCormack and the Roosevelt Era" (Ph.D. dissertation, Boston University Graduate School, 1976).

Graff, Helen E. "Henry T. Rainey - An American Statesman" (Master's thesis, State University of Iowa, 1933).

Green, Matthew Nathaniel, "Speakers of the House of Representatives and the Exercise of Legislative Leadership" (Ph.D. dissertation, Yale University, 2004).

_____. "Presidents and Personal Goals: The Speaker of the House and Non-Majoritarian Leader" (Unpublished Paper, Catholic University of America, 2005).

Grim, Mark Sillers, "The Political Career of John Bell" (Master's thesis, University of Tennessee, 1930).

Harrington, Fred Harvey, "The Life of N.P. Banks to 1861" (Ph.D. dissertation, New York University, 1937).

Hasenfus, William A., "Managing Partner: Joseph W. Martin, Jr., Republican Leader of the United States House of Representatives, 1939-1959" (Ph.D. dissertation, Boston College, 1986).

Heacock, Walter J., "William Brockman Bankhead: A Biography" (Ph.D. dissertation, University of Wisconsin, 1952).

Hechler, Kenneth W., "Insurgency: Personalities and Politics of the Taft Era" (Ph.D. dissertation, Columbia University, 1940).

Helms, James Marvin, Jr., "The Early Career of Nathaniel Macon: A Study in 'Pure Republicanism'" (Ph.D. dissertation, University of Virginia, 1962).

Henry, Milton Lyman, Jr., "Henry Winter Davis: Border State Radical" (Ph.D. dissertation, Louisiana State University, 1974).

Hizer, Trenton Eynon, "Virginia is Now Divided: Politics in the Old Dominion, 1820-1833" (Ph.D. dissertation, University of South Carolina, 1997).

Ifkovic, John William, "Jonathan Trumbull, Junior, 1740-1809: A Biography" (Ph.D. dissertation, University of Virginia, 1974).

Jacobsen, John Gregory, "Jackson's Judges: Six Appointments Who Shaped a Nation" (Ph.D. dissertation, The Graduate College at the University of Nebraska, 2004).

Klein, Larry Dean, "Henry Clay, Nationalist" (Ph.D. dissertation, University of Kentucky, 1977).

Kubik, William J., Jr., "Political Parties and the Committee System in the House of Representatives" (Ph.D. dissertation, The University of Rochester [New York], 1995).

Lacy, Alex B., "Jefferson and Congress: Congressional Method and Politics, 1801-1809" (Ph.D. dissertation, University of Virginia, 1963).

Laney, Ray Stanley, "Sam Rayburn, Legislator" (Master's thesis, East Texas State College, 1962).

Leemhuis, Roger Phillip, "James L. Orr: The Civil War and Reconstruction Years" (Ph.D. dissertation, The University of Wisconsin at Madison, 1970).

Lindquist, Elizabeth K., "Langdon Cheves (South Carolina)" (Master's thesis, The University of Chicago, 1922).

Little, Dwayne Lee, "The Political Leadership of Speaker Sam Rayburn" (Ph.D. dissertation, University of Cincinnati, 1970).

Lopez, Robert Rudy, "The House in Transition, 1905-1946: From 'Czarism' to Committee Government" (Ph.D. dissertation, University of Colorado at Boulder, 1998).

Malone, Preston St. Clair, "The Political Career of Charles Frederick Crisp" (Ph.D. dissertation, University of Georgia, 1962).

Maness, Lonnie Edward, "Henry Clay and the Problem of Slavery" (Ph.D. dissertation, Memphis State University, 1980).

Marsh, Richard Dean, "James K. Polk and Slavery" (Master's thesis, University of North Texas, 1977).

McDonald, Timothy Gregory, "Southern Democratic Congressmen and the First World War, August 1914-April 1917: The Public Record of Their Support for or Opposition to Wilson's Policies" (Ph.D. dissertation, University of Washington, 1961).

Moore, Richard Randall, "In Search of a Safe Government: A Biography of R.M.T. Hunter of Virginia" (Ph.D. Dissertation, University of South Carolina, 1993).

Morley, Margaret Ruth, "The Edge of Empire: Henry Clay's American System and the Formulation of American Foreign Policy, 1810-1833" (Ph.D. dissertation, University of Wisconsin, 1972).

Morrison, Geoffrey Fahy, "A Political Biography of Champ Clark" (Ph.D. dissertation, St. Louis University, 1972).

Parks, Norman L., "The Career of John Bell of Tennessee in the United States House of Representatives" (Ph.D. dissertation, Vanderbilt University, 1942).

Peterson, Sanford William, "The Genesis and Development of Parliamentary Procedure in Colonial America, 1609-1801" (Ph.D. dissertation, Indiana University, 1983).

Rager, Scott William, "The Fall of the House of Cannon: Uncle Joe and His Enemies, 1903-1910" (Ph.D. dissertation, University of Illinois, Urbana-Champaign, 1991).

Rigali, James Henry, "Restoring the Republic of Virtue: The Presidential Election of 1824" (Ph.D. dissertation, University of Washington, 2004).

Roberts, Carey Michael, "Men of Much Faith: Progress and Declension in Jeffersonian thought, 1787-1800" (Ph.D. dissertation, University of South Carolina, 1999).

Romano, Michael John, "The Emergence of John Nance Garner as a Figure in National Politics, 1924-1941" (Ph.D. dissertation, St. John's University [New York], 1974).

Shaffer, Wade Lee, "The Richmond Junto and Politics in Jacksonian Virginia" (Ph.D. dissertation, The College of William & Mary, 1993).

Shanks, Alexander Graham, "Sam Rayburn and the New Deal, 1933-1936" (Ph.D. dissertation, The University of North Carolina at Chapel Hill, 1965).

Shannon, Jasper B., "Henry Clay as a Political Leader" (Ph.D. dissertation, University of Wisconsin, Madison, 1934).

Spann, Edward K., "John W. Taylor, the Reluctant Partisan: 1784-1854" (Ph.D. dissertation, New York University, 1957).

Van Hollen, Christopher, "The House Rules Committee, 1933-1951: Agent of Party and Agent of Opposition" (Ph.D. dissertation, Johns Hopkins University, 1951).

Wicks, Aaron E., "Leadership Selection in the United States House of Representatives" (Ph.D. dissertation, The University of Rochester [New York], 2001).

Winkler, James R., "The Political Economy of Henry Clay" (Ph.D. dissertation, Fordham University, 1969).

Zhou, Baodi, "Thomas S. Foley and the Politics of Wheat: United States Wheat Trade with Japan, China, and the Soviet Union, 1965-1986" (Ph.D. dissertation, Washington State University, 1999).

Official Government Documents and Publications

"American State Papers: Documents, Legislative and Executive" (Washington: Published by Gales and Seaton; thirty-eight volumes, 1832-61).

"Celebration of the Rededication of Congress Hall: Addresses of Hon. Woodrow Wilson, President of the United States and Hon. Champ Clark, Speaker of the House of Representatives, at Philadelphia, Pa. October 25, 1913" House Document No. 272, 63rd Congress, 1st Session (1913).

Cobb, Howell, "Speech of Mr. Cobb, of Georgia, on the Tariff Bill. Delivered in the House of Representatives of the United States, May 3, 1844" (Washington: Printed by Blair and Rives, 1844).

"Dividing Line Between Georgia and Florida [Report from Mr. Philip Pendleton Barbour of the Committee on the Judiciary]" House Report 204, 20th Congress, 1st Session (1828).

Foster, Thomas, and George Cochran, "Eulogies Delivered in the Senate and House of Representatives of the United States on the Life and Character of Hon. John C. Calhoun, of South Carolina, Hon. Henry Clay, of Kentucky, and Hon. Daniel Webster, of Massachusetts" (Washington: Foster Cochran, 1853).

Great Britain. Parliament, "An Exact Abridgement of the Records in the Tower of London, from the Reign of King Edward the Second, unto King Richard the Third, of all the Parliaments Holden in each kings reign, and the several acts in every Parliament: together with the names and titles of all the Dukes, Marquesses, Earls, Viscounts, and Barons, summoned to every of the said Parliaments. Collected by Sir Robert Cotton, knight and baronet. Rev., Rectified in Sundry Mistakes, and Supplied with a Preface, Marginal Notes, several omissions, and exact tables, both of the special matters, great officers, speakers, nobles and other persons therein Contained. By William Prynne, Esquire, a bencher of Lincolns Inne" (London: Printed for William Leake, stationer, at the Crown in Fleetstreet, between the two Temple gates, 1657).

Hinds, Asher Crosby, "Precedents of the House of Representatives, Including References to Provisions of the Constitute, the Laws, and Decisions of the United States Senate" (Washington, D.C.: Government Printing Office; 11 volumes, 1907-08).

"History of the United States House of Representatives, 1789-1994. Printed under the Supervision of the Committee on House Administration" (Washington, D.C.: Government Printing Office, 1994).

"Joseph Gurney Cannon: Proceedings in the House of Representatives on the Eightieth Anniversary of His Birth" (House Document 1092, Sixty-fourth Congress, First Session {1916}).

"Journal of the House of Representatives of the United States: Being the First Session of the Twenty-third Congress, Begun and Held at the City of Washington, December 2, 1833, and in the Fifty-eighth Year of the Independence of the United States" (Washington: Printed by Gales & Seaton, 1833).

"Journals of the Continental Congress, 1774-1789. Edited from the Original Records in the Library of Congress by Worthington Chauncey Ford, Chief, Division of Manuscripts" (Washington: Government Printing Office; thirty-four volumes, 1904-37).

"Lieut. James M. Gilliss. Mr. Bocock, from the Committee on Naval Affairs, made the Following Report [on the petition of Lieut. James M. Gilliss for increased pay]" (House Report 165, 35th Congress, 2nd Session {1859}).

"Memorial Addresses on the Life and Character of Charles Frederick Crisp (Late a Representative from Georgia), Delivered in the House of Representatives and Senate, Fifty-Fourth Congress, Second Session. Published by Order of Congress" (Washington, D.C.: Government Printing Office, 1897).

"Memorial Services held in the House of Representatives of the United States, Together with Remarks presented in Eulogy of Nicholas Longworth, late a Representative from Ohio" (House Document 373, Seventy-second Congress, 1st Session {1932}).

"Memorial Services Held in the House of Representatives of the United States, Together With Remarks Presented in Eulogy of Henry T. Rainey, Late a Representative from Illinois, Seventy Fourth Congress, First Session" (Washington, D.C.: Government Printing Office, 1936).

"Naval Contracts and Expenditures. Mr. Bocock, from the Select Committee on Naval Contracts and Expenditures, made the following Report [on the subject of Contracts and Expenditures in the Navy Department]" (House Report 184, 35th Congress, 2nd Session {1859}).

"Register of Debates in Congress, Comprising the Leading Debates and Incidents" of the Sessions of Congress (Washington: Printed and Published by Gales and Seaton; twenty-nine volumes, 1825-37).

"Report of the Secretary of the Treasury to the House of Representatives, Relative to a Provision for the Support of Public Credit of the United States, in Conformity to a Resolution of the Twenty-first Day of September, 1789. Presented to the House on Thursday the 14th Day of January, 1790. Published by Order of the House of Representatives" (New York: Printed by Francis Childs and John Swain, 1790).

"Speakers of the House: Elections, 1913-2007," *CRS Report for Congress*, 29 January 2007.

"Speech Delivered by the Hon. Henry Clay, in the House of Representatives, of the United States, on Friday, the Eight Day of January, 1813, on the Bill for Raising an Additional Military Force of Twenty Thousand Men for One Year" (Washington City: Published at the Office of the National Intelligencer, 1813).

"Speeches Delivered in the House of Representatives, January 19, 1888, on the Presentation by the State of Massachusetts to the National Government of Portraits of Ex-Speakers Sedgwick, Varnum, and Banks. Published by Order of Congress" (Washington: Government Printing Office, 1888).

"Speech of Hon. John Bell, of Tennessee, on Non-Intervention. Delivered in the Senate of the United States, April 13, 1852" (Washington: Printed at the Congressional Globe Office, 1852).

"Supreme Court of the United States [Report of Mr. Philip Pendleton Barbour of the Committee on the Judiciary]" House Report 34, 20th Congress, 2nd Session (1829).

"The Cannon Centenary Conference: The Changing Nature of the Speakership" House Document 108-204, 108th Congress, 2nd Session (Washington, D.C.: Government Printing Office, 2004).

"The Debates and Proceedings in the Congress of the United States; with an Appendix, Containing Important State Papers and Public Documents, and All the Laws of a Public Nature; with a Copious Index" (Washington: Printed and Published by Gales and Seaton; forty two volumes, 1834-56).

"The Speaker of the House: House Officer, Party Leader, and Representative," *CRS Report for Congress*, 29 January 2007.

US House, "Memorial Addresses on the Life and Character of Charles Frederick Crisp (late a Representative from Georgia), Delivered in the House of Representatives and Senate, Fifty-fourth Congress, Second Session. Published by Order of Congress" (Washington: Government Printing Office, 1897).

_____, Committee on Rules, "A History of the Committee on Rules" (Washington, D.C.: Government Printing Office, 1983).

U.S. Senate, "Obituary Addresses on the Occasion of the Death of the Hon. Henry Clay, a Senator of the United States from the State of Kentucky" (Washington: R. Armstrong, 1852).

Manuscript Collections

James Barbour Papers, New York Public Library

James Gillespie Blaine Papers, Library of Congress

Henry Clay Papers, Library of Congress

Abraham Lincoln Papers, Library of Congress

Richard Peters, Jr., Papers, the Historical Society of Pennsylvania, Philadelphia

Andrew Stevenson Papers, Library of Congress

Charles Sumner Papers, Harvard University

Records of the United States House of Representatives, RG 233, The National Archives, Washington, D.C.

Newspapers Consulted

The following newspapers were consulted when researching the material in this book:

Daily National Intelligencer (Washington, D.C.)
Niles' Register
Richmond Enquirer (Virginia)
The New York Times
The New York Tribune
The New York World
The Washington Post
The Washington Post and Times-Herald